ASPLOS XVIII

Eighteenth International Conference on Architectural Support for Programming Languages and Operating Systems

AF849763

March 16–20, 2013
Houston, Texas, USA

Sponsored by:
SIGARCH
SIGPLAN
SIGOPS

Association for Computing Machinery

With Support from:

NSF, ARM, Google, Microsoft Research, VMware, Cavium, DE Shaw & Co, Facebook, Hewlett-Packard, Intel, Oracle Labs, Qualcomm, Texas Instruments, AMD, and IBM Research

Association for
Computing Machinery

Advancing Computing as a Science & Profession

The Association for Computing Machinery
2 Penn Plaza, Suite 701
New York, New York 10121-0701

ISBN: 978-1-4503-1870-9

Additional copies may be ordered prepaid from:

ACM Order Department
PO Box 30777
New York, NY 10087-0777, USA

Phone: 1-800-342-6626 (USA and Canada)
+1-212-626-0500 (Global)
Fax: +1-212-944-1318
E-mail: acmhelp@acm.org
Hours of Operation: 8:30 am – 4:30 pm ET

Printed in the USA

Message from the Chairs

It is our great pleasure to welcome you to the Eighteenth International Conference on Architectural Support for Programming Languages and Operating Systems — ASPLOS 2013! This year's conference continues and reinforces the ASPLOS tradition of publishing innovative multidisciplinary research spanning the boundaries of hardware, computer architecture, compilers, languages, operating systems, networking, and applications.

This year, authors submitted 193 papers, 12% more than last year when 172 papers were submitted, and 7% more than in 2010, the previous record year, when 180 papers were submitted. PC members co-authored 22 submissions. The following ten topic keywords were marked by at least 20 submissions: compilation, parallelization and optimization (40 submissions), programming models (32), OS scheduling and resource management (31), OS abstractions (29), testing and debugging (27), power/energy/thermal management (27), memory optimizations (25), heterogeneous architectures (24), parallel programming languages (23), and virtualization (21).

The 2013 ASPLOS Program Committee (PC) consisted of 35 members; each member was assigned 18 submissions, a workload of four more papers than the previous year. As in previous years, the Program Chair recruited an External Review Committee (ERC) whose expertise complemented that of the PC. The 2013 ERC consisted of 63 members, assigned 5 papers each. Additionally, 90 sub reviewers prepared 143 reviews. In total, we received 943 reviews, an average of 4.89 reviews per paper. 90% of submissions received at least five reviews, and all received at least four.

As in previous years, we employed two rounds of reviews. A significant difference this year was that no papers were rejected after the first round. The two phases were employed merely to spread out the review workload and to allocate reviewer expertise based on first-round reviews. After a three-day author response period, the PC and ERC members entered online discussion lasting about a week. The online discussion, moderated by paper discussion leaders assigned to each paper, was unusually lively. The discussion resulted in 71 papers being selected for deliberation at the physical PC meeting. During the entire review and selection process, scores alone were never used to reject a submission.

The PC gathered in Berkeley, CA, on Nov. 1, 2012, for a one-day meeting. Three committee members were unable to attend, mostly due to travel disruptions from the Hurricane Sandy. These members participated in online discussions prior to the meeting. The meeting followed the protocol of allocating a fixed amount of time for the discussion of each paper. If a consensus was not reached, the paper advanced to a discussion phase, which had the form of small groups composed of paper reviewers and other relevant PC members. In the late afternoon, these groups reported back to the PC with arguments for or against accepting the paper. PC and ERC members volunteered to shepherd 7 papers to ensure reviewer comments were properly addressed. The PC-authored submissions were not discussed at the meeting (see below). PC members with conflicts left the room during discussions, as is customary. Vivek Sarkar, the General Chair, attended the PC meeting as an observer and handled conflicts involving the Program Chair.

In the end, the PC and ERC accepted 44 papers, 7 more than the previous year. The acceptance rate is 22.8%, compared to 21.5% the previous year.

The 22 PC-authored submissions were reviewed only by the ERC. The ERC discussed and accepted these submissions in an online discussion, conducted mostly prior to the physical PC meeting. The ERC held the PC submissions to the same conference standard as other papers. Preliminary acceptance decisions, done by the ERC before the PC meeting, were calibrated against the papers accepted at the PC meeting with the help of the Program and General Chairs. In the end, 5 PC submissions were accepted. The acceptance rate was the same as for non-PC submissions.

We want to extend special thanks to Roxana Infante, the Program Chair's administrative assistant, for taking care of all logistics related to the PC meeting. We also want to thank UC Berkeley graduate students Mangpo Phitchaya Phothilimthana, for writing a genetic programming algorithm that prepared a paper discussion schedule minimizing the number of times a PC members had to leave the room due to conflicts; Shaon Barman, for processing data from the submission web site; and Sarah Chasins, for helping us moderate the PC meeting by taking notes and keeping careful track of time.

The success of a major conference like ASPLOS very much depends on the hard work of all members of the organizing committee who volunteer their time in this service. We especially want to thank all PC and ERC members for their thoughtful reviews and extensive online discussions. The Workshops Chair, Barbara Chapman, Tutorials Chair, Alan Cox, and Provocative Ideas Chair, Milind Kulkarni, did an excellent job in complementing the main conference program with stimulating technical events. The Sponsorship Chair, Kunle Olukotun, and Finance Chair, Michael Swift, worked tirelessly in their engagement with industry partners, and were able to obtain support from fourteen corporations. We thank Jeremy Singer and Vincent Cavé for their contributions as Publicity Chair and Web Chair respectively, and are especially grateful to Zoran Budimlic for all his efforts as Local Arrangements Chair. A special thank you goes to Kathryn O'Brien of Rice University for her hard work in co-organizing the banquet at the Houston Museum of Natural Science.

We are grateful to our sponsors, ACM SIGARCH, ACM SIGPLAN, and ACM SIGOPS, and to the ASPLOS steering committee for giving us the opportunity to organize this conference, and for providing guidance and historical perspective. Many thanks to the corporations who generously supported this conference — ARM, Google, Microsoft Research, and VMWare at the Gold level, Cavium, DE Shaw & Co, Facebook, Hewlett Packard, Intel, Oracle Labs, Qualcomm Research, and Texas Instruments at the Silver level, and AMD and IBM Research at the Bronze level. Finally, we wish to thank the authors and all the participants who make ASPLOS a unique and vibrant technical forum every year.

Ras Bodik
ASPLOS'13 Program Chair
University of California, Berkeley

Vivek Sarkar
ASPLOS'13 General Chair
Rice University

Table of Contents

Session 4: Keynote

Session Chair: Vivek Sarkar *(Rice University)*

Session 5: Architecture I

Session Chair: Kai Shen *(University of Rochester)*

Session 6: Performance Analysis

Session Chair: Karin Strauss *(Microsoft Research)*

Session 7: Security

Session Chair: Rusty Sears *(Microsoft)*

Session 8: Compilation I

Session Chair: Milo Martin *(University of Pennsylvania)*

Session 13: Architecture II

Session Chair: Emmett Witchel *(University of Texas, Austin)*

ASPLOS 2013 Conference Organization

General Chair: Vivek Sarkar *(Rice University, USA)*

Program Chair: Rastislav Bodik *(University of California, Berkeley, USA)*

Workshops Chair: Barbara Chapman *(University of Houston, USA)*

Tutorials Chair: Alan Cox *(Rice University, USA)*

Local Arrangements Chair: Zoran Budimlic *(Rice University, USA)*

Web Chair: Vincent Cavé *(Rice University, USA)*

Publicity Chair: Jeremy Singer *(University of Glasgow, UK)*

Finance Chair: Michael Swift *(University of Wisconsin - Madison, USA)*

Sponsorship Chair: Kunle Olukotun *(Stanford University, USA)*

Steering Committee:
Doug Burger *(Microsoft)*
George Candea *(EPFL, Switzerland)*
Rajiv Gupta *(University of California, Riverside, USA)*
Timothy Harris *(Oracle)*
Graham Hutton *(University of Nottingham, UK)*
Todd Mowry *(Carnegie Mellon University, USA)*
Michael Scott *(University of Rochester, USA)*
David Wood *(University of Wisconsin, USA)*

Program Committee:
Ali Reza Adl-Tabatabai *(Facebook)*
Sarita Adve *(University of Illinois at Urbana-Champaign, USA)*
Ole Agesen *(VMWare)*
Todd Austin *(University of Michigan, USA)*
Calin Cascaval *(Qualcomm)*
Hassan Chafi *(Oracle Labs)*
Byung-Gon Chun *(Yahoo!)*
Jason Cong *(University of California, Los Angeles, USA)*
Brian Demsky *(University of California, Irvine, USA)*
Bryan Ford *(Yale University, USA)*
Ada Gavrilovska *(Georgia Institute of Technology, USA)*
Steven Gribble *(University of Washington, USA)*
Kim Hazelwood *(Google)*
David Mazieres *(Stanford University, USA)*
Jonathan McCune *(Carnegie Mellon University, USA)*
Andrew Myers *(Cornell University, USA)*
Michael O'Boyle *(University of Edinburgh, UK)*

Program Committee (continued):

Mark Oskin *(University of Washington, USA)*
Keshav Pingali *(University of Texas, Austin, USA)*
Florentina Popovici *(Google)*
Rodric Rabbah *(IBM)*
P. (Saday) Sadayappan *(Ohio State University, USA)*
Tim Sherwood *(University of California, Santa Barbara, USA)*
Tajana Simunic Rosing *(University of California, San Diego, USA)*
Karin Strauss *(Microsoft Research)*
Edward Suh *(Cornell University, USA)*
Nathan Tallent *(PNNL, USA)*
Olivier Temam *(INRIA Saclay, France)*
Adam Welc *(Oracle Labs)*
Thomas Wenisch *(University of Michigan, USA)*
David Wentzlaff *(Princeton University, USA)*
Emmett Witchel *(University of Texas, Austin, USA)*
Nickolai Zeldovich *(Massachusetts Institute of Technology, USA)*
Xiaolan Zhang *(IBM)*
Lin Zhong *(Rice University, USA)*

External Review Committee:

Glenn Ammons
Krste Asanovic
Luiz Barroso
Ricardo Bianchini
Peter Bodik
Michael Bond
Mihai Budiu
Sebastian Burckhardt
Doug Burger
Barbara Chapman
Trishul Chilimbi
E Christopher Lewis
Nirav Dave
John Davis
Peter Dinda
Natalie Enright Jerger
Mattan Erez
David Gay
Dan Grossman
Tim Harris
Gernot Heiser
Urs Holzle
Wilson Hsieh
Galen Hunt
Norm Hutchinson
Hiroshi Inoue
Mary Jane Irwin
Suresh Jagannathan
Aamer Jaleel
Sam King
Christos Kozyrakis
Doug Lea
Calvin Lin
Geoff Lowney
Shan Lu
Dimitrios Lymberopoulos
Milo Martin
Maged Michael
Mark Moir
Greg Morrisett
Todd Mowry
Satish Narayanasamy
Ed Nightingale
Ravi Rajwar
Jose Renau
Majd Sakr
Karu Sankaralingam
Jiri Schindler
Russell Sears
Kai Shen
Armando Solar-Lezama
Greg Steffan
Per Stenstrom
Steven Swanson
David Tarditi
Bill Thies
Bhuvan Urgaonkar
T.N. Vijaykumar
Carole-Jean Wu
Antonia Zhai
Youtao Zhang
Ben Zorn
Willy Zwaenepoel

Additional reviewers:

Hrishikesh Amur
J. Anderson
Owen Arden
Amittai Aviram
Jason Boles
Kevin Brown
Jared Casper
Sivaramakrishnan Krishnamoorthy Chandrasekaran
Sunita Chandrasekaran
Mason Chang
Walter Chang
Jinsuk Chung
Curtis Dunham
Yong Hun Eom
Joel Galenson
Mohammad Ghodrat
Mohammadali Ghodrat
Justin Gottschlich
Miles Gould
Dominik Grewe
Ramakrishna Gummadi
Karthik Gururaj
Mohammad Hammoud
M. Amber Hassaan
Byron Hawkins
Matthew Hicks
Owen Hofmann
Anup Holey
Sungpack Hong
Tim Hsiau
Muhuan Huang
Akanksha Jain
Min Jeong
Peter Kessler
Kunal Korgaonkar
Hyoukjoong Lee
Andrew Lenharth
Kai Li
Sen Li
Xiaozhu Lin
Chunyue Liu
Abid Malik
Mike Marty
Vineeth Mekkat
Rupesh Nasre
Ragavendra Natarajan
Rajib Nath
Donald Nguyen
Brian Norris
Guilherme Ottoni
Peizhao Ou
Manoj Plakal
Gilles Pokam
Louis-Noel Pouchet
Dan Powell
Alex Protopopescu
Dimitris Prountzos
Moinuddin Qureshi
Pradeep Ramachandran
Raghavan Raman
Suhail Rehman
Tiark Rompf
Yaoping Ruan
Ben Serebrin
Zon-Yin Shae
Tatiana Shpeisman
Mark Silberstein
Jeremy Singer
Abhayendra Singh
Richard Strong
Arvind Sujeeth
Michael Sullivan
Nishant Totla
Jagannathan Venkatesh
Andreas Voellmy
Cheng Wang
Zheng Wang
Youfeng Wu
Bingjun Xiao
Yuanzhong Xu
Jinseok Yang
Jieming Yin
Piero Zappi
Danfeng Zhang
Fan Zhang
Peng Zhang
Bo Zhao
Haoqiang Zheng

ASPLOS 2013 Sponsors & Supporters

Sponsors: SIGARCH, ACM SIGPLAN, ACM SIGOPS

Gold Supporters: NSF, ARM, Google, Microsoft Research, vmware

Silver Supporters: Cavium, D E Shaw & Co, facebook, hp, intel, Oracle Labs, Qualcomm Research Silicon Valley, Texas Instruments

Bronze Supporters: AMD, IBM Research

GPUDet: A Deterministic GPU Architecture

Hadi Jooybar[1] Wilson W. L. Fung[1] Mike O'Connor[2] Joseph Devietti[3] Tor M. Aamodt[1]
University of British Columbia[1] Advanced Micro Devices, Inc. (AMD)[2] University of Washington[3]
jooybar@ece.ubc.ca, wwlfung@ece.ubc.ca, mike.oconnor@amd.com, devietti@cs.washington.edu, aamodt@ece.ubc.ca

Abstract

Nondeterminism is a key challenge in developing multithreaded applications. Even with the same input, each execution of a multithreaded program may produce a different output. This behavior complicates debugging and limits one's ability to test for correctness. This non-reproducibility situation is aggravated on massively parallel architectures like graphics processing units (GPUs) with thousands of concurrent threads. We believe providing a deterministic environment to ease debugging and testing of GPU applications is essential to enable a broader class of software to use GPUs.

Many hardware and software techniques have been proposed for providing determinism on general-purpose multi-core processors. However, these techniques are designed for small numbers of threads. Scaling them to thousands of threads on a GPU is a major challenge. This paper proposes a scalable hardware mechanism, GPUDet, to provide determinism in GPU architectures. In this paper we characterize the existing deterministic and nondeterministic aspects of current GPU execution models, and we use these observations to inform GPUDet's design. For example, GPUDet leverages the inherent determinism of the SIMD hardware in GPUs to provide determinism within a wavefront at no cost. GPUDet also exploits the Z-Buffer Unit, an existing GPU hardware unit for graphics rendering, to allow parallel out-of-order memory writes to produce a deterministic output. Other optimizations in GPUDet include deterministic parallel execution of atomic operations and a workgroup-aware algorithm that eliminates unnecessary global synchronizations.

Our simulation results indicate that GPUDet incurs only 2× slowdown on average over a baseline nondeterministic architecture, with runtime overheads as low as 4% for compute-bound applications, despite running GPU kernels with thousands of threads. We also characterize the sources of overhead for deterministic execution on GPUs to provide insights for further optimizations.

Categories and Subject Descriptors C.1.4 [*Processor Architectures*]: Parallel Architectures—GPU Architecture; D.1.3 [*Programming Techniques*]: Concurrent Programming

General Terms Design, Performance, Reliability

Keywords GPU, Deterministic Parallelism

ASPLOS'13, March 16–20, 2013, Houston, Texas, USA.

1. Introduction

Massively parallel processors are designed to run thousands of threads. The energy efficiency of these processors has driven their widespread popularity for many inherently-parallel applications, such as computer graphics. We anticipate that increasing demands for energy efficiency will motivate a broader range of applications with more complex data structures and inter-task communication to use these processors.

Unfortunately, developing parallel applications that can utilize such architectures is hampered by the challenge of coordinating parallel tasks, especially in ensuring that a parallel program behaves correctly for every possible combination of interactions among these tasks. With the thousands of threads required to utilize current massively parallel architectures like GPUs, the number of interactions to consider is substantial. Nondeterminism makes this challenge even harder, because it thwarts attempts to reproduce anomalous behavior or to provide guarantees about future executions.

Providing deterministic execution for GPU architectures is a crucial aid for simplifying parallel programming at scale. Determinism simplifies the debugging process by making program behavior reproducible for a given input. Determinism is also useful once code is deployed, to reproduce bugs that manifest in production settings. Finally, determinism amplifies the power of testing, by providing a guarantee that once a particular input has passed its tests, those tests will continue to pass in the future. Current nondeterministic parallel architectures provide no such guarantee, which allows testing to provide only probabilistic guarantees.

The key challenge of determinism is providing these properties with acceptable performance overhead. To this end, different levels of determinism have been proposed in the literature [35]. We are proponents of *strong determinism*, which provides determinism even in the presence of data races. Some deterministic schemes require data-race freedom [35], offering determinism in a more limited context but with lower performance overheads. In contrast, a strongly deterministic system makes no assumptions about the program it is running, which is well-suited to dealing with the buggy programs that need determinism the most. The programmability of GPUs can benefit greatly from strong determinism.

1.1 Debugging with a Deterministic GPU

Many existing GPU workloads are embarrassingly parallel applications free of inherent data-races. It may be tempting to dismiss the benefit of deterministic execution on GPUs for these applications. However, these applications usually feature complex data tiling to improve data locality. Subtle mistakes during development can result in nondeterministic bugs that are hard to detect. A deterministic GPU allows programmers to analyze such bugs more effectively with a consistent output.

Indeed, race conditions have appeared in GPGPU algorithms from the published literature. To illustrate how a deterministic GPU can simplify debugging, we use a buggy version of breadth-first-search (BFS) graph traversal distributed by Harish and Narayanan [21] (BFSr). Below is a simplified version of the kernel function in BFSr, which contains a race condition.

```
0: __global__ void BFS_step_kernel(...) {
1:   if( active[tid] ) {
2:     active[tid] = false;
3:     visited[tid] = true;
4:     foreach (int id = neighbour_nodes) {
5:       if( visited[id] == false ) {
6:         cost[id] = cost[tid] + 1;
7:         active[id] = true;
8:         *over=true;
9: } } } }
```

Presumably, this kernel is designed to traverse one level of the breadth-first-search nodes during each kernel launch. Each thread (`tid` = thread ID) is assigned a node in the graph. In each kernel launch (at each step), each thread updates the cost of its neighbouring nodes (`cost[id]`) that have not been visited, and sets their active flag (`active[id]`), which indicates these nodes should update their own neighbours during the next kernel launch. A race condition can occur since a thread can be reading its `active[tid]` and `cost[tid]` (at line 1 and 6) while its neighbour is updating these locations (at line 6 and 7). This causes `cost[id]` to be updated nondeterministically, which can lead to incorrect output. Harish and Narayanan have discovered the race conditions in this code and have posted a corrected version, which is now part of the Rodinia benchmark suite [14].

With a deterministic GPU, the programmer can observe the same incorrect output across different runs. This allows him to set a watch point in a GPU debugger at the location in `cost[]` that has an incorrect output value. The programmer can then pause the execution at every modification to this location and identify the threads responsible for the incorrect output value. Notice that this approach will not work with a nondeterministic GPU. The programmer cannot be sure that the race condition would occur at the same memory location in the second run via the debugger. This difficulty with nondeterministic parallel architecture has motivated the supercomputing community to create extensive logging tools that capture activities across the entire system, and analyze the (enormous) logs for errors [3]. We argue that providing a deterministic GPU to programmers is a more effective solution.

1.2 Our Contribution: GPUDet

This paper introduces GPUDet, which is the first deterministic massively parallel architecture. GPUDet provides strong determinism for current-generation GPU architectures. GPUDet leverages the approach suggested by Bergan et al. [6] for multi-core CPUs. In this approach, threads are executed in an isolated memory space, communicating with other threads only at deterministic, fixed intervals. Thread isolation is realized by appending all stores to a private buffer instead of directly updating global memory. Thread updates are made globally visible via a commit process which leverages existing GPU Z-Buffer hardware to execute in a deterministic but highly parallel fashion. Read-modify-write operations that need to be made globally visible have their execution deferred until this communication phase. GPUDet executes these operations in parallel and maintains a deterministic order among them by leveraging the ordering property in existing GPU memory systems.

Our key contributions in this paper are:

1. We propose GPUDet, the first hardware model for a fully deterministic GPU architecture.
2. We characterize the inherently deterministic and nondeterministic aspects of the GPU execution model and propose optimizations to GPUDet that leverage these inherent deterministic properties.

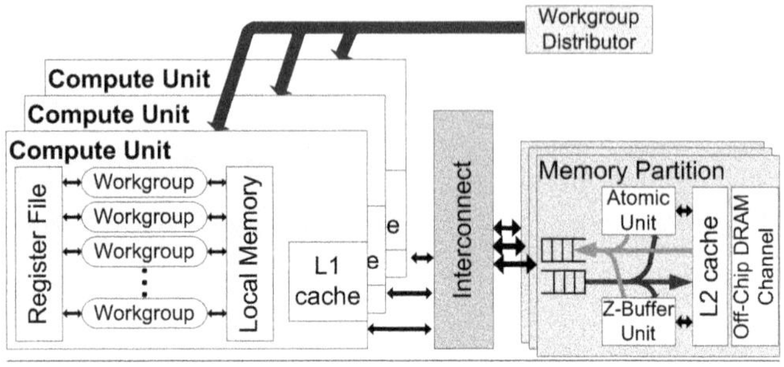

Figure 1. Baseline GPU Architecture

3. Our design exploits existing GPU hardware for Z-buffering to accelerate deterministic parallel committing of store buffers.
4. We introduce a workgroup-based quantum formation algorithm to enable larger quanta, which better amortized the overheads of quantum formation.
5. We exploit the point-to-point ordering in GPU memory subsystem to regain parallelism within each compute unit for read-modify-write operations that are executed in serial mode.

The rest of the paper is organized is follows. Section 2 summarizes our baseline GPU architecture and discusses sources of nondeterminism in GPUs. Section 3 summarizes existing techniques for providing deterministic execution and highlights the challenges in applying them on GPUs. Section 4 describes GPUDet. Section 5 presents a comprehensive evaluation of GPUDet. Section 6 discusses the related work. Section 7 concludes the paper.

2. Baseline Architecture

This section summarizes the details of our baseline GPU architecture relevant to deterministic execution on GPUs. Figure 1 shows an overview of our baseline GPU architecture modeled after the NVIDIA Fermi GPU architecture [32]. In this paper, we use OpenCL [24] terminology. However, to make the paper easier to read we use *thread* instead of *work item*. A GPU program (CUDA [33] or OpenCL [24]) starts running on the CPU and launches parallel compute kernels onto the GPU for processing. Each kernel launch consists of a hierarchy of threads organized in equal-sized *workgroups*. All threads in a kernel launch execute the same *kernel function*, while each thread may follow a unique execution path (with some performance penalty). Threads within a workgroup can synchronize quickly via *workgroup barriers* and communicate via an on-chip scratch-pad memory called the *local memory*. Communication among threads in different workgroups occurs through *global memory* located in off-chip DRAM. Each thread has exclusive access to its own *private memory* for non-shared data.

Our GPU microarchitecture consists of a set of compute units that access multiple partitions (i.e., channels) of off-chip DRAM via an interconnection network. Each compute unit can sustain up to 1536 threads in its register file. It has a scratch-pad memory that is partitioned among the different workgroups that run concurrently on the unit. The large register file allows a compute unit to freely context switch between different threads to tolerate long-latency accesses to global memory. The *workgroup distributor* on the GPU ensures that a compute unit has sufficient hardware resources to sustain all threads in a workgroup before dispatching the entire workgroup onto the unit. A GPU program may launch a kernel with more threads than the GPU hardware may execute concurrently. In this case, the GPU hardware starts executing as many workgroups as on-chip hardware resources permit, and dispatches the remaining ones as resources are released by the workgroups that have finished execution.

2.1 SIMT Execution Model

GPU architectures use Single-Instruction, Multiple-Data (SIMD) hardware for enhancing computational efficiency. Rather than exposing the SIMD hardware directly to the programmer, GPUs employ a Single-Instruction, Multiple-Threads (SIMT) execution model [29]. It groups scalar threads specified by the programmer into SIMD execution groups called *wavefronts* [2] (warps [33] in NVIDIA nomenclature). Threads in a wavefront execute in lockstep on the SIMD hardware. Since each thread can follow a unique execution path, a wavefront may *diverge* after a branch. The GPU hardware automatically serializes the execution of subsets of threads that have diverged to different control flow paths. Each wavefront has a SIMT stack [15, 20] maintaining the different control flow paths that still need to be executed. This allows for nested control flow divergence.

2.2 Memory Subsystem

Individual scalar accesses to global memory from threads in a wavefront are coalesced into wider accesses to 32, 64, or 128-byte chunks. The L1 data cache services one coalesced access per cycle. It caches data from both global memory and private memory, but with different policies. It acts as a writeback cache for accesses to private memory. Writes to global memory evict any line that hits in the L1 cache to make the memory updates visible to all compute units. However, the GPU hardware does not maintain coherence among the L1 data caches in different compute units. Each unit is responsible for purging stale data from its L1 cache.

Accesses that miss at the L1 cache are sent to the corresponding memory partition that contains the requested data. Each memory partition is responsible for its portion of the memory space. It contains a slice of the shared L2 cache. Accesses that miss at the L2 cache slices are in turn serviced by the off-chip DRAM controlled by the partition.

To support a rich set of synchronization primitives, the GPU programming model provides atomic operations, which are read-modify-write operations that update a single 32/64-bit word in the global memory. The wavefront sends each operation to its corresponding memory partition as with global memory accesses. Atomic operations are executed at the memory partitions with a set of specialized atomic operation units that operate directly on the L2 cache slices.

2.3 Sources of Nondeterminism in GPU Architectures

The standalone-accelerator nature of current GPU architectures helps isolate them from some sources of nondeterminism, like interrupt handlers and context switches, present in more general-purpose architectures. However, these sources will likely be increasingly relevant to future GPU architectures as GPUs become more general-purpose. To illustrate that nondeterminism exists on GPUs, we have developed GPU-Racey, a CUDA deterministic stress test, based on CPU deterministic stress test Racey [22]. Racey computes a signature that is extremely sensitive to the relative ordering of memory accesses among threads. Across multiple runs, it should generate different signatures on a nondeterministic system, and the same signature on a deterministic system. Running GPU-Racey on real GPU hardware (a Quadro FX 5800 and a Tesla C2050) with two or more concurrent wavefronts (warps) produces nondeterministic outputs on different runs. While the exact sources of nondeterminism in commercial GPUs are undocumented, we have postulated several potential sources.

First, each GPU usually consists of multiple clock domains [34], with each domain running at its optimal frequency. The synchronizer circuits interfacing between these domains can introduce nondeterministic delays to cross-domain messages due to phase drifting among the different clocks [38]. This source of nondeterminism may be exacerbated in the future as more aggressive power management features such as dynamic voltage and frequency scaling (DVFS) are introduced to GPU architectures.

Second, the access timing to off-chip memory on a GPU depends on the physical location of the data. Accesses to different memory partitions have an observable delay difference [45]. With the GPU shared by many different processes in the system, it is improbable for the GPU driver to starting in the same memory partition for every run of an application. The variance in DRAM cells may also encourages more adaptive refreshing techniques that change the refreshing interval according to the dynamic status of different cells [30]. This introduces nondeterministic delays for DRAM accesses.

Third, arbitration/scheduling units with uninitialized states can introduce nondeterminism by ordering thread execution or memory requests in an application differently between different runs. This includes the hardware wavefront schedulers in each compute unit, the workgroup distributor and the arbiters in the interconnection network. Although these units are reset to a known initial state at power up, the operating system is unlikely to reset them between kernel launches. This makes the states of these units dependent on the previously executed workload, which is usually not predictable.

Finally, as circuit process technology scales, transient faults in memory cells have become increasingly common. Transient failure in either on-chip or off-chip memory can trigger recover routines randomly [32], thus introducing nondeterministic latencies to memory accesses.

3. GPU Deterministic Execution: Background and Challenges

Many hardware and software techniques have been proposed for providing determinism on general-purpose multi-core processors [4, 6, 7, 16, 17, 23, 31, 35]. However, these techniques are designed for systems supporting tens, not thousands, of threads. Issues of serialization, global synchronization and per-thread fixed costs have much greater impact at GPU-scale than at CPU-scale.

In this section, we first summarize the deterministic multiprocessor schemes CoreDet and Calvin [6, 23], which serve as a basis for GPUDet. We then discuss the major challenges these prior approaches face in scaling up to work on GPU architectures. We have chosen to start with Calvin and CoreDet over more recent proposals because their simplicity – particularly Calvin's in-order pipeline design that avoids hardware speculation – is a good match for current GPU architectures. Furthermore, subsequent improvements in deterministic execution hardware provide lighter-weight synchronization operations [17], but do not address the scaling challenges inherent in making GPU architectures deterministic. Incorporating these subsequent improvements with GPUDet would improve performance for the applications that have frequent communications among threads.

3.1 Background: CoreDet and Calvin

CoreDet [6] is a compiler and accompanying runtime system that provides *strong determinism* for multithreaded programs. A multithreaded program compiled with CoreDet always produces the same result, even if the program contains data races. Calvin [23] is a processor design that provides deterministic execution, using an algorithm very similar to CoreDet's but incorporating the specifics of multi-core hardware. We provide a Calvin-centric overview as its hardware implementation is most similar to the GPUDet approach.

The basic mechanism both schemes use to enforce determinism is described in Figure 2. The execution of the program is divided into *quanta*, deterministically-sized sequences of instructions, e.g. every 1000th instruction executed by a wavefront marks the start of a new quantum. Each quantum is in turn composed of three phases. The first phase is *parallel mode*, wherein each processor executes in isolation. Calvin's special coherence protocol ensures that a processor sees only its own writes but not those of remote processors. In effect, each processor executes a single-threaded program which is inherently deterministic. At the end of parallel mode, all processors enter a global barrier before transitioning into *commit mode*. In commit mode the writes from each processor are made globally visible, using a deterministic parallel commit algorithm that maps well to GPU hardware (Section 4.4.1). Another global barrier separates commit mode from *serial mode*, during which atomic operations (which cannot execute correctly under the relaxed-consistency coherence protocol of parallel mode) execute in a deterministic, serial order. A final global barrier ends the current quantum and allows a new quantum's parallel mode to begin.

3.2 Deterministic GPU Execution Challenges

The first challenge for deterministic execution on the GPU is the **lack of private caches and cache coherence**. A GPU's multiplexing of hundreds of threads onto a single first-level cache means that Calvin's mechanism of using private caches to provide isolation between threads is not readily employable. Physically or logically partitioning each cache for use amongst hundreds of threads would dramatically reduce the cache's effectiveness. Even if per-thread private caches were available, the lack of cache coherence in a GPU's per-core caches rules out Calvin's modified coherence protocol as a way of providing low-overhead thread isolation. Implementing isolation in software (as in CoreDet) allows physical resources to be shared but has high runtime overhead.

Another major concern in building deterministic GPUs is dealing with **very large numbers of threads**. This in turn leads to a number of related problems. Large numbers of threads make the global barriers inherent in the CoreDet/Calvin deterministic execution algorithms much more expensive. Relatedly, atomic operations require serialization in the Calvin and CoreDet models, so their presence in a GPU kernel can quickly erode performance. By serializing thousands of threads, an atomic operation has effectively many orders of magnitude higher cost when run deterministically than when run nondeterministically.

The GPU hardware features various hardware mechanisms to efficiently manage thousands of threads. These mechanisms need to be extended accordingly to support deterministic execution. Specifically, with the **SIMT execution model**, arbitrarily pausing a scalar thread that has exhausted its instruction quota while permitting the others to proceed causes the wavefront to diverge. Handling this divergence requires substantial modification to the SIMT hardware and the extra determinism-induced divergence lowers the SIMD hardware utilization.

Finally, GPU kernels have different program properties than multithreaded CPU programs. Executing larger quanta is a natural solution to amortize expensive global barriers and atomic operations, and works well in the CPU space where threads are long-lived. Unfortunately, GPU kernels often contain a **large number of short-running threads**, making global barriers both expensive *and* frequent. GPU threads tends to synchronize frequently within a workgroup to communicate via the on-chip scratch-pad memory. This form of **hierarchical, localized communication** fits poorly with the infrequent global communication model in the CoreDet/Calvin deterministic execution algorithms. GPU threads also typically exhibit **less locality** than CPU threads, particularly in terms of memory accesses: frequently-used values are instead cached in a GPU's large register files or scratch-pad memory. This reduced locality makes Calvin's cache-based isolation mechanism a poor fit for GPU kernels.

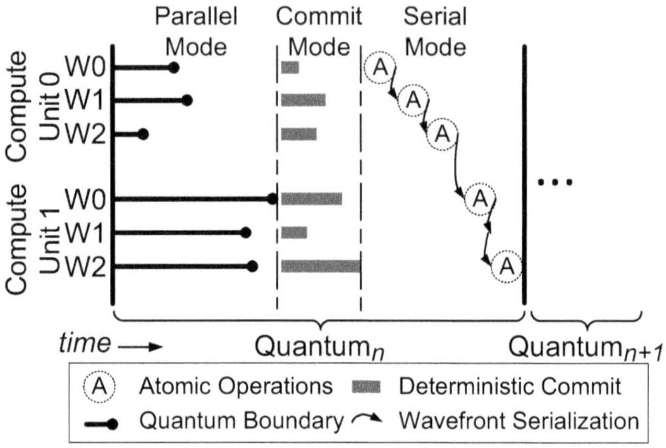

Figure 2. GPUDet-base architecture. Vertical lines show the global synchronization before the start of each mode. Wavefront 1 (W1) of compute unit 1 has been skipped in the serial mode since it has not reached an atomic operation in the $quantum_n$.

4. GPUDet

In this section, we present GPUDet, the first hardware proposal that provides strong determinism for deterministic massively parallel architecture with thousands of concurrent threads. We design GPUDet starting with a naive adaptation of the deterministic multiprocessor schemes from CoreDet/Calvin onto the GPU. This scheme divides GPU kernel execution into *quanta*. Each quantum has three phases: parallel mode, commit mode and serial mode as illustrated in Figure 2. GPUDet features optimizations for each mode, leveraging the inherent determinism in the GPU architecture as well as common-case GPU program behavior to recover more parallelism while reducing complexity required to support deterministic execution.

For parallel mode, GPUDet exploits the inherent determinism of current SIMT architectures to provide deterministic interaction among threads within a wavefront at no cost (Section 4.1). GPUDet also introduces a novel wavefront-aware quantum formation algorithm to eliminate unnecessary global synchronizations and replace them with local, deterministic synchronizations (Section 4.2). The store buffers that provide isolated execution among deterministic wavefronts are described in Section 4.3. For commit mode, GPUDet extends the Z-Buffer hardware designed for graphics rendering to accelerate its deterministic parallel commit algorithm (Section 4.4). For serial mode, it exploits the point-to-point ordering in the GPU's memory subsystem to reduce the amount of serialization required in this mode (Section 4.5). Section 4.6 discusses limitations in GPUDet's current design.

4.1 Deterministic Wavefront

The deterministic execution algorithm used in CoreDet and Calvin imposes determinism by pausing the execution of threads at deterministic intervals for communication [6, 23]. A naive GPU adaptation of this scheme would involve executing each scalar thread in isolation during the parallel mode and pausing the thread when it has exhausted its instruction count quota for the quantum. As mentioned in Section 3.2, this behavior interacts poorly with the implicit synchronizations of threads within a wavefront imposed by the SIMT execution model. Example 1 shows the execution of a wavefront with 4 threads (T0 to T3) through a branch hammock. The wavefront diverges at line `B`. In response, the SIMT stack deactivates T2 and T3 to execute line `C` with only T0 and T1 active. After executing line `C`, T0 and T1 have exhausted their instruction

Example 1 Thread-level isolation introduces divergence in SIMT architecture. In this example, each thread may execute up to 3 operations per quantum. The number of operations executed by each thread is shown beside each line of the code.

```
                                   T0  T1  T2  T3
A: v = 1;                      \\  1   1   1   1
B: if( threadIdx.x < 2 ){      \\  2   2   2   2
C:    v = input[threadIdx.x];  \\  3   3   2   2
D: }                           \\
E: output[threadIdx.x] += v;   \\  4   4   3   3
```

count quota for the quantum, and enter the global barrier for commit mode. A deadlock has occurred, because this global barrier is also waiting for T2 and T3, which are in turn paused by the SIMT stack to reconverge with T0 and T1 for full SIMD execution at line E. The SIMT stack can be modified to resolve this deadlock, but doing so introduces extra complexity and lowers the SIMD hardware utilization.

GPUDet eliminates these complexities and deadlock concerns altogether by exploiting the fact that the execution of the entire wavefront is inherently deterministic. Deterministic execution within a wavefront also eliminates the need to have thread-level isolation and allows threads in the same wavefront share a common store buffer. The inherent determinism of wavefront execution arises from two properties: 1) Pausing the execution of a wavefront causes each thread to execute a deterministic (but not necessarily equal) number of instructions, and 2) existing GPU architecture already handles data-races between threads within a wavefront.

As described in Section 2.1, the control flow of each wavefront, and the activity of its threads at every dynamic instruction, are controlled by its SIMT stack. The SIMT stack of every wavefront has deterministic initial state, since all wavefronts execute at the start of the kernel program. As the wavefront executes in parallel mode, its SIMT stack is updated to handle any branch divergence that occurs. This update is deterministic, because every thread in the wavefront is executing with input data from a deterministic global memory state produced by the previous quantum round. Since the SIMT stack has a deterministic initial state and it is updated deterministically, we can infer that the SIMT stack always maintains a deterministic state.

The deterministic SIMT stack provides deterministic control flow for the wavefront. More importantly, it ensures that the activity of each thread in the wavefront is deterministic for every dynamic instruction. This means that a wavefront can pause after any dynamic instruction to end its parallel mode for communication. Each thread in the wavefront may have executed a different amount of work in the parallel mode due to divergence, but the amount executed by each thread is always deterministic.

Data-races can occur between threads within a wavefront, but these data-races are reproduced deterministically on current SIMT hardware [25], a property we exploit in GPUDet. Data-races that occur between threads executing different dynamic instructions are always ordered deterministically, because instructions from the same wavefront are executed in-order and the control flow of each wavefront is deterministic as per the above discussion. Data-races that occur between threads at the same dynamic memory instruction are ordered by the coalescing unit, which combines the scalar memory accesses from threads within a wavefront into accesses to wider memory chunks. When multiple threads in a wavefront write to the same location the coalescing unit generates only one memory access for the location and chooses one of the threads' store values. To ensure determinism, GPUDet relies upon the fact that the coalescing unit selects the same thread's store value for a given access pattern. A NVIDIA patent [26] describes a way to deterministically handle the write collision based on thread IDs (e.g. sending data of the thread with largest thread ID). Samuli and Tero [25] have exploited this deterministic behavior to optimize their software rasterization engine for the Fermi GPU architecture [32]. We have verified this observation on current GPU hardware as well as our simulation infrastructure with the GPU-Racey stress test described in Section 2.3. The deterministic interaction of threads within a wavefront enables GPUDet to use a per-wavefront store buffer (described in Section 4.3) for execution isolation.

4.2 Quanta Formation

At certain points of execution GPUDet pauses thread execution to commit store buffers. In order to have deterministic results, these points should be selected deterministically. In other words, execution of threads should be paused at the exact same instructions in different runs of a program. These termination points are called *quantum boundaries* in this paper. This section describes the quantum formation algorithm and how GPUDet determines quanta boundaries for each wavefront.

GPUDet divides the program execution into quanta similar to previous work [6, 23, 35]. Each wavefront is allowed to execute a deterministic number of instructions during the parallel mode in each quantum. To avoid deadlocks and to handle atomic operations, a wavefront may end its parallel mode before reaching its instruction limit. The following are the events that can cause a wavefront to end its parallel mode:

Instruction Count. A wavefront ends its parallel mode once it finishes executing a fixed number of instructions. This number is the *quantum size.*

Atomic Operations. Atomic operations are handled in GPUDet like they are in CoreDet. A wavefront ends its parallel mode whenever it reaches an atomic operation to execute the operation in serial mode.

Memory Fences. GPUs provide memory fence instructions for programmers to impose ordering on memory operations. Similar to CoreDet/Calvin, a fence instruction causes a wavefront in GPUDet to end its parallel mode to commit its store buffer in commit mode.

Workgroup Barriers. The GPU architecture provides workgroup-level synchronization operations called workgroup barriers. As discussed in Section 2, threads inside a workgroup cannot exit a workgroup barrier before all other threads in the same workgroup have reached the barrier. Some of these other wavefronts may have exhausted their instruction count limit before reaching the workgroup barrier and are waiting at the global barrier for transition into commit mode. To prevent a deadlock in this case, the wavefront at the workgroup barrier should end its parallel mode to unblock the other wavefronts.

Execution Complete. When a wavefront finishes kernel execution before exhausting its instruction count limit, it ends its parallel mode.

Figure 3 shows the breakdown of these events for our GPU applications (more details in Section 5) running on GPUDet with this baseline quantum formation logic. In this figure, GPUDet is configured to have quantum size = 200 instructions. In ATM, CL and HT, wavefronts usually end their quanta by reaching an atomic operation. In AES, HOTSP, LPS and SRAD, most wavefronts end their quanta at workgroup barriers. In BFSr, BFSf and CFD, wavefronts end more then 50% of their quanta at the end of a kernel program, illustrating the short-running thread challenge discussed in Section 3.2. Collectively, these events constrain the number of instructions a wavefront may execute in each quantum, and thus limit the effectiveness of increasing quantum size to amortize the synchronization overhead at each quantum.

With the above observations, we have designed workgroup-aware logic to determine the end of parallel mode of each quantum.

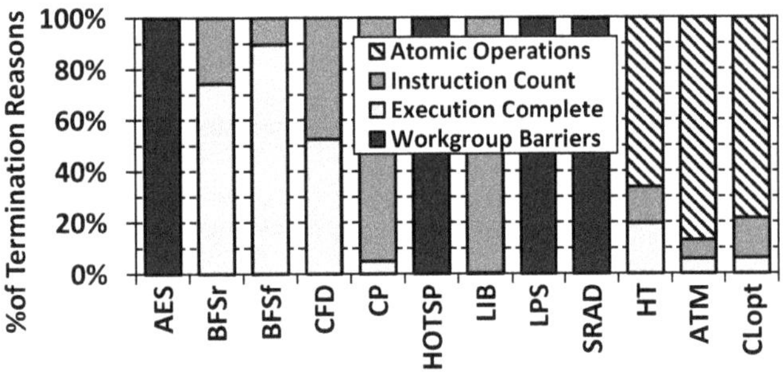

Figure 3. Breakdown of events that causes a wavefront to end its quantum in GPUDet with baseline quantum formation logic.

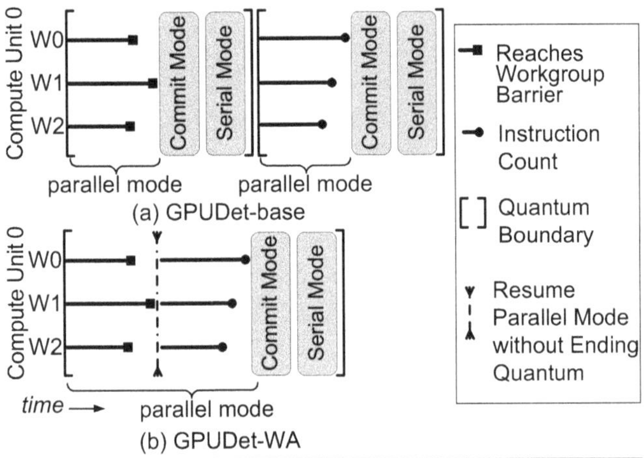

Figure 4. GPUDet quantum formation. (a) GPUDet-base behavior toward quantum termination events. (b) Workgroup-aware quantum formation of GPUDet (GPUDet-WA) allows wavefronts of one workgroup to continue the execution in parallel mode after all reaching workgroup barrier.

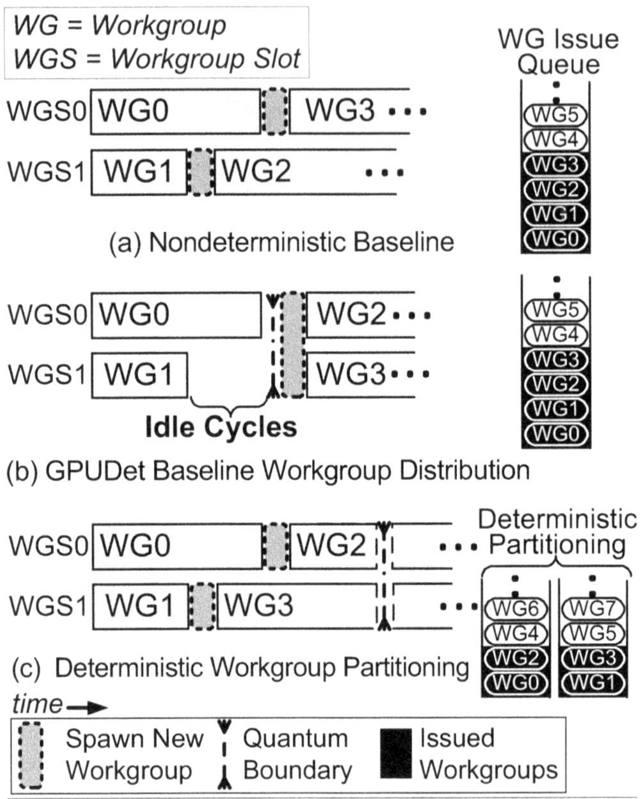

Figure 5. Workgroup distribution

In Section 4.2.1 and Section 4.2.2, we describe this workgroup-aware quantum formation logic with two optimizations. One optimization allows a wavefront to execute beyond a workgroup barrier without ending its parallel mode; the other permits the GPU to issue a new workgroup within a quantum.

4.2.1 Workgroup-Aware Quantum Formation

Our workgroup-aware quantum formation logic (GPUDet-WA) extends the parallel mode illustrated in Figure 2 with an intermediate *wait-for-workgroup* mode. A wavefront advances to this wait-for-workgroup mode after encountering one of the termination events listed in Section 4.2 and waits for other wavefronts in the same workgroup to arrive. In this intermediate mode, each wavefront can deterministically observe the states of other wavefronts in the same workgroup. This allows all wavefronts in a workgroup to collectively decide the next mode.

Figure 4 illustrates how this mechanism reduces synchronization overhead by eliminating an unnecessary quantum boundary introduced by a workgroup barrier. This mechanism, called *Barrier Termination Avoidance* (BTA), allows wavefronts to continue execution past certain quantum boundary formation conditions improving load balance when the quantum size is increased. In this figure W0, W1 and W2 belong to one workgroup. In Figure 4 all wavefronts of the workgroup have been terminated by reaching a workgroup barrier. In the baseline GPUDet (Figure 4(a)), wavefronts will end their quantum and wait for the global synchronization before start of commit mode. However, GPUDet wavefront aware quantum formation (GPUDet-WA) allows the wavefronts to exit the barrier and resume the parallel mode without ending the quantum (BTA). Since reaching all the wavefronts of workgroup is compulsory to exit the barrier, the wavefronts would not be able to exit the barrier if a wavefront in that workgroup stopped execution before the barrier. To avoid the resulting deadlock condition, all of the wavefronts of the workgroup finish the parallel phase if any of them have stopped their parallel mode before the barrier (e.g., reaching instruction limit).

A similar scenario arises when all wavefronts of the workgroup are terminated by reaching the end of their kernels. In this case, GPUDet launches a new workgroup and the execution continues in the parallel phase helping to ameliorate the impact of load imbalance between workgroups and gaining larger quanta.

4.2.2 Deterministic Workgroup Distribution

In Section 2, we described how a hardware workgroup distributor assigns a new workgroup to a compute unit whenever it has a free "slot" (subset of wavefronts with size of workgroup). This distribution of workgroups to compute units occurs both at the start of a kernel launch and when a running workgroup has finished execution.

Since the commit order of wavefronts is defined by how they are assigned to hardware wavefront slots, any change in this assignment will affect the commit order and hence the execution results. To achieve deterministic results, workgroups should be distributed among compute units deterministically. GPUDet has two different schemes to achieve deterministic workgroup distribution.

In the default scheme illustrated in Figure 5(b), GPUDet spawns workgroups only at the start of each quantum. The state of the whole system is deterministic when a quantum starts, so when employing this policy the workgroup distributor has deterministic information about free workgroup slots. To ensure determinism, workgroups are assigned to free slots deterministically based on hardware slot ID. To achieve this, GPUDet enters a special *work distribution mode* right before entering the parallel mode. Workgroups are spawned only in this work distribution mode. All wavefronts stay in this mode until the workgroup distributor finishes assigning all free workgroup slots on all compute units with new workgroups. A deterministic set of free slots and of remaining workgroups results in spawning a deterministic set of workgroups.

Although implementation of the default workgroup distribution scheme in GPUDet is simple, it performs poorly when the kernel launch consists of short-running threads. If new workgroups are only issued in work distribution mode, then the number of instructions executed by a wavefront in one quantum will be limited by the amount of work per workgroup. This leads to load imbalance when some workgroups have more work than others.

To address this problem, we have proposed a *Deterministic Workgroup Partitioning* technique (DWP) that allows workgroups to be issued deterministically in the middle of parallel mode. To prevent nondeterministic workgroup distribution inside parallel mode, GPUDet partitions the issue-pending workgroups among hardware workgroup slots before starting parallel mode. Each workgroup slot can only be replenished with the workgroups in its partition. As workgroup partitioning is done in a deterministic state (at the start of each quantum round), the final workgroup partitioning is deterministic.

4.3 Per-Wavefront Store Buffer

In GPUDet, each wavefront has a private store buffer that contains all of its global memory writes from the parallel mode in the current quantum. The store buffer is located in the private memory of the wavefront, cached by the L1 data cache and written back to off-chip DRAM. It has been observed that in GPU kernel programs, data written to global memory is rarely accessed by the writer thread/wavefront again [19]. This insight suggests organizing the store buffer as a linear write log. Each entry in this write log represents a coalesced global memory write to a coalesced memory access size -128-Byte- chunk. It has an address field indicating the destination location of the chunk, a data field, and a 128-bit byte mask to indicate the valid portion in the data field. The store buffer has a Bloom filter that summarizes the addresses updated in the write log. Each coalesced global memory read in parallel mode first queries the Bloom filter with its chunk address. A hit in the Bloom filter triggers a linear search through the write log; a miss redirects the global memory read to the normal access sequence.

The cost of using a large Bloom filter to reduce false positives is amortized with a wavefront-shared store buffer. A 1024-bit Bloom filter only takes 8kB of storage per compute unit (assuming 48 wavefronts per unit). The Bloom filter of each wavefront can be stored in the register file space allocated to the wavefront. This eliminates any need for permanent storage at the expense of extra register file bandwidth and capacity.

4.4 Parallel Commit of Store Buffers

GPUDet commits the store buffers from all wavefronts into the global memory in the commit mode to allow wavefronts to communicate deterministically. We use the deterministic parallel commit algorithm used in CoreDet [6]. This algorithm tags the entries from the store buffer from a wavefront with a deterministic ID. This ID defines the commit order of this wavefront with respect to the other wavefronts. The wavefronts can attempt to commit the entries in their store buffers in parallel. The algorithm uses the deterministic ID to determine the final writer, in commit order, to each memory location, and guarantees that the location contains the value written by this wavefront after the commit mode. Currents GPUs have non-coherent private caches. To avoid reading stale data GPUDet flushes the L1 data caches after the commit mode. Supporting cache coherency on GPUs [39] would eliminate this overhead.

While CoreDet implemented this algorithm in software using fine-grained locks, we recognized that this algorithm is analogous to the Z-Buffer algorithm that controls the visibility of overlapped polygons in graphics rendering. GPUDet adopts the Z-Buffer Unit for graphics rendering to implement a hardware accelerated version of the deterministic parallel commit algorithm.

Currently, no GPU vendors have exposed any instruction for using the Z-Buffer Unit directly in general purpose programming models like CUDA and OpenCL. We believe exposing this unit in general purpose programming model will not be expensive in terms of area or complexity.

4.4.1 Z-Buffer Unit

Z-Buffer algorithm is designed to control the visibility of overlapped 3D objects displayed on screen. In graphics rendering, 3D objects are represented by triangles that are transformed according to a given camera view to be displayed. Each pixel rendered from a triangle is assigned a depth value representing its logical order with respect to pixels from other triangles. These depth values are stored in a set of memory locations called the *Z-Buffer*. A specialized hardware unit in the GPU, which we call the *Z-Buffer Unit*, manages the Z-Buffer. Using the depth values in the Z-Buffer, the Z-Buffer Unit prevents overlapped triangles from updating the colors of the pixels that have been updated by a foreground triangle. The Z-Buffer Unit allows out-of-order writes to produce a deterministic result. Namely, each pixel on the screen displays the color of the foremost triangle covering that pixel regardless of the order of the triangle updates.

There is little publicly-available information regarding the internal architecture of Z-Buffer Unit in current GPUs. The Z-Buffer Unit evaluated in this paper is inspired by the details disclosed in a patent by ATI Technologies [43]. As shown in Figure 1, there is a Z-Buffer Unit in each memory partition, each responsible for servicing the color update requests to the memory locations managed by the partition. Each Z-Buffer Unit contains a *request buffer* for keeping the status of the incoming requests. Each request contains a 128-byte aligned address to the chunk of pixels it attempts to update, together with 32 color values and 32 depth values. It also has a 128-bit byte mask indicating the valid values in the color update request. A color update request first tries to retrieve the latest depth values for its pixels from a cache for the depth values, called the *Z-cache*. The depth values from the request are then compared against the retrieved depth values. The Z-Buffer Unit then updates the color of the pixels that passes the comparison by sending write requests to the L2 cache, and updating the depth values in the Z-cache. A request that misses at the Z-cache allocates a block in the cache, locks the block and defers its comparison until the depth values are fetched. Requests hitting at a locked block are deferred similarly. The Z-Buffer Unit overlaps multiple color update requests to tolerate the Z-cache miss latency.

4.4.2 Deterministic Parallel Commit using Z-Buffer

To adopt the Z-Buffer Units for deterministic parallel commit of store buffers, GPUDet allocates a corresponding Z-Buffer for each writable global memory buffer. The allocation routine co-locates both depth and data of a memory location at the same memory partition. In commit mode, each wavefront publishes the entries in its store buffer by traversing through the linear write log. From each entry, it generates a color update request containing the buffered data, with the depth equal to the logical quantum ID concatenated with its hardware wavefront ID:

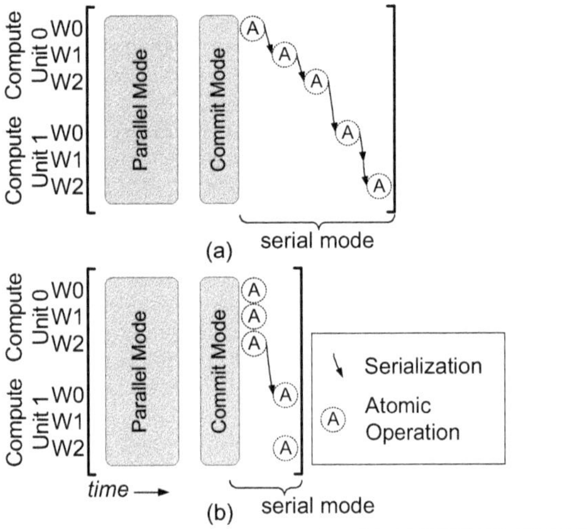

Figure 6. Serial mode in GPUDet. (a) Serializing execution of all atomic operations in GPUDet-base. (b) Overlapping execution time of atomic operations from each compute unit by GPUDet.

$$Depth\_value = -(quantum\_id \times 2^m) + wavefront\_id$$

Here, m is number of bits needed to represent the maximum number of wavefronts that can run concurrently on the hardware. We include the logical quantum ID in the depth to ensure that data from an earlier quantum is always overwritten by memory updates from a later quantum. Without the logical quantum ID, the depth values for all writeable locations in global memory must be reset to the largest positive integer at every quantum boundaries. With the quantum ID, GPUDet amortizes this overhead across a large number of quanta by resetting the Z-buffer only when the ID overflows.

4.5 Compute Unit Level Serialization

In serial mode, the wavefronts execute atomic operation in a deterministic serial order, with the operations updating the global memory directly. Each wavefront executes only one atomic operation in serial mode. Each atomic operation can take 100s of cycles to execute in the GPU's throughput-optimized memory subsystem. Our evaluation in Section 5.2.3 shows that this naive, wavefront-level serialization (W-Ser) significantly slows down applications that use atomic operations.

To recapture parallelism, GPUDet exploits the point-to-point ordering guaranteed by our GPU memory model and common in network-on-chip designs [44] to overlap the execution of atomic operations within a compute unit (CU-Ser). As long as the interconnection network guarantees point-to-point ordering, atomic operations from the same compute unit to the same memory partition will arrive in the original order. With little if any potential performance gain at stake, the memory partitions do not reorder accesses to the same memory location. By resetting the wavefront scheduler in each compute unit at the start of serial mode, GPUDet forces the unit to issue its atomic operations in a deterministic order. This order is preserved by the point-to-point ordering in the GPU memory subsystem. On the other hand, since there is no guaranteed ordering between requests from different cores, GPUDet has to serialize memory operations from different compute units.

Figure 6 demonstrates how this optimization reduces serialization overhead in GPUDet by eliminating serialization within each compute unit. In Figure 6(a), the atomic operations from all workgroup are executed serially. In Figure 6(b), each compute unit overlaps execution of their wavefronts in serial phase, so the serialization overhead is reduced by a factor of number of wavefronts in the compute unit.

4.6 Limitations

The current design of GPUDet does not enforce determinism in the use local memory (or shared memory in NVIDIA terminology). Local memory accesses update the on-chip scratch-pad memory directly and rely on the application to remove data-races via workgroup barriers. The wavefront scheduler at each compute unit can be modified to issue wavefronts in deterministic order. This modified scheduler will provide deterministic execution for local memory accesses even in the presence of data-race. We leave proper support for deterministic local memory accesses as future work.

Since the current Z-buffer design binds each 32-bit color pixel in memory with a depth value, the Z-buffer-based parallel commit algorithm is not directly applicable to applications with byte-granularity writes. An intermediate solution, without modifying the Z-Buffer Unit, is to commit (only) the store buffer entries with byte-granularity writes in the serial mode. We leave evaluation of this as future work. Note that the per-wavefront store buffer is already designed to support byte-granularity accesses. Each store buffer entry contains a 128-bit mask indicating the modified bytes, and the Bloom filter is only responsible for identifying accesses to the same 128-byte chunk.

5. Evaluation

We extended GPGPU-Sim 3.0.2 [5] to model a nondeterministic GPU architecture by randomizing the interconnect injection order of requests from different compute units. We evaluate the performance impact of GPUDet on a set of CUDA/OpenCL benchmarks (listed in Table 1) from Rodinia[14], Bakhoda et al.[5] and Fung et al.[19]. We ran each benchmark to completion. We do not exclude any benchmarks because of poor performance. We do exclude one benchmark that assumes workgroups are spawned in ascending ID order, and five benchmarks that contain hard-to-eliminate byte-granularity writes. We include a version of cloth simulation (CLopt) with a GPU-optimized work distribution scheme that transforms the non-coalesced memory accesses into coalesced accesses. This optimized version performs 30% faster than the original one on the nondeterministic baseline architecture. On GPUDet, this optimization significantly reduces the number of entries in the per-wavefront store buffers, lowering the overhead of each write-log search. It also generates fewer write-log searches by eliminating the aliased read-write accesses within a wavefront accessing different bytes in the same 128-bytes. These two effects cause CLopt to perform significantly better than CL on GPUDet (Section 5.3.1). We also include the version of BFS graph traversal with data-races (BFSr) from Section 1.1 as well as the corrected version (BFSf) from Rodinia [14]. Both BFSr and BFSf are modified to use 32-bit boolean flags to eliminate byte-granularity writes.

We used GPU-Racey (described in Section 2.3) to verify our nondeterminism extension to GPGPU-Sim, and to verify that our model of GPUDet can provide deterministic execution under this nondeterministic simulation framework.

Our modified GPGPU-Sim is configured to model a Geforce GTX 480 (Fermi) GPU [32] with the configuration parameters distributed with GPGPU-Sim 3.0.2. In our default GPUDet configuration, each Z-Buffer Unit runs at 650MHz, has a 16kB Z-cache, and a 16 entry request buffer. The per-wavefront store buffer uses a 1024-bit bloom filter, implemented with a Parallel Bloom Filter [37] with 4 sub-arrays each indexed with a different hash function. This default configuration assumes that each global barrier between parallel, commit, and serial modes in GPUDet takes zero cycles. Section 5.3.4 investigates the sensitivity of GPUDet's performance to various Z-cache sizes, smaller store buffer bloom fil-

Table 1. Benchmarks

Name	Abbr.
Without Atomic Operations	
AES Cryptography [5]	AES
BFS Graph Traversal (with Data-Race) [5]	BFSr
BFS Graph Traversal (Race-Free) [14]	BFSf
Computational Fluid Dynamics Solver [14]	CFD
Coulumb Potential [5]	CP
HotSpot [14]	HOTSP
LIBOR [5]	LIB
3D Laplace Solver [5]	LPS
Speckle Reducing Anisotropic Diffusion [14]	SRAD
With Atomic Operations	
Cloth Simulation [19]	CL
Cloth Simulation (Optimized)	CLopt
Hash Table [19]	HT
Bank Account [19]	ATM

ters, and higher global barrier latencies. Our modified version of GPGPU-Sim and the benchmarks are available online [1].

5.1 Overall Performance

To evaluate our system, we compare the execution time of the benchmarks on a baseline nondeterministic architecture (NONDET) and the optimized version of GPUDet. We configure the quantum size to 200 instructions. We increment the instruction count whenever a wavefront executes an instruction, regardless of how many threads in the wavefront execute that instruction. Figure 7 shows the total execution time of each application with GPUDet, normalized to execution time on a nondeterministic architecture. Our deterministic model causes about 105% performance penalty on average. The execution time of each application is broken down into time spent in parallel, commit and serial modes. Wavefronts spend the most time in parallel mode. We discuss the sources of performance overhead in parallel mode below. As discussed in Section 4.5, GPUDet only serializes the execution of atomic operations: applications without atomic operations (all except CLopt, HT, ATM) skip serial mode entirely.

We have found that some applications (CP, AES) perform slightly better with deterministic execution. A deeper inspection reveals that our workgroup distribution algorithm (Section 4.2.2) results in a more even distribution of workgroups compared to the baseline architecture. The baseline architecture tries to find the first free hardware slot to spawn a workgroup. This mechanism can cause uneven distribution at the very end of a kernel launch when all workgroups of one compute unit finish their executions within a short period. In this case, all remaining workgroups are assigned to the sole available compute unit. When other compute units become available, no workgroups are left to be assigned, and the compute units are underutilized (a similar observation was noted by Bakhoda et al [5]). For these applications, GPUDet's deterministic workgroup distribution will distribute workgroups more evenly, resulting in a small speedup.

5.2 Impact of GPUDet Optimizations

This section provides data to evaluate our optimization techniques discussed in Section 4.

5.2.1 Quantum Formation

To assess our proposed optimization techniques for quantum formation (Section 4.2) we implemented three versions of GPUDet shown in Figure 8. In the GPUDet-base configuration all optimizations are disabled. In the GPUDet-WA(BTA) the workgroup barrier optimization technique (Section 4.2.1) is enabled, allowing workgroups to synchronize without a quantum boundary. Finally, the GPUDet-WA(BTA+DWP) version additionally allows new workgroups to be spawned in parallel mode by deterministically partitioning of the workgroups (DWP) among workgroup slots (Section 4.2.2).

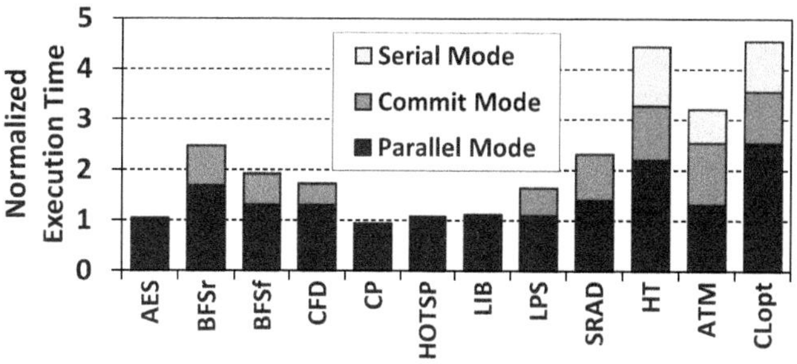

Figure 7. Breakdown of execution cycles. Normalized to NONDET execution time.

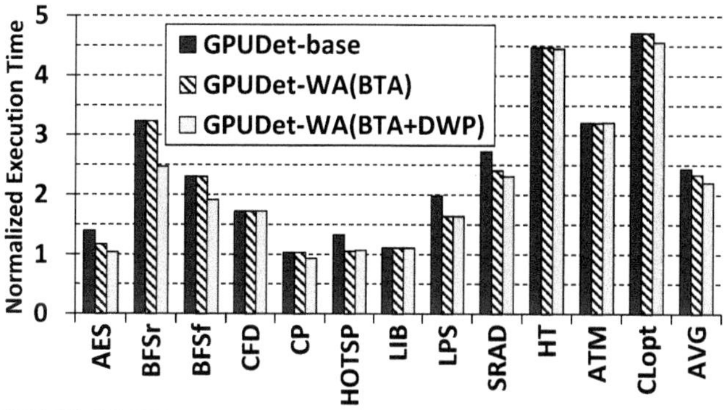

Figure 8. Performance impact of Barrier Termination Avoidance (BTA) and Deterministic Workgroup Partitioning (DWP) techniques. Bars Normalized to NONDET execution time.

Figure 8 shows that the barrier termination avoidance technique decreases the execution time by 4% on average over GPUDet-base. As expected, this improvement lies mostly with benchmarks that have frequent synchronization barriers (AES, HOTSP, LPS, SRAD). Figure 3 shows that encountering workgroup barriers is the dominant cause of quantum termination for these applications. Our experiments confirm that activating the barrier termination avoidance technique (GPUDet-WA(BTA)) forms 3.8× fewer quanta in these four benchmarks, improving their performance by 20% on average.

Figure 8 shows that applications with small kernel functions (BFSr, BFSf, CFD) benefit from spawning workgroups in parallel mode. Figure 3 confirms that most of the quanta in BFSr, BFSf and CFD are terminated by reaching the end of the kernel. The ability to start new workgroups deterministically in parallel mode (GPUDet-WA(BTA+DWP)) speeds up these applications by 19% on average.

5.2.2 Parallel Commit using Z-Buffer Unit

To evaluate the Z-Buffer Unit parallel commit algorithm, we implemented a lock-based version of committing the store buffer. The lock-based version simulates the software-based deterministic parallel commit algorithm proposed in CoreDet [6]. The algorithm locks the chunk of memory that corresponds to the store buffer entry address using atomic operations and performs the logical order priority comparisons and global memory updates in a mutually exclusive section. Although it has been reported that atomic operations contending for the same memory location can be up to 8.4× slower than non-atomic store operations in the Fermi architecture [40], in our evaluation we do *not* model this extra slowdown

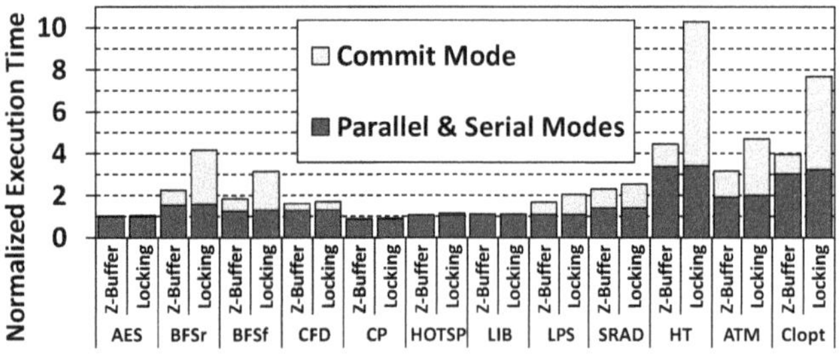

Figure 9. Execution time comparison of committing the store buffer between the Z-Buffer Unit parallel commit and the lock-based algorithms

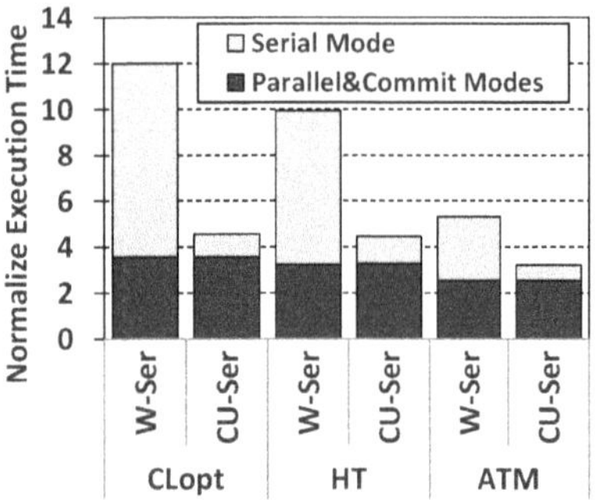

Figure 10. Execution time comparison between wavefront level (W-Ser) and compute unit level (CU-Ser) serialization of atomic operations (Section 4.5). Normalized to NONDET execution time

for the additional atomic operations required by the lock-based version.

Figure 9 shows the normalized execution time for both of the store buffer committing algorithms. The Z-Buffer Unit commit algorithm improves performance by 60% on average. Since spinning for a lock in compute units generates significantly more global memory accesses, it is expected that the applications with more accesses (e.g. HT) achieve more performance improvement by exploiting the Z-Buffer Unit commit algorithm. Figure 9 shows that the execution time of commit mode is decreased by 2.3× using the Z-Buffer Unit for the HT benchmark.

5.2.3 Serial Mode Optimization

Figure 10 evaluates the performance overhead of serial mode in GPUDet. Since only atomic operations are serialized, we omit benchmarks without atomic operations. W-Ser (wavefront level serialization) is the GPUDet-base configuration which serializes execution of all atomic operations. In CU-Ser (compute unit serialization), serialization is only performed among compute units by executing the atomic operations of a single compute unit in parallel. CU-Ser decreases overhead of serial mode by 6.1× for these applications.

5.3 Sensitivity Analysis

This section explores the performance impact of varying different GPUDet design parameters.

5.3.1 Quantum Size and Store Buffer Overhead

In this section we evaluate the effect of quantum size on performance. For better insight, we separate out the time spent in store buffer operations. Store buffer operations entail appending entries to store buffers for stores, and traversing store buffers for reply-

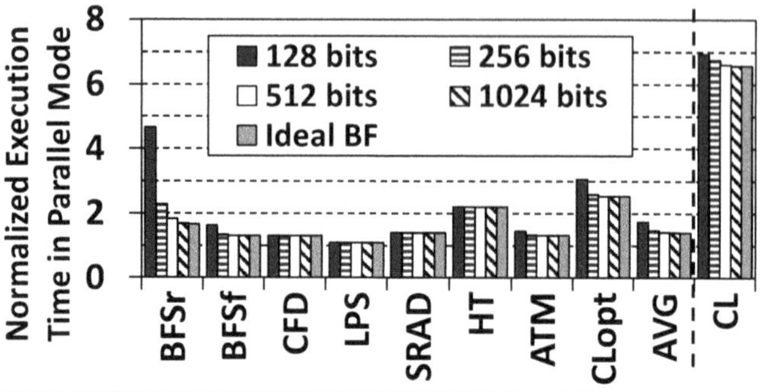

Figure 12. Execution cycles in parallel mode for various sizes of Bloom filter, normalized to NONDET execution. The AVG bar shows the average among all our benchmarks.

ing to loads. Figure 11 shows the execution time of GPUDet with quantum sizes of 100, 200, 600 and 1000 instructions.

Increasing quantum size has three kinds of effects on applications. For applications that have few stores to global memory (AES, CP, HOTSP and LIB) larger quanta improves performance. By increasing quantum size, we reduce the number of quantum boundaries, each of which involves expensive global synchronization.

For applications with frequent accesses to global memory (BFSr and BFSf), performance is degraded with increasing quantum size, because larger quanta lead to larger store buffers. Because GPUDet uses a linear write log traversal, load instructions hitting in store buffer must perform longer searches. Increasing the quantum size also has a side effect on the BFS benchmark. Since this benchmark is not work optimal [27] (it may do each task several times), the number of executed instructions varies in different configurations. In this application the number of redundant tasks depends on how frequently the execution results of each thread become visible to the other threads. Enlarging quantum size causes results to be visible less frequently, BFS runs more redundant tasks which decreases performance. Our experiments reveal that the number of executed instructions increases by 26% when the quantum size increases from 200 to 1000.

For the CL benchmark, the performance overhead of the linear write log is highly affected by the size of the quantum. We realized that in the Integrator, WriteBack and Driver Solver kernels [12] of this benchmark work is distributed block-wise among the threads, so wavefronts generate uncoalesced memory accesses. As described in Section 4.3, uncoalesced accesses generate many extra entries in the store buffer. Furthermore, due to Bloom filter aliasing, uncoalesced accesses result in unnecessary log traversals for load operations (Section 5.3.2). By using an interleaved distribution of work among the threads, we eliminated uncoalesced memory accesses in the CLopt application. Since eliminating uncoalesced accesses to the global memory is profitable for general GPU applications and it does not need substantial changes to CL source code, we have only included the optimized version of CL in our overall average.

5.3.2 Bloom Filter

Figure 12 evaluates the effect of Bloom filter size on performance. Since the Bloom filter configuration does not affect commit and serial modes, we present only the execution time of parallel mode. Figure 12 shows the execution time of the GPUDet architecture with 128, 256, 512 and 1024-bit Bloom filters, and an ideal Bloom filter which has no false positives. We only present the execution time of individual applications that use the store buffer frequently, but the average is for all our workloads. Figure 12 shows that for most of the applications (except BFSr and CL) a 256-bit Bloom fil-

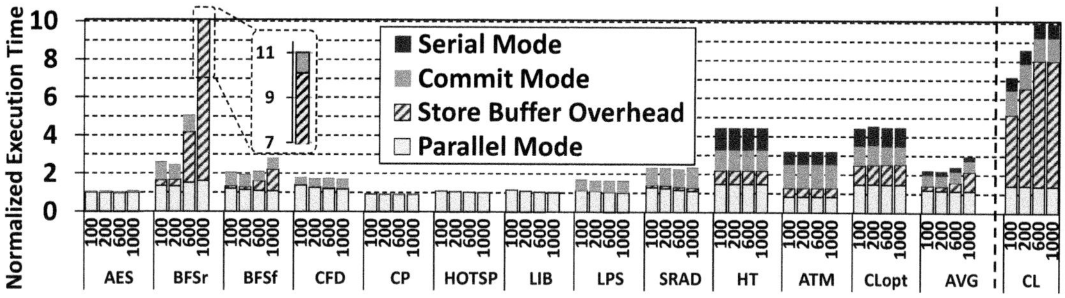

Figure 11. Sensitivity of GPUDet to quantum size. Execution time is normalized to NONDET. The unoptimized version of CL is not included in the average.

ter performs as well as ideal. Increasing Bloom filter size for BFSr reduces execution time because of a high number of store buffer entries in each quantum. For CL, because of the large number of uncoalesced accesses, the store buffer contains many 128B entries with sparsely-populated data portions. The large number of entries causes many loads to perform unnecessary log traversals.

5.3.3 Z-Buffer Unit

We assess the sensitivity of GPUDet to the size of the Z-cache (Section 4.4.1) by adjusting the size of cache for each memory partition from 8KB to 128KB. As expected, execution time decreases with increasing Z-cache size. However, since wavefronts spend most of their execution time in parallel and serial modes, the execution time decreases by less than 3% when the Z-cache is enlarged from 8KB to 128KB.

5.3.4 Global Synchronization Overhead

GPUDet needs global synchronization between each execution mode. We analysed the sensitivity of GPUDet to the cost of global synchronization. Our data illustrates that the overall performance degradation with a 100 cycles synchronization overhead is negligible. However increasing the overhead to 1000 cycles reduces overall performance by 22% over the instantaneous synchronization model.

6. Related Work

The most highly-related work to GPUDet are proposals for providing deterministic execution of general CPU programs [4, 6, 7, 16, 23, 31, 35]. These schemes provide determinism for general multithreaded code on commodity [4, 6, 7, 31, 35] or modified general-purpose multicore CPUs [16, 23]. A naive translation of these schemes to a GPU architecture would be highly inefficient due to the massive numbers of threads involved. For example, the global barriers inherent in many deterministic execution schemes ([4, 7, 16, 23, 31]) would not scale well with 1000s of threads. Kendo's [35] more scalable approach provides determinism for data-race-free programs only, which would scale better in a GPU environment but also reneges on many of the debugging benefits of other determinism techniques that can handle data races.

There has also been extensive work on deterministic programming languages ([9, 10, 13, 18, 36, 41]). Programs written in these languages are deterministic by construction, and incur little runtime overhead during execution at the expense of a restricted programming model. SHIM [18] is a deterministic version of MPI that provides determinism for message-passing programs. NESL [9] and Data Parallel Haskell [13] are pure functional languages that support data-parallel operations which are deterministic and implicitly parallel. Jade [36] is an imperative language that relies on programmer-supplied annotations to extract parallelism automatically while preserving sequential (and deterministic) semantics. StreamIt [41] is a language for streaming computations that enforces determinism by restricting communication between parallel stream kernels to occur only via FIFOs, though a later version of StreamIt allowed for out-of-band control messages that could flow both upstream and downstream without breaking determinism [42]. Deterministic Parallel Java [10] is a version of Java augmented with a type-and-effect system that proves non-interference between parallel fork-join tasks. None of these languages are directly applicable to current GPU programming models, which support a rich set of synchronization primitives via atomic operations on global memory.

A number of projects have looked at improving GPU programmability through hardware or software mechanisms. Kilo TM [19] showed that transactional memory can be incorporated into the GPU programming model at low cost. GRace [46] proposed a race detector for GPU programs, achieving low overhead via a combination of static analysis and runtime instrumentation. Boyer and Skadron [11] describe a GPU emulator that detects race conditions and bank conflicts for CUDA programs, though the emulation overheads are quite high compared to native execution. The PUG system [28] and GPUVerify [8] leverage the compact nature of GPU kernels to perform static race detection, occasionally requiring annotations from programmers to avoid false positives.

7. Conclusion

Nondeterminism in parallel architectures hampers programmers' productivity significantly as bugs can no longer be reproduced easily. We believe this non-reproducibility problem presents a key challenge to GPU software development, discouraging use of GPUs in broader range of applications.

In this paper we presented GPUDet, a proposal for supporting deterministic execution on GPUs. GPUDet exploits deterministic aspects of the GPU architecture to regain performance. Specifically, it uses the inherent determinism of the SIMD hardware in GPUs to provide deterministic interaction among threads within a wavefront. This amortizes the complexity of store buffers required to isolate the execution of each wavefront and works seamlessly with the existing SIMT execution model in GPUs. GPUDet uses a workgroup-aware quantum formation scheme that allows wavefronts in parallel mode to coordinate via workgroup barriers and to accept work from a deterministic workgroup distributor. GPUDet also extends the Z-Buffer Unit, an existing GPU hardware unit for graphics rendering, to deterministically commit store buffers in parallel. Finally, GPUDet eliminates the serialization required among atomic operations from the same compute unit by exploiting the implicit point-to-point ordering in the GPU memory subsystem.

Our simulation results indicate that these optimizations allow GPUDet to perform comparably against a nondeterministic baseline, despite running GPU kernels with thousands of threads. Our characterization of sources of overhead for deterministic execution on GPUs provides insights for further optimizations.

Acknowledgments

The authors would like to thank Inderpreet Singh, Tim Rogers, Henry Wong and the anonymous reviewers for their insightful feedback. We also thank Ayub Gubran for his work on developing the functional model for the Z-Buffer Unit in our simulator. This research was funded in part by grants from Advanced Micro Devices Inc., Qualcomm Inc., and the Natural Sciences and Engineering Research Council of Canada. Wilson W. L. Fung is supported by NVIDIA Graduate Fellowship Program.

References

[1] http://www.ece.ubc.ca/~aamodt/GPUDet.

[2] *White Paper — AMD Graphics Cores Next (GCN) Architecture*. AMD, June 2012.

[3] D. Arnold et al. Stack Trace Analysis for Large Scale Debugging. In *IPDPS*, 2007.

[4] A. Aviram, S.-C. Weng, S. Hu, and B. Ford. Efficient system-enforced deterministic parallelism. In *OSDI*, 2010.

[5] A. Bakhoda et al. Analyzing CUDA Workloads Using a Detailed GPU Simulator. In *ISPASS*, 2009.

[6] T. Bergan, O. Anderson, J. Devietti, L. Ceze, and D. Grossman. CoreDet: A Compiler and Runtime System for Deterministic Multithreaded Execution. In *ASPLOS*, 2010.

[7] T. Bergan, N. Hunt, L. Ceze, and S. D. Gribble. Deterministic Process Groups in dOS. In *OSDI*, 2010.

[8] A. Betts, N. Chong, A. F. Donaldson, S. Qadeer, and P. Thomson. GPUVerify: a verifier for GPU kernels. In *Proceedings of the 27th Annual ACM SIGPLAN Conference on Object-Oriented Programming, Systems, Languages, and Applications (OOPSLA'12)*. ACM, 2012.

[9] G. Blelloch. NESL: A Nested Data-Parallel Language (Version 3.1). Technical report, Carnegie Mellon University, Pittsburgh, PA, 2007.

[10] R. L. Bocchino, Jr., V. S. Adve, D. Dig, S. V. Adve, S. Heumann, R. Komuravelli, J. Overbey, P. Simmons, H. Sung, and M. Vakilian. A Type and Effect System for Deterministic Parallel Java. In *OOPSLA*, 2009.

[11] M. Boyer, K. Skadron, and W. Weimer. Automated Dynamic Analysis of CUDA Programs. In *Third Workshop on Software Tools for MultiCore Systems*, 2008.

[12] A. Brownsword. Cloth in OpenCL, 2009.

[13] M. M. T. Chakravarty, R. Leshchinskiy, S. Peyton Jones, G. Keller, and S. Marlow. Data Parallel Haskell: A Status Report. In *DAMP*, 2007.

[14] S. Che, M. Boyer, J. Meng, D. Tarjan, J. W. Sheaffer, S.-H. Lee, and K. Skadron. Rodinia: A Benchmark Suite for Heterogeneous Computing. In *IISWC*, 2009.

[15] B. W. Coon et al. United States Patent #7,353,369: System and Method for Managing Divergent Threads in a SIMD Architecture (Assignee NVIDIA Corp.), April 2008.

[16] J. Devietti, B. Lucia, L. Ceze, and M. Oskin. DMP: Deterministic Shared Memory Multiprocessing. In *ASPLOS*, 2009.

[17] J. Devietti, J. Nelson, T. Bergan, L. Ceze, and D. Grossman. RCDC: A Relaxed Consistency Deterministic Computer. In *ASPLOS*, 2011.

[18] S. A. Edwards and O. Tardieu. SHIM: A Deterministic Model for Heterogeneous Embedded Systems. In *EMSOFT*, 2005.

[19] W. W. L. Fung, I. Singh, A. Brownsword, and T. M. Aamodt. Hardware Transactional Memory for GPU Architectures. In *MICRO-44*, 2011.

[20] W. Fung et al. Dynamic Warp Formation and Scheduling for Efficient GPU Control Flow. In *MICRO*, 2007.

[21] P. Harish and P. J. Narayanan. Accelerating Large Graph Algorithms on the GPU Using CUDA. In *HiPC*, 2007.

[22] M. Hill and M. Xu. http://www.cs.wisc.edu/ markhill/racey.html, 2009.

[23] D. Hower, P. Dudnik, M. Hill, and D. Wood. Calvin: Deterministic or Not? Free Will to Choose. In *HPCA*, 2011.

[24] Khronos Group. OpenCL. http://www.khronos.org/opencl/.

[25] S. Laine and T. Karras. High-Performance Software Rasterization on GPUs. In *HPG*, 2011.

[26] G. H. Lars Nyland, John R. Nickolls and T. Mandal. United States Patent #8,086,806: Systems and methods for coalescing memory accesses of parallel threads (Assignee NVIDIA Corp.), April 2011.

[27] C. E. Leiserson and T. B. Schardl. A Work-Efficient Parallel Breadth-First Search Algorithm (or How to Cope with the Nondeterminism of Reducers). In *SPAA*, 2010.

[28] G. Li and G. Gopalakrishnan. Scalable SMT-Based Verification of GPU Kernel Functions. In *FSE*, 2010.

[29] E. Lindholm et al. NVIDIA Tesla: A Unified Graphics and Computing Architecture. *Micro, IEEE*, 2008.

[30] J. Liu, B. Jaiyen, R. Veras, and O. Multu. RAIDR: Retention-Aware Intelligent DRAM Refresh. In *ISCA*, 2012.

[31] T. Liu, C. Curtsinger, and E. D. Berger. DTHREADS: Efficient Deterministic Multithreading. In *SOSP*, 2011.

[32] *NVIDIA's Next Generation CUDA Compute Architecture: Fermi*. NVIDIA, October 2009.

[33] *NVIDIA CUDA Programming Guide v3.1*. NVIDIA Corp., 2010.

[34] *NVML API Reference Manual v3.295.45*. NVIDIA Corp., 2012.

[35] M. Olszewski, J. Ansel, and S. Amarasinghe. Kendo: Efficient deterministic multithreading in software. In *ASPLOS*, 2009.

[36] M. C. Rinard and M. S. Lam. The design, implementation, and evaluation of Jade. *ACM Trans. Program. Lang. Syst.*, 20(3), May 1998.

[37] D. Sanchez, L. Yen, M. D. Hill, and K. Sankaralingam. Implementing Signatures for Transactional Memory. In *MICRO*, 2007.

[38] S. R. Sarangi, B. Greskamp, and J. Torrellas. CADRE: Cycle-Accurate Deterministic Replay for Hardware Debugging. In *DSN*, 2006.

[39] I. Singh, A. Shriraman, W. W. L. Fung, M. O'Connor, and T. M. Aamodt. Cache Coherence for GPU Architectures. In *HPCA*, 2013.

[40] J. A. Stuart and J. D. Owens. Efficient Synchronization Primitives for GPUs. *CoRR*, abs/1110.4623, 2011.

[41] W. Thies, M. Karczmarek, and S. P. Amarasinghe. StreamIt: A Language for Streaming Applications. In *CC '02*, 2002.

[42] W. Thies, M. Karczmarek, J. Sermulins, R. Rabbah, and S. P. Amarasinghe. Teleport Messaging for Distributed Stream Programs. In *PPoPP*, 2005.

[43] T. J. Van Hook. United States Patent #6,630,933: Method and Apparatus for Compression and Decompression of Z Data (Assignee ATI Technologies Inc.), October 2003.

[44] S. Vangal et al. An 80-Tile Sub-100-W TeraFLOPS Processor in 65-nm CMOS. *IEEE Journal of Solid-State Circuits*, 43(1):29–41, Jan. 2008.

[45] H. Wong et al. Demystifying GPU microarchitecture through microbenchmarking. In *ISPASS*, 2010.

[46] M. Zheng, V. T. Ravi, F. Qin, and G. Agrawal. GRace: A Low-Overhead Mechanism for Detecting Data Races in GPU Programs. In *PPoPP*, 2011.

DeNovoND: Efficient Hardware Support for Disciplined Non-Determinism

Hyojin Sung, Rakesh Komuravelli, and Sarita V. Adve
Department of Computer Science
University of Illinois at Urbana-Champaign
{sung12, komuravl, sadve}@illinois.edu

Abstract

Recent work has shown that disciplined shared-memory programming models that provide deterministic-by-default semantics can simplify both parallel software and hardware. Specifically, the DeNovo hardware system has shown that the software guarantees of such models (e.g., data-race-freedom and explicit side-effects) can enable simpler, higher performance, and more energy-efficient hardware than the current state-of-the-art *for deterministic programs*. Many applications, however, contain non-deterministic parts; e.g., using lock synchronization. For commercial hardware to exploit the benefits of DeNovo, it is therefore necessary to extend DeNovo to support non-deterministic applications.

This paper proposes DeNovoND, a system that supports lock-based, disciplined non-determinism, with the simplicity, performance, and energy benefits of DeNovo. We use a combination of distributed queue-based locks and access signatures to implement simple memory consistency semantics for safe non-determinism, with a coherence protocol that does not require transient states, invalidation traffic, or directories, and does not incur false sharing. The resulting system is simpler, shows comparable or better execution time, and has 33% less network traffic on average (translating directly into energy savings) relative to a state-of-the-art invalidation-based protocol for 8 applications designed for lock synchronization.

Categories and Subject Descriptors B.3.2 [*Hardware*]: Memory Structures – Cache memories; Shared memory; C.1.2 [*Processor Architectures*]: Multiple Data Stream Architectures (Multiprocessors) – Parallel processors

Keywords shared memory, cache coherence, disciplined parallelism, memory consistency, non-determinism

1. Introduction

Shared-memory remains a popular programming model among multicore programmers and is the de facto model provided by multicore hardware. It is, however, increasingly evident that unbridled "wild" shared-memory programming environments that allow data races, ubiquitous non-determinism, unstructured parallelism, and complex memory consistency models make programming, debugging, testing, and maintaining software difficult [1, 32]. Recent software research has therefore proposed more *disciplined* shared-memory programming models that retain the advantage of a global address space, but make it easier to write safe parallel programs that are easier to debug, test, and maintain [4–6, 10–12, 14, 18, 19, 30, 39].

At the same time, providing hardware cache coherence and consistency that can scale in a power-efficient manner to hundreds of cores is also a significant challenge. There has recently been a surge in research by academics (see Section 7) and hardware companies [23, 26] to address this challenge in unconventional ways. In particular, the DeNovo hardware project observes that disciplined shared-memory programming models such as mentioned above can drive a holistic rethinking of the multicore memory hierarchy, providing more complexity-, performance-, and power-efficient hardware than the state-of-the-art *for deterministic programs* [17]. This paper shows that the benefits of disciplined programming and DeNovo can be extended to non-deterministic programs as well.

DeNovo has used Deterministic Parallel Java (DPJ) as an example disciplined programming model [11] to drive its design. DPJ provides the programmer with a novel region-based type and effects system to convey the read and write side-effects on shared-memory for every method. A type-checked DPJ program is guaranteed deterministic-by-default semantics. That is, unless non-determinism is explicitly requested, DPJ programs appear deterministic and with sequential semantics (the programmer can debug and test such a program as if it were sequential). Even when non-determinism is explicitly requested, DPJ provides strong safety guarantees; e.g., data-race-freedom, strong isolation, and sequential composition of deterministic code sections [12]. The DPJ compiler enforces these guarantees by checking that conflicting accesses from two concurrent tasks – the root cause of non-determinism – are always identified (as atomic) and always occur within explicitly marked atomic sections.

DeNovo has so far focused on deterministic programs, and shown that DPJ's information and guarantees can be exploited to provide a simpler and more efficient cache coherence protocol than the state-of-the-art MESI for such programs [17]. Specifically, DeNovo's protocol has the following advantages: (1) The implementation has no transient states and so is much easier to verify (verification is an order of magnitude faster) and much easier to extend (incorporating optimizations did not introduce any protocol state changes). (2) DeNovo does not rely on writer-induced invalidations; it therefore eliminates invalidation message traffic and does not require storage overhead for sharer lists in directories, removing a key source of unscalability. (3) DeNovo keeps coherence state at the granularity at which data is shared and so does not suffer from false sharing (the added state overhead is much less than the reduced directory state). Overall, compared to MESI, DeNovo is much simpler,

ASPLOS '13, March 16–20, 2013, Houston, Texas, USA.

performs comparably or better than MESI, and is more energy-efficient (since it reduces cache misses and network traffic) for a range of deterministic codes.

Although determinism is considered desirable for many application classes, there are many common codes that are non-deterministic or contain parts that are non-deterministic, most commonly through lock synchronization. For example, 21 out of 25 of the PARSEC and SPLASH-2 benchmarks contain locks in some parts. DeNovo currently cannot run such codes.[1] For commercial hardware to be able to exploit the benefits of DeNovo, it is imperative that we develop techniques to support non-deterministic codes with at least as much performance as conventional systems, without losing the benefits of DeNovo.

This paper explores exploiting disciplined programming models to develop simpler and more efficient hardware even for programs that contain non-determinism. We use DPJ's safe non-determinism model (with atomic sections replaced with locks), and show that simple additions to the DeNovo coherence protocol can support such non-determinism without giving up on DeNovo's previous advantages. We call the resulting system DeNovoND.

For deterministic programs, DeNovo achieves its benefits primarily by recognizing that DPJ explicitly provides the regions that could be potentially written in a parallel phase (e.g., DPJ's foreach or cobegin constructs) through its explicit effects. At the start of a new phase, DeNovo's cores execute compiler-inserted self-invalidations to all regions that could have write effects in the previous phase. Their caches therefore now have only valid data. If any of this data is updated in the next phase, DPJ's data-race-freedom guarantee ensures that only the writing core will read that data, ensuring up-to-date values for all reads. These observations eliminate the need for writer-induced invalidations, directories, and false sharing due to cache line driven protocols.

Unlike DeNovo, DeNovoND cannot assume that a parallel phase will have no conflicting accesses among concurrent tasks any more, but it knows that such accesses will be protected by the same lock (this lock may change in a different parallel phase). Further, such accesses are explicitly identified as atomic accesses in DPJ programs. Within a critical section, DeNovoND therefore tracks atomic writes through a signature which is conveyed to the next acquirer of the lock. The acquirer uses the signature to determine which data to invalidate in its cache. The strong guarantees given by DPJ enable an efficient implementation, while still providing freedom to express a variety of non-deterministic algorithms. Underlying the above is an implementation for a lock that does not require directories and a full-fledged MESI protocol – we use a distributed queue based implementation modeled after the Queue-on-Sync-Bit (QOSB) lock [20].

Overall, our system retains the advantages of DeNovo while significantly expanding the class of programs it supports without compromising performance. Specifically, for lock accesses, although DeNovo's coherence protocol state machine is extended to handle the distributed queue, it reuses the state bits from DeNovo's data accesses. For data accesses, again, no new externally visible states are added; the only support needed is a signature per core, the ability to transfer it to the next acquirer, and to use it for self-invalidation at subsequent reads. A bit per word at the L1 cache is used as an optimization. We continue to not have any directories, not have invalidations, and not incur false sharing.

We compared DeNovoND with a state-of-the-art MESI protocol for 11 benchmarks with lock synchronization. 3 of these spent more than 70% of their time in lock acquires, clearly requiring alternate synchronization techniques for reasonable parallel efficiency that are out of the scope of this work. We therefore focus on the remaining 8 benchmarks here, although we report results for the above 3 as well for completeness. We found that DeNovoND performs comparably or slightly better than MESI in terms of execution time. DeNovoND also shows 33% lower network traffic than MESI on average, which directly translates into energy savings. Performance optimizations previously proposed for DeNovo (for cache to cache and flexible granularity data transfer) [17] are applicable to DeNovoND as well without any additional changes, but are orthogonal to this work and not reported here. Thus, DeNovoND allows us to extend the benefits of DeNovo to include lock-based (safe) non-deterministic applications.

Our system shares commonalities with previous software distributed shared memory consistency models such as lazy release consistency [27], entry consistency [7], and scope consistency [22] as well as recent hardware shared-memory work that exploits data-race-freedom such as SARC [25]. However, none of those systems distinguish between deterministic and non-deterministic accesses in a way that is possible with our hardware/software co-designed approach, and so those systems cannot exploit the corresponding optimizations. Section 7 discusses the relationship of our work to prior work in more detail.

While DeNovoND takes a major step in exploiting software discipline in hardware for a larger class of programs, there is still much left to future work and outside the scope of one paper. Section 8 discusses future work to explore how to incorporate other key constructs (e.g., pipelined parallelism), and support more complex codes such as legacy codes and operating systems within this vision.

2. Background

2.1 Deterministic Parallel Java (DPJ)

DPJ is an extension to Java that enforces deterministic-by-default semantics via compile-time type checking [11, 12]. We first discuss DPJ without non-deterministic constructs [11]. DPJ provides parallel constructs of foreach and cobegin to express parallelism in a structured way as in many current languages (we refer to an iteration of a foreach loop or a parallel statement of a cobegin as a task). DPJ provides a new type and effect system for expressing common patterns of imperative, object-oriented programs. The DPJ programmer assigns every object field or array element to a named "region" and annotates every method with read and write "effects" summarizing the regions read and written by that method (a region can be non-contiguous in memory). The compiler uses this information to (i) type-check program operations in the region type system and (ii) ensure that no two parallel tasks interfere (conflict).

DPJ also provides parallel constructs that are potentially non-deterministic; i.e., foreach_nd and cobegin_nd [12]. These constructs allow conflicting accesses between their tasks, but require that such accesses be enclosed within atomic sections, their read and write effect declarations also include the atomic keyword, and their region types be declared as atomic. Note that there continue to be no conflicts allowed between a task from a deterministic parallel construct and any other concurrent (non-deterministic or deterministic) task. The compiler checks that all of the above constraints are satisfied by any type-checked program, again using a simple, modular type checking algorithm.

With the above constraints, DPJ is able to provide the following guarantees: (1) Data-race freedom. (2) Strong isolation of accesses in atomic section constructs and all deterministic parallel constructs; i.e., these constructs appear to execute atomically. (3) Sequential composition for deterministic constructs; i.e., tasks of a deterministic construct appear to occur in the sequential order

[1] The DeNovo work reports results for some of these benchmarks, but the parts with locks were either run sequentially or rewritten or not simulated [17].

implied by the program (even if they contain or are contained within non-deterministic constructs). (4) Determinism-by-default; i.e., any parallel construct that does not contain an explicit non-deterministic construct provides deterministic heap output for a given heap input. The above guarantees are strong – they not only ensure sequential consistency but also allow programmers to reason with very high-level strongly isolated and composable components such as complete foreach constructs and all atomic sections.

Although DPJ supports atomic sections, this paper assumes we can convert them to locks. This is possible because by default we can associate each atomic region with its own lock. For each atomic section, we can acquire locks for each atomic region that it accesses in a predefined order. This can be optimized in several ways; e.g., by coarsening the locks. An implementation of this algorithm is outside the scope of this paper. We therefore use hand inserted locks – for the applications we used, these locks were as provided in the original application.

2.2 DeNovo for Deterministic Codes

DeNovo divides the coherence problem into two parts:

(1) *No stale data:* A read should never see stale data in its private cache(s).

(2) *Locatable up-to-date data:* When a read misses in its private cache(s), it should know where to get an up-to-date copy of the data.

Above, *stale* and *up-to-date* are defined by the memory consistency model (sequential semantics, in our case). For (1), DeNovo recognizes that DPJ explicitly provides the regions that could be potentially written in a parallel phase (each DPJ parallel construct such as cobegin and foreach forms a phase, with an implicit barrier at the join). Before starting a new phase, a core issues compiler-inserted self-invalidations for all regions that could have write effects in the previous phase, eliminating all stale data from its private cache(s).[2] For data updated in the current phase, DPJ's data-race-freedom guarantee ensures that only the writing core will read that data, ensuring up-to-date values for all (private) cache hits. For (2), DeNovo uses a structure called the *registry* to keep track of one up-to-date copy of each cache line. This is analogous to a conventional directory, but unlike the latter, it does not track all sharers of a cache line (eliminating a source of unscalability). With systems with a shared last level cache, the data bank of the cache doubles as the registry storing the data or a pointer to it.

The DeNovo protocol has three states, *Registered*, *Valid*, and *Invalid*. These states are analogous to those in a conventional MSI directory protocol; *Registered* is similar to *M* with the line modified in a private cache and *Valid* is similar to *S*. The DeNovo protocol state transition diagram also resembles typical textbook pictures for MSI. A key difference, however, is that real implementations of MSI have tens of transient states to handle protocol races, introducing significant complexity and making verification difficult. In contrast, DeNovo has no transient states since it assumes race-free software, which eliminates virtually all races from the protocol hardware.

Next we describe the key aspects of the protocol's operation and refer to [17] for more details. For easier exposition, we assume a two level cache hierarchy with a shared L2 without loss of generality, and a line size of one word (this is relaxed below). A read hits in the L1 if the line is *Valid* or *Registered*. A read miss request goes to the registry (the shared L2) and either finds the data there or a pointer to the L1 that contains the data in *Registered* state. In the latter case, the request is routed to the registered data for service.

[2] This requires the cache to store region information as described in [17].

A write to data in *Registered* state at the L1 updates the data. A write to data in *Valid* or *Invalid* state at the L1 immediately transitions the data to *Registered* and updates it (no transients) and generates a registration request (and a writeback if needed). If the data is not registered elsewhere, the L2 immediately registers it and sends an acknowledgment. Otherwise, the L2 records the new registration and forwards the request to the previously registered core to relinquish its registration. Due to the data-race-free guarantee, registration transfer occurs only once in a phase (assuming no task migration, which can also be easily handled [17]), without any danger of protocol races.

Additionally, as an optimization, L1 contains *touched* bits that are set when the corresponding data is read. Due to data-race-freedom, it is guaranteed that no other core will write such data in that phase. Thus, "touched" data is up-to-date and does not need to be invalidated for the next phase. All self-invalidations occur at the end of the phase – regions with write effects in that phase are invalidated unless the data is registered or touched. Touched bits are reset after the invalidation, in preparation for the next phase.

The baseline word-based DeNovo protocol assumes equal address/tag allocation, communication, and coherence granularity, which is the granularity at which data-race-freedom is ensured. This granularity is a word for the applications evaluated. (Details about supporting sub-word (byte) granularity can be found in [17].) DeNovo further observes that any data that is marked *touched* or *Registered* is always up-to-date and can be freely copied from one cache to another without informing anyone (there is no directory tracking sharer lists). Thus, the word-based DeNovo protocol is easily enhanced to operate on larger communication and address/tag allocation granularities, while still maintaining coherence state at the word granularity.

A natural granularity for communication and allocation is a conventional cache line (e.g., 64 bytes), and the corresponding DeNovo protocol is referred to as the line based protocol. Here, a responding cache for a demand request sends a cache line worth of data (potentially with some words marked as invalid) and the valid words in the response message are merged with the local copy of the cache line of the requestor. These words are marked as *Valid*, but not *touched* (the *touched* bit is set when those words are actually read). DeNovoND is designed on top of this line-based protocol.

DeNovo has also explored more flexible communication granularities (more or less than one cache line) and direct L1 to L1 data transfers. These optimizations are simple with DeNovo and do not require any new states, but are difficult to incorporate in conventional protocols because they introduce even more transient states. The same optimizations can be directly applied to DeNovoND as well, again with no new states for DeNovoND. We do not study them here since they are orthogonal to the goal of this paper.

The DeNovo protocol we study additionally implements the optimization of write combining where multiple registration requests to words in a given cache line are combined into one request. This optimization was mentioned, but not implemented, in [17] to reduce write traffic. This optimization is not meaningful for conventional protocols since conventional store requests always operate on a full line while DeNovo registrations are for a word.

3. DeNovoND Design Overview

3.1 Basic Assumptions and Definitions

We assume all synchronization occurs through DPJ's parallel constructs (foreach, cobegin, and their nd versions) and through locks. We assume a barrier at the implicit join associated with the parallel constructs. We say all concurrent tasks of a given parallel construct – loop iterations in a foreach and parallel statements in a cobegin – form a *phase*.

For locks, we assume that an atomic section does not call a parallel construct, as is the case with all our applications. Thus, all operations of an atomic section occur within a single task and are enclosed within a lock acquire and release to the same lock variable (there may be nested locks to different lock variables). We refer to memory operations within such a lock acquire/release pair as occurring in a critical section protected by that lock variable.

For data accesses, we assume the ISA provides a mechanism by which loads and stores can be tagged as accessing atomic regions with atomic effects (e.g., with a bit in the op-code). The DPJ compiler has this information and can generate code with the bit set for such accesses. We refer to such accesses below as *atomic* accesses and to others as *non-atomic* accesses. Note that the former are regular data accesses from atomic sections and are not to be confused with atomic read-modify-writes or the C++ atomic keyword used for synchronization races.

Without loss of generality, we assume a two level cache hierarchy. We also assume a shared L2 cache. DeNovoND can be extended to deeper hierarchies and private last level caches in a straightforward way (similar to DeNovo [17]).

3.2 Memory Consistency Model

For a correct design, we must first understand the constraints imposed by the memory consistency model which specifies what value a read must return.

Informal model: DPJ provides a very strong consistency model. It guarantees sequential consistency and hence a total order over all memory operations (that is consistent with program order). A read must return the value of the last write to its location as defined by this total order. DPJ also enforces additional rules that further constrain this last write for data operations, simplifying reasoning for software and implementation for hardware as follows.

Non-atomic accesses: DPJ ensures that for a non-atomic access, there cannot be a conflicting access by another concurrent task in the same phase. Thus, for a non-atomic read, the last conflicting write is either from its own task or from a task in a previous phase. This is identical to DeNovo and we can use the identical implementation.

Atomic accesses: For atomic accesses as defined above, DPJ allows conflicting accesses among concurrent tasks, but ensures that all such accesses to a given location are in critical sections protected with the same lock. These critical sections must execute atomically, imposing a total order on all conflicting atomic accesses within a phase. A read therefore must return the value from the (unique) last conflicting write from a critical section in the current phase; if such a write does not exist, then the read must return the (unique) last conflicting write from the previous phase.

Formal model: We now state the model more formally. Note that this model is motivated as a specification for hardware and is therefore at a low level, in terms of individual reads and writes. DPJ programmers work at a higher level in terms of composition and serialization of higher level constructs (cobegin, atomic section, etc.) as described in Section 2.1. Our model can be stated in two parts for synchronization and data accesses respectively:

(1) Synchronization accesses are sequentially consistent. This implies a total order between phases and between critical sections to a given lock variable within a phase; this total order is consistent with program order.

(2) For conflicting data accesses, X and Y, we define a *happens-before* relation, denoted $\rightarrow_{hb}$ such that $X \rightarrow_{hb} Y$ iff

Type 1 edge: X's phase precedes Y's phase (by the total order in (1)), or

Type 2 edge: X and Y are in the same task, and X is before Y by program order, or

Type 3 edge: X and Y are atomic accesses in critical sections protected by the same lock variable, and X's critical section precedes Y's critical section (by the total order in (1)).

Then DPJ's guarantees ensure that $\rightarrow_{hb}$ orders all conflicting accesses, and hardware should ensure that a data read returns the value of the last conflicting write in $\rightarrow_{hb}$ order. For a non-atomic read, the last write is always ordered before it by a *type 1* or *type 2* $\rightarrow_{hb}$ edge. For an atomic read, the last write may be ordered before it by a *type 2* or *type 3* edge if such a write exists; otherwise, it is ordered by a *type 1* edge.

3.3 Data Coherence Mechanism

The coherence mechanism must simply ensure that a read returns the value from the write as defined by the consistency model. As with DeNovo, we divide the coherence mechanism into two components:

(1) *No stale data:* A read should never see *non-last* (stale) data in its private cache(s).

(2) *Locatable up-to-date data:* When a read misses in its private cache(s), it should know where to get the *last* (up-to-date) copy of the data.

Above, *last* is precisely defined by the happens-before order. For non-atomic accesses, both components above remain identical to DeNovo since the consistency model requirements are identical. For atomic accesses, the requirements are met as follows.

No stale data: For the first requirement of no stale data, we use self-invalidations as with DeNovo, thereby precluding the need for adding invalidation messages and directories with sharer lists. Additional self-invalidations are needed with DeNovoND only if there are conflicting atomic accesses among concurrent tasks in a phase (otherwise, DeNovo's self-invalidations at the start of a phase suffice). In the case of conflicting atomic accesses among concurrent tasks, we use the happens-before relation to determine *when* and *what* to self-invalidate as follows.

To determine when to self-invalidate, we note that a concurrent conflicting read must be in a critical section itself and must return the value of the last write also in a critical section protected by the same lock in the same phase (type 2 or 3 edge). Thus, it is sufficient to self-invalidate any time between the start of a critical section and an atomic read in that section.

To determine what to self-invalidate, we have several choices. We could invalidate the entire cache (which seems excessive) or only the atomic regions (for which we would need to keep extra state to identify in the cache). An alternative is for each core to update a signature that records all writes to atomic regions, and then to transfer this signature when the lock is acquired by another core. On a first atomic read to a location, the acquiring core needs to check the signature and self-invalidate the location if it is present in the signature. The acquiring core must forward the union of its signature and the signatures it has received to the next acquirer.

Locatable up-to-date data: For the second requirement of finding the value of the last write on a miss, we use ideas similar to DeNovo. On a write to valid or invalid data, the L1 cache sends a registration request to the L2. The registrations are required to complete before the lock release so that conflicting writes from critical sections are serialized in the right order (it is possible to postpone the registration completion until the next lock acquire). A read that misses in the cache simply goes to the registry (L2) to find the up-to-date value.

Thus we continue with only three states in the protocol as before: *Valid*, *Invalid*, and *Registered*. The extra work over DeNovo is to update the signature on atomic writes, send the signature on a lock transfer, and invalidate appropriately on atomic reads. Section 4.1 discusses each of these steps in more detail.

3.4 Distributed Queue-based Locks

Our distributed queue-based lock design is modeled after QOSB [20, 24], where the identities of the cores waiting for a lock are maintained in a queue of pointers distributed across the waiting cores' L1 caches and the L2 cache. All requests to a given lock are serialized at the corresponding shared L2 cache bank. The data portion of the L2 cache entry for a contended lock tracks the last requestor (i.e., the tail of the queue of waiters), referred to as *tailPtr*. When the L2 receives the next request for the lock, it forwards it to the current tail's L1. On receiving such a forwarded request, the L1 checks a bit in its copy of the lock word, called the *Locked* bit, to determine if the lock is still held or was unlocked. In the former case, the L1 stores the requestor's ID in another field of the lock word, referred to as *nextPtr*. In the latter case, the L1 responds to the requestor with its signature and transfers the lock, marking its own lock word *Invalid*. When a core releases a lock, its L1 checks its *nextPtr* – if not null, it transfers the lock (with the signature) to the *nextPtr* core; otherwise, it unsets its *Locked* bit. We allow eviction of lock words from the L1 and L2 caches by reusing the data portion of the lock words in the next level of the memory hierarchy to store lock queue information. This approach relies on using L2 data banks to store (non-data) metadata, which is similar to DeNovo's tracking of registration information for the *Registered* state. Section 4.2 discusses our implementation in more detail.

4. Implementation

This section discusses in detail how DeNovoND implements the memory consistency model and the coherence mechanism described in Section 3 using *access signatures* and the distributed queue-based lock mechanism. We also qualitatively discuss the hardware and performance overheads of the implementation.

4.1 Access Signatures for Coherence of Atomic Accesses

DeNovoND's memory consistency model requires that a read return the value of the last write preceding it, as ordered by the three types of *happens-before* edges described in Section 3. DeNovo already guarantees that a write ordered by a type 1 or type 2 edge is seen at a read (the former through self-invalidations at the start of a new phase and the latter through single core semantics). For a non-atomic read, a write is ordered only through the above two edge types; therefore, DeNovo already provides consistency for such reads. For atomic reads where a previous (atomic) write is ordered by a type 3 edge, however, DeNovoND must provide a new mechanism – it needs to track which data in atomic regions has been modified in a critical section in the current phase, as well as a mechanism to efficiently represent and transfer this information on a successful lock acquire.

We use an "access signature" for the purpose of tracking atomic writes. A signature is a compact representation of a set at the expense of precision. Its main functionality includes element insertion, membership query, and flash clear functions. DeNovoND implements the access signature as a small Bloom filter in hardware [9]. Due to its storage efficiency, simplicity, and low access latency, a hardware Bloom filter has been a popular solution for many areas including networking and transactional memory [13, 16].

For our Bloom filters, the keys are addresses accessed (i.e., atomic regions that have atomic effects in this phase), since we are interested only in modifications made to those addresses. The key domain dynamically changes between cores and phases, as a new set of atomic accesses occurs. To keep the false positive rate of Bloom filter reasonably low, the size of each Bloom filter should be determined based on the average size of the key domain. This turns out to be quite small in our case (256 bits suffice) since we only track atomic accesses in a given phase (later sections discuss

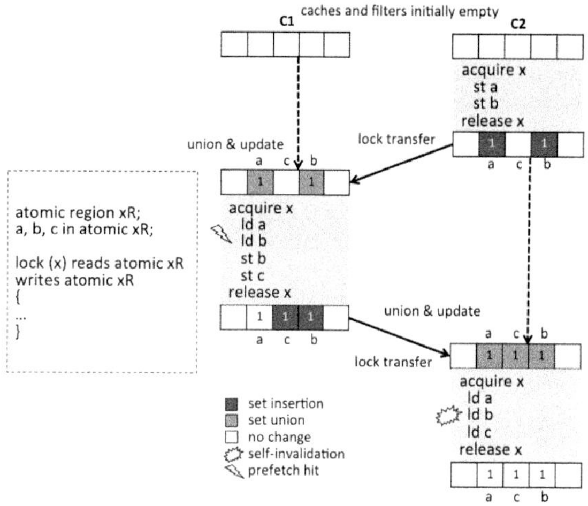

Figure 1: An example of propagating atomic writes using access signatures. Assume *a* and *b* are in the same cache line.

the size in more detail). We conservatively keep one filter per core to track all modifications across different critical sections (with different locks) on the same core. Thus, for a system with *n* cores, we have a total of *n* Bloom filters in the system.

The following uses Figure 1 as a running example to show how DeNovoND uses the Bloom filters. On the left, the figure shows DPJ style code depicting three variables, *a*, *b*, and *c* in atomic region *xR*. It then shows a critical section protected by lock *x* with atomic read and write effects on region *xR*. The right side of the figure shows an execution with two cores, *C1* and *C2*. *C2* acquires the lock for the critical section first, followed by *C1* and then *C2* again. The figure also shows the signatures at each core, assuming a perfect hash function.

On atomic writes: An atomic write (as determined by the op-code of the store instruction as discussed in Section 3) invokes the same cache protocol operations as in DeNovo. That is, if the word is not in *Registered* state at the L1, a registration request is sent to the L2. Additionally, the word is updated right away and any required writeback is sent to the L2 as well.

For DeNovoND, an atomic write additionally inserts the accessed address into its core's Bloom filter. To avoid repeating insertion of the same address to the Bloom filter, we can add an additional bit, called the "dirty bit," to mark a memory location already updated in a given phase. The "dirty bit" is set on the first atomic store request to a word in a phase, and all dirty bits get unset at the end of a phase. If a store finds the dirty bit already set, it means the word is already inserted into the core's Bloom filter and does not need to be inserted again. Since this is purely an optimization, we can piggyback the functionality of a dirty bit on other state bits described below (e.g., the *touched-atomic* bit) – this may result in some extraneous resets, but does not affect correctness and reduces extra state.

Thus, at the end of a critical section, all addresses modified in the section are recorded in the core's filter; i.e., their entries are non-zero. From Figure 1, every store request to *a*, *b*, and *c* in the lightly shaded critical sections updates the Bloom filter on *C1* and *C2*. The second critical section phase on *C2* does not update the Bloom filter since it does not have atomic writes.

On acquire/release: On an acquire, all modifications preceding the release associated with the acquire are made visible to the acquirer by transferring the access signature at the releaser. The releaser compresses and sends the Bloom filter at its core to the acquirer, when transferring the lock. The acquirer, on receiving the Bloom filter, updates its own Bloom filter by making a *union* of its local Bloom filter and the releaser's Bloom filter. Figure 1 shows the resulting Bloom filters at the beginning of each critical section, of which the lightly shaded entries come from the union operation. Note that we only send the signature, not the actual data. On acquire and release points, we also reset the "touched-atomic" and "prefetch" bits (as will be explained in detail below).

On atomic reads: Atomic reads need to conceptually consult the signatures obtained from remote releasers to determine if cached data is valid or stale. If the read is to a word in *Registered* state in the L1, then regardless of the signature state, the word is up-to-date in the cache and the read is a cache hit. If the word is *Invalid* in L1, then a normal read request is sent to L2. If the word is in *Valid* state, then it is also up-to-date if its address does not appear in the access signature. If the word is in *Valid* state and its address hits in the access signature, then it may or may not be up-to-date depending on whether it has been previously read in this critical section.

Specifically, if the word has already been read in this critical section, the previous read brought up-to-date data that is still valid (since no other core can write to the word during the same critical section). We identify this situation by using a *touched-atomic* bit that is set on the first read of the word in a critical section and reset at the release – more precisely, it needs to be reset only when the lock is handed off for another core's acquire (lock hand-off). Thus, a read to a word in *Valid* state with *touched-atomic* bit set is a cache hit.

Another case where a valid word may be up-to-date is when it is obtained as part of a cache line transfer for a demand access to another word in that line. We would like to take advantage of such a prefetch as with conventional cache lines and with DeNovo. If the word comes directly from the L2 or from memory, then it is definitely valid. If it comes from a remote cache, then it is valid if that word was marked as *touched-atomic* or *Registered* in the remote cache. In this case, we can conceptually add another bit called the "prefetch bit" which can be set for prefetched words with the above properties. These bits must be reset on the next lock hand-off or the next acquire, whichever happens first. A read that accesses a valid word with *prefetch* bit set is considered a cache hit. Although the *touched-atomic* and *prefetch* bits are separately motivated, both functions can be achieved by a single bit that we collectively refer to as the *touched-atomic* bit.

In summary, the *touched-atomic* bit of a word is set on the first read of the word in a critical section or for a word prefetched from L2/memory or from a remote L1 in *touched-atomic* or *Registered* state. The bit is reset on an acquire or lock hand-off, including the end of the phase. A read to *Valid* data with *touched-atomic* bit set or with an address that misses in the access signature is considered a hit. Otherwise, the *Valid* data is no longer up-to-date and must be marked invalid and a read miss request is issued.

In Figure 1, assume that variables *a* and *b* are in the same cache line. Then *C1*'s `load b` will be a hit since *C1*'s `load a` will bring in *b* as well and set its *touched-atomic* bit. On the other hand, `load b` in *C2*'s second critical section is a miss. This is because the preceding `load a` will read *a* in its own cache in *Registered* state and so will not prefetch *b* which is registered at *C1*.

Finally, we note that using a single, plain Bloom filter at each core to determine what to invalidate is inherently conservative. For example, it is possible that an address may have been updated before it had been last seen by a core but not updated again since then; our system will still invalidate the address on a read (in the same phase) from that core. In addition, false positives in a finite Bloom filter cause valid addresses to be invalidated if the filter entry is updated by another address mapped to the same entry. Another source of imprecision occurs when the signature is transferred well after the lock release occurs. Such a signature may include addresses to accesses after the release and before the subsequent acquire – these do not precede the acquire by happens-before and may lead to false positives and unnecessary invalidations. Our evaluation, however, showed that such cases did not occur often for applications with reasonable lock synchronization; nevertheless, we later discuss some approaches to mitigate such effects (Section 6).

End of phase actions: At the end of a phase, as with DeNovo, we insert self-invalidation instructions for all regions with writable effects in that phase. This includes atomic and non-atomic regions. Analogous to DeNovo, all data in such regions is invalidated unless it is registered or its *touched* bit (for non-atomic regions) is set or its *touched-atomic* bit (for atomic regions) is set. All *touched* and *touched-atomic* bits are reset at the end of the phase and all Bloom filters are cleared.

4.2 Lock Implementation

Tables 1a and 1b describe the state transitions for the L1 and L2 caches respectively for lock words, building on top of the DeNovo line protocol (as with DeNovo, the coherence states are at word granularity). We next discuss these in detail.

L1 transitions: There are two states at L1 for a lock word: *LockQ* and *Invalid*. The lock word transitions to *LockQ* on receiving a lock request from its core, and stays there until it transfers the lock (along with the access signature) to *nextPtr* or until the line is evicted. While in *LockQ* state, a bit in the data portion of the lock entry, called *Locked*, indicates whether the lock is held or released. Figure 2 shows the lock word layout at the L1 with a lock queue.

On a lock request by a core, its L1 sets the *Locked* bit for the corresponding word. If the word was already in *LockQ* state, the L1 informs the core of a successful lock acquire. If the previous state was *Invalid*, a lock request is sent to the L2 and the core is stalled (the cache does not service any further requests from the core) until the response is received.

On an unlock request to *LockQ* state, if *nextPtr* is not null, the L1 transfers the lock to the *nextPtr* core and transitions to *Invalid*. Otherwise, it unsets *Locked*. An unlock request to *Invalid* state generates a request to the L2. This request is simply a notification and does not bring back the cache line (the state stays *Invalid*).

An L1 in *LockQ* state may receive a remote lock request forwarded by the L2. If the *Locked* bit is set, the request is queued in *nextPtr*; otherwise, it is serviced immediately by transferring the lock and changing the state to *Invalid*. The L1 may also receive a remote lock request in *Invalid* state due to a previous writeback. If this request is only for the signature, it transfers the signature (along with an implicit lock transfer) to the remote requestor. If the request is for the lock as well, then it signifies a race between the L1's writeback and the remote request at the L2. In this case, L1 returns a Nack to the L2 – we discuss how the L2 responds to the Nack in detail below.

Eviction of lines with lock words at the L1 is similar to DeNovo's L1 evictions (not shown in Table 1a). The main difference is that the writeback message needs to indicate which words are in *LockQ* state so that the L2 can perform appropriate action as discussed below. Table 1a does not show any action for writeback requests generated by L2 for L1. This is because the L2 does not need to maintain inclusion with the L1 for lock words (similar to *Valid* data in DeNovo). The distributed lock queue constructed in the L1s stays valid and does not need to be rebuilt on an L2 writeback.

L2 transitions without L1 writebacks: The L2 has two states – *Invalid* and *Valid*. The main source of complexity at the L2 comes from L1 writebacks of *LockQ* words; we therefore first discuss L2 transitions without L1 writebacks, indicated by *WB*=0 in Table 1.

On a lock request in *Valid* state, the L2 forwards the request to its *tailPtr* core and updates the *tailPtr* with the requesting core's ID. A lock request in *Invalid* state allocates the line for the lock word, triggers a fetch from memory, and keeps the L2 in *Invalid* state. When the response returns, the L2 transitions to *Valid* and applies the actions for the *Valid* state to the lock request (i.e., forwards the

	Lock request from core *i*	Unlock request from core *i*	Response for lock request from core *i*	Remote lock request from core *k*
LockQ	set *Locked*	**if** *nextPtr* != null send response to *nextPtr*; go to *Invalid* **else** unset *Locked*	unstall core *i*; merge received signature	**if** *Locked* is set *nextPtr* := *k* **else** send response to core *k*; go to *Invalid*
Invalid	stall core *i*; update tag; go to *LockQ*; set *Locked*; send lock request to L2 (writeback if needed)	send unlock request to L2	X	**if** sig-only request send response to core *k* **else** send *Nack* to L2

(a) L1 cache for core *i*

	Lock request from core *i*	Unlock request from core *i*	Lock/Unlock/WB/Nack response from memory for core *i*	Lock writeback from core *i*	Nack from core *i* for core *k*
Valid	**if** *WB* == 0 fwd req to *tailPtr*; **else** // *WB* == 1 **if** *Locked* is not set send sig-only req to *lastAcquirer* for *i*; *WB* := 0 **else** // *Locked* is set **if** *firstWaiter* != null fwd req to *tailPtr* **else** *firstWaiter* := *i*; *tailPtr* := *i*	**if** *firstWaiter* != null send sig-only req to *i* for *firstWaiter*; *WB* := 0 **else** unset *Locked*	X	**if** *firstWaiter* == null copy *Locked* from WB message; *lastAcquirer* := *i*; *firstWaiter* := *nextPtr*; *WB* := 1; **else** // race **if** *Locked* is not set send sig-only req to *i* for *firstWaiter*	**if** *WB* == 0 *firstWaiter* := *k* **else** **if** *Locked* is not set send sig-only req to *lastAcquirer* for *k*; *lastAcquirer* := null **else** *firstWaiter* := *k*
Invalid	update tag; send data req to memory; (writeback if needed)	update tag; send data req to memory; (writeback if needed)	**if not** tag match allocate line; update tag; (writeback if needed) go to *Valid*; apply actions for Lock/Unlock/WB/Nack as specified in *Valid*	update tag; send data req to memory; (writeback if needed)	update tag; send data req to memory; (writeback if needed)

(b) L2 cache

Table 1: State transitions for a lock word. *X* indicates unreachable states.

request to *tailPtr*). If the line was deallocated between the request and the response due to eviction, another line is allocated and the above action taken.

An unlock request in *Valid* state can only occur if the unlocking L1 previously performed a writeback on the lock (i.e., *WB=1*), and so is discussed below.

Writebacks generated by the L2 to memory are similar to DeNovo. As we see below, all the lock queue related information needed at the L2 is maintained as part of the lock word in the L2 – on an L2 writeback, this information is simply preserved at memory and made available to the L2 for later use.

Handling L1 lock writeback at the L2: When the L2 receives a writeback from an L1, it must ensure that it stores all information needed to construct the lock queue that was stored at the L1. This information is stored in the data portion of the L2 along with the *tailPtr*. An L1 writeback containing a lock word can originate only from the head of the lock queue in *LockQ* state because other cores are either stalled on their lock request or invalidated after transferring the lock. The L2, therefore, stores the following information in its data portion on an L1 writeback from core *i* (Figure 2 illustrates the L2 data layout with example values before and after the writeback):[3]

WB: The *WB* bit is set to 1 to indicate that the lock has been evicted from the L1 of the head of the lock queue.

Locked: The *Locked* bit from the writeback message is copied into the L2 to indicate whether the lock was released (*Locked*=0) at the time of the writeback.

lastAcquirer: L2 sets *lastAcquirer* as *i*. This is used to forward the next lock requestor to core *i* to obtain the access signature.

firstWaiter: L2 copies *nextPtr* from the writeback message into its *firstWaiter* field to indicate the first element in the queue after the head. On a subsequent unlock, the lock must be transferred to the *firstWaiter* core if it is not null.

Next we revisit the transitions for various messages at the L2 when the *Valid* state has *WB*=1. On a lock request, if *Locked* is not set (writeback occurred after lock release), L2 forwards the request to the *lastAcquirer* core. This request is for the access signature only since we already know that the lock has been released. If *Locked* is set (writeback before release), then L2 checks if *firstWaiter* is null. If it is not null, then L2 queues the request by forwarding it to *tailPtr*. Otherwise, it sets *firstWaiter* to *i* since there is no other waiter in the queue.

Similarly for unlock requests, if *firstWaiter* is not null, L2 forwards the request of *firstWaiter* to *lastAcquirer* for the signature (and implicit lock transfer). Otherwise, the queue is empty. L2 resets *Locked*, indicating that the evicted head is unlocked now and is ready to transfer the lock.

Handling races: There can be a race between an L1 lock writeback from core *i* and a request for the same lock from another core *k*. Thus, before getting the writeback, the L2 can forward core *k*'s request to L1. In this case, L1 nacks the request back to L2, which takes the following actions depending on whether it has already received the writeback (last column of Table 1b):

[3] Storing these fields in the data bank of the L2 does not limit the number of cores that can be supported as we can increase the data size of a lock variable as needed.

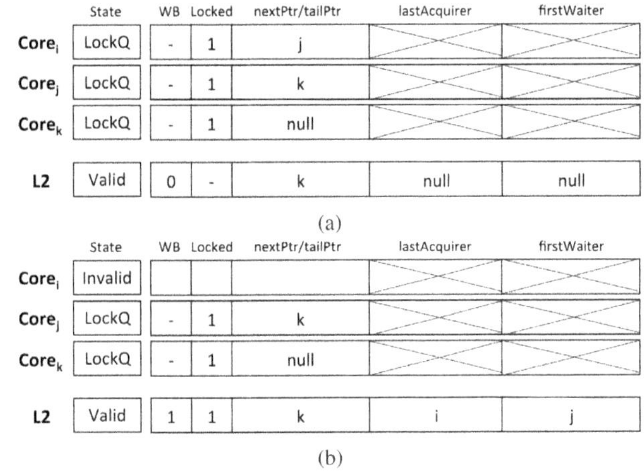

Figure 2: Example showing L1 and L2 data layout for the distributed queue-based lock (a) before writeback and (b) after writeback.

The Nack arrives before the writeback (WB=0): L2 simply sets *firstWaiter* to core *k*. When the writeback arrives, L2 finds its *firstWaiter* is not null and its request must be handled. If the *Locked* bit in the writeback is unset, L2 knows the lock was released and so can forward *firstWaiter*'s request to core *i* for signature transfer. If the *Locked* bit is set, then nothing needs to be done; the lock transfer to core *k* will occur when the *Unlock* arrives.
The Nack arrives after the writeback (WB=1): L2 services core *k*'s request using the information stored in the writeback; if *Locked* is not set, the request is forwarded to *lastAcquirer*. Otherwise, *k* is stored as the *firstWaiter*.

The above race is the only one that occurs in the lock protocol. It involves at most two cores and results in exactly one possible Nack message that the L2 immediately handles, with no deadlock or livelock causing actions.

4.3 Overheads

DeNovoND incurs the following overheads over DeNovo.
Hardware Bloom filter: There is one Bloom filter per core. A conservative upper bound for its size is the virtual memory size. In practice, an effective size can be empirically determined by measuring the number of atomic writes to distinct addresses in various applications. The size must also be large enough to have tolerable false positive rates. In our system, a relatively small size Bloom filter of only 256 bits worked well and provided performance similar to an infinite size Bloom filter for most cases. This is because the size of the key domain is restricted only to the addresses in atomic regions, and the filter is flash cleared at the end of a phase.

The quality of the hash function also impacts the efficiency of Bloom filters [42]. We experimented with two hash functions, multi-bit selection (similar to the one used in [16]) and H_3 (universal hash function that provides uniformly distributed hash values [15]), which showed consistent performance across applications. For our evaluation, we used H_3 which worked better with applications with high false positive rates. Finally, [16] has shown that Bloom filter operations of element insertion, membership query, and flash clear can be implemented very efficiently in hardware.
Storage overhead: Our distributed queue-based lock protocol reuses the L1 and L2 cache data banks to store the waiter queue information, incurring zero storage overhead for that purpose. It requires one additional state *LockQ* at L1 to distinguish between lock and data words. This does not result in any added storage overhead for L1 state as DeNovo already requires two bits per word for storing three states (*Invalid, Valid, and Registered*). With an additional *LockQ* state, we now have four states stored in two bits. The two L2 states for lock words can reuse the L2 per-word state bit of the baseline DeNovo protocol – lock words simply add new transitions to the existing L2 states, triggered by lock related messages. Thus, the lock protocol does not incur any additional storage overhead. The externally visible protocol states for data accesses also stay the same as for DeNovo. For efficient tracking of atomic writes, however, we added a *touched-atomic* bit per word in the L1 as an additional state bit (used only by the local core).
Communication and computation overhead: On acquire/release, the Bloom filter of the releaser is piggybacked on the lock transfer message. In order to minimize impact on network traffic, we can compress the Bloom filter using run-length encoding as in [16] or a Bloom-filter specific compression technique [38]. In our evaluations, we conservatively do not model such compression and charge the full 256 bits (32 bytes) of network traffic for the Bloom filter at a lock transfer. When a core receives a lock transfer message along with the signature, it needs to merge the received Bloom filter with its own before executing memory instructions in the critical section. The time for merging can be partially hidden by not blocking the execution until the first write/read instruction to an atomic region is issued.

For the distributed queue-based lock, there is an additional overhead for writeback messages which need to include an additional bit per word to indicate if the word is in *LockQ* state so that the L2 can perform appropriate lock related actions for this word. This overhead, however, can be compensated by observing that the writeback message does not have to contain full lock words, but only the *Locked* and *nextPtr* parts. The queue-based lock protocol also requires new state transitions in response to lock related messages; however, these do not introduce any new transient states or interact with the data protocol and can be separately verified.

5. Evaluation Methodology

5.1 Simulation Environment

For our evaluations, we use the Wind River Simics [34] full-system functional simulator to drive the Wisconsin GEMS detailed memory timing simulator [35] that we modified to implement our protocols. We also use the Princeton Garnet [3] interconnection network simulator to model network communication. To keep simulation times reasonable, as is common practice, we employ a simple, single-issue, in-order core model with blocking loads and 1 CPI for all non-memory instructions. (Note that DeNovoND does not require simple cores, but detailed timing simulation of a complex core would take an inordinate amount of time and we believe would not qualitatively affect our results.) We also assume 1 CPI for instructions executed inside the OS.

Table 2 shows the key parameters of our simulated systems. We simulate a multicore with 16 cores, a 64KB private L1 data cache per core (we do not model an Icache), a 16MB shared, NUCA L2 cache, and 4 memory controllers, all connected by a 2D mesh network. We configured the miss latencies to approximate those of the Nehalem processors [21]; e.g., a last-level shared cache miss (memory hit) costs 190 to 309 cycles on Nehalem (several of the latencies specify a range, depending on which L2 bank, remote L1 cache, or memory controller is accessed). We use the Bloom filter implementation shipped with GEMS [35] with the H_3 hashing function and 256 single-bit entries. We also simulated configurations with infinite Bloom filter entries for reference.

5.2 Simulated Systems

Our distributed queue-based lock is specifically designed for DeNovoND, reusing the coherence states of DeNovo, with no added transient states and limited race interactions. Implementing it on a conventional MESI-like protocol is possible, but will involve far more complexity to deal with interactions with the already existing numerous transient states and race conditions. On the other hand, comparing DeNovoND with distributed queue-based locks and MESI with conventional locking may not be fair to MESI. We therefore implemented simplified (idealized) queue-based locks that work for both MESI and DeNovo to isolate the effectiveness of access signatures. This idealized implementation maintains a "lock table" which is keyed by a lock variable address and maintains the waiter queue for each lock. Accesses to this table – creating an entry and grabbing the lock, adding a core to the waiter queue, waking up the first waiter in the queue, etc. – do not incur extra cycles. We also do not charge traffic overhead for lock and signature transfer for the idealized lock. Once a core is ready to release the idealized lock, lock transfer is instant and the next requestor wakes up immediately. Hence we evaluated the following systems:

MESI: We simulated MESI using idealized queue-based locks (MIL) and the `POSIX pthreads` mutex library (MPL). We modified the original implementation of MESI in GEMS [35] to support non-blocking writes for a fair comparison with DeNovoND where writes are non-blocking by default. Atomic instructions used in `pthreads` mutex codes are simulated using blocking store fences for correct execution.

DeNovoND: We simulated DeNovoND with idealized queue-based locks (DIL) and with distributed queue-based locks (DQL), both with a 256 bit Bloom filter (DIL-256 and DQL-256)) and, for reference, an infinite size Bloom filter (DIL-inf and DQL-inf). For DQL, operations on the lock incur latency consistent with table 2. For the signature transfer, we add a 256 bit (32 byte) payload to the lock transfer message and simulate network traffic and latency accordingly. This is conservative for DQL-256 since the signature could be compressed. It is aggressive but reasonable for DQL-inf since DQL-inf is intended to be a best case reference model.

5.3 Workloads

We evaluated 11 benchmarks with lock synchronization, taken from various suites to represent a range of behavior such as lock frequency, lock granularity, contention, critical section length, and shared working-set size. We evaluated *barnes* (16K particles), *ocean* (258×258), and *water* (512 molecules) from SPLASH-2 [45]; *fluidanimate* (35K particles) and *streamcluster* (8,192 points) from PARSEC 2.1 [8]; *tsp* (17 cities) as used in [12]; and *kmeans* (8,192 points, 24 dimensions, 16 centers), *ssca2* (2^{13} nodes), *genome* (256 nucleotides), *intruder* (1,024 traffic flows), and *vacation* (16,384 records) from STAMP [37].

The benchmarks from SPLASH-2 and PARSEC represent traditional applications designed and optimized to scale well with lock synchronization. The benchmarks from STAMP and *tsp*, however, were originally designed for hardware and software transactional memory. We ported them to use locks for our simulated systems. For short transactions, we directly replaced them with critical sections (*tsp*, *kmeans*, *ssca2*, and *intruder*). For longer transactions, we used finer-grained locks (*genome*, *vacation*).

We found that 3 out of the 6 transactional applications (*genome*, *intruder*, and *vacation*) spent > 70% of their execution time on lock acquire for all studied configurations. Clearly, parallelization using lock synchronization is inappropriate for these applications, for both MESI and DeNovoND. We therefore focus our results on the other 8 applications, referring to them as "lock-efficient" applications (Section 6.1). For completeness, we separately report results for the above three lock-inefficient applications (Section 6.2). We discuss optimizations to improve the performance of DeNovoND for the lock-inefficient applications, but fundamentally, these must be parallelized using different techniques for reasonable parallel speedups. Such techniques (including possibly transactional memory) are outside the scope of this work.

Core frequency	2GHz
# of cores	16
L1 data cache	64KB, 64 bytes (16 words) line size
L2 (16 banks, NUCA)	16MB, 64 bytes line
Memory	4GB, 4 on-chip controllers
L1 hit latency	1 cycle
L2 hit latency	29 to 61 cycles (bank-dependent)
Remote L1 hit latency	35 to 83 cycles
Memory hit latency	197 to 261 cycles
Network parameters	2D mesh, 16 bit flits
Bloom filter size	256 bits (infinite for reference)
hash function	4 H_3

Table 2: Simulated system parameters.

Finally, the lock-inefficient applications showed significant non-determinism in execution time. Although our timing simulations are deterministic, they depend on the state of the system when the application is started (the Simics checkpoint at the start of the application). For different state, the lock-inefficient applications showed varying results. We therefore ran each such application with five different checkpoints for each system and averaged the results (the same five checkpoints are used for all systems). We also report the results for the lock-efficient applications averaged across three different checkpoints, but these applications did not show much variability across their checkpoints.

6. Performance Results

6.1 Lock-Efficient Applications

Figure 3a shows the execution time for our 8 lock-efficient applications for the 6 configurations described in Section 5.2. All bars are normalized to MIL. Each bar is divided into compute time, stall time due to data memory accesses (henceforth referred to as *memory time*), barrier time, and lock acquire time. Since we model non-blocking lock releases, lock release time is negligible. Since our focus is on the memory system, Figure 3b blows up the memory time in each bar of Figure 3a, divided into stalls for L1 misses resolved at L2, a remote L1, or main memory. Since all modeled systems implement non-blocking stores, virtually all memory stalls are due to loads. Figure 4a presents network traffic for the same applications on MPL and DQL-256 (normalized to MPL), classified by the message type: load, store, queue lock/unlock, writeback, and invalidation. The queue lock/unlock traffic exists only in DQL-256 for transferring distributed queue-based locks with signatures. For MPL, the lock traffic is aggregated with the data load and store traffic. Note that only MPL incurs invalidation traffic. We do not show network numbers with other configurations because they are idealized, but we confirmed that the network results for DQL-256 stay qualitatively similar even when compared to MIL.

MIL vs. DIL-inf: For all 8 applications, DeNovoND shows the same or slightly better (up to 5%) execution time compared to MESI with idealized locks and infinite length Bloom filter. Focusing on memory time, again DIL-inf is either the same or better than MIL. For some applications, DIL is much better than MIL; e.g., 47% and 84% better for *kmeans* and *tsp* respectively. This is because MIL suffers from false sharing while DIL does not due to its per-word coherence state.

MPL vs. DQL-inf: Comparing the realistic lock implementations (but still with infinite Bloom filter size), we find that for all 8 applications, DQL-inf shows comparable or slightly better execution time than MPL. In fact, even compared to the idealized lock implementation in MIL, the execution time for DQL-inf is about the same or better in 7 of 8 cases and only 4% worse in the remaining case (*ssca2*). In terms of memory time, again DQL-inf is either comparable or sees large benefits due to the lack of false sharing relative to both MPL and MIL.

Impact of finite signatures: We next evaluate the impact of restricting the Bloom filter size: DIL-inf vs. DIL-256 and DQL-inf

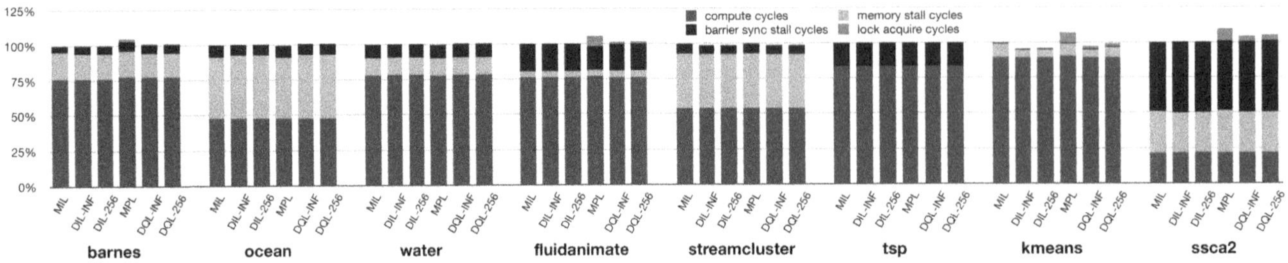

(a) Execution time.

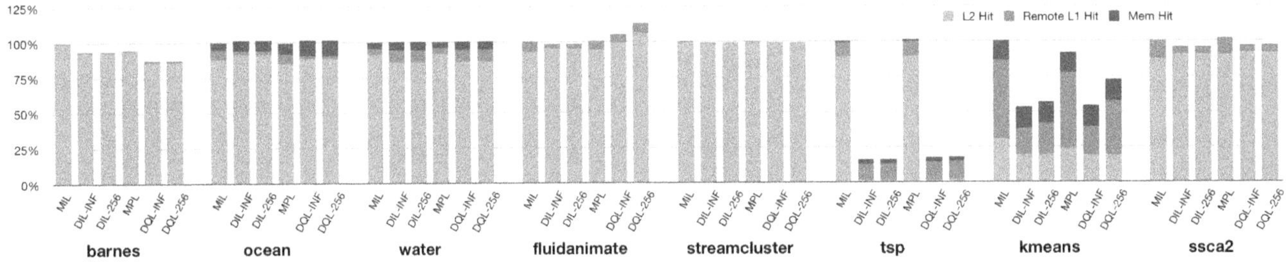

(b) Memory stall time.

Figure 3: Total execution time (a) and memory stall time (b) of lock-efficient applications on 6 configurations, normalized to MIL.

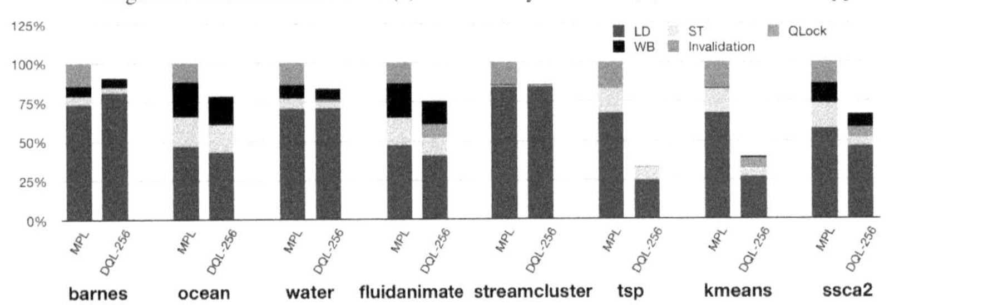

(a) Network traffic (lock-efficient).

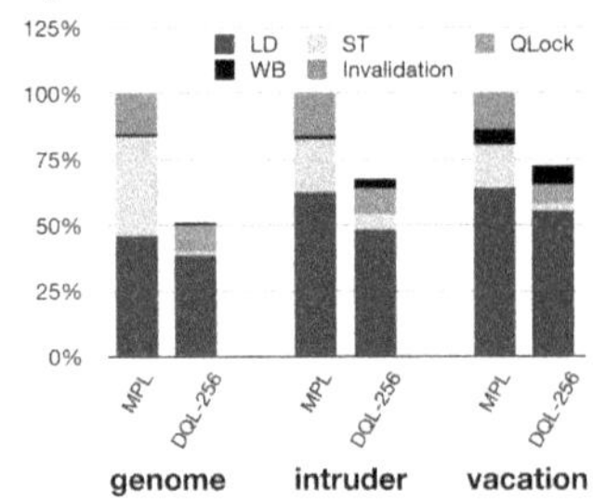

(b) Network traffic (lock-inefficient).

Figure 4: Network traffic of all applications on MPL and DQL-256, normalized to MPL.

vs. DQL-256. The 256 bit Bloom filters show virtually the same execution times as the infinite length filters. In terms of memory time, the two Bloom filter sizes are similar for 6 of the 8 applications. For *fluidanimate* and *kmeans*, however, the 256 bit filter shows a degradation. For *kmeans*, memory time for DQL-256 continues to remain significantly better than for both MESI configurations (20% or more better), but for *fluidanimate*, it is worse by 13% (the only application where this is the case).

Fluidanimate and *kmeans* show the above behavior due to a confluence of a few subtle effects. First, both use critical sections where an atomic region address that is read is also written. Often an atomic region address read by a core was also last written by the same core (either in the previous phase or in a previous critical section). If this address is still in the core's cache in modified (for MESI) or registered (for DeNovoND) state, then the read will be a hit for both MESI and DeNovoND. Otherwise, if the address was written back, the read will be a miss for both MESI and DeNovoND. The difference between the protocols arises for any other atomic region addresses that come along with such a read miss as part of the same cache line. If the same core reads such an address in a subsequent critical section without an intervening write by another core, then MESI will still hit in the cache but DeNovoND will have to check against the Bloom filter. This could require a self-invalidation since the corresponding Bloom filter bit may be set, resulting in an extra miss over MESI. A smaller Bloom filter exacerbates this problem since it also results in false positives on the key domain. Further, the effect is more noticeable in DQL than in DIL because *fluidanimate* and *kmeans* have fine-grained locks – these locks pollute the cache and cause more replacements, exacerbating the above effect.

Network traffic: Figure 4a shows that for all the applications, DQL-256 has much lower traffic than MPL (33% on average, 67% maximum). This directly translates into energy reduction.

The primary sources of these savings in DeNovoND are as follows: (1) DeNovoND does not incur any traffic for invalidations, a significant effect in all applications. (2) Store traffic is reduced in some applications because store requests in DeNovoND do not bring in the cache line – they directly write into the L1 word and only send out a registration request for that word (multiple registrations for a given line are combined and sent on the network as mentioned in Section 2.2). (3) The net reduction in load misses (memory time) due to the lack of false sharing (Figure 3b) directly leads to lower load traffic in several applications. (4) Load traffic is further reduced because a load response only contains valid or registered words of a cache line. Since coherence state is preserved per word, some words may be invalid at the servicing cache.

A source for increased network traffic in DeNovoND is the 32 byte signature with all lock transfers. Figure 4a shows that this is small in all our applications. It can be further reduced through compression techniques mentioned in Section 4.3.

Summary: Overall, our results show that for these applications, the access signature mechanism allows DeNovoND to enjoy all the benefits of DeNovo even in the presence of lock-based synchronization. Further, the signature size needed is small (32 bytes).

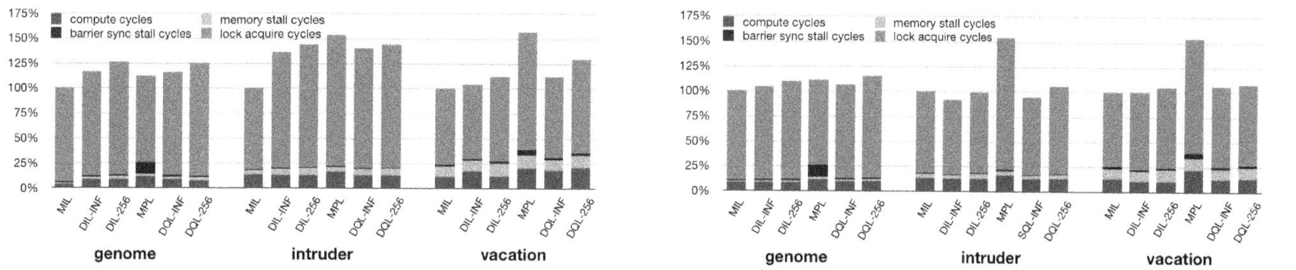

(a) Baseline.

(b) "Write-Once" Atomic Region and Signature Clearing.

Figure 5: Total execution time of lock-inefficient applications on six configurations: (a) baseline, (b) with "write-once" atomic region optimization and signature clearing (threshold=99%) applied, normalized to the MESI with idealized locks (MIL) configuration.

6.2 Lock-Inefficient Applications

The lock-inefficient applications spend more than 70% of their time on lock acquires, but are presented here for completeness. Figure 5a shows their execution times analogous to Figure 3a. There are several ways in which these applications differ from the lock-efficient ones. First, as mentioned earlier, they are dominated by lock acquire time and so need a significantly different algorithm for parallelization and/or synchronization. These applications were originally designed to study transactional memory. Some of them use patterns for which lock-free synchronization is commonly used. Supporting such forms of parallelism and synchronization is outside the scope of this paper, but forms a key part of our future work.

Second, as discussed in Section 5.3, these applications show significant non-determinism. Although we report results averaged over five runs starting from five different Simics checkpoints (the same five checkpoints for each system), the variability makes comparing different systems difficult.

Third, we find that compute time varies across different systems for each of these applications. Although not shown here, a significant fraction of compute time comes from the OS (e.g., due to frequent memory allocations), forming the main source of the compute time variation. (The lock-efficient applications have negligible OS compute time.) Our results must therefore be understood in the context of the above caveats.

MIL vs. DIL-inf: For all three applications, DIL-inf shows observably worse performance than MIL (16% for *genome*, 36% for *intruder*, and 5% for *vacation*). A large part of the performance difference appears to come from acquire time; e.g., DIL-inf spends 40% more cycles waiting for lock acquisition than MIL with *intruder*. Though memory time is a very small portion, it affects acquire time by increasing the time spent within critical sections. Our detailed results show that DIL-inf suffers from higher memory time than MIL, especially for *genome* and *intruder*.

The higher memory time above occurs due to an access pattern where an address is written only once in a phase and then read several times. Specifically, *genome* and *intruder* use list and hash table data structures that store "data" or "key-data" pairs of each entry as a field of the entry object – in these programs, the data is initialized when a new element is inserted (within a critical section) but never modified afterwards. A core may read this data later in different critical sections – DeNovoND will self-invalidate on such reads since it does not know if there was an intervening write since the last read. MESI, on the other hand, will hit on such reads if they happen close enough to exploit temporal locality.

Section 6.2.1 discusses how we can use software information to remedy the above situation. We believe, however, that a better solution to this problem is a better synchronization construct – using locks for such reads is overkill. Such constructs in the context of DeNovo and DeNovoND are a key part of our future work.

MPL vs. DQL-inf: DQL-inf performs slightly worse than MPL with *genome* for the same reason as the comparison between MIL and DIL-inf. DQL-inf outperforms MPL with *intruder* and *vacation* – for these applications, MPL has significantly higher acquire time than MIL. MPL's pthread locks, however, are inherently inefficient with high lock contention; therefore, this is not a fair comparison for MESI. Thus, little can be deduced here except perhaps that DeNovoND performance seems to be in the same range as MESI (this inability to draw a conclusion is an inherent artifact of the problem studied).

Impact of finite signatures: With smaller Bloom filter sizes, false positives exacerbate the impact of the conservative invalidations described above; for *genome* and *intruder* – DIL-256 and DQL-256 perform worse than DIL-inf and DQL-inf by 4% to 10%.

Vacation does not suffer from the conservative invalidations of *genome* and *intruder*, but reveals a different source of inefficiency with smaller signatures. Figure 5a shows DIL-256 is 8% worse than DIL-inf, while DQL-256 is 17% worse than DQL-inf for this application. This is mainly due to its large working set of atomic data, which can increase the false positive rate if a Bloom filter is too small. In addition, *vacation* has only one phase without any barriers in between; thus the Bloom filters get filled up for a long period without clearing. This further exacerbates the false positive rate, resulting in unnecessary self-invalidations and higher memory times. Section 6.2.1 describes an optimization technique called signature clearing to deal with this issue.

Network traffic: Figure 4b shows network traffic of the lock-inefficient applications on MPL and DQL-256. DQL-256 generates less network traffic (up to 48%) than MPL for all three applications for reasons similar to that for the lock-efficient applications. In addition, with relatively high lock contention, repeated accesses to lock variables can generate increasingly higher network traffic in MPL. In contrast, distributed queue-based lock request/response traffic scales in proportion to the number of lock transfers.

6.2.1 Optimizations

Handling "write-once" atomic data: As with the case with *intruder* and *genome*, once a new entry is created and then inserted into a data structure (list, hash table, etc.), the "data" portion of the entry may remain read-only for the entire execution while other fields of the entry are modified as the structure grows or shrinks. In this case, classifying the "data" as atomic makes every self-invalidation after the very first one (the memory location may have been used and freed before) unnecessary.

DeNovoND can safely get rid of these invalidations by identifying such atomic accesses as made to a "write-once" atomic region. In addition to general information about atomic regions and effects, software can allow such "write-once" atomic data to be marked differently by using a special region ID or a special op-code for the write. Then DeNovoND can exploit it to prevent such data from being self-invalidated as follows. If the data is known to be in a "write-once" atomic region, DeNovoND does not reset its *touched-atomic* bit on lock transfer; therefore, when the data is accessed (read) again later, it is treated as if it has been already accessed in the same critical section (with *touched-atomic* bit set) and will not be self-invalidated, thereby eliminating several subsequent misses.

The write-once annotation can be considered to be a generalization of *final* variables in Java; a final variable can only be initialized once, either at the time of declaration or by the constructor of the class in which it is declared [40]. Our write-once variables must be written (at most) once per parallel phase.

Signature clearing: Depending on the atomic write-set size in a phase, the fixed-size hardware Bloom filter may get saturated (all bits set) before the phase is over. This drives the false positive rate very high, resulting in many unnecessary self-invalidations. Saturated Bloom filters can be flash-cleared by a simple hardware operation, but it also requires flushing out atomic words in the cache. Also, the fact that a signature has been cleared in the releaser should be propagated to the acquirer so that the acquirer can update its cache according to the new version of the Bloom filter. We implemented a signature clearing algorithm that carries a vector of clearing counters per core. When signature clearing is triggered on a core, its counter is incremented. The vector of clearing counters is transferred on a lock transfer along with the access signature. The acquirer compares the received vector with its own, and performs signature clearing if there exists an element in the received vector that has a larger counter than the corresponding element in its own vector. Before the lock is transferred again, the vector is updated to have up-to-date values.

Performance impact: Figure 5b presents execution times analogous to figure 5a, but with the above optimizations applied.

For *genome*, all DeNovoND protocols now perform comparable to the MESI counterpart. Our detailed results show large reductions in memory time from the write-once optimization (118% to 151%). Since this reduction mainly comes from atomic accesses within critical sections, lock contention also improved. *Intruder* shows similarly dramatic results in memory time improvement with consequently large improvements in execution time for the DeNovoND configurations; acquire time is reduced by 36 to 42%, memory time by 56 to 76%, and overall execution time by 43% on average.

For *vacation*, DIL-256 and DQL-256 (protocols with finite Bloom filters) show performance benefits from signature clearing; DIL-256 and DQL-256 were 17% and 8% worse than DIL-inf and DQL-inf respectively without signature clearing. With signature clearing, with 99% filter saturation percentage as the trigger for clearing, the difference is reduced to 5% and 2%.

Overall, the optimizations are quite effective, making the DeNovoND protocols comparable or better than the corresponding MESI protocols even for the lock-inefficient applications.

7. Related Work

There has been much research on improving the performance of memory consistency models by guaranteeing consistency only at synchronization points. Our work is closest to that of lazy release consistency (LRC) [27], entry consistency (EC) [7], and scope consistency (ScC) [22]. A key focus of these models is saving invalidation network traffic by postponing propagation of modified data until an acquire. LRC maintains consistency of all shared data at every lock transfer. EC attempts to reduce traffic by requiring programmers to bind every shared object with a lock, and transferring only the bound data objects on a lock transfer. ScC attempts to relax the strict and explicit bindings between data and lock in EC; instead, it uses "consistency scope" to implicitly associate data and the acquire/release pair protecting the data. DeNovoND is similar in that it also assumes a software guarantee for data-race freedom and association of atomic regions and sections. However, a key difference between DeNovoND and the above models is that the latter are designed for software distributed shared memory, keeping coherence information at a coarse-grained page granularity and storing information about modified data in data structures in user space. DeNovoND focuses on tightly coupled multicores with different trade-offs. In particular, DeNovoND implements a much simplified yet effective scheme for tracking modified atomic locked data in hardware, while leveraging the feature of the baseline system (no invalidation traffic) for non-atomic data.

REFLEX [33] employs software distributed shared memory with release consistency to make it easier to program low-power smartphones. It uses either eager or lazy update propagation depending on the initiating core's power profile. While REFLEX concentrates on adapting release consistency for low power on heterogeneous systems, DeNovoND is a more general solution that addresses complexity, performance, and power.

The recent SARC coherence protocol [25] also exploits the data-race-free programming model, but their goal is to improve the conventional directory-based protocol [2]. SARC self-invalidates "tear-off, read-only" (TRO) copies of data to save power. However, SARC does not eliminate directory storage overhead or reduce protocol complexity like DeNovoND and its baseline system. Also, the concept of touched bit, which plays an important role in DeNovo and DeNovoND is not present in SARC.

Other efforts to improve coherence achieve one or more of our goals at the expense of other goals. [31] introduces more complexity for self-invalidations and [36] requires writes to go to a shared cache if there are potential conflicts. SWEL [41] and Atomic Coherence [44] rely on specific interconnect substrates to simplify their protocols. Rigel [28] and Cohesion [29] propose systems with accelerators using a hybrid memory model based on shared memory, and employ software-driven invalidation for coherence. However, Rigel eagerly writes back all dirty lines to the global shared cache at phase boundaries, causing potentially unnecessary and bursty network traffic. DeNovoND self-invalidates potentially stale blocks only, avoiding this unnecessary traffic. Cohesion does not address existing limitations of software and directory-based hardware coherence mechanisms. Its software coherence issues extra coherence instructions wasting cycles and network bandwidth since its coherence tracking is conservative and coarse-grained, while the hardware directory-based protocol has the same current complexity and scalability issues. In contrast, DeNovoND starts from a simple protocol and makes it easy to add various optimizations to improve performance and energy further without complicating the protocol.

We leverage much prior work on Bloom filters, which have recently been widely used for access tracking [16, 43, 46]. Typical prior such usage, however, uses filters in the range of 1K to 2K bits. DeNovoND is able to achieve competitive performance with 256 bits, with commensurately lower space and computation overheads, since its key domain is limited to atomic addresses.

8. Conclusion

This paper takes a significant step towards a vision for complexity-, performance-, and energy-efficient multicores enabled by disciplined shared-memory programming practices. Prior work on DeNovo showed how this vision could be achieved for deterministic programs. This paper develops DeNovoND, a system that additionally supports disciplined non-determinism with minimal additional overheads and complexity relative to DeNovo.

DeNovoND exploits a previously developed software-level guarantee that non-deterministic (atomic) data accesses are distinguishable and protected by a lock. The key insight is to use small and simple hardware Bloom filters to track and communicate such accesses across lock transfers, preserving DeNovo's previous advantages of no transient states, directory overhead, invalidation messages, or false sharing. Underlying the data transfer mechanism is a distributed queue-based lock mechanism that uses the cache data banks to construct a lock-waiter queue, without additional state bits or directory storage.

DeNovoND provides comparable or better performance than MESI with the lock-efficient programs studied here. Further, network traffic is significantly reduced, impacting energy. We also identified some patterns in lock-inefficient code that did not work as well with DeNovoND – we showed optimizations to mitigate those effects, but believe the correct solution lies in alternate forms of synchronization for such codes.

As future work, we plan to explore broadening the scope of our vision of hardware-software co-design rooted in disciplined programming to embrace further programming patterns such as pipelined parallelism and "lock-free" data structures, as well as support complex codes such as legacy codes and operating systems. Our ability to easily extend DeNovo to embrace lock based codes gives us further confidence in generalizing this vision.

Acknowledgments

This work was supported in part by Intel Corp. and Microsoft Corp. through the Universal Parallel Computing Research Center at Illinois, Intel Corp. through the Illinois-Intel Parallelism Center, and the National Science Foundation under grant CCF-1018796.

References

[1] S. Adve and H.-J. Boehm. Memory Models: A Case for Rethinking Parallel Languages and Hardware. *CACM*, Aug. 2010.

[2] S. Adve and M. Hill. Weak Ordering - A New Definition. In *ISCA*, 1990.

[3] N. Agarwal, T. Krishna, L.-S. Peh, and N. Jha. GARNET: A Detailed On-Chip Network Model inside a Full-System Simulator. In *ISPASS*, 2009.

[4] M. Allen, S. Sridharan, and G. Sohi. Serialization Sets: A Dynamic Dependence-based Parallel Execution Model. In *PPoPP*, 2009.

[5] Z. Anderson, D. Gay, R. Ennals, and E. Brewer. SharC: Checking Data Sharing Strategies for Multithreaded C. In *PLDI*, 2008.

[6] E. D. Berger, T. Yang, T. Liu, and G. Novark. Grace: Safe Multithreaded Programming for C/C++. In *OOPSLA*, 2009.

[7] B. Bershad, M. Zekauskas, and W. Sawdon. The Midway Distributed Shared Memory System. In *Compcon Digest of Papers.*, 1993.

[8] C. Bienia. *Benchmarking Modern Multiprocessors*. PhD thesis, Princeton University, 2011.

[9] B. H. Bloom. Space/Time Trade-offs in Hash Coding with Allowable Errors. *CACM*, 13:422–426, 1970.

[10] R. D. Blumofe, C. F. Joerg, B. C. Kuszmaul, C. E. Leiserson, K. H. Randall, and Y. Zhou. Cilk: An Efficient Multithreaded Runtime System. In *PPoPP*, 1995.

[11] R. Bocchino, Jr., V. Adve, D. Dig, S. Adve, S. Heumann, R. Komuravelli, J. Overbey, P. Simmons, H. Sung, and M. Vakilian. A Type and Effect System for Deterministic Parallel Java. In *OOPSLA*, 2009.

[12] R. L. Bocchino, Jr., S. Heumann, N. Honarmand, S. V. Adve, V. S. Adve, A. Welc, and T. Shpeisman. Safe Nondeterminism in a Deterministic-by-Default Parallel Language. In *POPL*, 2011.

[13] F. Bonomi, M. Mitzenmacher, R. Panigrahy, S. Singh, and G. Varghese. An Improved Construction for Counting Bloom Filters. In *ESA*, 2006.

[14] Z. Budimlić, M. Burke, V. Cavé, K. Knobe, G. Lowney, R. Newton, J. Palsberg, D. Peixotto, V. Sarkar, F. Schlimbach, and S. Taşirlar. Concurrent Collections. *Sci. Program.*, 18(3-4), Aug. 2010.

[15] J. L. Carter and M. N. Wegman. Universal classes of hash functions (extended abstract). In *STOC*, 1977.

[16] L. Ceze, J. Tuck, J. Torrellas, and C. Cascaval. Bulk Disambiguation of Speculative Threads in Multiprocessors. In *ISCA*, 2006.

[17] B. Choi, R. Komuravelli, H. Sung, R. Smolinski, N. Honarmand, S. V. Adve, V. S. Adve, N. P. Carter, and C.-T. Chou. DeNovo: Rethinking the Memory Hierarchy for Disciplined Parallelism. In *PACT*, 2011.

[18] J. Devietti, B. Lucia, L. Ceze, and M. Oskin. DMP: Deterministic Shared Memory Multiprocessing. In *ASPLOS*, 2009.

[19] A. Ghuloum, E. Sprangle, J. Fang, G. Wu, and X. Zhou. Ct: A Flexible Parallel Programming Model for Tera-Scale Architectures, 2007.

[20] J. R. Goodman, M. K. Vernon, and P. J. Woest. Efficient Synchronization Primitives for Large-Scale Cache-Coherent Multiprocessors. In *ASPLOS*, 1989.

[21] D. Hackenberg, D. Molka, and W. E. Nagel. Comparing Cache Architectures and Coherency Protocols on x86-64 Multicore SMP Systems. In *MICRO*. IEEE, 2009.

[22] L. Iftode, J. P. Singh, and K. Li. Scope Consistency: A Bridge between Release Consistency and Entry Consistency. In *SPAA*, 1996.

[23] Intel. The SCC Platform Overview, 2010.

[24] A. Kägi, D. Burger, and J. R. Goodman. Efficient Synchronization: Let Them Eat QOLB. In *ISCA*, 1997.

[25] S. Kaxiras and G. Keramidas. SARC Coherence: Scaling Directory Cache Coherence in Performance and Power. *IEEE Micro*, 2010.

[26] S. Keckler, W. Dally, B. Khailany, M. Garland, and D. Glasco. GPUs and the Future of Parallel Computing. *IEEE Micro*, 31:7–17, 2011.

[27] P. Keleher, A. L. Cox, and W. Zwaenepoel. Lazy Release Consistency for Software Distributed Shared Memory. In *ISCA*, 1992.

[28] J. H. Kelm, D. R. Johnson, M. R. Johnson, N. C. Crago, W. Tuohy, A. Mahesri, S. S. Lumetta, M. I. Frank, and S. J. Patel. Rigel: An Architecture and Scalable Programming Interface for a 1000-core Accelerator. In *ISCA*, 2009.

[29] J. H. Kelm, D. R. Johnson, W. Tuohy, S. S. Lumetta, and S. J. Patel. Cohesion: A Hybrid Memory Model for Accelerators. In *ISCA*, 2010.

[30] M. Kulkarni, K. Pingali, B. Walter, G. Ramanarayanan, K. Bala, and L. P. Chew. Optimistic Parallelism Requires Abstractions. In *PLDI*, 2007.

[31] A. Lebeck and D. Wood. Dynamic Self-Invalidation: Reducing Coherence Overhead in Shared-Memory Multiprocessors. In *ISCA*, 1995.

[32] E. A. Lee. The Problem with Threads. *IEEE Computer*, 39(5), 2006.

[33] F. X. Lin, Z. Wang, R. LiKamWa, and L. Zhong. Reflex: Using Low-Power Processors in Smartphones without Knowing Them. In *ASPLOS*, 2012.

[34] P. Magnusson, M. Christensson, J. Eskilson, D. Forsgren, G. Hallberg, J. Hogberg, F. Larsson, A. Moestedt, and B. Werner. Simics: A Full System Simulation Platform. *Computer*, 35:50–58, 2002.

[35] M. M. K. Martin, D. J. Sorin, B. M. Beckmann, M. R. Marty, M. Xu, A. R. Alameldeen, K. E. Moore, M. D. Hill, and D. A. Wood. Multifacet's General Execution-driven Multiprocessor Simulator (GEMS) Toolset. *SIGARCH Computer Architecture News*, 2005.

[36] S. L. Min and J.-L. Baer. Design and Analysis of a Scalable Cache Coherence Scheme Based on Clocks and Timestamps. *TPDS*, 1992.

[37] C. C. Minh, J. Chung, C. Kozyrakis, and K. Olukotun. STAMP: Stanford Transactional Applications for Multi-Processing. In *IISWC*, 2008.

[38] M. Mitzenmacher. Compressed Bloom Filters. In *PODC*, 2001.

[39] M. Olszewski, J. Ansel, and S. Amarasinghe. Kendo: Efficient Deterministic Multithreading in Software. In *ASPLOS*, 2009.

[40] Oracle. Java Language and Virtual Machine Specifications.

[41] S. H. Pugsley, J. B. Spjut, D. W. Nellans, and R. Balasubramonian. SWEL: Hardware Cache Coherence Protocols to Map Shared Data onto Shared Caches. In *PACT*, 2010.

[42] D. Sanchez, L. Yen, M. D. Hill, and K. Sankaralingam. Implementing Signatures for Transactional Memory. In *MICRO*, 2007.

[43] A. Shriraman, S. Dwarkadas, and M. L. Scott. Flexible Decoupled Transactional Memory Support. In *ISCA*, 2008.

[44] D. Vantrease, M. H. Lipasti, and N. Binkert. Atomic Coherence: Leveraging Nanophotonics to Build Race-Free Cache Coherence Protocols. In *HPCA*, 2011.

[45] S. C. Woo, M. Ohara, E. Torrie, J. P. Singh, and A. Gupta. The SPLASH-2 Programs: Characterization and Methodological Considerations. In *ISCA*, 1995.

[46] L. Yen, J. Bobba, M. R. Marty, K. E. Moore, H. Volos, M. D. Hill, M. M. Swift, and D. A. Wood. LogTM-SE: Decoupling Hardware Transactional Memory from Caches. In *HPCA*, 2007.

Parallelizing Data Race Detection

Benjamin Wester[†*]

[†]Facebook
bwester@fb.com

David Devecsery[*] Peter M. Chen[*]
Jason Flinn[*] Satish Narayanasamy[*]

[*]University of Michigan
{ddevec,pmchen,jflinn,nsatish}@umich.edu

Abstract

Detecting data races in multithreaded programs is a crucial part of debugging such programs, but traditional data race detectors are too slow to use routinely. This paper shows how to speed up race detection by spreading the work across multiple cores. Our strategy relies on *uniparallelism*, which executes time intervals of a program (called *epochs*) in parallel to provide scalability, but executes all threads from a single epoch on a single core to eliminate locking overhead. We use several techniques to make parallelization effective: dividing race detection into three phases, predicting a subset of the analysis state, eliminating sequential work via transitive reduction, and reducing the work needed to maintain multiple versions of analysis via factorization. We demonstrate our strategy by parallelizing a happens-before detector and a lockset-based detector. We find that uniparallelism can significantly speed up data race detection. With 4× the number of cores as the original application, our strategy speeds up the median execution time by 4.4× for a happens-before detector and 3.3× for a lockset race detector. Even on the same number of cores as the conventional detectors, the ability for uniparallelism to elide analysis locks allows it to reduce the median overhead by 13% for a happens-before detector and 8% for a lockset detector.

Categories and Subject Descriptors D.4.7 [*Operating Systems*]: Organization and Design; D.4.8 [*Operating Systems*]: Performance

General Terms Design, Performance

Keywords Data race detection, Uniparallelism

1. Introduction

The prevalence of multicore processors has led to an increased use of multithreaded programs. In such programs, several threads of execution share a single address space and coordinate their accesses to shared variables via synchronization operations, such as locks and condition variables.

Multithreaded programs are subject to a variety of concurrency bugs, of which a particularly pernicious type are *data races* [5]. A data race occurs when two threads access the same memory location without being ordered by a synchronization operation and at least one access is a write. Data races tend to be nondeterministic and difficult to debug, and they can lead to severe problems at runtime [20, 31]. Even enumerating the possible behaviors of programs with data races is difficult—the C and C++ language specifications explicitly leave the behavior of such programs undefined [4], and the Java specification for such programs is extremely complex and currently has known bugs [41].

To address this problem, researchers have developed tools to detect data races in multithreaded programs. We focus in this paper on dynamic data race detectors; static race detectors also exist but currently suffer from an excess of false positives. During development, data race detectors can help programmers find and eliminate data races. During production, data race detectors can try to avoid racy executions or can stop the program before it generates incorrect or arbitrary output.

The main problem preventing the widespread use of dynamic data race detectors is their high overhead, especially for tools that can operate on arbitrary binaries. For example, Intel Inspector incurs an average of 233× slowdown for the SPLASH-2 benchmarks [38], and Google's ThreadSanitizer (happens-before mode) incurs an average of 29× slowdown for a series of unit tests [40]. Even research systems that operate on managed code are slow, e.g., FastTrack [15], a state-of-the-art, precise race detector, imposes an average of 8.5× slowdown on the execution time of Java programs. The high overhead of these tools arises from needing to instrument and analyze each potentially-racy memory operation.

Several strategies have been explored to reduce the overhead of data race detection. One approach is to rely on custom hardware [11, 24, 33, 51], but such support is not yet available on commodity processors. Another approach is to tolerate false negatives (i.e., miss detecting some data races), such as by sampling only a portion of the execution [6, 22] or data space [13], by refining the granularity of detection at the cost of missing the first race on a variable [50], or by detecting the outcome of races rather than the race itself [43]. A third approach is to tolerate false positives (i.e., report some events that are not data races), such as by increasing the granularity of detection [46].

This paper presents a new strategy for accelerating a data race detector by enabling it to run in parallel across multiple cores. Surprisingly, not only does our method of parallelization scale well with increasing cores, it also usually reduces the overhead of data race detection even when run on the original number of cores. Our strategy relies on *uniparallelism* [44], which executes time intervals of a program (called *epochs*) in parallel, but executes all threads from a single epoch on a single core. To enable parallel execution of epochs, we run a lightweight program replica that conducts little race analysis, and we use this copy to predict future application and partial analysis state. Executing epochs across cores increases performance via parallelism. Executing all threads from a single epoch on one core increases performance by eliminating the need for the analysis code to acquire and release locks.

ASPLOS'13, March 16–20, 2013, Houston, Texas, USA.

We demonstrate how to adapt two traditional data race detectors (happens-before and lockset) to run in a uniparallel environment. Each detector must be restructured into three phases: the first phase runs epochs in sequence and predicts a subset of the analysis state, the second phase runs epochs in parallel and performs the bulk of the analysis, and the third phase merges together the results of the parallel phase. The second phase detects races that occur within a particular epoch, and the third phase detects races that occur across epochs.

We find that uniparallelism can significantly speed up data race detection. With 4× the number of cores as the original application, our strategy speeds up the median execution time by 4.4× for a happens-before detector and 3.3× for a lockset race detector. Even on the same number of cores as the conventional detectors, the ability for uniparallelism to elide analysis locks allows it to reduce the median overhead by 13% for a happens-before detector and 8% for a lockset detector.

In this paper, we make several novel contributions to the area of race detection and parallel program analysis. First, we show how running multiple epochs in parallel can parallelize race detection, even though detecting races for one epoch depends on the analysis done in prior epochs. We show how race detection in general can be restructured into three phases: one that predicts a subset of the analysis state, a second that runs the bulk of the analysis, and a third that resolves the symbolic expressions that were logged in the second phase. Second, we show how two classic race detectors (based on happens-before and lockset) can be reimplemented in this architecture. In particular, we show how to partition the work of those race detectors effectively into phases, reduce the amount of deferred work through transitive reduction, and reduce the amount of work needed to deal with unknown initial states through lockset factorization. Third, we show how uniparallelism reduces the overhead of fine-grained analyses such as race detection by eliminating locking overhead. Finally, we demonstrate that parallel race detection scales on commodity hardware.

2. Parallel race detection

It is challenging to parallelize fine-grained program analyses such as race detection. Typically, the analysis is done synchronously with the program, so the speeds of the program and analysis are linked. In addition, some race detectors have strong dependencies between instructions, i.e., the analysis of an instruction depends upon the analysis of prior instructions.

One way to parallelize a race detector is to run the application on more cores and run the race detector along with the scaled application. There are three problems with this approach. First, many applications cannot easily take advantage of more cores. Second, as we show in Section 6, applications that can adapt to more cores do not necessarily scale well, especially when run with race detection. Finally, a developer may want to debug the original application rather than an application that has been scaled to use more cores.

Another way to parallelize race detection is to instrument an application to log memory accesses and then feed the trace to multiple threads that perform data race detection. The problem with this approach is that the memory access logger must monitor every memory operation, and this may become a performance bottleneck without hardware support [7].

Our goal is to parallelize race detection in a way that does not suffer from these problems. Specifically, we would like to parallelize race detection without modifying the application, and we would like the parallel race detector to scale well to more cores even if the original application does not scale well. To achieve this goal, we use a previously proposed technique called uniparallelism [44].

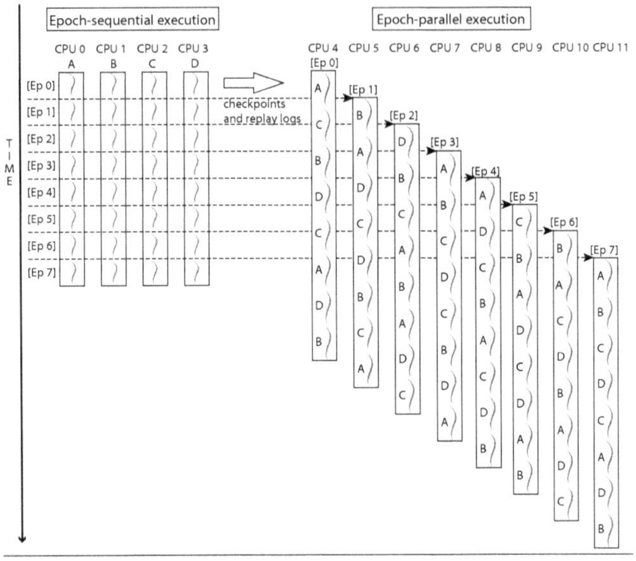

Figure 1. Uniparallelism

We first present an overview of uniparallelism in the next section; we then describe how we apply it to race detection.

2.1 Background: uniparallelism

Uniparallelism operates on unmodified applications. It achieves parallelism via a technique called epoch parallelism [29] (also called master/slave speculative parallelization [52] and predictor/executor approach [42]).

In epoch parallelism, the application is divided into distinct time intervals, called *epochs*. The goal of epoch parallelism is to run these epochs in pipelined fashion, where later epochs start before earlier ones finish. Epochs are isolated in their own address space, and the program's semantics are equivalent to a sequential execution: e.g., writes to local memory or files in one epoch are visible to epochs that logically occur later. With more cores available, the pipeline can be deeper and more epochs can run in parallel.

An immediate question that arises is: "How can a later epoch start before an earlier epoch finishes?" Starting epochs early in this manner depends on *predicting* the starting state of that epoch. The predicted state includes the architectural state of the process (the entire address space and all thread registers) as well as the relevant system state (e.g., so that file accesses are consistent). To generate these predictions, epoch parallelism runs a second execution of the application. This second execution runs normally, executing epochs sequentially. In this paper, we refer to this execution as the *epoch-sequential execution*, in contrast with the pipelined execution, which we refer to as the *epoch-parallel execution*. Figure 1 depicts these two executions.

Three properties must be true for epoch parallelism to work. First, the epoch-sequential execution must run ahead of the epoch-parallel execution, so it can predict the starting state of future epochs. In our work, we provide this property by performing most of the work of race detection only in the epoch-parallel execution. Since the work performed for race detection is much greater than the work to execute the original program, the epoch-sequential execution quickly outpaces the epoch-parallel execution.

Second, the state predictions generated by the epoch-sequential execution must *usually* be correct. While incorrect predictions do not affect correctness, they do reduce performance. If the predicted ending state for an epoch (generated by the epoch-sequential execution) does not match the actual ending state (generated by the epoch-parallel execution), the system must flush the pipeline of any epochs that depend on the incorrect prediction, and the epoch-sequential execution must restart from the last committed state (this is called a *rollback*). At any given time, the epoch that is currently the oldest in the pipeline is non-speculative and can release output; all other epochs are speculative and will be discarded in a rollback. Each rollback causes the pipeline to be flushed, which reduces parallelism and wastes the CPU time spent on the flushed epochs. Epoch parallelism ensures the accuracy of the predicted state in the common case via *online replay* [19]. The epoch-sequential execution logs most sources of nondeterminism, and the logged values are replayed during the epoch-parallel execution. Logged events include all synchronization operations (e.g., all `pthread` operations) and input received from system calls (e.g., disk and network I/O). All synchronization operations are replayed in a way that obeys the happens-before partial order of synchronization objects observed during recording.

Although the order of shared-memory accesses can also be nondeterministic, these accesses are too expensive to log and replay. However, since both executions use the same happens-before order of synchronization objects, shared-memory accesses can cause the epoch-sequential and epoch-parallel executions to diverge only when there is a data race [35]. In fact, many data races may not cause rollbacks because they do not affect the state of the program [25]. Programs with frequent data races may cause frequent rollbacks, but the speed of race detection is not critical for such programs because even a slow race detector can find races easily if they occur often.

Third, the system must detect when the state predicted by the epoch-sequential execution is incorrect. Previous epoch-parallel systems detect incorrect predictions by comparing the memory state of the two executions. However, we observe that a useful synergy exists when epoch parallelism is used to parallelize race detection. Since the prediction can only be incorrect when a prior epoch contains a data race, no memory comparison is required if a sound data race detector has determined that all prior epochs are race free.

Putting it all together, epoch parallelism runs the application twice: an epoch-sequential execution to generate predictions of future epoch states, and an epoch-parallel execution to conduct the race analysis. Although the epoch-parallel execution takes place in an unusual, pipelined manner, it is nonetheless a legitimate, real execution of the application. Its computation and output are identical to an execution in which the epochs are stitched together sequentially, because the ending state of an epoch matches the starting state of the next epoch (otherwise the system will rollback), and output is released only as epochs commit.

Uniparallelism is a further refinement of epoch parallelism in which all threads for a given epoch execute on the same core via timeslicing. Threads are scheduled onto the core non-preemptively, switching only when needed to follow the happens-before order determined by the epoch-sequential execution. Uniparallelism was motivated by the observation that some properties, such as deterministic record and replay [44] or the enforcement of specific thread orders [43], are much less expensive to achieve on a single processor than they are on a multiprocessor. Section 2.3 explains how uniparallelism can increase the efficiency of race detection, even when run on the same number of cores as a conventional detector.

2.2 Parallelizing the analysis

While uniparallelism increases the degree of parallelism for an application, it is not at all obvious how one can use epoch parallelism to parallelize the work of detecting races for that application. A key requirement of uniparallelism is that the epoch-sequential execution must run faster than the epoch-parallel execution, and this occurs only because the epoch-sequential execution is not encumbered by the work of detecting races. This means that the state needed to detect races (*analysis state*) is not generated or maintained by the epoch-sequential execution and hence is not part of the predicted state used to start epochs in the epoch-parallel execution (*application state*). For example, for happens-before race detectors, the epoch-sequential execution should not maintain the vector clocks for each variable, and for lockset-based race detectors, the epoch-sequential execution should not maintain the locksets for each variable. Otherwise, it would run as slowly as the epoch-parallel execution and would no longer be able to run ahead to predict states for future epochs.

Our strategy for parallelizing the analysis of the application is to divide it into three phases: the epoch-sequential phase, the epoch-parallel phase, and the commit phase. The bulk of the work is performed in the epoch-parallel phase; the epoch-sequential phase predicts a subset of the analysis state used in the epoch-parallel phase; and the commit phase carries out work that cannot be performed by the epoch-parallel phase because the epoch-parallel phase starts with incomplete state. This section describes these phases independently of the race detection algorithm; Sections 3 and 4 detail how we divide the work of specific race detectors into these phases.

2.2.1 Epoch-sequential phase

The epoch-sequential phase of race detection runs in the epoch-sequential execution. Its purpose is to predict a *subset* of the analysis state at the beginning of each epoch. The epoch-parallel phase can then use this predicted state when it analyzes each epoch in the epoch-parallel execution. Predicting a subset of the analysis state is similar to how the epoch-sequential execution predicts the state of the application at the beginning of each epoch. As with application state, the subset of analysis state is generated twice: once in the epoch-sequential phase to form the prediction, and another time in the epoch-parallel phase to maintain this state and to verify the prediction for the next epoch.

The work done in the epoch-sequential phase must meet three requirements. First, the subset of analysis state must be self-contained: updating the state subset must not depend on analysis state outside the subset.

Second, the work done in the epoch-sequential phase must be lightweight so that the epoch-sequential execution can continue to run ahead of the pipelined epoch-parallel execution. All events in the application that modify the analysis state in the subset must be instrumented and analyzed during the epoch-sequential phase, so the subset should ideally be chosen so that most instructions do not require it to be updated.

Third, the predicted analysis state should usually match the analysis state generated in the epoch-parallel execution, since mispredicted values cause rollbacks and thereby reduce performance. Recall that we guarantee that the application states generated in the epoch-sequential and epoch-parallel executions match for race-free programs by logging and replaying all sources of non-determinism except data races. Similarly, to avoid mispredictions in race-free programs due to mismatches in predicted analysis state, in our designs we ensure that all executions consistent with a happens-before order of synchronization operations will generate the same values for the subset of analysis state.

2.2.2 Epoch-parallel phase

The epoch-parallel phase of race detection runs as part of each epoch in the epoch-parallel execution. This work is pipelined along with the epochs and hence scales with increasing cores. To achieve the greatest scalability, most race detection work should occur in this phase.

Unfortunately, all the work of race detection cannot take place in the epoch-parallel phase because detecting races in one epoch depends on the analysis of prior epochs. Race detection algorithms are stateful: the analysis state gathered by analyzing prior epochs is required to correctly detect all races involving the current epoch. As a trivial example, identifying a race that spans epochs requires analysis state from both epochs. Further, even if the racing pair of accesses occurs within the same epoch, a race detector may require analysis state from prior epochs to identify the pair as racing. For example, with a lockset-based race detector, analyzing a variable access depends on knowing the set of locks that are held by a thread, which depends on the synchronization actions of prior epochs.

Some of the analysis state needed by the epoch-parallel phase is predicted by the epoch-sequential phase. However, state outside this subset is not known when the epoch starts. When the epoch-parallel phase needs to evaluate an expression that contains unknown state, it logs a symbolic form of the expression and defers the evaluation of this expression until the commit phase.

2.2.3 Commit phase

Because the epoch-sequential phase predicts only a subset of the analysis state, the epoch-parallel phase of race detection starts each epoch with incomplete information and may thus be unable to perform all the work of race detection. For example, it is too slow for the epoch-sequential phase to update state on each variable access, so the epoch-parallel phase will not be able to identify races that depend on the analysis state for a variable at the beginning of an epoch. To finish the work of race detection that was unable to be completed in the epoch-parallel phase, we add a final phase of race detection, which we call the commit phase.

The commit phase for an epoch E occurs after all prior epochs have been committed (i.e., commit phases execute sequentially). At this time, the complete analysis state at the beginning of epoch E is known, having been generated by the commit phases of the epochs prior to E. The commit phase can then use this complete analysis state to resolve all unclassified events from the epoch and to generate the complete analysis state for the end of epoch E.

Because the commit phase occurs after the epoch has finished, races detected during this phase are detected later than they would have been detected by a conventional on-the-fly detector. For some uses of race detection, this delay has no effect. For example, race detection could be used on a production system to provide fail-stop behavior for races, and the delay has no effect because speculative output is not released until the commit phase completes. However, for debugging, developers may want to recover the program's state at the time of the access rather than at the end of the epoch. For such a use case, the epoch could be replayed to the racing instruction via the same log used to synchronize the epoch-parallel execution with the epoch-sequential execution [35].

2.3 Eliding analysis locks

In addition to scaling race detection to more cores, uniparallelism can reduce the overhead of race detection even when using the same number of cores. To understand how, one must first consider how the code used to detect races is itself multithreaded. Race detectors read and write analysis state, and this state is shared across threads when the detector is analyzing a multithreaded program. Even if the original program contains no races, the race detector must be written carefully to avoid introducing races on this analysis state. For example, two threads may concurrently read an application variable without causing a data race, but the analysis code for these two events may update analysis state (e.g., a lockset) and must therefore not execute concurrently. As another example, analyzing accesses to separate variables may result in updating the same analysis state, and these updates must not execute concurrently.

A conventional way to provide atomicity for parallel analysis code is to use locks. The epoch-sequential phase of analysis uses this strategy to provide atomicity. However, acquiring and releasing locks can add significant overhead [10], especially when analyzing high-frequency events such as memory accesses.

An advantage of uniparallelism is that it guarantees atomicity for the race detection code that analyzes program events without needing the code to acquire and release locks. Only a single thread from each epoch executes at a time, and different epochs do not share analysis state (until the commit phase, which is run sequentially). Therefore, locks can easily be elided by restricting the code points at which context switches can occur (i.e., as is done in uniparallelism where such switches occur only during synchronization operations). Section 6 shows that eliminating the lock acquisitions and releases for the epoch-parallel phase can reduce the total CPU time needed for the epoch-parallel phase and thereby reduce the overhead of race detection.

In summary, race detection benefits from uniparallelism in two distinct ways. First, epoch parallelism allows race detection to scale well with increasing numbers of cores, even if the underlying program itself does not scale. Second, the refinement of uniparallelism elides locks around analysis code to decrease the cost of race detection for equivalent numbers of cores.

2.4 Synergy between race detection and uniparallelism

It is possible to completely separate the design of race detection from that of uniparallelism, but doing so ignores the synergies that are made possible by co-designing the two. For example, one can implement any race detector by dividing it into two parts: logging of events and analysis of events. One could then run this detector in a uniparallel style without modification: the epoch-parallel phase would log the events and the commit phase would analyze the logged events. While this implementation is amenable to all detectors, it is not scalable—the bulk of the work, i.e., the analysis of those operations, would be done sequentially in the commit phase. For performance to scale well with increasing cores, we must move more of the work into the epoch-parallel phase. Sections 3 and 4 show how we adapt the race detection algorithm for use in a uniparallel execution style.

Just as adapting a race detector to uniparallelism has benefits, so too does adapting the uniparallel execution system to the race detector. Uniparallelism depends on predicting application state (and analysis state, when used for program analysis). These predictions are guaranteed to be correct if there are no data races, since the uniparallel execution replays the happens-before relationship from the epoch-sequential execution. Prior uniparallel systems had to check these predictions by comparing the memory state of the epoch-sequential and epoch-parallel executions [44]. However, no memory comparison is needed when uniparallelism is used to parallelize a sound race detector because the race detector itself can detect potential mispredictions. We take advantage of this observation when parallelizing a sound, happens-before race detector by eliding this memory comparison.

3. Parallel happens-before

There are two main approaches used by race detectors: (1) detect when conflicting memory accesses are not ordered by the happens-before relationship [18] and (2) detect when a program violates a particular locking discipline [39]. This section shows how to parallelize a happens-before race detection algorithm. We examine how to parallelize FastTrack [15], a state-of-the-art precise detection algorithm, as a representative example of happens-before detectors (several other detection algorithms are closely related [3, 6, 11, 16, 32]). Section 4 describes how we parallelize the other approach to race detection by examining a locking-discipline detector.

Overview: We parallelize FastTrack by instrumenting only synchronization operations, such as lock/unlock and fork/join, in the epoch-sequential phase so that their happens-before order can be predicted. Each epoch in the thread-parallel phase additionally instruments memory accesses (i.e., it runs the full FastTrack algorithm), though some race checks cannot be evaluated for lack of data from earlier epochs. Those checks are logged for later evaluation in the commit phase.

3.1 Conventional detection

Happens-before race detectors find accesses (at least one of which is a write) to the same memory location that are not ordered with respect to the happens-before relation of program actions [18]. The happens-before relation is the least-restrictive partial order that obeys the following rules: (1) An event in one thread *happens before* a subsequent event in the same thread; and (2) a release of a synchronization object (e.g., lock) *happens before* a subsequent acquisition of that synchronization object. The happens-before relation is a partial order and is therefore transitive. It can be used with any synchronization operation such as locks, condition variables, barriers, atomic accesses, etc.. Creating a new thread can be modeled as the parent thread releasing a synchronization object and the new thread acquiring that object.

Race detectors process memory accesses and synchronization events in some serial order that is consistent with the happens-before relation; this serial order is usually determined by feeding events to the race detector as they occur in real time. When discussing the ordering of events, we specifically note when we are referring to the happens-before order. Otherwise, we are referring to the serial order in which events are processed.

As is common for happens-before race detectors, FastTrack guarantees detection only of the first race on each variable [3, 8, 15, 16, 32]. Detecting the first race on each variable is sufficient for common uses of race detection, e.g., treating data races as exceptions in production [12, 21] and trying to fix or annotate all races when debugging [1]. Our parallel happens-before detector preserves this detection guarantee.

FastTrack uses *vector clocks* [14, 23] to precisely model the happens-before relationship of an execution[1]. A vector clock (VC) is a vector of N logical clocks, each of which represents a logical time for one of the N threads in the program. VCs are updated by merge and increment operations. A thread *merges* VC_b into VC_a by setting each element of VC_a to the maximum of its current value and the value of the corresponding element in VC_b. A thread i *increments* a VC by incrementing element i of that VC.

We associate a VC with each thread and each synchronization object. The VC for a thread tracks its local logical time and shows which logical times in other threads *happen before* the current instant in the thread's execution. The VC for a synchronization object shows which logical times in each thread *happened before* all releases to the object. When a thread acquires a synchronization object, the synchronization object's VC is merged into the thread's VC. When a thread releases a synchronization object, the thread's VC is merged into the synchronization object's VC, then the thread's VC is incremented.

As each memory access is handled, the detector checks to see if the access races with any previous access. It is sufficient to check that: (1) on a read of the variable, the read must *happen after* the last write to the variable, and (2) on a write, the write must *happen after* the last write of the variable as well as the last read of the variable by each thread. To implement these checks, we maintain for each variable a read-VC and a write-VC, which store the local logical clocks for a subset of the last read and write to the variable by each thread. A thread performs a check by comparing the read-VC and/or write-VC to the thread's VC. If each element of the variable's VC is less than or equal to the corresponding element of the thread's VC, then the check succeeds. Otherwise, the detector declares a race on the variable. After checking for a race, the variable's VC(s) are updated. On a write, the thread resets the read-VC and write-VC by setting all elements to zero, then writes its own logical time to its element in the write-VC (preserving only the last write). On a read, the thread writes its logical time to its element in the read-VC (preserving the last write and all other reads). If the read *happens after* all previous reads, the thread may also overwrite all other elements in the read-VC with zero (preserving only the last write and read).

3.2 Epoch-sequential phase

The first task in designing a parallel happens-before race detector is to decide what part of the analysis state to predict in the epoch-sequential phase. Recall that predicting this part of the analysis state should be much cheaper than the full race predictor, yet the partial state being predicted should enable the epoch-parallel phase to do most of the work of race detection.

It is instructive to consider the two extreme approaches we could take, neither of which work well. If the epoch-sequential phase predicted *all* analysis state, it would be as slow as the full race detector and the predictions would come too late to start new epochs. At the other extreme, if the epoch-sequential phase predicted *no* analysis state, each epoch would start without knowing any vector clocks values. Since VCs always evolve by merging, incrementing, or setting individual elements, no concrete VC values could be generated by the epoch-parallel phase, and the entire task of race detection would need to be deferred until the commit phase (when the VC values at the start of the epoch have been determined).

In our design, the epoch-sequential phase predicts the VCs for threads and synchronization objects, but it does not predict the read-VCs or write-VCs for variables. We generate this state by instrumenting only the synchronization operations. This subset of the analysis meets the criteria stated in Section 2.2.1. It is self-contained, since the VCs for threads and synchronization objects depend only on other VCs for threads and synchronization objects (and not on VCs for variables). It is lightweight, since variable accesses comprise the vast majority of events that need to be monitored. It will usually match the analysis state generated by the epoch-parallel execution—online replay forces the epoch-parallel execution to follow the happens-before order logged during the epoch-sequential execution, so the prediction of this analysis state can only diverge on a data race (which are rare and will be detected).

3.3 Epoch-parallel phase

The epoch-parallel phase performs most of the work of race detection. All program events, synchronization operations and memory accesses, are instrumented and handled using the full FastTrack algorithm. It starts with the predicted VCs for threads and synchronization objects and continues to maintain these during the epoch.

The epoch-parallel phase does *not* know the initial state of each variable's read-VC and write-VC at the beginning of the epoch, since these are not predicted by the epoch-sequential phase. We treat the whole write-VC and each unknown element of the read-VC as a symbolic variable. Whenever the race detection algorithm

[1] FastTrack represents most VCs using a sparse array rather than a naïve array. Although our implementation follows this same approach, we present the algorithm here without distinguishing whether a VC is represented sparsely or naïvely.

needs to evaluate an expression containing symbolic elements from read-VCs or write-VCs, it logs a symbolic form of the expression and defers its evaluation until the commit phase (when the initial read-VCs and write-VCs are known). This can occur when the detector compares a thread VC with a read-VC and/or write-VC in order to check for races.

When an epoch begins, the write-VCs and all elements of the read-VCs are symbolic, and all checks must be deferred. When a thread reads a variable and updates the thread's element in the read-VC, that index takes on a concrete value. Once all elements of a read-VC become concrete, the VC as a whole becomes concrete, and all comparisons against it can be evaluated immediately rather than being deferred. When a thread writes a variable, the entire read-VC and write-VC are given concrete values. Further comparison of that variable in the epoch can be evaluated immediately.

The system described up to this point defers an excessive amount of checks to be handled in the commit phase. We can use transitive reduction [28, 49] as an optimization to reduce the number of checks that must be deferred. Once a check has verified that an access b *happens after* a prior access a, we can henceforth assume that the check succeeded, even if that check is deferred because it involves a symbolic value. (If a deferred check later fails, it would reveal the first race on the variable, and finding subsequent races on that variable is not required.) Any subsequent access c that *happens after* b can therefore be assumed to *happen after* a. This reasoning often allows checks to be evaluated immediately, even when the read-VC and write-VC contain symbolic values. We use transitive reduction in two circumstances.

First, we do not need to log a check for a read that *happens after* a prior read in that epoch; we need only log checks for concurrent reads. Consider a read r_2 that *happens after* read r_1 in the same epoch. r_2 can race with the last write of a previous epoch only if r_1 also raced, so r_2 needs only to be checked against writes in the current epoch, and these checks can be evaluated immediately. When a read is handled, the detector compares the concrete portions of the read-VC to the thread's VC to decide if the read is concurrent with other reads in the epoch.

Second, consider a thread i that synchronizes (either directly or transitively) with another thread j during the epoch, i.e., thread i's VC happens after some event by thread j in this epoch. By transitivity, accesses by thread i after this point *happen after* all accesses in prior epochs by thread j. If thread i synchronizes with *all* threads during the epoch, subsequent accesses by thread i are guaranteed to happen after all accesses in prior epochs by all threads. In this situation, the detector need only check against races in the current epoch, and these checks can be evaluated immediately by examining the concrete values in the read-VCs and write-VCs.

As a result of these optimizations, we can determine a maximum bound on the number of checks per variables that can be deferred. In a process with N threads, there can be at most N concurrent reads, and there can be only a single first write. Hence, at most $N + 1$ checks can be deferred per variable. In particular, when all reads to a variable are totally ordered (e.g., data is thread-local or is protected by a lock), only 2 checks are deferred.

3.4 Commit phase

The commit phase performs the operations that were deferred during the epoch-parallel phase. Commit phases occur in program order, so the commit phase for one epoch has access to the concrete values of the final, complete analysis state for the prior epoch. In particular, it has access to concrete read-VC and write-VC values for the beginning of its epoch. It uses these concrete values to evaluate the symbolic expressions logged during the epoch-parallel phase and any symbolic values in the analysis state.

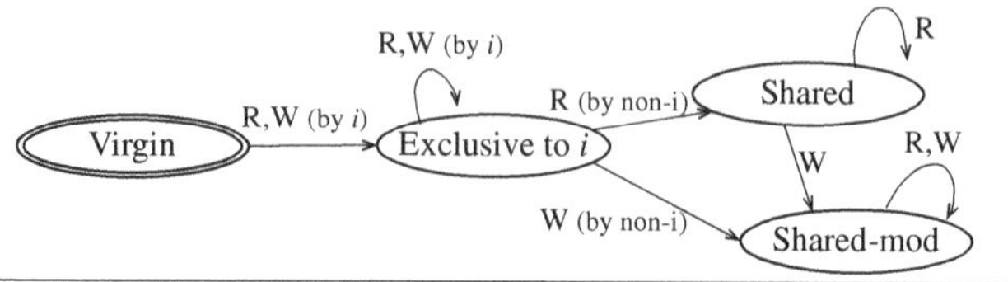

Figure 2. Eraser sharing state machine.

4. Parallel lockset

Another common approach to race detection is one based on *locksets* [39]. Lockset-based race detectors find potential races by looking for violations of a particular locking discipline. For example, a race may be declared for variables whose accesses are not consistently protected by at least one lock. Most lockset-based predictors are neither sound nor precise—they may miss real races and report false ones. Lockset detectors are nonetheless useful because they may find potential races that did not appear in the monitored execution.

We use the Eraser algorithm for lockset-based race detection [39]. Eraser tracks the *sharing state* of each variable according to the state machine shown in Figure 2. When a new variable is allocated, it starts in the *virgin* state. When the variable is first accessed, it transitions to the *exclusive* state and remains there until a different thread accesses it. If a different thread reads the variable, it transitions to the *shared* state; if a different thread writes the variable, it transitions to the *shared-modified* state.

The sharing state of a variable determines how the variable's lockset is updated. In the virgin state, the lockset is initialized to the set containing all locks in the program; it remains at this initial value while in the exclusive state. When the variable enters or is accessed in the shared or shared-modified states, its lockset is intersected with the locks currently held by the accessing thread (which we call the *thread lockset*). A race is declared if a variable's lockset is empty while the variable is in the shared-modified state. Eraser allows unlocked accesses to variables while they are being initialized by a single thread and to variables that are only read.

As described in Section 2.2, we split the task of race detection into three phases: epoch-sequential, epoch-parallel, and commit.

Overview: We instrument only synchronization and memory allocation in the epoch-sequential execution to predict each thread's lockset. The epoch-parallel execution adds memory access instrumentation, allowing it to track a superset of the true lockset for each variable. The commit phase merges a variable's lockset with that of previous epochs to reconstruct the actual lockset.

4.1 Epoch-sequential phase

The epoch-sequential phase predicts the thread locksets, but it does not predict the lockset or sharing state of each variable. To generate these predictions, synchronization and memory allocation operations are instrumented. This predicted subset of analysis state meets the criteria stated in Section 2.2.1. It is self-contained since thread locksets do not depend on variable states or variable locksets. It is lightweight since lock acquisitions and releases are much less frequent than variable accesses. It will usually match the analysis state generated by the epoch-parallel execution since the two executions can only diverge due to a data race. Because Eraser may miss data races, we verify that the predicted analysis state matches the analysis state generated by the epoch-parallel phase by comparing their values at the end of each epoch. In contrast, the parallel happens-before detector does not compare values because it identifies all data races.

	Initial sharing state {`ex_sh, owner, modified`}	
	{`EX, NONE or` i`, *`}	{`SH, *,` m_{init}} or {`EX,` $\neq$ `NONE` $\wedge \neq i$`, *`}
after access 1 (by thread i)	{`EX,` i`, FALSE`} $lockset = ALL$	{`SH, *,` $m_{\text{init}} \vee wr_1$} $lockset = LS_{\text{init}} \cap TLS_1$
after access 2 (by thread i)	{`EX,` i`, FALSE`} $lockset = ALL$	{`SH, *,` $m_{\text{init}} \vee wr_1 \vee wr_2$} $lockset = LS_{\text{init}} \cap TLS_1 \cap TLS_2$
after access 3 (by thread j)	{`SH, *,` wr_3} $lockset = TLS_3$	{`SH, *,` $m_{\text{init}} \vee wr_1 \vee wr_2 \vee wr_3$} $lockset = LS_{\text{init}} \cap TLS_1 \cap TLS_2 \cap TLS_3$
after access 4 (by thread k)	{`SH, *,` $wr_3 \vee wr_4$} $lockset = TLS_3 \cap TLS_4$	{`SH, *,` $m_{\text{init}} \vee wr_1 \vee wr_2 \vee wr_3 \vee wr_4$} $lockset = LS_{\text{init}} \cap TLS_1 \cap TLS_2 \cap TLS_3 \cap TLS_4$

Table 1. The two versions of analysis state maintained by epoch-parallel phase. The first version of analysis state assumes the initial sharing state is `EX`, and is owned either by `NONE` or by thread i (the thread that first accesses the variable in the epoch). The second version of analysis state covers all other conditions. wr_a is true iff access a is a write. TLS_a denotes the set of locks held by the accessing thread at the time of access a. LS_{init} and m_{init} denote the initial value of the variable's lockset and modification status. * means the value is ignored.

4.2 Epoch-parallel phase

The epoch-parallel phase performs most of the work of race detection. Synchronization, memory allocation, and memory access operations are all instrumented in this phase. An epoch starts with the predicted set of locks held by each thread and continues to maintain these during the epoch. However, the epoch-parallel phase does *not* know the initial value of each variable's lockset or sharing state, since these are not predicted by the epoch-sequential phase.

Not knowing the variables' initial sharing states has the potential to drastically slow down the epoch-parallel phase. The updates to a variable's lockset depends on the sharing state, so not knowing the sharing state forces the race detector to maintain multiple versions of each variable's lockset. For an application with N threads, there are $N + 3$ states in the sharing state machine: one exclusive state per thread, virgin, shared, and shared-modified. In the worst case, each state would cause the race detector to maintain the variable locksets differently, and this would require the race detector to perform $(N+3)$ times as many lockset manipulations as a conventional implementation.

Fortunately, by encoding and *factoring* the sharing state carefully, we eliminate most of this extra overhead. Instead of $N + 3$ versions of the sharing state and lockset, we maintain only two versions, and we need to manipulate only one version per variable access.

We encode the sharing state of a variable as a 3-tuple: {`ex_sh, owner, modified`}. The `ex_sh` field denotes whether the variable is exclusive to a single thread (`EX`) or shared by multiple threads (`SH`). If `ex_sh` is `EX`, then the `owner` field denotes which thread has accessed the variable, and `modified` is `FALSE` (the virgin state is handled as a special case of `EX` in which `owner` is NONE). If `ex_sh` is `SH`, `owner` is ignored, and the `modified` field denotes whether or not the variable has been modified while shared.

Table 1 shows how we maintain the sharing state and lockset for a variable, despite not knowing the initial sharing state or lockset. We maintain two versions of analysis state, which correspond to two possible categories of initial values for the sharing state. Conceptually, we maintain both versions of the sharing state and choose the correct one when the true sharing state at the beginning of the epoch is committed by the prior epoch. However, as we will show, our implementation needs only to update a single lockset and modified bit per access.

The first version of analysis state assumes the initial sharing state is `EX`, and `owner` is either `NONE` or the thread that first accesses the variable in the epoch. We call this *version-EX* because the first access in the epoch results in `ex_sh=EX`. The second version of analysis state is used for all other situations, i.e., it assumes the initial sharing state is `SH`, or it is `EX` and `owner` is a thread other than the one that first accesses the variable in the epoch. We call this *version-SH* because the first access in the epoch results in `ex_sh=SH`.

Consider the first access (in the epoch) to the variable by some thread i and all subsequent accesses by thread i that occur before some other thread accesses the variable. This sequence of accesses has different effects on the two versions of sharing state. For version-EX, this sequence of accesses leaves `ex_sh=EX`, `owner=`i, `modified=FALSE`, and `lockset=ALL`. For version-SH, this sequence of accesses leaves `ex_sh=SH`; the `modified` variable starts accumulating disjunctions of whether the access is a write or read; and the variable's lockset starts accumulating intersections of the accessing thread's lockset. Since disjunction and intersection are associative, we maintain these as a function of a symbolic value (m_{init} or LS_{init}) and a concrete value (e.g., in Table 1 after access 2, the initial values are m_{init} and LS_{init}, and the concrete values are $(wr_1 \vee wr_2)$ and $(TLS_1 \cap TLS_2)$). Note that, during this sequence of accesses, the epoch-parallel phase needs only to maintain the `modified` bit and the lockset for version-SH, since the `modified` bit and lockset for version-EX are not changing.

If a second thread accesses the variable in the epoch, we continue to maintain version-EX and version-SH. Since two threads have accessed the variable, `ex_sh=SH` in both versions. However, the value of `modified` and lockset continue to differ between the versions: in version-EX, these values are independent of the first sequence of accesses; in version-SH, these values depend on the first sequence of accesses. We minimize the number of operations needed to maintain `modified` and lockset for the two versions by factoring them into the disjunction (for `modified`) or intersection (for the lockset) of up to three expressions: the value at the beginning of the epoch (a symbolic value), a disjunction or intersection from the first thread's sequence of accesses (e.g., $TLS_1 \cap TLS_2$ in Table 1) and a disjunction or intersection from the accesses after the second thread accesses the variable (e.g., $TLS_3 \cap TLS_4$ in Table 1). With this factorization, we only need to manipulate a single instance of `modified` and lockset for each variable access.

4.3 Commit phase

The commit phase uses the final values for the lockset and sharing state from the prior epoch to generate the final values for the current epoch. It chooses between version-EX and version-SH based on the final values of `ex_sh` and `owner` from the prior epoch and the thread that first accessed the variable in the current epoch. If version-SH is chosen, it computes the final version of `modified` and lockset by merging in (via disjunction or intersection) the final value of `modified` or lockset from the prior epoch. After computing the final values for the analysis state, the commit phase detects if a race occurred on any variable accessed during this epoch by checking if any variable with `ex_sh=SH` has an empty lockset.

5. Implementation

Our execution system is based on the same infrastructure used in DoublePlay [44]. DoublePlay runs a 32-bit PAE Linux 2.6 kernel that has been heavily modified to provide uniparallelism. It uses online replay [19] to synchronize the epoch-parallel execution with the epoch-sequential execution, and it executes each epoch of the epoch-parallel execution on a single core. It also uses a custom version of glibc 2.5.1 to provide user-space logging for deterministic replay.

Race detectors need to analyze synchronization operations, memory management calls, and memory accesses. We intercept synchronization operations and memory management calls via dynamic library interposition. In particular, intercepting `malloc` calls allows lockset detectors to reinitialize analysis state on a new allocation. We intercept memory accesses by instrumenting loads and stores via a custom LLVM compiler pass. At default optimization levels, LLVM omits explicit loads and stores to variables whose references are proven not to escape the function. Consequently, we do not analyze accesses to these variables. For type-safe programs, these variables are guaranteed to be private to the thread. Since memory errors (e.g., buffer overflows) lead to undefined behavior and our race detector (like most such tools) runs in the address space of the instrumented process, such errors should be detected and fixed by other tools prior to running our detector.

For both happens-before and lockset race detectors, only the epoch-parallel execution needs to monitor loads and stores. For simplicity, we run the same program executable in both the epoch-sequential and the epoch-parallel execution, and the instrumentation checks a global variable to determine whether or not to analyze each instruction. The happens-before detector inlines this check within program instructions. The lockset detector (which compares the two executions' memory images) performs this check in its own function and additionally zeroes each new stack frame when it is allocated. A faster, though more complicated, strategy would be to run different program executables in the two executions [42]: the epoch-sequential execution would use a version without load/store instrumentation; the epoch-parallel execution would use a version with load/store instrumentation. We leave this for future work.

External libraries must either be compiled with instrumentation or have their functions annotated. We implement annotations for `glibc` through wrapper functions that explicitly invoke the handlers for analyzing loads and stores. For all other libraries, we compile a version with instrumentation.

Because race detectors analyze multithreaded programs, their analysis code must carefully handle the shared analysis state. Our analysis code uses spinlocks to provide atomicity at low latency in the common case. Analysis variables on a single cache line are guarded by the same lock to reduce inter-cache traffic. We provide a pool of spinlocks and hash the memory address being analyzed to select which spinlock to use. The pool contains 1024 spinlocks—large enough to avoid lock contention. These spinlocks are used by the conventional race detectors and the epoch-sequential phase of our race detector. The epoch-parallel phase instead ensures atomicity of the analysis code by running on a single core (Section 2.1).

For both happens-before and lockset detectors, all program memory is shadowed by analysis state, which is organized by a single-level page table with 4 MB pages. The baseline space overhead for the conventional and parallel happens-before detectors is twice the size of the program state; the baseline space overhead for the conventional and parallel lockset detectors is the size of the program state. Both parallel detectors use copy-on-write to minimize additional space overhead for the analysis state used by concurrent epochs; the amount of this additional space overhead is proportional to the number of epochs executing in parallel and the working set of each epoch.

The happens-before detectors find races with byte granularity. To minimize the analysis state and reduce the overhead of race detection, we compress the analysis state using a design similar to Valgrind's Memcheck [27]. We initially shadow entire four-byte words as single units. The first time an individual byte is accessed, we duplicate the word's analysis state and start shadowing each byte separately. The lockset detectors shadow and detect races with (fixed) word granularity without any compression.

6. Evaluation

This section evaluates experimentally the performance and scalability of our parallel happens-before and lockset race detectors. We compare the performance of our parallel race detectors with conventional happens-before and lockset detectors. The conventional detectors use the same race detection algorithms as the parallel detectors, which are based on FastTrack [15] and Eraser [39]. They use the same analysis infrastructure (LLVM) as the parallel detectors but run as normal multithreaded processes rather than using the uniparallel infrastructure. The main body of the analysis code is the same for conventional and parallel detectors, except that the parallel detectors do extra work to split the work across the epoch-sequential, epoch-parallel, and commit phases, while the conventional detectors acquire and release locks to guarantee atomicity for the analysis code. We compare the performance of all race detectors (both parallel and conventional) against uninstrumented versions of each benchmark that perform no race detection.

All experiments were performed on an 8-core workstation with 4 dual-core 2.4 GHz Intel Xeon CPUs (12 MB cache) and 6 GB RAM. We evaluate performance on five applications from the modified SPLASH-2 benchmark suite [48] (water-n^2, lu, ocean-contig, fft, radix) and one parallel application (pbzip2). The SPLASH-2 applications are CPU and memory intensive and contain little I/O. Pbzip2 is used to compress an 8 MB file, with multiple threads compressing different blocks of the file in parallel. We prefetch this file in advance to keep the application from becoming I/O-bound. We configure each application to use two worker threads; this allows us to evaluate scalability up to a 4:1 ratio of cores to threads; experiments with four worker threads had similar results up to the maximum ratio (2:1) on our platform. We exclude many of the other SPLASH-2 benchmarks because they contain frequent data races. The performance of a race detector is most important for programs that are mostly race-free and that run for an extended amount of time before encountering a data race (frequent races can be detected quickly even with a slow detector). When a race is detected, our detector records the event, but does not otherwise alter the execution of the target program.

We adjust the workload sizes so that each SPLASH-2 program executes in about 2 minutes on a single core when no race detection is used; pbzip2 take about 1 minute to run. For some applications, we scale the execution by looping through program's main computation multiple times. We also modify some applications to make periodic system calls, which allows our infrastructure to break long-running epochs.[2] All measurements are the mean of at least 4 samples of a benchmark's overall execute time. All graphs show 90% confidence intervals.

6.1 Overhead

We start by evaluating the performance of the conventional and parallel race detectors on a system with one core per worker thread (i.e., two cores total). Figure 3 shows the overhead of each detector, normalized to the execution time of the original application run without any race detector. For each application, the left bar shows

[2] The deterministic replay system we used ends epochs only at synchronous preemption points.

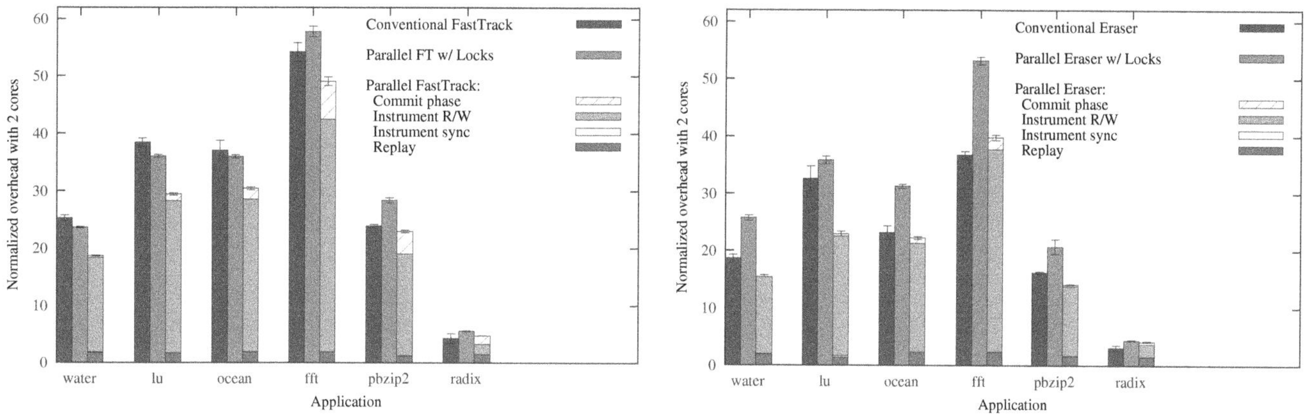

(a) Happens-before (b) Lockset

Figure 3. Overhead of race detection. Overhead values are normalized to the application's running time without race detection. For each application, the left bar shows the overhead of the conventional race detector; the right bar shows the overhead of the parallel race detector; and the middle bar shows the overhead the parallel race detector would have if it did not benefit from eliding analysis locks. The workloads shown use two worker threads and are run on two cores for both detectors.

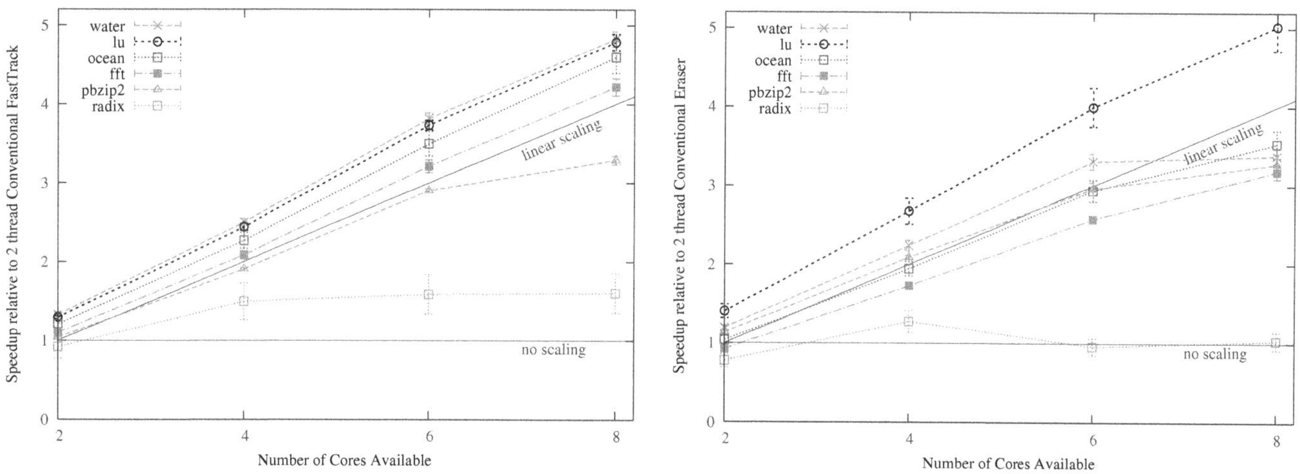

(a) Happens-before (b) Lockset

Figure 4. Scaling race detection via uniparallelism. Speedup is shown relative to the performance of the conventional race detector when run on two cores.

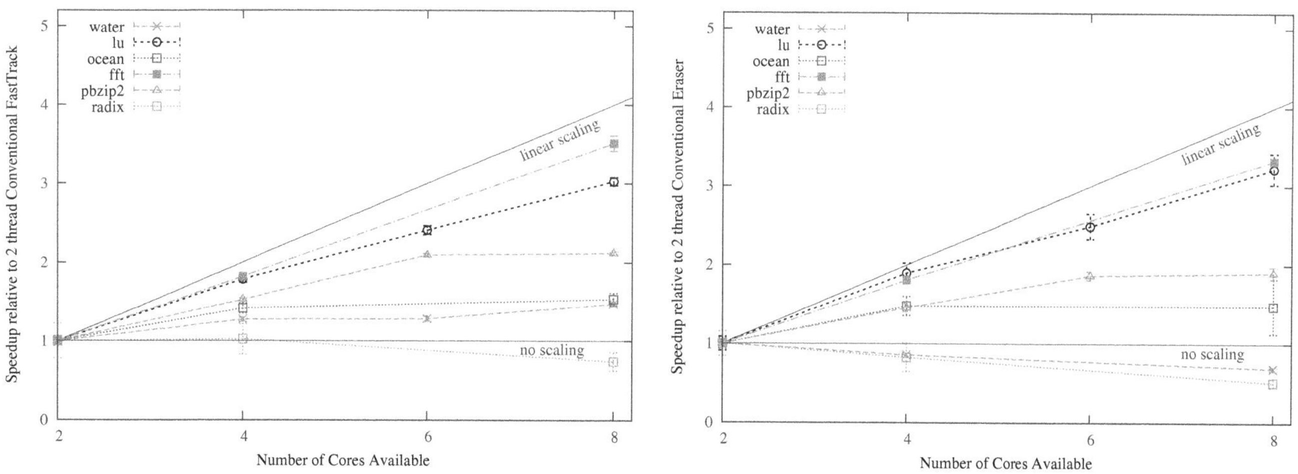

(a) Happens-before (b) Lockset

Figure 5. Scaling conventional race detection by increasing the number of worker threads in the application. Speedup is shown relative to the performance of a 2-thread application using the conventional race detector. In all cases, the number of worker threads in the application is equal to the number of cores used.

the overhead of the conventional race detector, and the right bar shows the overhead of the parallel race detector. The middle bar shows the overhead the parallel race detector would have if it did not benefit from eliding analysis locks.

Overhead varies widely between applications, depending on how frequently they access memory. Radix stands out as having the lowest overhead for race detection, due to radix's relatively low ratio of non-stack memory accesses to computation. As we will see later, radix's low overhead leaves little room for improvement via parallelization.

The middle bars in Figure 3 shows the overhead the parallel race detector would have if it needed to acquire and release analysis locks. Such a detector is slower than the conventional detector, since it takes extra work to parallelize an algorithm. For the lockset detector, lockset factorization greatly reduces the amount of extra work that needs to be done by the parallel detector.

The right bars in Figure 3 show that uniparallelism's ability to elide analysis locks usually gains back the extra overhead caused by parallelizing the algorithm. In fact, eliding analysis locks usually allows the parallel detectors to outperform the conventional ones, even when run on the same number of cores.

Overall, when both are run on the same number of cores, the parallel happens-before detector is 25% faster to 9% slower than the conventional detector (median 13% faster), and the lockset-based detector is 28% faster to 29% slower than the conventional detector (median 8% faster).

The rightmost bar in Figure 3 breaks the overhead for the parallel detectors into several components. *Replay* shows the time added to replay the application via uniparallelism without performing analysis on the replaying run. *Instrument sync* shows the time added to analyze synchronization operations in the epoch-sequential phase. *Instrument read/write* shows the time added to analyze memory accesses. *Commit phase* shows the time added to maintain and process the log of work that is deferred during the epoch-parallel phase.

We measured the overhead added by each component by incrementally enabling components of the instrumentation. For example, we measured overall running time with replay enabled but no instrumentation or commit; then we measured the running time with replay and instrumented synchronization calls but no read/write instrumentation or commit; etc.

As expected, most overhead comes from analyzing memory accesses. This overhead parallelizes well because the work to analyze memory accesses can be performed in the epoch-parallel phase. Commit phases for multiple epochs execute sequentially in our system, so they are a potential scalability bottleneck; however, Figure 3 shows that the commit phase is usually a small fraction of the overall overhead. For the happens-before detector, transitive reduction reduces the number of checks that are deferred to the commit phase; for the lockset detector, the commit phase has little work to do for each variable that was accessed in the epoch. Analyzing synchronization operations is done in the epoch-sequential phase in both detectors and could therefore be a scalability bottleneck, but Figure 3 shows that it adds a negligible amount to runtime.

6.2 Scalability

Our primary goal is to parallelize race detection across the available cores in the system. For benchmarks with two worker threads, we conduct experiments on 2, 4, 6, and 8 cores.

Figure 4 shows the speedup of our race detectors as we scale between 2 and 8 cores. Each point shows the speedup relative to the running time of the conventional race detector on 2 cores. The happens-before race detector parallelizes well for all applications except radix: with 8 cores, the median speedup over a 2-core conventional race detector is 4.4× (range is 1.6-4.8×). Parallel lockset also scales well for all applications except radix, but begins to reach scalability limits at 6 cores: with 6 cores, the median speedup over a 2-core conventional race detector is 3.0× (range is 1.0-4.0×). The lockset-based detector scales less well than the happens-before detector because the lockset detector adds less amount of overhead, so there is less room for improvement when scaling to more cores. The limiting factor to scaling is the the infrastructure we use to instrument the epoch-sequential execution. Because we run the same executable in both epoch-sequential and epoch-parallel executions, the epoch-sequential execution must perform some work on each memory access (viz., it must detect that it is running in the epoch-sequential execution and decide not to analyze the memory access). This per-access instrumentation causes the epoch-sequential execution to take about 3-5× as long as the original application. To scale the overhead lower than this, the epoch-sequential execution could use a different executable that eliminated this check [42].

For comparison, we show the speedup for two hypothetical parallel versions of the conventional detectors. First, the *linear scaling* lines in Figures 4 show the ideal speedup of the conventional detectors on 2 cores, assuming it could scale proportionally with available cores.

Second, we evaluate another strategy for parallelizing conventional detectors, which is to scale the application itself to use more cores. Figure 5 shows the speedup of this strategy, relative to the running time of the 2-thread application with a conventional race detector on 2 cores. Figure 5 shows that this strategy does not scale as well as our parallel detectors, in part because the applications themselves do not scale perfectly. Besides poorer scalability, there are two other downsides to this strategy. First, it works only for applications that can be easily configured to use more cores. Second, this strategy works only if the scaled application exhibits the same bugs as the original application. In contrast, parallelizing the race detectors via uniparallelism can achieve speedups on the original application, and it does not require the application itself to scale.

7. Related Work

Many researchers have studied how to detect data races dynamically via software techniques [2, 8, 9, 12, 15, 16, 32, 34, 35, 39, 50] and hardware techniques [11, 24, 30, 33, 51]. Despite much progress, dynamic data race detection remains expensive on commodity hardware, especially when analyzing unmanaged code.

Epoch parallelism was first used by Zilles and Sohi [52], who called it master/slave speculative parallelization. In their work, a fast, approximate version of a program to speed up a slow, correct version of the program. Others have since used epoch parallelism to parallelize some program analyses, such as data cache simulation [47], dynamic information flow tracking [29, 37], memory safety checks [17, 42], and program assertions [42]. Like us, Ruwase, et al. track symbolic values during an epoch and resolve them with concrete values when earlier epochs finish [37].

Uniparallelism, which is a variant of epoch parallelism, was first used by Veeraraghavan, et al. to implement a fast, deterministic replay system for multithreaded programs [44]. They used uniparallelism to minimize thread switches and thereby reduce the amount of nondeterminism that need to be logged. We use uniparallelism to eliminate thread switches while running analysis code, which reduces overhead by eliminating lock acquisitions and releases.

Veeraraghavan, et al. also used uniparallelism to design an *outcome-based* data race detector [43]. This algorithm detects races by running multiple replicas with different schedules and comparing their results [30]. Their outcome-based race detectors has low overhead but allows false negatives because it fails to detect races that do not affect the state at the end of the epoch. In contrast, we use uniparallelism to accelerate two classic types of data race detectors, namely happens-before and lockset analysis.

To our knowledge, ours is the first work that parallelizes conventional data race detectors on commodity hardware in a scalable way. Other researchers have split race detection across two processors by decoupling the monitoring of memory accesses from the race analysis of those accesses [7, 36], but this approach requires hardware support to reduce the overhead of instrumenting memory accesses and shipping logs to other processors. Uniparallelism allows us to parallelize both the instrumentation and analysis of memory accesses, and it reduces interprocessor communication by allowing these two tasks to run on a single processor for each epoch.

One benefit we gain from uniparallelism is its ability to provide mutual exclusion around analysis code without the overhead of acquiring and releasing locks. There are several other ways to provide mutual exclusion when analyzing multithreaded programs. The most common approach is to use coarse or fine-grained locking [12, 26, 38, 40], but this leads to significant overhead for race detectors because they need to acquire and release locks frequently and because they write analysis data even when reading application variables [45]. Using lock-free data structures can reduce this overhead, but these structures are more complicated to use than locks and cannot easily be applied in every situation (e.g., RaceTrack [50] uses lock-free lookups into a shared table, but it must lock when adding entries). Other researchers have proposed using hardware support for transactional memory to achieve the performance of fine-grained analysis locks [10]. Through uniparallelism, our system achieves the simplicity of a single lock, still allows analysis code to run in parallel, and eliminates the overhead of acquiring and releasing any locks. Our results show that eliding locks in this manner can significantly speed up race detection; this same approach could be used to speed up other high-frequency analyses.

8. Conclusions

This paper has shown how to speed up race detection via uniparallelism. Uniparallelism executes epochs across cores to increase parallelism, and it executes each epoch on a single core to reduce analysis locking overhead. We divide race detectors into three phases to enable them to run in a uniparallel environment: the epoch-sequential phase predicts a subset of the analysis state, the epoch-parallel phase carries out the bulk of the analysis, and the commit phase resolves symbolic expressions logged during the epoch-parallel phase.

We demonstrated our strategy by parallelizing a happens-before race detector and a lockset-based race detector. Each detector required unique optimizations to work well across the three phases: the happens-before detector used transitive reduction to reduce the work that must be deferred to the commit phase, and the lockset-based detector used lockset factorization to reduce the work needed to maintain multiple lockset versions during the epoch-parallel phase.

Our results showed that race detection can be parallelized effectively via uniparallelism. With 4× the number of cores as the original application, our strategy sped up the median execution time by 4.4× for a happens-before detector and 3.3× for a lockset race detector. Even on the same number of cores as the conventional detectors, the ability for uniparallelism to elide analysis locks allowed it to reduce the median overhead by 13% for a happens-before detector and 8% for a lockset detector.

We believe that many of the lessons learned in parallelizing data race detection can be applied to other heavyweight analyses of multithreaded programs. Analyses that can be restructured into the above three phases can benefit from uniparallelism, as long as most work can be done in the epoch-parallel phase. For any analysis, a key aspect of this restructuring is selecting the subset of the analysis to predict in the epoch-sequential phase. In addition, analyses that frequently acquire and release locks will benefit from the ability of uniparallelism to elide those locks.

Acknowledgments

We would like to thank all the anonymous reviewers for their valuable feedback and suggestions. This work has been supported by the National Science Foundation under award CNS-0905149 and by Intel Corp.. Satish Narayanasamy is supported by NSF CAREER award CNS-1149773. The views and conclusions contained in this document are those of the authors and should not be interpreted as representing the official policies, either expressed or implied, of NSF, Intel, Facebook, the University of Michigan, or the U.S. government.

References

[1] S. Adve. Data races are evil with no exceptions. *Communications of the ACM*, 53(11):84, November 2010.

[2] S. V. Adve, M. D. Hill, B. P. Miller, and R. H. B. Netzer. Detecting data races on weak memory systems. In *Proc. 1991 International Symposium on Computer Architecture*, pages 234–243.

[3] U. Banerjee, B. Bliss, Z. Ma, and P. Petersen. A theory of data race detection. In *2006 Workshop on Parallel and Distributed Systems: Testing and Debugging*, pages 69–78.

[4] H.-J. Boehm and S. V. Adve. Foundations of the C++ concurrency memory model. In *Proc. 2008 ACM Conference on Programming Language Design and Implementation*, pages 68–78.

[5] H.-J. Boehm and S. V. Adve. You Don't Know Jack About Shared Variables or Memory Models. *Communications of the ACM*, 55(2): 48–54, February 2012.

[6] M. D. Bond, K. E. Coons, and K. S. McKinley. Pacer: Proportional detection of data races. In *Proc. 2010 ACM Conference on Programming Language Design and Implementation*, pages 255–268.

[7] S. Chen, B. Falsafi, P. B. Gibbons, M. Kozuch, T. C. Mowry, R. Teodorescu, A. Ailamaki, L. Fix, G. R. Ganger, B. Lin, and S. W. Schlosser. Log-Based Architectures for General-Purpose Monitoring of Deployed Code. In *2006 Workshop on Architectural and System Support for Improving Software Dependability*.

[8] J.-D. Choi, K. Lee, A. Loginov, R. O'Callahan, V. Sarkar, and M. Sridharan. Efficient and precise datarace detection for multithreaded object-oriented programs. In *Proc. 2002 ACM Conference on Programming Language Design and Implementation*, pages 258–269.

[9] J.-D. Choi, B. P. Miller, and R. H. B. Netzer. Techniques for debugging parallel programs with flowback analysis. *ACM Transactions on Programming Languages and Systems*, 13(4):491–530, October 1991.

[10] J. Chung, M. Dalton, H. Kannan, and C. Kozyrakis. Thread-Safe Dynamic Binary Translation Using Transactional Memory. In *Proc. 2008 Symposium on High Performance Computer Architecture*, pages 279–289.

[11] J. Devietti, B. P. Wood, K. Strauss, L. Ceze, D. Grossman, and S. Qadeer. RADISH: Always-on sound and complete race detection in software and hardware. In *Proc. 2012 International Symposium on Computer Architecture*, pages 201–212.

[12] T. Elmas, S. Qadeer, and S. Tasiran. Goldilocks: A race and transaction-aware Java runtime. In *Proc. 2007 ACM Conference on Programming Language Design and Implementation*, pages 245–255.

[13] J. Erickson, M. Musuvathi, S. Burckhardt, and K. Olynyk. Effective data-race detection for the kernel. In *Proc. 2010 Symposium on Operating Systems Design and Implementation*, pages 151–162.

[14] C. J. Fidge. Timestamps in message-passing systems that preserve the partial ordering. *Australian Computer Science Communications*, 10 (1):56–66, February 1988.

[15] C. Flanagan and S. N. Freund. FastTrack: Efficient and precise dynamic race detection. In *Proc. 2009 ACM Conference on Programming Language Design and Implementation*, pages 121–133.

[16] A. Itzkovitz, A. Schuster, and O. Zeev-Ben-Mordehai. Toward integration of data race detection in DSM systems. *Journal of Parallel and Distributed Computing*, 59(2):180–203, November 1999.

[17] K. Kelsey, T. Bai, C. Ding, and C. Zhang. Fast Track: A software system for speculative program optimization. In *Proc. 2009 International Symposium on Code Generation and Optimization*, pages 157–168.

[18] L. Lamport. Time, clocks, and the ordering of events in a distributed system. *Communications of the ACM*, 21(7):558–565, July 1978. ISSN 0001-0782.

[19] D. Lee, B. Wester, K. Veeraraghavan, S. Narayanasamy, P. M. Chen, and J. Flinn. Respec: Efficient online multiprocesor replay via speculation and external determinism. In *Proc. 2010 International Conference on Architectural Support for Programming Languages and Operating Systems*, pages 77–90.

[20] N. G. Leveson and C. S. Turner. An Investigation of the Therac-25 Accidents. *IEEE Computer*, 26(7):18–41, July 1993.

[21] B. Lucia, L. Ceze, K. Strauss, S. Qadeer, and H.-J. Boehm. Conflict exceptions: Simplifying concurrent language semantics with precise hardware exceptions for data-races. In *Proc. 2010 International Symposium on Computer Architecture*, pages 210–221.

[22] D. Marino, M. Musuvathi, and S. Narayanasamy. LiteRace: Effective sampling for lightweight data-race detection. In *Proc. 2009 ACM Conference on Programming Language Design and Implementation*, pages 134–143.

[23] F. Mattern. Virtual time and global states of distributed systems. In *Proc. 1988 International Workshop on Parallel and Distributed Algorithms*.

[24] A. Muzahid, D. Suárez, S. Qi, and J. Torrellas. SigRace: Signature-based data race detection. In *Proc. 2009 International Symposium on Computer Architecture*, pages 337–348.

[25] S. Narayanasamy, Z. Wang, J. Tigani, A. Edwards, and B. Calder. Automatically Classifying Benign and Harmful Data Races Using Replay Analysis. In *Proc. 2007 ACM Conference on Programming Language Design and Implementation*, pages 22–31.

[26] N. Nethercote and J. Seward. Valgrind: A Framework for Heavyweight Dynamic Binary Instrumentation. In *Proc. 2007 ACM Conference on Programming Language Design and Implementation*, pages 89–100.

[27] N. Nethercote and J. Seward. How to shadow every byte of memory used by a program. In *Proc. 2007 ACM Conference on Virtual Execution Environments*, pages 65–74.

[28] R. H. B. Netzer. Optimal Tracing and Replay for Debugging Shared-Memory Parallel Programs. In *1993 ACM/ONR Workshop on Parallel and Distributed Debugging*.

[29] E. B. Nightingale, D. Peek, P. M. Chen, and J. Flinn. Parallelizing security checks on commodity hardware. In *Proc. 2008 International Conference on Architectural Support for Programming Languages and Operating Systems*, pages 308–318.

[30] A. Nistor, D. Marinov, and J. Torrellas. Light64: Lightweight hardware support for data race detection using systematic testing of parallel programs. In *Proc. 2009 International Symposium on Microarchitecture*, pages 541–552.

[31] K. Poulsen. Tracking the blackout bug. Technical report, SecurityFocus, April 2004. http://www.securityfocus.com/news/8412.

[32] E. Pozniansky and A. Scheuster. Efficient on-the-fly data race detection in multithreaded C++ programs. In *Proc. 2003 ACM Symposium on Principles and Practice of Parallel Programming*, pages 179–190.

[33] M. Prvulovic and J. Torrellas. ReEnact: Using thread-level speculation mechanisms to debug data races in multithreaded codes. In *Proc. 2003 International Symposium on Computer Architecture*, pages 110–121.

[34] P. Ratasaworabhan, M. Burtscher, D. Kirovski, B. Zorn, R. Nagpal, and K. Pattabiraman. Detecting and tolerating asymmetric races. In *Proc. 2009 ACM Symposium on Principles and Practice of Parallel Programming*, pages 173–184.

[35] M. Ronsse and K. D. Bosschere. RecPlay: A fully integrated practical record/replay system. *ACM Transactions on Computer Systems*, 17 (2):133–152, May 1999. ISSN 0734-2071.

[36] O. Ruwase, S. Chen, P. B. Gibbons, and T. C. Mowry. Decoupled Lifeguards: Enabling Path Optimizations for Dynamic Correctness Checking Tools. In *Proc. 2007 ACM Conference on Programming Language Design and Implementation*, pages 245–255.

[37] O. Ruwase, P. B. Gibbons, T. C. Mowry, V. Ramachandran, S. Chen, M. Kozuch, and M. Ryan. Parallelizing Dynamic Information Flow Tracking. In *Proc. 2008 ACM Symposium on Parallelism in Algorithms and Architectures*, pages 35–45.

[38] P. Sack, B. E. Bliss, Z. Ma, P. Petersen, and J. Torrellas. Accurate and efficient filtering for the Intel Thread Checker race detector. In *Proc. 2006 Workshop on Architectural and System Support for Improving Software Dependability*, pages 34–41.

[39] S. Savage, M. Burrows, G. Nelson, P. Sobalvarro, and T. Anderson. Eraser: A dynamic data race detector for multithreaded programs. *ACM Transactions on Computer Systems*, 15(4):391–411, November 1997.

[40] K. Serebryany and T. Iskhodzhanov. ThreadSanitizer: Data race detection in practice. In *Proc. 2009 Workshop on Binary Instrumentation and Applications*, pages 62–71.

[41] J. Sevcik and D. Aspinall. On Validity of Program Transformations in the Java Memory Model. In *Proc. 2008 European conference on Object-Oriented Programming*, pages 27–51.

[42] M. Süßkraut, T. Knauth, S. Weigert, U. Schiffel, M. Meinhold, and C. Fetzer. Prospect: A compiler framework for speculative parallelization. In *Proc. 2010 International Symposium on Code Generation and Optimization*, pages 131–140.

[43] K. Veeraraghavan, P. M. Chen, J. Flinn, and S. Narayanasamy. Detecting and surviving data races using complementary schedules. In *Proc. 2011 ACM Symposium on Operating Systems Principles*, pages 369–384.

[44] K. Veeraraghavan, D. Lee, B. Wester, J. Ouyang, P. M. Chen, J. Flinn, and S. Narayanasamy. DoublePlay: Parallelizing sequential logging and replay. In *Proc. 2011 International Conference on Architectural Support for Programming Languages and Operating Systems*, pages 15–26.

[45] E. Vlachos, M. L. Goodstein, M. A. Kozuch, S. Chen, B. Falsafi, P. B. Gibbons, and T. C. Mowry. ParaLog: Enabling and Accelerating Online Parallel Monitoring of Multithreaded Applications. In *Proc. 2010 International Conference on Architectural Support for Programming Languages and Operating Systems*, pages 271–284.

[46] C. von Praun and T. R. Gross. Object race detection. In *Proc. 2001 ACM Conference on Object-Oriented Programming, Systems, Languages, and Applications*, pages 70–82.

[47] S. Wallace and K. Hazelwood. SuperPin: Parallelizing dynamic instrumentation for real-time performance. In *Proc. 2007 International Symposium on Code Generation and Optimization*, pages 209–220.

[48] S. C. Woo, M. Ohara, E. Torrie, J. P. Singh, and A. Gupta. The SPLASH-2 programs: Characterization and methodological considerations. In *Proc. 1995 International Symposium on Computer Architecture*, pages 24–36.

[49] M. Xu, M. D. Hill, and R. Bodik. A regulated transitive reduction (RTR) for longer memory race recording. In *Proc. 2006 International Conference on Architectural Support for Programming Languages and Operating Systems*, pages 49–60.

[50] Y. Yu, T. Rodeheffer, and W. Chen. RaceTrack: Efficient detection of data race conditions via adaptive tracking. In *Proc. 2005 ACM Symposium on Operating Systems Principles*, pages 221–234.

[51] P. Zhou, R. Teodorescu, and Y. Zhou. HARD: Hardware-assisted lockset-based race detection. In *Proc. 2007 Symposium on High Performance Computer Architecture*, pages 121–132.

[52] C. Zilles and G. Sohi. Master/slave speculative parallelization. In *Proc. 2002 International Symposium on Microarchitecture*, pages 85–96.

Cooperative Empirical Failure Avoidance for Multithreaded Programs

Brandon Lucia and Luis Ceze
{blucia0a,luisceze}@cs.washington.edu
University of Washington, Department of Computer Science and Engineering
http://sampa.cs.washington.edu

Abstract

Concurrency errors in multithreaded programs are difficult to find and fix. We propose Aviso, a system for avoiding schedule-dependent failures. Aviso monitors events during a program's execution and, when a failure occurs, records a history of events from the failing execution. It uses this history to generate schedule constraints that perturb the order of events in the execution and thereby avoids schedules that lead to failures in future program executions. Aviso leverages scenarios where many instances of the same software run, using a statistical model of program behavior and experimentation to determine which constraints most effectively avoid failures. After implementing Aviso, we showed that it decreased failure rates for a variety of important desktop, server, and cloud applications by orders of magnitude, with an average overhead of less than 20% and, in some cases, as low as 5%.

Categories and Subject Descriptors D.1.3 [*Concurrent Programming*]: Parallel programming; D.2.5 [*Testing and Debugging*]: Error handling and recovery

General Terms Algorithms, Reliability

Keywords concurrency, cooperative failure avoidance

1. Introduction

Concurrency errors in multithreaded programs can lead to nondeterministic *schedule-dependent failures*, which are failures that arise from interactions between threads that are unforeseen by programmers during development. Such interactions can be characterized by sequences of synchronization operations and accesses to data that the threads share. Atomicity violations, a common type of schedule-dependent failure, occur when one thread's access to shared state is incorrectly permitted to interleave between a pair of accesses in another thread. Ordering violations, another type of schedule-dependent failure, take place when operations in different threads occur in an order that leads to a failure.

Most prior work dealing with concurrency errors has focused on their *detection*, which typically involves identifying patterns of memory accesses specific to certain bug types. Unfortunately, even with state-of-the-art tools, concurrency bugs remain in deployed code and cause costly, schedule-dependent failures.

Recent research is exploring the *avoidance* of schedule-dependent failures. Avoidance work seeks to determine the sequences of operations most likely to lead to buggy behavior and to prevent those sequences from executing. This general idea has had several incarnations. For example, prior work proposed the use of hardware to prevent atomicity violations [12, 13] and to bias execution towards tested behavior [27, 28]. Other avoidance work used memory-protection-based techniques [21, 22] and relied on programmer annotations to modify strategic points in a program [26].

These recent efforts have made progress toward more reliable concurrent systems, but they fall short in several ways. Some require significant programmer effort, which may be better spent patching the faulty program. Many cater only to certain types of bugs, and several require complex, expensive changes to hardware.

Failure avoidance systems face many complex challenges. Systems must monitor program execution to collect the information needed to identify likely failures. This monitoring must be efficient because failure avoidance is most useful in deployed systems, where performance is paramount. Systems also require precise techniques to identify failures using the collected data and mechanisms to influence the program's execution to avoid failures; as with monitoring, such mechanisms must be efficient. Furthermore, systems should avoid failures without requiring modifications to hardware or changes to the way programmers write their programs.

We overcome these challenges in this work. Our main contribution is a *novel, automated technique for avoiding schedule-dependent failures*. We develop an efficient system for collecting relevant program events at run-time in deployed software. When a program instance fails, we use the information collected by our system to generate hypotheses about what caused the failure. Then, leveraging the fact that we often have a number of deployed instances of the same software, we develop a predictive statistical model and an empirical framework to identify which hypothesis is most likely to be correct. Based on that hypothesis, we influence future program executions by perturbing the thread schedule to avoid subsequent failures.

We implement these ideas in Aviso, a distributed framework that coordinates many deployed instances of a program to cooperatively learn how to prevent failures. Our system works on commodity hardware with minimal impact on software and the development process. Our evaluation on several real-world desktop, server, and cloud applications shows that Aviso effectively and efficiently improves software reliability. In one test, Aviso reduced the failure rate of a buggy version of Memcached, a popular key-value store, by two orders of magnitude. Fixing the bug took developers about a year and their fix imposed about 7% performance overhead [1]. Aviso worked without developer intervention and in minutes found an effective constraint that imposed only a marginally higher overhead of about 15%.

The remainder of this paper describes Aviso in greater detail. Section 2 provides background that explains how Aviso avoids schedule-dependent failures. Section 3 reviews Aviso's design

ASPLOS'13, March 16–20, 2013, Houston, Texas, USA.

goals and architecture, while Section 4 relates how Aviso decides which events to monitor during an execution and how events and failures are to be monitored. We describe how Aviso generates candidate constraints after a failure in Section 5 and how it determines which candidate constraint effectively prevents failures as well as inter-system constraint sharing in Section 6. Section 7 provides implementation details. Sections 8–10 evaluate and characterize Aviso, contrast it with prior work, and summarize our findings.

2. Schedule-Dependent Failures

A program's execution experiences a schedule-dependent failure when threads execute a particular sequence of events that leads to a crash, contract violation (*e.g.*, assertion), or state corruption. Schedule-dependent failures are the result of programming errors, such as absent or incorrectly used synchronization.

Figure 1(a) illustrates how a programming error leads to a failure using an example from AGet-0.4, a multithreaded download accelerator. Figure 1(a) shows a snippet of a failing multithreaded execution. The failure is an atomicity violation: Thread 1 writes bytes to a file (`pwrite(...)` on line 116) and then adds the number of bytes written to the file to a shared counter (incrementing `bwritten` on line 121). The failure occurs when Thread 2 asynchronously reads the value of `bwritten` on line 41, between the call to `pwrite()` and the increment that follows. The programmer has omitted synchronization operations in Thread 2, permitting that thread to read an intermediate value. Note that if Thread 2's read was delayed, and Thread 1's update was allowed to proceed, the failure could have been avoided.

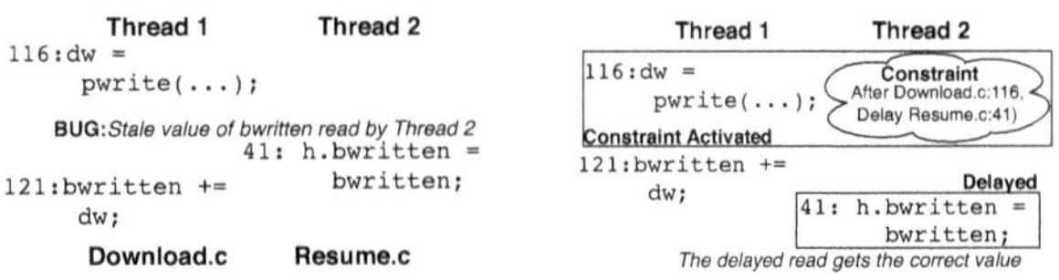

(a) **A failing execution.** The failure occurs when Thread 2 reads a stale value of `bwritten`.

(b) **Avoiding the failure.** The constraint delays Thread 2, reordering operations to avoid the failure.

Figure 1. A schedule-dependent failure in AGet-0.4.

2.1 Bug Depth

Recent concurrency testing work [3] formally characterized concurrency errors using the notion of *bug depth*. A bug's depth is the minimum number of pairs of program events that must occur in a particular order for that bug to manifest a failure [3]. Note that a single *bug* can lead to different *failures* under different execution schedules. A different set of event pair orderings is necessary to manifest each different failure and a failure occurs only if all its necessary orderings are satisfied. Typically, most schedules do not satisfy all orderings required to cause any particular failure, so executions usually do not fail.

This fact poses a key challenge to multithreaded testing. To expose a bug during testing by causing a failure, systems must enforce a number of orderings on the execution schedule that is greater than or equal to the bug's depth. The larger the bug's depth, the more work is needed to ensure that a failure occurs [3]. The bug in Figure 1(a) has depth 2 because two pairs of events must execute in a particular order for the failure to manifest: Thread 2's read must follow Thread 1's `pwrite` call and must precede Thread 1's `bwritten` update. If the first ordering were not upheld, Thread 2 would correctly see the value of `bwritten` before any of Thread 1's operations. If the second ordering were not upheld, Thread 2 would correctly see the result of Thread 1's operations.

2.2 The Avoidance-Testing Duality

In this work, we make the observation that a failure caused by a bug of *any* depth can be avoided by perturbing just *one* pair of events in the sequence that leads to the failure. Given a chain of pairs of events that must be ordered to manifest a failure in testing, perturbing the schedule to reorder any of the pairs "breaks the chain", preventing that failing schedule from occurring. This observation suggests a duality between testing for schedule-dependent failures and avoiding them: testing requires enforcing *all* of a conjunction of pair orderings to exercise a failing schedule; avoidance requires reordering events in *any* of those pair orderings to avoid a failing schedule. Avoiding a particular failing schedule leads the execution to a new schedule. Avoidance is successful if the new schedule does not lead to a failure, which is likely the case since there are typically significantly more failure-free schedules than schedules with failures.

Figure 2(a) illustrates bug depth. The circles are program events and the arrows represent pair orderings necessary to lead to a failure. There are d orderings, so assuming the figure shows the fewest possible orderings for the bug to cause a failure, the bug has depth d. Figure 2(b) contrasts testing and failure avoidance. Exposing a bug during testing requires satisfying a conjunction of d pair orderings, whereas the failure is avoided if a single pair of events is reordered.

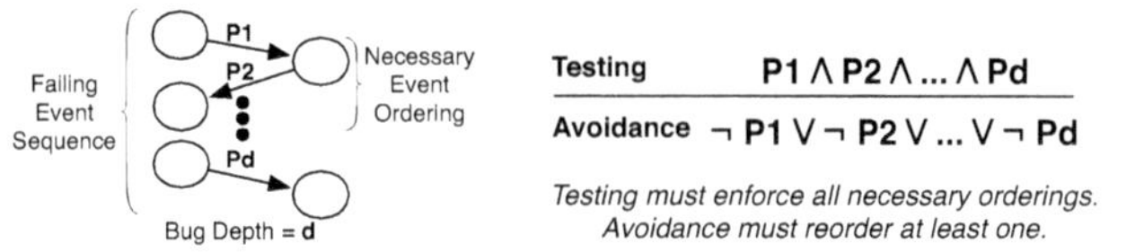

(a) **Pair orderings necessary for the failure to occur**. There are d orderings, so the bug responsible for the failure has depth d (assuming the figure shows the fewest orderings for the bug to cause a failure).

(b) **Contrasting testing with failure avoidance.** Testing aims to expose bugs, so *all* orderings must be satisfied. Avoidance aims to prevent failures by reorderings the events in *any* ordering.

Figure 2. The Avoidance-Testing Duality.

3. System Overview

This section provides an overview of Aviso's system architecture and design constraints. We then walk through Aviso's failure avoidance mechanism with an example, and explain how Aviso facilitates *cooperative*, *empirical* failure avoidance in a community of software instances.

3.1 System Architecture

Figure 3 presents Aviso's four components: (1) the profiler, (2) the compiler, (3) the runtime system, and (4) the framework.

Profiler and Compiler. After development, the programmer runs Aviso's profiler, which determines what program operations to monitor. The profiler sends an event profile to Aviso's compiler. The compiler uses the event profile to add event-handling runtime calls to the binary and links the binary to the Aviso runtime to produce and Aviso-enabled executable.

Runtime. The Aviso runtime system monitors and keeps a short history of events during program execution. The runtime also watches for failures and alerts the framework when they occur. Periodically during execution and when execution fails, the runtime sends its event history to the framework. The runtime can also perturb the execution schedule using *schedule constraints* (see below) that it receives from the framework.

Framework. Aviso-enabled executables run in the Aviso framework and the two communicate via a simple messaging API. The framework collects event histories and failure information sent by the runtime. It generates schedule constraints from this information and sends them to the runtime when Aviso-enabled executables start running. The framework selects constraints to send using a statistical model that predicts which constraint is most likely to avoid failures; it builds the model using aggregated history and failure information. By aggregating information from and sending constraints to many program instances, the framework enables program instances to cooperatively avoid failures.

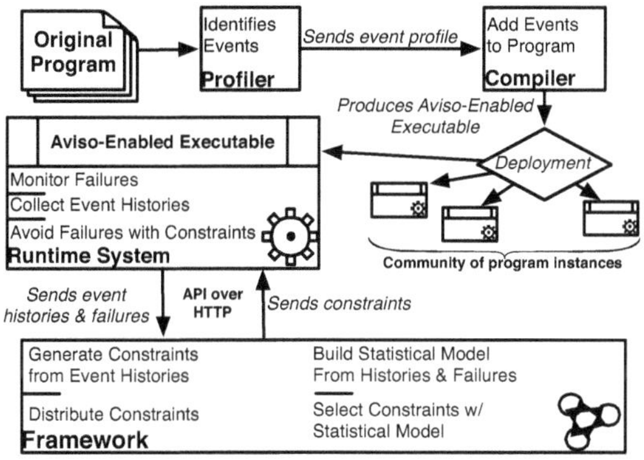

Figure 3. Aviso's components. The compiler and profiler find and instrument events. The runtime system monitors events and failures and avoids events. The framework generates constraints, selects likely effective constraints using a statistical model and shares effective constraints in a community of software instances.

3.1.1 Design Requirements

Our goal is to build a system that is general enough to avoid failures due to a broad class of concurrency errors in a deployment setting. This goal presents us with conflicting design constraints: For the sake of generality, the runtime should monitor as many program operations as possible, to capture a large variety of failure behaviors. However, monitoring imposes a time and space overhead, and building a system intended for use in deployment necessitates high performance. Aviso should find effective constraints quickly and permit as few failures as possible. To do so Aviso must leverage *prediction* to identify effective constraints without having to directly observe their impact on the program's behavior. Aviso is additionally constrained because programmer time is valuable and understanding and fixing concurrency errors is difficult, error-prone, and time consuming. Our system should require as little as possible from the programmer.

3.2 Avoiding Failures with Schedule Constraints

Aviso leverages the avoidance-testing duality introduced in Section 2.2 to avoid failures. Aviso uses *schedule constraints* to perturb an execution's thread schedule with the goal of reordering events in the execution whose original order leads to a failure.

A constraint is based on a pair of events observed by Aviso in a failing program execution. It is "activated" when the first event in its pair executes. When a constraint is active and a thread tries to execute the second event in the constraint's pair, Aviso delays the thread, reordering some events in the execution. If the original order of the reordered events was necessary for a failure to occur, reordering the events will avoid the failure. Such reorderings are the key to Aviso's failure avoidance mechanism. We provide more details on avoidance in Section 5.2.

Figure 1(b) shows how Aviso uses a constraint to avoid a failure. The constraint is made from a pair of events: the first event is Thread 1's `pwrite` call at Download.c, line 116, and the second event is Thread 2's read of `bwritten` at Resume.c, line 41. When the first event is executed, the constraint is activated. While the constraint is active, Thread 2 attempts to execute the second event, and it is delayed. During this delay, Thread 1's `bwritten` update executes atomically with its `pwrite` call, preventing the failure. Later, when Thread 2 resumes execution, it reads the correct value of `bwritten`.

3.3 Cooperative Empirical Failure Avoidance

Aviso is an *empirical* failure avoidance system. When a failure occurs, it generates a set of constraints from its event history (see Section 5). Each constraint is a *hypothesis* about how to prevent the failure. Aviso decides which constraints are most likely to avoid failures and instructs program instances to use those constraints. It is an *empirical system* because it uses a combination of predictive statistical modeling and experimentation to select effective constraints. As Aviso observes more execution behavior, it refines its model, improving its selections. The details of constraint selection are described in Section 6.

Aviso is also a *cooperative* failure avoidance system. It leverages communities of computers running the same program to select effective constraints in two ways. First, Aviso's statistical model is built using information drawn from a community of program instances. Second, Aviso distributes constraints to all members of a community. A constraint that consistently avoids failures for some members can be distributed to other members, sharing its benefit.

4. Monitoring Events and Failures

Aviso's profiler identifies program operations relevant to concurrent program behavior. The compiler inserts event-handling runtime calls into Aviso-enabled executables before each operation. Aviso works on deployed programs, so determining which operations should be treated as events determines the overhead of event handling. Aviso uses static and dynamic analyses to prune the detected set of events. Aviso's runtime traces events during execution and monitors for failures.

4.1 Identifying Relevant Program Events

Aviso focuses on concurrency errors, so we restrict our attention to events related to concurrency. There are three types of events that Aviso monitors: (1) synchronization events, (2) signal events, and (3) sharing events. *Synchronization events* are lock and unlock operations, thread spawn, and join operations that can be identified by matching synchronization library (*e.g.*, `pthread`) calls. Aviso can handle other types of synchronization, as well (*e.g.*, CAS) if the programmer identifies them as sychronization.

Signal events are functions that handle signals. They are of interest because signals may be delivered and handled asynchronously. Signal events are identified by instrumenting signal handler registration functions (*e.g.*, `signal()`) and functions that explicitly wait for signal delivery (*e.g.*, `sigwait()`).

Sharing events are more difficult to identify because they cannot be identified by looking only at syntactic properties of a program. Instead, Aviso identifies sharing events using a *sharing profiler* before application deployment, *i.e.*, during testing. The sharing profiler monitors threads' accesses to shared data. When a thread accesses data that has been accessed by another thread during the execution, the operation the thread is executing is considered to be a sharing event. Sharing events are reported by the profiler and inserted into the deployment binary by Aviso's instrumenting compiler. Aviso identifies events by their instruction address and the call stack when the event occurs.

4.2 Pruning and Instrumenting Events

Handling events too frequently leads to high performance overheads. To mitigate that issue, we use two techniques to reduce the number of handled events. First, our instrumenting compiler uses *dominance pruning* to eliminate instrumentation of some events. Second, our runtime system uses *online pruning* to limit the number of events that are handled.

Dominance Pruning (Static) Analysis. When compiling a function and before optimization, Aviso's compiler computes the set of dominators for each instruction. We use the computed dominance relationships to prune the set of candidate events. Given a pair of events (p, q), if p dominates q, then for every execution of q, there was a prior execution of p. Hence, tracking only p captures nearly as much information as tracking both p and q. In this situation, we remove q from the set of candidate events. If p and q are far apart in the code, dominance pruning might discard useful events. However, our analysis did not pose problems in our experiments for several reasons. First, dominance pruning does not apply to synchronization events, and synchronization events often occur near sharing events. Second, we identify sharing events using profiling, which is approximate; dominance pruning makes the approximation only slightly less precise. Third, dominance pruning operates at function granularity, limiting the distance between p and q to the length of a function at most. Fourth, if events are far apart, the dominance relation still conveys information about the interleaving of events along certain control flow paths. This information is less precise but still useful to prevent failures.

Online Pruning. To further reduce overheads, Aviso uses *online pruning* to adaptively reduce the number of events handled. During execution, Aviso tracks the interval between consecutive events. If two events occur within $1\mu s$ of one another, they likely encode redundant information, and Aviso discards the second of the two. Discarding events is, in effect, dynamically coalescing a sequence of events that occur within $1\mu s$ of one another into a single event, represented by the first in the sequence.

4.3 Tracing Important Program Events

When generating schedule constraints, Aviso focuses on pairs of events that occurred in a single failing program execution. When an execution fails due to a concurrency bug, the event sequence that caused the failure must have occurred during that execution. Aviso focuses on program events that occurred just before the failure. These events are likely to be related to the failure because *some* code point must have trigger the failure (*e.g.*, caused a crash, emitted buggy output, violated a contract, *etc.*); these events must have occurred occurs shortly before the symptom of the failure was manifested. This observation suggests that a backward scan over a trace of events from the point of failure is likely to encounter the events involved in the failure.

We therefore designed the Aviso runtime to maintain a totally ordered history of events recently executed by any thread, called the *Recent Past Buffer*, or RPB, for the execution. The RPB is a fixed-size queue; the size could vary across implementations, but it should be on the order of hundreds of events. We used an RPB that holds at most 1000 events from each thread. Across most of our experiments, we saw an average event frequency of around $500\mu s$, so each thread's RPB covers about the last 0.5s of its execution. Half a second is likely to be long enough to capture events related to a failure, as prior work suggests that such events often occur over short windows of execution [10, 11, 13]. When an event is executed, the oldest event in the RPB is dequeued and discarded, and the newest event is enqueued. When a failure occurs, the RPB contains a history of the execution's final moments and is likely to include the events that led to the failure.

4.4 Monitoring Program Failures

For crashes and assertion failures, the runtime preserves the RPB before the program terminates. For other failures, Aviso monitors for *ad hoc* failure conditions and preserves the contents of the RPB when failure conditions are met.

The best way to detect non-crash failures depends on the failure's symptom. Identifying arbitrary failures automatically is a difficult problem, and doing so comprehensively is outside the scope of this work. However, simple solutions often work well; *e.g.*, validating output is often adequate. In our tests with Memcached, we added an assertion that encodes a simple data structure invariant, preventing the use of deallocated storage. Section 8.1 describes our experience adding failure monitors to programs for the subset of our tests that required it.

In general, given an error report that describes a failure's symptom, an *ad hoc* failure monitor can be added to the Aviso framework to handle any failure diagnosis criteria. Using failure monitors is not always necessary – Aviso deals with fail-stop errors by default. When necessary, adding failure monitors is less risky and onerous than patching code or writing a workaround [26].

5. Generating Constraints and Avoiding Failures

After a failure, the framework examines the RPB and enumerates event pairs that could potentially have led to the failure. For each pair, it generates a *candidate constraint* that perturbs the thread schedule around the events in the pair. A candidate is *effective* if its perturbation avoids a failure. The framework selects candidate constraints to make available to future program executions that can use them to avoid failure. In Section 6 we discuss how Aviso selects effective candidates.

5.1 Generating Candidate Constraints

We take a straightforward approach to selecting event pairs to generate constraints. The framework considers pairs of events in execution order in the RPB, (B, A), that were executed by different threads. It selects these pairs under the constraint that between B and A no event was executed by the thread that executed B. Note that between events in a pair, other uninvolved threads may execute other unrelated events.

Figure 4 illustrates the process of enumerating event pairs. Notice that Thread 1's first execution of E is not part of a pair because it is immediately followed by B in the same thread. Also notice that Thread 2's F and Thread 3's X form a pair in spite of their separation by Thread 1's executions of E.

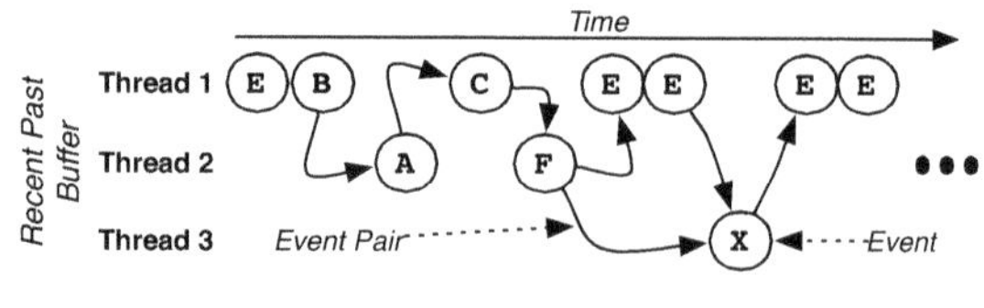

Figure 4. Enumerating pairs from a failing execution's RPB. There are three threads, and time proceeds left to right. Circles are events, and arcs between events are event pairs. Arcs for duplicate pairs are omitted. The figure shows a single 10-event window of events, but selection occurs for all 10-event windows.

To limit the number of constraints generated, we rely on the assumption that events that comprise effective constraints occur within a short window; we consider only event pairs separated by fewer than 10 events in the RPB. This assumption is reasonable for several reasons. First, prior work on finding and avoiding concurrency bugs [8, 12, 13, 18, 24, 25] suggests that the events involved in schedule-dependent failures often occur within a short window of the program's execution (*i.e.*, hundreds or thousand of instructions). Second, each event in the RPB represents a span of the program's execution, not a single instruction. Due to our online pruning approach (Section 4.2), two consecutive events in the same thread are at least $1\mu s$ apart, meaning that each event can represent thousands of instructions. Hence, a 10-event window covers a part of the execution large enough to contain useful event pairs.

5.2 Avoiding Failures

Each event pair corresponds to a schedule constraint. The first event in the pair is the constraint's "activation event", and the second event is the "delay event".

When a program instance starts, the framework makes a set of constraints available to the program instance. Every constraint starts as inactive. Inactive constraints have no effect on the program's execution. When a constraint's activation event is executed, the constraint is *instantiated*, and added to a set of active constraints. The runtime system records the ID of the thread that executed the activation event as the "activator" in the constraint instance. A thread may have at most one instance of a constraint active, but if several different threads execute a constraint's activation event, each thread will instantiate its own instance of the constraint. Figure 5 illustrates the constraint activation process.

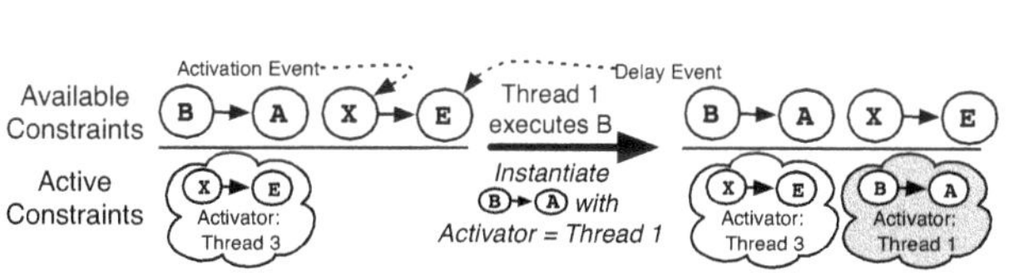

Figure 5. Constraint Activation. *Available constraints* are those that Aviso has made available to the execution. *Active constraints* are constraint instances that have been instantiated and can trigger delays. The large, central arrow signifies Thread 1 executing event B. To the left of the arrow there are no instances of the constraint (B, A); event B is its activation event, so when B is executed an instance of the constraint is added to the Active Constraints set (shaded cloud). Aviso records that Thread 1 is the instance's activator in the instance.

When a thread executes the constraint's delay event, Aviso decides whether to perturb the execution. To do so, it compares the executing thread to the activator of each constraint instance. If the thread executing the delay event is the same as the activator of a constraint instance, Aviso does nothing and execution continues. If it is different, Aviso delays that thread's execution. The delay perturbs the execution schedule by permitting threads other than the delayed one to continue their execution ahead of the delayed event. The reordering of these other threads' events with the delayed event is Aviso's strategy for preventing failures, as we described in Section 3.

5.2.1 Practical Issues with Constraints

There are several practical issues related to pair-based constraints.

Delay Length. Events delayed by constraints cannot be delayed indefinitely without impeding forward progress. Delays must be long enough to reorder events that would lead to failures, but short enough that their impact on performance is tolerable. We empirically determined that $1ms$ achieved this balance well across our benchmarks: any shorter and Aviso was unable to prevent failures in some cases; any longer and performance degraded without improvement in failure avoidance. We show data in Section 8 that further support our choice of delay length.

Composing Constraints. It is important that Aviso not be limited to preventing only one failure due to one bug at a time. Most programs have more than one bug. Each bug may lead to a different failure. To deal with this problem, Aviso can make a collection of constraints available to threads, each with different activation and delay events. When any constraint's activation event is encountered, the executing thread instantiates that constraint. Threads can instantiate multiple different constraints simultaneously to avoid multiple different classes of failures. Section 6 describes how Aviso decides when multiple constraints should be available to be instantiated.

5.2.2 Why Do Event Pairs Make Effective Constraints?

Section 2 discussed the relationship between schedule-dependent failures and bug depth: if we invert one of the d event pair orderings necessary for a bug of depth d to cause a failure, we prevent the failure. In general, Aviso is effective if it generates constraints that reorder such events, like the one in the center part of Figure 6. We now describe how Aviso can use the constraint in Figure 6 to avoid two concrete classes of failures – atomicity violations and ordering violations.

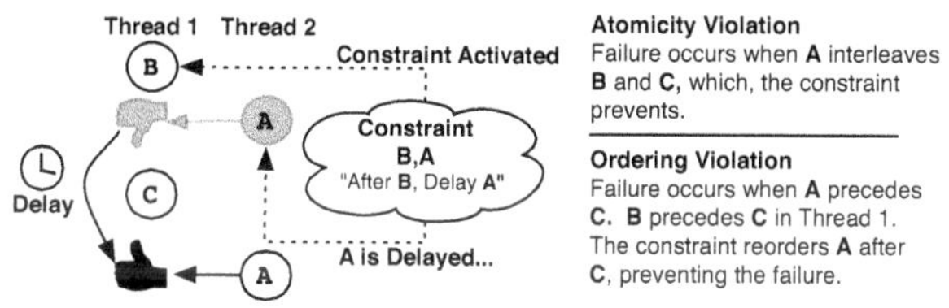

Figure 6. How a constraint avoids a failure. The constraint is shown in the cloud and is made from events B and A; when a thread executes B, the constraint is instantiated. When another thread executes A, it is delayed. The left side shows an execution snippet that can be viewed as both an atomicity violation and an ordering violation.

Avoiding Atomicity Violations. Figure 6 shows how constraints avoid atomicity violations. It depicts two threads with Thread 1 executing events B and C, which should not be interleaved by other events. Thread 2 is executing event A. The atomicity violation occurs if A happens between B and C. Note that there are two points in the execution where the failure can occur – just after A executes or just after C executes. In either case, the constraint prevents the failure. When Thread 1 executes B, it instantiates the constraint. When Thread 2 tries to execute A, it is delayed. During the delay, Thread 1 safely executes C. The delay prevents the failure by reordering A after C, rather than between B and C.

Avoiding Ordering Violations. Figure 6 also shows how constraints avoid ordering violations. To view the figure as an ordering violation, assume a failure occurs when Thread 2 executes A before event C.

Avoiding ordering failures is challenging because when the failure manifests, execution may fail just after C or just after A. If the program fails just after A, C will never execute and will therefore not appear in the RPB after the failure, so the Aviso framework will be unable to use it to form a constraint. To handle these failures, Aviso relies on the presence of a third event, B, executed by the same thread as C (Thread 1). In failing runs, B executes just before C would have and is added to the RPB. When A executes and the failure occurs, B is in the RPB followed by C. If

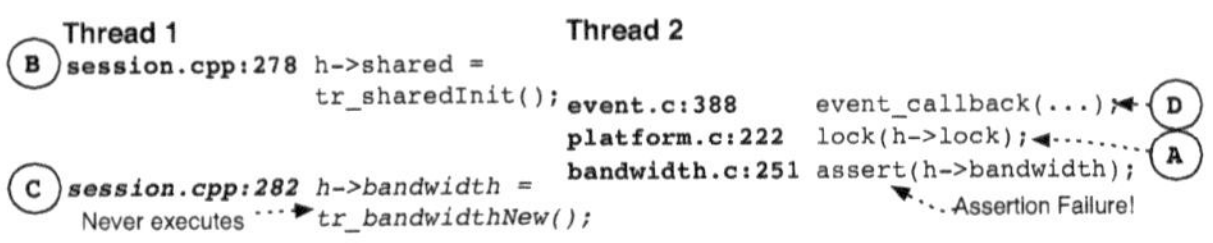

(a) **A failing execution.** Events are identified by the labeled circles.

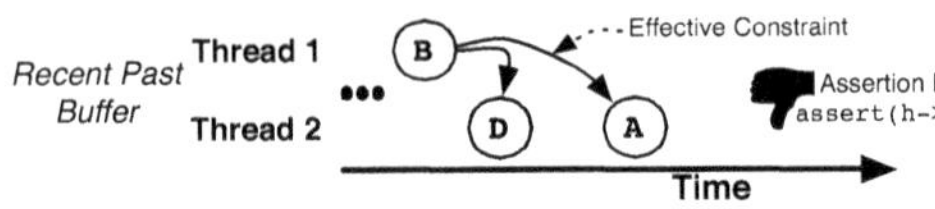

(b) **The RPB just after the failure.** Arcs indicate the event pairs Aviso enumerates and uses to generate constraints. The dashed arrow indicates that the pair (B, A) corresponds to a constraint that effectively avoids the failure by delaying Thread 2's execution of A until after Thread 1 executes B.

Figure 7. A use-before-initialization failure from Transmission and the constraint that avoids it.

C had executed, it would have immediately followed A. Hence, A following B in the RPB of a failing run indicates that the incorrect ordering of A and C is likely to have occurred.

The constraint in the figure is formed from B and A. When Thread 1 executes B, it activates the constraint. Later, when Thread 2 tries to execute A, it is delayed by the constraint. The delay gives C a chance to execute, preceding A. When the delay expires, A executes after C, avoiding the failure.

5.3 Constraint Generation Example: Transmission

Figure 7 illustrates a failure that can occur when Transmission-1.42 is starting up. Figure 7(a) shows an execution of the events that lead to a failure. The execution fails when Thread 2 reaches `assert(h->bandwidth)` at `bandwidth.c:251` before Thread 1 assigns `h->bandwidth` at `session.cpp:282`. In this situation, `h->bandwidth` is uninitialized, so the assertion fails.

Figure 7(b) shows an RPB snippet immediately after the execution fails. The way the constraint avoids the failure corresponds directly to the ordering violation situation in Figure 6. The constraint delays A (Thread 2's lock acquire at `platform.c:222`), making it execute after C (Thread 1's assignment at `session.cpp:282`). This reordering prevents a failure because `h->bandwidth` is initialized by Thread 1 before the assertion executes.

6. Selecting and Distributing Constraints

After an execution fails, the Aviso framework generates a large set of candidate constraints to assess which can prevent failures. It *selects* the constraints most likely to avoid failures and *distributes* them to new program instances when they start up.

6.1 Selecting Constraints

Aviso selects constraints using a two-part statistical model. The first part of the model is the *event pair model* that represents properties of event pairs, as they occur in correct and failing executions. The second part, the *failure feedback model*, empirically determines which constraints are most effective by tracking each constraint's impact on the program's failure rate. As Aviso progressively observes more failing and non-failing program runs, its models improve, yielding better selections.

6.1.1 Event Pair Model

The event pair model represents each constraint with a vector of features. The value of each of these features is different for each constraint and is derived from execution behavior observed by Aviso in failing and non-failing executions. The magnitude of a constraint's feature vector determines how likely the constraint is to be effective.

There are two main concerns related to the event pair model: (1)Collecting the information that goes into building the model; and (2)Describing and computing the features' values for each pair.

Collecting Model Information The event pair model synthesizes information in RPBs from both non-failing and failing program executions. When Aviso collects an RPB, it updates the event pair model by recomputing each constraint's feature values.

The model uses the information in RPBs from failing program executions. In Section 5 we described how Aviso collects post-failure RPBs to generate constraints. Aviso uses those RPBs to update its event pair model. Aviso also collects RPBs from non-failing program executions. To do so, Aviso samples the state of the RPB very rarely during correct executions. At a uniformly randomized interval between 0.1s and 20s, Aviso interrupts execution, captures the state of the RPB, and uses it to update the event pair model. Note that if Aviso samples an RPB, just before a failure occurs, the RPB may contain events related to the failure. To keep these events out of its set of correct RPBs, Aviso waits a fixed period of 5s before incorporating the correct run RPB into its model. If in the interim the execution fails, the sampled RPB is discarded.

Features Aviso represents each constraint with a vector of three features: *ordering invariance*, *co-occurrence invariance*, and *failure correlation*. Feature values are between 0 and 1. We engineered our feature representation so that larger feature values indicate a constraint is more likely to prevent a failure.

Ordering Invariance (OI) helps identify constraints whose events occur in one order in non-failing runs, but the opposite order in failing runs. Given a constraint built from a pair of events, (B, A), its $OI_{B,A}$ value is:

$$OI_{B,A} = \frac{\sum_{c \in CorrectRuns} f^c_{A,B}}{\sum_{c \in CorrectRuns} f^c_{A,B} + f^c_{B,A}}$$

where $f^c_{x,y}$ represents the number of times the pair x, y appears in the RPB sampled from correct run c. Note that the value of OI is larger if (A, B) occurs much more often in correct runs than (B, A). A large OI value suggests (B, A) is anomalous in correct runs and therefore related to the failure. Hence, perturbing the execution around (B, A) is more likely to avoid the failure.

Co-Occurrence Invariance (CI) identifies constraints whose pairs of events tend not to occur together in non-failing runs, but occur together in failing runs. Given a constraint built from a pair of events, (B, A), its $CI_{B,A}$ value is:

$$CI_{B,A} = 1.0 - \frac{\sum_{c \in CorrectRuns} f^c_{B,A}}{\sum_{c \in CorrectRuns} [\sum_{y \neq A} f^c_{B,y} + \sum_{x \neq B} f^c_{x,A}]}$$

Note that the fraction part of CI is large if B and A occur together frequently in non-failing runs, or if B and A occur with other events infrequently in non-failing runs. Both of these conditions suggest the pair (B, A) is *not* an anomaly in non-failing runs. We invert the sense of the fractional term subtracting it from 1.0. As a result, the value of CI is larger if B and A more often occur in non-failing executions in pairs with different events, rather than with one another.

Failure Correlation (FC) identifies pairs of events that occur frequently in failing executions. Given a constraint built from a pair of events, (B, A), its $FC_{B,A}$ value is:

$$FC_{B,A} = \frac{F_{B,A}}{F}$$

where F is the total number of failing executions and $F_{B,A}$ is the total number of failing executions in which (B, A) occurred at least once. A large FC value suggests that B and A tend to occur consistently in failing executions and are therefore related to the failure; therefore perturbing the execution around (B, A) is likely to avoid the failure.

FC is unlike CI and OI in two ways. First, CI and OI are computed based on RPBs from non-failing executions; FC is computed using data from failing executions. Second, unlike CI and OI, FC is computed using $F_{B,A}$ and F – numbers of executions, rather than numbers of occurrences of pairs (*e.g.*, $f^c_{B,A}$). This is because the frequency of a pair unrelated to a failure in a failing execution may be different because the execution terminated early due to the failure. Such differences act as noise in our model. Instead, our method for computing FC factors out this source of noise.

6.1.2 Failure Feedback Model

The second mechanism Aviso uses to select constraints is the failure feedback model. This model records the failure rate, FR, observed for each constraint. The model also records the failure rate with no constraints available. If the program's failure rate is low (*i.e.*, many non-failing runs, few failing runs) when a particular constraint is active, it is likely that that constraint helps avoid failures more than others.

Every time the program terminates, the failure feedback model is updated. If the program exited normally, Aviso increments the model's record of the number of non-failing runs for all constraints available to the program instance during that execution. If the program fails, Aviso updates the model's record of the number of failing runs.

Dealing with Long-Running Programs To keep the failure feedback model up to date, programs send Aviso a message indicating success or failure when they terminate. However, long-running programs like servers terminate infrequently. If an constraint is effectively preventing failures, the program may run indefinitely. In this case, Aviso might *never* update the failure feedback model to reflect the success of the constraint. To handle long-running programs, we add a facility to Aviso to record "logical time" ticks. To use logical time, we rely on the programmer to add markers to the code that represent progress in the application. Each call sends the framework a message, telling it to increment the non-failing execution count of each constraint the program is using; hence, a logical time tick in a long-running program is effectively a "non-failing run". We found these calls trivial to insert, even into large and unfamiliar programs. For example, in our experiments with Apache and Memcached, we incremented logical time after 1,000 and 10,000 requests were processed, respectively.

6.1.3 Combined Avoidance Likelihood Model

The framework selects constraints by querying its *combined avoidance likelihood model*, which incorporates both the failure feedback model and the event pair model. The combined avoidance likelihood model is a probability distribution with an entry for each constraint. The value of an constraint's entry is the likelihood that it is effective as predicted by the event pair model, scaled by an exponential function of the constraint's observed failure rate, as recorded in the failure feedback model. Concretely, the amount of probability mass contributed by an constraint is:

$$P_{B,A} = \underbrace{(CI_{B,A} \times OI_{B,A} \times FC_{B,A})}_{\text{Event Pair Model}} \times \underbrace{e^{r_1 \times (1.0 - FR_{B,A}) - r_2} + s}_{\text{Failure Feedback Model}}$$

where r_1, r_2 are parameters of the exponential function used in the model and s is a smoothing factor that keeps the model defined and bounded by 0 and 1. We chose $r_1 = 8$, $r_2 = 0.7$, and $s = 0.001$. These choices cause the function to peak when $FR = 0$ and bottom out at 0.001 (s).

The intuition behind the combined model is the following. The event pair model is *predictive* – the model's features encode our inductive bias, and data (RPBs) refine the model's predictions. The failure feedback uses *feedback* to scale predictions made by the event pair model. The scaling factor varies exponentially with the constraint's failure rate – constraints that fail often are exponentially less likely to be drawn than ones that fail rarely or never. As failures and non-failing runs occur, Aviso refines its models. Over time, effective constraints' probabilities in the combined model grow and ineffective constraints' probabilities decrease.

Figure 8 illustrates the combined model. Failure correlation (FC) is computed based on RPBs from observed failures. Cooccurrence invariance (CI) and Order invariance (OI) are computed based on RPBs sampled from correct execution. The failure feedback model maintains failure rate values for each constraint, computed by monitoring constraint failures. Aviso uses the combined model to select constraints according to a probability function composed of the event pair and failure feedback models, as shown.

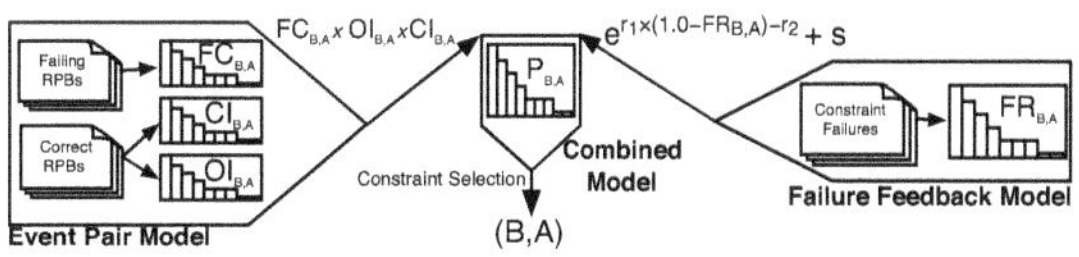

Figure 8. Aviso's statistical model. The event pair model tracks feature values for each constraint. The failure feedback model tracks constraints' failure rates. The combined model is comprised of the other two, yielding a selection probability for each constraint.

6.2 Distributing Constraints

All constraints start equally likely to be drawn. As program instances run, Aviso samples non-failing RPBs and stores them as the program runs. When the program fails, the framework generates constraints. The framework initializes the event pair model using the stored RPBs and the combined model assigns each constraint an initial probability based on the event pair model. The failure feedback model is ignored at this point because before any executions, all constraints' failure rates are undefined. Later, when a program instance starts, it queries Aviso for constraints. Aviso selects a constraint and sends it to the instance.

Aviso periodically instructs program instances to run with no constraints to establish the application's baseline failure rate. Initially, Aviso sends no constraint 10% of the time; the rate drops to 1% after seeing enough executions without any constraints to establish 95% statistical confidence that the observed baseline failure rate is within 5% of its actual value, assuming a binomial distribution of failures.

We continuously compute χ^2 statistics for each constraint to determine the significance of the difference of the constraint's observed failure rate and the baseline failure rate. We use a 2x2 contingency table and consider a difference to be significant if the χ^2 test indicates it to be with at least 95% probability. When a constraint that significantly decreases the failure rate is identified, Aviso uses that constraint 75% of the time. However, Aviso continues to draw constraints from the combined model for two reasons: (1) it is important to keep the baseline failure rate up to date; constraints may *lose* their significance if the baseline rate changes. (2) there may be other constraints with larger significant decreases in failure rate; halting its exploration, Aviso may settle for a non-optimal constraint.

6.2.1 Handling Multiple Failures

Up to this point, our discussion has assumed that all failures can benefit from a common pool of constraints. However, programs are likely to have more than one type of failure, stemming from more than one bug. Aviso also deals with multiple failures. The key is to maintain a separate model for each *failure class*. A failure class is identified by the content of the RPB at the point of failure. When a failure occurs, the post-failure RPB is compared to the RPBs collected from failures in each failure class, using symmetric set difference. The RPB is assigned to the class to which it is most similar, unless it is not at least 80% similar to any class, in which case a new failure class is created.

When a program instance starts and queries the framework for constraints, Aviso selects a constraint from each failure class according to its own model. The program instance is then sent one constraint per class. The constraint-less failure rate information is shared across classes. On a failure or successful run, all classes' models are updated.

There may be two unrelated failures that occur with similar RPBs. If the failures are assigned to the same class, only one constraint will be applied to starting program instances. As a result, it is possible that only one failure or the other will be prevented. We accommodate this situation by allowing Aviso to split a failure class in two if no constraint significantly decreases the failure rate after a fixed number of experiments. The purpose of this process is to select two constraints for what was previously a single failure class and thereby prevent both failures.

7. System Implementation

We built a complete implementation of Aviso including the profiler, instrumenting compiler, runtime system, and the constraint selection and avoidance-sharing framework[1]. We implemented the sharing profiler using PIN [14]. Dominance pruning and event placement were implemented in LLVM [9]. The framework and runtime were implemented from scratch.

7.1 Framework Implementation

The framework was implemented in about 3000 lines of Go code. The statistical models and constraint generation were implemented from scratch in the framework.

The framework exposes a messaging API. The API provides calls for the runtime to query for constraints, to send RPBs for sampled, non-failing periods and after failures occur, and to send logical time ticks. The API works over the network, via HTTP. The framework and runtime-enabled program instances form a distributed system that implements Aviso. Using HTTP as the messaging protocol for the distributed system makes it flexible, portable, and suitable for use in cloud environments such as Google AppEngine or Amazon EC2. Furthermore, its simple interface lets the framework be trivially replicated and lets replicas be load balanced for further scalability. Replicas' statistical models could be kept consistent via consensus, or simply operate independently.

7.2 Runtime Implementation

We implemented the runtime in a library with an event handling API. Synchronization, signal and sharing events make calls to the API. When a thread makes an event call, it records the event with a timestamp in a thread-local queue. When the thread ends, the timestamped events are serialized to a file. Timestamps are collected at nanosecond resolution using `clock_gettime`'s `CLOCK_MONOTONIC` clock. We use thread-local event queues and timestamps to collect events because they are faster than an earlier version of our system, which used a serializing event queue shared across threads.

Constraints are shared object plugins to the runtime. Each exposes a factory method to instantiate its constraint. When the program starts up, the runtime receives constraint descriptions as text. The runtime uses a simple, custom, templated code generator to produce C++ code from the text. We then call out to gcc to compile the code to a shared library that is loaded by the program. Program instances cache compiled constraints, so code generation and compilation need only be performed once; subsequent executions that call for the same constraint can reuse the previously generated constraint plugin.

The runtime was built for concurrent performance. Its only shared data structure is the state associated with active constraints; everything else is thread-local. Accesses to the shared structure are rare: each thread has a thread-local list of events that may require an access to the shared structures. The common case is for a thread executing an event to check its list and continue without accessing the shared structure. Only when a thread hits an event involved in a constraint must it consult the shared structure. This arrangement minimizes the chance that Aviso's data-structures will lead to serialization and poor performance.

8. Evaluation

We evaluate Aviso along several dimensions. First, we show Aviso's efficacy in avoiding failures. Second, we show that Aviso's overheads are reasonable both during data collection and when actively avoiding failures. Third, we characterize Aviso's constraint selection process. Finally, we characterize the Aviso's dynamic behavior.

8.1 Experimental Setup

We evaluated Aviso using several buggy parallel programs.

Out-of-the-Box Benchmarks. Our main results are based on experiments with one cloud application, one server application, and one desktop application made to run with Aviso "out of the box".

Memcached-1.4.4 is an in-memory key value store with an atomicity violation that leads to data-structure corruption and lost updates under heavy update load. We added a single assertion that detects the data-structure corruption when a thread writes to a deallocated table cell and aborts execution. The data-structure invariant that our assertion checks is the cause of the lost updates, but the assertion is oblivious to the lost update problem; to write the assertion, a programmer would not need to understand the lost update failure. We manually added a single Aviso call to the server to send a logical time update every 10,000 requests. Inserting this call was trivial even without being familiar with the codebase. For profiling, we initialized a key-value store with 10 keys storing integers that 8 threads accessed. We used a mix of accesses that was 90% reads and 10% updates. For tests, we used a 10-key store and the same thread count and operation mix.

Apache-2.0.46 is a web server with atomicity violations in its in-memory cache subsystem that lead to crashes when concurrently servicing many php script requests. Our server setup is Apache with mod_php loaded, in-memory caching enabled, and serving the time of day via a php script. We added a single Aviso call to send a logical time update every 10,000 requests. As with Memcached, inserting the call was trivial. For profiling, we used `ApacheBench` to issue 1,000 requests from 8 concurrent request threads for a static `html` page, then 1,000 requests from 8 threads for our php time server. For tests, we let the server run continuously until a fail-

[1] Aviso will be available for download at the authors' website.

ure. We sent time-of-day requests in groups of 10,000. To vary the workload, each group of requests was sent by a number of threads uniformly randomly chosen to be between 2 and 8.

AGet-0.4 (Figure 1) is a download accelerator with an atomicity violation in its signal handler that leads to output corruption. To detect failures, we manually added an assertion that aborts when it detects output corruption. The assertion compares a count of bytes written to the downloaded file to the sum of per-thread byte counts. The symptom of the failure is that these counts are not equal. Note that adding this assertion did not require understanding how to *prevent* the failure. We needed to understand only that the number of written bytes reported by AGet should match the number of bytes in the output file. To profile AGet, we downloaded a 1MB file using 8 threads from a local network resource twice, once letting it complete and once interrupting it with `SIGINT`. To test AGet, we started downloading a 700MB Linux image and interrupted the download with a `SIGINT` after 1s.

Schedule-patched Benchmarks. To further demonstrate Aviso's applicability, we conducted experiments with two other desktop programs. Unlike our first three benchmarks, we altered these two programs to amplify their failure rate. We applied patches that use sleep statements to lead execution toward failing schedules, similar to prior work [5, 27, 28]. These schedule patches are *not* essential – Aviso could be applied without them; we used them to facilitate experiments. Despite the patches, these results show Aviso's effectiveness for several reasons. First, the program is unchanged except for a single call to `usleep`. Second, the increased failure rate does not affect constraint generation or selection, except to reduce the time required for both. Third, events involved in the failure are identical in the patched and non-patched versions.

Transmission-1.42 (Figure 7) is a bittorrent client with a use-before-initialize error that leads to an assertion failure. To profile Transmission, we downloaded a Linux iso torrent without the schedule-altering patch. We ran tests on Transmission by running with the schedule-altering patch applied and downloading a non-existent torrent, which triggers the failure, causing a crash.

PBZip2-0.9.1 is a compression utility with a use-after-free error that leads to a crash. To profile PBZip2, we ran it under our profiler and first compressed, then decompressed, a 10MB text file. We experimented with PBZip2 by compressing a 250MB file. Aviso diagnosed the failure by watching for crashes and failed assertions.

8.2 Bug Avoidance Efficacy

Our main finding is that Aviso made our benchmarks fail less frequently, as shown on the plots in Figure 9. The plots show *on a log scale* the number of failures observed in our experiments for Aviso and for the baseline without Aviso, as well as a theoretical worst case. The slope at a point on a curve is the instantaneous failure rate at that point.

For all benchmarks, Aviso's curve is lower than the baseline, indicating a decrease in the number of failures experienced. In Apache's case, Aviso decreased the number of failures exhibited in our experiments by *two orders of magnitude*. Memcached saw a decrease in failures of more than an order of magnitude. Other cases had less pronounced decreases, but still benefited from Aviso.

These data elucidate how Aviso searches for the most effective constraint. For the first few runs of the program, the number of failures for Aviso is commensurate with the number for the baseline. During these first runs, Aviso is building and refining its statistical model. After a few runs, Aviso's model guides it to an effective constraint. At this point, the slope of the curve becomes flatter than the baseline, *i.e.*, Aviso begins to consistently choose a constraint or constraints that avoid failures.

	Performance Overhead	
	Coll. Only	**Coll. & Avoid**
Transmission	8.8%	29.5%
AGet	26.2%	30.7%
PBZip2	2.6%	5.5%
Memcached	17.3%	16.7%
Apache	12.1%	15.9%

Table 1. Aviso's runtime overheads. These overheads are relative to baseline execution when collecting events only and when collecting events and avoiding failures.

8.3 Performance

Table 1 shows that Aviso's runtime overhead is low. Column 2 is the overhead of event monitoring only. The overhead ranges from less than 3% for PBZip2 to 26.2% for AGet, with an average overhead of 13.4%. These results show that when Aviso is only collecting information, the performance overhead is tolerable.

Collection and Avoidance Overhead. Column 4 shows the combined overhead of event monitoring and avoidance. Avoiding failures does not prohibitively increase Aviso's overhead. For Memcached, the overhead is about the same as that of event collection alone; for Transmission, our worst case increase, the overhead is 20.7% greater than the overhead of event collection.

PBZip2 has very low overhead for both event collection and avoidance because threads spend a majority of the execution in a compression routine in `libbz2`. Avoidance adds little to the overhead because the most effective constraint for PBZip2 involves events that execute during shutdown; constraint activation checks and delays need only occur during shutdown, so they do not impede the execution.

AGet's event collection overhead is high relative to our other benchmarks because a majority of the program's execution is in a tight loop that includes two event calls. AGet's avoidance overhead is only slightly higher than its collection overhead because the events involved in the constraints that Aviso found effective execute only during signal handling. The increased overhead is due to an increase in constraint activation checks, not delays.

Memcached's overhead is nearly the same for both collection and avoidance: the constraints that Aviso found effective are not activated in the program's common case. The events involved in effective constraints execute only when the number of digits in the number stored in one of Memcached's table cells increases, which occurs rarely.

The key finding, then, is that when collecting events only, Aviso imposes a low performance penalty. When avoiding failures, the overhead is only slightly higher.

Contrasting Improved Reliability with Aviso's Overhead The data show that Aviso's overhead is non-negligible. These overheads are acceptable for two main reasons. First, the increase in reliability comes immediately and without the need for the programmer to understand how to fix the program. Patches are hard to write correctly, and hand-written patches may introduce bugs or degrade performance. For example, Memcached developers left the failure we studied unpatched for nearly a year after its initial report. They cited a 7% performance "regression" as one roadblock to committing a patch [1]. Aviso imposes a roughly similar performance overhead (16.7%) to the manually crafted solution and decreases the rate at which the failure occurs by nearly two orders of magnitude. Aviso does not require the programmer to understand how to fix the bug, let alone correctly patch the code to fix it. Furthermore, because Aviso operates automatically the gap between the first failure and Aviso's failure avoidance is a few minutes rather than the year required for the manual patch.

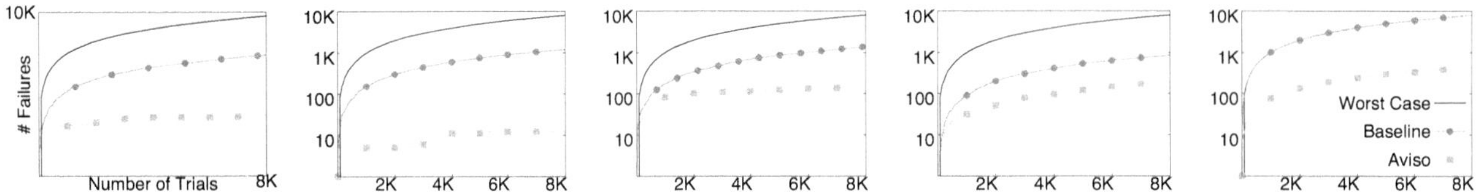

(a) Memcached (b) Apache (c) AGet (d) PBZip2 (e) Transmission

Figure 9. Aviso's improvement in reliability. We show data for (a)Memcached, (b)Apache, (c)AGet, (d)PBZip2, and (e)Transmission. The x-axis shows execution time in number of trials – logical time ticks for servers, executions for standalone applications. We ran each program for 8000 trials. The y-axis shows the the number of failures that have occurred at a given point in time *on a log scale*. The top (black) curve shows the worst case: every execution is a failure. The middle (red) curve shows the reliability of the baseline, compiled and run completely without Aviso. The bottom (green) curve shows the reliability with Aviso.

Second, Aviso's performance overhead saves programs from the potentially severe costs associated with failures. For example, Memcached's failure is a lost update that permits the store to be periodically corrupted but to continue executing. In safety-critical applications, data corruption is likely worse than performance degradation. Aviso provides the option of avoiding Memcached's data corruption at the cost of a modest performance hit.

8.4 Constraint Generation and Selection

Figure 10 characterizes how Aviso generates and selects constraints. Figure 10(a) shows that Aviso needs to experiment with only a small fraction of the constraints it generates to find effective constraints. Notice that the lower portion of the bars is considerably smaller than the upper portion: Aviso made only a small fraction of constraints available to program instances. Aviso effectively avoids failures, so this result shows that it selects effective constraints without having to observe many program instances.

Figure 10(b) shows that the number of constraints that Aviso makes available to program instances is small and for most of our benchmarks, most of the execution time was spent using a single effective constraint. These data reinforce the findings from Figure 10(a), *i.e.*, Aviso finds effective constraints after selecting and distributing only a few using its statistical model.

For Apache, Memcached, and AGet, the constraint represented by the bottom bar segment was used by Aviso for 92-99.7% of the execution time during our tests. For PBZip2, the bottom two bar segments account for nearly 80% of execution time; Aviso chose between these two constraints a majority of the time. These frequently chosen bottom segments all represent constraints that led to a statistically significant decrease in failure rates.

In concert with Figure 10(a), this result illustrates how Aviso works: Aviso initially selects effective constraints without having to experiment with them or directly observe their impact on failure rates. It chooses good constraints without experimenting by using its predictive event pair model. After initially selecting a constraint that turns out to be effective (*i.e.*, the event pair model's prediction was a good one), the failure feedback model biases Aviso to select the same constraint again. The data directly show this phenomenon. For example, in Apache's case, Aviso selected 16 different constraints, experimented with each, and observed their impact on the failure rate. The 16th turned out to be effective, preventing nearly all future occurrences of the failure. Due to the constraint's success, the failure feedback model ensured it was subsequently selected.

Aviso selects and tests constraints differently for Transmission than for the other benchmarks. Transmission's lower 14 bar segments provided a significant decrease in the failure rate. Aviso used one of these 14 constraints for about 85% of execution time.

The data in Figure 10(c) explain why Transmission is different and help further characterize Aviso's event pair model. The bar height shows the ratio of the total number of constraints generated during our experiments to the total number of pairs in the event pair model that were observed in sampled correct RPBs. We call this ratio the *coverage* of the model. If the event model has fewer pairs than constraints – *i.e.*, has low coverage – it is likely to predict effective constraints poorly. If the model has more pairs, it is more likely to be useful in assigning meaningful selection probabilities to more constraints. Note that coverage may exceed 1.0 if pairs in the model never show up in a post-failure RPB.

Transmission's model coverage is zero. The structure of Transmission's failure explains why: the failure occurs very early in the program's execution. The event pair model is primarily built from RPBs sampled from portions of correct execution. Transmission crashes early, so no RPBs are sampled, and the event pair model is of little use. Transmission's zero model coverage explains why Aviso was forced to experiment with more different constraints. Instead of predicting effective constraints, Aviso relied on the results of its experiments – the failure feedback model – to determine which constraints worked best.

Our other benchmarks had event pair models with higher coverage. Apache's model contained nearly the same number of pairs as there were constraints. Memcached and AGet also had models with high coverage. Looking back to Figures 10(a) and (b), the impact of higher model coverage is clear. For benchmarks with higher model coverage, the fraction of constraints used is lower and the fraction of execution time spent using a small number of effective constraints is higher.

In summary, Figure 10 shows that when Aviso's statistical model has observed enough correct execution behavior, it makes good predictions, and Aviso is effective. If the model has low coverage, Aviso still selects effective constraints using its failure-feedback model.

8.5 Characterizing Dynamic Behavior

Using an instrumented version of the Aviso runtime, we characterized its dynamic behavior. For these experiments, we fixed a few runtime parameters: we chose the constraint used most frequently by Aviso during our main experiments, and we used a single fixed-size input. For PBZip2, we used the 250MB input file. For AGet, we downloaded a Linux image and interrupted execution (without crashing). For Apache, we issued 1M requests from 8 concurrent request threads. For Transmission, we downloaded a Linux image torrent, while for Memcached, we ran 80,000 client requests.

Figure 10(d) plots the rolling average time between events in μs during our experiments. These data justify Aviso's delay length. Recall that to avoid failures, events must be reordered by delays. In order to reorder events, events must be delayed long enough to allow an event in another thread to execute. The data show that the delay time is longer than the average inter-event time of

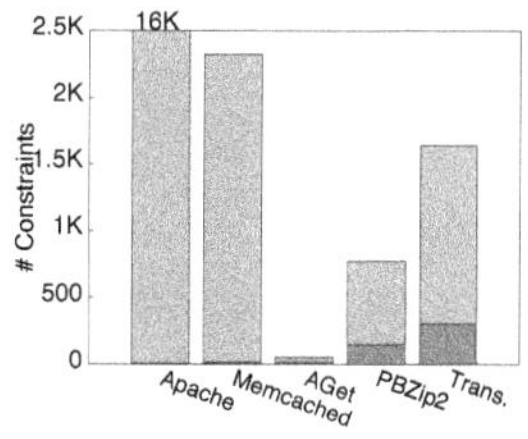

(a) **Characterizing constraint generation.** The bar height represents the total number of constraints generated after any failure that occurred during our experiments. The lower, red segment shows the number of constraints that were actually made available to a program instance by Aviso.

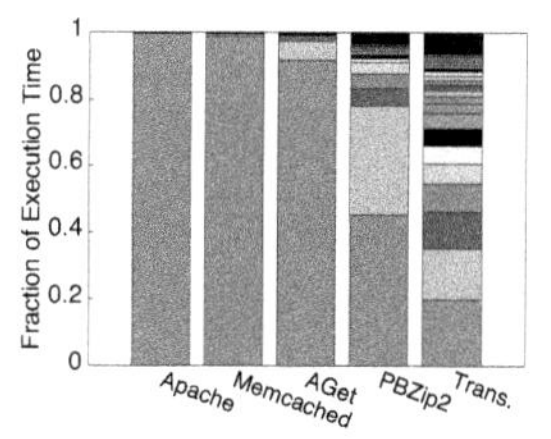

(b) **Characterizing constraint selection.** Each bar corresponds to a different benchmark. Each segment corresponds to a different constraint. The height of a segment represents the fraction of execution time during vetting that ran with that segment's constraint. The total number of segments in a bar is the number of constraints Aviso experimented with.

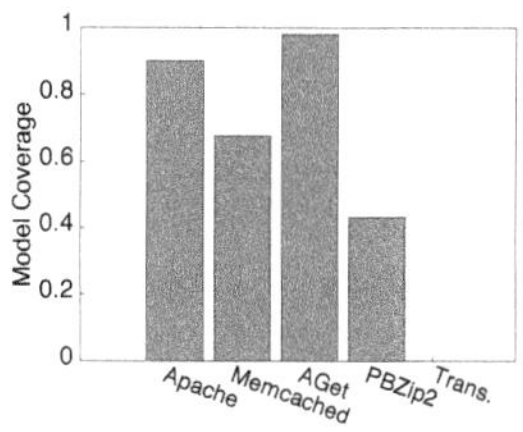

(c) **Characterizing of Model Coverage.** Bar height represents model coverage: the ratio of the total number of constraints generated to the total number of pairs in the event pair model that were observed in sampled correct RPBs.

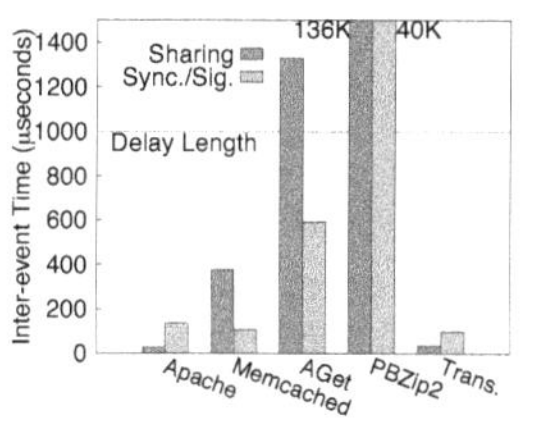

(d) **Characterizing inter-event time.** Bars show rolling average time between events in μs. The left (red) bar reflects sharing events and the right (green) bar, synchronization and signal events. Longer intervals mean events are less frequent. The horizontal line shows Aviso's delay length.

Figure 10. Characterizing Aviso's behavior.

most benchmarks. In the average case, a delay will reorder some events. Despite PBZip2's large average inter-event time, Aviso's delay length is adequate because the length of the interval between events involved in the failure is less than the delay length.

The data in Figure 10(d) also help explain Aviso's overheads. For PBZip2, the average time between events is several orders of magnitude larger than for other applications. The length of the interval makes sense because PBZip2 spends most of its time in a compression library call. It is likely that PBZip2's long time between events contributes to the low overhead reported in Table 1. Each of the other benchmarks has a shorter interval between events than PBZip2. Correspondingly, the event collection overheads in Table 1 for the other benchmarks are slightly higher than PBZip2's.

AGet, with the highest performance overhead, has several events on its inner loop. We expected these events to result in a short interval between events, explaining its overhead. However, as Figure 10(d) shows, AGet's inter-event interval was moderately *longer* than most other cases. Table 2 shows data that explain AGet's performance and further characterizes Aviso.

The data in the table illustrate several different sources of overhead: excessively frequent events, leading to many discarded events; constraint activation checks; and delays due to constraints. AGet's overhead is likely to come from frequent constraint activation checks. In AGet, 1 out of every 3 events requires the extra computation of a constraint activation check. In contrast, 0.4% of

	Sharing Events		**Sync/Sig Events**		**Constraints**		
	# Evts	# Discard	# Evts	# Discard	# Chks	# Strt	# Delays
Apache	44.6M	37.9M	1.5M	34K	27K	65	56
Memcached	200K	13K	1.2M	204K	87K	16	87
AGet	46K	0	92K	2	46K	5	40
PBZip2	227	0	1042	4	81	8	8
Transmission	10.6M	5.0M	2.0M	5	96	1	1

Table 2. Aviso's dynamic behavior. Columns 2 and 3 show the total number of sharing events and the number of sharing events discarded due to online pruning. Columns 4 and 5 show the total number and number discarded of synchronization and signaling events. Column 5 shows the number of times an event in an available constraint executes, requiring a check to see if the event activates the constraint. Column 6 shows the number of times a check actually leads to a constraint's instantiation. Column 7 shows the number of times an event is delayed by a constraint.

Apache's and 7.25% of Memcached's events required such checks. Constraint activation checks require holding a lock and accessing shared state, so they are more costly than those that do not.

The data in Table 2 show that a large fraction of Apache's events (over 80%) were discarded due to online pruning. The high rate of discards suggests that events are frequent; the very short inter-event time shown in Figure 10(d) corroborates this fact. Intuitively, such high-frequency events seem like a performance problem; however, Apache's event frequency did not impose excessive overhead – around 15%. Most of Apache's events did not require activation checks, instantiations, or delays. As a result, its events were inexpensive, requiring just a few access to thread-local memory. The absence of complex computation or serialization on global state is likely the reason for Apache's low overhead.

Delays were very infrequent across all our benchmarks, occurring mostly in uncommon case code. In PBZip2 8 worker threads delayed a cleanup thread. In Transmission, a delay during startup code prevented a use-before-initialization error. In Apache, a delay during a request cache flush prevented a crash. In AGet, a delay during signal handling prevented a crash. In Memcached, a delay during a rare-case update prevented data corruption.

To summarize, delays were not a problem in our tests because they were infrequent and in rare-path code. Event frequency alone did not dictate performance, although having very infrequent events seemed to lead to lower overhead (*e.g.*, PBZip2). Constraint activation checks seemed to be a more costly source of overhead than we expected, especially when events were frequent (*e.g.*, AGet).

9. Related Work

There has been a great deal of recent work on techniques dealing with software failures. Due to space constraints, we focus here on work that deals with concurrency-related failures.

Loom [26] is a system for patching concurrency bugs in running programs. Loom is like Aviso in that it aims to prevent failures between when a failure occurs, and when a patch is released. Aviso differs from Loom in an important and fundamental way: Loom requires the user to understand the *cause* of a failure well-enough to write a work-around. Aviso is automated, requiring nothing from the programmer in most cases to produce a work-around constraint. For some non-fail-stop errors, the user must recognize a bug's *symptom*, which is easier than understanding the cause.

There has been a lot of work on avoiding atomicity violations [4, 12, 13, 21, 22]. Isolator [21] and ToleRace [22] prevent single-variable atomicity violations, but do not handle the broader class of failures addressed by Aviso. AFix [4] produces bytecode patches that fix atomicity bugs. AFix is like Aviso in that it eliminates the need to think about a failure's cause. Unlike Aviso it is limited to atomicity errors. Atom-Aid [13] and ColorSafe [12] address single- and multi-variable atomicity bugs. These systems are unlike Aviso in that they only handle atomicity bugs, and need special hardware support. Other systems have proposed using hardware support to force executions to adhere to tested schedules [27, 28]. These systems are similar to Aviso in that they aim to prevent concurrency-related failures. They differ in that they use hardware, and can ensure reliability only in tested situations. Aviso avoids failures even in untested code. Dimmunix [7] and Communix [6] provide automated deadlock immunity for Java programs. Like Aviso these systems identify and avoid failures mostly automatically, and Communix systems share failure avoidance capability. These systems are limited in that they only address deadlocks.

Determinism [2, 15, 17] enforces one event interleaving in every execution. Aviso also affects event orderings. Aviso differs in that it does not restrict the interleaving of the entire program. Instead, all possible executions are permitted, except where restricted by constraints.

Avoiding Other Failures There is other work on failure avoidance not specifically for concurrency. Rx [20] uses checkpointing to recover from failures. Aviso differs from Rx in that it avoids failures, rather than just failing and recovering, and Aviso does not require checkpointing support. Failure-oblivious computing [23] permits execution to continue after a failure. This technique works well for some non-critical errors, but is otherwise of limited use.

Exterminator [16] was among the first to explore what it called "collaborative bug correction", inspiring Aviso's cooperative approach to failure avoidance. Unlike Aviso, Exterminator focuses on avoiding failures due memory errors (*e.g.*, buffer overflows, etc.), not concurrency errors, and it does so with just slightly higher overheads than Aviso (25% average runtime overhead).

ClearView [19] identifies invariants, and when they are violated produces a patch preventing future violations. ClearView is similar to Aviso in that it provides avoidance by avoiding behavior observed in failing runs. ClearView and Aviso both monitor their impact to determine the most effective strategy (constraints in Aviso, and patches in ClearView). Aviso differs in that it does not use invariants, and focuses on concurrency.

10. Conclusions

We presented Aviso, a system that automatically avoids concurrency-related program failures by empirically determining fault-free execution schedules. Aviso leverages a community of instances of a program and uses statistical techniques to quickly determine which program events (and their order) are the culprit of a failure. We built Aviso in software only (not relying on special hardware), and our evaluation showed that Aviso increases reliability significantly (orders of magnitude reduction in failure rate in some cases) and leads to overheads acceptable in real production runs. As our future work, we will explore expanding our statistical model to incorporate quality of service criteria, and using Aviso to implement speculative, empirically tuned performance optimizations.

Acknowledgments

We thank the members of the UW Sampa group and the anonymous reviewers for their feedback and help. We also thank Tony Fader and Adrian Sampson for their early contributions. This work was supported in part by the National Science Foundation under grants CCF-1064497 and CCF-1016495, and gifts from Microsoft.

References

[1] Issue 127: incr/decr operations are not thread safe. http://code.google.com/p/memcached/issues/detail?id=127.

[2] T. Bergan et al. Coredet: a compiler and runtime system for deterministic multithreaded execution. In *ASPLOS*, 2010.

[3] S. Burckhardt, P. Kothari, M. Musuvathi, and S. Nagarakatte. A Randomized Scheduler with Probabilistic Guarantees of Finding Bugs. In *ASPLOS*, 2010.

[4] G. Jin et al. Automatic atomicity-violation fixing. In *PLDI*, 2011.

[5] G. Jin, A. Thakur, B. Liblit, and S. Lu. Instrumentation and sampling strategies for Cooperative Concurrency Bug Isolation. In *OOPSLA*, 2010.

[6] H. Jula, P. Tozun, and G. Candea. Communix: A collaborative deadlock immunity framework. In *DSN*, 2011.

[7] H. Jula, D. M. Tralamazza, C. Zamfir, and G. Candea. Deadlock immunity: Enabling systems to defend against deadlocks. In *OSDI*, pages 295–308, 2008.

[8] B. Kasikci, C. Zamfir, and G. Candea. Data races vs. data race bugs: telling the difference with portend. In *ASPLOS '12*, 2012.

[9] C. Lattner and V. Adve. LLVM: A Compilation Framework for Lifelong Program Analysis & Transformation. In *CGO*, 2004.

[10] S. Lu, S. Park, E. Seo, and Y. Zhou. Learning from Mistakes - A Comprehensive Study on Real World Concurrency Bug Characteristics. In *ASPLOS*, 2008.

[11] S. Lu, J. Tucek, F. Qin, and Y. Zhou. AVIO: Detecting Atomicity Violations via Access Interleaving Invariants. In *ASPLOS*, 2006.

[12] B. Lucia, L. Ceze, and K. Strauss. ColorSafe: Architectural Support for Debugging and Dynamically Avoiding Multi-Variable Atomicity Violations. In *ISCA*, 2010.

[13] B. Lucia, J. Devietti, K. Strauss, and L. Ceze. Atom-Aid: Detecting and Surviving Atomicity Violations. In *ISCA*, 2008.

[14] C.-K. Luk et al. Pin: Building Customized Program Analysis Tools with Dynamic Instrumentation. In *PLDI*, 2005.

[15] P. Montesinos, L. Ceze, and J. Torrellas. DeLorean: Recording and Deterministically Replaying Shared-Memory Multiprocessor Execution Efficiently. In *ISCA*, 2008.

[16] G. Novark, E. D. Berger, and B. G. Zorn. Exterminator: automatically correcting memory errors with high probability. In *PLDI '07*, 2007.

[17] M. Olszewski, J. Ansel, and S. Amarasinghe. Kendo: efficient deterministic multithreading in software. In *ASPLOS*, 2009.

[18] S. Park, S. Lu, and Y. Zhou. CTrigger: Exposing Atomicity Violation Bugs from Their Hiding Places. In *ASPLOS*, 2009.

[19] J. H. Perkins et al. Automatically patching errors in deployed software. In *SOSP*, 2009.

[20] F. Qin, J. Tucek, J. Sundaresan, and Y. Zhou. Rx: treating bugs as allergies—a safe method to survive software failures. In *SOSP*, 2005.

[21] S. Rajamani et al. Isolator: Dynamically ensuring isolation in concurrent programs. In *MICRO*, 2009.

[22] P. Ratanaworabhan et al. Detecting and tolerating asymmetric races. In *IEEE Transactions on Computers*, 2011.

[23] M. Rinard et al. Enhancing server availability and security through failure-oblivious computing. In *OSDI*, 2004.

[24] Y. Shi et al. Do I use the wrong definition? defuse: definition-use invariants for detecting concurrency and sequential bugs. In *OOPSLA*, 2010.

[25] H. Volos, A. J. Tack, M. M. Swift, and S. Lu. Applying transactional memory to concurrency bugs. In *ASPLOS 2012*, 2012.

[26] J. Wu, H. Cui, and J. Yang. Bypassing races in live applications with execution filters. In *OSDI*, 2010.

[27] J. Yu and S. Narayanasamy. A Case for an Interleaving Constrained Shared-Memory Multi-Processor. In *ISCA*, 2009.

[28] J. Yu and S. Narayanasamy. Tolerating concurrency bugs using transactions as lifeguards. In *MICRO*, 2010.

Parasol and GreenSwitch: Managing Datacenters Powered by Renewable Energy *

Íñigo Goiri, William Katsak, Kien Le†, Thu D. Nguyen, and Ricardo Bianchini

Department of Computer Science
Rutgers University
{goiri,wkatsak,lekien,tdnguyen,ricardob}@cs.rutgers.edu

Abstract

Several companies have recently announced plans to build "green" datacenters, i.e. datacenters partially or completely powered by renewable energy. These datacenters will either generate their own renewable energy or draw it directly from an existing nearby plant. Besides reducing carbon footprints, renewable energy can potentially reduce energy costs, reduce peak power costs, or both. However, certain renewable fuels are intermittent, which requires approaches for tackling the energy supply variability. One approach is to use batteries and/or the electrical grid as a backup for the renewable energy. It may also be possible to adapt the workload to match the renewable energy supply. For highest benefits, green datacenter operators must intelligently manage their workloads and the sources of energy at their disposal.

In this paper, we first discuss the tradeoffs involved in building green datacenters today and in the future. Second, we present Parasol, a prototype green datacenter that we have built as a research platform. Parasol comprises a small container, a set of solar panels, a battery bank, and a grid-tie. Third, we describe GreenSwitch, our model-based approach for dynamically scheduling the workload and selecting the source of energy to use. Our real experiments with Parasol, GreenSwitch, and MapReduce workloads demonstrate that intelligent workload and energy source management can produce significant cost reductions. Our results also isolate the cost implications of peak power management, storing energy on the grid, and the ability to delay the MapReduce jobs. Finally, our results demonstrate that careful workload and energy source management can minimize the negative impact of electrical grid outages.

Categories and Subject Descriptors C.m [*Computer Systems Organization*]: Miscellaneous; D.4.1 [*Operating Systems*]: Process Management—Scheduling

Keywords Renewable energy, batteries, scheduling, datacenters.

* This work was partially supported by NSF grant CSR-1117368, and the Rutgers Green Computing Initiative. †Kien Le is now with A10 Networks.

ASPLOS'13, March 16–20, 2013, Houston, Texas, USA.

1. Introduction

Datacenters range from small sets of servers in machine rooms to several thousands of servers housed in warehouse-size installations [23, 44]. One may find the former datacenters at universities and enterprises, and the latter at Internet service companies like Google and Microsoft. Collectively, datacenters consume a massive amount of energy. Estimates for 2010 indicate that datacenters consume around 1.5% of the total electricity used world-wide [23]. This translates into high carbon emissions as most of this energy is produced using fossil fuels. A 2008 study estimated world-wide datacenters to emit 116 million metric tons of carbon, slightly more than the entire country of Nigeria [31].

Given these emissions and increasing societal awareness of climate change, governmental agencies, non-profits, and the public at large are starting to demand cleaner products and services. As a result, several companies have announced plans to build "green" datacenters, i.e. datacenters partially or completely powered by renewable energy such as solar or wind energy. These datacenters will either generate their own renewable energy (self-generation) or draw it directly from an existing nearby plant (co-location). For example, Apple is building a 20MW solar array for its North Carolina datacenter [6]. McGraw-Hill has recently completed a 14MW solar array for its datacenter [7]. Green House Data and AISO are two small cloud service providers that operate entirely on renewable energy [1, 15]. Other examples can be found in [8].

We argue that it is irrelevant whether these companies are investing in co-located or self-generated renewable energy for market positioning, public relations, cost, or environmental reasons. The fact is that they are expecting benefits from these investments. For example, companies may be able to attract customers who value their investments in renewables. Moreover, despite their decreasing-but-still-high capital costs, exploiting solar and/or wind energy in datacenters may reduce overall energy costs [11], peak grid power costs [34], or both [12]. We expect that an increasing number of companies will see benefits in exploiting renewables.

However, we do *not* argue that co-location or self-generation is the best approach for all datacenter operators. For example, Google prefers to invest in renewables by financing new plants and pumping the produced energy into the electrical grid. Rather, we argue that co-location or self-generation will be the approach of choice for many operators, as suggested by [1, 6–8, 15].

Co-location and self-generation are interesting from a research perspective as well: solar and wind energy are intermittent, which requires approaches for tackling the energy supply variability. One approach is to use batteries and/or the electrical grid as a backup for the renewable energy. It may also be possible to adapt the workload (the energy demand) to match the renewable energy supply [2, 11, 12, 24, 25]. For highest benefits, green datacenter operators must intelligently manage their workloads and the sources of energy at their disposal. For example, when the workload is deferrable (i.e., it can be delayed within a time bound), it may be appropriate to delay some of the load, and store the freed-up renewable energy in the batteries for later use (e.g., to shave an expected load peak when the renewable energy is not available). As far as we know, current green datacenter operators do not manage their energy sources and workloads in this manner.

We set out to build software and hardware to explore these issues. This paper describes some of our main efforts. First, we collect data from a large number of sources to quantify the tradeoffs involved in building solar- and/or wind-powered datacenters today and in the future. We pay particular attention to the evolving space requirements and capital costs of these technologies. We speculate that today's space requirements and capital costs may be cut in half in the 2020-2030 time frame.

Second, we present Parasol, a solar-powered micro-datacenter that we have built as a research platform. Parasol comprises a small container, a set of solar photovoltaic (PV) panels, batteries, and a grid-tie. The container houses two racks of energy-efficient servers and networking equipment. Parasol uses air-side economizer cooling (or simply "free cooling") whenever outside temperatures are low enough, and regular air conditioning otherwise.

Third, we describe GreenSwitch, our framework and system for scheduling workloads and selecting the source of energy to use (solar, battery, and/or grid) at each point in time. GreenSwitch is based on (1) predictions of future renewable energy availability; (2) predictions of future computational load; (3) the current amount of energy stored in the batteries; (4) analytical models of workload behavior, battery use, and electricity cost; and (5) the characteristics of the green datacenter and the prices of the grid energy and peak power. GreenSwitch seeks to minimize the overall cost of electricity, while respecting the characteristics of the workload and battery lifetime constraints. GreenSwitch can also be used to manage workloads and energy sources during electrical grid outages.

Fourth, we perform a large number of real day-long experiments with Parasol and MapReduce (Hadoop) workloads. We consider both deferrable and non-deferrable workloads. Our results demonstrate that smart workload and energy source management can indeed produce significant reductions in cost and carbon footprint. In contrast to prior work on leveraging batteries, e.g. [14], we find that batteries may not be as cost-effective when the system also includes a solar array and the ability to store energy on the grid ("net metering"). Our results also isolate the impact of peak power management, net metering, and the ability to delay the MapReduce jobs. Finally, our results demonstrate that careful workload and energy source management can minimize the negative impact of grid outages on the overall performance of a workload.

Through GreenSwitch, Parasol is the first green datacenter prototype to dynamically manage workload demands, multiple energy sources (renewable energy, batteries, and grid), and multiple energy stores (batteries and net metering), all at the same time. Throughout the paper, we mention important effects that we would have missed if we had used simulations or a simpler prototype in our study.

We conclude that green datacenters represent an increasingly interesting topic from many perspectives. We hope that Parasol and GreenSwitch will entice other researchers to consider these datacenters. In fact, we plan to enable other research groups to use Parasol from their remote sites through virtualization.

2. Related Work

Viability of green datacenters. Many recent papers have focused on datacenters that generate their own renewable energy [2, 3, 10–12, 24–26, 28, 29, 37, 39]. This paper adds to this body of work.

Ren *et al.* evaluated various ways for datacenters to incorporate renewable energy: self-generation, off-site generation feeding into the grid, power purchase agreements feeding into the grid, and renewable energy certificates [34]. They found that *both self-generation and off-site generation can lower costs*, as well as lower carbon footprints. In addition, they found self-generation to be the best approach when carbon reduction targets are moderate (up to 30%), especially due to its ability to reduce peak grid power cost.

Unfortunately, Ren *et al.* considered a low and constant grid energy price ($0.05/kWh), which made self-generation relatively expensive in comparison. A major benefit of self-generation is its ability to lower energy costs significantly under the pervasive off-peak/on-peak energy pricing. Had Ren *et al.* considered this type of pricing, and energy prices that are more representative of North America and Europe (e.g., $0.07-$0.14/kWh in the US [43]), they would have seen a larger range of scenarios where self-generation is cheaper than other approaches.

In contrast with this prior study, our analysis of viability focuses on the space requirements and capital costs of self-generation with wind and solar, now and in the future.

In a well-known blog post [17], James Hamilton from Amazon.com criticized Apple's 20MW solar array as consuming too much space for the amount of energy it will provide.

We agree with Hamilton's observations; solar energy currently consumes a significant amount of space and is still expensive. However, we take a broader perspective. First, as we illustrate in this paper, these space requirements and costs will continue to decrease quickly in the future. Second, many datacenters do not consume anywhere near maximum power most of the time. Third, many datacenter operators may want to draw only a moderate fraction of the energy consumed by their datacenters from renewables. Fourth, wind requires less space and lower capital expenditures than solar, and may provide a better alternative. (Although Parasol is solar-powered, our approaches for managing workloads and energy sources applies to any other technology that produces variability. Obviously, our approaches work best when this variability can be accurately predicted.) Finally, even when operators decide to leverage renewable energy for reasons other than electricity costs or the environment, the bottom line is that their workloads and energy sources must be managed properly for maximum benefits. Understanding how to do this management is a key goal of this paper.

Real implementations of green datacenters. Researchers from UMass at Amherst have built Blink [37], a cluster of 10 laptop motherboards powered by two micro wind turbines and two solar panels. They used batteries only as a small 5-minute energy buffer.

Blink faces the energy variability we study in this paper. Blink tackles it by modulating the motherboards' duty cycle, as it is completely off the electrical grid. In contrast, we study approaches that manage the workload (when it is deferrable or there is a grid outage) and energy sources, including larger batteries and the grid.

HP Labs has recently described a datacenter that is partially powered by a PV solar array [3]. The datacenter is also grid-tied, so that the grid can compensate for the lack of solar energy. For cooling, the datacenter uses outside air combined with standard air conditioners. They focused solely on workload management.

Although their datacenter is conceptually similar to Parasol, they only experimented with a small part of it, 4 servers. In addition, their workload management did not consider grid energy costs, peak grid power costs, or having batteries and the grid at the same time. Without considering these factors, they could not estimate the total cost savings that green datacenters can provide. Also importantly, their paper does not include any details about their workload management models/algorithms.

Managing workloads in green datacenters. Researchers have proposed to schedule batch jobs to maximize the use of renewable energy [11, 12, 24]. In contrast, Krioukov *et al.* proposed to adjust the quality of the replies provided to users in interactive workloads [25]. For datacenters that run a mix of interactive and batch workloads, Aksanli *et al.* proposed to adapt the amount of batch processing dynamically [2]. Liu *et al.* took the same approach [29]. In addition, they used modeling of the energy cost and the revenue from running batch jobs to derive their workload scheduling.

We consider deferrable (e.g., batch) and non-deferrable (e.g., interactive) workloads in green datacenters. Our management of deferrable workloads is similar to that in [11, 12], as we study the same types of electricity costs. However, for this type of workload, our decisions select the energy source in tandem with the workload schedule. For non-deferrable workloads, our management simply selects the energy source. These previous papers did not consider active energy source management, e.g. the renewable energy is always fully used when enough load is available, and wasted otherwise. Moreover, none of these papers considered net metering, and only [12] considered peak grid power costs.

Managing energy sources in datacenters. Researchers have explored the use of batteries in datacenters [13, 14, 22, 40, 45]. These studies show that batteries and other forms of energy storage can lower both the capital cost of the power delivery infrastructure and the operating cost of a datacenter.

However, none of these papers considered renewable energy or net metering. In addition, almost in their entirety, these studies focused on non-deferrable workloads with available grid power. We consider both deferrable and non-deferrable workloads, as well as grid outages. Interestingly, our results suggest that batteries may be less effective at lowering operating costs in the presence of solar energy and net metering, especially for non-deferrable workloads.

Finally, Li *et al.* have proposed an architecture in which two sets of servers draw power from different sources (e.g., from the grid or from a wind farm) [28]. In their setup, energy source management translates into migrating workloads between the two sets. We argue that their architecture is less flexible and incurs more (performance and energy) overheads than that of Parasol.

3. Tradeoffs in Greening Datacenters

In this section, we discuss the tradeoffs, space requirements, and capital costs involved in greening datacenters, using data from numerous sources. We start by comparing co-location and self-generation to grid-centric approaches. We then discuss how the space requirements and costs of solar and wind have evolved over time, and our expectations for the future.

Grid-centric vs co-location/self-generation. Grid-centric approaches include power purchase agreements and off-site generation contracted by the datacenter operator [34]. In these approaches, the renewable energy is generated at locations with an abundance of the renewable fuel (e.g., windy areas of the midwest in the US), and fed into the electrical grid. Another advantage is that the datacenter operator need not operate or maintain the renewable power plant. However, the power conversions (DC/AC), voltage transformations, and transmission over long distances may incur energy losses of up to 15% [20]. Moreover, in off-site generation, the datacenter operator may incur grid-transmission charges (e.g., the price of 5% of the produced energy) imposed by power utilities [34]. Further, in grid-centric approaches, the datacenter is completely dependent on the availability of the grid or on diesel generators. Grid outages occur frequently in developing countries (e.g., India)

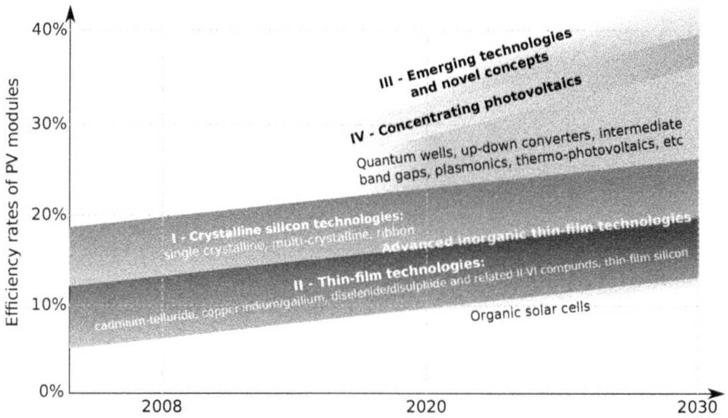

Figure 1. Solar PV efficiency over time. Reproduced from [21].

and in locations of developed countries that are prone to natural disasters (e.g., winter storms in the East of the US).

Co-location and self-generation incur much lower losses (5% or less), as the power undergoes fewer conversions/transformations and is not transmitted over long distances. There are also no additional charges and a lower dependence on the grid or diesel generators (although they do require batteries and/or a grid-tie, for when energy is needed but not enough renewable energy is available). Unfortunately, these approaches do have drawbacks. In co-location, the location of the renewable plant may not be ideal for a datacenter. In self-generation, the location that is ideal for the datacenter may not be so for the renewable plant. Moreover, in self-generation, the datacenter operator is responsible for the operation and maintenance of the renewable plant.

As aforementioned, previous studies [11, 12] have found that self-generation can lower overall electricity costs, as its capital costs can be amortized relatively soon. Comparing self- and off-site generation in terms of electricity costs, a recent study [34] found that the best approach depends on the carbon reduction target.

The above discussion suggests that no approach is perfect, so different operators may make different choices (e.g., Google and Apple). In terms of research, self-generation with solar and/or wind has become a hot topic, as discussed in the previous section.

Solar and wind are two promising sources of green energy for datacenters, as (1) they are more broadly available world-wide than hydroelectric energy; (2) they cause less environmental disruption than hydroelectric energy; and (3) they do not have the waste storage problem of nuclear energy. However, solar and wind have traditionally incurred large space requirements and capital costs.

Space and cost of solar energy. A key factor determining the space requirements of solar PV energy is its efficiency, i.e. the percentage of the sunlight energy that is transformed into electricity. Figure 1 plots the evolution of the efficiency of the different solar PV technologies over time [21]. Note that the efficiency of today's most affordable PV technology (multi-crystalline silicon) hovers around 15% and may increase to 25% by 2030. With other technologies, efficiency is likely to exceed 40%. This future increase in efficiency would represent a 50+% reduction in space requirements.

Another key issue is the "capacity factor", i.e. the percentage of the maximum theoretical solar energy production (24hrs of maximum sunlight every day) that is actually produced. Capacity factors vary depending on latitude and weather. For example, Erfurt (Germany), Princeton (US), Canberra (Australia), and Phoenix (US) have capacity factors of roughly 12.5%, 15.5%, 16.5%, and 24%, respectively [33]. A location with a capacity factor of 24% requires half of the space of a location with a 12% factor.

To make the discussion concrete, consider an example datacenter in which each rack consumes 8.8kW (40 200W 1U servers and a PUE of 1.1), the average power utilization is 33%, and the datacen-

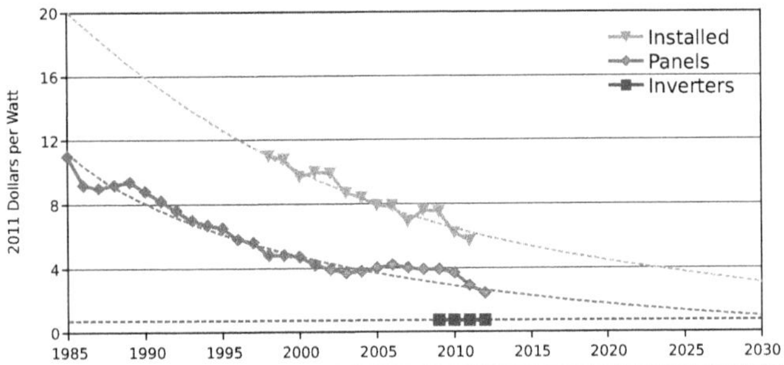

Figure 2. Solar PV capital costs over time without incentives [38, 41]. The data points represent actual average costs, whereas the dashed lines are our approximations of the historical trends. Our cost estimates for the distant future are admittedly speculative.

ter operator wants to produce 50% of the energy it needs from solar in New Jersey (15.5% capacity factor). Moreover, note that the area of a 235W DC solar panel is 17.64 square feet, and it produces a maximum of 202W AC after the de-rating we see in Parasol. Under these conditions, the amount of space required would be roughly 47x larger than the space taken by the racks (each standard rack takes 5.81 square feet, but we multiply this area by 3 to account for clearences in the front and back of the rack). The full calculation is $47 = 8800W/(202W \cdot 15.5\%) \cdot 17.64ft^2/17.43ft^2/(1/33\% \cdot 1/50\%)$. In the 2020-2030 range, we expect these requirements to decrease to roughly 24x. For racks of energy-efficient servers like those of Parasol (80 25W 0.5U servers and a PUE of 1.1), the space requirements are roughly 12x (now) and 6x (future). These requirements seem manageable at least by small/medium datacenters. For example, our predictions suggest that powering 10 racks of our energy-efficient servers (under the assumptions above) will likely require covering only 6 parking spaces with solar panels.

In terms of capital costs, solar energy has become substantially cheaper over time. Figure 2 plots the average final installed capital cost per Watt, and the average capital cost of inverters and panels, over time [38, 41]. The installed cost includes the panels, inverters, and all soft costs, such as permits and labor. Installed costs have decreased by roughly 50% since 1998. Governmental incentives reduce these costs even further. For example, current federal and state incentives in the US can lower installed costs by 40-60%.

The figure also plots dashed curves that approximate the historical data. (Admittedly, we are taking liberties here, as these curves reflect historical trends only, rather than expected technology-, market-, or governmental policy-driven cost changes. Nevertheless, the curves are accurate for the available data.) According to them, the installed cost could decrease by almost 50% by 2030. These trends are in stark contrast to the average cost of grid energy in the US, which has increased by 30+% since 1998 [43].

Section 6 quantifies these costs by computing how long it would take to amortize the installed capital cost of a solar array. Specifically, our experiments suggest amortization periods between 4.8 and 7.1 years, assuming governmental incentives of 60%. In the 2020-2030 time frame, these periods could be less than 2.4 and 3.6 years, assuming that incentives and grid electricity prices remain at the same levels as today. Obviously, these amortization period estimates for the distant future are highly speculative at this point.

Space and cost of wind energy. When a single turbine suffices, wind has lower space requirements than solar. For example, a 1MW wind turbine requires 11000 square feet [32]. In addition, wind has a higher capacity factor than solar in reasonably windy places. For example, the average wind capacity factor for the East of the US is 26%, whereas in the Mountain states it is 33% [42]. Assuming the East capacity factor, 1MW of wind requires roughly 12x less space than 1MW of solar. However, in larger installations, the wind turbines must be placed far apart, causing their overall space requirements to substantially exceed those of solar [30].

In terms of capital costs, wind is 2x-3x cheaper than solar [18].

Despite its small size, Parasol only uses solar energy because winds are not strong enough at our location.

Summary. The above data and trends suggest that self-generation using solar and/or wind energy will become increasingly attractive.

4. Design and Implementation of Parasol

In this section, we describe and justify our design of Parasol as a research platform. We start with the physical infrastructure, then describe its IT hardware and software. At the end of the section, we justify each of our design decisions and mention a few mistakes.

Physical infrastructure. Parasol comprises a small custom container, a set of fixed solar panels, batteries and a grid-tie, a free cooling unit, and a direct-expansion air conditioner (HVAC). The container lies on a steel structure placed on the roof of our building, and houses two 42U racks of energy-efficient IT equipment. Each of our servers takes half-U space, so two racks can host up to 150 of them (some rack space is needed for networking and other gear).

The 16 polycrystalline solar panels are mounted on top of the steel structure and shade the container from the sun most of the time. Each panel produces up to 235W DC. The DC power is transformed into AC using two SMA Sunny Boy 2000HF-US inverters placed inside the container. The panels produce up to 3.2kW of AC power (after derating). Parasol is also equipped with 32kWh of lead-acid batteries controlled by two SMA Sunny Island 5040-US charge controllers. In addition, Parasol is connected to the electrical grid and can be configured to net meter any excess solar energy. In typical on-grid solar setups, the batteries are only discharged during grid power outages. However, we have identified configuration parameters to the inverters and charge controllers that allow us (almost) full control of every source of energy available to Parasol. We can dynamically change the setting of these parameters according to our management goals. As discussed in Section 6, these changes have to be done in stages to prevent instability.

For cooling, Parasol uses the Dantherm Flexibox 450 free cooling unit, TKS 3000 free cooling controller, iA/C 19000 HVAC, and two relays that we introduced (1) to properly coordinate the free cooling unit and the HVAC; and (2) to completely shut down the HVAC when the free cooling is on. Parasol uses free cooling whenever the outside temperature is lower than a programmable threshold (27°C by default). The TKS controller modulates the fan speed according to a temperature sensor inside the container and the threshold. The free cooling unit consumes between 8W and 410W depending on fan speed. When the outside temperature exceeds the threshold, the controller closes the damper, turns the free cooling unit off, and turns the HVAC on. How often the HVAC compressor runs depends on the temperature of its internal sensor and the threshold. The HVAC consumes between 100W and 2.3kW. Under very low temperatures (less than 5°C by default), the HVAC activates its internal 3-kW heater.

To distribute power to the IT equipment, we use 3 Raritan Dominion PX PDUs, which monitor the energy drawn from each outlet and can turn the outlet on/off. Parasol also includes power meters, and temperature, humidity, and air quality sensors.

Figure 3 shows the steel structure, the container, and the solar panels. The steel structure is 8'×22', whereas the container is 7'×12'. The batteries are in the white enclosures on the right side of the photo. The HVAC can be seen on the long side of the container, whereas the exhaust damper can be seen to the left of the container's door. The free cooling unit (not shown) is on the short side of the container in the wall opposite to the damper.

Figure 3. Outside view of Parasol.

Figure 4 shows the layout of the inside of Parasol in scale. The servers face the free cooling unit on the left side of the figure, and expel hot air towards the exhaust damper on the right side. The straight dashed line represents a partition we introduced to create a "cold aisle" in front of the servers. Most of the rest of the container is the "hot aisle". To completely seal the cold aisle, we also placed a partition at the top of the racks (not shown). This top partition leaves the Sunny Boys in the hot aisle. The snake shaped duct brings conditioned air to the cold aisle, when the free cooling unit is off and the damper is closed.

IT hardware. Parasol currently hosts 64 Idotpc Atom-based servers, each of which has a Mini-ITX Motherboard with a dual-core Atom D525MW processor, 4GB of memory, one 250GB hard disk, and one 64GB solid-state drive. Each server consumes between 22W and 30W. To connect the servers, we use 2 low-power 1Gbps Ethernet switches (Cisco SG300-52), each with 52 ports and a power range of 24W to 42W. We will add more of these servers, switches, and PDUs in the near future.

Parasol also includes a quad-core Xeon server with 16GB of memory and 1TB of RAIDed disk space. This server receives and stores all the monitoring data collected from Parasol.

Software. Section 5 describes GreenSwitch. We have also built an energy-management daemon (not used in this paper) for Parasol. The daemon aggressively manages the energy consumption of the IT equipment by sending servers to sleep whenever they are not needed. For example, the daemon transitions inactive servers to the S3 ACPI state after a threshold amount of idle time. Our modified version of the SSH utility wakes up the servers.

Parasol uses Ganglia [35] for collecting and processing all monitoring data. We collect energy consumption or production data from every component (including inverters, cooling units, and PDUs) and quantify the losses in power conversion/distribution. With these data, we compute the Power Usage Efficiency (PUE) at each point in time. We also collect temperature, humidity, air flow, and air quality measurements in different locations. Finally, we monitor the utilization of the servers' CPUs, memories, and disks.

Justification. Our desire to study free cooling (beyond the scope of this paper) is the main reason we place the servers on the roof. Had we placed the servers inside our building, the building's central air conditioning would interfere with our experiments. Based on historical temperature data, we expect Parasol to run on free cooling more than 92% of the time at our location.

We designed the container to be large enough to house a non-trivial number of servers and the auxiliary equipment (inverters and charge controllers), but small enough that it would be cheaper and could be placed just about anywhere. Its internal layout creates a

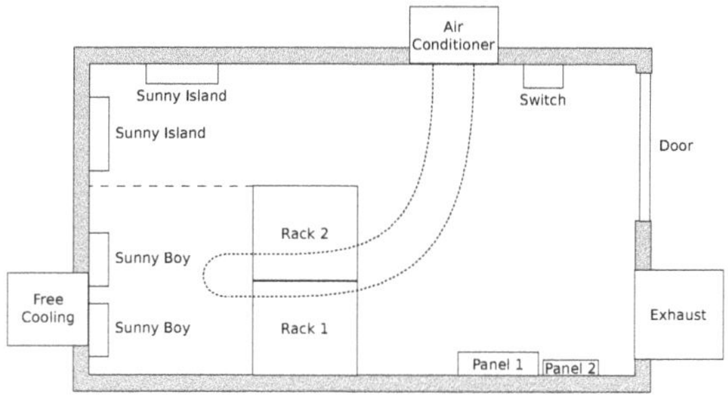

Figure 4. Inside view of Parasol.

small, sealed cold aisle, and a "wind-tunnel" effect between the free cooling unit, the servers, and the damper. The location of the HVAC is not ideal, requiring the air duct. A better location would have been the opposite wall, near the free cooling unit.

The steel frame is larger than the container, so that it can support a larger number of solar panels and the (heavy) batteries. We wanted enough panels to cover at least 30% of the energy consumption of Parasol; through aggressive power management, we expect to achieve this goal easily. The frame is raised to avoid interfering with roof maintenance and the roof's drain system.

Importantly, note that our goal was *not* to design a scaled down version of a warehouse-sized datacenter. Our concept of datacenter is substantially broader, including smaller server installations found in universities and many enterprises, for example. For these installations, it is typically acceptable not to have batteries or backup diesel generators for grid outages. (We included relatively large batteries in Parasol to investigate their use in lowering electricity costs in the face of solar energy and net metering, as we do in this paper.) Moreover, the research we envision on Parasol is independent of most of its physical characteristics. Strictly in terms of its design, Parasol can be seen as a modular datacenter (e.g., [19]) that uses solar energy and free cooling, or as a datacenter for off-grid deployments (possibly in isolated areas).

Our choice of Atom-based servers stems from our desire to study the tradeoffs between wimpy and high-performance servers, as a function of workload (beyond the scope of this paper). For instance, for our Hadoop workloads, our wimpy servers consume 5x less power than comparable Xeon-based servers, while running 4.8x slower. We also considered purchasing ARM-based servers, but those were not yet available at the time.

Finally, our IT equipment runs on AC power, which requires converting the DC power produced by the solar panels and drawn from our batteries. This conversion causes small energy losses (2% on average). We considered a design in which all IT equipment would run on DC power, which would require conversion of the power coming from the grid. Ultimately, we decided that AC power would likely make it easier to find the equipment we wanted.

5. Design and Implementation of GreenSwitch

In this section, we describe GreenSwitch, our model-based framework and system for managing workloads and energy sources in green datacenters. We divide the presentation into two parts: (1) management activities and objectives; and (2) analytical models, and associated optimization goals and solution procedures.

5.1 Management Activities and Objectives

Figure 5 illustrates the GreenSwitch components. The *predictor* predicts the workload and the renewable energy production. The *solver* takes these predictions and the current battery charge level as input, and outputs a workload schedule and an energy source schedule. The solver produces schedules that drive the use of energy by the system. The *configurer* effects the changes prescribed

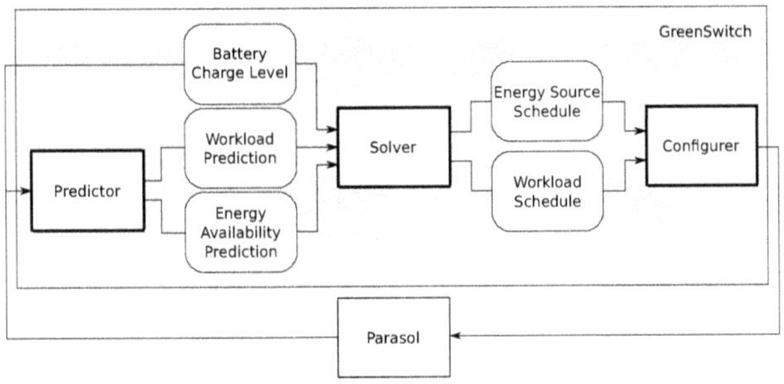

Figure 5. GreenSwitch architecture. Rectangles with round edges are data structures. Rectangles with square borders are processes.

by the solver in the two schedules. The changes may involve transitioning some servers between power states and/or changing the configuration of the energy sources. Monitoring data from the datacenter flows back to inform the predictor in its next iteration.

Note that the configurer is the only part of GreenSwitch that is specific to the system GreenSwitch is supposed to control (e.g., Hadoop); the other components are independent of this system and can be reused without modification. The configurer can be easily adapted to control other systems that provide an energy management interface.

GreenSwitch runs periodically. By default, a full iteration of it occurs every 15 minutes, which enables it to properly control peak grid power consumption. (Power utilities typically compute peak grid power consumption in windows of 15 minutes.) However, GreenSwitch checks the production of solar energy every 3 minutes (by default). During each of these checks, it decides to run a full iteration if there has been an unexpected change in energy production. Specifically, GreenSwitch is conservative and runs a full iteration if it detects a change that is larger than the maximum change we observe in any 15-minute interval on clear days.

Next, we discuss each component of GreenSwitch.

Predictor. The predictor produces predictions of the workload and renewable energy availability for the next "scheduling horizon" (1 day by default, representing the maximum delay a job might experience) at the granularity of shorter "epochs" (1 hour by default, which is the granularity of our solar predictions).

For its **workload prediction**, the predictor can use any method for predicting future loads in terms of the average power they will require in each epoch of the next horizon. Our current implementation assumes that the future will be similar to the past. Specifically, the predictor computes the average power using an exponentially weighted moving average of the average power consumed in the past. It predicts that this average power will be required in every epoch of the horizon. It progressively corrects any inaccuracies in its predictions in its following iterations. Obviously, workloads with repeating patterns could benefit from more sophisticated prediction approaches, e.g. time-series analysis. However, the workloads we have considered so far do not have this property. If necessary, it is easy to replace our current workload prediction implementation with a more sophisticated one.

For its **renewable energy availability prediction**, the predictor can use any model of the availability of solar and/or wind energy. Our implementation uses the method from [12] to predict solar energy. The method combines the model from Sharma *et al.* [36] with the approach for improving accuracy from Goiri *et al.* [11].

Sharma's model recognizes that the solar energy generation is inversely related to the amount of cloud cover, and is expressed as: $E_p(t) = B(t)(1 - CloudCover)$, where $E_p(t)$ is the amount of energy predicted for time t, $B(t)$ is the amount of energy expected under ideal sunny conditions for time t, and $CloudCover$ is the forecasted percentage cloud cover. For the cloud cover information, we use forecasts from Intellicast.com. We set $B(t)$ to the amount of energy generated on the day with the highest energy generation from the previous month.

Unfortunately, weather forecasts are sometimes wrong, which may lead to inaccurate predictions. To improve accuracy, we apply a second method, which computes $CloudCover$ from the amount of energy generated in the previous epoch. GreenSwitch compares the accuracy of the two methods, and uses the most accurate one to predict the remainder of the horizon. For example, at the beginning of epoch t, GreenSwitch computes $CloudCover$ for the next epoch using (1) the weather forecast, and (2) the energy produced in epoch $t-1$. At the beginning of epoch $t+1$, it compares the accuracy of the two methods and uses it to predict the remainder of the horizon. At time $t+2$, the process repeats.

Solver. The solver uses the predictions, information on the amount of energy stored in the batteries, and the models detailed in Section 5.2 to produce a workload schedule and an energy source schedule.

The solver can handle two metrics (grid electricity cost and performance degradation), two types of grid electricity cost (energy and peak power), two types of workload (deferrable and non-deferrable), three energy sources (solar, battery, and grid), two grid availability scenarios (grid is always up and grid goes down during the execution of the workload), and three energy storage scenarios (net metering only, batteries only, and batteries plus net metering).

The optimization metrics deserve more explanation. The grid electricity costs reflect the types of charges that utilities may impose. Datacenters often pay a different grid energy price, i.e. a dollar amount per kWh of consumed grid energy, during an off-peak period (e.g., at night) than during an on-peak period (e.g., daytime). In addition, datacenters often pay for their peak grid power consumption, i.e. a dollar amount per kW of grid power at the highest period of grid power usage. To compute the peak charges, utilities typically monitor the average grid power consumption within 15-minute windows during each month. They define the maximum of these averages as the peak grid power for the month.

The performance degradation metric assesses how much of a workload the system has processed over time.

The metric we seek to optimize depends on the workload and the availability of grid electricity. Under deferrable workloads, when the grid is up, we schedule the workload and the use of the energy sources to minimize the grid electricity cost. When the grid goes down, we still schedule both workload and energy sources, but seek to minimize the performance degradation (compared to having the grid up) during the outage. Under non-deferrable workloads, our management objective becomes restricted to scheduling the use of the energy sources to minimize the grid electricity cost.

Workload and energy source schedules. The workload schedule determines how much energy should be consumed in each epoch. For non-deferrable workloads, the workload schedule always matches the workload prediction, so that jobs are not delayed due to GreenSwitch. For deferrable workloads, GreenSwitch has more flexibility to spread the computation around, as long as jobs can still complete within their time bounds.

The energy source schedule determines how much energy to draw from each source in each epoch.

Configurer for Hadoop. In our implementation, GreenSwitch manages a slightly modified version of Hadoop. The modification enables energy management by implementing three server power states: active, decommissioned, and sleep. Active and sleep (the S3 state) are self-explanatory. The decommissioned state is an intermediate state that prevents new jobs from starting on the server. We configure our Hadoop setup to the Covering Subset scheme [27], i.e. we store a full copy of the dataset on the smallest possible

Parameter	Meaning	Default Value
$Load_t$	Average required IT power	N/A
$Workload_t$	Average offered IT load (power)	N/A
T	Length of the scheduling horizon	24 hours
$MaxPower$	Maximum IT power (servers and switches)	$64 \times 30W + 2 \times 42W$
$CoverPower$	Typical power consumption of the Covering Subset and switches	$8 \times 28W + 30W + 24W$
$LoadGreen_t$	Amount of green power to be used for the load	N/A
$LoadBrown_t$	Amount of grid power to be used for the load	N/A
$LoadBatt_t$	Amount of battery power to be used for the load	N/A
$BattGreen_t$	Amount of green power to be used for charging batteries	N/A
$NetGreen_t$	Amount of green power to be used in net metering	N/A
$Brown_t$	Amount of grid power to be used for any purpose	N/A
$BattBrown_t$	Amount of grid power to be used for charging batteries	N/A
$CapBatt_0$	Battery charge level in the first epoch	85%
$Duration$	Length of each epoch	15 minutes
β	Energy losses in batteries	10%
$BattMaxCharge$	Maximum charge rate of batteries	8kW
$MaxCapBatt$	Maximum battery capacity	32 kWh
γ	Minimum battery charge level	65%
$BEnergyPrice_t$	Grid energy price	\$0.08/kWh (off-peak), \$0.13/kWh (on-peak)
$BPeakPrice_t$	Peak grid power price	\$13.61/kW/month
α	Percentage of retail price paid in net metering	40%
$PreviousPeak$	Maximum grid power consumed so far	N/A
$MaxPeak$	Maximum peak grid power	N/A
$Load_t^{up}$	Average required IT power when the grid is up	N/A
$Load_t^{down}$	Average required IT power to be used when the grid is down	N/A

Table 1. Model parameters, meanings, and default values. N/A = not applicable.

number of servers; any server out of the Covering Subset can be sent to sleep without affecting data availability.

The configurer has two settings: server energy management on and off. When energy management is off, the configurer does not power-manage any servers. When energy management is on, the configurer abides by the workload schedule by transitioning servers between the three Hadoop server power states. Specifically: (1) it transitions any active server that need not be active but still stores data required by running jobs to the decommissioned state. In a following iteration, if the data stored at the decommissioned server is no longer needed, the configurer transitions it to the sleep state; (2) it transitions any active server that need not be active and does not store relevant data to sleep state; and (3) it transitions sleeping servers to the active state if they are required for computation during an iteration. The configurer keeps the Covering Subset active at all times.

To abide by the energy source schedule, the configurer uses the following actuators: activate/deactivate grid; change maximum current drawn from the grid (which affects the maximum power drawn from the grid); and start/stop charging the batteries. These actuators represent different settings of the parameters of the Sunny Island charge controllers. Interestingly, these actuators must be used carefully to avoid instability. For example, one cannot quickly transition from battery charging with solar energy to net metering, as this causes the inverter to shut down. Thus, this transition needs to be performed in steps, with some idle time in between the steps. Note that *such behaviors are simply overlooked in simulation or with simple prototypes* that do not include real charge controllers.

5.2 Models, Optimization, and Solution Approach

We now describe the solver's models of workload and energy sources. Next, we formulate the optimization problems that the solver implements, and discuss how it instantiates and solves them. Table 1 lists the models' parameters, meanings, and default values.

Modeling workloads. Let us start by defining $Load_t$ to be the average IT power the datacenter will consume in epoch t. (We leave the modeling and management of the cooling power for future work, since we only recently completed Parasol's cooling setup.) We also define $Workload_t$ as the amount of offered computational load (measured in terms of average power per epoch, including the Covering Subset) in epoch t.

We should execute the full workload during the horizon (T), so

$$\sum^{t \in T} Load_t = \sum^{t \in T} Workload_t \quad (1)$$

We can be more specific about this relationship, depending on the type of workload. When the workload is non-deferrable, the offered load must be executed without delay, i.e.

$$\forall t \in T : Load_t = Workload_t \quad (2)$$

When it is deferrable, the offered load can be delayed within T

$$\forall t \in T : \sum_{t'=1}^{t'=t} Load_{t'} \leq \sum_{t'=1}^{t'=t} Workload_{t'} \quad (3)$$

There are also a couple of constraints on $Load_t$. First, the average power during an epoch cannot be higher than the maximum power the load can consume ($MaxPower$), i.e.

$$\forall t \in T : Load_t \leq MaxPower \quad (4)$$

In addition, the power consumption has to be at least that of the servers in the Covering Subset ($CoverPower$), i.e.

$$\forall t \in T : Load_t \geq CoverPower \quad (5)$$

Relating the workload modeling back to the inputs and outputs to the solver, $Load$ represents the workload schedule that the solver produces, whereas $Workload$ is the workload prediction that GreenSwitch feeds to the solver.

Modeling energy sources. In the most general scenario, three sources can be used to power the system: renewable ($LoadGreen$), grid ($LoadBrown$), or battery ($LoadBattery$). Thus,

$$\forall t \in T : Load_t = LoadGreen_t + LoadBrown_t + LoadBatt_t \quad (6)$$

The renewable power ($AvailGreen$) may be used for multiple purposes: running the workload ($LoadGreen$), charging the batteries ($BattGreen$), and/or net metering ($NetGreen$). Thus,

$$\forall t \in T : LoadGreen_t + BattGreen_t + NetGreen_t \leq AvailGreen_t \quad (7)$$

Similarly, the grid ($Brown$) can be used to power the workload ($LoadBrown$) and/or charge the batteries ($BattBrown$).

$$\forall t \in T : LoadBrown_t + BattBrown_t = Brown_t \quad (8)$$

The modeling of the batteries is more involved. First, we must account for the fact that batteries incur losses, i.e. only a percentage (β) of the energy we store in them will be available for later use. We define the current capacity of the batteries ($CapBatt$) as:

$$\begin{aligned}\forall t \in T : CapBatt_t = CapBatt_{t-1} + \\ Duration \cdot \beta(BattGreen_{t-1} + BattBrown_{t-1}) - \\ Duration \cdot LoadBatt_{t-1}\end{aligned} \tag{9}$$

where $Duration$ is the length of each epoch t.

Second, we must formalize the constraints on the batteries. We cannot use more energy than what they have stored, so

$$\forall t \in T : Duration \cdot LoadBatt_t \leq CapBatt_t \tag{10}$$

They have a maximum charge rate ($BattMaxCharge$) in kW:

$$\forall t \in T : BattGreen_t + BattBrown_t < BattMaxCharge \tag{11}$$

They have a maximum capacity ($MaxCapBatt$):

$$\forall t \in T : CapBatt_t \leq MaxCapBatt \tag{12}$$

Third, we must ensure that leveraging the batteries as an energy source does not harm their lifetime. For this, we follow the analysis of Govindan *et al.* [14], which demonstrates that one can avoid reducing the batteries' lifetime by limiting the depth of discharge to a percentage ($CapBatt_0 - \gamma$) of the maximum capacity at all times. (We derive the proper γ in Section 6.) Thus,

$$\forall t \in T : CapBatt_t \geq \gamma MaxCapBatt \tag{13}$$

Fourth, we must account for operational modes that are not supported in typical solar installations. Specifically, we cannot charge the batteries with solar energy and do net metering at the same time.

$$\forall t \in \{T | BattGreen_t > 0\} : NetGreen_t = 0 \tag{14}$$

In addition, we cannot use the batteries and do net metering at the same time.

$$\forall t \in \{T | LoadBatt_t > 0\} : NetGreen_t = 0 \tag{15}$$

We cannot draw from the grid to power the load at the same time as doing net metering.

$$\forall t \in \{T | LoadBrown_t > 0\} : NetGreen_t = 0 \tag{16}$$

We cannot charge and discharge the batteries at the same time.

$$\forall t \in \{T | LoadBatt_t > 0\} : BattGreen_t + BattBrown_t = 0 \tag{17}$$

Finally, we must ensure that all parameters are ≥ 0.

Relating the energy source modeling back to the solver, $AvailGreen$ (renewable energy prediction) and $CapBatt$ (current battery capacity) are inputs, whereas $LoadGreen$, $LoadBrown$, $LoadBatt$, $BattGreen$, $NetGreen$, and $BattBrown$ represent the energy source schedule that the solver produces as an output.

Modeling the peak grid power usage. We define $PreviousPeak$ as the maximum grid power (averaged over 15-minute intervals) consumed from the beginning of the current month until the start of the current horizon. We also define $MaxPeak$ as the highest grid power consumption ($Brown$) since the beginning of the current month, i.e. $Brown$ and $PreviousPeak$ must be no higher than $MaxPeak$.

$$\begin{aligned}\forall t \in T : Brown_t \leq MaxPeak \\ PreviousPeak \leq MaxPeak\end{aligned} \tag{18}$$

Optimization goals. Under the constraints above, we now define our optimization goals: #1 minimize the grid electricity cost, when the grid is up; and #2 minimize the performance degradation (compared to the execution with the grid up), when the grid is down.

To model goal #1, we recognize that the cost of the grid electricity may have both energy and peak power components. We define the energy price per kWh as $BEnergyPrice$, and the peak power price per kW as $BPeakPrice$. When we feed green energy into the grid, we get paid a percentage (α) of the current retail price of the energy by the utility, i.e. $\alpha BEnergyPrice$. For example, the utility may pay the full retail price ($\alpha = 1$) or just the wholesale price ($\alpha < 1$). Thus, we model the first goal as:

$$\begin{aligned}min(\sum^{t \in T}(BEnergyPrice_t \cdot Duration \cdot Brown_t - \\ \alpha BEnergyPrice_t \cdot Duration \cdot NetGreen_t) + \\ BPeakPrice \cdot (MaxPeak - PreviousPeak))\end{aligned} \tag{19}$$

When the grid is down, goal #1 above does not make sense. In this case, optimization goal #2 becomes active. We model it as:

$$min \sum^{t \in T}(|T| - t)(Load_t^{up} - Load_t^{down}) \tag{20}$$

where $Load_t^{up}$ is the last workload schedule for epoch t before the grid outage, and $Load_t^{down}$ is the workload schedule to be used in epoch t during the outage. Since no new work can reach the datacenter during the outage, we define $Workload_t$ as $Load_t^{up}$ for all t. As the workload and energy predictions tend to be more accurate in the near future, goal #2 minimizes the performance degradation ($Load_t^{up} - Load_t^{down}$) while promoting early load execution ($|T| - t$).

Instantiating the models. Before solving the optimization problems, we need to instantiate the model's parameters. We instantiate them with values from Parasol, GreenSwitch, and our experimental setup. Specifically, we instantiate $MaxPower$, $CoverPower$, $BattMaxCharge$, and $MaxCapBatt$ with Parasol data. In addition, we instantiate $Workload$ with the GreenSwitch workload prediction, and $AvailGreen$ with its solar energy prediction. We also instantiate $Duration$ with the common-case duration of each epoch in GreenSwitch. In our experiments, we study multiple scenarios. When the datacenter is exposed to both grid energy and peak power charges, we instantiate $BEnergyPrice$ and $BPeakPrice$ with real values for those prices. When disregarding peak grid power, we set $BPeakPrice$ to \$0/kW. When considering non-deferrable workloads, we use the constraint defined by Equation 2 above, whereas for deferrable workloads we use Equation 3. To mimic scenarios without batteries, we set $\forall t \in T : LoadBatt_t + BattBrown_t + BattGreen_t = 0$. For scenarios without the grid, we set $\forall t \in T : Brown_t = 0$. For different net metering rates, we adjust α. We set $CapBatt_0$ to an initial battery charge.

Solving the optimization problems. Let us start with the grid electricity cost problem. Although Equation 19 is linear, the solver cannot use simple Linear Programming (LP), because the constraints in Equations 14–17 are non-linear. Fortunately, these constraints can be linearized into Mixed Integer LP (MILP) formulations. We solve the MILP problem efficiently using the Gurobi solver [16].

For goal #2, the solver (1) zeroes all parameters relating to the grid; (2) removes Equation 1, as we may not be able to run the entire workload without the grid; (3) changes γ to 21%. This value is the sum of the battery capacity needed to protect against the largest possible workload misprediction for an epoch (6%, corresponding to the full power of the cluster), and the lowest battery charge level before the charge controllers start to shut down (15%); (4) uses the last workload schedule before the grid outage as the first workload prediction during the outage; and (5) uses MILP to compute the new workload and energy source schedules.

6. Experimental Evaluation

In this section, we describe the remaining details of our methodology and the results of our experiments.

6.1 Methodology

Experimental setup. We run our experiments on Parasol. The 64 servers run our modified version of Hadoop. GreenSwitch runs on one of these servers. We also use a Xeon-based client located in another building to submit the Hadoop jobs. Each of our experiments runs for 23 hours and 15 minutes, starting at 12:00am, so that we have 45 minutes to prepare the next experiment.

Unless we state otherwise, all experiments with solar energy also use net metering. We consider systems with and without batteries. One can think of the system without batteries as a conventional on-grid solar-powered system, i.e. batteries are only used when the electrical grid is out. Another way to think about it is as a system without any batteries whatsoever. When batteries are not used or not present, solar energy deficits are compensated with grid energy, and solar energy surpluses are stored on the grid via net metering.

Our experiments with solar energy are exposed to real weather conditions, making it hard to compare two experiments directly. Fortunately, for non-deferrable workloads, we can first run the GreenSwitch experiment on the real system. Then, using this experimental data, we can manually mimic the no-battery schedule under the same workload and solar energy conditions. We cannot use the same trick for deferrable workloads, because the GreenSwitch schedules interact. For both types of workload, we can compare the GreenSwitch results to a grid-only datacenter setup, i.e. no solar energy, no batteries, and modified Hadoop (which does server energy management, but never defers workloads).

Workloads. We study two widely different Hadoop traces, called "Facebook" and "Nutch". Facebook comes from a larger trace of 600 machines at Facebook [4]. The original trace was collected from May to October 2009, and contains roughly 1 million jobs. We use the Statistical Workload Injector for MapReduce (SWIM) [5] to generate a scaled-down version of the trace for 24 hours on 64 machines. In the resulting trace, each job comprises 2–1190 map tasks and 1–63 reduce tasks. There are roughly 5500 jobs and 68000 tasks. The map phase of each job takes 25–13000 seconds, whereas the reduce phase takes 15–2600 seconds. Jobs have inputs of 64MB–74GB and outputs of up to 4GB. These characteristics lead to a cluster utilization of 27%.

Nutch is the indexing part of the Web search system in CloudSuite [9]. The trace consists of 2000 jobs that index groups of pages previously fetched from our Web domain. Each job runs 42 map tasks and 1 reduce task. Each map phase takes 15–40 seconds, whereas the reduce phase takes 150 seconds. On average, each job touches 85MB of data. Jobs arrive according to a Poisson distribution with mean inter-arrival time of 40 seconds. These characteristics lead to a cluster utilization of 32%.

We run these workloads in the deferrable and non-deferrable modes. The workloads require 8 servers in their Covering Subsets.

Instantiating the models. We use the default values in the third column of Table 1 to instantiate our models. We have already explained all these default values, except for $BEnergyPrice$, $BPeakPrice$, α, $CapBatt_0$, β, and γ.

In terms of electricity prices ($BEnergyPrice$, $BPeakPrice$), we assume on-peak/off-peak pricing, the most common type of variable grid energy pricing. In this scheme, energy costs less during off-peak times (11pm–9am) than during on-peak times (9am–11pm). We use the energy prices charged by the main utility at our location: \$0.13/kWh (on-peak) and \$0.08/kWh (off-peak). This utility charges for peak grid power at \$13.61/kW. By default, we assume that the utility pays the wholesale energy price of 40% (α) of the retail price [43] for net metering. However, we also consider the scenario where the utility pays the retail price ($\alpha = 100\%$).

Finally, we start our experiments with the batteries at 85% of their capacity ($CapBatt_0$), because it takes substantially longer to reach higher charge levels. We computed the battery energy losses (β) from our experiments with Parasol. We calculated the minimum acceptable charge level (γ) from the maximum depth of discharge, using the same approach as [14]. Specifically, we first profiled one year of solar energy production from a local farm to compute the expected number of battery charge/discharge cycles in a system like Parasol. From this data, we find that 90+% of the days would require 2 discharges or less. Assuming a desired lifetime of 4 years, 2 discharges per day translates into 2920 discharges. According to the model in Figure 3b of [14], a maximum depth of discharge of 20% is required to achieve 2920 discharges. So, $\gamma = 85\% - 20\% = 65\%$.

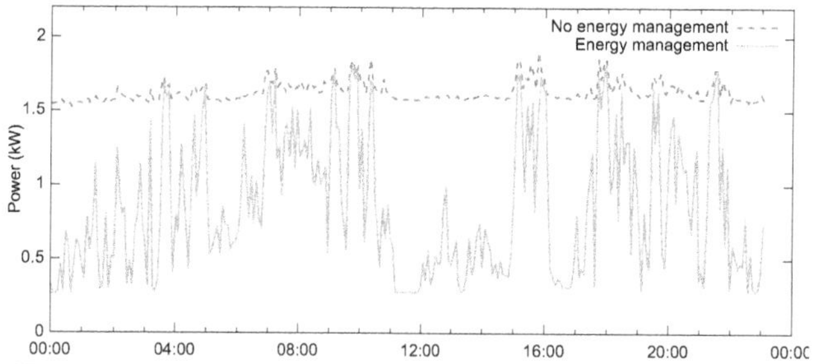

Figure 6. Power with/without energy management for Facebook.

6.2 Experimental Results

This section presents our experimental results. We first compare our modified version of Hadoop to standard Hadoop to establish a baseline. Second, we quantify the accuracy of GreenSwitch's workload and solar energy predictions. Third, we evaluate GreenSwitch's management of the energy sources for a non-deferrable workload. Fourth, we evaluate GreenSwitch's management of workload and energy source for a deferrable workload. Fifth, we study different energy storage scenarios. Sixth, we evaluate GreenSwitch's management of peak grid power draw. Seventh, we study the impact of different amounts of solar energy. Eighth, we consider a different workload. Finally, we show results for a grid outage scenario.

Energy management in Hadoop. We start by comparing the energy consumption of our modified Hadoop to that of the original Hadoop implementation for the Facebook trace in the non-deferrable mode. The modified Hadoop computes the number of active servers to fully pack them with the available map tasks (each server can run 3 maps and 1 reduce concurrently).

Figure 6 shows the power consumed by the trace over time with (modified Hadoop) and without (Hadoop) server energy management. Note that the power consumption without energy management is almost flat, because our servers have a small dynamic power range. The execution becomes much more energy proportional when energy management is in effect. Overall, we find that our modifications to Hadoop enable energy savings of 41%. The savings are higher (roughly 50%) for the Nutch trace in the non-deferrable mode. (We do not consider deferrable workloads in this comparison, because original Hadoop is incapable of leveraging the ability to delay jobs.) Given these positive results, we use our modified Hadoop as the baseline for comparison from now on.

Accuracy of workload and solar energy predictions. To assess the accuracy of our predictions, we compare them to the actual workload and solar energy production for each epoch of the experiments we describe below. These comparisons show average workload prediction errors of 36% 1 hour ahead, and 51% 3 hours ahead, when the workload is non-deferrable. For deferrable workloads, these numbers are 31% and 48%, respectively. In terms of solar energy predictions, these average errors are 13% and 14%, respectively. We do not evaluate the GreenSwitch predictions more

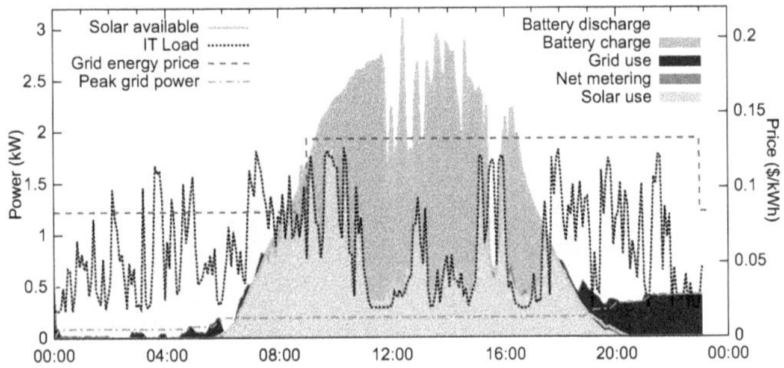

Figure 7. Energy source management for non-deferrable Facebook.

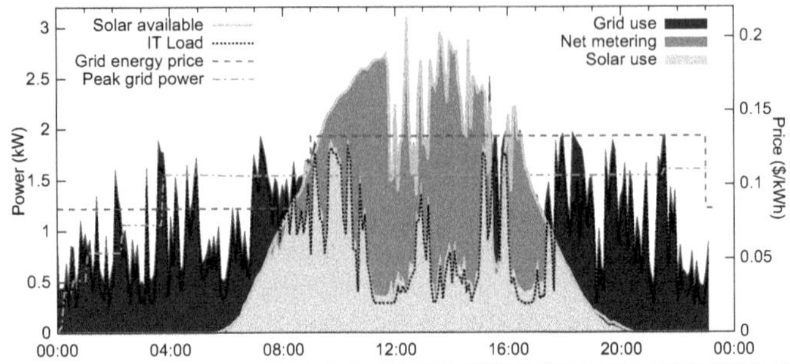

Figure 8. No-battery, non-deferrable Facebook (re-colored).

thoroughly because our methods for producing them are not contributions of our work. Importantly, GreenSwitch is able to quickly detect and adapt to workload and solar energy mispredictions, due to its frequent iterations (3-15 minutes).

Energy source management for a non-deferrable workload. Figure 7 illustrates the GreenSwitch execution of the Facebook trace in the non-deferrable mode on July 17, 2012. The fill colors represent the use of the different energy sources, whereas the lines going across the figure are the solar energy production (full), the IT load (dots), the grid energy price (dashes, Y-axis on the right), and the current peak grid power draw (dashes-dots). Recall that GreenSwitch seeks to minimize the grid electricity cost when the grid is up, and that GreenSwitch schedules the entire workload within a maximum of 1 horizon.

First, we can see that the amount of produced solar energy varied significantly during the day, especially 11am–2pm and 3pm–4pm, due to cloudy conditions. Second, the solar energy was enough to power the workload and charge the batteries. Despite their energy losses, GreenSwitch decided to charge the batteries to attempt to avoid using grid energy while it was still expensive (until 11pm). Third, when there was no solar energy, GreenSwitch drew energy from both the batteries and the grid in many cases. (Recall that GreenSwitch prevents the battery charge level to fall below 65% for lifetime reasons.) Early on, GreenSwitch predicted that it would not have enough battery energy to run the load until solar energy was available. Consequently, it sought to consume grid energy. At night, it again predicted not to have enough battery capacity, and resorted to grid energy. Throughout the day, GreenSwitch was able to limit the increase in the peak grid power by using batteries and/or solar energy. However, it was unable to prevent a slight increase of the peak grid power, as its control of the grid draw (done through a limit on current) is not accurate enough. Note that *this effect would not be seen under simulation or with a simple prototype* that does not include a real grid-tie.

To quantify the electricity cost savings, we compare the use of the energy sources in this figure to those when batteries are not used or not present at all (Figure 8). Because of the difficulty in comparing experiments (Section 6.1), Figure 8 simply re-colors Figure 7 with the colors we would see in the absence of GreenSwitch.

Comparing the executions shows that GreenSwitch reduced the grid energy cost by 73%, the peak grid power cost by 78%, and the overall grid electricity cost by 75%. Despite these high savings, it may be difficult to amortize the capital cost of the batteries ($0.21/Wh in the US [38]) during their lifetime. Specifically, GreenSwitch discharged the battery once per day (to the maximum depth of discharge) in this experiment, extending the batteries' lifetime to 8 years. Under these conditions, the cost of the batteries would have to be roughly 1.8x lower for us to amortize it in 8 years.

A more positive comparison is between a solar-powered system without batteries (same behavior as in Figure 8) and a grid-only datacenter. This comparison shows that the electricity cost savings accrued by the solar-powered system (66%) could amortize its installed capital cost ($2.28/W with incentives) in 7 years.

Workload and energy source management for a deferrable workload. We now consider the GreenSwitch behavior assuming that the jobs in the Facebook trace are deferrable. Figure 9 shows this behavior on July 1, 2012 in the same format as the previous figures. The white filling represents solar energy that was produced but lost due to inefficiency.

The figure shows a significant drop in solar energy production between 4pm and 6pm. We can see also that the energy consumption was low when solar energy was not available. The reason is that deferring load allows GreenSwitch to send more servers to the sleep state; only the servers in the Covering Subset (and the switches) stay active. When there was no solar energy, GreenSwitch drew energy from the batteries, since they stored enough capacity for the load. Another observation is that the available solar energy was enough to power the workload, charge the batteries, and do significant net metering. In the deferrable mode, the workload consumes less energy due to batching effects (better utilization of fewer active servers). The amount of net metering was high for this workload, because it took a relatively small amount of solar energy to fully recharge the batteries. A final observation is that losses (e.g., inverters, PDUs) were significant at lower power consumption, e.g. at night. This is why the fill color goes higher than the load curve in the figure. The same effect can be seen in other figures but it is not as pronounced as when the load is low. Again, *this effect is typically overlooked* (in favor of constant losses) in simpler setups.

As mentioned above, we cannot compare two experiments with solar energy directly. However, we can compare the results of this experiment to those of a grid-only datacenter. This comparison shows that the solar setup with batteries produced a *profit* of 9% in grid electricity cost, deriving from GreenSwitch's ability to intelligently schedule workload and energy source use. Since there was only 1 discharge (down to 70% charge), the batteries' lifetime would be roughly 9.5 years. GreenSwitch would be able to amortize the cost of the solar setup and batteries in 7.6 years.

When we run this workload with solar energy but without batteries (on June 30, 2012), GreenSwitch was able to reduce the grid electricity cost by 96%, compared to a grid-only datacenter. We could amortize the installed capital cost of this setup in 4.8 years.

Since deferrable loads illustrate the ability of GreenSwitch to manage workloads (as well as energy sources), we use this type of workload from now on unless we explicitly state otherwise.

Energy storage approaches. We now turn to investigating the GreenSwitch behavior under different energy storage assumptions. We run experiments with (1) net metering (utility pays wholesale prices) but no batteries; (2) batteries but no net metering; and (3) both batteries and net metering (utility pays retail prices). The behavior of net metering with retail prices but no batteries is that in experiment (1). Recall that the results we presented above (Figure

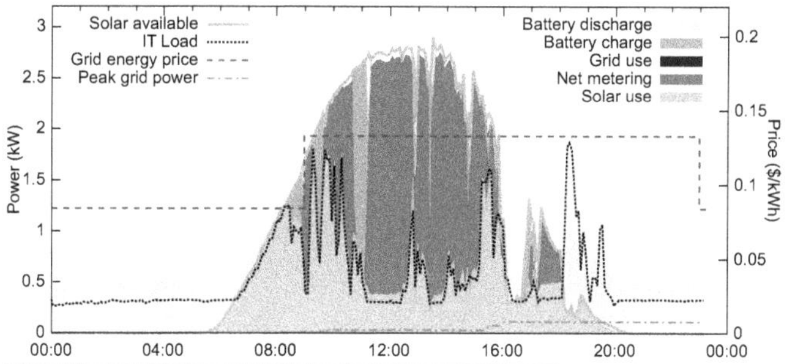

Figure 9. Workload and energy source management for deferrable Facebook.

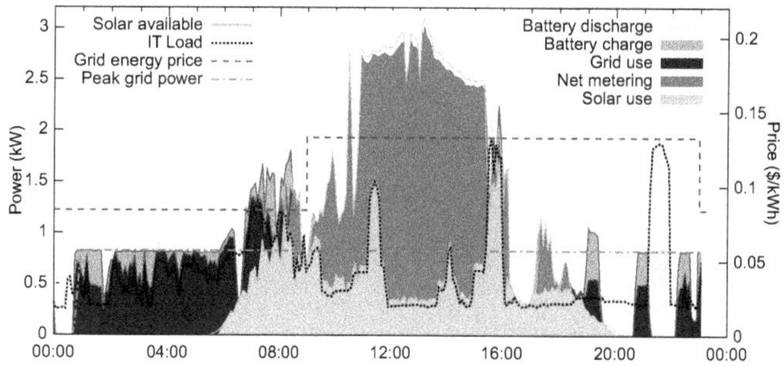

Figure 10. Net metering pays retail energy prices for deferrable Facebook.

7) assume the remaining option: both batteries and net metering (utility pays wholesale prices).

Experiment (1) exhibits the obvious behavior, i.e. GreenSwitch delayed the workload until solar energy become available. Any excess solar energy got net metered. When solar energy was not available, GreenSwitch kept only the servers in the Covering Subset (and switches) in the active state, and used grid energy.

Experiment (2) is more interesting. Since net metering was not available, GreenSwitch consumed energy from the batteries when solar energy was not enough to power the load. However, GreenSwitch did not delay the entire workload until solar energy was available. As it predicted that it would be able to fully recharge the batteries from solar energy later, it scheduled some of the load for the night time.

Finally, in experiment (3), net metering becomes extremely attractive, especially during on-peak hours. For this reason, GreenSwitch net metered all of the excess solar energy. When solar energy was not available, GreenSwitch consumed grid energy when it was cheap, and battery energy when it was expensive. Figure 10 shows these behaviors. Note that GreenSwitch still had to schedule the use of the grid during on-peak hours. The reason is that it predicted not to have enough battery capacity to handle the load during the night.

Unfortunately, we cannot directly compare the electricity costs of these experiments since they were run on different days (June 30, July 9, and July 10, 2012 respectively). However, it is clear that setups that do not require batteries have a major capital cost advantage. For example, under the same weather conditions, the electricity cost savings from setup (1) would be smaller than from using both net metering and batteries. But the capital cost of setup (1) is much lower, if the datacenter can be down during grid outages.

Peak grid power charges. Another important issue is how effective GreenSwitch is at limiting the peak grid power draw. When it disregards these charges, GreenSwitch is more willing to increase the peak grid power, especially when energy is cheap. For the Facebook trace in the non-deferrable mode, the peak grid draw reached 1854W, when GreenSwitch disregarded the peak grid power charges. When it managed the peak grid draw, the peak reached only 408W. This represents a savings in peak power cost of 78%. In the deferrable mode, the peak grid draw reached 711W when GreenSwitch disregarded the peak charges. When it accounted for those charges, the peak reached only 114W; an 84% savings in peak power cost.

These significant savings demonstrate the importance of explicitly managing this aspect of the electricity cost.

Solar energy availability. To see the impact of different weather conditions, consider Figure 11, which corresponds to the Facebook workload in the deferrable mode on a cloudy day (July 13, 2012). Compare this figure with Figure 9, the same workload on a sunny day. On the sunny day, there was no need to use grid energy. On the cloudy day, there was. From its energy predictions, GreenSwitch expected that it would not have enough solar energy to execute the entire workload and charge the batteries. Thus, it decided to use cheap grid energy to compensate. Based on this experiment, the batteries would last 10+ years, whereas it would take 9.2 years to amortize the capital costs of the solar setup and batteries.

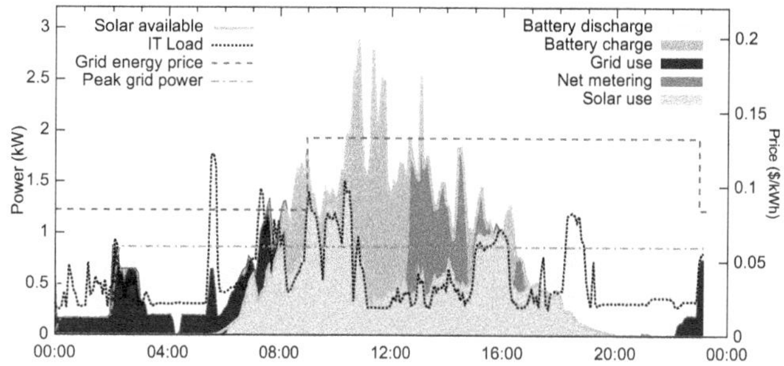

Figure 11. Deferrable Facebook on July 13, 2012.

We also experimented with the same workload, without batteries, on a cloudy day with a thunderstorm (July 18, 2012). This experiment led to an amortization period of 5.4 years for the solar setup, compared to a grid-only datacenter. An ever worse day (rain the whole day) led to an amortization period of 7 years.

These comparisons show that GreenSwitch is capable of nicely adapting to weather conditions.

Nutch. To demonstrate that our results are similar for widely different workloads, we experimented with Nutch assuming that its jobs are non-deferrable. Figures 12 and 13 show the results with and without energy source management, respectively. Since this workload is in the non-deferrable mode, the latter result is the re-colored version of the original experiment.

These results show that GreenSwitch's energy source management reduced the grid energy cost by 66%, the peak grid power cost by 49%, and the overall grid electricity cost by 59%. As for the Facebook trace, these are significant savings. Also like Facebook, the batteries' lifetime would be 9.5 years. However, their capital cost would have to be 2x lower to be amortized in their lifetimes. Comparing a system without batteries to a grid-only datacenter, we find that the grid electricity cost savings (66%) would amortize the installed capital cost of the solar setup after 7.1 years.

Grid outage. Our final experiment demonstrates the GreenSwitch behavior during a grid outage. Recall that GreenSwitch turns to minimizing performance degradation when the grid goes down. Figure 14 shows the behavior of our system for the Facebook trace in the deferrable mode. We assume that the outage occurs at 12am, following the experiment in Figure 10. Note that the day of the outage (July 19, 2012) was mostly cloudy.

The GreenSwitch workload schedule nicely matched the behavior we would have seen had the grid stayed up. Specifically,

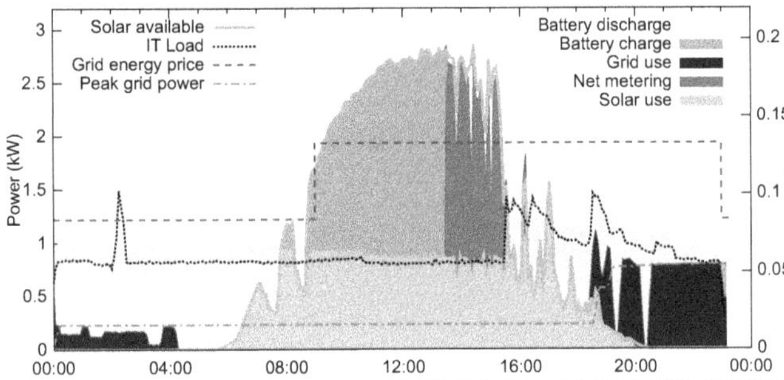

Figure 12. Non-deferrable Nutch workload.

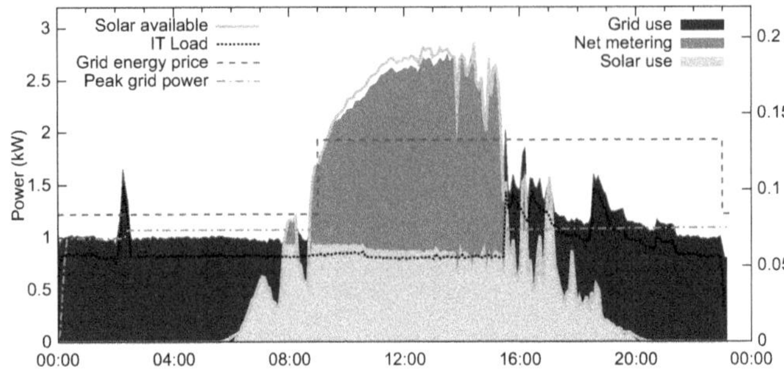

Figure 13. No battery, non-deferrable Nutch (re-colored).

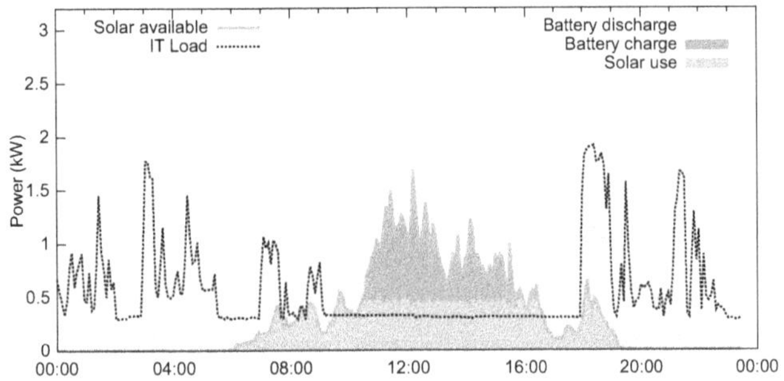

Figure 14. Grid outage on July 19, 2012.

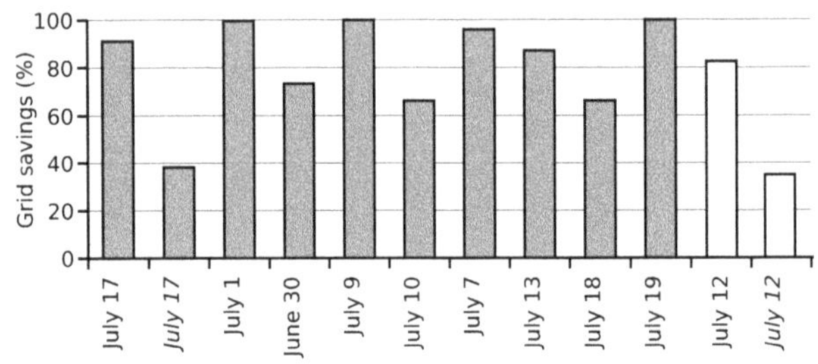

Figure 15. Grid energy reductions compared to grid-only. Repeated date = re-colored result. Gray bars = Facebook; white bars = Nutch.

GreenSwitch intended to execute most of the load early, when the grid energy was cheap, while net metering most of the solar energy for a high retail price. When the grid went down, GreenSwitch kept a similar schedule, executing the entire workload during the day and leaving the battery at 45% capacity.

Reductions in carbon footprint. Figure 15 shows the GreenSwitch reductions in grid energy use compared to a grid-only datacenter for each of the experiments we described above. From left to right, the experiments appear in the order they were discussed above. We identify each experiment by the date when it was run (repeated dates correspond to re-colored results). The two bars furthest to the right are for Nutch, whereas the others are for Facebook. It is clear that GreenSwitch is extremely successful at reducing footprints for both workloads, in some cases completely eliminating any grid energy use (100% reductions). The minimum reduction is 36%.

Summary of results. The results above suggest several interesting observations:

- GreenSwitch's aggressive management of all energy sources (including batteries) during normal operation can produce significant reductions in grid electricity cost and consumption.
- Although GreenSwitch produces the lowest grid electricity costs when batteries are available, their capital cost is a burden for non-deferrable workloads. Specifically, their cost would have to be 1.8x–2x lower to be amortized during their lifetime. Our experiments suggested lifetimes between 8 and 10 years.
- Given the flexibility to delay loads, GreenSwitch can produce integrated workload and energy source schedules that even more significantly lower electricity costs. These schedules enable GreenSwitch to amortize the cost of the batteries, but a solar setup without batteries is still superior.
- The installed capital cost of a solar setup without batteries can be amortized in 4.8–7.1 years in our experiments.
- The GreenSwitch benefits are robust to different renewable energy profiles and workloads. However, every part of GreenSwitch is required, especially its management of peak grid power.
- GreenSwitch is beneficial during grid outages as well, enabling the system to minimize performance degradations.

7. Discussion

Parasol most likely differs from any existing datacenter as: (1) it uses solar energy, batteries, and net metering, whereas most datacenters only draw electricity from the grid and use batteries solely until diesel generators become fully active after a power outage; (2) it uses low-power servers, whereas most datacenters use more powerful servers; and (3) its number of servers (150 max) is comparable to those of datacenters found in universities and enterprises, but tiny compared those of the warehouse-scale datacenters that host popular Internet services.

Despite these differences, our experience and results should be useful in practice for several reasons. First, Parasol exemplifies the type of green datacenter one may choose to deploy at universities, enterprises, or remote locations. Second, GreenSwitch tackles the set of issues and tradeoffs one may face in managing energy sources and workloads in green datacenters of any size. Third, low-power servers are energy-efficient for many workloads (including those in this paper). Moreover, the fact that they incur higher execution times is often not a major concern, especially when the workload is deferrable. Fourth, the electricity cost savings, grid energy savings, amortization periods, and battery lifetimes we report are relative to the size of Parasol. Thus, scaling Parasol (and its workload) proportionally to larger setups (e.g., by doubling the number of servers, the number of solar panels, and the battery capacity) would likely produce similar GreenSwitch results. Obviously, warehouse-scale datacenters are more complex than just a large multiple of Parasol, so the results could be quite different for those systems.

8. Conclusions

In this paper, we presented (1) an analysis of the main tradeoffs involved in powering datacenters with solar and/or wind energy; (2) the design and justification for a research platform, called Parasol, that powers a micro-datacenter with solar energy; (3) a system, called GreenSwitch, for managing workload execution and energy source use in a datacenter powered by solar energy; and (4) a detailed evaluation of GreenSwitch. We discussed many issues that we faced solely because of our use of a real green datacenter prototype. We conclude that the use of renewable energy in datacenters may become increasingly appealing over time, which will likely encourage more initiatives such as Parasol and GreenSwitch.

Based on our experience with our real systems and to extrapolate from the results we presented in this paper, we are currently implementing a simulator that will accurately mimic Parasol and GreenSwitch for longer periods, e.g. a year. The simulator will also enable comparisons against an "offline optimal" version of GreenSwitch that has complete future knowledge of renewable energy production and workload. In the future, we plan to enable other researchers to use Parasol remotely by dedicating servers to their efforts and virtualizing our energy sources.

Acknowledgements

We would like to thank David Meisner and Anand Sivasubramaniam for comments that helped us improve this paper. We are also indebted to Joan Stanton, Heidi Szymanski, Jon Tenenbaum, Chuck Depasquale, SMA America, and Michael J. Pazzani for their extensive help in building/funding Parasol.

References

[1] AISO.net. Web Hosting as Nature Intended, 2012. http://www.aiso.net/.

[2] B. Aksanli et al. Utilizing Green Energy Prediction to Schedule Mixed Batch and Service Jobs in Data Centers. In *HotPower*, 2011.

[3] M. Arlitt et al. Towards the Design and Operation of Net-Zero Energy Data Centers. In *ITherm*, 2012.

[4] Y. Chen et al. The Case for Evaluating MapReduce Performance Using Workload Suites. In *MASCOTS*, 2011.

[5] Y. Chen et al. Statistical Workload Injector for MapReduce, 2012.

[6] Data Center Knowledge. Apple Plans 20MW of Solar Power for iDataCenter, 2012. http://www.datacenterknowledge.com/archives/-2012/02/20/apple-plans-20mw-of-solar-power-for-idatacenter/.

[7] Data Center Knowledge. Data Centers Scale Up Their Solar Power, 2012. http://www.datacenterknowledge.com/archives/2012/05/14/-data-centers-scale-up-their-solarpower/.

[8] EcobusinessLinks. Green Hosting - Sustainable Solar & Wind Energy Web Hosting, 2012. http://www.ecobusinesslinks.com/-green_webhosts/.

[9] EPFL. CloudSuite, 2012. http://parsa.epfl.ch/cloudsuite/cloudsuite.html.

[10] D. Gmach et al. Capacity Planning and Power Management to Exploit Sustainable Energy. In *CNSM*, 2010.

[11] I. Goiri et al. GreenSlot: Scheduling Energy Consumption in Green Datacenters. In *Supercomputing*, 2011.

[12] I. Goiri et al. GreenHadoop: Leveraging Green Energy in Data-Processing Frameworks. In *EuroSys*, 2012.

[13] S. Govindan et al. Leveraging Stored Energy for Handling Power Emergencies in Aggressively Provisioned Datacenters. In *ASPLOS*, 2012.

[14] S. Govindan, A. Sivasubramanian, and B. Urgaonkar. Benefits and Limitations of Tapping into Stored Energy For Datacenters. In *ISCA*, 2011.

[15] Green House Data. An Economically Responsible Data Center, 2012. http://www.greenhousedata.com/.

[16] Gurobi Optimization, Inc. Gurobi Optimizer 5.0, 2012. http://www.gurobi.com.

[17] J. Hamilton. I Love Solar Power But..., 2012. http://perspectives.-mvdirona.com/2012/03/17/ILoveSolarPowerBut.aspx.

[18] P. Hearps and D. McConnell. Renewable Energy Technology Cost Review. Technical report, Melbourne Energy Institute, 2011.

[19] IBM. Portable Modular Data Center, 2012. http://www-935.ibm.com/services/us/igs/flexible-design.html.

[20] International Electrotechnical Commission. Efficient Electrical Transmission and Distribution. Technical report, 2007.

[21] International Energy Agency. Technology Roadmap – Solar Photovoltaic Energy. Technical report, 2010.

[22] V. Kontorinis et al. Managing Distributed UPS Energy for Effective Power Capping in Data Centers. In *ISCA*, 2012.

[23] J. Koomey. Growth in Data Center Electricity Use 2005 to 2010, 2011. Analytic Press.

[24] A. Krioukov et al. Integrating Renewable Energy Using Data Analytics Systems: Challenges and Opportunities. *Bulletin of the IEEE Computer Society Technical Committee*, 2011.

[25] A. Krioukov et al. Design and Evaluation of an Energy Agile Computing Cluster. Technical Report EECS-2012-13, UC Berkeley, 2012.

[26] K. Le et al. Cost- And Energy-Aware Load Distribution Across Data Centers. In *HotPower*, 2009.

[27] J. Leverich and C. Kozyrakis. On the Energy (In)efficiency of Hadoop Clusters. In *HotPower*, 2009.

[28] C. Li, A. Qouneh, and T. Li. iSwitch: Coordinating and Optimizing Renewable Energy Powered Server Clusters. In *ISCA*, 2012.

[29] Z. Liu et al. Renewable and Cooling Aware Workload Management for Sustainable Data Centers. In *SIGMETRICS*, 2012.

[30] M. Love. Land Area and Storage Requirements for Wind and Solar Generation to Meet the US Hourly Electrical Demand. Master's thesis, Department of Mechanical Engineering, University of Victoria, 2003.

[31] J. Mankoff, R. Kravets, and E. Blevis. Some Computer Science Issues in Creating a Sustainable World. *IEEE Computer*, 41(8), 2008.

[32] National Renewable Energy Laboratory. Wind Farm Area Calculator, 2012. http://www.nrel.gov/analysis/power_databook/calc_wind.php.

[33] PVOutput.org. PV Outputs, 2012. http://www.pvoutput.org.

[34] C. Ren et al. Carbon-Aware Energy Capacity Planning for Datacenters. In *MASCOTS*, 2012.

[35] F. D. Sacerdoti et al. Wide Area Cluster Monitoring with Ganglia. In *Cluster*, 2003.

[36] N. Sharma et al. Cloudy Computing: Leveraging Weather Forecasts in Energy Harvesting Sensor Systems. In *SECON*, 2010.

[37] N. Sharma et al. Blink: Managing Server Clusters on Intermittent Power. In *ASPLOS*, 2011.

[38] SolarBuzz. Solar market research and analysis, 2011. http://www.-solarbuzz.com/facts-and-figures.

[39] C. Stewart and K. Shen. Some Joules Are More Precious Than Others: Managing Renewable Energy in the Datacenter. In *HotPower*, 2009.

[40] R. Urgaonkar et al. Optimal Power Cost Management Using Stored Energy in Data Centers. In *SIGMETRICS*, 2011.

[41] US Department of Energy. 2010 Solar Technologies Market Report. Technical report, 2011.

[42] US Department of Energy. 2010 Wind Technologies Market Report. Technical report, 2011.

[43] US Energy Information Administration. Electricity prices, 2012. http://www.eia.gov/.

[44] US Environmental Protection Agency. Report to Congress on Server and Data Center Energy Efficiency, 2007.

[45] D. Wang et al. Energy Storage in Datacenters: What, Where, and How much? In *SIGMETRICS*, 2012.

Power Containers: An OS Facility for Fine-Grained Power and Energy Management on Multicore Servers

Kai Shen* Arrvindh Shriraman† Sandhya Dwarkadas* Xiao Zhang§ Zhuan Chen*

* University of Rochester † Simon Fraser University § Google

{kshen, sandhya, zchen}@cs.rochester.edu ashriram@cs.sfu.ca xiaozhang@google.com

Abstract

Energy efficiency and power capping are critical concerns in server and cloud computing systems. They face growing challenges due to dynamic power variations from new client-directed web applications, as well as complex behaviors due to multicore resource sharing and hardware heterogeneity. This paper presents a new operating system facility called "power containers" that accounts for and controls the power and energy usage of individual fine-grained requests in multicore servers. This facility relies on three key techniques—1) online model that attributes multicore power (including shared maintenance power) to concurrently running tasks, 2) alignment of actual power measurements and model estimates to enable online model recalibration, and 3) on-the-fly application-transparent request tracking in multi-stage servers to isolate the power and energy contributions and customize per-request control. Our mechanisms enable new multicore server management capabilities including fair power capping that only penalizes power-hungry requests, and energy-aware request distribution between heterogeneous servers. Our evaluation uses three multicore processors (Intel Woodcrest, Westmere, and SandyBridge) and a variety of server and cloud computing (Google App Engine) workloads. Our results demonstrate the high accuracy of our request power accounting (no more than 11% errors) and the effectiveness of container-enabled power virus isolation and throttling. Our request distribution case study shows up to 25% energy saving compared to an alternative approach that recognizes machine heterogeneity but not fine-grained workload affinity.

Categories and Subject Descriptors D.4.1 [*Operating Systems*]: Process Management—Multiprocessing/multiprogramming/multitasking; D.4.8 [*Operating Systems*]: Performance—Measurements, Modeling and prediction

General Terms Design, Experimentation, Measurement, Performance, Reliability

Keywords Multicore, power modeling, power virus, hardware counters, server and cloud computing, operating system

1. Introduction

Designers of data centers and server systems place high priority on improving energy efficiency, controlling peak power draw, and monitoring resource usage anomalies. Online applications are continuously evolving with new features and some rely on end users to supply content or even content-generating code. For instance, cloud computing platforms run user applications at third-party hosting centers. Online collaboration software (such as the WeBWorK homework management system [37]) allows users (teachers in WeBWorK) to supply scripting programs to run at servers. The workload diversity and dynamic client-directed processing result in large power fluctuations on modern multicore processors with substantial hardware resource sharing and increasing power proportionality [8]. Our measurements found that the idle power is only about 5% of the total CPU package power on a recent Intel SandyBridge processor (the idle power proportion is 32% when counting the full machine power consumption).

Modern processors also exhibit highly varying power consumption during execution, depending on the scope and level of activity in the CPU cores as well as in uncore components such as the memory interconnect. At the same (full) CPU utilization on our SandyBridge processor, a cache/memory-intensive application consumes 49% more power than a CPU spinning program does. On these machines, extreme power-consuming tasks (or "power viruses") [19] may appear accidentally or be devised maliciously. Isolating per-client power attribution to identify such tasks so as to cap the system power draw in a fair fashion is highly desirable. Further, recognizing the energy usage of individual requests helps inform the full costs of web use, under grid power as well as renewable energy sources [35]. Additionally, the economics of incremental upgrades, along with low-power specialization, lead to widespread heterogeneity in server clusters. Exploiting the diverse workload affinity to heterogeneous platforms is beneficial for realizing high energy efficiency.

This paper presents a new operating system facility, called *power containers*, to account for and control the power and energy usage of individual requests in multicore servers. Previous research (particularly, Resource Containers [6], Magpie [7], and our hardware counter modeling [32, 33]) has recognized the need for profiling and isolating per-request resource usage in a server. However, they do not include power or energy as a resource. Fine-grained power and energy management on multicore servers is challenging due to their complex relationship with resource utilization. Concurrent task executions, varying power consumption among resources, and dynamic hardware component sharing in a multicore processor lead to complex per-task power behaviors. Request executions in a concurrent, multi-stage server contain fine-grained activities with frequent context switches, and direct power measurements on such spatial and temporal granularities are not available on today's systems. Hence, request-level power and energy management requires agile, low-cost control to ensure isolation and achieve efficiency.

The characterization of request power and energy behaviors provides a detailed understanding of the server system power profile, and facilitates fine-grained attribution of energy usage to clients and their individual requests. We develop three key techniques to support our power containers facility:

- We attribute the multicore power consumption to individual tasks running concurrently on a multicore system. We extend previous event-driven power models [9, 10, 25] to capture shared multicore maintenance power and dynamically attribute it to actively running tasks at runtime. For low overhead, the power accounting is performed independently at each CPU core without global coordination.
- Power modeling inaccuracy [26] may result from different characteristics between calibration workloads and production workloads, particularly for unusually high-power applications. Online power measurements can help recalibrate power modeling but measurement results often arrive with some delays. We align power measurements and modeling estimates using signal processing cross-correlation.
- Utilizing an application-transparent, online request context tracking mechanism, we isolate the power consumption contribution of each individual request, and enable client/request-oriented accounting of power and energy usage. Online request context tracking also allows the selective adoption of power and energy control mechanisms for certain requests. Such resource accounting and control is also desirable in cloud computing, especially for those (like the Google App Engine) that do not adopt heavy virtual machine-based isolation.

Our power containers enable the first-class management of multicore server power and energy resources in new ways. In particular, we can pinpoint the sources of power spikes and anomalies, and further condition the request power consumption in a fair fashion—throttling the execution of power viruses (using processor duty-cycle modulation) while allowing normal requests to run at full speed. Furthermore, we improve energy efficiency in a heterogeneous environment through container heterogeneity-aware load distribution. Specifically, request energy profiles on different machines are used to understand each request's cross-machine relative energy affinity and direct its execution accordingly. The rest of this paper will present the design and implementation of our power containers and evaluate its accuracy and effectiveness in several management case studies.

2. Related Work

Power Measurement and Modeling Per-hardware-component power can be measured through elaborate embedded instruments (as in LEAP [27]). However, it is difficult to directly measure per-core power on a multicore chip due to shared use of components such as cache and memory interconnect. Bellosa [9] estimated the processor and memory power using a linear model on hardware event counts. Additional research has supported event-based power phase modeling [10, 25]. On the negative side, McCullough *et al.* [26] identified high power model errors due to multicore complexities and hidden device states. Event-based power modeling has also been included in processor designs like the IBM POWER7 [38] and Intel SandyBridge [30]. Most recently, Huang *et al.* [24] proposed a firmware-level power proxy that estimates per-core power by utilizing specialized activity counters in the IBM POWER7+ chip hardware. Direct measurement or hardware event-based modeling alone is limited by their inability to identify and isolate software-level concurrent resource principals in server and cloud computing environments.

System-Level Energy Accounting By coordinating the external power measurement with interrupt-triggered program sampling, Flinn and Satyanarayanan [16] were able to profile the energy usage of application processes and procedures. Chang *et al.* [12] further enhanced the statistical sampling accuracy using energy-driven sampling intervals. ECOSystem [39] is a unified framework of whole-system energy accounting to support energy management policies. In ECOSystem, the CPU power consumption is assumed to be constant during busy periods. Quanto [18] combined the information of component power states, high-resolution energy metering, and causal tracking of system activities to profile energy usage in embedded network devices. The Cinder operating system [31] employed new control abstractions (isolation, delegation, and subdivision) to account for and manage energy in mobile devices. In comparison to these techniques, our work tackles the challenges of power attribution in two new dimensions—over shared-resource multicore processors and among concurrently running fine-grained requests.

Data Center Power Management In light of the load burstiness at large-scale service sites, Chase *et al.* [13] and Pinheiro *et al.* [29] proposed to consolidate services to a subset of servers at load troughs while the remaining servers can be shut down to conserve energy usage. In terms of data center power provisioning, Fan *et al.* [15] and Govindan *et al.* [20] suggested that the power provisioning should take into account the independence as well as correlation of power fluctuations at individual servers. PowerNap [28] enables fast transitioning between active state and minimum-power nap state, which results in very low server idle power. Research [14, 23] has also recognized the energy effects of load placement in a heterogeneous server cluster. Our power containers are complementary to these techniques. In particular, we enable more fine-grained (request-level) multicore server power tracking and control, a need not addressed by previous techniques.

3. Design and Implementation

We propose a new operating system facility that accounts for and controls the power and energy usage of individual requests in a multicore server. We tackle the challenges of power attribution and control in two new dimensions—1) over concurrent executions on a shared-resource multicore and 2) among fine-grained requests in a multi-stage server application. To tackle the first challenge, we model per-task power consumption from core-level activities and shared multicore chip power (Section 3.1). In addition, we align online power measurements and modeling estimates to recalibrate the power model for better accuracy (Section 3.2). To tackle the second challenge, we build operating system mechanisms (Section 3.3) to track multi-stage request executions on-the-fly, account for request power and energy usage, and apply request-grained power control. We also present container-enabled new multicore server power and energy analysis and management cases (Section 3.4).

3.1 Power Attribution to Concurrent Tasks

While previous work has extensively explored system power modeling [9, 10, 25, 26, 38] and devised on-chip power estimation registers [30], their focus is largely on coarse-grained whole system or full processor power. Since multiple tasks may run concurrently in a multicore system and each task may belong to a distinct user request, there is a clear need for separate accounting. We present new techniques to attribute the power consumption to individual tasks running concurrently on a multicore system. This section focuses on the processor and memory power attribution while the I/O resource accounting will be briefly discussed in Section 3.3.

Our first approach follows Bellosa [9]'s model in that the processor/memory power consumption is linearly correlated with the frequency of relevant hardware events. Example metrics of interests include the core utilization or the ratio of non-halt core cycles over elapsed cycles ($\mathcal{M}_{\text{core}}$), retired instructions per CPU cycle ($\mathcal{M}_{\text{ins}}$), floating point operations per cycle ($\mathcal{M}_{\text{float}}$), last-level cache requests per cycle ($\mathcal{M}_{\text{cache}}$), and memory transactions per cycle ($\mathcal{M}_{\text{mem}}$). The constant power term ($\mathcal{C}_{\text{idle}}$) in the linear relationship represents the idle power consumed when zero values for all metrics are observed. The remaining *active* (full minus idle) power can be modeled as:

$$\begin{aligned}\mathcal{P}_{\text{active}} = \mathcal{C}_{\text{core}} \cdot \mathcal{M}_{\text{core}} + \mathcal{C}_{\text{ins}} \cdot \mathcal{M}_{\text{ins}} + \mathcal{C}_{\text{float}} \cdot \mathcal{M}_{\text{float}} \\ + \mathcal{C}_{\text{cache}} \cdot \mathcal{M}_{\text{cache}} + \mathcal{C}_{\text{mem}} \cdot \mathcal{M}_{\text{mem}}\end{aligned} \quad (1)$$

where $\mathcal{C}$'s are coefficient parameters for the linear model that can be calibrated offline (once for each target machine configuration). Equation 1 models the full system active power if $\mathcal{M}$'s capture the summed event metrics over all cores. We can also use it to account for the active power of an individual task if $\mathcal{M}$'s capture the metrics on the CPU core where the target task is currently running.

We implement such event-based power accounting in the operating system. Each core performs accounting for its local task independently without cross-core synchronization or coordination. We acquire per-core system metrics ($\mathcal{M}$'s) online by reading processor hardware counters and computing relevant event frequencies. The continuous maintenance of the power model and hardware counter statistics requires periodic counter sampling. We configure the core-local Programmable Interrupt Controller for threshold-based event counter overflow interrupts. Specifically, we set the interrupt intervals to a desired number of non-halt core cycles. *Non-Halt* cycle-based triggers have the benefit of suppressing the interrupts when the CPU core has no work to do (so it can continuously stay in the low-power idle state).

The above approach assumes that the power accounting for a task only depends on core-level physical events. On a multicore chip with intricately shared hardware resources, however, chip-wide environmental factors also affect per-core power accounting. In particular, the maintenance of shared multicore resources (including clocking circuitry, voltage regulators, and other uncore units [21]) consumes some active power as long as one core is running, which does not change proportionally with core-level event rates. Figure 1 illustrates this symptom using a simple CPU spinning microbenchmark. This workload scales perfectly on a multicore so all event metrics scale proportionally with the CPU core utilization. The Equation 1 model would suggest a linear relationship between the core utilization and power. However, measurements on the quad-core SandyBridge machine show that the power increment from idle to one utilized core is substantially larger than further power increments, which suggests an active power component that does not scale with core-level physical events. The same experiment on a dual-socket machine (with two dual-core Woodcrest processors) shows that the power increments from idle to two utilized cores are higher than further increments. This indicates that both sockets become active when two cores are utilized, which matches the Linux operating system (used in our experiments)'s multicore scheduling policy that maximizes performance.

We evenly attribute the chip maintenance power at each time instant to the currently running tasks. The system utilization level fluctuates over time in production server environments [8]. Proper accounting and attribution of shared chip maintenance power is challenging because one task's share may change depending on activities (or the lack thereof) on other cores. We use a new metric $\mathcal{M}_{\text{chipshare}}$ ($0.0 \leq \mathcal{M}_{\text{chipshare}} \leq 1.0$) to denote the proportion of a given task's share of on-chip maintenance power. If a core is busy while all siblings are idle, the full chip power should be attributed to

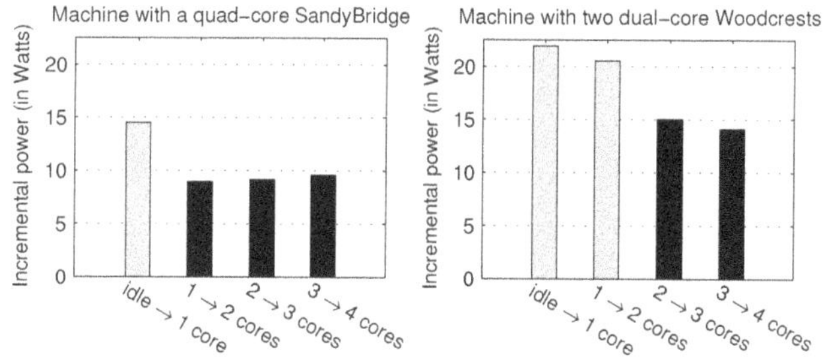

Figure 1. Incremental (per-core) power consumption increases on two machines (one with a quad-core SandyBridge processor and the other with two dual-core Woodcrest processors).

the task on the busy core ($\mathcal{M}_{\text{chipshare}}=1.0$). If multiple ($k$) cores are busy, then each running task on one of the busy cores has $\mathcal{M}_{\text{chipshare}}=\frac{1.0}{k}$. Our new active power model adds the shared chip maintenance power to the original model:

$$\begin{aligned}\mathcal{P}_{\text{active}} = \mathcal{C}_{\text{core}} \cdot \mathcal{M}_{\text{core}} + \mathcal{C}_{\text{ins}} \cdot \mathcal{M}_{\text{ins}} + \mathcal{C}_{\text{float}} \cdot \mathcal{M}_{\text{float}} \\ + \mathcal{C}_{\text{cache}} \cdot \mathcal{M}_{\text{cache}} + \mathcal{C}_{\text{mem}} \cdot \mathcal{M}_{\text{mem}} \\ + \mathcal{C}_{\text{chipshare}} \cdot \mathcal{M}_{\text{chipshare}}\end{aligned} \quad (2)$$

Unlike the core-level event metrics that can be simply acquired through hardware counters on the CPU core, the chip power share $\mathcal{M}_{\text{chipshare}}$ does not correspond to any processor hardware counter. Further, precise sharing information in a dynamic system depends on time-synchronized global activities across multiple cores. In our implementation, each core independently makes an approximate estimation in order to avoid expensive global coordination or cross-core interrupts. We discretize the computation of $\mathcal{M}_{\text{chipshare}}$ over time intervals that match the hardware counter sampling periods for collecting core-level events. We approximate the number of busy sibling cores using the sum of the latest core utilization ratios at all siblings on the multicore chip. Formally, on an n-core processor, the task currently running on CPU core c has:

$$\mathcal{M}_{\text{chipshare}}(c) = \mathcal{M}_{\text{core}}(c) \cdot \frac{1}{1 + \sum_{1 \leq i \leq n, i \neq c} \mathcal{M}_{\text{core}}(i)}, \quad (3)$$

where $\mathcal{M}_{\text{core}}(x)$ indicates the core utilization ratio on CPU core x.

We check a sibling's core utilization by reading its most recent hardware counter sample in memory. We do so without any cross-core synchronization for efficiency. Note that each core performs independent sampling at non-halt cycle-triggered interrupts, which stop when the core is idle. Therefore an idle sibling may have stale sample statistics. To address this problem, we check whether the OS is currently scheduling the idle task on a sibling core and consider its current activity rate as zero if so.

Our discussion so far applies to the power modeling of a single multicore chip. On a multi-socket machine with more than one multicore chips, each chip's power will be modeled using our approach described above and the full power will include the power from all multicore chips on the machine.

3.2 Measurement Alignment for Recalibration

Despite the wide uses of event-based power models [9, 10, 25, 38], we found that large errors may arise in practice. Recent research [26] has also raised questions on the accuracy of event-based power models. Beyond superficial problems like insufficient coverage of modeled events, significant modeling inaccuracy also results from differing characteristics between calibration workloads and production workloads. This is particularly the case for unusually high power-consuming production workloads that demand careful

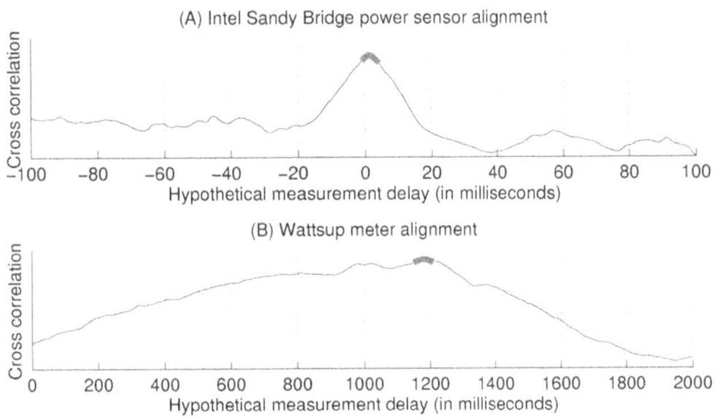

Figure 2. Measurement/model alignment cross-correlation for the Intel SandyBridge on-chip power meter (A) and a Wattsup power meter (B). High correlation peaks are specially marked.

attention in server system power management. To address the modeling inaccuracy, we utilize online power measurements to adjust and recalibrate the offline-constructed power models.

While whole-system power can be measured through off-the-shelf meters, measurement results may arrive with some lag time due to the meter reporting delay and data I/O latency (*e.g.*, through a USB interface). On the other hand, processor event counter-based power models can be maintained at the much shorter latency of reading CPU registers and computing simple statistics. In order to use the power measurements to identify modeling errors and recalibrate the model, the measurement results and modeling estimates need to be properly aligned.

While a poorly calibrated power model may not accurately predict the power consumption, it may still identify power transitions and phases quite well. In other words, aligned power measurements should follow the fluctuation patterns of real-time power model estimates. We therefore employ a signal processing approach to align measurement samples and model estimates. Specifically, we compute the cross-correlation metric between measurement and model power samples at different hypothetical measurement delays. A higher cross-correlation would indicate better matching of the measurement/model fluctuation patterns.

Formally, let $\mathcal{P}_{\text{measure}}(1)$, $\mathcal{P}_{\text{measure}}(2)$, $\cdots$ be the sequence of recent power measurement samples ($\mathcal{P}_{\text{measure}}(1)$ is the most recent). Let $\mathcal{P}_{\text{model}}(1)$, $\mathcal{P}_{\text{model}}(2)$, $\cdots$ be the sequence of recent modeling samples at the same sampling frequency. Then the cross-correlation at a hypothetical measurement delay t is:

$$\text{Cross-corr.}(t) = \sum_{i=1}^{\text{number of matching samples}} \mathcal{P}_{\text{measure}}(i) \cdot \mathcal{P}_{\text{model}}(i+t). \quad (4)$$

Figure 2 shows a case example of alignment cross-correlation over hypothetical measurement delays. The highest point of the correlation curve (specially marked in the figure) indicates the likely measurement delay. Our results show about 1 msec delay for the Intel SandyBridge on-chip power meter and about 1.2 second (1200 msecs) delay for a Wattsup power meter. Longer delay for the Wattsup meter is due to its coarse-grained measurements and data propagation latency through an external USB connection. Figure 3 shows the aligned measurement/model power samples for the Intel SandyBridge on-chip power meter. Note that the measured power (whether using the SandyBridge's power meter or using off-chip instruments) is for the whole system, necessitating the per-core/per-request model we have designed for fine-grained online control.

Aligned power measurements can identify modeling errors for the currently running workload and help recalibrate our multicore

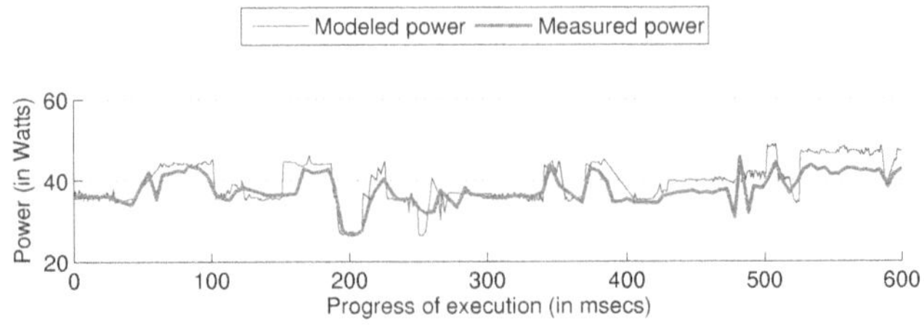

Figure 3. Aligned measurement/model power traces for the Intel SandyBridge on-chip power meter.

power model in Equation 2. The recalibration intuitively means adding new online samples of aligned system metrics and corresponding power measures to the original offline model parameter calibration. We perform online least-square-fit linear regression to recalibrate the model parameters when new online samples are available. Our parameter recalibration includes both offline workload samples and current online measurements, weighed equally in the square error minimization target. The short measurement delay (about 1 msec) for the SandyBridge on-chip power meter makes it suitable for real-time model adjustment and power control.

3.3 Request Power Accounting

We construct operating system mechanisms to support request-level power containers in a server system. Our first goal is to account for request power consumption and cumulative energy usage. Our second goal is to enable request-specific power and energy control (*e.g.*, speed throttling) according to request-level policies on resource usage and quality-of-service. The online control requires each request's power container to be maintained *on-the-fly*—while the request executes.

Our OS support tracks request execution contexts so that power-relevant metrics can be properly attributed and control mechanisms can be properly applied. A request context coincides with a process (or thread) context in some cases. However, a request execution may flow through multiple processes in a multi-stage server. For instance, a PHP web processor propagates the request context into a database thread through a socket message. Such a socket connection can be *persistent* in a high-throughput server when each server process can repeatedly serve multiple requests and one socket connection is reused by multiple request propagations over time. The past approach of Resource Containers [6] requires applications to explicitly pass request context bindings across server stages. Google's Dapper tracing infrastructure [34] assumes that applications use a unified RPC framework that can be easily instrumented. Magpie [7] recognizes request context propagations in a server system but it does so out-of-band, which is sufficient for trace analysis but not for applying per-request power control online.

The X-Trace framework [17] is closest to our needs of system-level in-band request context tracking. However, X-Trace was designed for general network systems tracing and we specifically target high-throughput server systems. We highlight two particular differences. First, our request tracking is implemented entirely in the operating system requiring no application change. While the X-Trace propagation primitives provide flexible application control, our transparent mechanism can easily support a large variety of complex (even closed-source) server applications. We achieve application transparency by recognizing key request propagation channels in server systems. Fundamentally, the operating system may recognize request context propagation events as those that indicate causal dependences through data and control flows, specifically, socket communications, IPCs, and process forking. OS-only management, however, cannot track user-level request stage transfers in an event-driven server or a server that employs user-level threads. This is an important limitation, but our mechanism is applicable to a large number of real-world server applications that do not employ an event-driven model (for easier programming with threads and processes) or user-level threads (to avoid performance anomalies due to complex user/kernel thread mapping and lack of full visibility by the OS scheduler and I/O management). Past research [11] suggests that some user-level request stage transfers may be OS-observable by trapping accesses to critical synchronization data structures. We leave its implementation for possible future work. We include a variety of applications supported by our framework in our evaluation in Section 4.2.

We also make efforts to support request tracking over a persistent socket connection in high-throughput servers. We tag each socket message with the sender's request context identifier. We store the identifier in a new TCP option field for protocol compatibility (it will be safely ignored if the message reaches a different machine that does not support our request container mechanism). If the message arrives at the destination socket but the receiver has not made the `read()` call, the message has to be buffered. In a naive implementation, the destination socket simply inherits the request context tag of the buffered message and the receiver will acquire the socket's request context when it calls `read()`. This, however, is unsafe in a persistent connection when the context tag for a new request may arrive before the previously arrived message is read by a receiver (in which case the receiver incorrectly inherits the new request context). Therefore, multiple data segments in a socket buffer must be individually tagged with the corresponding request context. A receiver process will inherit the proper context according to the data it reads.

Our implementation builds on our past work of server system hardware counter modeling [32, 33], with new mechanisms for power and energy accounting. During the course of a request execution, our system samples cumulative processor hardware event counters including elapsed non-halt CPU cycles, retired instructions, floating point operations, last-level cache reference counts, and memory transactions. It samples at multiple moments and calculates the counter metric for each period between consecutive sampling. To maintain per-request event metrics, we sample the counter values at the request context switch time to properly attribute the before-switch and after-switch event counts to the respective requests. A request context switch on a CPU occurs in two scenarios—1) when two processes bound to different request contexts switch on the CPU; 2) when the running process receives a new context binding (*e.g.*, by an arriving socket message). Figure 4 illustrates a captured request execution and power and energy attribution in a realistic multi-stage server application containing Apache PHP processing, MySQL database, and various external file manipulation processes.

In addition to context switch sampling, we sample at periodic interrupts (triggered by a desired number of non-halt core cycles) to capture fine-grained behavior variations that affect power. With per-request event sampling, our power model in Equation 2 specifies the contribution from collected metrics to the request power. Beyond the processor/memory power, our full system power accounting also considers power-consuming peripheral devices for disk and network I/O. The OS can identify requests responsible for I/O operations by tracking the requests that consume the data received at I/O interrupts. With the estimation of request power at each sampling period, the cumulative energy usage can be simply calculated as the integral of power consumption over time.

3.4 Container-Enabled Management

By identifying and isolating the power and energy contribution of individual requests in the multicore server, we enable new first-class management of server power and energy resources for efficiency and fairness. We present two particular management cases here.

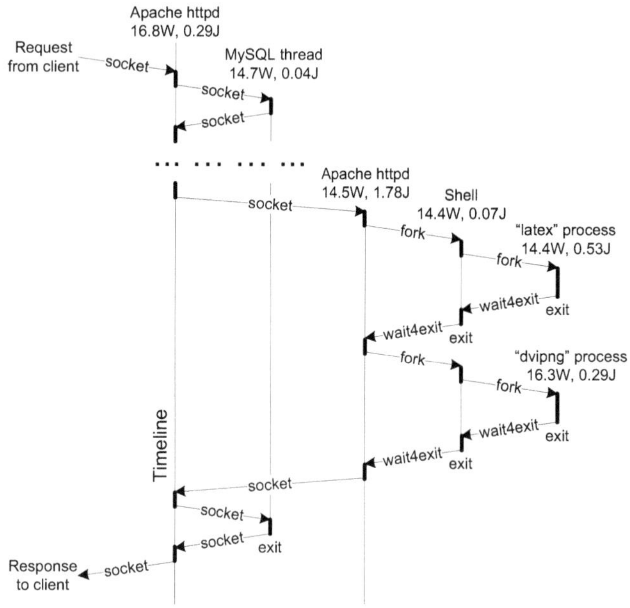

Figure 4. A captured request execution that involves Apache PHP processing, MySQL database, and various external operations on content and image rendering. We mark the attributed power (in Watts) and energy (in Joules) at each request stage. This request is from the WeBWorK online homework system [37]. Identified data and control flows between server components are marked with arrows. Darkened portions of a component timeline indicate active executions (while the rest represent blocking waits).

Fair Request Power Conditioning The infrastructure cost to provision for the system peak power usage is substantial in data centers [15, 22]. While research has looked into cluster-wide load management to control system power [15, 20], a complementary effort would be to condition each server's power consumption to a target level. The system power consumption can be controlled by throttling CPU execution. Specifically, on Intel processors, the OS can specify a portion (a multiplier of 1/8 or 1/16) of regular CPU cycles as duty cycles. During each non-duty-cycle period (on the order of microseconds [1]), the processor is effectively halted and no memory operations are issued. This would lead to fewer activities (including memory transactions) and consequently lower power consumption, at the cost of slower application execution. The duty-cycle modulation can be independently adjusted on a per-core basis. It also exhibits a simple (approximately linear) relationship between the duty-cycle level and active power consumption, which eases the control policy decision.

CPU duty-cycle modulation can control surging power consumption. However, indiscriminate full-machine throttling would lead to slowdowns of all running requests regardless of their power use. In particular, the occurrence of a power virus could force speed reductions on all concurrently running normal requests. Our power container provides two mechanisms to enable power conditioning in a fair fashion—1) request power accounting can detect sources of power spikes; 2) container-specific power control can precisely throttle execution of power-hungry requests. In practice, we maintain a power consumption target for each request. Those that exceed the specified target will be subject to request-specific CPU duty-cycle modulation while other requests will run at full speed. In our implementation, we apply a particular CPU duty-cycle modulation level to a given request execution according to its power consumption. We also track the request power consumption variations after each periodic counter sampling (typically once per millisecond), and then change the CPU duty-cycle level if desirable. When the CPU core switches to run another request, the core duty-cycle level will be adjusted according to the policy setting and power consumption of the new request.

Heterogeneity-Aware Request Distribution Past work has tackled the problem of energy management in a server cluster, primarily through server consolidation [13, 15, 20, 29] to shut down unneeded machines at load troughs. A production server cluster may contain different models of machines because it is not economical to upgrade all servers at once in a data center. Another possible reason is that each of the machine models has unique characteristics desired in certain workload scenario. In a heterogenous server cluster, the load placement and distribution on available machines (probably after consolidation) may affect the system energy efficiency. Previous research [14, 23] has recognized the importance of energy efficiency optimization in a heterogeneous system. However, heterogeneity-aware request distribution across multicore servers is further made difficult by the need to identify workload cross-machine energy usage tradeoffs during concurrent multicore executions. Our power containers directly address this challenge by capturing fine-grained request energy usage profiles, which can later enable the preferential placement of each request on a machine where its relative energy efficiency is high.

A request container can be maintained over multiple machines in a server cluster using socket message-based request context propagation described in Section 3.3. When a socket message crosses the machine boundary, we tag it with local request statistics including the cumulative runtime, cumulative energy usage, and most recent power usage. Additional information about request execution control may also be included. By tagging request messages, a dispatcher machine can pass container identifier and control policy settings to the server machines. By tagging response messages, server machines can pass cumulative power and energy usage information to the dispatcher machine for comprehensive resource accounting.

3.5 Overhead Assessment

We implemented a prototype power container facility including per-request hardware counter sampling, power modeling, and statistics maintenance in Linux 2.6.30. Online container maintenance introduces overhead in the system. A container maintenance operation typically includes reading the hardware counter values, computing modeled power values, and updating request statistics. We measure its overhead on a machine with a quad-core SandyBridge processor. Results show that one container maintenance operation takes about 0.95 μsec. If the maintenance (hardware counter sampling) occurs at the frequency of once every millisecond (sufficiently fine-grained for many accounting and control purposes), the overhead is only around 0.1%.

Besides the overhead, the hardware counter sampling and statistics maintenance also produces additional activities (and energy usage) that do not belong to the inherent application behaviors. This behavior, called the *observer effect*, introduces perturbation in the generated power and energy profiles. We measure the maintenance-induced event metrics and find that an average container maintenance operation uses 2948 cycles, 1656 instructions, 16 floating point operations, 3 last-level cache references, and no measurable memory transactions. Assuming all four cores are busy (1/4 chip share), the average energy usage for a container maintenance is about 10 micro-Joules according to our active power model. To mitigate the observer effect in the collected statistics, we subtract the maintenance-induced additional event counts from the measured event counts of each sampling period.

The measurement alignment and model recalibration (Section 3.2) also introduce online overhead. The measurement alignment does not need to occur frequently because the measurement lag time on a given system is unlikely to change dynamically. Our least-square fit model recalibration requires linear algebra computation that consumes about 16 μsecs per calibration. Its online overhead is negligible if it is performed at a rate of no more than once every 10 msecs.

For container power control, configuring the CPU duty-cycle level requires reading and then writing a control register. The read/write operations take about 265 and 350 cycles respectively, or less than 0.2 μsec on a 3.0 GHz machine.

Note that the reported overhead above is incurred on a per-CPU-core (hardware counter sampling, container maintenance, and duty-cycle adjustment) or whole-system basis (model recalibration), rather than for each request in the system. In particular, the hardware counter sampling only occurs for the request that is running on the CPU core at the moment of sampling. Active requests that are not currently running only consume space (but not CPU runtime) costs. This is important for the scalability of our system.

We also report the memory space cost of our system. In our implementation, the state of an active power container is encapsulated in a 784-byte data structure that includes cumulative event counters and statistics, locks, flags, and a reference counter. The data structure is released when all tasks linked to the container exit (when the reference counter is zero) so it does not leak in a long-running server. The space cost is modest and it should not affect the server scalability even if thousands of active power containers exist in the server at the same time.

4. Experimental Evaluation

Our evaluation uses three different machines. The first is a multichip/multicore machine with two dual-core (four cores total) Intel Xeon 5160 3.0 GHz "*Woodcrest*" processors. Two cores on each processor chip share a single 4 MB L2 cache. The second machine contains two six-core (12 cores total) Intel Xeon L5640 ("L" for low-power) 2.26 GHz "*Westmere*" processors. The six cores on each processor chip share a 12 MB L3 cache. The third machine contains a quad-core Intel Xeon E31220 3.10 GHz "*SandyBridge*" processor. The four cores share an 8 MB L3 cache. The three processors were publicly released in 2006, 2010, and 2011 respectively. Both Westmere and SandyBridge processors utilize the recent 32 nm technology. We configure hardware event counting registers on each processor to assemble the input metrics for our power model in Equation 2.

We employ two power measurement instruments. First, each machine uses a Wattsup meter that reports the whole machine power once a second. The Wattsup measurements are fed back to the target machine through the USB interface. In addition, we use the on-chip power meter available on the SandyBridge machine, which measures power for the processor socket package including all cores, the uncore components (e.g., Last-Level-Caches), the memory controller, and quickpath interconnects. The SandyBridge meter tracks many (order of 100) microarchitecture events and applies active energy costs to each event [30]. Specifically, it reports accumulated energy once per millisecond and the power is then calculated as the rate of energy changes. Our evaluations sample the SandyBridge power once every 10 milliseconds. Note that the SandyBridge on-chip meter does not report per-core power and it cannot identify and isolate concurrent resource principals in a server environment.

The full power includes a constant idle power consumed when the server exhibits no activity. On the SandyBridge machine, the idle power (26.1 Watts) is about 32% of the full machine power at an observed high load scenario. The idle power ratio goes down to 5% if we only consider the CPU package power (including uncore components, the memory controller, and quickpath interconnects), indicating excellent energy proportionality [8] for the processor sub-system. We note that the idle power is of little interest to modeling or resource provisioning since it is a constant. Including it in the power metric would make modeling errors look artificially small. Therefore we present most evaluation results on the active (full minus idle) power. When using the SandyBridge on-chip power meter, we report the full power reading since its idle component is very small.

The rest of this section will first present the power model calibration results. We will then evaluate the accuracy of our request power and energy accounting using several realistic applications. We will also present two power container-enabled server management case studies—fair request power conditioning and heterogeneity-aware request distribution.

4.1 Power Model Calibration

Our multicore server model in Section 3.1 requires offline calibration to acquire the coefficient parameters. This calibration is performed once for a target machine configuration but is subject to measurement-based online recalibration as described in Section 3.2. We design a set of microbenchmarks that stress different parts of the system (including raw CPU spin, CPU spin with high instruction rate, CPU spin with high floating point operations, high last-level cache access, high memory access, high disk I/O, high network I/O, and a benchmark with a mixture of different workload patterns). For each microbenchmark, we use several different load levels (100%, 75%, 50%, and 25% of the peak load) to produce calibration samples. We use the least-square-fit linear regression to calibrate the coefficients for Equation 2.

As an example, we list the coefficient parameters of the calibrated offline model for the SandyBridge machine. While a model coefficient $\mathcal{C}$ is not intuitively meaningful, $\mathcal{C}\cdot\mathcal{M}^{\max}$ (where $\mathcal{M}^{\max}$ is the maximum observed value for the metric for the whole machine including all cores) represents the maximum active power impact of the metric—

$$
\begin{aligned}
\mathcal{C}_{\text{idle}} &= 26.1 \text{ Watts;}\\
\mathcal{C}_{\text{core}}\cdot\mathcal{M}^{\max}_{\text{core}} &= 33.1 \text{ Watts;}\\
\mathcal{C}_{\text{ins}}\cdot\mathcal{M}^{\max}_{\text{ins}} &= 12.4 \text{ Watts;}\\
\mathcal{C}_{\text{cache}}\cdot\mathcal{M}^{\max}_{\text{cache}} &= 13.9 \text{ Watts;}\\
\mathcal{C}_{\text{mem}}\cdot\mathcal{M}^{\max}_{\text{mem}} &= 8.2 \text{ Watts;}\\
\mathcal{C}_{\text{chipshare}}\cdot\mathcal{M}^{\max}_{\text{chipshare}} &= 5.6 \text{ Watts;}\\
\mathcal{C}_{\text{disk}}\cdot\mathcal{M}^{\max}_{\text{disk}} &= 1.7 \text{ Watts;}\\
\mathcal{C}_{\text{net}}\cdot\mathcal{M}^{\max}_{\text{net}} &= 5.8 \text{ Watts.}
\end{aligned}
$$

4.2 Request Model Evaluation

Our evaluation uses the following server and cloud computing workloads:

- *RSA-crypto* is a synthetic security processing workload. Each request runs multiple RSA encryption/decryption procedures from OpenSSL 0.9.8g. It contains three types of requests: each uses one of the three encryption keys provided as examples in OpenSSL.
- *Solr* [2] is a popular, open-source search platform from the Apache project. It uses the Lucene Java search library as the core for full-text indexing and searching. The search server runs within a Servlet container such as Tomcat. Our deployment uses Solr 3.6.1 and Tomcat 6.0.35 software. We construct a search workload from the Wikipedia data dumps [5]. Our workload has the raw data size of 5.6 GB and indexed data size of 1.7 GB that the Solr search server runs on. The indexed data fits into the memory of our search server. Client queries in our workload are generated by randomly selecting and sequencing article titles in the Wikipedia data dump.
- *WeBWorK* [37] is a web-based teaching application hosted at the Mathematical Association of America and used by over 240 colleges and universities. WeBWorK lets teachers post science problems for students to solve online. It is unique in its *user (teacher)-created content*—considered by some a distinctive "Web 2.0" feature [36]. Our installation runs Apache 2.2.8 web server, a variety of Perl PHP modules, and MySQL 5.5.13 database. Tests are driven by around 3,000 teacher-created problem sets (ranging from pre-calculus to differential equations) and user requests logged at the real site.
- *Stress*, or Stressful Application Test [3], is a benchmark that runs the Adler-32 checksum algorithm over a large segment of memory with added floating point operations. It stresses the CPU core units, floating point unit, and cache/memory accesses simultaneously. It generates higher-than-normal power consumption, particularly on our Westmere processor-based machine. We adapted it to a server-style workload with requests each running for about 100 msecs.
- *GAE-Vosao*. Google App Engine (GAE) provides a Platform-as-a-Service cloud computing infrastructure that enables users to build, maintain, and scale web applications. We install the GAE Java software development kit including a Java web server that simulates the GAE runtime environment with a local datastore. On our local GAE setup, we deploy the Vosao content management application [4], which supports collaborative building of dynamic web sites. Our tests use a workload that models the collaborative web content editing using the published revision history of the "Harry Potter" article at Wikipedia. We adopt a 9:1 read/write ratio to mimic the typical higher rate of reads in a mixed read/write scenario.
- *GAE-Hybrid* contains a mixture of GAE-Vosao requests and some artificial GAE-based power viruses. Our power virus design is not optimized as in previous work [19]. Instead, our goal is to show the impact of a very simple power virus that one can easily create. Specifically, our power virus (about 200 lines of Java code) repeatedly writes one of every four bytes over a 16-MByte block. Our measurements find that this workload pattern keeps the cache/memory and instruction pipelining units simultaneously busy. We also use statically allocated data blocks to minimize the impact of Java garbage collection. In our hybrid workload composition, approximately half the load is generated by Vosao requests and power viruses respectively.

Most of our workloads contain only open-source software. One exception is the GAE Java web server, which is released in the form of Java byte code by Google.

Figure 5 shows the measured active power consumption for all the application workloads on the three machines. Our experiments employ a test client that can send concurrent requests to the server at a desired load level. We show results at two load levels—peak load when the target server is fully utilized, and half load when the server utilization is about 50%.

WeBWorK uses multi-stage server architectures including the database. The web server in WeBWorK also pools many request executions on each worker process. Both the Solr search engine and Google App Engine (GAE) workloads run on the Java virtual machine and use Servlets. Our power container facility properly tracks individual request activities and attributes request power consumption during concurrent multicore execution. Figure 6 shows the dis-

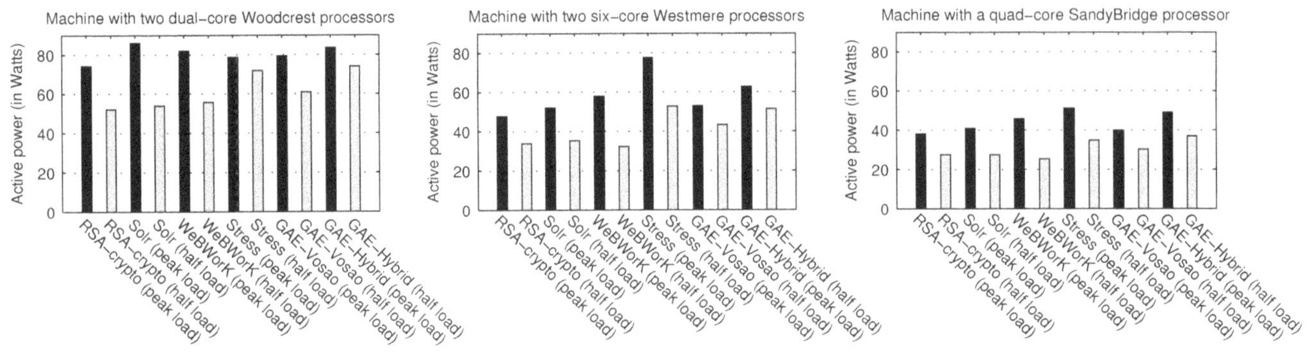

Figure 5. Measured active power of application workloads on three machines and two load levels.

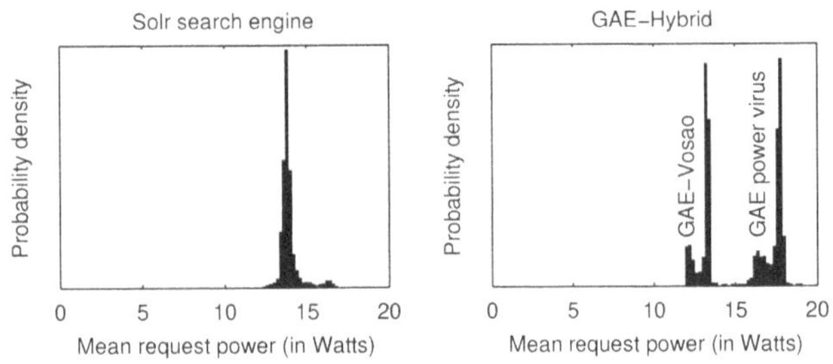

Figure 6. Mean request power distributions (in histograms) for the Solr search engine and GAE-Hybrid workloads on the SandyBridge machine. The mean power for a request is its average power consumption over the course of the request execution. For the GAE-Hybrid workload, we label the major distribution masses for Vosao and power virus requests respectively. Results were collected when each workload runs at half server load. We intentionally do not show the quantitative Y values (histogram heights) in the figures because these values have no inherent meaning and they simply depend on (inversely proportional to) the width of each bin in the distribution histogram.

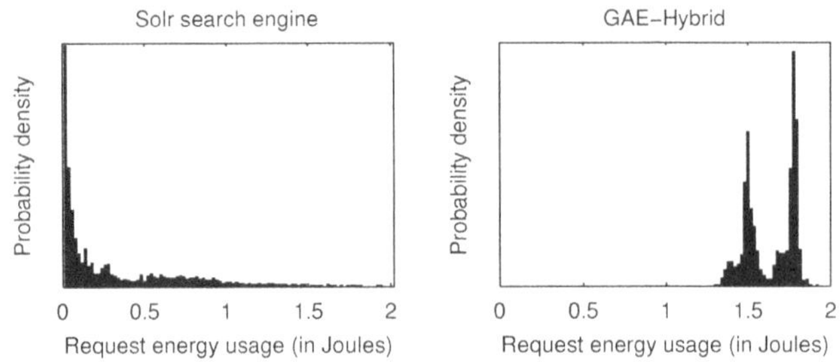

Figure 7. Request energy usage distributions (in histograms) for the Solr search engine and GAE-Hybrid on the SandyBridge machine.

tributions of mean request power for Solr and GAE-Hybrid (mixture of GAE-Vosao and power viruses) workloads on the SandyBridge machine. We observe varying request power consumption for the GAE workload. Specifically, power viruses consume substantially higher power than Vosao requests due to their intense CPU/memory activities. Figure 7 further shows the request energy usage distributions. The varying request energy usage is due both to request power variation (primarily for GAE-Hybrid) and to their execution time difference (primarily for Solr).

Validation By Summing Request Energy Usage A direct validation of our power container modeling is infeasible without a way to measure power attribution to concurrently running tasks on a hardware resource-sharing multicore. Even if such a measurement mechanism exists, it must coordinate with fine-grained request activities (particularly, frequent context switches) to directly measure the power profile for individual requests. Given such difficulties, we adopt an indirect validation approach. Our power containers can profile the energy usage of all request executions that fall into a given time duration. The sum of all request energy usage, divided by the time duration, will produce an estimate of the average system power consumption. We validate the accuracy of our request power and energy profiles by comparing this estimate against measured system power.

During this experiment, we identified some substantial background processing by the Google App Engine (GAE) that presents no traceable connections to application request executions. We suspect that these background processes are related to the GAE security management, although we are unable to verify without access to the GAE source code. We account for the resource usage of these background processes in a special power container and include it in our energy usage sum.

To understand the benefits of our proposed techniques, we compare the validation accuracy over three different approaches:

- Approach #1 (described in Section 3.1) employs a linear power model on core-level event metrics. It does not consider the shared chip maintenance power.
- Approach #2 (also presented in Section 3.1) additionally accounts for the multicore chip maintenance power and attributes it to concurrent requests.
- Approach #3 (presented in Section 3.2) further employs measurement-aligned online model recalibration to mitigate the power model errors.

Validation results in Figure 8 show that our techniques are effective in producing accurate request power and energy profiles. Across all workloads, the approach of only modeling core-level events exhibits 29%, 41%, and 20% worst-case validation errors for the three machines respectively. Attributing shared multicore power reduces the worst-case validation errors to 18%, 35%, and 13% for the three machines. The measurement-aligned online model recalibration further reduces the worst-case errors to 8%, 9%, and 6% on the three machines. The measurement-aligned recalibration is particularly effective in improving the request profiling accuracy of high-power workloads like Stress.

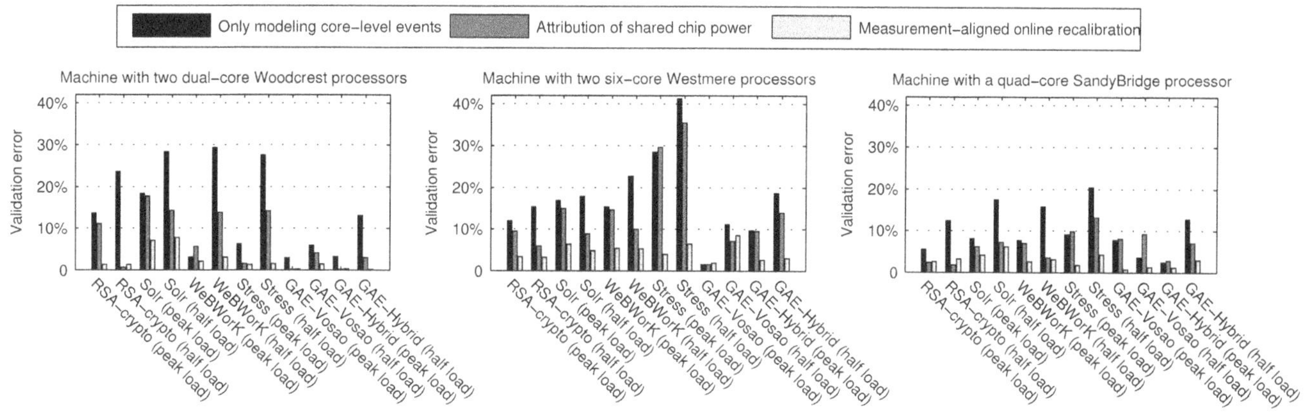

Figure 8. The accuracy of different approaches to estimate system active power from aggregate profiled request energy usage. The error is defined as $\frac{|\text{aggregate profiled request power} - \text{measured system active power}|}{\text{measured system active power}}$.

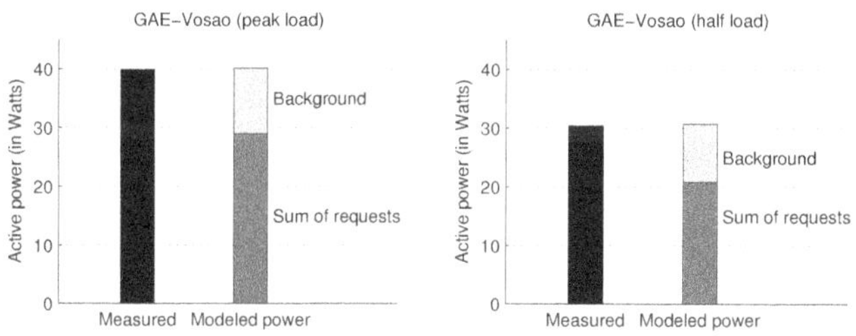

Figure 9. Resource usage of background processes in Google App Engine systems (GAE-Vosao peak load and half load) on the machine with a quad-core SandyBridge processor.

Our evaluation also allows us to understand the significance of GAE background processing on the total system resource usage. Figure 9 illustrates the modeled active power due to sum of requests and due to background processes respectively for GAE-Vosao on our SandyBridge machine. Our power model shows that almost one third of the total system active power can be attributed to background processing in a GAE system.

Prediction At New Request Composition The above validation shows that nearly all measured energy usage is accounted for and attributed. However, it does not validate whether the request power and energy attribution is properly done. We address this issue by validating power prediction at new request compositions. Specifically, we can learn the energy profiles of different types of requests from a running system. By assembling such per-request energy profiles, we can predict the system power in new, hypothetical workload conditions (different composition/ratios of request types, as well as different request rates). A successful validation of this prediction would indicate that the profiled per-request energy usage was accurate. Here we assume that the energy usage for each type of request does not change from the profiled system to new workload conditions. Note that this assumption does not hold for workloads (like Stress) that exhibit dynamic behaviors at different resource contention levels on the multicore.

For comparison, we consider two alternative approaches to predicting system active power at hypothetical request compositions/rates. The *request-rate-proportional* approach simply assumes that all requests have a uniform effect on the total system energy usage so the active power consumption is exactly proportional to the request rate. The other approach, *CPU-utilization-proportional*, assumes that the active power consumption is proportional to the CPU utilization level. Note that this approach requires profiling the CPU usage of individual requests through careful request context tracking [6, 7].

We perform evaluation on new RSA-crypto and WeBWorK workload conditions by changing their request type composition. For RSA-crypto, the original workload contains requests with three different encryption keys. The new workload only contains requests with the largest key among the three. For the WeBWorK application, the original problem-solving workload includes thousands of science problem sets used in the real site. We consider a new workload with only the 10 most popular problem sets. Figure 10 shows the predicted power and measured power at several load levels between median and high load. Results show that our request energy profile-enabled prediction achieves higher accuracy than the two alternatives (particularly at high load). Our approach has up to 11% prediction error, compared to up to 19% error for the CPU-utilization-proportional approach and up to 56% error for the request-rate-proportional approach.

4.3 Fair Request Power Conditioning

We evaluate the effectiveness of fair power conditioning using container-specific CPU throttling (presented in Section 3.4). We experiment with our Google App Engine (GAE)-enabled cloud computing workloads. The GAE-Vosao workload fully utilizes all four cores on the SandyBridge machine. In the middle of the experimentation, we inject high-power requests to mimic power viruses. Our GAE power viruses arrive in a sporadic fashion at an average rate of one per second. Each power virus occupies a CPU core for about 100 msecs. Figure 11(A) shows that the introduction of power viruses lead to substantial power spikes. We apply our container-based fair power conditioning with a system active power target of 40 Watts. If all four cores are being utilized, the per-core active power target is 10 Watts when the system is fully busy. Figure 11(B) shows that our request container-enabled power conditioning can effectively keep power consumption at or below the target level despite the power viruses. It does so by throttling the core running the request that contains the power virus.

While capping the full system power, we further show that the CPU speed adjustment has been applied fairly to each request. Figure 12 plots the applied CPU duty-cycle ratio and original request power (before throttling) for each request. Since a request power consumption may fluctuate over its execution, different duty-cycle levels may be applied over time. We show the time-averaged duty-

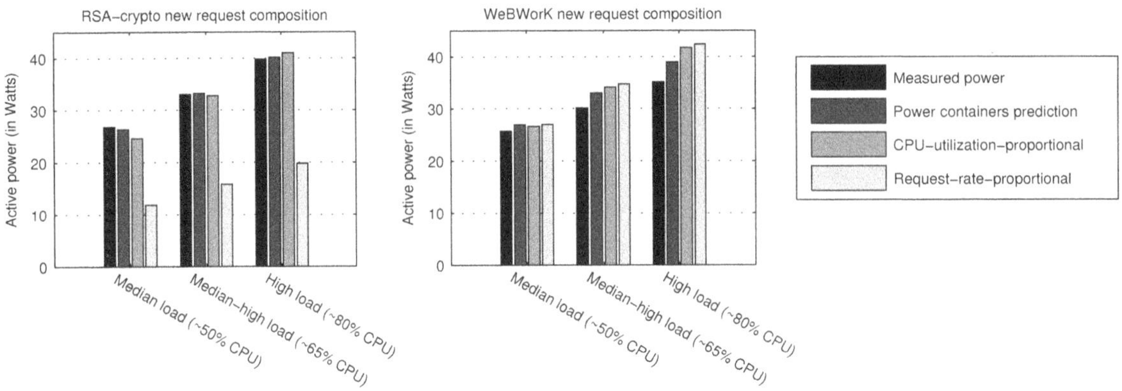

Figure 10. Accuracy of our power containers-produced request energy profiles (and alternative approaches) to predict power at new workload conditions. Experiments were performed on the SandyBridge machine.

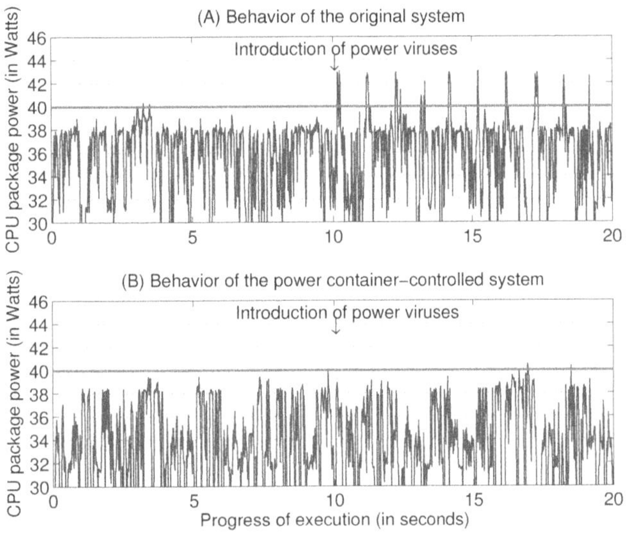

Figure 11. Measured power for original and power-conditioned executions of Google App Engine with power viruses. Experiments were performed on the SandyBridge machine and power is measured using its on-chip power meter. Power viruses are introduced at the 10-second time.

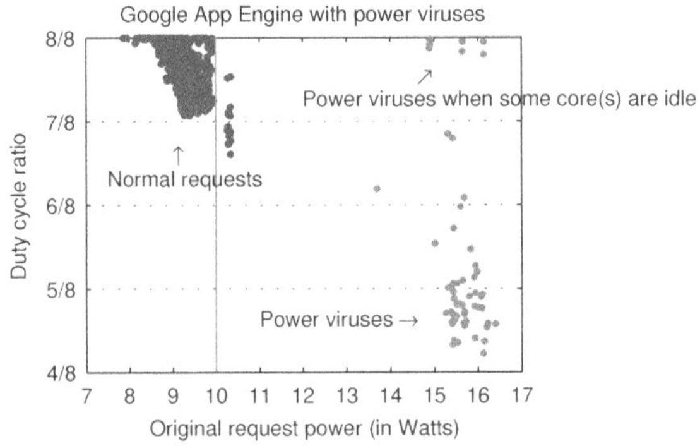

Figure 12. Original power and duty-cycle throttling for Google App Engine with power viruses. Each point represents a sample request. X-coordinate indicates the original (before throttling) request power consumption. Y-coordinate indicates the CPU duty-cycle ratio applied to the request.

cycle ratio for each request. We also estimate its power consumption in the original system (assuming a linear relationship between active power and CPU duty-cycle level). Results show that low-power GAE-Vosao requests suffer minor CPU speed slowdown (averaged at about 2%). At the same time, the power viruses are subject to substantial (33% on average) slowdown. It may appear surprising that a few power viruses (at Figure 12's top-right corner) are not significantly throttled. This is because they happen to run when some CPU core(s) are idle so each request at the time has a higher-than-10 Watts budget when maintaining the whole system power target of 40 Watts.

Without our container-enabled fair power conditioning, alternatively the peak power can be reduced through full-machine throttling. A full-machine duty-cycle level of 7/8 would be required for such throttling, leading to about 13% slowdown of all requests (low-power normal requests as well as power viruses).

4.4 Heterogeneity-Aware Request Distribution

We evaluate container profiling-enabled energy-efficient request distribution in a heterogeneous server cluster (presented in Section 3.4). We start by assessing the energy efficiency heterogeneity across different machines. While recent processors (*e.g.*, SandyBridge) are generally more energy-efficient than older models (*e.g.*, Woodcrest), some applications or application requests may see more substantial cross-machine energy efficiency difference than others do. Our energy container profiling can quantify such workload-specific relative energy efficiency. Figure 13 shows the cross-machine (SandyBridge over Woodcrest) active energy usage ratio for different workloads. In this evaluation and analysis, we measure the active energy usage that does not include the idle power consumption. We consider the constant idle power as part of the fixed system overhead that is of little interest to our adaptive energy management. Figure 13 shows that the cross-machine energy usage ratio can be as high as 0.91 (for the Stress workload) and as low as 0.22 (for RSA-crypto). When distributing some load from SandyBridge to Woodcrest becomes necessary, placing a Stress request on Woodcrest would be four times more energy-efficient than placing a RSA-crypto request.

We evaluate request distribution over a small heterogeneous cluster consisting of two machines—the newer (more energy-efficient) SandyBridge and the older Woodcrest-based machine

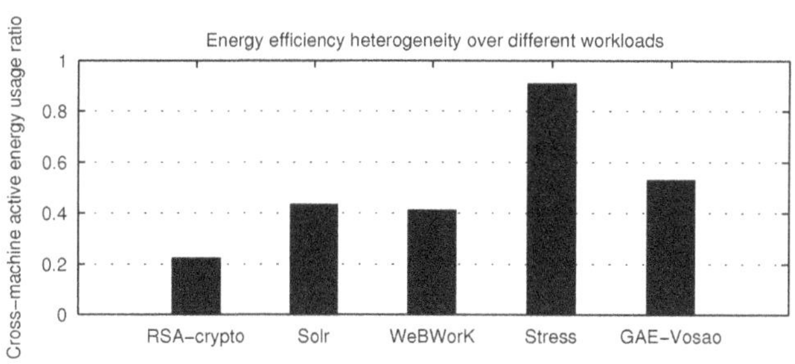

Figure 13. Cross-machine active energy usage ratio (energy usage on SandyBridge over that on Woodcrest) for different workloads. The energy usage on each machine is measured at the peak load level.

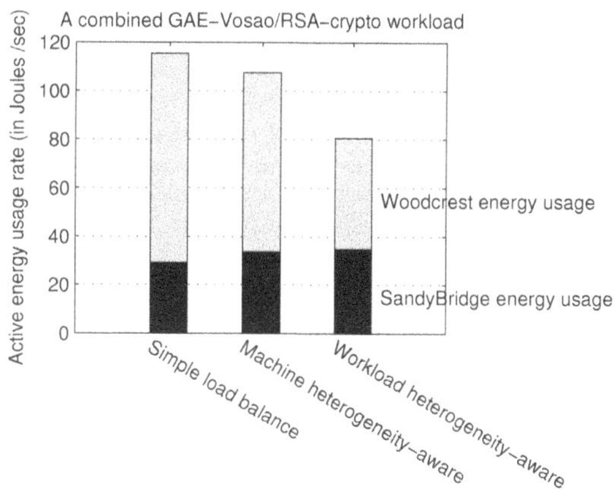

Figure 14. Measured active energy usage rate under three request distribution approaches in a heterogeneous server cluster. Usage for the two machines are marked in different colors.

from our experimental platform. Our goal is to achieve low overall system energy usage without overloading the more energy-efficient machine. We compare three load distribution approaches:

- *Simple load balance* balances the server load by directing an equal amount of load to each of the two machines. It is oblivious to the energy efficiency heterogeneity in the cluster.
- *Machine heterogeneity-aware* approach loads up the more energy-efficient SandyBridge to a healthy high utilization (about 70% CPU utilization to prevent overloading) before loading Woodcrest. It is oblivious to workload energy profiles so it distributes the exact same input request composition to both machines.
- *Workload heterogeneity-aware* approach also first loads up the more energy-efficient SandyBridge. Beyond that, it recognizes the request energy usage profiles using our power containers and it preferentially places requests with higher relative energy efficiency (lower energy usage ratio in Figure 13) on SandyBridge.

Our experiment utilizes a combined GAE-Vosao and RSA-crypto workload (with an approximately 50%–50% load composition). The volume of incoming work in our experiment is the maximum volume that can be supported (without excessive timeout) under the simple load balance. Figure 14 shows the energy usage rate under the three load distribution approaches. Our workload heterogeneity-aware approach saves 30% in combined two-machine energy usage compared to the simple load balance. The saving is 25% compared to the machine heterogeneity-aware approach that cannot recognize diverse workload-to-machine affinity. Our container-enabled request distribution achieves these energy savings by preferentially loading each machine with requests of high relative energy efficiency.

Beyond high energy efficiency, our workload heterogeneity-aware approach also maintains high performance. Table 1 shows the average request response time for GAE-Vosao and RSA-crypto under the three request distribution approaches. Both heterogeneity-aware approaches achieve good performance by keeping the machines under healthy utilization levels. The simple load balance suffers from poor performance because it fails to consider machine heterogeneity and overloads the Woodcrest machine.

Load distribution approach	GAE-Vosao	RSA-crypto
Simple load balance	537 msecs	1,728 msecs
Machine heterogeneity-aware	159 msecs	66 msecs
Workload heterogeneity-aware	131 msecs	50 msecs

Table 1. Average request response time for the two applications under three request distribution approaches in a heterogeneous server cluster.

5. Conclusion

This paper presents an operating system facility (power containers) to account for and control the power and energy usage of individual requests in multicore servers and cloud computing platforms. Power containers utilize an online per-core power estimation model that includes cross-core environmental effects, measurement-aligned online recalibration, and mechanisms within the operating system to isolate request-level power for accounting and control. Our system incurs low overhead (on the order of 0.1% for a typical setup). Validation shows that with the help of online re-calibration, the acquired request power and energy usage profiles can be aggregated to match measured system power (with no more than 9% error) and predict system power at new, hypothetical workload request compositions (with no more than 11% error).

Power containers enable the OS to better manage online applications with dynamic power profiles as well as new hardware platforms with resource sharing and heterogeneity. When running a Google App Engine-based cloud computing workload, our power containers can cap the system power in a fair fashion—throttling power viruses (using processor duty-cycle modulation) while allowing normal requests to run at almost full speed. Further, the acquired request energy profiles enable energy-efficient request distribution on heterogeneous server clusters, saving up to 25% energy usage compared to an alternative approach that recognizes machine heterogeneity but not fine-grained workload affinity.

Acknowledgments

This work was supported in part by the U.S. National Science Foundation grants CNS-0834451, CCF-1016902, CNS-1217372, CCF-1217920, CNS-1239423. Kai Shen was also supported by a Google Research Award. Arrvindh Shriraman was supported by the Canadian NSERC Discovery grant, CRD 614093/569226, and Strategic 612142.

References

[1] Intel Core2 Duo and Dual-Core thermal and mechanical design guidelines. http://www.intel.com/design/core2duo/documentation.htm.

[2] Apache Solr search server. http://lucene.apache.org/solr/.

[3] Stressful application test. http://code.google.com/p/stressapptest.

[4] Vosao content management system. http://www.vosao.org.

[5] Wikipedia data dumps. http://dumps.wikimedia.org/enwiki/.

[6] G. Banga, P. Druschel, and J. Mogul. Resource containers: A new facility for resource management in server systems. In *Third USENIX Symp. on Operating Systems Design and Implementation (OSDI)*, pages 45–58, New Orleans, LA, Feb. 1999.

[7] P. Barham, A. Donnelly, R. Isaacs, and R. Mortier. Using Magpie for request extraction and workload modeling. In *6th USENIX Symp. on Operating Systems Design and Implementation (OSDI)*, pages 259–272, San Francisco, CA, Dec. 2004.

[8] L. Barroso and U. Hölzle. The case for energy-proportional computing. *IEEE Computer*, 40(12):33–37, Dec. 2007.

[9] F. Bellosa. The benefits of event-driven energy accounting in power-sensitive systems. In *ACM SIGOPS European Workshop*, pages 37–42, Kolding, Denmark, Sept. 2000.

[10] R. Bertran, M. Gonzalez, X. Martorell, N. Navarro, and E. Ayguade. Decomposable and responsive power models for multicore processors using performance counters. In *24th ACM Int'l Conf. on Supercomputing (ICS)*, pages 147–158, Tsukuba, Japan, June 2010.

[11] A. Chanda, A. Cox, and W. Zwaenepoel. Whodunit: Transactional profiling for multi-tier applications. In *Second EuroSys Conf.*, pages 17–30, Lisbon, Portugal, Mar. 2007.

[12] F. Chang, K. I. Farkas, and P. Ranganathan. Energy-driven statistical sampling: Detecting software hotspots. In *Second Workshop on Power-Aware Computer Systems*, pages 110–129, Cambridge, MA, Feb. 2002.

[13] J. S. Chase, D. C. Anderson, P. N. Thakar, A. M. Vahdat, and R. P. Doyle. Managing energy and server resources in hosting centers. In *18th ACM Symp. on Operating Systems Principles (SOSP)*, pages 103–116, Banff, Canada, Oct. 2001.

[14] B.-G. Chun, G. Iannaccone, G. Iannaccone, R. Katz, G. Lee, and L. Niccolini. An energy case for hybrid datacenters. In *Workshop on Power Aware Computing and Systems*, Big Sky, MT, Oct. 2009.

[15] X. Fan, W.-D. Weber, and L. Barroso. Power provisioning for a warehouse-sized computer. In *34th Int'l Symp. on Computer Architecture (ISCA)*, pages 13–23, San Diego, CA, June 2007.

[16] J. Flinn and M. Satyanarayanan. Energy-aware adaptation for mobile applications. In *17th ACM Symp. on Operating Systems Principles (SOSP)*, pages 48–63, Kiawah Island, SC, Dec. 2001.

[17] R. Fonseca, G. Porter, R. H. Katz, S. Shenker, and I. Stoica. X-Trace: A pervasive network tracing framework. In *4th USENIX Symp. on Networked Systems Design and Implementation (NSDI)*, Cambridge, MA, Apr. 2007.

[18] R. Fonseca, P. Dutta, P. Levis, and I. Stoica. Quanto: Tracking energy in networked embedded systems. In *8th USENIX Symp. on Operating Systems Design and Implementation (OSDI)*, pages 323–338, San Diego, CA, Dec. 2008.

[19] K. Ganesan, J. Jo, W. L. Bircher, D. Kaseridis, Z. Yu, and L. K. John. System-level max power (SYMPO): a systematic approach for escalating system-level power consumption using synthetic benchmarks. In *19th Int'l Conf. on Parallel Architecture and Compilation Techniques (PACT)*, pages 19–28, Vienna, Austria, Sept. 2010.

[20] S. Govindan, J. Choi, B. Urgaonkar, A. Sivasubramaniam, and A. Baldini. Statistical profiling-based techniques for effective power provisioning in data centers. In *4th EuroSys Conf.*, pages 317–330, Nuremberg, Germany, Apr. 2009.

[21] V. Gupta, P. Brett, D. Koufaty, D. Reddy, S. Hahn, K. Schwan, and G. Srinivasa. The forgotten 'uncore': On the energy-efficiency of heterogeneous cores. In *USENIX Annual Technical Conf.*, Boston, MA, June 2012.

[22] J. Hamilton. Where does the power go in high-scale data centers? Keynote speech at SIGMETRICS, June 2009.

[23] T. Heath, B. Diniz, E. V. Carrera, W. Meira Jr., and R. Bianchini. Energy conservation in heterogeneous server clusters. In *10th ACM Symp. on Principles and Practice of Parallel Programming (PPoPP)*, pages 186–195, Chicago, IL, June 2005.

[24] W. Huang, C. Lefurgy, W. Kuk, A. Buyuktosunoglu, M. Floyd, K. Rajamani, M. Allen-Ware, and B. Brock. Accurate fine-grained processor power proxies. In *45th Int'l Symp. on Microarchitecture (MICRO)*, pages 224–234, Vancouver, Canada, Dec. 2012.

[25] C. Isci and M. Martonosi. Phase characterization for power: Evaluating control-flow-based and event-counter-based techniques. In *12th Int'l Symp. on High-Performance Computer Architecture (HPCA)*, pages 121–132, Austin, TX, Feb. 2006.

[26] J. C. McCullough, Y. Agarwal, J. Chandrasheka, S. Kuppuswamy, A. C. Snoeren, and R. K. Gupta. Evaluating the effectiveness of model-based power characterization. In *USENIX Annual Technical Conf.*, Portland, OR, June 2011.

[27] D. McIntire, K. Ho, B. Yip, A. Singh, W. Wu, and W. Kaiser. The low power energy aware processing (LEAP) embedded networked sensor system. In *5th Int'l Conf. on Information Processing in Sensor Networks*, pages 449–457, Nashville, TN, Apr. 2006.

[28] D. Meisner, B. Gold, and T. Wenisch. PowerNap: Eliminating server idle power. In *14th Int'l Conf. on Architectural Support for Programming Languages and Operating Systems (ASPLOS)*, pages 205–216, Washington, DC, Mar. 2009.

[29] E. Pinheiro, R. Bianchini, E. V. Carrera, and T. Heath. Dynamic cluster reconfiguration for power and performance. In *Compilers and Operating Systems for Low Power*, pages 75–93, 2003.

[30] E. Rotem, A. Naveh, D. Rajwan, A. Ananthakrishnan, and E. Weissmann. Power Management Architecture of the 2nd Generation Intel Core microarchitecture, formerly codenamed Sandy Bridge. In *Hot Chips: A Symposium on High Performance Chips*, Aug. 2011.

[31] A. Roy, S. M. Rumble, R. Stutsman, P. Levis, D. Mazières, and N. Zeldovich. Energy management in mobile devices with the Cinder operating system. In *6th EuroSys Conf.*, pages 139–152, Salzburg, Austria, Apr. 2011.

[32] K. Shen. Request behavior variations. In *15th Int'l Conf. on Architectural Support for Programming Languages and Operating Systems (ASPLOS)*, pages 103–116, Pittsburg, PA, Mar. 2010.

[33] K. Shen, M. Zhong, S. Dwarkadas, C. Li, C. Stewart, and X. Zhang. Hardware counter driven on-the-fly request signatures. In *13th Int'l Conf. on Architectural Support for Programming Languages and Operating Systems (ASPLOS)*, pages 189–200, Seattle, WA, Mar. 2008.

[34] B. H. Sigelman, L. A. Barroso, M. Burrows, P. Stephenson, M. Plakal, D. Beaver, S. Jaspan, and C. Shanbhag. Dapper, a large-scale distributed systems tracing infrastructure. Technical report, Google, Apr. 2010.

[35] C. Stewart and K. Shen. Some Joules are more precious than others: Managing renewable energy in the datacenter. In *Workshop on Power Aware Computing and Systems*, Big Sky, MT, Oct. 2009.

[36] C. Stewart, M. Leventi, and K. Shen. Empirical examination of a collaborative web application. In *IEEE Int'l Symp. on Workload Characterization*, Seattle, WA, Sept. 2008.

[37] The Mathematical Association of America. WeBWorK: Online homework for math and science. http://webwork.maa.org/.

[38] M. Ware, K. Rajamani, M. Floyd, B. Brock, J. C. Rubio, F. Rawson, and J. B. Carter. Architecting for power management: The IBM POWER7 approach. In *16th Int'l Symp. on High-Performance Computer Architecture (HPCA)*, Bangalore, India, Jan. 2010.

[39] H. Zeng, C. S. Ellis, A. R. Lebeck, and A. Vahdat. ECOSystem: Managing energy as a first class operating system resource. In *10th Int'l Conf. on Architectural Support for Programming Languages and Operating Systems (ASPLOS)*, pages 123–132, Boston, MA, Oct. 2002.

Paragon: QoS-Aware Scheduling for Heterogeneous Datacenters

Christina Delimitrou
Stanford University
cdel@stanford.edu

Christos Kozyrakis
Stanford University
kozyraki@stanford.edu

Abstract

Large-scale datacenters (DCs) host tens of thousands of diverse applications each day. However, interference between colocated workloads and the difficulty to match applications to one of the many hardware platforms available can degrade performance, violating the quality of service (QoS) guarantees that many cloud workloads require. While previous work has identified the impact of heterogeneity and interference, existing solutions are computationally intensive, cannot be applied online and do not scale beyond few applications.

We present Paragon, an online and scalable DC scheduler that is heterogeneity and interference-aware. Paragon is derived from robust analytical methods and instead of profiling each application in detail, it leverages information the system already has about applications it has previously seen. It uses collaborative filtering techniques to quickly and accurately classify an unknown, incoming workload with respect to heterogeneity and interference in multiple shared resources, by identifying similarities to previously scheduled applications. The classification allows Paragon to greedily schedule applications in a manner that minimizes interference and maximizes server utilization. Paragon scales to tens of thousands of servers with marginal scheduling overheads in terms of time or state.

We evaluate Paragon with a wide range of workload scenarios, on both small and large-scale systems, including 1,000 servers on EC2. For a 2,500-workload scenario, Paragon enforces performance guarantees for 91% of applications, while significantly improving utilization. In comparison, heterogeneity-oblivious, interference-oblivious and least-loaded schedulers only provide similar guarantees for 14%, 11% and 3% of workloads. The differences are more striking in oversubscribed scenarios where resource efficiency is more critical.

Categories and Subject Descriptors C.5.1 [Computer System Implementation]: Super (very large) computers; D.4.1 [Process Management]: Scheduling
Keywords Datacenter, cloud computing, heterogeneity, interference, scheduling, QoS

1. Introduction

An increasing amount of computing is performed in the cloud, primarily due to cost benefits for both the end-users and the operators of datacenters (DC) that host cloud services [4]. Large-scale providers such as Amazon EC2 [13], Microsoft Windows Azure [43], Rackspace [33] and Google Compute Engine [17] host tens of thousands of applications on a daily basis. Several companies also organize their IT infrastructure as private clouds, using management systems such as VMware vSphere [41] or Citrix XenServer [47].

ASPLOS'13, March 16–20, 2013, Houston, Texas, USA.

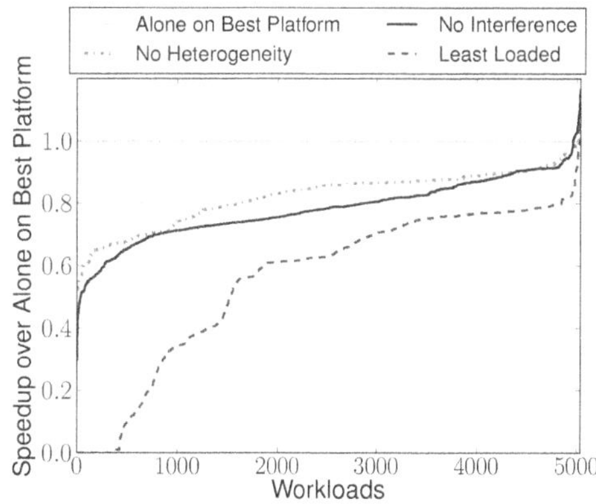

Figure 1: Performance degradation for 5,000 applications on 1000 EC2 servers with heterogeneity-oblivious, interference-oblivious and baseline least-loaded schedulers compared to ideal scheduling (application runs alone on best platform). Results are ordered from worst to best-performing workload.

The operator of a cloud service must schedule the stream of incoming applications on available servers in a manner that achieves both fast execution (user's goal) and high *resource efficiency* (operator's goal), enabling better scaling at low cost. This scheduling problem is particularly difficult as cloud services must accommodate a diverse set of workloads in terms of resource and performance requirements [4]. Moreover, the operator often has no a priori knowledge of workload characteristics. In this work, we focus on two basic challenges that complicate scheduling in large-scale DCs: *hardware platform heterogeneity* and *workload interference*.

Heterogeneity occurs because servers are gradually provisioned and replaced over the typical 15-year lifetime of a DC [4, 19, 23, 27, 31]. At any point in time, a DC may host 3-5 server generations with a few hardware configurations per generation, in terms of the specific speeds and capacities of the processor, memory, storage and networking subsystems. Hence, it is common to have 10 to 40 configurations throughout the DC. Ignoring heterogeneity can lead to significant inefficiencies, as some workloads are sensitive to hardware configurations. Figure 1 shows that a heterogeneity-oblivious scheduler will slow applications down by 22% on average, with some running nearly 2x slower (see Section 4 for methodology). This is not only suboptimal from the user's perspective, but also for the DC operator as workloads occupy servers for significantly longer.

Interference is the result of co-scheduling multiple workloads on a single server to increase utilization and achieve better cost efficiency. By co-locating applications a given number of servers can host a larger set of workloads (better scalability). Alternatively, by packing workloads in a small number of servers when the overall load is low, the rest of the servers can be turned off to save energy. The latter is needed because modern servers are not energy-proportional and consume a large fraction of peak power even at low utilization [3, 4, 25, 29]. Co-scheduled applications may interfere negatively even if they run on different processor cores because they share caches, memory channels, storage and networking devices [18,

28, 32]. Figure 1 shows that an interference-oblivious scheduler will slow workloads down by 34% on average, with some running more than 2x slower. Again, this is undesirable for both users and operators. Finally, a baseline scheduler that is both interference and heterogeneity-oblivious and schedules applications to least-loaded servers is even worse (48% average slowdown), causing some workloads to crash due to resource exhaustion on the server.

Previous work has showcased the potential of heterogeneity and interference-aware scheduling [27, 28]. However, techniques that rely on detailed application characterization cannot scale to large DCs that receive tens of thousands of potentially unknown workloads every day [9]. Most cloud management systems have some notion of contention or interference-awareness [20, 32, 39, 40, 46]. However, they either use empirical rules for interference management or assume long-running workloads (e.g., online services), whose repeated behavior can be progressively modeled. In this work, we target both heterogeneity and interference and assume no a priori analysis of the application. Instead, we leverage information the system *already* has about the large number of applications it has previously seen.

We present *Paragon*, an online and scalable datacenter scheduler that is heterogeneity and interference-aware. The key feature of Paragon is its ability to quickly and accurately classify an unknown application with respect to heterogeneity (which server configurations it will perform best on) and interference (how much interference it will cause to co-scheduled applications and how much interference it can tolerate itself in multiple shared resources). Paragon's classification engine exploits existing data from previously scheduled applications and offline training and requires only a minimal signal about a new workload. Specifically, it is organized as a low-overhead recommendation system similar to the one deployed for the Netflix Challenge [6], but instead of discovering similarities in users' movie preferences, it finds similarities in applications' preferences with respect to heterogeneity and interference. It uses singular value decomposition to perform collaborative filtering and identify similarities between incoming and previously scheduled workloads.

Once an incoming application is classified, a greedy scheduler assigns it to the server that is the best possible match in terms of platform and minimum negative interference between all co-scheduled workloads. Even though the final step is greedy, the high accuracy of classification leads to schedules that satisfy both user requirements (fast execution time) and operator requirements (efficient resource use). Moreover, since classification is based on robust analytical methods and not merely empirical observation, we have strong guarantees on its accuracy and strict bounds on its overheads. Paragon scales to systems with tens of thousands of servers and tens of configurations, running large numbers of previously unknown workloads.

We implemented Paragon and evaluated its efficiency using a wide spectrum of workload scenarios (light, high, and oversubscribed). We used Paragon to schedule applications on a private cluster with 40 servers of 10 different configurations and on 1000 exclusive servers on Amazon EC2 with 14 configurations. We compare Paragon to a heterogeneity-oblivious, an interference-oblivious and a state-of-the-art least-loaded scheduler. For the 1000-server experiments and a scenario with 2500 workloads, Paragon maintains QoS for 91% of workloads (within 5% of their performance running alone on the best server). The heterogeneity-oblivious, interference-oblivious and least-loaded schedulers offer such QoS guarantees for only 14%, 11%, and 3% of applications respectively. The results are more striking in the case of an oversubscribed workload scenario, where efficient resource use is even more critical. Paragon provides QoS guarantees for 52% of workloads and bounds the performance degradation to less than 10% for an additional 33% of workloads. In contrast, the least-loaded scheduler dramatically degrades performance for 99.9% of applications. We also evaluate Paragon on a Windows Azure and a Google Compute Engine cluster and show similar gains. Finally, we validate that Paragon's classification engine achieves the accuracy and bounds predicted by the analytical methods and evaluate various parameters of the system.

The rest of the paper is organized as follows. Section 2 describes the analytical methods that drive Paragon. Section 3 presents the implementation of the scheduler. Section 4 presents the experimental methodology and Section 5 the evaluation of Paragon. Finally, Section 6 discusses related work and Section 7 concludes the paper.

2. Fast & Accurate Classification

The key requirement for heterogeneity and interference-aware scheduling is to quickly and accurately classify incoming applications. First, we need to know how fast an application will run on each of the tens of server configurations available. Second, we need to know how much interference it can tolerate from other workloads in each of several shared resources without significant performance loss and how much interference it will generate itself. Our goal is to perform online scheduling for large-scale DCs without any a priori knowledge about incoming applications. Most previous schemes address this issue with detailed but offline application characterization or long-term monitoring and modeling approaches [28, 32, 39]. Instead, Paragon takes a different perspective. Its core idea is that, instead of learning each new workload in detail, the system leverages information it already has about applications it has seen to express the new workload as a combination of known applications. For this purpose we use collaborative filtering techniques that combine a minimal profiling signal about the new application (e.g., a minute's worth of profiling data on two servers) with the large amount of data available from previously scheduled applications. The result is fast and highly accurate classification of incoming applications with respect to both heterogeneity and interference. Within a minute of its arrival, an incoming workload can be scheduled efficiently on a large-scale cluster.

2.1 Collaborative Filtering Background

Collaborative filtering techniques are frequently used in recommendation systems. We will use one of their most publicized applications, the Netflix Challenge [6], to provide a quick overview of the two analytical methods we rely upon, Singular Value Decomposition (SVD) and PQ-reconstruction (PQ) [34]. In this case, the goal is to provide valid movie recommendations for Netflix users given the ratings they have provided for various other movies.

The input to the analytical framework is a sparse matrix A, the *utility matrix*, with one row per user and one column per movie. The elements of A are the ratings that users have assigned to movies. Each user has rated only a small subset of movies; this is especially true for new users which may only have a handful of ratings or even none. While there are techniques that address the cold start problem, i.e., providing recommendations to a completely fresh user with no ratings, here we focus on users for which the system has some minimal input. If we can estimate the values of the missing ratings in the sparse matrix A, we can make movie recommendations: suggest that users watch the movies for which the recommendation system estimates that they will give high ratings with high confidence.

The first step is to apply singular value decomposition (SVD), a matrix factorization method used for dimensionality reduction and similarity identification. Factoring A produces the decomposition to matrices U, V and Σ.

$$A_{m,n} = \begin{pmatrix} a_{1,1} & a_{1,2} & \cdots & a_{1,n} \\ a_{2,1} & a_{2,2} & \cdots & a_{2,n} \\ \vdots & \vdots & \ddots & \vdots \\ a_{m,1} & a_{m,2} & \cdots & a_{m,n} \end{pmatrix} = U \cdot \Sigma \cdot V^T$$

where

$$U_{m\times r} = \begin{pmatrix} u_{11} & \cdots & u_{1r} \\ u_{21} & \cdots & u_{2r} \\ \vdots & \ddots & \vdots \\ u_{m1} & \cdots & u_{mr} \end{pmatrix}, V_{n\times r} = \begin{pmatrix} v_{11} & v_{12} & \cdots & v_{1n} \\ \vdots & \vdots & \ddots & \vdots \\ v_{r1} & v_{r2} & \cdots & v_{rn} \end{pmatrix}$$

$$\Sigma_{r\times r} = \begin{pmatrix} \sigma_1 & \cdots & 0 \\ \vdots & \ddots & \vdots \\ 0 & \cdots & \sigma_r \end{pmatrix}$$

are the matrices of left and right singular vectors and the diagonal matrix of singular values.

Dimension r is the rank of matrix A and it represents the number of similarity concepts identified by SVD. For instance, one similarity concept may be that certain movies belong to the drama category, while another may be that most users that liked the movie "Lord of the Rings 1" also liked "Lord of the Rings 2". Similarity concepts are represented by singular values (σ_i) in matrix Σ and the confidence in a similarity concept by the magnitude of the corresponding singular value. Singular values in Σ are ordered by decreasing magnitude. Matrix U captures the strength of the correlation between a row of A and a similarity concept. In other words, it expresses how users relate to similarity concepts such as the one about liking drama movies. Matrix V captures the strength of the correlation of a column of A to a similarity concept. In other words, to what extend does a movie fall in the drama category. The complexity of performing SVD on a $m \times n$ matrix is $min(n^2m, m^2n)$. SVD is robust to missing entries and imposes relaxed sparsity constraints to provide accuracy guarantees. Density less than 1% does not reduce the recommendation accuracy [38].

Before we can make accurate score estimations using SVD, we need the full utility matrix A. To recover the missing entries in A, we use PQ-reconstruction. Building from the decomposition of the initial, sparse A matrix we have $Q_{m\times r} = U$ and $P^T_{r\times n} = \Sigma \cdot V^T$. The product of Q and P^T gives matrix R which is an approximation of A with the missing entries. To improve R, we use Stochastic Gradient Descent (SGD), a scalable and lightweight latent factor model [7, 24, 26, 44] that iteratively recreates A:

$\forall r_{ui}$, where r_{ui} an element of the reconstructed matrix R

$\epsilon_{ui} = r_{ui} - q_i \cdot p_u{}^T$

$q_i \leftarrow q_i + \eta(\epsilon_{ui} p_u - \lambda q_i)$

$p_u \leftarrow p_u + \eta(\epsilon_{ui} q_i - \lambda p_u)$

until $|\epsilon|_{L_2} = \sqrt{\sum_{u,i} |\epsilon_{ui}|^2}$ becomes marginal.

In the process above η is the learning rate and λ is the regularization factor. The complexity of PQ is linear with the number of r_{ui} and in practice takes up to a few ms for matrices with $m, n \sim 1,000$. Once the dense utility matrix R is recovered we can make movie recommendations. This involves applying SVD to R to identify which of the reconstructed entries reflect strong similarities that enable making accurate recommendations with high confidence.

2.2 Classification for Heterogeneity

Overview: We use collaborative filtering to identify how well an incoming application will run on the different hardware platforms available. In this case, the rows in matrix A represent applications, the columns server configurations (SC) and the ratings represent normalized application performance on each server configuration.

As part of an offline step, we select a small number of applications, a few tens, and profile them on all different server configurations. We normalize the performance results and fully populate the corresponding rows of A. This only needs to happen once. If a new configuration is added in the DC, we need to profile these applications on it and add a column in A. In the online mode, when a new application arrives, we profile it for a period of 1 minute on any two server configurations, insert it as a new row in matrix A and use the process described in Sec. 2.1 to derive the missing ratings for the other server configurations.

Metric	Applications (%)			
	ST	MT	MP	IO
Selected best SC	86%	86%	83%	89%
Selected SC within 5% of best	91%	90%	89%	92%
Correct SC ranking (best to worst)	67%	62%	59%	43%
90% correct SC ranking	78%	71%	63%	58%
50% correct SC ranking	93%	91%	89%	90%
Training & best SC match	28%	24%	18%	22%

Table 1: Validation metrics for heterogeneity classification.

In this case, Σ represents similarity concepts such as the fact that applications that benefit from SC1 will also benefit from SC3. U captures how an application correlates to the different similarity concepts and V how an SC correlates to them. Collaborative filtering identifies similarities between new and known applications. Two applications can be similar in one characteristic (they both benefit from high clock frequency) but different in others (only one benefits from a large L3 cache). This is especially common when scaling to large application spaces and several hardware configurations. SVD addresses this issue by uncovering hidden similarities and filtering out the ones less likely to have an impact on the application's behavior.

The size of the offline training set is important as a certain number of ratings is necessary to satisfy the sparsity constraints of SVD. However, over that number the accuracy quickly levels off and scales well with the number of applications thereafter (smaller fractions for training sets of larger application spaces). For our experiments we use 20 and 50 offline workloads for a 40 and 1,000-server cluster respectively. Additionally, as more incoming applications are added in A the density of the matrix increases and the recommendation accuracy further improves. Note that online training is performed only on two SCs. This not only reduces the training overhead compared to exhaustive search but since training requires dedicated servers, it also reduces the number of servers necessary for it. In contrast, if we attempted to classify applications through exhaustive profiling, the number of profiling runs would equal the number of SCs (e.g., 40). For a cloud service with high workload arrival rates, this would be infeasible to support, underlining the importance of keeping training overheads low, something that Paragon does.

Classification is very fast. On a production-class Xeon server, this takes 10-30 msec for thousands of applications and tens of SCs. We can perform classification for one application at a time or for small groups of incoming applications (*batching*) if the arrival rate is high without impacting accuracy or speed.

Performance scores: We populate A with normalized scores that represent how well an application performs on a server configuration. We use the following performance metrics based on application type:

(a) *Single-threaded workloads:* We use instructions committed per second (IPS) as the initial performance metric. Using execution time would require running applications to completion in the profiling servers, increasing the training overheads. We have verified that using IPS leads to similar classification accuracy as using full execution time. For multi-programmed workloads we use aggregate IPS.

(b) *Multithreaded workloads:* In the presence of spin-locks or other synchronization schemes that introduce active waiting, aggregate IPS can be deceiving [1, 42]. We address this by periodically polling low-overhead performance counters, to detect changes in the register file (read and writes that would denote regular operations other than spinning) and weight-out of the IPS computation such execution segments. We have verified that scheduling with this "useful" IPS leads to similar classification accuracy as using full execution time. When workloads are not known, or multiple workload types are present "useful" IPS is used to drive the scheduling decisions.

The choice of IPS as the base of performance metrics is influenced our current evaluation which focuses on single-node CPU, memory and I/O intensive programs. The same methodology holds for higher-level metrics, such as queries per second (QPS), which cover complex multi-tier workloads as well.

Validation: We evaluate the accuracy of heterogeneity classification on a 40-server cluster with 10 SCs. We use a large set of single-threaded, multi-threaded, multi-programmed and I/O-bound workloads. For details on workloads and server configurations, see Section 4. The offline training set includes 20 applications selected randomly from all workload types. The recommendation system achieves 24% performance improvement for single-threaded, 20% for multi-threaded, 38% for multi-programmed, and 40% for I/O workloads on average, while some applications have a 2x performance difference. Table 1 summarizes key statistics on the classification quality. Our classifier correctly identifies the best SC for 84% of workloads and an SC within 5% of optimal for 90%. The predicted ranking of SCs is exactly correct for 58% and almost correct (single reordering) for 65% of workloads. In almost all cases 50% of SCs are ranked correctly by the classification scheme. Finally, it is important to note that the accuracy does not depend on the two SCs selected for training. The training SC matched the top performing configuration only for 20% of workloads.

We also validate the analytical methods. We compare performance predicted by the recommendation system to performance obtained through experimentation. The deviation is less than 3.8% on average.

2.3 Classification for Interference

Overview: There are two types of interference we are interested in: interference that an application can *tolerate* from pre-existing load on a server and interference the application will *cause* on that load. We detect interference due to contention on shared resources and assign a score to the sensitivity of an application to a type of interference. To derive sensitivity scores we develop several microbenchmarks, each stressing a specific shared resource with tunable intensity. We run an application concurrently with a microbenchmark and progressively tune up its intensity until the application violates its QoS, which is set at 95% of the performance achieved in isolation. Applications with high tolerance to interference (e.g., sensitivity score over 60%) are easier to co-schedule than applications with low tolerance (low sensitivity score). Similarly, we detect the sensitivity of a microbenchmark to the interference the application causes by tuning up its intensity and recording when the performance of the microbenchmark degrades by 5% compared to its performance in isolation. In this case, high sensitivity scores, e.g., over 60% correspond to applications that cause a lot of interference in the specific shared resource.

Identifying sources of interference (SoI): Co-scheduled applications may contend on a large number of shared resources. We identified ten such sources of interference (SoI) and designed a tunable microbenchmark for each one. SoIs span resources such as memory (bandwidth and capacity), cache hierarchy (L1/L2/L3 and TLBs) and network and storage bandwidth. The same methodology can be expanded to any shared resource.

Collaborative filtering for interference: We classify applications for interference tolerated and caused, using twice the process described in Sec. 2.1. The two utility matrices have applications as rows and SoIs as columns. The elements of the matrices are the sensitivity scores of an application to the corresponding microbenchmark (sensitivity to tolerated and caused interference respectively). Similarly to classification for heterogeneity, we profile a few applications offline against all SoIs and insert them as dense rows in the utility matrices. In the online mode, each new application is profiled against two randomly chosen microbenchmarks for one minute and its sensitivity scores are added in a new row in each of the matrices. Then, we use SVD and PQ reconstruction to derive the missing entries and the confidence in each similarity concept. This process performs accurate and fast application classification and provides information to the scheduler on which applications should be assigned to the same server (see Sec. 3.2).

Metric	Percentage (%)
Average sensitivity error across all SoIs	5.3%
Average error for sensitivities $< 30\%$	7.1%
Average error for sensitivities $< 60\%$	5.6%
Average error for sensitivities $> 60\%$	3.4%
Apps with $< 5\%$ error	ST: 65% MT: 58%
Apps with $< 10\%$ error	ST: 81% MT: 63%
Apps with $< 20\%$ error	ST: 90% MT: 89%
SoI with highest error	
for ST: L1 i-cache	15.8%
for MT: LLC capacity	7.8%
Frequency L1 i-cache used as offline SoI	14.6%
Frequency LLC cap used as offline SoI	11.5%
SoI with lowest error	
for ST: network bandwidth	1.8%
for MT: storage bandwidth	0.9%

Table 2: Validation metrics for interference classification.

Validation: We evaluated the accuracy of interference classification using the single-threaded and multi-threaded workloads and the same systems as for the heterogeneity classification. Table 2 summarizes some key statistics on the classification quality. Our classifier, achieves an average error of 5.3% in estimating both tolerated and caused interference across all SoIs. For high values of sensitivity, i.e., applications that tolerate and cause a lot of interference, the error is even lower (3.4%), while for most applications (both single-threaded and multi-threaded) the errors are lower than 5%. The SoIs with the highest errors are the L1 instruction cache for single-threaded workloads and the LLC capacity (L2 or L3) for multi-threaded workloads. The high errors are not a weakness of the classification, since both resources are profiled adequately, but rather of the difficulty to consistently characterize contention in certain shared resources [28]. On the other hand, network and storage bandwidth have the lowest errors, primarily due to the fact that we used CPU and memory intensive workloads for this evaluation.

2.4 Putting It All Together

Overall, Paragon requires two short runs ($\sim$1 minute) on two SCs to classify incoming applications for heterogeneity. Another two short runs against two microbenchmarks on a high-end SC are needed for interference classification. We use a high-end SC to decouple server features from interference analysis. Running for 1 minute provides some signal on the new workload without introducing significant profiling overheads. In Section 3.4 we discuss the issue of workload phases, i.e., transient effects that do not appear in the 1 minute profiling period. Next, we use collaborative filtering to classify the application in terms of heterogeneity and interference, tolerated and caused. This cumulatively requires a few msec even when considering thousands of applications and several tens of SCs or SoIs. The classification for heterogeneity and interference is performed *in parallel*. For the applications we considered, the overall profiling and classification overheads are 1.2% and 0.09% on average.

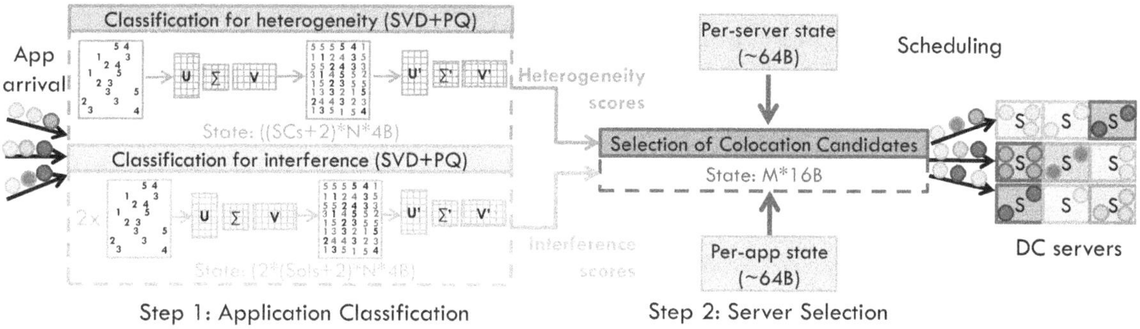

Figure 2: The components of Paragon and the state maintained by each component. Overall, the state requirements are marginal and scale linearly or logarithmically with the number of applications (N), servers (M) and configurations.

Using analytical methods for classification has two benefits; first, we have *strong analytical guarantees* on the quality of the information used for scheduling, instead of relying mainly on empirical observations. The analytical framework provides low and tight error bounds on the accuracy of classification, statistical guarantees on the quality of colocation candidates and detailed characterization of system behavior. Moreover, the scheduler design is workload independent, which means that the analytical or statistical properties the scheme provides hold for any workload. Second, these methods are *computationally efficient*, *scale well* with the number of applications and SCs, do not introduce significant training and decision overheads and enable exact complexity evaluation.

3. Paragon

3.1 Overview

Once an incoming application is classified with respect to heterogeneity and interference, Paragon schedules it on one of the available servers. The scheduler attempts to assign each workload to the server of the best SC and colocate it with applications so that interference is minimized for workloads running on the same server. The scheduler is online and greedy so we cannot make holistic claims about optimality. Nevertheless, the fact that we start with highly accurate classification helps achieve very efficient schedules. The interference information allows Paragon to pack applications on a subset of servers without significant performance loss[1]. The heterogeneity information allows Paragon to assign to each SC only applications that will benefit from its characteristics. Both these properties lead to faster execution, hence resources are freed as soon as possible, making it easier to schedule future applications (more unloaded servers) and perform power management (more idling servers that can be placed in low-power modes).

Fig. 2 presents an overview of Paragon and its components. The scheduler maintains per-application and per-server state. Per-application state includes information for the heterogeneity and interference classification of every submitted workload. For a DC with 10 SCs and 10 SoIs, we store 64B per application. The per-server state records the IDs of applications running on a server and the cumulative sensitivity to interference (roughly 64B per server). The per-server state needs to be updated as applications are scheduled and, later on, complete. Paragon also needs some storage for the intermediate and final utility matrices and temporary storage for ranking possible candidate servers for an incoming application. Overall, state overheads are marginal and scale logarithmically or linearly with the number of applications (N) and servers (M). In our experiments with thousands of applications and servers, a single server could handle all processing and storage requirements of scheduling[2].

We present two methods for selecting candidate servers; a fast, greedy algorithm that searches for the optimal candidate and a statistical scheme of constant runtime that provides strong guarantees on the quality of candidates as a function of examined servers.

3.2 Greedy Server Selection

In examining candidates, the scheduler considers two factors: first, which assignments minimize negative interference between the new application and existing load and second, which servers have the best SC for this workload. Decisions are made in this order; first identifying servers that do not violate QoS and then selecting the best SC between them. This is based on the observation that interference typically leads to higher performance loss than suboptimal SCs.

The greedy scheduler strives to minimize interference, while also increasing server utilization. The scheduler searches for servers whose load can tolerate the interference caused by the new workload and vice versa, the new workload can tolerate the interference caused by the server load. Specifically it evaluates two metrics, $D_1 = t_{server} - c_{newapp}$ and $D_2 = t_{newapp} - c_{server}$, where t is the sensitivity score for tolerated and c for caused interference for a specific SoI. The cumulative sensitivity of a server to caused interference is the sum of sensitivities of individual applications running on it, while the sensitivity to tolerated interference is the minimum of these values. The optimal candidate is a server for which D_1 and D_2 are exactly zero for all SoIs. This implies that there is no negative impact from interference between new and existing applications and that the server resources are perfectly utilized. In practice, a good selection is one for which D_1 and D_2 are bounded by a positive and small ϵ for all SoIs. Large, positive values for D_1 and D_2 indicate suboptimal resource utilization. Negative D_1 and/or D_2 imply violation of QoS and identify poor candidates that should be avoided.

We examine candidate servers for an application in the following way. The process is explained for interference tolerated by the server and caused by the new workload (D_1) and is exactly the same for D_2. Given the classification of an application, we start from the resource that is most difficult to satisfy (highest sensitivity score to caused interference). We query the server state and select the server set for which D_1 is non-negative for this SoI. Next, we examine the second SoI in order of decreasing sensitivity scores, filtering out any servers for which D_1 is negative. The process continues until all SoIs have been examined. Then, we take the intersection of candidate server sets for D_1 and D_2. We now consider heterogeneity. From the set of candidates we select servers that correspond to the best SC for the new workload and from their subset we select the server with $min(||D_1 + D_2||_{L1})$.

.4pt plus 2pt minus 4pt[1]Packing applications with minimal interference should be a property exhibited by any optimal schedule.

.4pt plus 2pt minus 4pt[2]Additional scheduling servers can be used for fault-tolerance.

As we filter out servers, it is possible that at some point the set of candidate servers becomes empty. This implies that there is no single server for which D_1 and D_2 are non-negative for some SoI. In practice this event is extremely unlikely, but is supported for completeness. We handle this case with backtracking. When no candidates exist the algorithm reverts to the previous SoI and relaxes the QoS constraints until the candidate set becomes non empty, before it continues. If still no candidate is found backtracking is extended to more levels. Given M servers, the worst-case complexity of the algorithm is $O(M \cdot SoI^2)$, since theoretically backtracking might extend all the way to the first SoI. In practice, however, we observe that for a 1000-server system, 89% of applications were scheduled without any backtracking. For 8% of these, backtracking led to negative D_1 or D_2 for a single SoI and for 3% for multiple SoIs. Additionally, we bound the runtime of the greedy search using a timeout mechanism, after which the best server from the ones already examined is selected in the way previously described (best SC and minimum interference deviation). In our experiments timeouts occurred in less than 0.1% of applications and resulted in a server within 10% of optimal.

3.3 Statistical Framework for Server Selection

The greedy algorithm selects the best server for an application - or a near-optimal server. However, for very large DCs, e.g., 10-100k servers, the overhead from examining the server state in the first step of the search might become high. Additionally, the results depend on the active workloads and do not allow strict guarantees on the server quality under any scenario. We now present an alternative, statistical framework for server selection in very large DCs based on sampling, which has constant runtime and enables such guarantees.

Instead of examining the entire server state we sample a small number of servers. We use cryptographic hash functions to introduce randomness in the server selection. We hash the scores of tolerated interference of each server using variations of SHA-1 [22] as different hash functions (h_j) for each SoI to increase entropy. The input to a h_j is a sensitivity score for an SoI and the output a hashed value of that score. Outputs have the same precision as inputs (14bits). This process is done once, unless the load of a server changes. When a new application arrives, we obtain candidate servers by hashing its sensitivity scores to caused interference for each SoI. For example, the input to h_1 for SoI 1 is a. The output will be a new number, b which corresponds to server ID u. Re-hashing b obtains additional IDs of candidate servers. This produces a random subset of the system's servers. After a number of re-hashes the algorithm ranks the examined servers and selects the best one. Candidates are ranked by *colocation quality*, which is a metric of how suitable a given server is for a new workload. For candidate i, colocation quality is defined as:

$$Q_i = [sign(\sum^{SoIs}(t-c)_i)]|1 - ||t-c||_1| =$$
$$[sign(\sum_{k=1}^{SoIs}(t(k)-c(k))_i)]|1 - \sum_{k=1}^{SoIs}|t(k)-c(k)|_i|$$

t is the original, unhashed sensitivity to tolerated interference for a server and c the original sensitivity to caused interference for the new workload. The $sign$ in Q_i reflects whether a server preserves (positive) or violates QoS (negative). The L1 norm of $(t-c)$ reflects how closely the server follows the application's requirements and is normalized to its maximum value, 10, which happens when for all ten SoIs $t = 100\%$ and $c = 0$. High and positive Q_i values reflect better candidates, as the deviation between t and c is small for all SoIs. Poor candidates have small Q_i or even negative when they violate QoS in one or more SoIs. Quality is normalized to the range $[0, 1]$. For example, for unnormalized qualities in the range

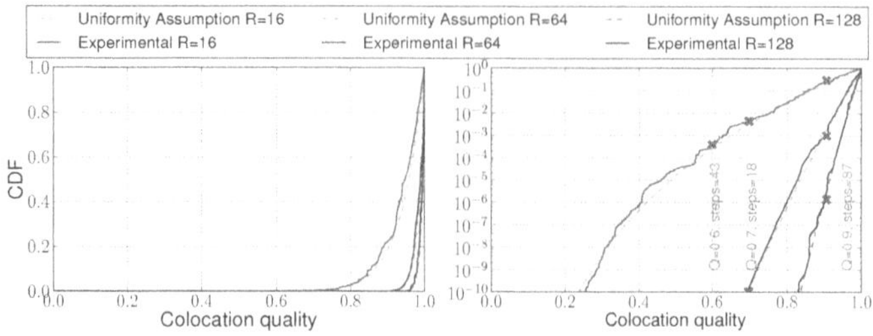

Figure 3: Colocation quality distribution ($F(x) = x^R$, where $R = 16, 64$ and 128). Fig. 3b shows the comparison between the greedy algorithm and the statistical scheme for three colocation candidates of $Q = 0.6, 0.7$ and 0.9.

$[-1.2, 0.8]$ and a candidate with $Q = -1.0$, the normalized quality will be: $\frac{(-1.0+|min|)}{|max|+|min|} = 0.2/2 = 0.1$.

We now make an assumption on the distribution of quality values, which we verify in practice. Because of the way candidate servers are selected and the independence between initial workloads, Q_i's approximate a uniform distribution, for problems with tens of thousands of servers and applications. Figure 3a shows the CDF of measured quality for 16, 64 and 128 candidates and the corresponding uniform distributions ($F(x) = x^R$, where R the number of candidates examined) in a system with 1,000 servers. In all cases, the assumption of uniformity holds in practice with small deviations. When we exceed 128 candidates (1/8 of the cluster) the distribution starts deviating from uniform. We have observed that for even larger systems, e.g., a 5,000-server Windows Azure cluster, uniform distributions extend to larger numbers of candidates (up to 512) as well. The probability of a candidate having quality a is $Pr(a) = a^R$. For example, for 128 candidates there is a 10^{-6} probability that no candidate will have quality over 0.9.

We now compare the statistical scheme with the greedy algorithm (Figure 3b). While the latter finds a server with quality Q after a random number of steps, the statistical scheme provides strong *guarantees* on the number of candidates required for the same quality. For example, for a candidate with $Q = 0.9$, the greedy algorithm needs 87 steps, but cannot provide ad hoc guarantees on the quality of the result, while the statistical scheme guarantees that for the same requirements, with 64 candidates, there is a 10^{-3} chance that no server has $Q \geq 0.9$. The guarantees become stricter as the distribution gets skewed towards 1 (more candidates). Therefore, although the statistical scheme cannot guarantee optimality, it shows that examining a small number of servers provides strict guarantees on the obtained quality and makes scheduling efficiency workload independent.

In our 1,000-server experiments, the overhead of the greedy algorithm is marginal (less than 0.1% in most cases), while the statistical scheme induces 0.5-2% overheads due to the computation required for hashing. Because at this scale the greedy algorithm is faster, all results in this work are obtained using greedy search. However, for problems of larger scale the statistical scheme can be more efficient.

3.4 Discussion

Workload phases: Application classification in Paragon is performed once for each new workload, using the information from its 1 minute profiling. It is possible that some applications will go through various phases that are not captured during profiling. Hence, the schedule will be suboptimal. We detect such workloads by monitoring their performance scores (e.g., IPS) during execution. If the monitored performance deviates significantly and for long periods of time from the performance predicted by the classification engine, the application may have changed behavior. Upon detection we do one

Server Type	GHz/sockets/cores/ L1(KB)/LLC(MB)/mem(GB)						#
Xeon L5609	1.87	2	8	32/32	12	24 DDR3	1
Xeon X5650	2.67	2	12	32/32	12	24 DDR3	2
Xeon X5670	2.93	2	12	32/32	12	48 DDR3	2
Xeon L5640	2.27	2	12	32/32	12	48 DDR3	1
Xeon MP	3.16	4	4	16/16	1	8 DDR2	5
Xeon E5345	2.33	1	4	32/32	8	32 FB-DIMM	8
Xeon E5335	2.00	1	4	32/32	8	16 FB-DIMM	8
Opteron 240	1.80	2	2	64/64	2	4 DDR2	7
Atom 330	1.60	1	2	32/24	1	4 DDR2	5
Atom D510	1.66	1	2	32/24	1	8 DDR2	1

Table 3: Main characteristics of the servers of the local cluster. The total core count is 178 for 40 servers of 10 different SCs.

of the following. First, we can avoid scheduling a large number of other workloads on the same server as the interference information for this workload is likely incorrect. Second, if there is a migration mechanism available (process or VM migration), we can clone the workload, repeat the classification from its current execution point and evaluate whether re-scheduling to another server is beneficial. Note that migration can involve significant overheads if the application operates on significant amounts of state. Section 5 includes an experiment where workload behavior experiences different phases. We assume that there exists an underlying mechanism, such as vShpere [41], that performs the live migration.

Suboptimal scheduling: A second concern apart from application phases is suboptimal scheduling, either due to the greedy selection algorithm which assigns applications to servers in a per-workload fashion, or due to pathological behavior in application arrival patterns. Suboptimal scheduling can be detected exactly as the problem of workload phases and can potentially be resolved by re-scheduling several active applications. Although re-scheduling was not needed for the examined applications, Paragon provides a general methodology to detect such deviations and leverage mechanisms like VM migration to re-schedule the sub-optimally scheduled workloads.

Latency-critical applications and workload dependencies: Finally, Paragon does not explicitly consider latency-critical applications or dependencies between application components, e.g., a multi-tier service, such as search or webmail, where tiers communicate and share data. One differentiation in this case comes from the metrics the scheduler must consider. It is possible that the interference classification should use microbenchmarks that aim to degrade the per-query latency as opposed to the workload's throughput. Another differentiation comes from the possible workload scenarios. One scenario can involve a latency-critical application running as the primary process, e.g., memcached, and the remaining server capacity being allocated to best-effort applications, such as analytics or background processes using Paragon. A different scenario is one where a throughput-bound distributed workload, e.g., MapReduce runs with high priority and the remaining server capacity is used by instances of a latency-critical application. Paragon does not currently enforce fine-grain priorities between application components or user requests, or optimize for shared data placement, which might be beneficial for these scenarios. There is related work on this topic [20] and we will consider how it interacts with Paragon in future work.

4. Methodology

Server systems: We evaluated Paragon on a small local cluster and three major cloud computing services. Our local cluster includes servers of ten different configurations shown in Table 3. We also show how many servers of each type we use. Note that these configurations range from high-end Xeon systems to low-power Atom-based boards. There is a wide range of core counts, clock frequencies and memory capacities and speeds present in the cluster.

For the cloud-based clusters we used exclusive (reserved) server instances, i.e., no other users had access to these servers. We verified that no external scheduling decisions or actions such as auto-scaling or workload migration are performed during the course of the experiments. We used 1,000 servers on Amazon EC2 [13] with 14 different SCs, ranging from small, low-power, dual-core machines to high-end, quad-socket, multi-core servers with hundreds of GBs of memory. All 1,000 machines are private, i.e., there is no interference in the experiments from external workloads. We also conducted experiments with 500 servers on Windows Azure [43] with 8 different SCs and 100 servers on Google Compute Engine [17] with 4 SCs.

Schedulers: We compared Paragon to three alternative schedulers. First, a baseline scheduler that preserves an application's core and memory requirements but ignores both its heterogeneity and interference profiles. In this case, applications are assigned to the *least-loaded* (LL) machine. Second, a *heterogeneity-oblivious* (NH) scheme that uses the interference classification in Paragon to assign applications to servers without visibility in their SCs. Finally, an *interference-oblivious* (NI) scheme that uses the heterogeneity classification in Paragon but has no insight on workload interference. The overheads for the heterogeneity and interference-oblivious schemes are the corresponding classification and server selection overheads.

Workloads: We used 29 single-threaded (ST), 22 multi-threaded (MT) and 350 multi-programmed (MP) workloads and 25 I/O-bound workloads. We use the full SPEC CPU2006 suite and workloads from PARSEC [8] (*blackscholes, bodytrack, facesim, ferret, fluidanimate, raytrace, swaptions, canneal*), SPLASH-2 [45] (*barnes, fft, lu, ocean, radix, water*), BioParallel [21] (*genenet, svm*), Minebench [30] (*semphy, plsa, kmeans*) and SPECjbb (*2, 4 and 8-warehouse instances*). For multiprogrammed workloads, we use 350 mixes of 4 applications, based on the methodology in [36]. The I/O-bound workloads are data mining applications, such as clustering and recommender systems [34], in Hadoop and Matlab running on a single-node. Workload durations range from minutes to hours. For workload scenarios with more than 426 applications we replicated these workloads with equal likelihood (1/4 ST, 1/4 MT, 1/4 MP, 1/4 I/O) and randomized their interleaving.

Workload scenarios: To explore a wide range of behaviors, we used the applications listed above to create multiple workload scenarios. Scenarios vary in the number, type and inter-arrival times of submitted applications. The load is classified based on its relation to available resources; low: the required core count is significantly lower than the available processor resources; high: the required core count approaches the load the system can support but does not surpass it; and oversubscribed: the required core count often exceeds the system's capabilities, i.e., certain machines are oversubscribed.

For the *small-scale* experiments on the local cluster we examine four workload scenarios. First, a *low load* scenario with 178 applications, selected randomly from the pool of workloads, which are submitted with 10 sec inter-arrival times. Second, a *medium load* scenario with 178 applications, randomly selected as before and submitted with inter-arrival times that follow a Gaussian distribution with $\mu = 10$ sec and $\sigma^2 = 1.0$. Third, a *high load* scenario with 178 workloads, each corresponding to a sequence of three applications with varying memory loads. Each application goes through three phases; first medium, then high and again medium memory load. Workloads are submitted with 10 sec intervals. Finally, we examine a scenario, where 178 randomly-chosen applications arrive with 1 sec intervals. Note that the last scenario is an *over-subscribed* one. After a few seconds, there are not enough resources in the system

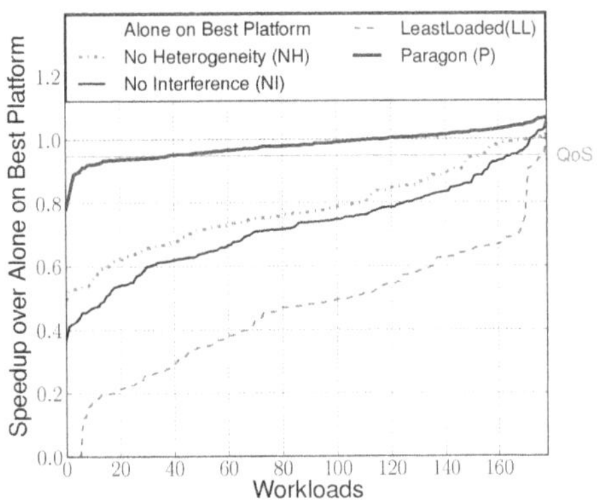

Figure 4: Performance impact from scheduling with Paragon for *medium load*, compared to heterogeneity and/or interference-oblivious schedulers. Application arrival times follow a Gaussian distribution. Applications are ordered from worst to best.

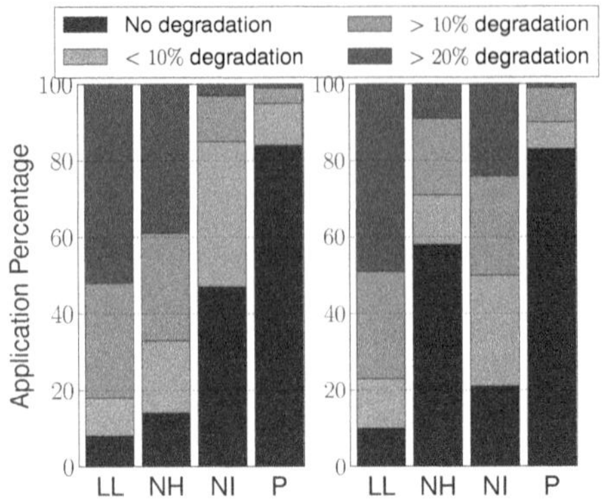

Figure 5: Breakdown of decision quality for heterogeneity (left) and interference (right) for the medium load on the local cluster. Applications are divided based on performance degradation induced by the decisions made by each of the schedulers.

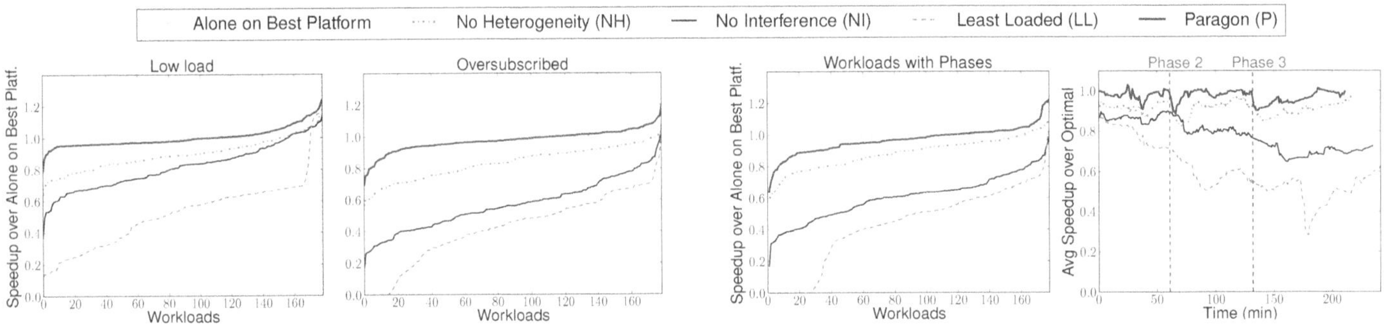

Figure 6: Performance comparison between the four schedulers for three workload scenarios: low, oversubscribed and workloads with phases (Fig. 6(a, b, c)) and performance over time for the scenario where workloads experience phases (Fig. 6d).

to execute all applications concurrently, and subsequent submitted applications are queued.

For the *large-scale* experiments on EC2 we examine three workload scenarios; a *low load* scenario with 2,500 randomly-chosen applications submitted with 1 sec intervals, a *high load* scenario with 5,000 applications submitted with 1 sec intervals and an *oversubscribed scenario* where 7,500 workloads are submitted with 1 sec intervals and an additional 1,000 applications arrive in burst (less than 0.1 sec intervals) after the first 3,750 workloads.

5. Evaluation

5.1 Comparison of Schedulers: Small Scale

QoS guarantees: Figure 4 summarizes the performance results across the 178 workloads on the 40-server cluster for the *medium load* scenario where application arrivals follow a Gaussian distribution. Applications are ordered in the x-axis from worst to best-performing workload. The y-axis shows the performance (execution time) normalized to the performance of an application when it is running in the best platform in isolation (without interference). Each line corresponds to the performance achieved with a different scheduler. Overall, Paragon (P) outperforms the other schedulers, in terms of preserving QoS (95% of optimal performance), and bounding performance degradation when QoS requirements cannot be met. 78% of workloads maintain their QoS with Paragon, while the heterogeneity-oblivious (NH), interference-oblivious (NI) and least-loaded (LL) schedulers provide similar guarantees only for 23%, 19% and 7% of applications respectively. Even more, for the case of the least-loaded scheduler some applications failed to complete due to memory exhaustion on the server. Similarly, while the performance degradation with Paragon is smooth (94% of workloads have less than 10% degradation), the other three schedulers dramatically degrade performance for most applications, in almost linear fashion with the number of workloads. For this scenario, the heterogeneity and interference-oblivious schedulers perform almost identically, although ignoring interference degrades performance slightly more. This is due to workloads that arrive at the peak of the Gaussian distribution, when the cluster's resources are heavily utilized. For the same workloads, Paragon limits performance degradation to less than 10% in most cases. This figure also shows that few workloads experience speedups compared to their execution in isolation. This is a result of cache effects or instruction prefetching between similar co-scheduled workloads. We expect positive interference to be less prevalent for a more diverse application space.

Scheduling decision quality: Figure 5 explains why Paragon achieves better performance. Each bar represents a percentage of applications based on the performance degradation they experience due to the quality of decisions of each of the four schedulers in terms of platform selection (left) and impact from interference. Blue bars reflect good and red bars poor scheduling decisions. In terms of platform decisions, the least-loaded scheduler (LL) maps applications to servers with no heterogeneity considerations, thus it significantly degrades performance for most applications. The heterogeneity-oblivious (NH) scheduler assigns many workloads to suboptimal SCs, although fewer than LL, as it often steers workloads to high-end SCs that tend to tolerate more interference. However, as these servers become saturated, applications that would benefit from them are scheduled suboptimally and NH ends up making poor quality assignments afterwards. On the other hand, the schedulers that account for heterogeneity explicitly (interference-oblivious (NI) and Paragon (P)) have much better decision quality. NI induces no degradation to 47% of workloads and less than 10% for an additional 38%. The reason why NI does

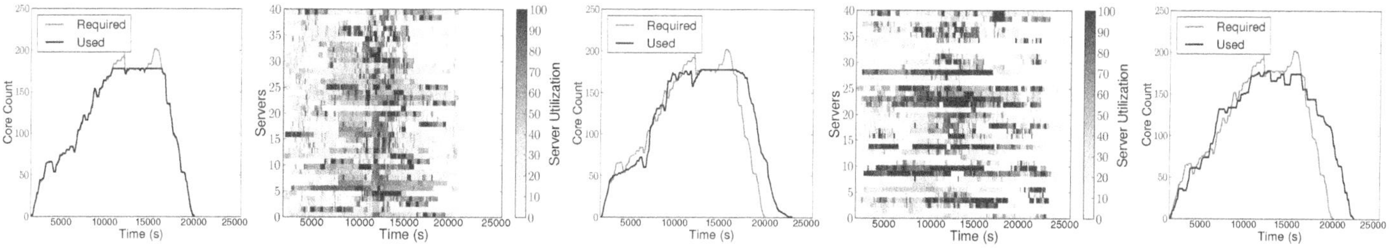

(a) Paragon (b) No Interference (c) Least-Loaded

Figure 7: Comparison of activity and utilization between Paragon, the interference-oblivious and the least-loaded scheduler. Plots show the required and allocated core count at each moment. We also show heat maps of server utilization over time for Paragon and the interference-oblivious scheme.

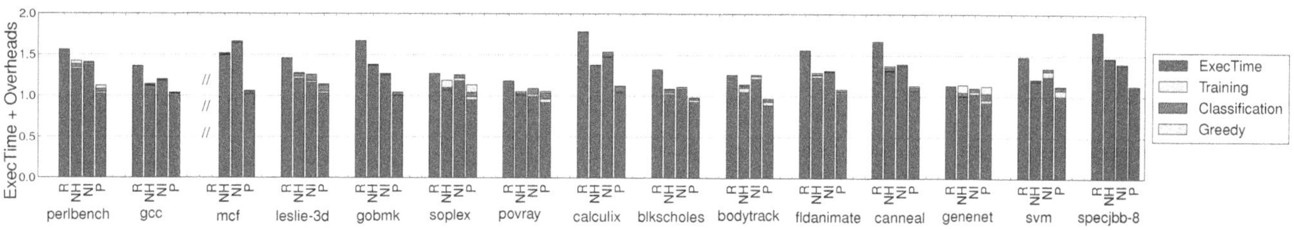

Figure 8: Execution time breakdown for selected single-threaded and multithreaded applications in the medium load scenario.

not behave better in terms of platform selection is that it has no input on interference, therefore it assigns most workloads to the best SCs. As these machines become saturated, destructive interference increases and performance degrades, although, unlike NH, which selects a random SC next, NI selects the SC that is ranked second for a workload. Finally, Paragon outperforms the other schedulers and assigns 84% of applications to their optimal SC.

The right part in Figure 5 shows decision quality with respect to interference. LL behaves the worst for similar reasons, while NI is slightly better than LL since it assigns more applications to high-end SCs, that are more likely to tolerate interference. NH outperforms NI as expected, since NI ignores interference altogether. Paragon assigns 83% of applications to servers that induce no negative interference. Considering both graphs establishes why Paragon significantly outperforms the other schedulers, as it has better decision quality both in terms of heterogeneity and interference.

Other workload scenarios: Figure 6 compares Paragon to the three schedulers for the other three scenarios; low load, oversubscribed, and workloads with phases. For low load, performance degradation is small for all schedulers, although LL degrades performance by 46% on average. Since the cluster can easily accommodate the load of most workloads, classifying incoming applications has a smaller performance impact. Nevertheless, Paragon outperforms the other three schedulers and achieves 99% of optimal performance on average. It also improves resource efficiency during low load by completing the schedule faster. For the oversubscribed scenario, Paragon guarantees QoS for the largest workload fraction, 75% and bounds degradation to less than 10% for 99% of workloads. In this case, accounting for interference is much more critical than accounting for heterogeneity as the system's resources are fully utilized.

Finally, for the case where workloads experience phases, we want to validate two expectations. First, Paragon should outperform the other schedulers, since it accounts for heterogeneity and interference (66% of workloads preserve their QoS). Second, Paragon should adapt to the changes in workload behavior, by detecting deviations from the expected IPS, re-classifying the offending workloads and re-scheduling them if a more suitable server is available. To verify this, in Fig. 6d we show the average performance for each scheduler over time. The points where workloads start changing phases are denoted with vertical lines. First, at phase change, Paragon induces much less degradation than the other schedulers, because applications are assigned to appropriate servers to begin with. Second, Paragon recovers much faster and better from the phase change. Performance rebounces to values close to 1 as the deviating workloads are re-scheduled to appropriate servers, while the other schedulers achieve progressively worse average performance.

Resource allocation: Ideally, the scheduler should closely follow application resource requirements (cores, cache capacity, memory bandwidth, etc.) and provide them with the minimum number of servers. This improves performance (applications execute as fast as possible without interference) and reduces overprovisioning (number of servers used, periods for which they are active). The latter particularly extends to the DC operator, as it reduces both capital and operational expenses. A smaller number of servers needs to be purchased to support a certain load (capital savings). During low load, many servers can be turned off to save energy (operational savings).

Figure 7a shows how Paragon follows the resource requirements for the medium load scenario shown in Figure 4. The green line shows the required core count of active applications based on arrival rate and ideal execution time and the blue line the allocated core count by Paragon. Because the scheduler tracks application behavior in terms of heterogeneity and interference it is able to follow their requirements with minimal deviation (less than 3.5%), excluding periods when the system is oversubscribed and the required cores exceed the total number of cores in the system. In comparison, NI (Figure 7b) and similarly for NH, either overprovisions or oversubscribes servers, resulting in increased execution time; per-application and for the overall scenario. Finally, Figure 7c shows the resource allocation for the least-loaded scheduler. There is significant deviation, since the scheduler ignores both heterogeneity and interference. All cores are used but in a suboptimal manner. Hence, execution times are increased for individual workloads and the overall scenario. Total execution time increases by 28%, but more importantly per-application time degrades, which is harmful both for users and DC operators.

Server utilization: In Figure 7 we also plot heat maps of the server utilization over time for Paragon and the interference-oblivious scheduler. Server utilization is defined as average CPU utilization across the cores of a server. For Paragon, utilization is high in the mid-

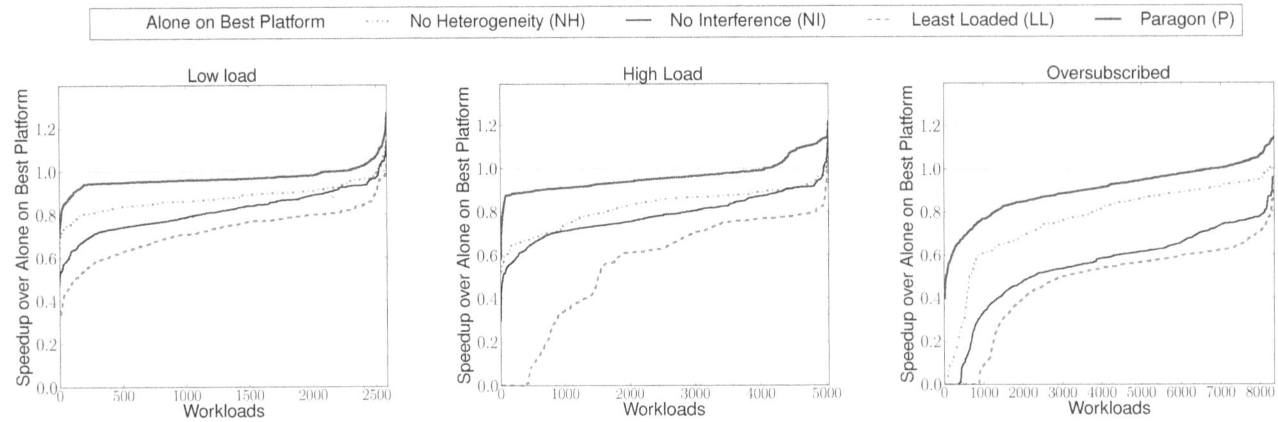

Figure 9: Performance comparison between the four schedulers, for three workload scenarios on 1,000 EC2 servers.

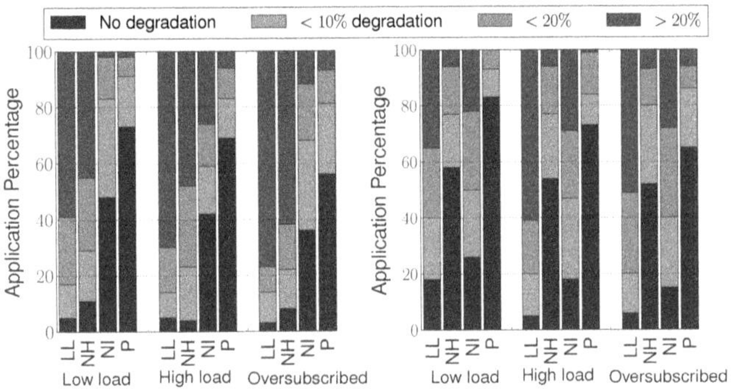

Figure 10: Breakdown of decision quality in terms of heterogeneity (left) and interference for the three EC2 scenarios.

dle of the scenario when many applications are active (47% higher than without colocation), and returns to zero when the scenario finishes. In this case, resource usage improves without performance degradation due to interference. On the other hand, NI keeps server utilization high in some servers and underutilizes others, while violating per-application QoS and extending the scenario's execution time. This is undesirable both for the user who gets lower performance and for the DC operator, since the high utilization in certain servers does not translate to faster execution time, adhering scalability to servicing more workloads.

Scheduling overheads: Finally, we evaluate the total scheduling overheads for the various schemes. These include the overheads of offline training, classification and server selection using the greedy algorithm. Figure 8 shows the execution time breakdown for selected single-threaded and multi-threaded applications. These applications are representative of workloads submitted throughout the execution of the medium load scenario. All bars are normalized to the execution time of the application in isolation in the best SC. Training and classification for heterogeneity and interference are performed in parallel so there is a single bar for each, for every workload. There is no bar for the least-loaded scheduler for *mcf*, since it was one of the benchmarks that did not terminate successfully. Paragon achieves lower execution times for the majority of applications and close to optimal. The overheads of the recommendation system are low; 1.2% for training and 0.09% for classification. The overheads of the greedy algorithm are less than 0.1% in most cases with the exceptions of *soplex* and *genenet* that required extensive backtracking which was handled with a timeout. Overall, Paragon performs accurate classification and efficient scheduling within 1 minute of the application's arrival, which is marginal for most workloads.

5.2 Comparison of Schedulers: Large scale

Performance impact: Figure 9 shows the performance for the three workload scenarios on the 1,000-server EC2 cluster. Similar to the results on the local cluster, the *low load* scenario, in general, does not create significant performance challenges. Nevertheless, Paragon outperforms the other three schemes, it maintains QoS for 91% of workloads and achieves on average 0.96 of the performance of a workload running in isolation in the best SC. When moving to the case of *high load*, the difference between schedulers becomes more obvious. While the heterogeneity and interference-oblivious schemes degrade performance by an average of 22% and 34% and violate QoS for 96% and 97% of workload respectively, Paragon degrades performance only by 4% and *guarantees QoS* for 61% of workloads. The least-loaded scheduler degrades performance by 48% on average, while some applications do not terminate (crash). The differences in performance are larger for workloads submitted when the system is heavily loaded and becomes oversubscribed. Although, we simply queue applications in FIFO order until resources become available, Paragon bounds performance degradation (only 0.6% of workloads degrade more than 20%), since it co-schedules workloads that minimize destructive interference. We plan to incorporate a better admission control protocol in the scheduler in future work.

Finally, for the oversubscribed case, NH, NI and LL dramatically degrade performance for most workloads, while the number of applications that do not terminate successfully increases to 10.4%. Paragon, on the other hand, provides strict QoS guarantees for 52% of workloads, while the other schedulers provide similar guarantees only for 5%, 1% and 0.09% of workloads respectively. Additionally, Paragon limits degradation to less than 10% for an additional 33% of applications and maintains performance degradation moderate (no cliffs in performance such as for NH in applications [1-1000]).

Decision quality: Figure 10 shows a breakdown of the decision quality of the different schedulers for heterogeneity (left) and interference (right) across the three experiments. LL induces more than 20% performance degradation to most applications, both in terms of heterogeneity and interference. NH has low decision quality in terms of platform selection, while NI causes performance degradation by colocating unsuitable applications. The errors increase as we move to scenarios of higher load. Paragon decides optimally for 65% of applications for heterogeneity and 75% for interference on average, significantly higher than the other schedulers. It also constrains decisions that lead to larger than 20% degradation due to interference to less than 8% of workloads. The results are consistent with the findings for the small-scale experiments.

Resource allocation: Figure 11 shows why this deviation exists.

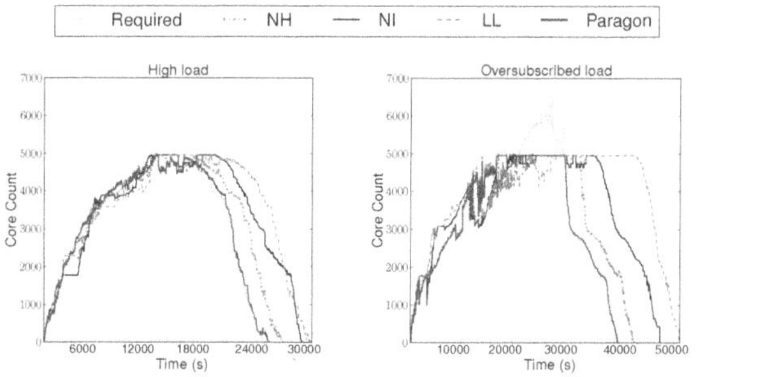

Figure 11: Comparison of required and performed core allocation between Paragon and the other three schedulers for the three workload scenarios on EC2. The total number of cores in the system is 4960.

We omit the graph for low load where deviations are small and show the high and oversubscribed scenarios. The yellow line represents the required core count based on the applications running at a snapshot of the system, while the other four lines show the allocated core count by each of the schedulers. Since Paragon optimizes for increased utilization within QoS constraints, it follows the application requirements closely. It only deviates when the required core count exceeds the resources available in the system. NH has mediocre accuracy, while NI and LL either significantly overprovision the number of allocated cores, or oversubscribe certain servers. There are two important points in these graphs: first, as the load increases the difference in execution time exceeds the optimal one, which Paragon approximates with minimal deviation. Second, for higher loads, the errors in core allocation increase dramatically for the other three schedulers, while for Paragon the average deviation remains constant, excluding the part where the system is oversubscribed.

Windows Azure & Google Compute Engine: We validate our results on a 500-server Azure and a 100-server Compute Engine (GCE) cluster. We run a scenario with 2,500 and 500 workloads respectively. Due to space reasons we omit the performance figures for these experiments, however, in both cases the results are consistent with what was noted for EC2. In Azure, Paragon achieves 94.3% of the performance in isolation and maintains QoS for 61% of workloads, while the other three schedulers provide the same guarantees for 1%, 2% and 0.7% of workloads. Additionally, this was the only time where NI outperformed NH, most likely due to the wide variation between SCs which increases the importance of accounting for heterogeneity. In the GCE cluster, which has only 4 SCs, workloads exhibit mediocre benefits from heterogeneity-aware scheduling (7% over random), while the majority of gains comes from accounting for interference. Overall, Paragon achieves 96.8% of optimal performance and NH 90%. The consistency between experiments, despite the different cluster configurations and underlying hardware, shows the robustness of the analytical methods that drive Paragon.

6. Related Work

We discuss work relevant to Paragon in the areas of DC scheduling, VM management and workload rightsizing. We also present related work from scheduling for heterogeneous multi-core chips.

Datacenter scheduling: Recent work on DC scheduling has highlighted the importance of platform heterogeneity and workload interference. Mars et al. [27, 28] showed that the performance of Google workloads can vary by up to 40% due to heterogeneity even when considering only two SCs and up to 2x due to interference even when considering only two co-located applications. In [27], they present an offline scheme that used combinatorial optimization to select the proper SC for each workload. In [28], they present an offline, two-step method to characterize the sensitivity of workloads to memory pressure and the stress each application exercises to the memory subsystem. Govindan et al. [18] also present a scheme to quantify the effects of cache interference between consolidated workloads, although they require access to physical memory addresses. Finally, Nathuji et al. [32] present a control-based resource allocation scheme that mitigates the effects of cache, memory and hardware prefetching interference of co-scheduled workloads. In Paragon, we extend the concepts of heterogeneity and interference-aware DC scheduling in several ways. We provide an online, highly-accurate and low-overhead methodology that classifies applications for both heterogeneity and interference across multiple resources. We also show that our classification engine allows for efficient, online scheduling without using computationally intensive techniques which require exhaustive search between colocation candidates.

VM management: VM management systems such as vSphere [41], XenServer [47] or the VM platforms on EC2 [13] and Windows Azure [43] can schedule diverse workloads submitted by a large number of users on the available servers. In general, these platforms account for application resource requirements which they learn over time by monitoring workload execution. Paragon can complement such systems by making efficient scheduling decisions based on heterogeneity and interference and detecting when an application should be considered for migration (re-scheduling).

Resource management and rightsizing: There has been significant work on resource allocation in virtualized and non-virtualized large-scale DCs, including Mesos [20], Rightscale [35], resource containers [2], Dejavu [39] and the work by Chase et al. [10]. Mesos performs resource allocation between distributed computing frameworks like Hadoop or Spark [20]. Rightscale automatically scales out 3-tier applications to react to changes in the load in Amazon's cloud service [35]. Dejavu serves a similar goal by identifying a few workload classes and based on them, reuses previous resource allocations to minimize reallocation overheads [39]. Zhu et al. [48] present a resource management scheme for virtualized DCs that preserves SLAs and Gmach et al. [16] a resource allocation scheme for DC applications that relies on the ability to predict their behavior a priori. In general, Paragon is complementary to resource allocation and rightsizing systems. Once such a system determines the amount of resources needed by an application (e.g., number of servers, memory capacity, etc.), Paragon can classify and schedule it on the proper hardware platform in a way that minimizes interference. Currently, Paragon focuses on online scheduling of previously unknown workloads. We will consider how to integrate Paragon with a rightsizing system for scheduling long running, 3-tier services in future work.

Scheduling for heterogeneous multi-core chips: Finally, scheduling in heterogeneous CMPs shares some concepts and challenges with scheduling in heterogeneous DCs, therefore some of the ideas in Paragon can be applied in heterogeneous CMP scheduling as well. Fedorova et al. [14] discuss OS level scheduling for heterogeneous multi-cores as having the following three objectives: optimal performance, core assignment balance and response time fairness. Shelepov et al. [37] present a scheduler that exhibits some of these features and is simple and scalable, while Craeynest et al. [11] use performance statistics to estimate which workload-to-core mapping is likely to provide the best performance. DC scheduling also has similar requirements as applications should observe their QoS, resource allocation should follow application requirements closely and fairness between co-scheduled workloads should be preserved. Given the increasing number of cores per chip and co-scheduled tasks, techniques such as those used for the classification engine of Paragon can be applicable when deciding how to schedule applications to heterogeneous cores as well.

7. Conclusions

We have presented Paragon, a scalable scheduler for DCs that is heterogeneity and interference-aware. Paragon is derived from validated analytical methods, such as collaborative filtering and it quickly and accurately classifies incoming applications with respect to platform heterogeneity and workload interference. Classification uses minimal information about the new application and relies mostly on information from previously scheduled workloads. The output of classification is used by a greedy scheduler to assign workloads to servers in a manner that maximizes application performance and optimizes resource usage. We have evaluated Paragon with both small and large-scale systems. Even for very demanding scenarios, where heterogeneity and interference-agnostic schedulers degrade performance for up to 99.9% of workloads, Paragon maintains QoS guarantees for 52% of the applications and bounds degradation to less than 10% for an additional 33% out of 8500 applications on a 1,000-server cluster. Paragon preserves QoS guarantees while improving server utilization, hence it benefits both the DC operator, who achieves perfect resource use and the user, who gets the best performance. In future work we will consider how to couple Paragon with VM management and rightsizing systems for large-scale datacenters.

Acknowledgements

We sincerely thank our shepherd, Byung-Gon Chun for his useful comments and feedback. We also thank John Ousterhout, Mendel Rosenblum, Daniel Sanchez, Jacob Leverich, David Lo, and the anonymous reviewers for their feedback on earlier versions of this manuscript. This work was partially supported by a Google directed research grant on energy proportional computing. Christina Delimitrou was supported by a Stanford Graduate Fellowship.

References

[1] A. Alameldeen, D. Wood. "IPC Considered Harmful for Multiprocessor Workloads". *In IEEE Micro, July/Aug. 2006.*

[2] G. Banga, P. Druschel, J. Mogul. "Resource containers: a new facility for resource management in server systems". *In Proc. of OSDI, 1999.*

[3] L. Barroso. "Warehouse-Scale Computing: Entering the Teenage Decade". *ISCA Keynote, SJ, June 2011.*

[4] L. A. Barroso, U. Holzle."The Datacenter as a Computer". *Synthesis Series on Computer Architecture, May 2009.*

[5] L. A. Barroso and U. Holzle."The Case for Energy- Proportional Computing". *Computer, 40(12):33–37, 2007.*

[6] R. M. Bell. Y. Koren, C. Volinsky."The BellKor 2008 Solution to the Netflix Prize". Technical report, AT&T Labs, Oct 2007.

[7] L. Bottou. "Large-Scale Machine Learning with Stochastic Gradient Descent". *In Proc. of COMPSTAT 2010.*

[8] C. Bienia, et al. "The PARSEC benchmark suite: Characterization and architectural implications". *In Proc. of PACT, 2008.*

[9] B. Calder, et al. "Windows Azure Storage: A Highly Available Cloud Storage Service with Strong Consistency". *In Proc. of SOSP, 2011.*

[10] J. Chase, D. Anderson, et al. "Managing Energy and Server Resources in Hosting Centers". *In SIGOPS, 35(5):103–116, 2001.*

[11] K. Craeynest, et al. "Scheduling Heterogeneous Multi-Cores through Performance Impact Estimation (PIE)". *In Proc. of ISCA, 2012.*

[12] J. Dean and S. Ghemawat. "MapReduce: Simplified Data Processing on Large Clusters". *In Proc. of OSDI, SF, 2004.*

[13] Amazon Elastic Compute Cloud.`http://aws.amazon.com/ec2/`

[14] A. Fedorova, D. Vengerov, D. Doucette. "Operating System on Heterogeneous Core Systems". *In Proc. of OSHMA, 2007.*

[15] S. Ghemawat, H. Gobioff, S.-T Leung . "The Google File System". *In Proc. of SOSP, NY, 2003.*

[16] D. Gmach, J. Rolia, et al. "Workload Analysis and Demand Prediction of Enterprise Data Center Applications". *In Proc. of IISWC, 2007.*

[17] Google Compute Engine. `cloud.google.com/compute`

[18] S. Govindan, et al. "Cuanta: Quantifying effects of shared on-chip resource interference for consolidated virtual machines. *In Proc. of SOCC, 2011.*

[19] J.R. Hamilton. "Cost of Power in Large-Scale Data Centers". `http://perspectives.mvdirona.com`

[20] B. Hindman, et al. "Mesos: A Platform for Fine-Grained Resource Sharing in the Data Center". *In Proc. of NSDI, 2011.*

[21] A. Jaleel, M. Mattina, B. Jacob. "Last Level Cache (LLC) Performance of Data Mining Workloads On a CMP - A Case Study of Parallel Bioinformatics Workloads". *In Proc. of* 12th *HPCA, TX, 2006.*

[22] J. Katz and Y. Lindell. "Introduction to Modern Cryptography". *Chapman & Hall/CRC Press, 2007.*

[23] C. Kozyrakis, A. Kansal, et al. "Server Engineering Insights for Large-Scale Online Services". *In IEEE Micro, vol.30, no.4, July 2010.*

[24] K. Kiwiel. "Convergence and efficiency of subgradient methods for quasiconvex minimization". *Math. Programming, Springer, 2001.*

[25] J. Leverich, C. Kozyrakis. "On the Energy (In)Efficiency of Hadoop Clusters". *In Proc. of HotPower, October 2009.*

[26] J. Lin, A. Kolcz. "Large-Scale Machine Learning at Twitter". *In Proc. of SIGMOD, Scottsdale, 2012.*

[27] J. Mars, L. Tang, R. Hundt. "Heterogeneity in "Homogeneous" Warehouse-Scale Computers: A Performance Opportunity". In IEEE CAL, July-December 2011.

[28] J. Mars, L. Tang, et al. "Bubble-Up: Increasing Utilization in Modern Warehouse Scale Computers via Sensible Co-locations". *In Proc. of MICRO-44, Brazil, December 2011*

[29] D. Meisner, C. Sadler, L. A. Barroso, et al. "Power Management of On-line Data-Intensive Services". *In Proc. of ISCA, SJ, June 2011.*

[30] R. Narayanan, B. Ozisikyilmaz, et al. "MineBench: A Bench- mark Suite for DataMining Workloads". *In Proc. of IISWC, 2006.*

[31] R. Nathuji, C. Isci, E. Gorbatov. "Exploiting platform heterogeneity for power efficient data centers". *In Proc. of ICAC, 2007.*

[32] R. Nathuji, et al. "Q-Clouds: Managing Performance Interference Effects for QoS-Aware Clouds". *In Proc. of EuroSys, 2010.*

[33] Rackspace. `http://www.rackspace.com/`

[34] A. Rajaraman and J. Ullman. "Textbook on Mining of Massive Datasets", 2011.

[35] Amazon EC2: Rightscale. `https://aws.amazon.com/solution-providers/isv/rightscale`

[36] D. Sanchez, C. Kozyrakis. "Vantage: Scalable and Efficient Fine-Grain Cache Partitioning". *In Proc. of ISCA, SJ, 2011.*

[37] D. Shelepov, J. Saez, et al. "HASS: A Scheduler for Heterogeneous Multicore Systems". *In OSP, vol. 43, 2009.*

[38] J. Sun, Y. Xie, H. Zhang, C. Faloutsos. "Less is More: Compact Matrix Decomposition for Large Sparse Graphs". *In Proc. of SDM, 2007.*

[39] N. Vasic, et al. "DejaVu: Accelerating Resource Allocation in Virtualized Environments". *In Proc. of ASPLOS, London, 2012.*

[40] vMotion™. `http://www.vmware.com/products/vmotion`

[41] VMWare vSphere. `http://www.vmware.com/products/vsphere/`

[42] T. Wenisch, et al. "SimFlex: Statistical Sampling of Computer System Simulation". *In IEEE MICRO, vol. 26, no. 4, Jul-Aug 2006.*

[43] Windows Azure. `http://www.windowsazure.com/`

[44] I. Witten, E. Frank et al. "Data Mining: Practical Machine Learning Tools and Techniques". M. Kaufmann, 3rd Edition.

[45] S. Woo, M. Ohara, et al. "The SPLASH-2 Programs: Characterization and Methodological Considerations". *In Proc. of the 22nd ISCA, 1995.*

[46] Xen Hypervisor 4.0. `http://www.xen.org/`

[47] XenServer. `http://www.citrix.com/products/xenserver/overview.html`

[48] X. Zhu, et al. "1000 Islands: An Integrated Approach to Resource Management for Vurtualized Datacenters". *In Cluster Computing Journal, 2009.*

ReQoS: Reactive Static/Dynamic Compilation for QoS in Warehouse Scale Computers

Lingjia Tang Jason Mars
University of California, San Diego
{lingjia, mars}@cs.ucsd.edu

Wei Wang Tanima Dey Mary Lou Soffa
University of Virginia
{wwang,td8h,soffa}@virginia.edu

Abstract

As multicore processors with expanding core counts continue to dominate the server market, the overall utilization of the class of datacenters known as *warehouse scale computers* (WSCs) depends heavily on colocation of multiple workloads on each server to take advantage of the computational power provided by modern processors. However, many of the applications running in WSCs, such as websearch, are user-facing and have quality of service (QoS) requirements. When multiple applications are co-located on a multicore machine, contention for shared memory resources threatens application QoS as severe cross-core performance interference may occur. WSC operators are left with two options: either disregard QoS to maximize WSC utilization, or disallow the co-location of high-priority user-facing applications with other applications, resulting in low machine utilization and millions of dollars wasted.

This paper presents **ReQoS**, a static/dynamic compilation approach that enables low-priority applications to adaptively manipulate their own contentiousness to ensure the QoS of high-priority co-runners. ReQoS is composed of a profile guided compilation technique that identifies and inserts markers in contentious code regions in low-priority applications, and a lightweight runtime that monitors the QoS of high-priority applications and reactively reduces the pressure low-priority applications generate to the memory subsystem when cross-core interference is detected. In this work, we show that ReQoS can accurately diagnose contention and significantly reduce performance interference to ensure application QoS. Applying ReQoS to SPEC2006 and SmashBench workloads on real multicore machines, we are able to improve machine utilization by more than 70% in many cases, and more than 50% on average, while enforcing a 90% QoS threshold. We are also able to improve the energy efficiency of modern multicore machines by 47% on average over a policy of disallowing co-locations.

Categories and Subject Descriptors B.3.3 [*Hardware*]: Memory Structures—Performance Analysis and Design Aids; D.3.4 [*Programming Languages*]: Processors—code generation, run-time environments, compilers, optimization; D.4.8 [*Operating Systems*]: Performance—measurements, monitors

General Terms Performance, Algorithms, Measurement

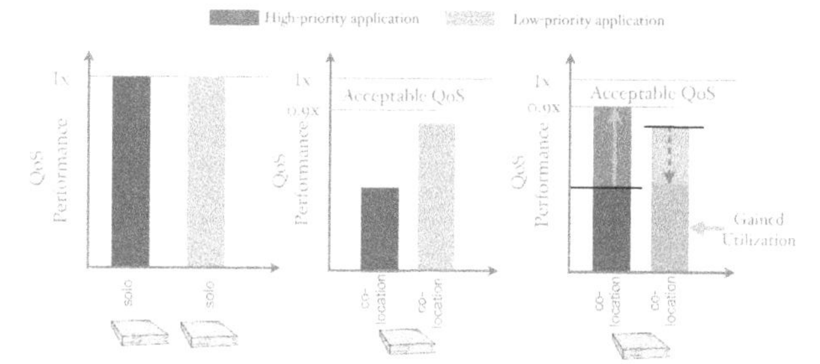

(a) Disallow Colocation. Low Utilization, Peak QoS (2 servers)
(b) Allow Colocation. High Utilization but significant QoS degradation (1 server)
(c) ReQoS Enable "Safe" Colocation, High Utilization, Acceptable QoS (1 server)

Figure 1. Goal of **ReQoS**

Keywords datacenter; warehouse scale computers; quality of service; contention; cross-core interference; compiler; dynamic techniques; online adaptation; runtime systems; multicore

1. Introduction

Web-service companies such as Google, Yahoo, Amazon, and Microsoft host large-scale data intensive applications that require nothing less than a *Warehouse Scale Computer* (WSC) [3] to run. These WSCs house hundreds to thousands of machines to provide the computing resources needed to serve millions of users. To limit the cost of ownership of WSCs, these machines are composed of commodity components that are cheap and easily replaceable, often 2 to 4 server grade processors per machine, and 4 to 12 cores per chip. The cores of a single chip share memory subsystem resources such as caches and bandwidth to the main memory on the machine. When multiple applications are running simultaneously on a multicore machine, resources sharing and contention among cores can result in a significant amount of performance interference. This interference leads to a significant problem for the service level requirements of user facing web-service applications [19, 33].

User facing *latency-sensitive* applications must provide a predictable and sometimes strictly defined *quality of service* (QoS). To avoid the constant unpredictable threat that shared resource contention poses to application QoS, datacenter operators and system designers typically disallow co-locations of latency-sensitive jobs with other jobs. This unnecessary *over-provisioning* of compute resources reduces the overall utilization of WSCs, recently reported to be below 30% on average [22], and results in an unnecessarily high cost and a large environmental footprint for a given set of web-service workloads.

Improving the utilization of multicore processors in light of QoS constraints has been identified as an important goal by prior work. However, the problem is far from solved in real-world deployments. A number of novel hardware solutions have been proposed [12, 13, 27, 28, 30, 36] to address contention and performance fairness. However, these solutions are not readily deployable and high cost may hinder their adoption in production. Contention aware scheduling has also been proposed in prior work [2, 4, 7, 11, 15, 23, 34, 37]. However, these techniques assume that a balanced set of contentious and non-contentious jobs are available to maximize utilization and can only select co-run schedules of these jobs. When contentious workloads must co-run, one approach that has largely been unexplored in prior work is to dynamically *change* the contentious nature of applications.

The goal of this work is to manage contention directly by manipulating the contentiousness of co-running applications to ensure high quality of service and high utilization, *irrespective* to the co-run schedule. This goal is summarized in Figure 1. As opposed to disallowing the co-location of high-priority and low-priority applications to guarantee QoS, as shown in 1(a), or simply allowing co-locations and suffering performance interference, as shown in 1(b), we aim to enable "safe" co-locations between potentially contentious low-priority applications with high-priority applications, shown in 1(c), by providing a software mechanism to manipulate contentiousness directly.

Recently, compilation has been proposed to provide a mechanism to indeed modify the contention characteristics of applications to attenuate the interference caused to co-running applications [32] by applying transformations to stagger the memory request rate of contentious code regions. This approach effectively trades the performance of low-priority applications for the QoS of high-priority applications to facilitate co-location and has shown to be particularly useful within the ecosystem of applications in WSCs as the workloads and infrastructure in a WSC are typically owned by the same web-service company, such as Google, Microsoft, Yahoo and Apple. However, there are three critical limitations of this approach, all of which stem from the fact that the code transformations are decided before runtime and applied statically:

1. The performance sacrificed to ensure the "niceness" of the low-priority application is overly conservative as it persists regardless of whether it is in fact co-running with a high-priority application that is indeed sensitive to contention.
2. Specific QoS goals cannot be targeted and the self-adaptation of the low-priority application to ensure a QoS goal is not possible. With a static approach, the resulting QoS of the high priority application when co-located is variable and unpredictable.
3. A significant tuning effort is required for each low-priority application as it is based entirely on the particular contentious characteristics of the application.

To address these three challenges and best accomplish the goal outlined in Figure 1, a *reactive* dynamic approach is needed to effectively detect contention at runtime and adaptively adjust the contentious nature of an application based on the amount of contention that is actually occurring. Such an approach addresses each of the three limitations noted. In designing this reactive approach, we aim to ensure its deployability in WSCs by providing a lightweight software solution that does not incur high performance overheads and is unobtrusive in that it does not require changes to the current production system software stack in deployment. In this paper, we present **ReQoS**, a static/dynamic compilation approach for adaptively manipulating application contentiousness online to increase WSC utilization while enforcing application QoS.

ReQoS is composed of two co-designed components: the **RQ-Compiler** and **RQ-Runtime**. First, our RQ-Compiler uses a profiling approach similar to that proposed in prior work [32] to identify the code regions in low-priority applications that aggressively demand memory resources and may cause resource contention. Then, as opposed to statically pessimizing the contentious region, our RQ-Compiler applies a code marking technique on those regions. The marking technique has been co-designed with the RQ-Runtime to enable the flexible and reactive manipulation of the code regions' contentiousness. Dynamically, the RQ-Runtime uses a novel software-only technique to detect when contention has caused QoS degradations and adaptively throttles down the memory request rate by injecting short naps in the contentious code regions of the low-priority application. The degree of nap insertion applied to the contentious code regions of the low-priority application is dynamically determined based on the severity of observed QoS degradation of the high-priority application, resulting in more drastic responses to higher levels of contention. As contention lessens dynamically, naps are reduced, increasing the execution rate of the low-priority application to maximize machine utilization. Keep in mind that when the application executes code not identified as contentious, these naps do not occur. In performing this execution rate manipulation, cores that would otherwise remain idle are utilized.

To the best of our knowledge, this paper is the first to enable the direct modification of the contentiousness of low-priority applications dynamically to ensure the QoS of high priority applications. Specifically, this paper makes the following contributions:

- **The RQ-Compiler** - We present a compilation approach that enables the adaptive manipulation of contentiousness of the low-priority application. The RQ-Compiler identifies the contentious code regions of an application and inserts hooks in these regions that are used to invoke runtime manipulation.
- **The RQ-Runtime** - We present a runtime system that continuously monitors the QoS of high-priority applications, detects when contention is occurring dynamically, and directs the manipulation of the contentiousness of low-priority applications based on an adaptation policy.
- **`Simple` and `Targeted` Adaptation Policies** - We present two adaptation policies, `simple`, which provides a "knob" that controls whether the online response to contention emphasizes higher utilization or higher QoS, and for when a specific QoS threshold is available, `targeted`, that dynamically self tunes to the specified QoS target while maximizing utilization.
- We present a thorough evaluation of ReQoS and each of its adaptation policies including a phase level analysis demonstrating how ReQoS adapts during execution to ensure application QoS.

Using ReQoS on SPEC2006 and SmashBench workloads on a Quad Core Intel Nehalem machine, we are able to improve utilization by more than 70% in many cases, and more than 50% on average, while enforcing a 90% QoS threshold. We are also able to improve the energy efficiency of modern multicore machines by 47% on average over a policy of disallowing co-locations. Comparing to prior work [32], ReQoS improves utilization by 51% on average while providing similar QoS improvement.

The rest of the paper is organized as follows: Section 2 presents the overview of ReQoS. Section 3 presents our compilation technique to instrument markers to identified contentious code regions to invoke dynamic adaptation. Section 4 presents the runtime and policies for dynamic contention detection and reaction. Section 5 presents the evaluation. Section 6 presents prior work and Section 7 concludes.

2. ReQoS Overview

ReQoS provides a software mechanism that automatically and adaptively regulates the pressure that a low-priority *batch* appli-

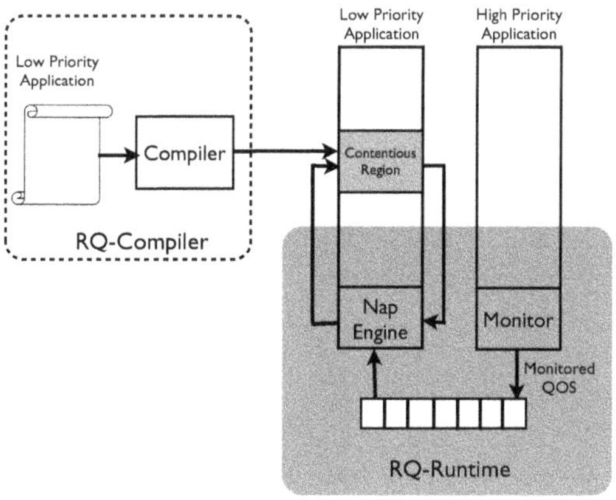

Figure 2. ReQoS Overview

cation applies to the shared memory subsystem resources to ensure the QoS of high-priority *latency-sensitive* applications. As shown in Figure 2, ReQoS consists of two components: The RQ-Compiler, and RQ-Runtime.

2.1 RQ-Compiler

The RQ-Compiler is a static profile-driven compiler approach that uses a performance counter based profiling analysis to identify contentious code regions and insert markers on those regions to steer the runtime adaptation. This profiling allows us to pinpoint the potentially problematic code regions for accurate dynamic contention detection with a small runtime overhead. As shown in Figure 2, the inserted markers trigger the RQ-Runtime, via the *Nap Engine*, when contentious code regions are executed. These triggers call upon the runtime to directly manipulate the rate of memory accesses generated by the low-priority application through the Nap Engine interface. The binaries produced by the RQ-Compiler can also be run without the RQ-Runtime. In this case, the inserted markers are benign, and the application runs as normal. The overhead of having these markers present in the binary is minimal. A full evaluation of the overhead is presented in Section 5. The RQ-Compiler and the profiling analysis used to identify contentious code regions are described in detail in Section 3.

2.2 RQ-Runtime

The RQ-Runtime is responsible for monitoring the QoS of high-priority applications, detecting when a low-priority application interferes with the performance of the high-priority application, and dynamically deciding the degree of memory access rate reduction to apply to alleviate the performance interference. As shown in Figure 2, a lightweight dynamic runtime that monitors application QoS is attached to the high-priority application. This runtime periodically reports an application's QoS through a shared memory buffer. The Nap Engine that is attached to the application binary of the low-priority application reads the most recent QoS reports from this buffer to steer the online contention response. The RQ-Runtime and the adaptive policies are described in detail in Section 4.

Figure 2 also illustrates how ReQoS is used in the context of a WSC. All low-priority applications in the WSC are compiled with a flag denoting that it is a low-priority application. The applications are then compatible for execution with ReQoS enabled. When these applications are scheduled to co-run with a high-priority application, QoS monitoring is turned on, and the Nap Engine enacts the adaptation policy.

2.3 ReQoS in the OS

ReQoS can be integrated into the OS by implementing the RQ-Runtime as a module that is compiled into the OS and allowing the application markers to trigger the runtime via system calls for ReQoS. However, while contention aware scheduling approaches can naturally be realized as OS techniques, the dynamic manipulation of the contentiousness of specific code regions can best be realized using user-mode runtime systems as the cost to invoke the runtime in user-mode is an order of magnitude more efficient than suffering an OS context switch for each runtime invocation. These context switches can become overbearing especially when considering the frequency of invocations during detection and the fine grain feedback control mechanisms discussed in Section 4.

3. Compiling for ReQoS

In this section we present RQ-Compile, our static compilation to enable dynamic contention mitigation and QoS improvement at runtime. The RQ-Compile process is illustrated in Figure 3. To compile a low-priority application, we first identify its contentious code regions using a profiler that scores the contentious nature of code regions as they execute. We then insert markers in those regions that periodically invoke the RQ-Runtime. Because markers target the problematic regions, the runtime engine is only triggered when the contentious regions are executing, minimizing the runtime overhead.

3.1 Profiling to Identify Contentious Code

Our profiling analysis provides dynamic scoring of sequences of executed code for its contentious nature using a prediction model based on prior work [32]. The model uses the memory resource usage of a code region to predict the severity of the performance interference the code may cause when co-running with other applications. The more aggressively a code region consumes the shared memory resources such as caches and memory bandwidth when executing, the more likely it is to be contentious for the resource when co-running. To collect the memory resource usage information of a code region, the profiler samples performance monitoring units (PMUs) during runtime. Using the prediction model based on the performance counter sampling, the profiler dynamically calculates the contention score of a code region, identifies contentious code regions that aggressively demand shared memory resources and thus most likely to cause contention and performance degradation when co-running with other applications.

The prediction model takes several important shared resources including shared caches, memory bandwidth and prefetchers into consideration. Our general linear model is as follows:

$$C = a_1 \times LLC\_usage + b_1 \times BW\_usage + c_1 \times Pref\_usage, \quad (1)$$

where C is the contention score indicating the amount of the potential degradation a code region may cause to its co-runners. LLC is the shared last level cache; BW is memory bandwidth and $Pref$ is the prefetchers.

After identifying the appropriate performance counters, we apply multiple regression to determine the appropriate model coefficients for our experimental platform (Section 5.1) using **SmashBench** [19], a suite of contentious kernels developed within Google to span a spectrum of contentious memory access patterns and working set sizes. The established model is as follows:

$$\begin{aligned} C = {} & 1.663 \times (L2LinesIn/ns - L3LinesIn/ns) \\ & + 8.890 \times L3LinesIn/ns + 0.044, \end{aligned} \quad (2)$$

where $L2LinesIn$ is the number of cache lines brought in for the last level private cache (L2) and $L3LinesIn$ for the shared last level cache (L3). The difference between the two measures the

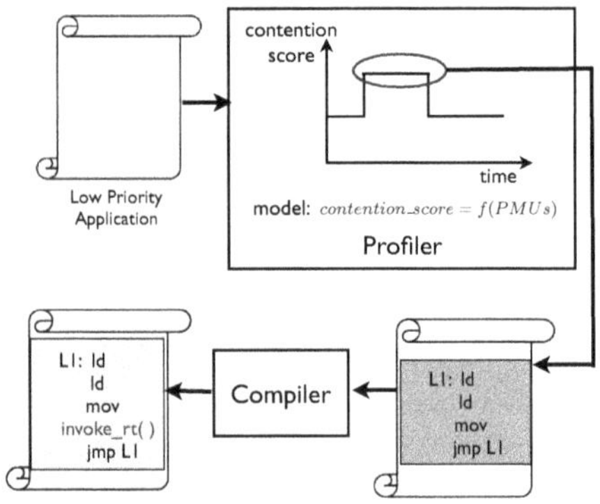

Figure 3. ReQoS Compilation

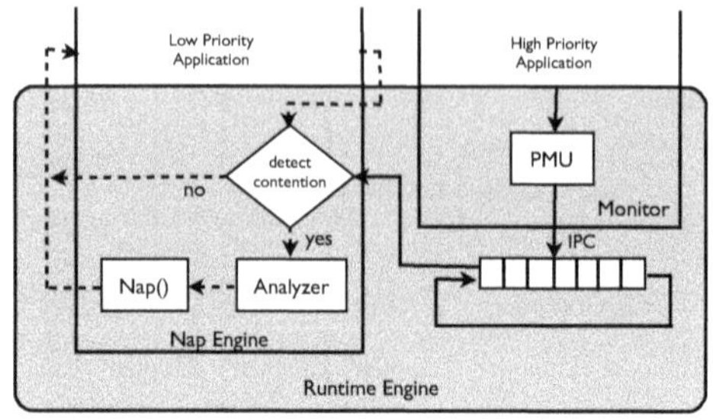

Figure 4. ReQoS Runtime Architecture

amount of data coming from the shared cache instead of the main memory, including the traffic generated by L2 prefetchers. It is used as a proxy to measure the shared cache usage. $L3LinesIn$ is used to measure the memory bandwidth consumption. The coefficients of each term in Equation 2 demonstrate the relative impact of bandwidth contention and LLC contention, implying that memory bandwidth contention may have a more dominating impact on performance degradation on this platform.

3.2 Compiling Contentious Code

Our profiler identifies the contentious code regions based on the PMU model and applies instrumentation to these regions. The instrumentation facilitates the dynamic manipulation and adaptation of a code region's contentiousness. To identify these contentious regions, during profiling, performance counters (L2 and L3 cache lines in rate) are sampled every 1 `ms` and the contention score is calculated using Equation 2. To correlate the contention score to the corresponding static code regions, the number of instructions retired in each 1 `ms` execution interval is also sampled and recorded. After the profiling run, a PIN [18] tool is used to replay the execution. Based on the recorded instruction profile, our PIN tool identifies the hottest basic blocks that are executed during each 1 `ms` execution interval and assigns the corresponding contention score to these basic blocks. The PIN tool then selects the basic blocks with a high contention score.

After these highly contentious basic blocks are identified, we instrument markers, *invoke_rt( )*, to the contentious code, shown in Figure 3. At runtime, these markers invoke the RQ-Runtime to dynamically decide the throttling policy. To minimize the potential overhead of frequent calls to the runtime, we have implemented a number of optimizations. Most notably, we use a self-tuning global checker that allows the call to the runtime to be executed only after sufficient execution iterations of the same basic block. This is especially helpful when a large number of markers are inserted in the critical path of execution. Instead of executing the function call every time, an increment and compare is executed in the average case.

4. The ReQoS Runtime

ReQoS combines both static compilation and dynamic adaptation. The profiling and static compilation enable the dynamic engine to manipulate the execution of the low-priority application. They also assist the diagnosis of contention and trigger the runtime only when problematic code regions are executing. As neither the particular co-locations of high-priority applications and low-priority applications nor how sensitive the high-priority application may be to resource contention are known statically, it is desirable to have a runtime approach that can adjust the amount of throttling dynamically. In this section, we present RQ-Runtime, our runtime engine that detects the QoS degradation of high-priority applications due to resource contention online, and adaptively manipulates the contentiousness of the low-priority applications to mitigate the degradation.

4.1 Runtime

Figure 4 illustrates the design for RQ-Runtime. The runtime engine is composed of two main components: *Monitor* and *Nap Engine*. The Nap Engine is linked into the low-priority application and the Monitor is either linked into, or attached to the PID of, the high-priority application. The Nap Engine and the Monitor communicate through a shared memory buffer.

[Monitor] The Monitor is responsible for monitoring the QoS of high-priority applications. The monitor is capable of using various performance metrics. In our implementation we use instruction-per-cycle (IPC) as a proxy for QoS. The IPC is often used in production datacenters as a QoS proxy because it is readily available using hardware performance counters and can be sampled with little overhead. For example, Google Wide Profiling (GWP) is currently deployed in Google's fleet to collect IPC and other counters for performance monitoring and debugging [26]. The Monitor uses a *periodic probing* technique, leveraging a timer interrupt to sample the hardware performance counters every 1 `ms`, and storing the recent sequence of IPC samples in a circular buffer in the shared memory. As we show in Section 5, this period probing technique incurs a minimal overhead (often less than 1%).

[Nap Engine] Based on the monitored QoS, the Nap Engine detects resource contention and QoS degradation, and accordingly reacts by deciding the appropriate execution rate reduction for the low-priority application. The Nap Engine is only invoked by the instrumented markers when the low-priority application is executing the contentious regions. Instead of invoking the Nap Engine every time an instrumented contentious basic block is executing, a timer based on the time stamp register, read using the RDTSC instruction [1], is used in the instrumentation to only yield control from the low-priority application to the Nap Engine periodically (2 `ms` in our experiments). To further reduce the overhead of timer checking, we also use this timer to adapt the global checker mentioned in Section 3 by approximating the amount of runtime invocations to skip before reading the timestamp counter again. This approximation requires a simple calculation based on the time past since the prior invocations and is adaptively adjusted upon every timestamp read. Due in part to these optimizations, the overhead of invoking the Nap Engine is low, never exceeding 5%. The evaluation is presented in Section 5.

When invoked, the Nap Engine's main tasks are to firstly detect contention and QoS degradation based on the information provided by the Monitor, and secondly if contention is detected, analyzes and decides how to appropriately throttle down the low-priority application to mitigate the degradation. The Nap Engine controls the execution rate of a low-priority application by putting the execution of a contentious code region to epochal intermittent short "nap" mode.

Naps reduce the memory request rate and execution rate of the low-priority application and the pressure it puts on the shared memory subsystem. This in turn prioritizes the memory requests of the co-running high-priority application, and as a result, the QoS degradation it suffers due to the resource contention is greatly reduced or eliminated. The nap is implemented using nanosleep( ). Two main parameters that affect the behavior and the effectiveness of napping include the *frequency* and the *duration* of naps. The Nap Engine controls these parameters and decides whether and when a nap should occur (essentially how long the low-priority application should execute at a normal rate) and how long of a nap it should take to effectively improve the QoS of the co-running high-priority application. Because the Nap Engine can directly control these two parameters, it has a fairly accurate and predictable rate reduction control. Flexible policies and heuristics for contention detection and reaction can be implemented in RQ-Runtime, which are further discussed in the next section.

4.2 Detection and Reaction

In this section, we present two adaptation policies used in RQ-Runtime to detect resource contention and QoS degradation, and to reactively control the execution rate of the low-priority application to mitigate contention if necessary. It is challenging to design a software approach to detecting contention as it occurs. As we mentioned earlier, this is mostly due to the fact that contention in various hardware components such as shared caches and memory controllers is not exposed to the software. We design probabilistic empirical approaches to tackling the challenge of dynamic contention detection based on the online monitoring and feedback control. Once contention and QoS degradation are detected, the Nap Engine is also tasked to decide the appropriate rate reduction to apply to the low-priority application to reduce the QoS degradation.

In this work, we design two heuristics for the Nap Engine: `simple` and `targeted`. The `simple` heuristic directly relies on QoS monitoring information of the high-priority application and is designed to provide users with a flexible, tunable "knob" to manage the tradeoffs between QoS and utilization. For example, the heuristic can be configured to prioritize QoS and conservatively reduce utilization or prioritize utilization and risk the QoS. However, the `simple` heuristic does not strive for a strict QoS goal, such as improving the QoS of high-priority application to above 90% of its normal QoS when running alone. The `targeted` heuristic on the other hand, is designed to accommodate a pre-specified QoS target. `Targeted` makes the detection based on closely monitoring the impact of throttling of the low-priority application on the QoS and uses an analytical model to adjust the appropriate nap duration adaptively.

Algorithm 1: Nap_Engine (Heuristic 1: Simple)

Input : *threshold_low, threshold_high, nap_ratio_low, nap_ratio_mid, nap_ratio_high*

ipc = latest IPC sample from the shared IPC buffer;
if *(ipc < threshold_low)* **then**
  | *nap_duration* ← *nap_ratio_low* × *exec_duration* ;
else if *(ipc < threshold_high)* **then**
  | *nap_duration* ← *nap_ratio_mid* × *exec_duration* ;
else
  | *nap_duration* ← *nap_ratio_high* × *exec_duration* ;
end
nap(nap_duration);

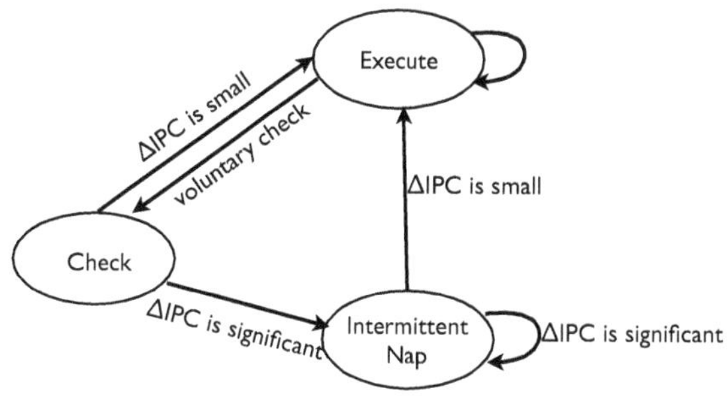

Figure 5. DFA for `Targeted` Heuristic

[Heuristic 1: Simple] The basic idea of `simple` is to detect and react purely based on the monitored QoS of the high-priority application. In our runtime implementation, we use instruction-per-cycle (IPC) as a proxy for QoS and `simple` adjusts the nap duration based on the dynamically monitored IPC. The details of our algorithm are described in Algorithm 1. When the contentious code region of a low-priority application (LP) is executing, the Nap Engine is invoked periodically (every `execution duration`). The Nap Engine then reads the latest IPC sample of the high-priority application (HP). Two thresholds (`threshold_low`, `threshold_high`) are used to bucket the monitored IPC into low, medium and high. The nap duration is decided based on which bucket the IPC is in. The lower the IPC, the longer the nap duration. In addition to IPC, application specific performance metrics such as query latency can also be monitored and bucketed. The rationale of this heuristic is that although many factors other than contention may cause QoS degradation (such as load fluctuations), we will conservatively throttle down the low-priority application once the QoS degradation of the high-priority application is observed. The parameter configurations (IPC thresholds and nap ratio) decide how QoS-biased (`conservative`) or utilization-biased (`optimistic`) the `simple` heuristic is. The sensitivity of those parameters is discussed in Section 5.

[Heuristic 2: Targeted] The primary design goal of `targeted` is to adaptively adjust the nap duration to improve the QoS to a user-specified goal (such as a minimum QoS of normalized 90% of a specific QoS target). The basic idea of `targeted` is to detect and react based on measuring how the QoS of high-priority application is affected by naps of low-priority applications. Figure 5 illustrates the logic of `targeted`. There are three basic states for a low-priority application (LP), which the Nap Engine tracks and controls. Periodically, the nap engine is invoked to analyze the QoS samples of the high-priority application (HP) and the analysis result triggers potential state transitions.

- `Intermittent nap state`. In this state, naps are inserted to throttle LP's execution rate. The QoS of the HP is sampled both when the LP is napping and when the LP wakes up from the nap and resumes executing. The difference between the two samples, *delta_IPC* is used to adjust the next nap duration. The bigger the difference, the more significant the impact of contention is, and the longer the nap duration should be. The detailed model of adapting the nap duration is shown later this section. When the IPC delta is smaller than the pre-specified QoS degradation threshold, it indicates that napping does not have a significant impact, and LP transition to the `execution state`.
- `Execution state`. In `execution state`, LP executes at the full rate with no naps inserted. However, LP does not stay in `execution state` indefinitely. A countdown is set to trigger

the transition to voluntary `check state` after a pre-specified execution period.

- `Check state`. The purpose of the `check state` is to periodically detect if contention occurs after a period of execution. The detection is similar to `intermittent nap state`. LP is put to nap for a short interval and then is run for a short interval. The difference of the IPC samples of HP during these two intervals is used to decide if contention is occurring. If so, LP transitions to the `intermittent nap state`; if not, the `execution state`.

Algorithm 2: Nap_Engine (Heuristic 2: Targeted)

```
Input : QoS_goal, conservative_factor, execute_period
if (LP_state == execution_state && execute_countdown > 0)
then
    execute_countdown − − ;
    return;          /* no napping, running ahead */ ;
else if (LP_state == execution_state &&
execute_countdown = 0) then
    nap(check_interval) ;
    ipc_nap ← read the average IPC of HP when LP is in the last napping
    duration from the shared IPC buffer ;
    LP_state ← check_state;  /* voluntarily nap for a short
    period to test if contention is back by checking
    delta_IPC */ ;
else if (LP_state == nap_state || LP_state == check_state) then
    ipc_exec ← read the average IPC of HP when LP is the execution
    interval from the shared IPC buffer ;
    delta_ipc ← (ipc_nap − ipc_exec)/ipc_nap ;
    if (delta_ipc < conservative_factor * (1 − QoS_goal)) then
        execute_countdown ← execute_period ;
        LP_state ← execution_state ;
        return; /* significant contention is not detected nap
        does not seem to have a big enough effect on IPC */
        ;
    else
        nap_duration ←
        calculate_duration(delta_ipc, QoS_goal) ;
        nap(nap_duration) ;
        ipc_nap ← read the average IPC of HP when LP is the last
        napping duration from the shared IPC buffer ;
        LP_state ← nap_state ;
    end
end
```

The algorithm for `targeted` heuristics is described in Algorithm 2. A parameter `conservative factor` is used to guard how close the monitored QoS degradation is to the pre-specified threshold (*delta_IPC*, for example) before the napping is used to throttle down the LP. Also in Algorithm 2, we estimate the appropriate nap duration based on the QoS goal (the degradation threshold QoS_{thresh}, such as 90% of the optimal QoS), the given $exec\_duration$ (how long LP executes between consecutive nap engine invocations) and the observed difference between IPC of HP when LP is napping (IPC_{nap}) and when LP is executing (IPC_{exec}). To estimate the appropriate nap duration we solve the following equation:

$$QoS_{thresh} = \frac{IPC_{nap} \times nap\_duration + IPC_{exec} \times exec\_duration}{IPC_{nap} \times (nap\_duration + exec\_duration)}, \quad (3)$$

where $exec\_duration$ is the duration of the execution interval between inserted intermittent naps.

5. Evaluation

In this section, we first valuate the effectiveness of our two heuristics in mitigating the QoS degradation due to resource contention and in improving machine utilization. We also take a deeper look into the dynamic behavior of ReQoS and its reaction to contentious phases throughout execution. We then compare ReQoS against the technique presented in prior work. Lastly, we evaluate the overhead and power efficiency of ReQoS.

Configurations	thresh_low	thresh_high	nap_ratio
util_biased	0.5	1.0	{0, 1, 2}
balanced	0.8	1.5	{0, 1, 2}
QoS_biased	0.5	1.0	{1, 2, 3}

Table 1. Three configurations for `simple` heuristic

5.1 Setup and Methodology

Our evaluation is conducted on a 2.67GHZ Quad Core *Intel Nehalem* processor with private L1/L2 caches, an 8MB last level cache (L3) shared by four cores and 4GB main memory. This platform runs Linux 2.6.29.6 and a customized GCC 4.4.6.

The workloads used in our evaluation include the `sledge` application from the **SmashBench** contentious kernel suite [19, 20] (developed at Google) and applications from SPEC CPU2006. All benchmarks are compiled using GCC at the O2 level. All SPEC applications are run using **ref** inputs. Each experiment is conducted three times to calculate the average performance. Benchmark runs are stable with a performance variance of 1% or less between runs. As shown in prior work [19, 32, 33], key large-scale Google workloads including web search, bigtable and ad-servlets degrade significantly due to memory resource contention such as shared caches and bandwidth (5%-40%), similar to the amount of degradation SPEC CPU2006 (especially several SPEC memory intensive benchmarks) suffer on this architecture. In addition, prior work [32] shows that throttling down low-priority applications using inserted naps at millisecond granularity has a similar effect of improving the performance of both SPEC and Google applications.

5.2 Effectiveness of ReQoS: QoS and Utilization

In this section, we evaluate the effectiveness of ReQoS using both `simple` and `targeted` heuristics and discuss the tradeoffs between the two heuristics.

5.2.1 Heuristic 1: Simple

As mentioned in Section 4.2, our `simple` heuristic provides "knobs" that control whether the emphasis of ReQoS is biased towards QoS or machine utilization. Table 1 presents the three configurations we use in our evaluation. These include `util_bias`, `balanced`, and `QoS_bias`, representing an emphasis on higher utilization, a balance between utilization and QoS, and higher QoS respectively. `Threshold_low`, `threshold_high` and `nap_ration` are parameters for Algorithm 1 to control the binning of monitored instructions-per-cycle (IPC) of the high-priority application and the nap duration of the low-priority application. In general the longer the nap ratio, the more throttling down the heuristic applies to the low-priority applications, and the more biased the heuristic is towards the QoS of high-priority applications.

Figures 6, 7 and 8 present the QoS of the high-priority applications when we apply ReQoS to their co-running low-priority applications with three configurations of `simple` heuristic. In each of these figures, the x-axis shows the high-priority applications and the y-axis shows their QoS when each of them is co-running with a low-priority application, normalized to its QoS performance when running alone on the machine. For each high-priority application, a cluster of four bars demonstrates four settings for the co-running low-priority application. The first bar shows the QoS of the high-priority application when it is co-running with the original low-priority application without the ReQoS. The rest of the three bars show its QoS when we apply ReQoS with three con-

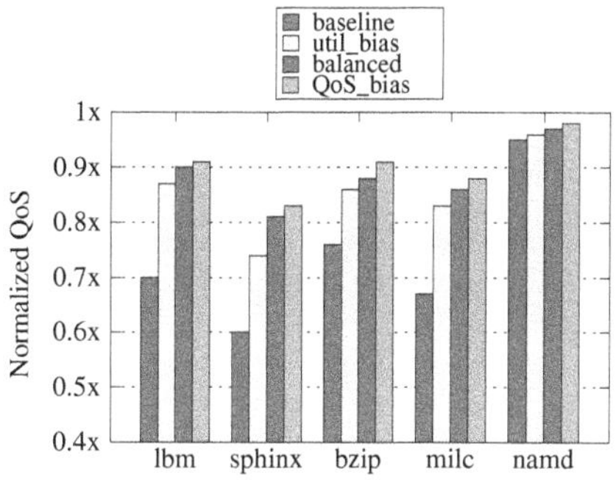

Figure 6. Normalized QoS of each benchmark co-running with `sledge` (`RQ_simple`)

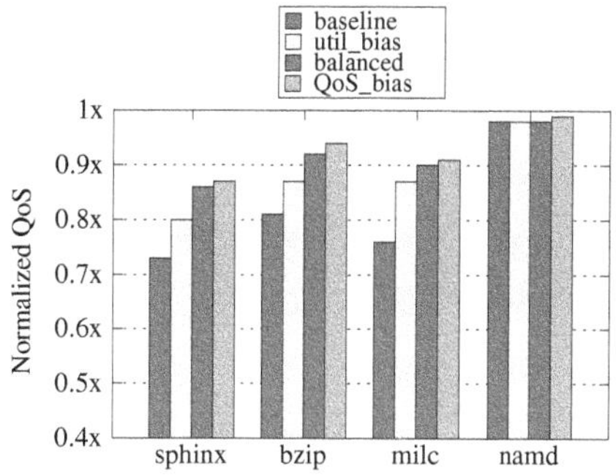

Figure 7. Normalized QoS of each benchmark co-running with `lbm` (`RQ_simple`).

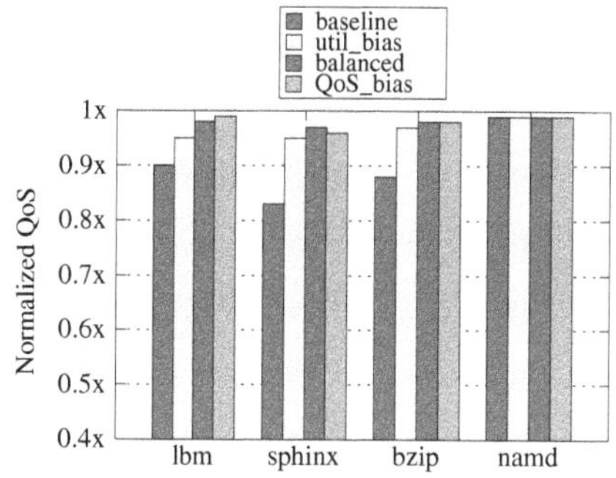

Figure 8. Normalized QoS of each benchmark co-running with `milc` (`RQ_simple`)

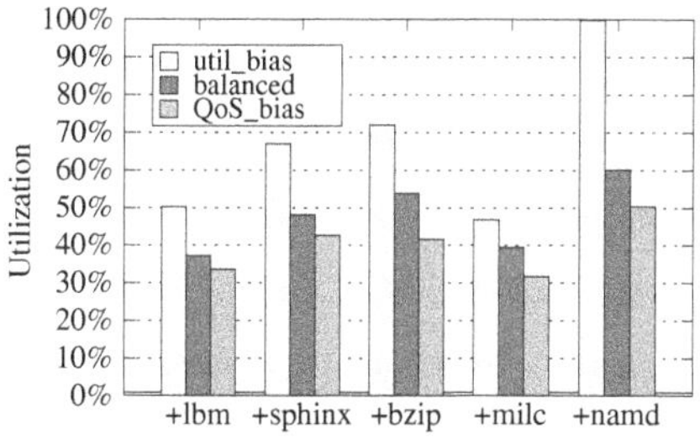

Figure 9. Utilization of `sledge` (`RQ_simple`)

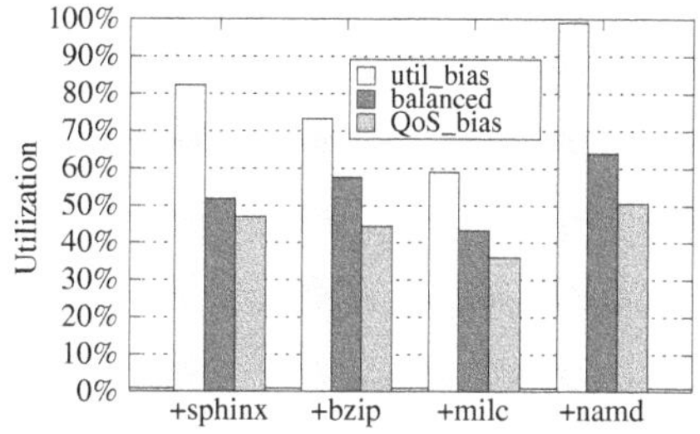

Figure 10. Utilization of `lbm` with each configuration. (`RQ_simple`)

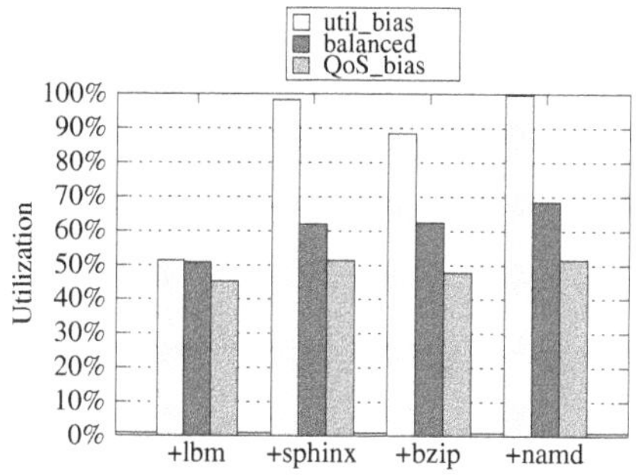

Figure 11. Utilization of `milc` with each configuration (`RQ_simple`)

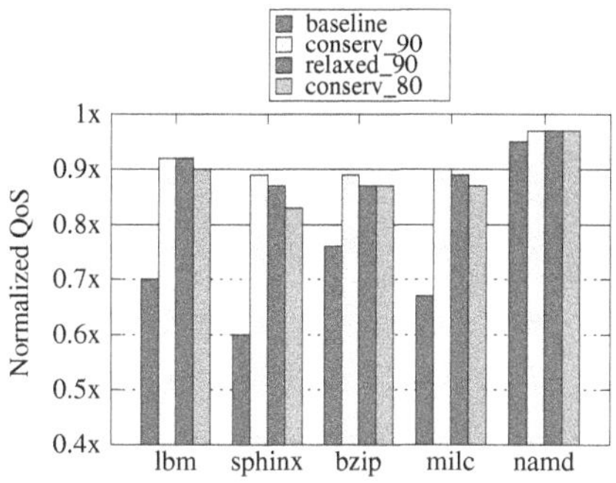

Figure 12. Normalized QoS of each benchmark co-running with `sledge` (`RQ_targeted`)

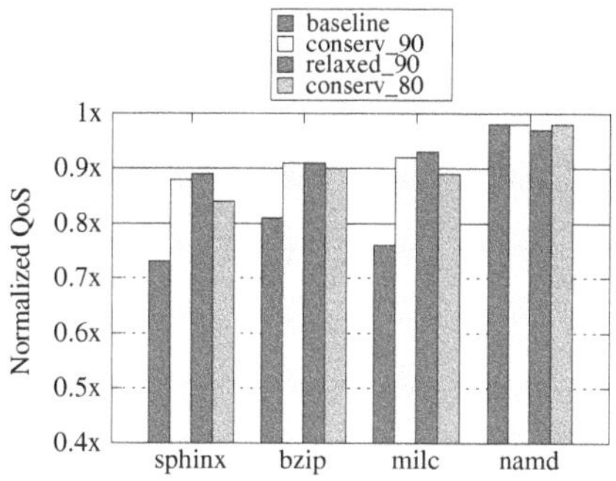

Figure 13. Normalized QoS of each benchmark co-running with `lbm` (`RQ_targeted`)

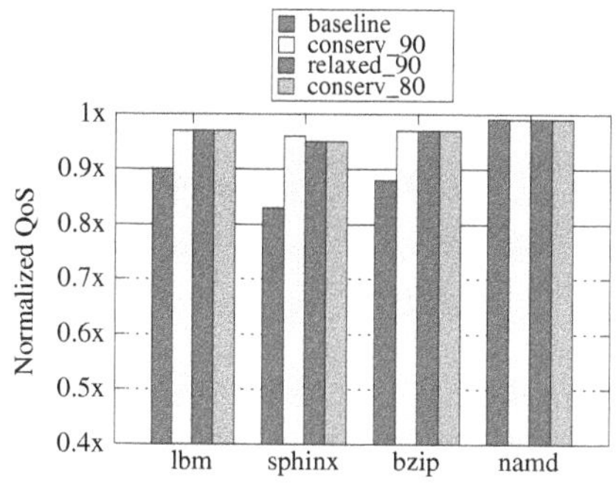

Figure 14. Normazlied QoS of each benchmark co-running with `milc` (`RQ_targeted`)

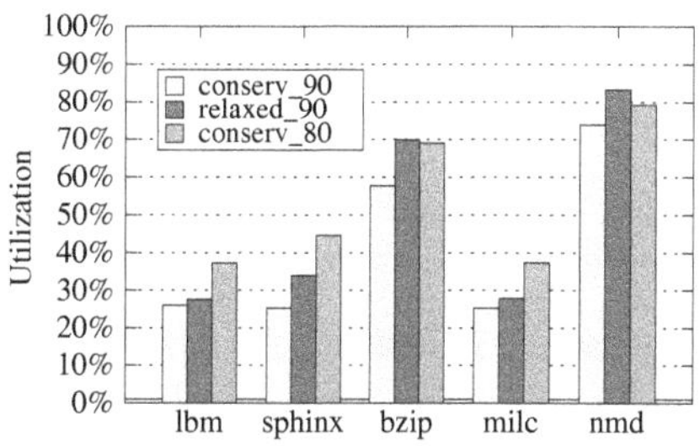

Figure 15. Utilization of `sledge` with each configuration (`RQ_targeted`)

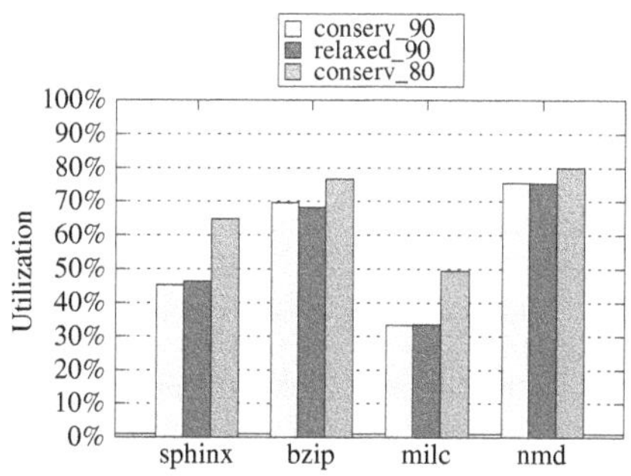

Figure 16. Utilization of `lbm` with each configuration (`RQ_targeted`)

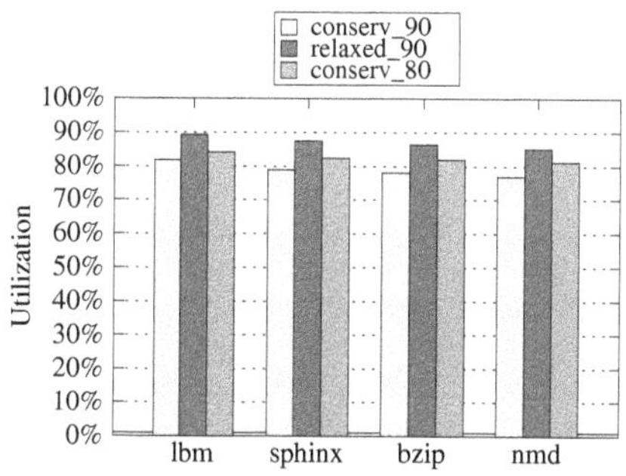

Figure 17. Utilization of `milc` with each configuration (`RQ_targeted`)

Configurations	ex_period(ms)	conserv_factor	QoS_goal
conservative_90	6	0.4	90%
relaxed_90	12	1.0	90%
conservative_80	9	0.4	80%

Table 2. Three configurations of `targeted` heuristic

figurations of the `simple` heuristic to its co-running low-priority application. Each of three low-priority applications, `sledge`, `lbm`, and `milc` is used in Figures 6, 7, 8 respectively. `Sledge` is a highly contentious kernel that contains two large arrays copying data back and forth between arrays with this sledgehammer pattern. `Lbm` and `milc` are top contentious benchmarks in the SPEC 2006 suite. The five high-priority applications in each graph present a wide range of sensitivity to contention in SPEC suite.

Figures 9, 10 and 11 show the corresponding utilization gained for each low-priority application. We measure the execution rate of the low-priority application normalized to its speed when running alone on that architecture to indicate the utilization of the computing resources used by the application. For example, 50% utilization for `lbm` indicates that `lbm` is now running at half of its speed when it is running alone.

From Figure 6-11, we observe that when applying ReQoS with our `simple` heuristic, the QoS of each high-priority application is significantly improved (by up to 26%) compared to simply allowing the co-location of both applications without ReQoS (first bars of each cluster in Figures 6, 7 and 8). Without ReQoS, such colocation of low- and high-priority applications would be disallowed due to the potentially significant QoS degradation. Compared to this commonly adopted approach of disallowing co-location, we gain a significant amount of utilization when allowing co-location with ReQoS, often more than 50%. Various configurations in `simple` heuristic also provide a wide range of options for balancing QoS and utilization. In this experiment, the utilization-biased configuration achieves significantly higher utilization than other two configurations, and the QoS of each high-priority application only slightly degrades. This demonstrates that the `simple` heuristic can be effective in improving QoS while gaining a significant amount of machine utilization.

5.2.2 Heuristic 2: Targeted

Our more sophisticated `targeted` heuristic enables a more precise enforcement to achieve the desired QoS requirements. This heuristic has effectively three "knobs," one for the specific QoS threshold to enforce, and the other two for how conservatively (strictly) this QoS threshold must be enforced (parameters `QoS goal`, `conservative factor` and `execution period` in Algorithm 2). With more conservative parameters, a larger amount utilization may be sacrificed; however, the application QoS is less likely to drop below the specified threshold. We explore this tradeoff in our evaluation.

Figures 12 – 17 are similar to those presented above. For this set of graphs we use our `targeted` heuristic with the three configurations presented in Table 2. The configurations `conserv_90`, `relaxed_90`, and `conserv_80` represent a conservative setting at a 90% QoS threshold, a relaxed setting at 90%, and a conservate setting at an 80% QoS threshold, respectively. Figures 12, 13 and 14 show the effect of using our `targeted` heuristic on the QoS of the high-priority applications. Note that two horizontal lines are drawn in each graph denoting the 90% and 80% QoS thresholds. Figures 15, 16 and 17 show the corresponding processor utilization gained for each configuration.

As shown in these figures, the `targeted` heuristic is quite effective in bringing the QoS of the high-priority applications to the desired QoS threshold, beating it in many cases and coming very close in the worst cases with our conservative settings. When using a relaxed setting, we observe a bump in the utilization, and our QoS target is often met. The decision as to how conservative or relaxed the QoS target is depends on the objectives and discretion of the application service provider and whether higher utilization is desired or stricter QoS polices are specified.

[Simple vs. Targeted] Our `simple` and `targeted` heuristics offer two options to application service providers: one providing the flexibility and the tradeoffs between utilization and QoS, the other allowing specifying a QoS target. When configured appropriately, the `simple` heuristic can perform quite well. However, it may require a significant amount of parameter tuning to search for the appropriate configuration if certain QoS level is required. The `targeted` does not require such parameter tweaking because it is self-tuning and feedback directed. More comparison between `simple` and `targeted` is presented in the following section.

5.3 Phase Level Behavior

We further evaluate the phase-level effectiveness of RQ-Runtime including our two heuristics in improving the QoS of high-priority applications and machine utilization.

[Improving QoS] Figure 18 presents the IPC of `sphinx` when it is running with the original `sledge`, comparing to its IPC when running with `sledge` on RQ-Runtime using the `simple` heuristic. The IPC samples are normalized to `sphinx`'s IPC profile when running alone to demonstrate the IPC degradation due to contention. In this experiment, `simple` heuristic is using `balance` configuration and `sphinx` is using `ref` input. To calculate the normalized IPC, we collect the IPC profiles of `sphinx` when it is running alone (solo) and running with `sledge`. IPC is sampled every 1 `ms` and all profiles of the entire execution of `sphinx` are down sampled to 1000 data points. The normalized IPC at point i is calculated as $\frac{IPC_{co-run\_i}}{IPC_{solo\_i}}$. Therefore, the closer the normalized IPC to 1, the less the degradation. In Figure 18, the line denoting the original `sledge` shows phase-level changes of the IPC degradation due to contention. For example, around samples 100 to 200, and 300 to 400, there are noticeable phases of degradation increase. The degradation is also less significant during the later half of the execution. Figure 18 clearly demonstrates the IPC improvement achieved by RQ-Runtime throughout the entire execution of `sphinx`. Instead of around 60%-70% of the normalized IPC when running with the original `sledge`, ReQoS improves the normalized IPC to above 80% during most of the execution.

Similar to Figure 18, Figure 19 presents `sphinx`'s normalized IPC when it is running with `sledge` using `targeted` heuristics (`conservative_90` configuration), also compared with its normalized IPC when running with the original `sledge`. Despite the distinctive phases of varying levels of degradation when running with the original `sledge` as discussed previously (for example, samples 100-200 and 300-400), `targeted` heuristic consistently achieves around 90% IPC for `sphinx` during the entire execution. This is different from the `simple` heuristic shown in Figure 18 where the improved normalized IPC fluctuates between 70% and 90%. This comparison highlights the difference between `simple` and `targeted` heuristics. While `simple` is effective in improving the QoS, `targeted` heuristic is effective in adapting, achieving and maintaining a stable QoS level as specified.

[Improving Utilization] Similar to Figures 18 and 19, Figures 20 and 21 present the normalized IPC of `sphinx` when it is running with the original `milc`, as well as `milc` with ReQoS. In Figures 20 and 21, the RQ-Runtime for `milc` uses the `simple` heuristic and `targeted` heuristic respectively. The normalized IPC of `sphinx` when running with the original `milc` demonstrates the phases with varying levels of contention and degradation. For example, during samples 600 to 800, the degradation is significantly

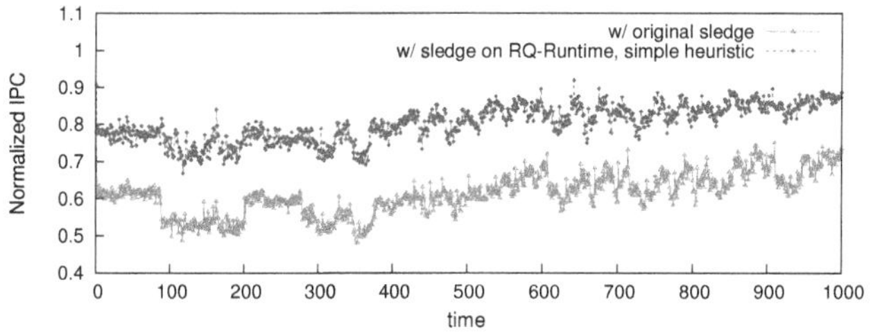

Figure 18. `Sphinx` normalized IPC with original `sledge` and with `simple sledge`

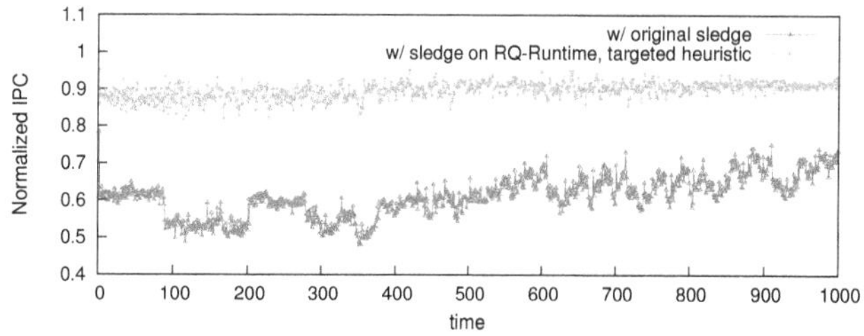

Figure 19. `Sphinx` normalized IPC with original `sledge` and with `targeted sledge`. Compared to `simple`, `targeted` heuristic is effective in achieving and maintaining a more stable QoS level as specified

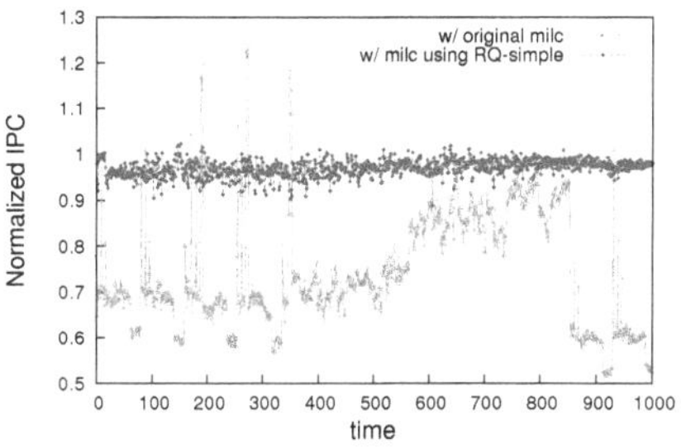

Figure 20. `Sphinx` normalized IPC with original `milc` and with `simple milc`

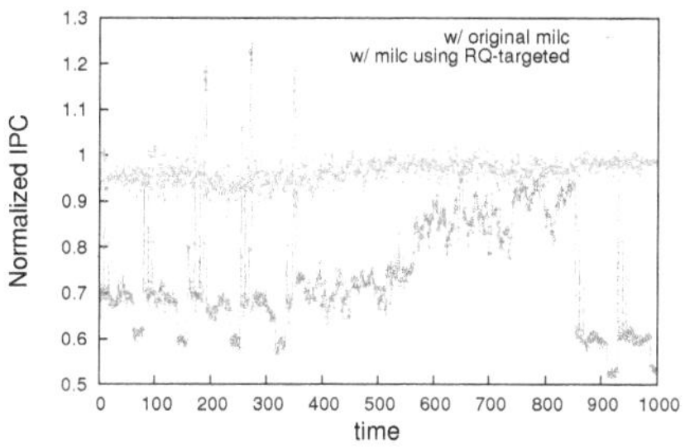

Figure 21. `Sphinx` normalized IPC with original `milc` and with `targeted milc`

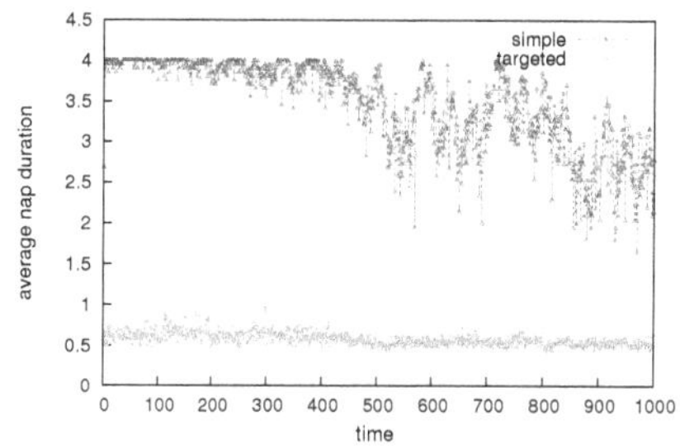

Figure 22. Average nap duration for `milc` with `simple` vs. `milc` with `targeted`. `Targeted` adaptively determines the necessary amount of napping, attaining higher utilization.

smaller (normalized IPC close to 1) than the rest of the execution. A few samples of normalized IPC are higher than 1 due to aliasing of downsampling. In this set of experiments, `targeted` heuristic is configured as `conservative_90`, meaning RQ-Runtime aims at less than 10% of the QoS degradation for `sphinx`. `Simple` heuristic is configured with `QoS_biased` configuration to achieve the similar QoS goal as `targeted`. Figures 18 and 19 demonstrate similar effectiveness of both heuristics. The QoS of `sphinx` is significantly improved after applying either heuristic to the co-running `milc`; the normalized IPC of `sphinx` is stable and between 0.9 and 1.

However, there is significant difference in nap duration with two heuristics. Figure 22 presents the corresponding average nap duration of `milc` for every 2 `ms`' execution, decided dynamically by RQ-Runtime based on dynamic contention detection. The longer the nap duration, the lower the utilization. Figure 22 shows that `simple` heuristic demonstrates certain adaptability. After sample 600 when the contention is not as significant, naps become shorter. However, when using the `targeted` heuristic, the nap duration is significantly shorter, and thus the utilization is much higher, while achieving similar QoS improvement as the `simple` heuristic. This demonstrates that `simple` heuristic may over-conservatively throttle down the low-priority application, while `targeted` heuristic can intelligently estimate and adaptively adjust the necessary amount of nap/throttling, attaining much higher utilization while achieving the QoS goal. This also demonstrates the importance of using dynamic feedback control (`targeted`) to prune the potential false positive contention detection instead of detecting purely on QoS degradation (`simple`).

5.4 Comparing to the prior art

Figures 23 and 24 compare the effectiveness of ReQoS against the state-of-the-art technique QoS-Compile [32]. Figure 23 presents the normalized QoS of high-priority applications when each of them is co-running with a low-priority application. The x-axis presents the workloads, each composed of a high-priority (HP) and a low-priority (LP) application. For example, `sphinx - lbm` denotes a HP application `sphinx` co-running with a LP application `lbm`. The first bar in each cluster of bars presents the QoS of the high-priority application running with the original LP application. The second and the third present its QoS when QoS-compile or ReQoS is applied to the LP application, respectively. C1 and C2 denote two configurations we use for QoS-Compile and ReQoS. For ReQoS, configuration 1 (C1) targets 80% QoS, and configuration 2 (C2) targets 90% QoS. Note that we can specify a QoS target in ReQoS and the RQ-Runtime can adaptively adjust the throttling to achieve the target. However, QoS-Compile does not have that functionality. To achieve a specified QoS, many trial runs of parameter tuning are needed. Here we carefully tune the configurations of QoS-Compile to achieve similar QoS improvement as ReQoS.

As Figures 23 and 24 demonstrate, while with careful tuning, QoS-Compile can be as effective as ReQoS in reducing contention and improving QoS, ReQoS attains significantly higher machine utilization than QoS-Compile. For example, for `sphinx-milc_C2`, ReQoS achieves 80% execution rate for `milc` as opposed to 40% using QoS-Compile while providing better QoS. On average, ReQoS attains 65% utilization compared to 43% by QoS-Compile, 51% better while providing similar QoS. This is mainly due to the fact that ReQoS can adaptively adjust the necessary throttling down as contention phase changes, avoiding unnecessary throttling down while maintaining stable QoS. However, QoS-compile determines the amount of throttling down statically. Even with tuning, it does not handle phase changes and may perform either over conservatively and waste utilization, or over-optimistically and fail to effectively mitigate degradation to achieve the QoS goal. In addition,

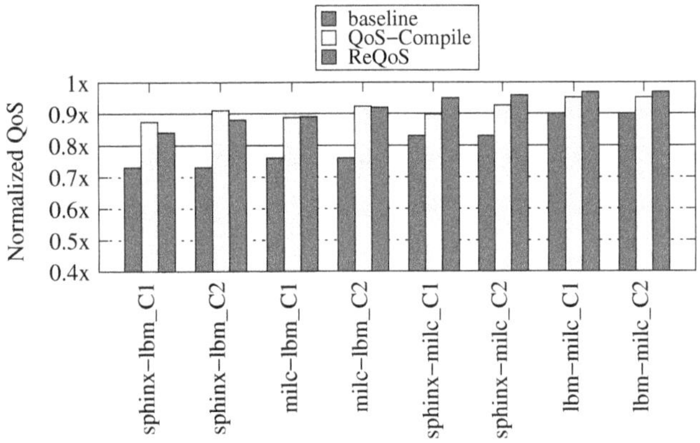

Figure 23. QoS of high-priority applications. When carefully tuned for each workload, QoS-Compile achieves similar QoS as ReQoS.

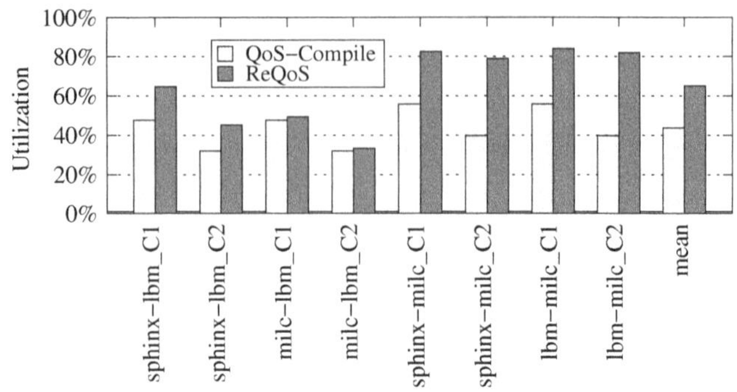

Figure 24. Utilization. ReQoS attains higher machine utilization than QoS-Compile.

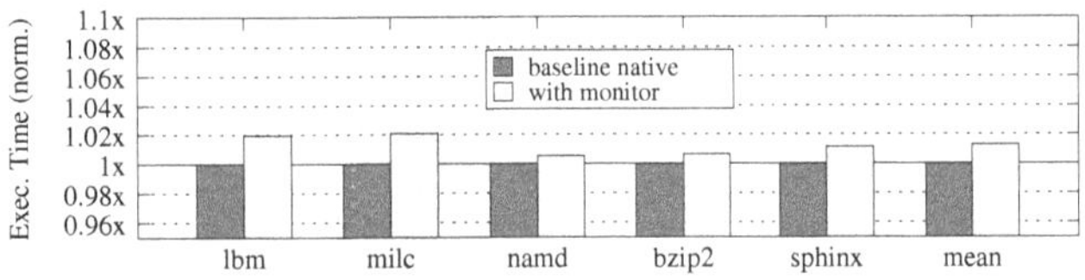

Figure 25. Overhead of monitoring for high-priority application.

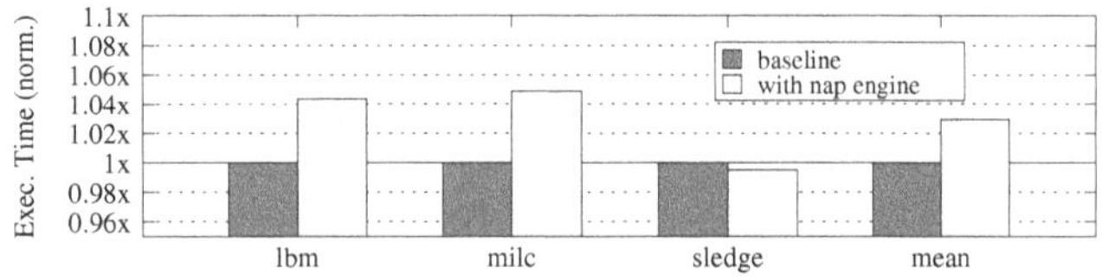

Figure 26. Overhead of nap engine for low-priority application.

due to its static nature, QoS-Compile also cannot adapt to new situations such as changes of the co-running high-priority applications or their QoS requirements. In comparison, ReQoS can adapt to these changes without any tuning.

5.5 Overhead

Figure 25 presents the performance costs of the monitoring the QoS of the high-priority application. The overhead is minimal. The overhead suffered by high-priority applications is less than 1% on average with a max of 2% in the cases of `milc` and `lbm`.

Figure 26 shows the performance overhead of invoking the Nap Engine to throttle down low-priority applications. The overhead of probing the Nap Engine is slightly more costly, approaching 5% for `milc`. However, the Nap Engine only causes overhead to the low-priority application, and thus the performance cost is not as important.

The low cost of our runtime approach for the high-priority application is due to the fact that the overhead of reading and recording performance counters at 1 `ms` granularity is minimal. The cost is slightly higher for the low-priority application because we add a lightweight check at the point of every compiler-inserted marker. However the runtime is only invoked when the marker is detected (when the identified contentious region is executing) instead of every 1 `ms`. Coarsening the granularity can further reduce these overheads; but the tradeoff must be made between a lower overhead and a higher penalty for potential delays in detecting contention as it occurs.

5.6 Energy Efficiency of ReQoS

Figure 27 presents the improved energy efficiency when allowing co-location with ReQoS. These experiments were performed using a P3 International Kill A Watt® power meter connected to our Quad Core Intel Nehalem machine to measure whole system watt consumption during execution. For each cluster of bars in the figure, the energy efficiency is calculated by the instructions processed per watt for a three minute time period after the machine wattage stabilizes during each run. The higher the bar, the more energy efficient. The x-axis shows the workloads, the high-priority and low-priority application pairs. The first bar for each workload shows the energy efficiency when using separate machines for low and high-priority applications; the second bar shows the energy efficiency of co-locating both high and low-priority applications using ReQoS with the `targeted` policy and the `conserv_90` configuration shown in Table 2. We observe a significant energy efficiency improvement for many workloads. Application pairs that include less contentious applications, such as `namd`, produce a greater benefit as there is less napping occurring. Meanwhile, highly contentious pairs, such as `sphinx-lbm`, show a more modest benefit. On average there is a 47% improvement of using ReQoS to allow co-location over using two separate machines for low- and high-priority applications.

5.7 Varying Architecture

To investigate the effectiveness of ReQoS across architectures, we performed experiments on a 2.6GHZs Quad Core AMD Phenom X4 system with 6MB last level cache and 3GB of main memory. This machine is also running Linux 2.6.29.6 and our customized GCC 4.4.6.

Figures 28 and 29 show the results for our `targeted` heuristic using the same configurations shown in Table 2. As shown in these figures, ReQoS is also quite effective on this platform. For both `lbm` and `milc` we achieve 80% to 90% utilization while significantly reducing the performance interference to our high-priority applications. The contentiousness of `sledge` is severe on this processor. For the `lbm-sledge` pair, we observe that when lowering the QoS threshold to 80% from 90%, we achieve more than 2x improvement for the utilization. Overall, as shown in Figure 28, our conservative settings meet and exceed our QoS requirements in all experiments,

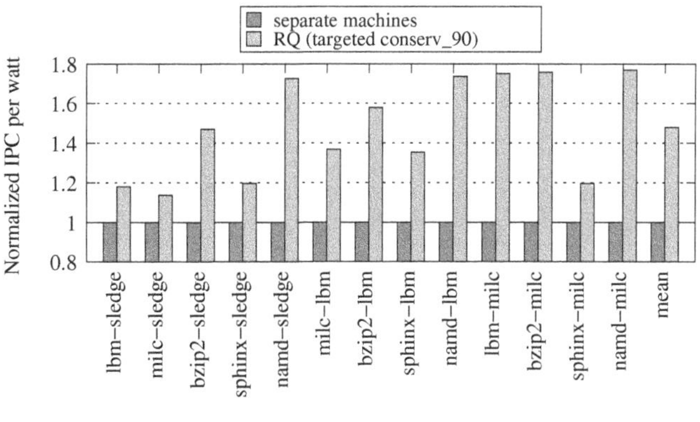

Figure 27. Energy efficiency of allowing co-location with ReQoS (`targeted`) vs. over-provisioning.

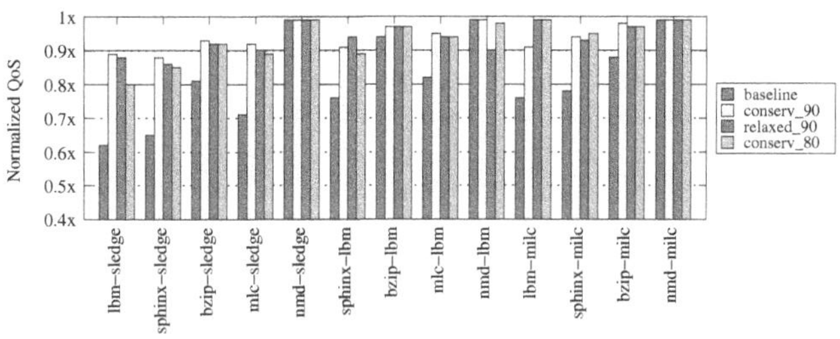

Figure 28. Effectiveness of `RQ_targeted` - QoS of each benchmark co-running with `sledge`, `lbm`, and `milc` on AMD X4

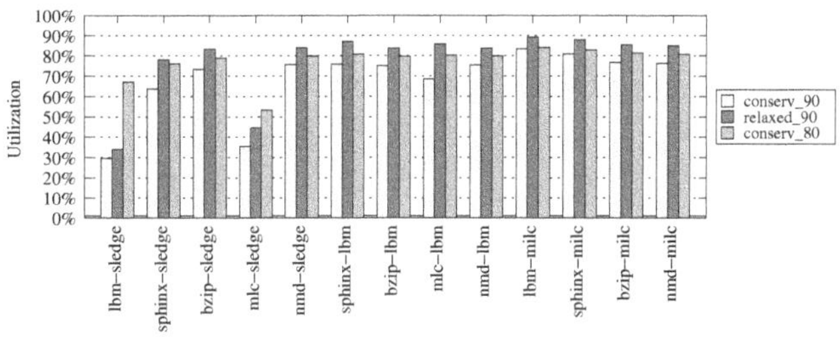

Figure 29. Effectiveness of `RQ_targeted` - Utilization of `sledge`, `lbm` and `milc` with each configuration on AMD X4

and our relaxed configuration satisfies the QoS constraint for the majority of the applications.

6. Related Work

Contention Aware Scheduling An important software approach to mitigating contention is contention aware scheduling [2, 4, 7, 11, 15, 23, 34, 37]. Our work is orthogonal and complementary to existing contention-aware scheduling approaches. The goal of scheduling is to, for a given set of applications, decide what applications should be co-running together to improve performance or performance isolation. The goal of ReQoS is to, for a given co-run schedule (a set of applications that are scheduled to run simultaneously), make sure that the high priority application achieves a pre-specified QoS goal by manipulating the contentiousness of low-priority applications. ReQoS can be used after the schedule is decided. To illustrate the difference, imagine a simple scenario where only two applications are available for scheduling and these applications do not "play nicely" together. In this situation, scheduling can either run these two appliations simultaneously (thus violating the QoS of the high-priority application), or only allow one to run to ensure QoS. ReQoS is complimentary in that it enables "safe colocation" by allowing two applications to run simultaneously and guaranteeing the QoS of the high-priority application. It is also important to note that, unlike ReQoS, prior work on contention-aware OS scheduling does not precisely guarantee application QoS. When the scheduler selects applications to co-run, the resulting QoS depends on the composition of the workloads. Different from scheduling, our approach does not require a balanced mix of high-contention and low-contention applications since we directly manipulate the contentiousness of an application to improve QoS. Even if only contentious co-runners are left to be scheduled our approach remains effective. Yang et al. present Redline [35], an OS technique to guarantee the QoS of interactive applications on time-sharing systems. However, we focus on contention among applications simultaneously executing across multiple cores. Software solutions to reduce cache contention using page coloring/remapping have also been proposed [5, 16, 29]. Most page coloring methods require significant modifications to the kernel and the knowledge of the cache design details.

QoS-compile Tang et al. [32] propose QoS-Compile, a state-of-the-art technique to statically throttle down the memory contentious regions to achieve the same goal as this paper. As shown in our evaluation (Section 5.4), because of its dynamic and reactive nature, ReQoS significantly outperforms QoS-Compile. Mars et al. [21] propose a shutter approach to detect contention, while our approach first identifies contentious code regions and then applies compilation techniques to those regions.

Researchers recently have started to explore using code transformations and restructuring to improve cache sharing and reduce contention on multicores [12, 13, 27, 28, 30, 36]. Most such research focuses on compilation techniques to improve cache sharing for a multi-threaded application. Differently, our approach manipulates how applications interact with each other in terms of contending for the memory resources. Hardware techniques such as cache/bandwidth partitioning and source throttling to improve performance and fairness on multicores have received much research attention [6, 8–10, 14, 17, 24, 25, 31]. These studies have shown promising future directions for hardware designers; however they require hardware changes and are not yet available in commodity chips.

7. Conclusion

In this work, we have shown that static compilation and dynamic adaptation can be combined to address the challenge of cross-core interference on the QoS of high-priority applications. We have presented ReQoS, a statically enabled dynamic compilation approach to improve machine utilization in WSCs by enabling the adaptive manipulation of the contentiousness of low-priority applications to ensure the QoS of high-priority co-runners. Using a profile guided compilation technique that identifies and inserts markers in contentious code regions, and a lightweight runtime that monitors the QoS of high-priority applications and reactively triggers short naps of low-priority applications when cross-core interference is detected we were able to improve utilization by more than 70% in many cases, and more than 50% on average, while enforcing a 90% QoS threshold. In this work, we argue that in addition to providing a compilation strategy for an application's individual performance, it is also desirable to include an application's "niceness" to other co-runners as a compilation objective, and show that ReQoS can significantly reduce performance interference to ensure application QoS.

8. Acknowledgements

We would like to thank the reviewers for their helpful feedback and suggestions. Lingjia Tang and Jason Mars were supported by Google research awards. This work was also partially supported by NSF CNS-0964627 and CNF-0811689 to the University of Virginia.

References

[1] Intel 64 and ia-32 architectures software developer's manual volume 2b: Instruction set reference, m-z.

[2] M. Banikazemi, D. Poff, and B. Abali. Pam: a novel performance/power aware meta-scheduler for multi-core systems. *SC '08: Proceedings of the 2008 ACM/IEEE conference on Supercomputing*, Nov 2008.

[3] L. Barroso and U. Hölzle. The datacenter as a computer: An introduction to the design of warehouse-scale machines. *Synthesis Lectures on Computer Architecture*, 4(1):1–108, 2009.

[4] M. Bhadauria and S. McKee. An approach to resource-aware co-scheduling for cmps. *ICS 2010*, Jun 2010.

[5] S. Cho and L. Jin. Managing distributed, shared l2 caches through os-level page allocation. *MICRO 39*, Dec 2006.

[6] E. Ebrahimi, C. Lee, O. Mutlu, and Y. Patt. Fairness via source throttling: a configurable and high-performance fairness substrate for multi-core memory systems. *ASPLOS 2010*, Mar 2010.

[7] A. Fedorova, M. Seltzer, and M. Smith. Improving performance isolation on chip multiprocessors via an operating system scheduler. *PACT 2007*, Sep 2007.

[8] F. Guo, Y. Solihin, L. Zhao, and R. Iyer. A framework for providing quality of service in chip multi-processors. *MIRCO 2007*, pages 343–355, 2007.

[9] A. Herdrich, R. Illikkal, R. Iyer, D. Newell, V. Chadha, and J. Moses. Rate-based qos techniques for cache/memory in cmp platforms. *ICS '09: Proceedings of the 23rd international conference on Supercomputing*, Jun 2009.

[10] R. Iyer, L. Zhao, F. Guo, R. Illikkal, S. Makineni, D. Newell, Y. Solihin, L. Hsu, and S. Reinhardt. Qos policies and architecture for cache/memory in cmp platforms. *SIGMETRICS '07: Proceedings of the 2007 ACM SIGMETRICS international conference on Measurement and modeling of computer systems*, Jun 2007.

[11] Y. Jiang, K. Tian, and X. Shen. Combining locality analysis with online proactive job co-scheduling in chip multiprocessors. *High Performance Embedded Architectures and Compilers*, pages 201–215, 2010.

[12] M. Kandemir, S. Muralidhara, S. Narayanan, Y. Zhang, and O. Ozturk. Optimizing shared cache behavior of chip multiprocessors. *Microarchitecture, 2009. MICRO-42. 42nd Annual IEEE/ACM International Symposium on DOI - UR -*, pages 505–516, 2009.

[13] M. Kandemir, T. Yemliha, S. Muralidhara, S. Srikantaiah, M. Irwin, and Y. Zhnag. Cache topology aware computation mapping for multicores. *PLDI '10*, Jun 2010.

[14] S. Kim, D. Chandra, and Y. Solihin. Fair cache sharing and partitioning in a chip multiprocessor architecture. *PACT 2004*, Sep 2004.

[15] R. Knauerhase, P. Brett, B. Hohlt, T. Li, and S. Hahn. Using os observations to improve performance in multicore systems. *IEEE Micro*, 28(3):54–66, 2008.

[16] J. Lin, Q. Lu, X. Ding, Z. Zhang, X. Zhang, and P. Sadayappan. Gaining insights into multicore cache partitioning: Bridging the gap between simulation and real systems. *HPCA 2008*, pages 367–378, 2008.

[17] F. Liu, X. Jiang, and Y. Solihin. Understanding how off-chip memory bandwidth partitioning in chip multiprocessors affects system performance. *HPCA 2010*, pages 1–12, 2010.

[18] C.-K. Luk, R. Cohn, R. Muth, H. Patil, A. Klauser, G. Lowney, S. Wallace, V. J. Reddi, and K. Hazelwood. Pin: building customized program analysis tools with dynamic instrumentation. PLDI '05, pages 190–200, New York, NY, USA, 2005. ACM.

[19] J. Mars, L. Tang, R. Hundt, K. Skadron, and M. L. Soffa. Bubble-up: Increasing utilization in modern warehouse scale computers via sensible co-locations. In *MICRO '11: Proceedings of The 44th Annual IEEE/ACM International Symposium on Microarchitecture*, New York, NY, USA, 2011. ACM.

[20] J. Mars, L. Tang, R. Hundt, K. Skadron, and M. L. Soffa. Increasing utilization in warehouse scale computers using bubble-up! *Special Issue: IEEE Micro's Top Picks from 2011 Computer Architecture Conferences*, 2012.

[21] J. Mars, N. Vachharajani, R. Hundt, and M. Soffa. Contention aware execution: online contention detection and response. *CGO '10: Proceedings of the 8th annual IEEE/ACM international symposium on Code generation and optimization*, Apr 2010.

[22] D. Meisner, B. Gold, and T. Wenisch. Powernap: eliminating server idle power. *ASPLOS '09: Proceeding of the 14th international conference on Architectural support for programming languages and operating systems*, Feb 2009.

[23] R. Nathuji, A. Kansal, and A. Ghaffarkhah. Q-clouds: managing performance interference effects for qos-aware clouds. *EuroSys '10*, Apr 2010.

[24] K. Nesbit, N. Aggarwal, J. Laudon, and J. Smith. Fair queuing memory systems. *MICRO 2006*, pages 208 – 222, 2006.

[25] M. Qureshi and Y. Patt. Utility-based cache partitioning: A low-overhead, high-performance, runtime mechanism to partition shared caches. *MICRO 39: Proceedings of the 39th Annual IEEE/ACM International Symposium on Microarchitecture*, Dec 2006.

[26] G. Ren, E. Tune, T. Moseley, Y. Shi, S. Rus, and R. Hundt. Google-wide profiling: A continuous profiling infrastructure for data centers. *IEEE Micro*, 30:65–79, 2010.

[27] S. Rus, R. Ashok, and D. Li. Automated locality optimization based on the reuse distance of string operations. CGO '11, pages 181 –190, Apr 2011.

[28] A. Sandberg, D. Eklöv, and E. Hagersten. Reducing cache pollution through detection and elimination of non-temporal memory accesses. *SC 2010*, Nov 2010.

[29] L. Soares, D. Tam, and M. Stumm. Reducing the harmful effects of last-level cache polluters with an os-level, software-only pollute buffer. *Micro 2008*, pages 258 – 269, 2008.

[30] S. Son, M. Kandemir, M. Karakoy, and D. Chakrabarti. A compiler-directed data prefetching scheme for chip multiprocessors. *PPoPP 2009*, Feb 2009.

[31] S. Srikantaiah, M. Kandemir, and M. Irwin. Adaptive set pinning: managing shared caches in chip multiprocessors. *ASPLOS XIII: Proceedings of the 13th international conference on Architectural support for programming languages and operating systems*, Mar 2008.

[32] L. Tang, J. Mars, and M. L. Soffa. Compiling for niceness: mitigating contention for qos in warehouse scale computers. In *Proceedings of the Tenth International Symposium on Code Generation and Optimization*, CGO '12, pages 1–12, New York, NY, USA, 2012. ACM.

[33] L. Tang, J. Mars, N. Vachharajani, R. Hundt, and M. L. Soffa. The impact of memory subsystem resource sharing on datacenter applications. In *ISCA*, pages 283–294, 2011.

[34] D. Xu, C. Wu, and P.-C. Yew. On mitigating memory bandwidth contention through bandwidth-aware scheduling. *PACT 2010*, Sep 2010.

[35] T. Yang, T. Liu, E. D. Berger, S. F. Kaplan, and J. E. B. Moss. Redline: first class support for interactivity in commodity operating systems. In *Proceedings of the 8th USENIX conference on Operating systems design and implementation*, OSDI'08, pages 73–86, Berkeley, CA, USA, 2008. USENIX Association.

[36] E. Zhang, Y. Jiang, and X. Shen. Does cache sharing on modern cmp matter to the performance of contemporary multithreaded programs? *PPoPP 2010*, pages 203–212, 2010.

[37] S. Zhuravlev, S. Blagodurov, and A. Fedorova. Addressing shared resource contention in multicore processors via scheduling. *ASPLOS 2010*, Mar 2010.

Production-Run Software Failure Diagnosis via Hardware Performance Counters

Joy Arulraj Po-Chun Chang Guoliang Jin Shan Lu
University of Wisconsin–Madison
{joy,pchang9,aliang,shanlu}@cs.wisc.edu

Abstract

Sequential and concurrency bugs are widespread in deployed software. They cause severe failures and huge financial loss during production runs. Tools that diagnose production-run failures with low overhead are needed. The state-of-the-art diagnosis techniques use software instrumentation to sample program properties at run time and use off-line statistical analysis to identify properties most correlated with failures. Although promising, these techniques suffer from high run-time overhead, which is sometimes over 100%, for concurrency-bug failure diagnosis and hence are not suitable for production-run usage.

We present PBI, a system that uses existing hardware performance counters to diagnose production-run failures caused by sequential and concurrency bugs with low overhead. PBI is designed based on several key observations. First, a few widely supported performance counter events can reflect a wide variety of common software bugs and can be monitored by hardware with almost no overhead. Second, the counter overflow interrupt supported by existing hardware and operating systems provides a natural and effective mechanism to conduct event sampling at user level. Third, the noise and non-determinism in interrupt delivery complements well with statistical processing.

We evaluate PBI using 13 real-world concurrency and sequential bugs from representative open-source server, client, and utility programs, and 10 bugs from a widely used software-testing benchmark. Quantitatively, PBI can effectively diagnose failures caused by these bugs with a small overhead that is never higher than 10 %. Qualitatively, PBI does not require any change to software and presents a novel use of existing hardware performance counters.

Categories and Subject Descriptors D.2.5 [*Software Engineering*]: Testing and Debugging; B.8.1 [*Performance and Reliability*]: Reliability, Testing, and Fault-Tolerance; D.1.3 [*Programming Techniques*]: Concurrent Programming

General Terms Reliability, Languages, Measurement

Keywords failure diagnosis, production run, performance counters, concurrency bugs

1. Introduction

1.1 Motivation

Software bugs are a major cause of production-run system failures. Software companies spend over 30% of development resources in testing [34], but still cannot eliminate all bugs from released software [15]. Things are getting worse in the multi-core era. The increasingly popular multi-threaded software has a huge state space that makes software testing even more difficult. Many bugs, including not only sequential bugs but also concurrency bugs, escape into the field, causing severe failures and huge financial loss [29, 35]. Diagnosing these failures is time consuming, because non-deterministic concurrency bugs are difficult to repeat and multi-threaded execution is difficult to reason about. Previous studies show that concurrency-bug failures often take developers weeks to months to diagnose [10, 24] and the released patches are 4 times more likely to be incorrect than those for sequential bugs [41]. To improve the quality of production-run software, effective failure-diagnosis tools are needed.

There are two major challenges for *production-run failure-diagnosis* tools: diagnostic capability and diagnostic performance.

Diagnostic capability Tools with good diagnostic capability should be able to accurately explain failures caused by a wide variety of bugs. Previous research [16, 21, 22, 25, 28] has found an effective approach for achieving good diagnostic capability. This approach collects program predicates, such as whether a branch is taken, during both success and failure runs of the program. It then uses statistical processing to identify predicates that are highly correlated with failure runs. The only concerns of this approach are designing predicates that can reflect common failure root causes and avoiding large run-time overhead in collecting predicates.

Diagnostic performance Tools with good diagnostic performance should incur small run-time *overhead* that is suitable for deployment. Although progress has been made, we are still far from addressing this challenge.

One potential approach is to use hardware support. Many techniques have been proposed that try to leverage hardware support to speed up bug detection [4, 23, 25, 31, 32, 40, 42, 45, 46]. Unfortunately, these solutions require hardware support that is not available in existing machines.

Another promising approach is *sampling* [16, 21, 22]. By randomly collecting a small portion of predicates in each run, the overhead can be significantly decreased. Unfortunately, this sampling approach does not work as well for diagnosing concurrency-bug failures as it does for sequential-bug failures. Diagnosing concurrency-bug failures requires interleaving-related predicates, such as whether two consecutive accesses to one variable come from the same thread. Collecting these predicates requires coordinating multiple threads and serializing global data-structure updates, which often incurs more than 100% of overhead even with very sparse sampling [16]. In addition, sampling can hurt the evaluation accuracy of interleaving-related predicates (see details in Section 4.3).

Furthermore, existing software-based monitoring and sampling techniques rely on code instrumentation [16, 21, 28]. This approach requires changes to program source code or binary code. It significantly increases the size of executables (by 11–123X in our experiments) and burdens code caches [38].

1.2 Contribution

This paper presents PBI, a system that leverages existing hardware performance counters to effectively diagnose production-run failures caused by a wide variety of sequential and concurrency bugs with negligible overhead. PBI does *not* rely on code instrumentation and makes no changes to the program source code or binary code.

Performance counters are special registers supported by hardware to monitor hardware performance events. Although widely used for performance tuning and architectural-design verification [7, 30], they have only had limited use in automated software-reliability tools for several reasons:

First, **limited information**. Only a limited and fixed set of performance-counter events can be monitored. For most of these events, hardware only provides the occurrence-count information. Interrupt-based counter access provides information about the instruction that triggered a counter overflow/increment. Unfortunately, interrupt-based access poses extra challenges as follows.

Second, **expensive access**. Although maintaining event counts by hardware has almost no overhead, accessing a counter by user-level software through interrupts does incur overhead.

Third, **noise and randomness**. The information about which instruction triggered a counter overflow is inevitably imprecise, containing noise due to out-of-order execution and imprecise interrupt delivery. Further, it is difficult to command interrupts to be raised at specific program locations. The instructions that raise counter interrupts in a program are quite random.

As a result, no previous work has used hardware performance counters for automated failure diagnosis. Some recent work uses performance counters in an inspiring yet limited way, either to provide hints [11] or to provide part of the information needed [36], for detecting a specific type of bugs (i.e., data races).

In this paper, we address the above challenges and design PBI based on several observations:

First, although only limited hardware events are supported, a couple of widely supported events can already reflect the occurrence of a wide variety of sequential bugs (e.g., branch-related events) and concurrency bugs (e.g., L1 cache coherence events). They can be used as program predicates to help PBI achieve good diagnostic capability (see details in Section 3).

Second, although every single counter access is relatively expensive, interrupt-based performance-counter access is a natural fit for predicate sampling. Specifically, the predicate evaluation is handled by hardware with high accuracy and almost no overhead; the sampling overhead is oblivious to predicate types (e.g., concurrency-bug predicates vs. sequential-bug predicates) or program structure (e.g., branch intensity); the sampling overhead can be controlled easily and drops to almost 0% during sparse sampling. This allows PBI to achieve much better diagnostic performance than instrumentation-based sampling (see details in Section 4).

Third, the noise in the performance-event profile can be filtered by statistical processing. The randomness in interrupt-based counter access is exactly needed for sampling-based failure diagnosis (see details in Sections 4 and 5).

Fourth, as PBI does **not** require code instrumentation, we can monitor programs independent of the programming language in which they are developed, with no increase in the code size.

Overall, this work has made several contributions:

- A novel way of using existing hardware performance counters that leverages their unique characteristics.
- A failure-diagnosis system that handles a wide variety of failures while requiring no changes to software and incurs low overhead that is suitable for production-run deployment.
- An evaluation of 13 real-world concurrency and sequential bugs from open-source server/client/utility programs, as well as 10 bugs from a widely used software-testing benchmark. The evaluation shows that PBI can effectively diagnose failures caused by these bugs, including several concurrency-bug failures that cannot be effectively diagnosed by previous work [16]. PBI failure diagnosis incurs only a small run-time overhead that is never higher than 10% for all applications, much faster than traditional concurrency-bug failure diagnosis techniques. The evaluation also reveals challenges and opportunities in using performance counters.

2. Background

2.1 Hardware Performance Counters

Counters and counter events A hardware *performance counter* is a register dedicated to monitoring *performance events*, such as cache misses and taken branches. Modern architectures usually support a small number of performance-counter registers and a relatively large number of performance events. Each register can be configured to monitor any supported performance event at run time.

The numbers of performance counters and supported performance events have both increased in recent years. Among Intel processors, Pentium Pro has only two counters supporting 98 events in 68 categories, while Nehalem (Core i7) has four counters per core supporting 325 events in 97 categories [19]. Some events such as retired instruction count are supported by almost all architectures; some events like load/store latency are only supported by a few architectures.

Accessing performance counters To monitor a performance event, the user first configures a counter register for that event. The event count can then be obtained by polling the counter periodically or during the handling of counter-overflow interrupt.

Performance counters can be maintained and accessed in different modes, including per-thread mode, per-core mode, and system-wide mode with operating system support. The OS can save performance-counter values for a thread during a context switch. This way, we can easily obtain per-thread statistics when multiple threads are sharing the same set of hardware counter registers.

In PBI, we access hardware performance counters through PERF [17], a profiling utility available in Linux kernel 2.6.31 and later versions. PERF provides a simple command-line interface. When a program is launched under PERF to monitor a specific event, PERF handles the performance counter-overflow interrupt and generates a log file that contains information related to every counter overflow, such as the program counter of the instruction associated with counter overflow and the event being counted.

2.2 Cooperative Bug Isolation

PBI shares a common program-sampling and statistical-processing philosophy with CBI [16, 21, 22], a state-of-the-art production-run failure-diagnosis framework. We present an overview of CBI below.

CBI performs source-to-source transformation of C programs and randomly samples the values of *predicates* at particular program points, called *instrumentation sites* or *sites*, across many success and failure runs of the software. It then uses statistical techniques to identify predicates that correlate with failures, which are referred to as *failure predictors*. The key components of CBI are:

Predicate design and evaluation Predicates are carefully designed to reflect common root causes of software bugs. To diagnose sequential-bug failures, CBI monitors three types of predicates. *Branch predicates* evaluate whether a branch is taken; *Return predicates* evaluate whether a function return value is zero, negative, or positive; *Scalar-pair predicates* evaluate whether a variable is smaller than, larger than, or equal to other in-scope variables.

CBI can hardly diagnose concurrency-bug failures. To address this problem, an extension of CBI called CCI [16] is proposed. CCI monitors three types of predicates related to thread interleaving. *CCI-Prev* predicates evaluate whether two successive accesses to a given location were by two distinct threads; *CCI-Havoc* predicates evaluate whether the value of a given location changes between two consecutive accesses by one thread; *CCI-FunRe* predicates evaluate whether two threads execute a function F in parallel.

Previous work has demonstrated that CBI and CCI predicates can effectively diagnose a wide variety of software failures. Among CCI predicates, CCI-FunRe has significantly worse diagnosis capability than the other two. Therefore, we will restrict the comparison of PBI to only CCI-Prev and CCI-Havoc predicates.

Predicate sampling To lower performance overhead, CBI uses an instrumentation-based sampling technique that randomly collects predicates from a small number of sites instead of all sites during every run. CCI has extended this scheme to support interleaving-related predicates. This extension sometimes incurs high overhead, causing more than 100% of overhead in some memory-intensive programs even with very sparse sampling [16].

At the end of each run, CBI generates a profile. The profile includes information for every predicate at all program sites indicating whether the predicate was ever observed in that particular run, and if observed, whether it was true or false. CBI assumes that the runs will be classified as success or failure runs by an automated tool or by the users themselves. PBI continues to use this assumption.

Statistical processing After collecting predicate samples from many success and failure runs, CBI framework uses a statistical model to measure each predicate's correlation with software failures. The correlation is quantitatively evaluated using two scores: *frequency* and *Increase*. *Frequency* measures the frequency of a predicate being observed true in a failure run. *Increase* measures how much more likely it is for a program to fail when a predicate is observed as *true* than when it is simply observed. The statistical model in CBI finally ranks the predicates based on the harmonic mean of *frequency* and *increase* scores. The top ranked predicates are reported as good failure predictors.

In the following sections, we will describe how PBI uses hardware performance counters to diagnose a wide variety of production-run software failures and provide a detailed comparison of PBI with CBI and CCI.

3. PBI Predicate Design

3.1 Design for Concurrency-bug Failures

3.1.1 MESI predicate design

Previous work has proposed extending cache-coherence protocols and L1 caches to help detect concurrency bugs [23, 31, 32]. Inspired by these studies, PBI utilizes cache-coherence related performance counter events to diagnose concurrency-bug failures.

Cache-coherence events are supported by performance counters in many modern microarchitectures, such as Intel Core i7 [19] and IBM Power 7 [1]. PBI uses eight cache-coherence events shown in Figure 1. When a hardware performance counter is configured with event code 0x40 (or 0x41) and unit mask 0x01, the counter will count every cache load (or store) that observes an Invalid cache-coherence state at its corresponding cache line just *before* the access is performed. We will refer to this performance-counter event as *I Event*. Similarly, we will refer to performance-counter events that count cache accesses that observe Modified, Exclusive, and Shared states, as *M Event*, *E Event*, and *S Event* respectively.

L1 Data Cache LOAD (STORE)	Event Code : 0x40 (41)
Unit mask	Description
0x01	L1 data cache access in I state
0x02	L1 data cache access in S state
0x04	L1 data cache access in E state
0x08	L1 data cache access in M state
perf record –event=r0140:u <program monitored>	

Figure 1. L1 data cache load and store events in Intel Nehalem along with a PERF command that monitors user-level (specified by ":u") load events in I state

PBI defines 4 MESI-predicates to diagnose concurrency-bug failures: an M-predicate, an E-predicate, an S-predicate and an I-predicate. Every memory-access instruction i in the application is a *site* for MESI-predicates. The I-predicate at i is denoted as $P_I(i)$. $P_I(i)$ is true when I Event is observed to occur at i at run time. The other MESI-predicates are similarly denoted and defined.

3.1.2 Diagnostic Potential of MESI predicates

Previous study [24] of real-world concurrency bugs has shown that atomicity violations and order violations are the two most common types of concurrency bugs, with the former contributing to almost 70% of non-deadlock concurrency bugs. We now assess the potential of MESI-predicates for diagnosing atomicity-violation failures, order-violation failures, and other concurrency-bug failures.

Atomicity violation Atomicity violation happens when a sequence of memory accesses in one thread is unserializably interleaved by memory accesses from another thread(s). Earlier studies [23, 24, 39] show that the majority of atomicity violations only involve one variable and can be categorized into 4 types as listed in Table 1.

We observe that the I-predicate and S-predicate can differentiate failure runs from success runs for all 4 types of atomicity violations. Therefore, we expect good diagnostic potential for failures caused by atomicity violations.

Order violation Order violation happens when the expected order between two groups of memory accesses from two threads are flipped. Order violation bugs are usually accompanied by abnormal values of MESI-predicates.

A real-world order violation in FFT is illustrated in Figure 2. Instruction A from thread 2 is expected to initialize the global variable Gend before B1 and B2 access Gend from thread 1. Unfortunately, without proper synchronization, A could execute after B1 and B2, causing wrong outputs. Failures caused by this bug can be diagnosed by the MESI-predicates at the site B2. Specifically, during success runs, B2 would observe a Shared state before its access of Gend. During most failure runs, with A executed after B1 and B2, B2 will observe an Exclusive state. During rare failure runs, when A executes between B1 and B2, B2 will observe an Invalid state. Clearly, the MESI-predicates can differentiate failure runs from success runs.

However, there is no guarantee that all order-violation failures can be diagnosed by MESI-predicates. In the example shown in Figure 2, if the program did not contain B2, MESI-predicates would fail to diagnose the failure. In that made-up scenario, A and B1 are the only two instructions involved in failures. They would both observe Invalid states during both success and failure runs.

ID	Failure-Inducing Interleaving	Value of Related Predicates: Failure run	Value of Related Predicates: Success run
RWR	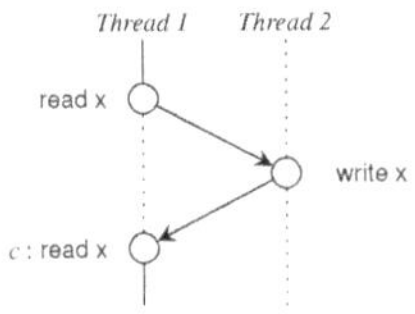	$P_I(c)$=TRUE	$P_I(c)$=FALSE
WWR	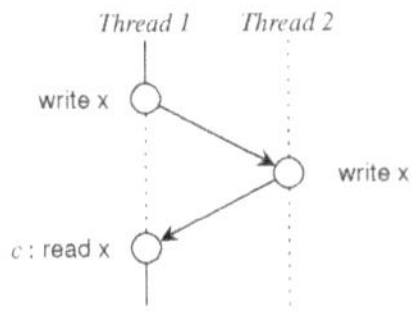	$P_I(c)$=TRUE	$P_I(c)$=FALSE
RWW	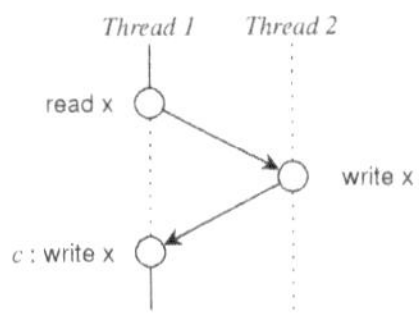	$P_I(c)$=TRUE	$P_I(c)$=FALSE
WRW	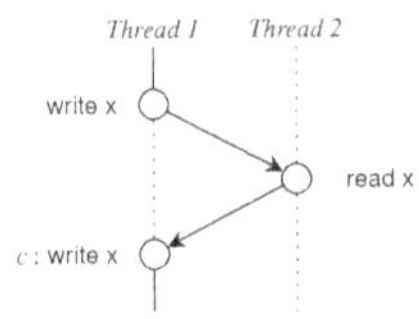	$P_S(c)$=TRUE	$P_S(c)$=FALSE

Table 1. Diagnostic potential of MESI predicates for different atomicity violations ("⟶" shows execution order. "x" is a shared memory location. In success runs, the two accesses to x from Thread 1 are *not* interleaved by the depicted access to x from Thread 2).

```
// Thread 1                              // Thread 2
printf ("End at %f", Gend); //B1         // Gend is uninitialized
...                                      // until here
printf ("Take %f", Gend−init); //B2      Gend = time(); //A
```

Figure 2. An order violation in FFT. Thread 2 should initialize Gend before thread 1 accesses it.

```
//Master Thread                  //Slave Thread
while(...){                      while(...){
  pos = my_pos; //W_good           pos+=4; //W_bad
  ...                              ...
}//many iterations                 log_read(pos); //R
                                 }// many iterations
```

Figure 3. A real-world bug in MySQL that is neither an atomicity violation nor an order violation [44]: during each iteration, *R* should read the value of pos defined by the Master thread (success run), instead of its own thread (failure run).

Other concurrency bugs Recent bug-detection work [44] and previous characteristics study have shown that some real-world concurrency bugs are caused by neither atomicity violation nor order violation, such as the bug shown in Figure 3. MESI-predicates are still effective for this rare bug as the *M*-predicate at site R will be a good failure predictor.

To summarize, we expect MESI-predicates to diagnose a wide variety of concurrency-bug failures by leveraging the difference in cache-coherence states observed between success and failure runs.

3.1.3 Predicate Evaluation

Evaluating MESI-predicates involves two steps: (1) run-time monitoring using PERF, and (2) off-line log analysis.

We configure PERF to collect user-level MESI-related performance counter events when the program is executed as shown in Figure 1. At run time, PERF handles every counter-overflow interrupt and logs down information like the instruction that caused the counter overflow and the performance event that was counted.

The log analysis is straightforward. While processing the log obtained from each run, we treat every instruction *i* that appears in the log as a *site*. We evaluate $P_e(i)$ to be true if *i* appears in the log with event type *e* (*e* is *M*, *E*, *S*, or *I*). Otherwise, we evaluate $P_e(i)$ to be false.

Ideally, we want to monitor all 8 MESI events in each run. In practice, the number of performance events that can be accurately monitored at the same time depends on hardware support. As most existing machines contain 1 – 8 hardware performance-counter registers in each core, only one event can be accurately monitored at a time in the worst case.

To ensure that PBI runs correctly on a wide range of machines, our current implementation monitors only one performance-counter event at a time. In each run, we randomly select one out of the 8 *MESI* events listed in Figure 1 to be monitored by PERF, and use the trace-analysis algorithm discussed above. Note that the failure-diagnosis accuracy will not be affected by this implementation decision, because each event is given an equal chance to be monitored in the long term. Our implementation can also be easily extended to collect more events in each run given hardware/OS support on some existing or future platforms.

3.1.4 Statistical Processing of MESI Predicates

PBI uses the statistical model developed in CBI to identify predicates that are highly correlated with failures. As discussed in Section 2.2, this statistical model assigns *frequency* and *increase* scores to each predicate. It then uses the harmonic mean of these two scores to rank the predicates. The top ranked predicates are considered as good failure predictors.

We compute these scores during the off-line analysis of PERF logs. The formulas used to calculate *frequency* and *increase* scores of a predicate $P_e(i)$ are provided in eqs. (1) and (2). $|expr|$ denotes the number of runs that satisfy the condition *expr*. *F* denotes the condition that a run has failed; $P_e(i)$ denotes the condition that a run has evaluated $P_e(i)$ to be true (*e* could be *M*, *E*, *S*, or *I* here); *i* denotes the condition that a run has observed site *i*.

$$\text{Frequency} = \frac{|\mathrm{P_e(i)}|}{|\mathrm{F}|} \tag{1}$$

$$\text{Increase} = \frac{|\mathrm{F\&P_e(i)}|}{|\mathrm{P_e(i)}|} - \frac{|\mathrm{F\&i}|}{|\mathrm{i}|} \tag{2}$$

3.1.5 Comparison with Software-based Predicates

CCI-Prev and CCI-Havoc are two predicates used by CCI to diagnose concurrency-bug failures. They treat every instruction *i* that accesses a heap/global variable as a *site*. When *i* is executed by a thread *t* to access a memory location *m*, CCI-Prev evaluates whether the last access to *m* is from thread *t* or not, and CCI-Havoc evaluates whether the value of *m* has changed between *i* and the last access of *m* in *t*. We briefly compare the diagnostic potential and overhead of these two predicates with PBI-MESI predicates.

```
//Thread 1          //Thread 2
tmp=Gcnt;
...                 printf("%d",Gcnt);
Gcnt=tmp+1;//s
```

(a) A success run
($P_{\text{CCIPrev}}(s)$=true,$P_I(s)$=false)

```
//Thread 1          //Thread 2
                    tmp=Gcnt
tmp=Gcnt;           ...
...                 Gcnt=tmp-1;
Gcnt=tmp+1;//s
```

(b) A failure run
($P_{\text{CCIPrev}}(s)$=true,$P_I(s)$=true)

Figure 4. Difference in diagnosing atomicity violations between PBI-MESI and CCI-Prev

BR instructions retired	Code: 0xC4
Unit mask	Description
0x20	Retired branches that are taken
0x10	Retired branches that are not-taken
perf record –event=r20C4:u <program monitored>	
perf record –event=r10C4:u <program monitored>	

Figure 5. Branch-retired events in Intel Nehalem along with PERF commands that monitor user-level branch taken and non-taken events

Diagnostic Potential CCI-Havoc can diagnose three out of four types of atomicity violation failures listed in Table 1. It cannot diagnose order-violation failures. When two writes from a thread are interleaved by a read from another thread (WRW violation), the failure-inducing interleaving does not cause any value change in the variable involved, and hence cannot be diagnosed by CCI-Havoc.

Similar to PBI-MESI, CCI-Prev can diagnose atomicity violations and some order violations. A key difference between CCI-Prev and PBI-MESI is that CCI-Prev does not differentiate read accesses from write accesses. For instance, the predicates of CCI-Prev cannot distinguish success runs from failure runs in the bug shown in Figure 4, while PBI-MESI can. This prevents CCI-Prev from diagnosing some atomicity-violation failures [16].

Diagnostic overhead To evaluate CCI-Prev and CCI-Havoc predicates, CCI maintains a table that records memory-access information for *every* heap/global variable touched by the program. The overhead is especially large for CCI-Prev where all threads share one table that records which thread has issued the most recent access to a variable. Synchronizing accesses to this table from different threads incurs large overhead.

In contrast, hardware completely takes care of monitoring MESI events for PBI. We do not need to maintain an auxiliary data structure like the memory-access table in CCI. Therefore, PBI can scale well to large multi-threaded software with large heap/global memory footprint and many heap/global accesses.

The main overhead of PBI-MESI is due to the counter-overflow interrupt. If we want to evaluate MESI predicates for *every* memory access, the interrupt overhead would be large.

Code-size overhead CCI needs to insert a predicate-evaluation function, which queries and updates the memory-access table, before every instruction that accesses heap/global variables. In contrast, PBI does not change the program at all.

3.2 Design for Sequential-bug Failures

3.2.1 Predicate Design

State-of-the-art failure-diagnosis systems [22, 33] have found that branch-related predicates are effective in diagnosing sequential-bug failures. Inspired by previous work, PBI uses branch-related performance counter events to diagnose sequential bugs.

Branch-related events are widely supported in modern microarchitectures [19]. PBI uses the "branches retired" events shown in Figure 5. When a counter is configured with event code 0xC4 and unit mask 0x20, it counts every retired conditional branch that is *taken*. We will denote this performance-counter event as *BT Event*. We apply the mask 0x10 to count the retired branches that are *not taken*, and denote that event as *BNT Event*.

PBI defines BT and BNT predicates to diagnose sequential-bug failures. Every branch instruction b is a *site* of BT and BNT predicates, denoted as $P_{BT}(b)$ and $P_{BNT}(b)$. $P_{BT}(b)$ is true when BT Event is observed to occur at b at run time. Similarly, $P_{BNT}(b)$ is true when BNT Event is observed to occur at b at run time.

3.2.2 Diagnostic Potential of BT Predicate

Previous work [22, 33] has shown that branch-related predicates are effective in diagnosing sequential-bug failures, because many sequential bugs are associated with abnormal control flows. For example, many semantic bugs are related to corner cases and wrong control flows [20]; many buffer-overflow bugs occur under incorrect boundary-condition checking; many dangling-pointer and double-free bugs occur due to incorrect conditions for memory deallocation. Overall, we expect PBI-BT and PBI-BNT predicates to possess good diagnostic capability for sequential-bug failures.

3.2.3 Predicate Evaluation and Statistical Processing

Similar to PBI-MESI predicates, evaluation of PBI-BT and PBI-BNT predicates are done using PERF. For each run, we configure PERF to monitor branch taken or branch not-taken event that occurs at user level using the commands shown in Figure 5. We process the log generated by PERF for each run, and evaluate $P_e(i)$ to be true if and only if i occurs in the log with event e (e is BT or BNT here).

The statistical model used to identify sequential-bug failure predictors is the same one used to identify concurrency-bug failure predictors, as described in Section 3.1.4.

3.2.4 Comparison with Software-based Predicates

Techniques designed to diagnose sequential-bug failures are much more mature than those designed for diagnosing concurrency-bug failures. We briefly compare the diagnostic potential and run-time overhead between CBI [21, 22] and PBI.

In general, traditional software-based techniques have better diagnostic potential for sequential-bug failures than PBI. The flexibility of software instrumentation allows tools like CBI to collect not only branch-related predicates, but also *Scalar* and *Return* predicates, as discussed in Section 2. In contrast, it is very difficult for PBI to support these two types of predicates that are not related to any performance event. Of course, PBI still has good diagnostic potential, as branch taken or not-taken information is among the most effective predicates for diagnosing sequential-bug failures [33].

To evaluate branch-related predicates, CBI instruments every branch. This overhead is not small for branch-intensive programs. However, the evaluation of predicates designed for diagnosing sequential-bug failures is much more lightweight than that of concurrency-related predicates.

In PBI, branch events are monitored by hardware with almost no overhead. However, handling counter-overflow interrupts incurs overhead. Modern microarchitectures provide several alternatives to monitor branch events. Special hardware registers like Last Branch Record [18] could be utilized to further improve the performance of PBI in future.

4. Predicate Sampling

4.1 PBI Sampling Scheme

Sampling is widely used to amortize the overhead of run-time monitoring [3, 16, 21, 22, 26]. It is traditionally achieved through software instrumentation. PBI also uses sampling to improve performance. Sampling in PBI is performed through performance counter-overflow interrupts rather than software instrumentation.

Two parameters in PERF affect the sampling rate of PBI. One is PERF's kernel parameter *perf_event_max_sampling_rate*. This parameter specifies the maximum number of samples allowed during a time slice before context switch. It is used to avoid too frequent overflow interrupts. PBI currently uses the default PERF setting of this parameter, 10^5. The other is PERF's command-line parameter "-c". When "−c *C*" is specified, PERF configures the underlying performance counter to trigger an interrupt approximately once every C occurrences of event instructions. In our evaluation, PBI changes this command-line parameter to adjust the sampling rate: larger value of *C* corresponds to sparser sampling. Note that when *C* is small, as we will see in Section 7, the effective sampling rate is much sparser than one out of C due to the throttling effect of *perf_event_max_sampling_rate*.

4.2 Diagnostic Potential of PBI Sampling

A poorly designed sampling scheme can hurt diagnostic potential. For instance, a naïve scheme that deterministically collects the first K predicates in every execution cannot diagnose failures whose root causes are in the later part of the execution, no matter how well the predicates are designed. To support effective failure diagnosis, every site should have a fair chance to be sampled. For example, CBI framework uses uniformly random sampling, where each site independently has an equal probability of being sampled.

At first glance, PBI sampling may not appear to be random enough for effective failure diagnosis. With a "-c C" configuration, in a deterministic computer system, PERF will be expected to collect a deterministic sequence of predicates for a program under a given input: the C-th predicate, the 2C-th predicate, and so on.

Interestingly, PBI sampling has inherent randomness in practice benefiting from non-determinism in modern hardware and operating systems, and the throttling effect of *perf_event_max_sampling_rate*. We evaluated this randomness using a microbenchmark as discussed below. The effectiveness of PBI in diagnosing different types of failures in real-world applications (Section 7) also reflects the randomness of PBI sampling to some extent. We could also introduce more randomness in PBI sampling, by inserting a random set of dummy memory-access/branch instructions at the beginning of a program. However, based on our experience, there is no need for extra randomness in PBI sampling.

Evaluating the randomness of* PBI *sampling We designed a microbenchmark to evaluate the randomness of sampling used in PBI. The microbenchmark contains 10^5 static branches. It is designed in a way that every branch will be executed and taken exactly once at run time. We configure PERF to sample the branch-taken event with a configuration of −c 100.

The microbenchmark is executed 10^5 times under the same configuration. If PERF deterministically collects samples every 100 instructions, as suggested by its command-line option, we would see a *wide* variance in the sampling frequency — some branches are sampled with 100% frequency and others are sampled with 0% frequency. Furthermore, we would see only 1% of the branches in the microbenchmark get sampled after 10^5 runs. The real results obtained from PERF contradict with these and address several important questions.

Is the sampling frequency uniform across sites? We observe in Figure 6 that the sampling frequency at different sites actually exhibits low variance in practice. Therefore, PBI sampling provides every program site with a fair chance for getting sampled.

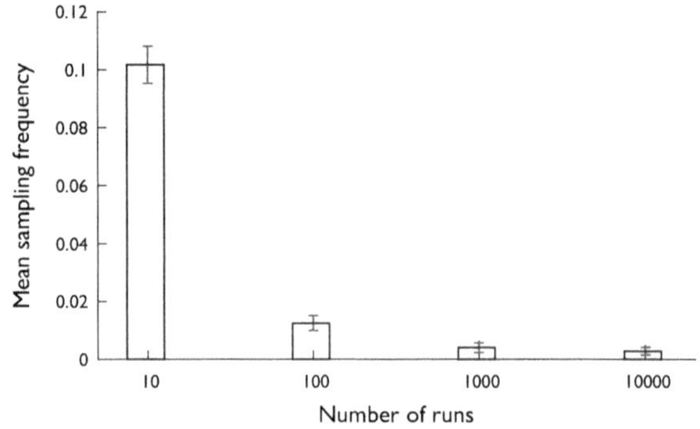

Figure 6. Variation of sampling frequency among all program sites. The sampling frequency of site *b* after N runs is the number of times a predicate is observed at *b* divided by *N*. The error bars represent standard deviation; shorter bars indicate more uniform sampling.

Can PERF *sampling eventually cover all sites?* The results from the microbenchmark study confirm that the answer is yes! With just 2.7% branch coverage in the microbenchmark after 10 runs, the coverage quickly reaches 81.8% after 10^3 runs. We obtain an almost ideal coverage of 97.5% after 10^4 runs.

We can also observe the throttling effect of *perf_event_max_sampling_rate* in Figure 6. With the −c 100 configuration, ideally the sampling rate should be around one out of 100. However, in practice, the observed mean sampling frequency is only about one out of 500.

We also designed microbenchmarks for other performance-counter events. The overall trend is the same as what we presented above for branch-taken event.

The above observations indicate that PERF sampling can support our sampling-based failure diagnosis framework well. We will revisit and confirm these observations in Section 7.

4.3 Comparison with Instrumentation-based Sampling

We compare PBI sampling with traditional instrumentation-based sampling with respect to overhead, accuracy and code-size increase.

Performance overhead Instrumentation-based sampling does not come for free as it needs to frequently check whether a predicate should be evaluated or skipped, as shown in Figure 7. The frequency and overhead of this checking varies across different sampling schemes. CBI performs this type of checking at the beginning of every acyclic code region. In addition to that, CCI needs an extra checking before every global/heap-memory access for thread-coordinated sampling, which is required by CCI-Prev predicates. CCI also needs bursty sampling [14] to effectively collect CCI-Prev and CCI-Havoc predicates, which adds further overhead.

Due to different sampling mechanisms, the *best-case* performance, which occurs under very sparse sampling, is different between PBI and traditional failure-diagnosis systems. PBI can achieve almost zero best-case overhead, when the sampling rate drops to zero. In contrast, CBI could have as large as 20% best-case overhead, depending on the control-flow structure of a program [21]. CCI could cause over 100% best-case overhead, depending on the memory-access density of a program [16].

PBI incurs substantially lower overhead at the same sampling rate when compared with CBI and CCI as it exploits hardware support. Further, it requires *fewer* runs to isolate failure predictors

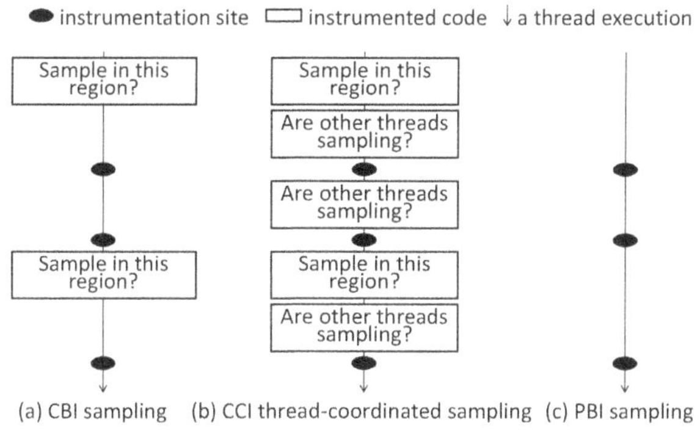

Figure 7. Different sampling schemes

under the same overhead constraint, as sampling can be done much more intensively.

Predicate-evaluation accuracy Sampling can affect the accuracy of predicate evaluation. In fact, this is a concern for many interleaving-related predicates. For example, when a memory location m is accessed for the first time in a sampling period, we cannot possibly know whether the preceding access to m is from the same thread or not. This dilemma is shared by all CCI predicates.

PBI sampling suffers much less from this problem. Hardware keeps monitoring the specified performance event without any gap, unless a cache-line is evicted while cache-related events are monitored. Normal cache-line eviction cycles are much longer than the sampling period in CCI, which is only 100 instructions by default for CCI performance concerns.

Code-size increase PBI sampling does not require any change to a program. In contrast, a significant amount of instrumentation is needed to support sampling in traditional systems. CBI framework prepares one fast version and one slow version for every acyclic region in a program to support its sampling scheme, which at least doubles the code size.

5. Detailed Issues

This section discusses several potential sources of inaccuracy in PBI failure diagnosis that we have not discussed.

Skid in counter-overflow interrupts Interrupt-based sampling is generally *imprecise*. Specifically, the last instruction retired prior to the service of a performance-event overflow interrupt may not be the instruction that actually triggered the interrupt. This gap between the instruction that actually triggered the interrupt and the instruction whose program counter gets collected is termed as *skid*. According to PERF documentation [17], the amount of skid for a particular event could vary, and can be up to dozens of instructions.

To better understand the impact of skid in failure diagnosis, we designed 3 microbenchmarks, each comprised of two threads. Each thread executes a loop that contains a store followed by a load from a shared variable. In each benchmark, different mixes of assembly instructions that do not access memory are inserted before and after the two shared-variable access instructions in the loop. The microbenchmarks contain 100, 200, and 600 static padding instructions respectively. We execute these benchmarks under PERF to monitor I Event. In theory, the padding instructions could never be associated with cache-access events. However, in practice, they appear in the PERF logs, which allows us to calculate the amount of skid.

After running each benchmark 1000 times, we have several observations. First, skid exists in all three benchmarks.

Second, the *variance* of skid for each instruction is very small. In fact, there is always a dominant amount of skid for an instruction. That is, more than 99% of PERF logs for a microbenchmark have a specific amount of skid. This dominant amount of skid is 8 in the first benchmark, and 1 in the second and third benchmarks. Given the existence of dominant skids, performance events that actually occurred at instruction i would mostly be reported at instruction s, and rarely be reported at other instructions s_1, s_2, etc. If i is a good failure predictor, PBI would still be able to identify s as a good failure predictor and filter out noise generated by s_1, s_2, and others, benefiting from the statistical processing of PBI.

Third, skids are usually not long, mostly within 10 assembly instructions. Therefore, the failure predictor detected by PBI can still guide developers to the actual bug location in the program.

We will revisit and further confirm these observations in our experiments on real world bugs presented in Section 7.

Hardware issues False sharing is a common concern for hardware-based concurrency-bug detection and diagnosis [23, 31, 32]. Since multiple shared variables could be placed in the same cache line, cache coherence states may not indicate how a shared variable is accessed by multiple threads. False sharing could affect the quality of PBI failure diagnosis. In our experiments, it has never affected the topmost failure predictor. More details will be presented in Section 7.3.4.

Thread migration and scheduling can also be sources of inaccuracy for hardware-based techniques. Since a thread's performance-counter values are saved by OS during context switches, they have relatively little impact on PBI. Failure diagnosis could be affected when multiple threads scheduled in the same core are executing simultaneously in SMT mode. In this case, shared-variable access interleavings may not cause any cache coherence traffic. If the multiple threads are scheduled to run one at a time, there would be no impact.

In summary, the accuracy of PBI could be affected by hardware and system issues in theory. In practice, although false sharing and skid effects are observed in our evaluation, we have never observed PBI fail in diagnosing a failure due to these two issues or other issues discussed above, as we will see in Section 7.

6. Methodology

We have evaluated PBI on 13 real-world software failures caused by concurrency and sequential bugs, and 10 failures caused by sequential bugs in a widely used software-testing benchmark print_tokens2[1]. These bugs all come from C/C++ programs, and represent different types of common root causes and failure symptoms, as shown in Table 2. All the experiments were performed on an Intel Core i7 (Nehalem) machine running Linux 3.2 kernel.

The experiments focus on evaluating the two design goals for PBI: diagnostic capability and diagnostic performance.

For applications with concurrency-bug failures, we perform a head-to-head comparison between PBI and the state-of-the-art instrumentation-based failure diagnosis tool CCI [16]. We have evaluated *all* the benchmarks examined in CCI paper (Table 2) under the same environment used for CCI. Our evaluation uses the same bug-triggering inputs for PBI and CCI. Further, we use two MySQL benchmarks that are not used in CCI work to evaluate PBI's capability of supporting C++ programs.

Following the evaluation methodology used in CCI, we added randomly executed thread yield calls in the source code to make

[1] Print_tokens2 is a tokenizer program in Siemens benchmark suite [13]. It includes a correct version and 10 buggy versions. Each buggy version contains a bug injected by benchmark designers to emulate common real-world sequential bugs, especially semantic bugs.

Program	KLOC	Root Cause	Failure Symptom	Runs Total	Runs Failed
Concurrency-Bug Failures					
Apache1	333	A.V.	corrupted log	1000	464
Apache2	333	A.V.	crash	1000	504
Cherokee	83	A.V.	corrupted log	1000	480
FFT	1.3	O.V.	wrong output	1000	416
LU	1.2	O.V.	wrong output	1000	480
Mozilla-JS1	107	A.V.	crash	1000	520
Mozilla-JS2	107	A.V.	wrong output	1000	511
Mozilla-JS3	107	A.V.	crash	1000	467
MySQL1	478	A.V.	crash	1000	576
MySQL2	478	A.V.	wrong output	1000	488
PBZIP2	2.1	A.V.	crash	1000	592
Sequential-Bug Failures					
BC	14.4	mem.	crash	1000	444
CUT	1.2	mem.	crash	1000	505
print_tokens2*	0.5	sem.	wrong output	1000	500

Table 2. General characteristics of buggy applications evaluated. "KLOC": program size in thousands of lines of code; "A.V.": atomicity violations; "O.V.": order violations; "mem.": memory bugs; "sem.": semantic bugs; Mozilla-JS: Mozilla JavaScript engine; *: print_tokens2 contains 10 versions, with 1 bug in each version.

the program fail more frequently. This is applied in the same way to our PBI and CCI experiments. The failure rate for each application is shown in Table 2. These random yields do *not* affect the quality of our evaluation, as they only increase the failure occurrence frequency. In real-world software deployment, the failure-occurrence frequency is usually low for concurrency bugs. In these scenarios, PBI users simply need to collect enough failure runs and combine them with a random subset of successful runs to obtain a mix of program runs similar to the mix we are evaluating.

For applications with sequential-bug failures, we have primarily used the input sets designed by the original developers. The developers of print_tokens2 have designed nearly 2000 inputs for it. For each version of print_tokens2, we executed each of these inputs once, and randomly took PERF logs generated by 500 success runs and 500 failure runs. We used the GNU Coreutils program dd to generate random bug-triggering inputs for BC and used bug-triggering inputs provided in bug reports for CUT. We attempted to compare PBI and CBI with respect to sequential-bug failure diagnosis. Unfortunately, we were unable to set up software libraries required by CBI on our machines due to configuration problems. As a result, we will only present a qualitative comparison between CBI and PBI.

PBI's experiments use the default PERF setting of *perf_event_max_sampling_rate* and a command-line "-c 3" configuration to control the sampling rate. This configuration provides a comparable sampling rate as that of CCI, which by default starts sampling at one out of 10,000 rate and each period lasts for 100 instructions. The impact of different "-c" configurations is evaluated and presented in Section 7.3.

7. Evaluation Results

Overall, PBI has successfully diagnosed all the 11 concurrency-bug failures and 10 out of 12 sequential-bug failures. PBI incurs low overhead in the range of 0.4–8.6% for all applications evaluated. In the following paragraphs, we will discuss about diagnostic capability, run-time overhead, parameter sensitivity, and other results in detail.

```
//Thread 1: start a new log          //Thread 2: writing to log
1.1 log_status = OPEN ;
...                                   2.1 if(log_status!=OPEN)
...                                   2.2 // skip logging
1.2 log_status = CLOSED ;
```

Figure 8. A WRW atomicity-violation bug in MySQL (skipping logging leads to a wrong output failure)

7.1 Diagnostic Capability Results

7.1.1 Concurrency bugs

For all the 11 concurrency-bug failures evaluated, PBI has identified predicates directly related to the failure root cause as its **topmost** failure predictor, as shown in the "diagnostic capability" column in Table 3. PBI identifies I-predicates as top predictors for 8 failures caused by atomicity violations. PBI also identifies E-predicates as top predictors for 2 failures caused by order violations (FFT and LU). Finally, PBI identifies an S-predicate as the top predictor for the MySQL2 failure caused by a WRW atomicity violation.

In contrast, there are 6 failures that CCI-Prev or CCI-Havoc fails to diagnose. This can be attributed to four reasons.

First, the current implementation of CCI cannot handle C++ programs, such as MySQL, because its underlying static analysis infrastructure [27] is designed for C programs. One of the MySQL failures is depicted in Figure 8. PBI successfully identifies the S-predicate on line 1.2 as the top failure predictor. We believe that CCI-Prev can also diagnose this failure, if it could use a C++-friendly static-analysis infrastructure.

Second, CCI-Havoc cannot diagnose failures caused by WRW atomicity violations, such as MySQL2 shown in Figure 8, or order violations, such as FFT and LU. The root cause of FFT and LU failures are similar to the one depicted in Figure 2. Since order violations usually do not cause a variable to change its value between two consecutive accesses in one thread, CCI-Havoc cannot diagnose FFT and LU failures. PBI E-predicates are usually good predictors for order-violation failures, as discussed in Section 3.1.2.

Third, sampling prevents CCI from diagnosing the Mozilla-JS1 failure whose root-cause code regions cannot fit into one sampling period, as discussed in Section 4.3. PBI successfully diagnosed this failure, because hardware has accurately tracked the cache-access history related to this failure.

Fourth, CCI-Prev fails to diagnose the Cherokee failure because it does not differentiate read accesses from write accesses. The Cherokee failure is similar to the one depicted in Figure 4.

In summary, PBI is effective in diagnosing a wide variety of concurrency-bug failures. It is also much more language independent than software instrumentation-based techniques.

7.1.2 Sequential bugs

For 10 out of 12 sequential-bug failures, PBI has successfully identified predicates that are directly related to the failure root causes within the top two failure predictors, as shown in Table 4.

An example of a successfully diagnosed sequential-bug failure is shown in Figure 9. This piece of code should return FALSE on line 6. However, it incorrectly returns TRUE there. As a result, whenever there is white-space character (' ') in the input, print_tokens2 will output an incorrect token in its text-parsing output. The topmost failure predictor reported by PBI is a BT predicate at line 4. As we can see, the predicate can help developers to quickly locate the root cause of the wrong output.

In CUT, the buggy code is enclosed by two nested if-conditions. Clearly, the inner-if is closer to the buggy code than the outer-if. However, in our experiments, the BT predicate at the outer-if is ranked first and the BT predicate at the inner-if is ranked second.

	Diagnosis Capability			Skid	Diagnosis Overhead			Avg. # samples in each run		
Program	PBI	CCI-P	CCI-H		PBI	CCI-P	CCI-H	PBI	CCI-P	CCI-H
Apache1	✓ 1(I)	✓ 1	✓ 1	1	0.4%	1.9%	1.2%	305051	127299	129907
Apache2	✓ 1(I)	✓ 1	✓ 1	0	0.4%	0.4%	0.1%	284936	192196	198902
Cherokee	✓ 1(I)	-	✓ 2	1	0.5%	0.0%	0.0%	29795	15966	5182
FFT*	✓ 1(E)	✓ 1	-	0	1.0%	121%	118%	7615	8875	8869
LU*	✓ 1(E)	✓ 1	-	1	0.8%	285%	119%	9541	51893	23356
Mozilla-JS1	✓ 1(I)	-	✓ 2	1	1.5%	800%	418%	111847	74707	38831
Mozilla-JS2	✓ 1(I)	✓ 1	✓ 1	1	1.2%	432%	229%	37851	77919	37162
Mozilla-JS3	✓ 1(I)	✓ 2	✓ 1	0	0.6%	969%	837%	11439	5501	1290
MySQL1	✓ 1(I)	-	-	0	3.8%	-	-	583597	-	-
MySQL2	✓ 1(S)	-	-	1	1.2%	-	-	299389	-	-
PBZIP2	✓ 1(I)	✓ 1	✓ 1	2	8.4%	1.4%	3.0%	312808	125668	124785

Table 3. Concurrency-bug failure diagnosis. "✓ n" indicates that the nth highest ranked predictor captures the root cause, while "-" indicates that neither of the top two predictors is useful. The E/S/I following "✓ n" indicates which MESI-predicate is the top predictor. *: For fair comparison, we use the same program configuration for CCI and PBI, which is different from that in the CCI work [16] for FFT and LU.

Program	Diagnosis Capability	Skid	Diagnosis Overhead
BC	✓ 1(BT)	1	6.1%
CUT	✓ 2(BT)	2	7.6%
print_tokens2 v1	-	-	8.6%
print_tokens2 v2	-	-	8.6%
print_tokens2 v3	✓ 1(BNT)	1	8.6%
print_tokens2 v4	✓ 1(BT)	2	8.6%
print_tokens2 v5	✓ 1(BT)	1	8.6%
print_tokens2 v6	✓ 1(BT)	2	8.6%
print_tokens2 v7	✓ 1(BT)	3	8.6%
print_tokens2 v8	✓ 1(BNT)	2	8.6%
print_tokens2 v9	✓ 1(BNT)	2	8.6%
print_tokens2 v10	✓ 1(BT)	3	8.6%

Table 4. Sequential-bug failure diagnosis. "✓ n" indicates that the nth highest ranked predictor captures the root cause, while "-" indicates that neither of the top two predictors is useful. The BT/BNT following "✓ n" indicates the predictor type.

```
// Print_tokens2 v7
if(ch == '\n')
  return (TRUE);
else if(ch == ' ')
// Bug: should return FALSE
  return (TRUE);
else
  return (FALSE);
```

Figure 9. A semantic bug in print_tokens2 v7

Our investigation shows that most test inputs that take the outer-if branch end up also taking the inner-if branch. In other words, once the BT predicate is observed at the inner-if site, it is mostly evaluated to be true. This causes a low *increase* score for the BT predicate at the inner-if site.

PBI fails to diagnose two print_tokens2 failures for different reasons. In v1, the buggy program does not contain any branch that is related to the software failure. In a function that is executed by every input, the program misses both the code that handles a special character in the input and the branch that checks whether the input contains that special character. As a result, BT and BNT predicates cannot help in diagnosing this program's failure at all. In v2, the buggy code is indeed enclosed by a branch. The BT predicate at this branch suffers a low *increase* score for a similar reason as that in CUT discussed above. So, the top ranked failure predictor is an *effect*, rather than the *cause* of the failure. We have also checked whether the above two failures can be diagnosed by CBI. Based on our understanding of CBI, it should be able to diagnose the failure of v2 through scalar predicates.

Summary The above results show that PBI can effectively diagnose a wide variety of concurrency and sequential bugs. Comparing with the state-of-the-art failure-diagnosis system, PBI has better diagnostic capability for the evaluated concurrency-bug failures and comparable capability for sequential-bug failures.

7.2 Diagnostic Performance Results

PBI has incurred only 0.4–8.6% overhead during its failure diagnosis for *all* the benchmarks. This performance is comparable with and in some cases (e.g., in BC) slightly better than CBI for sequential programs[2, 21], and is much better than CCI for multi-threaded programs. In fact, CCI incurs over 100% overhead for 5 out of the 9 concurrency-bug benchmarks it is applied to, as shown in the "diagnosis overhead" columns of Table 3.

To better understand the performance difference between PBI and CCI, we first confirmed that the number of samples collected by PBI and CCI are mostly comparable to each other, as shown in Table 3. We then evaluated the overhead of CCI under *very* sparse sampling mode (i.e., sampling rate is 0). As shown in Table 5, even with *no* predicate collected, the instrumentation-based sampling framework of CCI still incurs around or more than 100% overhead for 5 out of the 9 benchmarks it is applied to. This shows that counter-overflow based PBI sampling has a significant performance advantage over traditional instrumentation-based sampling techniques.

Program	CCI-Prev	CCI-Havoc
Apache1	0.4%	0.5%
Apache2	0.0%	0.0%
Cherokee	0.0%	0.0%
FFT	96%	102%
LU	112%	95%
Mozilla-JS1	608%	371%
Mozilla-JS2	254%	191%
Mozilla-JS3	884%	830%
PBZIP2	0.8%	2.3%

Table 5. Overhead of CCI under *very* sparse sampling mode

PBZIP2 is the only application where PBI has slightly larger overhead than CCI. The reason is that CCI does not instrument

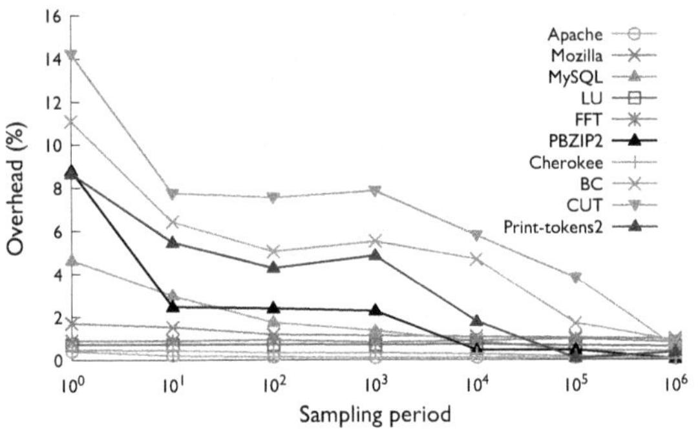

Figure 10. Overhead of PBI under different "-c" configurations

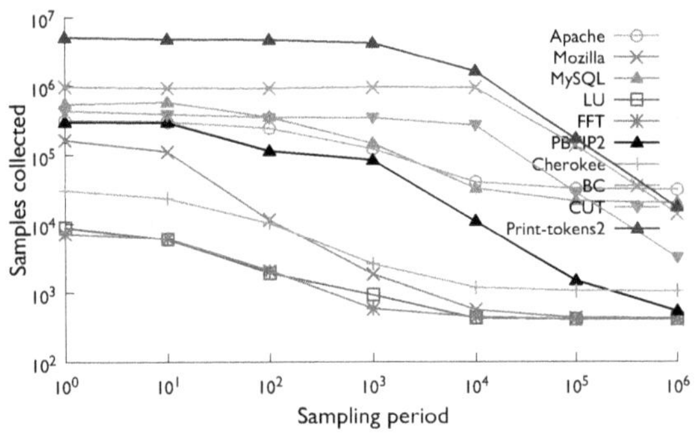

Figure 11. Samples collected by PBI under different "-c" configurations

the memory-intensive BZIP2 compression library used by PBZIP2. PBI monitors *all* user-level event occurrences, including those from library code. This causes extra overhead for PBI. In fact, when CCI is configured to monitor the compression library as PBI does, it incurs over 100% overhead even under very sparse sampling mode.

Unlike the CBI/CCI frameworks, PBI does not incur larger overhead during concurrency-bug failure diagnosis than during sequential-bug failure diagnosis. The reason is that PBI essentially uses the same mechanism to evaluate and sample its concurrency-related predicates and sequential-related predicates.

Note that the overhead of FFT and LU are different from what was originally reported in CCI work [16]. In the original CCI work, accesses to floating-point variables are not instrumented for FFT and LU. For a fair head-to-head comparison, we have reconfigured CCI to monitor floating-point variable accesses, similar to the monitoring done by PBI. In fact, even when CCI does not instrument floating-point instructions, CCI still has much worse performance than PBI. For example, CCI-Prev would still incur around 100% overhead for FFT and LU.

Summary PBI aims to leverage hardware performance counters to achieve low-overhead failure diagnosis that is suitable for production-run deployment. As we can see, PBI has successfully achieved this goal and made significant improvement over previous work.

7.3 Other Detailed Results

7.3.1 Parameter sensitivity

We have evaluated the variation of performance overhead and the number of samples collected by different "-c" configurations.

As we can see in Figure 10, the overhead of PBI reduces substantially as the sampling sparsity increases. In fact, the overhead drops significantly to around 1% for *all* benchmarks under the "-c 10^6" configuration. Of course, diagnostic capability would have to be sacrificed for reduced overhead. As shown in Figure 11, the number of collected samples also significantly drops as the sampling sparsity increases. As a result, many more runs will be needed to collect sufficient samples for PBI failure diagnosis.

Overall, hardware performance counters provide a naturally effective mechanism for PBI users to control the tradeoff between diagnostic performance and diagnostic capability. Furthermore, future work can adjust the sampling sparsity of PBI at run time to achieve more efficient and effective failure diagnosis.

7.3.2 Code size increase

Program	PBI	CCI-Prev	CCI-Havoc
Apache1	1X	65X	40X
Apache2	1X	123X	60X
Cherokee	1X	18X	11X
FFT	1X	64X	37X
LU	1X	69X	39X
Mozilla-JS1	1X	42X	28X
Mozilla-JS2	1X	36X	24X
Mozilla-JS3	1X	43X	29X
PBZIP2	1X	38X	37X

Table 6. Code size with respect to original binary

As shown in Table 6, CCI would increase the binary-code size by 11 to 123 times. Instead, PBI does not change program binary code at all, because it does not rely on code instrumentation for predicate evaluation and sampling.

7.3.3 Skid in real world bugs

Imprecise interrupt handling often causes *skid* between an instruction that triggered the performance-counter overflow and the instruction that is collected by PERF, as discussed in Section 5. Occasionally, the amount of skid could be up to dozens of instructions.

Fortunately, the statistical model used in PBI is capable of pruning noise caused by random skids. As shown in Table 3 and Table 4, all failure predictors have a skid of 0–2 binary instructions, except for two versions of print_tokens2 that have a skid of 3 instructions. These binary-instruction skids do *not* cause any skid at the source-code level. Further, in all cases where skid is observed, the instruction corresponding to the skid is not a memory-access or branch instruction. Therefore, we believe it would be easy for developers to identify the "actual" instruction where the failure predictor is located.

We validated the true location of failure predictor in all benchmarks using the padding-insertion technique described in Section 5.

7.3.4 Effect of false-sharing on PBI failure diagnosis

None of the topmost PBI failure predictors is affected by the cache-line false sharing problem discussed in Section 5. Further checking shows that the 2nd and 3rd ranked failure predictors in FFT and LU are actually due to false sharing. That is, success and failure runs have different patterns in accesses to two/more variables that are located in the same cache line. To some extent, they are also valid failure predictors, as long as the developers are aware of false sharing, which might be challenging. We verified that after changing the source code to avoid false sharing, these failure predictors are pruned out from PBI diagnosis results.

7.4 Limitations of PBI

PBI is not a panacea for production-run failure diagnosis. Although PBI has successfully diagnosed all the concurrency-bug failures in our experiments, it could fail to diagnose some concurrency-bug failures in practice, such as some order-violation failures discussed in Section 3.1.2. Its failure diagnosis could also be affected by hardware constraints, as discussed in Section 5. In addition, PBI is not as flexible as instrumentation-based tools. For example, given the limited types of performance events supported by hardware, PBI cannot support all types of predicates supported by CBI. As another example, instrumentation-based tools can easily skip certain instructions during its program monitoring, such as stack-variable accesses, floating-point instructions, or instructions from library code. It is difficult to achieve the same effect using hardware performance counters alone.

Like the CBI/CCI framework, PBI intentionally collects less information from each run to achieve better run-time performance. As a result, only failures that are observed for multiple times, which is a common pattern in production-run systems, can be diagnosed effectively by PBI. We believe that this tradeoff is worthwhile and suitable for production-run use, as also demonstrated by previous work [3, 16, 21, 22, 26]. Without sampling, program monitoring would incur too large an overhead to be deployed in the field. The production-run usage scenario also allows failures to easily repeat for many times for widely deployed software. In fact, for popular software [9], only failures that have bothered many users (or important users) are processed by developers.

Overall, PBI complements existing techniques and is useful for diagnosing real-world software failures. In practice, users can instruct PBI to collect and analyze MESI, BT, and BNT predicates to diagnose potential failures in single- and multi-threaded software.

8. Related Work

Due to space constraints, this section discusses some closely related work that has not been discussed in the earlier sections.

Using performance counters for software reliability Performance counters are useful for diagnosing system performance bottlenecks [5]. Recently, several interesting techniques have been proposed to help bug detection and software testing using performance counters.

One system [11] uses a performance-counter overflow as a signal to enable and disable a software-based race detector at run time. Specifically, it uses OTHER_CORE_L2_HITM event to count the number of times a cache line is loaded when it is stored in modified state within another core's private L2 cache. The count can imply the existence of conflicting accesses to shared variables.

RACEZ [36] uses Instruction_Retired event to collect samples of executed instructions and related register images. It also instruments the software to collect a trace of executed synchronization operations. During off-line analysis, it uses the the first trace to reconstruct memory-access samples and then combines the two traces to detect data races.

The above two systems have different goals from PBI. They are both designed to detect data races, not to diagnose failures. In fact, they would fail to diagnose many failures, because many concurrency bugs are not caused by data races. They will also incur many false positives in failure diagnosis, because many data races do not cause externally visible failures. Previous work [16] has shown that a race detector would cause 9–81 false positives for the benchmarks evaluated in Section 7. In contrast, PBI can diagnose failures caused by a wide variety of concurrency bugs. In addition, PBI has very few false positives (0 in our evaluation of concurrency-bug failure diagnosis), leveraging its statistical model and failure information. Furthermore, these two systems use performance counters differently from PBI. The first system only uses performance counter outputs as a hint to start traditional race detection; the second system still relies on software instrumentation to collect synchronization information. In contrast, PBI completely relies on performance counters to collect all the needed program-property information for failure diagnosis.

Eunomia [43] uses branch-related events and itlb_misses event to detect certain types of security attacks. It collects instruction and branch execution traces through performance counters. It then checks the trace to discover invalid instructions or infeasible control-flow paths caused by code-injection attacks. This tool does not target general software bugs, and cannot be used to diagnose general software failures.

Other recent works have proposed using branch-related performance counter events to measure code coverage during software testing [37] and using cache-hit/miss performance-counter events to help improve performance [30]. Similar to PBI, these tools all use performance counters to improve traditional techniques that are based on software instrumentation. But, these tools also have completely different goals and hence have very different designs from PBI.

Hardware support for bug detection Researchers have made several proposals [4, 23, 25, 31, 32, 40, 42, 45, 46] to speed up the detection of concurrency bugs and memory bugs by extending hardware. PBI has drawn inspiration from these works. At the same time, PBI is different from them because it uses existing hardware support.

Bug detection Sampling is a widely used technique to lower the overhead of run-time monitoring. Some previous bug-detection tools [3, 26] use software-based sampling techniques to give hot code paths smaller probability to be sampled than cold paths, which helps them detect data races with small overhead. PBI is different from these previous techniques, because its sampling does not require code instrumentation. In addition, as a failure diagnosis tool, PBI has different design goals and strengths from these race-detection tools as discussed above. PBI uses CBI's statistical model to measure each predicate's correlation with software failures. Statistical approaches have also been used before to detect general software bugs during in-house development and testing [6, 8, 12].

9. Conclusion

This paper presents PBI, a production-run failure-diagnosis system. PBI samples hardware performance-counter events at run time and uses statistical processing to discover event instructions closely related to failures. We evaluate PBI using 13 real-world bugs from representative open-source software and 10 bugs from a widely used software-testing benchmark. Our evaluation demonstrates that PBI can effectively diagnose software failures caused by a wide variety of concurrency and sequential bugs, including some failures that cannot be effectively diagnosed by previous work. Benefiting from hardware performance-counter sampling, PBI incurs less than 10% overhead for all the benchmarks, much faster than previous work in concurrency-bug failure diagnosis. PBI does not require any change to the monitored software, operating systems, or hardware. Future work can further improve PBI by exploring more types of performance events and combining instrumentation-based failure-diagnosis techniques with performance-counter based techniques.

Acknowledgments

We thank the anonymous reviewers for their insightful feedback which has substantially improved the content and presentation of this paper. We thank Mark Hill, Ben Liblit and Piramanayagam Nainar for their invaluable comments on PBI. We are grateful to

Stephane Eranian for useful discussions on PERF. We also thank Subhadip Ghosh and Dibakar Gope for their assistance in evaluating skid-related microbenchmarks. This work is supported in part by NSF grants CCF-1018180, CCF-1054616, and CCF-1217582; and a Claire Boothe Luce faculty fellowship. Any opinions, findings, and conclusions or recommendations expressed in this material are those of the authors and do not necessarily reflect the views of NSF or other institutions.

References

[1] V. R. I. Alex Mericas, Brad Elkin. Comprehensive pmu event reference - POWER7. https://www.power.org/events/Power7/.

[2] P. Arumuga Nainar. *Applications of Static Analysis and Program Structure in Statistical Debugging*. PhD thesis, University of Wisconsin – Madison, Aug. 2012.

[3] M. D. Bond, K. E. Coons, and K. S. McKinley. Pacer: Proportional detection of data races. In *PLDI*, 2010.

[4] L. Ceze, P. Montesinos, C. von Praun, and J. Torrellas. Colorama: Architectural support for data-centric synchronization. In *HPCA*, 2007.

[5] J. Demme and S. Sethumadhavan. Rapid identification of architectural bottlenecks via precise event counting. In *ISCA*, 2011.

[6] D. Engler, D. Y. Chen, S. Hallem, A. Chou, and B. Chelf. Bugs as deviant behavior: A general approach to inferring errors in systems code. In *SOSP*, pages 57–72, 2001.

[7] S. Eranian. Perfmon2, 2010. http://perfmon2.sourceforge.net.

[8] M. Ernst, A. Czeisler, W. G. Griswold, and D. Notkin. Quickly detecting relevant program invariants. In *ICSE*, 2000.

[9] K. Glerum, K. Kinshumann, S. Greenberg, G. Aul, V. Orgovan, G. Nichols, D. Grant, G. Loihle, and G. C. Hunt. Debugging in the (very) large: ten years of implementation and experience. In *SOSP*, 2009.

[10] P. Godefroid and N. Nagappan. Concurrency at Microsoft – an exploratory survey. In *Workshop on Exploiting Concurrency Efficiently and Correctly*, 2008.

[11] J. L. Greathouse, Z. Ma, M. I. Frank, R. Peri, and T. M. Austin. Demand-driven software race detection using hardware performance counters. In *ISCA*, 2011.

[12] S. Hangal and M. S. Lam. Tracking down software bugs using automatic anomaly detection. In *ICSE*, 2002.

[13] M. J. Harrold and G. Rothermel. Siemens Programs, HR Variants. http://www.cc.gatech.edu/aristotle/Tools/subjects/.

[14] M. Hirzel and T. M. Chilimbi. Bursty tracing: A framework for low-overhead temporal profiling. In *4th ACM Workshop on Feedback-Directed and Dynamic Optimization*, 2001.

[15] J. L. Lions et. al. ARIANE 5 Flight 501 Failure – report by the inquiry board. http://sunnyday.mit.edu/accidents/Ariane5accidentreport.html.

[16] G. Jin, A. Thakur, B. Liblit, and S. Lu. Instrumentation and sampling strategies for Cooperative Concurrency Bug Isolation. In *OOPSLA*, 2010.

[17] L. kernel developers. Perf profiling framework, 2012. https://perf.wiki.kernel.org/index.php/Main_Page.

[18] D. Levinthal. Performance analysis guide for intel processors. Intel manual, Feb. 2009. http://software.intel.com/sites/products/collateral/hpc/vtune/performance_analysis_guide.pdf.

[19] D. Levinthal. Ia-32 architectures software developers manual volume 3b: System programming guide, part 2. Intel manual, June 2009.

[20] Z. Li, L. Tan, X. Wang, S. Lu, Y. Zhou, and C. Zhai. Have things changed now?: an empirical study of bug characteristics in modern open source software. In *ASID*, 2006.

[21] B. Liblit, A. Aiken, A. X. Zheng, and M. I. Jordan. Bug isolation via remote program sampling. In *PLDI*, 2003.

[22] B. Liblit, M. Naik, A. X. Zheng, A. Aiken, and M. I. Jordan. Scalable statistical bug isolation. In *PLDI*, 2005.

[23] S. Lu, J. Tucek, F. Qin, and Y. Zhou. AVIO: detecting atomicity violations via access interleaving invariants. In *ASPLOS*, 2006.

[24] S. Lu, S. Park, E. Seo, and Y. Zhou. Learning from mistakes – a comprehensive study of real world concurrency bug characteristics. In *ASPLOS*, 2008.

[25] B. Lucia and L. Ceze. Finding concurrency bugs with context-aware communication graphs. In *MICRO*, 2009.

[26] D. Marino, M. Musuvathi, and S. Narayanasamy. Effective sampling for lightweight data-race detection. In *PLDI*, 2009.

[27] G. C. Necula, S. McPeak, S. P. Rahul, and W. Weimer. CIL: Intermediate language and tools for analysis and transformation of c programs. In *International Conference on Compiler Construction*, 2002.

[28] S. Park, R. W. Vuduc, and M. J. Harrold. Falcon: fault localization in concurrent programs. In *ICSE*, 2010.

[29] PCWorld. Nasdaq's Facebook Glitch Came From Race Conditions. http://www.pcworld.com/businesscenter/article/255911/nasdaqs_facebook_glitch_came_from_race_conditions.html.

[30] A. Pesterev, N. Zeldovich, and R. T. Morris. Locating cache performance bottlenecks using data profiling. In *EuroSys*, 2010.

[31] M. Prvulovic. Cord:cost-effective (and nearly overhead-free) order-reordering and data race detection. In *HPCA*, 2006.

[32] M. Prvulovic and J. Torrellas. Reenact: using thread-level speculation mechanisms to debug data races in multithreaded codes. In *ISCA*, 2003.

[33] R. Santelices, J. A. Jones, Y. Yu, and M. J. Harrold. Lightweight fault-localization using multiple coverage types. In *ICSE*, 2009.

[34] SDTimes. Testers spend too much time testing. http://www.sdtimes.com/SearchResult/31134.

[35] SecurityFocus. Software bug contributed to blackout. http://www.securityfocus.com/news/8016.

[36] T. Sheng, N. Vachharajani, S. Eranian, R. Hundt, W. Chen, and W. Zheng. Racez: a lightweight and non-invasive race detection tool for production applications. In *ICSE*, 2011.

[37] M. L. Soffa, K. R. Walcott, and J. Mars. Exploiting hardware advances for software testing and debugging (nier track). In *ICSE*, 2011.

[38] Uh, Gang-ryung, Cohn, Robert, Ayyagari, and Ravi. Analyzing dynamic binary instrumentation overhead. *WBIA at ASPLOS*, 2006.

[39] M. Vaziri, F. Tip, and J. Dolby. Associating synchronization constraints with data in an object-oriented language. In *POPL*, 2006.

[40] G. Venkataramani, B. Roemer, Y. Solihin, and M. Prvulovic. Memtracker: Efficient and programmable support for memory access monitoring and debugging. In *HPCA*, 2007.

[41] Z. Yin, D. Yuan, Y. Zhou, S. Pasupathy, and L. N. Bairavasundaram. How do fixes become bugs? In *FSE*, 2011.

[42] J. Yu and S. Narayanasamy. A case for an interleaving constrained shared-memory multi-processor. In *ISCA*, 2009.

[43] L. Yuan, W. Xing, H. Chen, and B. Zang. Security breaches as pmu deviation: detecting and identifying security attacks using performance counters. In *APSys*, 2011.

[44] W. Zhang, J. Lim, R. Olichandran, J. Scherpelz, G. Jin, S. Lu, and T. Reps. ConSeq: detecting concurrency bugs through sequential errors. In *ASPLOS*, 2011.

[45] P. Zhou, F. Qin, W. Liu, Y. Zhou, and J. Torrellas. iWatcher: Efficient Architecture Support for Software Debugging. In *ISCA*, 2004.

[46] P. Zhou, R. Teodorescu, and Y. Zhou. Hard: Hardware-assisted lockset-based race detection. In *HPCA*, 2007.

ConAir: Featherweight Concurrency Bug Recovery via Single-Threaded Idempotent Execution

Wei Zhang[1] Marc de Kruijf[1,2] Ang Li[1] Shan Lu[1] Karthikeyan Sankaralingam[1]

[1]Computer Sciences Department, University of Wisconsin–Madison [2]Google, Inc

{wzh,dekruijf,ali28,shanlu,karu}@cs.wisc.edu

Abstract

Many concurrency bugs are hidden in deployed software and cause severe failures for *end-users*. When they finally manifest and become known by *developers*, they are difficult to fix correctly. To support end-users, we need techniques that help software survive hidden concurrency bugs during production runs. To help developers, we need techniques that fix exposed concurrency bugs.

The state-of-the-art techniques on concurrency-bug fixing and survival only satisfy a subset of four important properties: compatibility, correctness, generality, and performance. We aim to develop a system that satisfies all of these four properties. To achieve this goal, we leverage two observations: (1) rolling back a *single* thread is sufficient to recover from most concurrency-bug failures; (2) reexecuting an *idempotent* region, which requires no memory-state checkpoint, is sufficient to recover from many concurrency-bug failures. Our system ConAir includes a static analysis component that automatically identifies potential failure sites, a static analysis component that automatically identifies the idempotent code regions around every failure site, and a code-transformation component that inserts rollback-recovery code around the identified idempotent regions.

We evaluated ConAir on 10 real-world concurrency bugs in widely used C/C++ open-source applications. These bugs cover different types of failure symptoms and root causes. Quantitatively, ConAir helps software survive failures caused by all of these bugs with negligible run-time overhead (<1%) and short recovery time. Qualitatively, ConAir can help recover from failures caused by unknown bugs. It guarantees that program semantics remain unchanged and requires no change to operating systems or hardware.

Categories and Subject Descriptors D.1.3 [*Programming Techniques*]: Concurrent Programming; D.2.5 [*Software Engineering*]: Testing and Debugging; D.4.1 [*Operating Systems*]: Process Management

Keywords idempotency, concurrency bugs, failure recovery, static analysis, bug fixing

1. Introduction

1.1 Motivation

Concurrency bugs are unsynchronized memory accesses in multi-threaded programs. Many concurrency bugs are hidden in production-run software, causing severe failures in the field with huge financial losses [30, 42, 48]. When they finally get known by developers, correctly fixing them takes substantial manual effort. Developers often need weeks, or even months, to design a concurrency-bug patch [20, 35] yet about 40% of released concurency-bug patches are incorrect, which are the most error-prone among all types of bug patches [56]. Therefore, it is critical to help *end-users* enable production-run software to *survive* failures caused by hidden concurrency bugs and help *developers fix* known concurrency bugs.

An ideal bug fixing and survival technique should have several key properties: *compatibility*, i.e. no OS/hardware modification; *performance*, i.e. small run-time overhead and fast failure recovery; *generality*, i.e. helping bugs with a wide variety of root-cause interleaving patterns without reliance on accurate bug detection; *correctness*, i.e. not generating results infeasible for original software.

Table 1 summarizes three solutions to this problem and outlines their differences for all these four properties. As shown in columns 2, 3, and 4, no existing technique can achieve all four properties at the same time. We now elaborate on these techniques.

	Auto. Fixing	Prohibiting Interleaving	Rollback Recovery	ConAir
Compatibility	✓	*	*	✓
Correctness	✓	✓	✓	✓
Generality	-	*	✓	✓
Performance	✓	*	*	✓

Table 1. A comparison among concurrency-bug fixing and survival techniques (✓: yes; -: no; *: cannot all be yes at the same time.)

The *automatic fixing* approach statically or dynamically adds synchronization into programs to eliminate *known* bug-triggering interleavings [23, 24, 39]. Although promising, a tool with this approach only fixes bugs with a specific root cause (e.g., atomicity violations [23]), because it requires different types of synchronization to eliminate buggy interleavings of different root-causes. Furthermore, by design, this approach does not help software survive hidden bugs. It only fixes known bugs based on accurate bug root-cause detection.

Proactively prohibiting certain types of interleavings at run time is a common approach to surviving hidden concurrency bugs [5, 29, 37, 43, 45, 46, 51, 55, 57, 58]. Techniques based on this approach only survive failures caused by certain types of interleavings, and tend to impose unnecessary serialization and performance loss on existing hardware. In rare cases, some techniques belonging to this

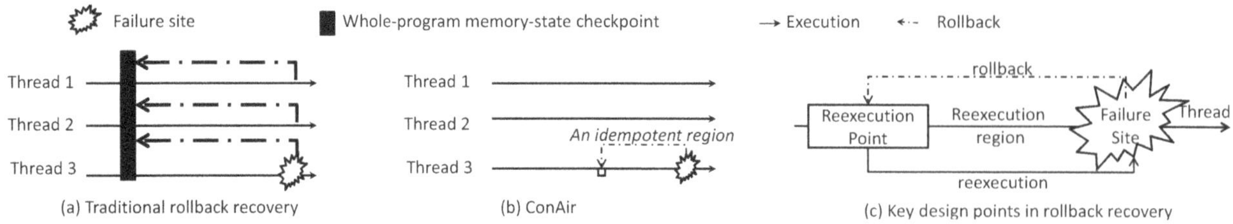

Figure 1. An overview of ConAir

approach may need programmer annotations to eliminate the effect of certain interleavings to maintain correctness.

The *rollback recovery* approach leverages the non-determinism of multi-threaded software to survive hidden concurrency bugs [44, 50, 53]. Without prohibiting any interleaving, it uses system checkpoint and rollback techniques to recover from failures, which is not limited to particular types of root causes. Unfortunately, existing techniques based on this approach require periodic *whole-program* checkpoint at run time and *whole-program* rollback for failure recovery. As a result, they require OS/hardware modifications to achieve good performance.

1.2 Contributions

This paper presents ConAir, a static tool that automatically inserts rollback-recovery code into multi-threaded software and allows software to recover from a wide variety of known and hidden concurrency bugs with little run-time overhead, as shown in Figure 1.

ConAir distinguishes itself from existing rollback-recovery systems by the following features:

1. **No multi-threaded rollback**. We observe that failures caused by most concurrency bugs can be recovered through rolling back just *one* thread, instead of all threads.
2. **No memory-state checkpointing**. We observe that failures caused by many concurrency bugs can be recovered by reexecuting an *idempotent* region surrounding the failure site. A code region is idempotent if it can be reexecuted for any number of times without changing the program semantics. More formal definition of idempotent regions is in Section 2.2.

The above observations help ConAir achieve the four properties listed in Table 1. The reexecution of single-threaded idempotent regions guarantees no change to program semantics (*correctness*)[1]. The rollback-recovery approach, by design, allows ConAir to recover from concurrency bugs caused by a wide variety of root causes (*generality*). By avoiding the need for checkpointing memory state and by avoiding coordination across threads, ConAir limits its run-time overhead (*performance*) and requires no modification to OS/hardware (*compatibility*).

ConAir can be used in two modes. In survival mode, ConAir can be applied to harden a multi-threaded program against hidden concurrency bugs. In fix mode, it can generate safe temporary patches for concurrency bugs whose root causes are unknown. This is helpful to developers who often know the failure symptom of a reported bug long before they understand the root cause of the bug.

We have evaluated ConAir by using 10 real-world concurrency bugs in open-source server and client software. These 10 bugs represent bugs of common root causes, including atomicity violations, order violations, and deadlocks, and bugs of common failure symptoms, including assertion violations, wrong outputs, segmentation faults, and hangs. Without any knowledge of these bugs, ConAir automatically hardens the software at 7 – 19185 statically identified potential failure sites per program. The hardened software runs almost as fast as the original software, with only 0 – 0.2% run-time overhead. Failures caused by 8 out of 10 bugs can always be successfully recovered. The other 2 bugs lead to wrong-output failures. If the output-correctness conditions are known to ConAir, failures caused by these 2 bugs can also be successfully recovered. The time taken for failure recovery varies and is between 8 microseconds and 17 milliseconds. ConAir also has its limitations, which will be discussed in Section 6.5.

[1] ConAir does not violate memory consistency model (see Section 2.2).

2. ConAir overview

The design of a rollback-recovery system for multi-threaded software includes three key components, as shown in Figure 1c: (1) how many threads participate in the rollback recovery; (2) where the failure site is in each participant thread; (3) what is the reexecution point in each participant thread. We take a novel approach to these components by leveraging our key observations. To address component (1), *unlike* previous work, only one thread participates in ConAir rollback recovery. Components (2) and (3) are synergistically handled by forming idempotent code-regions whose end-point is the failure site, and start-point serves as a natural reexecution point for the participant thread. This section develops these key observations of ConAir in detail, and uses these observations to explain its *generality*, *correctness*, *performance*, and *compatibility* properties.

Terminology The program location where software fails is called a *failure site*. The location where software could fail is called a *potential failure site*. Since we may never know whether a failure would occur at a particular location, sometimes the paper does not differentiate failure sites and potential failure sites. A previous study shows that 97% of non-deadlock concurrency bugs first encounter their failures in a single thread, which may then terminate the whole program [61]. We refer to the thread that first encounters the failure as the *failing thread*.

2.1 Single-threaded rollback to recover concurrency bugs

We first discuss the *generality* of single-threaded recovery and compare it with traditional multi-threaded recovery. This discussion does not consider the *correctness* issue, which is discussed in Section 2.2. Our discussion and conclusions are based on root-cause and error-propagation characteristics of real-world concurrency bugs.

Recovering atomicity-violation bugs Atomicity violations contribute to about 70% of real-world non-deadlock bugs [35]. They occur when two code regions R_1 and R_2 from two threads interleave unserializably, which violates the expected atomicity of one or both regions. Clearly, if we can rollback and reexecute any one involved thread, the execution of R_1 and R_2 will be serialized and the failure will be recovered. Therefore, to understand whether single-threaded

```
/*Thread 1*/    /*Thread 2*/
log=CLOSE;      if(log!=OPEN)
log=OPEN;           {//output failure}
```

(a) Violating WAW atomicity (Rollback Thread 2 to recover)

```
/*Thread 1*/    /*Thread 2*/
ptr=aptr;
tmp=*ptr;       ptr=NULL;
```

(b) Violating RAW atomicity (Rollback Thread 1 to recover)

```
/*Thread 1*/ /*Thread 2*/
if(ptr)
  fputs(ptr);   ptr=NULL;
```

(c) Violating RAR atomicity (Rollback Thd 1 to recover)

```
/*Thread 1*/                          /*Thread 2*/
cnt+=deposit1;
printf("Balance=%d",cnt);    cnt+=deposit2;
```

(d) Violating WAR atomicity (Rollback Thread 1 to recover)

Figure 2. Most failures caused by atomicity violations can be recovered by rolling back one thread, the failing thread (Different checkpoint/sandbox techniques may be needed to guarantee correctness.).

recovery works, we need to know whether the failing thread is involved in the unserializable interleaving.

We checked 51 real-world atomicity-violation bugs collected by a previous work [35]. About 92% of them cause failures in a thread that is involved in the unserializable interleaving and hence can potentially be recovered by single-threaded recovery.

The above observation can be better understood through bug examples shown in Figure 2. This figure depicts the most common types of real-world atomicity violations [33, 35, 52]. As we can see, an atomicity violation usually causes an involved thread to read an unexpected value from a shared variable, such as log in Figure 2a, ptr in Figure 2b and Figure 2c, and cnt in Figure 2d. This incorrect value quickly leads to a failure in that thread. Clearly, the failure can be recovered by rolling back and reexecuting that thread.

Recovering order-violation bugs Order violations contribute to nearly 30% of real-world non-deadlock concurrency bugs [35]. They occur when an operation A is expected to execute before an operation B, but instead executes after B due to lack of synchronization. Clearly, if we can rollback and reexecute the thread of B, the occurrence of B will be effectively delayed and the failure will be recovered. Since single-threaded recovery always rolls back the failing thread, we need to understand whether the thread of B is the failing thread.

We checked all 21 real-world order-violation bugs collected by a previous work [35]. We found that about 50%of order-violation bugs lead to failures in the thread of B, and hence can be recovered by the single-threaded recovery. Failures of the other bugs manifest in the thread of A and occasionally some other threads.

To better understand this observation, one can consider a common type of order-violation bugs: thread t_B reads a shared-variable V before V is initialized by thread t_A. In this case, the uninitialized value in V usually leads to a failure in t_B. By rolling back t_B, we can postpone the read of V until V is initialized.

Recovering deadlock bugs Deadlock contributes to about 40% of all concurrency bugs [31]. When a deadlock occurs, every thread involved is holding some resource that is blocking another thread. In a typical deadlock, making any thread release a resource will break the circular resource dependence. Clearly, rolling back any single failing thread can recover from a deadlock.

Summary Overall, rolling back a single thread (i.e., the failing thread) is effective to recover from most concurrency bugs: all deadlocks, almost all atomicity violations (47 among the 51 studied), and about half of the order violations (11 among the 21 studied).

2.2 Idempotent reexecution to recover concurrency bugs

In general, an idempotent region is a code region that can be reexecuted for any number of times without changing the program semantics. Figure 3 shows a code-snippet that is idempotent contrasted with one that is not. In general, such regions can have arbitrary start and end-points in the program, so long as the code in that region adheres to idempotency semantics.

We narrow the definition to make the regions amenable for bug recovery. In this work, an idempotent region always ends at a potential failure site. It does not contain any writes to shared

```
y=x+1;
z=x+y;
```

(a) An idempotent region

```
x=x+1;
z=x+y;
```

(b) Not an idempotent region

Figure 3. Idempotency

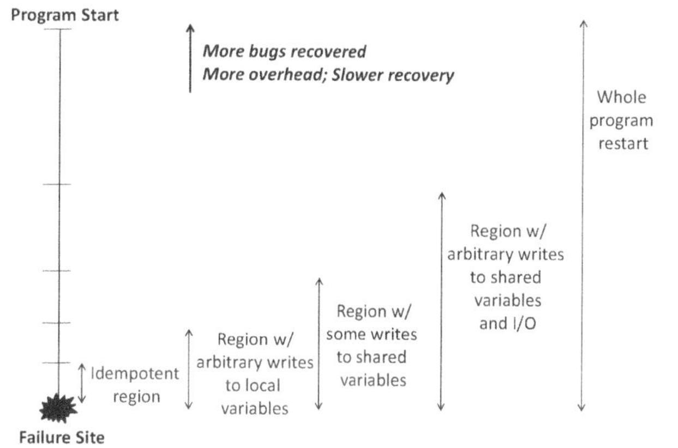

Figure 4. The tradeoff of reexecution-region design

variables, so that its single-threaded reexecution does not violate the memory-consistency model of hardware and system. It does not contain any I/O operations. It also does not contain any writes to local variables that could cause incorrect reexecution.

Using idempotent regions as reexecution regions can easily achieve *correctness* and good *performance*, because they can be correctly reexecuted without any checkpointing or logging. The only concern is that they may be too short to recover concurrency bugs. On the other hand, longer reexecution regions can recover more bugs, but also hurt *performance* and/or *compatibility* more, because they require more complicated rollback-reexecution techniques, such as sandboxing I/O events, buffering shared-variable modifications, and checkpointing local-variable values. Figure 4 sketches this trade-off and design space.

Fortunately, several empirical observations indicate that constraining reexecution regions to be free of idempotency-destroying operations does not eliminate the chance of recovering from concurrency-bug failures.

- I/O operations. Idempotent regions cannot contain any I/O operations. A study of real-world concurrency bugs shows that only about 15% of concurrency bugs' recovery involves I/O operations [54].
- Shared-variable writes. Idempotent regions cannot contain any write to shared variables. Fortunately, among all types of common concurrency bugs discussed earlier, only RAW and WAR atomicity violations (Figure 2b and Figure 2d) require reexecuting shared-variable writes to recover.

```
//assert(e)

  if(e){
  }else{
 Failure:

     __assert_fail(...);

  }
```
(a) Assertion Failures

```
//printf("..",e,..);

    if(Assert(e)){
    }else{
 Failure:
 //developers specify
 //Assert(...)
    }
    printf("..",e,..);
```
(b) Wrong Outputs

```
//tmp=*G_ptr;
  l_ptr=G_ptr;
  if(l_ptr>LowerBound){
  }else{
 Failure:


  }
  tmp=*l_ptr;
```
(c) Segmentation Faults

```
//pthread_mutex_lock(..);
  int ret = pthread_mutex_timedlock(..);
  if (ret!=ETIMEOUT ){
  }else{
 Failure:




  }
```
(d) Deadlock Failures

Figure 5. Failure sites for different types of failures (Some of them involve ConAir code transformation; LowerBound is 10,000 by default.)

- Local-variable writes that are not idempotent, such as the write to x in Figure 3b. No previous study has looked at this. Fortunately, one study of real-world concurrency bugs shows that most non-deadlock bugs have short error-propagation distances, often a handful of data/control dependence edges within one thread [61]. It is likely that many bugs' error-propagation does not involve such idempotency-destroying writes. As for deadlock bugs, they can be recovered by rolling back *any* single involved thread. It is likely that at least one thread can release a deadlock-inducing resource when rolling back its idempotent reexecution region[2].

To know the exact percentage of real-world failures that require each type of reexecution regions is difficult — most of the real-world concurrency bugs examined in previous work [35] have never been reproduced in a research environment. Therefore, we studied all the 26 bugs repeated and presented by 6 recently published works on concurrency-bug detection and prevention [23, 24, 49, 54, 60, 61]. Among these 26 bugs, 20 can be survived through single-threaded reexecution[3]. Among the reexecution regions of these 20 bugs, 16 are idempotent, 2 contain I/O operations, and 2 contain non-idempotent memory writes but no I/Os. Section 6 will present real-world failure examples that can be recovered by reexecuting idempotent regions in the failing thread.

Summary Traditional techniques mainly trend toward the right end of the reexecution-region design spectrum in Figure 4. Their focus of the failure-recovery universality inevitably leads to large run-time overhead and complicated/non-existing platform support.

This paper will explore the leftmost end of the design spectrum. We use idempotent regions as reexecution regions, and identify a reexecution point as the starting point of the idempotent region surrounding each failure site. Our design does not aim the universality of failure recovery. Instead, it aims to survive a significant portion of concurrency-bug failures with a wide variety of root causes at negligible overhead on existing platforms, which will allow easy adoption in production systems.

In the following, Section 3 presents a basic design and implementation of ConAir. Section 4 discusses further extensions and optimizations of ConAir, such as how to avoid useless recovery attempts and how to conduct inter-procedural recovery. Section 5 and Section 6 present the evaluation of ConAir.

3. ConAir design and implementation

ConAir framework includes three components:

1. A static analysis component that identifies failure sites in software (Section 3.1).
2. A static analysis component that identifies reexecution points for every failure site (Section 3.2).
3. A static code-transformation component that enables a multi-threaded program to survive concurrency bugs at the failure sites identified above through single-threaded rollback (Section 3.3).

ConAir does not aim to handle all possible software failures. Instead, it aims to handle common failures with a variety of failure symptoms and root causes with good run-time performance and no modification to the OS or hardware. ConAir also provides guarantee to never deviate from the original software semantics.

3.1 Failure site identification

Failure sites are where failures occur. Some failures may occur due to hidden bugs and some failures may have already manifested with their symptoms known to users/developers. To handle these two types of failures, ConAir operates in two modes: survival mode and fix mode. These two modes only differ in how the failure sites are identified.

3.1.1 Identifying failure sites in survival mode

Without any knowledge of hidden concurrency bugs, ConAir uses static analysis to identify program locations where common failures could occur. The following four types of failures are the most common among the real-world concurrency bugs [61].

Assertion failures. The assert macro is widely used by developers to specify critical program properties. In Linux systems, an assertion failure will cause the execution of __assert_fail(...). ConAir identifies the invocation of __assert_fail(...) as a (potential) failure site, as shown in Figure 5a.

Wrong outputs. Wrong output failures occur when software produces an incorrect output or fails to produce any output when an output is desired. Judging a wrong-output failure requires oracles specified by developers or users. The current prototype of ConAir can help recover from wrong-output failures, if developers can provide output oracles in the format of assert as shown in Figure 5b.

Segmentation-fault failures. A previous study [60] shows that most segmentation faults caused by concurrency bugs occur during the dereference of a heap/global pointer variable. Therefore, ConAir identifies every dereference of a heap/global pointer variable as a potential segmentation fault failure site, as shown in Figure 5c.

Deadlock failures. There are different ways to detect a deadlock failure. Some previous work [24] instruments Pthread library functions and reports deadlocks by catching cycles in the run-time resource-acquisition graph. Many real-world multi-threaded systems, such as MySQL [40], simply maintain a timer for each lock acquisition function and report a deadlock once the lock-acquisition times out. ConAir can work with any deadlock-detection mechanism: the detection code that reports a deadlock is treated as a (potential) failure site. Our current prototype assumes the time-out based

[2] Strictly speaking, idempotent code regions cannot contain lock functions. ConAir's techniques to solve this problem are discussed in Section 4.1.

[3] The 20/26 single-threaded recovery rate is lower than that among a larger set of real-world bugs presented in Section 2.1, because some papers [49, 60] use disproportionally large numbers of order-violation benchmarks.

deadlock detection. ConAir transforms every pthread_mutex_lock function into pthread_mutex_timedlock, and identifies failure sites accordingly as shown in Figure 5d. ConAir can handle customized lock functions, as long as the developers specify the prototypes of their lock, unlock, and timeout-lock functions.

ConAir does not require its failure-site identification to be sound or complete. Inevitably, many sites identified above never manifest as failures. Treating them as potential failure sites only causes negligible run-time overhead, as we will see in Section 6.2, benefiting from ConAir's low-overhead design. The above analysis can be easily customized to cover more types of failures or to focus on a smaller set of severe failures.

3.1.2 Identifying failure sites in fix mode

Fix mode can be used when users or developers encounter a non-deterministic failure with an *unknown* root cause. In this case, users or developers inform ConAir of the failure location. For example, when the bug shown in Figure 2b manifests, users or developers will observe a segmentation fault at the statement tmp=*ptr, which ConAir treats as the failure site.

3.2 Reexecution point identification

As discussed in Section 2.2, the placement of reexecution points and reexecution regions largely determines the system performance. ConAir uses idempotent regions as its reexecution regions during failure recovery. Each reexecution point is the starting point of an idempotent region, which ends at a potential failure site. This design makes ConAir lightweight and able to recover from many, although not all, concurrency-bug failures.

3.2.1 Principle of identifying idempotent regions

Identifying idempotent code regions is not trivial. A code region that is *not* idempotent in source code, such as x=x+1, could become idempotent in bitcode, such as $x_1=x_0+1$, due to variable renaming conducted by a compiler. A code region that is idempotent in bitcode could later become *not* idempotent in binary code due to physical-register allocation. Due to these challenges, there are usually two approaches to identifying idempotent code regions in the binary code. One is to rely on binary code analysis alone. Unfortunately, this could be very complicated for x86 code. The second approach, which is used by recent work [12], is to use a combination of bitcode/binary-code analysis and bitcode/binary-code transformation.

ConAir takes the second approach using the LLVM static analysis and code generation framework [27]. As discussed in Section 2.2, an idempotent region does not contain shared-variable writes, non-idempotent local-variable writes, or I/O operations. Following this, ConAir identifies an idempotent region as an LLVM bitcode region that contains none of the following *idempotency-destroying instructions*: (1) writes to global or heap variables; (2) writes to local variables that are not allocated in virtual registers[4]; (3) function-call instructions. This code region is guaranteed to be idempotent at bitcode level.

To guarantee the region is also idempotent in the binary code, ConAir performs two transformations. First, ConAir uses the −no−stack−slot−sharing flag for LLVM to generate the binary code. This flag guarantees that different virtual registers, when not allocated in physical registers, are allocated in different stack slots. Under this configuration, the code regions identified above will always conduct idempotent operations on memory states. The only concern is that these regions may modify the value of a physical register and cause the reexecution to read a different register value from the original execution. Therefore, ConAir saves the register image at the beginning of the code region and restores the register image right before a rollback. The register save and restore are conducted by setjmp and longjmp. They are both very lightweight, taking only a few nanoseconds.

[4] In LLVM, a virtual register is a variable in static single assignment form (SSA) [8]. It is statically assigned only once.

Alternative methods to identify idempotent code regions Some code regions that contain *idempotent-destroying operations* are still idempotent in binary code. For example, writing a stack variable v that is not allocated in virtual registers does not necessarily hurt the idempotency of a code region R, unless this write is preceded by a read of v that is not preceded by another write to v. As another example, some function calls do not hurt the idempotency. With more complicated analysis, we could identify more and longer idempotent regions in the future.

An alternative implementation decision is to modify the register allocator. A recent work [12] first identifies the boundaries of idempotent regions in LLVM bitcode, it then modifies the compiler back-end code generator to guarantee that idempotent bitcode is translated to idempotent binary code [12]. For our work, we took the setjmp/longjmp approach because it is easier to implement and is ISA independent. A production use of ConAir could employ either approach. The previous work [12] also splits the whole program into idempotent code regions, covering every instruction by idempotent regions. In contrast, our work only identifies idempotent regions that end at potential failure sites. This allows us to achieve negligible overhead ($< 1\%$) in our experiment (Section 6). On the contrary, previous work [12] could have more than 10% run-time overhead.

3.2.2 Algorithm of identifying idempotent regions

When a program does not contain any branch instruction, identifying reexecution points is straightforward. For every failure site f, we simply need to analyze statements one by one backwardly until we find the first statement s that is an *idempotency-destroying* instruction. The reexecution point is right after s.

Unfortunately, real programs always contain branch instructions and there could be multiple execution paths leading to a failure site f. Therefore, we have to identify an appropriate reexecution point along every path leading to f.

ConAir conducts a backward depth-first search from f. This static analysis starts with pushing the predecessors of f in the control-flow graph (CFG) into a work-list stack, and keeps processing the top statement in this stack as follows. (1) When the analysis encounters an idempotency-destroying operation, ConAir identifies a reexecution point right after this operation. ConAir then removes this statement from its work list. (2) When encountering the entrance of function containing f, ConAir identifies it as a reexecution point and removes it from its work list. This decision means that ConAir reexecution does not touch the caller of f. We will revisit this decision and discuss inter-procedural recovery in Section 4. (3) When encountering other statements, ConAir checks how many predecessors of this statement have not been visited. If there is none, ConAir removes this statement from the work list. Otherwise, ConAir pushes an unvisited predecessor of this statement to the top of its work list. ConAir stops its analysis when its work list is empty. At that point, all reexecution points for f are identified. The complexity of this analysis is linear to the static function size.

ConAir repeats the above algorithm for every failure site. Note that the reexecution points of different failure sites do not conflict with each other. That is, the reexecution region of a failure site f_1 will never get shortened by the reexecution points of another failure site f_2. The reason is that a reexecution point is always right after an idempotency-destroying operation or at the entrance of a function, which is the same for all failure sites.

```
1
2
3
4
5
6
7
8  if(e){
9  }else{
10
11
12
13
14     __assert_fail(..);
15 }
```

(a) Original code

```
1  __thread jmp_buf c;
2  __thread int RetryCnt=0;
3  ...
4  Reexecution:
5    setjmp(c);
6    ...
7    //reexecution region
8    if(e){
9    }else
10 Failure:
11     while(RetryCnt++<maxRetryNum){
12       longjmp(c,0);
13     }
14     __assert_fail(..);
15   }
```

(b) Transformed code

Figure 6. ConAir code transformation for assert(e)

3.3 Transformation at failure sites and reexecution points

After identifying failure sites and reexecution points, ConAir performs the following code-transformations that enable the multi-threaded software to recover from concurrency-bug failures.

At every reexecution point, ConAir inserts a setjmp (line 5 in Figure 6) to make sure our reexecution region is idempotent. Sometimes, multiple failure sites may share a common reexecution point. In these cases, ConAir makes sure to insert just one, instead of multiple, setjmp at the common reexecution point.

At every failure site, ConAir inserts a longjmp to rollback the execution to the reexecution point (line 12 in Figure 6). While restoring the register image c, longjmp automatically changes the program counter to the reexecution point where c was taken. This naturally accomplishes the control-flow rollback. ConAir supports multiple reexecutions through the loop on Line 11, because some failures may require several rounds of reexecution to recover. The loop-condition variable is a configurable threshold that prevents endless recovery attempts. Its default value is one million.

ConAir uses a *thread-local* variable to save the register image at every reexecution point (line 1 in Figure 6). At run time, this variable always keeps the register image taken at the most recent reexecution point in a thread. This guarantees that the program will roll back to the right reexecution point.

Deadlock recovery can potentially lead to a livelock problem. This occurs when multiple threads involved in the deadlock try to rollback at exactly the same time. This issue can be solved by putting a small random sleep at the failure site.

3.4 Discussion

Future work can extend ConAir by extending its failure-site identification. Some potential failure sites could be pruned, if we can statically prove that failures can never occur there. For example, analysis could know that NULL-pointer dereference may never occur at some places [6]. We can also use dynamic technique like ConSeq [61] to prune well tested potential failure sites. We can also enlarge the set of potential failure sites based on developers' annotations or automatically inferred specifications. For example, ConAir currently inserts an assertion before every fputs function call to check whether the parameter of fputs is NULL or not.

Future work can also explore other designs of the reexecution regions. For example, some regions that write shared variables can be correctly reexecuted with more sophisticated rollback or checkpoint techniques.

4. Optimizations and Extensions

This section discusses how we extend the basic design of ConAir to recover from more concurrency bugs and optimize the basic design to achieve better performance.

4.1 Extending reexecution regions for library functions

The basic design of ConAir reexecution regions is very stringent: it cannot contain any function calls. In the following, we extend the basic reexecution regions to include some library-function calls.

Why do we need to reexecute library functions? Some failures cannot be recovered unless some library-function calls are reexecuted. For example, if we do not allow a reexecution region to call pthread_mutex_timedlock, ConAir can never recover a deadlock failure shown in Figure 5d. In fact, a reexecution region has to include a call of pthread_mutex_lock to recover deadlock failures, which we will discuss later.

Which library functions can be correctly reexecuted? Some library functions can be correctly reexecuted by executing *compensation functions* at the failure site. For example, if a code region executes a malloc, we need to call a free at the failure site; if a code region executes a pthread_mutex_lock, we need to call a pthread_mutex_unlock at the failure site.

Some library functions cannot be easily reexecuted. For example, output functions in general are difficult to reexecute without system support. Reexecuting free or pthread_mutex_unlock could also be dangerous. Imagine a code region that frees an object that is allocated before this region starts or releases a lock that is acquired before this region starts. It is almost impossible to correctly reexecute this type of code regions.

Implementing library-function extension in ConAir Following the above observations, we allow ConAir reexecution regions to contain memory-allocation functions and lock functions. Other functions, such as free, unlock, and output functions, are still considered idempotency-destroying and cannot be included in any reexecution region.

To support this extension, three changes are made. First, ConAir instruments every call site of memory-allocation and lock functions to record which region is allocated and which lock is acquired. ConAir checks the return value of pthread_mutex_timedlock to know whether a lock is acquired. Second, ConAir needs to know which memory-regions/locks are acquired in the *current* reexecution region at a failure site. To support this, ConAir maintains an integer counter for each thread, which is increased by one at every reexecution point. At the return of every memory-allocation/lock function, ConAir stores the starting address of the newly allocated region or the address of the newly acquired lock, as well as the current counter value of this thread, into a per-thread vector maintained by ConAir. Before storing the new record, ConAir cleans the vector, if the current counter value is different from what is stored in the vector. Third, at each failure site, before the longjmp, ConAir inserts code to iterate through the vector, identify every region/lock that is allocated/acquired under the current counter value, and deallocate/free it.

The above extension guarantees the recovery correctness. Note that deallocating a memory region R or releasing a lock L at the failure site in thread t_1 does *not* affect the correctness of other threads. Since a reexecution region cannot contain writes to shared variables, other threads could not have obtained any pointer pointing to R. Furthermore, no other thread could have acquired L before t_1 releases it. Also note that reexecution regions do not contain any free or pthread_mutex_unlock functions. Therefore, we do not need to worry about an object/lock that is allocated/acquired and then freed/released during one reexecution region.

(a)	(b)	(c)	(d)

Reexecution:
 	
lock(&L);//blocked
	Reexecution:
	lock(&L0);
	lock(&L); //blocked
		Reexecution:
		tmp=tmp+1;
		assert(tmp);//violated
			Reexecution:
			tmp=global_x;
			assert(tmp);//violated

(a) Can**not** be recovered	(b) Could be recovered	(c) Can**not** be recovered	(d) Could be recovered

Figure 7. Some failure sites cannot be recovered by ConAir (The last line in each figure is a potential failure site)

4.2 Optimizations to remove unnecessary rollbacks

Some failures cannot be recovered by ConAir, such as those shown in Figure 7a and Figure 7c. We identify failure sites that are statically proven to be unrecoverable and remove any unnecessary rollback-reexecution code inserted by the basic ConAir algorithm described in Section 3.

Deadlock failure optimizations To recover from a deadlock failure, ConAir should at least release a lock originally held by the thread at the failure site, as shown in Figure 7b. Otherwise, other threads involved in this deadlock cannot possibly make progress during the recovery attempt, and hence ConAir has no chance to recover the deadlock. ConAir optimization follows this intuition. Each deadlock failure site f could correspond to different reexecution regions along different execution paths. ConAir checks whether there is a lock-acquisition operation inside at least one reexecution region of f. If there is none, no lock will be released at f and there is no chance for deadlock recovery. Therefore, ConAir removes the failure-recovery code at f. The current prototype of ConAir turns pthread_mutex_lock functions into pthread_mutex_timedlock functions when it identifies potential deadlock sites, as discussed in Section 3.1.1. Once ConAir identifies a failure site to be unrecoverable, the corresponding pthread_mutex_timedlock is turned back to pthread_mutex_lock.

Non-deadlock failure optimizations To recover from a non-deadlock failure, the reexecution conducted by ConAir should include at least one shared-variable read that can affect the evaluation outcome at the failure site, as shown in Figure 7d. Otherwise, the reexecution is guaranteed to fail again. Following this intuition, ConAir checks every non-deadlock failure site f. ConAir first uses intra-procedural static backward slicing to identify global/heap memory-read instructions that can affect f through data dependence and/or control dependence. ConAir then checks whether there is at least one such read instruction that is inside a reexecution region of f. If not, f is not recoverable and no failure-recovery code is inserted for it.

Our intra-procedural backward-slicing analysis is implemented in LLVM to analyze LLVM bitcode. Interestingly, our analysis is much simpler than general backward-slicing algorithms.

A major source of complexity in general slicing analysis is tracking data dependence through memory accesses, which requires pointers-alias analysis, as shown by the dotted line in Figure 8a.

ConAir does *not* have this concern. Recall that write instructions in a ConAir reexecution region only write to virtual registers (Section 3.2), such as the write to %0, %1, and %2 in Figure 8b. Therefore, when ConAir backward slicing encounters a read instruction r that does not read from a virtual register, such as line 2 in Figure 8b, ConAir simply *stops* tracking its data dependence. The reason is that the instruction that provides value for r must write to non-virtual-register locations (e.g., line 1 in Figure 8b) and do not belong to ConAir idempotent regions. Slicing outside an idempotent region, and hence a reexecution region, is useless for ConAir.

After removing all unrecoverable failure sites, ConAir also removes reexecution points that do not correspond to any failure site and finishes the optimization.

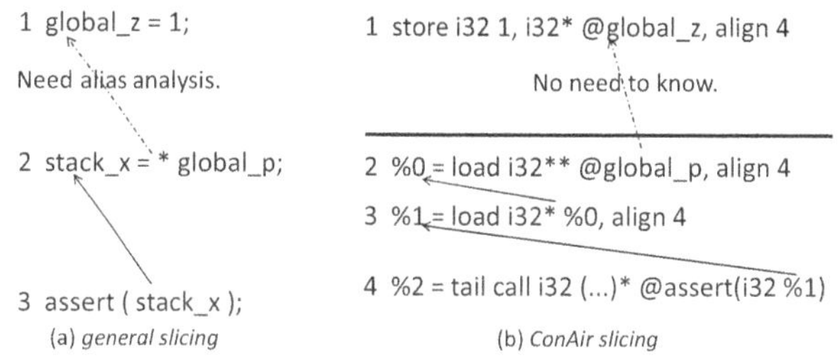

Figure 8. The difference between general slicing analysis and the slicing in ConAir (the stack_ prefix denotes stack variables; the global_ prefix denotes global variables; a solid arrow shows an easy-to-get dependence; a dotted arrow shows a difficult-to-get dependence; the thick line in (b) shows the reexecution-region boundary.)

4.3 Inter-procedural reexecution

The basic ConAir algorithm presented in Section 3 only attempts intra-procedural recovery. That is, the reexecution point for a failure site f is always in the function that contains f, referred to as foo. In this section, we discuss pushing reexecution points into the callers of f. We refer to this as *inter-procedural recovery*. Inter-procedural recovery can help recover from more failures, but can also hurt performance.

When is inter-procedural recovery correct? We should not attempt an inter-procedural recovery, if doing so would generate results infeasible for the original program. Following the discussion in Section 3.2, when there is no idempotency-destroying operation on a path between f and the entrance of foo, it is safe to extend the reexecution region into the caller of foo.

When can inter-procedural recovery help? Since a ConAir reexecution region cannot contain any modification to shared variables, parameters are the only ways for a caller to affect the execution outcome at f. Therefore, inter-procedural reexecution can potentially help the recovery of a non-deadlock failure, only when a parameter of foo is on the backward slice of f.

When do we need inter-procedural recovery the most? It is difficult to accurately predict when inter-procedural recovery will be needed without knowing the hidden bugs. Intuitively, imagine a path p between the entrance of foo and f. As discussed in Section 4.2, reexecuting p cannot help recover a non-deadlock failure at f, if p contains no shared-variable read that can affect the outcome of f. Similarly, reexecuting p cannot help recover a deadlock failure at f, if p contains no lock-acquisition functions. Therefore, we hypothesize that an inter-procedural recovery is most needed when such an *unrecoverable* path p exists.

Conditions of ConAir inter-procedural recovery Inter-procedural recovery could help recover more failures. However, it significantly slows down ConAir static analysis, which we will see in Section 6; it will also identify more reexecution points with more setjmp executed at run time, which incurs more overhead.

Based on these considerations, ConAir selects a failure site f for inter-procedural recovery when f satisfies all the following three conditions: (1) There is no idempotent-destroying operation on any path between the entrance of foo and f. This way, once selected for inter-procedural recovery, the recovery attempt of f is always conducted interprocedurally, no matter which path is followed in foo during the failure run. (2) At least one argument of foo is on the backward slice of f, when f is a non-deadlock failure site. This way, the inter-procedural reexecution can potentially help recover the failure. This parameter is referred to as a *critical parameter*. (3) At least one path between the entrance of foo and f is unrecoverable.

How to identify inter-procedural reexecution point? When a failure site f is identified for inter-procedural recovery, ConAir uses static analysis to find every function foo_1 that calls foo. Inside foo_1, we use the analysis described in Section 3.2.2 to look for reexecution points. This analysis starts from the instruction that pushes the critical parameter onto the stack of foo, when f is a non-deadlock site; it starts from the invocation of foo, when f is a deadlock site.

We then identify reexecution points just as during intra-procedural recovery (Section 3.2). Note that the setjmp and longjmp inserted at reexecution points and failure sites handle the program-counter register and the stack-frame registers. Therefore, no extra effort is needed for inter-procedural rollback.

While analyzing the caller of foo, we could decide to try inter-procedural recovery again. In our current prototype, we set a threshold of how many levels of inter-procedural recovery we would attempt for one initial failure site f. The default setting is 3. That is, to recover f inside a function foo, ConAir could at most rollback the execution to the callers' callers' caller of foo, referred to as foo_3. This threshold is configurable. It balances the recovery capability and run-time performance.

Theoretically, there could be a path between the entrance of foo_3 and f that does not contain any idempotent-destroying operations. Since we decide not to go further into the caller of foo_3, we could choose to set the reexecution point at the entrance of foo_3. However, this scheme could prevent failure sites inside foo_3 to attempt inter-procedural recovery. Therefore, in our current prototype, ConAir simply gives up the inter-procedural recovery attempt of f in that case and puts the reexecution point back to the entrance of foo. Note that, this case is extremely rare and has *never* occurred in any of the applications evaluated by us.

Other issues Our inter-procedural recovery analysis needs to work together with the intra-procedural recovery analysis discussed in Section 3 and the optimization analysis discussed in Section 4.2. ConAir first conducts intra-procedural analysis. This analysis could identify the entrance of foo as a reexecution point for a failure site f, referred to as RE_{intra}. ConAir then conducts inter-procedural recovery analysis. Once f is identified for inter-procedural recovery, ConAir safely removes the reexecution point RE_{intra}[5]. Finally, ConAir conducts its optimization analysis discussed in Section 4.2. This optimization is *only* applied to failure sites that conduct intra-procedural recovery. Failure sites that are selected for inter-procedural recovery usually have long reexecution regions. It is much harder to statically prove them to be unrecoverable.

5. Experimental Methodology

Our work aims to allow programs to recover from a significant portion of real-world concurrency-bug failures with a wide variety of root causes at low overhead on existing platforms. To empirically evaluate whether ConAir has achieved this goal, our experiments look at 10 real-world concurrency-bug failures in 10 open-source applications that have been widely used in previous bug detection

[5] This could cause some other failure sites in foo to conduct interprocedural recovery too, which is fine.

App.	App. Type	LOC	Failures	Causes
FFT	Scientific computing	1.2K	w. output	A/O Vio.#
HawkNL	Network library	10K	hang	deadlock
HTTrack	Web crawler	55K	seg. fault	O Vio.
MozillaXP	XPCOM: cross platform component object model	112K	seg. fault	O Vio.
MozillaJS	JavaScript engine	120K	hang	deadlock
MySQL1	Database server	681K	w. output	A Vio.
MySQL2	Database server	693K	assertion	A Vio.
Transmission	BitTorrent client	95K	assertion	O Vio.
SQLite	Database engine	67K	hang	deadlock
ZSNES	Game simulator	37K	assertion	O vio.

Table 2. Applications and Bugs (w. output: wrong output failures; A Vio.: atomicity violations; O Vio.: order violations; #: There are both order violations and atomicity violations in FFT.)

and avoidance research [23, 24, 49, 54, 60, 61]. They represent a wide variety of failure symptoms and root causes, as shown in Table 2. We will quantitatively evaluate whether ConAir can indeed recover failures with different root causes; what is the run-time overhead introduced by ConAir; how long it takes to recover a failure under ConAir; and the static-analysis complexity of ConAir.

We apply ConAir to analyze and transform each application twice, representing fix mode and survival mode respectively.

While applying ConAir in survival mode, ConAir needs **no** knowledge of failures or bugs. It automatically identifies potential failure sites as discussed in Section 3.1 and transforms software.

While applying ConAir in fix mode, ConAir assumes the knowledge of failure sites provided by developers or users who want to fix a particular failure they observed. This could be a specific assert that is violated; a particular pthread_mutex_lock that blocks the program; a particular memory-access instruction that causes a segmentation fault; or an output function that generates incorrect results. Note that ConAir needs **no** information about bug-triggering inputs, bug root-causes, or bug-detection results.

To evaluate whether the software can survive the manifestation of a bug, we insert sleeps into each program's buggy code regions to force the occurrence of the failure-inducing interleaving. Executed under this setting and failure-inducing inputs, the software in our benchmark set fails with almost 100% probability, if ConAir is not applied. After ConAir is applied, we execute the software under the same setting for 1000 times. We claim ConAir to have successfully recovered the failure if the hardened software executes correctly in all 1000 runs. To evaluate the run-time overhead, we execute the original program and the transformed programs under the same input (i.e., the bug-triggering input) for 20 times each, and calculate the average overhead. No sleep is inserted and software never fails during the run-time overhead measurement.

Among all types of failures, wrong-output failures cannot be recovered unless the users or developers annotate the correctness condition of an output. This condition is easily available in fix mode, but is not necessarily available in survival mode. To better understand the *worst*-case overhead of ConAir in the survival mode, ConAir treats every output function as a potential failure site, even though the correctness condition may be unavailable.

All the experiments are conducted on an 8-core Intel Xeon machine running Linux version 2.6.18 and using the LLVM 2.8 compiler.

6. Experimental Results

As shown in Table 3, ConAir recovers all the evaluated bugs. ConAir incurs no overhead in fix mode, and negligible overhead ($< 1\%$) in survival mode. In this section, we will explain the following experimental results in detail: (1) how ConAir effectively fixes bugs with known failure symptoms; (2) how ConAir transparently hardens

App.	Failure Recovered?		Overhead	
	fix	survival	fix	survival
FFT	✓	$\checkmark_c$	0%	0.0%
HawkNL	✓	✓	0%	0.0%
HTTrack	✓	✓	0%	0.0%
MozillaXP	✓	✓	0%	0.0%
MozillaJS	✓	✓	0%	0.0%
MYSQL1	✓	$\checkmark_c$	0%	0.1%
MYSQL2	✓	✓	0%	0.0%
SQLite	✓	✓	0%	0.0%
Transmission	✓	✓	0%	0.2%
ZSNES	✓	✓	0%	0.0%

Table 3. Overall bug recover results (✓: recovered; $\checkmark_c$: conditionally recovered; recovering these wrong-output failures requires annotations.)

```
1 //Thread 1
2 fprintf("Start %d",Init);
3 tmp=End;
4 assert(tmp>0);
5 fprintf("Stop %d, Total %d", tmp, tmp-Init);
```

```
1 //Thread 2
2 //End is 0 until below
3
4 End=time(NULL);
```

Figure 9. An atomicity/order violation in FFT that causes a wrong-output failure. If developers specify the output-correctness condition (e.g., the assert above), ConAir can help recover the failure.

multi-threaded software to survive hidden bugs; (3) how ConAir achieves negligible run-time overhead; (4) the fast failure recovery under ConAir; (5) the static analysis time of ConAir.

6.1 Failure recovery

6.1.1 Fix-mode failure recovery

In fix mode, ConAir is aware of the failure sites and failure symptoms. It inserts rollback-recovery code accordingly.

Among the non-deadlock bugs that are evaluated, five of them (FFT, HTTrack, MozillaXP, Transmission, and ZSNES) cause failures in a thread that reads a shared variable too early; FFT[6] and MySQL2 cause failures due to RAR atomicity violations; MySQL1 causes failures due to a WAW atomicity violation. ConAir can successfully recover failures caused by all of them.

Some failure recoveries only roll back a few instructions. For example, Figure 9 shows a bug in FFT. In this program, thread 1 could unexpectedly read End (line 3in Figure 9) before thread 2 updates it, causing either an order violation or an atomicity violation and a wrong-output failure. ConAir inserts a setjmp right before the assert, which helps FFT to recover this failure.

Two of these 10 bugs (Transmission and MozillaXP) require inter-procedural reexecution to recover. For example, Figure 10 depicts the MozillaXP bug. In MozillaXP, thread 1 could unexpectedly read mThd->state in function GetState before the global pointer mThd is initialized by thread 2. This could cause a segmentation-fault failure. ConAir inserts a pointer sanity check right before line 9 in GetState; it also identifies a reexecution point inside function Get and inserts setjmp there. Once ConAir sees an invalid pointer at line 9 in thread 1, the program will automatically jump back to before the invocation of GetState in Get. Eventually, thread 2 will initialize mThd and the program will succeed.

Deadlock recovery is slightly different from the recovery of non-deadlock bugs. Figure 11 shows a real-world deadlock bug in HawkNL. As we can see, thread 1 and thread 2 could acquire nlock and slock in reversed orders and lead to a deadlock. ConAir analyzes both threads. When ConAir considers Lock(&slock) (line 8) in thread 1 as a potential failure site, the reexecution region is very short due to the idempotency-destroying operation, driver->Close(). Since this region does not contain another lock acquisition function, ConAir considers it as unrecoverable and does not attempt any failure recovery in thread 1 (Section 4.2). When ConAir considers Lock(&nlock) (line 8) in thread 2 as a potential failure site, its reexecution region can go all the way back to before the invocation of Lock(&slock) (line 4) in thread 2. Since this region contains another lock-acquisition function, ConAir considers Lock(&nlock) in thread 2 as a recoverable failure site. ConAir turns it into a lock with timeout and inserts setjmp to the beginning of Shutdown function. At run time, once thread 2 times out at its attempt to acquire nlock, thread 2 will release slock and reexecute a large chunk of Shutdown. This effectively resolves the deadlock problem in HawkNL.

[6] FFT contains both order violations and atomicity violations.

```
1 //Thread 1
2 Get(){
3   ...
4   tmp=GetState(mThd);
5 }
6
7 GetState(THD *thd)
8 {
9   return(thd->state &
10      THREAD_DETACHED);
11 }
```

```
1 //Thread 2
2 //mThd is shared
3 //between two threads;
4 //it is 0 before
5 //initialized below.
6
7 InitThd(){
8
9   mThd =
10    CreateThd(..);
11 }
```

Figure 10. An order violation in Mozilla XPCOM.

```
1 //Thread 1
2 Close(){
3   ...
4   Lock(&nlock);
5
6   driver->Close();
7
8   Lock(&slock);
9   ...
10 }
```

```
1 //Thread 2
2 Shutdown(){
3   ...
4   Lock(&slock);
5   if(nSockets!=NULL){
6     int i=0;
7     if(nSockets[i]){
8       Lock(&nlock);
9       ...
10    }
11  }
12 }
```

Figure 11. A deadlock in HawkNL.

Summary ConAir can effectively fix concurrency bugs with a variety of root causes once the failure sites and symptoms are known.

6.1.2 Survival mode

In survival mode, ConAir is **not** aware of any bug. It automatically and systematically identifies potential failure sites and transforms the program accordingly.

As shown in Table 4, ConAir has identified and hardened 7 – 19185 static failure sites in each benchmark program. Naturally, ConAir identifies the fewest failure sites in the smallest programs (FFT and HawkNL) and the most failure sites in the largest programs (MySQL1 and MySQL2). In general, potential segmentation-fault sites dominate all types of potential failure sites, because ConAir identifies every heap/global pointer dereference as a potential segmentation-fault site. Potential deadlock sites are the fewest among all four types of failure sites, because only a lock operation that is enclosed by another lock operation with no write to shared variables in between is identified as a potential deadlock site that is recoverable by ConAir. HTTrack developers left many assertions in the program, leading to a large number of potential assertion-violation sites.

App.	Assertion Violation	Wrong Output	Seg. Fault	Dead-lock	Total
FFT	5	34	14	0	53
HawkNL	0	0	5	2	7
HTTrack	657	504	3146	0	4307
MozillaXP	1	117	6791	0	6909
MozillaJS	0	5	134	6	146
MYSQL1	119	3256	15791	19	19185
MYSQL2	518	2853	15498	21	18890
SQLite	0	25	47	1	73
Transmission	430	190	2151	0	2771
ZSNES	1	50	331	0	382

Table 4. Static failure sites hardened by ConAir

App.	Survival Mode		Fix Mode	
	Static	Dynamic	Static	Dynamic
FFT	56	24	5	5
HawkNL	7	7	1	1
HTTrack	3570	12995	3	4
MozillaXP	3647	2170	1	23
MozillaJS	144	6	1	1
MYSQL1	12494	215218	1	20
MYSQL2	13031	82394	1	30
SQLite	142	7	1	1
Transmission	2568	4425	3	8
ZSNES	321	32	1	2

Table 5. The number of reexecution points inserted by ConAir

These automatically identified potential failure sites include the failure sites of all the 10 bugs that are evaluated. Therefore, ConAir can help software successfully recover from these hidden bugs.

Note that survival-mode ConAir identifies every output functions, including fprintf, printf, application-specific functions, such as my_printf in MySQL and js_printf in Mozilla, and others as a potential site of wrong output. The current prototype of ConAir needs developers' specification to recover a wrong-output failure, as shown in Figure 9. We believe this effort is worthwhile for hardening critical outputs. Future work can also use likely-invariant inference tools [15] to infer such specifications for an output function, and automate the wrong-output failure recovery process.

Summary The above evaluation shows that ConAir is effective to help software survive failures caused by hidden bugs.

6.2 Runtime overhead

The run-time overhead of ConAir comes from four sources: (1) code inserted at every reexecution point; (2) extra condition-checking at the failure sites, such as sanity checking for pointers at potential segmentation-fault sites; (3) code inserted at call site of memory-allocation and lock functions. (4) using the −no−stack−slot−sharing LLVM linking flag. Among these four, the first one is the dominant source.

To understand the runtime overhead of ConAir, we have counted the number of reexecution points in the hardened programs.

As shown in Table 5, ConAir introduces 6 – 215218 dynamic reexecution points in survival mode. Considering that each reexecution point only takes a few nanoseconds to execute (a setjmp and a local counter increment), the low overhead of survival-mode ConAir is understandable. Naturally, the fix-mode ConAir introduces only a few reexecution points, as shown in Table 5. Its overhead is not perceivable.

There are mainly two reasons that ConAir only requires a relatively small numbers of reexecution points. First, the reexecution

App.	Non-Deadlock		Deadlock	
	Static	Dynamic	Static	Dynamic
FFT	2.0%	5.0%	N/A	N/A
HawkNL	50%	50%	33%	83%
HTTrack	42%	5.4%	N/A	N/A
MozillaXP	2.4%	1.7%	N/A	N/A
MozillaJS	0.0%	0.0%	50%	50%
MYSQL1	1.1%	8.2%	88%	99%
MYSQL2	0.46%	14.6%	91%	100%
SQLite	3.4%	0.0%	30%	71%
Transmission	4.5%	1.76%	N/A	N/A
ZSNES	6.8%	36.4%	N/A	N/A

Table 6. The percentage of reexecution points that are optimized (N/A: the non-optimized version has 0 reexecution point).

Application	ConAir Recovery		Restart
	Time (μs)	# Retries	Time (μs)
FFT	907	97	3189072
HawkNL	59	1	943
HTTrack	4237	474	10776
MozillaXP	17388	8432	207041
MozillaJS	44	1	472
MYSQL1	6014	575	26308
MYSQL2	8	1	836177
SQLite	86	1	1443
Transmission	6476	761	553109
ZSNES	1022	123	8643

Table 7. Failure recovery time (The experiments are conducted with small amount of noises inserted to help trigger the concurrency-bug failures).

points are identified according to potential failure sites. Different from previous work [12], ConAir does not aim to find a reexecution point for every instruction in the program. Instead, it targets on common failures of concurrency bugs. Second, ConAir optimization discussed in Section 4.2 has helped to remove failure sites that are not recoverable under ConAir and corresponding reexecution points.

To quantitatively demonstrates the optimization effect, we have tried to harden each program by survival-mode ConAir with and without ConAir optimization. As we can see in Table 6, the optimization effect is significant for deadlock reexecution points: 30–91% of static reexecution points can be optimized away. Many lock operations are not enclosed by another lock operation in its reexecution region, and hence are considered as not recoverable. In comparison, the optimization effect for non-deadlock reexecution points is not as significant. Fewer than 10% of static or dynamic reexecution points are optimized away for most benchmarks. The reason is that the optimization cannot eliminate any segmentation-fault reexecution points. In the current prototype of ConAir, the potential site of a segmentation fault is the dereference of a global/heap pointer variable. Since the reexecution regions of this type of failure sites always contain a read of global/heap variable (i.e., the pointer) that can affect the failure outcome, ConAir considers them un-optimizable. HTTrack has a large number of reexecution points that are not related to segmentation faults. Therefore, a significant number of its reexecution points are optimized away.

Summary Benefiting from its single-threaded idempotent reexecution design, its failure-oriented idempotent region identification, and its optimization analysis, ConAir can effectively improve the reliability of production-run software almost for free.

6.3 Recovery time

Recovery time affects the availability of production-run software. We quantitatively measure the failure-recovery time under ConAir, and compare it with the time of restarting the whole program.

Note that software restart almost always changes the program semantics perceived by users, unless it can log all the inputs and external signals, and sandbox I/O operations. In addition, the recovery time of software restart becomes worse with the workload getting larger. Instead, the recovery time of ConAir is largely oblivious of the workload. Therefore, the advantage of ConAir recovery in practice would be much more significant than the quantitative results presented below.

As shown in Table 7, the failure recovery in ConAir ranges between 8 microseconds and 17 milliseconds. In contrast, program restart could take as long as several seconds when the failure occurs at the end of a scientific computation (FFT). The recovery-time speedup of ConAir ranges from 8 times to over 100,000 times.

The ConAir recovery speed is mainly determined by the root cause of the failure. Failures caused by RAR atomicity violations (Figure 2c) are always fast to recover. The failing thread does not need to wait for any other thread. Once it reexecutes the read-after-read, the atomicity violation is immediately eliminated and the failure immediately recovers. That is why MySQL2 takes only 8 microseconds to recover. Deadlock bugs (HawkNL, SQLite and MozillaJS) also require relatively short recovery time. After one thread t_1 involved in the deadlock releases a lock at the failure site, another thread t_2 can almost immediately jumps out of the deadlock situation. The recovery time for t_1 will be determined by the critical region length of t_2. Failures caused by order violations usually require a relatively long time to recover. Take the MozillaXP bug shown in Figure 10 as an example. At run time, thread 1 reads mThd too early and has to rollback due to an invalid value in mThd. Rolling back thread 1 once may not recover the failure, because thread 1 has to wait for thread 2's progress. In our experiment, this rollback is conducted more than 8000 times until thread 2 initializes mThd. This is the main reason of the relatively long recovery time of HTTrack, MozillaXP, Transmission, and ZSNES.

Summary Our evaluation shows that ConAir supports fast failure recovery. It can help software survive failures with little impact to latency and availability.

6.4 Static analysis time

The static analysis and code transformation time of ConAir ranges from less than a second (FFT) to around 4 hours (MySQL). The majority of the time is spent in attempting inter-procedural failure recovery. In fact, the basic intra-procedural static analysis discussed in Section 3 and the optimization analysis discussed in Section 4.2 together take only 50 seconds for MySQL and fewer than 10 seconds for other benchmarks.

Summary The static analysis of ConAir is fast enough to process large real-world multi-threaded software. If the time budget is tight, ConAir users can disable the inter-procedural recovery analysis.

6.5 Limitations of ConAir

ConAir does not aim to recover all concurrency-bug failures, which inevitably requires much higher run-time overhead and/or complicated platform support. Specifically, ConAir cannot recover failures that require multi-threaded reexecution or very long reexecution regions, as discussed in Section 2.1. Fortunately, as also discussed in Section 2.1, many real-world concurrency bugs do not require multi-threaded reexecution or long reexecution to recover, and hence can benefit from ConAir. Finally, ConAir cannot recover software from a wrong-output failure, if developers do not provide output-correctness conditions.

7. Related Work

Many closely related works have been discussed in the earlier sections. This section presents other related works.

Concurrency bug detection Many techniques have been proposed to detect data races [14, 18, 47, 59], atomicity violations [5, 17, 33, 34], order violations [19, 36, 49, 57, 60], and others. Bug-detection tools help developers discover and understand the defects in software. ConAir has a different goal from bug-detection tools. It aims to recover concurrency-bug failures at run time without understanding the bug root causes.

Software checkpoint and replay Checkpoint and replay are useful techniques for failure diagnosis and recovery. Many techniques have been proposed to checkpoint and replay multi-threaded software deterministically or non-deterministically [1, 22, 26, 28]. To achieve good performance, these techniques often require sophisticated operating-system support or hardware support. ConAir only rolls back an idempotent region in one thread and does not require these sophisticated techniques.

Deterministic execution Deterministic systems [2, 3, 7, 32, 41] force a multi-threaded program to execute a deterministic interleaving under a given input. This promising approach still faces challenges, such as overhead, integration with system non-determinism, language design, etc. In general, these tools address different problems from ConAir. Even inside a deterministic run time, concurrency bugs can still occur and require recovery.

Rollback recovery As discussed in Section 1, several rollback-recovery systems have been built before, such as Rx [44], ASSURE [50], and Frost [53]. They all change operating systems to support whole program checkpoint and rollback. Rx changes the program environment during reexecution to handle deterministic bugs. ASSURE rolls back a failed software to an existing error-handling path. It is designed to mitigate the impact of deterministic bugs, and cannot help software generate correct results after the manifestation of a non-deterministic concurrency bug. Frost [53] proposes a novel solution to survive data races. With OS support, it executes multiple replicas of the program with complementary thread schedules at the same time. Periodically, it compares the states of different replicas and tries to survive state divergence caused by data races. In general, these systems all require checkpointing the whole program states and rolling back all threads during a failure. Consequently, they all require sophisticated changes to operating systems.

Microreboot [4] is a recovery technique that reboots only application components, instead of the whole program, when failures occur. To benefit from microreboot, the programmers have to manually separate their systems into components (groups of objects) that can be individually restarted, such as Enterprise Java Beans components in J2EE applications. ConAir shares a common high-level philosophy with microreboot of not rolling back the whole program. However, the similarity ends there. ConAir focuses on concurrency-bug failure recovery. It works on any C/C++ multi-threaded software without manual changes. It automatically identifies reexecution points and conducts automated code transformation.

Apart from rollback recovery, a recent work studies the phenomenon that some software is able to automatically recover from state corruption, because they overwrite the corrupted states with new input data. This type of software is called self-stabilizing programs [13]. To some extent, ConAir can transform a multi-threaded program to become self-stabilizing.

Idempotency While the idea of leveraging idempotency for recovery is not new [9–12, 16, 21, 25, 38], our work is the first to apply it towards the problem of recovery from concurrency bugs. Additionally, most previous work on idempotency has assumed hardware support for recovery with a focus on hardware exceptions [9, 21, 38], hardware faults [11, 16], and hardware mis-speculation [25]. Our technique requires no hardware support. While the general paradigm of idempotent processing [12], which allows programs to be executed entirely as sequences of idempotent regions, does not strictly require hardware support to enable various features, the authors' technique does *not* work for general multi-threaded programs. This technique allows an idempotent region to store to shared variables. Such a region cannot be considered idempotent in the presence of data races and hence their algorithm cannot be used. In addition, instead of splitting the entire program into idempotent regions, ConAir only identifies idempotent regions that end at potential concurrency-bug failure sites. This focused approach allows ConAir to achieve negligible overhead (<1%), while previous work could incur more than 10% overhead [12]. We furthermore do not limit ourselves to intra-procedural analysis and allow our static analysis to be applied inter-procedurally to maximize its effectiveness.

8. Conclusions

This paper presents ConAir, a static analysis and code transformation tool that helps fix and survive concurrency-bug failures through single-threaded recovery and idempotent processing. The evaluation using 10 real-world concurrency bugs shows that ConAir successfully helps software quickly recover from failures that cover a variety of symptoms and root causes. ConAir works well even when it has no knowledge about a bug.

ConAir is not designed to recover all failures, but is effective for a large number of common concurrency-bug failures. It only introduces negligible run-time overhead, less than 1% in our experiments. This good performance is achieved without any change to hardware or operating systems and is suitable for production-run deployment. ConAir's effectiveness is a result of a seemingly serendipitous property: short recovery regions are naturally idempotent. In future work, we hope to investigate whether automatic or programmer-aided transformations can help increase its coverage.

ConAir provides a novel use of existing assertions and error checking in programs. With ConAir, assertions and error-checking code no longer just passively observe system failures and errors. Instead, they actively help ConAir to recover software from failures and correct software internal errors. ConAir's creative use of assertions opens up the possibility of sanity checks in multi-threaded programs being useful in deployment and as a recovery tool beyond just a debugging tool. For the future work, we would like to investigate how well this works in the field on widely deployed and used code-bases. Also, we would like to understand developer issues in using such a paradigm.

ConAir introduces a perspective that many points in the design space of rollback/recovery are meaningful, with reexecution regions spanning from tens of instructions to the whole program. Future work can extend ConAir to explore other design points in this large design space.

Acknowledgments

We thank the anonymous reviewers for their invaluable feedback. We thank Prof. Mark Hill for his invaluable suggestions. We thank John T. Criswell for going above and beyond his responsibilities to answer our LLVM related questions. This work is supported by NSF grants CCF-0845751, CCF-1018180, CCF-1054616, CCF-1217582, a Google U.S./Canada PhD fellowship, and a Claire Boothe Luce faculty fellowship. Any opinions, findings, and conclusions or recommendations expressed in this material are those of the authors and do not necessarily reflect the views of NSF or other institutions.

References

[1] G. Altekar and I. Stoica. ODR: output-deterministic replay for multicore debugging. In *SOSP*, 2009.

[2] A. Aviram, S.-C. Weng, S. Hu, and B. Ford. Efficient system-enforced deterministic parallelism. In *OSDI*, 2010.

[3] T. Bergan, N. Hunt, L. Ceze, and S. D. Gribble. Deterministic process groups in dOS. In *OSDI*, 2010.

[4] G. Candea, S. Kawamoto, Y. Fujiki, G. Friedman, and A. Fox. Microreboot - a technique for cheap recovery. In *OSDI*, 2004.

[5] L. Chew and D. Lie. Kivati: Fast detection and prevention of atomicity violations. In *EuroSys*, 2010.

[6] R. Chugh, J. W. Voung, R. Jhala, and S. Lerner. Dataflow analysis for concurrent programs using datarace detection. In *PLDI*, 2008.

[7] H. Cui, J. Wu, J. Gallagher, H. Guo, and J. Yang. Efficient deterministic multithreading through schedule relaxation. In *SOSP*, 2011.

[8] R. Cytron, J. Ferrante, B. K. Rosen, M. N. Wegman, and F. K. Zadeck. Efficiently computing static single assignment form and the control dependence graph. *Trans. Program. Lang. Syst.*, 13(4), Oct. 1991.

[9] M. de Kruijf and K. Sankaralingam. Idempotent processor architecture. In *MICRO*, 2011.

[10] M. de Kruijf and K. Sankaralingam. Idempotent code generation: Implementation, analysis, and evaluation. In *CGO*, 2013.

[11] M. de Kruijf, S. Nomura, and K. Sankaralingam. Relax: an architectural framework for software recovery of hardware faults. In *ISCA*, 2010.

[12] M. de Kruijf, K. Sankaralingam, and S. Jha. Static analysis and compiler design for idempotent processing. In *PLDI*, 2012.

[13] Y. h. Eom and B. Demsky. Self-stabilizing java. In *PLDI*, 2012.

[14] J. Erickson, M. Musuvathi, S. Burckhardt, and K. Olynyk. Effective data-race detection for the kernel. In *OSDI*, 2010.

[15] M. Ernst, A. Czeisler, W. G. Griswold, and D. Notkin. Quickly detecting relevant program invariants. In *ICSE*, 2000.

[16] S. Feng, S. Gupta, A. Ansari, S. A. Mahlke, and D. I. August. Encore: low-cost, fine-grained transient fault recovery. In *MICRO*, 2011.

[17] C. Flanagan and S. N. Freund. Atomizer: a dynamic atomicity checker for multithreaded programs. In *POPL*, 2004.

[18] C. Flanagan and S. N. Freund. Fasttrack: efficient and precise dynamic race detection. In *PLDI*, 2009.

[19] Q. Gao, W. Zhang, Z. Chen, M. Zheng, and F. Qin. 2ndStrike: toward manifesting hidden concurrency typestate bugs. In *ASPLOS*, 2011.

[20] P. Godefroid and N. Nagappani. Concurrency at Microsoft – an exploratory survey. Technical report, MSR-TR-2008-75, Microsoft Research, May 2008.

[21] M. Hampton and K. Asanović. Implementing virtual memory in a vector processor with software restart markers. In *ICS*, 2006.

[22] D. R. Hower, P. Montesinos, L. Ceze, M. D. Hill, and J. Torrellas. Two hardware-based approaches for deterministic multiprocessor replay. *Commun. ACM*, 52(6), June 2009.

[23] G. Jin, L. Song, W. Zhang, S. Lu, and B. Liblit. Automated atomicity-violation fixing. In *PLDI*, 2011.

[24] H. Jula, D. Tralamazza, C. Zamfir, and G. Candea. Deadlock immunity: Enabling systems to defend against deadlocks. In *OSDI*, 2008.

[25] S. W. Kim, C.-L. Ooi, R. Eigenmann, B. Falsafi, and T. N. Vijaykumar. Exploiting reference idempotency to reduce speculative storage overflow. *ACM Trans. Program. Lang. Syst.*, 28(5), Sept. 2006.

[26] S. T. King, G. W. Dunlap, and P. M. Chen. Operating systems with time-traveling virtual machines. In *Usenix*, 2005.

[27] C. Lattner and V. Adve. LLVM: A compilation framework for lifelong program analysis & transformation. In *CGO*, 2004.

[28] D. Lee, B. Wester, K. Veeraraghavan, S. Narayanasamy, P. M. Chen, and J. Flinn. Respec: efficient online multiprocessor replayvia speculation and external determinism. In *ASPLOS*, 2010.

[29] Z. Letko, T. Vojnar, and B. Křena. AtomRace: data race and atomicity violation detector and healer. In *PADTAD*, 2008.

[30] N. G. Leveson and C. S. Turner. An investigation of the therac-25 accidents. *Computer*, 26(7):18–41, 1993.

[31] Z. Li, L. Tan, X. Wang, Y. Zhou, and C. Zhai. An empirical study of bug characteristics in modern open source software. In *ASID*, 2006.

[32] T. Liu, C. Curtsinger, and E. D. Berger. Dthreads: efficient deterministic multithreading. In *SOSP*, 2011.

[33] S. Lu, J. Tucek, F. Qin, and Y. Zhou. AVIO: detecting atomicity violations via access interleaving invariants. In *ASPLOS*, 2006.

[34] S. Lu, S. Park, C. Hu, X. Ma, W. Jiang, Z. Li, R. A. Popa, and Y. Zhou. MUVI: Automatically inferring multi-variable access correlations and detecting related semantic and concurrency bugs. In *SOSP*, 2007.

[35] S. Lu, S. Park, E. Seo, and Y. Zhou. Learning from mistakes – a comprehensive study of real world concurrency bug characteristics. In *ASPLOS*, 2008.

[36] B. Lucia and L. Ceze. Finding concurrency bugs with context-aware communication graphs. In *MICRO*, 2009.

[37] B. Lucia, J. Devietti, K. Strauss, and L. Ceze. Atom-aid: Detecting and surviving atomicity violations. In *ISCA*, 2008.

[38] S. A. Mahlke, W. Y. Chen, R. A. Bringmann, R. E. Hank, W.-M. W. Hwu, B. R. Rau, and M. S. Schlansker. Sentinel scheduling: a model for compiler-controlled speculative execution. *ACM Trans. Comput. Syst.*, 11(4), Nov. 1993.

[39] S. Misailovic, D. Kim, and M. Rinard. Parallelizing sequential programs with statistical accuracy tests. MIT-CSAIL-TR-2010-038.

[40] MySQL. Mysql 5.6 reference manual. http://dev.mysql.com/doc/refman/5.6/en/.

[41] M. Olszewski, J. Ansel, and S. Amarasinghe. Kendo: efficient deterministic multithreading in software. In *ASPLOS*, 2009.

[42] PCWorld. Nasdaq's Facebook Glitch Came From Race Conditions. http://www.pcworld.com/businesscenter/article/255911/ nasdaqs_facebook_glitch_came_from_race_conditions.html.

[43] S. Qi, N. Otsuki, L. O. Nogueira, A. Muzahid, and J. Torrellas. Pacman: Tolerating asymmetric data races with unintrusive hardware. In *HPCA*, 2012.

[44] F. Qin, J. Tucek, J. Sundaresan, and Y. Zhou. Rx: Treating bugs as allergies c a safe method to survive software failures. In *SOSP*, 2005.

[45] S. K. Rajamani, G. Ramalingam, V. P. Ranganath, and K. Vaswani. Isolator: dynamically ensuring isolation in comcurrent programs. In *ASPLOS*, 2009.

[46] P. Ratanaworabhan, M. Burtscher, D. Kirovski, B. G. Zorn, R. Nagpal, and K. Pattabiraman. Detecting and tolerating asymmetric races. In *PPOPP*, 2009.

[47] S. Savage, M. Burrows, G. Nelson, P. Sobalvarro, and T. Anderson. Eraser: A dynamic data race detector for multithreaded programs. *TOCS*, 1997.

[48] SecurityFocus. Software bug contributed to blackout. http://www.securityfocus.com/news/8016.

[49] Y. Shi, S. Park, Z. Yin, S. Lu, Y. Zhou, W. Chen, and W. Zheng. Do I use the wrong definition?: DefUse: definition-use invariants for detecting concurrency and sequential bugs. In *OOPSLA*, 2010.

[50] S. Sidiroglou, O. Laadan, C. Perez, N. Viennot, J. Nieh, and A. D. Keromytis. Assure: automatic software self-healing using rescue points. In *ASPLOS*, 2009.

[51] G. Upadhyaya, S. P. Midkiff, and V. S. Pai. Automatic atomic region identification in shared memory SPMD programs. In *OOPSLA*, 2010.

[52] M. Vaziri, F. Tip, and J. Dolby. Associating synchronization constraints with data in an object-oriented language. In *POPL*, 2006.

[53] K. Veeraraghavan, P. M. Chen, J. Flinn, and S. Narayanasamy. Detecting and surviving data races using complementary schedules. In *SOSP*, 2011.

[54] H. Volos, A. J. Tack, M. M. Swift, and S. Lu. Applying transactional memory to concurrency bugs. In *ASPLOS*, 2012.

[55] D. Weeratunge, X. Zhang, and S. Jagannathan. Accentuating the positive: atomicity inference and enforcement using correct executions. In *OOPSLA*, 2011.

[56] Z. Yin, D. Yuan, Y. Zhou, S. Pasupathy, and L. N. Bairavasundaram. How do fixes become bugs? In *FSE*, 2011.

[57] J. Yu and S. Narayanasamy. A case for an interleaving constrained shared-memory multi-processor. In *ISCA*, 2009.

[58] J. Yu and S. Narayanasamy. Tolerating concurrency bugs using transactions as lifeguards. In *MICRO*, 2010.

[59] Y. Yu, T. Rodeheffer, and W. Chen. RaceTrack: Efficient detection of data race conditions via adaptive tracking. In *SOSP*, 2005.

[60] W. Zhang, C. Sun, and S. Lu. ConMem: Detecting severe concurrency bugs through an effect-oriented approach. In *ASPLOS*, 2010.

[61] W. Zhang, J. Lim, R. Olichandran, J. Scherpelz, G. Jin, S. Lu, and T. Reps. ConSeq: Detecting concurrency bugs through sequential errors. In *ASPLOS*, 2011.

Transparent Mutable Replay for Multicore Debugging and Patch Validation

Nicolas Viennot Siddharth Nair Jason Nieh
Columbia University
nviennot@cs.columbia.edu, ssn2114@columbia.edu, nieh@cs.columbia.edu

Abstract

We present DORA, a mutable record-replay system which allows a recorded execution of an application to be replayed with a modified version of the application. This feature, not available in previous record-replay systems, enables powerful new functionality. In particular, DORA can help reproduce, diagnose, and fix software bugs by replaying a version of a recorded application that is recompiled with debugging information, reconfigured to produce verbose log output, modified to include additional print statements, or patched to fix a bug.

DORA uses lightweight operating system mechanisms to record an application execution by capturing nondeterministic events to a log without imposing unnecessary timing and ordering constraints. It replays the log using a modified version of the application even in the presence of added, deleted, or modified operations that do not match events in the log. DORA searches for a replay that minimizes differences between the log and the replayed execution of the modified program. If there are no modifications, DORA provides deterministic replay of the unmodified program.

We have implemented a Linux prototype which provides transparent mutable replay without recompiling or relinking applications. We show that DORA is useful for reproducing, diagnosing, and fixing software bugs in real-world applications, including Apache and MySQL. Our results show that DORA (1) captures bugs and replays them with applications modified or reconfigured to produce additional debugging output for root cause diagnosis, (2) captures exploits and replays them with patched applications to validate that the patches successfully eliminate vulnerabilities, (3) records production workloads and replays them with patched applications to validate patches with realistic workloads, and (4) maintains low recording overhead on commodity multicore hardware, making it suitable for production systems.

Categories and Subject Descriptors D.2.5 [*Software Engineering*]: Testing and Debugging; D.2.4 [*Software Engineering*]: Software/Program Verification; D.2.7 [*Software Engineering*]: Distribution, Maintenance, and Enhancement; D.4.5 [*Operating Systems*]: Reliability

Keywords Deterministic Replay, Mutable Replay, Multicore, Debugging

ASPLOS'13, March 16–20, 2013, Houston, Texas, USA.

1. Introduction

As applications grow in complexity, software bugs have become increasingly common and more difficult to reproduce, diagnose, and fix. Aggressive release schedules exacerbate the problem, resulting in frail software that requires patches to fix problems that occur in the field. Resolving a bug typically starts with reproducing it in a controlled environment. Because the common approach of conveying a bug report is often inadequate for tricky, nondeterministic bugs, record-replay has been developed to capture application bugs as they occur and deterministically replay the bug at a later time, removing the burden of repeated testing to reproduce the bug.

Despite an abundance of research on using record-replay systems for debugging [2, 3, 7, 11, 18, 19, 21, 22, 26, 27], most works have focused on bug reproducibility and have had limited or no support for diagnosing and fixing bugs. Debugging almost always requires modifying the program, whether by adding print statements, testing if a change fixes the problem, or some other method. However, previous record-replay systems do not allow the recorded execution to be replayed with any modifications to the application, with a couple exceptions. A handful of systems do allow some new code to be run in the middle of a recording, but they do not support changes to the application state [7, 12], which limits the utility of these systems for debugging and validating changes.

To address this problem, we introduce DORA, a mutable record-replay system which allows a recorded execution of an application to be replayed with a modified version of the application. Mutable record-replay provides a number of benefits for reproducing, diagnosing, and fixing software bugs. For instance, mutable record-replay can replay a version of the recorded application that is recompiled with debugging information, reconfigured to produce verbose log output, or modified to include additional code instrumentation such as print statements.

Mutable record-replay can also replay a recorded application execution of a production workload using a patched version of the application. This is useful for both application developers and system administrators. An application developer can use a recording of a bug when developing a fix. Replaying the recording on a modified application speeds up debugging and provides a novel way of validating bug fixes for nondeterminstic bugs, which can otherwise be time consuming and difficult. For example, a developer who writes a patch can test it by taking a recorded execution of the exploit on the original application and replaying it using the patched application to quickly verify that the patch closes the vulnerability instead of painstakingly regenerating the exploit for each attempted fix of the problem.

System administrators often worry that applying patches will break their applications. Mutable replay allows administrators to independently test patches on production workloads. An administrator can record the unpatched application in production, apply the patch to an offline version of the application, and then replay the recorded execution using the patched application. If the replay succeeds, the administrator will be more confident that the changes will not introduce regressions.

Mutable replay complements traditional quality assurance testing. Quality assurance provides broad coverage but fails to handle many corner cases, which is why bugs arise in production in the first place. In contrast, mutable replay isolates actual bugs that occur in production. These bugs can be timing and configuration dependent, so some surface very rarely. This coverage is often not possible with traditional testing due to nondeterministic program behavior. Furthermore, mutable replay provides fast turnaround time, enabling a bug to be replayed quickly and directly tested against application changes that attempt to fix the problem. This not only speeds up debugging, but also provides a way to validate bug fixes for nondeterminstic bugs, which can otherwise be much more time consuming and difficult.

DORA consists of three components: (1) a recorder that records application execution to a log, (2) a replayer that can replay a modified version of the application using the log, and (3) an explorer that uses the replayer to find the execution of the modified program that best corresponds to the log file. The recorder and replayer build upon our previous deterministic record-replay engine, Scribe [16].

The recorder operates primarily at the interface between applications and the operating system (OS) to transparently record an application's nondeterministic interactions. It avoids imposing unnecessary timing and ordering constraints that would hinder mutable replay with a modified application. To aid mutable replay, the recorder also logs deterministic interactions to detect and resolve any differences between the recorded application execution and the replay of a modified version of the application.

The replayer replays a previously recorded execution using a modified version of the application, matching events from the original log with the actions of the modified program. If the application used for replay is the same as the one recorded, the replayer provides deterministic replay of the unmodified application. However, if the replayed application's behavior diverges from the original's, the replayer gathers information for the explorer about the new code path the program was trying to execute and waits for instructions on how to proceed. Because it operates at the OS level like the recorder, the replayer has access to sufficient OS semantics to understand why a replay diverges from the original execution and can leverage these semantics to help the explorer.

The explorer evaluates several possible execution paths to find a successful mutable replay. It performs a best-first search for an execution of the modified program that is as close to the original execution as possible according to some cost function d. It begins by replaying a recorded execution on a modified program. When the replay diverges from the original execution, the explorer tries to determine why. For example, suppose the modified program made an unexpected `printf()` call. This could be a new call to produce debugging information, or it could simply occur earlier than expected because code was deleted. The explorer chooses the most promising possibility and communicates its decision to the replayer. This process repeats until a successful execution is found.

DORA is designed to handle an wide range of real-world programs, including multi-threaded applications. It can support a broad range of useful application changes, but cannot support arbitrary changes; major changes to the process layout or shared memory layout are not supported. Despite this limitation, DORA is useful in a wide range of real-world use cases for testing, debugging, and validating application changes. In fact, we even found a previously unknown bug in Apache using DORA [1]. DORA's usefulness in practice makes sense given that bug fixes tend to be relatively small and rarely change core application semantics [13, 29].

We have implemented a DORA Linux prototype that runs on commodity multicore hardware without changing, relinking, or recompiling applications or libraries. Our experimental results with over thirty different application changes show that DORA can (1) record unmodified real-world multi-threaded applications with less than 10% overhead on multicore hardware, (2) replay applications that have been reconfigured to produce verbose debugging output or modified with added debugging instrumentation, (3) replay real exploits on patched applications to verify that the patches close these vulnerabilities, and (4) replay benchmark workloads to validate application patches and version upgrades despite changes in thousands of lines of code.

We present the design, implementation, and evaluation of the DORA mutable replay system. Section 2 provides a definition of mutable replay. Section 3 describes the DORA recorder. Section 4 describes the DORA replayer. Section 5 describes the DORA explorer and presents an example illustrating the use of the system. Section 6 presents some of the guarantees that can be made about the system's behavior. Section 7 discusses limitations of the current system. Section 8 presents experimental results. Section 9 discusses related work. Finally, we present some concluding remarks and directions for future work.

2. Mutable Replay Concept

Since mutable replay is a previously undefined concept, we begin by presenting a definition. Let e be the recorded execution of some program P. Let E' be the set of possible executions of P', a modified version of P. A mutable replay of e on P' will then be an execution e' in E' such that the differences between e and e' are a result of the differences between P and P'.

The difference between two programs includes not only differences in their executables, but can also include changes in input and environment, such as environment variables, the file system, and host-related information. Note that there is not always a clear mapping from input in the original program to input in the modified program. For example, the original program could read more bytes from `stdin` than the modified program.

Since some executions in E' are intuitively preferable to others, we introduce the concept of a *d-optimal mutable replay*, an execution in E' that is optimal according to a cost function d. The cost function measures the difference between the original execution and the mutable replay. The value returned by d reflects the minimal cost of transforming the execution e_1 into a candidate execution e_2. A lower score is better, scores can be negative, and the score must be the lowest when e_1 is identical to e_2. A d-optimal mutable replay e_d of an execution e on P' satisfies $d(e, e_d) = min_{e' \in E'} d(e, e')$. There is always at least one d-optimal mutable replay for a given execution e and a program P'.

Finding the d-optimal mutable replay is undecidable in the general case. To show this, we first observe that finding the d-optimal mutable replay requires running P' because predicting the executions of a program is undecidable. Suppose P' has an added infinite loop at its beginning. Then, when running P', the replayer will loop infinitely since detecting an infinite loop is undecidable. Thus, finding the d-optimal replay is undecidable.

Even in the subset of cases in which finding a d-optimal mutable replay is decidable, it is still NP-hard with respect to the number of events in the log. Consider a program P' which only adds a `read()` system call of `n` bytes. There are $O(2^n)$ possible results of this call. In addition, arbitrary signals could be delivered between any two instructions. If the program is threaded, they are many possible thread interleavings. Since differences in signal delivery and thread interleaving could theoretically cause radically different behavior, and since determining the future execution of a program is undecidable, a mutable replayer must consider every possibility,

```
int main() {
  printf("%d\n", time(NULL));
  return 0;
}
```

Figure 1. Original program

```
int main() {
  FILE *out = fopen("output", "w");
  fprintf(out, "%d\n", time(NULL));
  return 0;
}
```

Figure 2. Modified program

which is infeasible. Thus, no mutable replay system can efficiently find a d-optimal mutable replay in all cases.

Fortunately, however, many useful changes to programs are modest in size and scope. In particular, bug fixes tend to be relatively small and rarely change core application semantics [13, 29]. The same is typically true of code instrumentation added to a program for debugging. Based on this observation, we designed DORA with a d function that has useful properties for testing and debugging. In this context, Section 8 shows that DORA is able to find d-optimal mutable replays in practice using real-world applications. Furthermore, Section 6 presents guarantees that can be made about the optimality of DORA's approximation algorithm.

A simple example may help further clarify the concept of mutable replay. Figure 1 shows a program that prints the current time in seconds to `stdout`. Figure 2 shows a modified version of the original program that instead writes the output to a file. Intuitively, we want the `gettimeofday()` call in the replay of the modified program to return the same time returned in the recorded execution of the original program. We will show that DORA does this, producing a d-optimal replay with the cost function described in Section 5.

3. Recorder

DORA's recorder builds upon our Scribe work on lightweight OS-level deterministic replay on multiprocessors [16]. The Scribe engine provides four key benefits for mutable replay. First, operating at the OS level avoids tracking low-level hardware nondeterminism that is unnecessary for application replay and would significantly complicate mutable replay. Second, DORA records the execution of system calls in a manner that enables system calls and their effects on the kernel to be fully executed during replay. As discussed in Section 4, this is essential for mutable replay because there are times when DORA must transition processes from controlled replay to live execution to enable mutable replay. Third, DORA's recorder can record the execution of multiple processes and threads with low overhead on production systems. Finally, DORA's recording is transparent to applications. It does not require changing, relinking, or recompiling applications or libraries, and it supports programs written in any programming language.

The recorder operates on a group of tasks (threads and processes), which we refer to as a *session*. DORA records interactions between the session and its external environment, such as incoming network packets and nondeterministic interactions between tasks, in a manner which accommodates application changes during replay. DORA also records deterministic information to help detect changes in an application's execution path during replay.

The recorder saves the recorded execution to a log file. Figure 3 shows the tail of the log file generated by running the simple program in Figure 1. We excluded 83 events related to program initialization, including `execve()` and C library bootstrapping events.

```
// 83 initialization events
--- cut ---
munmap(0xb76e1000, 968e) = 0
rdtsc = 000057ed322904cf
time(NULL) = 0x4f9bd2e7
fstat(1, 0xbff8d684) = 0
mmap(0, 1000, 3, 34, -1, 0) = 0xb76ea000
write(1, 0xb76ea000, 11) = 11
exit(0) = 0
```

Figure 3. Recorded log file of original execution

The last two initialization events are shown. The `rdtsc` event corresponds to seeding a random generator from the C library by reading the time stamp counter of the CPU. The log also includes several system calls and information about their arguments.

3.1 Nondeterministic Interactions

To replay an execution deterministically, the timing and ordering of nondeterministic interactions between tasks must be recorded. To enable mutable replay, DORA must also be resilient to changes in the application behavior which add or remove nondeterministic system calls. We highlight how key interactions involving system calls, signals, and shared memory are handled.

System calls. The ordering of system calls that access shared resources causes nondeterminism if at least one call modifies the resource. For instance, a `write()` and a `read()` on the same pipe are *related system calls* since they access a shared resource and their relative ordering matters. Preserving the order of related system calls during replay ensures that recorded racy behavior is maintained in the replay. To provide this deterministic behavior, DORA operates at the OS level to capture concurrency at the same level of granularity as the OS. DORA leverages kernel code that already serializes access to shared kernel objects to record and enforce a partial ordering of all related system calls. This is in contrast to previous approaches [11, 26] which impose a total ordering of system calls. Such approaches do not scale well for multicore and do not work for mutable replay. Application changes are likely to change the number and order of system calls, making a total ordering of system calls too restrictive for replaying an execution using a modified program.

Shared objects tracked by DORA include inodes, files, file-tables, memory maps, process credentials, process states, and system-wide properties such as the hostname and mount points. To keep track of access ordering, every resource is assigned a globally unique identifier and a serial number indicating the order of access. For each resource a system call accesses, DORA increments its serial number and records its identifier and serial number. This allow the replayer to deterministically reproduce the access sequence.

Signals. The delivery time of signals is another source of nondeterminism. Signals are normally delivered in two steps in the kernel. First, the sender process sends a signal to the target process, which is marked as having a signal pending. Second, the target process detects and handles the pending signal when it returns to user space from kernel space. If the target process is executing in user space on another core, an inter-processor interrupt will force it into kernel space, where it will detect the pending signal. Replaying this behavior can be challenging because it requires interrupting the target process at the exact same instruction as during its original execution. Previous approaches [5, 6, 9, 10] have relied on hardware providing a cycle accurate instruction counter [25], but this does not work for CPUs without such counters and does not work for mutable replay. Application changes are extremely likely to change the number and ordering of instructions, rendering the counter values useless.

To address this problem, DORA defers signal delivery to locations called *sync points*. Sync points are well-defined locations in an execution which deterministically cause the process to enter kernel space, such as system calls, traps due to division by zero, and page faults due to shared memory accesses, as discussed further below. By only delivering signals at sync points, DORA effectively converts asynchronous events into synchronous ones and does not require special hardware or application modifications. This also makes it much easier to replay using an application with modified signals. Note that this behavior complies with the POSIX semantics of signals.

Delaying signal delivery to sync points may introduce some latency in the application. However, our previous work on Scribe [16] shows that sync points occur quite frequently in common desktop and server applications. Our evaluation showed that deferred signals were delayed by less than 100 μs on average with a maximum delay of less than 1 ms, so this latency is generally imperceptible. Furthermore, the vast majority of signals were delivered immediately because the target process was already in a sync point when the signal was sent. This is not surprising given that processes often stay in a sync point for a prolonged period of time. For example, a process blocking on I/O in a system call is in a sync point. While a process is in a sync point, signals are delivered immediately and need not be deferred.

Shared memory. Shared memory accesses cause nondeterminism arising from the order in which threads and processes read and write to the same memory locations. Memory is shared either implicitly, as with threads that share an entire address space, or explicitly, as with processes that share a common memory mapping. Since processes typically access multiple locations on a page during a given time interval because of spatial and temporal locality, DORA tracks memory accesses at a page granularity by managing page ownership with the help of the hardware page protection mechanism. Each shared memory page is assigned an owner process or thread for some time interval. The owner can exclusively modify that page during that interval and treat it like private memory. Thus, DORA does not need to track every memory access during such periods. Transitioning page ownership from one process or thread to another is done using a concurrent read, exclusive write (CREW) protocol on memory pages with some optimizations [16].

To ensure that ownership transitions occur at precisely the same location in the execution during both record and replay, previous approaches [5, 6, 9, 10] have relied on cycle-accurate hardware instruction counters. An ordering this precise is not resilient to application changes, so it does not work for mutable replay. To address this problem, DORA defers ownership transitions until the owner reaches a sync point. As with system calls accessing shared resources, a memory event is logged for the thread that accesses shared memory. The event includes a page identifier and a per page serial number indicating the order of access; this process is similar to the one for system resources.

DORA implements this CREW protocol by creating a *shadow page table* for each thread, which is a private version of the shared page table. If a thread does not have ownership of a page, its shadow page table entry (PTE) access privilege bits are cleared. When a thread tries to access a page owned by another thread, it triggers a page fault, notifies the owner, and blocks until access is granted. Note that while the thread is blocked, it is in a sync point, so it can immediately release pages to other requesting threads, which prevents deadlock [16]. Once the page owner reaches a sync point in its execution, it transfers the page ownership to the thread requesting access, which then returns from its page fault handler. Recording performance can be negatively impacted for applications that exhibit an enormous number of ownership transitions. Nevertheless, DORA performs well for a wide range of real-world applications as shown in Section 8.

3.2 Additional Information for Mutable Replay

In traditional replay, all deterministic information need not be recorded because it will be regenerated during replay, but in mutable replay, the modified application may behave differently even in deterministic sections of code. DORA's recorder stores additional deterministic information in the log to help the replayer detect differences between the original and replayed executions as early as possible. Since DORA provides deterministic replay for unmodified applications, it does not need to record the additional deterministic information in production, but instead records such information afterwards by replaying the original execution and recording additional deterministic information as needed.

As part of this process, DORA records all system calls executed, not just those involved in nondeterministic interactions. DORA records the system call number, arguments, and return value for each system call. For arguments that are pointers, DORA follows the pointer chain to record the actual memory contents, which are used during replay to see if two system calls are equivalent. By recording memory contents instead of the pointer values, DORA is more tolerant of memory layout changes caused by application modifications.

DORA also records the virtual addresses of shared memory accesses, allowing the replayer to match shared memory access to detect divergence. However, this mechanism means that changes to the memory layout of writable shared memory affecting page boundaries can cause DORA to incorrectly replay data races. Fortunately, a recent study of common security patches indicates that a vast majority of application patches [13] do not make such changes.

Finally, when performing mutable replay, the modified application may introduce system calls that are nondeterministic and environment dependent. DORA addresses this issue by recording two additional types of information during the original recorded execution. First, DORA stores additional information for mutable replay to ensure that nondeterministic actions that occur during the modified application replay but not during the original recorded execution are consistent with the recorded execution. For example, DORA periodically records timing information to ensure that time-related functions are consistent. If a new `gettimeofday()` call is present in a replayed execution, the replayer can report a time that is consistent with other values replayed from the recorded execution. Second, DORA records other information about the execution environment so that new system calls in the modified application behave as they would have in the environment in which the program was recorded. For example, the recorder stores host information in case the modified application requests it with a new `uname()` or `gethostname()` call.

4. Replayer

DORA's replayer replays the originally recorded execution using either the original program or a modified program. It requires that the execution is replayed on a machine which supports all the recorded instructions. For example, a program that uses SSE instructions when it is recorded cannot be replayed on a machine without SSE instructions unless it is recompiled to use a different ISA. The replayer uses the recorded log file to generate a separate log file per task. Each task is replayed independently, but the replayer enforces the recorded order of access to shared resources.

A key aspect of the replayer is that it can transition a task or a group of tasks from controlled replay to normal execution. This feature is essential for mutable replay because a modified program may have new code to execute that is not part of the recorded execution. DORA can run such code at any time because it fully executes system calls and their effects on the kernel during replay. Many other replay systems only emulate the effects they have on userspace [11, 22], but this would prevent normal execution of the application from being enabled in the middle of replay.

As a task executes kernel code, the replayer compares the execution with what is expected in the log file. When the execution *matches* expected events in the log, the replayer ensures it behaves as it did in the original execution. System calls match if they have the same system call numbers and arguments. When an argument is a pointer to a buffer, DORA compares the contents of the buffers instead of the pointer addresses. Shared memory access events match if the access types and page addresses are the same. The replay ends successfully if all tasks terminate after consuming every recorded event. A replay that uses an unmodified application will always end successfully in this manner.

However, if a replaying task is about to execute a code path that does not correspond to the expected event, the replay has *diverged* from the log. The replayer conveys this to the explorer, which determines how the replayer should resolve the divergence. If the explorer determines that the replayer should continue replaying the current log, the unexpected event can be treated in number of different ways to try to resolve the divergence so that later events will match events in the log. For simplicity, DORA treats a divergence as one of two possible types of *mutations*, an *addition* or a *deletion*.

4.1 Additions

An addition is an event added to the program. For example, a program could be modified by adding code that includes a new system call. A new event is most often a system call, but it can also be a new signal or shared memory access. When executing an event not in the log file, DORA has three main responsibilities. First, it must decide when to execute the new event relative to events already in the log file. System calls, signals, and shared memory events are often racy with respect to other processes or threads, so there can be many possible orderings. Second, it must ensure that the semantics of the event are consistent with the semantics of the recorded execution. Finally, it is useful to be able to deterministically reproduce these decisions in subsequent replays, as explained in Section 5.

To handle these responsibilities, the replayer switches the process that encountered the addition from controlled replay into *direct mode*. Direct mode switches the respective process to normal execution and enables DORA's recorder to record the execution. This adds a new event to the log and orders it with respect to other events in the log. The resulting log can then be later deterministically replayed with the same modified program. Once the process completes the additional operation, it returns to regular replay mode; no other process has left regular replay mode. We discuss how this is done in further detail for new system calls, signals, and shared memory accesses.

System calls. When encountering a new system call, DORA executes the call and records the execution as discussed in Section 3. This is possible because the replayer fully executes system calls and their effects instead of just emulating them, ensuring that it is possible to switch a process to normal execution at any time. DORA further instruments various system calls to ensure that the new system call behaves consistently with the recorded execution. The specifics of this depend upon the semantics of the added system call. We highlight system calls that deal with three important types of issues: environmental or timing information, resource allocation, and sockets.

For system calls that request environmental information or timing information, DORA ensures that the return values are made consistent with the information in the original log. This includes `gettimeofday()` and `gethostname()`. For example, if a new `gethostname()` call is executed, DORA already recorded such environmental information and ensures that the name reported is the same as what was already recorded.

For system calls that request new resources, DORA ensures that assigned resources do not conflict with those used by the replayed execution. For example, if a new page in memory is allocated, DORA ensures that its address will not conflict with those used in the original program. If the system call manipulates an existing shared resource, the respective resource serial numbers are renumbered to account for the new event.

DORA simply executes new socket-related system calls during replay except when dealing with data streams originating from outside the session. To deal with data streams, such as external sockets, DORA registers fake backends to the corresponding file descriptor. Socket system calls related to those data streams will simply manipulate the recorded network data. For example, if a `read()` on a network socket is changed to a `recvmsg()` on the same socket, DORA provides the appropriate data. If a new `read()` from a socket tries to access more data than recorded, 0 is returned to indicate end of file.

Signals. When encountering a new signal, such as from a modified application with a new `kill()` call, DORA needs to determine when to deliver the signal to the target process. The replayer does this much as the recorder does. Like the recorder, the replayer defers signal delivery until the target process encounters a sync point. This ensures that signal delivery can be replayed deterministically during subsequent replays.

Shared memory. When encountering a new shared memory access, DORA needs to determine how to interleave the access with other accesses. As in recording, a page fault occurs when a replayed process tries to access a shared page that it does not own, and the process must acquire ownership of the page. Once the process obtains ownership and completes the memory access, it releases ownership to the previous owner at the next sync point to ensure that the access order in the original execution is respected. The new memory events are added to the log file and the original serial numbers are reordered as necessary to ensure that subsequent replays based on this log deterministically perform the memory access in the same way.

4.2 Deletions

A deletion corresponds to the removal of events from the original log file and implies that the unexpected event matches a later event in the log. The replayer deletes the intermediate events. There can be several possible matches for an event if the event occurs several times later in the original log. DORA identifies possible matches and reports each possible match to the explorer. Because it is expensive to process many events and it becomes increasingly unlikely to find a match that will result in a successful mutable replay if an extremely large number of events need to be deleted, DORA imposes a cap on the number of events it can remove for a deletion. The cap is 10,000 events in our implementation. We present further detail regarding deletions that involve system calls, signals, and shared memory accesses.

System calls. Most system calls do not have any side effects in the log file, so not executing a call itself is all that is necessary to delete it. If the system call involves a shared resource, DORA also renumbers the serial numbers for the resource so that its serial number sequence does not contain any gaps. Deleting system calls related to external sockets does not remove the incoming data, since it is preserved as part of the stream of data associated with the resource. Data that is not consumed from a deleted socket system call will eventually be consumed by other remaining or new system calls.

When a deleted system call was originally associated with the delivery of asynchronous events, the events must be relocated to other sync points. For example, consider a program that has a `SIGALRM` delivery scheduled on a `getpid()` sync point. If the new execution no longer calls `getpid()`, DORA must choose a new sync point at which to deliver the `SIGALRM` signal. DORA postpones the delivery of asynchronous events until the next sync point the application encounters. Choosing the next sync point is better than choosing the previous one because releasing page ownership prematurely would introduce spurious page faults in the application and could prevent DORA from respecting the original page access order. For example, suppose a thread writes to a page and then releases ownership of the page at the following sync point, which is on a system call. If the system call is removed and DORA moved the ownership release event to a previous sync point, it would occur before the access to the page. This access would then trigger a page fault and generate a new ownership acquisition event that may not respect the original ordering. Moving the release of ownership to the following sync point avoids this issue.

Signals. Deleting a signal involves deleting its source, which is typically a system call. System calls that deliver signals require additional consideration because their effects create multiple events in the log file. For example, removing a `kill()` system call must also remove the delivery of the corresponding signal. During recording, DORA associates delivered signals with their sources by using an incrementing global token used across the entire session. When a signal is about to be delivered, DORA waits for the source to be triggered or deleted, which respectively delivers the signal or omits the signal from being delivered.

Shared Memory. When deleting a shared memory access, the corresponding ownership acquisition event should not be executed. However, the previous owner still releases its page ownership so that its behavior is consistent with the original recorded execution. Asynchronous events associated with a deleted shared memory event are relocated to other sync points in the same manner as they are for system calls.

4.3 Going Live

In rare cases, the entire log file is consumed before the modified application terminates. This can occur when the original application crashes, but the patched application avoids crashing. The replayer allows the session to *go live* and entirely transition from controlled replay to live execution. This enables the user to validate the correctness of the patch. Since DORA faithfully replays kernel actions, the system is always in a state that allows it to transition to live execution. Linux namespaces [4] create a consistent environment for processes before and after they go live. Examples of this are demonstrated in Section 8.

5. Explorer

The explorer uses the replayer to search for a d-optimal replay. When the replay diverges, the explorer must determine how to proceed. If this was the first divergence, the explorer decides whether the replayer should consider the mutation as an addition or a deletion. If there were previous divergences, the explorer might also tell the replayer to reconsider a previously detected divergence and explore a different path. In this case, the explorer provides the replayer with a new log file. Thus, the replayer needs no knowledge of the exploration algorithm.

The explorer treats the problem of finding the best mutable replay as a search through a tree T of possible candidate executions from a start node e, the execution of the original program, to one of many goal nodes, which represent executions in E'. This problem is different from most other search problems because (1) expanding a node can result in an infinite loop, (2) there can be virtually infinite goal nodes, and (3) the paths to the goal nodes are not known beforehand because determining the possible executions of a program in advance is undecidable.

Since an exact search is undecidable in the general case and NP-hard even when it is decidable, DORA performs an inexact search using a modified uniform-cost search. For simplicity, DORA only considers additions and deletions. It does not consider, for example, input fuzzing or trying all possible racy paths. The algorithm performs the following steps:

1. Initialize T to contain the root node e.
2. Pick an unexplored execution in the tree with the lowest cost according to the cost function d.
3. Attempt to replay this execution on P'.
   (a) If this replay succeeds, this execution is selected and the exploration concludes.
   (b) Otherwise, the replay diverges on an unexpected event, and new nodes are added to the graph. One node represents an addition and the others correspond to each possible deletion. Each node has an associated log file so that nondeterminism in added system calls is reproduced exactly across replays. Go to step 2.

A useful feature of the explorer is that the end result of a replay up to a given node is recorded. Since this recording can be deterministically replayed, a mutable replay is easily reproducible. Furthermore, it is easy to compare two logs to see the differences between two executions. For example, a developer can compare the log of the originally recorded execution with the log of a mutable replay to understand how application modifications affected the replay.

For simplicity, we have implemented the explorer algorithm by replaying a new execution from the beginning of the log upon divergence. In reality, there is no inherent reason for executions to be replayed from the beginning since each child node's log only differs from its parent node's log after the point of divergence. For example, a checkpoint could be taken just before divergence occurs. Nodes created because of this divergence could replay from the checkpoint instead of from the beginning of execution [14, 15, 20].

While any function satisfying the properties specified in Section 2 can be used for d, we present a simple function that has useful properties for debugging purposes. Since matches are desirable and additions and deletions are undesirable, each match has a cost of $-M$ and each addition or deletion has a cost of $+1$, where $M > 1$. We use a value of 3 for M in our prototype, but the process of selecting a mutable replay was relatively insensitive to the specific value. Using a negative cost for matches means that the explorer is unlikely to backtrack after making many contiguous matches. This also means that the uniform-cost search is not guaranteed to find the optimal replay even amongst the nodes it considers (additions and deletions). We made this decision because the number of nodes it would need to consider to guarantee correctness is exponential. Since the future execution of a program is unknown, even potential executions which seem very unpromising could theoretically match many later events in the log file and obtain a very good score. Thus, the search would effectively become a breadth-first search if d could only return non-negative numbers. Event logs may have billions of events long, so this would not be feasible.

```
  munmap(0xb76e1000, 968e) = 0
  rdtsc = 000057ed322904cf
+ brk(NULL) = 0x9870000
+ brk(0x9891000) = 0x9891000
+ open("output", 577, 438) = 500
  time(NULL) = 0x4f9bd2e7
+ fstat(500, 0xbff8d674) = 0
- fstat(1, 0xbff8d684) = 0
  mmap(0, 1000, 3, 34, -1, 0) = 0xb76ea000
+ write(500, 0xb76ea000, 11) = 11
- write(1, 0xb76ea000, 11) = 11
  exit(0) = 0
```

Figure 4. Mutable replay of modified program

Example. To make this process more clear, we return to the example introduced in Section 2, in which a program that prints the time to `stdout` is modified to write the time to a file. Figure 4 illustrates how the explorer replays the modified program in Figure 2 using the recorded execution shown in Figure 3 of the original program in Figure 1. The explorer starts by replaying the original log file on the modified program. The complete original log file contains 90 events, but Figure 4 omits initialization events, such as `execve()` and bootstrapping code from the C library.

The replayer matches the first 85 events successfully, which are all system call events, resulting in a cost of -255. At this point, the replayer encounters a `brk()` that does not match the `time()` call in the original log file and diverges. Upon divergence, DORA can treat `brk()` as an added system call or search the original log for a `brk()` call and delete intermediate events. Since no other call to `brk()` occurs in the log file, only the addition path is considered, resulting in a cost of -254 and an additional node in the tree of candidate executions.

Following this algorithm, replayer adds two more system calls: another `brk()` and `open()`, resulting in a cost of -252. A `time()` call is executed and successfully matches the expected call in the original log, ensuring that the time returned in the replayed execution is the same as the time in the original log. The match lowers the cost of the execution path to -255.

The changed program then executes an `fstat(500, ...)` in the replaying execution. Although the system call number is the same as the `fstat(1, ...)` in the log, the file descriptors passed as the first argument are different. This is treated as a mismatch. No subsequent matching `fstat()` calls are in the log, so this is treated as an another addition, increasing the cost of the execution path to -254.

Next, the application diverges on the call to `mmap()` since it does not match `fstat(1, ...)`. For the first time in this example, the divergence can lead to a deletion or addition since there is a matching `mmap()` in the original log. The explorer creates two nodes, and explores the unexplored node with the lowest cost. In this case, these two nodes are the only unexplored nodes. The addition node costs -253 since there is a one point addition penalty. The deletion node costs -256 because there is a one point deletion penalty for removing one node and a three point bonus for matching `mmap()`. Therefore, the deletion node is selected. The addition and deletion of `fstat()` is effectively a *replacement* of the system call.

The modified program then runs a `write(500, ...)` in the replaying execution which is different from the `write(1, ...)` in the log. Although the function calls are the same, the file descriptors are different, so this is treated as a mismatch. Since no subsequent matching `write()` calls are in the file, this must be treated as an addition, increasing the cost of the execution path to -255.

Finally, the program calls `exit()`, which diverges from the `write(1, ...)` in the original log. The divergence can lead to an addition of `exit_group()` or a deletion of `write(1, ...)`, matching the `exit_group()` in the original log. The addition node costs -254, the deletion node costs -257, and the unexplored node which added `mmap()` costs -253. The deletion node is selected.

Since the end of the log file has been reached, the explorer has found a successful replay with a cost of -257 and terminates. In this case, the explorer has successfully found a d-optimal replay. Although the explorer cannot prove this, the optimality of this replay is evident given the nature of the application modification.

From this simple example, we can observe that small code changes may significantly impact the behavior interactions of the application with the kernel API. The `fopen()` library call internally calls `malloc()`, resulting in two new invocations to `brk()`. Thus, even minor changes to high-level source code can result in relatively large changes to the low-level executable code.

6. Properties

We can make several useful guarantees about the behavior of DORA for certain classes of application changes.

PROPERTY 1. DORA *deterministically replays the original execution if the program is unmodified.*

In other words, DORA performs traditional deterministic record-replay when the program is unchanged. This property also implies that DORA provides d-optimal mutable replay for all d for unmodified programs.

PROPERTY 2. *If all explored mutations are* safe, DORA *deterministically replays all events in the original execution with the modified program.*

For our d, a safe mutation is an addition that does not change any state which is read by the original execution. These additions may store state which is later read, but the original execution must not access this new data. This guarantee is quite useful for debugging because it implies that all behavior in the original program, including race conditions, will be preserved deterministically.

For example, a `printf()` changes the internal state of the program by modifying an internal buffer, but returns the program to its original state, assuming proper newlines. Therefore, adding a `printf()` to debug a race condition always preserves recorded races because it will not change the relative ordering of events in the log. DORA can also handle the creation of new files. Any new calls to `open()` will receive a file descriptor not used by the original execution, so DORA guarantees that the original behavior of the program will be unaffected.

As another example, consider memory changes, for both shared and private regions of memory. First, reading the value of a variable in memory is safe. This is true even if the read is from shared memory and triggers a page fault leading to a temporary ownership transition. Additionally, the program can allocate and write to pages that are unused by the original execution. To avoid conflicts, DORA always assigns new memory allocations to a reserved area that is isolated from the original memory mappings.

PROPERTY 3. DORA *does not guarantee deterministic replay when given a modified application with arbitrary modifications.*

As explained in Section 4, DORA does not evaluate all possible interleaving of additions. For example, when a `printf()` is added in two different threads without locking, the order in which the calls are executed is variable. DORA picks the first possibility it encounters during replay and enforces this ordering for subsequent replays. However, this ordering is not enforced across separate invocations of the explorer.

PROPERTY 4. DORA *can deterministically replay a mutable replay of a modified application.*

DORA's explorer outputs the replay it selects to a log file. Thus, DORA can deterministically replay the original execution of the explorer using the modified program. This enables exact reproduction of a previously found replay, allowing DORA to be used iteratively.

7. Limitations

DORA has several limitations as it has no knowledge of application semantics. As a result, it only supports replay across application changes that do not alter core application or execution semantics.

For example, an exploit might add a new entry to a MySQL database. This entry would be assigned a particular id by MySQL, and would affect the ids of all later entries. A patch that removes the exploit would also remove the created entry, resulting in a mismatch between the ids assigned during replay and the recorded assignments. DORA would not find a d-optimal mutable replay because the core semantics of the execution have changed.

Additionally, DORA currently does not effectively support major changes in the layout of shared memory. If objects are relocated from a page to another, DORA cannot always preserve the original access ordering since DORA manages shared memory at the page level. DORA could be modified to track objects instead of pages by instrumenting the application. Even without this functionality, however, DORA is able to handle some changes to MySQL, which heavily uses shared memory.

Finally, DORA currently does not support process/thread layout changes. For example, if an application was originally recorded with 10 threads running, and is now reconfigured to run with 5 threads as part of the application modification, DORA does not provide a way to find a good mutable replay. Similarly, DORA has difficulty with applications that use green threads as small code changes may result in radically different schedules.

Thus, there are some types of changes for which DORA will not find the d-optimal replay. Fortunately, DORA produces enough information for the user to identify when these conditions occur. This allows the user to distinguish behavior caused by an application change from behavior due to DORA's limitations and makes DORA a useful tool for debugging and validation.

These conditions may seem restrictive, but they are often not an issue in practice because patches rarely change core application semantics. In a study of 60 patches each for MySQL, Apache, OpenSSL, and Squid, 83% resulted in only minor changes to the application behavior. Analysis of various security patches showed that over 75% only changed applications in minor ways [13]. This makes sense, as patches often attempt to fix an edge case in an application.

8. Evaluation

We have implemented a prototype of DORA in Linux. The recorder and replayer run in kernel space while the explorer runs in user space. Although the prototype only instruments a subset of the Linux kernel API, we demonstrated the functionality of this prototype in diagnosing and fixing bugs and measured its performance overhead with nine widely used real-world, multi-process, and multi-threaded applications and 32 different application changes involving thousands of lines of code. For our experiments, we used version 2.6.35 of the Linux kernel, Python 2.6.6, Cython 0.14, and UnionFs-Fuse 0.23. Measurements were done on a set of HP DL360 G3 servers, each with dual 3.06 GHz Intel Xeon CPUs, 4 GB RAM, and dual 18 GB local disks.

We recorded a wide range of applications with various workloads that exhibited bugs, as listed in the third column of Table 2.

Name	apache-upgrade	redis-upgrade
Start Version	Apache 2.2.19	Redis 2.4.1
Upgrades	3 (2.2.20 - 2.2.22)	12 (2.4.2 - 2.4.13)
Commits	277	137
LOC	5179+, 388-	2942+, 1154-
Workload	`httperf 0.8`	`redis-benchmark`

Table 1. Application upgrades

We verified that DORA can deterministically replay the original recorded applications and then replayed the executions with modified applications. Section 8.1 shows that DORA can replay these workloads using reconfigured or modified applications with additional debugging or other instrumentation. Section 8.2 shows how DORA can replay the exploits in Table 2 using patched versions of the applications to help developers verify that the bug patches successfully resolve the problems. It also shows how DORA can replay the workloads listed in the last column of Table 2 using the patched versions of the applications to help system administrators verify that the patches do not introduce errors in production workloads. Section 8.3 shows that DORA can verify production workloads on a series of release upgrades for the applications listed in Table 1. Finally, Section 8.4 presents record-replay overhead for the production workloads.

8.1 Debugging and Diagnosis Techniques

We used a wide range of debugging and diagnosis techniques with the workloads listed in the third column of Table 2. Since our work focuses on diagnosing and fixing bugs, most of the problems involve known security vulnerabilities, as indicated by their Common Vulnerabilities and Exposures (CVE) identifiers. However, the apache-log scenario shows a previously unknown bug in Apache that we found with DORA, and the Redis scenario shows how to add retroactive logging without discussing a specific bug.

For each of these exploits, we show how DORA can be used to diagnose the cause of a bug. We consider debugging techniques an experienced developer might apply to identify the root cause of each problem. Table 3 lists the application changes needed to use various debugging and diagnosis techniques for each scenario. DORA successfully found the d-optimal replay for all of these application changes. Table 3 shows the needed replay mutations.

apache-log was originally intended to show how DORA could be used for retroactive logging, but ended up showing DORA finding a previously unknown Apache bug [1]. We wanted to use DORA to add user agent and referrer information to Apache log files, since these could provide useful usage statistics for a website administrator. Although the default Apache logging configuration will not log this information, DORA records all HTTP header information that the server receives. Thus, an administrator using DORA could modify a configuration file to include this information and replay the recorded execution with the modified configuration to generate the desired web server log.

However, doing this yields a log file with incorrectly truncated entries. This behavior was due to a previously unknown bug in Apache. In several places in code, Apache mistakenly assumes that a call to `write()` will either write the desired amount of bytes or fail, instead of checking the return value and calling `write()` until all the required bytes are written. We submitted a bug report and patch to Apache [1] which was accepted into the codebase.

apache-sec records an exploit of a heap overflow vulnerability that launches a denial of service attack against an Apache web server using only a handful of requests. By examining Apache's log, an experienced Apache developer will notice oddities in some of the requests, but will not have enough information to identify

Name	Description	Problem/Exploit Workload	Production Workload
apache-log	Apache 2.4.2 web server	Log format change (Apache Bug 53131)	`httperf 0.8` with 100KB web page
apache-sec	Apache 2.2.19 web server	DoS attack (CVE 2011-3192)	`httperf 0.8` with 100KB web page
exim	Exim 4.69 mail server	Privilege escalation (CVE 2010-4344)	Send 1000 1KB e-mail messages
mysql	MySQL 5.0.67 database server	Unauthorized access (CVE 2008-2079)	`sql-bench`
nginx	Nginx 0.8.14 web server	Crash server (CVE 2009-2629)	`httperf 0.8` with 100KB web page
proftpd	ProFTPD 1.3.0 ftp server	Crash server (CVE 2006-5815)	100 clients fetch 10MB file
redis	Redis 2.4.11 key-value store	Request with insufficient logging	`redis-benchmark` with 50 clients
squid	Squid 3.1.7 http proxy server	DoS attack (CVE 2010-3072)	`ab 2.3` with cached facebook.com
wget	wget 1.11.4 http client	Create arbitrary file (CVE 2010-2252)	100 requests to http://www.cnn.com

Table 2. Application scenarios

Name	Debugging Change	Replay Mutations
apache-log	Modify log format in configuration file	Add 1 `fstat()`, 1 `mmap()`, and 3 `write()` per request
apache-sec	Add print statements for debugging	Add 1 `fstat()`, 1 `mmap()` and then 2 `write()` per request
exim	Recompile with debugging options enabled	None
mysql	Add conditional print statements for debugging	Add 1 `fstat()`, 1 `mmap()`, 1 memory event, 12 `write()`
nginx	Change the config file to enable debug messages	Add 508 `write()`, delete 1064 syscalls
proftpd	Recompile with debugging options enabled	Add 1 `close()`
redis	Log erroneous client requests	Add 1 `open()`, at least 3 `write()` and 1 `close()` per request
squid	Save parsed requests to file	Add 1 `open()`, at least 10 `write()` and 1 `close()` per request
wget	Change language from Italian to Japanese	Replace 17 `write()`, 24 `mmap()`, 2 `open()`, and delete 5 syscalls

Table 3. Application modifications for debugging

the bug with the default logging settings. In particular, it would be helpful to have more information about the range headers of the requests. Using DORA, a developer can add print statements to Apache, replay, and recognize that the problem was due to incorrect handling of overlapping range headers. Five system calls were added for each request as a result of the additional print statements.

exim involves an exploit that crashes the mail server using a heap overflow vulnerability in a buggy string formatting function that allows attackers to execute arbitrary code. If this crash was recorded in the wild, it would be helpful to use GDB to analyze the program at the time of the crash. However, production servers are almost always optimized and compiled without debugging symbols. Thus, a traditional record-replay system would be unable to help. Using DORA, a developer can recompile the program, replay the exploit using the recompiled program, and hook GDB to the replayed program before it crashes. When investigating the stack trace, the nature of this attack becomes clear. No mutations were needed in the d-optimal replay, despite various memory layout changes to the program as a result of recompilation.

mysql involves an exploit which maliciously uses symlinks to elevate permissions to a database. By default, MySQL disables logging. Thus, a developer trying to discover how a malicious user gained access to a database will have no information about which commands were executed. Using DORA, the developer can modify the program to log executed commands, then replay the exploit using the modified program. This process can be repeated, allowing the developer to iteratively add print statements to different sections of the code and pinpoint the bug. To demonstrate this, we added enough print statements to identify the bug. DORA found the d-optimal replay, which had mutations of fourteen added system calls and a shared memory event.

nginx involves running Nginx, a high-performance HTTP server, and crashing one of its worker processes with a malicious HTTP request that uses a buffer underflow attack to execute arbitrary code. The default log does not show what actions were taken on each request, which makes debugging difficult. Using DORA, the developer can modify the configuration file to enable verbose logging and replay the exploit with the modified configuration. To generate verbose logs on a workload exhibiting the exploit, 508 `write()` calls were added and 1064 system calls were deleted.

proftpd records an exploit that crashes the FTP server by taking advantage of an off-by-one error to execute arbitrary code. As with the exim use case, GDB would be a helpful debugging tool, but a production server is unlikely to be compiled with debugging symbols. With DORA, a developer can recompile with the Makefile configuration for debugging, replay the exploit using the recompiled program, and hook GDB to the replayed program before it crashes. The resulting stack trace makes it easy to diagnose the problem. A replay mutation of adding 1 `close()` was needed to use the debugging configuration.

redis involves recording Redis, an in-memory key-value store often used in production applications as a caching layer on top of a general purpose database. This use case does not involve a specific bug but instead shows how a developer can add logging to Redis and replay this modification on the original recording, effectively turning on retroactive logging. Replay mutations of adding at least five system calls per request was needed. The number of additions varied based on the nature of the request. For instance, a malformed request triggered more logging than a proper request.

squid involves an exploit that crashes the Squid daemon by sending an empty Expect HTTP header parameter. The default request logging does not provide enough information about the header to determine the cause of the bug. Using DORA, a developer can modify the program to log each request to a file with the complete header information of the request, then replay a recording of the exploit with the modified program. This allows the developer to see that the requests which crash the server have empty header parameters and narrow down the bug to a very specific section of code. At least 12 system calls were added per request. The exact number varied depending on the type of request.

wget involves downloading a file from a malicious server that does a 301 redirect. A vulnerability in wget allows the server to choose the destination filename. Remote servers can create or overwrite arbitrary files and even execute arbitrary code by writing dotfile in a home directory. Because this behavior depends on a live server behaving in a particular way, this issue may be difficult to reproduce and debug if it is not noticed immediately. Additionally, to demonstrate the robustness of DORA, we suppose that an Italian developer observes this behavior and wants to show it to a Japanese developer who cannot reproduce the results because the server is no longer available. Using DORA, the second developer can replay wget in a different language, enabling collaborative debugging across international borders and language barriers. While this scenario is tongue-in-cheek, the translation use case is novel and has interesting applications. The replay involved replacing 43 system calls and deleting 5 system calls.

8.2 Patch Validation

For each bug exhibited by the workloads listed in the third column of Table 2, we replayed the bug-inducing workload on the patched application to verify that the patch successfully fixed the bug. Table 5 lists the number of lines of code added and deleted for each patch and the mutations needed for each replay. Redis is not included; since it did not involve an application bug, no patch was necessary. Table 5 shows three interesting points.

First, DORA found the d-optimal replay even with substantial patches of over 400 lines of code changed. The replay mutations that were needed to find the d-optimal replay varied. Many involved executing different system calls, but others involved changes in signal delivery and shared memory accesses. This demonstrates DORA's ability to replay despite a broad range of application modifications so long as the core application semantics remain the same.

Second, we show that production workloads can be replayed using patched applications to verify that the patch does not introduce errors into those workloads. For each workload listed in the last column of Table 2, DORA recorded the workload using the unpatched application, then found a d-optimal mutable replay using patched versions of each application. We examined the output of each mutable replay and verified that the patches did not change application behavior when running the workload. We also compared each original recorded log with the log of the corresponding mutable replay to verify that the patches did not change the application execution in unexpected ways. System administrators could use this technique to test patches before deploying them to have more confidence that they will not break their production systems.

Third, Table 5 shows that the go live feature of the replayer can be used to validate patches even when a recorded exploit crashes a process. The exploit for Nginx caused a worker to crash, and the Squid exploit crashed the entire application. In both cases, DORA does not replay the original `SIGSEGV` and allows the applications to go live and handle new requests. Although a worker process crashed in the proftpd scenario, DORA did not go live because the proftpd master forks a new worker per connection and is resilient to worker crashes, allowing subsequent requests to be replayed without going live.

8.3 Release Upgrades

To demonstrate another use case of DORA, we took two server applications and recorded them running the benchmarks we used as production workloads as listed in Table 1. We then replayed those executions over a series of 15 release upgrades to verify that the workloads continued to function correctly across upgrades. DORA found the d-optimal replay in all of these cases.

apache-upgrade consists of a series of upgrades of Apache over an 8 month timeframe from 2.2.19 (May 21, 2011) to 2.2.22 (Jan 30, 2012). The upgrades involved changes of more than 5000 lines of code and 277 separate commits. Using DORA, we recorded version 2.2.19 running httperf, then replayed the recording with each subsequent version. We repeated this process for versions 2.2.20 and 2.2.21. DORA successfully replayed all of these application changes. This required various add and delete mutations of `read()` and `brk()` calls. Note that we also tried this experiment starting with Apache 2.2.18, but DORA was unable to replay from that version due to core library modifications that caused large shared memory layout changes between Apache 2.2.18 and 2.2.19.

redis-upgrade consists of a series of upgrades of Redis over a 7 month timeframe from 2.4.1 (October 17, 2011) to 2.4.13 (May 2, 2012). The upgrades involved changes of more than 4000 lines of code in 137 separate commits. Using DORA, we recorded version 2.4.1 running redis-benchmark, then replayed the recording with each later version. We also repeated this experiment for version 2.4.2 and upgrades 2.4.3 to 2.4.13, version 2.4.3 and upgrades 2.4.13 to 2.4.4, and so on. DORA successfully replayed all of these application changes. They required add and delete mutations of 12 different system calls, including `open()`, `close()`, `read()`, `write()`, `mmap()`, `munmap()` and `time()` system calls.

Name	Recording Overhead	Storage Growth	Replay Speedup
apache-log	9.3%	31 KB/s	3.8x
apache-sec	4.8%	18 KB/s	1.9x
exim	4.3%	30 KB/s	7.2x
mysql	4.7%	9.6 KB/s	1.1x
nginx	9.7%	15 KB/s	2.2x
redis	2.6%	91 KB/s	1.3x
proftpd	4.1%	22 KB/s	2.6x
squid	8.2%	124 KB/s	1.2x
wget	2.2%	19 KB/s	11x

Table 4. Mutable replay performance

8.4 Performance

To quantify the performance costs of using DORA, we measured the runtime overhead of recording and replaying the production workloads listed in the last column of Table 2. Table 4 shows the overhead of recording the production workload with the unpatched application, the storage growth rate of recording, and the speedup when replaying the recording with the patched application. Unless otherwise noted, default configuration options were used for all applications. The standard deviations for all measurements were negligible.

The recording overhead in all cases was less than 10% even for CPU-bound workloads designed to stress application performance. For example, Squid performance was measured with a fully cached web page, resulting in a CPU intensive workload. Even with these unfavorable workloads, the results indicate that DORA can be used in production systems with modest overhead.

Similarly, the time to replay the original recording on the original application was in all cases faster than the original execution; in one case, it was over an order of magnitude faster. This is because DORA can bypass blocking system calls that sleep. Since production servers are likely to sleep more and service requests less frequently than in our benchmarks, replay speedup will be much higher in practice.

While recording, the log was streamed through `gzip` before being persisted to disk. The storage growth rates ranged from 10 KB/s to 130 KB/s. These storage requirements are modest considering our workloads. DORA would take almost three months to fill a 1 TB drive at the worst of these rates, which makes it an affordable and practical solution.

Name	Patch LOC +/-	Replay Mutations
apache-log	39+, 39-	Add 1 `write()` per truncated log entry
apache-sec	292+, 154-	Add 1 `write()` and replace 1 `writev()` per request
exim	7+, 0-	Delete 18 syscalls, add 29 syscalls
mysql	170+, 60-	Add 29 `lstat()`, delete 79 syscalls, add 1 `write()`, delete 15 and add 8 memory events
nginx	9+, 5-	Delete 1 `write()` and replace 1 `writev()` per request, then go live on crash
proftpd	17+, 3-	Delete 694 syscalls, add 38 syscalls, delete a `SIGSEGV`
squid	38+, 33-	Delete a `SIGSEGV`, 1 `close()`, 1 `stat()`, 1 `write()`, then go live
wget	43+, 12-	Replace 9 syscalls among `stat()`, `write()`, `open()`, `utime()`

Table 5. Application patches tested against exploits

9. Related Work

Many record-replay approaches have been proposed to improve bug reproducibility debugging [2, 3, 7, 11, 18, 19, 21, 22, 26, 27], but none allows for mutable replay. Some approaches propose relaxing the requirement of deterministic replay for performance reasons. For example, ODR [2] proposes only ensuring that the output is deterministically replayed for replay debugging. This is quite different from mutable replay, in which the output may change due to application changes.

Some record-replay systems can support a form of deterministic replay that may differ in limited ways from the original recorded execution. Crosscut [8] can reduce the information recorded in a log so that, for example, sensitive information can be purged before replay. Our previous work on Scribe [16] replays a recorded application execution until a specified point, and then transitions to live execution instead of replaying the rest of the log. Our previous work on Racepro [17] detects process races due to dependencies in the ordering of system calls by recording an application execution to a log, identifying a pair of system calls that may be racy, truncating the log at the occurrence of the pair of system calls, inverting their order, and then replaying the truncated log with the reordered system calls to detect process races. However, Racepro only supports changes that reorder system calls and does not support changes in the middle of replay. None of these approaches supports mutable replay, but mutable replay could be useful for some of these systems. For example, Racepro could use mutable replay to avoid replay divergence and more effectively detect process races. Another race detection tool [19] uses the iDNA [3] record-replay framework and would also benefit from mutable replay.

A few record-replay systems allow new code to be run while replaying a recorded execution [7, 12]. However, this new code cannot have any side effects on the program. If a replay diverges due to new code, these systems must rollback to a point prior to the divergence for the replay to continue. In contrast, DORA allows replay to continue even after divergence; side effects due to new code are preserved. Moreover, unlike DORA, these other approaches prevent application developers from leveraging existing configurable application functionality and instead require that developers learn a new complex system. Because these other approaches work at a VM level, they are fundamentally limited in their abilities to perform mutable replay and support the kind of application changes supported by DORA. Finally, none of these other approaches work on multicore or multiprocessor systems.

A concept of mutable replay was mentioned as a part of DSF [28], a Java-only framework for implementing distributed algorithms. DSF recognized that existing replay approaches did not allow adding print statements for debugging. DSF requires that all applications to be written using its framework, requires modification to the applications, and is primarily simulation-based. Furthermore, DSF presents no algorithms or mechanisms for actually doing mutable replay, and presents no experimental results demonstrating the ability to do mutable replay. More recently, a study has assessed the potential utility of mutable replay on real patches [13], though no mutable replay system or results are presented. DORA presents the first system that achieves transparent mutable replay, requires no application modifications, and demonstrates experimentally that mutable replay can be used with real applications.

Alternative techniques have been proposed to help with patch validation, one use case of mutable replay. Band-aid patching [23] and delta execution [29] instrument patches to identify portions of an application that have changed, execute both the unpatched and patched code paths either serially or in parallel, and select the results from one path or merge the results from both paths. However, these approaches incur substantial performance overhead. Many simple patches cannot be handled by these approaches, such as simple changes to data structures. Unlike DORA, these approaches do not allow patch validation on a recorded bug or offline patch validation on a production workload. Furthermore, they are designed for patch validation only and are not effective for debugging.

Self-healing systems have been proposed which record the occurrence of a bug, then automatically generate and apply a patch as a temporary fix to the problem [24]. DORA is complementary to these systems and can be used to verify that a generated patch successfully fixes problems that occurred in the original workload.

Finding a mutable replay has some similarities to the edit distance and longest common subsequence problems, which have applications to approximate string matching and bioinformatics. In those problems however, both sequences being used for matching are known in advance. In contrast, mutable replay must match a known execution log with an execution sequence that is not known in advance, so these algorithms cannot be directly applied.

10. Conclusions and Future Work

DORA introduces the concept of mutable record-replay and is the first transparent mutable record-replay system. It enables, for the first time, a recording of an application execution to be replayed using a modified version of the application for a large class of application changes. This is made possible by the use of lightweight operating system mechanisms to record and replay without imposing unnecessary timing and ordering constraints. DORA introduces an explorer that directs the replay mechanism to identify a mutable replay of the modified aplication that minimizes differences with the original unmodified application execution.

Our experimental results on a Linux prototype demonstrate that mutable replay is feasible across a wide range of real-world applications and application changes which can reach thousands of lines of code, even without support for major changes to core application semantics. We show that mutable replay is useful for enabling common debugging techniques not possible with previous record-replay systems. We also show that mutable replay enables validation of security patches against both exploits and production workloads. This is all accomplished without requiring source code modifications and with low recording overhead, enabling usage on production systems. These results demonstrate that mutable replay has the potential to enable new techniques for debugging and patch testing and validation, which can lead to substantial improvements in software reliability and developer productivity.

We hope to explore a number of directions in future work. While we have explored a few ways in which mutable replay can be used in multicore debugging and patch validation, DORA provides a foundation for exploring other uses of mutable replay as well. We have evaluated a particular cost function and exploration algorithm for mutable replay, but much more can be done to consider alternatives that may be particularly suited for other use cases. Furthermore, it would be beneficial to perform instrumentation at a higher level: if runtime systems like the Java Virtual Machine or the Ruby MRI were instrumented to work with DORA, mutable replay could be an even more effective tool to reproduce, diagnose, and fix software bugs for Web and mobile applications.

Acknowledgments

Oren Laadan and Dan Tsafrir provided helpful comments on earlier drafts of this paper. This work was supported in part by an IBM Faculty Award and NSF grants CNS-1018355, CNS-0905246, and CCF-1162021.

References

[1] Apache Bug 53131. `https://issues.apache.org/bugzilla/show_bug.cgi?id=53131`.

[2] G. Altekar and I. Stoica. ODR: Output-Deterministic Replay for Multicore Debugging. In *Proceedings of the 22nd ACM Symposium on Operating Systems Principles (SOSP '09)*, Nov. 2009.

[3] S. Bhansali, W.-K. Chen, S. de Jong, A. Edwards, R. Murray, M. Drinić, D. Mihočka, and J. Chau. Framework for Instruction-level Tracing and Analysis of Program Executions. In *Proceedings of the 2nd International Conference on Virtual Execution Environments (VEE '06)*, June 2006.

[4] E. W. Biederman. Multiple Instances of the Global Linux Namespaces. In *Proceedings of the Linux Symposium*, July 2006.

[5] T. C. Bressoud. TFT: A Software System for Application- Transparent Fault Tolerance. In *Proceedings of the 28th International Symposium on Fault-Tolerant Computing (FTCS '98)*, June 1998.

[6] T. C. Bressoud and F. B. Schneider. Hypervisor-Based Fault Tolerance. In *Proceedings of the 15th ACM Symposium on Operating Systems Principles (SOSP '95)*, Dec. 1995.

[7] J. Chow, T. Garfinkel, and P. M. Chen. Decoupling Dynamic Program Analysis from Execution in Virtual Environments. In *Proceedings of the USENIX Annual Technical Conference (USENIX '08)*, June 2008.

[8] J. Chow, D. Lucchetti, T. Garfinkel, G. Lefebvre, R. Gardner, J. Mason, S. Small, and P. M. Chen. Multi-stage Replay with Crosscut. In *Proceedings of the 6th International Conference on Virtual Execution Environments (VEE '10)*, Mar. 2010.

[9] G. W. Dunlap, S. T. King, S. Cinar, M. A. Basrai, and P. M. Chen. ReVirt: Enabling Intrusion Analysis Through Virtual-Machine Logging and Replay. In *Proceedings of the 5th Symposium on Operating Systems Design and Implementation (OSDI '02)*, Dec. 2002.

[10] G. W. Dunlap, D. G. Lucchetti, M. A. Fetterman, and P. M. Chen. Execution Replay of Multiprocessor Virtual Machines. In *Proceedings of the 4th International Conference on Virtual Execution Environments (VEE '08)*, Mar. 2008.

[11] Z. Guo, X. Wang, J. Tang, X. Liu, Z. Xu, M. Wu, M. F. Kaashoek, and Z. Zhang. R2: An Application-Level Kernel for Record and Replay. In *Proceedings of the 8th Symposium on Operating Systems Design and Implementation (OSDI '08)*, Dec. 2008.

[12] A. Joshi, S. T. King, G. W. Dunlap, and P. M. Chen. Detecting Past and Present Intrusions through Vulnerability-Specific Predicates. In *Proceedings of the 20th ACM Symposium on Operating Systems Principles (SOSP '05)*, Oct. 2005.

[13] I. Kravets and D. Tsafrir. Feasibility of Mutable Replay for Automated Regression Testing of Security Updates. In *Workshop on Runtime Environments, Systems, Layering and Virtualized Environments (RESoLVE)*, March 2012.

[14] O. Laadan and J. Nieh. Transparent Checkpoint-Restart of Multiple Processes on Commodity Operating Systems. In *Proceedings of the 2007 USENIX Annual Technical Conference*, June 2007.

[15] O. Laadan, R. A. Baratto, D. Phung, S. Potter, and J. Nieh. DejaView: A Personal Virtual Computer Recorder. In *Proceedings of the 21st ACM Symposium on Operating Systems Principles (SOSP '07)*, Oct. 2007.

[16] O. Laadan, N. Viennot, and J. Nieh. Transparent, Lightweight Application Execution Replay on Commodity Multiprocessor Operating Systems. In *Proceedings of the ACM International Conference on Measurement and Modeling of Computer Systems (SIGMETRICS '10)*, June 2010.

[17] O. Laadan, N. Viennot, C.-c. Tsai, C. Blinn, J. Yang, and J. Nieh. Pervasive Detection of Process Races in Deployed Systems. In *Proceedings of the 23rd ACM Symposium on Operating Systems Principles (SOSP '11)*, Oct. 2011.

[18] T. J. LeBlanc and J. M. Mellor-Crummey. Debugging Parallel Programs with Instant Replay. *IEEE Transactions on Computers*, 36(4), Apr. 1987.

[19] S. Narayanasamy, Z. Wang, J. Tigani, A. Edwards, and B. Calder. Automatically Classifying Benign and Harmful Data Races Using Replay Analysis. In *Proceedings of the ACM SIGPLAN 2007 Conference on Programming Language Design and Implementation (PLDI '07)*, June 2007.

[20] S. Osman, D. Subhraveti, G. Su, and J. Nieh. The Design and Implementation of Zap: A System for Migrating Computing Environments. In *Proceedings of the 5th Symposium on Operating Systems Design and Implementation (OSDI '02)*, Dec. 2002.

[21] S. Park, Y. Zhou, W. Xiong, Z. Yin, R. Kaushik, K. H. Lee, and S. Lu. PRES: Probabilistic Replay with Execution Sketching on Multiprocessors. In *Proceedings of the 22nd ACM Symposium on Operating Systems Principles (SOSP '09)*, Oct. 2009.

[22] Y. Saito. Jockey: a User-Space Library for Record-Replay Debugging. In *Proceedings of the 6th International Symposium on Automated Analysis-Driven Debugging (AADEBUG '05)*, Sept. 2005.

[23] S. Sidiroglou, S. Ioannidis, and A. D. Keromytis. Band-aid Patching. In *Proceedings of the 3rd workshop on on Hot Topics in System Dependability (HotDep '07)*, June 2007.

[24] S. Sidiroglou, O. Laadan, C. Perez, N. Viennot, J. Nieh, and A. D. Keromytis. ASSURE: Automatic Software Self-healing Using REscue points. In *Proceedings of the 14th International Conference on Architecture Support for Programming Languages and Operating Systems (ASPLOS '09)*, Mar. 2009.

[25] J. H. Slye and E. Elnozahy. Supporting Nondeterministic Execution in Fault-Tolerant Systems. In *Proceedings of the 26th International Symposium on Fault-Tolerant Computing (FTCS '96)*, June 1996.

[26] S. M. Srinivasan, S. Kandula, C. R. Andrews, and Y. Zhou. Flashback: A Lightweight Extension for Rollback and Deterministic Replay for Software Debugging. In *Proceedings of the USENIX Annual Technical Conference (USENIX '04)*, June 2004.

[27] D. Subhraveti and J. Nieh. Record and Transplay: Partial Checkpointing for Replay Debugging Across Heterogeneous Systems. In *Proceedings of the ACM International Conference on Measurement and Modeling of Computer Systems (SIGMETRICS '11)*, June 2011.

[28] C. Tang. DSF: A Common Platform for Distributed Systems Research and Development. In *Proceedings of the 10th ACM/IFIP/USENIX International Conference on Middleware (Middleware '09)*, Nov. 2009.

[29] J. Tucek, W. Xiong, and Y. Zhou. Efficient Online Validation With Delta Execution. In *Proceedings of the 14th International Conference on Architecture Support for Programming Languages and Operating Systems (ASPLOS '09)*, Mar. 2009.

Using Likely Invariants for Automated Software Fault Localization

Swarup Kumar Sahoo John Criswell Chase Geigle Vikram Adve

Department of Computer Science
University of Illinois at Urbana-Champaign
Urbana, Illinois USA
{ssahoo2,criswell,geigle1,vadve}@illinois.edu

Abstract

We propose an automatic diagnosis technique for isolating the root cause(s) of software failures. We use likely program invariants, automatically generated using correct inputs that are close to the fault-triggering input, to select a set of candidate program locations which are possible root causes. We then trim the set of candidate root causes using software-implemented dynamic backwards slicing, plus two new filtering heuristics: dependence filtering, and filtering via multiple failing inputs that are also close to the failing input. Experimental results on reported software bugs of three large open-source servers show that we are able to narrow down the number of candidate bug locations to between 5 and 17 program expressions, even in programs that are hundreds of thousands of lines long.

Categories and Subject Descriptors D.2.5 [*Software Engineering*]: Testing and Debugging—Debugging aids; B.8.1 [*Performance and Reliability*]: Reliability, Testing, and Fault-Tolerance

General Terms Algorithms, Performance, Reliability

Keywords Software reliability, Root cause, Testing, Debugging, Fault localization, Invariants, Bug Diagnosis, Program analysis

1. Introduction

Software bugs are *everywhere*. Not only do they infest software during development, but they escape our extermination efforts and enter production code. In addition to severe frustration to customers, software failures result in billions of dollars of lost revenue to service providers [4, 11, 38].

Given a program, *bug detection* is the problem of determining whether the program has bugs, preferably with test cases that trigger such bugs. Bug detection tools such as Valgrind [34], FindBugs [1], Fortify [2], Coverity [3], and many others are widely used in software development today.

Given a program and a "failing input," i.e., an input for which the program encounters a failure, *bug diagnosis*, or "debugging," is the problem of identifying the *reasons*, including the location, cause, and possible fixes for the failure. A key component of bug diagnosis is *fault localization*, the problem of identifying one or more possible locations in the program where code needs to be changed to prevent the failure. Fault localization is an important and time-consuming step in debugging software failures. Currently, bug diagnosis is mostly a manual process, either during development or, during production-run failures. The latter are especially difficult to diagnose because it is difficult to reproduce the failures at the developers' site and because privacy and economic concerns severely limit what information is available from the end-user's site [20]. Automating this diagnosis process can significantly increase programmer productivity and reduce software development costs.

There has been much previous work on this problem [5, 10, 12, 16, 24, 27, 28, 30, 41, 42, 44], but the overall problem is far from solved, and, to our knowledge, *no automated fault localization or bug diagnosis tools are used in real world development*. Simple statistical techniques such as Tarantula [26, 27] and Ochiai [5] turn out to be useful only in relatively few bugs, as our results show (see Section 8.3). Some tools [45] are slow and may not be suitable for large applications or for production-site diagnosis systems. Other tools [16, 24, 35, 41] may report too many source lines as potential root causes of the bug (i.e., report too many false positives) or often fail to report source lines containing the root cause (i.e., often have false negatives). Some tools [16] also may be impractical due to special hardware requirements. Others use systematic but unscalable techniques to compare the memory states of passing and failing runs [41]. In fact, for many of these approaches, it is not clear how they will scale to large, realistic programs.

Likely program invariants are a powerful tool for detecting and diagnosing software errors [18, 24, 35]. Informally, *likely program invariants* are program properties that are *observed* to hold in some set of successful executions but, unlike true invariants, may not necessarily hold for all possible executions.

By training likely program invariants on "good inputs," violations of these invariants in a failing run can identify deviations between good and bad runs (i.e., possible bug locations and their consequences). The tradeoff, however, is that they can also be violated on valid behaviors not captured in the training runs ("false positives") and, if the invariants are too broad, can miss bug locations ("false negatives"). Despite these tradeoffs, such invariants are powerful because they can capture properties *of the actual source code*, including properties that violate programmer intent (whereas programmer-written invariants or assertions in the code, will only express programmer intent), and, by observing patterns of behavior of program variables, (e.g., "the variable `month` lies between 1 and 12"), they can capture deep algorithmic properties which are captured in limited ways, if at all, by static analysis [17].

We propose a sophisticated approach combining likely program invariants with novel filtering techniques to narrow down a possible

ASPLOS'13, March 16–20, 2013, Houston, Texas, USA.

set of locations that have to be changed to eliminate a failure ("*candidate root causes*"). Our goal is to make this set as small as possible. We improve over previous work in two key ways.

First, all the previous invariant-based approaches except one [24] use general test inputs for training invariants, which has two serious disadvantages. One, using general test inputs makes the likely invariants very broad (e.g., observed value ranges of variables may be large) and not tailored to the specific failure, which can make them miss root causes. Two, because the code coverage from test inputs is often not high [32], root causes from the untested parts of the code can be missed (and the untested parts of the code are also likely to contain bugs). Our first key improvement over previous work is that we generate likely invariants by using a small set of training inputs *that are as close to the given failing input as possible*. Any of these invariants that fail during the failing run capture differences between the failing and passing runs. In this sense, our invariants can be seen as a way to isolate the differences between failing and similar passing runs, which is the original insight behind *Delta Debugging* [44], but the invariants in our approach are a much more lightweight (though less precise) method for comparing program states than the explicit state comparisons used in Delta Debugging. The invariant failures give us a set of program locations that may be candidate root causes of the failure.

Our second key improvement is that we use a more sophisticated series of filters, including two novel techniques, to filter out false positives. Filtering is important due to how our system creates invariants. *We consider it important not to miss the root cause, and instead prefer to generate many candidate root causes and then use sophisticated filtering techniques to eliminate false positives.* We therefore use a very *small* set of training inputs (e.g., only 8 inputs for each bug in our experiments, compared with hundreds or thousands in traditional approaches [18]), which yields much narrower invariants. Narrower invariants are more likely to be violated (leading to fewer false negatives), but many other spurious invariants may be violated as well (leaving a large number of false positives).

We therefore use a combination of novel and known techniques to eliminate the false positives from the initial candidates. We first use dynamic backward slicing to filter out invariants that do not influence the observed failure symptom. We then use two novel heuristics to further narrow down the root causes of failure. The heuristics are based on two observations. First, if an invariant on one instruction fails, then another instruction dependent on the first one may also be likely to have an invariant failure, but the underlying cause is the first, not the second. We remove the second from the candidate root causes and call this the *dependence filtering* step. For efficiency, this heuristic leverages the dynamic backward slicing directly. Second, if multiple similar inputs produce the same failure symptom, they are likely to have the same root cause, and therefore, we can focus on invariants that fail for all such inputs. Again, this heuristic directly leverages (indeed, simply reapplies) the previous steps, but for additional failing inputs.

In summary, the two key insights underlying our work are:

1. Generating likely invariants using training inputs close to the failing input is less likely to miss root causes than using invariants generated from a large number of unrelated inputs (e.g., test inputs); and
2. Using sophisticated filtering techniques can allow us to start with a large number of initial candidate root causes (reducing false negatives), and narrow them down to a small set of final locations (reducing false positives).

We evaluate our techniques experimentally using three large open-source servers: Squid, Apache web server and MySQL. These programs are far larger than those used in any previous study we know of except one [42]. We used eight previously reported bugs, including four memory corruption and four incorrect output bugs. We use an automated procedure to construct the passing and failing inputs that are "close" to the failing input. The results are extremely strong. Overall, we reduce the number of candidate root causes to a range of only 5–17 program expressions per bug, even in programs of hundreds of thousands of lines of code.[1] Moreover, each of the filtering steps proves important: slicing removes nearly 80% of false candidates, dependence filtering removes nearly 58% of the remaining false positives, and using multiple faulty inputs removes several more. Comparing our work against the Tarantula [26, 27] and Ochiai [5] approaches, which have been used for similar comparisons in previous work, we find that their approach is slightly better in the two best cases, but is extremely inconsistent, with thousands of candidate locations in 6 out of 8 cases.

To summarize, our main contributions are:

1. We present a novel invariant-based approach for fault localization, based on training the invariants with a small set of automatically constructed "good inputs" that are close to a given failing input. Our results show that this approach yields a more precise set of root causes than previous work.
2. We present novel heuristics for reducing false positives in the diagnosis results. These heuristics have valuable synergy with our core invariant strategy because they leverage the other analysis techniques, including input construction and dynamic backward slicing.
3. We evaluate our approach for real bugs in a larger and more realistic set of applications than all previous work except one.
4. Our results show that the approach is extremely effective at reducing the set of possible root causes, even in large programs, and that each of the filtering steps makes an important contribution in reducing this set.

The rest of the paper is organized as follows. Section 2 motivates and gives an overview of our invariant-based diagnosis framework. Section 3 describes the design of our invariant-based analysis. Sections 4 and 5 describe techniques that prune false positives. Section 6 briefly describes how the results of the diagnosis is presented to the programmer. Section 7 describes our experimental methodology and applications. Our experimental results are presented in Section 8. Related work is discussed in Section 9, and we describe future work and conclude in Section 10.

2. Overview of Our Approach

Some previous automated bug diagnosis techniques use program invariants [24, 30]. Others, such as Delta Debugging [12, 44], compare a failed execution of the program with a successful execution to identify the root causes of a failure. One drawback of Delta Debugging is that comparing individual dynamic statements or values between a failed and a successful run can be inefficient and unscalable. Instead, we can use program invariants to make an efficient comparison of the program runs. Thus, *our approach essentially combines these two prior approaches.*

Our approach needs the source code of the program, configuration files, a failing input and a deterministic detector (described in more detail in Section 7.2). Figure 1 gives a broad overview of our approach. The process begins with a program and a failing input, plus an optional grammar or *specification* specifying the possible tokens in valid program inputs (in the form of a lexical analyzer or tokenizer) and all possible replacement tokens for each input to-

[1] Although total program size is not a good metric of programmer effort in narrowing down a bug, it is a good metric for the difficulty faced by automated tools which must begin with the entire program.

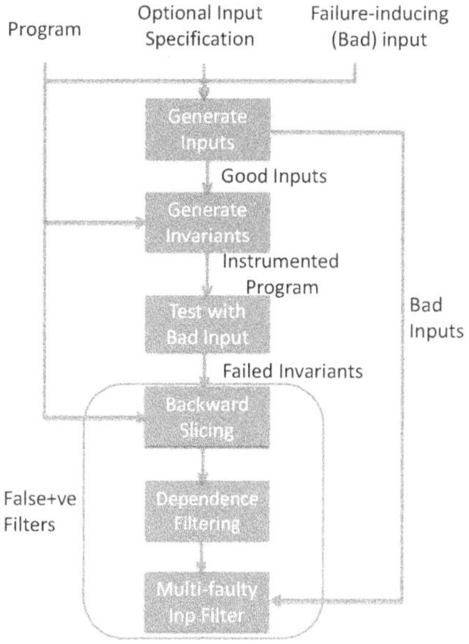

Figure 1. Diagnosis Tool Architecture

ken. The output is a set of source-level program expressions that identify locations of the possible root causes. Note that our current approach only uses the specification of tokens and their replacements, if available; it does not need any production rules of the input grammar. If this information about the grammar is not available, our approach falls back on an application-oblivious character-level rewriting algorithm, very similar to the tool, `ddmin` [45]. (A final step mapping invariants back to source program expressions is not shown.)

Program invariants are predicates that are guaranteed to hold for all possible inputs. Predicates observed to hold for some, but perhaps not all, program inputs are known as *likely invariants* [18]. Likely invariants can be extracted by monitoring the execution of the program for some desired set of program inputs; we refer to these as the *training runs*. If we extract likely invariants from some set of training runs of a program, instrument the program to test the likely invariants, and then execute it with the failing input, any invariants that fail are a strong indicator of differences from successful runs. Thus, we can use locations of failed invariants as an initial set of *candidate root causes* of the bug.

One key problem we must address in this work is that this initial set of candidate root causes is often very large, e.g., with hundreds of locations. We refer to all except the true locations of the root cause as *false positives*. The challenge is to filter down the set of candidates into as small a set of locations as possible. We use a series of dynamic analysis steps based on dynamic program slicing and dependence filtering to filter out as many false positives as possible.

We use the example in Listing 1 to illustrate the steps of our approach. This is a simplified version of some code in the MySQL database server which contains a buffer overflow bug. The buffer overflow occurs when a *Select* query contains a specific date between 0000-Jan-01 and 0000-Feb-28. The overflow occurs at line 31, when the `type_names` array is indexed with `weekday` for the aforementioned dates. The root cause of this bug is at line 10 in function `calc_daynr`. It uses an unsigned variable `year` to perform computation. When the value of `year` is 0, the decrement statement at line 10 results in a very large number and, consequently, the value of `temp` at line 13 also becomes a very large number. Finally, at line 14, the function returns a negative number; this value is used to calculate the day of the week in function `calc_weekday`, which, in turn, returns a negative value. Hence, when the return value is used as an index in line 31, it causes a buffer overflow and a program crash.

2.1 Likely Program Invariants

We use program invariants to find a set of candidate program instructions that are possible root causes of a failure. Given an input that triggers the bug, we derive a set of good inputs that are close to the failure inducing input in lexicographic distance, and do not trigger the bug. We do this automatically using a variant of the *ddmin* algorithm [45], using character-level or token-level rewriting depending on whether the specification (grammar tokens and replacements) are known. We then run the program with these good inputs to find a set of program invariants. The invariants we use are *range invariants* (described in Section 3.1.1). We limit our invariants to load, store or function return values, for reasons explained in Section 3.1. For example, we monitor the return value of functions such as `calc_daynr` and `calc_weekday`, as well as the loads of the three fields of `t` in the arguments to `calc_daynr`. For all good inputs, the return values of the two functions will be positive; this will be captured as likely invariants. When the program is run on the failure-inducing input, these two invariants (along with some other invariants) will fail as the return values of these functions will be negative. This will give us a number of candidate locations which can be root causes.

Overall, this step generated 95 failed invariants for this particular bug in MySQL. While this is far too large to report to programmers, it is still an impressively low number (especially considering that we are using one of the simplest possible types of invariants, ordinary ranges). This is strong evidence that the overall approach based on invariants constructed from nearby good inputs is promising.

2.2 Dynamic Program Slicing

Most failed invariants are not root causes of the bug. For example, some failed invariants are on instructions that do not compute any values that affect (directly or transitively) the instruction at which the symptom occurs. We can eliminate any such instruction from the set of possible root causes.

Dynamic backwards slicing [48] is a technique that can precisely determine which instructions affected a particular value in a single execution of a program. We start from the statement which causes the symptom (in this example, the invalid array element access) and find the statements in the execution that could have affected that statement, either via data flow or control flow. This set of statements is exactly the dynamic backward slice. We then remove all the failed invariants which are not part of this slice from the set of possible root causes.

In the part of the code shown in Listing 1, there are actually no failed invariants for the failing execution (though there are fairly many in other parts of the program). However, imagine that statements 25 and 26 had generated failed invariants. They would have been false positives since they are not the root cause of the failure. However, these statements are not part of the dynamic backward slice because they do not affect the value at the symptom, and so they would have been filtered out from the candidate set. Note that both function returns are part of the dynamic backward slice and would be included in the candidate set.

For this bug, this step removes about 62% of the failed invariants, reducing the candidate count from 95 to 36.

2.3 Dependence Filtering

Another source of false positives is error propagation. If a faulty instruction that is the bug's root cause triggers an invariant fail-

```
long calc_daynr(uint year,uint month,uint day)
{
  long delsum;
  int temp;

  if (year == 0 && month == 0 && day == 0)
    return (0); /* Skip errors */
  delsum= (long)(365L*year+31*(month-1)+day);
  if (month <= 2)
      year--;
  else
    delsum-= (long) (month*4+23)/10;
  temp=(int) ((year/100+1)*3)/4;
  return (delsum+(int) year/4-temp);
}

int calc_weekday(long daynr, bool first_week_day)
{
  return ((int)((daynr+5L+(first_week_day ? 1L : 0L)) % 7));
}

bool make_date_time(TIME_FORMAT *format, M_TIME *t,
                timestamp_type type, String *str)
{
   str->length(0);
   if (l_time->neg)
     str->append('-');
 ...
  weekday= calc_weekday(calc_daynr(t->year,t->month,
                                  t->day),0);
  str->append(loc->d_names->type_names[weekday],
       strlen(loc->d_names->type_names[weekday]),
                                      system_charset_info);
 ...
}
```

Listing 1. Source Code Example

ure, then any instruction using the faulty value computed by that instruction may also trigger an invariant failure. Such subsequent invariant failures are not indicative of a root cause; they merely occur because the erroneous value is propagating through subsequent computation.

Using this observation, we have devised a heuristic called *dependence filtering* to further reduce the set of candidate root causes. This heuristic uses the data flow graph and control dependence graph formed during the previous dynamic slicing step to eliminate any instruction with a failed invariant that depends on another instruction with a failed invariant, *with no intervening passing invariants*. This policy is explained in Section 5.1.

For the example bug, when we build the dynamic dependence graph starting from the failing array indexing statement, the failed invariants of `calc_daynr` and `calc_weekday` will lie on one path to the symptom. Since the result of `calc_daynr` is directly used by `calc_weekday` with no intervening instructions that have invariants, the error at `calc_weekday` is likely to be propagated from `calc_daynr`, and we exclude the return value of `calc_weekday` as a candidate.

This step removes about 55% of the 36 remaining candidate root causes, leaving only about 16 candidates.

2.4 Filtering Using Multiple Failing Inputs

Note that once the invariants have been computed, the remaining steps above (finding failing invariants; dynamic backward slicing; dependence filtering) all happen using a single failing input. However, we can construct multiple inputs similar to the original input that also cause the program to fail with exactly the same symptom. (We do this using the same variant of the ddmin algorithm.) Since these new bad inputs result in the same failure, it is very likely that the root cause will be the same. We can therefore *repeat the last three steps above* for each such failing input. The root cause should be included in the final candidates generated for all these inputs. We can then take the intersection of these sets to find the final set of candidates. For this bug, this step reduced the final set of candidates by 25% from 16 to 12.

The tool will first present the set of candidate locations from the final step to the developer for analysis. If the developer cannot find the root cause among them, then the tool will present the other candidate root causes in the order depending upon the number of other failing inputs in which they appear. If the root cause cannot still be identified, then the tool will present root causes from previous steps in this order - dependence filtering, slicing and likely invariants.

Overall, our diagnosis has narrowed down the possible location of the bug *to 16 locations in a program of over 1 million total lines of code* for this bug since the root cause of this bug cannot be found in the final step but can be found among the candidate locations after the dependence filtering step. Moreover, for each of these locations, we have fairly detailed information about the ranges of program values seen in the successful executions and the corresponding actual values from the failing runs which fall outside those ranges. This is an extremely effective result because it should vastly simplify the task of the programmer in debugging the error.

2.5 Feedback to the Programmer

Each candidate invariant in the final or non-final set represents an instruction that may indicate the location of a root cause of the failure. Recall, however, that we only track invariants on load, store and return instructions. This means that the actual location of a bug may be anywhere in the maximal sub-expression rooted at a load, store or return that does not itself contain any load, store or return. (We call this a *pure, local sub-expression*). Therefore, the tool additionally computes the maximal pure, local sub-expression rooted at each candidate root cause and presents it back to the programmer.

For the example bug, the invariant on the return value of `calc_daynr` indicates the location of the root cause, but the true location is somewhere in the body of that function. (Note that the entire function body is pure and local, after register promotion of local stack variables.) Therefore, the tool would present to the programmer the subset of the body of the function that is used to compute the return value in the failing run, i.e., lines 6, 8, 9, 10, 13 and 14. Of course, the negative return value in the failing run is a huge clue that `temp` at line 14 must be a large value. `temp` is computed from `year`, and `year` is computed by decrementing the incoming parameter value. This can only produce a large value by overflowing. Thus, the decrement of `year` is the true root cause.

2.6 Program Analysis Infrastructure

Our system uses the LLVM Compiler Infrastructure [29] to analyze and transform programs. LLVM supports multiple languages, including C and C++. Its intermediate representation (the LLVM IR) represents a program as a set of functions; each function is a set of basic blocks with an explicit, statically known control-flow graph. Scalar variables are kept in Static Single Assignment (SSA) form [13], making definition-use chains explicit. Other variables (e.g., C arrays and structs) are kept in non-SSA form; scalar fields of structures and array elements are accessed using RISC-like load and store instructions.

3. Diagnosis with Invariants

We make some assumptions about the inputs and the programs being diagnosed. First, we assume that the inputs to the program can be described by some formal *specification* (specifying the possible tokens in valid program inputs and all possible replacement tokens) suitable for driving an input generation algorithm based on the *ddmin* approach for minimizing failure-inducing inputs [45]. This specification, however, is optional. If the specification is not available, we can use our default specification-independent character-level rewriting approach for input generation. Second, we assume that the program includes a set of *deterministic detectors* to detect failures. For example, memory safety errors can manifest in non-deterministic ways, but we can use detectors like SAFECode [14], Valgrind [34] or SoftBound [33] to ensure that they provide the same symptom every time they are triggered. These detectors are only used offline after a failure is detected; the detectors are not used, and therefore add no overhead, in production runs of the program. For incorrect output errors, we assume that programmer-inserted assertions can be used for detection (these are often available at development time) or "known outputs" are available (e.g. from nightly testing, different version of the application) for failure detection. Also, these detectors can be used online during development time, since overhead is not an issue during development time. Failure detectors are further discussed in Section 7.2.

The input to our diagnosis is a program, required configuration files, the "failing input" that triggered the failure, and the failure symptom detected by some deterministic detector.

3.1 Constructing Candidate Root Causes

When a program fails on a particular input but succeeds for an input that is very similar (i.e., close) to the failing input, there are likely to be relatively few differences in behavior between those two executions; the key insight behind the Delta Debugging work is that these differences can help narrow down the root cause(s) of the failure. Our goal is to perform this narrowing automatically. If we can construct a set of such good inputs, then we can automatically extract behavior patterns that are common to these inputs. If the execution with the failing input violates any of these behavior patterns, that violation is a powerful indicator of the possible root cause(s) of the failure.

3.1.1 Likely Range Invariants

In this work, we use a simple form of program invariants — likely range invariants. A *likely range invariant*, or range invariant for short, is a range of values computed by some program instruction in the monitored runs. For example, if an instruction `load int* %p` is always observed to return a value in the range between -5 and 10 (denoted [-5,+10]) in some set of executions, then that range represents a range invariant for that instruction. A range invariant can be *tested* in future runs by instrumenting the program to compare the value computed by the instruction to see whether or not it falls within the range.

Range invariants are attractive because they capture concisely the observed values of program variables and instructions. They are also efficient to generate and monitor. The number of such invariants is linear in the size of the program (unlike e.g., invariants comparing pairs of variables). Although other data and control invariants are likely to be useful in identifying candidate root causes, we leave it to future work to explore such choices.

Since programs can have many instructions, we limit our monitoring of invariants to load, store, and function return instructions. For example, an assignment statement, `A[i] = a + b * B[j];` may have an error anywhere in the expression, but we only monitor the load of `B[j]` and the store to `A[i]` (there are no loads/stores of a and b as they are register promoted locals). This means we cannot narrow down the location of an error to anything smaller than an entire subexpression terminating in a load or store, but we expect this granularity to be ample for programmers to pinpoint the root causes of a failure. It may not be obvious why we monitor loads as well as stores when loads almost always return values from previous stores. We do so because it allows us to detect errors in array index expressions, such as `A[i]` or `B[j]` above.

We extract range invariants from training runs using the good inputs generated from the original failing input. We generate invariants only for instructions that are executed by at least one of the good inputs. We then instrument the program to test those invariants and re-execute the instrumented program using the failing input. If a particular range invariant is violated, i.e., the relevant instruction produced a value outside the observed range, we assume that the relevant instruction may contain the bug, i.e., we consider it to be a candidate root cause of the failure.

3.1.2 False Positives

The technique used to extract likely invariants can affect the accuracy and the number of candidate root causes. When a large number of arbitrary program inputs are used to extract range invariants (e.g., all inputs used during software testing), the ranges obtained are likely to be wide. *This makes it less likely that such a range invariant will be violated during a particular failing run,* which means that the root cause of a failure may not be included in the initial set of candidate root causes. This was the approach taken by previous systems [16, 24].

Instead, we construct "good" inputs that are (a) result in execution whose control flow and intermediate program values are as close to that of the failing run as possible and, (b) few in number, and use those to extract range invariants. Using such good inputs has two benefits. First, it ensures that the behavior of the training runs will be as close to the failing run as possible, and so tends to isolate the differences that might be the causes of the failure. Moreover, it allows us to use a very small set of training inputs (e.g., only 8 as opposed to thousands, as used in prior work [18]). For example, consider a bug in MySQL that is triggered by an uncommon `Date` field in a Query *SELECT DATE_FORMAT("0000-01-01",'%W %d %M %Y') as a;*. Constructing invariants using a general set of inputs would include queries for INSERT, DELETE, SELECT, JOIN, etc., most of which are likely to have very different behaviors from the failing input. One would need a large number of such inputs to be representative of program behavior. Using a small number of inputs that are variations of the previous query with different `Date` fields that do not trigger the error requires a much smaller set of inputs to represent the behavior we are seeking.

Using only a few such good inputs makes the invariants narrower (e.g., smaller ranges for range invariants), which is both good and bad. It is good because it makes it more likely that the different behavior will result in a failed invariant. It is bad because it may cause a large number of invariants to fail. Since we aim to identify the root cause(s) of a failure, it is important not to miss the root cause and so the benefit far outweighs the disadvantage. One key goal of this work, therefore, is to compensate for the disadvantage, i.e., to filter out the false positives, reducing the final set of reported candidates as much as possible without eliminating the true root causes. Filtering techniques we employ are described in detail in Section 5.

As explained earlier, success of our approach depends upon generating good inputs with similar execution behavior like program control flow and intermediate values as that of the failing input and training invariants using those inputs. Hence, the first step of our overall process is to construct such a set of "good" inputs which is discussed in next Section.

3.2 Input Construction

Algorithm 1 Deletion-based Input Generation

```
function INP-GEN-DELETE(input, num)
    GoodInputs ← a set of good inputs from ddmin algorithm
    return good-inp-gen (GoodInputs, num)
end function

function GOOD-INP-GEN(inputs, num)
    Initialize queue GoodInpQ with inputs
    while GoodInpQ ≠ ∅ do
        goodInput ← removeFront (GoodInpQ)
        add goodInput to GoodInputList
        find-good-inp (goodInput, length (goodInput))
    end while
    sort GoodInputList based on edit-distance
    return first num elements of GoodInputList
end function

function FIND-GOOD-INP(input, n)
    Split input into n subsets of equal size
    for each subset s do
        if s is a good input then
            enqueue(GoodInputQ, s)
        end if
        if complement of s is a good input then
            enqueue(GoodInputQ, complement of s)
        end if
    end for
    if n/2 > 1 then
        find-good-inp (input, n/2)
    end if
end function
```

The first step of our overall process is to create inputs with similar execution behavior by constructing a set of "good" inputs that are as close to the failing input as possible. By "good," we mean that the inputs do not trigger a failure with any of the detectors in the program.[2]

We have designed two input generation algorithms that construct such similar good inputs by systematically modifying parts of a small failing input (they can also be used to generate additional failure-triggering, or bad, inputs by modifying the criteria they use for selecting which inputs to return). These algorithms use two different approaches to generate inputs–one uses a deletion based approach described as *inp-gen-delete* in Algorithm 1, and the other uses a replacement based approach described as *inp-gen-replace* in Algorithm 2. The second approach is more powerful but requires input specification to perform token-level rewriting. The first approach is a fallback character-level rewriting approach in case a specification is not available. Both *inp-gen-delete* and *inp-gen-replace* take an input (e.g., the input that triggers the bug) and the number of desired good inputs and return a set of good (or failure-inducing) inputs.

The deletion approach initially uses *ddmin* [45] (a systematic procedure for generating minimal inputs that also produces good and bad inputs as a side-effect) to generate a few good inputs. Since, in many cases, *ddmin* produces too few good inputs, we also use *good-inp-gen* (a variation of the original *ddmin* algorithm) to produce more good inputs. This function starts by removing single characters and then removes exponentially more characters from the input as it tries to find more good inputs. Like *ddmin*, this also tries both a substring and its complement to increase the likelihood of quickly finding good inputs. The algorithm can determine whether an input is good or bad by running the application on the input and determining if the input triggers the same fault as the original failure-inducing input. After the good inputs are generated, *good-inp-gen* sorts the inputs in the order based on its edit-distance from the original failure-inducing input and returns a pre-defined number of elements from the front of the list.

Both *ddmin* and *good-inp-gen* do not require knowledge of the input specification, so they are easy to deploy. However, by utilizing the specification, we can create a more powerful input generator. An example of such a generator is *inp-gen-replace* which needs an input specification specifying the possible tokens in valid program inputs and all possible replacement tokens for each input token. This generator uses the specification to identify tokens for each terminal in the input. It then systematically generates many variations for each token depending upon the type of the token (note that, in Algorithm 2, there is a *mk<type>Variations()* function to generate inputs for each type of token). For example, *mkStrVariations()* systematically divides strings into 2^i parts for various values of i and then replaces each character with some other characters, which runs in time proportional to the size of the string. Similarly, *mkIntVariations()* systematically creates different integer values which differ by 2^i from the original value for various values of i. For grammar symbol tokens which are not of any special type, we replace them with their matching tokens depending upon the input specification rules. For example, a token for an aggregate function in MySQL like MAX can be replaced by matching tokens like MIN, AVG, and SUM. Then, we generate inputs by combining the different replacement values for each token. Currently, we generate inputs each of which contain variations of only one token, as exponential blow-up is possible if we consider variations of many tokens in each input.

While building an input generator that utilizes an optional input specification may seem onerous, we believe that it can be made

[2] We expect that the approach would work even if such inputs trigger other unknown failures because our main requirement is to isolate differences that avoid triggering the failure being diagnosed. We have not encountered this situation so far.

Algorithm 2 Replacement-based Input Generation

```
function INP-GEN-REPLACE(input, num)
    GoodInput ← a good input from ddmin or original input
    return inp-replace-input-gen (GoodInput, num)
end function

function INP-REPLACE-INPUT-GEN(input, num)
    GoodInputs ← ∅
    for each token t in the input do
        if t is string then
            newInputs ← mkStrVariations (input, t)
        else if t is integer then
            newInputs ← mkIntVariations (input, t)
        else if t is float then
            newInputs ← mkFloatVariations (input, t)
            ...
        else if t is grammar symbol then
            newInputs ← mkSymbolVariations (input, t)
        end if

        newGood ← subset of newInputs that are good inputs
        GoodInputs ← GoodInputs ∪ newGood
    end for

    sort GoodInputs based on edit-distance
    return first num inputs in GoodInputs
end function
```

practical. We have already implemented it for MySQL, Squid and Apache bugs. First, it should be possible to build "input generator generator" tools (in the same vein as tools like Lex, Yacc and Bison) that semi-automate the creation of input generators. Such a tool would take, as input, the optional specification and a set of functions to generate new strings by replacing individual tokens; the output would be a program that generates inputs for that specification. Second, many programs use standardized input grammars (e.g., all web servers use the HTTP protocol grammar; many databases use the SQL grammar). Once an input generator has been created for a input grammar, it can be reused by many applications using that grammar (since all of them will also use the same specification). Third, creating an input generator is a one-time effort. For large applications that are used over many years, the short-term effort to create an input generator should yield long-term savings in bug diagnosis time. Finally, we currently need only the specification of input tokens (lexical analyzer) and their possible replacements; the individual production rules of the grammar are unnecessary. Programs with complex inputs, like MySQL databases and compilers, have explicit tokenizers which drive their parsers, and it is not be very difficult to use this for our input construction algorithm. The first author implemented this for MySQL. It was not difficult, even though he is not a MySQL developer. In the worst case, we can fall back on the default specification-independent character-level rewriting approach of Algorithm 1 or other fuzzing-based input generation techniques [9, 19].

These algorithms are likely to produce many good inputs since the number of good inputs are likely to much more than failure-inducing inputs. (Both algorithms filter out invalid inputs by examining the output of the execution.) We can also use a variation of these algorithms to construct some failure-inducing bad inputs as well. We select bad inputs instead of good inputs in the appropriate steps to do this.

By constructing inputs close to the original input, and yet avoiding the original failure, these algorithms carefully try to create inputs which minimize the differences between the failing and non-failing executions, thus increasing the likelihood of better diagnostic accuracy. The algorithms presented here are just two possible input generation algorithms; other algorithms may work, too. We also observe that multiple input generators can be used in a single debugging session to provide a variety of inputs.

4. Dynamic Backwards Slicing

We can first discard invariants on values that *do not* affect the behavior of the faulting instruction. We use dynamic backwards slicing starting from the failure symptom to find these values. Dynamic backwards slicing traces a program's execution and then finds the precise set of instructions that directly or indirectly influenced the result of a given value in that execution [48]. For each execution of the program that triggers the failure symptom, we compute the dynamic backward slice of the symptom. Only failing invariants for instructions on this slice are retained. Our dynamic slicing system handles both data-flow and control-flow dependences when computing the dynamic backwards slice. Supporting control-dependence allows our tool to find failed invariants on values that control whether pieces of code relevant to the bug are executed.

Most dynamic backwards slicing systems have two phases [48]: in the first phase, they instrument the code to record, in a trace file at run-time, sufficient information to find the backwards slice of any value. In the second phase, an analysis uses the execution trace to create a program dependence graph that can be used to find which computations affected the result of a value within that specific program execution. Since an execution trace is used, dynamic backwards slicing is precise; it will not include values that did not influence the computation in question [48].

We have implemented a dynamic backwards slicing compiler pass called *Giri*. Giri is very similar to Zhang and Gupta's No Preprocessing with Caching (NPwC) algorithm [48] in that it does not precompute a complete program dependence graph from the trace; instead, it consults the trace only on demand to compute the dynamic backwards slice of a variable and caches the result in memory for subsequent queries.

Giri takes advantage of the LLVM IR to reduce the size of the trace file. LLVM IR represents a program as a set of functions; each function is a set of basic blocks with an explicit, statically known control-flow graph [29]. Scalar variables are kept in Static Single Assignment (SSA) form [13], making the definition-use chains explicit [29]. Other variables (e.g., C arrays and structs) are kept in non-SSA form; scalar struct fields and array elements are accessed using RISC-like load and store instructions [29].

Giri instruments code so that it records three different pieces of information during the first phase: (a) basic block exits; (b) memory accesses and their addresses; and (c) function calls and returns. Using these values and the LLVM program representation (which holds all scalar temporaries in Static Single Assignment (SSA) form), Giri can easily construct the precise dynamic backward slice in the second phase.

Giri's instrumentation works as follows. First, Giri adds an instruction to each basic block that creates a record in the trace when the basic block has finished execution. These trace records are used in the second phase to determine which branches were taken dynamically during the program's execution. Note that recording each basic block's execution (as opposed to recording each individual instruction's execution) suffices since all other instructions in a basic block must have executed before the basic block's last instruction.

Second, Giri instruments the program to record the memory locations accessed by all loads, stores, and select C library functions. During the second phase, when it encounters a load instruction while finding the backwards slice, Giri can use the trace to find the store that created the value that the load read from memory. Giri can then continue backtracking from the store to find instructions influencing the loaded value. Note that consulting the trace isn't required for finding the sources of values used by most LLVM instructions. Since most instructions operate on SSA scalar values, the input operands to those instructions can be determined from the explicit SSA graph in the LLVM IR representation of the program.

Finally, Giri instruments a program to record the execution of function calls and function returns. Having this information in the trace allows Giri to match up formal and actual arguments and caller/callee return values during the second phase for both direct and indirect function calls.

Giri calculates dynamic control dependences as follows: when Giri first adds instructions from a dynamic execution of a basic block to the backwards slice, it uses static control-dependence analysis [13] to determine which value forced the execution of that basic block. Giri will then find the most recent execution of the instruction generating that value and add it to the backwards slice.

By using the LLVM IR to reduce the trace size, our tool's traces are relatively small (43 to 144 MB in our experiments), making the use of more sophisticated optimizations unnecessary. To speed up the second phase, we perform one important optimization on the trace file. Giri performs a forward scan through the trace, recording the memory regions that have been modified by store instructions. If a load instruction is encountered that accesses a memory location not defined by a store (e.g., a non-modified global variable), it is given a special marking. This marking is used during backwards searches of the trace file to prevent tracing back to the beginning of the trace for loads without a defining store. Other optimizations are possible but are not implemented presently.

5. Filtering False Positives

In practice, dynamic backward slicing reduces the number of candidate root causes by a large amount (nearly 58%) but still leaves a fairly large number to be analyzed. We propose two new techniques to filter out false positives from the remaining set. One of these takes advantage of the dynamic tracing information, which allows us to filter invariants using the dynamic dependence graph (DDG), which is the union of the dynamic dataflow graph and the control dependence graph. The second one takes advantage of our input construction capability to identify candidates that appear to explain the symptom for multiple failing inputs that are only slightly different from the original one.

5.1 Dependent Chains of Failures

We observe that the result of an anomalous computation (i.e., one that violates an invariant) can cause dependent instructions to produce anomalous values. For example, if the variable x fails a range invariant because it is negative when it was expected to be non-negative, then the result of a subsequent computation using x (such as 2*x) that was expected to be non-negative will be negative, too, potentially failing its range invariant. The real culprit, however, is the first failure; the second failure is just a false positive and not an independent buggy location.

We can filter out such false positives by identifying dependent chains of failing invariants using the DDG. The DDG is a graph $G(N, E)$, where the set of nodes N is the set of instructions executed in a given run of a program, and E is the set of edges $n_i \rightarrow n_j$ such that n_i is an instruction that generates a value that is an operand of n_j or n_j is control dependent on n_i. Graph G must be acyclic since it represents data flow and control dependence within a dynamic sequence of instructions. Conceptually, this graph can be constructed easily from the dynamic trace together with the program, since together they identify the complete set of CPU operations, loads and stores, and the dependencies between them.

We can use a standard depth-first-search traversal on this graph to look for cases where a failed invariant is dependent on a previous failed invariant. However, not all instructions have invariants computed for them. We therefore look for direct paths between two failed invariants without any intervening passing invariants, $n_1 \rightarrow n_2 \rightsquigarrow \ldots \rightsquigarrow n_{k-1} \rightarrow n_k$, $k \geq 2$, where (a) n_1 and n_k both have invariants that failed; and either (b) $k = 2$, or (b′) all instructions n_i, $2 \leq i \leq k-1$, do not have any passing invariants at all. In other words, there are no intervening invariants between n_1 and n_k at all. We then simply drop n_k from the set of candidate root causes under the argument that it "went bad" simply because n_1 went bad, as discussed above, i.e., it was not an independent bug location. Of course, n_1 may itself get dropped if it is, in turn, dependent on some previous instruction that had a failed invariant. Observe that the key case we are excluding with this rule is when there is a *passing* invariant between n_1 and n_k. Intuitively, we are "trusting" the invariants to distinguish correct values from erroneous ones. If an instruction has a passing invariant, we assume that it did not produce an erroneous value, and therefore a later dependent instruction that has a failed invariant may be an independent source of an error.

In practice, computing the DDG explicitly is unnecessary. Recall that the dynamic backward slicing algorithm, Giri, traverses the union of the dynamic dataflow graph and the control dependence graph of the execution. We piggyback directly on Giri to identify dependence chains. Giri essentially uses depth-first search (DFS) on the union of the two graphs to construct the backward slice. Every time Giri visits an instruction I, we check if I had an invariant and, if so, whether that invariant failed or passed. If I failed an invariant, we traverse I's parents in the depth-first-search tree (which corresponds to the chain of users) until we arrive at an ancestor instruction, A_I, that has a passing invariant. We mark all intervening instructions between A_I and I for later filtering. We also stop this ancestor traversal if we arrive at a failed invariant and mark it for later filtering. This ensures that we never need to process any instruction (i.e., mark it and recursively traverse its parents) more than once during the ancestor traversals, though we may arrive at it as many times as there are incoming operands (i.e., incoming edges in the DDG). This ensures that the total time for this dependence filtering pass is linear in the number of edges in the DDG.

At the end of this algorithm, we filter out all remaining candidate instructions that were marked for filtering. In practice, this pass is also very effective at eliminating false positives. It is unfortunately possible, however, that this pass may occasionally eliminate a true root cause itself. In particular, it is possible that I_2 depends on I_1, both have failed invariants, but I_1 was actually a false positive while I_2 was a true root cause. However, we expect this behavior to be rare with sufficient training.

5.2 Multiple Failure-inducing Inputs

Although we found that the number of remaining candidate root causes after dependence filtering tends to be fairly low (e.g., in the range of 7-18, reduced from hundreds originally), we can do better for some bugs without new mechanisms. We observe that, using essentially the same methodology that we used for nearby good inputs, we can construct additional failure-inducing inputs that are close to the original one *and produce the same failure symptom as the original one*. For each such input, since the failure symptom is the same *and* the inputs are very similar to the original one by construction, the true root cause of the failure is very likely to be the same.

This insight leads to the following simple strategy. Construct a set of additional failure-inducing inputs close to the original one that produce the same failure symptom. Repeat the previous analysis for each such new input: (1) identify all failing invariants when executing with that input (using the invariants previously extracted using the set of good inputs); (2) filter out invariants not on the dynamic backward slice of the failure symptom; and (3) filter out invariants using the dependence filtering step above. This process gives a set of candidate invariants for this failing input. Compute the intersection of these sets from all the failing inputs. That intersection yields the set of invariants that are candidate root causes for all failing inputs and is the final output of our analysis.

6. Generating Programmer Results

Each candidate invariant in the final set represents an LLVM instruction that may indicate the location of a root cause. Recall, however, that we only track invariants on load, store and return instructions. This means that we must identify the entire subexpression rooted at a load, store or return for the programmer.

We identify the operations involved in the subexpression using a simple traversal of the Dynamic Dependence Graph. We could place invariants on these subexpression values to remove parts of the subexpression that are not the root cause, but we do not have this implemented at present. Once all LLVM instructions within the subexpression are identified, our analysis maps them back to source statements using debug information.

7. Experimental Methodology

7.1 Applications

In our experiments, we used three widely-used servers: the Squid HTTP proxy server, the MySQL database server, and the Apache HTTP web server. MySQL, which has about a million lines of code, is by far the largest application used to evaluate automatic diagnosis algorithms in the literature to date, except in the Triage work [42]. All these servers communicate with clients using well-defined protocols with well-defined grammars amenable to our input construction algorithm.

7.2 Software Bugs and Failure Detectors

We selected 8 real software bugs for these three server programs. We were limited in two ways. First, we needed bugs that we could reproduce using information in the bug reports for versions of the software that we could compile with LLVM on a current Linux system. Second, our current implementation cannot handle concurrency bugs as we need a deterministic detector. Our implementation also cannot handle missing code bugs (usually uninitialized variable bugs) because the root cause may not be effectively identified by range invariants. We expect they will need control flow invariants, which are outside the scope of this work. Hence, out of 12 such bugs, we omitted four "missing code" bugs; we plan to investigate control flow invariants for diagnosing such bugs in future.

Table 1 describes in detail the eight bugs we used. The first column provides a name for each bug for identification, using which we refer to the bugs later. The second column shows the name of the application and version which contains the bug. The third column provides the number of lines of code (in units of 1000 lines). The next column shows the failure symptom of the bug: four bugs were memory safety errors; the rest were incorrect output bugs. The last column provides a brief description of each bug.

The selected bugs have different root causes. For example, some bugs occur due to integer overflow or loss of precision. One buffer overflow bug occurred due to the use of an unsigned intermediate value for some computation. buffer overflow bug occurred when a buffer length was incorrectly computed for some specific inputs. In another bug, using an incorrect MySQL object type for a MySQL item causes a segmentation fault.

The difficulty of fault localization will depend upon many properties of the bug. Table 2 lists some important properties of these 8 bugs. The second column shows the unique, static number of source lines of code that are executed for the failure-inducing input. We first use the program trace to determine the LLVM instructions that are executed during the failing run, and then use LLVM debug metadata information to map them to their corresponding program source lines. For some LLVM instructions, debug metadata may be missing due to optimizations. We count one source line for each such instruction. All the bugs require execution of thousands of lines of source code before resulting in the failure symptom. The number of executed source lines is an indicator of the difficulty of fault localization. Note that the complexity of fault localization for an automated tool will also depend upon the size or lines of code of the complete application. The next three columns specify another important property which can impact the difficulty of diagnosis process – the distance from the symptom to the root cause. The third column gives the distance from symptom to root cause along the dynamic slice in terms of number of dynamic LLVM instructions. LLVM instructions are simple instructions, each of which translates to approximately 2-3 x86 instructions on average [6]. The next two columns show the static number of source lines and functions corresponding to these dynamic LLVM instructions. The root causes for incorrect output bugs are sometimes far from the symptom. More importantly, the intervening statements along the slice span several different functions, increasing the difficulty of the fault localization process. Note that these numbers do not include many other intervening statements and functions which are outside the path from root cause to symptom. Our approach, on the other hand, is agnostic to the distance of root cause from symptom, unlike other previous work like Triage [42].

Table 2. Bug Characteristics which may Impact Difficulty of Diagnosis.

#Bug	Static #LOC executed in failed run	Distance (Dyn #LLVM inst)	Distance (Static #LOC)	Distance (Static #Functions)
Bug-1	6927	12	6	2
Bug-2	9822	18	7	3
Bug-3	9982	86	27	10
Bug-4	11308	4	4	2
Bug-5	7874	124	41	17
Bug-6	7835	114	36	17
Bug-7	9835	429	16	5
Bug-8	6217	32780	6	2

We do not use automated detectors for our experiments. For each memory safety error, we manually inserted program assertions at the program point where a tool like SAFECode would have detected a memory safety error. For each incorrect output error, we manually inserted an assertion at the program point just before the server starts processing the incorrect output to send it to the client. In both cases, the assertions serve both as detectors and as starting points for dynamic backwards slicing.

Although we use manually inserted detectors, we expect that insertion of automatic detectors will be feasible in practice. One of the most important use cases for our tool is automated testing (e.g., such as nightly testing, which is widely used), which already makes use of automatic failure detectors, including "known good outputs" that identify wrong-output errors. For memory safety errors or integer numerical errors, we can also use a tool like SAFECode [14] or IOC [15], which precisely detect the symptoms of the failure. For incorrect output errors outside automated testing, comparison with the output of a different version of the application or other equivalent software may also work as a detector. Alternatively, we can fall back on programmer-inserted assertions for detection.

7.3 Good and Bad Input Construction

Our proposed diagnosis approach begins with these steps:

1. Compute a small failure-inducing input from the original failure-inducing input that fails with the same symptom.

Table 1. Software Bugs Used In The Experiments.

Bug#	Application	LOC	Symptom	Bug Description
Bug-1	Squid 2.3	70K	buffer overflow	Incorrect computation of buffer length leads to buffer overflow
Bug-2	MySQL 5.1.30	1019K	buffer overflow	Use of unsigned variable causes integer overflow which leads to buffer overflow
Bug-3	MySQL 5.1.30	1019K	Incorrect output	Wrong algorithm to convert microsecond field to integer results in incorrect value
Bug-4	MySQL 5.1.23a	1054K	buffer overflow	Use of a negative number along with an aggregate function results in seg fault
Bug-5	MySQL 5.0.18	949K	Incorrect output	Loss of precision in a sequence of computation results in wrong value
Bug-6	MySQL 5.0.18	949K	Incorrect output	Overflow during decimal multiplication results in garbage output
Bug-7	MySQL 5.0.15	937K	Incorrect output	Loss of data when inserting big values in a table
Bug-8	Apache 2.2	225K	buffer overflow	For particular value of output size, buffer overflow occurs

2. Construct a small set of good inputs that are close to the small failure-inducing input.
3. Construct a small set of additional failure-inducing inputs that fail with exactly the same symptom as the original failing input.

For step 1, we already had fairly small failure-inducing inputs available from the bug reports for six of the eight bugs. For the remaining two bugs, we slightly reduced the inputs by hand by applying an algorithm similar to *ddmin* [45], but this reduction is not critical to our results. For steps 2 and 3, we constructed 8 good and 8 bad inputs for the server bugs using the input construction algorithms described in Section 3.2. For the Apache bug (bug-8), our current approach could not generate additional bad inputs, as only very few specific input values could trigger the failure. To determine if an input was a good input, we tested the input on the buggy version of the application and on a version of the application with the bug fixed.[3] If the fixed application returned errors on the input, we assumed the input was grammatically incorrect and threw it out. All other inputs either did not trigger the bug and produced identical output on both the buggy and fixed versions of the application (i.e., were deemed as good inputs) or produced correct output in the fixed version but triggered the bug in the buggy version (i.e., were deemed as bad inputs). This approach allowed us to categorize inputs for incorrect output bugs sans an automated error detector.

It should be noted that our approach does not require "minimal" failure-inducing input. In many cases, developers already have reduced inputs which should suffice for our approach. The inputs from the bug reports we used in experiments were small but not necessarily minimal. An earlier empirical study [37] of over 260 randomly selected bugs in six different server applications (including some stateful servers) found that most bugs could be reproduced with 3 or fewer inputs. If the inputs are very large, tools like ddmin [45], delta debugging [12, 44], and C-Reduce [36] do a good job of minimizing the inputs for many classes of applications. Hence, it will not be hard to get small enough inputs for most bugs for successful diagnosis.

8. Experimental results

In this section, we evaluate the effectiveness of our approach. In particular, we investigate (a) whether our approach can find the true root causes of bugs; and (b) how many false positives it generates. For the purpose of this evaluation, we use the following definition of root cause: for each bug, we use the correct patch in the bug reports to identify the minimal statements which should be changed or deleted to remove the failure symptom. (The only cases where new lines of code are added are to replace some existing lines, since we do not include missing-code bugs in our experiments.) We say all these statements are part of the root cause, and we say our approach is successful if it can identify all these statements.

[3] This was purely for experimental evaluation; in practice, any other suitable approach like automated memory-error detectors, programmer-inserted assertions or comparison with known-output can be used to determine whether the failure symptom is avoided or not.

We used the LLVM-2.6 compiler [29] infrastructure to compile the programs, to extract invariants and compute dynamic backward slices. We conducted the experiments on Linux 2.6 on a machine with a dual-core Intel ® Core ™ 2 Duo CPU running at 3 GHz with 4 MB cache and 8 GB of RAM.

The time for the complete diagnosis depends on the trace size and program size. For these bugs, total diagnosis time varied from around 8 minutes up to 4 hours depending upon the application. For two bugs, we believe it took an excessively long time because our slicing implementation is not optimized. We expect to see many fold improvements in the execution time after a few optimizations.

The detailed experimental results using automated input generation are presented in Table 3. The first column in the table lists the bug numbers from Table 1. The second column shows the total number of invariants that are generated and inserted by our system. The third column shows the total number of failed invariants by the original failure-triggering input. For memory bugs where failure occurs soon after root cause, there may not be any invariant present between the root cause and failure symptom to catch divergent behavior. Failure location can give a strong clue about root cause for such cases. Hence, for such kinds of bugs, we also count the program statement at the failure location as a candidate root cause and include it in this column. The fourth column shows the number of failed invariants that are on the dynamic backward slice. The fifth column shows the number after the dependence filtering step, and the sixth column shows the number after the filtering using multiple failure-inducing inputs. The final column shows the maximum number of source lines corresponding to all the expression trees which the developer needs to analyze to fix the bug depending upon which latest step contains the root cause. The last column shows whether the candidates after the final multiple inputs filtering step includes the root cause or not.

Note that a single candidate sub-expression at the LLVM level may span multiple source code lines. Therefore, the number of source statements is, in general, larger than the number of final candidate locations. We believe, however, that the difficulty of the programmer's final task is best measured by the number of candidate locations they have to understand, and not simply the total number of source code lines. In particular, the number of source lines highly depends on the idioms the programmer uses rather than the fundamental nature of the candidate computations: a relatively simple sub-expression may span two or more lines of code or a complex computation may be expressed in a single compact statement. For this reason, we measure the effectiveness of our analysis primarily by the number of candidate locations and secondarily by the number of source statements they represent.

8.1 Number of Candidate Root Causes

From the results, it is clear that dynamic backward slicing is effective in reducing the number of candidate root causes, consistently removing nearly 80% of the false positives. In three cases, it reduces them by factors of 6 (Bug 6) and 10 (Bug 1 and 8).

The dependence filtering step is also very effective in reducing the remaining false positives. On average, it removes nearly 58%

Table 3. Number of Reported Root Causes

Bug#	#Invs	Failed Invs	Slice	Dependence filter	Multiple faulty inputs	Src-expr-tree	Root Cause in final step?
Bug-1	3358	357	30	9	9	49	Yes
Bug-2	5917	95	36	16	12	48	No
Bug-3	5942	93	27	9	6	64	Yes
Bug-4	6847	156	44	14	8	28	Yes
Bug-5	4566	130	34	18	17	89	Yes
Bug-6	4652	83	13	7	5	26	Yes
Bug-7	5836	153	35	17	11	152	Yes
Bug-8	2295	120	12	6	6	171	Yes

of the false positive candidate root causes, in one case (Bug 1) removing nearly 70% of them.

The last filtering step, using multiple faulty inputs, has less consistent benefits. In some cases (Bugs 1 and 5), it has only a small effect or no effect at all. In other cases, the benefit is quite substantial (Bugs 2, 3, 4 and 7), especially considering that it comes after a series of other highly effective filters.

8.2 Efficacy at Finding True Root Causes

As Table 3 shows, when using all of the false positive filters, our tool included the root cause in the final list of candidates for 7 of the 8 bugs. Our approach could not narrow down the root cause for Bug 2 among the program expressions in the final filtering step. However, the root cause is still included in the candidate set after the dependence filtering step. Hence, developers need to analyze 16 candidate program expressions instead of 12 expressions to find the exact root cause. We found that diagnosis for this bug is very sensitive to input. When we tried a different set of training inputs, the final step was able to identify the root cause, essentially because the training runs produced a more precise set of invariants.

There are at least two strategies to deal with such "false negative" cases. The programmer can investigate the final suggestions first and, when all are eliminated, ask the tool for other suggestions. The tool could present the penultimate set of 16 locations (4 additional locations compared to initial 12 locations) in this case, and the user would investigate four more locations to find the bug. Second, the tool could be made more effective with a better input generation algorithm which can identify the root cause for all cases.

Note that our approach is more likely to identify root causes of bugs, including Bug 2, than invariants extracted using general inputs. For example, using our input construction algorithm, we are able to find the root cause for Bug 1, where a large input field (a *username*) with many special characters (as in a ftp request like *ftp : //usernam\\\\\\\\\\\\\\\\\\\\\\\\\\\\\\: pass@ftp.cs.wisc.edu*) causes a segmentation fault. Each special character needs three times the buffer size compared to normal characters; however, the code incorrectly allocates less buffer size leading to a buffer overflow. If we use a general set of training inputs, the invariant ranges on the buffer length would be wider and bug-independent, making them less effective. More specifically, if any HTTP training input contained a larger *username* field than the failure-inducing input, the analysis would miss the root cause. However, our invariants with a better and focused training set could find the root cause through invariants on buffer length.

It is also important to note that our approach missed the most ideal invariant failure which could have accurately pinpointed the root cause in bug-7. This happens because the value on which invariant fails is not used in any computation, hence it gets filtered out. However fortunately, a different, but related invariant fails which was able to identify the actual root cause.

For bugs 7 and 8, the number of source lines are comparatively larger as a few expression trees inside large functions accounted for a much larger number of source lines. However, this approach

Table 4. Tarantula/Ochiai Results

Bug	Tarantula	Ochiai	Our Approach
Bug-1	[6 - 5266]	[2 - 5255]	49
Bug-2	[34 - 34]	[34 - 34]	48
Bug-3	[55 - 9409]	[55 - 9409]	64
Bug-4	[776 - 9847]	[694 - 9762]	28
Bug-5	[1 - 19]	[1 - 16]	89
Bug-6	[5680 - 6878]	[5678 - 6876]	26
Bug-7	[8 - 6060]	[8 - 6060]	152
Bug-8	[28 - 5372]	[1 - 5357]	171

still results in a significant reduction considering the fact that over 9000 and 6000 static source lines are executed by these two bugs respectively. For example, the six LLVM-level expressions of bug-8 mapped to 2, 11, 15, 35, 92, and 115 source-level statements respectively (note that some of the expressions overlap). The root-cause was in the third expression spanning only 15 source lines. The latter two, very high numbers, greatly skewed the average, and both are false positives. For this bug, we could not apply the last filtering step as our current approach was not able to create additional bad inputs. Similarly, three large false-positive expressions increase the final number of source lines for bug-7 significantly though the expression containing the true root-cause consists of 16 source lines. Further elimination of false positives would greatly bring down the average number of source lines in these bugs as well. Moreover, we would like to add a second pass of invariants and filtering that evaluates individual *intermediate values within expressions* to narrow down the root causes internal to these expressions. This should greatly bring down the final number of source statements reported to the programmer.

8.3 Comparison with Tarantula and Ochiai

The Tarantula [26, 27] and Ochiai [5] statistical approaches, while simplistic in nature, are powerful methods that allow for reproduction in a reasonable amount of time and serve as a good baseline for software bug diagnosis. These two approaches work by performing an analysis of executed program statements for a given set of inputs. Specifically, they record for each input whether or not the faulty behavior was induced and the statements which were executed. This results in a vector for each program statement whose elements are 1 if the statement executed for a given input and 0 if it did not. These vectors are compared against a success/failure vector whose elements are 1 if the program exhibited the failure and 0 if it did not. A similarity coefficient is computed using each approach's namesake formula, where each a_{ij} is a counter for the number of elements in the source line vector with value i whose corresponding element in the success/failure vector has value j.

$$tarantula = \frac{\frac{a_{11}}{a_{11}+a_{01}}}{\frac{a_{11}}{a_{11}+a_{01}} + \frac{a_{10}}{a_{10}+a_{00}}}$$

$$ochiai = \frac{a_{11}}{\sqrt{(a_{11}+a_{01}) * (a_{11}+a_{10})}}$$

Program statements are then ranked in decreasing order by this similarity score. The basic principle serves to identify which program statements are highly correlated with program failures. We include Ochiai in our comparison because this similarity metric has been found to give better empirical results [5]. We have implemented these approaches using the LLVM compiler system, leveraging the trace files generated by Giri.

Table 4 lists, for each of our bugs, the range of source lines a programmer would have to inspect to find the root cause. We computed this by determining the similarity metric for each source line, ranking them, and then counting all statements that had a higher ranking than the root cause. In most cases, the Tarantula or Ochiai formulas will calculate many source lines as having the same similarity; this is reflected by the ranges offered, where the best case occurs if the root cause is listed at the top of the list of ties, and the worst case when it is listed at the bottom.

We see that the statistical correlation method of bug diagnosis' effectiveness varies dramatically depending on the type of bugs analyzed. In particular, when analyzing bugs that involve program control-flow divergence (such as Bug 5), we see that the Tarantula and Ochiai approaches perform notably well, but in cases where the same root cause is executed under both successful and failure-inducing inputs (such as Bug 6), we see results that are much less impressive, as one would expect. This highlights an important shortcoming of the correlation-based approaches: they fail to accurately account for cases where there is an absence of control flow divergence that leads to failure-inducing behavior. In our sampling of all bugs, the statistical methods only performed well on 2 out of 8 bugs—our approach provides much more consistent behavior.

8.4 Summary and Limitations

In summary, the analysis tool is able to identify only 5 to 17 candidate root cause expressions for all 8 bugs in three programs, one of which is millions of lines long. These results indicate that bug-specific likely invariants and dynamic backwards slicing, combined with our novel filtering techniques, can be extremely effective in helping programmers diagnose the root causes of failures.

Our current implementation also has some limitations. First, it cannot effectively handle missing code bugs like missing initialization and concurrency bugs as explained earlier. Second, various stages of the approach depend on robust input generation, as seen in one bug that was diagnosed with one set of inputs but, with another set, the root cause was dropped by the "multiple faulty inputs" filter. Also, for Bug 2, in an early version of our system that had *insufficient* training, dependence filtering removed the root cause because it was directly dependent on a false positive. This behavior has not happened since we improved the automated input generation procedure. Similarly, the "multiple faulty inputs" filter in an early version of our system removed the root cause for Bug 3, but this did not occur with improved input generation. Finally, we do not yet generate invariants for function arguments, which can make some of our expression trees unnecessarily large.

We can also combine our approach with other static and dynamic analysis approaches e.g., Tarantula. Moreover, our analysis computes but does not report a lot of valuable information (like the invariant failures and values) that could further assist diagnosis bugs. Such post-processing is outside the scope of this work.

9. Related Work

Delta debugging [12, 44] compares a successful and a failing run for fault localization but does not scale to larger programs due to inaccurate mapping of program states. Recent work on program execution indexing and memory indexing [41, 43] has greatly improved delta debugging's diagnostic accuracy. However, these techniques compute causal paths instead of root causes, and previous work [39, 40] shows 45% of the computed causal paths miss the root cause. Previous work [39, 40] also states that if a different input is used for a failing run, it can give inaccurate causal paths. Also, when copying state from a correct run to a faulty run, it may be necessary to copy more than the faulty state, thus resulting in false positives. It is also not clear how this approach will scale for larger programs and larger program traces.

DIDUCE [24] was the first work to use invariants for bug diagnosis; it used a variant of range invariants to find root causes. Pytlik et.al. [35] used invariants for fault localization of Siemens benchmark suite without much success possibly due to the fact that they used general test inputs to generate invariants. Statistical techniques like Tarantula and others [5, 26, 27] use differences in control flow between successful and failing runs and rank the statement based on a suspiciousness criteria. Liblit et. al. [30] developed more efficient methods to use statistical techniques with much lower overhead. However, these stand-alone techniques can result in too many false positives. Mariani et. al. [31] filter out invariants which are also violated in successful executions as false-positives, which may be less effective with good training.

Dynamic slicing has also been used for bug diagnosis; failure inducing chop [23] used both forward and backward slicing. Triage [42] combines differences in control flow between successful and failing runs with dynamic backward slicing. We improve upon these techniques by combining dynamic slicing with invariants similar to the work by Dimitrov et. al. [16]. We improve upon Dimitrov et. al. [16] in that our techniques to reduce false positives are not ad hoc, our system does not require special hardware support, and our system utilizes control dependence which, while it can increase false positives, is needed for diagnosing certain bugs [47].

BugAssist's [28] approach of using MAX-SAT solvers for fault localization is more systematic than ours. Execution perturbations [25, 46] have been used to find root causes for small programs. We do not believe that these techniques alone will scale to larger programs. Our approach is orthogonal to these approaches and can be combined with them to improve diagnostic accuracy.

Fuzzing techniques [9, 19] have previously been used to randomly modify inputs to create new inputs. Recent advances in symbolic execution and dynamic test generation techniques [21] have given rise to a new form of testing called whitebox fuzzing technique [22] to create inputs for discovering new software bugs. Artzi et. al. [7, 8] also developed techniques to automatically generate test cases using a form of concolic testing which they used for fault localization of PHP applications using known statistical techniques. Our emphasis is the opposite: our focus is more on effective fault localization techniques than on input generation. We generate inputs by modifying input according to an input specification. Our strategy is less general, but more scalable for larger programs. We also showed that using similar inputs in an invariants-based framework can, in fact, increase diagnosis accuracy by localizing faults which will be missed by using general test inputs. However, our tool could use these techniques to generate inputs for applications in which our input generation algorithms do not yield good results.

Finally, our work, to the best of our knowledge, performs diagnosis on much larger applications than any previous automated diagnosis technique except Triage [42].

10. Future Work and Conclusions

We have proposed a new automated bug diagnosis approach that combines invariant-based diagnosis, delta debugging, and dynamic backward slicing to compute an accurate set of possible root causes. Our system automatically constructs good inputs which are similar to the failure-inducing input to develop better invariants that are more likely to find root causes. We also proposed two new heuristics that play an important role in reducing false positives. The overall procedure is able to narrow down the root causes of bugs in large, real-world applications to only 5–17 program expressions, even in programs with hundreds of thousands of lines of code.

In the future, we plan to make our automated input construction algorithms more robust and evaluate it with more applications and bugs. We also plan to investigate new and other existing program analysis techniques to reduce false positives further, and new invariants which can capture a wider variety of bugs like concurrency bugs and missing code bugs.

Acknowledgments

We gratefully acknowledge the support by NSF contracts CCF 08-11693 and CNS 12-19080 for this work.

References

[1] Website. http://findbugs.sourceforge.net/.

[2] Website. http://www.hpenterprisesecurity.com/products/hp-fortify-software-security-center/hp-fortify-static-code-analyzer/.

[3] Website. http://www.coverity.com/products/coverity-save.html.

[4] NIST: National Institute of Standards and Technology. Software errors cost U.S. economy $59.5 billion annually: NIST assesses technical needs of industry to improve software-testing. June 2002.

[5] R. Abreu, P. Zoeteweij, and A. J. van Gemund. An evaluation of similarity coefficients for software fault localization. In *12th Pacific Rim International Symposium on Dependable Computing(PRDC)*, 2006.

[6] V. Adve, C. Lattner, M. Brukman, A. Shukla, and B. Gaeke. LLVA: A low-level virtual instruction set architecture. In *Proc. ACM/IEEE Int'l Symp. on Microarch. (MICRO)*, page 205, Washington, DC, USA, 2003. IEEE Computer Society.

[7] S. Artzi, J. Dolby, F. Tip, and M. Pistoia. Directed test generation for effective fault localization. In *Proceedings of the 19th international symposium on Software testing and analysis*, ISSTA '10.

[8] S. Artzi, J. Dolby, F. Tip, and M. Pistoia. Practical fault localization for dynamic web applications. In *Proceedings of the 32nd ACM/IEEE International Conference on Software Engineering*, 2010.

[9] D. L. Bird and C. U. Munoz. Automatic generation of random self-checking test cases. *IBM Systems Journal*, 22(3):229 –245, 1983.

[10] M. Bond. *Diagnosing and Tolerating Bugs in Deployed Systems*. PhD thesis, University of Texas at Austin, 2008.

[11] R. N. Charette. Why Software Fails. *Spectrum, IEEE*, 42(9):42–49, September 2005.

[12] H. Cleve and A. Zeller. Locating causes of program failures. In *ICSE*, 2005.

[13] R. Cytron, J. Ferrante, B. K. Rosen, M. N. Wegman, and F. K. Zadeck. Efficiently computing static single assignment form and the control dependence graph. *ACM Trans. on Prog. Langs. and Systs. (TOPLAS)*, pages 13(4):451–490, October 1991.

[14] D. Dhurjati, S. Kowshik, and V. Adve. SAFECode: Enforcing alias analysis for weakly typed languages. In *ACM SIGPLAN Conference on Programming Language Design and Implementation*, 2006.

[15] W. Dietz, P. Li, J. Regehr, and V. Adve. Understanding Integer Overflow in C/C++. In *International Conference on Software Engineering*, June 2012.

[16] M. Dimitrov and H. Zhou. Anomaly-based bug prediction, isolation, and validation: an automated approach for software debugging. In *ASPLOS*, 2009.

[17] D. Engler, B. Chelf, A. Chou, and S. Hallem. Checking system rules using system-specific, programmer-written compiler extensions. In *Proceedings of the 4th conference on Symposium on Operating System Design & Implementation - Volume 4*, OSDI'00, 2000.

[18] M. D. Ernst, J. Cockrell, W. G. Griswold, and D. Notkin. Dynamically discovering likely program invariants to support program evolution. *IEEE Trans. Software Eng.*, 2001.

[19] J. E. Forrester and B. P. Miller. An empirical study of the robustness of windows nt applications using random testing. In *Proceedings of the 4th conference on USENIX Windows Systems Symposium*, 2000.

[20] K. Glerum, K. Kinshumann, S. Greenberg, G. Aul, V. Orgovan, G. Nichols, D. Grant, G. Loihle, and G. C. Hunt. Debugging in the (very) large: ten years of implementation and experience. In *SOSP*, 2009.

[21] P. Godefroid, N. Klarlund, and K. Sen. Dart: directed automated random testing. In *Proceedings of the 2005 ACM SIGPLAN conference on Programming language design and implementation*, PLDI '05, 2005.

[22] P. Godefroid, M. Y. Levin, and D. A. Molnar. Automated whitebox fuzz testing. In *Network Distributed Security Symposium (NDSS)*. Internet Society, 2008.

[23] N. Gupta, H. He, X. Zhang, and R. Gupta. Locating faulty code using failure-inducing chops. In *ASE*, 2005.

[24] S. Hangal and M. S. Lam. Tracking down software bugs using automatic anomaly detection. In *Proceedings of the International Conference on Software Engineering*, 2002.

[25] D. Jeffrey, N. Gupta, and R. Gupta. Effective and efficient localization of multiple faults using value replacement. In *ICSM*, 2009.

[26] J. Jones, M. Harrold, and J. Stasko. Visualization of test information to assist fault localization. In *Proceedings of the 24th international conference on Software engineering*, 2002.

[27] J. A. Jones and M. J. Harrold. Empirical evaluation of the tarantula automatic fault-localization technique. In *ASE*, 2005.

[28] M. Jose and R. Majumdar. Cause clue clauses: error localization using maximum satisfiability. In *PLDI*, 2011.

[29] C. Lattner and V. Adve. LLVM: A compilation framework for lifelong program analysis and transformation. In *Proc. Conf. on Code Generation and Optimization*, 2004.

[30] B. Liblit, M. Naik, A. X. Zheng, A. Aiken, and M. I. Jordan. Scalable statistical bug isolation. In *Proc. ACM SIGPLAN Conf. on Programming Language Design and Implementation (PLDI)*, 2005.

[31] L. Mariani, F. Pastore, and M. Pezze. Dynamic analysis for diagnosing integration faults. *IEEE Transactions on Software Engineering*, 37:486–508, 2011.

[32] A. Mockus, N. Nagappan, and T. T. Dinh-Trong. Test coverage and post-verification defects: A multiple case study. In *International Symposium on Empirical Software Engineering and Measurement*, 2009.

[33] S. Nagarakatte, J. Zhao, M. M. Martin, and S. Zdancewic. Softbound: highly compatible and complete spatial memory safety for c. *SIGPLAN Not.*, 44(6):245–258, 2009.

[34] N. Nethercote and J. Seward. Valgrind: A program supervision framework. *Electronic notes in theoretical computer science*, 89(2), 2003.

[35] B. Pytlik, M. Renieris, S. Krishnamurthi, and S. P. Reiss. Automated fault localization using potential invariants. *In Proceedings of the Workshop on Automated and Algorithmic Debugging*, 2003.

[36] J. Regehr, Y. Chen, P. Cuoq, E. Eide, C. Ellision, and X. Yang. Test-case reduction for c compiler bugs. In *Submission*, 2012.

[37] S. K. Sahoo, J. Criswell, and V. Adve. An empirical study of reported bugs in server software with implications for automated bug diagnosis. In *ICSE*, 2010.

[38] D. Scott. Making smart investments to reduce unplanned downtime. *Tactical Guidelines TG-07-4033, Gartner Group*, March 1999.

[39] W. N. Sumner and X. Zhang. Automatic failure inducing chain computation through aligned execution comparison. In *Technical Report 08-023, Purdue University*, 2008.

[40] W. N. Sumner and X. Zhang. Algorithms for automatically computing the causal paths of failures. In *FASE*, 2009.

[41] W. N. Sumner and X. Zhang. Memory indexing: canonicalizing addresses across executions. In *FSE*, 2010.

[42] J. Tucek, S. Lu, C. Huang, S. Xanthos, and Y. Zhou. Triage: diagnosing production run failures at the user's site. In *SOSP*, 2007.

[43] B. Xin, W. N. Sumner, and X. Zhang. Efficient program execution indexing. In *PLDI*, 2008.

[44] A. Zeller. Isolating cause-effect chains from computer programs. In *SIGSOFT '02: FSE*, 2002.

[45] A. Zeller and R. Hildebrandt. Simplifying and isolating failure-inducing input. *IEEE Transactions on Software Engineering*, 2002.

[46] X. Zhang, N. Gupta, and R. Gupta. Locating faults through automated predicate switching. In *ICSE*, 2006.

[47] X. Zhang, N. Gupta, and R. Gupta. A study of effectiveness of dynamic slicing in locating real faults. *Empirical Software Engineering*, 2007.

[48] X. Zhang, R. Gupta, and Y. Zhang. Precise dynamic slicing algorithms. In *Proceedings of the 25th International Conference on Software Engineering*, 2003.

The Rise of the Expert Amateur:

DIY Culture and the Evolution of Computer Science

Eric Paulos
University of California, Berkeley
Berkeley Center for New Media (BCNM) and Electrical Engineering Computer Science
paulos@berkeley.edu

Abstract

We are at an important technological inflection point. Most of our computing systems have been designed and built by professionally trained experts (i.e. us – computer scientists, engineers, and designers) for use in specific domains and to solve explicit problems. Artifacts often called "user manuals" traditionally prescribed the appropriate usage of these tools and implied an acceptable etiquette for interaction and experience. A fringe group of individuals usually labeled "hackers" or "amateurs" or "makers" have challenged this producer-consumer model of technology by creating novel hardware and software features to "improve" our research and products while a similar creative group of technicians called "artists" have redirected the techniques, tools, and tenets of accepted technological usage away from their typical manifestations in practicality and product. Over time the technological artifacts of these fringe groups and the support for their rhetoric have gained them a foothold into computing culture and eroded the established power discontinuities within the practice of computing research. We now expect our computing tools to be driven by an architecture of open participation and democracy that encourages users to add value to their tools and applications as they use them. Similarly, the bar for enabling the design of novel, personal computing systems and "hardware remixes" has fallen to the point where many non-experts and novices are readily embracing and creating fascinating and ingenious computing artifacts outside of our official and traditionally sanctioned academic and industrial research communities.

But how have we as "expert" practitioners been influencing this discussion? By constructing a practice around the design and development of technology for task based and problem solving applications, we have unintentionally established such work as the status quo for the human computing experience. We have failed in our duty to open up alternate forums for technology to express itself and touch our lives beyond productivity and efficiency. Blinded by our quest for "smart technologies" we have forgotten to contemplate the design of technologies to inspire us to be smarter, more curious, and more inquisitive. We owe it to ourselves to rethink the impact we desire to have on this historic moment in computing culture. We must choose to participate in and perhaps lead a dialogue that heralds an expansive new acceptable practice of designing to enable participation by experts and non-experts alike. We are in the milieu of the rise of the "expert amateur". We must change our mantra -- not just performance, completeness, and usability but openness, usefulness and relevancy to our world, its citizens, and our environment.

This talk will explore elements of the DIY and maker culture and its relevancy to research questions across computational hardware, languages, and systems. Ultimately, this talk will outline and argue for expanding the design territory and potential opportunities for all of us to collaborate and benefit as a society from this cultural movement.

Categories and Subject Descriptors: H.5.m Miscellaneous

Keywords: Do-It-Yourself, DIY, Citizen Science, New Media, Maker

Speaker Bio

Eric Paulos is the Director of the Living Environments Lab and an Assistant Professor in the Berkeley Center for New Media (BCNM) and Electrical Engineering Computer Science Department (EECS) at UC Berkeley. Previously, Eric held the Cooper-Siegel Associate Professor Chair in the School of Computer Science at Carnegie Mellon University (CMU) where he was faculty within the Human-Computer Interaction Institute with courtesy faculty appointments in the Robotics Institute and in the Entertainment Technology Center. Prior to CMU, Eric was a Senior Research Scientist at Intel Research in Berkeley, California where he founded the Urban Atmospheres research group. His areas of expertise span a deep body of research territory in urban computing, sustainability, green design, environmental awareness, social telepresence, robotics, physical computing, interaction design, persuasive technologies, and intimate media. Eric received his PhD in Electrical Engineering and Computer Science from UC Berkeley where he helped launch a new robotic industry by developing some of the first internet tele-operated robots including Space Browsing helium filled blimps and Personal Roving Presence devices (PRoPs). Eric is also the founder and director of the Experimental Interaction Unit and a frequent collaborator with Mark Pauline of Survival Research Laboratories.

ASPLOS'13, March 16–20, 2013, Houston, Texas, USA.
ACM 978-1-4503-1870-9/13/03.

Computational Sprinting on a Hardware/Software Testbed

Arun Raghavan* Laurel Emurian* Lei Shao‡
Marios Papaefthymiou† Kevin P. Pipe†‡ Thomas F. Wenisch† Milo M. K. Martin*

* Dept. of Computer and Information Science, University of Pennsylvania
† Dept. of Electrical Engineering and Computer Science, University of Michigan
‡ Dept. of Mechanical Engineering, University of Michigan

Abstract

CMOS scaling trends have led to an inflection point where thermal constraints (especially in mobile devices that employ only passive cooling) preclude sustained operation of all transistors on a chip—a phenomenon called "dark silicon." Recent research proposed computational sprinting*—exceeding sustainable thermal limits for short intervals—to improve responsiveness in light of the bursty computation demands of many media-rich interactive mobile applications. Computational sprinting improves responsiveness by activating reserve cores (parallel sprinting) and/or boosting frequency/voltage (frequency sprinting) to power levels that far exceed the system's sustainable cooling capabilities, relying on thermal capacitance to buffer heat.*

Prior work analyzed the feasibility of sprinting through modeling and simulation. In this work, we investigate sprinting using a hardware/software testbed. First, we study unabridged sprints, wherein the computation completes before temperature becomes critical, demonstrating a 6.3× responsiveness gain, and a 6% energy efficiency improvement by racing to idle. We then analyze truncated sprints, wherein our software runtime system must intervene to prevent overheating by throttling parallelism and frequency before the computation is complete. To avoid oversubscription penalties (context switching inefficiencies after a truncated parallel sprint), we develop a sprint-aware task-based parallel runtime. We find that maximal-intensity sprinting is not always best, introduce the concept of sprint pacing, *and evaluate an adaptive policy for selecting sprint intensity. We report initial results using a phase change heat sink to extend maximum sprint duration. Finally, we demonstrate that a sprint-and-rest operating regime can actually outperform thermally-limited sustained execution.*

Categories and Subject Descriptors C.1.4 [*Parallel architectures*]: mobile processors

Keywords computational sprinting; thermal-aware computation

1. Introduction

The anticipated end of CMOS voltage (a.k.a. Dennard) scaling has led to an inflection point in computer system design. In the past, chip designers could deliver value by exploiting transistor counts that double with near-constant total chip power each technology generation. Technology trends indicate that in the future, although transistor dimensions will likely continue to scale for at least another decade, power density will grow with each generation at a rate that far outstrips improvements in our ability to dissipate heat [11, 15, 18, 20, 48, 52]. This conundrum has led many researchers and industry observers to predict the advent of "dark silicon", *i.e.*, that much of a chip must be powered off at any time [11, 12, 18, 20, 26, 37, 48, 52]. Thermal constraints are particularly acute in hand-held and mobile devices that are restricted to passive cooling; dark silicon is already a reality in mobile chips like the Apple A5, where half of chip area is dedicated to accelerators that are active only some of the time.

Whereas the thermal constraints that underlie dark silicon loom as a significant industry challenge, they create an opportunity to rethink how we use chip area to deliver value. Many interactive applications are characterized by short bursts of intense computation punctuated by long idle periods waiting for user input [8, 47, 54]. Media-intensive mobile applications, such as mobile visual search [2, 3, 23], handwriting and character recognition [17, 35], and augmented reality [53], often fit this pattern. For short bursts of computations found in such applications, one approach to improve responsiveness on thermally-constrained devices is to transiently exceed a chip's sustainable thermal limits to deliver a brief but intense burst of computation.

Our prior work proposed *computational sprinting* [45], which activates reserve cores (parallel sprinting) and/or boosts frequency and voltage (frequency sprinting) to power levels that exceed the system's sustained cooling capabilities (*i.e.*, the thermal design power or TDP) by an order of magnitude or more. Sprinting exploits *thermal capacitance*, the property that materials can buffer significant heat as they rise in temperature and subsequently dissipate this heat to the ambient after the sprint. Recent chips from Intel and AMD already exploit such phenomena with limited forms of frequency sprinting. For example, Intel's second-generation "Turbo Boost" exceeds the sustainable chip power by 25% for tens of seconds [46].

Previously, we explored the feasibility of computational sprints that exceed sustainable thermal limits by an order of magnitude through a combination of modeling and simulation [45]. In this paper, we describe and measure a concrete implementation of computational sprinting in a hardware/software testbed that supports both parallel and frequency sprinting, offering a maximum sprint intensity that exceeds sustainable power levels by a factor of five. The testbed comprises a conventional quad-core Core i7 desktop system, in which we remove the chip's heat sink to engineer a system with a 10 W TDP—just enough cooling to sustain the indefinite operation of a single core at the lowest configurable operating frequency. At the maximum sprint intensity, with four cores at maximum configurable frequency drawing over 50 W, chip temperature will rise to cause overheating in mere seconds. However, this temperature rise is not instantaneous, but extends over a few seconds because of the inherent thermal capacitance of the copper heat spreader and chip package; we exploit this brief interval to sprint. We implement a software runtime system to monitor and control the platform and execute a suite of image processing and vision workloads to investigate computational sprinting on this testbed.

ASPLOS'13, March 16–20, 2013, Houston, Texas, USA.

We first study *unabridged sprints*—those sprints that can be completed within the thermal capacitance limits of our testbed. We show that the thermal capacitance of the heat spreader is sufficient to allow a few seconds of 5× sprints over the platform's sustainable thermal dissipation, resulting in an average improvement in responsiveness of 6.3× over sustainable execution. We also analyze the energy impact of sprinting and find that even for a chip that has not been designed for sprinting, using parallel sprinting can result in a net energy efficiency gain relative to sustainable operation. This somewhat counterintuitive result stems from the relatively high background power required to activate even a single core (*e.g.*, last-level cache and other "uncore" logic), so the incremental performance benefit of activating additional cores more than offsets the additional energy consumption. Furthermore, by completing the computation more quickly, the system can enter idle mode more quickly. Our analysis indicates that the energy efficiency advantages of sprinting grow as idle power decreases. Hence, although there is already a more than ten-to-one ratio between peak and idle power in the testbed's chip, even lower idle power remains desirable in chips designed with sprinting in mind.

Overall, when sprints can complete within thermal capacitance limits, the sprinting policy is relatively straightforward on the testbed: for best responsiveness, sprint with all cores at maximum frequency and voltage; for best energy efficiency, sprint with all cores at the minimum operating frequency and voltage. However, experiments reveal that optimal sprinting policy becomes much more complicated when the thermal capacitance is insufficient to complete all work during a sprint. We call sprints that must end due to thermal limits *truncated sprints*.

We study two aspects of truncated sprints. First, we study the *oversubcription penalty* of post-sprint execution. When a parallel sprint is truncated, execution switches to reach a sustainable operating mode by disabling all but one core and migrating all still-active threads to be multiplexed on a single core. This coarse-grain multiplexing by the operating system can lead to substantial slowdown relative to simply running the entire computation on a single thread, particularly when threads synchronize frequently [9, 25, 28, 29, 50]. If the post-sprint execution period is large relative to the sprint, then sprinting can result in a net slowdown; both energy and responsiveness would have been better if the system had never attempted to sprint at all. This effect is most pronounced on one workload, where the oversubscription penalty is nearly 2×. We show that converting the workload to use a sprint-aware task-based work-stealing parallel runtime can serve as a general strategy to eliminate this oversubscription penalty. In this sprint-aware runtime, worker threads simply cease claiming new tasks and instead put themselves to sleep as thermal capacity nears exhaustion.

Addressing the oversubscription problem ensures that sprinting will not result in performance worse than sustainable single-core execution. Nevertheless, simply sprinting at maximum intensity is not always best. Rather, experiments show that maximum responsiveness requires *sprint pacing* in which a sprint intensity is selected such that the computation completes just as the thermal capacitance is exhausted. Optimum sprint pacing depends on the interplay of available thermal capacitance, the amount of work to be completed, and the power/performance characteristics of the platform and workloads. Measured results indicate that the best static sprint intensity can be determined *a posteriori* once the amount of work to complete is known. However, as the required length of a sprint is often uncertain, *a priori* sprint pacing (*e.g.*, based on predicting task lengths) may not be feasible. Instead, we propose a dynamic pacing scheme in which sprints are initiated at maximum intensity, but then frequency (and voltage) are reduced after half of the thermal capacitance has been consumed. Although straightforward, this policy provides the maximum responsiveness for short sprints while providing the benefits of sprinting to a wider range of computation lengths than maximum-intensity sprinting alone.

Prior work suggested incorporating phase change materials into the chip packaging to extend maximum sprint duration with the additional thermal capacitance available in the latent heat of a phase transition [45]. We report on experiences with augmenting the testbed with a phase change heat sink placed on top of the package, demonstrating a 6× extension in sprint duration.

Finally, we consider the implications of computational sprinting for long-running computations that greatly exceed the maximum sprint duration. Although intuition might suggest such computations call for sustained execution within the thermal limit, we find that a staccato *sprint-and-rest* operating regime is both faster and more energy efficient. Sprint-and-rest outperforms thermally-constrained sustained operation because energy efficiency is maximized by activating all useful cores, thus amortizing the fixed costs of operating at all.

To summarize, this paper is the first to explore aspects of sprinting on an actual hardware testbed (Section 2), and the paper's experimental findings include:

- Showing that existing sources of thermal capacitance are sufficient for 5× intensity sprints for up to a few seconds of duration (Section 3.1).
- Demonstrating that parallel sprinting can actually improve energy efficiency (Section 3.2).
- Identifying the potential inefficiencies of truncating sprints and proposing a sprint-aware task-based runtime as a remedy (Section 4.2).
- Introducing the concept and opportunity of *sprint pacing* and proposing an initial adaptive sprint pacing policy implemented in the software runtime (Section 4.3).
- Reporting our experiences with augmenting the testbed with a phase-change heat sink (Section 5).
- Demonstrating that sprint-and-rest outperforms thermally constrained (sustained) execution for long-running computations (Section 6).

2. Sprinting Testbed Hardware

In contrast to earlier simulation-based studies [45, 49], this paper investigates computational sprinting using a testbed built from a real system. We modify a current desktop system to act as a proxy for a hypothetical future thermally-limited mobile system. Avoiding simulation overcomes modeling artifacts and simulation time constraints [38], but it is imperfect in that our study is limited to existing chips/platforms, which have not been designed with sprinting in mind.

To evaluate sprinting, a chip must offer an operating point where its peak power greatly exceeds the sustainable power dissipation of its cooling system (*i.e.*, the platform's TDP). Existing mobile chips have been designed with peak power envelopes easily dissipated via passive cooling, and hence are not appropriate for our study. Instead, as a proxy for the thermal characteristics of a future sprint-enabled device, we create a sprinting testbed system using a multi-core desktop-class chip and adjust its cooling environment to create an appropriate ratio between the chip's peak power and the platform's sustainable TDP (in our case, 5:1). A further advantage of using a modern desktop chip is that such chips already have documented support to allow software to control power states and monitor chip energy and temperature.

Testbed implementation. We engineer the thermal environment of our testbed such that it can sustain indefinitely (without overheating) a single-core running at the lowest configurable fre-

(a) Testbed setup

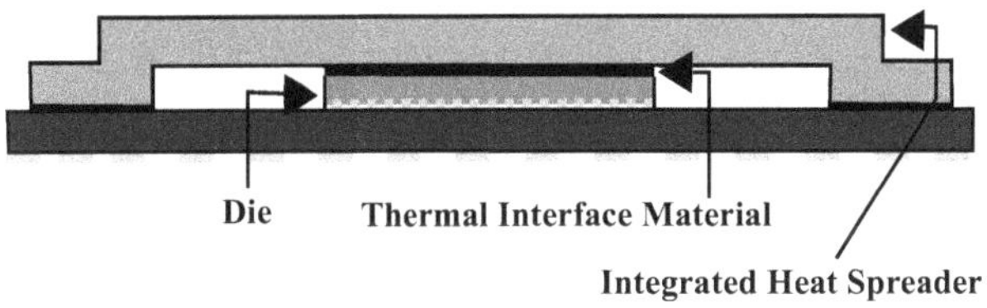

(b) Package internals

Figure 1. Testbed setup and package cut-away.

quency, but all higher power operating points are not sustainable and hence represent various intensities of sprinting. We build the testbed from a system with an Intel Core i7 2600 quad-core "Sandy Bridge" chip. We remove the heat sink and place a small variable-speed fan several inches above the exposed package, as shown in Figure 1(a). By tuning the fan speed, we can adjust the testbed's sustainable TDP. For this chip, single-core operation at 1.6 GHz (the lowest user-selectable frequency/voltage setting) draws 9.5 W. We tune the fan speed such that under sustained execution, die temperature saturates at 75° C (just under the rated junction temperature limit of 78° C). Although we had hoped to demonstrate sprinting using purely passive cooling, unfortunately, operating even a single core at minimum configurable frequency/voltage dissipates more power than can be sustained without a fan.

To control sprinting, we disable the chip's own frequency management and instead explicitly control the chip's operating point using the software ACPI interface to enable/disable cores and select frequency/voltage. With all cores executing at highest configurable frequency (3.2 GHz), this chip draws approximately 50 W. This setting represents our most intense sprinting mode (5× higher power than sustainable operation). In our experimental results, we use the chip's energy measurement facility to report package-level energy consumption and the on-die temperature sensors to report die temperature. We validated these energy readings by calibrating against measured wall-socket power. After each experiment, we wait until the temperature returns to the idle temperature before conducting the next experiment. Each experiment is repeated multiple times; we present average results over these runs.

Thermal capacitance from the integrated heat spreader. Sprinting leverages thermal capacitance to support brief operation at modes with unsustainable power dissipation. Like a mobile system, the testbed has no heatsink that would serve as a natural source of thermal capacitance for sprinting to exploit. It does, however, have an integrated heat spreader (IHS), which is a copper plate inside the package that is attached directly to the die via a thin thermal interface material, as illustrated in Figure 1(b). The traditional role of the IHS is to spread the heat: (*i*) on the die (to reduce hot spots) and (*ii*) from the die to the entire top of the package (to facilitate cooling), so the IHS is typically larger than the die.

The copper IHS provides sufficient thermal capacitance for sprinting. Given its dimensions (32 mm × 34 mm × 2 mm [4]) and the density (8.94 g/cc) and specific heat of copper (0.385 J/gK), we estimate its total heat capacity to be 7.5 J/K. When the system idles, its temperature settles at roughly 50° C. Thus, during sprinting, for a temperature swing of 25° C to a maximum temperature of 75° C, the IHS can store 188 J of heat. Therefore, in theory, the IHS present in this off-the-shelf package enables 4.7 s of sprinting at 40 W over sustainable TDP (50 W total). As we will show later, because lateral heat spreading is not instantaneous with the IHS, the actual achievable sprint duration at maximum intensity is somewhat less than this simple calculation suggests. We explore extending this sprint duration by augmenting the testbed with a phase change heat sink to increase thermal capacitance in Section 5.

The testbed relies on the thermal capacitance of the heat spreader for sprinting, and chips in mobile devices have typically not employed heat spreaders. However, the Apple A5X chip used in the third-generation iPad tablet does employ a heat spreader [13]. In addition, the dual-core A5X has a die size of 162 mm^2, which is nearly as large as the 216 mm^2 die of the quad-core Core i7 used in the testbed (albeit on 45 nm for the A5X vs. 32 nm for the Core i7). Perhaps the largest difference is that the peak power draw of the A5X chip is nowhere near the 50 W or more of the Core i7. Correspondingly, both the idle power and the power of using just one core of the Core i7 is substantially higher than the A5X. Based on this comparison and process scaling trends [11, 18, 20, 48, 52], a future mobile chip with more cores than can sustainably operate within the thermal constraints of a mobile device seems entirely plausible.

Effects not captured in the testbed. In addition to the thermal effects captured in the testbed (which are the focus of this paper), sprinting also places requirements on energy supply, including the voltage regulator, sufficient pins to carry the necessary peak electrical current, and power supply (which would be a battery in a mobile device). Prior work discusses these challenges and potential solutions [45], including ultra-capacitor/battery hybrids to meet peak current demands [39, 42, 44]. In our testbed, the electrical supply is already provisioned to sustain the chip's peak power, and hence is a non-issue. We do not address the electrical challenges or reliability/wearout implications of sprinting in this paper.

3. Unabridged Sprints

Computational sprinting is relatively easy to manage when sprints are *unabridged*, that is, when the parallel work can be completed entirely during the sprint without exhausting the system's thermal capacitance. This section explores the responsiveness and energy efficiency of unabridged sprints; we turn to the more complex case of truncated sprints in Section 4.

3.1 Responsiveness Benefits of Sprinting

Our testbed is able to sprint due to the thermal capacitance available in the copper mass of the integrated head spreader. Section 2 provides a back-of-the-envelope estimate for this capacitance as 188 J, which suggests a maximum sprint duration of 4.7 s at peak intensity. We compare this estimate against repeated trials of sprinting with all four cores at maximum configurable frequency (3.2 GHz) to establish the actual maximum sprint duration at peak. This operating mode dissipates approximately 5× the power of the sustainable single-core 1.6 GHz mode (50 W vs. 9.5 W) and can potentially improve responsiveness by 8× (2× frequency and 4× cores).

Kernel	Description
`sobel`	Edge detection filter; parallelized with OpenMP
`disparity`	Stereo image disparity detection; adapted from [51]
`segment`	Image feature classification; adapted from [51]
`kmeans`	Partition-based clustering; parallelized with OpenMP
`feature`	Feature extraction (SURF) from [14]
`texture`	Image composition; adapted from [51]

Table 1. Parallel workloads used to evaluate sprinting.

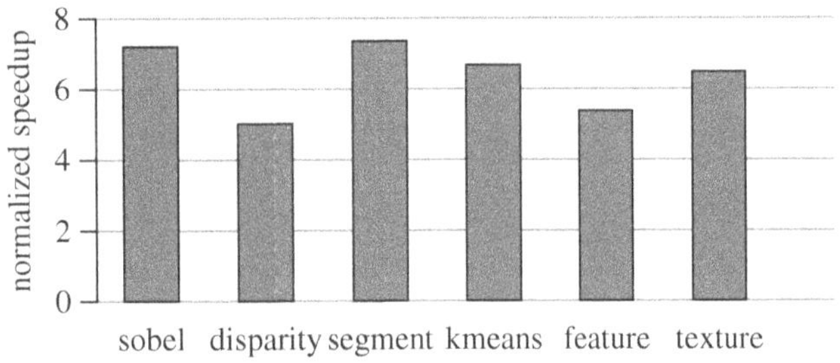

Figure 2. Speedup benefits of unabridged sprinting using four cores at 3.2 Ghz over a single-core 1.6 Ghz baseline.

For each trial, we allow the system to cool to a nominal of approximately 50° C and sprint until the system reaches our safe temperature threshold of 75° C as measured by internal on-die temperature sensors.

We find that the testbed can sprint for at most three seconds at maximum intensity. The actual sprinting capability of the testbed is lower than the total thermal capacity of the bulk-copper heat spreader suggesting a delay in lateral heat spreading [34]—the temperature rise during sprints is so rapid that significant temperature gradients persist. Given the thermal conductivity of copper (between 300 and 400 W/mK), heat will spread only 16 mm to 19 mm during a 3 s sprint, which is insufficient to reach the corners of the heat spreader from the center of the die. As we show later in our study of truncated sprints, reducing sprint intensity allows more time for heat to spread, allowing more thermal capacitance to be utilized before the critical temperature is reached.

To explore the practical benefits of unabridged sprints in real workloads, we configure the work size for our parallel workloads (see Table 1) to complete before the thermal limit is reached. Figure 2 shows the responsiveness benefits of maximum-intensity sprints (four cores at 3.2 GHz) in terms of speedup over the sustainable single-core 1.6 GHz baseline. On average, sprinting provides a 6.3× benefit over the baseline. In essence, sprinting allows this system to complete in just a few seconds what would have taken fifteen seconds or more if constrained to operate only in sustainable (non-sprinting) mode.

To better understand the testbed's thermal behavior, Figure 3 shows its power and temperature response over time. Each graph has two lines, which correspond to the same computation being performed in sustainable (single-core) and maximum-intensity sprint mode for the `sobel` workload. At time zero (on the x-axis), the power in sustainable mode (dotted line) rises from the idle-draw of 4.5 W to 9.5 W (Figure 3(a)), causing a gradual increase in temperature (Figure 3(b)); the computation completes after 26 s, at which time the power level drops back to idle and the temperature begins to fall. Under sprinting (solid line), power jumps initially to 50 W, which causes the temperature to rise precipitously. In fact, the temperature rise is so large that the leakage power of the chip grows over the duration of the sprint, causing power to increase further to a peak of 55 W. After a few seconds, the computation completes, the chip returns to idle, and temperature falls quickly (although not as quickly as it rose).

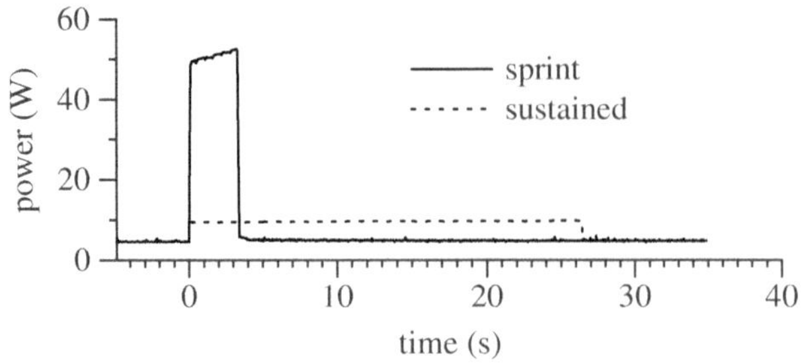

(a) Power

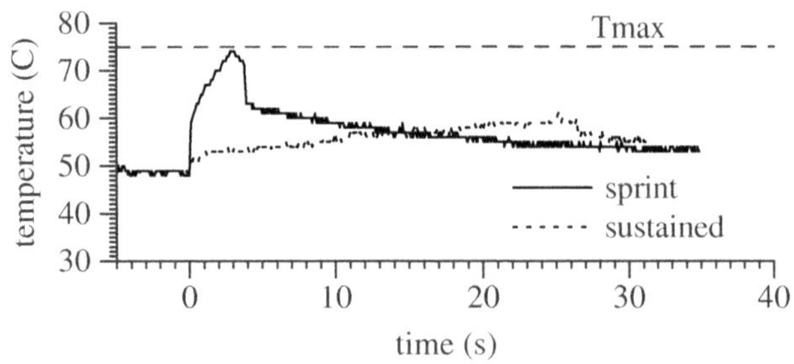

(b) Temperature

Figure 3. Chip power and thermal behavior for sustained and sprinting operation.

3.2 Energy Impacts of Sprinting

Energy consumption is a critical metric especially for battery-powered devices, so sprinting may not be an attractive option if it uses more energy than slower sustained execution. Perhaps counter-intuitively, however, we find sprinting can actually result in net gains in energy efficiency by (*i*) amortizing the fixed uncore power consumption over a larger number of active cores and (*ii*) capturing race-to-idle effects. Our conclusions stand in contrast to our previously published predictions from simulation-based analysis of computational sprinting [45], which neglected uncore power and hence suggested that sprinting might at best be energy neutral.

When considering energy implications, there are two distinct knobs available for sprinting: the number of cores and the clock frequency. Increasing the clock frequency requires increasing voltage as well, leading to a super-linear increase in energy consumption. In contrast, we find that increasing the number of cores results in a sub-linear energy increase, consistent with previously published estimates [6]. For the chip in our testbed, all but one core can be disabled (clock and power gated) but the last-level cache and ring interconnect are always powered and active unless the system has been suspended to DRAM. In this chip, this background power draw is substantial and largely independent of the number of active cores. Thus, activating all four cores requires only 2× more power than single-core operation. For any platform in which background/static power dissipation is substantial, using more cores will improve energy efficiency and responsiveness for unabridged sprints by amortizing these fixed overheads (provided the workload performance scales with the number of cores). On our testbed, four-core sprints dominate configurations that use fewer cores, hence, we omit such configurations from our results.

Whereas our responsiveness analysis in the preceding section considered only the most intense possible sprint, incorporating all cores at maximum frequency/voltage, because of the super-linear power increase of voltage/frequency scaling, we also con-

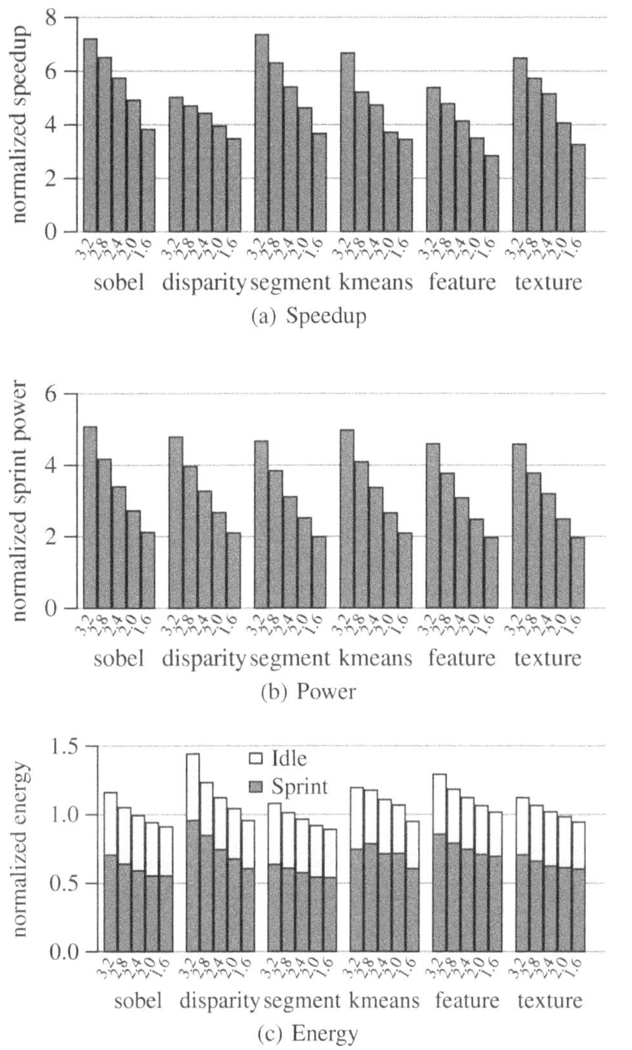

Figure 4. Speedup, power, and energy (normalized to the one-core 1.6 GHz sustainable baseline) for four cores across frequencies.

sider sprinting with lower frequencies to improve energy efficiency. Figure 4 shows the responsiveness, power, and energy implications of sprinting with all four cores at various frequency/voltage levels. The left-most bar in each group of Figure 4(a) shows the same speedup (6.3× on average) with a maximum-intensity four-core 3.2 GHz sprint that was presented earlier in Figure 2. The corresponding bars in Figure 4(b) show the 5× power increase for such a sprint. As the frequency is lowered, the responsiveness improvements decrease, but power decreases relatively more.

Figure 4(c) shows the energy implications of each sprint. We apportion energy into two components. The lower portion of the bar depicts the energy consumed during the sprint itself; because of the non-linear relationship between performance and power under frequency/voltage scaling, higher frequency sprints consume more energy. The upper portion of each bar depicts the energy consumed as a result of idle power dissipated after the end of the sprint until the work would have completed under sustainable single-core execution. By measuring energy consumption over the period of the slower, sustainable execution, we facilitate a fair efficiency comparison.

Ignoring idle energy for a moment, we see that even sprinting at maximum intensity reduces the energy consumed during the computation. The background power conserved by finishing sooner more than compensates for the super-linear cost of voltage scaling, reducing energy up to 30%. At lower frequencies, this potential energy savings grows to nearly 40%. Similar race-to-idle effects have been observed previously [5, 7, 21, 22, 33, 36, 40].

Unfortunately, chips continue to dissipate power even when idle. By finishing earlier, the chip must idle for longer [40]; thus we must also consider the top segment of each bar, which adds the energy consumed during the additional idle time. For the 3.2 GHz four-core sprint, once the idle energy is included, the total energy is 21% higher than the sustainable baseline. However, when we consider the lowest-frequency four-core sprint, we find an energy efficiency gain of 6% even when including idle energy. Hence, when sprint intensity is selected appropriately, sprinting can improve energy efficiency as well as responsiveness even on today's chips. Finally, we note that, even though the chip idle power is already less than one tenth of its peak, there is still ample motivation to optimize idle power further: the energy efficiency advantages of sprinting grow rapidly as idle power vanishes. With several emerging mobile architectures seeking to aggressively reduce idle power (*e.g.*, NVIDIA Tegra 3's vSMP/4-plus-1 [41] and ARM's big.LITTLE multicores [24]), we see substantial potential for sprinting as an energy saver as well as a responsiveness enabler.

4. Truncated Sprints

Ideally, all sprints would be unabridged, completing before available thermal capacitance is exhausted. However the system must avoid overheating for computations that cannot be completed entirely within a sprint while aiming to preserve some of the responsiveness benefits of sprinting.

This section first describes the software for truncating sprints to avoid overheating by throttling frequency and disabling all but one core. Next, we observe that for some workloads, the naive approach to completing work after truncation, *i.e.*, migrating threads to be multiplexed on a single core, can result in significant degradation in performance and energy efficiency. We explore mitigating these effects using a sprinting-aware task-based parallel runtime. Finally, we motivate *sprint pacing* by showing that the most responsive mode of sprinting is not always maximum-intensity sprints, but instead is sprinting at the most intense rate that still allows the sprint to remain unabridged.

4.1 Implementing and Evaluating Sprint Truncation

The testbed software monitors die temperature using a thread to query the on-die temperature sensor every 100 ms. Although implemented as a user-level thread in our testbed prototype, ultimately this functionality would likely be integrated into the operating system's dynamic thermal management facility. When the die temperature reaches T_{max}, the software truncates the sprint by: (*i*) pinning all threads to a single core to force the operating system to migrate the threads, (*ii*) disabling the now-idle cores, and (*iii*) changing the frequency of the single core to the lowest configurable frequency. The testbed software implements these steps using system calls and the standard Linux ACPI interface.

To explore the behavior of sprint truncation, we reconfigure the workloads to run longer so that the computation exceeds the available thermal capacitance for sprinting. Figure 5 shows the impact of sprint truncation on the power and temperature of the chip over time for both sustained execution and a truncated sprint. As before, temperature rises sharply when sprinting begins from the idle state at time zero. Once the temperature reaches the T_{max} value of 75° C, the runtime system invokes sprint truncation, which results in the abrupt drop in power from 55 W to 9.5 W. In response, the temperature stops rising, as the system's power consumption now matches the rate of cooling dissipation. In fact, the temper-

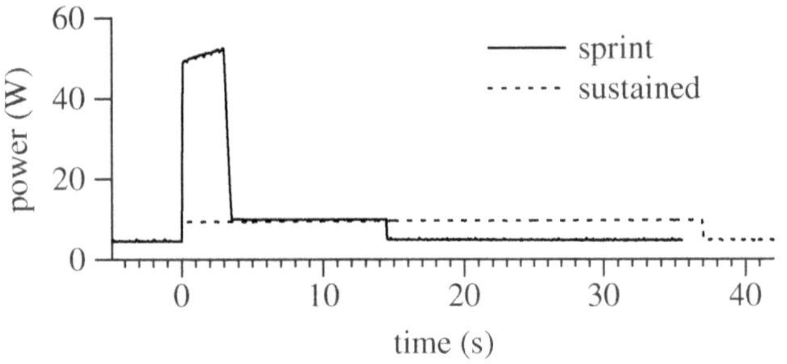

(a) Power

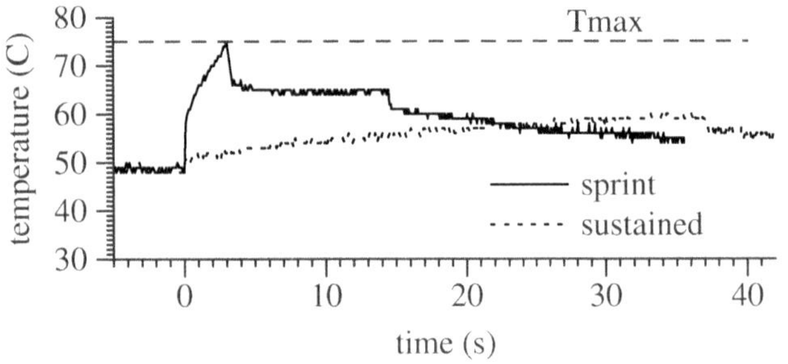

(b) Temperature

Figure 5. Power and thermal response for truncated sprints.

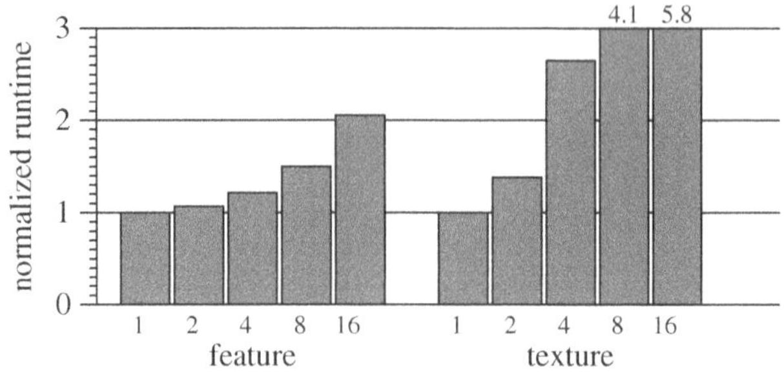

Figure 7. Runtime penalty from oversubscription with increasing numbers of threads on a single core.

ature drops initially as the heat spreads throughout the die, package, and surrounding components. After truncation, the computation continues in sustainable mode with all threads multiplexed on a single active core at minimum frequency. The system's thermal response matches that of the sustained computation during this interval. When the computation completes, the remaining core becomes idle, and the chip begins to cool.

Performance and energy penalties of sprint truncation. To evaluate the impact of sprint truncation, we vary the length of each computation and measure responsiveness across sprint intensities. In Figure 6, each group of bars shows the execution time (Figure 6(a)) or energy (Figure 6(b)) for maximum-intensity sprinting for varying computation lengths normalized to a non-sprinting system. The segments of each bar indicate the fraction of time spent in sprint (bottom segment), sustained (middle segment), and idle modes (top segment). Unsurprisingly, as the computation length increases beyond the sprint capacity, larger and larger fractions of time are spent computing in sustained mode. Correspondingly, the impact of sprinting on execution time (and thus responsiveness) and energy is smaller for longer computations as less time is spent sprinting. One seeming anomaly is that truncated sprinting is actually slower than the sustained baseline for two workloads (`feature` and `texture`), which we address next.

4.2 Mitigating Overheads of Truncated Sprints

Sprint truncation results in all active threads being multiplexed on the single remaining core, which leads to a net slowdown in some workloads relative to the sustainable baseline (Figure 6(a)). Although it is expected that long-running computations would receive little benefit from an initial sprint, the observed degradation is highly undesirable as ideally sprinting would "do no harm" to long-running computations. The observed degradation in these workloads is a result of multiplexing all threads on a single core. The resulting oversubscribed system is prone to known pathologies from contention on synchronization, load imbalance, convoying, and frequent context switches [9, 25, 28, 29, 50].

Demonstrating the penalty of oversubscription. To demonstrate the performance penalty of oversubscription, Figure 7 shows the performance impact of spawning N threads but pinning them to a single core. As the amount of oversubscription increases, so does the penalty. Although most of the workloads are not sensitive to oversubscription (omitted for brevity), the effect is particularly pronounced in `texture`, where we see a penalty of over 2.5× for a four-to-one oversubscription ratio. The penalty is as high as 5.8× for 16 threads.

Conventional approaches to mitigating the penalty of oversubscription. This well-known phenomenon has several typically prescribed mitigation approaches. One approach—avoiding the problem of oversubscription by spawning only as many threads as cores—is not applicable because sprint truncation changes the number of available cores while the computation is executing. Another mitigating approach is to tailor shared-memory synchronization primitives (locks and barriers) to yield the processor instead of busy waiting. We explored various implementations and our reported results already include user-level synchronization primitives that `yield()` after spinning for 1000 cycles. These primitives reduced the prevalence of the oversubscription penalty, but extra context switches are still required and the penalty remains for two workloads due to their frequent use of barrier synchronization. Another approach is to have programs dynamically adjust the number of active threads [50], which is the approach we build upon here.

Sprint-aware task-based parallel runtime to mitigate oversubscription penalties. Efficient sprint truncation requires an efficient mechanism to dynamically change the number of active software threads. To provide such a mechanism, we look toward task-queue based worker thread execution frameworks [1, 10, 16, 19, 30, 50], in which applications are decomposed into tasks and the program is oblivious to the actual number of worker threads. In such frameworks, the tasks created by the application are then assigned to thread queues. Worker threads first look for tasks to execute in their local task queue. Upon the absence of a local task, workers "steal" tasks from other threads' task queues. The core-oblivious nature of the task-based model, coupled with its automatic load balancing via task stealing facilitates dynamically changing the number of worker threads. Reducing the number of threads is as simple as having a worker thread go to sleep once it has completed its current task.

We mitigate oversubscription penalties with a sprint-aware task-stealing runtime framework (similar to Intel's Threading Building Blocks [1]). Before dequeuing another task to execute, a thread first queries a shared variable that indicates the number of worker threads that should be active. If the desired number of active threads is lower than the worker thread's identifier, the worker thread exits. Any pending tasks in that thread's queues will eventually be stolen and executed by the worker thread running on the single remaining core after a sprint is truncated. The same monitor thread that other-

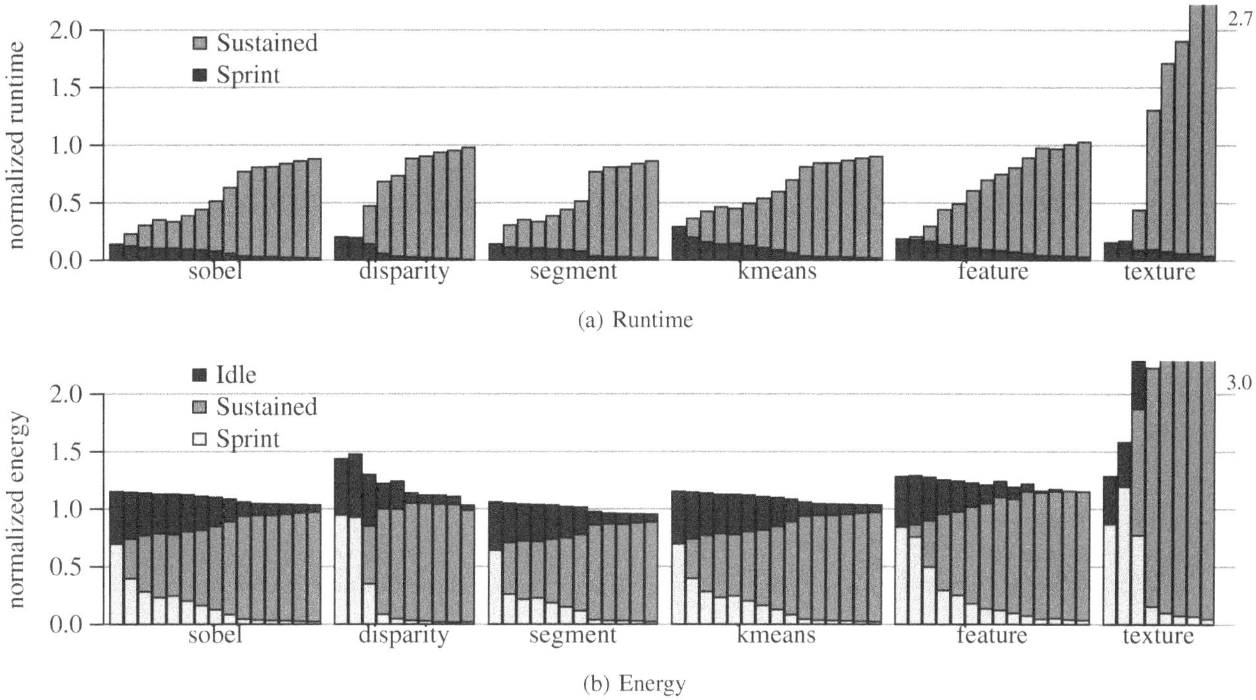

Figure 6. Runtime and energy spent during sprinting, sustained, and idle modes for 4-core sprints at 3.2 Ghz (normalized to the one-core 1.6 Ghz baseline.) Bars represent increasing computation lengths from left to right.

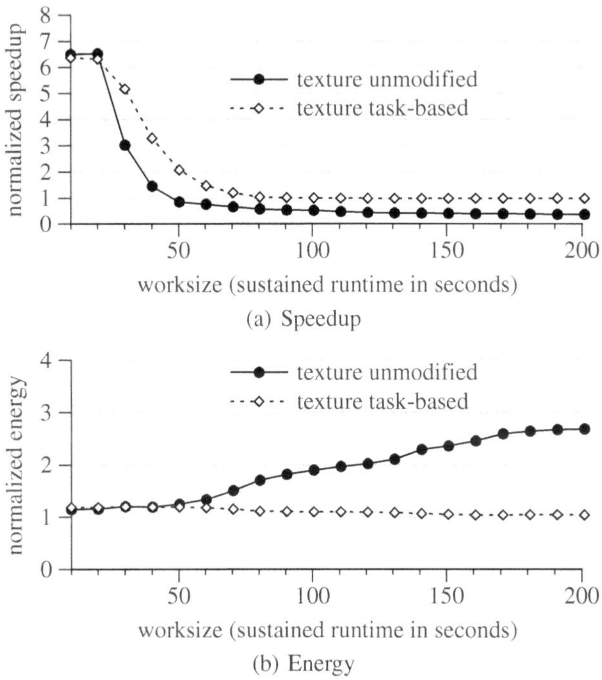

Figure 8. Speedup and energy comparison of the unmodified threaded and task-based implementations of `texture`.

wise handles sprint termination is responsible for setting the desired number of active threads by writing to the shared variable. This task-based mechanism does not replace the existing thread migration and core disabling mechanism; that mechanism is still needed in case a thread is executing a long task, which must be suspended and migrated to avoid overheating. However, the task-based policy ensures that eventually all but one worker thread will be put to sleep, thus avoiding the oversubscription penalty for the remainder of the computation.

To evaluate the effectiveness of this approach, we create a variant of the `texture` workload rewritten for this task-based parallelism model. Figure 8 shows the sprint truncation behavior of the original multi-threaded version of `texture` and the task-based variant for various computation lengths. Both versions have similar responsiveness when the computation is short and the sprint is unabridged. However, whereas the performance of the original multi-threaded version of `texture` falls well below that of the sustainable baseline, the task-based `texture` variant converges to it. This experiment indicates that a sprint-aware task-based runtime can eliminate the inefficiencies of sprint truncation, allowing for robust "do no harm" sprinting.

4.3 Sprint Pacing

Section 3 concluded that for unabridged sprints, sprinting at maximum intensity is best to improve responsiveness. However, when maximum-intensity sprinting results in sprint truncation, the choice of sprint intensity is not so simple. Figure 9 shows responsiveness benefits over a sustainable baseline for four-core sprints across frequencies ranging from 3.2 GHz to 1.6 GHz. For short computations (the far left of the graph), maximum-intensity sprinting maximizes responsiveness; for large computations, the responsiveness is no better than sustainable execution. However, for intermediate computation lengths, the optimal sprinting mode is not always maximum sprint intensity. In such cases—just as in human runners—it is better to sprint at a slower pace for longer than to sprint at maximum pace for an extremely short duration. This observation motivates the need for a *sprint pacing policy*.

Benefits of paced sprinting. To better understand the opportunity for sprint pacing, consider the difference in maximum sprint

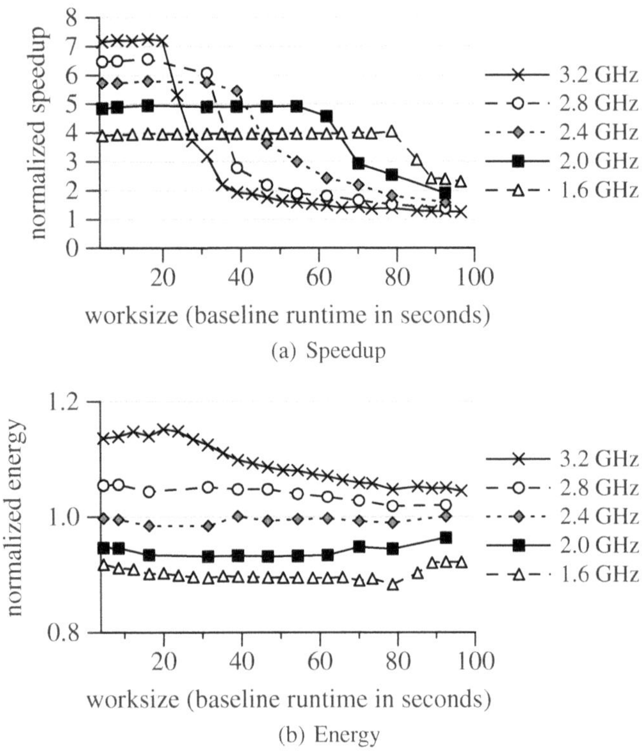

Figure 9. Speedup and energy versus size of computation for sprinting with four cores at different differences.

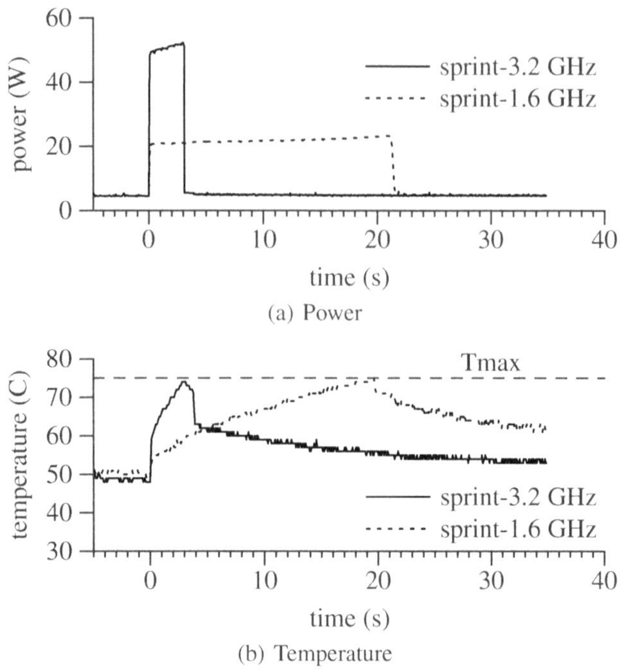

Figure 10. Power and thermal response for sprinting with four cores at 1.6 GHz.

duration for four cores at 3.2 GHz vs. 1.6 GHz, illustrated with power and temperature curves in Figure 10. The responsiveness advantage due to doubling frequency is 2× at best. However, the maximum sprint duration at 1.6 GHz is 6.3× longer than the 3.2 GHz sprint, implying that a 1.6 GHz sprint can complete over 3× more work. The less intense sprint completes more work for three reasons. First, lowering frequency and voltage results in a more energy efficient operating point, so the thermal capacitance consumed per unit of work is lower. Second, the longer sprint duration allows more heat to be dissipated to ambient during the sprint. Third, as we discussed previously, maximum intensity sprints are unable to fully exploit all thermal capacitance in the heat spreader because the lateral heat conduction delay to the extents of the copper plate is larger than the time for the die temperature to become critical. By sprinting less intensely, more time is available for heat to spread and more of the heat spreader's thermal capacitance can be exploited.

Toward a sprint pacing policy. The most critical impact on sprint pacing policy is the length of the computation, and we envision two general approaches to sprint pacing. The first approach is *predictive sprint pacing* in which the length of the computation is predicted to select a near-optimal sprint pace. Such a prediction (*e.g.*, [27]) could be performed by the hardware, operating system, or with hints from the application program directly. In the absence of such a prediction, an alternative approach is *adaptive sprint pacing* in which the pacing policy dynamically adapts the sprint pace to capture the best-case benefit for short computations, but moves to a less intense sprint mode to extend the length of computations for which sprinting improves responsiveness. Figure 11 shows the behavior of a simple adaptive sprint policy that sprints at full intensity until half of the thermal capacity is consumed, after which it switches to less intense and more power-efficient sprints by keeping all four cores active but throttling their frequency to 1.6 GHz. As shown in the graph, this policy captures the benefits of sprinting for short computations but maintains some responsiveness gains for longer computations. Although the dynamic policy falls short of an *a priori* selection of the best sprint intensity for some computation lengths, it is robust in that it provides benefits over a larger range of computation lengths.

Other parameters that may impact sprint pacing policies. The optimal sprint pace is potentially impacted by other factors. Although the most basic factor is the length of the computation, other factors include the performance and power impact of both the clock frequency and the number of cores [31, 32, 43]. For example, a workload that has poor parallel scaling may benefit more from higher frequency than additional cores. In our four-core testbed with workloads that scale well, we found such effects were not significant, but they will likely become more critical in the future as the number of cores on a chip increases.

5. Extending Sprints using Latent Heat

Thus far, this paper has examined policy approaches to mitigating the impacts of limited sprint duration. A complementary approach to increase sprinting effectiveness is to engineer a system that supports longer sprints by including more thermal capacitance. Instead of leveraging only the specific heat of conventional materials, prior work proposed using the latent heat of a phase change material (PCM) to add thermal capacitance to a sprinting system [45]. Latent heat has the advantage that it can absorb substantial heat without a change in temperature. Whereas each gram of copper in the heat spreader can absorb 11.5 J over a 30° C rise, many phase change materials used for heat storage can absorb 200 J per gram or more [55].

To test the potential of phase change materials to extend sprint duration, we perform proof-of-concept experiments using our testbed. We are unaware of a readily available PCM designed to meet the needs of computational sprinting (e.g., stability over numerous rapid thermal cycles with a melting point within the relevant temperature range), so we test paraffin (BW-40701 from BlendedWaxes, Inc.) which has a melting point of 54° C. Because paraffin has poor thermal conductivity (0.2 W/mK), we infuse it

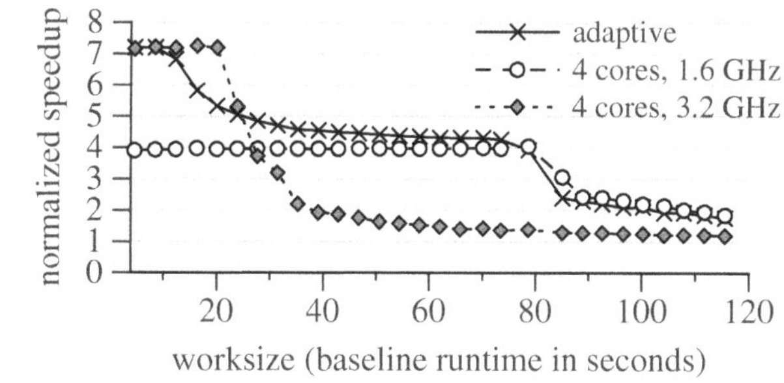

(a) Speedup

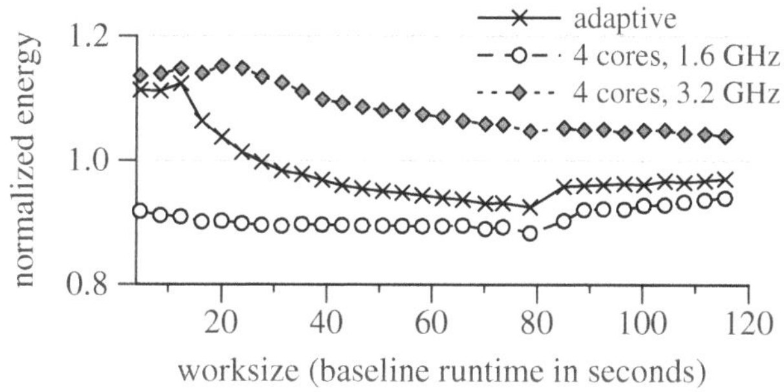

(b) Energy

Figure 11. Speedup and energy for sprinting based on an adaptive allocation of sprint budget between the most responsive and most energy efficient schemes.

(a) Phase change material on top of the package

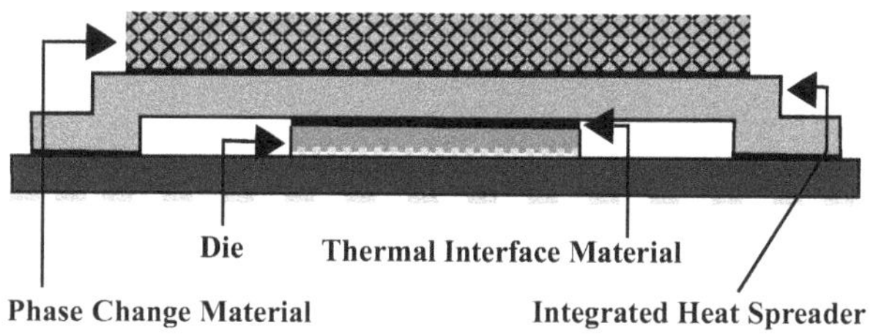

(b) Cross-section of phase change material on the package

Figure 12. Testbed augmented with phase-change material.

in 0.9 g of Doucel aluminum foam (bulk thermal conductivity of 5 W/mK). To prevent leakage, we enclose the paraffin/foam structure in a 4.2 cm × 4.2 cm × 0.3 cm box of 0.013 cm thick copper weighing 4 g. We then mount this enclosure on the processor socket using screws to provide firm attachment and improve interfacial heat transfer. Figure 12 illustrates our setup.

Figure 13 shows the thermal response of sprinting with four cores at 1.6 GHz on this modified testbed, isolating the effects of each of the labeled components. Adding the copper container and aluminum foam alone (labeled empty foam) increases thermal capacitance due to the additional specific heat and nearly doubles the baseline (air) sprint duration (37 s vs. 20 s). With the addition of 4 g of PCM (wax), the testbed can sprint for 120 s—6× over the baseline. The flattening in the PCM temperature curve is a consequence of the PCM melting. Given the latent heat of paraffin wax (200 J/g), 4 g of such material can absorb about 800 J of heat when melting, corresponding to an additional 40 s of sprint duration at 20 W. However, the observed sprint extension exceeds this estimate largely due to the additional heat dissipated to the ambient over this duration, and to a smaller extent, due to the specific heat of the wax.

To further distinguish the contribution of latent heat from specific heat, we replace the PCM with an equal weight of water (and a plastic cap to prevent the water from evaporating), and observe a sprint duration of 50 s. As the specific heat of water (4.2 J/gK) is higher than that of paraffin (2 J/gK), we conclude that the latent heat of the PCM indeed accounts for the substantial sprint extension. Although our experiments confirm that using PCM can be an effective approach for extending sprint duration, significant opportunity remains for engineering more effective PCM materials and composites, especially if incorporated directly within the package.

6. Sprint-and-Rest for Extended Computations

Whereas introducing additional thermal capacitance facilitates longer sprints, maximum sprint duration remains finite. In the

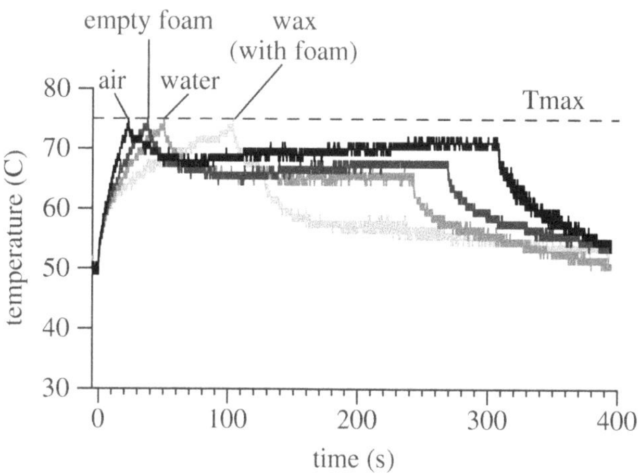

Figure 13. Comparison of sprinting thermal response with and without PCM.

previous sections, we have analyzed sprint policy as a function of workload size while considering only a single sprint. In this section, we consider whether sprinting can also be beneficial for extended (even indefinite) computations.

Over the long run, the average power consumption of a platform is constrained by the heat dissipation of the cooling solution (*i.e.*, the platform's TDP). The obvious way to execute a long-running computation is to select a sustainable operating mode that consumes less power than the TDP (in which case the chip can operate indefinitely). However, in a sprint-enabled system, one can also consider an operating regime that alternates between sprint and rest periods. Provided (*i*) the sprint periods are short enough to remain within temperature bounds and (*ii*) the rest periods are long enough to dissipate the accumulated heat, such a sprint-and-rest mode of operation is also sustainable indefinitely. That is, sprint-

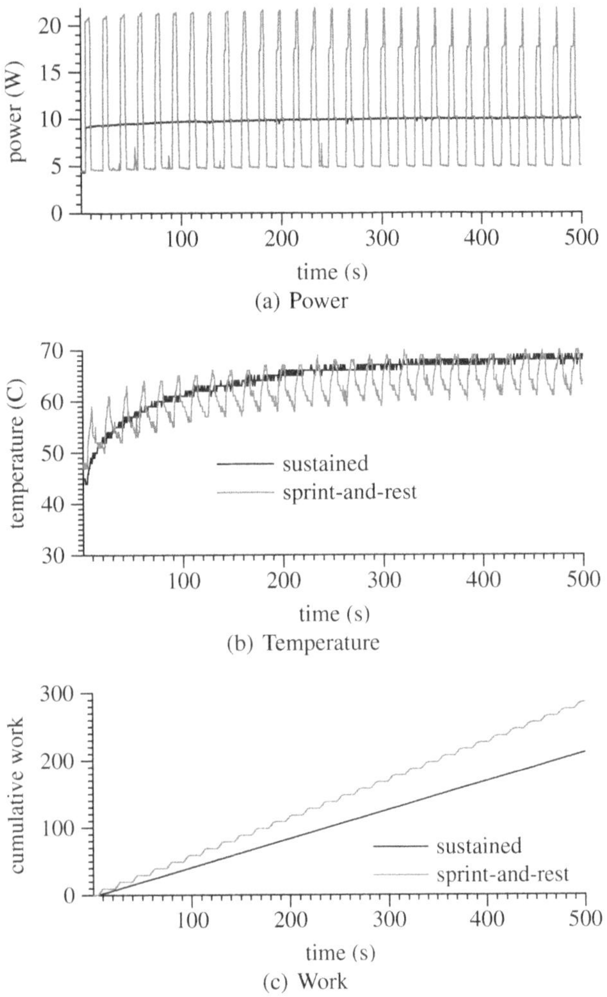

Figure 14. Comparison of power, temperarature, and cumulative work done with sprint-and-rest and sustained computation.

and-rest is sustainable as long as the average (but not necessarily instantaneous) power dissipation over a sprint-and-rest cycle is at or below the platform's sustainable power dissipation.

We contrast conventional sustainable operation using a single-core at 1.6 GHz and sprint-and-rest operation with four cores at 1.6 GHz. For the sprint-and-rest mode to be sustainable, its average power draw must be at or below the 9.5 W dissipation of the single-core mode. On our testbed, a four-core 1.6 GHz sprint consumes 20 W, while idling consumes 4.5 W. Hence, the maximum sustainable sprint-to-rest ratio is 1:2.1. We conservatively choose a ratio of 1:2.5, with a sprint duration of 5 s followed by a rest period of 12.5 s. We repeat this cycle over several minutes and measure temperature fluctuations, power, and the total work completed.

Counterintuitively, we found that this sprint-and-rest mode provides *higher* performance despite marginally lower average power consumption than the sustainable baseline. Figure 14 shows power, temperature, and cumulative completed work over several minutes. The power plot (Figure 14(a)) shows the staccato instantaneous power pattern of sprint-and-rest operation. The temperature plot (Figure 14(b)) reveals temperature increases for both modes—with sprint-and-rest following a sawtooth pattern—but both modes converge to a temperature below the 75° C threshold. Careful examination of the power plot reveals a slight upward trend for the power consumption of both sustained and sprint-and-rest execution, due to temperature-dependent leakage. The cumulative work plot (Figure 14(c)) demonstrates the performance advantage of sprint-and-rest; despite the stair-step pattern of forward progress, sprint-and-rest completes work at an average rate 35% higher than single-core sustained. Hence, sprint-and-rest provides both greater performance and better energy-efficiency than steady sustained operation.

Sprint-and-rest outperforms TDP-constrained sustained operation because the instantaneous energy efficiency of quad-core operation is better than single-core operation; operating all four cores provides quadruple the performance at double the power. This benefit arises because quad-core operation amortizes the fixed power costs of operating the chip over more useful work. Sprint-and-rest will provide a net efficiency gain whenever the instaneous energy-efficiency ratio of sprint vs. sustainable operation exceeds the sprint-to-rest time ratio required to cool. The advantages of sprint-and-rest grow if the idle power of the chip is reduced. We expect that similar observations may hold for chips that provide other kinds of performance-power assymetry, for example, due to heterogeneous cores. On the other hand, repeated thermal cycling introduced by sprint-and-rest can affect the reliability of the chip and potentially cause thermal stress in packaging components like solder bumps. We leave an analysis of reliability to future work.

7. Conclusions

Finding ways to deliver value to customers from dark silicon may be one of the defining challenges of the next decade of computer architecture research. Computational sprinting offers one such value proposition for bursty interactive applications by transiently activating dark silicon to deliver performance when end users need it most—when they are waiting for their device to respond.

Whereas prior work argued for the feasibility and potential of computational sprinting in theory, in this paper we reduce it to practice through experimentation on a concrete hardware/software sprinting testbed. We have shown that even though our testbed is constructed with an existing chip that was not designed with sprinting in mind, sprinting can provide not only substantial gains in responsiveness, but in fact also provides net energy efficiency gains by racing to idle. Even for extended computations, we find that a thermally constrained sprint-enabled chip achieves better performance through sprint-and-rest operation rather than sustained execution. The central insight underlying these counterintuitive results is that chip energy efficiency is maximized by activating all useful cores—disregarding thermal limits—to best amortize the fixed costs of operating at all. Moreover, our results provide ample motivation for chip designers to further optimize idle power; although many chips already achieve 10-to-1 ratios between peak and idle power, our results indicate that further overall energy efficiency gains of nearly 40% could be achieved by driving down idle power.

Our study demonstrates the synergy between task-based work-stealing parallelism and sprinting; by dissociating parallel work from specific threads, we give the runtime the freedom it needs to manage sprint pacing and avoid oversubscription penalties for truncated sprints. We have performed an investigation of sprint pacing, demonstrating the benefits of adaptive pacing, but anticipate rich opportunities for further innovation as chips scale in heterogeneity and number of cores. Finally, we have shown the first experimental results that phase change materials can indeed extend sprint durations, which may open a myriad of avenues for innovation in packaging and thermal management.

Acknowledgments

This work was supported in part by NSF grants CCF-0644197, CCF-0815457, CCF-1161505 and CCF-1161681. The authors would like to thank Yatin Manerkar and the anonymous reviewers for their feedback.

References

[1] Threading Building Blocks. URL `http://threadingbuildingblocks.org`.

[2] Nokia Point and Find, 2006. URL `http://www.pointandfind.nokia.com`.

[3] Google Goggles, 2009. URL `http://www.google.com/mobile/goggles`.

[4] 2nd Generation Intel Core Processor Family Desktop and Intel Pentium Processor Family Deskop, and LGA1155 Socket, 2011. URL `http://www.intel.com/content/dam/doc/guide/2nd-gen-core-lga1155-socket-guide.pdf`.

[5] S. Albers and A. Antoniadis. Race to Idle: New Algorithms for Speed Scaling with a Sleep State. In *Proceedings of the Twenty-Third Annual ACM-SIAM Symposium on Discrete Algorithms*, 2012.

[6] O. Azizi, A. Mahesri, B. C. Lee, S. J. Patel, and M. Horowitz. Energy Performance Tradeoffs in Processor Architecture and Circuit Design: A Marginal Cost Analysis. In *Proceedings of the 37th Annual International Symposium on Computer Architecture*, June 2010.

[7] P. Bailis, V. J. Reddi, S. Gandhi, D. Brooks, and M. I. Seltzer. Dimetrodon: Processor-level Preventive Thermal Management via Idle Cycle Injection. In *Proceedings of the 48th Design Automation Conference*, June 2011.

[8] G. Blake, R. G. Dreslinski, T. Mudge, and K. Flautner. Evolution of Thread-Level Parallelism in Desktop Applications. In *Proceedings of the 37th Annual International Symposium on Computer Architecture*, June 2010.

[9] M. Blasgen, J. Gray, M. Mitoma, and T. Price. The Convoy Phenomenon. *ACM SIGOPS Operating Systems Review*, 13, April 1979.

[10] R. D. Blumofe, C. F. Joerg, B. C. Kuszmaul, C. E. Leiserson, K. H. Randall, and Y. Zhou. Cilk: An Efficient Multithreaded Runtime System. In *Proceedings of the 5th ACM SIGPLAN Symposium on Principles and Practice of Parallel Programming (PPOPP)*, July 1995.

[11] S. Borkar and A. A. Chien. The Future of Microprocessors. *Communications of the ACM*, 54(5):67–77, 2011.

[12] K. Chakraborty. *Over-provisioned Multicore Systems*. PhD thesis, University of Wisconsin, 2008.

[13] Chipworks. The New iPad: A Closer Look Inside, Mar. 2012. URL `http://www.chipworks.com/en/technical-competitive-analysis/resources/recent-teardowns/2012/03/the-new-ipad-a-closer-look-inside/`.

[14] J. Clemons, H. Zhu, S. Savarese, and T. Austin. MEVBench: A Mobile Computer Vision Benchmarking Suite. In *Proceedings of the IEEE International Symposium on Workload Characterization*, Sept. 2011.

[15] Computing Community Consortium. 21st Century Computer Architecture: A Community Whitepaper, Mar. 2012. URL `http://cra.org/ccc/docs/init/21stcenturyarchitecturewhitepaper.pdf`.

[16] G. Contreras and M. Martonosi. Characterizing and Improving the Performance of Intel Threading Building Blocks. In *Proceedings of the IEEE International Symposium on Workload Characterization*, Sept. 2008.

[17] B. Erol, E. Antunez, and J. J. Hull. PACER: Toward a Cameraphone-based Paper Interface for Fine-grained and Flexible Interaction with Documents. In *Proceedings of the International Symposium on Multimedia*, 2009.

[18] H. Esmaeilzadeh, E. Blem, R. S. Amant, K. Sankaralingam, and D. Burger. Dark Silicon and the End of Multicore Scaling. In *Proceedings of the 38th Annual International Symposium on Computer Architecture*, June 2011.

[19] M. Frigo, C. E. Leiserson, and K. H. Randall. The Implementation of the Cilk-5 Multithreaded Language. In *Proceedings of the SIGPLAN 1998 Conference on Programming Language Design and Implementation*, June 1998.

[20] S. H. Fuller and L. I. Millett. Computing Performance: Game Over or Next Level? *IEEE Computer*, 44(1):31–38, Jan. 2011.

[21] A. Gandhi, M. Harchol-Balter, R. Das, and C. Lefurgy. Optimal Power Allocation in Server Farms. In *Proceedings of the 2009 ACM SIGMETRICS Conference on Measurement and Modeling of Computer Systems*, June 2009.

[22] M. Garrett. Powering Down. *Queue*, 5(7):16–21, 2007.

[23] B. Girod, V. Chandrasekhar, D. M. Chen, N.-M. Cheung, R. Grzeszczuk, Y. Reznik, G. Takacs, S. S. Tsai, and R. Vedantham. Mobile Visual Search. *IEEE Signal Processing Magazine*, July 2011.

[24] P. Greenhalgh. Big.LITTLE Processing with ARM Cortex-A15 & Cortex-A7: Improving Energy Efficiency in High-Performance Mobile Platforms, Sept. 2011.

[25] A. Gupta, A. Tucker, and S. Urushibara. The Impact of Operating System Scheduling Policies and Synchronization Methods of Performance of Parallel Applications. In *Proceedings of the 1991 ACM Sigmetrics Conference on Measurement and Modeling of Computer Systems*, May 1991.

[26] N. Hardavellas, M. Ferdman, B. Falsafi, and A. Ailamaki. Toward Dark Silicon in Servers. *IEEEMICRO*, 31(4):6–15, July 2011.

[27] C. J. Hughes, P. Kaul, S. V. Adve, R. Jain, C. Park, and J. Srinivasan. Variability in the Execution of Multimedia Applications and Implications for Architecture. In *Proceedings of the 28th Annual International Symposium on Computer Architecture*, July 2001.

[28] F. R. Johnson, R. Stoica, A. Ailamaki, and T. C. Mowry. Decoupling Contention Management from Scheduling. In *Proceedings of the 15th International Conference on Architectural Support for Programming Languages and Operating Systems*, Mar. 2010.

[29] L. I. Kontothanassis, R. W. Wisniewski, and M. L. Scott. Scheduler-Conscious Synchronization. *ACM Transactions on Computer Systems*, 15(1):3–40, Feb. 1997.

[30] D. Lea. A Java Fork/Join Framework. In *Proceedings of the ACM Java Grande 2000 Conference*, 2000.

[31] J. Li and J. F. Martínez. Power-Performance Considerations of Parallel Computing on Chip Multiprocessors. *ACM Transactions on Architecture and Code Optimization*, 2(4):397–422, Dec. 2005.

[32] J. Li and J. F. Martinez. Dynamic Power-Performance Adaptation of Parallel Computation on Chip Multiprocessors. In *Proceedings of the 12th Symposium on High-Performance Computer Architecture*, Feb. 2006.

[33] X. Li, Z. Li, F. David, P. Zhou, Y. Zhou, S. Adve, and S. Kumar. Performance Directed Energy Management for Main Memory and Disks. In *Proceedings of the 11th International Conference on Architectural Support for Programming Languages and Operating Systems*, Oct. 2004.

[34] Y. Li, B. C. Lee, D. Brooks, Z. Hu, and K. Skadron. CMP Design Space Exploration Subject to Physical Constraints. In *Proceedings of the 12th Symposium on High-Performance Computer Architecture*, Feb. 2006.

[35] G. Loudon, O. Pellijeff, and L. Zhong-Wei. A Method for Handwriting Input and Correction on Smartphones. In *Proceedings of the 7th International Workshop on Frontiers in Handwriting Recognition*, 2000.

[36] D. Meisner, B. T. Gold, and T. F. Wenisch. PowerNap: Eliminating Server Idle Power. In *Proceedings of the 14th International Conference on Architectural Support for Programming Languages and Operating Systems*, Mar. 2009.

[37] R. Merritt. ARM CTO: Power Surge Could Create 'Dark Silicon'. *EE Times*, Oct. 2009. URL `http://www.eetimes.com/electronics-news/4085396/ARM-CTO-power-surge-could-create-dark-silicon`.

[38] F. J. Mesa-Martinez, E. K. Ardestani, and J. Renau. Characterizing Processor Thermal Behavior. In *Proceedings of the 15th International Conference on Architectural Support for Programming Languages and Operating Systems*, Mar. 2010.

[39] A. Mirhoseini and F. Koushanfar. HypoEnergy: Hybrid Supercapacitor-Battery Power-Supply Optimization for Energy

Efficiency. In *Proceedings of the Conference on Design, Automation and Test in Europe*, Mar. 2011.

[40] A. Miyoshi, C. Lefurgy, E. Van Hensbergen, R. Rajamony, and R. Rajkumar. Critical Power Slope: Understanding the Runtime Effects of Frequency Scaling. In *Proceedings of the 2002 International Conference on Supercomputing*, June 2002.

[41] *Variable SMP (4-PLUS-1TM) A Multi-Core CPU Architecture for Low Power and High Performance*. NVIDIA, 2011.

[42] L. Palma, P. Enjeti, and J. Howze. An Approach to Improve Battery Run-time in Mobile Applications with Supercapacitors. In *34th Annual IEEE Power Electronics Specialist Conference*, volume 2, June 2003.

[43] S. Park, W. Jiang, Y. Zhou, and S. Adve. Managing Energy-Performance Tradeoffs for Multithreaded Applications on Multiprocessor Architectures. In *Proceedings of the 2007 ACM SIGMETRICS Conference on Measurement and Modeling of Computer Systems*, June 2007.

[44] M. Pedram, N. Chang, Y. Kim, and Y. Wang. Hybrid Electrical Energy Storage Systems. In *Proceedings of the 2010 International Symposium on Low Power Electronics and Design*, 2010.

[45] A. Raghavan, Y. Luo, A. Chandawalla, M. C. Papaefthymiou, K. P. Pipe, T. F. Wenisch, and M. M. K. Martin. Computational Sprinting. In *Proceedings of the 17th Symposium on High-Performance Computer Architecture*, Feb. 2012.

[46] E. Rotem, A. Naveh, D. Rajwan, A. Ananthakrishnan, and E. Weissmann. Power Management Architecture of the 2nd Generation Intel Core Microarchitecture, Formerly Codenamed Sandy Bridge. In *Hot Chips 23 Symposium*, Aug. 2011.

[47] A. Shye, B. Scholbrock, and G. Memik. Into the Wild: Studying Real User Activity Patterns to Guide Power Optimizations for Mobile Architectures. In *Proceedings of the 42nd International Symposium on Microarchitecture*, Nov. 2009.

[48] M. B. Taylor. Is Dark Silicon Useful? Harnessing the Four Horsemen of the Coming Dark Silicon Apocalypse. In *Proceedings of the 49th Design Automation Conference*, June 2012.

[49] A. Tilli, A. Bartolini, M. Cacciari, and L. Benini. Don't Burn Your Mobile! Safe Computational Re-Sprinting via Model Predictive Control. In *Proceedings of the Eighth IEEE/ACM/IFIP International Conference on Hardware/Software Codesign and System Synthesis*, 2012.

[50] A. Tucker and A. Gupta. Process Control and Scheduling Issues for Multiprogrammed Shared-Memory Multiprocessors. In *Proceedings of the 12th ACM Symposium on Operating System Principles*, 1989.

[51] S. K. Venkata, I. Ahn, D. Jeon, A. Gupta, C. Louie, S. Garcia, S. Belongie, and M. B. Taylor. SD-VBS: The San Diego Vision Benchmark Suite. In *Proceedings of the IEEE International Symposium on Workload Characterization*, Sept. 2009.

[52] G. Venkatesh, J. Sampson, N. Goulding, S. Garcia, V. Bryksin, J. Lugo-Martinez, S. Swanson, and M. B. Taylor. Conservation Cores: Reducing the Energy of Mature Computations. In *Proceedings of the 15th International Conference on Architectural Support for Programming Languages and Operating Systems*, Mar. 2010.

[53] D. Wagner and D. Schmalstieg. Making Augmented Reality Practical on Mobile Phones, Part I. *Computer Graphics and Applications, IEEE*, 29(3):12–15, 2009.

[54] L. Yan, L. Zhong, and N. Jha. User-Perceived Latency Driven Voltage Scaling for Interactive Applications. In *Proceedings of the 41st Design Automation Conference*, June 2005.

[55] B. Zalbaa, J. M. Marina, L. F. Cabezab, and H. Mehling. Review on Thermal Energy Storage with Phase Change: Materials, Heat Transfer Analysis and Applications. *Applied Thermal Engineering*, 23(3):251–283, 2003.

DeAliaser: Alias Speculation Using Atomic Region Support

Wonsun Ahn Yuelu Duan Josep Torrellas
University of Illinois at Urbana-Champaign
http://iacoma.cs.uiuc.edu

Abstract

Alias analysis is a critical component in many compiler optimizations. A promising approach to reduce the complexity of alias analysis is to use speculation. The approach consists of performing optimizations assuming the alias relationships that are true most of the time, and repairing the code when such relationships are found not to hold through runtime checks.

This paper proposes a general alias speculation scheme that leverages upcoming hardware support for transactions with the help of some ISA extensions. The ability of transactions to checkpoint and roll back frees the compiler to pursue aggressive optimizations without having to worry about recovery code. Also, exposing the memory conflict detection hardware in transactions to software allows runtime checking of aliases with little or no overhead. We test the potential of the novel alias speculation approach with Loop Invariant Code Motion (LICM), Global Value Numbering (GVN), and Partial Redundancy Elimination (PRE) optimization passes. On average, they are shown to reduce program execution time by 9% in SPEC FP2006 applications and 3% in SPEC INT2006 applications over the alias analysis of a state-of-the-art compiler.

Categories and Subject Descriptors C.1.2 [*Processor Architectures*]: Multiple Data Stream Architectures — MIMD processors; D.3.4 [*Programming Languages*]: Processors — Compilers, Optimization

General Terms Algorithms, Design, Performance.

Keywords Alias Analysis, Atomic Region, Transactional Memory, Compiler Optimization.

1. Introduction

Recently, there has been a flurry of activity in the industry to integrate support for transactional memory into processors, in the hopes of making parallel programming more tractable. Several mechanisms or machines now provide architectural support for transactions, such as Intel's Transactional Synchronization Extensions [2], IBM's Bluegene/Q [1], IBM's POWER architecture [3], AMD's Advanced Synchronization Facility [10], and Azul's Vega [11].

Interestingly, transactions can be leveraged for a completely different purpose — to aid the compiler generate better code. In particular, they can enable more aggressive code motion transformations. Code motion forms the basis of most redundancy elimination optimizations, such as Loop Invariant Code Motion (LICM), Global Value Numbering (GVN), Dead Store Elimination (DSE), and Partial Redundancy Elimination (PRE). In these optimizations, the compiler attempts to move a computation to a location where it is less frequently executed, or to a location where it can be eliminated by proving redundancy. However, code motion is prevented when there is an intervening memory access in its span that potentially aliases with the computation.

Unfortunately, proving that such intervening memory accesses do not alias is a notoriously difficult problem, especially in the presence of pointers. The general problem of proving the aliasing properties of a program, or alias analysis, has been of much interest. Many researchers have worked on it over the years [6, 16, 17, 24, 37, 42], making important progress. However, the difficulty has been that there is a trade-off between precision and efficiency, and the most accurate algorithms have too high space and time complexity to gain general use [18]. Indeed, alias analysis is hard even from a theoretical point of view [9, 19, 22, 34, 36].

Luckily, the use of transactions, or atomic regions, can be a game-changer in the field of alias analysis. There are two reasons for this. First, transactions provide the ability to checkpoint and buffer modified memory state — since they have to guarantee commit atomicity. Second, they provide the ability to perform alias checks of memory state accessed by the transaction against other memory accesses — since they have to guarantee isolation. The former allows the compiler to perform code motion speculatively, based on assumptions about aliasing and without having to worry about recovery. The latter allows the compiler to check these assumptions at runtime with little or no overhead. For this to be feasible, however, we need to extend the hardware-software interface for transactions, making them more *permeable* to software.

In this work, we apply these insights to build a form of alias speculation that can be used by the compiler to perform aggressive optimizations that were not previously possible. Unlike conventional alias analyses, which need to prove aliasing properties, we only need to determine that the aliasing properties are true "most of the time". We can detect the cases when they are incorrect at runtime, and just roll back the execution in those rare cases.

Admittedly, this is not the first time that speculation has been adopted for alias analysis. Speculation has been used in the past in a purely software setting [31], or with the help of hardware in the Itanium Advanced Load Address Table (ALAT) [14, 25, 26] and the Transmeta data speculation support [15, 21]. However, past work has not fully taken advantage of what transactions can potentially offer, including the ability to (i) move store accesses (in addition to load accesses) and (ii) perform multiple optimizations with differing code motion spans in the same atomic region.

Specifically, the ALAT does not use atomic regions, and is only used to speculatively hoist loads across aliasing stores. Moreover, the compiler must place a check instruction at each location in the code where the original load was. Equally important, the compiler

ASPLOS'13, March 16–20, 2013, Houston, Texas, USA.

is in charge of generating the recovery code, which is complex and hampers subsequent optimization and code generation passes.

Transmeta is closest to our proposal in that it supports checkpointing hardware. It provides alias detection hardware to hoist loads to hide load latencies. However, its Code Morphing Software (CMS) x86 binary translator is also limited in that it does not support the movement of store accesses. Moreover, the existing literature on CMS does not explain how multiple optimizations with differing code motion spans could be performed within a single atomic region. In fact, there is only a cursory introduction of the alias-checking instructions in the literature. The specifics of what optimizations are performed and how they are realized is not discussed.

In this paper, we propose a more powerful and flexible environment for alias speculation. The main contributions of this work are as follows:

- It proposes, for the first time, to expose the alias checking capabilities present in upcoming transactional memory systems for the purpose of alias speculation. It also proposes a set of novel ISA extensions to enable this.
- It shows how to do speculative code motion in two new ways. The first one involves moving stores. The second one performs multiple optimizations with differing code motion spans inside the same atomic region.
- It is the first paper to evaluate the benefits of alias speculation using atomic regions in the context of a source-level compiler and not a binary translator. It evaluates LICM, GVN, and PRE optimizations enhanced with alias speculation on the LLVM compiler [23]. They result in an average speedup of 9% in SPEC FP2006 programs and 3% in SPEC INT2006 programs over the baseline LLVM alias analysis.

This paper is organized as follows: Section 2 gives a background; Section 3 presents our alias speculation approach; Section 4 describes our compiler implementation; Section 5 presents examples of optimizations and experimental results; Section 6 discusses applying the approach to other environments; and Section 7 lists related work.

2. Background: Code Motion & Atomic Regions

2.1 Code Motion

Code motion involves moving a piece of code from its original location to a more desirable one, often to minimize the frequency of execution at runtime. Code motion is crucial for many compiler optimizations. A popular example of code motion optimization is Loop Invariant Code Motion (LICM). Other optimizations such as Partial Redundancy Elimination (PRE), Global Value Numbering (GVN), Common Subexpression Elimination (CSE), and Dead Store Elimination (DSE) implicitly involve code motion. For example, in CSE, the compiler moves the redundant expression to the site of the original expression to perform the elimination. If there are any aliasing accesses in the code motion span, the optimization is denied.

The aliasing properties that need to be followed by code motion can be summarized in a few correctness rules. In the following, we describe these rules and apply them to a few optimizations, namely LICM, GVN, and PRE.

2.1.1 Correctness Rules

If code motion M is to be performed on expression E, the following rules need to be followed between the set of addresses read and written by E (R_E and W_E), and the set of address read and written by loads and stores in the code motion span (R_M and W_M).

- **Read Motion Rule ($R_E \cap W_M = \emptyset$).** The values read by E must remain invariant. If a location read by E is updated in the code motion span, E may generate a wrong value in its moved location.
- **Write Motion Rule ($W_E \cap R_M = \emptyset \wedge W_E \cap W_M = \emptyset$).** The value written by E must not be used by any load in the code motion span. Otherwise, the load may produce a wrong value. Also, the code motion must not cause E or any store in its span to write a stale value. If E is moved before an aliasing store, that will cause that store to write a stale value. If E is moved after an aliasing store, that will cause E to write a stale value.

2.1.2 LICM

LICM involves either *hoisting* an expression in the body of a loop to the preheader of the loop, or *sinking* an expression in the body of a loop to the exit block of the loop [41]. If there is a load that repeatedly loads from the same location, the load is hoisted. If there is a load that loads from different locations but the loaded value is not used inside the loop, the load is sunk and only the last load is executed. In both cases, the loaded location should not be modified by any store in the loop (**Read Motion Rule**).

If there is a store instruction in the loop that repeatedly stores to the same location, LICM attempts to promote that location to a register. In effect, this *sinks* the store to the exit block of the loop. For this to be legal, the stored value must not be accessed by any load in the loop and must not be overwritten by any store in the loop (**Write Motion Rule**).

2.1.3 GVN/PRE

GVN attempts to eliminate redundant expressions by assigning a value number to each expression, which is stored in a map, and replacing an expression with a value if it can find one with the same number [5]. PRE also attempts to eliminate redundant expressions but it can eliminate them even when they are partially redundant, meaning that they are redundant only on certain paths to the expression. In this case, PRE makes those expressions fully redundant by performing code motion across the control flow graph [20]. LLVM utilizes a PRE algorithm based on static single assignment (SSA) form that performs GVN simultaneously [40].

Both GVN and PRE are subject to the **Read Motion Rule** in that the value of the expression that is being moved must not change in the course of code motion.

2.2 Hardware Support for Atomic Regions

There are several recent examples of mechanisms or machines that support atomic regions, namely Intel's Transactional Synchronization Extensions [2], IBM's Bluegene/Q [1], IBM's POWER architecture [3], AMD's Advanced Synchronization Facility [10], and Azul's Vega [11]. Atomic regions allow programmers to demarcate a region of code that is guaranteed to execute in isolation with respect to other threads and commit its outcome atomically. Its goal is to help parallel programming. We wish to use the same hardware support for the purpose of alias speculation.

All atomic region implementations incorporate two primitives that are necessary to guarantee atomicity and isolation: checkpointing with speculative buffering and conflict detection. The first primitive takes a register checkpoint at the beginning of an atomic region and buffers all writes to memory. If isolation is compromised before the end of the atomic region, the buffered writes are discarded and the register checkpoint restored. If isolation is successful, the buffered writes are made visible to other threads all at once when the atomic region commits.

The conflict detection primitive guarantees isolation by keeping track of addresses read in the atomic region (the read-set) and written in the atomic region (the write-set). All remote memory accesses check the read-set and the write-set for memory conflicts that compromise the isolation of the atomic region. The read-set and write-set are typically recorded by setting speculatively read (SR) bits and speculatively written (SW) bits in a cache. There is one SR bit and one SW bit per each cache line to record whether that line belongs to the read-set and/or write-set of an atomic region. Besides conflict detection, SW bits are also used to mark cache lines that need to be buffered for rollback purposes. This type of cache organization is called a speculative cache.

In this paper, we assume an atomic region implementation using a speculative cache. However, our proposal can be applied to any hardware-based atomic region implementation.

3. Proposed Alias Speculation Approach

3.1 Overview

We propose to make hardware support for atomic regions more permeable to software through ISA extensions for the purposes of alias speculation. Specifically, we want to expose to software the *memory conflict detection* facility of atomic region hardware that is hidden under the covers in current transactional memory systems. Currently, the conflict detection hardware is only used to guarantee the isolation of a transaction with respect to remote accesses. We wish to repurpose this hardware to detect memory conflicts, or aliases, between accesses of the *same thread*, and expose this hardware to the software to perform alias checks.

To leverage this new capability, pairs of references that do not alias "most of the time" are speculated upon during compile time as not aliasing. The compiler communicates its assumptions to the hardware using our new ISA extensions. After the assumptions have been communicated, the alias detection hardware is in charge of automatically verifying them at runtime. Verification failure results in the atomic region being rolled back and a version of the code without speculation being executed in place of the atomic region. This approach allows the compiler to perform code movements and optimizations that were previously impossible.

In designing the new ISA extensions and compiler algorithms, we want to achieve four goals:

- The movement of both loads and stores should be supported.
- All optimizations that can be improved through alias speculation should be enabled to their fullest extent possible.
- The optimizations should be achieved with as little instrumentation overhead as possible.
- The ISA extensions should only expose pre-existing hardware structures and functionality that is required for transactions, and not add significant complexity to the hardware.

A key design decision is where to place the atomic regions, since it dictates which pairs of aliased accesses can be speculated upon. Note that placing atomic regions carelessly results in performance degradation due to frequent rollbacks or the overhead of the atomic region instructions themselves. Hence, we decide to place atomic regions around loops. Wrapping loops in atomic regions provides ample range for optimizations such as LICM and PRE to perform large-scale redundancy elimination. Also, the benefit from optimizations performed inside loops accumulates at each iteration, and can easily offset the overhead of atomic region instrumentation. This is hard to attain in straight-line code.

Once we place an atomic region around a given loop, we want to enable as many code motions as possible. The code motions might span the entire loop, as in the case of LICM, or they might span a subset of instructions in the loop, as in the case of GVN and PRE. For each code motion, we need to make sure that the moved expression does not alias with any intervening loads or stores that can compromise the correctness rules laid out in Section 2.1.1. Specifically, for each code motion span M, ideally we need to know the read (R_M) and write (W_M) sets, to check that they do not alias illegally with the R_E and W_E of the moved expression E.

In reality, existing transactional memory hardware keeps track of just two sets of addresses for an atomic region: the set of addresses read (R_{AR}) and those written (W_{AR}) in the atomic region (AR). Alias checking against R_{AR} and W_{AR} instead of against R_M and W_M always guarantees correctness, since $R_M \subseteq R_{AR}$ and $W_M \subseteq W_{AR}$ always holds. However, the imprecision of the check can result in extraneous failures at runtime and frequent rollbacks of the atomic region. In the end, the cost of rollbacks can prevent some optimizations from being performed.

We propose to mitigate the problem of imprecision by manipulating the Speculative Read (SR) bits of a transaction at will, so that they constitute read address sets other than R_{AR}. However, we must be prepared to give up on isolation guarantees for the atomic region. R_{AR} is only needed for conflict detection and isolation of the atomic region. Since we are not using the atomic region for synchronization purposes like in transactional memory, we can give up on isolation and repurpose the SR bits to mark only read addresses that we want to monitor for alias checking.

Note that we still need the transaction's atomicity guarantees, since we must be able to roll back the atomic region on alias speculation failure. Hence, we are forbidden from manipulating the Speculative Written (SW) bits because we still need to buffer writes for checkpointing and rollback. The implications of forfeiting isolation on the rest of the system are discussed later in Section 6.2.

In the next sections, we discuss how to reduce conservatism by manipulating the SR bits and using special check instructions.

3.2 DeAliaser ISA Extensions

Table 1 shows the new Instruction Set Architecture (ISA) extensions that we add for DeAliaser. The instructions are categorized into three types: those that control the placement of atomic regions, those that control what memory locations are monitored for alias checking, and those that check the monitored locations.

Controlling Atomic Regions. The instructions *begin_atomic_opt* and *end_atomic_opt* begin and end an atomic region for optimization. The atomic region created by these instructions is exactly the same as a regular atomic region in transactional memory, except that the operation of the SR bits is changed. Now, regular loads do not set SR bits; only the special loads described below do so.

A rollback of the atomic region triggers a jump to a program counter (PC) given as an operand to *begin_atomic_opt*. It is the PC of the safe version: a conservative replica of the code in the atomic region that does not assume any speculation, and is always safe to execute. This safe version support is standard in all transactional systems.

Controlling Monitored Locations. The set of cache lines with the SR bit set and the set of cache lines with the SW bit set are the set of monitored read and write locations, respectively. The *load.r* instruction loads data into a register and sets the SR bit of the line in the cache containing the data. The *clear.r* instruction takes an address and clears the SR bit of the line in the cache corresponding to that address. Therefore, the *load.r* and *clear.r* instructions start and end the monitoring of a loaded location. With them, we can flexibly expand and shrink the set of read-monitored locations as the need arises for alias checking. This gives us the freedom to alias check multiple spans of code motion.

We do not have the corresponding operations for SW bits. DeAliaser cannot manipulate them because they are used for determining what to roll back if the atomic region fails. Thus, we cannot control the set of write-monitored locations, which is always the entire set of locations written by the atomic region so far. This can be a source of imprecision when doing alias checks.

Checking Monitored Locations. The *storechk.(r/w/rw)* and *loadchk.(r/w/rw)* instructions, in addition to storing to a location or loading from it, perform a check of the speculative bits in the cache line containing the location. The instruction postfix indicates which speculative bit is checked: *r* checks the SR, *w* checks the SW, and *rw* checks both. If the checked bit is set (or at least one of the two checked bits is), the hardware signals an alias check failure. A check failure means that this store or load access does alias with a monitored location, violating a *no alias* assumption made by the compiler. This results in a rollback of the atomic region and a jump to the safe version.

The *storechk.(r/w/rw)* instructions set the SW bit as is required of all store instructions, and they do so after performing the checks. Notably, the *loadchk.r* and *loadchk.rw* instructions also set the SR bit after the checks, and this is by design. They are designed in this way because the SR bit only needs to be checked by a load instruction when it *also* wants to set it immediately afterwards, as will be seen later.

Instruction	Description
begin_atomic_opt PC	Begins an atomic region for optimization. It creates a new register checkpoint and starts buffering memory accesses. *PC* is the program counter of the beginning of the safe version.
end_atomic_opt	Ends an atomic region for optimization. It commits all buffered accesses.

(a)

Instruction	Description
load.r r1, addr	Loads location *addr* into register *r1* just like a regular load. In addition, it sets the SR bit in the cache line containing *addr* for monitoring.
clear.r addr	Clears the SR bit in the cache line containing *addr*, hence ending monitoring.

(b)

Instruction	Description
storechk.(r/w/rw) r1, addr	Stores register *r1* into location *addr* just like a regular store. In addition, it checks the SR bit, the SW bit, or both in the cache line containing *addr*, depending on whether the postfix of the opcode is *r*, *w*, or *rw*. If the checked bit (or at least one of the two checked) is set, the atomic region is rolled back and execution jumps to the safe version.
loadchk.(r/w/rw) r1, addr	Loads location *addr* into register *r1* just like a regular load. In addition, it checks the SR bit, the SW bit, or both in the cache line containing *addr*, depending on the postfix of the opcode. If the checked bit (or at least one of the two checked) is set, the atomic region is rolled back and execution jumps to the safe version. Lastly, *loadchk.r* and *loadchk.rw* set the SR bit after it is checked.

(c)

Table 1. Extensions to the ISA to control atomic regions (a), control monitored locations (b), and check monitored locations (c).

3.3 Alias Speculation and Code Motion

The way a conventional compiler applies the code motion rules of Section 2.1.1 is necessarily conservative because of two reasons. First, even if the rules hold "most of the time", the compiler must guarantee correct execution for the corner cases. Secondly, even if the rules hold all the time, static analyses are fundamentally limited in what they can prove.

We use DeAliaser to circumvent having to prove the rules. Instead, we check them at runtime, thereby enabling more code motion at compile time. DeAliaser checks a modified version of the set of rules which, while sometimes more conservative, is still sufficient to guarantee the original set of rules. We explain how the rules are modified and checked for four types of code motion optimizations that are allowed by DeAliaser: hoisting loads, sinking loads, hoisting stores, and sinking stores. We also describe how to sink the *clear.r* instructions introduced by DeAliaser itself, in order to minimize overhead. Refer to Figure 1 while we go over each case.

Figure 1(a) illustrates how each code motion optimization is performed by example. For each case, the left hand side shows the code in its original state and the right hand side shows it after transformation. The moved instruction itself is marked in bold, and the register operands for all instructions are omitted for brevity. In each example, the loads and stores in grey denote the instructions that are checked by DeAliaser for aliasing against the instruction moved. Of these, the light grey ones are those checks that are performed and are necessary for correctness, while the dark grey ones are those checks that are performed as a side effect because of the imprecision in the DeAliaser hardware, and are not necessary for correctness. The table in Figure 1(b) describes each motion optimization in more general terms. Column 2 in the table lists the compiler actions that need to be performed after each motion. Column 3 describes how the alias checks guarantee the correctness of the motion. Finally, Column 4 states whether the alias checks are precise.

For the purposes of explanation, we adopt the following terminology. As before, M is the set of instructions in the span of the code motion performed on expression E, which are loads and stores that *may alias* with E. R_E is the address read by the moved load and W_E is the address written by the moved store. R_M and W_M are the set of addresses read and written, respectively, by accesses in M. $R_{Monitored}$ and $W_{Monitored}$ are the set of read and written addresses, respectively, currently being monitored in the atomic region. As mentioned before, $R_{Monitored}$ can be expanded or shrunk using the *load.r*, *loadchk.r*, *loadchk.rw*, and *clear.r* instructions. However, $W_{Monitored}$ is always the entire set of addresses written in the atomic region so far. Finally, we refer to a load or a store that sets the SR or SW bits as a *monitored* load or store; a load or a store that checks the bits is a *checking* load or store.

3.3.1 Hoisting Loads

In the top left example of Figure 1(a), we hoist *load A* above *store X*. After hoisting a load, we must monitor all the stores that may-alias in the span M of the motion. Our transformation involves: changing the hoisted load to *loadchk.r*, changing all the store instructions in M that may alias with the load to *storechk.r*, and placing a *clear.r* at the end of M to stop monitoring the load. We use *loadchk.r* instead of *load.r* to detect any interference with another unrelated code motion optimization. Specifically, if that other optimization had a monitored load that aliased with our load, both loads would set the same bit. Then, the first *clear.r* operation found would clear the SR bit, incorrectly turning off monitoring for both loads. With *loadchk.r*, we ensure that we detect this problem when we start monitoring, and roll back the atomic region.

The **Read Motion Rule** for moving loads ($R_E \cap W_M$) is trivially guaranteed, as shown in Figure 1(b). This is because checking against the set of addresses written by M using *storechk.r* instructions, referred to as $W(chk.r)_M$ in the table, is equivalent by construction to checking against W_M. The checks are not only correct but precise, since a *storechk.r* check failure always means that the rule was violated. The only potential source of extraneous rollbacks comes from the use of the *loadchk.r* instruction. We will see that

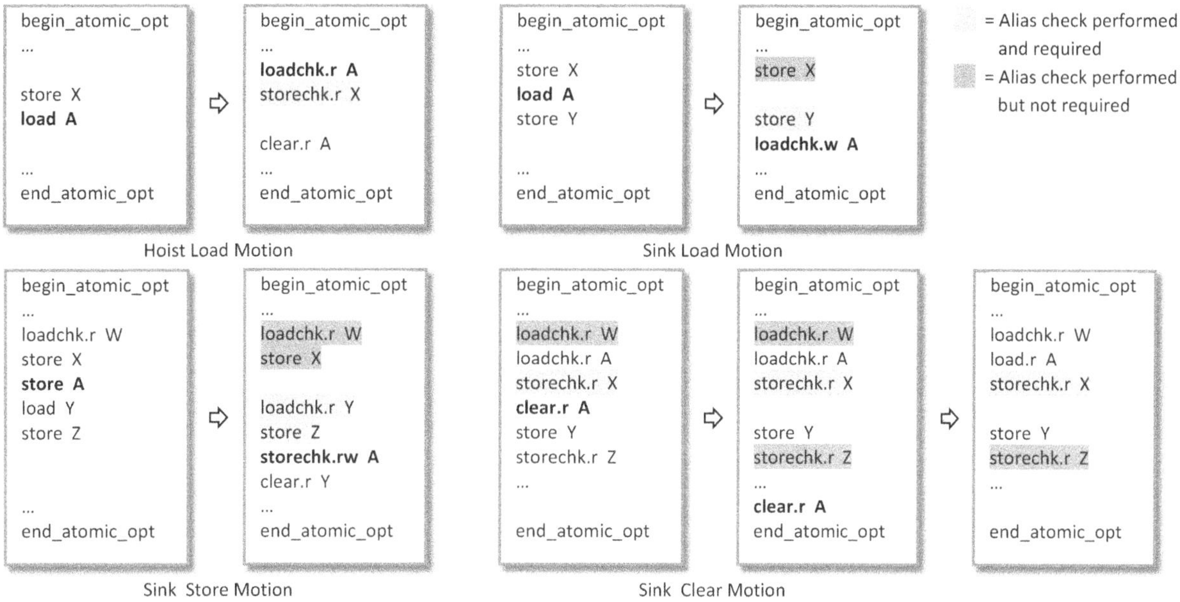

(a)

Code Motion	Action	Correctness Guarantee	Precise?
Hoist Load	Change *load* to *loadchk.r*. Change all may-alias stores in M to *storechk.r*. Insert *clear.r* at end of span to stop monitoring.	$R_E \cap W_M = R_E \cap W(chk.r)_M = \emptyset$	Yes
Sink Load	Change *load* to *loadchk.w*.	$R_E \cap W_{Monitored} = \emptyset, W_{Monitored} \supseteq W_M$	No
Hoist Store	Change all may-alias loads in M to *loadchk.w*. Change all may-alias stores in M to *storechk.w*.	$W_{Monitored} \cap R(chk.w)_{AR} = \emptyset \wedge W_{Monitored} \cap W(chk.w)_{AR} = \emptyset$, $W_{Monitored} \supseteq W_E, R(chk.w)_{AR} \supseteq R_M$, $W(chk.w)_{AR} \supseteq W_M$	No
Sink Store	Change *store* to *storechk.r/w/rw* depending on whether you are speculating on load aliases, store aliases, or both. If speculating on load aliases, change all may-alias loads in M to *loadchk.r* (unless they are already *loadchk.r/rw*). For all newly monitored loads, insert *clear.r* to stop monitoring after the store.	$W_E \cap R_{Monitored} = \emptyset \wedge W_E \cap W_{Monitored} = \emptyset$, $R_{Monitored} \supseteq R_M, W_{Monitored} \supseteq W_M$	No
Sink Clear	If *clear.r* is sunk to end of atomic region, remove it. Change *loadchk.r* to *load.r* or vice versa for affected monitored loads.	Expanding a monitoring span never compromises correctness.	No

(b)

Figure 1. Code motions supported by DeAliaser shown through examples (a) and explained in general terms (b).

the *loadchk.r* can often be converted to a check-less *load.r* when sinking *clear* instructions.

3.3.2 Sinking Loads

In the top right example of Figure 1(a), we sink *load A* below *store Y*. The initial code also includes an earlier *store X*. Our transformation involves changing the sunk load to *loadchk.w*. This load now checks that it does not alias with any of the writes executed in the atomic region so far. This includes the *store Y*, but it also includes all the previous stores in the atomic region such as *store X*. As shown in Figure 1(b), since M covers a subset of the instructions in the atomic region, the **Read Motion Rule** ($R_E \cap W_M$) is trivially guaranteed to be enforced. However, the check is not precise, potentially leading to extraneous rollbacks.

3.3.3 Hoisting Stores

We do not show an example of hoisting stores because of space limitations, but we still describe the actions performed and correctness guarantees in Figure 1(b). After hoisting the store, all may-alias loads in M are changed to *loadchk.w* instructions and all may-alias stores in M are changed to *storechk.w* instructions.

These transformations guarantee the **Write Motion Rule** ($W_E \cap R_M \wedge W_E \cap W_M$) for stores, but with potentially significant imprecision. In Section 3.3.1, we could selectively monitor hoisted loads by changing the load to *load.r* or *loadchk.r* and setting the SR bit. The same cannot be done with stores and SW bits, however, and we have no choice but to check all written locations since the beginning of the atomic region ($W_{Monitored}$) — instead of just W_E. Also, since SW bits cannot be cleared, we cannot stop monitoring at the end of M. If there are any *loadchk.w*, *loadchk.rw*, *storechk.w*, or *storechk.rw* instructions after the end of M, DeAliaser still performs the checks. Hence, we check against the entire set of locations accessed with *loadchk.w/rw* (called $R(chk.w)_{AR}$ in the table), or *storechk.w/rw* (called $W(chk.w)_{AR}$ in the table) in the atomic region following the hoisted store.

Hoisting stores is the code motion that suffers the most from imprecision. Fortunately, most compiler optimizations in use today do not use it.

3.3.4 Sinking Stores

In the bottom left example of Figure 1(a), we sink *store A* below *load Y* and *store Z*. The initial code also includes two earlier instructions: a *loadchk.r* and a store. Our transformation involves three parts. First, we change the sunk store to the appropriate flavor of *storechk.r/w/rw* instruction, depending on whether the motion is speculating on load aliases, store aliases, or both. Second, if we are speculating on load aliases, we change all the may-alias loads in M to *loadchk.r*. If some of these loads are already *loadchk.r/rw*, we do not change them. Third, we place *clear.r* instructions immediately after the *storechk.r/w/rw* for all the newly monitored loads, to stop monitoring after the store.

Figure 1(b) shows the correctness guarantee for this motion speculating on both load and store aliases. The ones for speculating on either only loads or only stores are obtained by simply removing one term. We see that the **Write Motion Rule** ($W_E \cap R_M \wedge W_E \cap W_M$) is trivially guaranteed because the set of addresses accessed in M is a subset of monitored addresses.

This check is not precise. The monitored stores are all the writes before the sunk store. The monitored loads are all the *loadchk.r/rw* ones before the sunk store, including those that were in the original code before the transformation. In Figure 1(a), we see that there are unnecessary checks against *loadchk.r W* and *store X*.

3.3.5 Sinking Clears

After all the movement of loads and stores is done, the last step is to remove overhead by sinking the *clear.r* instructions that have been added in the process. They are either sunk to a less frequently executed location or to the end of the atomic region, where they can be trivially eliminated. As we sink a *clear.r*, we are expanding the monitoring span of a *load.r* or *loadchk.r/rw* and this is always correct.

As the *clear.r* instructions are moved and eliminated, some *loadchk.r* instructions that used to interfere with each other no longer do. In this case, the *loadchk.r* instructions can be safely converted to *load.r* instructions. For example, consider the bottom right example of Figure 1(a). Initially, *loadchk.r A* had to be checked against *loadchk.r W* to make sure *clear.r A* does not clear the SR bit set by the latter erroneously. Once *clear.r A* is eliminated, *loadchk.r A* can safely be converted to *load.r A*. Now *load.r A* no longer checks against *loadchk.r W* and, therefore, can no longer cause extraneous rollbacks.

Vice versa, movement of *clear.r* instructions can cause *load.r* instructions that used to not interfere with each other to do so and in these cases, they have to be reverted back to *loadchk.r* instructions.

3.3.6 Discussion

Even though having only a single set of SR and SW bits in the atomic region leads to some imprecision, the imprecision is controlled by manipulating the SR bits and also by checking only relevant memory accesses. Importantly, correctness is still guaranteed even when there are multiple code motions. For the optimizations and applications that we studied, our experience is that this imprecision does not significantly restrict code motion or cause extraneous failures.

Also, having just one SR and SW bit per cache line leads to another type of imprecision — that due to false sharing. But false sharing does not compromise the correctness of our transformations; at worst, it causes extraneous rollbacks. The only case that needs special attention is when a *loadchk.r* instruction is converted to a *load.r* instruction because it does not interfere anymore with other *loadchk.r/rw* or *load.r* instructions. One might mistakenly think that proving a *no alias* relationship between two loads is sufficient to guarantee non-interference. But even if two loads do not alias per se, they might alias through false sharing. Hence, converting *loadchk.r* instructions based on the no alias assumption may still cause a problem when the *clear.r* is executed. Therefore, the compiler needs to either take false sharing into account when performing the conversion or not perform the conversion.

The only case where instructions are added for instrumentation purposes (other than *begin_atomic_opt* and *end_atomic_opt*) is when *clear.r* instructions are needed. In addition, even these can often be eliminated by sinking them to the end of the atomic region. Consequently, DeAliaser introduces negligible instrumentation overhead.

Overall, the DeAliaser design successfully allows multiple code motions inside an atomic region while minimizing instrumentation overhead. At the same time, the added hardware complexity over transactions is kept very small.

3.4 Application of Code Motion to Optimizations

While there are numerous compiler optimizations that can benefit from DeAliaser, we focus on LICM, GVN, and PRE to demonstrate its usefulness. These optimizations are already implemented as optimization passes in the LLVM compiler that we use for evaluating our scheme. GVN and PRE are performed simultaneously, as part of a single GVN/PRE pass. Hence, from here on, we use GVN to refer to the GVN/PRE pass with both optimizations.

LICM involves the hoisting and sinking of loads, and the sinking of stores, as described in Section 2.1.2. Hoists are moved to the preheader of the loop and sinks to the exit block of the loop. Since atomic regions are instrumented around loops, the span of code motion and the span of the atomic region are often identical, namely the loop. In this case, R_M and W_M are simply the entire set of memory locations read or written in the atomic region, and $R_{Monitored}$ and $W_{Monitored}$ are equivalent to these. According to the Hoist Load, Sink Load, and Sink Store rows of Figure 1(b), this means that no imprecision is introduced due to the alias checks. Also, since monitoring always ends at the end of the atomic region, *clear.r* instructions can always be eliminated.

GVN/PRE involves the hoisting and sinking of loads in order to eliminate computation of identical expressions, or to find the location where an expression can be computed less frequently. Unlike LICM, the code motion done by GVN might not span the entire loop if the redundancy is found within the body of the loop. Hence, imprecision in the alias checks may lead to some conservatism. However, in the applications studied, we find that this conservatism does not lead to any significant restriction in optimizations. Also, like in LICM, we are almost always able to eliminate the *clear.r*.

3.5 Transforming a Loop for Optimization

Before a loop can be optimized using DeAliaser, it needs to be instrumented with an atomic region. For this, *begin_atomic_opt* is inserted at the preheader of the loop and an *end_atomic_opt* is inserted at the exit block of the loop, so that the loop is enwrapped completely in an atomic region. Also, a safe version replica of the loop is created before any speculative optimizations are done. The safe version has no speculation, and no atomic regions are required. The failure of alias checks at any point in the atomic region triggers a rollback and a jump to the safe version. Once the safe version completes, execution jumps to the code after the loop.

The failure of an atomic region can also come from the overflow of the hardware resources that buffer the speculative writes and the read-monitored locations. To prevent overflows, we perform loop blocking, which reduces the footprint of an atomic region. After blocking, an atomic region is placed around the inner blocked loop. In the rare case where an atomic region still overflows, it can roll back and execute the safe version just like in the case of check failure.

3.6 Illustrative Example of LICM and GVN

We finish with an example of DeAliaser using LICM and GVN to optimize a loop. Figure 2(a) shows the initial loop. To see the capabilities of DeAliaser, assume that (i) a and b may alias with *p and *s; and (ii) *p, *q, and *s may alias with each other. Ideally, we would like to perform three code motion optimizations: 1) use LICM to hoist $b + 10$ to the beginning of the loop; 2) use

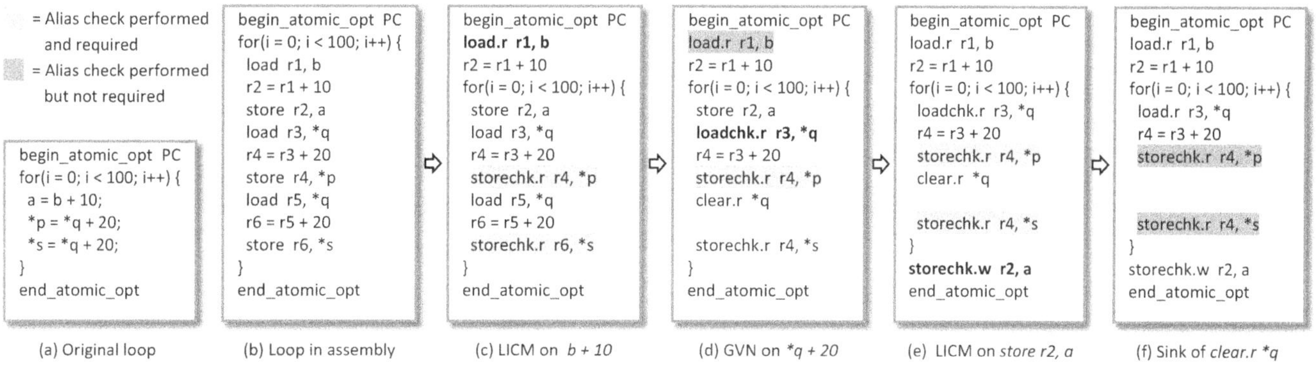

Figure 2. Example of a loop optimized with LICM and GVN using alias speculation through DeAliaser. Assume that (i) *a* and *b* may alias with **p* and **s*; and (ii) **p*, **q*, and **s* may alias with each other.

GVN to remove the second redundant computation of $*q + 20$; and 3) use LICM to sink the store to a to the end of the loop. Unfortunately, without DeAliaser, the compiler cannot perform any of these optimizations because of potential aliasing.

With DeAliaser, the compiler can do them all. To see how, we start with the original loop in assembly, as shown in Figure 2(b). The next few charts show each of the steps of the transformation in sequence. At each step, we show the moved memory access in bold, and the memory accesses checked by DeAliaser against the moved access in gray, using the same conventions as in Figure 1(a).

Figure 2(c) uses LICM to hoist $b + 10$ to the beginning of the loop. As per Section 3.3.1, we change all the store instructions in the loop that may alias to *load b* to *storechk.r*. This includes *store *p* and *store *s*. We change *load b* to *load.r b* rather than *loadchk.r b* because there is no other code motion optimization that can interfere. Also, we do not place a *clear.r* because it would go to the end of the loop.

Figure 2(d) uses GVN to remove the second, redundant $*q +$ 20. We hoist the second *load *q* and its computation above the *storechk.r *p*. The two hoisted instructions are combined with the ones that generated the same expression. In this load hoist, we do not change any stores because the one in the code motion span was already *storechk.r *p*. However, we need to replace the hoisted, combined *load *q* with *loadchk.r *q*. We use *loadchk.r* instead of *load.r* since it may alias with *load.r b* through false sharing (even if the compiler alias analysis thinks otherwise). In addition, we place the *clear.r *q* at the end of the code motion span.

Figure 2(e) uses LICM to sink *store a* to the end of the loop. Based on our assumptions in the example, we only need to speculate on store aliases. Hence, as per Section 3.3.4, the *store a* is sunk and replaced with *storechk.w a*. This instruction will be checked against all the stores in the loop.

Finally, Figure 2(f) reduces overhead by sinking and then eliminating the *clear.r *q* instruction. As per Section 3.3.5, we need to consider all the relevant new instructions added to the monitoring span of *loadchk.r *q*. We are including *storechk.r *s*, which may now produce extraneous failures. We are also adding *storechk.r *p* from *other* iterations, which may also create extraneous failures. Finally, because we have removed the *clear.r*, we can again use *load.r *q* rather than *loadchk.r *q*. The reason we had used *loadchk.r *q* was to ensure that the *clear.r* did not reset the SR bit set by *load.r b*. Retaining *loadchk.r *q* can only generate extraneous failures.

Beyond the false sharing issue with *load.r b*, the sinking and removal of *clear.r* is the only motion that adds imprecision to the checks. This motion is performed in the hope that the two stores will not alias with the load of $*q$ at runtime. However, if this does not turn out to be so, the *clear.r* must stay where it is.

Overall, the example shows how the compiler can leverage DeAliaser to perform multiple code motions in a single atomic region. A loop iteration started with 9 instructions and ended up with 4. Not a single instrumentation instruction was added.

4. Compiler Implementation

4.1 The Cost-Benefit Model

Until now, we have focused on how DeAliaser enables optimizations. But an equally important question is when are these optimizations beneficial. One can use heuristics for this purpose [12], but a more precise method is to profile the application. Fortunately, we can leverage the same hardware support that we use for DeAliaser to collect a profile with high efficiency. To decide whether to optimize a particular loop using DeAliaser, we estimate the following measures, in number of dynamic instructions for the average execution of the AR:

D: Number of instructions in the AR after applying DeAliaser.
I: Number of DeAliaser instrumentation instructions in the AR.
r: AR rollback rate.
R: Reduction in AR instructions through DeAliaser application.

For DeAliaser to be desirable, it should be that $R > I + D \times r$. It means that the benefit of the optimizations enabled by DeAliaser should outweigh the overhead due to instrumentation and rollbacks due to failures.

The number of dynamic instructions in an atomic region and the number of dynamic instructions reduced by optimizations can be obtained by branch profiling [43] or by taking measurements using hardware performance counters while profiling. DeAliaser instruction overhead is the two instructions *begin_atomic_opt* and *end_atomic_opt* at the beginning and end of the loop, plus any *clear.r* instructions that could not be eliminated.

There are two reasons why an atomic region can roll back: buffer overflows and alias speculation failures. We can eliminate virtually all of the buffer overflows through loop blocking. We measure the rate of remaining rollbacks due to speculation failures by maintaining two counters per atomic region while profiling: a success counter that is incremented at each successful commit and a failure counter that is incremented at every jump to the safe version.

We perform the optimizations incrementally for each code motion that requires speculation, and take profiling measurements to decide whether the motion was beneficial. All loops in an application can be profiled simultaneously in a single run. Hence, the number of profiling runs needed is the maximum number of speculative optimizations performed for a single loop.

4.2 Compiler Support

We modified the LLVM compiler [23] release 2.8 to implement DeAliaser. Considering how much effort it takes to correctly implement a complex alias analysis, the modifications that we did are quite straightforward. We performed four tasks in the compiler. One was to write a blocking pass for loops. We also wrote a pass that inserts loops in atomic regions, and creates the safe versions for the loops. Next, we modified the optimization passes to perform speculative code motions within the atomic regions and insert DeAliaser alias checking instructions appropriately. Lastly, we wrote a simple profiler pass that adds success and failure counters for each atomic region and generates a profile.

5. Evaluation

5.1 Experimental Setup

For our experiments, we use the applications in the SPEC INT2006 and SPEC FP2006 suites, except for *416.gamess* and *481.wrf*, which are in Fortran and our infrastructure does not handle well. We compile the applications using the modified LLVM compiler and, for each of the applications, produce three types of binaries: *BaselineAA*, *DSAA*, and *DeAliaser*.

BaselineAA is built by running LICM and GVN in sequence, using the default *Basic Alias Analysis* provided with the LLVM compiler, after running the standard -O3 set of optimizations. Basic Alias Analysis is what most applications compiled by LLVM use today. It is an aggressive, yet scalable alias analysis that uses knowledge about heap, stack, and global memory allocations, and structure field information.

DSAA is built by running LICM and GVN using the *Data Structure Alias Analysis*, which was first proposed by Lattner et al. [24]. Data Structure Alias Analysis is the most advanced alias analysis that has been implemented on LLVM and is shown to be more precise [24] than either Steensgaard's [37] or Andersen's [6] alias analyses. It is a heap-cloning algorithm that is flow-insensitive but context-sensitive and field-sensitive. It does unification to reduce memory usage, but we find that it is still not able to compile certain programs due to memory overflows. In fact, it fails to compile four benchmarks, namely *400.perlbench*, *403.gcc*, *483.xalancbmk*, and *445.gobmk*, with 4 GB of memory (the limit on our systems). Hence, we are not able to show results using *DSAA* for these four codes.

DeAliaser is built by running LICM and GVN using DeAliaser support to speculate on aliases. The Basic Alias Analysis is run before speculating using DeAliaser, to filter out the easily-provable alias relationships. Only the remaining may-aliases after running the Basic Alias Analysis are candidates for speculation. Also, loops with many iterations are blocked appropriately so that they do not overflow the speculative cache.

We run the applications on a cycle-level architecture simulator based on SESC [35], and built on top of Pin [27]. We model a uniprocessor desktop with an out-of-order core extended with DeAliaser instructions, and two levels of caches. The simulator simulates all latencies in detail, including memory latencies. It simulates the speculation resources needed to enable atomic regions. We use SR and SW bits at the granularity of cache lines, which is 64 bytes. Table 2 shows the parameters of the hardware.

The speculative L1 cache buffers all the speculatively-written data within an atomic region, as well as all the read-monitored cache lines (those with SR=1). The SR bit and SW bit in each cache line can be accessed and controlled by the DeAliaser ISA extensions. If the L1 cache overflows or an alias check fails, the atomic region is rolled back and the safe version is executed. Speculatively written cache lines are either marked non-speculative when the atomic region commits or are invalidated if the atomic region aborts. Read-monitored cache lines are unmarked when the atomic region either commits or aborts, or when a *clear.r* instruction is executed. In one of the experiments, we also use word-granularity SR and SW bits.

```
Processor:
  2-issue wide, out-of-order superscalar
  Functional units: 2 Int, 1 Ld/St, 1 Br, 2 FP
  I-window: 44 entries; Ld/St queue: 26 entries
Speculative L1 Cache:
  Round trip: 2 cycles
  Size, line, assoc.: 32KB, 64B, 8-way
  Speculative Rd/Wr bits: line granularity
L2 Cache:
  Round trip: 10 cycles
  Size, line, assoc.: 512KB, 64B, 8-way
Memory round trip: 300 cycles; Bus with: 32B
```

Table 2. Parameters of the hardware simulated.

We also use the simulator mentioned above to run the alias profiling phase for *DeAliaser*. We use the *train* input set provided in SPEC CPU2006 for profiling, and the *ref* input set for performance measurement. For the programs we tested, we find that the results of alias analysis profiling are not very sensitive to the input set.

5.2 Optimization Examples

We start the evaluation by showing two examples of real code where *DeAliaser* produces more efficient code than *BaselineAA* or *DSAA*. Figure 3 shows one loop in *433.milc* optimized using LICM, and Figure 4 shows another loop in *410.bzip2* optimized using a combination of LICM and GVN. In both cases, we show the loop before and after applying *DeAliaser*.

```
for(i=0;i<3;i++) {
  for(j=0;j<3;j++) {
    ...
    br=b->e[j][0].real;
    ...
    c->e[i][j].real=cr;
  }
}
```

(a)

```
for(i=0;i<3;i++) {
  ...
  br0=b->e[0][0].real;
  br1=b->e[1][0].real;
  br2=b->e[2][0].real;
  ...
  c->e[i][0].real=cr0;
  c->e[i][1].real=cr1;
  c->e[i][2].real=cr2;
}
```

(b)

```
begin_atomic_opt(Safe_Loop_PC)
load.r real0, b->e[0][0].real;
load.r real1, b->e[1][0].real;
load.r real2, b->e[2][0].real;
for(i=0;i<3;i++) {
  ...
  br0 = real0;
  br1 = real1;
  br2 = real2;
  ...
  storechk.r cr0, c->e[i][0].real
  store      cr1, c->e[i][1].real
  store      cr2, c->e[i][2].real
}
end_atomic_opt
```

(c)

Figure 3. Loop in function mult_su3_na(...) of *433.milc* before transformation (a), after loop unrolling (b), and after applying *DeAliaser* with LICM (c).

BaselineAA, *DSAA*, and *DeAliaser* unroll the loop in Figure 3(a) three times, to produce the singly-nested loop in Figure 3(b). After

Benchmark	Dynamic Instructions				Code Optimized Inside Loop	
	BaselineAA or *DSAA*	DeAliaser		Reduction (%)	BaselineAA or *DSAA*	DeAliaser
		Total	Overhead			
433.milc	448	343	2	23	Calculations of addresses for field $real$ in $b \rightarrow e[0][0]$, $b \rightarrow e[1][0]$, $b \rightarrow e[2][0]$ hoisted.	All hoists in BaselineAA. Loads of field $real$ in $b \rightarrow e[0][0]$, $b \rightarrow e[1][0]$, $b \rightarrow e[2][0]$ hoisted.
401.bzip2	950	905	5	5	None.	Load of address for $s \rightarrow tt$ hoisted. Redundant load of field $s \rightarrow cftab[uc]$ removed.

Table 3. Analysis of the examples shown in Figure 3 and Figure 4.

this, *BaselineAA* and *DSAA* are able to hoist out the address computations for the fields in $b \rightarrow e[0][0]$, $b \rightarrow e[1][0]$, and $b \rightarrow e[2][0]$, but not the loads of the fields themselves. The address computations can be hoisted because the dimensions of b are statically defined, but the loads cannot be hoisted because *BaselineAA* and *DSAA* cannot prove that they do not alias with the updates to the fields in $c \rightarrow e[i][0]$. *DeAliaser* places an atomic region around the entire loop and speculatively hoists the loads. We show the code in Figure 3(c). There is a single *storechk.r* to $c \rightarrow e[i][0]$. It turns out that b and c are always distinct locations.

```
for (i = 0; i < nblock; i++) {
  uc = (UChar)(s->tt[i] & 0xff);
  s->tt[s->cftab[uc]] |= (i << 8);
  s->cftab[uc]++;
}
```

(a)

```
for (i = 0; i < nblock; i+=50) {
  begin_atomic_opt(Safe_Loop_PC)
  load.r r1, &(s->tt[0]);
  for (ii = i; ii < i+50 && ii < nblock; ii++) {
    uc = (UChar)(r1[ii] & 0xff);
    load.r r2, s->cftab[uc];
    r3 = r1[r2];
    r3 |= (ii << 8);
    storechk.r r3, r1[r2];
    r2++;
    store r2, s->cftab[uc];
  }
  end_atomic_opt
}
```

(b)

Figure 4. Loop in subroutine BZ2_decompress() of *401.bzip2* before (a) and after (b) applying *DeAliaser* with LICM and GVN.

For *401.bzip2* in Figure 4(a), there is not much that *BaselineAA* or *DSAA* can do in terms of LICM or GVN, in spite of the visibly-redundant computations $s \rightarrow tt$ and $s \rightarrow cftab[uc]$. Neither analysis can prove that the store to $s \rightarrow tt[s \rightarrow cftab[uc]]$ does not alias with the loads for either of these expressions. However, in Figure 4(b), *DeAliaser* can perform both LICM and GVN after blocking the loop and placing an atomic region around the inner loop.

Through LICM, *DeAliaser* hoists the load of $s \rightarrow tt$ out of the loop and stores the value into r1, which gets reused across iterations. Also, through GVN, it stores the value of the first load of $s \rightarrow cftab[uc]$ into r2 and reuses it in place of the second redundant load. In the process, the aliasing store to $s \rightarrow tt[s \rightarrow cftab[uc]]$ is replaced with a *storechk.r* and the moved loads are replaced with *load.r* instructions. The store to $s \rightarrow cftab[uc]$, which is in the span of LICM for the load of $s \rightarrow tt$, is proven not to alias with that load by the Basic Alias Analysis. Therefore, it is left as is. Also, *clear.r* instructions are introduced for each monitored load to mark when the monitoring ends, and they are eventually eliminated.

Specifically, the *clear.r* for $s \rightarrow tt$ is placed at the end of the loop, where the monitoring ends, and is trivially removed. The *clear.r* for $s \rightarrow cftab[uc]$ is originally placed at the location where the redundant load used to be, which is right before *r2++*, but is also sunk out of the loop and eliminated. This is possible because even though the monitored load always aliases with $store\ r2, s \rightarrow cftab[uc]$, the latter instruction is a regular store and does not check the SR bit. As mentioned, the instruction could remain a regular store and not get converted to a *storechk.r* thanks to the Basic Alias Analysis. This is a good example of cooperation between runtime alias speculation and static alias analysis to achieve the best outcome.

Table 3 presents an analysis of the optimizations performed on these two loops. Columns 2-5 show what effect optimizations have on the average dynamic instruction count of each atomic region. Column 2 refers to the dynamic instruction count when compiled using the *BaselineAA* or *DSAA* configurations (they do not actually contain atomic regions, but we count the corresponding region of code). Column 3 refers to the dynamic instruction count when compiled using the *DeAliaser* configuration. Column 4 shows how many instructions in Column 3 are for the purposes of enabling the *DeAliaser* optimization, such as *begin_atomic_opt*, *end_atomic_opt*, *clear.r*, and instructions needed to block the loop. Column 5 shows the percentage of instruction reduction for *DeAliaser* when compared to *BaselineAA/DSAA*. For both loops, applying *DeAliaser* results in a reduction in the number of instructions, namely 23% for *433.milc* and 5% for *401.bzip2*. Columns 6-7 show the actual code movements that occur for the *BaselineAA/DSAA* and *DeAliaser* configurations.

5.3 Alias Analysis Results

Figure 6 measures the quality of alias analysis responses generated by each alias analysis configuration, when paired with the LICM pass. The results shown are the percentage of queries that return a *may alias*, *no alias*, or *must alias* response among the total set of queries thrown by the LICM client pass. In the figure, *B*, *D*, and *A* refer to the *BaselineAA*, *DSAA*, and *DeAliaser* configurations, respectively. For *DeAliaser*, *no alias* means that the profiler recommended a speculation be performed, although during the execution, we may suffer occasional aborts.

We are unable to show bars for *400.perlbench*, *403.gcc*, *443.gobmk*, and *483.xalancbmk* for *DSAA* due to reasons mentioned in Section 5.1. For these benchmarks, we use the *BaselineAA* results when calculating the averages. This methodology is used throughout the evaluation.

Alias analyses return a *may alias* response when they can neither prove that a pair of references must alias nor not alias. Hence, the fraction of *may alias* responses is a measure of their imprecision. In the figure, we see that *DeAliaser* leads to a drastic reduction in the fraction of *may alias* responses in all of the benchmarks. All of the *may alias* responses eliminated are translated into *no alias* responses, thereby recommending code motion for LICM. We also see that *DeAliaser* is not able to eliminate all of the *may alias* responses. This is because some pairs of references actually do *may alias* during execution — that is, they reference the same location a noticeable number of times. Finally, recall that DeAliaser is un-

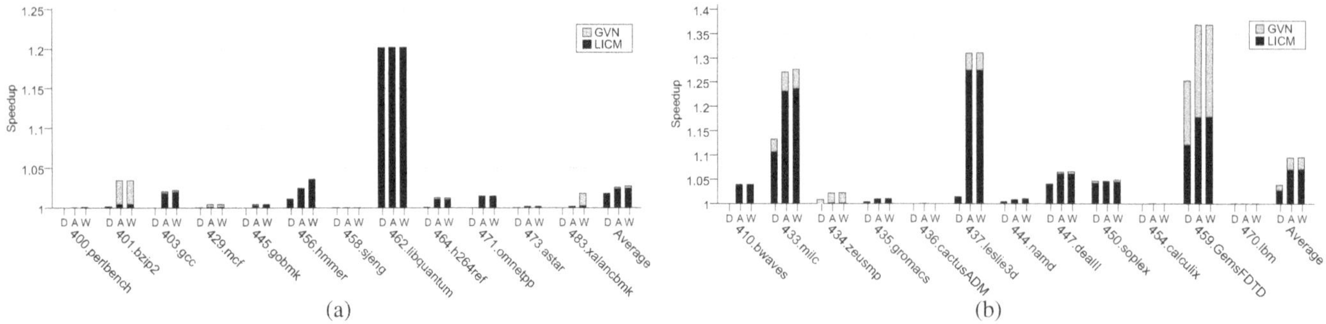

Figure 5. Speedups of *DSAA* (D), *DeAliaser* (A), and word-granularity *DeAliaser* (W) over *BaselineAA* for SPEC INT2006 (a) and SPEC FP2006 (b).

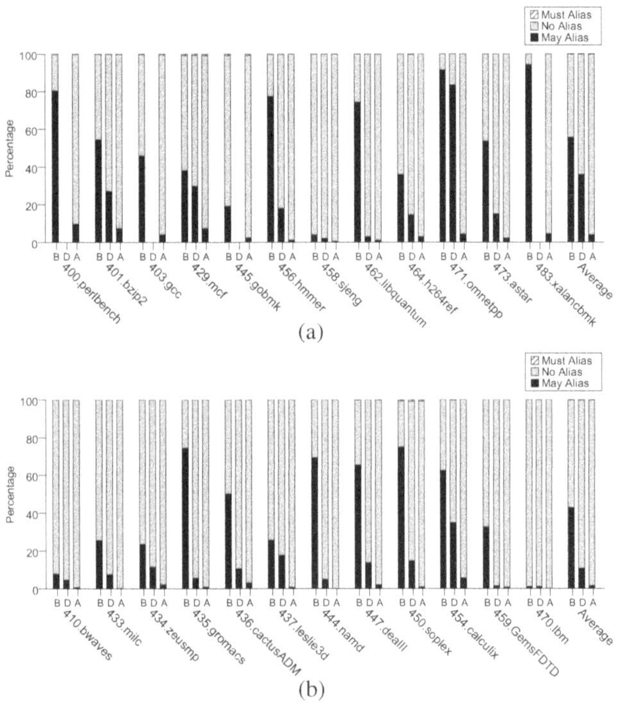

Figure 6. Fraction of alias queries performed by LICM that return a *may alias*, *no alias*, or *must alias* response for SPEC INT2006 (a) and SPEC FP2006 (b). In the figure, B, D, and A stand for *BaselineAA*, *DSAA*, and *DeAliaser*.

able to conclude for sure that two references alias with each other. Hence, some of the remaining *may aliases* in the *DeAliaser* bars may correspond to pairs of references that *must alias*.

The results for GVN are omitted in the interest of space, but follow the same trend.

5.4 Performance

To assess the impact of DeAliaser, we report the execution speedups (Figure 5) and the reduction in dynamic instruction count (Figure 7). Figure 5 shows the benchmark execution speedups measured using our architectural simulator. We show the speedups of *DSAA* (D), *DeAliaser* (A), and word-granularity *DeAliaser* (W) over *BaselineAA*. Word-granularity *DeAliaser* is like *DeAliaser* except that, to detect aliased accesses, caches keep speculative read and write bits *per word*. The speedups are broken down into the contribution of LICM and GVN.

The figure shows that *DeAliaser* enables significant speedups in multiple benchmarks, beyond what can be provided using *DSAA*. On average, *DeAliaser* speeds-up SPEC FP2006 benchmarks by 9% and SPEC INT2006 benchmarks by about 3% over *BaselineAA*. On the other hand, *DSAA* manages an average of 4% for SPEC FP2006 and 2% for SPEC INT2006. In both configurations, most of the speedups come from LICM, although GVN also has a significant impact in benchmarks such as *401.bzip2* and *459.GemsFDTD*.

There is barely any difference between the speedups achieved using word-granularity SR and SW bits and those using line-granularity bits. The granularity of access bits determines the accuracy of alias checks performed by hardware; larger granularity can cause them to return an aliased result due to false sharing. This can potentially stifle optimizations by returning less accurate information. However, the results show that having one SR and SW bit per word is unnecessary, when using 64-byte cache lines.

In general, better alias analysis may not necessarily translate into better performance. This is because even a single alias inside a loop can prevent code optimization. In addition, even if the analysis can prove that none of the references alias with each other, there simply might not be opportunities for optimization in that loop.

Figure 7 shows the reduction in the dynamic instruction count of the benchmarks categorized by non-memory, load, and store instructions. *B*, *D*, and *A* again refer to the *BaselineAA*, *DSAA*, and *DeAliaser* configurations. We can see that, across the benchmarks, the reduction in the instruction count is loosely correlated with the speedups. On average, *DeAliaser* reduces the instruction count by 9% in the SPEC FP2006 benchmarks and by about 3% in the SPEC INT2006 benchmarks over *BaselineAA*.

The most marked reduction is in the number of load instructions. The hoisting of load instructions that read loop-invariant values from memory is responsible for the majority of the reduction. There is also some reduction in non-memory instructions, especially in *437.leslie3d*. This is due to the movement of the address calculation for matrix element accesses.

Store instructions show some reduction in *437.leslie3d* and *433.milc*. This is due to two reasons. The first one is the sinking of stores to the exit of the loop. The second one is the reduction in register pressure due to having computation moved out of the loop, leading to fewer spills. However, register spills can also be increased with LICM, by increasing the live ranges of the registers that contain the values of hoisted loads. This was the case in *459.GemsFDTD*, but the reduction in load instructions more than made up for it.

5.5 Atomic Region Aborts

In our *DeAliaser* experiments so far, the use of the cost-benefit model of Section 4.1 has resulted in very few atomic region aborts. To study a more aggressive environment, we scrap the model and

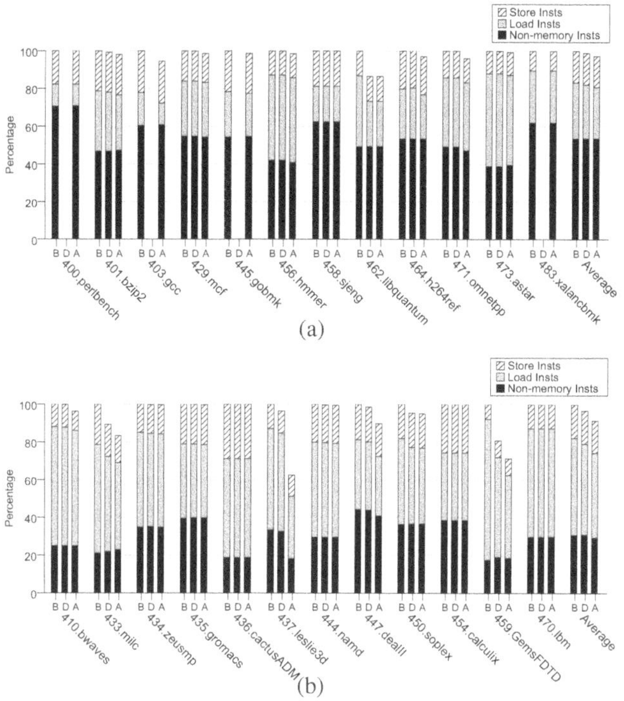

Figure 7. Dynamic instruction count of *BaselineAA* (B), *DSAA* (D), and *DeAliaser* (A) after LICM and GVN for SPEC INT2006 (a) and SPEC FP2006 (b). The bars are broken down by category and normalized to *BaselineAA*.

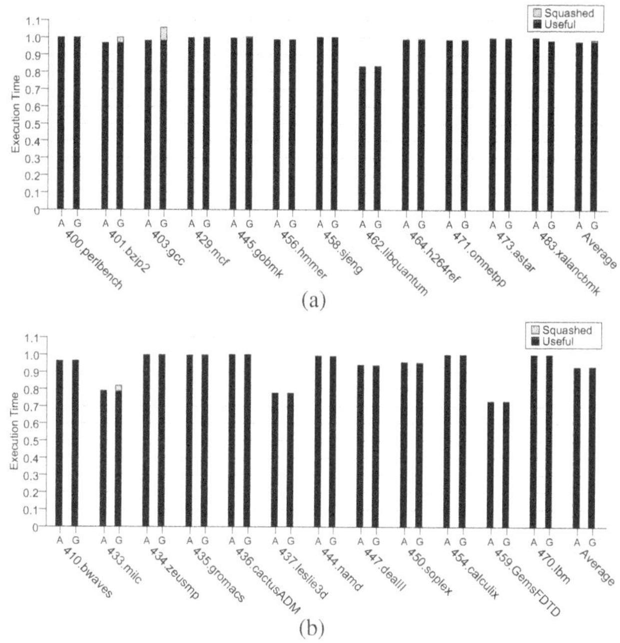

Figure 8. Execution time of *DeAliaser* (A) and *DeAliaser_Aggressive* (G) for SPEC INT2006 (a) and SPEC FP2006 (b). The bars are broken down by category and normalized to *BaselineAA*.

speculate on all alias pairs that *may alias*, regardless of the cost. We call this configuration *DeAliaser_Aggressive*.

The resulting execution time is shown in Figure 8, alongside that of the original *DeAliaser*, normalized to *BaselineAA*. The *Useful* component of each bar is the time spent making forward progress, while the *Squashed* component is the time spent executing instructions that are aborted due to aliasing. We see that the *Useful* component does not show any change from *DeAliaser* to *DeAliaser_Aggressive*, meaning that barely any new optimizations were enabled. This was expected, given that there was preciously little remaining *may alias* results to speculate upon (Figure 6). However, the few new optimizations that are enabled sometimes do cause abort overhead in *401.bzip2*, *403.gcc*, and *433.milc*. For some benchmarks, it is important for the compiler to have a cost model in order to avoid slowdowns.

5.6 Commit Latency Sensitivity

For our performance results in Section 5.4, we assumed that both *begin_atomic_opt* and *end_atomic_opt* take just a single cycle to complete. In different systems, these instructions may take different times and, in particular, the *end_atomic_opt* that commits an atomic region, could take significantly more time. In Figure 9, we do a sensitivity study on how much our speedups depend on commit latency. In the figure, (A), (B), and (C) show the speedups of *DeAliaser* over *BaselineAA* when assuming commit latencies of 1, 10, and 100 cycles, respectively. The figure shows that the speedups for SPEC FP2006 benchmarks barely change even as we increase the commit latency to 100 cycles, but SPEC INT2006 benchmarks are more sensitive. At 100 cycles, the average speedup for SPEC INT2006 is halved. This is because SPEC FP2006 benchmarks have much larger atomic regions, which are better able to amortize commit overhead, as can be seen next.

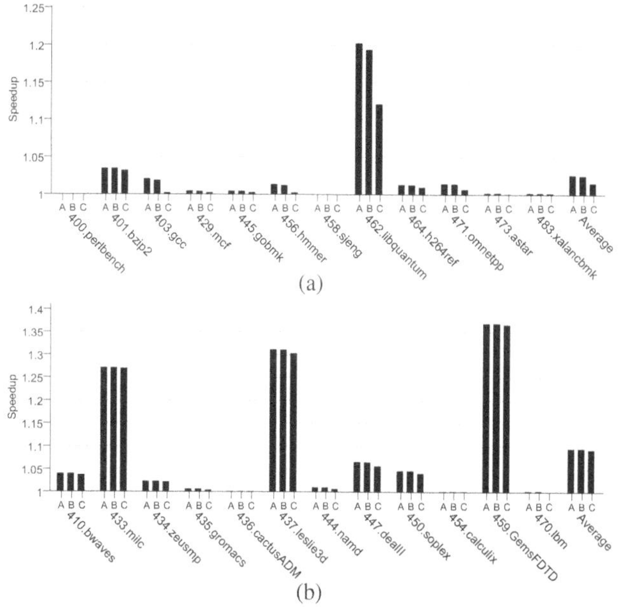

Figure 9. Speedups of *DeAliaser* with commit latencies 1 cycle (A), 10 cycles (B), and 100 cycles (C) over *BaselineAA* for SPEC INT2006 (a) and SPEC FP2006 (b).

Benchmark	Coverage(%)	Dynamic Instructions per Atomic Region							L1 Occ. (%)
		BaselineAA	DSAA		DeAliaser		ALAT		
			Insts	Reduc.(%)	Insts	Reduc.(%)	Insts	Reduc.(%)	
401.bzip2	9	933	933	0	734	21	930	0	2
403.gcc	23	439	439	0	337	23	440	0	2
429.mcf	9	1228	1228	0	1053	14	1207	2	0
445.gobmk	12	1229	1229	0	1082	12	1218	1	2
456.hmmer	8	8580	8535	1	6935	19	7787	9	1
462.libquantum	69	1401	1122	20	1124	20	1405	0	2
464.h264ref	8	848	843	1	549	35	811	4	1
471.omnetpp	73	3185	3185	0	3014	5	3028	5	5
473.astar	4	528	528	0	426	19	623	-18	19
483.xalancbmk	1	1171	1171	0	1073	8	1171	0	4
INT Average	18	1702	1674	2	1434	16	1628	4	4
410.bwaves	72	6261	6259	0	5941	5	6101	3	1
433.milc	54	16027	13150	18	11113	31	14620	9	6
434.zeusmp	5	9005	8811	2	8415	7	8879	1	7
435.gromacs	3	2592	2514	3	2257	13	2566	1	4
436.cactusADM	0	3072	3072	0	1228	60	2282	26	1
437.leslie3d	58	5331	5113	4	1853	65	3739	30	4
444.namd	38	24907	24757	1	24574	1	24915	0	14
447.dealII	36	2713	2607	4	1957	28	2362	13	2
450.soplex	25	1377	1121	19	1104	20	1395	-1	5
454.calculix	0	1002	995	1	882	12	995	1	3
459.GemsFDTD	64	28270	20054	29	15571	45	26776	5	21
FP Average	29	8379	7371	12	6241	26	7885	6	6

Table 4. Average dynamic instruction statistics per atomic region for each benchmark.

5.7 Characterization

In this section, we characterize the runtime behavior of the atomic regions instrumented by *DeAliaser*. Dynamic atomic regions are characterized in terms of coverage, instruction count, and hardware speculation and conflict detection resources needed. The data is shown in Table 4. In the table, there are three benchmarks missing (*400.perlbench*, *458.sjeng*, and *470.lbm*) because *DeAliaser* does not instrument any atomic regions.

Column 2 of the table shows the percentage of dynamic instructions that were covered with atomic regions. We can see that the average is 18% for SPEC INT2006 and 29% for SPEC FP2006. Column 3 shows the dynamic instruction count per atomic region for *BaselineAA* after performing LICM and GVN. As mentioned before, *BaselineAA* does not actually contain atomic regions, but we count the number of instructions in the corresponding loop. We can see that we start with sizable atomic regions. The average size is 1702 instructions for SPEC INT2006 and 8379 instructions for SPEC FP2006. This is desirable, to amortize atomic region instrumentation overhead.

Columns 4-5 show information pertaining to the average atomic region in *DSAA*: Column 4 shows the dynamic instruction count, and Column 5 shows the percentage of instruction reduction compared to *BaselineAA*. Columns 6-7 shows the same information for *DeAliaser*. The dynamic instruction count for *DeAliaser* includes overhead for DeAliaser instrumentation and loop blocking. For the vast majority of cases, the only DeAliaser instrumentation required was the *begin_atomic_opt* and *end_atomic_opt* instructions. With *DeAliaser*, we obtain average instruction reductions of 16% for SPEC INT2006 and 26% for SPEC FP2006. For *DeAliaser* to show good speedups, both the instruction reduction percentage and the coverage have to be high. This occurs in *462.libquantum*, *433.milc*, *437.leslie3d*, and *459.GemsFDTD*.

Columns 8-9 show, for comparison, dynamic instruction count and percentage of instruction reduction had we used an ALAT. Although the ALAT can perform all the load hoisting optimizations done by *DeAliaser*, it also requires lots of extra alias check instructions such as ld.c or chk.a to be performed, which cancel out much of the instruction reduction from optimization. This results from the fact that a ld.c or chk.a check instruction must be placed at the original location of every hoisted load. Sometimes, this even leads to a net increase in the total number of instructions. It occurs because the hoisting induces register spills.

Column 10 shows the average fraction of the 32KB speculative L1 cache that is used per atomic region to buffer speculatively written lines and read-monitored lines. In many cases, the L1 occupancy rate is very small compared to the size of the atomic region. For example, *456.hmmer* has 6935 instructions per atomic region, but the occupancy rate is just 1%. In a typical transaction used in transactional memory, most of the lines that need to be buffered are speculatively read lines, since usually loads are more prevalent than stores. In the case of *DeAliaser*, read-monitored lines are only a small fraction of the lines read in the atomic region, which helps reduce the footprint.

6. Discussion

6.1 Limitations due to Imprecision

In Section 3.3, we discussed the potential limitations of DeAliaser due to having just a single set of SR and SW bits to monitor memory locations, and not being able to manipulate SW bits due to rollback requirements. These limitations make the alias checks more imprecise by stifling optimizations.

Adding extra hardware to the upcoming transactional memory systems can help in easing some of these limitations. One addition with significant impact would be to add support for one extra monitored write set, decoupled from rollback requirements, that the compiler can freely manipulate. This can be easily done by adding one extra SW bit per cache line to mark monitored write locations. With this, the precision of alias checks for load sinking, store hoisting, and store sinking that use the $W_{Monitored}$ set would be dramatically improved (refer to Figure 1(b)).

Beyond this, adding more hardware to increase the number of monitored read or write sets can progressively increase the precision of alias checks. Ideally, we would like as many monitored sets as the number of code motions. This can be accomplished with one SR and SW bit-pair in cache lines for each code motion. However, a more efficient implementation may be to use hardware signatures that encode addresses (e.g., [28, 38, 39]).

6.2 Isolation Issues

Repurposing the SR bits for load monitoring means forfeiting the isolation semantics of atomic regions. Let us refer to the atomic regions created using DeAliaser's *begin_atomic_opt* instruction as *opt* atomic regions, and those created using the conventional Transactional Memory (TM) *begin_atomic* instruction as *sync* atomic regions. The issue arises when a remote processor's write conflicts with an address read by a local *opt* atomic region with a non-monitored load. Since the local SR bit is not set, the local *opt* atomic region would still commit, compromising isolation.

The simple solution to this problem is not to use *opt* atomic regions for the synchronization purposes that *sync* atomic regions serve in TM. An atomic region should be used for either optimization or synchronization, but not both.

But what if an *opt* atomic region is nested inside a *sync* atomic region? If nested atomic regions are flattened, as is done in many current systems, manipulation of the SR bits in the inner atomic region would compromise the isolation of the outer *sync* atomic region. To avoid this problem, nested *opt* atomic regions should automatically trigger a jump to the safe version with no DeAliaser instrumentation.

What if a *sync* atomic region is nested inside an *opt* atomic region? To avoid compromising the isolation of the inner *sync* atomic region, all the loads in the inner atomic region should set the SR bit. This would make sure that any read memory conflict in the inner atomic region would trigger a rollback. While this may increase the chances of alias speculation failure in the outer *opt* atomic region, correctness is guaranteed. If the increase in failure rate is too high, it would be detected in the profiling phase and the *opt* atomic region would not be instrumented.

Adding hardware support for maintaining a monitored read set separate from the speculative read set (e.g., by adding one extra bit in each cache line separate from the SR bit) solves this issue.

6.3 Applying to Dynamic Compilation

Although our discussion has focused on the LLVM static compiler, we believe that there is fertile ground for applying alias speculation to dynamic compilers. Dynamic compilers have largely avoided complex alias analyses such as Data Structure Alias Analysis because of the unacceptable compilation overhead. However, a dynamic analysis such as the one in DeAliaser that leverages profiling information is a perfect fit for application to dynamic compilers. Moreover, as discussed in Section 4.1, DeAliaser profiling imposes only a very small overhead.

7. Related Work

7.1 Optimizations using Atomic Regions

Speculative code optimizations in atomic regions have been applied to control speculation over a hot trace of code [15, 29, 30, 32]. When these traces of code are generated to enable on-the-fly optimization of uops translated from machine instructions [7, 8, 15, 29], the atomic regions are also used to support precise exceptions at the machine level. In addition, atomic regions are a good way of hiding code movements, which might violate the machine memory model, from other processors. With this support, a compiler can enforce a strict memory model like sequential consistency on a relaxed-consistency machine, and still attain high performance [4]. Continued interest in atomic regions has also led to work that proposes ways to deal with the limitation of hardware speculation resources, either through short rollbacks [8] or smart monitoring of the resources [7].

7.2 Alias Speculation

There is a significant body of work that attempts to perform alias analysis speculatively, relying on runtime checks to verify them in similar ways as DeAliaser. These checks can either be done purely in software [31], or with the assistance of special hardware such as in Itanium's Advanced Load Address Table (ALAT) [14, 25, 26] and in Transmeta's binary translator [15, 21].

The ALAT is a hardware table that monitors accesses to memory locations. It is used for hoisting load instructions across potentially aliasing stores. A check instruction is placed at the location of the original load that verifies in hardware that no intervening stores aliased with the hoisted load. Since the span of code motion is clearly demarcated by the hoisted load and the check, precise alias checks on multiple code motions are naturally supported. However, the need to perform recovery in software prevents certain optimizations from being performed and the engineering complexity discourages compiler writers from implementing aggressive optimizations. Also, the frequency of check instructions cost both performance and energy.

Perhaps the work that bears the most resemblance to ours is the work on Transmeta's Code Morphing Software (CMS) binary translator [15, 21]. Just like DeAliaser, CMS leverages atomic regions to perform alias speculation. Load hoisting is used to overlap load latencies with computation in their statically-scheduled VLIW hardware. However, it is unclear from the ISA extensions that the company published, how multiple spans of code motion can be supported inside a single atomic region. This support is crucial for aggressive optimization. Moreover, to our knowledge, the exact details of how CMS takes advantage of those extensions have never been published in the literature. In addition, note that neither CMS or the ALAT supports the movement of stores.

In this paper, we discuss many compiler as well as hardware aspects of the problem of doing alias speculation using atomic regions and propose a solution that can move both loads and stores in a general way. We also discuss ways to minimize imprecision in the face of multiple code motions inside an atomic region.

Another related approach has been to have the hardware monitor alias speculation violations and silently patch up the state when it happens, unbeknownst to software and even without having to rollback execution, such as in CRegs [13] and in the Store-Load Address Table (SLAT) [33]. While this is an attractive idea, the complexity of patching up the state is analogous to the job of generating recovery code in the compiler, and doing this in hardware clearly has its limits. Hence, the optimization that they support is limited to speculative register promotion.

8. Conclusions

This paper proposed, for the first time, to expose the alias checking capabilities present in upcoming transactional memory systems for the purpose of alias speculation. This is accomplished with a set of novel instructions and hardware extensions. We call our approach DeAliaser. The paper also presented how these instructions are used in a source-level compiler to enable (i) code motion on both loads and stores, and (ii) multiple code motions in a single atomic region with minimal loss of precision. The latter is crucial for aggressive optimization. DeAliaser's capabilities are attained by simply exposing the existing checkpointing and memory conflict checking facilities of atomic regions to the compiler. No significant hardware complexity was added to existing atomic regions.

We evaluated LICM, GVN, and PRE optimizations enhanced for DeAliaser in the LLVM compiler. Our work resulted in an average application speedup of 9% for SPEC FP2006 benchmarks and 3% for SPEC INT2006 benchmarks, over the application of the baseline LLVM alias analysis. We also showed a detailed characterization of the atomic regions formed by DeAliaser, and examples of real code where the optimizations happened.

Acknowledgements

This work was supported in part by NSF under grants CCF-1012759 and CNS-1116237, and by Intel under the Illinois-Intel Parallelism Center (I2PC).

References

[1] *IBM System Blue Gene Solution: Blue Gene/Q Application Development Manual*. IBM Corp., March 2012.

[2] *Intel Architecture Instruction Set Extensions Programmig Reference*. Intel Corporation, February 2012.

[3] *POWER ISA Transactional Memory*. IBM Corp., December 2012.

[4] W. Ahn, S. Qi, J.-W. Lee, M. Nicolaides, X. Fang, J. Torrellas, D. Wong, and S. Midkiff. BulkCompiler: High-Performance Sequential Consistency through Cooperative Compiler and Hardware Support. In *International Symposium on Microarchitecture*, December 2009.

[5] B. Alpern, M. N. Wegman, and F. K. Zadeck. Detecting Equality of Variables in Programs. In *Symposium on Principles of Programming Languages*, January 1988.

[6] L. O. Andersen. *Program Analysis and Specialization for the C Programming Language*. PhD thesis, Univ. of Copenhagen, 1994.

[7] E. Borin, Y. Wu, M. Breternitz, and C. Wang. LAR-CC: Large Atomic Regions with Conditional Commits. In *International Symposium on Code Generation and Optimization*, April 2011.

[8] E. Borin, Y. Wu, C. Wang, W. Liu, M. Breternitz, Jr., S. Hu, E. Natanzon, S. Rotem, and R. Rosner. TAO: Two-level Atomicity for Dynamic Binary Optimizations. In *International Symposium on Code Generation and Optimization*, April 2010.

[9] V. T. Chakaravarthy. New Results on the Computability and Complexity of Points–to Analysis. In *International Symposium on Principles of Programming Languages*, January 2003.

[10] J. Chung, L. Yen, S. Diestelhorst, M. Pohlack, M. Hohmuth, D. Christie, and D. Grossman. ASF: AMD64 Extension for Lock-Free Data Structures and Transactional Memory. In *International Symposium on Microarchitecture*, December 2010.

[11] C. Click. Azul's Experiences with Hardware Transactional Memory. In *HP Labs Workshop on Transactional Memory*, January 2009.

[12] J. Da Silva and J. G. Steffan. A Probabilistic Pointer Analysis for Speculative Optimizations. In *International Conference on Architectural Support for Programming Languages and Operating Systems*, October 2006.

[13] P. Dahl and M. O'Keefe. Reducing Memory Traffic with CRegs. In *International Symposium on Microarchitecture*, December 1994.

[14] X. Dai, A. Zhai, W.-C. Hsu, and P.-C. Yew. A General Compiler Framework for Speculative Optimizations Using Data Speculative Code Motion. In *International Symposium on Code Generation and Optimization*, March 2005.

[15] J. Dehnert et al. The Transmeta Code Morphing Software: Using Speculation, Recovery, and Adaptive Retranslation to Address Real-Life Challenges. In *International Symposium on Code Generation and Optimization*, March 2003.

[16] A. Diwan, K. S. McKinley, and J. E. B. Moss. Type-based Alias Analysis. In *International Conference on Programming Language Design and Implementation*, May 1998.

[17] R. Ghiya, D. Lavery, and D. Sehr. On the Importance of Points-to Analysis and Other Memory Disambiguation Methods for C Programs. In *International Conference on Programming Language Design and Implementation*, June 2001.

[18] M. Hind. Pointer Analysis: Haven't We Solved this Problem Yet? In *Workshop on Program Analysis for Software Tools and Engineering*, June 2001.

[19] S. Horwitz. Precise Flow-insensitive May-alias Analysis is NP-hard. *ACM Transactions on Programming Languages and Systems*, January 1997.

[20] R. Kennedy, S. Chan, S.-M. Liu, R. Lo, P. Tu, and F. Chow. Partial Redundancy Elimination in SSA Form. *ACM Transactions on Programming Languages and Systems*, May 1999.

[21] A. Klaiber. The Technology Behind Crusoe Processors. Technical report, Transmeta, January 2000.

[22] W. Landi. Undecidability of Static Analysis. *ACM Letters on Programming Language System*, December 1992.

[23] C. Lattner and V. Adve. LLVM: a Compilation Framework for Lifelong Program Analysis Transformation. In *International Symposium on Code Generation and Optimization*, March 2004.

[24] C. Lattner, A. Lenharth, and V. Adve. Making Context-Sensitive Points-to Analysis with Heap Cloning Practical For The Real World. In *International Conference on Programming Language Design and Implementation*, June 2007.

[25] J. Lin, T. Chen, W.-C. Hsu, and P.-C. Yew. Speculative Register Promotion Using Advanced Load Address Table (ALAT). In *International Symposium on Code Generation and Optimization*, March 2003.

[26] J. Lin, T. Chen, W.-C. Hsu, P.-C. Yew, R. D.-C. Ju, T.-F. Ngai, and S. Chan. A Compiler Framework for Speculative Analysis and Optimizations. In *International Conference on Programming Language Design and Implementation*, June 2003.

[27] C.-K. Luk, R. Cohn, R. Muth, H. Patil, A. Klauser, G. Lowney, S. Wallace, V. J. Reddi, and K. Hazelwood. Pin: Building Customized Program Analysis Tools with Dynamic Instrumentation. In *International Conference on Programming Language Design and Implementation*, June 2005.

[28] C. Minh, M. Trautmann, J. Chung, A. McDonald, N. Bronson, J. Casper, C. Kozyrakis, and K. Olukotun. An Effective Hybrid Transactional Memory System with Strong Isolation Guarantees. In *International Symposium on Computer Architecture*, June 2007.

[29] N. Neelakantam, D. R. Ditzel, and C. Zilles. A Real System Evaluation of Hardware Atomicity for Software Speculation. In *International Conference on Architectural Support for Programming Languages and Operating Systems*, March 2010.

[30] N. Neelakantam, R. Rajwar, S. Srinivas, U. Srinivasan, and C. Zilles. Hardware Atomicity for Reliable Software Speculation. In *International Symposium on Computer Architecture*, June 2007.

[31] A. Nicolau. Run-Time Disambiguation: Coping with Statically Unpredictable Dependencies. *IEEE Transactions on Computers*, May 1989.

[32] S. Patel and S. Lumetta. rePLay: A Hardware Framework for Dynamic Optimization. *IEEE Transactions on Computers*, June 2001.

[33] M. Postiff, D. Greene, and T. Mudge. The Store-load Address Table and Speculative Register Promotion. In *International Symposium on Microarchitecture*, December 2000.

[34] G. Ramalingam. The Undecidability of Aliasing. *ACM Transactions on Programming Language System*, September 1994.

[35] J. Renau, B. Fraguela, J. Tuck, W. Liu, M. Prvulovic, L. Ceze, S. Sarangi, P. Sack, K. Strauss, and P. Montesinos. SESC Simulator, January 2005. http://sesc.sourceforge.net.

[36] N. Rinetzky, G. Ramalingam, M. Sagiv, and E. Yahav. On the Complexity of Partially-flow-sensitive Alias Analysis. *ACM Transaction on Programming Language System*, May 2008.

[37] B. Steensgaard. Points-to Analysis in Almost Linear Time. In *International Symposium on Principles of Programming Languages*, January 1996.

[38] J. Torrellas, L. Ceze, J. Tuck, C. Cascaval, P. Montesinos, W. Ahn, and M. Prvulovic. The Bulk Multicore Architecture for Improved Programmability. *Communications of the ACM*, December 2009.

[39] J. Tuck, W. Ahn, L. Ceze, and J. Torrellas. SoftSig: Software-Exposed Hardware Signatures for Code Analysis and Optimization. In *International Conference on Architectural Support for Programming Languages and Operating Systems*, January 2008.

[40] T. Vandrunen and A. L. Hosking. Value-based Partial Redundancy Elimination. In *Compiler Construction*, March 2004.

[41] K. R. Wadleigh and I. L. Crawford. *Software Optimization for High Performance Computing: Creating Faster Applications*. Prentice Hall, 2000.

[42] R. P. Wilson and M. S. Lam. Efficient Context-sensitive Pointer Analysis for C programs. In *International Conference on Programming Language Design and Implementation*, June 1995.

[43] Y. Wu and J. R. Larus. Static Branch Frequency and Program Profile Analysis. In *International Symposium on Microarchitecture*, November 1994.

Regularities Considered Harmful: Forcing Randomness to Memory Accesses to Reduce Row Buffer Conflicts for Multi-Core, Multi-Bank Systems

Heekwon Park*
Computer Science Department
University of Pittsburgh
parkhk@cs.pitt.edu

Seungjae Baek*
Computer Science Department
University of Pittsburgh
baeksj@cs.pitt.edu

Jongmoo Choi
Department of Computer Science
Dankook University
choijm@dankook.ac.kr

Donghee Lee
School of Computer Science
University of Seoul
dhl_express@uos.ac.kr

Sam H. Noh
School of Computer & Information Engineering
Hongik University
samhnoh@hongik.ac.kr

Abstract

We propose a novel kernel-level memory allocator, called M^3 (M-cube, Multi-core Multi-bank Memory allocator), that has the following two features. First, it introduces and makes use of a notion of a memory container, which is defined as a unit of memory that comprises the minimum number of page frames that can cover all the banks of the memory organization, by exclusively assigning a container to a core so that each core achieves bank parallelism as much as possible. Second, it orchestrates page frame allocation so that pages that threads access are dispersed randomly across multiple banks so that each thread's access pattern is randomized. The development of M^3 is based on a tool that we develop to fully understand the architectural characteristics of the underlying memory organization. Using an extension of this tool, we observe that the same application that accesses pages in a random manner outperforms one that accesses pages in a regular pattern such as sequential or same ordered accesses. This is because such randomized accesses reduces inter-thread access interference on the row-buffer in memory banks. We implement M^3 in the Linux kernel version 2.6.32 on the Intel Xeon system that has 16 cores and 32GB DRAM. Performance evaluation with various workloads show that M^3 improves the overall performance for memory intensive benchmarks by up to 85% with an average of about 40%.

Categories and Subject Descriptors B.3.1 [*Memory Structures*]: Semiconductor Memories—Dynamic memory (DRAM); D.4.2 [*Operating Systems*]: Storage Management—Allocation/deallocation strategies; D.4.2 [*Operating Systems*]: Storage Management—Main memory; D.4.8 [*Operating Systems*]: Performance—Measurements

General Terms Algorithms, Design, Experimentation, Measurement, Performance

Keywords Row-buffer conflict, Memory management, Randomized algorithm, Memory container, Analysis tool

* This work was done when these authors were doctorate students at Dankook University in the Republic of Korea (South Korea).

ASPLOS'13, March 16–20, 2013, Houston, Texas, USA.

1. Introduction

A recent distinct trend in computer architecture is that of multi-core support as exemplified by the Intel Core i7 [3], AMD Opteron [1] and ARM Cortex-A15 [2]. In order to take advantage of the increased computation of multi-core chips, computer systems commonly come with a vast amount of main memory. These trends require us to revisit the internal policies and mechanisms of today's operating systems.

In this paper, we rethink the memory allocation issue in light of these architectural trends. In particular, we look into how memory can be allocated more efficiently by alleviating the row-buffer conflict problem from an operating system standpoint. The row-buffer conflict problem has been looked into primarily as an architecture problem [9, 31, 34]. To the best of our knowledge, this study is the first to present an operating system based solution.

Before presenting an outline of our solution, let us look at the source of the row-buffer conflict. A row-buffer is essentially a cache area in a memory bank [34]. A row-buffer conflict occurs when a core alternatively accesses different page frames mapped to the same bank or when several cores access the bank simultaneously. This leads to significant performance degradation [14, 20, 26, 28, 33].

Our operating system solution to the row-buffer conflict is a novel kernel-level memory allocator, which we refer to as M^3 (M-cube, Multi-core Multi-bank Memory allocator), that takes two distinct approaches. The first is to allocate page frames to a core from different banks as much as possible. To this end, we introduce the notion of a memory container, which, for now, can be thought of as a unit of memory formed from a collection of distinct, non-overlapping pages. Then each core is assigned a memory container such that when a core requests for memory, the request is serviced within the assigned memory container.

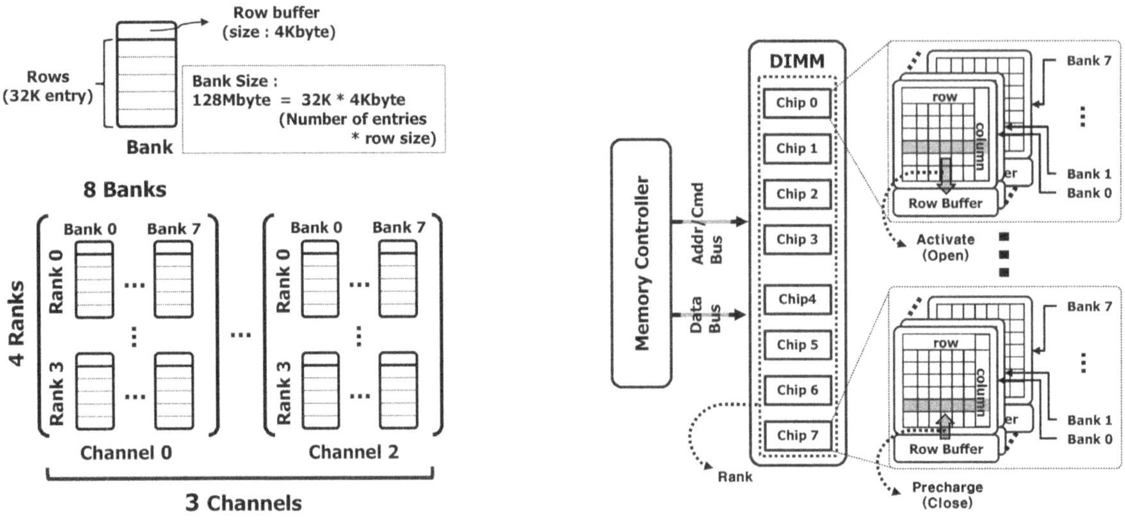

(a) Conceptual memory organization

(b) Physical memory module

Figure 1. Memory organization consisting of multiple channels, ranks, and banks

The second approach is to randomize memory accesses. This may, at first, sound counter-intuitive, but we show that sequential memory accesses or accesses that show regularities such as references with patterned intervals tend to aggravate the row-buffer conflict. To alleviate such effects, we propose a memory allocation algorithm that randomizes the actual accesses at the memory bank level. Note that the memory references generated by the threads are not the ones being randomized, but that randomization is being forced upon only at the memory bank level. We devise a downward search and individual page frame management scheme to implement such an algorithm in an efficient manner.

To understand the effect of regularities and randomness and to realize the notion of a memory container, a full understanding of the underlying memory organization is necessary. To this end, we develop an analysis tool that allows us to infer the relationships between page frames and the various components that make up the physical main memory.

We implement M^3 in the Linux kernel version 2.6.32 on a system that consists of two Intel XEON x5570 processors with four cores on each processor (a total of 16 cores with the hyperthreading technology enabled), 32GB DDR3 main memory, and 3.6TB SAS disks. Using six benchmarks, we conduct various experiments that show that M^3 can improve the total execution time by up to 85.2% with an average of 39.7% for memory-intensive benchmarks and by up to 7.8% with an average of 1.3% for CPU or I/O intensive benchmarks. Also, we conduct experiments using the PARSEC benchmark that demonstrates the spectrum of performance improvements of M^3 according to the characteristics of applications.

The contributions of our work can be summarized as follows:

- **Randomness for the Better:** We make a non-intuitive observation that in multi-core and multi-bank systems, a [1]randomized memory access pattern yields better performance than a regular pattern.
- **M^3 design:** The notion of a memory container and a randomizing algorithm are devised so that the operating system can efficiently randomize page frame accesses.
- **Memory organization analysis tool:** A tool that exposes the mappings between page frames and memory components such as channels, ranks, and banks is presented.
- **Real implementation:** Performance gains of our proposal are quantitatively evaluated through real implementation based experiments with various types of workloads.

[1] Henceforth, unless specifically mentioned, when we refer to randomizing or randomized memory accesses, this refers to memory accesses being randomized at the memory bank level and not at the thread level.

The rest of the paper is organized as follows. In the next section, we describe the architectural background and related work. The memory organization analysis tool is presented in Section 3, and the effects of access patterns on the row-buffer conflict are discussed in Section 4. The design and implementation details of M^3 are elaborated in Section 5. In Section 6, we present the performance evaluation results. Finally, conclusions are presented in Section 7.

2. Background

In this section, we first describe the general structure of memory organizations adopted in modern PCs and server systems. Then, we discuss how the page frame allocation decision of operating systems affects memory parallelism. Finally, we survey previous research related to our work.

2.1 Memory Organization and Row-Buffer

Figure 1(a) depicts the conceptual structure of a memory organization. It consists of multiple channels, which is divided into multiple ranks. Each rank is further divided into multiple banks, and each bank consists of a set of rows and a row-buffer. For instance, in our experimental system, the IBM X3650 M2 system, there are 3 channels, 4 ranks per channel, and 8 banks per rank. Each bank has 32K rows, whose size is 4KB, making the size of each bank 128MB.

In reality, the memory organization complexity goes even a step further as shown in Figure 1(b) [11, 12]. A memory module such as a DIMM (Dual In-line Memory Module), which is directly mounted on a printed circuit board, consists of multiple memory chips, and the chips within a DIMM comprise a rank. Then, a rank contains multiple banks. In our experimental system, a rank is composed of 8 chips similar to the one in Figure 1(b). Also, data stored in a bank of the rank is distributed into the 8 chips that can be referenced in parallel. In other words, the aggregation of the bank 0s in the 8 chips of Figure 1(b) corresponds to bank 0

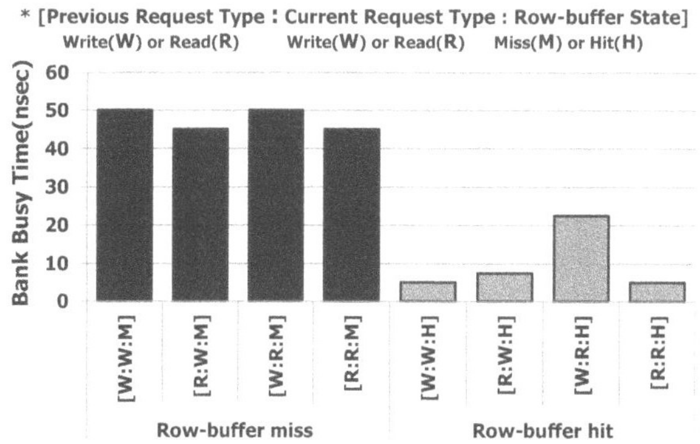

Figure 2. Row-buffer hit and conflict overhead

in Figure 1(a). Hereafter, all discussions are presented using the organization of Figure 1(a) since the issues tackled in this paper can be fully discussed using this conceptual structure.

As previously mentioned, there is a row-buffer for each bank, the size of which is the same as a row. A row-buffer is a cache area used to exploit spatial locality. When a memory request is triggered by a core, the DRAM controller first checks the row-buffer of the bank related to the requested address. If data is cached in the row-buffer, the request can be served immediately from the row buffer. This is called a row-buffer hit. Otherwise, upon a row-buffer miss the DRAM controller performs the precharge and activate operations. The precharge operation is a step to write back data of the row-buffer into the original row. The activate operation is a step to load the entire data from the row that contains the requested address into the row-buffer. After the two operations, the request is served from the row-buffer. This whole scenario is called a row-buffer conflict. Note that even though the request size from a core is a CPU cache line width (for instance, 64B), the DRAM controller loads the entire row into the row buffer (for instance, 4KB) anticipating that the next request will be serviced from the same row.

Row-buffer conflicts eliminate the caching effect of the row-buffer and incur significant precharging and activating overhead, resulting in substantial delays and energy consumption. To assess the overhead more quantitatively, we plot Figure 2 using raw data borrowed from previous papers [9, 13]. Note that the bank busy time, which is defined as the time spent by a bank to service the memory request issued to that bank, depends not only on the row-buffer state, but also on the previous/current request types. For example, `[W:W:H]` takes $5ns$ while `[W:R:H]` and `[W:W:M]` take 22.5 and $50ns$, respectively. Although there are some variations, this figure consistently shows that the row-buffer conflict degrades memory access latency by 2 to 5 times. The eventual goal of our study is in reducing row-buffer conflicts through an operating system approach.

2.2 Operating System Challenges

For main memory management, traditional operating systems use two abstractions, virtual memory and physical memory. As NUMA (Non-Uniform Memory Access) architecture such as Intel's Nehalem QPI (QuickPath Interconnect) [3] and AMD's hypertransport technology [1] gains attention, some operating systems are incorporating the local and remote memory concepts into their abstractions. For instance, the recent Linux kernel employs the notion of a *node*, which is simply a range of physical memory considered local, and it tries to allocate page frames to a core from a local node to some extent taking into account the physical memory layout in it's allocation decision [7, 10].

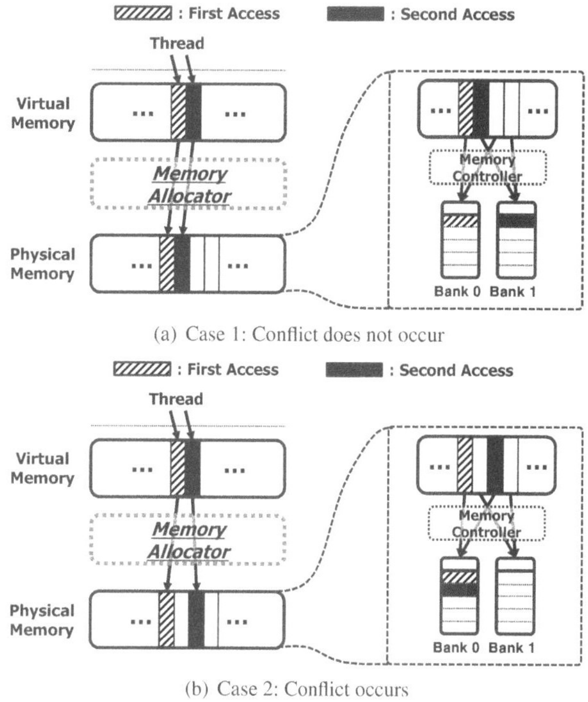

(a) Case 1: Conflict does not occur

(b) Case 2: Conflict occurs

Figure 3. Effects of page frame allocation decision on the row-buffer conflict. (a) Case 1: page frames are allocated from different banks, (b) Case 2: page frames are allocated from a same bank.

We argue, through this paper, that to decrease row-buffer conflict and to make full use of the memory parallelism supported by recent memory organizations, the allocator must understand and take into account the physical memory organization when making its allocation decisions. As an example, consider Figure 3 where we assume that there is an application that alternatively accesses two virtual pages. Allocating page frames for this application could be done in one of two ways: one, by allocating the pages from different banks as depicted in Figure 3(a) as Case 1, and the other, by allocating from the same bank as depicted in Figure 3(b) as Case 2. Then, naturally, Case 2 is expected to cause more row-buffer conflicts than Case 1. In this manner, though both cases are allocating for the same virtual pages, understanding the physical memory organization may allow the allocator to allocate in such a way that row-buffer conflicts may be alleviated.

Note that the mapping between virtual pages and physical page frames are governed by the kernel-level memory allocator, while the mapping between page frames and banks are managed by the memory controller. Developing a row-buffer conflict aware memory allocator is the main objective of this paper. This is discussed in detail in Sections 4 and 5. Understanding the characteristics of the memory organization is an essential prerequisite for our allocator design, and this is discussed in Section 3.

2.3 Related Work

A large number of research have been conducted with aims to increase the effect of the row-buffer and to enhance memory parallelism. One approach is based on memory partitioning at the channel level [19], rank level [4, 35] and the bank level [14]. More specifically, Jeong et al. propose to partition the internal memory banks between cores to isolate their access streams and eliminate locality interference [14]. Muralidhara et al. suggest application-

Algorithm 1 Pseudo code of analysis tool

```
1:  procedure ANALYZER_CORE(start_of_mem, end_of_mem)
2:      *CL_1 ← First cache line from start_of_mem
3:      *CL_2 ← Second cache line from start_of_mem
4:      CACHE_CONTROL(start_of_mem, end_of_mem, Uncached)
                ▷ Set uncached mode from start_of_mem to end_of_mem
5:      repeat                  ▷ Iterate through all test memory area
6:          i ← 0
7:          Begin_time ←STOPWATCH( )

8:          while i < 500 do            ▷ Repeat sufficient number of times
9:              *CL_1 ← *CL_2 + i
10:             *CL_2 ← *CL_1 + i
                ▷ To prevent out-of-order execution at CPU and memory controller
11:             i ← i + 1
12:         end while

13:         End_time ←STOPWATCH( )
14:         RECORD_TIME(End_time − Begin_time)
15:         CL_2 ← Next cache line
16:     until CL_2 ≤ end_of_mem
17: end procedure
```

aware memory channel partitioning to decrease inter-application interference in the memory system [19].

Another approach is using memory request scheduling. Rixner et al. design the FR-FCFS (First Ready, First Come First Serve) scheduling algorithm that prioritizes memory requests that hit in the row-buffers of DRAM banks over other requests to exploit the locality of the row-buffer [25, 26]. Mutlu and Moscibroda present the STFM (Stall-Time Fair Memory) scheduler to equalize the DRAM-related slowdown experienced by each thread due to interference from other threads sharing the DRAM memory system [20]. Kaseridis et al. describe the complex structure of memory organization in many-core systems and propose a fair memory hashing scheme to control the maximum number of row-buffer hits [15].

Other notable approaches have also been studied. Zhang et al. propose a permutation-based page interleaving scheme to mitigate row-buffer conflicts by exploiting data access locality in the row-buffer [34]. Yoon et al. design an adaptive-granularity memory system that effectively combines fine-grained and coarse-grained memory accesses to improve performance and energy savings [33]. They also suggest an OS support that augments the virtual memory interface to allow software to specify the preferred access granularity for each page.

Sudan et al. introduce a new data placement scheme based on micro-pages, where chunks from different pages are collocated in a row-buffer to improve the overall utilization of the row buffer contents, consequently reducing memory energy consumption and access time [28]. Lee et al. propose mechanisms to maximize DRAM bank-level parallelism by arranging memory requests to be serviced in parallel in different DRAM banks [17]. Kim et al. design TCM (Thread Cluster Memory) scheduling that employs multiple different memory scheduling policies for different threads based on the threads' memory access and interference characteristics [16].

Our approach differs from all previous studies in that it is a purely OS-level approach not requiring any hardware modifications or special support. Though Jeong et al. propose an approach that may be realized at the operating system level, their study is limited to a simulator and is not conducted on a real system [14]. More importantly, however, to the best of our knowledge, our paper is the first to apply randomness in the page frame allocation decision to reduce row-buffer conflicts.

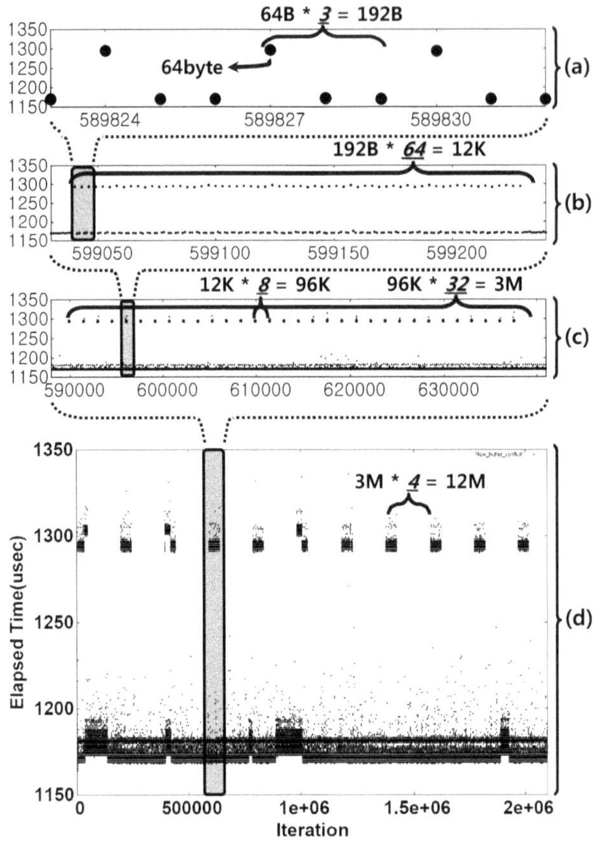

Figure 4. Analysis results

3. Memory Organization Analysis

In this section, we first explain the pseudo code for our memory organization analysis tool. Then, we discuss the analysis results and elaborate on the mappings between page frames and the various DRAM components such as the channels, ranks, and banks.

3.1 Analysis Algorithm

To reduce row-buffer conflicts from the operating system level, we need to understand how page frames are mapped into the memory organization. However, such information is not readily available. Hence, we develop an analysis tool that can help explore the detailed internal structure of the memory organization. While designing the tool, we consider its portability so that it may be used not only for our experimental system, but with other systems as well.

Algorithm 1 presents the pseudo code used by the tool. Basically, it repeatedly accesses two variables, namely `CL_1` and `CL_2`. The first variable has a fixed physical address (the first available physical address of node 1, which is 16GB in size in this experiment), while the second has a non-fixed address that is incremented by the cache line size (64B) at each iteration. The elapsed time of each iteration is measured as shown in line 7 and 13. The elapsed time is used to infer the memory organization and the row-buffer conflict, in particular.

In addition, we employ the following three techniques to enhance the accuracy of the analysis. First, we set the CPU cache mode as uncacheable, as expressed in line 4, to guarantee that each access is serviced at the memory module. This setting is done only for the memory area starting from `start_of_mem` to `end_of_mem`, while all other variables and instructions remain cacheable, so that these other factors will have minimum effect on the execution of the

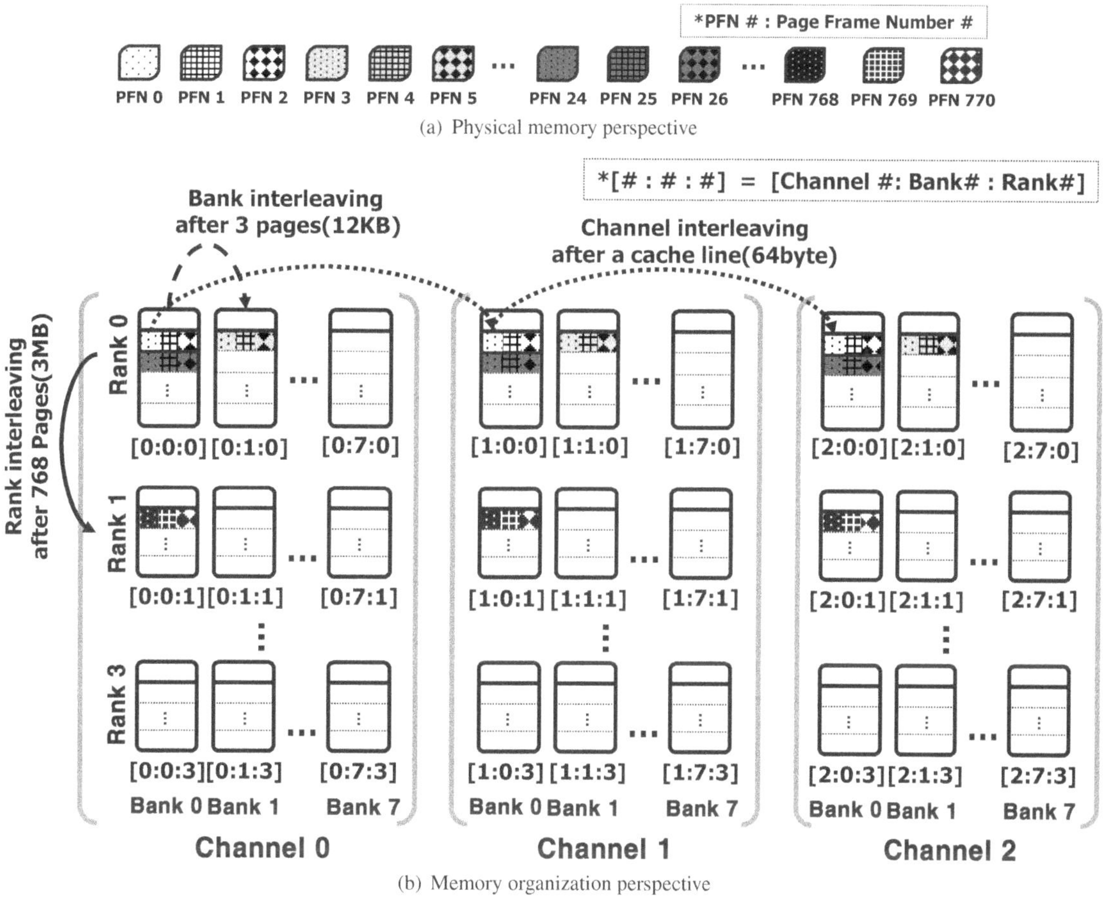

Figure 5. Relationship between physical memory and memory organization

algorithm. Second, at each iteration, we access the two variables numerous times to cancel out measurement noise such as sudden bus contention and inter-command delay. Specifically, for our experiments, we access them 500 times as shown in line 8. Third, we make the two variables mutually dependent, as denoted in lines 9 and 10. This avoids various optimizations such as out-of-order execution in the core or request scheduling in the memory controller so that the instructions in the code are executed as we want them executed.

3.2 Analysis Results

Figure 4 shows the analysis results. In the figure, the x-axis is the iteration number of the repeat statement, while the y-axis is the measured elapsed time. Note that the physical address of the second variable, that is CL_2, is incremented by the cache line size of 64 bytes. Hence, the x-axis also represents the sequence of physical memory addresses. That is, the $\mathtt{i}_{th}$ iteration corresponds to the physical memory address of "the address of the second cache line + 64 × i".

Figure 4 depicts four graphs, each depicting, from bottom to top, smaller and smaller ranges. Specifically, Figure 4(d), the bottom-most figure, ranges from 0 to 2,000,000 (roughly 128MB size), Figure 4(c) zooms in on the 590,000-640,000 portion of Figure 4(d). Again, Figure 4(b) shows a portion of iterations of Figure 4(c), while Figure 4(a) shows that of Figure 4(b). In other words, we zoom in the results from Figure 4(d) to Figure 4(a) to examine them from a finer-grained viewpoint.

Now let us first discuss Figure 4(a). This figure reveals that the measured elapsed time has a distinct pattern for every 3 addresses. Specifically, the first address shows higher elapsed time than the latter two addresses due to the row-buffer conflict. It implies that at the first address, CL_1 and CL_2 are located at the same bank, while at the second and third addresses, they are at different banks. Note that our experimental system has 3 channels. Hence, we can infer that channel interleaving is performed with the cache line unit.

Figure 4(b) shows that the pattern observed in Figure 4(a) occurs continuously 64 times. When we convert this number into memory size, we get 12KB from a calculation of 64B×3×64. Since the row size is 4KB in our system [18], we can infer that three consecutive rows are managed in the same manner.

Now let us turn the discussion to Figure 4(c). This figure shows that the 12KB pattern described in Figure 4(b), reoccurs in 96KB memory size intervals. Note that our system has 8 banks, and as 12×8=96, we can deduce that bank interleaving is configured in three row units. In addition, Figure 4(c) shows that the 96KB pattern is repeated 32 times within the memory size of 3MB (96KB×32).

Finally, Figure 4(d) shows that the 3MB pattern of Figure 4(c) reoccurrs in 12MB intervals. Since our system has 4 ranks, we can deduce that rank interleaving is performed in 3MB units. The 12MB pattern is repeated until the end of memory is reached.

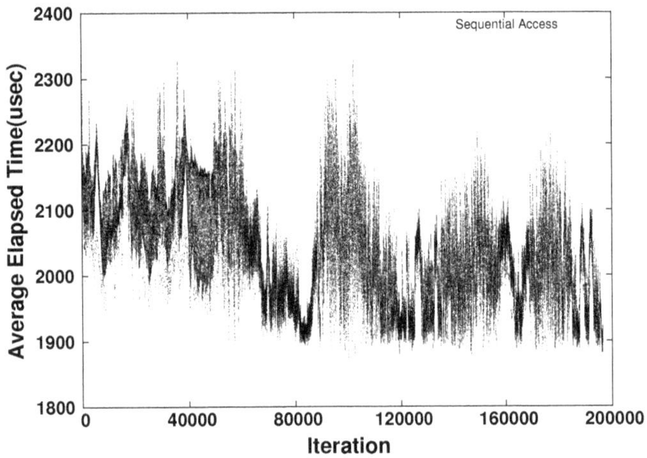

Figure 6. Row-buffer conflicts with 4 cores: sequential access pattern

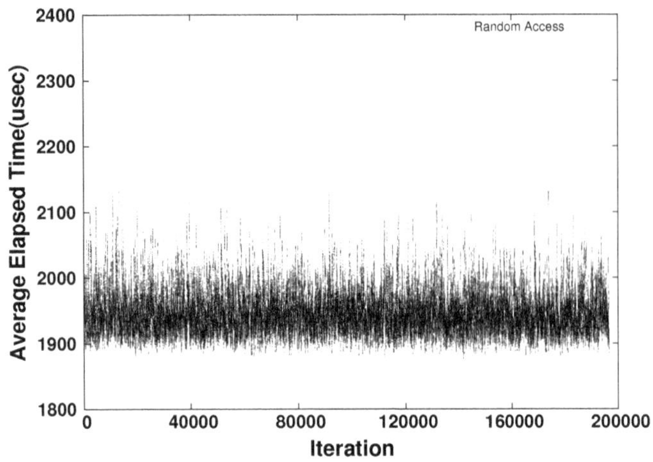

Figure 7. Row-buffer conflicts with 4 cores: random access pattern

3.3 Implication

From the analysis results discussed in Section 3.2, we can figure out how page frames are mapped into rows as illustrated in Figure 5. The observation of Figure 4(a) indicates that page frame 0 is distributed into three banks, namely `[0:0:0]`, `[1:0:0]` and `[2:0:0]` where the notation refers to `[channel number: bank number: rank number]`. In other words, channel interleaving is done with the cache line unit. Also, from Figure 4(b), we can conjecture that page frames 1 and 2 are mapped in the same way as page frame 0.

Bank interleaving discussed in Figure 4(c) suggests that page frames 3, 4, 5 are mapped into banks `[0:1:0]`, `[1:1:0]`, `[2:1:0]`, page frames 6, 7, 8 into banks `[0:2:0]`, `[1:2:0]`, `[2:2:0]`, and so on, until page frames 21, 22, and 23 are mapped to bank 7. Then, page frames 24, 25, 26 are mapped back at bank 0 and are mapped again into banks `[0:0:0]`, `[1:0:0]`, `[2:0:0]` in round-robin fashion. This round-robin is repeated 32 times as discussed in Figure 4(c). After 32 repetitions, rank interleaving is utilized. So, page frames 768, 769, 770 are mapped into banks `[0:0:1]`, `[1:0:1]`, `[2:0:1]`. These arrangements continue up to page frame 3071, which is mapped into banks `[0:7:3]`, `[1:7:3]`, `[2:7:3]`, the last bank of each channel. The page frames that are mapped into every bank up to this point make up the 12MB interval as observed in Figure 4(d). The next page frame 3072 then, is again mapped into banks `[0:0:0]`, `[1:0:0]`, `[2:0:0]`, starting a new 12MB interval.

Figure 5 makes it possible to discuss the results observed in Figure 4 more clearly. Assume that the `CL_1` variable is located in page frame 0, while `CL_2` is in page frame 24. Then, execution of the code generates the pattern observed in Figure 4(a). On the other hand, when `CL_2` is in page frame 27 or 768, the code does not cause a row-buffer conflict leading to the lower elapsed time ranging from 1150 to 1200.

The findings from the analysis can be summarized as follows. First, channel interleaving is conducted in the CPU cache line unit, not the page frame unit. Of course, one can change this configuration so that the page frame is used as the channel interleaving unit. However, modern computer systems prefer cache line interleaving since it can obtain memory parallelism even with a single page frame. Second, some consecutive page frames are mapped into the same row; 3 consecutive frames in our system. Put it another way, a single page frame is distributed into several rows, 3 in our particular case, leading to higher parallelism and thus, better performance. Third, rank interleaving is performed in a relatively large unit; 3MB in our system. Finally, a memory area of 12MB size can cover all banks with a minimum number of page frames in our system. These findings are used as guidelines when designing the memory container as discussed in the next section.

4. Regularity Considered Harmful

As the number of cores increase, the row-buffer conflict problem becomes more serious. In a single core system, the row-buffer conflict occurs only when an application accesses two different page frames located on identical banks at the same time. However, in a multiple core system, the conflict also happens when two or more cores access those page frames concurrently. This means that row-buffer aware page frame allocation will become more important in a multi-core system.

To evaluate the behavior of the row-buffer under multiple cores, we modify the code presented in Algorithm 1. Specifically, we make the following two changes. First, we set the two variables so that they are located in the same cache line. Then, their addresses are incremented by the cache line size at each iteration. With this change, row-buffer conflict will not occur should the code be executed by itself on a single core. The other change is that we now run the modified code concurrently on 4 cores with each instance of the code having a different starting physical address incremented by 12MB from the previous core. For instance, if core 0 has a start address of X, then core 1 has a start address of $X + 12$MB, and core 2, $X + 24$MB, and so on. Recall from Figure 5 that 12MB is the memory range that covers all banks from `[0:0:0]` to `[2:7:3]`. Consequently, all four threads start accessing memory from the same bank and the memory accesses also progress in the same order.

Figure 6 presents the experimental results. The x-axis is the iteration number, while the y-axis is the average of the elapsed times measured for the 4 cores. The results show that row-buffer conflicts occur in a large number of iterations. When all 4 cores are involved in a conflict, the elapsed time becomes the highest.

Figure 6 also shows that some ranges of iterations result in higher conflicts than other ranges. For instance, conflicts are rare in the 70,000 to 90,000 range, while most of the iterations in the 90,000 to 110,000 range result in high conflicts. Overall, we see a fluctuation in the intensity of conflicts. This phenomenon, however, is counter-intuitive. To elaborate, the threads executing on the four cores started referencing from the same bank, which should result in a row-buffer conflict, and since the threads are executing with the same rate of progress, the conflicts should, with high probability, be occuring over and over. Hence, we should be seeing an almost flat graph, not a graph that fluctuates as shown in Figure 6.

The explanation for this fluctuation is the interference induced by external events such as interrupt handling and scheduling. These external events trigger delays at the cores handling the events disrupting the progress of the threads. This leads to asynchrony among the cores releaving them of conflicts for some time period. However, as these events continue to occur the timing among the cores become synchronized again leading to conflicts. Hence, this pattern of synchrony and asynchrony repeats itself as the execution continues.

One feasible solution to avoid conflicts among cores is memory partitioning. For instance, from Figure 5, we can partition memory vertically (banks 0 and 1 to core 0, banks 2 and 3 to core 1, and so on) or horizontally (rank 0 to core 0, rank 1 to core 1, and so on). The essential benefit of this partitioning is that it can completely remove conflicts among cores.

However, there are problems in applying memory partitioning into operating systems. First, it reduces memory parallelism such as bank interleaving or rank interleaving. Second, it raises the scalability issue as the number of cores increase. Third, it brings up the availability issue since it cannot support large consecutive page frames that may be requested by the kernel, say, for example, by the device driver. For instance, if we partition banks 0 and 1 into core 0, in the experimental platform that we use, we would not be able to service requests demanding more than 6 consecutive frames as each bank retains only 3 successive pages. Finally, when an application is migrated from a core to another core for CPU load balancing, which is frequently adopted in modern operating systems, conflict among the cores will again occur. In this case, conflicts can be more serious as the total number of banks accessible by a core has now been reduced via partitioning.

Let us now see how random memory access patterns affect row-buffer conflicts. For this purpose, we again modify the code used for the previous experiment such that a random number generator is used to make sure that each core has a different access pattern and that each address is accessed no more than once. Note that in this case, we are randomizing memory references at the application level.

The experimental results using the randomly accessing code are presented in Figure 7. The results show that most iterations do not cause row-buffer conflicts and that conflicts where all 4 cores are involved are non-existent. The average elapsed time of all iterations of Figure 7 is 1925, while that of Figure 6 is 2052. This implies that random accesses mitigate conflicts better then sequential patterns.

Our sensitivity analysis reveals that the worsen elapsed time of the sequential pattern is due to correlated conflicts, which we define as a set of successive conflicts. In the sequential pattern, once a reference iteration causes a conflict, the next reference iteration is likely to cause another conflict. In contrast, in the random pattern, since the addresses accessed by consecutive iterations are independent of each other, the next conflict probability is constant at "$1/total\_number\_of\_banks$". Note that correlated conflicts occur not only in sequential patterns, but also in any pattern with regularities such as accesses with the same stride or patterned intervals.

This observation is also applicable to the page frame allocation pattern in operating systems. An operating system can govern the allocation pattern to make it regular or random, and we expect that the former will cause a larger number of correlated conflicts than the latter.

5. M^3 Design and Implementation

The observations discussed in the previous sections inspire us to develop a novel kernel-level memory allocator called M^3 (M-cube, Multi-core Multi-bank Memory allocator). In this section, we elaborate on two features of M^3, specifically the memory container and the randomized algorithm.

5.1 Memory Container

To reduce row-buffer conflict, page frames allocated to each individual thread should come from distinct banks as much as possible. For this purpose, we introduce the notion of a memory container, which is defined as a unit of memory that comprises the minimum number of page frames that can cover all the banks of the memory organization. (Recall that we were able to find this using the analysis tool described in Section 3, and that this number is 12MB for our experimental platform.)

M^3, then, divides the entire memory into multiple memory containers, with a memory container being exclusively assigned to a core. When an application requests a page frame, M^3 serves the request from the memory container of the core that is executing the application. Requests for page frames from other applications running on different cores will be allocated from the memory container assigned to that core. Deallocation is also performed within the memory container frame.

Note that the notion of a memory container combined with random allocation will tend to disperse page frame allocation among the banks that comprise the memory container. This is because when a page is allocated from a particular bank, the probability of allocating a page from that same bank decreases on the next allocation attempt. The reason the probability decreases is because the number of pages belonging to a particular bank is constant within a single memory container, and with random allocation, each page has equal probability of being allocated. Hence, once a page is allocated from a particular bank, then the probability of that same bank being selected on the next allocation attempt is reduced by the probability of a page being selected.

When a core uses up all the page frames from the assigned memory container, M^3 assigns a new available memory container to the core. When the allocated page frames are freed, the page frames are released to the memory container that owns the page frames. If the number of available memory containers become insufficient, the swapping mechanism is triggered to free page frames so that more memory containers can be generated. In our current implementation, the swapping mechanism provided in Linux is used as is. Hence, the pages reclaimed may be a part of several different memory containers. It may be possible to modify the swap mechanism so that pages belonging to the same memory container are reclaimed together for better management of memory containers. This, however, is left for future work.

As mentioned previously, the ideal memory container size, by definition, is 12MB for our experimental system, since 12MB is the size that covers all banks with the minimum number of page frames, as already discussed in Figure 5. In the experimental study conducted in Section 6, however, we set the size of the memory container to 4MB. This was a choice that we made to make M^3 as generic as possible so that it can be deployed in a wide range of existing systems. Hence, there are roughly 8000 memory containers in our system.

5.2 Randomized Algorithm

Even though the memory container can reduce row-buffer conflict in a single core, there still exists conflicts among multiple cores. As discussed in Section 4 random allocation can have a positive effect on reducing conflicts among cores. To realize randomness, M^3 replaces the buddy algorithm [8, 21, 22], which is utilized in various modern operating systems including the Linux kernel considered in this paper, with a randomizing algorithm that we describe below.

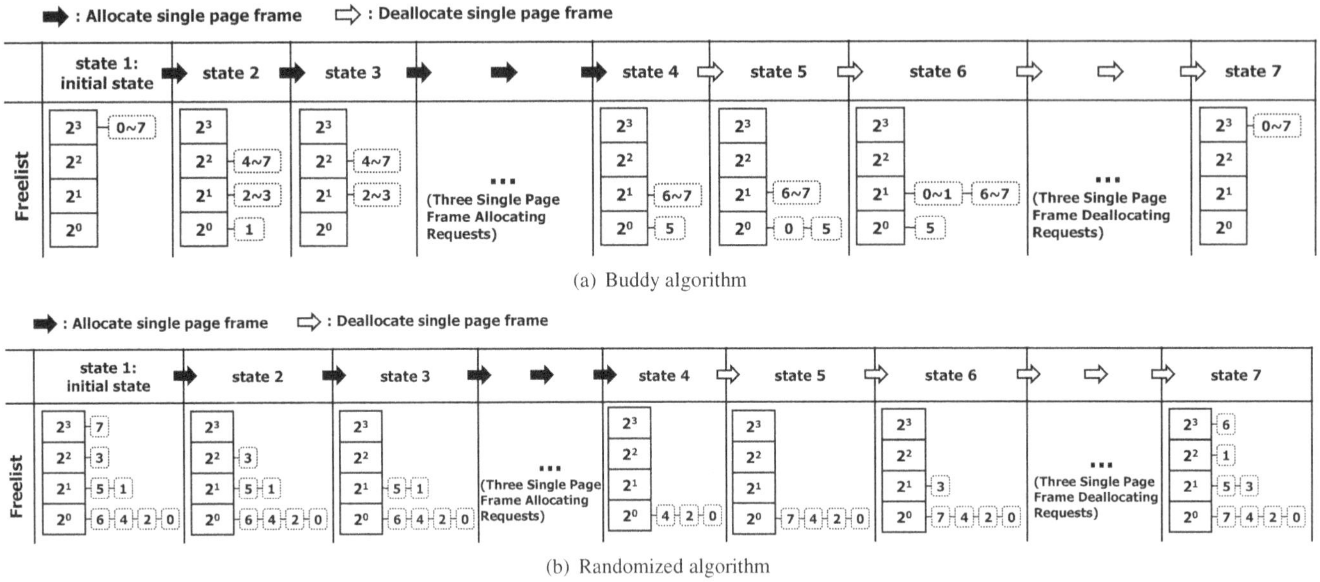

Figure 8. Comparison between buddy and our randomized algorithm

Figure 8(a) presents the structure of the buddy algorithm and its operational example. In the figure, we assume that physical memory consists of 8 page frames. As shown in Figure 8(a), the buddy algorithm uses a set of doubly linked list data structures called the freelist. The freelist is constructed in multiple levels labeled (bin) 2^0, 2^1, ...,2^i, ..., where, at level 2^i, 2^i number of consecutive page frames are treated as a single unit. We refer to this single unit as a buddy group. The buddy algorithm utilizes two key operations, splitting and coalescing. The former is used to satisfy a memory request as suitably as possible, while the latter is used to reconstruct a buddy group.

At the initial stage of our study, we considered using the buddy algorithm for managing each memory container. However, we detected its tendency to allocate page frames in a regular pattern. Let us discuss this issue using a walk-through example as demonstrated through states 1 to 7 in Figure 8(a). State 1 shows the initial state, where all 8 page frames are free. Assume that five requests arrive, where each request wants a single page frame. Then, the buddy algorithm searches upward from the lowest level, recursively splitting, if necessary. In this case, the allocation sequence of page frames becomes $0 \rightarrow 1 \rightarrow 2 \rightarrow 3 \rightarrow 4$, and the resulting memory state is shown in state 4.

Now, assume that the allocated page frames are freed in order. Then, the buddy algorithm, again, coalesces recursively, as necessary, leading to state 7. If five allocation requests are made again, the allocation sequence at this time again becomes $0 \rightarrow 1 \rightarrow 2 \rightarrow 3 \rightarrow 4$. Indeed, the buddy algorithm allocates page frames in a regular manner. Even if the initial state is different, it shows partial regularities since it searches upward from the lowest level, making the possibility of allocating a buddy page frame from a recently allocated one high. If we choose the buddy algorithm to manage each memory container, each core will have a tendency to access memory in a regular pattern, incurring more correlated conflicts as discussed in Section 4.

One straightforward way to integrate randomness into the buddy algorithm is to use a random number generating function to select a candidate page frame for allocation. However, as such a function would need to exist independent of the buddy layer, it could possibly become a source of considerable operational overhead as page frame allocation is one of the most frequently invoked operations in the kernel. Furthermore, extra effort must be made to manage consecutive pages at the buddy layer as randomness is introduced. Finally, forced randomness will cause more splitting and coalescing operations to be invoked, resulting in significant overhead.

To overcome these problems, we introduce two new concepts into the buddy algorithm; one is individual page frame management and the other is a downward search. To elaborate on our proposed randomized algorithm, we make use of Figure 8(b), which shows that we use the same data structure as the buddy algorithm. Downward search refers to the fact that to find a candidate page frame for allocation, the randomized algorithm performs searching downward from the highest level, not upward as the buddy algorithm does. For example, upon a single page allocation request at initial state 1, page 7, which is at the highest level, would be allocated resulting in state 2.

Let us now discuss individual page frame management. Note in Figure 8(b) that every page frame in the freelist is being managed individually. This is in contrast to the buddy algorithm where the freelist is managed per buddy group, which is composed of one or more page frames, as shown in Figure 8(a). Management of the freelist as single page frames tells us that each page may be allocated individually. However, the location of the page allows us to convey a double meaning. Specifically, each bin (2^0, 2^1, and so on, represented as solid line boxes in the freelist) of the freelist represents the same meaning as that of the conventional buddy algorithm; that is, it tells of the existence of consecutive multiple pages that can be allocated. For example, at state 2 in Figure 8(b), bin 2^2 with page 3 on its list indicates that 2^2 consecutive pages (pages $0 \sim 3$) are allocatable, while bin 2^1 with pages 5 and 1 on its list indicates that two consecutive pages (pages 0, 1 and pages 4, 5) can be allocated together. Note that this meaning conveyed by the bin is in addition to the fact that each of the pages may be allocated as a single page frame.

Let us discuss the characteristics of the randomized algorithm using examples as presented in Figure 8(b). State 1 is the initial state, where all free page frames are managed individually. Assume that five requests for a single page frame arrive. The randomized algorithm performs searching downward and allocates page frames

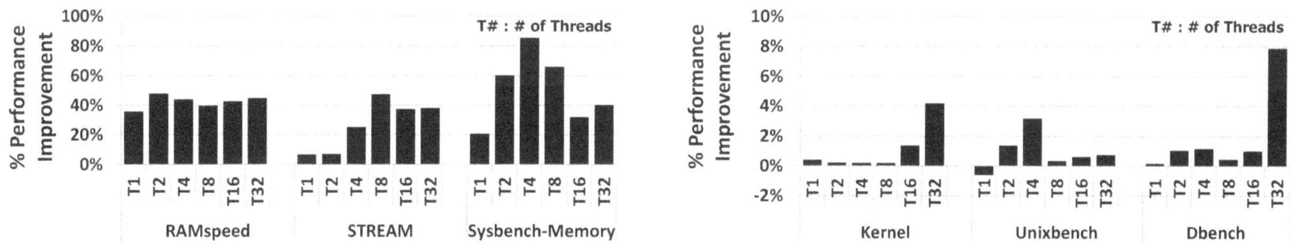

(a) Memory intensive benchmark results

(b) CPU or I/O intensive benchmark results

Figure 9. Performance impact of different workload characteristics

Table 1. Characteristics of programs in PARSEC

Program	Application Domain	Working Set
blackscholes	Financial analysis	Small
bodytrack	computer vision	Medium
canneal	Engineering	Unbounded
dedup	Enterprise storage	Unbounded
facesim	Computer animation	Large
ferret	Similarity search	Unbounded
fluidanimate	Computer animation	Large
freqmine	Data mining	Unbounded
streamcluster	Machine learning	Medium
swaptions	Computational finance	Medium
vips	Media processing	Medium
x264	Media processing	Medium

from the highest level. Hence, the allocation sequence becomes $7 \rightarrow 3 \rightarrow 5 \rightarrow 1 \rightarrow 6$, where state 4 becomes the memory state after there allocations.

Now, assume that the allocated page frames are freed in order. Then, the randomized algorithm puts the released page frame at the lowest level and ascends it to the higher level if its buddy is free. The ascending operation works just like the coalescing operation, except that it manages each frame individually, not merging them into a buddy group. State 7 shows the final state after serving the five deallocation requests. Note that even if the memory state is the same (page frames from 0 to 7 are all free), the data structure shown in states 1 and 7 are different. From state 7, if the same five requests arrive again, the allocation sequence this time becomes $6 \rightarrow 1 \rightarrow 5 \rightarrow 3 \rightarrow 7$, which is not the same as the sequence from state 1. Note also that the freeing sequence becomes a seed for a different allocation sequence. For example, if the freeing sequence were $6 \rightarrow 7 \rightarrow 1 \rightarrow 3 \rightarrow 5$ for the above example, the subsequent allocation sequence would become $6 \rightarrow 3 \rightarrow 1 \rightarrow 5 \rightarrow 7$, which also differs from the previous allocation sequences.

The walk-through example shows the merits of downward search and individual management. Downward search enables the allocated page frames to be dispersed in a random fashion. Furthermore, it allows the allocation order to be determined not only by the programming logic but also by the deallocation sequence increasing randomness even further. Individual management makes it possible to efficiently integrate randomness into the buddy algorithm without paying additional overhead for splitting and coalescing. Note that in the randomized algorithm, the coalescing/splitting operation is also carried out when an allocation/deallocation for multiple page frames is requested.

6. Performance Evaluation

In this section, we first describe the experimental setup and the seven benchmarks that represent a variety of workload characteristics. Then, we present the overall performance results and discuss how the characteristics affect the performance of M^3.

6.1 Experiment Environment

Our experimental system is an IBM x3650 M2 server system that consists of two Intel XEON x5570 quad core processors (when we turn on the hyperthreading capability, each processor can have at most 8 cores), 32GB DDR3 main memory and eight 2.5 inch SAS disks of 450GB capacity each. On this hardware platform, we implement the M^3 allocator on the Linux kernel version 2.6.32.

To evaluate the performance of M^3, we use the following seven benchmarks that can be categorized into three groups. The first group consists of memory intensive benchmarks, specifically, Stream, Sysbench-memory and Ramspeed. The Stream benchmark is a synthetic benchmark used for measuring sustainable memory bandwidth in high performance systems [27]. The Sysbench-memory benchmark is a memory allocation and transfer speed benchmark [29]. The Ramspeed benchmark is a utility to measure cache and memory performance of computer systems [24].

The second group consists of CPU or I/O intensive benchmarks that include Kernel Compile, Dbench and Unixbench. The Kernel Compile builds a new kernel image by compiling the Linux kernel version 2.6.32 and by linking the compiled objects. The Dbench benchmark is a file system benchmark that generates a workload similar to the commercial Netbench benchmark [5]. The Unixbench benchmark is a general-purpose benchmark designed to evaluate the performance of a Unix-like system, integrating CPU and file I/O tests as well as system behavior under various user loads [30].

The final group is the PARSEC benchmark that was designed to represent diverse application domains [6]. It is composed of 12 programs, whose characteristics are summarized in Table 1 [6, 23, 32]. In terms of intensity, canneal, facesim, fluidanimate and streamcluster are categorized as memory intensive, while the others as CPU or I/O intensive.

6.2 Experimental Results

Figure 9(a) shows the performance improvements owing to M^3 for the three memory intensive benchmarks. To evaluate the multi-core effects, we run the benchmarks with various number of threads. Depending on the configuration, performance is improved by as little as 6.5% to as much as 85.2% compared to the original Linux kernel that uses the buddy algorithm. Specifically, the average improvements are 26.6%, 50.4%, and 42.1% for the Stream, Sysbench-memory and Ramspeed benchmark, respectively.

The performance improvement is obtained from two sources. The first is by applying the randomized algorithm. As already dis-

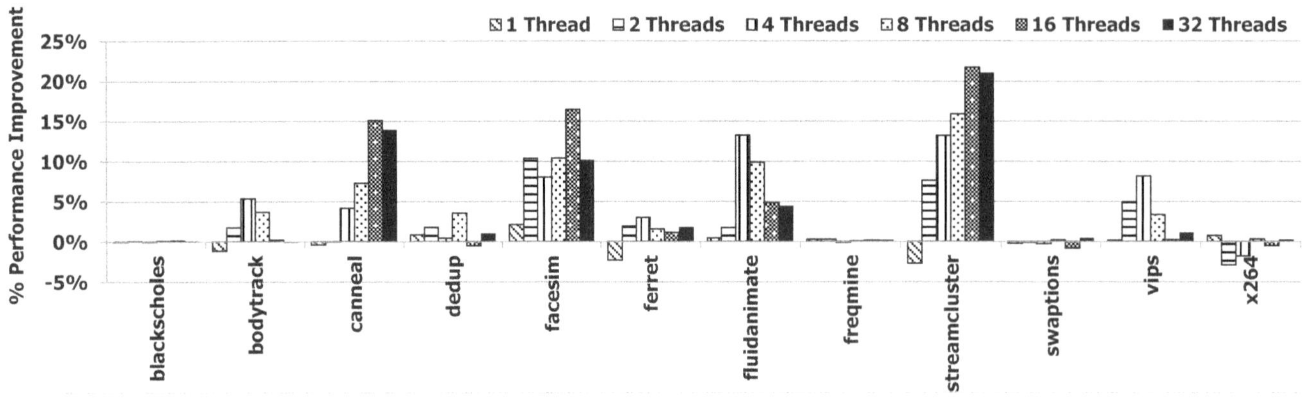

Figure 10. PARSEC benchmark results

cussed in Figures 7 and 8, random access patterns have a positive effect on performance. The second source is the memory container. Without the memory container, pages frames would be allocated into cores in an interleaved manner, failing to achieve memory parallelism in the core while still generating references with regularities.

Experimental results for the three CPU and I/O intensive benchmarks are shown in Figure 9(b). As expected, the improvements are not that considerable since memory references of these benchmarks are only a small portion of the overall benchmark performance. However, from these results, we can deduce that memory container management, individual page frame management, and downward search work efficiently without incurring noticeable overhead.

Figure 10 presents the PARSEC benchmark results. According to the characteristics of the programs, performance improvements show different aspects. For programs that intensively access a large memory range such as canneal, facesim, fluidanimate, and streamcluster, the improvements are up to 21.7% with an average of 10.4%. The results of other programs can be classified into two groups. The first group that includes blackscholes, freqmine, swaptions and x264, does not show noticeable performance differences since they already have irregular access patterns at the application-level [28]. The second group, which are the remaining programs, shows improvements of up to 8.2% with an average of 2.2%.

While analyzing the results, in particular, we found an interesting comparison between our results and the results presented by Sudan et al. [28]. In their work, Sudan et al. proposed micro-pages that collocates hot cache blocks from different page frames into a row-buffer to improve the overall utilization of the row buffer contents. Their approach differs from ours in that it tries to optimize the cases where small data are accessed heavily while ours tries to optimize cases where large data are accessed in regular patterns. Hence, according to the characteristics of the programs, the two approaches show contrasting improvements. Specifically, the blackscholes, swaptions and vips show relatively better improvements in the approach by Sudan et al., while canneal, facesim and streamcluster improves more with our approach. Since the two approaches are orthogonal, we speculate that integrating the two will result in even more positive effects on performance.

7. Conclusions

In this paper, we proposed M^3, a novel kernel-level memory allocator for multi-core, multi-bank systems. It was developed with two goals in mind. The first is to dedicate multiple banks to a core as much as possible so as to maximize memory parallelism, while the second is to reduce cases where multiple cores access the same bank at the same time. To achieve the first goal, the notion of a memory container was devised. For the second goal, we introduced a randomizing memory allocation algorithm. To the best of our knowledge, this is the first study that enforces randomness in page frame allocation decisions to reduce row-buffer conflicts.

We are considering two research directions as future work. One direction is analyzing the randomized algorithm more formally. We think that a single page frame allocation can be done in $O(1)$ time complexity, while it takes $O(\log n)$ in the original buddy algorithm. We are also investigating other issues related to M^3 such as fragmentation and lock contention. Another direction is a more thorough study of memory isolation techniques. We believe that with the cooperation of the memory controller, operating systems can partition memory more effectively so that it can completely eliminate row-buffer conflicts between cores.

Acknowledgments

We thank the anonymous ASPLOS reviewers for comments that helped improved this paper. This work was supported by the National Research Foundation of Korea(NRF) grant funded by the Korea government(MEST) (No. 2012R1A2A2A01014233) and (No. 2012R1A2A2A01045733).

References

[1] AMD Multi-core, http://www.amd.com.

[2] ARM Cortex-A9 Processor, http://www.arm.com.

[3] Intel Multi-core Technology, http://www.intel.com.

[4] J. H. Ahn, N. P. Jouppi, C. Kozyrakis, J. Leverich, and R. S. Schreiber. Future Scaling of Processor-Memory Interfaces. In *Proceedings of the Conference on High Performance Computing Networking, Storage and Analysis*, SC '09, pages 42:1–42:12, 2009.

[5] Benchmark. Linux Benchmark Suite Home Page. `http://lbs.sourceforge.net/`.

[6] C. Bienia, S. Kumar, J. P. Singh, and K. Li. The PARSEC Benchmark Suite: Characterization and Architectural Implications. In *Proceedings of the 17th International Conference on Parallel Architectures and Compilation Techniques*, PACT '08, pages 72–81, 2008.

[7] M. J. Bligh, M. Dobson, D. Hart, and G. Huizenga. Linux on NUMA Systems. In *Proceedings of the Linux Symposium*, pages 295–306, 2004.

[8] G. S. Brodal, E. D. Demaine, and J. I. Munro. Fast Allocation and Deallocation with an Improved Buddy System. *Acta Informatica*, 41:273–291, March 2005.

[9] H. Choi, J. Lee, and W. Sung. Memory Access Pattern-Aware DRAM Performance Model for Multi-core Systems. In *Proceedings of the*

2011 IEEE International Symposium on Performance Analysis of Systems & Software, ISPASS '11, pages 66 –75, 2011.

[10] M. Corrêa, A. Zorzo, and R. Scheer. Operating System Multilevel Load Balancing. In *Proceedings of the 2006 ACM Symposium on Applied Computing*, SAC '06, pages 1467–1471, 2006.

[11] B. K. Ganesh Balakrishnan, Ralph M. Begun. Understanding Intel Xeon 5600 Series Memory Performance and Optimization in IBM System x and BladeCenter Platforms. White paper, IBM, May 2010.

[12] Hewlett-Packard. DDR3 Memory Technology, Technology Brief, 3rd edition. White paper, HP, April 2012.

[13] JEDEC. JEDEC Standard : DDR3 SDRAM Specification. White paper, JEDEC, July 2012. `http://www.jedec.org/standards-documents/docs/jesd-79-3d`.

[14] M. K. Jeong, D. H. Yoon, D. Sunwoo, M. Sullivan, I. Lee, and M. Erez. Balancing DRAM Locality and Parallelism in Shared Memory CMP Systems. In *Proceedings of the IEEE 18th International Symposium on High-Performance Computer Architecture*, HPCA-18 '12, pages 1–12, 2012.

[15] D. Kaseridis, J. Stuecheli, and L. K. John. Minimalist Open-page: A DRAM Page-mode Scheduling Policy for the Many-core era. In *Proceedings of the 44th Annual IEEE/ACM International Symposium on Microarchitecture*, MICRO-44 '11, pages 24–35, 2011.

[16] Y. Kim, M. Papamichael, O. Mutlu, and M. Harchol-Balter. Thread Cluster Memory Scheduling: Exploiting Differences in Memory Access Behavior. In *Proceedings of the 43rd Annual IEEE/ACM International Symposium on Microarchitecture*, MICRO-43 '10, pages 65–76, 2010.

[17] C. J. Lee, V. Narasiman, O. Mutlu, and Y. N. Patt. Improving Memory Bank-level Parallelism in the Presence of Prefetching. In *Proceedings of the 42nd Annual IEEE/ACM International Symposium on Microarchitecture*, MICRO-42 '09, pages 327–336, 2009.

[18] Micron Technology. DDR3 SDRAM RDIMM : MT18JSF25672PD 2GB. White paper, Micron, July 2010. `http://www.micron.com/products/dram-modules/`.

[19] S. P. Muralidhara, L. Subramanian, O. Mutlu, M. Kandemir, and T. Moscibroda. Reducing Memory Interference in Multicore Systems via Application-Aware Memory Channel Partitioning. In *Proceedings of the 44th Annual IEEE/ACM International Symposium on Microarchitecture*, MICRO-44 '11, pages 374–385, 2011.

[20] O. Mutlu and T. Moscibroda. Stall-Time Fair Memory Access Scheduling for Chip Multiprocessors. In *Proceedings of the 40th Annual IEEE/ACM International Symposium on Microarchitecture*, MICRO-40 '07, pages 146–160, 2007.

[21] I. P. Page and J. Hagins. Improving the Performance of Buddy Systems. *IEEE Transactions on Computers*, 35:441–447, May 1986.

[22] J. L. Peterson and T. A. Norman. Buddy Systems. *Communications of the ACM*, 20:421–431, June 1977.

[23] K. K. Pusukuri, R. Gupta, and L. N. Bhuyan. Thread Tranquilizer: Dynamically Reducing Performance Variation. *ACM Transactions on Architecture and Code Optimization*, 8(4):46:1–46:21, January 2012.

[24] Ramspeed. Ramspeed Benchmark. `http://alasir.com/software/ramspeed/`.

[25] S. Rixner. Memory Controller Optimizations for Web Servers. In *Proceedings of the 37th Annual IEEE/ACM International Symposium on Microarchitecture*, MICRO-37 '04, pages 355–366, 2004.

[26] S. Rixner, W. J. Dally, U. J. Kapasi, P. Mattson, and J. D. Owens. Memory Access Scheduling. In *Proceedings of the 27th Annual International Symposium on Computer Architecture*, ISCA-27 '00, pages 128–138, 2000.

[27] STREAM. STREAM Benchmark. `http://www.cs.virginia.edu/stream`.

[28] K. Sudan, N. Chatterjee, D. Nellans, M. Awasthi, R. Balasubramonian, and A. Davis. Micro-pages: Increasing DRAM Efficiency with Locality-Aware Data Placement. In *Proceedings of the 15th International Conference on Architectural Support for Programming Languages and Operating Systems*, ASPLOS-15 '10, pages 219–230, 2010.

[29] SysBench. Sysbench: A System Performance Benchmark. `http://sysbench.sourceforge.net/`.

[30] UnixBench. UnixBench: A Fundamental High-level Linux Benchmark Suite. `http://www.tux.org/pub/tux/benchmarks/System/unixbench/`.

[31] D. Wang, B. Ganesh, N. Tuaycharoen, K. Baynes, A. Jaleel, and B. Jacob. DRAMsim: A Memory System Simulator. *ACM SIGARCH Computer Architecture News*, 33(4):100–107, November 2005.

[32] W. Wang, T. Dey, J. Mars, L. Tang, J. W. Davidson, and M. L. Soffa. Performance Analysis of Thread Mappings with a Holistic View of the Hardware Resources. In *Proceedings of the 2012 IEEE International Symposium on Performance Analysis of Systems & Software*, ISPASS '12, pages 156–167, 2012.

[33] D. H. Yoon, M. K. Jeong, and M. Erez. Adaptive Granularity Memory Systems: A Tradeoff between Storage Efficiency and Throughput. In *Proceedings of the 38th Annual International Symposium on Computer Architecture*, ISCA-38 '11, pages 295–306, 2011.

[34] Z. Zhang, Z. Zhu, and X. Zhang. A Permutation-based Page Interleaving Scheme to Reduce Row-buffer Conflicts and Exploit Data Locality. In *Proceedings of the 33rd Annual ACM/IEEE International Symposium on Microarchitecture*, MICRO-33 '00, pages 32–41, 2000.

[35] H. Zheng, J. Lin, Z. Zhang, E. Gorbatov, H. David, and Z. Zhu. Mini-rank: Adaptive DRAM Architecture for Improving Memory Power Efficiency. In *Proceedings of the 41st Annual IEEE/ACM International Symposium on Microarchitecture*, MICRO-41 '08, pages 210–221, 2008.

Cyrus: Unintrusive Application-Level Record-Replay for Replay Parallelism

Nima Honarmand, Nathan Dautenhahn, Josep Torrellas, Samuel T. King
Department of Computer Science
University of Illinois at Urbana-Champaign
Urbana, IL
{honarma1, dautenh1, torrella, kingst}@illinois.edu

Gilles Pokam, Cristiano Pereira
Intel
Santa Clara, CA
{gilles.a.pokam, cristiano.l.pereira}@intel.com

Abstract

Architectures for deterministic record-replay (R&R) of multithreaded code are attractive for program debugging, intrusion analysis, and fault-tolerance uses. However, very few of the proposed designs have focused on maximizing replay speed — a key enabling property of these systems. The few efforts that focus on replay speed require intrusive hardware or software modifications, or target whole-system R&R rather than the more useful application-level R&R.

This paper presents the first hardware-based scheme for unintrusive, application-level R&R that explicitly targets high replay speed. Our scheme, called *Cyrus*, requires no modification to commodity snoopy cache coherence. It introduces the concept of an on-the-fly software Backend Pass during recording which, as the log is being generated, transforms it for high replay parallelism. This pass also fixes-up the log, and can flexibly trade-off replay parallelism for log size. We analyze the performance of Cyrus using full system (OS plus hardware) simulation. Our results show that Cyrus has negligible recording overhead. In addition, for 8-processor runs of SPLASH-2, Cyrus attains an average replay parallelism of 5, and a replay speed that is, on average, only about 50% lower than the recording speed.

Categories and Subject Descriptors C.0 [**General**]: Hardware/Software Interfaces; C.1.2 [**Processor Architectures**]: Multiple Data Stream Architectures (Multiprocessors) - MIMD Processors; D.1.3 [**Programming Techniques**]: Concurrent Programming - Parallel Programming; D.1.3 [**Programming Techniques**]: Concurrent Programming - Parallel Programming; D.4.0 [**Operating Systems**]: General; D.4.1 [**Operating Systems**]: Process Management - Threads

Keywords Deterministic Replay, Application-level Parallel Replay, Unintrusive Hardware-Assisted Recording, Source-only Recording, Backend Log Processing

1. Introduction

Deterministic Record-Replay (R&R) seeks to monitor the execution of a program (or a set of programs) and exactly reproduce it on a subsequent execution. R&R has broad uses in at least program debugging [1, 15, 33], where, for example, a concurrency bug can be reproduced, intrusion analysis [10, 14], where an intrusion can be traced back to an attacker's actions, and fault-tolerant, highly-available systems [9, 32], where a backup machine can resume where the primary failed. This paper focuses on R&R for multithreaded applications on multiprocessor machines. In such a scenario, R&R typically involves recording all the non-deterministic events that occurred during the initial execution — i.e., application inputs and memory access interleavings. Then, during replay, logged inputs are provided to the application at the correct times, and the memory accesses are forced to interleave in the same manner as in the log.

There are several proposals of schemes for R&R of multithreaded programs. On the one hand, there are those that do not require any special hardware [2, 5, 10, 11, 18, 27, 28, 32–34], typically relying on the OS, compiler and/or run-time libraries for recording and replaying. Being software-only solutions, these systems are relatively inexpensive to implement but tend to run slowly during recording. Other schemes record with the aid of some special hardware module [3, 7, 13, 23–26, 30, 31, 35–37]. These systems add negligible overhead during recording, but can be expensive to implement. In addition, some schemes R&R the whole machine's execution (e.g., [3, 13, 23]), while there are others that only R&R a single or a group of applications running on the machine (e.g., [24, 25, 33]). Typically, it is the latter (application-level R&R) that the users actually need rather than the former (whole-system R&R). In addition, recreating the whole machine state during replay is often very hard and, to work correctly, needs to deal with many non-portable operating system and hardware issues of the platform. Application-level R&R, in contrast, tends to be more portable and adds less overhead.

Different R&R schemes attempt to optimize different metrics. Traditionally, hardware-based R&R schemes have attempted to minimize log size requirements. Software-based schemes, instead, have focused on minimizing the overhead of recording — in some cases, even at the cost of potentially having to replay multiple times [2, 28]. Very few schemes have focused on maximizing replay speed — most notably DeLorean/Capo [23, 24], DoublePlay [34], and Karma [3]. All three use *parallel replay* mechanisms for this purpose.

Each of the three previous systems has shortcomings that could limit its practicality. Specifically, DeLorean/Capo uses transactional record and replay hardware, which requires a redesign of current commodity processor hardware. Karma provides whole-system R&R rather than application-level R&R. As indicated above, this is not what users typically need and, in addition, it is hardly portable. In addition, Karma requires augmenting the cache coherence protocol messages — which we want to avoid. Finally, DoublePlay is a software-based scheme, which requires modifying and recompiling the application, marking its synchronizations.

This is unfortunate, given that fast replay is a key enabling property for R&R systems. For example, debugging can be more productive if buggy executions can be quickly replayed to the point of the bug. Similarly, intrusion analysis can benefit from extensive on-the-fly analysis of how the attack is taking place. Finally, in fault tolerance, a backup machine has to quickly catch up with a failed one to provide hot replacement.

To attain effective low-overhead R&R, we believe that, in addition to providing fast parallel replay, the system needs to: (i) support *application-level* R&R, and (ii) rely on *unintrusive* hardware design. In particular, it should avoid system-level hardware changes such as any changes to the cache coherence protocol. We believe this is fundamental for acceptance of R&R hardware. Since most multiprocessors today use snoopy cache coherence, we require our design to be compatible with (and not modify) snoopy protocols.

In this paper, we make the following contributions:

• We present the first hardware-based approach for unintrusive, application-level R&R that explicitly targets high-speed replay. The approach, called *Cyrus*, requires no modification to commodity snoopy cache coherence.

• Cyrus introduces the concept of an on-the-fly software *Backend Pass* during recording which, as the log is being generated, consumes it and transforms it. This pass fixes-up the log, which has incomplete information due to our recording requirements of only application-level interactions and no cache coherence protocol changes. In addition, the backend pass exposes a high degree of parallelism for replay. Finally, as the backend pass produces the final log, it can also flexibly trade-off replay parallelism for log size.

• We modified the Linux kernel to control and virtualize a simulated version of the Cyrus hardware. Our results show that Cyrus adds negligible recording overhead, even with the backend pass. In addition, for 8-processor runs of SPLASH-2, Cyrus attains an average replay parallelism of 5 (in terms of the length of the critical instruction path), and a replay speed that is, on average, only about 50% lower than the recording speed.

The rest of the paper is organized as follows: Section 2 discusses background issues and challenges in R&R; Section 3 presents Cyrus' architecture; Section 4 describes implementation issues; Sections 5 and 6 evaluate Cyrus; Section 7 discusses related work; and Section 8 concludes the paper.

2. Background and Key Challenges

2.1 Background on Deterministic R&R

Deterministic Record-Replay (R&R) consists of monitoring the execution of a multithreaded application on a parallel machine, and then exactly reproducing the execution later on. R&R requires recording all the non-deterministic events that occur during the initial execution. They include the inputs to the execution (e.g., return values from system calls) and the order of the inter-thread communications (i.e., the interleaving of the inter-thread data dependences). Then, during replay, the logged inputs are fed back to the execution at the correct times, and the memory accesses are forced to interleave according to the log.

To accomplish application-level R&R, we leverage previous work, Capo [24], which describes how the OS virtualizes the R&R structures. A Replay Sphere is the single application (or group of applications) that we want to R&R in isolation from the rest of the system. Each sphere has an Input Log and a Memory Log.

The Memory Log collects the order of the data dependences between threads. To collect such orders, we can use a software-only solution that relies on the runtime or operating system. Alternatively, we can use a hardware-assisted scheme that relies on a special hardware module. This approach has the advantage of recording with negligible performance overhead, even for applications with frequent inter-thread data dependences. Hardware-assisted schemes typically use cache coherence transactions to detect inter-thread dependences.

To reduce the amount of state that needs to be collected in the Memory Log, most of the recent proposals of hardware-assisted schemes [3, 13, 23, 24, 30, 35] log the amount of work that a thread does between communications, rather than the communications themselves. Specifically, each entry in the log records the number of consecutive operations executed by a processor between inter-thread dependences. These groups of instructions or memory accesses are known as *chunks*, *episodes* or *blocks*. The entry also has information on what other block(s) in the log depend on this one. During replay, inter-thread dependences are enforced by executing these blocks in the proper order.

Most of the proposed block-based recording schemes encode the execution in a fairly serial form that can take away much of the parallelism that existed in the original execution. Specifically, some schemes log a total order of blocks [23, 24, 30], while others use Scalar Lamport Clocks (SLC) [17] to order blocks [13, 35]. In a basic design with SLCs, when a processor detects an inter-thread data dependence, it terminates its current block and assigns to it a scalar clock value (usually called *timestamp*). The recording mechanism guarantees that if an instruction in block *B2* depends on an instruction in block *B1*, then *B2* receives a timestamp strictly larger than that of *B1*. This way of using timestamps creates many unnecessary block ordering constraints which hide the original parallelism.

To recover lost parallelism, DeLorean uses speculative execution of blocks in parallel [23]. Karma [3], instead, records the block orders as a directed acyclic graph (DAG) of blocks. In the general case, each block has multiple predecessor and successor blocks, and parallel replay is possible.

Karma, however, is a whole-system R&R scheme that has been designed around a directory-based cache coherent system. It augments the coherence messages with timestamps and some new fields. It relies on the availability of explicit invalidation acknowledgements in directory protocols.

2.2 Key R&R Challenges

Our goal is to develop a useful and easy-to-implement R&R hardware scheme. Such a scheme needs to: (i) support application-level R&R rather than whole-system R&R, (ii) avoid changes to system-level multiprocessor hardware, especially changes to the snoopy cache coherence protocol, and (iii) enable highly-parallel replay.

In this section, we elaborate on the challenges that these three requirements pose. Our general approach matches current proposals [3, 13, 23, 24, 30, 35]: we use the cache coherence transactions to detect dependences between threads, and each entry in the log records the number of consecutive instructions executed by a processor between dependences.

2.2.1 Challenge 1: Application-Level R&R

The main difficulty in performing application-level R&R is that many of the cache coherence transactions observed in the machine are potentially unrelated to the application being recorded; they are due to the OS or to other applications. Consequently, an application-level R&R scheme has to identify these unrelated transactions and prevent them from inhibiting correct replay. This is unlike a whole-system R&R scheme.

Figure 1 shows this problem for a three-processor machine. As we run the application, we may observe coherence transactions between processors executing the application being recorded (e.g., transaction (1)). However, we may also observe transactions between the application being recorded and the OS (transaction (2)), between two OS threads (transaction (3)), and even between the application (or OS) and an application that is *not* being recorded (transactions (4) and (5)).

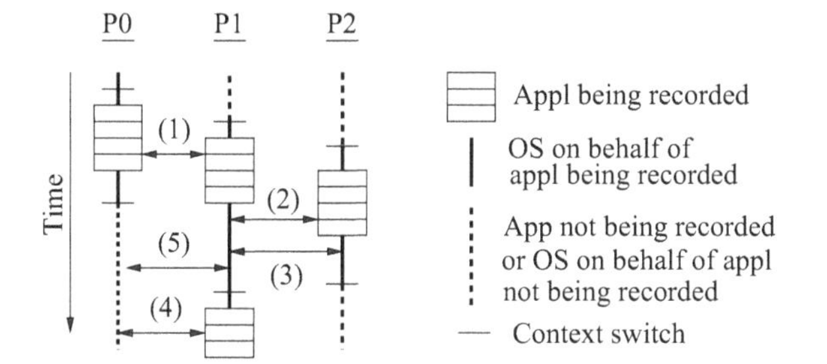

Figure 1. Difficulties in capturing inter-thread dependences in application-level R&R.

Some of these communication events are unrelated to the application and can make the log inconsistent and cause replay divergence. They result from a variety of causes. One is interaction between OS and application threads, possibly through common buffers, and between OS threads. Another is the presence of hardware prefetchers, which may move unpredictable data and change its coherence state. Another effect is the processor issuing speculative loads, which access unpredictable data. In addition, the presence of context switches adds further uncertainty: a transaction may move data from a cache where the owner thread has been preempted. Should we record it? Finally, the Bloom filters [4] used in many R&R schemes to help detect dependences between threads [13, 23, 30] compound the problem: the events may be false positive dependences due to address aliasing in the signature.

2.2.2 Challenge 2: Unintrusive Hardware

The second challenge of an R&R scheme is the need to avoid changes to system-level hardware and, in particular, any changes to the cache coherence protocol. This paper focuses on snoopy coherent systems because they are the most commonly used approach today. In this environment, we must not augment the coherence protocol with new messages or even new fields in existing messages. This is because the timing of the messages is an integral part of the protocol design and any timing changes will require protocol re-validation.

A key consequence of this requirement is that the R&R scheme must record inter-thread dependences *from the dependence source only*. To see why, consider Figures 2(a)-(c). In these charts, processor *P1* initiates a request, which causes *P0* to supply a cached line and/or to invalidate it. These are dependences that need to be recorded in the R&R log. However, snoopy protocols provide incomplete information. Specifically, while the requesting processor (*P1*) includes its ID in the coherence transaction, the processor at the dependence source (*P0*) does not supply its ID in Figure 2(c) because there is no response message; in addition, *P0* may or may not provide its ID in Figures 2(a)-(b). This is unlike directory-based protocols, where there are explicit request and response messages that include the sender ID.

Hence, in any dependence, only the R&R module at the source processor (*P0*) knows about it and logs it; we have to assume that

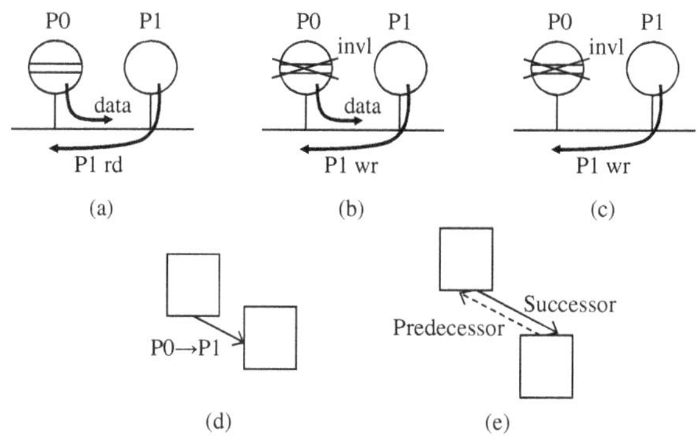

Figure 2. Keeping a snoopy cache coherence protocol unmodified requires recording dependences from the dependence source only.

the R&R module at the destination processor (*P1*) is completely unaware of the dependence. Any replay system must be able to reconstruct the execution from a log with only dependences of the form shown in Figure 2(d) instead of bidirectional successor and predecessor information as in Figure 2(e).

2.2.3 Challenge 3: Replay Parallelism

Parallelism is fundamental to high-speed replay, which in turn will enable new uses of this technology. To expose maximum parallelism, the log must encode the dependences between blocks across threads. Also, for each dependence, the source and destination block boundaries should be *as close as possible* to the dependence's source and destination references, respectively.

3. Unintrusive App-Level R&R for Replay Parallelism

3.1 Main Idea

We propose a new general approach to address the previous challenges and deliver hardware-unintrusive, application-level R&R for replay parallelism. Our approach is called *Cyrus*. We use the mechanisms of Capo [24] to record input logs (Section 4.2). As for the memory log, to support application-level R&R, the hardware judiciously avoids logging certain types of interprocessor interactions. Moreover, to keep the cache coherence protocol unmodified, the hardware logs the dependence only on the source processor. The result of these two constraints is a log with some dependences that still need to be fixed-up or discarded, and with unidirectional dependence information only.

Consequently, as the log is being dumped into memory, an on-the-fly software *Backend Pass* consumes it and transforms it into the final log. This backend pass performs three actions: (i) fixes-up and discards some of the dependences to correctly implement application-level replay; (ii) transforms the unidirectional dependences into bi-directional ones for ease of replay; and (iii) produces a log that enables a high degree of parallelism during replay. In addition, the backend pass can flexibly produce a log with the desired tradeoff between degree of replay parallelism and log size.

Figure 3 shows the system. We consider this backend pass to be a fundamental enabler of a hardware-assisted R&R scheme that is hardware-unintrusive, supports application-level R&R and allows a maximum (and also settable) degree of replay parallelism. In the following, we show how Cyrus addresses each of the challenges.

3.2 Application-Level R&R

To understand which interprocessor dependences need to be recorded for application-level R&R, consider the model of Figure 4(a). At

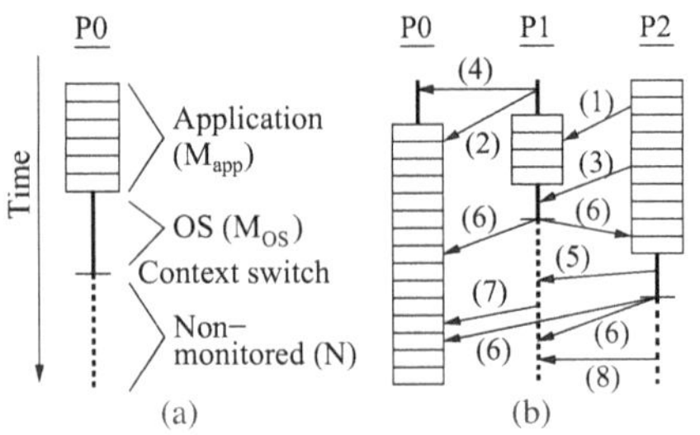

Type of Interaction		Type of Dependence	Cyrus Action	Example
$srcM$	$srcM_{app} \rightarrow dstM_{app}$	Correct	Record	(1)
	$srcM_{OS} \rightarrow dstM_{app}$	Correct	Record	(2)
	$srcM_{app} \rightarrow dstM_{OS}$	Early or Unrelated	Record & Defer/Discard	(3)
	$srcM_{OS} \rightarrow dstM_{OS}$	Early or Unrelated	Record & Defer/Discard	(4)
	$srcM \rightarrow dstN$	Unrelated	Record & Defer/Discard	(5)
M-preemption in context switch		Serialization (Multiple)	Record & Defer/Discard	(6)
$srcN$	$srcN \rightarrow dstM$	Correct, Early or Unrelated	Ignore	(7)
	$srcN \rightarrow dstN$	Unrelated	Ignore	(8)

(c)

Figure 4. Characterizing the types of interprocessor interactions.

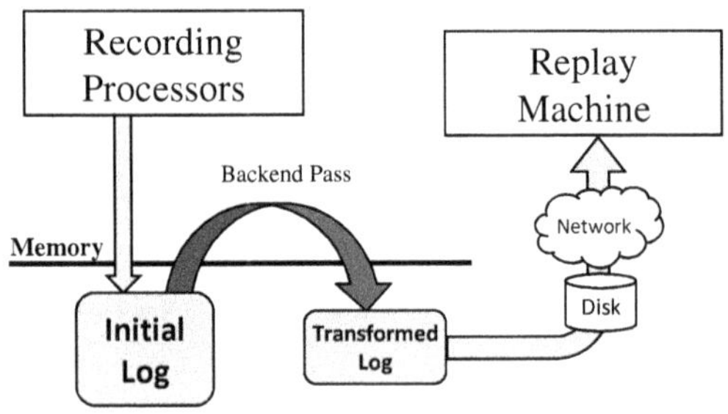

Figure 3. Overview of the Cyrus system.

any given time, a processor may run a process that is being recorded or one that is not. We call such times *M* and *N* for monitored and non-monitored, respectively. During the *M* time, the processor may run application code (M_{app} time) or OS code on behalf of the application (M_{OS} time).

In this environment, there are several types of interactions between a source and a destination processor. The destination processor (*dst*) is the one that initiates a coherence action and receives a response — e.g., it misses in its cache or sends an invalidation. The source processor (*src*) is the one that sends the response. Figure 4(c) shows the types of interactions possible, together with the corresponding type of dependence involved, the action taken by Cyrus, and a dependence example from Figure 4(b). In the next few paragraphs, we describe each of the interactions and how Cyrus handles them.

We start by describing the interactions where the source is a processor running a monitored process (*srcM*), as shown in the first group of entries in Figure 4(c). If the destination is a processor running monitored application code ($srcM_{app} \rightarrow dstM_{app}$ or $srcM_{OS} \rightarrow dstM_{app}$), this is a correct dependence within the recorded application — the recorded application misses in the cache or sends an invalidation. Therefore, Cyrus records it in the log.

If the destination is running the OS on behalf of a monitored application ($srcM_{app} \rightarrow dstM_{OS}$ or $srcM_{OS} \rightarrow dstM_{OS}$), two cases are possible. One is that the OS is accessing data that will later be accessed by the monitored application code (i.e., it is effectively prefetching the data); the other case is that the OS is accessing data that is unrelated to the monitored program and happens to be in the source processor's cache. In the first case, we must record this correct dependence that is detected *early*; in the second case, we must discard it. Since Cyrus does not know which case it is, it conservatively records it in the initial log. Later, the backend pass will find which case it is, and either set the destination of the dependence to be the next M_{app} block running on the destination processor (an action called "deferring the dependence"), or discard it. In Figure 4(c), we call this action "Record & Defer/Discard".

Finally, if the destination processor is running a non-monitored process ($srcM \rightarrow dstN$), the action pertains to unrelated data, and does not need to be recorded. However, for ease of implementation as we will see, Cyrus records it as in the previous case.

The next row in Figure 4(c) corresponds to a context switch where an *M* process is preempted. After the preemption, data left in the cache may be requested by other processors. To avoid having to log such interactions, in a context switch, Cyrus conservatively records one dependence from this processor to every other processor in the machine. This is called a *serialization* because it effectively serializes the last block of the current processor prior to the context switch before the current block of every other processor. Cyrus records such dependences in the initial log and the backend pass will defer or discard them. Specifically, any such dependence will be discarded if no monitored process ever runs on the destination processor.

The final two rows in Figure 4(c) correspond to when the source is a non-monitored process (*srcN*). In this case, a $srcN \rightarrow dstM$ interaction can be correct, early or unrelated, while a $srcN \rightarrow dstN$ interaction is unrelated. Cyrus ignores each of these dependences. This behavior is correct since any such dependence is guaranteed to be superseded by one of the serialization dependences described above.

Overall, as shown in Figure 4(c), to ensure correct application-level recording, Cyrus only needs to log events when a processor running the application or OS code of a *monitored* process is: (i) either the *source* of a dependence (i.e., at the request of another processor, it provides a line from its cache or invalidates a line from its cache) or (ii) suffers a context switch. Still, we need a later pass to fix or discard certain dependences.

3.3 Unintrusive Recording Hardware

The Cyrus hardware is shown at a high level in Figure 5. Each core has a *Race Recording Unit* (RRU) associated with the cache controller. For simplicity, we show the RRU for a system with a single-level cache hierarchy. In this design, the RRU observes the bus transactions, and is also informed of processor requests and cache evictions.

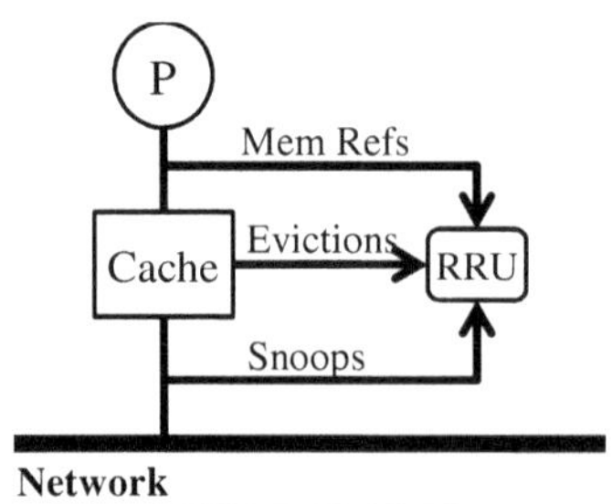

Figure 5. High-level view of the Cyrus hardware.

To keep the design unintrusive, we require that it does not change the cache coherence protocol in any way — including, for snoopy schemes, not adding new fields to messages. As explained

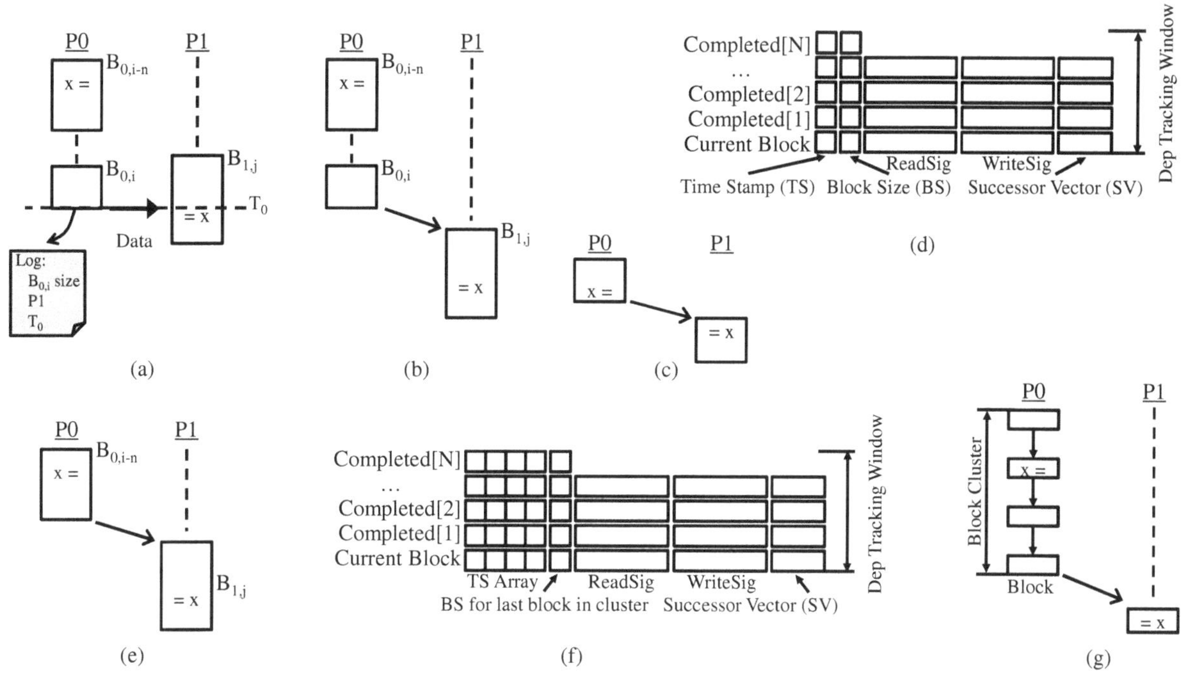

Figure 6. Recording dependences in Cyrus.

in Section 2.2.2, the implication for snoopy schemes is that, when an interprocessor dependence takes place, only the source processor knows about it and can record it.

Consequently, Cyrus operates as follows. When a processor (P_0) executing a block ($B_{0,i}$) of a monitored process observes a bus transaction to which its cache needs to respond (by invalidating a line and/or providing a line), the RRU hardware is signaled. The RRU terminates $B_{0,i}$ and (in a naive design) creates a local log entry composed of: $B_{0,i}$'s block size (BS) in number of instructions, the ID of the processor that initiated the transaction (the dependence's destination processor), and the current time. Cyrus counts time as the number of bus transactions so far, which is known by and is consistent across all processors. We call such number the Time Stamp (TS). The destination processor is unaware that a dependence has been recorded.

This information is all that Cyrus needs to log, and requires no modification to the coherence protocol. However, to ease the replay, we will need to have bidirectional dependence information as in Figure 2(e). Such information is generated from the initial log by the backend pass and is stored in the final log (Section 3.5).

3.4 Replay Parallelism

With the naive approach described, the log records an inter-thread dependence between the blocks that are running when the coherence action is detected. This approach enables only limited replay parallelism. For example, consider Figure 6(a), where processor P_0 writes to variable x in block $B_{0,i-n}$ and processor P_1 reads x in block $B_{1,j}$ at time T_0. The figure also shows the log entry. Since the coherence action occurs while P_0 is executing block $B_{0,i}$, the logged entry implies a dependence and a replay order between blocks $B_{0,i}$ and $B_{1,j}$ as in Figure 6(b) — even though the source of the dependence is much earlier, and the destination is deep inside the destination block. To extract maximum parallelism, we would like the log to represent the execution as in Figure 6(c), where processors P0 and P1 overlap their execution as much as possible.

To approach this ideal capability, Cyrus can be designed to use a small Maximum Block Size and to track multiple blocks at a time. The idea is for the RRU to keep information for the most recent N completed local blocks. These completed blocks plus the currently-running block form the *Dependence-Tracking Window*, from which dependence sources are tracked. Each of these blocks (except for the oldest one) has a read and a write signature register (ReadSig and WriteSig), which hash-encode with a Bloom filter [4] the addresses of the lines read or written by the block (Figure 6(d)). When the local cache responds to an incoming coherence request, the hardware checks the address of the request against the signatures in reverse order, starting with the ones for the currently-running block. When one of the signatures matches the address, we know that the corresponding block was the source of the dependence, and record it. This allows us to precisely place the source of the dependence in the right block. If none of the signatures matches the address, the oldest of the N completed blocks is assumed to source the dependence.

If the currently-running block is the source of the dependence, it is terminated. In this case, all the blocks are shifted up, the old one is written to the log, and a new one starts. With this support, the log records the example dependence as in Figure 6(e), where the source of the arrow is closer to the source access. This enables more replay parallelism. Karma [3] uses this approach for N=1.

Figure 6(d) shows other fields of each entry in the dependence-tracking window, which we will discuss later.

Unfortunately, even this enhanced approach has some shortcomings. To have a large dependence-tracking window, N needs to be high, which means that many pairs of costly signatures are needed. The alternative is to increase the block size, therefore needing a lower N. In this case, however, the source of the dependence may be far from the end of the source block, and the destination of the dependence may be far from the beginning of the destination block. In the worst case, the source and destination references are separated by twice the maximum block size.

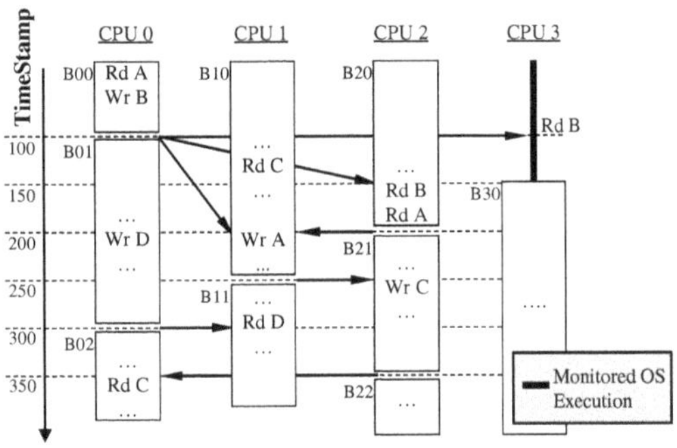

(a) Execution

CPU	TID	TS	SIZE	Successor Vector			
0		100		-	200	150	100
0		300		-	300	0	0
0		370		-	0	0	0
1		250		0	-	250	0
1		360		0	-	0	0
2		200		0	200	-	0
2		350		350	0	-	0
2		390		0	0	-	0
3		385		0	0	0	-

(b) Initial Log

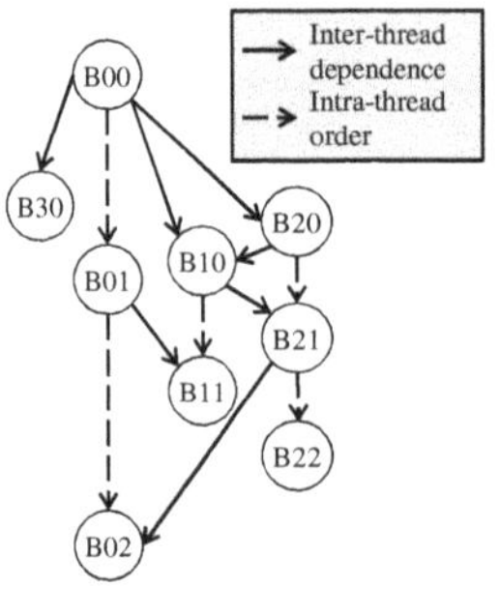

CPU	TID	SIZE	PTV				STV			
0			-	0	0	0	-	1	1	1
0			-	0	0	0	-	1	0	0
0			-	0	1	0	-	0	0	0
1			1	-	1	0	0	-	1	0
1			1	-	0	0	0	-	0	0
2			1	0	-	0	0	1	-	0
2			0	1	-	0	1	0	-	0
2			0	0	-	0	0	0	-	0
3			1	0	0	-	0	0	0	-

(c) MaxPar

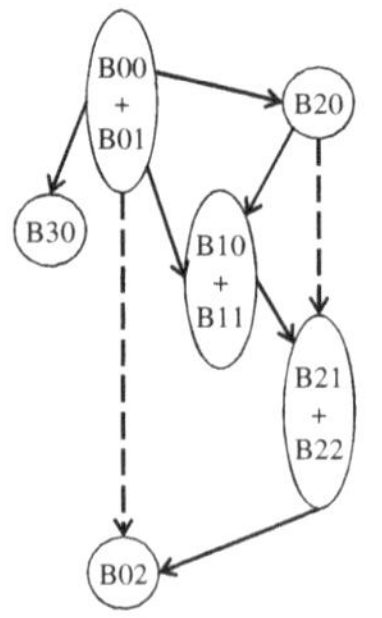

CPU	TID	SIZE	PTV				STV			
0			-	0	0	0	-	1	1	0
0			-	0	1	0	-	0	0	0
1			1	-	1	0	0	-	1	0
2			1	0	-	0	0	1	-	0
2			0	1	-	0	1	0	-	0
3			1	0	0	-	0	0	0	-

(d) Stitched

TID	SIZE

(e) Serial

TID	SIZE

(f) StSerial

Figure 7. Example of execution and resulting Cyrus logs. The table in (b) depicts the initial block data dumped by the processors, while the other tables show the results of the different backends, encoding the corresponding DAGs. In the tables, dashes indicate entries corresponding to dependencies to the processor itself. These are never used.

To address this problem, Cyrus introduces the concept of *Block Clusters*. Block clusters use the observations that: (i) to reduce the separation between the beginning of the destination block and the destination reference, we need small blocks; and (ii) to reduce the separation between the source reference and the end of the source block, we need a large dependence-tracking window which, to be cheap, needs large blocks. Hence, in block clusters, we use small blocks and *combine them to make them appear* as large blocks. In practice, reducing the separation in (i) is more important than in (ii). The reason is that any separation in (i) directly slows down the replay execution relative to the recorded execution.

With block clusters, we use a small block size, but we group multiple consecutive blocks into a cluster for the purpose of tracking dependence sources. The RRU's dependence-tracking window contains multiple block clusters. Each one has a *single* ReadSig and WriteSig signature pair that contains the addresses accessed by all the blocks in the cluster. If the address of an incoming coherence transaction matches the signature, then the source of the dependence is assumed to be the *last* block of the cluster.

Figure 6(f) shows the case of four blocks per cluster. When a block executes and exhausts its maximum size without recording a dependence, its termination time stamp is stored in TS[i] and the next block in the cluster starts. Note that for such blocks, Cyrus does not need to store the size explicitly because it is known to be the maximum block size. When a dependence is found in the running cluster's signatures, the running block is assumed to be the source; that block is terminated, its time stamp and size (BS) are saved, and the cluster is terminated. All the cluster information is shifted up and a new cluster is started. Future dependence sources found in the signatures of any cluster in the RRUs dependence-tracking window, are assigned to the last block in that cluster.

With this support, Cyrus provides a large dependence tracking window, and at the same time, reduces the distance between the beginning of the destination block and the destination reference. This is seen in Figure 6(g). The result is more replay parallelism.

3.5 Backend Software Pass

The initial log generated by the recorder has unidirectional dependence information only, and contains some dependences that need to be fixed-up or discarded for application-level R&R. To correct these issues, a backend software pass processes the log, creating a final log that is highly amenable to parallel replay. In addition, the backend pass can format the log for different tradeoffs between replay parallelism and log size.

3.5.1 Transforming the Log

Each entry of the initial log contains the following base information for one block: the ID of the CPU that executed the block and the block's termination time stamp (TS). In addition, if this is the last block of a cluster that sourced dependences, the information also includes the block size (BS) in number of instructions, and successor vector (SV). The latter has one entry for each of the other processors in the machine. SV entry *i* is either null or has the TS when the current cluster sourced a dependence to processor *i*. If the cluster sourced multiple dependences to processor *i*, SV[i] has the TS of the earliest one — which is the most conservative.

Figures 7(a) and (b) show an example execution with 4 processors and the resulting initial log, respectively. Each row in Figure 7(b) indicates a block dumped by the corresponding processor. In all of the tables in Figure 7, TID is the ID of the thread to which the block belongs. It is provided by the OS driver that controls the RRU. The hardware itself is oblivious to the notion of threads (Section 4.2).

For simplicity, we assume one block per cluster and two clusters. In Figure 7(a), we can see that, as soon as a processor sources a dependence for a datum accessed in the current block, it terminates the block. If the dependent datum has not been accessed in the current block but in past blocks, the current block is not terminated. For example, at TS=200, CPU1 performs "Wr A". Since this access does not conflict with block B01 of CPU0, B01 is not cut and the dependence is assigned to B00, instead.

In Figure 7(a), all the dependences are Correct ones except for the one from CPU0 to CPU3, which is an Early or an Unrelated one. In the figure, CPU3 is initially executing the OS on behalf of the monitored process. The OS accesses variable *B*, creating a dependence with processor 0, which terminates its block B00. According to Cyrus's operation, it has to record the dependence, and rely on the backend pass to either defer it or discard it. Since, as shown in the figure, CPU3 later executes block B30 of the monitored application, the backend pass sets the destination of the dependence to be B30 — i.e., defers the dependence. This is required for correctness, as block B30 could next silently access variable *B*. If, instead, CPU3 never executes any block of the monitored application, the backend pass discards the dependence.

Similarly, if the OS preempts a monitored thread (i.e., on a context switch), it uses the programming interface of the RRU (Section 4.2) to create Serialization dependences with all other processors; they are eventually deferred or discarded by the backend pass.

As the backend pass processes each entry of the initial log, fixing up and discarding dependences, it also records, in each dependence's destination block, which other block is the source. Encoding such bidirectional dependence information will enable parallel replay. Hence, it incrementally builds the dependence DAG that captures all the necessary ordering of blocks for a deterministic replay.

To encode the resulting DAG in the final log, we adopt and generalize the representation used by Karma [3], in which, instead of representing dependences as source-destination block pairs, we use a token-based representation. Assume a dependence between block B1 of processor P1 to block B2 of processor P2. To enforce the dependence during the replay, the log will have B1 send a token to P2 after its execution, and B2 wait for a token from P1 before starting. Both source and destination are processor numbers rather than block numbers.

Our baseline backend pass algorithm and the resulting transformed log are called *MaxPar* because they expose maximum replay parallelism obtainable from the initial log. An entry in the MaxPar log contains the following information for a block: the IDs of the CPU and thread that executed it, its size, the Successor Token Vector (STV), and the Predecessor Token Vector (PTV). The STV is a bit vector with as many bits as other processors. Bit *i* is set if a successor of the block is in processor *i*. The PTV is an array of counters with as many entries as the STV. Entry *i* counts the number of predecessors that the block has in processor *i*. For our example, the resulting MaxPar log and execution DAG are shown in Figure 7(c).

With the MaxPar log, replay will involve processors executing in parallel, synchronizing only on dependences — figuratively passing tokens between them. In the following, we outline the MaxPar algorithm and then consider other algorithms.

3.5.2 MaxPar: Algorithm for Maximum Parallelism

In this discussion, we call a block *open* while it still has unresolved successors or predecessors, and *resolved* otherwise. After a block becomes resolved, the backend can write it to the transformed log as soon as all of the previous blocks of the same processor are written. After writing, we say the block is *retired*.

Figure 8 shows the high-level pseudocode of the algorithm. Each processor is represented by a proxy object. A proxy keeps track of its open blocks in a chronologically ordered list. Also, it keeps a data structure (called *waitingList*) for blocks of other proxies that, according to their Successor Vectors (SV), have unresolved successors in this proxy.

The algorithm processes blocks in batches of consecutive blocks from the same processor. When a new block is added to proxy *P*, its SV is checked, and for each successor, the block is added

```
AddBatch(batch, proxy):
  for each block b in the batch
    for each valid successor processor s in b.sv
      /* call sp the proxy for processor s */
      add b to sp.waitingList[proxy]
  foreach other proxy op in the system:
    foreach block b in proxy.waitingList[op]
      find dep
      /* dep is the block in proxy that is the successor of b */
      if (dep is not NULL)
        remove b from proxy.waitingList
        mark this dependence as resolved in b
        update b.STV and dep.PTV
  if enough time has passed since last trimming
    Trim()
Trim():
  for each proxy p in the system
    for each block b in p
      if b is old enough and all its predecessors are retired
        write b to the transformed log
        remove b from p
MaxPar():
  while (there are batches)
    batch ← next batch
    AddBatch(batch, proxies[batch.cpu])
```

Figure 8. High-level description of the MaxPar algorithm.

to the *waitingList* of the proxy for that successor. Next, since a new batch has been added to *P*, blocks in the *waitingList* of *P* are checked to see if their dependences can be resolved. To resolve a dependence that was recorded at time *t*, the open blocks of *P* are binary-searched to find the first block whose time stamp is larger than *t*. This block is the destination of the dependence. The dependence is recorded by setting the appropriate entry in the STV of the source block and incrementing the corresponding entry in the PTV of the destination block. As dependences are resolved, periodically, a trimming pass is run to retire the resolved blocks from the proxies by writing them to the transformed log. Before writing a block to the log, MaxPar tries to merge it with the previous block of the same processor, if that does not reduce the recorded parallelism. Specifically, assume that the previous block is B_0 and the current block is B_1. If B_0 has no successors (other than B_1) and B_1 has no predecessors (other than B_0), merging B_0 and B_1 will not change the recorded parallelism.

There are some details that are not shown in Figure 8. One difficulty is how to tell whether all the predecessors of a given block have been seen and resolved. Processors dump their block data independently and in batches (not one by one) and it is quite possible that when a block is dumped, some of its predecessors are still in their respective processors.

The solution here is to make sure block data do not indefinitely reside in processor buffers and will be dumped if they have been around for a preset amount of time, called *Maximum Silence Period* (or MSP) — e.g., 100000 timestamp units. Consider block B_i of proxy P_i. With the above guarantee, which we call the *Bounded Silence* guarantee, if the maximum timestamp of all the blocks dumped so far is larger than $B_i.ts + MSP$, then we know for sure that all the predecessors of B_i have also been dumped and their dependencies have been resolved (please recall that the predecessors of B_i have smaller timestamps than B_i itself). At this time, we can consider B_i to be *old enough* (Figure 8) to be retired.

Another important question concerns Early or Unrelated dependencies (See the table in Figure 4). Assume B_i records P_j as a successor but, since P_j is not running any monitored threads, it will not dump any blocks for a long time (or maybe forever). How should the recorded dependence be resolved?

To handle this case, again, we use the Bounded Silence guarantee. If B_i recorded the dependence at time t and P_j dumps no blocks before time $t + MSP$, then it is guaranteed that no monitored block existed on P_j at time t. Hence, it suffices to attribute the dependence to the next dumped block of P_j, or it can be safely discarded if P_j never dumps. The token-based representation enables an efficient implementation in this case. Each proxy, P_j in this example, has a vector of counters which count the number of Early dependences from other processors (P_i in this case). Let us call this vector the Early Token Vector. At time $B_i.ts + MSP$, B_i can consider its dependence resolved and send an Early token to P_j by incrementing entry i of the Early Token Vector in P_j. When the next block of P_j is dumped, the counters in the Early Token Vector are added to the PTV of that block and then they are reset.

The MSP-based techniques described above imply that, at time $B_i.ts + MSP$, B_i is *old enough* (term used in Figure 8) to be retired, since all of its predecessors and successors are guaranteed to have been resolved by that time.

3.5.3 Trading-off Replay Parallelism for Log Size

As the backend pass generates the final log, it can transform it in ways that affect the size of the log and the potential for parallelism in its replay. This provides substantial flexibility (Figure 9). For example, when R&R is used for on-line intrusion analysis or fault tolerance, it typically requires high-speed replay. In this case, the log format should be such that it enables highly-parallel replay. Such format is MaxPar. On the other hand, when R&R is used for (off-line) software debugging, replay speed is less important. Hence, we likely prefer a format that needs less log space at the expense of offering less parallelism. Such format is called *Stitched*. This format is also suitable for intrusion analysis or fault tolerance when the application is I/O- or memory-intensive. This is because, in such scenarios, replay is typically faster than recording. Finally, when small log size is paramount, even at the expense of replay speed, the *Serial* or *StSerial* formats should be used. In the following, we discuss these formats.

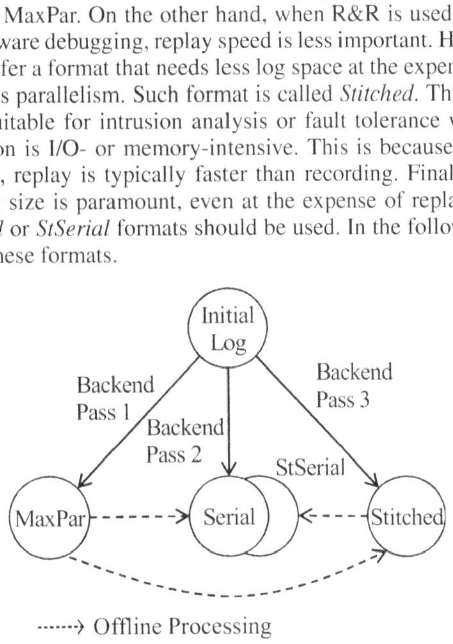

Figure 9. Flexibility of the backend pass.

Stitched: Reduced Parallelism. The Stitched format uses less log space than MaxPar, but it offers less parallelism for replay. Compared to MaxPar, Stitched merges consecutive blocks of an application thread into a *Stitched* block as long as this process does not introduce cycles in the graph.

Accurately detecting cycles on-the-fly can be computationally intensive. There are conservative techniques that can be used instead. One such technique involves using Lamport Scalar Clocks. Specifically, each block is assigned a clock that should be strictly larger of those of its predecessors. While merging a sequence of consecutive blocks into a stitched block *SB*, the algorithm watches the clock values of the all the predecessors of the blocks in *SB*. As long as all of these predecessors have clock values not larger than that of the first block in *SB*, no cycle can be created and we can safely merge the blocks. If, however, one of the predecessors of the next block to stitch violates this condition, we stop merging and start a new block sequence.

Figure 7(d) shows the Stitched execution DAG and log for the example in Figure 7(a). Compared to the MaxPar algorithm (Figure 7(c), we have combined blocks into bigger blocks, hence reducing the number of log entries but also decreasing the parallelism of the DAG available to the replayer.

Serial: Sequential Replay. When having a very small log is very important, even at the expense of any parallelism in the replay, we use the Serial format. In this case, we create a total order of blocks. This format is generated with a simple topological sort on the dependence DAG. It can be generated either on-the-fly in the backend or off-line after the MaxPar log has been created. Each serial log entry only needs to contain the thread ID and the size of a block — the rest of the information is unnecessary.

Figure 7(e) shows the Serial execution DAG and log for the example in Figure 7(a). Compared to the MaxPar algorithm (Figure 7(c)), we have created a total order of blocks, disabling any parallel replay, but substantially reducing the log size.

StSerial: Stitched Sequential Log. Finally, we can reduce the log size even more if we apply the Serial algorithm to a DAG generated by Stitcher. The result is called StSerial. Compared to MaxPar, we reduce both the number of log entries and the size of each of them. The replay is also serial. Figure 7(f) shows the StSerial execution DAG and log for the example in Figure 7(a).

Advanced Uses. Other flexible uses of the backend pass are possible. One use is for the backend to dynamically change the format of the log at different phases of a program's execution. This scenario may be useful when R&R is used in online-replay scenarios (e.g., fault tolerance) where a secondary server follows the execution of a primary one. To reduce the bandwidth required to transfer the log from the primary to the secondary server, the backend may usually use the Stitched format. However, in sections of the program when fast replay is needed (perhaps because the execution becomes compute intensive), the backend may switch to MaxPar.

Once can also think of a transformation to reduce the number of processors in the log. The transformation involves combining the entries from two or more processors into one. In practice, this transformation is unlikely to be useful since (i) it does not change the number of log entries and just reduces the size of PTV and STV, and (ii) the replay can already be done with fewer processors than used for recording, even with an unmodified log; we only need that a replay processor execute blocks from multiple recording ones.

4. Implementation Issues

4.1 Race Recording Unit (RRU) Design

The Cyrus hardware consists of a *Race Recording Unit* (RRU) associated with the cache controller of each processor (Figure 5). When a processor is executing a monitored process, if its cache observes a bus transaction that induces a dependence with data previously accessed by the processor, the RRU records that dependence.

Figure 10 shows the hardware inside the RRU. It has four components: Tracked Block-Cluster Buffer, Block-Cluster Buffer, Time Counter, and Eviction Signature. The Time Counter is the global clock, obtained by counting the number of coherence transactions on the bus. It has the same value in all the cores.

The Tracked Block-Cluster Buffer (TBCB) implements the dependence-tracking window described in Section 3.4. It contains information about several block clusters: the currently-running one

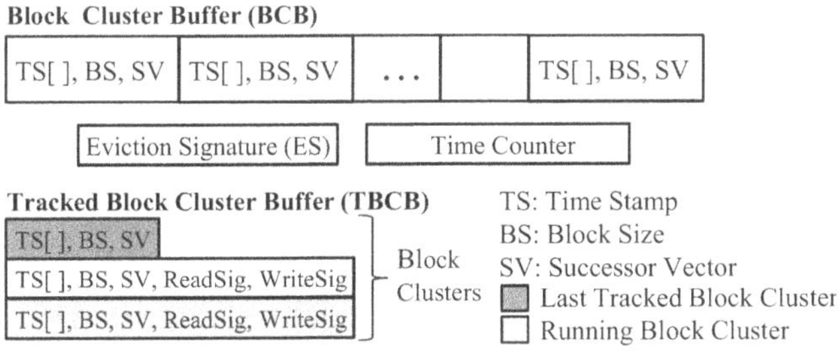

Figure 10. Race Recording Unit (RRU) design.

(*Running* in Figure 10) and the N most recently-completed ones. Of these, the earliest one is called *Last Tracked* in Figure 10. All block clusters in the TBCB except for the Last Tracked one have read and write signature registers. These registers hash-encode and accumulate with a Bloom filter [4] the addresses of all the lines read or written by all the blocks in the corresponding block cluster.

To understand how the TBCB works, assume first that there is no cache overflow; we consider cache evictions later. When a request on the bus *hits in a cache*, the cache's RRU checks the requested address against the signature registers in its TBCB — a bus write is checked against read and write signatures, while a bus read only against write signatures. The checks are performed in order, starting with the signatures of the Running cluster and proceeding to older clusters. The goal is to find which cluster is the latest source of the dependence.

If there is a hit in the signatures of the Running cluster, the current time stamp is saved in the cluster's Successor Vector (SV) entry for the requesting processor. Moreover, the cluster terminates and the current block size is saved in the cluster's BS field. In addition, the whole TBCB is shifted upward, pushing the contents of the Last-Tracked cluster into the Block-Cluster Buffer and a new Running block cluster begins.

If, instead, there is a hit in the signatures of an older cluster in the TBCB, we save the current time stamp in that cluster's SV entry for the requesting processor. Finally, if instead, the request does not hit in any signature, we conservatively assume that the Last Tracked cluster is the source of the dependence. In this case, we save the current time stamp in that cluster's SV entry for the requesting processor. In all cases, if the corresponding SV entry is already set to a smaller timestamp, we do not update it.

The case when processor P0 writes a variable, then P1 reads it and then P2 reads it, correctly triggers the logging of a dependence P0→P2 (in addition to P0→P1). The reason is that, although the P2 read does not induce any coherence operation on P0's cache, P0's cache hits and, as a result, P0's write signatures are checked. If the P0 write occurred during its Last Tracked cluster, there is no signature, but Cyrus still records a dependence by default. This would be conservative (although correct) if P0 had only read, not written. Fortunately, recording conservative dependences so far in the past is not expected to hurt replay parallelism.

If the current block in the Running cluster reaches its maximum size without sourcing a dependence, it terminates, saving the current time stamp in the corresponding TS field of the Running cluster. Then, a new block starts. If all the blocks of the Running cluster have been exhausted, the cluster terminates, and the whole TBCB is shifted upward. As information on an old cluster is displaced from the tail of the TBCB, it is dumped into the Block Cluster Buffer (Figure 10). When the Block Cluster Buffer is about to fill up, its contents are appended to the tail of an in-memory buffer provided by the operating system (Section 4.2).

4.1.1 Eviction Signature

Caches suffer line evictions. In the design presented, when a cache evicts a line, its RRU loses the ability to record inter-processor dependences on data from that line. Indeed, future bus transactions on that line would not find the data in the cache and, therefore would not trigger checks in the dependence-tracking window.

To eliminate this problem, when a clean or dirty line is evicted from a cache, Cyrus hash-encodes and accumulates its address into the RRU's Eviction Signature (ES) (Figure 10). Then, when a transaction is observed on the bus, Cyrus checks if the address hits in the cache or in the ES. If it hits in at least one, Cyrus proceeds with checking the block clusters in the TBCB.

The ES should be regularly cleared to avoid collecting many addresses that could cause address aliasing. Fortunately, every time that the OS preempts a thread that is being monitored, the local RRU records a Serialization dependence with all other processors in the system (Section 3.2). At that point, the ES can be cleared. Also if, at any time, the ES contains too many addresses, Cyrus simply terminates the current block, records a dependence from it to all the other processors, and clears the ES.

4.2 OS Design for R&R

Figure 11 shows the overall architecture of our R&R system, where the dashed boxes indicate the Cyrus extensions. We base our design on that of Capo [24]. The Replay Sphere Manager (RSM) is the basic kernel module that controls R&R. We organize the OS extensions according to the sources of non-determinism. Hence, we have two components: one for input non-determinism and one for memory-interleaving non-determinism.

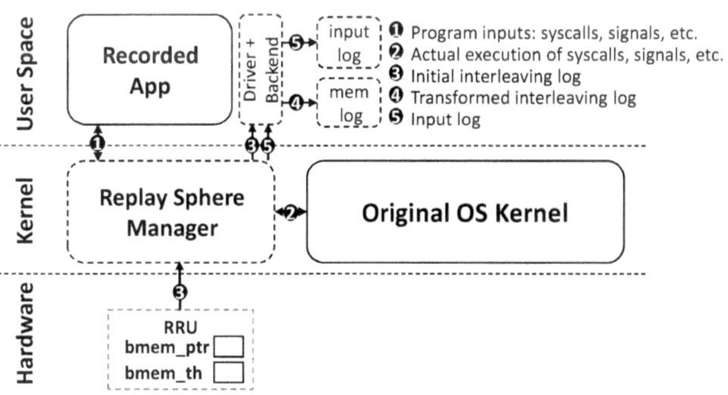

Figure 11. Overall architecture of our R&R system, where the dashed boxes are the Cyrus extensions. The numbers correspond to the generation of logs during recording.

We use a driver program to launch a R&R sphere to perform record or replay. In record mode, the RSM generates the input log, while the RRUs generate the memory-interleaving log. The data transfers proceed as shown with numbers in the figure. As the initial memory interleaving log is generated, the backend pass runs on a dedicated processor and transforms it. In replay mode, the driver reads the input and memory interleaving logs and passes them to the RSM, which consumes them. In addition, the RSM uses performance counters to detect block termination, as we will see.

4.2.1 Input Non-Determinism Module

This module is similar to Capo's [24]. There are four different sources of input non-determinism that Cyrus handles: system calls, data copied to/from the user address space, signals, and non-deterministic processor instructions. Unlike Capo, which uses `ptrace`, we have implemented this component as a Linux kernel module to improve the performance and make it easier to integrate with the memory-interleaving module. Since this module uses per-thread data structures, it is easy to support multiple replay spheres simultaneously.

4.2.2 Memory-Interleaving Non-Determinism Module

Using the RRU at Record Time. As the RRU generates the log, it dumps it into an OS-allocated block of memory called *bmem*. The RRU offers a minimal interface for the OS to manage and virtualize the hardware during recording. This interface contains: (i) a pointer to bmem (*bmem_ptr*), and (ii) a threshold register that indicates the point at which bmem is about to overflow (*bmem_th*). When bmem_th is reached, an interrupt is triggered, and a new bmem is allocated.

The OS manages the per-thread bmem areas and virtualizes these hardware registers, so that different threads can use the hardware without mixing up their data. In particular, this involves making sure that a valid bmem_ptr is configured before recording begins, allocating a fresh bmem when the previous one is full, and ensuring that, on a context switch, all the recorded data is dumped into the bmem and a Serialization dependence is recorded. This is done by writing to a RRU-specific control register. Also, the OS appends to each bmem buffer the ID of the thread to which the blocks in the buffer belong. Thus, the RRU itself does not need to know about threads.

Enforcing the Recorded Interleavings during Replay. The OS is able to recreate the recorded interleavings by allowing each block to start its execution only after all of its predecessors have executed. For this, it uses mechanisms to detect block termination and to synchronize predecessor/successor blocks.

To detect block termination, Cyrus uses performance counters similar to those available in commodity processors. The replaying thread configures the counter so that an interrupt is triggered when the number of instructions executed equals the needed block size. Cyrus assumes synchronous and precise interrupts for this, i.e., the interrupt is generated just before the first instruction of the next block is executed.

To synchronize predecessor/successor blocks, Cyrus uses a software solution. When a block finishes, it should send tokens to its successors, and before the next block starts, it should wait for enough tokens from its predecessors. Cyrus implements this in the RSM (i.e., in the OS and without modifying the application code) using software semaphores. There is a semaphore for each (P_i, P_j) pair of different record-time processors. This semaphore represents tokens sent from P_i to P_j. After a block terminates, the OS first sends tokens to the appropriate semaphores for its successors. It then reads the next block from the memory-interleaving log and for each recorded predecessor, it uses the appropriate semaphore to wait until enough tokens are received from that predecessor.

5. Evaluation Setup

For our evaluation, we augmented the Linux 3.0.8 kernel with a Replay Sphere Manager (RSM). The OS drives and virtualizes the Cyrus architecture modeled with the Simics [22] full-system simulator. The OS changes include the input non-determinism module and the memory-interleaving non-determinism module that manage the two logs.

We use Simics to model an x86-based chip multiprocessor with a single level of private caches that are kept coherent using a snoopy-based MESI cache coherence protocol. Table 1 shows the parameters of the architecture. Unless explicitly specified, we perform the parallel record and replay runs with our applications running on 8 processors. The backend pass uses one additional processor. The baseline RRU configuration uses blocks with at most 4K instructions. It has 2 tracked block clusters (N = 1), and hence

Processor and Memory System Parameters	
Chip multiprocessor	Bus-based with snoopy MESI protocol 8 proc. for application; 1 for backend
Processor	Single issue, x86 ISA 2GHz clock
L1 Cache	64KB size, 64B line, 4-way assoc. 1 cycle hit, 2-bit LRU replacement
L1 Cache Miss Latency	10-cycle round-trip to another L1 100-cycle round-trip to memory
Cyrus Parameters	
Read & write signature	4×512bits & 4×256bits H3 Bloom filter
Eviction signature	4×512bits H3 Bloom filter
# Tracked block-clusters	2
# Blocks per block cluster	16
Maximum block size	4K instructions
Block cluster buffer (BCB)	8 entries

Table 1. Parameters of the simulated hardware.

we only need one pair of signatures per RRU. We use 16 blocks per cluster. We execute 10 applications from the SPLASH-2 suite, which we run from beginning to end.

6. Evaluation

6.1 Recording & Backend Overhead

We first examine the initial log size and whether it can become a bottleneck for Cyrus. Figure 12 shows the growth in the rate of the *initial log* generation as the number of processors increases. This is a temporary log and, hence, it is not compressed. The time unit in this figure is 1K cycles of total execution time (i.e., 0.5 μsec assuming a 2GHz clock). On a system with 8 processors, this means 8K-cycles worth of instruction execution. As seen in the figure, on average, the logging rate grows about linearly with the number of processors. However, a simple calculation shows that even with 8 processors, the average log generation rate is less than 29 MByte/sec. This is far less than the bandwidth of the system bus in current machines (which is typically on the order of several GByte/sec). For this reason, it is not likely that the initial log generation can become a bottleneck.

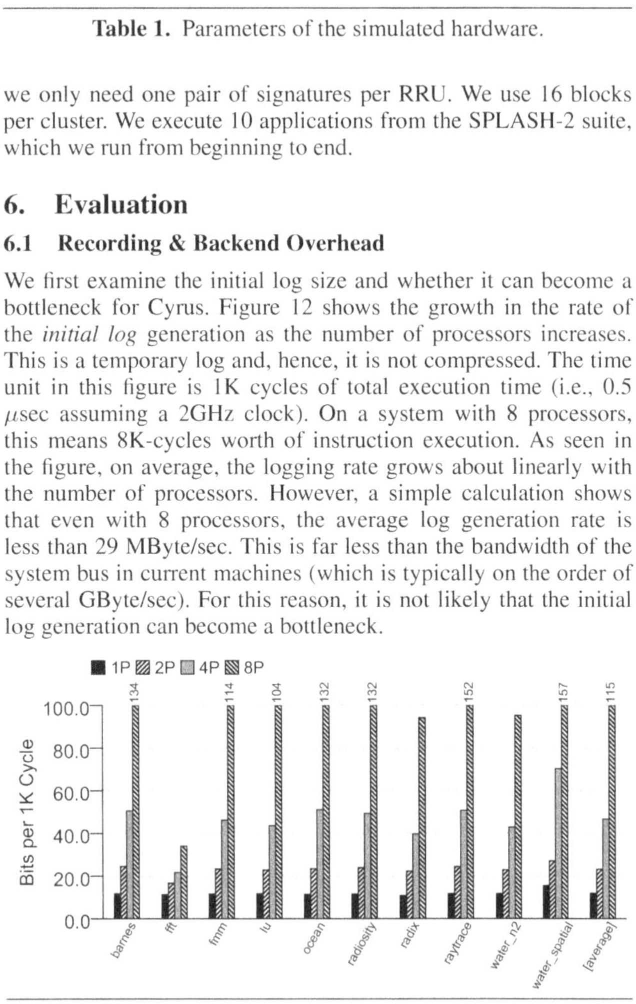

Figure 12. Initial log size for different numbers of processors, shown in terms of the number of bits generated per 1K cycles of total execution time.

Figure 13 examines the overhead of recording with and without the backend. The figure compares the execution time of the benchmarks when the Cyrus hardware is not enabled (*NoMemLog*), when Cyrus records the memory-interleaving log (*MemLog*), and when, in addition, the backend pass runs (*MemLog+Backend*). In all cases, the RSM is recording the input non-determinism log. For each benchmark, the bars are normalized to *NoMemLog*. The applications execute with 8 processors.

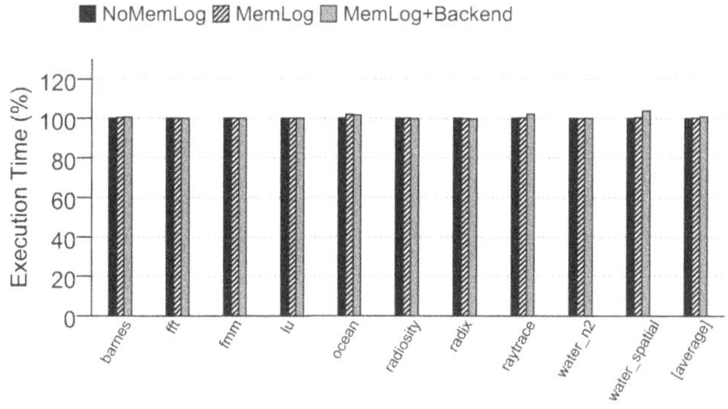

Figure 13. Overhead of recording with and without the backend pass for 8-processor runs.

The figure shows that the overhead of recording the memory-interleaving log, either with or without the backend pass, is negligible. The backend pass induces little overhead because it uses a dedicated processor. While this fact increases the system cost, it allows Cyrus' R&R to be non-intrusive to the hardware.

6.2 Comparing Different Backend Pass Algorithms

We now compare the different Cyrus' backend pass algorithms. We compare the available replay parallelism and the log size of the Serial, StSerial, Stitched, and MaxPar formats (Figures 14 and 15). To estimate the available replay parallelism, we use the Normalized Inverse Critical Path Length (NICPL) of the dependence graph in the log. To measure the NICPL of a benchmark, we start by computing the length of the longest chain of dependences (in terms of number of instructions) in the log. This is the critical path length. Then, we divide the critical path length obtained with a fully-serial log like Serial or StSerial (which is the number of instructions in the benchmark) by the critical path length obtained with a given log. The result is the NICPL of the log. Thus, a higher NICPL value indicates more parallelism in the recorded dependence graph.

Figure 14 compares the NICPL values for the Serial, StSerial, Stitched, and MaxPar formats. We can see that, on average, MaxPar and Stitched provide a replay parallelism of 5 and 3, respectively. Most of the applications can benefit considerably from MaxPar and, to a lesser extent, from Stitched.

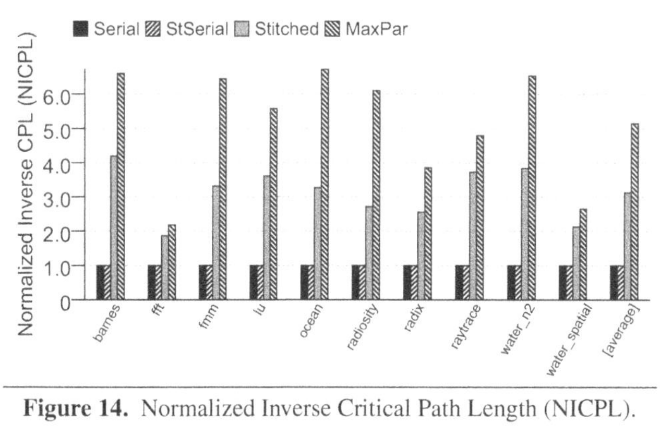

Figure 14. Normalized Inverse Critical Path Length (NICPL).

Figure 15 shows the resulting size of the logs. We compressed the logs with bzip2 and report the number of bits used per 1K instructions. We see that, on average, MaxPar and Stitched generate about 2 bits/Kinstruction, while Serial and StSerial generate 1 bit/Kinstruction. Stitched is not capable of considerably reducing the log size over MaxPar's because, as mentioned in Section 3.5.2, MaxPar already merges many of the recorded blocks while retaining maximum parallelism. On the other hand, StSerial is only slightly more space efficient than Serial. Finally, the figure shows that water_spatial produces large log files. This is because it synchronizes frequently, which creates many small blocks.

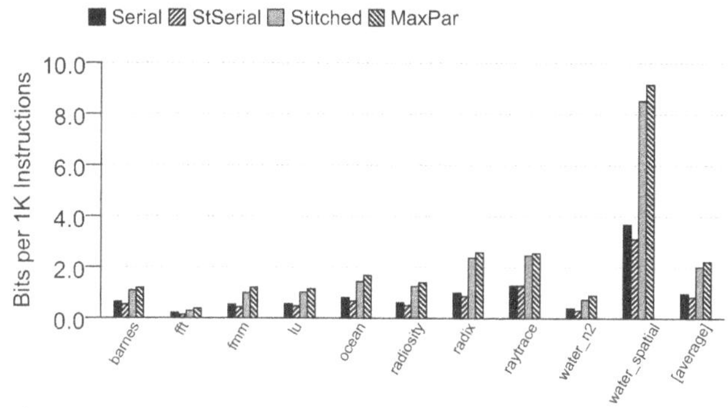

Figure 15. Log size in bits per 1K instructions.

Overall, comparing MaxPar to Serial, we conclude that, with a 2x bigger log, MaxPar delivers a 5x higher parallelism. This is likely to be a very good tradeoff in some R&R applications. On the other hand, Stitched is not a desirable design point. With a 2x bigger log than Serial, it only delivers a 3x higher parallelism. StSerial is only slightly better than Serial.

6.3 Replay Execution Time

We now compare the replay execution time of the benchmarks under a variety of scenarios. We start with the MaxPar log with different block sizes. Figure 16 shows the replay execution time for maximum block sizes equal to 1K, 4K, 16K, and 64K instructions. In all cases, there are 2 block clusters and 64K instructions per cluster. Thus, there are 64, 16, 4, and 1 blocks per cluster, respectively. The plot is normalized to the execution time of recording with 64K-instruction blocks (the recording time for all the other scenarios is practically the same). We can see that, in general, replay execution time is comparable to recording time, even for these communication-intensive benchmarks. On average, with 1K blocks, replay takes only 50% longer than recording, while with 4K blocks, it takes only 60% longer. As we increase the block size, replay time increases. This is largely because there is less replay parallelism with big blocks.

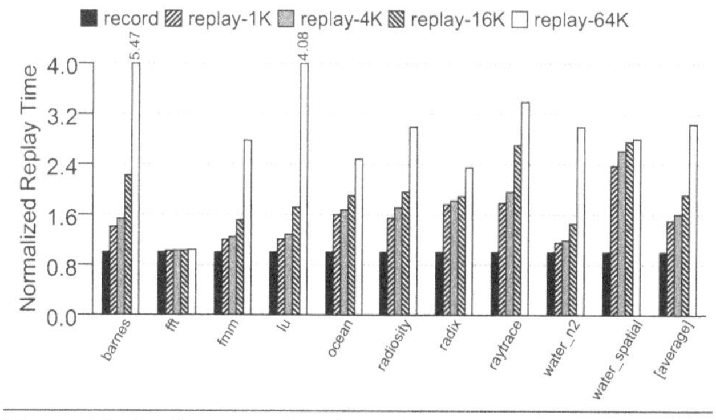

Figure 16. Replay execution time with the MaxPar log for different block sizes.

Figure 17 shows how the logs of the different backends (MaxPar, Stitched, StSerial, and Serial) affect the replay execution time. For this experiment, we use the baseline RRU configuration of Section 5. As usual, the figure shows the replay times normalized to the recording execution time. As expected, the less-parallel logs cause an increase in the replay execution time. On average, we see that with MaxPar and Stitched, it takes about 60% and 100% longer, respectively, to replay than to record. Replaying in StSerial and Serial takes, on average, about 7 and 12 times longer, respectively, than recording. The relative speeds of MaxPar, Stitched, and StSerial largely match the parallelism numbers provided by the NICPLs in Figure 14. Serial, however, is much slower. The reason is that, in the current implementation, Serial does not try to merge blocks before writing them to the log, since this may cause replay deadlocks (we omit the discussion of why this is the case in the interest of space). Hence, it has a high overhead passing tokens, which is done with semaphores.

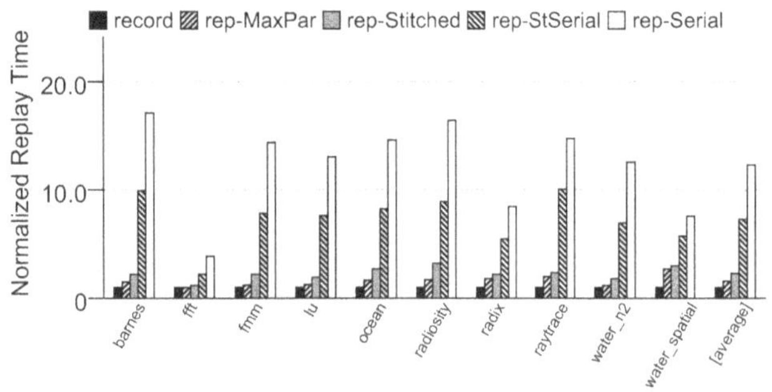

Figure 17. Replay execution time with logs from different backends for a 4K block size.

An important feature of application-level R&R is the ability to replay on machines that have different architectures and, in particular, different processor counts than the recording machine. In Figure 18, we show the effect of using fewer processors to replay than were used to record. The recording run used 8 processors, while the replay executes a MaxPar log on 8, 4, 2 or 1 processors. In each case, the 8 threads of the application have to be multiplexed over the available number of processors and synchronize by passing tokens around. The figure compares the execution times normalized to the recording time. As shown in the figure, the replay becomes progressively slower, but not exceedingly so. The amount of slowdown is a function of the number of replay processors as well as the parallelism that existed in the original execution and was captured in the MaxPar log.

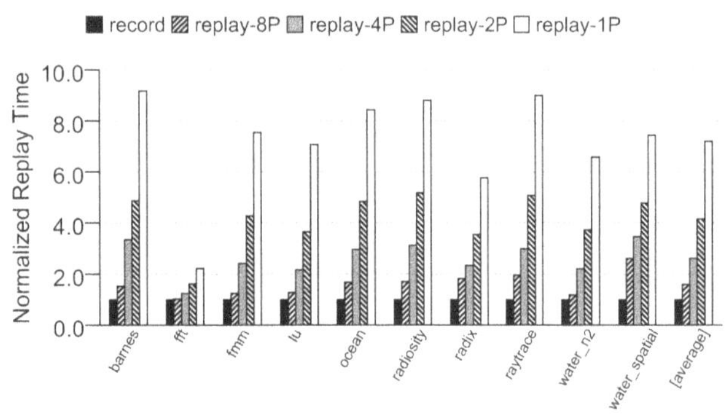

Figure 18. Replay execution time with a lower processor count than during recording.

Finally, Figure 19 breaks down the execution time of replay with the MaxPar log. For each benchmark, the bars are normalized to 100 and broken down into: time spent executing user mode instructions (*user*), time when the OS is executing on behalf of the application, such as servicing system calls (*kernel*), overhead associated with handling the input log (*input log overhead*), overhead associated with handling the memory interleaving block log (*block log overhead*), time spent waiting for tokens from predecessor blocks (*wait for pred*), and time that could not be classified as one of the above (*other*). The latter is mostly application-level load imbalance — e.g., when some application threads are waiting on a barrier while other threads have not yet arrived at that barrier.

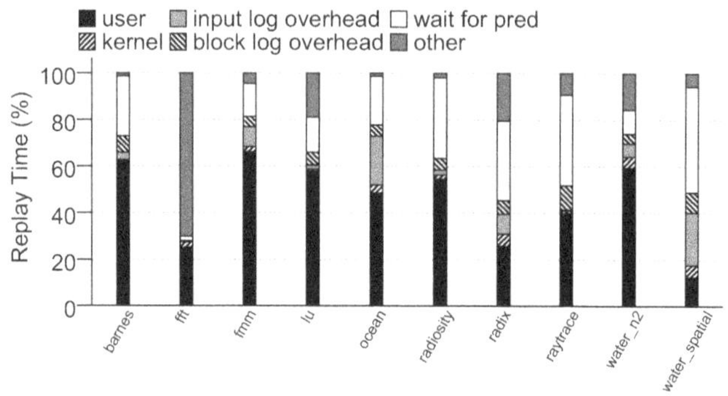

Figure 19. Breakdown of the replay execution time with the MaxPar log for 4K blocks.

The figure shows that the benchmarks exhibit very different behaviors. However, if we focus on the overheads — i.e., the categories other than *user* and *kernel* — we see that *other* and *wait for pred* are often dominant. The *other* category typically implies that there is load imbalance, and little can be done. For example, FFT has a long initialization phase that causes load imbalance. The *wait for pred* category appears in many benchmarks. They suffer considerable slowdowns just because of waiting for tokens. This suggests focusing on recording more parallelism, possibly with more aggressive techniques. Also, utilizing special hardware support (rather than using semaphores and an all-software solution) for token passing during replay may significantly reduce this overhead for some applications.

6.4 Dependence-Tracking Window Analysis

In this section, we compare different organizations of the dependence-tracking window, using replay parallelism (i.e., NICPL) as our metric. Figure 20 shows the NICPLs for different designs, represented as $I \times J \times K$, where I is the number of block clusters (including the last one, with no signatures), J is block size, and K is the number of blocks per block cluster. Recall that the tracked window size equals $I \times J \times K$.

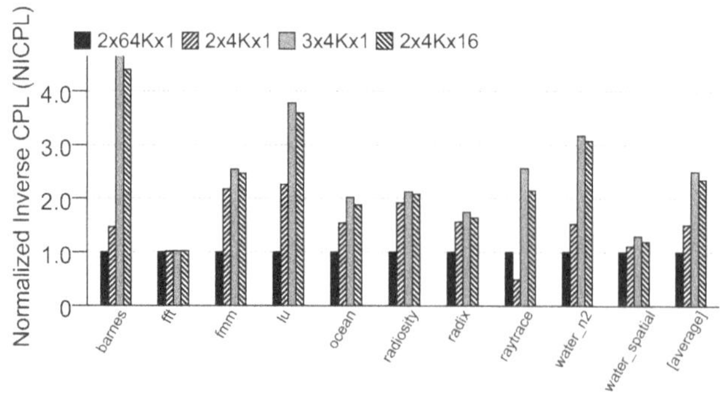

Figure 20. Effect of different organizations of the dependence-tracking window on parallelism. $I \times J \times K$ stands for I block clusters, J block size, and K blocks per cluster.

In the figure, higher bars are better. The figure is normalized to the NICPL of $2 \times 64K \times 1$, which can track a window of 128K. If we reduce the block size to 4K (second bar), we increase the NICPL even though the window is now only 8K. This design is better because small blocks improve parallelism. If we increase the number of clusters to 3 while keeping the block size to 4K (third bar), we improve NICPL significantly because the tracked window increases to 12K, but at the cost of an extra set of signatures. Finally, if we keep the clusters to 2 and the block size to 4K but use 16 blocks per cluster (last bar), we have nearly the same NICPL. We have a less precise tracking with only 2 clusters, but have a larger tracked window size. Moreover, we need no extra signatures. This is the most competitive design and we use it as default.

7. Related Work

Deterministic R&R has been the subject of a vast body of research work. Software-based solutions assume no special hardware support. Instead, they rely on modified runtime libraries, compilers, operating systems and virtual-machine monitors to capture sources of non-determinism. Russinovich and Cogswell [32] propose to modify the OS scheduler to record thread interleaving in a uniprocessor. Recap [27] takes a compiler-based approach, where the compiler inserts some code before every read operation that may touch shared data. LeBlanc and Mellor-Crummey [18] use Reader-Writer locking for shared memory accesses to log an execution. Agora [12] uses write-once memory and a history log for maintaining the correct state of a program. DejaVu [8] records the scheduling decisions of a Java Virtual Machine to enable deterministic replay of multi-threaded Java applications on uniprocessors. Bressoud and Schneider [5] and ReVirt [10] use a modified hypervisor to replay single processor virtual machines. Dunlap et al. [11] extend ReVirt to multiprocessor virtual machines. Flashback [33] focuses on application-level R&R for debugging, and captures only the interactions between the application being debugged and the operating system, like system calls and signals, instead of logging everything. PinPlay [29] is another software-only approach based on the Pin dynamic instrumentation system. It uses Pin for both recording and replay. Scribe [16] uses the virtual-memory page-level access control mechanisms to capture the interleaving of shared memory accesses. Although the paper reports reasonable overheads for system applications with low levels of sharing, it is not clear how it will perform for sharing- and synchronization-intensive programs.

These software-based approaches are either inherently designed for uniprocessor executions or suffer significant slowdown when applied to multiprocessor executions. DoublePlay [34] made efforts to make replay on commodity multiprocessors more efficient. It timeslices multiple threads on one processor and then runs multiple time intervals on separate processors. Hence, it only needs to record the order in which threads in each time interval are timesliced on the corresponding processor. This technique eases logging by only requiring the logger to record the order in which the time slices are executed within a time interval. However, DoublePlay uses an additional execution to create checkpoints off which multiple time intervals can be run in parallel. It also needs to use modified binaries (in particular, a modified libc) for efficient execution.

ODR [2] and PRES [28] are probabilistic replay techniques for reproducing concurrency bugs. The idea is to record only a subset of non-deterministic events required for deterministic replay (to reduce the recording overhead) and use a replayer that searches the space of possible executions to reproduce the same application output or bug, respectively. Respec [20] targets online replay scenarios. It records a subset of non-deterministic events and uses the online replay run to provide external determinism. The idea is to retry the execution from the last checkpoint when a divergence happens. Like DoublePlay [34], it needs to use modified binaries.

Hardware-based solutions usually use hardware to record memory races to reduce the overhead of R&R for multiprocessor executions. Past work on memory race recording has largely concentrated on directory-based schemes (e.g., [3, 13, 23, 24, 36, 37]). There is work on snoopy protocols [26, 30, 31], but the designs require modifications to the cache coherence protocol hardware. Specifically, Strata [26] requires that all the processors agree to start a new stratum (or logging epoch) at regular intervals. This is done by augmenting the messages with a Log Stratum bit, which can be set by the processor initiating the miss or by a processor that provides the data. Strata uses a recording approach that requires that all processors record an entry in their logs at the same time, which does not scale well with the processor count. In the MRR [30] and CoreRacer [31] systems, every time that a block commits, the event is broadcasted with a bus transaction. The design uses Lamport clocks to order the blocks and does not provide much parallelism.

FDR [36] and RTR [37] are among the very first race recording techniques proposed. They record dependences between pairs of instructions and, thus, can record parallel dependence graphs. However, they are full-system techniques and rely on modified directory protocols. Also, recording dependences between pairs of instructions can produce large logs and increase associated overhead. To reduce this overhead, block-based techniques [7, 13, 23, 24, 30, 31, 35] have been proposed, but they are not designed for parallel replay and require changes to the coherence protocol. DeLorean [23] and Capo [24] are block-based techniques that use speculative multithreading hardware to achieve replay parallelism.

Karma [3] is the first block-based R&R technique that explicitly targets replay parallelism without relying on speculative hardware. It is a whole-system (rather than application-level) R&R scheme for directory protocols. It records bidirectional dependences between source and destination blocks and, hence, makes some modifications to the cache coherence messages. The design allows two blocks to be tracked, an idea we build on in this paper. Karma allows the blocks to grow beyond conflicts, similar to the Stitched logs presented in this paper. The paper reports replay speeds within 19%-28% of vanilla runs (i.e., without R&R). The authors make, however, several simplifying assumptions about the mechanisms used for recording non-deterministic input events, and for handling memory logs, which need care in a realistic, OS-aware implementation of R&R. It is also difficult to extrapolate their results to an application-level scheme like Cyrus. It is also unclear how their replay mechanism can be extended to application-only replay, and to cases where the recording and replaying machines have different numbers of processors.

BugNet [25] records user processes by storing the result of load instructions in a hardware-based dictionary. This is enough to handle both input and memory-interleaving non-determinism and allows each thread to be replayed independently. However, BugNet still needs a solution to record inter-thread dependences, for which it uses FDR [36]. Lee et al. [19, 21] augment this technique by using offline symbolic analysis to reconstruct the inter-thread dependences. This technique is mostly suitable for debugging, since the analysis is, in general, a slow process.

8. Concluding Remarks

This paper presented Cyrus, the first hardware-based approach for unintrusive, application-level R&R that explicitly targets high replay speed. It introduces the concept of an on-the-fly software backend pass during recording which, as the log is being generated, transforms it. This backend pass fixes-up the log, which has incomplete information due to our recording requirements of only application-level interactions and no coherence protocol changes.

It also exposes the recorded parallelism and can flexibly trade-off replay parallelism for log size. Cyrus had negligible recording overhead. In addition, for 8-processor runs of SPLASH-2, it attained an average replay parallelism of 5, and a replay speed that was, on average, only about 50% lower than the recording speed. The backend pass was highly flexible and added negligible overhead.

While it is conceivable that a single-threaded backend can become a bottleneck as the number of processors increases, we did not find it to be so in our experiments (as evidenced by Figure 13). Also, when such a backend becomes a bottleneck, we can parallelize it and allocate more than one processor to it. This should only be necessary for considerably large systems and workloads that actively use many processors and generate many blocks. It should be emphasized that compute- and sharing-intensive applications such as SPLASH2 programs represent the worst case for Cyrus. Less demanding *system* workloads, such as databases and web servers, that create smaller memory logs, are considerably easier to handle.

Although we motivated Cyrus using bus-based snoopy systems, it can be easily adapted to other coherence schemes. Cyrus uses source-only recording, which is crucial for parallel application-level R&R. Moreover, it uses the number of bus transactions as the time source. The same time source can be used in any coherence scheme where all the processors see all of the requests in the same order (e.g., address-broadcast tree of Sun's Starfire [6] or the ring-based design of Intel's SandyBridge processors [38]). Alternatively, in many modern CMPs, there are chip-level-consistent clock sources that can be used as the time stamp (e.g., the uncore clock that synchronizes the on-die interconnect of recent Intel systems).

For directory-based designs, where such time sources are not available, the local time stamp of the requesting processor can be piggybacked on the request message. Then, the sourcing processors can save this time stamp in their successor vectors — hence, implementing source-only recording. This requires some changes in the format of the coherence requests. Fortunately, compared to bus-based designs, such changes are relatively easy to make in directory-based systems.

Acknowledgements

This work was supported in part by NSF under grants CCF-1012759, CNS-1116237, CNS-0834738, and CNS-0831212; Intel under the Illinois-Intel Parallelism Center (I2PC) and the ISTC for Secure Computing; and AFOSR MURI grant FA9550-09-01-0539.

References

[1] H. Agrawal et al. An Execution-Backtracking Approach to Debugging. *IEEE Software*, 8(3), May 1991.

[2] G. Altekar and I. Stoica. ODR: Output-deterministic replay for multicore debugging. In *Symposium on Operating Systems Principles*, 2009.

[3] A. Basu et al. Karma: Scalable deterministic record-replay. In *Int. Conference on Supercomputing*, 2011.

[4] B. Bloom. Space/Time Trade-Offs in Hash Coding with Allowable Errors. *Communications of the ACM*, 11(7), July 1970.

[5] T. Bressoud and F. Schneider. Hypevisor-based fault-tolerance. *ACM Transactions on Computer Systems*, 14(1), Feb 1996.

[6] A. Charlesworth. Starfire: Extending the SMP Envelope. *IEEE Micro*, 18(1), Jan. 1998.

[7] Y. Chen et al. LReplay: A pending period based deterministic replay scheme. In *Int. Symposium on Computer Architecture*, 2010.

[8] J.-D. Choi and H. Srinivasan. Deterministic replay of Java multithreaded applications. In *Symposium on Parallel and Distributed Tools*, 1998.

[9] B. Cully et al. Remus: High availability via asynchronous virtual machine replication. In *USENIX Symposium on Networked Systems Design and Implementation*, 2008.

[10] G. W. Dunlap et al. ReVirt: Enabling intrusion analysis through virtual-machine logging and replay. In *Symposium on Operating Systems Design and Implementation*, 2002.

[11] G. W. Dunlap et al. Execution replay of multiprocessor virtual machines. In *Int. Conference on Virtual Execution Environments*, 2008.

[12] A. Forin. Debugging of heterogeneous parallel systems. In *Workshop on Parallel and Distributed Debugging*, 1988.

[13] D. R. Hower and M. D. Hill. Rerun: Exploiting Episodes for Lightweight Memory Race Recording. In *Int. Symposium on Computer Architecture*, 2008.

[14] S. T. King and P. M. Chen. Backtracking intrusions. In *Symposium on Operating Systems Principles*, 2003.

[15] S. T. King et al. Debugging operating systems with time-traveling virtual machines. In *USENIX Annual Technical Conference*, 2005.

[16] O. Laadan et al. Transparent, lightweight application execution replay on commodity multiprocessor operating systems. In *SIGMETRICS Int. Conference on Measurement and Modeling of Computer Systems*, 2010.

[17] L. Lamport. Time, clocks, and the ordering of events in a distributed system. *Communications of the ACM*, 21(7), July 1978.

[18] T. J. LeBlanc and J. M. Mellor-Crummey. Debugging Parallel Programs with Instant Replay. *IEEE Trans. Comput.*, 36(4), Apr. 1987.

[19] D. Lee et al. Offline symbolic analysis for multi-processor execution replay. In *Int. Symposium on Microarchitecture*, 2009.

[20] D. Lee et al. Respec: Efficient online multiprocessor replayvia speculation and external determinism. In *Int. Conference on Architectural Support for Programming Languages and Operating Systems*, 2010.

[21] D. Lee et al. Offline symbolic analysis to infer Total Store Order. In *Int. Symposium on High Performance Computer Architecture*, 2011.

[22] P. S. Magnusson et al. Simics: A Full System Simulation Platform. *IEEE Computer*, 35(2), February 2002.

[23] P. Montesinos et al. DeLorean: Recording and Deterministically Replaying Shared-Memory Multiprocessor Execution Efficiently. In *Int. Symposium on Computer Architecture*, 2008.

[24] P. Montesinos et al. Capo: A software-hardware interface for practical deterministic multiprocessor replay. In *Int. Conference on Architectural Support for Programming Languages and Operating Systems*, 2009.

[25] S. Narayanasamy et al. BugNet: Continuously Recording Program Execution for Deterministic Replay Debugging. In *Int. Symposium on Computer Architecture*, 2005.

[26] S. Narayanasamy et al. Recording shared memory dependencies using strata. In *Int. Conference on Architectural Support for Programming Languages and Operating Systems*, 2006.

[27] D. Z. Pan and M. A. Linton. Supporting reverse execution for parallel programs. In *Workshop on Parallel and Distributed Debugging*, 1988.

[28] S. Park et al. PRES: Probabilistic replay with execution sketching on multiprocessors. In *Symposium on Operating Systems Principles*, 2009.

[29] H. Patil et al. PinPlay: A framework for deterministic replay and reproducible analysis of parallel programs. In *Int. Symposium on Code Generation and Optimization*, 2010.

[30] G. Pokam et al. Architecting a chunk-based memory race recorder in modern CMPs. In *Int. Symposium on Microarchitecture*, 2009.

[31] G. Pokam et al. CoreRacer: A practical memory race recorder for multicore x86 TSO processors. In *Int. Symposium on Microarchitecture*, 2011.

[32] M. Russinovich and B. Cogswell. Replay for concurrent non-deterministic shared-memory applications. In *Programming Language Design and Implementation*, 1996.

[33] S. M. Srinivasan et al. Flashback: a lightweight extension for rollback and deterministic replay for software debugging. In *USENIX Annual Technical Conference*, 2004.

[34] K. Veeraraghavan et al. DoublePlay: Parallelizing sequential logging and replay. In *Int. Conference on Architectural Support for Programming Languages and Operating Systems*, 2011.

[35] G. Voskuilen et al. Timetraveler: Exploiting acyclic races for optimizing memory race recording. In *Int. Symposium on Computer Architecture*, 2010.

[36] M. Xu et al. A "flight data recorder" for enabling full-system multiprocessor deterministic replay. In *Int. Symposium on Computer Architecture*, 2003.

[37] M. Xu et al. A regulated transitive reduction (RTR) for longer memory race recording. In *Int. Conference on Architectural Support for Programming Languages and Operating Systems*, 2006.

[38] M. Yuffe et al. A fully integrated multi-CPU, GPU and memory controller 32nm processor. In *Int. Solid-State Circuits Conference*, 2011.

Why You Should Care About Quantile Regression

Augusto Born de Oliveira
Sebastian Fischmeister
Dept. of Electrical and Computer Eng.
University of Waterloo
Waterloo, ON, Canada
{a3olivei,sfischme}@uwaterloo.ca

Amer Diwan
Google Inc.
Mountain View, CA, USA
diwan@google.com

Matthias Hauswirth
Faculty of Informatics
University of Lugano
Lugano, Switzerland
Matthias.Hauswirth@usi.ch

Peter F. Sweeney
IBM T.J. Watson Research Center
Yorktown Heights, NY, USA
pfs@us.ibm.com

Abstract

Research has shown that correctly conducting and analysing computer performance experiments is difficult. This paper investigates what is necessary to conduct successful computer performance evaluation by attempting to repeat a prior experiment: the comparison between two Linux schedulers.

In our efforts, we found that exploring an experimental space through a series of incremental experiments can be inconclusive, and there may be no indication of how much experimentation will be enough. Analysis of variance (ANOVA), a traditional analysis method, is able to partly solve the problems with the previous approach, but we demonstrate that ANOVA can be insufficient for proper analysis due to the requirements it imposes on the data.

Finally, we demonstrate the successful application of quantile regression, a recent development in statistics, to computer performance experiments. Quantile regression can provide more insight into the experiment than ANOVA, with the additional benefit of being applicable to data from any distribution. This property makes it especially useful in our field, since non-normally distributed data is common in computer experiments.

Categories and Subject Descriptors D.4.8 [*OPERATING SYSTEMS*]: Performance

Keywords Scheduling, Latency, Performance Evaluation, ANOVA, Quantile Regression

1. Introduction

Both academia and industry use performance evaluation to identify bottlenecks and to evaluate innovations. Unfortunately, performance evaluation is difficult and error prone because it requires (1) profound knowledge of hidden factors that on the surface seem irrelevant to the experiment [11, 18], and (2) deep understanding of statistical methods used to analyze the data from the experiment [22]. This paper sheds light on both of these difficulties by attempting to reproduce a prior experiment: the comparison between two Linux schedulers.

The two Linux schedulers we considered are the current mainline scheduler, the Completely Fair Scheduler (CFS) [16], and the current contender, the BFS [14]. The CFS concentrates on maximizing throughput on a wide range of platforms, while the BFS aims to maximize interactivity by reducing latency. A current hot debate is which of the two schedulers is superior to the other and under which conditions. To help resolve the debate, the Linux community came up with experiments to measure scheduling latency and computing throughput to identify the best scheduler for interactive platforms.

Our results show that while we were able to repeat prior experiments for these schedulers, we were unable to reproduce the community's conclusions based on the results. By this we mean that when we attempted to generalize the prior experiment, we encountered a series of contradictions. For example, in one experiment, CFS had superior latency and throughput to BFS while a minor change suddenly reversed the decision for both. After conducting a series of experiments, we were not only unable to reach a decisive conclusion, but also unable to determine when enough experimentation had been done.

Trying to produce a reproducible experiment, we applied textbook experimental design and analysis techniques, namely factorial design and analysis of variance [17] (ANOVA). Through a factorial design, researchers can clearly define an experimental space, and through ANOVA they can draw conclusions that apply in that space. We found that while this was effective for some metrics, it was inapplicable for others because they failed to satisfy the necessary assumptions for applying the technique.

Next, we applied a new statistical technique to our experiment: quantile regression [12]. Quantile regression allows researchers to analyse data in greater detail than ANOVA, without requiring the data to satisfy specific statistical properties. While ANOVA focuses on the mean, quantile regressions allow the quantification of factor effects on any given quantile (e.g., the median, or the 99th percentile) of the metric of interest. Our experiments with quantile regression led to correct and reproducible results.

This paper is organized as follows: Section 2 presents the scheduler comparison used as a base for the rest of the paper. Section

ASPLOS'13, March 16–20, 2013, Houston, Texas, USA.

3 describes the benchmark and the platforms used in experimentation. Section 4 demonstrates the pitfalls of unstructured experimentation. Section 5 presents our factorial design, and demonstrates both the strengths and weaknesses of ANOVA. Section 6 demonstrates the successful use of quantile regression. Section 7 describes a series of other pitfalls encountered in our experimentation. Section 8 discusses related work, and Section 9 concludes.

2. Background

In this paper, we compare two Linux schedulers — the Completely Fair Scheduler (CFS), and the BFS — to investigate the difficulty in measuring and analysing computer performance. The Linux scheduler is important, since it potentially affects the performance of platforms ranging from cellphones to large data centers. The CFS [16], Linux's official scheduler since 2007, aims to be a unified solution for all target platforms, scaling to a large processor count. The BFS [14] was created in 2009 to minimize scheduling latency, trying to yield better performance in interactive systems.

The release of the BFS led several developers on the Linux Kernel Mailing List to conduct independent experiments to measure the performance of both schedulers [6]. BFS proponents argue that its focus on lowering scheduling latency yields better interactivity and responsiveness on commodity hardware; a claim that experimenters could verify through scheduling latency benchmarks. Furthermore, CPU and mixed-load benchmarks can measure scheduler overhead, predicting applications' throughput under the BFS.

Initial attempts to verify the effectiveness of the BFS were inconclusive, and after some discussion, a kernel developer released the Latt [1] benchmark. Latt measures scheduling latency while generating CPU load; this ensures the scheduler treats the benchmark process as it would a typical interactive application. Section 3.1 describes Latt. Even with the acceptance of Latt by both sides of the discussion, all experimentation conducted was unstructured and unscientific; unsurprisingly, the kernel developers did not come to a consensus, and the BFS and the CFS are both under concurrent development. We use Latt for all experiments in this paper, since it adequately measures scheduling latency, and is already accepted and used by kernel developers, precluding the need for revalidating it. Using Latt is also important because of our goal of reproducing the unstructured experiments that the kernel developers conducted.

3. Experimental Setup

Through a series of experiments, we attempt to determine how the BFS and the CFS compare in terms of latency and throughput.

3.1 Latt

Latt is composed of a server thread and a set of one or more client threads. Figure 1 shows the control flow of Latt. At the start of execution, the server thread spawns the client threads, and opens a pipe (a stream for interprocess communication found in UNIX-like systems) to each of them. The client threads then block trying to read from the pipe. At random intervals, the server thread then writes a *wakeup request timestamp* to each of the pipes, freeing the client threads. As soon as the clients finish reading that timestamp, they collect a *woken up timestamp*. The difference between the woken up and the wakeup request timestamps is the time during which the client thread was ready to execute but did not receive the processor, i.e., the scheduling latency.

As soon as each client collects the woken up timestamp, they perform a compression task. This is to avoid scheduler heuristics that may prioritize client threads for consistently releasing the processor before using their full share of CPU time. Latt registers the time to complete these compression operations, and depending on the load of the system, these measurements serve as a surrogate for throughput[1]. The user can configure the number of clients and the size of the data to compress. There must be at least one client (so that latency measurements are collected), but the compression size may be zero, meaning that the client threads perform no work, and Latt only collects latency information.

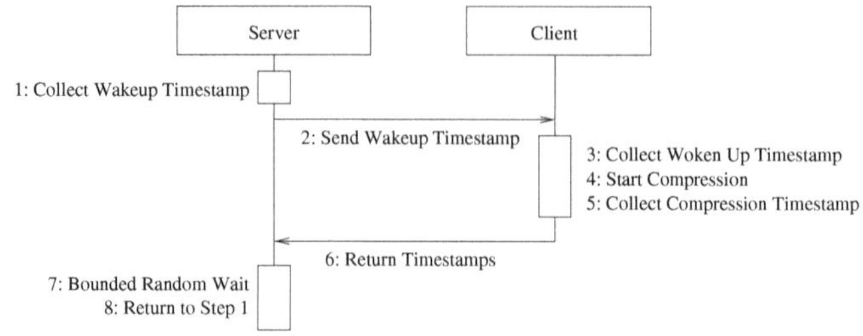

Figure 1. Control flow of the Latt benchmark.

Latt thus collects two metrics, scheduling latency (in microseconds) and client throughput (in bytes compressed per microsecond). The lower the latency measurement, the more responsive an interactive system will be. The higher the client throughput, the faster a user would expect a CPU-bound task to complete.

Measuring latency and client throughput in isolation is unrealistic; to solve that, Latt permits defining arbitrary background loads, by taking an arbitrary program as a parameter. Latt collects measurements for as long as that background load executes. For example, if `sleep 30` is passed as a parameter, Latt will collect latency and client throughput data for 30 seconds, resulting in multiple measurements per execution. The background load parameter guarantees that data collection happens only while the load executes (the loads used in our experiments are described in the next section).

By default, Latt outputs only aggregate statistics (such as the mean and standard deviation) of its latency and client throughput measurements. To enable in-depth data analysis, we modified Latt to output each individual latency and client throughput measurement. Our implementation of this feature allocates a large buffer in the beginning of execution and only writes the data to disk once the background load completes, thus minimizing interference on the metrics of interest. Furthermore, in addition to latency and client throughput data, we collected end-to-end execution time measurements for each execution, to analyze the effect of each scheduler on the background load execution time.

3.2 Background Load Configurations

We used three different load configurations: *idle*, *compile*, and *encode*. To differentiate the schedulers under a wide range of conditions, we chose loads that represented the spectrum from an idle system to one executing a multi-threaded, CPU-bound load. As described earlier, Latt receives each of these loads as a command line parameter.

The idle load blocks on a timer for a set amount of time, using no CPU time. This load serves to establish a baseline for the metrics on an idle system. The command passed to Latt for this load is `sleep 30`.

The compile load consists of compiling the *xz v5.0.3* [20] open-source compression utility using *GCC 4.6.3*. It is a single threaded load, consisting of a mix of CPU and I/O operations. The command passed to Latt is `./configure; make`.

The encode load is based on *x264 v0.120.x* [21], an open-source H.264 video encoder. It is a multi-threaded, CPU-bound load. The

[1] This approach is problematic, and Section 7 discusses its shortcomings.

command passed to Latt is `x264 -B 2000 soccer_4cif.y4m -threads 4`. The input file to the encoder is a freely-distributable test sequence [23].

3.3 Experimental Platforms

We used two different computers for the experiments. A Core 2 machine, consisting of a 2.4GHz Intel Core 2 Quad Q6600 with 3GB of RAM, and a P4 machine, consisting of a 2.0GHz Intel Pentium 4 with 512MB of RAM. The P4 machine was chosen to measure latency behavior on a slower processor, on which the scheduler choice may prove more significant. Both machines executed version 3.2.7 of the Linux kernel, with BFS version 416. The distribution used was Arch Linux, and only essential software executed during data collection (most notably, no graphical interface was used during benchmarks). Since these machines required remote access, their network connection was active throughout benchmarking. The relatively long running time of the benchmarks and the fact that the machine rejected connections except on the remote terminal port minimize any network interference on the metrics of interest.

4. Repeating Prior Experiments

Our first experiments started in an attempt to replicate experiments described in the Linux Kernel Mailing list. The goal of all experiments in this section is to determine how the schedulers compare in terms of latency and end-to-end performance. The initial intuition (according to the developers involved in the discussion) is that the BFS yields better latency, but the CFS yields better end-to-end times. We will now test this intuition with a sequence of experiments, using information gained along the way to determine the next step.

All results presented in this section were collected on the Core 2 machine. For each experiment, the machine boots into the kernel with the appropriate scheduler, executes the benchmark, and offloads the data to a network server. Figures 2(a) and 2(b) show box plots of the latency and end-to-end times under both schedulers for all experiments described in this section. The data set for each experiment consists of ten separate executions of Latt, each of which yields several latency samples and one end-to-end sample. The three horizontal lines in each box represent the upper quartile, the median, and the lower quartile. The lower and upper whiskers extend to the last value within 1.5 times the interquartile range of the lower and upper quartile, respectively. Dots represent outliers that are outside this range. The cross ($\times$) represents the mean value of each distribution. Note that the y-axis on Figure 2(a) is in a logarithmic scale.

4.1 Experiment 1: Idle

The first experiment was conducted on an idle system. Latt executed a single client thread, which performed no compression, and we used the idle load. The goal of this experiment was to ascertain if there was a significant performance difference between the schedulers in a system with no load. This experiment also serves to establish that the method used by Latt provides reliable data, that is, the experiment is repeatable.

The plot for Experiment 1 in Figure 2(a) confirms the intuition that the average latency under the BFS is lower than that of the CFS. Nevertheless, even the worst case under CFS is below $30\mu s$ (much lower than the human-perceptible 100ms [3]). The standard deviation under both schedulers is very low (under $3\mu s$ for both schedulers), which suggests Latt's method for measuring latency is robust, at least in an idle system.

This experiment confirms the expectations of the developer of the BFS, but the latency behavior measured with this unrealistic load may not be observed in real applications. Therefore, investigating how the schedulers behave under load is still necessary.

4.2 Experiment 2: Compile

The goal of this experiment is to evaluate the different schedulers under more realistic conditions than in Experiment 1. This experiment has all the same conditions of Experiment 1, except for the use of the compile load instead of the idle load.

The plot for Experiment 2 in Figure 2(a) shows that, under these conditions, the BFS has a higher mean latency and higher variance than the CFS. These results contradict the previous experiment *and* the initial claim. However, this could be a scheduling artifact: the lack of work in the Latt client threads may be causing the CFS to prioritize them over all others, since it queues threads by spent processor time. This, in turn, leads to artificially low latency measurements. Adding load to the Latt clients could confirm this hypothesis.

4.3 Experiment 3: Compile with Compression

The goal of this experiment is to check whether increasing load in the Latt client threads will affect latency measurements. To accomplish this, we changed two parameters from the last experiment: we increased the number of clients in Latt from 1 to 8, and each client compressed 64kb of data. In a real application, latency-sensitive threads also perform work, which is approximated by the compression functions in Latt.

The plot for Experiment 3 in Figure 2(a) shows that the increase in the number of client threads and the addition of compression to their work cycles causes a reversal in the results from the previous experiment, and now confirm the initial claim once again. In contrast to the previous experiment, now the BFS has better average latency and better worst-case latency than the CFS. The CFS' highest latency measurement approaches 60ms, which is significantly closer to the human perceptible threshold than the BFS' worst observed case. If latencies of 60ms are observed in these relatively powerful desktop systems, the perceptible threshold of 100ms will likely be surpassed on slower processors, such as those found on mobile systems.

While the conditions of this experiment represent a more realistic environment than the previous experiments, the CPU may not have been fully utilized (due to I/O operations in the background load, and the fact that Latt contains sleep cycles). Therefore, the behavior of the two schedulers under full CPU load requires further investigation. Since interactive systems intermittently go through temporary periods of full utilization, making a conclusion at this point could be premature.

4.4 Experiment 4: Encode

The goal of this experiment is to compare the schedulers under full CPU load. To accomplish this, we modified the parameters of last experiment by using the encode background load instead of the compile load. Preliminary experiments showed this multi-threaded background load to fully utilize the CPU on the Core 2 machine.

Figure 2(b) shows end-to-end execution times for all experiments. The BFS has a lower execution time than the CFS for this experiment, contradicting yet again the initial claim and the previous two experiments. Figure 2(a) shows latency was also lower for the BFS than for the CFS.

With these additional results, there is still insufficient evidence to choose a scheduler based on either metric. To attempt to explain the reversal in end-to-end time performance, we decided to collect idleness data; if the BFS is utilizing the CPU at the same rate as the CFS, then overhead associated with scheduling may be causing the observed discrepancy in end-to-end time. Since the encode load

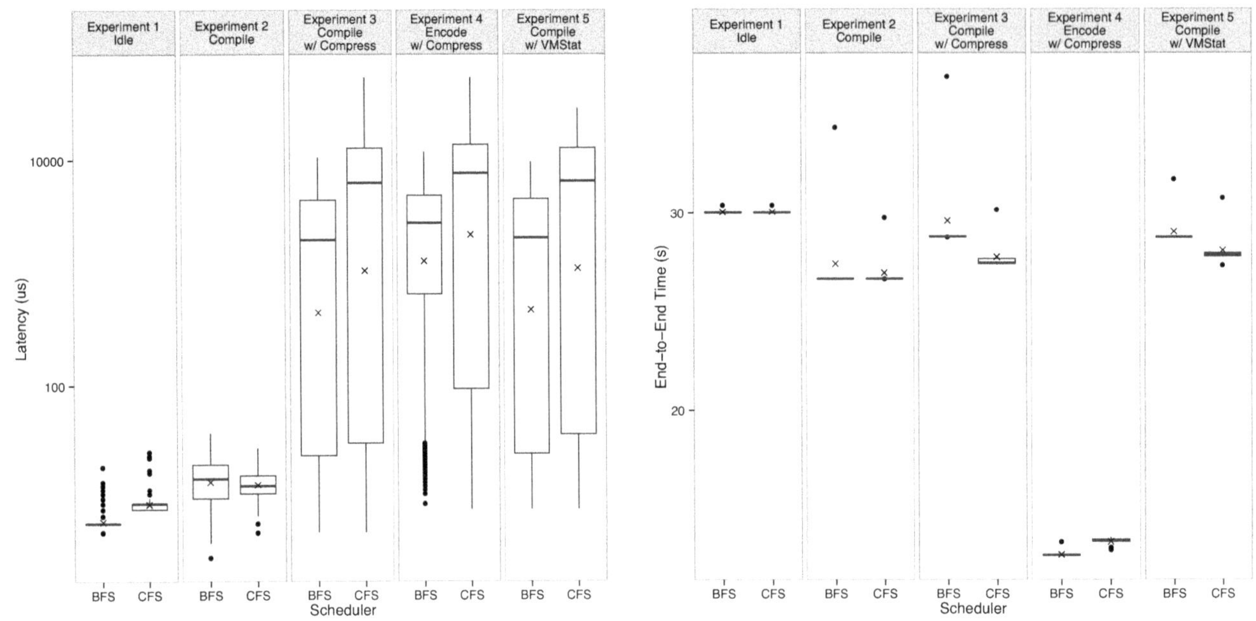

(a) Latency

(b) End-to-End Times

Figure 2. Results of the sequential experiments.

requires fewer scheduling decisions, this overhead would not be as pronounced.

4.5 Experiment 5: Compile with Idleness Data

The goal of this experiment is to revisit Experiment 3, with the addition of the idleness data collection. We added calls to the *VMStat* Linux utility to Latt, so that every time Latt collected a latency sample, it used VMStat to collect an idleness value. We instrumented Latt to buffer idleness data in memory, along with latency and client throughput data.

The last plot on Figure 2(a) shows that, while the overall conclusion is the same from Experiment 3 — the BFS has better average and worst-case latency — the worst-case latency for the CFS decreased by nearly 50%, from 53,370μs to 28,530μs. The latency behavior of the BFS, on the other hand, remained the same. This change in behavior was later revealed to be caused by a probe effect specific to the CFS, caused by a scheduling policy introduced in late 2010 (the `CONFIG_SCHED_AUTOGROUP` kernel option). Section 7 includes details on this effect.

4.6 Discussion

The unstructured experiments demonstrated that several factors affect both the latency and the end-to-end time behavior of both schedulers: the background load, the Latt client load, and the presence of VMStat calls in Latt. Unfortunately, they also led to a series of contradictions, and no clear conclusion as to what scheduler has a better latency or end-to-end performance. Worst of all, there is no indication of when these sequential experiments would converge to a conclusion.

There was, however, a significant difference between schedulers on all experiments, and the changes in experimental conditions affected both metrics on both schedulers. We used Kruskal-Wallis tests [17][2] to analyze the data in two ways: first, we verified that the latency and end-to-end time distributions differed between schedulers for all experiments ($P < 0.01$), second, we verified that latency and end-to-end time distributions for each scheduler differed between experiments ($P < 0.01$). Since the schedulers differ, there must be a correct scheduler choice under each operating condition.

An important question to answer is "when have you experimented enough to draw conclusions?" To answer this question, we realized we needed to more systematically explore the factors affecting our metrics. Using traditional design and analysis of experiments, we can delimit our experimental space and, if analysis is successful, draw conclusions about the performance of each scheduler.

[2] The Kruskal-Wallis test is a non-parametric test used to verify if two or more samples belong to the same distribution.

5. Factorial Design

We now use established statistical methods to try to successfully compare the performance of the two schedulers. Factorial experiment design, coupled with ANOVA [9, 15, 17] allows isolating the effect of factors on response variables — latency, client throughput, and end-to-end times — measuring not only the magnitude of their individual effects, but also any interaction between factors. In this section we will demonstrate how ANOVA can be insightful when used correctly, but can also produce misleading results when used incorrectly.

Analysis of Variance (ANOVA)

A statistical analysis method that partitions the variability in a data set into its component parts.

Output: A model of the mean of the response variable as a linear function of factor levels.

Distribution Assumptions: Normally and independently distributed errors with constant variance.

We used a two-level full factorial design [17] for our experiments. In this design, the experimenter varies the factors between two levels — low and high — and executes experiments containing all combinations of levels for all factors. This experiment design assumes that the factors are fixed, and allows quantifying not only the effect of factors in isolation but also their interactions. Table 1 shows the factors and levels explored in this design. All of the factors listed here measurably affected the latency in the experiments described in Section 4, and the machine factor was added to ensure results were not exclusive to the Core 2 machine used in the previous experiments. We fixed the Latt client number at eight and the compression size at 64kb, since those were the only conditions under which realistic latency measurements were collected. We omitted the sleep load for the same reason. Measuring latency in an idle system would lead to unrealistic results as demonstrated in Section 4.1.

Factor	Low Lvl.	High Lvl.
Scheduler	BFS	CFS
Machine	Core 2	P4
VMStat	off	on
Load	compile	encode

Table 1. Factors and their levels.

Exp.	Scheduler	Machine	VMStat	Load
3	CFS	Core 2	off	compile
	BFS	Core 2	off	compile
4	CFS	Core 2	off	encode
	BFS	Core 2	off	encode
5	CFS	Core 2	on	compile
	BFS	Core 2	on	compile

Table 2. Factors and their levels for the sequential experiments.

The set of factors and levels specified above define our *experimental space*. For this full factorial design, experiments will consist of executing every combination of factor levels (a total of 16 combinations) five separate, non-consecutive times. This number of runs provided us with enough data for a robust analysis, since all effects were measured with a high significance level; if this were not the case, we would collect more data to improve the statistical power of the test (i.e., reduce the odds of a false negative). To ensure that the measurement error is distributed uniformly across all factor levels, we randomized the order of the execution of the trials.

Table 2 shows how the last three experiments from the previous section consist of a six trial subset of the full-factorial design. By simultaneously varying all factors in a series of automated experiments, the full-factorial design will allow us to reach general conclusions without having to sequentially explore the experimental space one factor at a time.

The analysis of the results consists of creating a linear model of the data, relating the factors to one response variable at a time using linear regression. Linear regression is a method to calculate the best fitting linear mathematical model to a data set, and assumes normally distributed, independent observations. The resulting model will be of the form

$$y = \beta_0 + \beta_1 x_1 + \beta_2 x_2 + \ldots + \beta_k x_k + \ldots + \beta_{12} x_1 x_2 + \ldots + \beta_{ik} x_i x_k + \ldots + \epsilon \quad (1)$$

where y is the response variable, which is related to k factors, each with a level x_i and a coefficient β_i, where $i = 1, \ldots, k$. Terms of the form $\beta_{12} x_1 x_2$ allow the modeling of interactions between factors. Higher-level interactions (between three or more factors) can also be included in the model. The ϵ term is a random error component that incorporates other sources of variability (uncontrolled factors and measurement error). This model describes a hyperplane in the k-dimensional space of the k factors, and β_0 is the intercept for the plane, i.e., where the plane crosses the response variable dimension when all $x_i = 0$.

More intuitively, let x_1 represent the scheduler factor. We attribute indicator values to its levels: -1 for low (BFS) and +1 for high (CFS). The scheduler effect β_1 will then be *half* the expected change in the mean response variable when the scheduler factor is modified and all other factors are unchanged. In other words, the low indicator value $x_1 = -1$, will subtract the value of β_1 from the response variable, the high indicator value $x_1 = +1$, will add it; hence β_1 is half the total expected change in the response value when x_1 changes from -1 to $+1$. A positive β_i signifies positive feedback on the response variable with an increasing value of x_i; a negative β_i signifies a negative feedback under the same conditions.

There are a number of pre-requisites that the underlying distribution of the data must meet for the linear regression modeling to be successful, namely that (1) the error is normally distributed, (2) the error is independently distributed, i.e., one observation does not affect the probability of any other, and (3) the error has mean zero and constant variance. If a linear model adequately approximates the data set, ANOVA will allow us not only to quantify the impact of the factor on the response variable, but also to quantify unexplained variation. This is particularly useful in settings where hidden factors are commonplace, since a large aggregated effect by hidden factors may indicate the need for further experimentation. If these assumptions are broken, the true significance level (i.e., the probability of a false positive) of any statistical tests performed with the model (e.g., testing the statistical significance of a factor) will differ from what calculations report, generally with a loss of statistical power (i.e., the chance of a false negative increases).

Any factors that affect the response variables but were *not* controlled (i.e., do not appear in Table 1) will cause variability that is not attributable to any factor or factor interaction. In ANOVA, this variability will be indistinguishable from any other source of error (such as random measurement error). Experimenters should strive to minimize the amount of error, so that as much variability as possible is adequately explained. The smaller the error, the smaller the effects that will be detectable.

5.1 End-to-End Times

To demonstrate the use of linear regression and ANOVA, we apply them to the end-to-end time data from our experiment. We first verify that the assumptions of ANOVA are not violated, by checking whether the residuals — the distance, or error, by which each observation differs from what the model estimates it should be — are normal, and do not present a pattern or heterogeneous variance. Residual plots verify these properties, by relating the response variable values predicted by the model (plotted on the x-axis) with their distance from the actual, measured values that compose our data set (y-axis). In other words, for any combination of factor levels (values of the x_i variables) a value of y can be calculated (i.e., the model can predict a response value for a factor level combination). The residuals are simply the differences between these predicted values and the values that were experimentally observed for each combination of factor levels. Residual plots should show no discernible pattern when there is no systematic error (e.g., from faulty experimentation or analysis). Figure 3 shows that the residuals for this data have no discernible pattern or widely heterogeneous variances. A normal probability plot of the residuals (omitted for

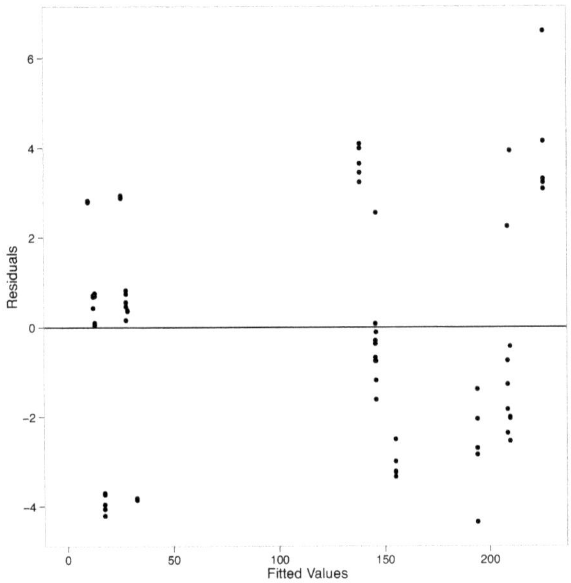

Figure 3. Residual plot for the linear model of end-to-end time response variable, showing no error patterns.

brevity) showed that the normality assumption held. Therefore, linear regression produced a model with a good fit, and we can be confident in the conclusions drawn from ANOVA. The more pronounced residual (with a value higher than 6) did not adversely affect the model[3].

Table 3 shows the ANOVA results for end-to-end times. The source column lists the source factor for the variability. The effect column lists the values of β_i calculated by linear regression, and the boundaries of their 95% confidence interval. The sum of squares column shows the total variability attributable to each factor (i.e., the higher the sum of squares attributed to each factor, the more variability was caused by that factor). The p-value column shows the statistical significance of each factor's effect. For example, a significance level of 0.01 means that a factor is significant (i.e., has a non-zero effect) at the 99% confidence level. The statistical significance of an effect does not indicate its magnitude, which is captured by the β_i model coefficients (c.f., the effects column).

The residuals (shown in the last row of Table 3) allow us to quantify the effect of all uncontrolled factors that affected end-to-end times in this experiment. The residual sum of squares, 545, is an upper bound on the variability attributed to the sum of all hidden factors. This value is negligible in comparison to the machine factor (with a sum of squares of 493,851, three orders of magnitude greater). Therefore, for this experiment, in this design space, the effect of controlling for any further factors will be negligible and we can conclude that enough experimentation has been conducted. The residuals are also used in calculating the explained variability (or the R^2 statistic) of a model; in this case, the explained variability is of 99.8%. This means that, out of the total variability observed in the data set (total sum of squares) 0.2% is caused by error (residual sum of squares), and the remaining 99.8% is attributable to one of the factors or a combination of them.

To interpret the results of the ANOVA table, we focus on the effect estimate column. The effect estimate for the machine factor (78.6s) clearly shows that it is the defining factor for end-to-end times, with a main effect estimate far larger than that of any other main factor. The estimate of the interaction between the machine and load (19.7s) can be interpreted as follows: depending on the machine, the load factor affects end-to-end times at a different rate. In other words, changing the load type incurs a larger increase in end-to-end time on the slower machine than on the faster one. Several other factors and interactions are statistically significant at the 99% confidence level (i.e., have p-values lower than 0.01) but have comparatively negligible effects.

Most notably, these results show that the scheduler factor, despite being statistically significant, had a relatively negligible impact on the execution time of the benchmark. This means that (1) if end-to-end time is the user's only concern, then the scheduler choice will be inconsequential and (2) end-to-end time does not differentiate these two schedulers. Thus, end-to-end time is a poor metric to benchmark these two schedulers' performance, unlike it has been discussed in the Linux community.

Factor	Effect (s)			Sum Sq.	p-value
	Low 95%	Estimate	High 95%		
machine	77.9	78.6	79.2	493,851	< 0.01
load	11.4	12.0	12.6	11,497	< 0.01
sched	2.5	3.1	3.7	764	< 0.01
vmstat	2.4	3.0	3.6	725	< 0.01
machine:load	19.1	19.7	20.3	31,004	< 0.01
machine:sched	2.4	3.1	3.7	750	< 0.01
machine:vmstat	2.3	3.0	3.6	708	< 0.01
load:sched	1.4	2.0	2.7	333	< 0.01
load:vmstat	1.0	1.7	2.3	219	< 0.01
sched:vmstat	-0.1	0.5	1.1	19	> 0.05
Residuals				545	

Table 3. ANOVA results for end-to-end times.

5.2 Latency

Although ANOVA works well for end-to-end time measurements, our main interest is the worst-case of the latency response variable. We now apply ANOVA to latency, and again, must verify if the method applies. Figure 4 shows a latency histogram for the following combination of factor levels: CFS scheduler, the Core 2 machine, no VMStat, and the compile load. This distribution is highly non-normal, which, in turn, can cause residuals to also be non-normal; this is the first indication that linear regression is inapplicable.

Figure 5 shows the residuals plotted against the fitted values. In contrast to Figure 3, we see a clear pattern of increasing variability as the latency values themselves increase. While this problem can be mitigated by transforming the data into a form with constant variance and then applying ANOVA to the transformed data, these residuals are also not normally distributed. Figure 6, a normal probability plot of the residuals, demonstrates this; if the residuals were normal, they would lie alongside the solid, horizontal line — which indicates a perfectly normal distribution — following no discernible pattern. Non-normality of residuals causes errors in the significance of the estimated coefficients, and is difficult to resolve through data manipulation. The application of linear regression on the latency data resulted in a poorly fitting model, with an explained variability of 12.19%.

If we were to ignore these warning signs and attempt to choose a scheduler using this analysis, we would be basing our decision on a problematic model. The effect for the scheduler factor (i.e., the β_i value corresponding to the scheduler choice) given by this poorly fitting model is of 796μs ($\pm$69 at a 95% confidence level). Consider, then, the plot for Experiments 4 in Figure 2(a), where the difference in mean latency between the CFS and the BFS is of

[3] We used Cook's distance, a metric designed to quantify the influence of outliers on a model, to verify this [17].

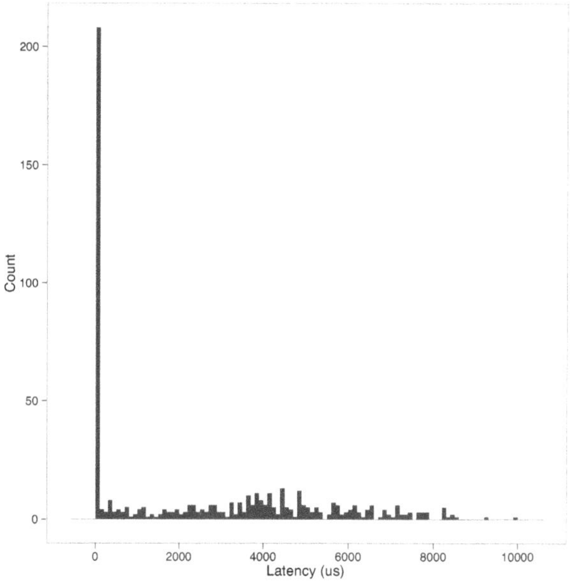

Figure 4. Example of non-normal latency behavior on the Core 2 machine, under the CFS, with no VMStat and the compile load.

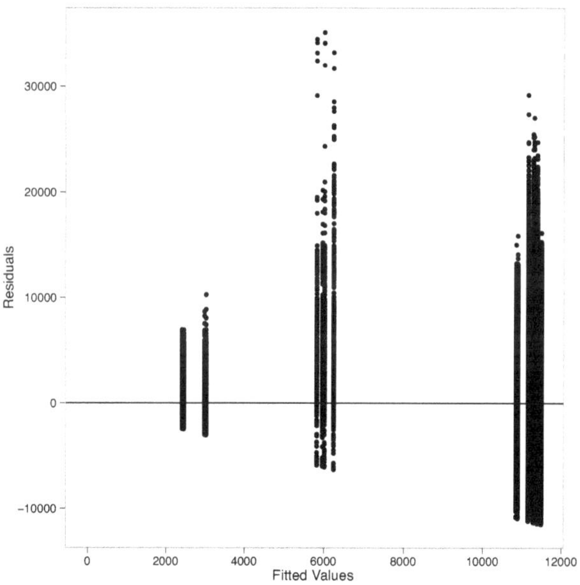

Figure 5. Residual plot for the linear model of the latency response variable, showing heterogeneous error variance.

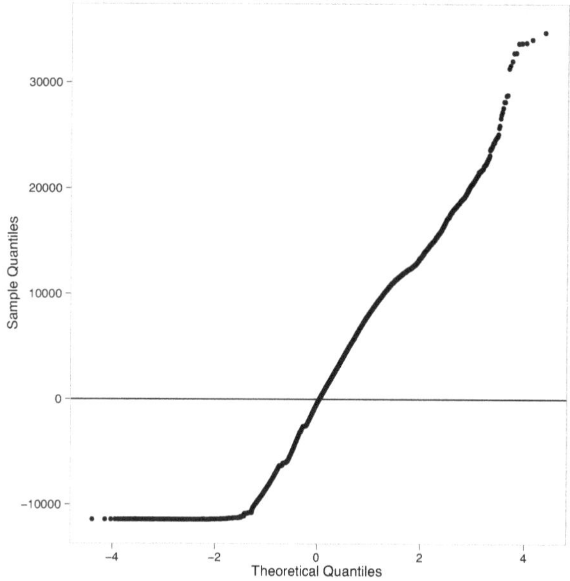

Figure 6. Normal residual plot for the linear model of the latency response variable, showing non-normal errors.

$5453\mu s$; Experiments 3 and 5 show similar differences. The conditions of Experiments 3 through 5 are in this experimental space, so the results of those experiments should be approximated by this model. However, the model suggests that, on average, a change in mean latency of approximately $1600\mu s$ would be observed by a change of scheduler. That is a severe underestimation, and might lead to incorrect conclusions.

Most important of all, however, is the fact that the worst-case latency is of special importance for latency-critical applications. This means that using linear regression, a method to model means, would not allow the analysis of the effects on the right tail of the response variable distribution, providing instead an incomplete picture containing only the mean latency value. As we will show in Section 6, the scheduler effect discussed before will be even more conservative, if the worst-case is of any interest. Since the non-normal data seen here is common in computer experiments [4, 7, 19], a different analysis method is needed. We now apply quantile regression to analyse this same data set, determining each factors' effects on worst-case behavior, with the added bonus of not requiring normally distributed data.

6. Quantile Regression

Quantile regression [12], like linear regression, is a method to model the effect of factors on a response variable. The main difference between the two methods is that, while linear regression models effects on the mean of the response variable, quantile regression can model the effect of factors on *any given quantile*, such as the median or the 99th percentile. By performing multiple quantile regressions on different quantiles of a data set, a researcher can quantify the effect of a factor all along the response variable's probability distribution, and get a more detailed idea of how it is affected by the factors of interest.

Quantile Regression
An optimization-based statistical method to model the effect of factors on *arbitrary* quantiles.
Output: A model of any quantile of the response variable as a linear function of factor levels.
Distribution Assumptions: None.

Although the probability distribution of a performance metric will depend on many factors (such as processor speed), the effect of factors on this distribution can be more complex than a simple change in its mean. Indeed, factors may affect only *part* of the overall distribution. Consider a hypothetical CPU-bound benchmark. The best case performance of this benchmark occurs when it is entirely in cache at the beginning of measurements; in this case, memory latency is irrelevant to performance. In other executions, it may be partially cached or entirely out of the cache; in these scenarios, memory latency will affect performance to different extents. Applying linear regression in this scenario (investigating memory latency as a factor) would lead to a model of the mean behavior, overlooking the fact that memory latency affects *different quantiles of the response variable at different rates*. Quantile regression, on the other hand, is able to capture these details.

Linear quantile regression models are very similar to the linear models described in Equation 1. They take the form

$$Q_y(\tau|X) = \beta_0(\tau) + \beta_1(\tau)x_1 + \beta_2(\tau)x_2 + \ldots + \beta_k(\tau)x_k + \ldots + \beta_{12}(\tau)x_1x_2 + \ldots + \beta_{ik}(\tau)x_ix_k \quad (2)$$

where $\tau \in [0, 1]$ is the quantile of interest[4] of the response variable y, X is the combination of factor levels, and $Q_y(\tau|X)$ is the τth conditional quantile of the response variable y (i.e., the τth quantile of y given factor levels X). As with the linear model, the β_i coefficients represent the expected change in the conditional quantile as the corresponding factor levels change.

Quantile regression also differs from linear regression in that it is non-parametric, that is, it does not assume anything about the distribution of the error component. This is because parameter estimates are only affected by the local behavior of the response variable near each quantile of interest. While the application of linear regression on our non-normal latency data yielded an incorrect model because the data failed to meet requirements, we now demonstrate that quantile regression can successfully analyse the same data set.

To quantify the effect of each factor at different points on the latency probability distribution, we apply ten quantile regressions to the dataset: nine from the 10th percentile through the 90th percentile at equal intervals, then one at the 99th percentile. Coefficients were estimated for all factors and interactions up to the four-factor interaction. Figure 7 shows all main factors, the scheduler by machine interaction, and the intercept. The intercept, or the $\beta_0(\tau)$ coefficient, does not depend on factors to affect the response variable; it can be thought of as the baseline latency at each of those quantiles before factor effects are applied. The x-axis shows the quantiles of the latency probability distribution, and the y-axis shows the magnitude of effects at each of those quantiles. A black line is plotted through the estimated effects, and the grey band denotes the 95% confidence interval for the effects. For example, consider the machine factor subplot in the figure. This factor has no effect at the 10th percentile (0.1 on the x-axis). Towards the right of the plot, the effect of this factor starts to grow, ultimately reaching 5,594.5μs at the 99th percentile. This means that, all else being equal, a change from the Core 2 machine to the P4 will increase the value of the 99th percentile of the response variable by approximately 11,189μs (as with ANOVA in Section 5, the net increase is doubled due to the coding used for factor levels). Similarly, a negative effect like the scheduler by machine interaction will cause a quantile to decrease in value.

The first observation of note is the significant effect of the scheduler on latency. The scheduler subplot in Figure 7 shows that this factor has no effect below the 40th percentile, but then its effect gradually increases with each percentile, eventually reaching 2,244.1μs at the 99th percentile. The difference between the BFS and the CFS near the worst-case latency will therefore be of approximately 4,488.2μs. While this latency may seem to be low, it accounts for *more than 10% of the single worst-case latency observed in all our factorial design trials*, which was of 41,164μs. A 10% improvement in worst-case latency would make a significant interactivity impact in a mobile system that operates near the 100ms threshold.

Table 4 provides a list of all effects on the 99th percentile, the highest percentile shown in Figure 7. Similarly to Table 3, which presented the ANOVA results for the end-to-end time, the effects column lists the expected change in the 99th conditional percentile when each factor level changes and all else remains equal, accompanied by the high and low boundaries of their 95% confidence interval. The statistical significance of each effect is shown in the p-value column. At this extreme percentile, the machine has the largest effect, closely followed by the scheduler by machine interaction, and then the scheduler main effect. We can conclude that, if the user is concerned about the worst-case latency, then the BFS will provide better performance.

Figure 7 and Table 4 permit further conclusions. Latency, for most quantiles, is independent of the load factor; Figure 2(a) also shows this, where the difference between the latency measured in Experiment 3 (compile load) and 4 (encode load) was minimal. The difference between the two experiments is concentrated in the lower quantiles, where most of the load factor's effect is located. We can also observe that the VMStat factor, while largely indistinguishable from zero, becomes more pronounced after the 90th percentile. Table 4 shows that interactions with the VMStat factor are also significant at that quantile. Figure 2(a) for Experiment 5 already indicated this, where adding VMStat significantly decreased the worst-case latency of the CFS.

To summarize, quantile regression (1) allowed us to analyze a data set that linear regression failed to model correctly, and (2) provided a higher level of detail than linear regression ever could. The first point is important because non-normality is common in computer science experimental data; ANOVA yielded a poor model because of the non-normality and different variances in the latency data, while quantile regression provided insight into the data despite these properties. The second point is important because when researchers have more than a model of mean response (or indeed, simply a test of whether samples originate from the same distribution), they can gain more insight from their experiments. For example, the fact that the scheduler has an increasingly larger effect as latency values increase — making it very important for worst-case latency analysis — would be impossible to detect through ANOVA or any form of analysis that focuses on the response mean.

[4] The τth quantile of a distribution y is the smallest observed value in y such that the probability of obtaining smaller values of y is τ.

Factor	Effect (μs) Low 95%	Estimate	High 95%	p-value
machine	5,199.7	5,594.5	5,989.3	0.000
sched	1,849.3	2,244.1	2,639.0	0.000
vmstat	-947.9	-553.0	-158.2	0.021
load	-342.0	52.9	447.7	0.825
sched:machine	-5,087.5	-4,692.6	-4,297.8	0.000
sched:vmstat	-940.7	-545.9	-151.0	0.022
machine:vmstat	68.7	463.5	858.3	0.053
load:vmstat	-101.0	293.9	688.7	0.220
machine:load	-114.0	280.9	675.7	0.241
sched:load	-668.6	-273.8	121.1	0.254
sched:machine:vmstat	215.5	610.4	1,005.2	0.011
sched:machine:load	82.7	477.5	872.3	0.046
machine:load:vmstat	-636.5	-241.6	153.2	0.314
sched:load:vmstat	-232.6	162.3	557.1	0.499
sched:machine:load:vmstat	-602.827	-208.000	186.828	0.386

Table 4. Quantile regression coefficients for the 99th percentile.

7. Further Pitfalls

While we conducted the experiments for this paper, several experimentation pitfalls became obvious. This section discusses those pitfalls and their proposed solutions.

Autogroup as a Hidden Factor The experiment described in Section 4.5 demonstrated how a small, seemingly innocuous change of experimental conditions can significantly affect results. In that case, the addition of VMStat calls to Latt caused a significant change in latency behavior. This was caused by the autogroup option in the Linux kernel (named `CONFIG_SCHED_AUTOGROUP` in the configuration options), which causes the CFS to schedule processes in the same TTY as a group.

We confirmed this hidden factor with Apache's *ab* benchmark. The *ab* benchmark is an automated HTTP client that measures how many requests per second Apache can serve. To demonstrate this hidden effect, we executed Apache and *ab* in two configurations: (1) in the same TTY, and (2) in different TTYs. Figure 8 shows that, while there was no evidence of a change in the mean execution time (verified with a t-test, $P > 0.05$), executing *ab* in the same TTY as Apache caused the best observed execution time under the CFS to decrease by 1.37s, and the worse case to increase by 0.33s, that is, the spread of measured values seemed to increase. This was verified through an F-test, which showed that the ratio between the *variances* of the two CFS distributions was approximately 0.2. In other words, autogroup made the execution time variance measurably larger for the CFS. On the other hand, this does not hold for the BFS ($P > 0.05$ for both t and F-tests), as it ignores the autogroup kernel option. It is reasonable to assume that some server administrators are unknowingly measuring unrealistic performance because of this hidden scheduling artifact.

Incorrect Surrogate Metrics During our experiments, Latt's client throughput metric proved to be a poor surrogate for application throughput. We found that an execution of Latt could have a lower mean client throughput, but a higher end-to-end time than another execution, which can be easily interpreted as a fault in Latt. The surprising result is due to the fact that Latt does not tally time spent in the server thread, and therefore, the client throughput metric only captured a part of the total execution time of the benchmark. After discovering this, we started using the end-to-end time of a useful computation (compilation or video encoding) to provide a reliable metric of throughput.

Choice of Background Load "Clean room" experimentation may lead to incorrect or misleading results, as shown by the latency measurements for Experiments 1 and 2 in Section 4. By keeping the processor largely idle, the idle load yielded latency data that did not distinguish the two schedulers. Similarly, having a single Latt client perform no work failed to yield realistic latency data. Because of this, we encourage the exploration of the experimental space with a focus on determining not only what factors affect the response variable, but also how the response variable behaves at the different levels of those factors.

8. Related Work

Several researchers have investigated the difficulty of correctly evaluating computer performance. Mytkowicz et al. [18] demonstrate that seemingly innocuous experimental setup details, such as the UNIX environment size or the benchmark link order, can have a significant impact on performance. Harji et al. [8] show that the Linux kernel has had a series of performance affecting issues, and that papers that present data measured on Linux could contain incorrect results. Kalibera et al. [11] show that random symbol names generated by a compiler lead to different memory layouts at run time, and, consequently, random variations in performance. In this paper, we describe encounters with several hidden factors, and demonstrate the pitfalls of conducting sequential, undesigned experiments in their presence. We demonstrate that, for a fixed experimental space, ANOVA can be used to quantify the total effect of hidden factors and assist in determining when they have been sufficiently controlled.

Other previous work has argued that more statistical rigor is needed in computer science. Vitek and Kalibera [22] report that in PLDI'11, a selective conference where experimental results are commonly published, 39 of the 42 papers that published experimental results did not report a measure of uncertainty in their data, making the need for more rigorous statistical analysis in computer science clear. Kalibera and Jones [10] raise a similar point, presenting a random effects model tailored to computer experiments, while also noting that current textbook approaches may be insufficient in the field. Georges et al. [5] argue for the use of statistically rigorous analysis methods, however, they only go so far as ANOVA, which we show here to be insufficient in some cases.

Due to its relatively recent development, quantile regression is also gaining acceptance in other fields. Cade and Noon [2] present the method to ecologists, and Koenker and Hallock [13] demon-

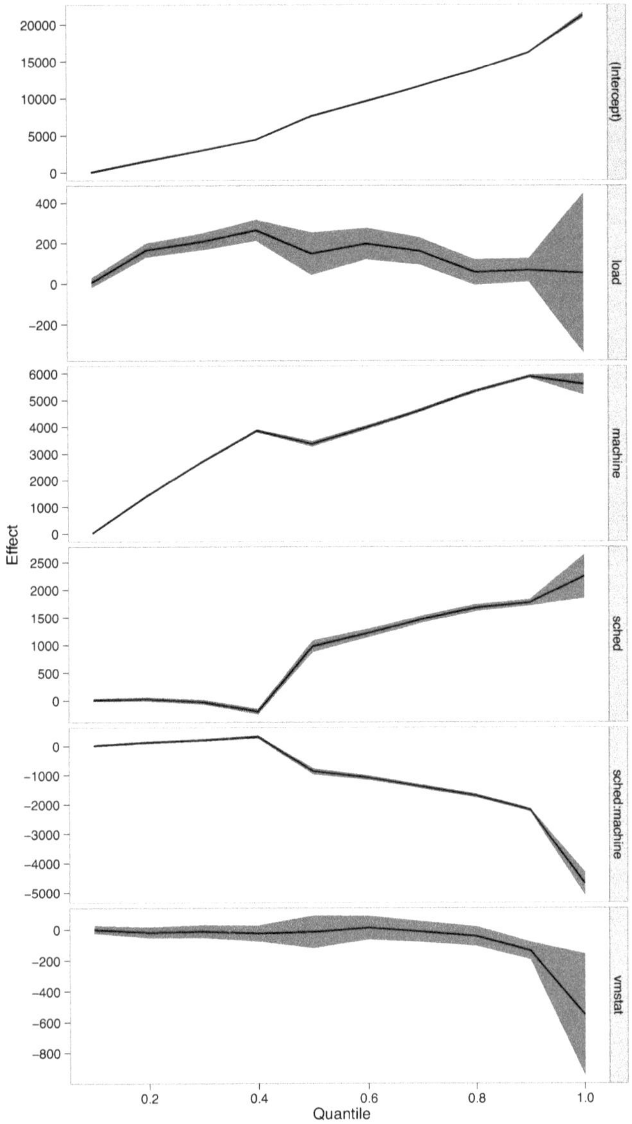

Figure 7. Quantile regression effects for the most relevant factors for the latency response variable.

strate the method to econometricians. We hope that this paper will serve a similar purpose in experimental computer science.

9. Conclusion

Computer performance evaluation is essential to industry and academia alike. However, past research demonstrates that both collecting and analysing performance data is not a trivial process. In this paper, we investigate what is necessary to conduct a successful performance experiment.

First, we attempted to replicate an undesigned experiment, and failed to reach satisfactory conclusions. Instead, a series of contradictions left us with no indication of when we would have conducted enough experiments. Then, we applied textbook design and analysis of experiments with mixed results; while ANOVA worked well for one metric, it failed to provide insight on another.

Finally, we successfully applied quantile regression, a recent development in statistics, to the non-normal data set, and gained insights that ANOVA (or indeed any statistical tool that focuses solely on the mean value) would have failed to provide. We believe that quantile regression is a useful tool for computer scientists, given the abundance of data to which methods that assume normality do not apply.

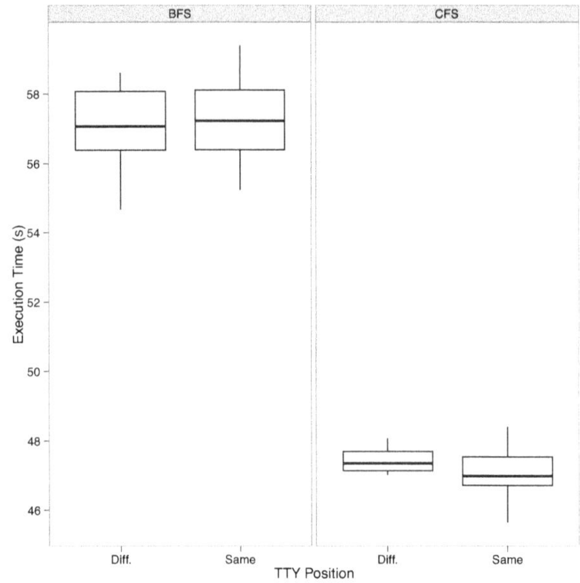

Figure 8. Effect of autogroup on the *ab* benchmark.

Acknowledgments

This research was supported in part by NSERC DG 357121-2008, ORF-RE03-045, CFI 20314, CMC, and the industrial partners associated with these projects.

References

[1] J. Axboe. Latt benchmark. http://git.kernel.dk/?p=latt.git;a=summary.

[2] B. S. Cade and B. R. Noon. A gentle introduction to quantile regression for ecologists. *Frontiers in Ecology and the Environment*, 1(8):412–420, 2003.

[3] S. K. Card, A. Newell, and T. P. Moran. *The Psychology of Human-Computer Interaction*. L. Erlbaum Associates Inc., Hillsdale, NJ, USA, 1983. ISBN 0898592437.

[4] M. E. Crovella and A. Bestavros. Self-similarity in world wide web traffic: evidence and possible causes. *IEEE/ACM Trans. Netw.*, 5(6): 835–846, Dec. 1997. ISSN 1063-6692. doi: 10.1109/90.650143. URL http://dx.doi.org/10.1109/90.650143.

[5] A. Georges, D. Buytaert, and L. Eeckhout. Statistically rigorous Java performance evaluation. In *Proceedings of the 22nd Annual ACM SIGPLAN Conference on Object-oriented Programming Systems and Applications*, OOPSLA '07, pages 57–76, New York, NY, USA, 2007. ACM. ISBN 978-1-59593-786-5. doi: http://doi.acm.org/10.1145/1297027.1297033. URL http://doi.acm.org/10.1145/1297027.1297033.

[6] Gmane. Linux Kernel Mailing List - BFS vs. mainline scheduler benchmarks and measurements. http://thread.gmane.org/gmane.linux.kernel/886319.

[7] M. Harchol-balter. The effect of heavy-tailed job size distributions on computer system design. In *Proc. of ASA-IMS Conf. on Applications of Heavy Tailed Distributions in Economics*, 1999.

[8] A. S. Harji, P. A. Buhr, and T. Brecht. Our troubles with linux and why you should care. In *Proceedings of the Second Asia-Pacific Workshop on Systems*, APSys '11, pages 2:1–2:5, New York, NY, USA, 2011.

ACM. ISBN 978-1-4503-1179-3. doi: 10.1145/2103799.2103802. URL `http://doi.acm.org/10.1145/2103799.2103802`.

[9] R. Jain. *The Art of Computer Systems Performance Analysis: Techniques for Experimental Design, Measurement, Simulation, and Modeling*. Wiley-Interscience, New York, 1991.

[10] T. Kalibera and R. Jones. Quantifying performance changes with effect size confidence intervals. Technical Report 4–12, University of Kent, June 2012. URL `http://www.cs.kent.ac.uk/pubs/2012/3233`.

[11] T. Kalibera, L. Bulej, and P. Tuma. Benchmark precision and random initial state. In *Proceedings of the 2005 International Symposium on Performance Evaluation of Computer and Telecommunications Systems (SPECTS)*, pages 853–862. SCS, 2005.

[12] R. Koenker and J. Bassett, Gilbert. Regression quantiles. *Econometrica*, 46(1):pp. 33–50, 1978. ISSN 00129682. URL `http://www.jstor.org/stable/1913643`.

[13] R. Koenker and K. F. Hallock. Quantile regression. *Journal of Economic Perspectives*, 15(4):143–156, Fall 2001.

[14] C. Kolivas. FAQS about BFS. v0.330. http://ck.kolivas.org/patches/bfs/bfs-faq.txt.

[15] D. J. Lilja. *Measuring Computer Performance: A Practitioner's Guide*. Cambridge University Press, 2000.

[16] I. Molnar. Design of the CFS scheduler. http://people.redhat.com/mingo/cfs-scheduler/sched-design-CFS.txt.

[17] D. C. Montgomery. *Design and Analysis of Experiments*. John Wiley & Sons, 2006. ISBN 0470088109.

[18] T. Mytkowicz, A. Diwan, M. Hauswirth, and P. F. Sweeney. Producing wrong data without doing anything obviously wrong! In *Proceedings of the 14th International Conference on Architectural Support for Programming Languages and Operating Systems*, ASPLOS '09, pages 265–276, New York, NY, USA, 2009. ACM. ISBN 978-1-60558-406-5. doi: http://doi.acm.org/10.1145/1508244.1508275. URL `http://doi.acm.org/10.1145/1508244.1508275`.

[19] V. Paxson and S. Floyd. Wide area traffic: the failure of poisson modeling. *IEEE/ACM Trans. Netw.*, 3(3):226–244, June 1995. ISSN 1063-6692. doi: 10.1109/90.392383. URL `http://dx.doi.org/10.1109/90.392383`.

[20] Tukaani Project. The .xz file format. http://tukaani.org/xz/format.html.

[21] VideoLAN. x264. http://www.videolan.org/developers/x264.html.

[22] J. Vitek and T. Kalibera. Repeatability, Reproducibility, and Rigor in Systems Research. In *Proceedings of the Ninth ACM International Conference on Embedded Software*, EMSOFT '11, pages 33–38, New York, NY, USA, 2011. ACM. ISBN 978-1-4503-0714-7. doi: 10.1145/2038642.2038650. URL `http://doi.acm.org/10.1145/2038642.2038650`.

[23] Xiph.Org Foundation. Xiph.org Video Test Media. http://media.xiph.org/video/derf/.

STABILIZER: Statistically Sound Performance Evaluation

Charlie Curtsinger Emery D. Berger

Department of Computer Science
University of Massachusetts Amherst
Amherst, MA 01003
{charlie,emery}@cs.umass.edu

Abstract

Researchers and software developers require effective performance evaluation. Researchers must evaluate optimizations or measure overhead. Software developers use automatic performance regression tests to discover when changes improve or degrade performance. The standard methodology is to compare execution times before and after applying changes.

Unfortunately, modern architectural features make this approach unsound. Statistically sound evaluation requires multiple samples to test whether one can or cannot (with high confidence) reject the null hypothesis that results are the same before and after. However, caches and branch predictors make performance dependent on machine-specific parameters and the exact layout of code, stack frames, and heap objects. A single binary constitutes just one sample from the space of program layouts, regardless of the number of runs. Since compiler optimizations and code changes also alter layout, it is currently impossible to distinguish the impact of an optimization from that of its layout effects.

This paper presents STABILIZER, a system that enables the use of the powerful statistical techniques required for sound performance evaluation on modern architectures. STABILIZER forces executions to sample the space of memory configurations by repeatedly re-randomizing layouts of code, stack, and heap objects at runtime. STABILIZER thus makes it possible to control for layout effects. Re-randomization also ensures that layout effects follow a Gaussian distribution, enabling the use of statistical tests like ANOVA. We demonstrate STABILIZER's efficiency ($< 7\%$ median overhead) and its effectiveness by evaluating the impact of LLVM's optimizations on the SPEC CPU2006 benchmark suite. We find that, while `-O2` has a significant impact relative to `-O1`, the performance impact of `-O3` over `-O2` optimizations is indistinguishable from random noise.

Categories and Subject Descriptors C.4 [*Performance of Systems*]; D.2.0 [*Software Engineering*]: General; D.3.4 [*Programming Languages*]: Compilers

Keywords Randomization, Measurement Bias, Performance Evaluation

ASPLOS'13, March 16–20, 2013, Houston, Texas, USA.

1. Introduction

The task of performance evaluation forms a key part of both systems research and the software development process. Researchers working on systems ranging from compiler optimizations and runtime systems to code transformation frameworks and bug detectors must measure their effect, evaluating how much they improve performance or how much overhead they impose [7, 8]. Software developers need to ensure that new or modified code either in fact yields the desired performance improvement, or at least does not cause a performance regression (that is, making the system run slower). For large systems in both the open-source community (e.g., Firefox and Chromium) and in industry, automatic performance regression tests are now a standard part of the build or release process [25, 28].

In both settings, performance evaluation typically proceeds by testing the performance of the actual application in a set of scenarios, or a range of benchmarks, both before and after applying changes or in the absence and presence of a new optimization, runtime system, etc.

In addition to measuring *effect size* (here, the magnitude of change in performance), a statistically sound evaluation must test whether it is possible with a high degree of confidence to reject the *null hypothesis*: that the performance of the new version is indistinguishable from the old. To show that a performance optimization is statistically significant, we need to reject the null hypothesis with high confidence (and show that the direction of improvement is positive). Conversely, we aim to show that it is not possible to reject the null hypothesis when we are testing for a performance regression.

Unfortunately, even when using current best practices (large numbers of runs and a quiescent system), the conventional approach is unsound. The problem is due to the interaction between software and modern architectural features, especially caches and branch predictors. These features are sensitive to the addresses of the objects they manage. Because of the significant performance penalties imposed by cache misses or branch mispredictions (e.g., due to aliasing), their reliance on addresses makes software exquisitely sensitive to memory layout. Small changes to code, such as adding or removing a stack variable, or changing the order of heap allocations, can have a ripple effect that alters the placement of every other function, stack frame, and heap object.

The impact of these layout changes is unpredictable and substantial: Mytkowicz et al. show that just changing the size of environment variables can trigger performance degradation as high as 300% [22]; we find that simply changing the link order of object files can cause performance to decrease by as much as 57%.

Failure to control for layout is a form of *measurement bias*: a systematic error due to uncontrolled factors. All executions constitute just one sample from the vast space of possible memory layouts. This limited sampling makes statistical tests inapplicable, since they depend on multiple samples over a space, often with a known distribution. As a result, it is currently not possible to test whether a code modification is the direct cause of any observed performance change, or if it is due to incidental effects like a different code, stack, or heap layout.

Contributions

This paper presents STABILIZER, a system that enables statistically sound performance analysis of software on modern architectures. To our knowledge, STABILIZER is the first system of its kind.

STABILIZER forces executions to sample over the space of all memory configurations by efficiently and repeatedly randomizing the placement of code, stack, and heap objects at runtime. We show analytically and empirically that STABILIZER's use of randomization makes program execution independent of the execution environment, and thus eliminates this source of measurement bias. Re-randomization goes one step further: it causes the performance impact of layout effects to follow a Gaussian (normal) distribution, by virtue of the Central Limit Theorem. In many cases, layout effects dwarf all other sources of execution time variance [22]. As a result, STABILIZER often leads to execution times that are normally distributed.

By generating execution times with Gaussian distributions, STABILIZER enables statistically sound performance analysis via parametric statistical tests like ANOVA [11]. STABILIZER thus provides a push-button solution that allows developers and researchers to answer the question: does a given change to a program affect its performance, or is this effect indistinguishable from noise?

We demonstrate STABILIZER's efficiency ($< 7\%$ median overhead) and its effectiveness by evaluating the impact of LLVM's optimizations on the SPEC CPU2006 benchmark suite. Across the SPEC CPU2006 benchmark suite, we find that the `-O3` compiler switch (which includes argument promotion, dead global elimination, global common subexpression elimination, and scalar replacement of aggregates) does not yield statistically significant improvements over `-O2`. In other words, the effect of `-O3` versus `-O2` is indistinguishable from random noise.

We note in passing that STABILIZER's low overhead means that it could be used at deployment time to reduce the risk of performance outliers, although we do not explore that use case here. Intuitively, STABILIZER makes it unlikely that object and code layouts will be especially "lucky" or "unlucky." By periodically re-randomizing, STABILIZER limits the contribution of each layout to total execution time.

Outline

The remainder of this paper is organized as follows. Section 2 provides an overview of STABILIZER's operation and statistical properties. Section 3 describes the implementation of STABILIZER's compiler and runtime components, and Section 4 gives an analysis of STABILIZER's statistical properties. Section 5 demonstrates STABILIZER's avoidance of measurement bias, and Section 6 demonstrates the use of STABILIZER to evaluate the effectiveness of LLVM's standard optimizations. Section 7 discusses related work. Finally, Section 8 presents planned future directions and Section 9 concludes.

2. STABILIZER Overview

This section provides an overview of STABILIZER's operation, and how it provides properties that enable statistically rigorous performance evaluation.

2.1 Comprehensive Layout Randomization

STABILIZER dynamically randomizes program layout to ensure it is independent of changes to code, compilation, or execution environment. STABILIZER performs extensive randomization: it dynamically randomizes the placement of a program's functions, stack frames, and heap objects. Code is randomized at a per-function granularity, and each function executes on a randomly placed stack frame. STABILIZER also periodically *re-randomizes* the placement of functions and stack frames during execution.

2.2 Normally Distributed Execution Time

When a program is run with STABILIZER, the effect of memory layout on performance follows a normal distribution because of layout re-randomization. Layout effects make a substantial contribution to a program's execution. In the absence of other large sources of measurement bias, STABILIZER causes programs to run with normally distribution execution times.

At a high level, STABILIZER's re-randomization strategy induces normally distributed executions as follows: Each random layout contributes a small fraction of total execution time. Total execution time, the sum of runtimes with each random layout, is proportional to the mean of sampled layouts. The *Central Limit Theorem* states that "the mean of a sufficiently large number of independent random variables ... will be approximately normally distributed" [11]. With a sufficient number of randomizations (30 is typical), and no other significant sources of measurement bias, execution time will follow a Gaussian distribution. Section 4 provides a more detailed analysis of STABILIZER's effect on execution time distributions.

2.3 Sound Performance Analysis

Normally distributed execution times allow researchers to evaluate performance using *parametric* hypothesis tests, which provide greater *statistical power* by leveraging the properties of a known distribution (typically the normal distribution). Statistical power is the probability of correctly rejecting a false null hypothesis. Parametric tests typically have greater power than non-parametric tests, which make no assumptions about distribution. For our purposes, the null hypothesis is that a change had no impact. Failure to reject the null hypothesis suggests that more samples (benchmarks or runs) may be required to reach confidence, or that the change had no impact. Powerful parametric tests can correctly reject a false null hypothesis—that is, confirm that a change did have an impact—with fewer samples than non-parametric tests.

2.4 Evaluating Code Modifications

To test the effectiveness of any change (known in statistical parlance as a *treatment*), a researcher or developer runs a program with STABILIZER, both with and without the change. Each run is a sample from the treatment's *population*: the theoretical distribution from which samples are drawn. Given that execution times are drawn from a normally distributed population, we can apply the Student's t-test [11] to calculate the significance of the treatment.

The null hypothesis for the t-test is that the difference in means of the source distributions is zero. The t-test's result (its *p-value*) tells us the probability of observing the measured difference between sample means, assuming both sets of samples come from the same source distribution. If the p-value is below a threshold α (typically 5%), the null hypothesis is rejected; that is, the two source distributions have different means. The parameter α is the probability of committing a type-I error: erroneously rejecting a true null hypothesis.

It is important to note that the t-test can detect *arbitrarily small* differences in the means of two populations (given a sufficient number of samples) regardless of the value of α. The difference in means does not need to be 5% to reach significance with $\alpha = 0.05$. Similarly, if STABILIZER adds 4.8% overhead to a program, this does not prevent the t-test from detecting differences in means that are smaller than 4.8%.

2.5 Evaluating Compiler and Runtime Optimizations

To evaluate a compiler or runtime system change, we instead use a more general technique: analysis of variance (ANOVA). ANOVA takes as input a set of results for each combination of benchmark and treatment, and partitions the total variance into components: the effect of random variations between runs, differences between benchmarks, and the collective impact of each treatment across all benchmarks [11]. ANOVA is a generalized form of the t-test that is less likely to commit type I errors (rejecting a true null hypothesis) than running many independent t-tests. Section 6 presents the use of STABILIZER and ANOVA to evaluate the effectiveness of compiler optimizations in LLVM.

Evaluating Layout Optimizations. All of STABILIZER's randomizations (code, stack, and heap) can be enabled independently. This independence makes it possible to evaluate optimizations that target memory layout. For example, to test an optimization for stack layouts, STABILIZER can be run with only code and heap randomization enabled. These randomizations ensure that incidental changes, such as code to pad the stack or to allocate large objects on the heap, will not affect the layout of code or heap memory. The developer can then be confident that any observed change in performance is the result of the stack optimization and not its secondary effects on layout.

3. STABILIZER Implementation

STABILIZER uses a compiler transformation and runtime library to randomize program layout. STABILIZER performs its transformations in an optimization pass run by the LLVM compiler [17]. STABILIZER's compiler transformation inserts the necessary operations to move the stack, redirects heap operations to the randomized heap, and modifies functions to be independently relocatable. STABILIZER's runtime library exposes an API for the randomized heap, relocates functions on-demand, generates random padding for the stack, and re-randomizes both code and stack at regular intervals.

3.1 Building Programs with Stabilizer

When building a program with STABILIZER, each source file is first compiled to LLVM bytecode. STABILIZER builds Fortran programs with `gfortran` and the `dragonegg` GCC plugin, which generates LLVM bytecode from the GCC front-end [27]. C and C++ programs can be built either with `gcc` and `dragonegg`, or LLVM's `clang` front-end [26].

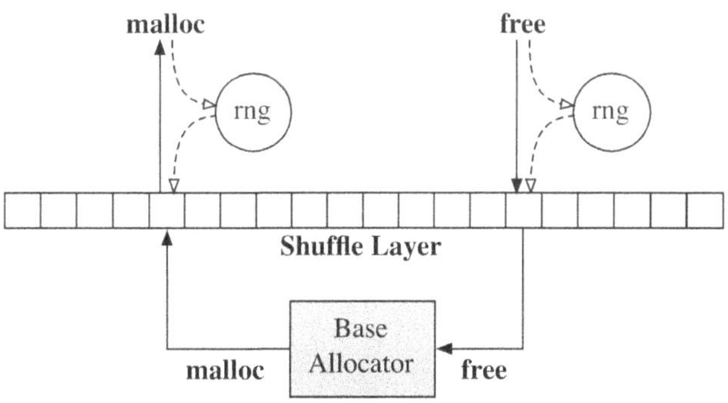

Figure 1. STABILIZER efficiently randomizes the heap by wrapping a deterministic base allocator in a shuffling layer. At startup, the layer is filled with objects from the base heap. The `malloc` function generates a random index, removes the indexed object from the shuffling layer, and replaces it with a new one from the base heap. Similarly, the `free` function generates a random index, frees the indexed object to the base heap, and places the newly freed object in its place.

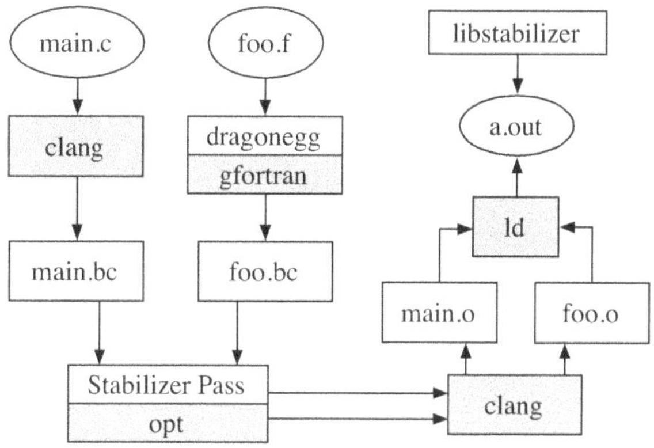

Figure 2. The procedure for building a program with STABILIZER. This process is automated by the `szc` compiler driver.

The compilation and transformation process is shown in Figure 2. This procedure is completely automated by STABILIZER's compiler driver (`szc`), which is compatible with the common `clang` and `gcc` command-line options. Programs can easily be built and evaluated with STABILIZER by substituting `szc` for the default compiler/linker and enabling randomizations with additional flags.

3.2 Heap Randomization

STABILIZER uses a power of two, size-segregated allocator as the base for its heap [33]. Optionally, STABILIZER can be configured to use TLSF (two-level segregated fits) as its base allocator [19]. STABILIZER was originally implemented with the DieHard allocator [3, 24]. DieHard is a bitmap-based randomized allocator with power-of-two size classes. Unlike conventional allocators, DieHard does not use recently-freed memory for subsequent allocations. This lack of reuse and the added TLB pressure from the large virtual address space can lead to very high overhead.

While STABILIZER's base allocators are more efficient than DieHard, they are not fully randomized. STABILIZER randomizes the heap by wrapping its base allocator in a shuffling layer built with HeapLayers [4]. The shuffling layer consists of a size N array of pointers for each size class. The array for each size class is initialized with a fill: N calls to `Base::malloc` are issued to fill the array, then the array is shuffled using the Fisher-Yates shuffle [10]. Every call to `Shuffle::malloc` allocates a new object `p` from `Base::malloc`, generates a random index `i` in the range $[0, N)$, swaps `p` with `array[i]`, and returns the swapped pointer. `Shuffle::free` works in much the same way: a random index `i` is generated, the freed pointer is swapped with `array[i]`, and the swapped pointer is passed to `Base::free`. The process for `malloc` and `free` is equivalent to one iteration of the inside-out Fisher-Yates shuffle. Figure 1 illustrates this procedure. STABILIZER uses the Marsaglia pseudo-random number generator from DieHard [3, 18].

The shuffled heap parameter N must be large enough to create sufficient randomization, but values that are too large will increase overhead with no added benefit. It is only necessary to randomize the index bits of heap object addresses. Randomness in lower-order bits will lead to misaligned allocations, and randomized higher order bits impose additional pressure on the TLB. NIST provides a standard statistical test suite for evaluation pseudorandom number generators [2]. We test the randomness of values returned by libc's `lrand48` function, addresses returned by the DieHard allocator, and the shuffled heap for a range of values of N. Only the index bits (bits 6-17 on the Core2 architecture) were used. Bits used by branch predictors differ significantly across architectures, but are typically low-order bits generally in the same range as cache index bits.

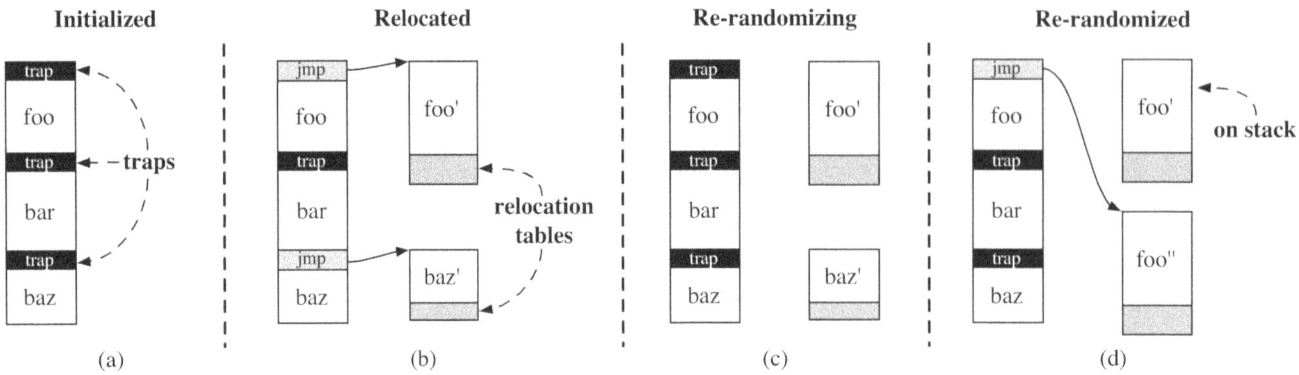

Figure 3. *(a)* During initialization, STABILIZER places a trap instruction at the beginning of each function. When a trapped function is called, it is relocated on demand. *(b)* Each randomized function has an adjacent relocation table, populated with pointers to all referenced globals and functions. *(c)* A timer triggers periodic re-randomizations (every 500ms by default). In the timer signal handler, STABILIZER places traps at the beginning of every randomized function. *(d)* Once a trapped function is called, STABILIZER walks the stack, marks all functions with return addresses on the stack, and frees the rest (`baz'` is freed in the example). Any remaining functions (`foo'`) will be freed after a future re-randomization once they are no longer on the stack. Future calls to `foo` will be directed to a new, randomly located version (`foo''`).

The `lrand48` function passes six tests for randomness (Frequency, BlockFrequency, CumulativeSums, Runs, LongestRun, and FFT) with $> 95\%$ confidence, failing only the Rank test. DieHard passes these same six tests. STABILIZER's randomized heap passes the same tests with the shuffling parameter $N = 256$. STABILIZER uses this heap configuration to randomly allocate memory for both heap objects and functions.

3.3 Code Randomization

STABILIZER randomizes code at function granularity. Every transformed function has a *relocation table* (see Figure 3(b)), which is placed immediately following the code for the function. Functions are placed randomly in memory using a separate randomized heap that allocates executable memory.

Relocation tables are not present in a binary built with STABILIZER. Instead, they are created at runtime immediately following each randomly located function. The sizes of functions are not available in the program's symbol table, so the address of the next function is used to determine the function's endpoint. A function refers to its adjacent relocation table with a PC-relative offset. This approach means that two randomly located copies of the same function do not share a relocation table.

Some constant floating point operands are converted to global variable references during code generation. STABILIZER converts all non-zero floating point constants to global variables in the IR so accesses can be made indirect through the relocation table.

Operations that convert between floating-point and integers do not contain constant operands, but still generate implicit global references during code generation. STABILIZER cannot rewrite these references. Instead, STABILIZER adds functions to each module to perform int-to-float and float-to-int conversions, and replaces the LLVM `fptosi`, `fptoui`, `sitofp`, and `uitofp` instructions with calls to these conversion functions. The conversion functions are the only code that STABILIZER cannot safely relocate.

Finally, STABILIZER renames the `main` function. The STABILIZER runtime library defines its own main function, which initializes runtime support for code randomization before executing any randomized code.

Initialization. At compile time, STABILIZER replaces the module's libc constructors with its own constructor function. At startup, this constructor registers the module's functions and any constructors from the original program. Execution of the program's constructors is delayed until after initialization.

The `main` function, defined in STABILIZER's runtime, overwrites the beginning of every relocatable function with a software breakpoint (the `int 3` x86 instruction, or `0xCC` in hex); see Figure 3(a). A pointer to the function's runtime object is placed immediately after the trap to allow for immediate relocation (not shown).

Relocation. When a trapped function is executed, the STABILIZER runtime receives a `SIGTRAP` signal and relocates the function (Figure 3(b)). Functions are relocated in three stages: first, STABILIZER requests a sufficiently large block of memory from the code heap and copies the function body to this location. Next, the function's relocation table is constructed next to the new function location. STABILIZER overwrites the beginning of the function's original base address with a static jump to the relocated function (replacing the trap instruction). Finally, STABILIZER adds the function to the set of "live" functions.

Re-randomization. STABILIZER re-randomizes functions at regular time intervals (500ms by default). When the re-randomization timer expires, the STABILIZER runtime places a trap instruction at the beginning of every live function and resumes execution (Figure 3(c)). Re-randomization occurs when the next trap is executed. This delay ensures that re-randomization will not be performed during the execution of non-reentrant code.

STABILIZER uses a simple garbage collector to reclaim memory used by randomized functions. First, STABILIZER adds the memory used by each live functions to a set called the "pile." STABILIZER then walks the stack. Every object on the pile pointed to by a return address on the stack is marked. All unmarked objects on the pile are freed to the code heap.

3.4 Stack Randomization.

STABILIZER randomizes the stack by adding a random amount of space (up to 4096 bytes) between each stack frame. STABILIZER's compiler pass creates a 256 byte stack pad table and a one-byte stack pad index for each function. On entry, the function loads the index-th byte, increments the index, and multiplies the byte by 16 (the required stack alignment on `x86_64`). STABILIZER moves the stack down by this amount prior to each function call, and restores the stack after the call returns.

The STABILIZER runtime fills every function's stack pad table with random bytes during each re-randomization. The stack pad

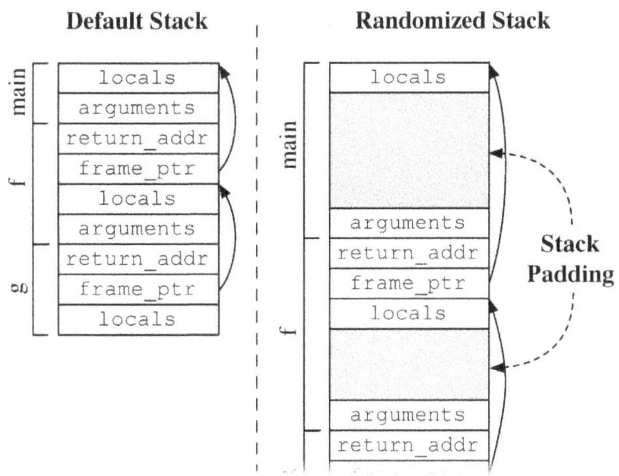

Figure 4. STABILIZER randomizes the stack by adding up to a page of random padding at each function call. Functions are instrumented to load a pad size from the stack pad table. STABILIZER periodically refills this table with new random values to re-randomize the stack.

index may overflow, wrapping back around to the first entry. This wraparound means functions may reuse a random stack pad several times between re-randomizations, but the precise location of the stack is determined by the stack pad size used for each function on the call stack. This combination ensures that stack placement is sufficiently randomized.

3.5 Architecture-Specific Implementation Details

STABILIZER runs on the x86, x86_64 and PowerPC architectures. Most implementation details are identical, but STABILIZER requires some platform-specific support.

x86_64

Supporting the x86_64 architecture introduces two complications for STABILIZER. The first is for the jump instructions: jumps, whether absolute or relative, can only be encoded with a 32-bit address (or offset). STABILIZER uses `mmap` with the `MAP_32BIT` flag to request memory for relocating functions, but on some systems (Mac OS X), this flag is unavailable.

To handle cases where functions must be relocated more than a 32-bit offset away from the original copy, STABILIZER simulates a 64-bit jump by pushing the target address onto the stack and issuing a return instruction. This form of jump is much slower than a 32-bit relative jump, so high-address memory is only used after low-address memory is exhausted.

PowerPC and x86

PowerPC and x86 both use PC-relative addressing for control flow, but data is accessed using absolute addresses. Because of this, the relocation table must be at a fixed absolute address rather than adjacent to a randomized function. The relocation table is only used for function calls, and does not need to be used for accesses to global data.

4. STABILIZER Statistical Analysis

This section presents an analysis that explains how STABILIZER's randomization results in normally distributed execution times for most programs. Section 5 empirically verifies this analysis across our benchmark suite.

The analysis proceeds by first considering programs with a reasonably trivial structure (running in a single loop), and successively weakens this constraint to handle increasingly complex programs.

We assume that STABILIZER is only used on programs that consist of more than a single function. Because STABILIZER performs code layout randomization on a per-function basis, the location of code in a program consisting of just a single function will not be re-randomized. Since most programs consist of a large number of functions, we do not expect this to be a problem in practice.

Base case: a single loop. Consider a small program that runs repeatedly in a loop, executing at least one function. The space of all possible layouts l for this program is the population L. For each layout, an iteration of the loop will have an execution time t. The population of all iteration execution times is E. Clearly, running the program with layout l for 1000 iterations will take time:

$$T_{random} = 1000 * t$$

For simplicity, assume that when this same program is run with STABILIZER, each iteration is run with a different layout l_i with execution time t_i (we refine the notion of "iteration" below).

Running this program with STABILIZER for 1000 iterations will thus have total execution time:

$$T_{stabilized} = \sum_{i=1}^{1000} t_i$$

The values of t_i comprise a sample set x from the population E with mean:

$$\bar{x} = \frac{\sum_{i=1}^{1000} t_i}{1000}$$

The central limit theorem tells us that $\bar{x}$ must be normally distributed (30 samples is typically sufficient for normality). The value of $\bar{x}$ only differs from $T_{stabilized}$ by a constant factor. Multiplying a normally distributed random variable by a constant factor simply shifts and scales the distribution. The result remains normally distributed. Therefore, for this simple program, STABILIZER leads to normally distributed execution times. Note that the distribution of E was never mentioned—the central limit theorem guarantees normality regardless of the sampled population's distribution.

The above argument relies on two conditions. The first is that STABILIZER runs each iteration with a different layout. STABILIZER actually uses wall clock time to trigger re-randomization, but the analysis still holds. As long as STABILIZER re-randomizes roughly every n iterations, we can simply redefine an "iteration" to be n passes over the same code. The second condition is that the program is simply a loop repeating the same code over and over again.

Programs with phase behavior. In reality, programs have more complex control flow and may even exhibit phase-like behavior. The net effect is that for one randomization period, where STABILIZER maintains the same random layout, one of any number of different portions of the application code could be running. However, the argument still holds.

A complex program can be recursively decomposed into subprograms, eventually consisting of subprograms equivalent to the trivial looping program described earlier. These subprograms will each comprise some fraction of the program's total execution, and will all have normally distributed execution times. The total execution time of the program is thus a weighted sum of all the subprograms. A similar approach is used by SimPoint, which accelerates architecture simulation by drawing representative samples from all of a program's phases [13].

Because the sum of two normally distributed random variables is also normally distributed, the program will still have a normally distributed execution time. This decomposition also covers the case

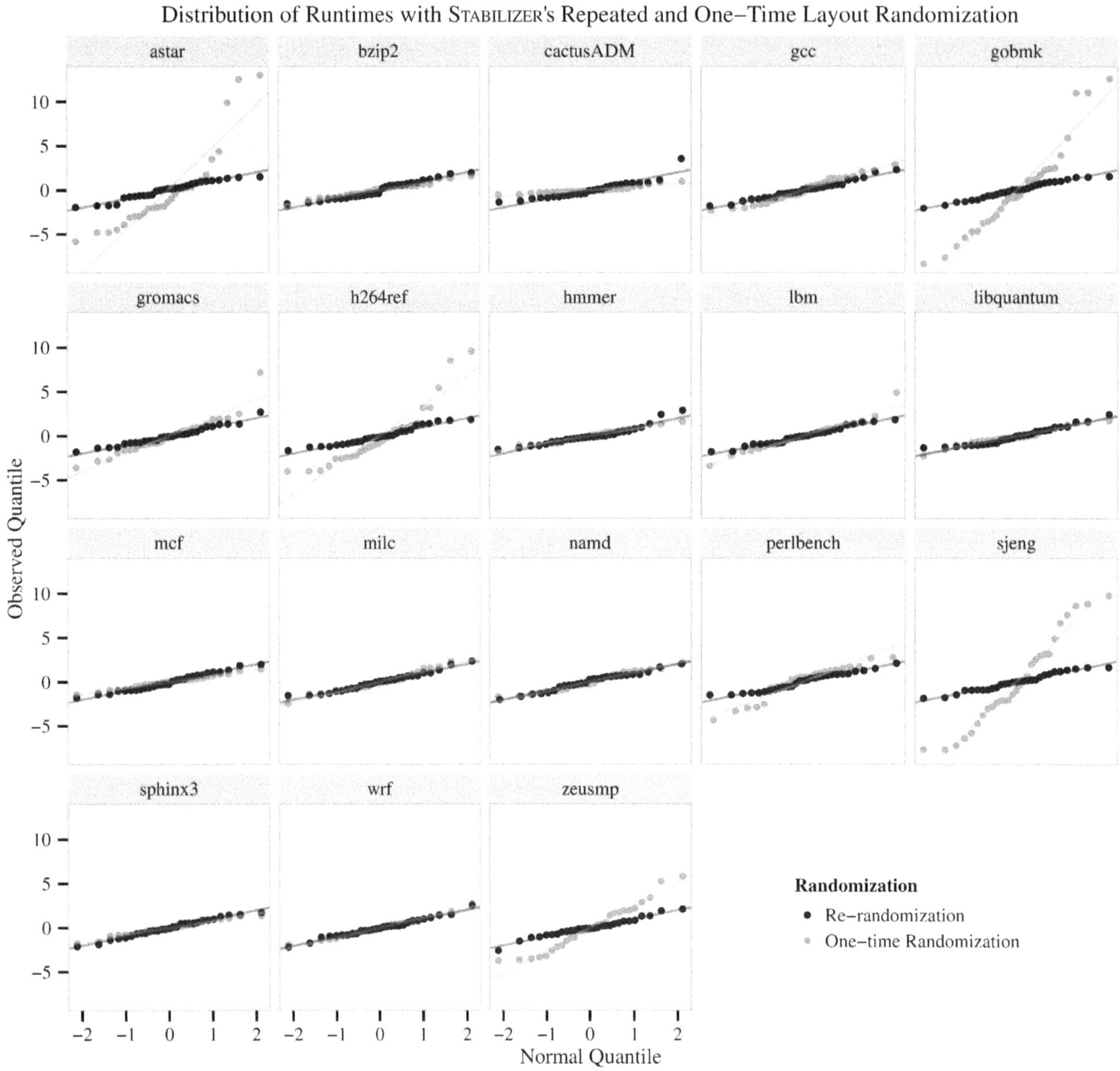

Figure 5. Gaussian distribution of execution time: Quantile-quantile plots comparing the distributions of execution times to the Gaussian distribution. Samples are shifted to a mean of zero, and normalized to the standard deviation of the re-randomized samples. Solid diagonal lines show where samples from a Gaussian distribution would fall. Without re-randomization, `astar`, `cactusADM`, `gromacs`, `h264ref`, and `perlbench` have execution times that are not drawn from a Gaussian distribution. With re-randomization, all benchmarks except `cactusADM` and `hmmer` conform to a Gaussian distribution. A steeper slope on the QQ plot indicates a greater variance. See Section 5.1 for a discussion of these results.

where STABILIZER's re-randomizations are out of phase with the iterations of the trivial looping program.

Heap accesses. Every allocation with STABILIZER returns a randomly selected heap address, but live objects are not relocated because C/C++ semantics do not allow it. STABILIZER thus enforces normality of heap access times as long as the program contains a sufficiently large number of short-lived heap objects (allowing them to be effectively re-randomized). This behavior is common for most applications and corresponds to the generational hypothesis for garbage collection, which has been shown to hold in unmanaged environments [9, 21].

STABILIZER cannot break apart large heap allocations, and cannot add randomization to custom allocators. Programs that use custom allocators or operate mainly small objects from a single large array may not have normally distributed execution times because STABILIZER cannot sufficiently randomize their layout.

5. STABILIZER Evaluation

We evaluate STABILIZER in two dimensions. First, we test the claim that STABILIZER causes execution times to follow a Gaussian distribution. Next, we look at the overhead added by STABILIZER with different randomizations enabled.

All evaluations are performed on a dual-core Intel Core i3-550 operating at 3.2GHz and equipped with 12GB of RAM. Each core has a 256KB L2 cache. Cores share a single 4MB L3 cache. The system runs version 3.5.0-22 of the Linux kernel (unmodified) built

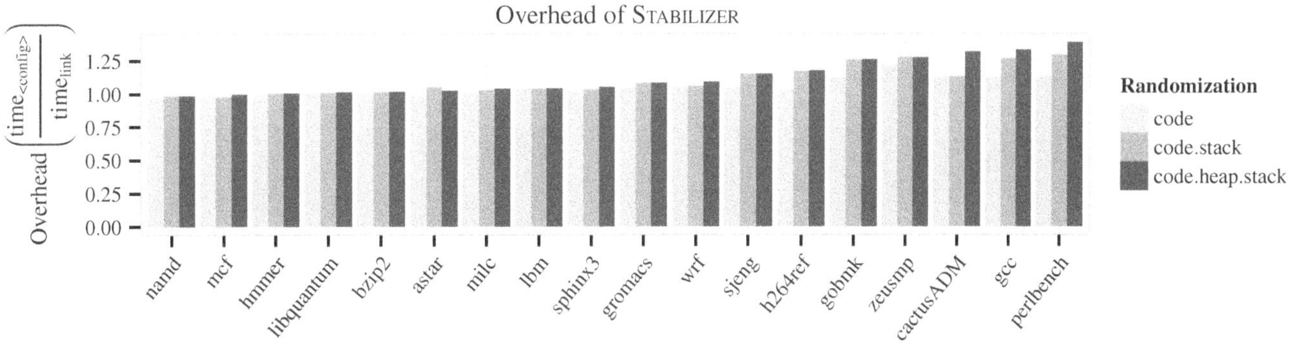

Figure 6. Overhead of STABILIZER relative to runs with randomized link order (lower is better). With all randomizations enabled, STABILIZER adds a median overhead of 6.7%, and below 40% for all benchmarks.

for `x86_64`. All programs are built using `gcc` version 4.6.3 as a front-end, with `dragonegg` and LLVM version 3.1.

Benchmarks. We evaluate STABILIZER across all C benchmarks in the SPEC CPU2006 benchmark suite. The C++ benchmarks `omnetpp`, `xalancbmk`, `dealII`, `soplex`, and `povray` are not run because they use exceptions, which STABILIZER does not yet support. We plan to add support for exceptions by rewriting LLVM's exception handling intrinsics to invoke STABILIZER-specific runtime support for exceptions. STABILIZER is also evaluated on all Fortran benchmarks, except for `bwaves`, `calculix`, `gamess`, `GemsFDTD`, and `tonto`. These benchmarks fail to build on our system when using `gfortran` with the LLVM plugin.

5.1 Normality

We evaluate the claim that STABILIZER results in normally distributed execution times across the entire benchmark suite. Using the Shapiro-Wilk test for normality, we can check if the execution times of each benchmark are normally distributed with and without STABILIZER. Every benchmark is run 30 times each with and without STABILIZER's re-randomization enabled.

Table 1 shows the p-values for the Shapiro-Wilk test of normality. Without re-randomization, five benchmarks exhibit execution times that are not normally distributed with 95% confidence: `astar`, `cactusADM`, `gromacs`, `h264ref`, and `perlbench`. With re-randomization, all of these benchmarks exhibit normally distributed execution times except for `cactusADM`. The `hmmer` benchmark has normally distributed execution times with one-time randomization, but not with re-randomization. This anomaly may be due to `hmmer`'s use of alignment-sensitive floating point operations.

Figure 5 shows the distributions of all 18 benchmarks on QQ (quantile-quantile) plots. QQ plots are useful for visualizing how close a set of samples is to a reference distribution (Gaussian in this case). Each data point is placed at the intersection of the sample and reference distributions' quantiles. Points will fall along a straight line if the observed values come from the reference distribution family.

A steeper slope on the QQ plot indicates a greater variance. We test for homogeneity of variance using the Brown-Forsythe test [11]. For eight benchmarks, `astar`, `gcc`, `gobmk`, `gromacs`, `h264ref`, `perlbench`, `sjeng`, and `zeusmp`, re-randomization leads to a statistically significant decrease in variance. This decrease is the result of *regression to the mean*. Observing a very high execution time with re-randomization would require selecting many more "unlucky" than "lucky" layouts. In two cases, `cactusADM` and `mcf`, re-randomization yields a small but statistically significant increase in variance. The p-values for the Brown-Forsythe test are shown in Table 1.

Result: STABILIZER nearly always imposes a Gaussian distribution on execution time, and tends to reduce variance.

5.2 Efficiency

Figure 6 shows the overhead of STABILIZER relative to unrandomized execution. Every benchmark is run 30 times in each configuration. With all randomizations enabled, STABILIZER adds a median overhead of 6.7%.

Most of STABILIZER's overhead can be attributed to reduced locality. Code and stack randomization both add additional logic to function invocation, but this has limited impact on execution time. Programs run with STABILIZER use a larger portion of the virtual address space, putting additional pressure on the TLB.

With all randomizations enabled, STABILIZER adds more than 30% overhead for just four benchmarks. For `gobmk`, `gcc`, and `perlbench`, the majority of STABILIZER's overhead comes from stack randomization. These three benchmarks all have a large number of functions, each with its own stack pad table (described in Section 3).

	Shapiro-Wilk		Brown-Forsythe
Benchmark	Randomized	Re-randomized	
`astar`	**0.000**	0.194	**0.001**
`bzip2`	0.789	0.143	0.078
`cactusADM`	**0.003**	**0.003**	**0.001**
`gcc`	0.420	0.717	**0.013**
`gobmk`	0.072	0.563	**0.000**
`gromacs`	**0.015**	0.550	**0.022**
`h264ref`	**0.003**	0.183	**0.002**
`hmmer`	0.552	**0.016**	0.982
`lbm`	0.240	0.530	0.161
`libquantum`	0.437	0.115	0.397
`mcf`	0.991	0.598	**0.027**
`milc`	0.367	0.578	0.554
`namd`	0.254	0.691	0.610
`perlbench`	**0.036**	0.188	**0.047**
`sjeng`	0.240	0.373	**0.000**
`sphinx3`	0.727	0.842	0.203
`wrf`	0.856	0.935	0.554
`zeusmp`	0.342	0.815	**0.000**

Table 1. P-values for the Shapiro-Wilk test of normality and the Brown-Forsythe test for homogeneity of variance. A p-value less that $\alpha = 0.05$ is sufficient to reject the null hypothesis (indicated in bold). Shapiro-Wilk tests the null hypothesis that the data are drawn from a normal distribution. Brown-Forsythe tests whether the one-time randomization and re-randomization samples are drawn from distributions with the same variance. Boldface indicates statistically significant non-normal execution times and unequal variances, respectively. Section 5.1 explores these results further.

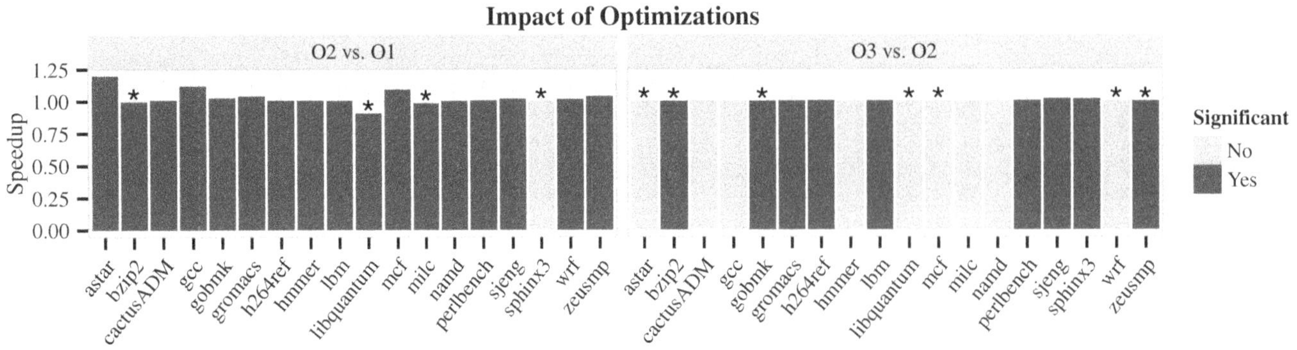

Figure 7. Speedup of -O2 over -O1, and -O3 over -O2 optimizations in LLVM. A speedup above 1.0 indicates the optimization had a positive effect. Asterisks mark cases where optimization led to slower performance. Benchmarks with dark bars showed a statistically significant average speedup (or slowdown). 17 of 18 benchmarks show a statistically significant change with -O2, and 9 of 18 show a significant change with -O3. In three cases for -O2 and three for -O3, the statistically significant change is a performance *degradation*. Despite per-benchmark significance results, the -O3 data do not show significance across the entire suite of benchmarks, and -O2 optimizations are only significant at a 90% level (Section 6.1).

The increased working set size increases cache pressure. If STABILIZER allowed functions to share stack pad tables, this overhead could be reduced. STABILIZER's heap randomization adds most of the overhead to `cactusADM`. This benchmark allocates a large number of arrays on the heap, and rounding up to power of two size classes leads to a large amount of wasted heap space.

STABILIZER's overhead does not affect its validity as a system for measuring the impact of performance optimizations. If an optimization has a statistically significant impact, it will shift the mean execution time over all possible layouts. The overhead added by STABILIZER also shifts this mean, but applies equally to both versions of the program. STABILIZER imposes a Gaussian distribution on execution times, which enables the detection of *smaller* effects than an evaluation of execution times with unknown distribution.

Performance Improvements

In four cases, STABILIZER (slightly) improves performance. `astar`, `hmmer`, `mcf`, and `namd` all run faster with code randomization enabled. We attribute this to the elimination of branch aliasing [15]. It is highly unlikely that a significant fraction of a run's random code layouts would exhibit branch aliasing problems. It is similarly unlikely that a significant fraction of random layouts would result in large performance improvements. The small gains with STABILIZER suggest the default program layout is slightly worse than the median layout for these benchmarks.

6. Sound Performance Analysis

The goal of STABILIZER is to enable statistically sound performance evaluation. We demonstrate STABILIZER's use here by evaluating the effectiveness of LLVM's -O3 and -O2 optimization levels. Figure 7 shows the speedup of -O2 and -O3, where speedup of -O3 is defined as:

$$\frac{\text{time}_{-O2}}{\text{time}_{-O3}}$$

LLVM's -O2 optimizations include basic-block level common subexpression elimination, while -O3 adds argument promotion, global dead code elimination, increases the amount of inlining, and adds global (procedure-wide) common subexpression elimination.

Execution times for all but three benchmarks are normally distributed when run with STABILIZER. These three benchmarks, `hmmer`, `wrf`, and `zeusmp`, have p-values below $\alpha = 0.05$ for the Shapiro-Wilk test. For all benchmarks with normally distributed execution times, we apply the two-sample t-test to determine whether -O3 provides a statistically significant performance improvement over -O2, and likewise for -O2 over -O1. The three non-normal benchmarks use the Wilcoxon signed-rank test, a non-parametric equivalent to the t-test [32].

At a 95% confidence level, we find that there is a statistically significant difference between -O2 and -O1 for 17 of 18 benchmarks. There is a significant difference between -O3 and -O2 for 9 of 18 benchmarks. While this result is promising, it does come with a caveat: `bzip2`, `libquantum`, and `milc` show a statistically significant *increase* in execution time with -O2 optimizations. The `bzip2`, `gobmk`, and `zeusmp` benchmarks show a statistically significant performance degradation with -O3.

6.1 Analysis of Variance

Evaluating optimizations with pairwise t-tests is error prone. This methodology runs a high risk of erroneously rejecting the null hypothesis (a type-I error). The parameter $\alpha = 0.05$ is the probability of observing the measured speedup, given that the optimization actually has no effect. Figure 7 shows the results for 36 hypothesis tests, each with a 5% risk of a false positive. We expect $36 * 0.05 = 1.8$ of these tests to show that an optimization had a statistically significant impact when in reality it did not.

Analysis of variance (ANOVA) allows us to test the significance of each optimization level over all benchmarks simultaneously. ANOVA relies on a normal assumption, but has been show to be robust to modest deviations from normality [11]. We run ANOVA with the same 18 benchmarks to test the significance of -O2 over -O1 and -O3 over -O2.

ANOVA takes the total variance in execution times and breaks it down by source: the fraction due to differences between benchmarks, the impact of optimizations, interactions between the independent factors, and random variation between runs. Differences between benchmarks should not be included in the final result. We perform a one-way analysis of variance within subjects to ensure execution times are only compared between runs of the same benchmark.

For the speedup of -O2, the results show an F-value of 3.235 for one degree of freedom (the choice between -O1 and -O2). The F-value is drawn from the F distribution [11]. The cumulative probability of observing any value drawn from $F(1) > 3.235 = 0.0898$ is the p-value for this test. The results show that -O2 optimizations are significant at a 90% confidence level, but not at the 95% level. The F-value for -O3 is 1.335, again for one degree of freedom. This gives a p-value of 0.264. We fail to reject the null hypothesis and must conclude that compared to -O2, -O3 *optimizations are not statistically significant*.

System	Base Randomization code	stack	heap	Fine-Grain Randomization code	stack	heap	Implementation recompilation	dynamic	re-randomization
Address Space Layout Randomization [20, 29]		✓	✓					✓	
Transparent Runtime Randomization [35]		✓	✓					✓	
Address Space Layout Permutation [16]	✓	✓	✓	✓				✓	
Address Obfuscation [5]	✓	✓	✓	✓	✓		✓	✓*	
Dynamic Offset Randomization [34]	✓			✓*			✓	✓	
Bhatkar *et al.* [6]	✓	✓	✓	✓	✓		✓	✓	
DieHard [3]			✓			✓		✓	✓
STABILIZER	✓	✓	✓	✓	✓	✓	✓	✓	✓

Table 2. Prior work in layout randomization includes varying degrees of support for the randomizations implemented in STABILIZER. The features supported by each project are marked by a checkmark. Asterisks indicate limited support for the corresponding randomization.

7. Related Work

Randomization for Security. Nearly all prior work in layout randomization has focused on security concerns. Randomizing the addresses of program elements makes it difficult for attackers to reliably trigger exploits. Table 2 gives an overview of prior work in program layout randomization.

The earliest implementations of layout randomization, Address Space Layout Randomization (ASLR) and PaX, relocate the heap, stack, and shared libraries in their entirety [20, 29]. Building on this work, Transparent Runtime Randomization (TRR) and Address Space Layout permutation (ASLP) have added support for randomization of code or code elements (like the global offset table) [16, 35]. Unlike STABILIZER, these systems relocate entire program segments.

Fine-grained randomization has been implemented in a limited form in the Address Obfuscation and Dynamic Offset Randomization projects, and by Bhatkar, Sekar, and DuVarney [5, 6, 34]. These systems combine coarse-grained randomization at load time with finer granularity randomizations in some sections. These systems do not re-randomize programs during execution, and do not apply fine-grained randomization to every program segment. STABILIZER randomizes code and data at a fine granularity, and re-randomizes during execution.

Heap Randomization. DieHard uses heap randomization to prevent memory errors [3]. Placing heap objects randomly makes it unlikely that use after free and out of bounds accesses will corrupt live heap data. DieHarder builds on this to provide probabilistic security guarantees [23]. STABILIZER can be configured to use DieHard as its substrate, although this can lead to substantial overhead.

Predictable Performance. Quicksort is a classic example of using randomization for predictable performance [14]. Random pivot selection drastically reduces the likelihood of encountering a worst-case input, and converts a $O(n^2)$ algorithm into one that runs with $O(n \log n)$ in practice.

Randomization has also been applied to probabilistically analyzable real-time systems. Quiñones et al. show that random cache replacement enables probabilistic worst-case execution time analysis, while maintaining good performance. This probabilistic analysis is a significant improvement over conventional hard real-time systems, where analysis of cache behavior relies on complete information.

Performance Evaluation. Mytkowicz et al. observe that environmental sensitivities can degrade program performance by as much as 300% [22]. While Mytkowicz et al. show that layout can dramatically impact performance, their proposed solution, *experimental setup randomization* (the exploration of the space of different link orders and environment variable sizes), is substantially different.

Experimental setup randomization requires far more runs than STABILIZER, and cannot eliminate bias as effectively. For example, varying link orders only changes inter-module function placement, so that a change of a function's size still affects the placement of all functions after it. STABILIZER instead randomizes the placement of every function independently. Similarly, varying environment size changes the base of the process stack, but not the distance between stack frames.

In addition, any unrandomized factor in experimental setup randomization, such as a different shared library version, could have a dramatic effect on layout. STABILIZER does not require *a priori* identification of all factors. Its use of dynamic re-randomization also leads to normally distributed execution times, enabling the use of parametric hypothesis tests.

Alameldeen and Wood find similar sensitivities in processor simulators, which they also address with the addition of non-determinism [1]. Tsafrir, Ouaknine, and Feitelson report dramatic environmental sensitivities in job scheduling, which they address with a technique they call "input shaking" [30, 31]. Georges et al. propose rigorous techniques for Java performance evaluation [12]. While prior techniques for performance evaluation require many runs over a wide range of (possibly unknown) environmental factors, STABILIZER enables efficient and statistically sound performance evaluation by breaking the dependence between experimental setup and program layout.

8. Future Work

We plan to extend STABILIZER to randomize code at finer granularity. Instead of relocating functions, STABILIZER could relocate individual basic blocks at runtime. This finer granularity would allow for branch-sense randomization. Randomly relocated basic blocks can appear in any order, and STABILIZER could randomly swap the fall-through and target blocks during execution. This approach would effectively randomize the history portion of the branch predictor table, eliminating another potential source of bias.

STABILIZER is useful for performance evaluation, but its ability to dynamically change layout could also be used to improve program performance. Searching for optimal layouts *a priori* would be intractable: the number of possible permutations of all functions grows at the rate of $O(N!)$, without accounting for space between functions. However, sampling with performance counters could be used to detect layout-related performance problems like cache misses and branch mispredictions. When STABILIZER detects these problems, it could trigger a complete or partial re-randomization of layout to try to eliminate the source of the performance issue.

9. Conclusion

Researchers and software developers require effective performance evaluation to guide work in compiler optimizations, runtime libraries, and large applications. Automatic performance regression tests are now commonplace. Standard practice measures execution times before and after applying changes, but modern processor architectures make this approach unsound. Small changes to a program or its execution environment can perturb its layout, which affects caches and branch predictors. Two versions of a program, regardless of the number of runs, are only two samples from the distribution over possible layouts. Statistical techniques for comparing distributions require more samples, but randomizing layout over many runs may be prohibitively slow.

This paper presents STABILIZER, a system that enables the use of the powerful statistical techniques required for sound performance evaluation on modern architectures. STABILIZER forces executions to sample the space of memory configurations by efficiently and repeatedly randomizing the placement of code, stack, and heap objects at runtime. Every run with STABILIZER consists of many independent and identically distributed (i.i.d.) intervals of random layout. Total execution time (the sum over these intervals) follows a Gaussian distribution by virtue of the Central Limit Theorem. STABILIZER thus enables the use of parametric statistical tests like ANOVA. We demonstrate STABILIZER's efficiency ($< 7\%$ median overhead) and its effectiveness by evaluating the impact of LLVM's optimizations on the SPEC CPU2006 benchmark suite. We find that the performance impact of `-O3` over `-O2` optimizations is indistinguishable from random noise.

We encourage researchers to download STABILIZER to use it as a basis for sound performance evaluation: it is available at `http://www.stabilizer-tool.org`.

Acknowledgments

This material is based upon work supported by the National Science Foundation under Grant No. 1012195-CCF and the PROARTIS FP7 Project (European Union Grant No. 249100). The authors gratefully acknowledge Peter F. Sweeney, David Jensen, Daniel A. Jiménez, Todd Mytkowicz, Eduardo Quiñones, Leonidas Kosmidis, Jaume Abella, and Francisco J. Cazorla for their guidance and comments. We also thank the anonymous reviewers for their helpful comments.

References

[1] A. Alameldeen and D. Wood. Variability in Architectural Simulations of Multi-threaded Workloads. In *HPCA '03*, pp. 7–18. IEEE Computer Society, 2003.

[2] L. E. Bassham, III, A. L. Rukhin, J. Soto, J. R. Nechvatal, M. E. Smid, E. B. Barker, S. D. Leigh, M. Levenson, M. Vangel, D. L. Banks, N. A. Heckert, J. F. Dray, and S. Vo. SP 800-22 Rev. 1a. A Statistical Test Suite for Random and Pseudorandom Number Generators for Cryptographic Applications. Tech. rep., National Institute of Standards & Technology, Gaithersburg, MD, United States, 2010.

[3] E. D. Berger and B. G. Zorn. DieHard: Probabilistic Memory Safety for Unsafe Languages. In *PLDI '06*, pp. 158–168. ACM, 2006.

[4] E. D. Berger, B. G. Zorn, and K. S. McKinley. Composing High-Performance Memory Allocators. In *PLDI '01*, pp. 114–124. ACM, 2001.

[5] S. Bhatkar, D. C. DuVarney, and R. Sekar. Address Obfuscation: an Efficient Approach to Combat a Broad Range of Memory Error Exploits. In *USENIX Security '03*, pp. 8–8. USENIX Association, 2003.

[6] S. Bhatkar, R. Sekar, and D. C. DuVarney. Efficient Techniques for Comprehensive Protection from Memory Error Exploits. In *SSYM '05*, pp. 271–286. USENIX Association, 2005.

[7] S. M. Blackburn, A. Diwan, M. Hauswirth, A. M. Memon, and P. F. Sweeney. Workshop on Experimental Evaluation of Software and Systems in Computer Science (Evaluate 2010). In *SPLASH '10*, pp. 291–292. ACM, 2010.

[8] S. M. Blackburn, A. Diwan, M. Hauswirth, P. F. Sweeney, et al. TR 1: Can You Trust Your Experimental Results? Tech. rep., Evaluate Collaboratory, 2012.

[9] A. Demers, M. Weiser, B. Hayes, H. Boehm, D. Bobrow, and S. Shenker. Combining Generational and Conservative Garbage Collection: Framework and Implementations. In *POPL '90*, pp. 261–269. ACM, 1990.

[10] R. Durstenfeld. Algorithm 235: Random Permutation. *Communications of the ACM*, 7(7):420, 1964.

[11] W. Feller. *An Introduction to Probability Theory and Applications*, volume 1. John Wiley & Sons Publishers, 3rd edition, 1968.

[12] A. Georges, D. Buytaert, and L. Eeckhout. Statistically Rigorous Java Performance Evaluation. In *OOPSLA '07*, pp. 57–76. ACM, 2007.

[13] G. Hamerly, E. Perelman, J. Lau, B. Calder, and T. Sherwood. Using Machine Learning to Guide Architecture Simulation. *Journal of Machine Learning Research*, 7:343–378, Dec. 2006.

[14] C. A. R. Hoare. Quicksort. *The Computer Journal*, 5(1):10–16, 1962.

[15] D. A. Jiménez. Code Placement for Improving Dynamic Branch Prediction Accuracy. In *PLDI '05*, pp. 107–116. ACM, 2005.

[16] C. Kil, J. Jun, C. Bookholt, J. Xu, and P. Ning. Address Space Layout Permutation (ASLP): Towards Fine-Grained Randomization of Commodity Software. In *ACSAC '06*, pp. 339–348. IEEE Computer Society, 2006.

[17] C. Lattner and V. Adve. LLVM: A Compilation Framework for Lifelong Program Analysis & Transformation. In *CGO '04*, pp. 75–86. IEEE Computer Society, 2004.

[18] G. Marsaglia. Random Number Generation. In *Encyclopedia of Computer Science, 4th Edition*, pp. 1499–1503. John Wiley and Sons Ltd., Chichester, UK, 2003.

[19] M. Masmano, I. Ripoll, A. Crespo, and J. Real. TLSF: A New Dynamic Memory Allocator for Real-Time Systems. In *ECRTS '04*, pp. 79–86. IEEE Computer Society, 2004.

[20] I. Molnar. Exec-Shield. `http://people.redhat.com/mingo/exec-shield/`.

[21] D. A. Moon. Garbage Collection in a Large LISP System. In *LFP '84*, pp. 235–246. ACM, 1984.

[22] T. Mytkowicz, A. Diwan, M. Hauswirth, and P. F. Sweeney. Producing Wrong Data Without Doing Anything Obviously Wrong! In *ASPLOS '09*, pp. 265–276. ACM, 2009.

[23] G. Novark and E. D. Berger. DieHarder: Securing the Heap. In *CCS '10*, pp. 573–584. ACM, 2010.

[24] G. Novark, E. D. Berger, and B. G. Zorn. Exterminator: Automatically Correcting Memory Errors with High Probability. *Communications of the ACM*, 51(12):87–95, 2008.

[25] The Chromium Project. Performance Dashboard. `http://build.chromium.org/f/chromium/perf/dashboard/overview.html`.

[26] The LLVM Team. Clang: a C Language Family Frontend for LLVM. `http://clang.llvm.org`, 2012.

[27] The LLVM Team. Dragonegg - Using LLVM as a GCC Backend. `http://dragonegg.llvm.org`, 2013.

[28] The Mozilla Foundation. Buildbot/Talos. `https://wiki.mozilla.org/Buildbot/Talos`.

[29] The PaX Team. The PaX Project. `http://pax.grsecurity.net`, 2001.

[30] D. Tsafrir and D. Feitelson. Instability in Parallel Job Scheduling Simulation: the Role of Workload Flurries. In *IPDPS '06*. IEEE Computer Society, 2006.

[31] D. Tsafrir, K. Ouaknine, and D. G. Feitelson. Reducing Performance Evaluation Sensitivity and Variability by Input Shaking. In *MASCOTS '07*, pp. 231–237. IEEE Computer Society, 2007.

[32] F. Wilcoxon. Individual Comparisons by Ranking Methods. *Biometrics Bulletin*, 1(6):80–83, 1945.

[33] P. R. Wilson, M. S. Johnstone, M. Neely, and D. Boles. Dynamic Storage Allocation: A Survey and Critical Review. *Lecture Notes in Computer Science*, 986, 1995.

[34] H. Xu and S. J. Chapin. Improving Address Space Randomization with a Dynamic Offset Randomization Technique. In *SAC '06*, pp. 384–391. ACM, 2006.

[35] J. Xu, Z. Kalbarczyk, and R. Iyer. Transparent Runtime Randomization for Security. In *SRDS '03*, pp. 260–269. IEEE Computer Society, 2003.

A Study of the Scalability of Stop-the-world Garbage Collectors on Multicores *

Lokesh Gidra, Gaël Thomas, Julien Sopena and Marc Shapiro
LIP6-INRIA
Université Pierre et Marie Curie
4 place Jussieu, Paris, France
firstname.lastname@lip6.fr

Abstract

Large-scale multicore architectures create new challenges for garbage collectors (GCs). In particular, throughput-oriented stop-the-world algorithms demonstrate good performance with a small number of cores, but have been shown to degrade badly beyond approximately 8 cores on a 48-core with OpenJDK 7. This negative result raises the question whether the stop-the-world design has intrinsic limitations that would require a radically different approach. Our study suggests that the answer is no, and that there is no compelling scalability reason to discard the existing highly-optimised throughput-oriented GC code on contemporary hardware. This paper studies the default throughput-oriented garbage collector of OpenJDK 7, called Parallel Scavenge. We identify its bottlenecks, and show how to eliminate them using well-established parallel programming techniques. On the SPECjbb2005, SPECjvm2008 and DaCapo 9.12 benchmarks, the improved GC matches the performance of Parallel Scavenge at low core count, but scales well, up to 48 cores.

Categories and Subject Descriptors D.4.2 [*Software*]: Garbage collection

General Terms Experimentation, Performance

Keywords Garbage collection; NUMA; multicore

1. Introduction

Contemporary hardware with large memories and high core counts creates new challenges for garbage collectors (GCs). To achieve the best possible performance, throughput-oriented GCs traditionally use a stop-the-world design, in which the collector pauses the application threads during the whole collection to prevent concurrent memory accesses from the application. Stop-the-world is the simplest design and is relatively easy to combine with advanced techniques [12]. In contrast, a concurrent GC does not pause the application, but is much more complex: as it runs in parallel with application code, it requires complicated fine-grain synchronisation with the GC and costly code instrumentation to intercept reference mutations [1, 7, 16, 24, 27, 28].

According to some authors, for instance Iyengar et al. [11], stop-the-world collectors are not adequate on large machines because their pause time increases with available memory. This reasoning ignores the counter-balancing effect that large machines also come with many cores, translating to more parallelism. If efficiently exploited, this parallelism should reduce the pause time. However, our previous study [10] shows that the performance of the stop-the-world GCs available in OpenJDK 7 degrades beyond about 8 GC threads, taking over one-third of total application time at maximum parallelism (one GC thread for each of 48 hardware cores). This performance issue questions the design of stop-the-world collectors: are they intrinsically unable to scale with the number of cores, and thus, is it now time to pay the price of concurrent collectors to collect large heaps?

The result of our study suggests that the answer is no, at least on an off-the-shelf 48-core NUMA machine.[1] Our study is based on Parallel Scavenge [21], the stop-the-world throughput-oriented collector used by default in OpenJDK 7. We show that its bad performance with a lot of cores is not intrinsic to its design, but is due to two bottlenecks, which we correct using well-established parallel programming techniques:

- **Lack of NUMA-awareness.** Many objects are allocated on a single node, overloading it, during execution of both the application and the GC code. To correct this issue, we compare three different approaches to balancing memory access among nodes. The first one focuses on balance only. The other two have a secondary goal of also improving spatial locality, by attempting to place objects on the node where they are used.
- **A heavily contended lock inside the parallel phase of Parallel Scavenge.** To avoid this bottleneck, we remove the lock: (i) by replacing a queue with a lock-free one, and (ii) by simplifying the synchronisation protocol to begin and terminate the GC's parallel phase.

The resulting GC, called NAPS, for Numa-Aware Parallel Scavenge, distributes live objects among nodes in a balanced way, and

* This research is supported in part by ANR projects Prose (ANR-09-VERS-007-02) and ConcoRDanT (ANR-10-BLAN 0208).

[1] A NUMA (Non Uniform Memory Access) architecture is a multicore architecture where memory access latency depends on the locations of the physical memory and the core that accesses it. It consists of several *nodes*, each containing either one single core, as in the Tile-Gx processor family of Tilera, or several cores connected by a bus, as in the Magny-Cours of AMD. Nodes are connected by a network that we call the *interconnect*, on which several *memory controllers* are also connected.

ASPLOS'13, March 16–20, 2013, Houston, Texas, USA.

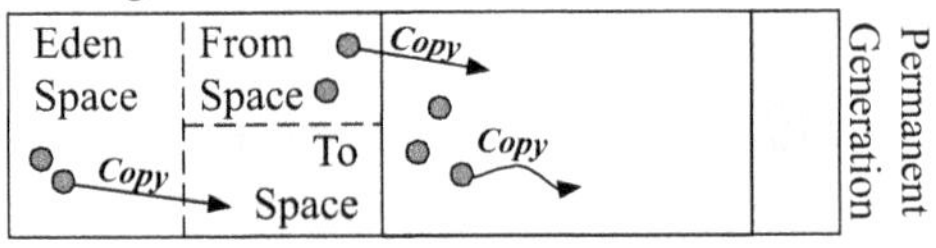

Figure 1. Memory Layout of Parallel Scavenge

completely avoids any locking during the parallel phase of the collection.

Our approach deliberately uses the simplest possible techniques, resulting in fewer than 1000 modified lines of code. This result shows that a careful adjustment of a small portion of the code is sufficient to solve a known problem, for which a more drastic redesign is often proposed.

Our evaluation is based on the applications from three industry-standard benchmark suites, SPECjbb2005 [25], SPECjvm2008 [26] and DaCapo-9.12 [4], on a 48-core AMD Magny-Cours machine with eight nodes. Our results show that:

- NAPS scales well with the number of cores. At constant heap size, the collection time of NAPS decreases with the number of cores, for applications with high memory requirements. As compared to Parallel Scavenge, NAPS never degrades performance.
- As a side-effect of balancing the memory access among nodes, in addition to the improved collection time, NAPS improves application time by up to 28%. The combination of GC-time improvement and better application performance doubles the throughput of SPECjbb2005, the most memory-intensive application in our evaluation.
- We observe that the major improvement comes from balancing memory access among nodes, which eliminates the top bottleneck to scaling GC. Beyond 32 cores, improving memory locality also becomes important, in order to decrease the load on the interconnect. In contrast, thanks to improved memory locality, the effect of decreasing memory access latency, is marginal.

The rest of the paper is organised as follow. Section 2 describes the design of Parallel Scavenge. Section 3 describes its bottlenecks and how we solve them. Section 4 reports the evaluation results and discusses their implications. Section 5 presents an overview of related work, and Section 6 concludes the paper.

2. Parallel Scavenge

This section describes Parallel Scavenge, the baseline of our study. Parallel Scavenge is the default GC of OpenJDK's HotSpot virtual machine and is the one that provides the best performance when the number of cores increases [10]. It is a *stop-the-world* collector. To achieve the best performance, it combines several advanced GC techniques: generational, copying and compacting [12]. A major advantage of the stop-the-world design is that integrating these advanced techniques is straightforward.

2.1 Overview

Empirical studies across a wide range of applications and languages show that "most objects die young:" a recently-allocated object has a greater probability of becoming garbage than one that already survived GCs [2, 13, 31]. A generational collector exploits this by segregating the heap into multiple generations, and by collecting the young generation more frequently than the older one(s).

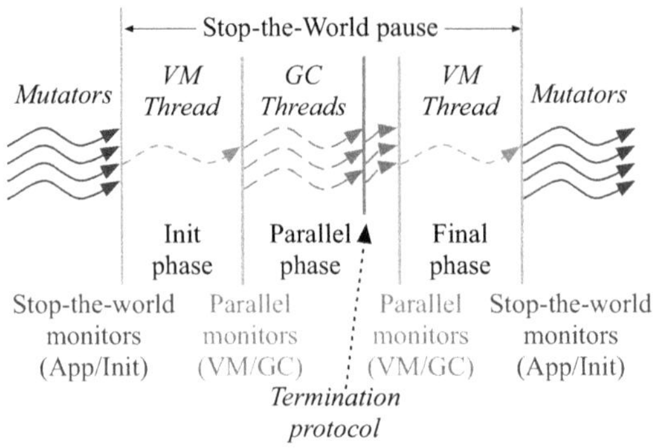

Figure 2. Phases of Parallel Scavenge

As presented in Figure 1, Parallel Scavenge defines three generations: a small *young* generation; a larger *old* generation; and a *permanent* generation, similar to the old one, but much smaller.

The young generation of Parallel Scavenge is divided into three spaces, an *eden space* and two *survivor spaces*, called *from-space* and *to-space*. When a mutator, i.e., an application thread, allocates an object, it resides initially in the eden space. If an object survives the first collection, the GC copies it to one of the survivor spaces, and, if it survives the second collection, the GC copies it to the old generation. Thus, an object must survive a complete cycle between two collections before being promoted to the old generation.

The old and the permanent generations consist each of a single space. The old space contains objects that were promoted from the young generation, and the permanent space the Java classes only.

2.2 Allocation

To avoid synchronisation between the mutators at each allocation, a mutator first allocates, for its exclusive use, a large memory chunk from the eden space called a Thread-Local Allocation Buffer (TLAB). Thereafter, it allocates objects from its TLAB, without synchronisation, using a bump pointer. Similarly, promoting an object to the survivor space or to the old generation allocates from Promotion-Local Allocation Buffers (PLAB), which are allocated from the to-space and the old generation.

2.3 Young generation collection

A young-generation collection is triggered when an allocation fails both to find space in the current TLAB and to get a new TLAB from the eden space.

When a young-generation collection begins, the eden space contains the most-recently allocated objects, the from-space contains those that survived the previous collection, and the to-space is empty. As illustrated in Figure 1, a young-generation collection copies live objects from eden space to to-space, and from from-space to old generation. At the end of a young-generation collection, eden space and from-space contain dead objects only, and are thus considered empty. At this point, from- and to-space are swapped: the from-space of the last collection becomes the to-space for the next one, and vice-versa.

As illustrated in Figure 2, Parallel Scavenge consists of several phases. First, mutators are paused at the stop-the-world barrier. During the initialisation phase, a single thread, called the VM thread, prepares GC tasks, which are executed in the parallel phase by the GC threads. A *Termination Protocol* detects that all GC threads have terminated the parallel phase; after which a barrier suspends the GC threads and wakes up the VM thread. In the final phase, the VM thread mainly resizes the heap and wakes up the mutators.

2.3.1 Synchronisation mechanism

As synchronisation between threads is a common performance bottleneck on a multicore machine [15], we describe how it is implemented and used in Parallel Scavenge. Parallel Scavenge uses monitors for this purpose. A monitor contains both a condition variable, to suspend and wake up threads, and a lock to prevent concurrent accesses to shared data. Furthermore, since the condition variable of a monitor is a shared variable, it is protected by the associated lock.

Parallel Scavenge uses two monitor pairs: *the stop-the-world pair* and the *parallel pair*. The *stop-the-world pair* suspends the mutators and wakes up the VM thread at the beginning of the collection, and vice-versa at the end. It consists of the App monitor, to synchronise the mutators, and the Init monitor, to synchronise the VM thread. The *parallel pair* suspends the VM thread and wakes up the GC thread at the beginning of the parallel phase, and vice-versa at the end. It consists of the VM monitor to synchronise the VM thread; and the GC monitor to synchronise the GC threads, and to protect data shared between the GC threads.

2.3.2 Initialisation phase

Being a stop-the-world collector, Parallel Scavenge has to ensure that all mutators are paused at the beginning of a collection. The stop-the-world monitor pair coupled with a counter to know the number of suspended mutators serves this purpose. As soon as all the mutators are suspended, the VM thread initialises the queue of GC tasks. Then, the VM thread synchronises with the GC threads: it wakes up all the GC threads that are waiting on the GC monitor, and suspends itself by waiting on the VM monitor.

2.3.3 Parallel phase

A GC thread fetches tasks from the global queue of GC tasks using the GC monitor's lock of the parallel pair to avoid concurrent fetches. In the case of young-generation collection, there are three kinds of tasks: root tasks, steal tasks and a single final task. Root tasks contain the entry points of the object graph. Steal tasks are used to balance the load between the GC threads. They are ordered in the queue after the root tasks, and are fetched by GC threads once they have fetched all the root tasks. The final task is used to elect a leader to coordinate the end of the parallel phase.

Root tasks. A root task provides an entry point into the graph of live objects. This includes static variables, mutator stacks, and inter-generation references. A GC thread performs a breadth-first traversal (BFT) of the graph of live objects, starting from the addresses provided by the root tasks.

For each object that a GC thread reaches, it creates a copy in the PLAB appropriate for the object's age, and installs a forwarding pointer to the new object in the old object's header. To avoid copying the same object concurrently with another thread, the GC thread uses an atomic compare-and-swap (CAS) instruction to install the forwarding pointer. Then, the GC thread pushes all the references contained in the object into a local *BFT queue*, which is implemented as a lock-free bounded queue, backed by an overflow stack. After this, the GC thread repeatedly pops a reference from its BFT queue, which it processes in the same way. When its BFT queue is empty, the GC thread goes back to the global task queue, popping either another root task, or eventually a steal task.

Steal tasks. As the sub-graph reachable from a root task depends on mutator activity, the load of the GC threads could be unbalanced, resulting in some GC threads remaining idle, while others still have a large amount of work. To better balance the load, an idle GC thread "steals" a reference from a randomly-chosen BFT queue and processes the corresponding sub-graph.[2] To avoid conflicting concurrent accesses to a BFT queue, the queue owner pushes and pops from the queue head, whereas other GC threads pop (steal) from the tail.

A GC thread may be unable to steal, either because the parallel graph traversal is terminated, or because its random choice never picked an overloaded GC thread even though one exists. To handle the second case, the GC thread does not directly leave the steal task. Instead, after a number of unsuccessful steal attempts, it enters a *termination protocol*. It first atomically increments a global thread counter in order to indicate to other GC threads that it is in the termination protocol. Then, the GC thread actively polls the global thread counter in a bounded loop. If the counter reaches the number of GC threads, this means that all BFT queues are empty and therefore that the parallel phase is terminated. In this case, the GC thread leaves the termination protocol. Otherwise, if the counter has not reached the number of GC threads in the bounded loop, the GC thread "peeks" into the other BFT queues. If all queues are empty, the GC thread also leaves the termination protocol, otherwise, it atomically decrements the global thread counter and continues to steal.

Final task. The final task aims to ensure that no GC thread is modifying the heap when the VM thread restarts. Once a GC thread has left the termination protocol, it again attempts to pop a task from the task queue. Since there is a single final task, only one GC thread succeeds. It thereby becomes the leader, and coordinates the other GC threads using the parallel monitors (VM and GC). We call it the final thread.

The other GC threads find the task queue empty. They increment a global thread counter protected by the GC monitor. Then, they wake up the final thread and suspend themselves on the same monitor. Conversely, the final thread waits on the GC monitor, until the global thread counter reaches the number of GC threads. Once this is done, the final thread wakes up the VM thread using the VM monitor. This constitutes entry into the final phase, where the VM thread is the only one running.

Note that, in the normal case studied here, this final synchronisation is redundant with the termination protocol because both ensure that all the GC threads have terminated their steal tasks. It is required only in specific configurations (out of scope here) where there are no steal tasks.

2.3.4 Final synchronisation phase

The main purpose of the final phase is to adapt the sizes of the spaces and the generations. The sophisticated resizing policy of Parallel Scavenge is essential for performance, because it adapts the heap size to the needs of the application, based on factors such as space usage and/or time taken by the collection cycle. In Parallel Scavenge, resizing is cheap, as it consists of simply adjusting a set of pointers.

Once this is done, the VM thread resumes the mutators using the stop-the-world monitor pair. It wakes up the mutators with the App monitor, and then sleeps, awaiting the next collection with the Init monitor.

2.4 Old-generation collection

If an object promotion fails at any stage of a young-generation collection because the old space is full, this indicates that the old generation needs to be collected. The GC thread that suffers the promotion failure sets a flag and continues the parallel phase. After the parallel phase, if the flag is set, the VM thread starts an old-generation collection. As Parallel Scavenge directly allocates in the

[2] Stealing is done from the queue only. The overflow stack is accessed solely by the owning thread.

old generation large objects that do not fit in the young one, an old-generation collection can also start during an allocation from the mutator.

Old-generation collection uses a two-phase mark-compact algorithm. In the first phase, the GC threads mark in parallel the live objects starting from the roots. In the second phase, the GC threads compact in parallel live objects by sliding them into holes created by dead objects.

Before each phase, the VM thread initialises the task queue with appropriate tasks, then starts the parallel phase. The parallel phase terminates using the same mechanism as the young generation: with the termination protocol and with the final task. They are executed twice, once for the marking and once for the compacting phase.

3. Bottlenecks and optimisations

We now analyse some of the bottlenecks experienced by Parallel Scavenge on large multicores. For each one, we describe the solution that we implement. This information is summarised in Table 1. Our experimental evaluation, presented in Section 4, shows that our optimisations improve GC scalability substantially.

3.1 Synchronisation Primitives

Parallel Scavenge uses locks to synchronise access to internal shared data structures, such as the GC task queue and the condition variables. To implement lock acquisition, Parallel Scavenge first attempts a fast-path atomic compare-and-swap (CAS) instruction, spinning for some number of iterations. If this fails, the mutator falls back to a slow path using Posix synchronisation primitives. CAS works fine for a small number of threads, as the fast path generally succeeds. However, as observed by Lozi et al. [15], on a large multicore, lock performance collapses under contention; this is particularly severe when spinning on CAS. To avoid this issue, we study the code to find the most contended locks, which we fix as explained next.

3.1.1 Lock-free GC task queue

Issue. Parallel Scavenge synchronises access to the task queue by using the GC monitor's lock. At the beginning of the parallel phase, all the GC threads access the task queue at the same time. The lock becomes contended, and its performance degrades drastically. Many GC threads wait for a long duration, preventing them from participating in the parallel phase, sometimes for the whole duration of a collection.

Solution. The task queue has First-In-First-Out semantics. In Parallel Scavenge, it is implemented as a singly-linked list. To avoid the performance collapse caused by lock acquisition, we implement the task queue with a Michael-Scott lock-free queue [18]. Recall that the VM thread enqueues tasks during the initialisation phase, which are dequeued during the parallel phase. Thus, there is no concurrency between enqueue and dequeue operations, but only between dequeues. Therefore, the VM thread enqueues without synchronisation, and GC threads dequeue using atomic CAS operations.

3.1.2 Lazy GC parking

Issue. When a GC thread executes the final task, all GC threads request the GC monitor's lock in order to synchronise the end of the parallel phase. However, this lock request immediately follows the termination protocol, and therefore all the GC threads reach this point at roughly the same time. As a consequence, the lock gets contended and its performance collapses.

Solution. To avoid this issue, we remove the GC monitor's lock. The lock was used for three purposes: first, to protect the task queue; second, to protect the global thread counter which is used for the barrier at the end of the parallel phase; and third, to protect the associated condition variable of the GC monitor, which is used to suspend the GC threads.

The first use is already taken care by the lock-free task queue. For the second case, we remove the redundant synchronisation in the final task (see Section 2.3.3). Instead of waiting for the other GC threads, the final thread simply wakes up the VM thread, and then suspends itself. Other GC threads suspend themselves without any synchronisation. After this change, the global thread counter is not required anymore.

For the last case, we replace the condition variables of VM and GC monitors with Linux's `futex_wait` calls [9]. A `futex_wait` has the semantics of an atomic compare-and-sleep, and does not require acquiring a lock.

However, our modifications potentially introduce a new race condition if a GC thread gets preempted after the termination protocol, but before suspending itself. In this scenario, the VM thread may wake up the mutator threads, a new collection may begin and the VM thread may wake up the GC threads to begin the new parallel phase. If the delayed GC thread suspends itself on the futex at this step, it will never be woken up by the VM thread, leading to a deadlock.

This is not a problem in Parallel Scavenge because, during the whole execution of the final task, the GC threads own the lock of the GC monitor. Acquiring this lock is required to wake up the GC threads with the GC monitor to begin the new parallel phase. Therefore, the GC threads inevitably suspend themselves before receiving the wake up notification. However, this condition does not hold in NAPS, because the GC monitor does not exist anymore.

To solve this problem, we use a timestamp, which is incremented atomically by the VM thread before the parallel phase. To suspend itself, a GC thread uses the futex to atomically check whether the timestamp has been modified before sleeping. If it was not modified, the futex call suspends the GC thread. Otherwise, it returns, and the GC thread directly enters the new parallel phase, thus avoiding the deadlock.

3.2 NUMA heap

When the garbage collector scans an object, this implies that it was not scanned previously in the same garbage collection cycle. Thus, GC does not benefit from hardware data caches, and accesses physical memory mostly, stressing the memory controllers. GC also stresses the interconnect between the nodes for remote accesses. These two hardware components saturate if their load is too high. In this section, we study the factors that impact performance of memory access, and consider three alternative heap layouts aiming to optimise memory placement.[3]

3.2.1 Influence of memory placement

In order to propose efficient memory layout for NUMA hardware, we first evaluate the scalability impact of four different memory placements on our 48-core/8-node AMD machine. This experiment measures the impact of memory access imbalance and locality, the main factors that impact performance [5].

Figure 3 summarises this evaluation. It contains one curve per placement algorithm, plotting the speedup in completion time of a fixed number of operations executed by a varying number of threads. Each operation consists of sequentially reading from a thread-local buffer that does not fit in the CPU caches, triggering a physical memory access. Threads are pinned on the nodes with a round-robin policy. The curves are as follows:

[3] Similar techniques already existed in Parallel Scavenge, but their implementation was flawed, as discussed.

Bottleneck	Optimisation name	Optimisation description
Heavily contended GC lock (3.1)	Lock-free GC task queue	GC task queue lock-free
	Lazy GC parking	GC thread sleeps lazily at end of parallel phase
NUMA heap (3.2)	Interleaved space	Balances the memory access between the nodes
	Fragmented space	Balance the memory accesses and improve the spatial locality
	Segregated space	Node-local collection

Table 1. Summary of proposed optimisations

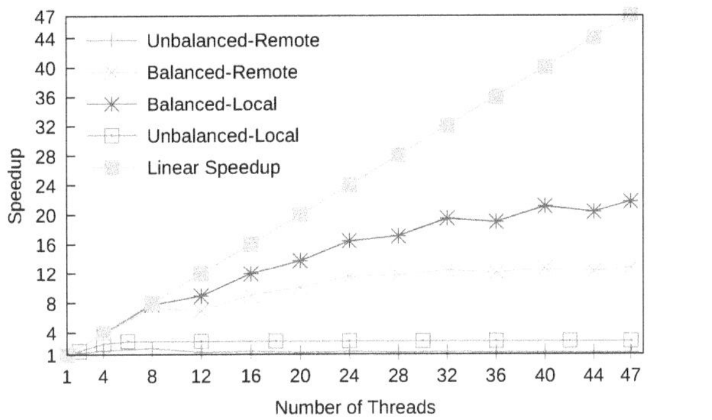

Figure 3. Influence of the memory placement.

- **Unbalanced-Remote.** All the buffers are allocated on Node 0. Access is (i) remote (except for the threads running on Node 0), and (ii) unbalanced.
- **Balanced-Remote:** The pages of the buffer are allocated to the nodes in round robin. Access is (i) mostly remote, and (ii) perfectly balanced.
- **Balanced-Local:** The buffers are allocated on the same node as its corresponding thread. Access is (i) local only, and (ii) perfectly balanced.
- **Unbalanced-Local.** The threads are first pinned on Node 0, and only these ones participate. The curve is extended beyond Node 0 by adding idle threads. Access is (i) local only, and (ii) unbalanced.

As shown in Figure 3, the performance of *Unbalanced-Remote* improves until 8 threads only, whereas *Balanced-Remote* continues to improve up to 32 threads. We conclude that when load is unbalanced, fewer threads suffice to saturate the machine (either the memory controllers and/or the interconnect between the nodes). This experiment shows that balancing the load has a huge impact on scalability. Comparing *Unbalanced-Remote* with *Unbalanced-Local* shows that balancing load is a higher priority than improving locality.

Furthermore, *Balanced-Remote* stops improving beyond 32 threads, whereas *Balanced-Local* continues to improve up to 40 threads, and has significantly better results. We conclude that improving memory locality constitutes a secondary scalability objective, once balancing access among nodes has been taken care of.

3.2.2 Memory access imbalance

Issue. The memory access imbalance issue mainly concerns eden space, because of the conjunction of two things: the kernel's memory allocation policy; and a sequential pattern of memory initialisation by the application, as we explain next.

Parallel Scavenge reserves a large virtual memory range for the heap using the `mmap` system call. No physical pages are initially allocated to an `mmap`ped region; the first time a virtual page is accessed, the kernel allocates a physical page on demand. The kernel's allocation policy preferentially allocates a physical page from the same node that triggered the fault [14]. Thereafter, a virtual address range remains associated to the same physical node.

Many applications start with a single-threaded initialisation phase, which consumes most of the eden space. Because of the kernel allocation policy, these objects are all allocated on the same physical node, the one executing the initialisation thread. The physical pages mapped to the eden space remain on that same node thereafter, causing this node to suffer memory access imbalance. This allocation pattern is typical of the *Unbalanced-Remote* case discussed earlier.

This issue can also occur with the other spaces when threads create large objects. Parallel Scavenge allocates these objects directly in the old space, also leading to the mapping of large part of the virtual space to a single node.

Interleaved spaces. To address this issue, we introduce interleaved spaces, whose pages are mapped from different nodes with a round robin policy. By balancing memory allocation among the nodes, we expect that interleaved spaces will also balance memory access. Our experiments in Section 4 support this hypothesis.

3.2.3 Memory locality and access balance

Issue. Interleaved spaces balance the load but do not address memory locality. However, as shown by comparing the curves *Balanced-Remote* and *Balanced-Local* in Figure 3, excessive remote access can be a scalability bottleneck. Therefore, we introduce two heap layouts that balance load and secondarily improve memory locality.

Fragmented spaces. Fragmenting consists of dividing a space into multiple fragments, where each fragment is a virtual address range that gets all its physical pages from a single node. Under this policy, a thread allocates an entire TLAB or PLAB from the fragment associated with the node where it is executing.

Fragmented spaces improve locality for the mutators because: (i) a thread mostly accesses objects that it allocated recently, and (ii) the operating system avoids migrating threads between nodes. It also helps to improve locality for the GC, because objects are copied to the memory node of the GC thread that performs the copy.

Fragmented spaces also solve the issue of memory access imbalance caused by the initialisation phase of the application, because the page allocation policy of each fragment is fixed, and thus insensitive to the application's allocation pattern. Additionally, in conjunction with the work-stealing mechanism, fragmented spaces help to balance memory accesses among the nodes. Work-stealing ensures that every GC thread copies roughly the same number of bytes; hence it eventually balances the distribution of objects among nodes, even if the objects were initially allocated on a single node (we pin GC threads, spreading them across all the nodes in round robin).

However, fragmented spaces do not help to balance memory access in the specific case where the application allocates objects according to a master-slave pattern, in which a master thread allocates the objects for the slaves. With a fragmented space, objects

Space type	Load balancing	Mutator locality			GC locality				
		First	Later Access		Eden	Survivor		Old/Permanent	
		Access	New	Promoted	Scan	Copy	Scan	Copy	Scan
Parallel Scavenge	−	+	−	−	−	−	−	−	−
Interleaved space	+	−	−	−	−	−	−	−	−
Fragmented space	∼	+	+	−	−	+	−	Not Applicable‡	
Segregated space	∼	+	+	+	+	+	+	Not Applicable‡	

‡ Our simple algorithms are not adequate for compacting spaces.

Table 2. Load balancing vs. locality properties

will all be allocated on the master node, leading to an unbalance of the accesses. After a collection, the balance will be re-establish, but, as threads mostly access recently-allocated objects, interleaved spaces are better. The only of the applications that we evaluated to exhibit this pattern is H2.

Segregated spaces. A segregated space is a fragmented space that is restricted to being accessed by GC threads running on the same node. This is achieved by: (i) restricting work-stealing to GC threads that run on the same node; and (ii) by disallowing a GC thread from accessing a remote object. When a GC thread discovers a reference to an object located on some other node, rather than scanning it itself, it sends a "scan" message to the GC threads running on remote node.

Segregated spaces ensure perfect memory locality, at the cost of exchanging messages between nodes. Moreover, segregated spaces solve the issue of memory access imbalance caused by the the initialisation phase of the application, using the same approach as described earlier for fragmented spaces. However, since segregated spaces never move an object between nodes, if the allocation rate of different mutator threads is asymmetric, object placement will remain unbalanced.

3.2.4 Summary of the space policies

Our analysis of load-balancing vs. locality trade-offs is summarised in Table 2. For a given space type, the second column identifies whether the approach is systematically good (+) or bad (−) for load balancing, or if we observe that it is good (∼) due to the memory allocation pattern of the applications. The other columns depict the locality properties, for the mutator and the GC respectively. For the mutator, we distinguish the mutator's initialisation phase (First) from the rest of the execution (accesses to new and promoted objects). For GC, we distinguish the different generations, and within each generation, between scanning and copying the object.

Mutator locality is improved by locating newly-allocated objects on the mutator's execution node (First Access, Later access/New) and by copying objects to their node of use (Later Access/Promoted). GC locality is improved by scanning objects located in the node where the GC thread runs (Scan), and by copying objects towards the node where the GC thread runs (Copy).

3.3 Implementation details

Parallel Scavenge already provides interleaved and fragmented spaces through a command line option. However, this implementation is inefficient on our hardware. To provide evidence of the problem, we evaluate a 4.5 min.-run of SPECjbb2005, our most memory-intensive application, with 48 GC threads and 48 mutators. In this test, activating the fragmented-space option slows Parallel Scavenge down even more (63.6 GB/s with fragmented spaces, vs. 98.4 GB/s in the default configuration, a slowdown of 35%). We explain the issues hereafter.

The resizing problem. The fragmented spaces of Parallel Scavenge raise two different issues. First, in the Parallel Scavenge fragmented spaces, each fragment is $1/N^{\text{th}}$ of the size of the space (where N is the number of nodes). Therefore, an allocation might fail prematurely when a single fragment is full, even though there is still space in other fragment(s). This totally invalidates the decisions of the resizing policy, and can lead to many useless collections. In our SPECjbb test, we observe that the number of collections triggered with fragmented spaces is almost twice the number without (325 collections versus 177).

Second, resizing a space is substantially more expensive. As the spaces and generations are contiguous in virtual memory, resizing requires many remappings. Each remapping triggers two system calls, one to free the physical pages from their virtual addresses, and another one to re-associate the virtual address range to a different memory node. This cost increases with the number of remapped pages, i.e., with the size of the fragmented space. In our SPECjbb test, we observe that roughly 20% of collection time is spent in resizing.

Solution. Our own implementation of fragmented spaces leverages the difference between virtual and physical memory. We initially reserve a very large virtual space for the heap, and use allocation counters to control the number of physical bytes actually allocated in a space. This large virtual memory reservation is possible on a 64-bit machine because the virtual address space is sufficiently large.

We avoid invalidating the resizing policy by making the virtual memory size of each fragment equal to the total size of the space it belongs to. This ensures that allocation from a space does not fail until its allocation counter reaches the assigned limit. Thus, NAPS triggers collection at exactly the heap size specified by the resizing policy, and does not invalidate its decisions.

We avoid the cost of system calls by reserving the maximal possible heap size. Each space and each fragment have a fixed address range, and their pages are mapped according to the memory policy configured during the initialisation of the virtual machine. As we pre-reserve the maximal size for each space, and therefore for each fragment, spaces and fragments can grow or shrink safely, without any remapping.

4. Evaluation

This section analyses the effect of our optimisations on GC pause time and on application throughput, using representative applications from standard benchmark suites (SPECjbb2005, SPECjvm-2008 and DaCapo).

4.1 Experimental Setup

4.1.1 Hardware and Operating System

We conduct our experiments on a machine with four AMD Opteron 6172 sockets, each consisting of two nodes. Each node consists of six cores (2.1 GHz clock rate). The nodes are connected to each other by HyperTransport links, with a maximum distance of two hops. In total there are 48 cores, carrying 96 GB of RAM consisting of 8 memory nodes. The system runs a Linux 3.0.0 64-bit kernel.

Application	Heap Size (GB)	Description
SPECjbb2005	3.5	Business logic service application
XML Transform	1	Transforms an XML tree
XML Validation	2	Validates an XML tree
Compiler.Sunflow	2	Compiles Sunflow Java code
Crypto AES	1	Runs AES algorithm
Eclipse	0.5	Java editor
Tradesoap	0.5	Business logic service application

Table 3. Applications used in the evaluation

<table>
<tr><th></th><th></th><th>Baseline</th><th>Inter.</th><th>Fragm.</th><th>Segr.</th></tr>
<tr><td rowspan="4">Nn-Loclty</td><td>Eden</td><td rowspan="4">≥0.7</td><td rowspan="4">≥0.7</td><td rowspan="2">≥0.7</td><td>0.0 0.0 0.0</td></tr>
<tr><td>From</td><td>0.0 0.0 0.0</td></tr>
<tr><td>To</td><td>0.0 0.0 0.0</td><td>0.0 0.0 0.0</td></tr>
<tr><td>Old</td><td>≥0.7</td><td>≥0.7</td></tr>
<tr><td rowspan="4">Imbalance</td><td>Eden</td><td>2.6 2.6 1.9</td><td rowspan="4">≤0.3</td><td>0.1 0.6 0.5</td><td>0.1 0.6 0.64</td></tr>
<tr><td>From</td><td rowspan="3">≤0.3</td><td rowspan="3">≤0.3</td><td>0.2 0.2 0.4</td></tr>
<tr><td>To</td><td rowspan="2">≤0.3</td></tr>
<tr><td>Old</td></tr>
</table>

Table 4. Non-locality (remote access ratio) and imbalance (standard deviation of remote access). Left to right in each column: SpecJBB2005, XML Transform and TradeSoap.

4.1.2 Benchmarks

We base our evaluation on the applications from three benchmark suites. As these applications use much less memory than our available memory, each experiment sets a heap size that is very close to the application's working set size in order to focus on the garbage collector. As we measure the throughput of the garbage collector, i.e., the number of bytes collected per second, the size of the heap has only a small impact on our result.

Table 3 summarises the applications we evaluate. We discard the less memory-intensive applications of the suites, because they are impacted only marginally by GC performance.

SPECjbb2005 is a business logic service-side application. It emulates a three-tier client/server system, with emphasis on the middle tier [25]. This benchmark runs for a fixed amount of time (configured by the user) and measures application throughput, i.e., the number of operations per second.

The benchmark allocates a warehouse for each worker thread. We run a warm-up round of 30 s with 40 warehouses, then a final round of four minutes with 48 warehouses. We use a heap size of 3.5 GB to execute this application. This is the benchmark with the largest working set, and therefore the one that stresses GC the most.

SPECjvm2008 is a suite of real-life and area-focused applications [26]. Depending on benchmark settings, an iteration runs either for some number of operations per mutator thread and measures application time, or for some amount of time and measures throughput. We use the first setting. We discard scientific applications as they do not generate sufficient work to trigger the GC more than once or twice. Therefore, from this suite, we only evaluate XML Transform, XML Validation, Crypto AES and Compiler.Sunflow. We use a heap of 1 GB for XML Transform and Crypto AES, and 2 GB for the other two.

DaCapo is a set of real-life applications, aimed at evaluating the performance of different components of a Java Virtual Machine [4]. Each application in this suite contains a predefined, fixed-sized workload. Because of their small working sets (between 100 and 500MB), the DaCapo applications do not stress the GC: at 48 cores, each GC thread has only a few kilo-bytes to collect. Still, we present the results of two representative applications from this suite, Eclipse and Tradesoap, to study the effects of our optimisations on less memory-intensive applications. They both require a 500 MB heap.

4.2 Analysis of individual optimisations

This section discusses the performance impact of each optimisation. We focus on three applications for this analysis: SPECjbb-2005, XML Transform from SPECjvm, and Tradesoap from DaCapo. We choose these three because they represent very different working sets, from small for Tradesoap to large for SPECjbb-2005. For XML Transform, we run two iterations, each consisting of 40 operations per mutator; for Tradesoap, we run 10 iterations with *large* workload size. We execute each experiment three times and report the average. The standard deviation between the three runs is not significant.

In order to focus on the performance of the garbage collector as the number of cores increases, we keep the memory allocated constant by setting the number of application threads to 48. We measure GC scalability by varying the number of GC threads from one to 48, in steps of eight.

- **Table 4** evaluates, for the three applications (left to right: SpecJBB2005, XML Transform and TradeSoap), memory access non-locality and memory access imbalance. Non-locality is defined as the fraction of memory accesses during collection that are remote. For example, 0.7 means that 70% of GC accesses are remote, whereas 0.0 means that all GC access is local. Imbalance is measured as the standard deviation over the ratio of number of accesses to a node divided by the total number of accesses. For example, an imbalance of 0.1 means that the standard deviation is small and thus the load is balanced, whereas an imbalance of 2.6 reports a large standard deviation, and thus the load is highly unbalanced.
- **Figure 4** plots GC throughput, i.e., the total amount of memory allocated by the application, divided by the total amount of time spent in GC. The throughput characterises the pause time of the applications independently from the number of allocated bytes. This shows the effects of our optimisations on GC performance.
- **Figure 5** plots completion time of Tradesoap and XML Transform (lower is better) and throughput for SPECjbb (higher is better). This shows the effects of our optimisations on the GC and on the application in combination.
- **Figure 6** highlights the effect of our optimisations on the application, in addition to the GC effect, by plotting the difference between completion time and GC pause time. We report curves for XML Transform only. We discard SPECjbb because it is not possible to isolate application improvement from GC improvement with a fixed duration run. We discard Tradesoap as it uses very little memory to show any significant results.

4.2.1 Interleaved spaces

Impact on garbage collection. Recall, from Section 3, that many applications initialise using a single thread, which maps the physical pages of the eden space to a single node. For example, with SPECjbb2005, at the time of first collection, we observe that 95% of the eden space's pages were allocated from a single node. As shown in Table 4, all three applications suffer from this problem, and memory access is highly unbalanced between the nodes. Interleaved spaces solve this problem by completely avoiding load imbalance.

As shown in Figure 4.a, we observe that with 48 threads, interleaving improves GC throughput for SpecJBB2005 approximately by 75% as compared to Parallel Scavenge. XML Trans-

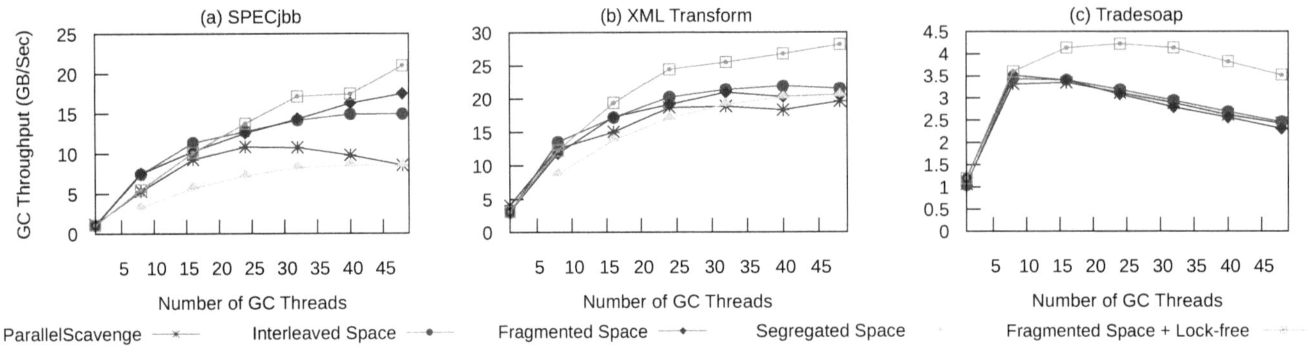

Figure 4. Impact of each of the optimisations on GC throughput

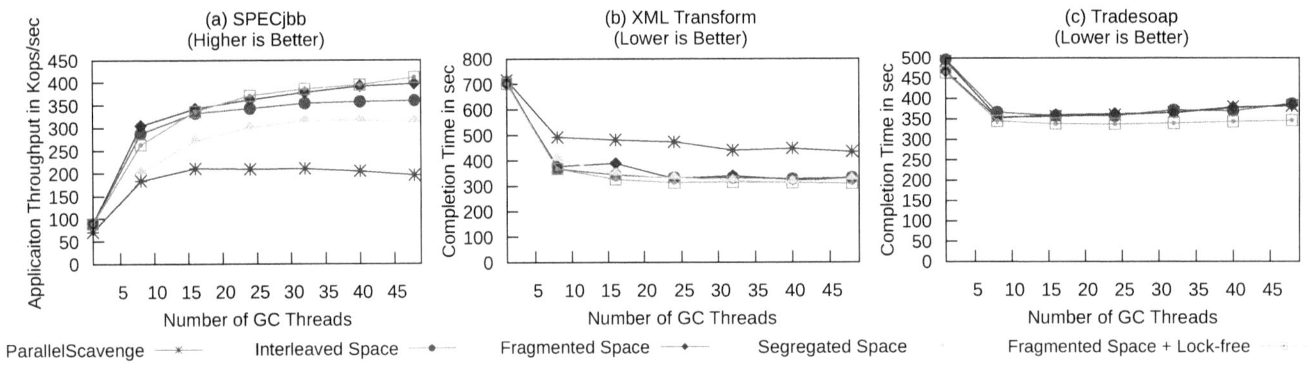

Figure 5. Impact of each of the optimisations on application performance

form demonstrates exactly the same situation, with GC throughput increasing by roughly 10% at 48 cores (Figure 4.b). Since this application allocates less memory, the GC spends less time in graph traversal, and therefore, the effect of interleaved spaces is less significant. In Tradesoap, we observe that even though pages are mainly allocated from two nodes in the beginning, and that the application suffers from a high imbalance (see Table 4), using an interleaved space only leads to a 1% improvement (Figure 4.c). This is because the heap is very small and graph traversal is dominated by the time spent in synchronising the threads.

We thus conclude that balancing memory accesses between the nodes has a high impact on the garbage collector for memory intensive applications and that the impact is less if the GC threads don't have enough memory to collect.

Impact on application. Better balancing memory access among nodes also impacts the application. Figures 5 and 6 show this phenomenon. For example, after excluding GC time, XML Transform runs 26% faster when using interleaved spaces. This shows that both the application and the GC are hampered by an imbalance of the memory accesses between the nodes. Overall, the results show that load balancing has a high impact on both application and GC, especially if the application is memory-intensive, such as SPECjbb.

4.2.2 Fragmented and segregated spaces

In our next experiment, we use either fragmented or segregated space for all the spaces of the young generation. However, we still use interleaved spaces for the old and permanent generations, as these generations use a compacting algorithm. Zhou and Demsky [32] propose a NUMA-aware compaction algorithm, but this is out of our scope. Furthermore, our results show that using a fragmented

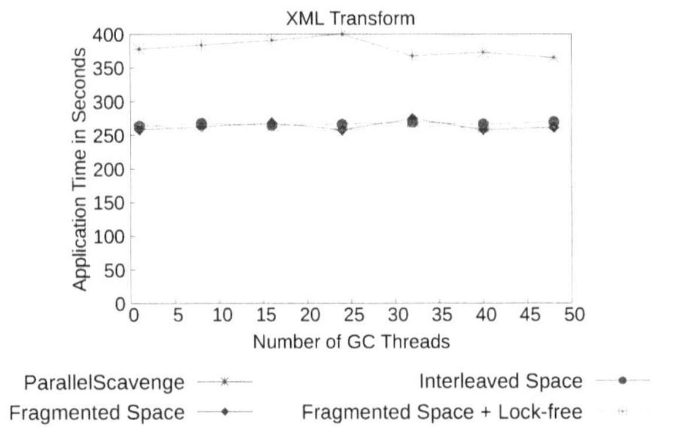

Figure 6. Application improvement not including GC.

space for the other generations is not required to make the garbage collector scale.

Fragmented spaces. Table 4 shows that fragmented spaces reduce the memory access imbalance as compared to Parallel Scavenge. For this reason, except for SPECjbb with more than 32 cores, fragmented and interleaved spaces give roughly the same improvement as compared to Parallel Scavenge (see Figure 4). For the same reason, using fragmented space leads to the same application improvement (see Figure 6).

Fragmented spaces improve locality by eliminating remote access when objects are copied to the to-space (see Table 4). They also improve locality of the application since instead of allocating objects on random nodes, as in the case of interleaved space, an object is allocated on the node that triggers the allocation. Despite this locality improvement, Figures 4, 6 and 5 show that the performance of the GC and of the application is almost the same with either an interleaved space or a fragmented space, when the GC uses less than 32 threads. This result shows that remote access latency has only a small impact on the GC and on the application.

However, in SPECjbb, fragmented spaces improve GC performance with more than 32 GC threads, as compared to interleaved spaces (Figure 4.a). As presented in Section 3.2, good memory locality helps scalability when the load is balanced. This property explains why SPECjbb is unable to scale beyond 32 cores with interleaved spaces, whereas it continues to scale with fragmented spaces. This phenomenon is not visible in XML Transform and Tradesoap, as their heap sizes are smaller and thus, the number of memory accesses is smaller during the collection.

To summarise, we conclude that memory latency due to remote access has little impact on the GC and the application. However, increasing locality is necessary to let the GC scale.

Segregated spaces Segregated spaces require at least one thread on each node to process the received messages, and is thus plotted with at least 8 threads. Furthermore, we cannot use segregated spaces in Tradesoap, as Tradesoap uses a lot of weak references and our segregated space implementation is unable to process them in parallel.

Table 4 shows that segregated spaces eliminate remote access when objects are scanned or copied in the young generation. The table also depicts that segregated spaces are as beneficial as fragmented spaces in reducing memory imbalance. These properties explain that, as shown in Figure 4.a and 4.b, segregated spaces scale up to 48 cores.

However, segregated spaces do not perform as well as fragmented spaces. We observe on SPECjbb that 12% of the scanned objects do not belong to the node where they are discovered during scanning. Moreover, for each remote object, the scanning thread sends the object reference to a remote queue, causing an inter-node cache miss. Thereafter, a thread on the remote node, updates the location of the reference in the scanning thread's node, after copying the object; this causes another inter-node cache miss. Therefore, we believe that this extra overhead compensates any benefit due to better locality, and hence hampers the performance. We did not investigate it further, which would be an interesting extension to this work.

4.2.3 Lock-free task-queue and lazy thread parking

Individual impact. The lock-free task-queue decreases the synchronisation cost at the beginning of the parallel phase, and lazy thread parking at the end. As synchronisation overhead is most noticeable when the heap is small, this is where we expect the effect of this improvement to be most visible.

Unexpectedly, better synchronisation has an important effect on all the three applications (see Figure 4). As compared to fragmented spaces, our synchronisation optimisations improve the performance of SPECjbb, XML Transform and Tradesoap by 23%, 40% and 34% respectively, when using 48 GC threads. For XML Transform and Tradesoap, this improvement is large mainly because the time to traverse the object graph is small. For SPECjbb, the most memory intensive application, optimising the synchronisation also begins to have a significant impact after 24 GC threads and is required to make the GC scale up to the 48 cores. Indeed, without it, beyond 24 GC threads, the bouncing of the lock's cache line between the cores of the GC threads becomes significant and hampers performance by saturating the interconnect [15]. The lightweight synchronisation protocol avoids this overload.

Combined impact. Combined with the fragmented heap, the synchronisation optimisations let SPECjbb and XML Transform scale up to 48 GC threads. It is not the case for Tradesoap as its heap is small and adding more GC threads only increases contention on the cache lines that contain the objects.

	Parallel Scavenge	NAPS
SPECjbb	105 ms	49 ms
Compiler.Sunflow	108 ms	80 ms
XML Transform	14 ms	9.2 ms
XML Validation	80 ms	55 ms
Crypto AES	25.6 ms	9 ms
Eclipse	17.8 ms	13 ms

Table 5. Individual pause time

As compared to Parallel Scavenge, the pause time reduction due to fragmented spaces combined with lock optimisations translates to a total application time improvement of 9% in Tradesoap and 28% in XML Transform, and improved throughput of SPECjbb-2005 by more than twice at 48 GC threads (see Figure 5).

4.3 Scalability

NAPS uses fragmented spaces in the young generation and interleaved spaces in the others, as this combination provides the best performance. Figure 7 compares throughput of Parallel Scavenge and NAPS, i.e., total amount of memory allocated during the whole execution divided by total pause time. It would be unfair to compare throughput across applications, since GC performance depends not only on the number of allocated bytes, but also on the number of objects that survives their collection.

Observation 1: NAPS improves performance and scalability over Parallel Scavenge in all cases, except Compiler.Sunflow where both collectors roughly provide the same performance. This shows that the bottlenecks that we have identified are real.

Observation 2: The performance of NAPS continues to increase up to 48 cores with the 5 memory-intensive applications, except Crypto AES. Furthermore, by adding more GC threads, the performance of NAPS never degrades, except for Eclipse which is, along with Tradesoap, the least memory-intensive applications of the evaluated applications. For Crypto AES, NAPS stops scaling after 24 threads, and for Eclipse it degrades after 32 GC threads. For these applications, the number of objects that survive their collection is small, either because the application mostly allocates objects that die quickly (Crypto AES), or because the application requires a small heap (Eclipse).

Observation 3: The Table 5 reports, for each of the applications, the pause time of a single collection pause. As we can see, NAPS reduces the individual pause times, by up to 2.8 times in the best case. These results confirm that using a scalable stop-the-world collector improves the responsiveness of the application.

Conclusion: From these three observations, we conclude that a stop-the-world GC, such as NAPS, is able to scale almost linearly up to 48 GC threads, provided it has enough memory to collect. Moreover, using a scalable stop-the-world GC actually decreases the pause time and helps in improving the responsiveness of applications.

5. State of the Art

There has been much research on concurrent garbage collection, mainly targeting real-time applications [6, 17, 22, 23]. These collectors have been evaluated on eight cores and two nodes at most. The evaluation of Immix, a recent stop-the-world collector, has the same limitation [3]. This is insufficient to expose the problems that

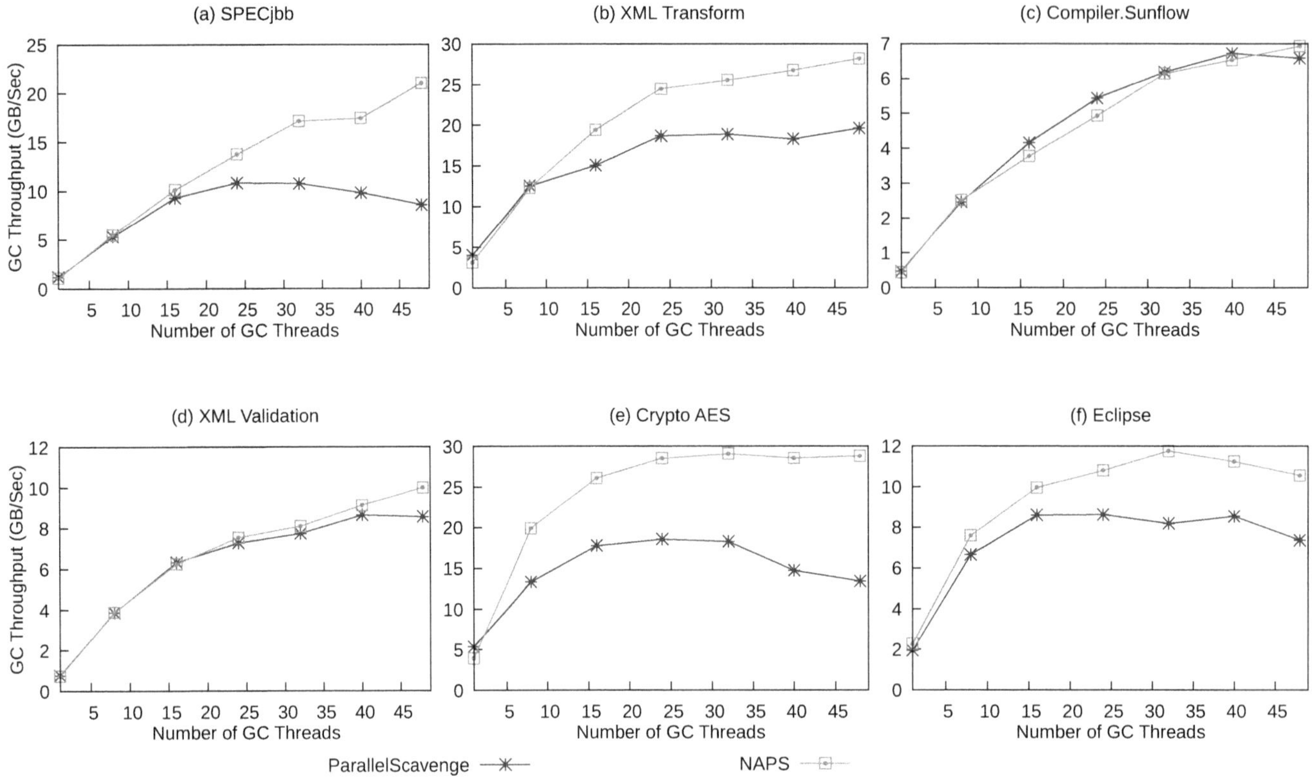

Figure 7. GC Throughput of Parallel Scavenge and NAPS.

arise in large multicores. For intance, Gidra et al. [10] show that Garbage First [6] collapses after 20 cores.

Zhou and Demsky [32] propose a new parallel mark-and-compact collector targeting the TILE-Gx microprocessor family, for which each core is a memory node [30]. It focuses on increasing memory locality, while balancing memory access across the nodes, by balancing the allocations at each node, during compaction. We do not implement such an algorithm, because we believe it will not impact performance on our hardware, in which memory-load balance is the main bottleneck, not the locality. It would be interesting to compare this algorithm with NAPS on a TILE-Gx processor, to isolate which part of the improvement is caused by improving memory locality, and which by balancing memory-load.

Ogasawara [20] and Tikir and Hollingsworth [29] ensure that an object is copied to the memory node where it is accessed most of the time. These algorithms improve application locality, but do not improve GC locality. Again, these algorithms target memory locality, not memory-load balance, the bottleneck on our hardware.

There is considerable amount of work on efficient load balancing among GC-threads. Flood et al. [8] propose a per-object work stealing technique using lock-free double ended queues, also used by Marlow et al. [17]. This is the scheme implemented in OpenJDK 7. Our experiments show that this algorithm is well-adapted to our hardware platform, since, by balancing the load across GC threads, it balances copies across nodes, and hence balances the load across the memory controllers. Oancea et al. [19] associate work-lists to dedicated partitions of the heap. Only the owner of a work-list (the worker thread that works exclusively on that work-list) traces the objects in the corresponding heap partition. For load balancing, workers take ownership of whole work-lists, rather than of individual objects. We believe that stealing a whole work-list is too coarse, and will result in unbalanced memory-load.

A widely-used technique to improve locality and concurrency is to use thread-local heaps [1, 7, 16, 24, 27]. In such GCs, an object is first allocated in a thread-local heap, and gets migrated to a shared global heap only when it gets referenced from the shared heap. This heap layout ensures that a thread-local heap collection can execute concurrently with the application threads on other cores. These algorithms do not focus on efficient collection of the shared heap on large-scale multicore hardware. Moreover, even if the read barrier optimisation of Sivaramakrishnan et al. [24] is applied, applications must still pay the price of a write barrier.

Iyengar et al. [11] states that "Stop-the-World garbage collection is a fundamental fault line in the design of managed runtime environments [because] such stop-the-world techniques become untenable for online processing application [when the heap size grows]". Our results do not support this statement; on the contrary, well-established parallel computing techniques appear to be sufficient to enable stop-the-world collectors to scale on multicore hardware.

6. Conclusion

This paper studies the problem of scalability of throughput-oriented GCs on multicore hardware. We present how we can fix these bottlenecks using well-established parallel programming techniques, and show that they were not caused by the stop-the-world design, but by some of the mechanisms that were not planned for contemporary NUMA multicores with tens of cores. Our evaluation suggests that today, there is no conceptual reason to believe that the pause time of a stop-the-world GC will increase with the increasing number of cores and memory size of multicore hardware. It leads to the conclusion that the costly and complex fine-grain synchronisation of concurrent GCs are not yet required for throughput-oriented

GCs: to achieve good performance, and to scale with the increasing number of cores and heap size.

As a future work, we will explore how we can make segregated spaces perform better by avoiding most of the inter-node messages. We propose to make the old generation fragmented, which will enable us to identify most of the references in their home nodes locally.

Acknowledgement

We would like to thanks our anonymous reviewers for their insightful comments and suggestions.

References

[1] T. A. Anderson. Optimizations in a private nursery-based garbage collector. In *ISMM '10*, pages 21–30. ACM, 2010.

[2] A. W. Appel. Simple generational garbage collection and fast allocation. *SP&E*, 19(2):171–183, 1989.

[3] S. M. Blackburn and K. S. McKinley. Immix: a mark-region garbage collector with space efficiency, fast collection, and mutator performance. In *PLDI '08*, pages 22–32. ACM, 2008.

[4] S. M. Blackburn, R. Garner, C. Hoffmann, A. M. Khang, K. S. McKinley, R. Bentzur, A. Diwan, D. Feinberg, D. Frampton, S. Z. Guyer, M. Hirzel, A. Hosking, M. Jump, H. Lee, J. E. B. Moss, A. Phansalkar, D. Stefanović, T. VanDrunen, D. von Dincklage, and B. Wiedermann. The DaCapo benchmarks: Java benchmarking development and analysis. In *OOPSLA '06*, pages 169–190. ACM, 2006.

[5] M. Dashti, A. Fedorova, J. Funston, F. Gaud, R. Lachaize, B. Lepers, V. Quema, and M. Roth. Traffic management: A holistic approach to memory placement on numa systems. In *ASPLOS '13*. ACM, 2013.

[6] D. Detlefs, C. Flood, S. Heller, and T. Printezis. Garbage-first garbage collection. In *ISMM '04*, pages 37–48. ACM, 2004.

[7] D. Doligez and X. Leroy. A concurrent, generational garbage collector for a multithreaded implementation of ml. In *POPL '93*, pages 113–123. ACM, 1993.

[8] C. H. Flood, D. Detlefs, N. Shavit, and X. Zhang. Parallel garbage collection for shared memory multiprocessors. In *JVM '01*, pages 21–21. USENIX Association, 2001.

[9] H. Franke and R. Russell M. K. Fuss, futexes and furwocks: Fast userlevel locking in linux. In *Ottawa Linux Symposium, OLS '02*, pages 479–495, 2002.

[10] L. Gidra, G. Thomas, J. Sopena, and M. Shapiro. Assessing the scalability of garbage collectors on many cores. In *SOSP Workshop on Programming Languages and Operating Systems, PLOS '11*, pages 1–5. ACM, 2011.

[11] B. Iyengar, G. Tene, M. Wolf, and E. Gehringer. The collie: a wait-free compacting collector. In *ISMM '12*, pages 61–72. ACM, 2012.

[12] R. Jones, A. Hosking, and E. Moss. *The garbage collection handbook: the art of automatic memory management*. Chapman & Hall/CRC, 1st edition, 2011.

[13] H. Lieberman and C. Hewitt. A real-time garbage collector based on the lifetimes of objects. *CACM*, 26(6):419–429, 1983.

[14] LinuxMemPolicy. What is linux memory policy? http://www.kernel.org/doc/Documentation/vm/numa_memory_policy.txt, 2012.

[15] J.-P. Lozi, F. David, G. Thomas, J. Lawall, and G. Muller. Remote Core Locking: migrating critical-section execution to improve the performance of multithreaded applications. In *USENIX ATC '12*, pages 65–76. USENIX Association, 2012.

[16] S. Marlow and S. Peyton Jones. Multicore garbage collection with local heaps. In *ISMM '11*, pages 21–32. ACM, 2011.

[17] S. Marlow, T. Harris, R. P. James, and S. Peyton Jones. Parallel generational-copying garbage collection with a block-structured heap. In *ISMM '08*, pages 11–20. ACM, 2008.

[18] M. M. Michael and M. L. Scott. Simple, fast, and practical non-blocking and blocking concurrent queue algorithms. In *PODC '96*, pages 267–275. ACM, 1996.

[19] C. E. Oancea, A. Mycroft, and S. M. Watt. A new approach to parallelising tracing algorithms. In *ISMM '09*, pages 10–19. ACM, 2009.

[20] T. Ogasawara. NUMA-aware memory manager with dominant-thread-based copying GC. In *OOPSLA '09*, pages 377–390. ACM, 2009.

[21] OpenJDK Memory. Memory management in the Java hotspot™ virtual machine. Technical report, Sun Microsystems, 2006.

[22] F. Pizlo, D. Frampton, E. Petrank, and B. Steensgaard. Stopless: a real-time garbage collector for multiprocessors. In *ISMM '07*, pages 159–172. ACM, 2007.

[23] F. Pizlo, L. Ziarek, P. Maj, A. L. Hosking, E. Blanton, and J. Vitek. Schism: fragmentation-tolerant real-time garbage collection. In *PLDI '10*, pages 146–159. ACM, 2010.

[24] K. Sivaramakrishnan, L. Ziarek, and S. Jagannathan. Eliminating read barriers through procrastination and cleanliness. In *ISMM '12*, pages 49–60. ACM, 2012.

[25] SPECjbb2005. SPECjbb2005 home page. http://www.spec.org/jbb2005/, 2012.

[26] SPECjvm2008. SPECjvm2008 home page. http://www.spec.org/jvm2008/, 2012.

[27] B. Steensgaard. Thread-specific heaps for multi-threaded programs. In *ISMM '00*, pages 18–24. ACM, 2000.

[28] G. Tene, B. Iyengar, and M. Wolf. C4: the continuously concurrent compacting collector. In *ISMM '11*, pages 79–88. ACM, 2011.

[29] M. M. Tikir and J. K. Hollingsworth. NUMA-aware Java heaps for server applications. In *IPDPS '05*, pages 108–117. IEEE Computer Society, 2005.

[30] Tilera. TILE-Gx processor family. http://www.tilera.com/products/processors/TILE-Gx_Family, 2012.

[31] D. Ungar. Generation scavenging: A non-disruptive high performance storage reclamation algorithm. In *SDE '84*, pages 157–167. ACM, 1984.

[32] J. Zhou and B. Demsky. Memory management for many-core processors with software configurable locality policies. In *ISMM '12*, pages 3–14. ACM, 2012.

Discerning the Dominant Out-of-Order Performance Advantage: Is it Speculation or Dynamism?

Daniel S. McFarlin
Carnegie Mellon University
dmcfarlin@cmu.edu

Charles Tucker Craig Zilles
University of Illinois at Urbana-Champaign
{cetucker,zilles}@illinois.edu

Abstract

In this paper, we set out to study the performance advantages of an Out-of-Order (OOO) processor relative to in-order processors with similar execution resources. In particular, we try to tease apart the performance contributions from two sources: the improved schedules enabled by OOO hardware speculation support and its ability to generate different schedules on different occurrences of the same instructions based on operand and functional unit availability. We find that the ability to express good static schedules achieves the bulk of the speedup resulting from OOO. Specifically, of the 53% speedup achieved by OOO relative to a similarly provisioned in-order machine, we find that 88% of that speedup can be achieved by using a single "best" static schedule as suggested by observing an OOO schedule of the code. We discuss the ISA mechanisms that would be required to express these static schedules.

Furthermore, we find that the benefits of dynamism largely come from two kinds of events that influence the application's critical path: load instructions that miss in the cache only part of the time and branch mispredictions. We find that much of the benefit of OOO dynamism can be achieved by the potentially simpler task of addressing these two behaviors directly.

Categories and Subject Descriptors D.3.4 [**Software**]: Programming Languages–*Processors:Compilers, Optimization*, C.0 [**Computer Systems Organization**]: General–*Hardware/software interfaces*

General Terms Performance

Keywords Optimization; Speculation; Dynamic Scheduling

1. Introduction

The current state of parallel programming has unleashed a tension of design criteria on modern general-purpose CPUs. There are neither so few nor so many parallel programs that either parallel or single-thread performance can be marginalized. Instead CPU designers must design chips with high single-thread performance, but vigilantly maximize performance/area and performance/watt.

One important design decision that plays centrally in this trade-off is the choice between in-order and out-of-order instruction scheduling by the hardware. GPUs and lower-end processors have demonstrated the performance/area and performance/watt advantages of in-order, but currently out-of-order (OOO) designs hold the mindshare for achieving peak single-thread performance.

We perceive, however, that there are two potential sources for the performance advantage between the hardware OOO schedules and compiler-generated schedules as executed by in-order machines:

1. the OOO has few constraints other than true dependencies and functional unit availability to constrain schedule generation, whereas existing ISAs prevent the expression of some *speculative* schedules by compilers.
2. OOO can execute the same instructions in different schedules at different points of the execution, reacting to the specific events observed during each execution. We'll call this advantage *dynamism*.

Little effort has been directed at quantifying the contributions of each of these effects, but we believe that this is an important question. Specifically, if the difference between OOO and in-order is largely not the result of dynamism, but rather due to the inability of the compiler to express the desired schedule given the available ISA interface, this is something that can be addressed by further ISA development.

To this end, this paper reports a study we undertook to characterize the relative importance of dynamism in OOO and better understand the schedule differences between in-order and OOO schedulers.

This paper makes the following contributions:

- We demonstrate that most (on average 88%) of the OOO's performance advantage is due to the speculation support that enables the formation of high quality schedules.
- We show that the OOO's remaining performance advantage from dynamism is predominantly from its ability to deploy different schedules in the immediate locus of a cache miss or branch misprediction.
- We quantify the ability of a complexity-effective, "off-the-shelf" solution for cache miss recovery coupled with a simple mechanism for misprediction recovery to cover the remaining performance gap to the OOO.
- We provide recommendations for realizing performance competitive in-order designs given current technology and workload trends.

The remainder of the paper is organized as follows: Section 2 elaborates on the need for the present work. Section 2.1 examines the motivation for the strong tendency towards OOO designs in industry and the factors limiting the performance competitiveness of in-order designs. In Section 2.2 we employ a criticality framework to

ASPLOS'13, March 16–20, 2013, Houston, Texas, USA.

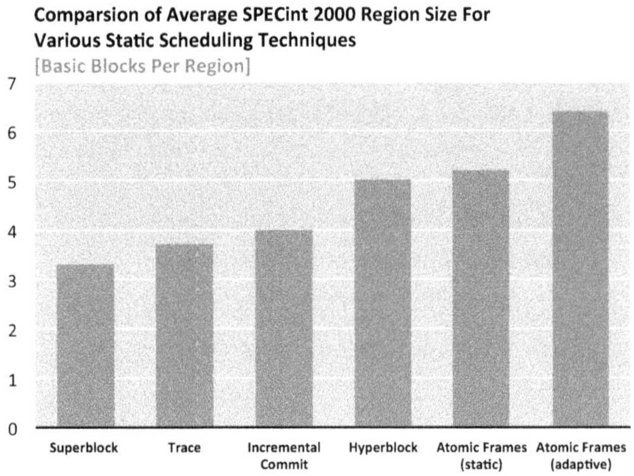

Figure 1. Average region size achieved by top-performing scheduling techniques for in-order machines.

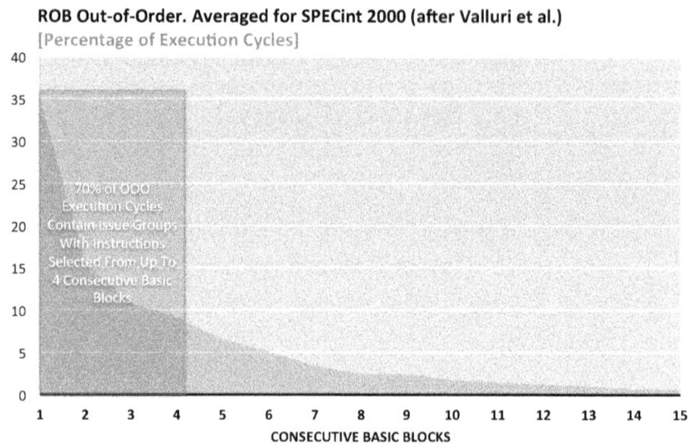

Figure 2. The basic block overlap ability of a representative out-of-order design.

explore the theoretical and practical implications of dynamism on performance and provide intuition as to its principle and we argue, limited advantages over the OOO's baseline speculation support. Section 3 looks at our methodology for quantifying the relative contributions of dynamism and speculation to OOO performance; the presentation and discussion of our results appear in Sections 4 and 5. The rich history of the in-order vs. OOO debate along with the challenges academia and industry encountered in trying to match the OOO's performance are explored in Section 6. We conclude in Section 7.

2. Background/Motivation

Previous work has observed that OOO scheduling hardware tends to spend most of its time scheduling the same small subset of the static program, and moreover tends to create the same cycle-by-cycle schedule repeatedly. Caching these schedules is the motivation for Execution Caching [47], to allow the scheduler to be shut down (which they argue produces power savings) some of the time.

Our work extends this intuition in several ways. First, previous work has been in terms of actual architectural implementations, which tends to mask the theoretical limitations of static scheduling with implementation details. We seek conclusions applicable more generally to statically scheduled architectures. In addition, we want to tease apart the OOO performance advantage to see whether an aggressive in-order design has any hope of matching its performance, and what sorts of features it would require to do so.

2.1 The Perceived Out-of-Order Performance Advantage

Despite some of the well-known advantages offered by in-order designs (usually lower power, higher frequency, and reduced HW complexity), Out-of-Order designs dominate general purpose computing and are proliferating into domains where OOO designs were conventionally seen as poorly suited e.g. transaction processing [41], data/control-plane processing [20] and the embedded space [16]. While direct comparisons between in-order and OOO designs are difficult, OOO designs seem to consistently provide higher single-thread performance relative to comparably provisioned in-order designs [22].

The common explanation for the IO/OOO performance disparity is that the OOO is inherently better at exploiting memory-level parallelism as even the most sophisticated static schedule is hobbled by the stall-on-use/head-of-line blocking problem inherent to cache misses in IO designs [2, 22]. In contrast, the enduring trend over several generations of OOO designs is their ability to tolerate an ever increasing number of longer latency cache misses; Intel's 22nm Ivy Bridge boasts a window size nearly twice that of the 45nm Penryn [24]. Indeed, given the ever increasing complexity and non-determinism of the memory hierarchy, the MLP advantage seems to be what is motivating the trend towards OOO designs. Recent in-order processors have explicitly incorporated HW features to "buy back" [28] this loss of MLP relative to the OOO including run-ahead execution (Power6) and Subordinate scout threading (Rock) [22]. Yet, a recent in-order design that combined a sophisticated run-ahead scheme, advanced prefetchers, register checkpointing, and gated store-buffer with a good compiler was still some 42% slower than a comparably provisioned OOO design [22]. Why?

Figures 1 and 2 highlight a major challenge for in-order designs in matching the OOO: the OOO's ability to simultaneously execute instructions from a consistently larger number of consecutive basic blocks. Figure 1 compares the average region size (number of basic blocks) found by some of the best performing static scheduling techniques documented in the literature when applied to SPECint 2000. Trace Scheduling [42], Superblock [21] and Hyperblock [17, 37] are all well known, often profile-driven global scheduling techniques employed by static compilers. Incremental Commit/Non-Atomic Traces [51] and Atomic Frames [36] are techniques employed by runtimes to dynamically optimize binaries; the first three techniques require modest amounts of HW support; the last two require fairly aggressive HW implementations with the adaptive version of Atomic Regions continually re-optimizing certain regions based on performance/event counters.

Excluding Atomic Frames, the first four scheduling techniques produce regions of, on average, between 3.3 and 5 basic blocks in size. How does this compare to the OOO? Figure 2 shows that overlapping the execution of instructions from 4 basic blocks is only sufficient to account for about 70% of the OOO's execution cycles; the OOO spends the remaining 30% of its execution cycles issuing instructions derived from 5 or more consecutive basic blocks. Note Figure 2's "long tail"; even overlapping the execution of instructions from 6 consecutive basic blocks, comparable to the overlap achieved by the best performing Atomic Frames variant, only accounts for about 82% of the OOO's execution cycles.[1] Adding yet another consecutive basic block (a region size increase of 16%) contributes only another 3% improvement to coverage. Furthermore, the emerging performance trend of static scheduling

[1] Architectures such as TRIPS [17] and the Region Slip variant of rePlay [45] provide for the overlapping of Hyperblocks and Atomic Frames, respectively, at the cost of substantially increased hardware, runtime and compiler complexity as well as costlier misspeculation penalties

techniques for SPECint 2006 is not particularly encouraging; [43] reports that the average region size for global trace scheduling fell about 15%, from 3.7 basic blocks to 3.2 basic blocks.

While this data re-affirms the well-known need for hardware support for software speculation, state-of-the-art static scheduling techniques that rely on such support still fail to match the dynamic schedules produced by the OOO. We argue that the primary enabler for the higher quality, dynamic schedules is the OOO's more general and better provisioned speculation support facilities (very large ROB, renamer, larger Load/Store Queue, dynamic/adaptive memory disambiguation) [49] and the generally lower cost of misspeculation; the OOO can more readily adapt to data misspeculation [10] while its finer-grained commit and cheaper recovery mechanisms give it an edge over Non-Atomic Traces and Atomic Frames [9, 45]. Consequently, a combination of HW support for software speculation, some form of non-blocking instruction issue and, as will be demonstrated, the ability to recover from mispredicts is necessary to close the performance gap. To the best of our knowledge, no industrial or academic design has explored the theoretical desirability and practical necessity of this combination.

2.2 Scheduling vs. Dynamism

It is easy to attribute the benefits of OOO almost entirely to dynamism, that is the ability of OOO to generate schedules at runtime based on the actual path taken by the code and execution latencies of the operations. In this section, we attempt to tease apart what OOO provides to understand which component could potentially be provided by simpler mechanisms.

Path Specificity:

Because out-of-order performs scheduling after branch prediction it gets the benefit of scheduling based on the predicted path. This creates a important practical distinction between out-of-order and in-order when the predictability of a branch exceeds the branch's bias. Consider, for example, the following code:

Block A is terminated by a branch that can flow to either block B or block C. Each basic block contains a collection of instructions with dependencies, which result in the schedule for each basic block to be narrower than the machine's width. There is, however, potential for overlap between basic blocks (*i.e.*, the critical path through the whole application is not the sequence of critical paths through each basic block).

On an out-of-order machine, if block B is predicted to follow block A, then the instructions from block B will be intermingled with those from block A. Similarly, if the path from block A to block C is predicted, then C's instructions will be intermingled with block A.

Of course, many compilers are capable of hoisting instructions across basic block boundaries, often using ILP scheduling techniques like superblock scheduling. What ILP scheduling techniques accomplish is to statically pick a path for optimization (*e.g.*, the path from block A to B) and hoist instructions from block B into block A. Using this technique, when the code executes the path from A to B, it can achieve schedule quality similar to that of the out-of-order machine. When the path from A to C is taken, however, the collection of instructions from block B that were hoisted to block A are wasted work and we have achieved no overlap between C and A [2]. This is not a serious problem if the the path from A to B is much more frequent than the path from A to C. Furthermore, the behavior of the A to C path with an ILP scheduling compiler is much like the behavior of the out-of-order machine when it predicts incorrectly to follow the path from A to B when the path A to C is needed; in this case, the out-of-order will hoist much of B before the branch in A is resolved at which point C will need to be fetched, likely resulting in no overlap between A and C.

In short, an ILP compiler typically achieves good overlap in proportion with the bias of the branch, while the out-of-order does so in proportion to the predictability of the branch. This results in a significant advantage for the out-of-order because branch predictability is almost always higher than branch bias, sometimes significantly so.

Variable Latency:

Tolerance of long latency operations is an often touted strength of out-of-order processors, but it is important to recognize that static scheduling — through techniques like modulo scheduling — can effectively tolerate long latencies as well. The key advantage of out-of-order is two-fold: first, in its ability to tolerating variable latency, and, second, in how this interacts with path specificity.

While most instructions on modern machines have a fixed latency, some instructions, notably load instructions, have a variable latency. This variable latency is important when it potentially affects the critical path. Consider the following three scenarios:

Scenario A: (off the critical path)

```
(int *)A[N];
int C[N];

for (int i = 0 ; i < N ; i ++) {
  C[i] = *A[i];
}
```

This code exhibits a "spine and ribs" structure where the loop carried dependence (`i++`) forms the critical path and the work of the loop (a serial dependence chain of two loads and store) are a rib hanging off that spine. Because the variable latency — the second load — is on the rib (and hence off the critical path) a compiler for an in-order machine could theoretically schedule the consumers of that load for its worst case latency. This would achieve the same performance as the out-of-order, because there is little benefit to completing the spines early.

Scenario B: (on the critical path)

```
int A[N], index = 0;

for (int i = 0 ; i < N ; i ++) {
  index = A[index];
}
```

In this code example, we can pack the code as tight as possible. The critical path will always go through the loads, no matter what their latency.

Scenario C: (the critical path is a function of latency)

What is particularly challenging for static scheduling to deal with is when the critical path through a region is a function of whether an access hits or misses in the cache. Below is a simple, illustrative example of this consisting of 4 loads. The data dependence graph for this code is shown in Figure 3(a).

```
z = p1->x->z + p2->x->z;
```

In this code, how the second pair or loads should be scheduled depends on which loads miss, so that we can overlap misses. Figure 3(b) shows a scenario where the `p1->x->z` load should be scheduled last so that both misses overlap, and Figure 3(c) shows the complementary scenario that benefits from the other ordering. This is a situation where there is no substitute for dynamism.

[2] Alternatively, we could hoist some instructions from both B and C into block A, but typically machine width and functional unit limitations prevent us from hoist as many instructions from either path if we choose to hoist from both.

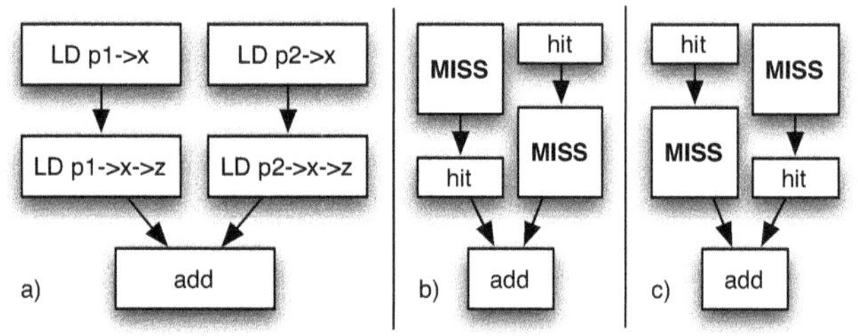

Figure 3. Scenario C variable latency code example: a) data dependence graph, b) `p1->x` and `p2->x->z` miss, c) `p2->x` and `p1->x->z` miss.

Early Branch Resolution:

While it doesn't happen frequently, an OOO machine has the potential to overlap branch misprediction latency with other execution. In the code that follows, the branch on `b` does not depend on the computation before it, so it can be resolved in parallel with the computation.

```
p->y ++;
if (b) {
    ...
```

Achieving this overlap can be challenging for in-order machines because branches generally must be placed at the end of their basic block (to demarcate which instructions belong in the block), which also constrains their place in the schedule. Two solutions to this problem are available. On the software side, the pre-branch computation can be pushed down onto both downstream paths at the cost of code replications. On the hardware side, "prepare-to-branch" mechanisms [29] have been proposed that separate the computation of a branch outcome from the branch's role as a basic block boundary; IBM's Cell processor is a recent example employing such a mechanism [19]

Branch Misprediction:

One of the fundamental advantages of dynamic scheduling over static schedules is that ability of the dynamic scheduler to "ramp up" after and during a branch mispredict. Specifically, the dynamic scheduler has superior recovery from branch mispredicts as it is able to respond to actual instruction readiness that occurs during and after the mispredict recovery period rather than the readiness assumptions encoded in a static schedule. The main insight here is that the ILP instructions hoisted by the static scheduler between a critical path producer and consumer to cover non-unit latencies can in fact extend the critical path when these non-unit latencies have already been covered (in part or in full) by the misprediction recovery latency. Once the correct path instructions hit the execute stage, a statically scheduled machine must still churn through the non-critical hoisted instructions before reaching the critical path consumer despite the consumer's immediate readiness upon misprediction recovery; a dynamically scheduled machine has no such limitation and can immediately execute the critical path consumer.

We illustrate this phenomenon through two examples excerpted from SPEC2000 Integer benchmarks and visualized in Figures 4 and 5. Each figure follows the same convention:

- Time flows from left to right
- Instructions that issue in the same cycle are shown in the same column
- Non critical path instructions are denoted by a label of the form `ILP[0-9]+`
- **A** shows the in-order, linear instruction sequence as emitted by the compiler; Critical path instructions are identified by decorated borders
- **B** shows an execution trace of the dynamically scheduled code (OOO) when the fall-through is correctly predicted
- **C** shows an execution trace of the statically scheduled code (VLIW with packets shown as rounded rectangles) when the fall-through is correctly predicted
- **D** shows an execution trace of the dynamically scheduled code (OOO) when the fall-through is mispredicted
- **E** shows an execution trace of the statically scheduled code (VLIW) when the fall-through is mispredicted

All examples have consumers of loads located in the fall-through path of a conditional branch. Both the dynamic scheduler and static scheduler are able to cover the load-to-use latency of the loads by hoisting instructions from the fall-through-path after the branch but before the consumer. In the common case of a correct branch prediction (not-taken), the dynamic schedule and the static schedule execute in the same number of cycles. The real disparity in performance comes in the event of a branch misprediction. The load prior to the branch executes in the same cycle in both schedules. Assume that both redirect the front-end at the same time and both incur the same mispredict penalty. In both cases, the L1 hit latency is covered by the time to redirect the front-end. In other words, for both scheduling techniques, the consumer of the load is ready to execute as soon as it enters the window. In the parlance of Fields criticality [14], the consumer of the load issued prior to the mispredicted branch is fetch critical.

The delinquent execution of `r0` in **E** relative to **D** in Figure 4 (derived from `gap`) shows the performance difference between the two scheduling techniques; the dynamic scheduler is able to immediately execute the consumer of `LD(A)` (it is the oldest, ready instruction in the window). In contrast, the static schedule that enters the window after the branch misprediction recovery consists of instructions that were hoisted to cover the L1-hit latency but this latency has already been covered by the mispredict latency. As a result, these hoisted instructions now prevent the immediate execution of the load's consumer.

Though the branch mispredict latency extends the critical path length for both the dynamically and statically scheduled versions, the hoisted instructions in the static schedule now further extend the critical path length by delaying the use of a critical, ready instruction. In other words, a static schedule to cover the L1-hit latency along the critical path is now penalized by the L1-hit latency. An extension of this scenario occurs when, with sufficient profiling, the static scheduler schedules for an L2 hit and is able to find sufficient ILP to cover the L2-hit latency. In this case, the execution of the use of the L2-hit is delayed by 10 cycles (the mispredict recovery latency) when the redirected instruction stream finally reaches the execute stage.

Figure 5 derived from `eon` demonstrates that this problem is compounded by the presence of cascading loads *i.e.*loads that feed other loads. In this example, `r0 = LD(A)` feeds `r1 = LD(r0)` before a conditional branch. The consumer of `r1` is after the conditional branch. As in example 1, in the case of a correctly predicted fall-through, the performance of the static schedule is identical to that of the dynamic schedule; the static schedule initiates `r0 = LD(A)` before the conditional branch and pushes the use of `r0(r1 = LD(r0))` beneath the branch. The L1-hit latency of `LD(A)` is covered by hoisted instructions; the L1-hit latency of `LD(r0)` is similarly covered. With an L1-hit latency of 4 cycles, the path to `r1` from `LD(A)` is 8 cycles. As in Example 1, both scheduling techniques experience a mispredict. For the OOO, `LD(A)` and `LD(r0)`

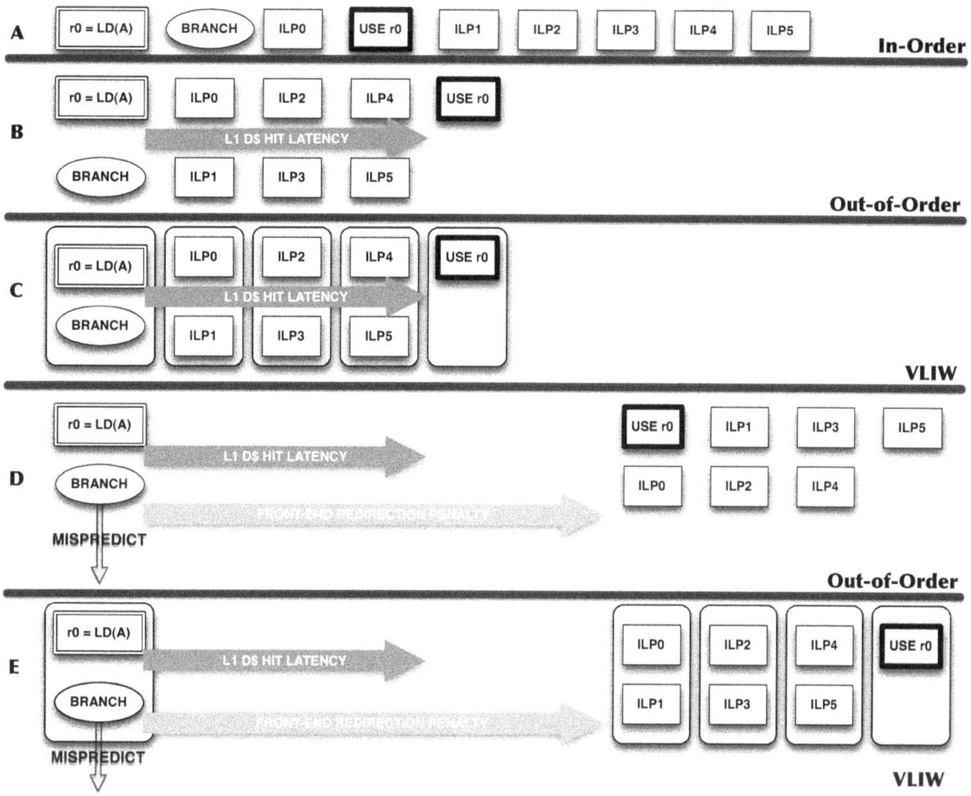

Figure 4. Misprediction recovery latency covers L1-hit latency

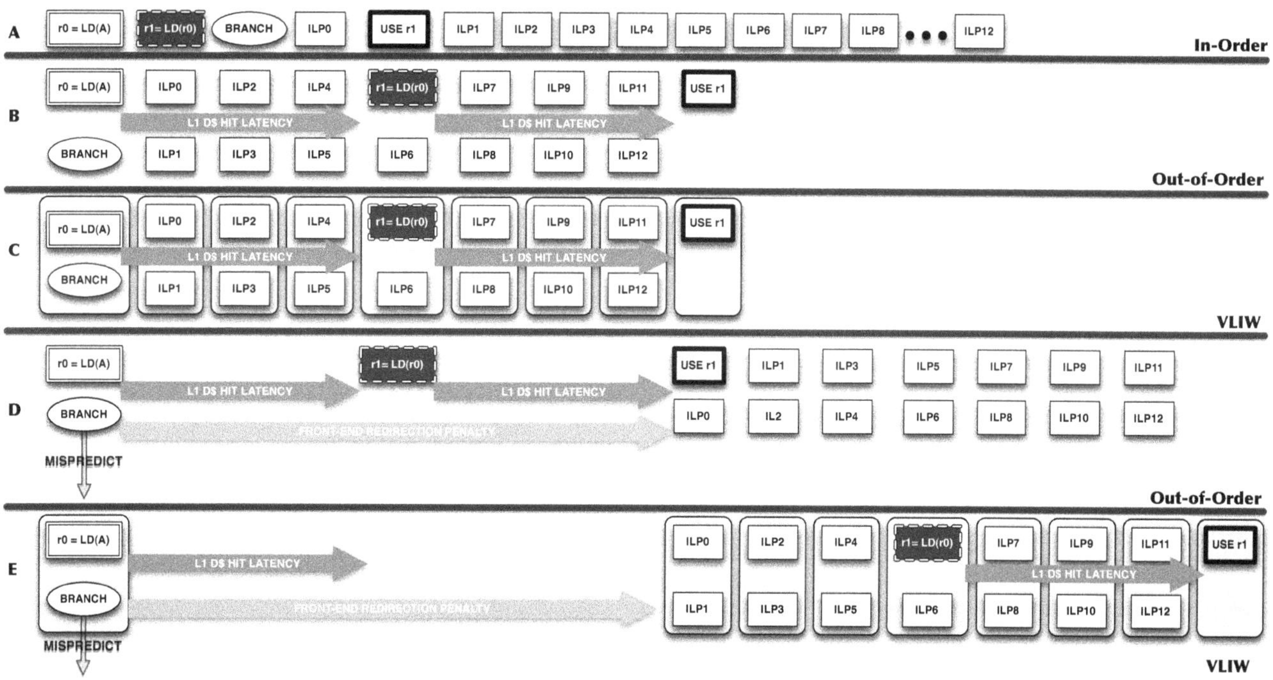

Figure 5. Misprediction recovery latency covers L1-hit latencies of a Load chain

can both execute in the shadow of the mispredict recovery. When the correct path instructions finally enter the window, `LD(r0)`, as the oldest, ready instruction executes immediately. In contrast, because the static schedule has pushed the `r1 = LD(r0) => USE r1` chain below the branch and hoisted ILP instructions to cover the L1-hit latencies for `r0 = LD(A)` and `r1 = LD(r0)`, the execution of `r1` is delayed by 8 cycles.

3. Experimental Method

In an attempt to separate the speculation and dynamism aspects of OOO execution, we have developed a simulator framework that allows us to run a benchmark on the simulator configured as an OOO processor and capture the dynamic schedules used, identify a dominant schedule for each region, and replay these schedules in a second in-order execution. In this section, we describe our choice of benchmarks (Section 3.1), how we collect the dynamic schedules (3.2), how we replay these schedules

It should be noted that this work is a limit study of sorts. Specifically, we make no attempt to describe the mechanisms that would be necessary to produce these schedules nor the architectural features that would be necessary to encode these schedules. We do, however, think that a useful mental model for the system under study is a machine like the Transmeta Crusoe [9], which consisted of a VLIW processor coupled with the CMS dynamic binary translator. Our study can be viewed as investigating the potential for a futuristic dynamic optimizer provided it was not constrained in the static schedules it could generate and it could effectively profile the execution so as to generate relevant schedules.

In addition to scheduling code, such a dynamic optimizer is capable of applying other optimizations (*e.g.*, converting a store-to-load forwarding into a register communication) that can reduce the program's critical path and/or number of executed operations. While these transformations are valuable and could potentially improve the performance of an optimized in-order execution past a traditional out-of-order, we will not consider those here because they would only make our goal of understanding the role dynamism plays in OOO execution by obfuscating where performance is coming from.

3.1 Benchmarks

Because the largest benefits of OOO have historically come from non-numeric programs[3], we focus on integer programs, from the SPECint 2000 benchmark suite, in this work. For our Alpha-based simulation framework, our executables are compiled using the DEC C Alpha compiler (V5.9- 005), with peak optimizations enabled for the 4-wide, in-order DEC Alpha 21164, but no profile feedback.

For each experiment, we run several checkpoints from each benchmark in SPECint 2000. Each run executes for 2 million instructions to warm up caches and branch predictors then execution time is measured for the next 10 million instructions.

3.2 Harvesting Schedules

Generating our static schedules is a two step process. In the first step, we run our OOO simulator and collect a trace of the schedule as it was scheduled by the OOO machine. To make the selection of a dominant schedule tractable, we find dominant schedules for various regions of code and then *stitch* them back together. Thus, as we collect the trace, we break it into *snippets* of code, terminating snippets at backwards branches and function returns. Each time a snippet is captured, we record the cycle that an instruction executed relative to the first instruction of each snippet (which executed in cycle 0 by definition). Due to the nature of the OOO, it is common for instructions to have negative offsets. We also record the PC and the offset of the first instruction of the next snippet, which we use as a *stitching point* when we attempt to put the snippets back together.

We aggregate all of the snippets from all of the checkpoints of a given benchmark and post-process them together. The first step is to discard any schedules that embed a mispredicted branch; we found that these schedules are too pessimistic to assume as our static schedule. Second, any time the stitching point has a negative offset (*e.g.*, when the first instruction of a subsequent snippet happens to execute before the first instruction of this schedule), we set the stitching offset to zero to avoid a deadlock in our simulations. After these two transformations, we simply select the most common schedule (*i.e.*, the mode) to be our static schedule. This schedule along with its *key* – the sequence of PCs in program order that make up the schedule – are entered into a "database" which is used in the subsequent simulation. Together these snippets provide more than 99.999% coverage of our simulated dynamic instruction stream.

As our "region formation" heuristic is very simple, it has some known shortcomings. First, it often results in short snippets. This is largely mitigated by overlapping the schedule of snippets through the stitching discussed below. Tight loops with high trip counts have the potential to be more problematic. Our methodology can underestimate the performance of such loops because it is constrained to produce code with integer initiation intervals. For example, a loop with 5 instructions will result in an initiation interval of 2, where a compiler, by unrolling this loop could pack 4 iterations into 5 cycles.

3.3 Replaying Dominant Schedules

We have modified the front end of our simulator to allow us to replay these dominant schedules as if they were static schedules provided by a compiler. At the fetch stage of our timing simulator, we exploit the functional-first nature of our timing simulator to examine the upcoming dynamic trace of instructions to generate a key and select the appropriate snippet. By construction, none of our snippet keys are a prefix of any other, so this lookup process is a simple one. In this way, we construct a short queue of snippets and their schedules.

We combine the snippet schedules into a composite schedule by placing each successive schedule's cycle 0 at the insertion point indicated by the previous schedule and populating the composite schedule. Because our snippet schedules are selected independently, there is the potential that we selected a snippet schedule that never executed with the schedule for the snippet before it. As a result, this naive stitching can result in unrealizable schedules due to oversubscribing the width of the machine or by violating data dependencies. If one of these violations is detected, the insertion point is "bumped" forward a cycle and the process is repeated. In principle, most of this work could be done offline, but as our post-processor doesn't actually decode the instructions and hence cannot detect dependence violations, it was simplest to implement this as part of the front end. Most notably, stitching is performed in the front end with no awareness of dynamic events like branch mispredictions or cache misses, so is performed the same way each time for a given sequence of basic blocks.

Our simulator framework lacks support for feeding wrong-path instructions into our timing model. When our predictor model indicates a mispredicted branch, we stall fetch of subsequent instructions until the branch hits an execute unit (and resolves), after which fetch begins again. We use the same approach for all simulations.

[3] Numeric programs often have extensive instruction-level parallelism, more regular control flow, and simpler memory-access patterns (*e.g.*, fewer pointer-based data structures) which make traditional compiler optimization more successful resulting in very competitive performance on in-order machines.

Front end	4-wide fetch (no I$ modeled)
	10-cycle branch mispredict
	GShare (16b index, 16b history)
	Cascading Indirect Predictor
	2K-entry target buffer
	16-entry RAS
Execution	Maximum 4 of: 4 Int (1 cycle simple, 5 mul/div) 2 FP (4 simple, 20 complex) 2 Load/Store (1 AGEN/TLB) + cache latency)
	64 entry window
Back end	128 entry ROB
	4-wide commit
L1$	32KiB, 64B line, 4-way LRU, 3 cycles
L2$	256KiB, 64B line, 8-way LRU, 25 cycles
DRAM	150 cycle latency, 16B/cycle
iCFP	64 entry slice buffer

Table 1. Simulated machine parameters

As previously noted our snippet coverage is almost but not quite 100%. So as to be not too pessimistic with the less than 0.00001% of the total instructions that aren't covered by snippets, dynamic scheduling is used for these instructions in the simulator. We don't, however, allow the execution of these instructions to overlap with snippets before or after them, which means our handling of these instructions is likely conservative.

3.4 Processor Model

Our processor model is configured to approximate the resources and latencies in modern OOO processors [34], as shown in Table 1.

In order to support pre-scheduled code in the simulator, we need to make a handful of simplifications and modifications to the processor model's front end. First, as previously noted, we use a functional-first methodology which lacks support for injecting wrong-path instructions into the execution. The impact of this limitation is mitigated by the fact that we are studying the relative performance of the pre-scheduled runs to a baseline (OOO) and all runs incur this limitation.

Second, it would be difficult to accurately model the instruction cache performance of the pre-scheduled runs, so we assume a perfect instruction cache. This has little impact on the baseline runs because our benchmarks have relatively small instruction working sets, but may result in some over-prediction of performance for the the pre-scheduled runs which will necessarily require some amount of code replication in order to achieve the desired static schedules in the presence of control flow.

Third, we perform branch prediction using the PC of branches as they appear in the original execution stream. In a real system, any place code has been replicated, each of those static instances would likely index into different places in the branch predictor. This separation can have negative (*e.g.*, longer training times, more predictor aliasing) and positive (*e.g.*, the streams may be more predictable when separated) affects. We cannot, however, consider this in our simulation infrastructure because our snippets selection is derived from future path information such that many snippet branches are completely biased. By using prediction based on the original program stream, we can ensure that our performance results are not benefiting from any prediction anomalies.

When branch mispredictions occur, their penalties are enforced at the point where the branch was scheduled; that is, post-branch cycles of the schedule are not fetched until the branch itself has executed. This does not however prevent right-path instructions that were scheduled above the branch to execute in parallel with the branch resolution as if they had been hoisted above the branch by the compiler. We are not, however, able to model the contention from wrong path instructions that the compiler might also have desired to hoist above the branch.

3.5 Avoiding Cache Miss-Induced Stalls

Continual Flow Pipelining [46] was originally proposed to give an existing OOO processor a larger effective window without growing complex structures. It does this by "slicing out" instructions transitively dependent on (and stalled by) a load miss (or equivalently any other high-latency event) into a separate queue and re-inserting them in the back-end when the load miss returns. In-order retire still requires that these sliced instructions hold ROB slots, but other resources (physical registers, reservation station slots) can be used for independent work. Notably, this does not allow for load/store queue entries to be reclaimed; dependencies through both registers and memory must be identified to slice out the correct instructions. Once the load miss comes back, the design "rallies", leveraging existing superscalar / SMT front-end hardware to dovetail the slice contents with the fresh instructions still being fetched.

In-order architectures rarely actually stall the processor when they encounter a cache miss ("stall on load"). Instead, they they allow independent instructions to proceed in the pipeline in parallel with the cache fill, but only up to the first instruction which uses the missing memory value, at which point they must stall ("stall on use").

In iCFP (in-order Continual Flow Pipelining) [22], this slice-out mechanism requires the much the same speculative-execution support an OOO does (ROB or equivalent result-buffering queue, load-store alias detection / avoidance), but allows the processor to make independent progress by not stalling on the first use of the result. Instead, iCFP poisons the result of the load and adds it to the slice buffer, and any later instruction that uses a poisoned value is sliced / poisoned in turn. When the miss returns, instructions are re-issued from the slice buffer in parallel to fresh instructions from the front-end (in the usual super-scalar fashion), potentially exposing new misses and MLP.

Since we assume the same speculation support in our experimental machine, iCFP makes an excellent compliment, and allows us to effectively extract another schedule in the shadow of a cache miss. Our implementation slices out the poisoned portions of each issue group into a FIFO, and always rallies to the head of that queue when any miss returns. Rallied issue groups are allowed to merge with fresh groups if they fit together, though no dependence checking is required for this merge due to the use of poison bits. See section 4.1 for its performance impact.

4. Results

In an effort to understand the roles that speculation and dynamism play in contributing to OOO performance, we first attempt to measure their relative contributions by measuring what fraction of OOO performance can be achieved through the OOO's speculation support without its ability to schedule dynamically (Section 4.1). We then move on to understand in what ways does dynamism contribute the remaining performance and to what degree do mechanisms that provide dynamism in the specific circumstances where it most benefits us can substitute for the general dynamism mechanism that is OOO execution (Section 4.2).

4.1 Speculation vs. Dynamism

To understand what fraction of baseline performance is contributed by OOO execution, we begin by comparing the performance of the baseline OOO to a comparably provisioned in-order superscalar, with both machines executing the traditionally compiled code. The

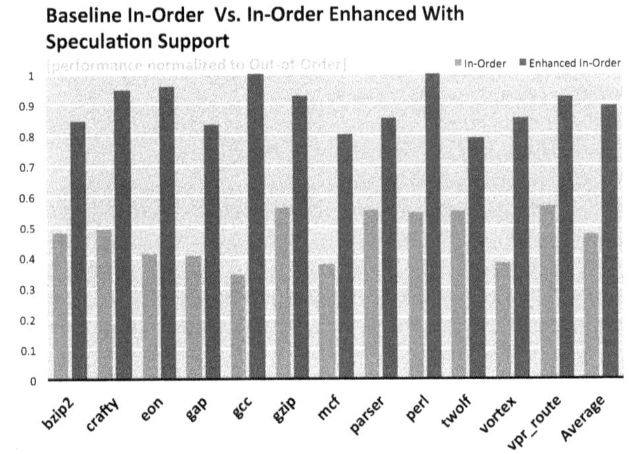

Figure 6. Performance Comparison of the Baseline In-Order and the In-Order Enhanced With Support for Software Speculation

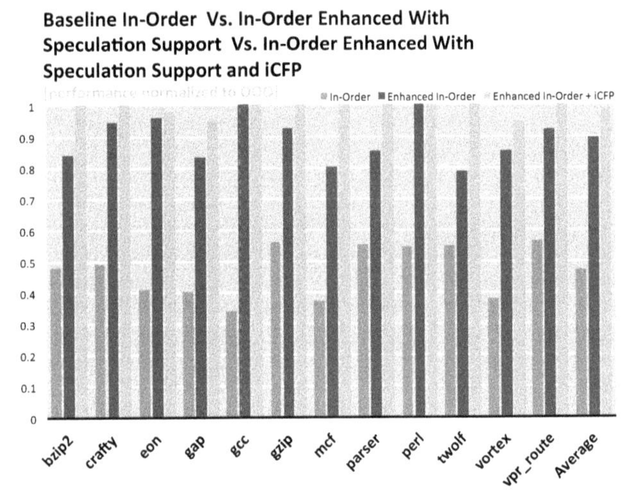

Figure 7. Performance Comparison of the Baseline OOO and the In-Order Enhanced With Support for Software Speculation and iCFP

in-order performance (normalized to the OOO) is shown in the left-most bar of Figure 6. We find the in-order machine to achieve, on average, 47% of the performance of the OOO, which is consistent with previous results [22]. This same work suggests that coupling a comparably provisioned in-order with an advanced run-ahead mechanism, iCFP is only sufficient to reach 57% of the OOO's performance, for the integer programs currently under investigation.

The pre-scheduled code exploits the speculation support of an out-of-order without benefiting from dynamism. Running the pre-scheduled code on the same in-order processor model results in substantially higher performance. As shown in the right bars of Figure 6, the pre-scheduled code achieves 89% of the OOO performance compared to the baseline in-order's 47%. From this data, it appears that it is OOO's ability to generate aggressive schedules, and not its ability to vary these schedules based on dynamic events, which is responsible for most of its performance advantage. Specifically, speculation provides roughly 79% of the gap between the in-order and OOO baselines.

4.2 Understanding Dynamism

By comparing the execution schedules produced by the OOO simulator with that of the pre-scheduled in-order, we observed two situations that seem to contribute the bulk of the performance discrepancy: re-scheduling in the locus of a cache miss and in the locus of a branch misprediction. In an attempt to quantify their relative contributions as well as to understand to what degree these types of dynamism could be captured by mechanisms that are potentially simpler than a general out-of-order mechanism, we undertook two further experiments.

First, we enhanced our simulator to implement a simple implementation of in-order Continual Flow Pipelining (CFP) [22], as described in Section 3.5. The dynamism that iCFP provides is very specialized and at a relatively course granularity. If there are no cache misses, iCFP has no impact on the execution. Upon a cache miss, the program is split into two streams, a miss-dependent stream and a miss-independent stream. Each of these streams retains its existing schedule, but these schedules can slip with respect to each other.

In spite of the somewhat simplistic nature of this dynamism, it seems to provide exactly what the pre-scheduled in-order execution requires. With iCFP, the pre-scheduled code can, on average, achieve 99% of the performance of the OOO, as is shown in Figure 7. We find that this makes a lot of sense. The pre-scheduled code already encodes the code re-ordering that is required for common case good performance, so the fact that iCFP does nothing in the absence of a cache miss is not a problem.

However, even in this configuration, the performance of `eon`, `gap` and `vortex` still lags behind the OOO by 2%, 4.9% and 5.2% respectively. We attribute this performance deficit to the in-order's inferior "recovery after branch mispredict" behavior described in detail in Section 2.2 with visualizations of such behavior excerpted from `eon`, `gap` and `vortex`. As an expedient, we found that simply executing the next 20 instructions after a branch mispredict on the dynamic scheduler enabled these benchmarks to match the OOO's performance; no more than 4% of the total instruction count is directed towards the dynamic scheduler in this manner. We further observed that the schedules discovered by the dynamic scheduler were remarkably stable suggesting a simple software only solution to this performance issue: branch-after-mispredict in which the front-end is redirected to an alternate version of the correct path schedule which is optimized for the instruction readiness that occurs during the mispredict recovery interval.

We also note (but do not show) that the combination of iCFP and speculative scheduling support actually enables the enhanced in-order to surpass the performance of the OOO in some cases. This is due to the fact that while waiting for misses to return, the Execute stage in the enhanced in-order only stalls when the ROB is full. In contrast, the OOO is compelled to stall when the Instruction Queue is full; practical designs generally feature Instruction Queues that have a fraction (typically less than half) of the number of entries contained in the ROB [24].

5. Discussion

The performance of our simulated machine with these harvested schedules suggests that the dynamic flexibility of a full-blown OOO processor is (expensive) over-kill and shows us some of the architectural features a more statically-scheduled processor needs to achieve similar performance.

5.1 Benefit of Dynamism

The primary advantage of a dynamic scheduler is that it can schedule for the dynamically-exposed critical path, without having to store and retrieve those schedules. The OOO gets many schedules from a single set of instructions, while our in-order requires explicit schedules to be provided for every cache-miss and branch-mispredict that it schedules after. While it seems likely that not all of these schedules contribute significantly to performance, the front-end which can support this combinatorial explosion of schedules may be infeasible. We expect that profile-guided JIT compilation could identify the critical misses and mispredicts, and even provide reasonable code-growth, but these does not eliminate our need for low-latency access to a second (or third, or fourth) schedule to execute in the shadow of these unlikely events. The trade off of dynamic scheduling is thus between bringing several schedules to the execution core, or generating them on-site.

5.2 What mechanisms do inorders need to generate OOO-like schedules?

Given the above, there are two pieces of the in-order architecture that are missing.

The first is a scheme for decorating the instruction stream with secondary schedules, to be used in the event of unexpected long-latency events. In the case of a cache miss, this is akin to a "branch-on-cache-miss" where control is revectored based on the hit signal from the data cache similar to the mechanisms proposed in [23] and [1]. This obviously has little advantage if the schedule cannot see the use before the miss returns in addition to the more general problem of generating good miss-handling routines. The other mechanism is a "branch-on-branch-mispredict", where the schedule injected in the front end of the machine might be different, based on whether that path was predicted correctly, or it was the result of a re-steer.

The second piece of the puzzle is a mechanism for doing software alias speculation. The OOO uses a load-store queue to great effect, dynamically teasing out dependencies through memory, which allows for dynamic schedules that are aggressive where a compiler must be conservative. A non-faulting memory instruction, combined with a "branch-on-alias" would allow for the common-case execution to reap the benefits of not-always-safe load hoisting without sacrificing correctness. An OOO may also employ alias-prediction hardware, but the overhead of software scheduling adaptation in the presence of often-aliasing instructions may be prohibitively expensive, so this prediction mechanism may still be desirable (akin to branch prediction) in the in-order design.

6. Related Work

There is an extensive and venerable body of literature focusing on the fundamental advantages and disadvantages of dynamically scheduled hardware particularly in the context of attempting to match the OOO's performance with less complex hardware [4, 7, 30, 38, 44, 50]. While insightful and prescient in many respects especially regarding the scalability of dynamically scheduled hardware, the small memory footprints and low branch complexity of the programs used for comparison purposes in these studies make it challenging for the reader to discern what contribution dynamism, independent of speculation support mechanisms, makes to overall performance. Follow-on studies examined the static vs. dynamic scheduling issue in the context of the emerging memory wall and power-constrained but performance-intensive platforms [15, 39]. These works make strong arguments for a middle-ground between statically and dynamically scheduled hardware particularly due to perceived impending circuit limitations on OOO cycle times as well as concerns over object compatibility with the proposed simpler hardware.

Industry R&D [12] and academia [13] were exploring this middle-ground between statically and dynamically scheduled hardware, ("quasi-dynamic scheduling" in the parlance of rePLay[35]) while contemporaneous commercial processors at two extremes were the Itanium [40] and Transmeta processors [27]. Both the Itanium and Transmeta designs provide extensive hardware support for software speculation; data and control speculation are facilitated by associative structures and non-trapping instructions that the software can manipulate and query. Recovery from misspeculation differs in that the Transmeta design features automatic HW rollback [9] while Itanium exposes explicit rollback and recovery to software. Subsequently, Itanium designs have refined/expanded their HW structures to permit more control and data speculation [31] and the most recently announced version has greater HW support for dynamism [48] in a manner explored by [6]. We also note the encouraging trend of expanded HW support for software speculation, specifically the HW transactional memory systems in IBM's BlueGene/Q and Intel's forthcoming Haswell architecture [25].

Some form of transactional memory or HW atomicity is typically required [33] for quasi-dynamic scheduling but even a limited form combined with specialized functional units can facilitate performance comparable to a narrow-window OOO [8]. Though we do not address it in this work, quasi-dynamic and static scheduling all suffer from the region boundary issue that does not afflict the OOO; the OOO's ability to rotely eliminate control-flow and object code barriers to hoisting instructions is difficult to match both in theory [45, 49] and practice [17]. Matching the OOO's performance requires, at a minimum, the immensely challenging task of devising good predictors that function on large regions [17] while the HW support required to "region slip" is non-trivial.

Coping with memory operations remains problematic for both static and quasi-dynamically scheduled machines as they are typically compelled to stall on the use of an unready register. Simply finding sufficient instructions to cover load-to-use latency on an in-order can be a challenge and can introduce complications as seen in the mispredict recovery examples above. Some proposed solutions include dispatching instructions to latency-specific queues based on latency information encoded into the instructions at compile time [18] to more dataflow oriented ISAs and associated HW [32] though all come at the cost of significantly higher HW complexity and instruction encoding bloat.

Solutions for handling variable latency loads in general purpose in-orders range from the extremely aggressive hardware prefetchers, software prefetching support and runahead execution of the Power6 [5] to more modest compiler-inserted prefetch threads which use an idle SMT context [26]. An excellent overview of runahead techniques that occupy the middle ground between these extremes is provided by [3]. We chose iCFP [22] due to its recentness, its focus on in-order processors and the merits of its "rally" and "advance" modes which collectively enable it to outperform most rival techniques in the literature. We found iCFPs treatment of implementation issues equally compelling, though probably the greatest challenge facing runahead techniques is validation/verification. Finally, the microarchitectural substrate required to implement iCFP (multiple, checkpointed register files, advanced store queue, etc) could also provide HW support for software data and control speculation if these mechanisms were exposed at the ISA level.

Lastly, the observation that the OOO continually generates high quality schedules has motivated several research efforts to capture/re-use these schedules or to allow a compiler/runtime to indicate when dynamic schedules should be generated. The major motivation in this regard has been energy savings, [47, 49], generally at the cost of performance degradation though off-the-critical-path HW rescheduling of ROB traces in [34] yields a performance speedup over the baseline OOO. It must be noted that these approaches invariably execute a significant percentage of their instructions via the dynamic scheduler (upwards of 70%, 45% and 20% for [34, 47, 49] respectively) rather than executing the captured OOO traces on the in-order HW . Our own experiments suggest that even executing only 5% of `bzip2`'s instructions via the dynamic scheduler enhanced performance by 18% relative to executing all instructions on the in-order HW. Finally, a novel and inspirational use of captured OOO schedules was demonstrated in [11] in which programs destined to run on an in-order architecture were first passed through a simulated OOO-version of the architecture, their traces captured and then appropriately patched up (in the form of compensation code for control/data misspeculation) to run directly on the in-order architecture.

7. Conclusions

Out-of-Order processors generally attain higher performance on control intensive integer code than in-order designs, including those with hardware support for software speculation. Conventional wisdom for this disparity in performance is the OOO's ability to avoid head-of-line blocking and exploit far-flung memory-level parallelism; collectively we call this ability "dynamism"; the major enabler for dynamism is the OOO's general-purpose, well-provisioned speculation support mechanisms e.g. large ROB, renamer, Load/Store Queue etc which can rollback speculative state at lower cost than even the most advanced in-order designs. We demonstrated that nearly 88% of the speedup attained by the OOO over an in-order design can be attributed to these speculation support mechanisms alone. Of the remaining performance differential, a complexity-effective run-ahead mechanism, iCFP, was sufficient to close the gap to the OOO in most cases. The final 1-2% performance gap was found to be in the in-order's inability to match the OOO's recovery after a branch mispredict; we proposed and qualified a simple mechanism for addressing this deficiency.

8. Acknowledgments

We are deeply indebted to Naveen Neelakantam and Sara Baghsorkhi, both of Intel Corp., for reviewing an early draft of this work. We also thank the anonymous reviewers for their insightful comments and suggestions. Daniel S. McFarlin was supported by an National Defense Science and Engineering Graduate Fellowship.

References

[1] B. A. Babaian, S. K. Okunev, and V. Y. Volkonsky. Critical path optimization–unload hard extended scalar block. USPTO 6584611, 2001.

[2] R. D. Barnes, J. W. Sias, E. M. Nystrom, S. J. Patel, J. N. Navarro, and W.-m. W. Hwu. Beating in-order stalls with "flea-flicker" two-pass pipelining. *IEEE Trans. Comput.*, 55(1):18–33, Jan. 2006.

[3] A. T. Brian Kreskamp, Pablo Montesinos. Enhancing mlp: Runahead execution and related techniques. IACOMA Technical Report 512, 2005.

[4] M. Butler and Y. Patt. An investigation of the performance of various dynamic scheduling techniques. In *Proceedings of the 25th annual international symposium on Microarchitecture*, MICRO 25, pages 1–9, Los Alamitos, CA, USA, 1992. IEEE Computer Society Press.

[5] H. W. Cain and P. Nagpurkar. Runahead execution vs. conventional data prefetching in the ibm power6 microprocessor. In *ISPASS*, pages 203–212, 2010.

[6] L. Carter, W. Chuang, and B. Calder. An epic processor with pending functional units. In H. Zima, K. Joe, M. Sato, Y. Seo, and M. Shimasaki, editors, *High Performance Computing*, volume 2327 of *Lecture Notes in Computer Science*, pages 445–448. Springer Berlin / Heidelberg, 2006.

[7] P. P. Chang, W. Y. Chen, S. A. Mahlke, and W.-m. W. Hwu. Comparing static and dynamic code scheduling for multiple-instruction-issue processors. In *Proceedings of the 24th annual international symposium on Microarchitecture*, MICRO 24, pages 25–33, New York, NY, USA, 1991. ACM.

[8] A. Deb, J. M. Codina, and A. González. Softhv: a hw/sw co-designed processor with horizontal and vertical fusion. In *Proceedings of the 8th ACM International Conference on Computing Frontiers*, CF '11, pages 1:1–1:10, New York, NY, USA, 2011. ACM.

[9] J. C. Dehnert et al. The Transmeta Code Morphing Software: Using Speculation, Recovery, and Adaptive Retranslation to Address Real-life Challenges. In *Proceedings of the International Symposium on Code Generation and Optimization*, pages 15–24, 2003.

[10] J. Doweck. Inside Intel Core Microarchitecture and Smart Memory Access. Intel Whitepaper, 2006.

[11] M. Dupré, N. Darch, and O. Teman. VHC: Quickly Building an Optimizer for Complex Embedded Architectures. In *Proceedings of the International Symposium on Code Generation and Optimization*, pages 53–64, 2004.

[12] K. Ebcioglu and E. R. Altman. DAISY: Dynamic compilation for 100% architectural compatibility. In *Proceedings of the 24th Annual International Symposium on Computer Architecture*, pages 26–37, June 1997.

[13] B. Fahs et al. Performance Characterization of a Hardware Framework for Dynamic Optimization. In *Proceedings of the 34th Annual IEEE/ACM International Symposium on Microarchitecture*, Dec. 2001.

[14] B. A. Fields, S. Rubin, and R. Bodik. Focusing processor policies via Critical-Path prediction. In *Proceedings of the 28th Annual International Symposium on Computer Architecture*, pages 74–85, July 2001.

[15] J. Fritts and W. Wolf. Evaluation of static and dynamic scheduling for media processors. In *Proceedings of the 2nd Workshop on Media Processors and DSPs*, Micro '00, 2000.

[16] J. S. Gardner. Mips aptiv cores hit the mark. *Microprocessor Report*, May 2012.

[17] M. Gebhart, B. A. Maher, K. E. Coons, J. Diamond, P. Gratz, M. Marino, N. Ranganathan, B. Robatmili, A. Smith, J. Burrill, S. W. Keckler, D. Burger, and K. S. McKinley. An evaluation of the trips computer system. In *Proceedings of the 14th international conference on Architectural support for programming languages and operating systems*, ASPLOS '09, pages 1–12, New York, NY, USA, 2009. ACM.

[18] J. P. Grossman. Cheap out-of-order execution using delayed issue. In *Proceedings of the International Conference of Computer Design*, CD 2000, pages 549 – 551, 2000.

[19] M. Gschwind, H. P. Hofstee, B. Flachs, M. Hopkins, Y. Watanabe, and T. Yamazaki. Synergistic processing in cell's multicore architecture. *IEEE Micro*, 26(2):10–24, Mar. 2006.

[20] T. R. Halfhill. Netlogic doubles up xlp. *Microprocessor Report*, April 2011.

[21] M. Heffernan. *Data-Dependency Graph Transformations for Instruction Scheduling*. PhD thesis, Massachusetts Institute of Technology, 2007.

[22] A. Hilton, S. Nagarakatte, and A. Roth. icfp: Tolerating all-level cache misses in in-order processors. *IEEE Micro*, 30(1):12–19, Jan. 2010.

[23] M. Horowitz, M. Martonosi, T. C. Mowry, and M. D. Smith. Informing memory operations: Providing memory performance feedback in modern processors. In *In Proceedings of the 23rd Annual International Symposium on Computer Architecture*, pages 260–270, 1996.

[24] Intel. Intel 64 and ia-32 architectures optimization reference manual. Intel Technical Manual, 2012.

[25] Intel. Intel architecture instruction set extensions programming reference. Intel Technical Manual, 2012.

[26] D. Kim and D. Yeung. Design and evaluation of compiler algorithms for pre-execution. In *Proceedings of the 10th international conference on Architectural support for programming languages and operating systems*, ASPLOS-X, pages 159–170, New York, NY, USA, 2002. ACM.

[27] A. Klaiber. The Technology Behind Crusoe Processors. Transmeta Whitepaper, Jan. 2000.

[28] H. Q. Le, W. J. Starke, J. S. Fields, F. P. O'Connell, D. Q. Nguyen, B. J. Ronchetti, W. M. Sauer, E. M. Schwarz, and M. T. Vaden. IBM POWER6 microarchitecture. *IBM J. Res. Dev.*, 51:639–662, November 2007.

[29] D. J. Lilja. Reducing the branch penalty in pipelined processors. *Computer*, 21(7):47–55, July 1988.

[30] C. E. Love and H. F. Jordan. An investigation of static versus dynamic scheduling. In *Proceedings of the 17th annual international symposium on Computer Architecture*, ISCA '90, pages 192–201, New York, NY, USA, 1990. ACM.

[31] C. McNairy and D. Soltis. Itanium 2 processor microarchitecture. *IEEE Micro*, 23(2):44–55, Mar. 2003.

[32] R. Nagarajan, S. K. Kushwaha, D. Burger, K. S. McKinley, C. Lin, and S. W. Keckler. Static placement, dynamic issue (spdi) scheduling for edge architectures. In *Proceedings of the 13th International Conference on Parallel Architectures and Compilation Techniques*, PACT '04, pages 74–84, Washington, DC, USA, 2004. IEEE Computer Society.

[33] N. Neelakantam, R. Rajwar, S. Srinivas, U. Srinivasan, and C. Zilles. Hardware atomicity for reliable software speculation. In *Proceedings of the 34th International Symposium on Computer Architecture*, pages 174–185, 2007.

[34] O. Palomar, T. Juan, and J. J. Navarro. Reusing cached schedules in an out-of-order processor with in-order issue logic. In *Proceedings of the 2009 IEEE international conference on Computer design*, ICCD'09, pages 246–253, Piscataway, NJ, USA, 2009. IEEE Press.

[35] S. J. Patel and S. S. Lumetta. rePLay: A Hardware Framework for Dynamic Optimization. *IEEE Transactions on Computers*, 50(6):590–608, 2001.

[36] S. J. Patel, T. Tung, S. Bose, and M. M. Crum. Increasing the size of atomic instruction blocks using control flow assertions. In *Proceedings of the 33rd annual ACM/IEEE international symposium on Microarchitecture*, MICRO 33, pages 303–313, New York, NY, USA, 2000. ACM.

[37] N. Ranganathan, R. Nagarajan, D. Jimnez, D. Burger, S. W. Keckler, and C. Lin. Combining hyperblocks and exit prediction to increase front-end bandwidth and performance. Technical report, 2002.

[38] B. R. Rau. Dynamically scheduled vliw processors. In *Proceedings of the 26th annual international symposium on Microarchitecture*, MICRO 26, pages 80–92, Los Alamitos, CA, USA, 1993. IEEE Computer Society Press.

[39] K. W. Rudd and M. J. Flynn. Instruction-level parallel processors-dynamic and static scheduling tradeoffs. In *Proceedings of the 2nd AIZU International Symposium on Parallel Algorithms / Architecture Synthesis*, PAS '97, pages 74–, Washington, DC, USA, 1997. IEEE Computer Society.

[40] H. Sharangpani and K. Arora. Itanium processor microarchitecture. *IEEE Micro*, 20(5):24–43, Sept. 2000.

[41] J. L. Shin, H. Park, H. Li, A. Smith, Y. Choi, H. Sathianathan, S. Dash, S. Turullols, S. Kim, R. Masleid, G. Konstadinidis, R. T. Golla, M. J. Doherty, G. Grohoski, and C. McAllister. The next-generation 64b sparc core in a t4 soc processor. In *ISSCC*, pages 60–62, 2012.

[42] G. Shobaki. *Optimal Global Instruction Scheduling Using Enumeration*. PhD thesis, University of California Davis, 2006.

[43] G. Shobaki, K. Wilken, and M. Heffernan. Optimal trace scheduling using enumeration. *ACM Trans. Archit. Code Optim.*, 5(4):19:1–19:32, Mar. 2009.

[44] M. D. Smith, M. Horowitz, and M. S. Lam. Efficient superscalar performance through boosting. In *Proceedings of the 5th International Conference on Architectural Support for Programming Languages and Operating Systems*, pages 248–259, 1992.

[45] F. Spadini, B. Fahs, S. Patel, and S. S. Lumetta. Improving quasi-dynamic schedules through region slip. In *Proceedings of the international symposium on Code generation and optimization: feedback-directed and runtime optimization*, CGO '03, pages 149–158, Washington, DC, USA, 2003. IEEE Computer Society.

[46] S. T. Srinivasan, R. Rajwar, H. Akkary, A. Gandhi, and M. Upton. Continual flow pipelines. In *Proceedings of the 11th international conference on Architectural support for programming languages and operating systems*, ASPLOS-XI, pages 107–119, New York, NY, USA, 2004. ACM.

[47] E. Talpes and D. Marculescu. Execution cache-based microarchitecture power-efficient superscalar processors. *IEEE Trans. Very Large Scale Integr. Syst.*, 13(1):14–26, Jan. 2005.

[48] S. Undy. Poulson: An 8 core 32nm next generation intel itanium processor, 2011.

[49] M. G. Valluri, L. K. John, and K. S. McKinley. Low-power, low-complexity instruction issue using compiler assistance. In *Proceedings of the 19th annual international conference on Supercomputing*, ICS '05, pages 209–218, New York, NY, USA, 2005. ACM.

[50] D. W. Wall. Limits of instruction-level parallelism. *SIGARCH Comput. Archit. News*, 19(2):176–188, Apr. 1991.

[51] M. T. Yourst and K. Ghose. Incremental commit groups for non-atomic trace processing. In *Proceedings of the 38th annual IEEE/ACM International Symposium on Microarchitecture*, MICRO 38, pages 67–80, Washington, DC, USA, 2005. IEEE Computer Society.

Iago Attacks: Why the System Call API is a Bad Untrusted RPC Interface

Stephen Checkoway
Johns Hopkins University
s@cs.jhu.edu

Hovav Shacham
UC San Diego
hovav@cs.ucsd.edu

Abstract

In recent years, researchers have proposed systems for running trusted code on an untrusted operating system. Protection mechanisms deployed by such systems keep a malicious kernel from directly manipulating a trusted application's state. Under such systems, the application and kernel are, conceptually, peers, and the system call API defines an RPC interface between them.

We introduce *Iago attacks*, attacks that a malicious kernel can mount in this model. We show how a carefully chosen sequence of integer return values to Linux system calls can lead a supposedly protected process to act against its interests, and even to undertake arbitrary computation at the malicious kernel's behest.

Iago attacks are evidence that protecting applications from malicious kernels is more difficult than previously realized.

Categories and Subject Descriptors D.4.6 [*Operating Systems*]: Security and Protection

General Terms Security

Keywords Iago attacks, system call, Overshadow

1. Introduction

The prospect of running trusted tasks or processes on an untrusted operating system is a tantalizing one. Legacy operating systems are complicated and possibly untrustworthy systems, and retargeting an application written for a legacy OS to run on another, supposedly secure new OS may be prohibitively expensive. Retargeting is also not an option if we wish to provide trusted facilities (such as keyboard input [18]) to legacy applications.

But how is it possible to protect a task from the operating system running it? Every interaction between a userland process and the outside world is mediated by the kernel. A malicious kernel could lead a trusted process astray by falsifying its inputs. Furthermore, the kernel runs at higher privilege on the processor, and is specifically charged with managing application memory. A malicious kernel could read an application's secrets from memory, or cause an application to misbehave arbitrarily by modifying its program code.

In the last few years, researchers have proposed systems intended to achieve precisely the objective above: to run trusted code on an untrusted operating system. These proposed systems insinuate a supervisory module at high privilege that cooperates with the trusted application to isolate and protect it from the potentially malicious kernel. The supervisory module may derive its privilege from trusted hardware, as in XOMOS [14] and Flicker [15–17], or from running as a hypervisor, as in Overshadow [6, 22].

ASPLOS'13, March 16–20, 2013, Houston, Texas, USA.

Listing 1. A Linux program that can be completely compromised by an Iago attack.

```
#include <stdlib.h>
int main() {
    void *p = malloc(100);
}
```

In this paper, we give evidence that protecting applications from malicious kernels is more difficult than previously realized. For concreteness, we make particular reference to the design of Overshadow. We stress, however, that it is not our intention to single out Overshadow. Instead, we consider an abstract Overshadow-style system that prevents a malicious kernel from manipulating the protected application's memory and other resources. Under such a system, the application and kernel are, conceptually, peers, and the system call API defines an RPC interface between them. We illustrate this conceptual relationship in Figure 1, on the next page.

In our main contribution, we describe attacks that a malicious kernel can mount in this model. Specifically, we show how a carefully chosen sequence of integer return values to Linux system calls can lead a supposedly protected process astray. In many cases, including Linux programs as simple as that given in Listing 1, our attacks induce *arbitrary computation* in the protected program. (See Section 4.3 for details of our attack on the program in Listing 1.) We call our attacks *Iago attacks* because our malicious kernel convinces the application to act against its interests simply by communicating with it.

Some of the systems listed above, such as Flicker, provide only a narrow interface between the trusted component and the untrusted OS, and may therefore not be vulnerable to Iago attacks. The stated design goal of other systems listed above — notably, Overshadow — is protecting legacy applications that make general-purpose system calls and run on untrusted legacy operating systems such as Linux.

Overshadow The Overshadow system, proposed by Chen et al. [6] at ASPLOS 2008, allows legacy applications to run, without modification, on an untrusted kernel.

The fundamental technique introduced by Overshadow is *cloaking*. When the application is running, its memory is mapped normally. At other times, including when the kernel handles a system call on the application's behalf, the application's memory is encrypted and authenticated. Encryption keeps the kernel from reading application memory, and authentication keeps the kernel from modi-

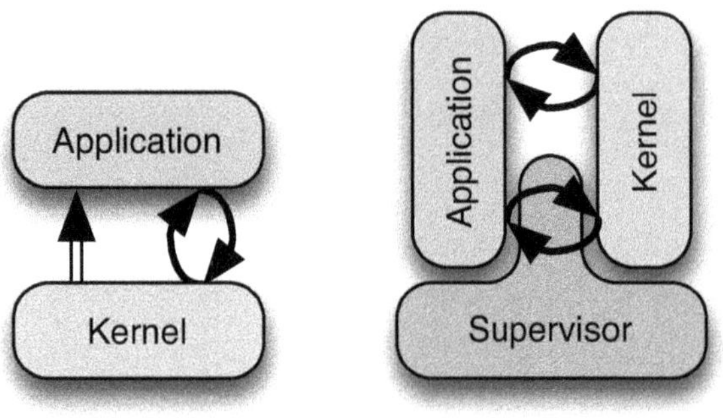

(a) Unprotected **(b)** Protected

Figure 1. Software stack abstraction for (a) unprotected systems and (b) systems protected by an Overshadow-like mechanism. In an unprotected system, the application communicates with the kernel via system calls. Additionally, the kernel is free to read and write application memory at will. In a protected system, the application and kernel are peers which communicate either directly via system calls, as with an unprotected system, or through supervisor intermediation. At no point is the kernel able to directly read or write protected application memory.

fying application memory. The Overshadow monitor interposes on application-kernel switches to swap between the two views. Overshadow uses virtualization to make cloaking efficient.

A sophisticated system of shims for system calls marshals data between the application and the kernel. Some system calls are modified extensively; for example, Overshadow applications use `mmap()` instead of `read()` and `write()` for secure file I/O. Other system calls, such as `getpid()`, are considered safe and not interposed on [6, Section 6.1].

As we noted above, the Overshadow system's stated security goal is to run general-purpose legacy applications, unmodified, on arbitrary untrusted kernels. Overshadow's authors write:

> Overshadow protects *legacy* applications from the commodity operating systems running them ... it requires *no changes* to existing operating systems or applications ... Overshadow is backwards-compatible, protecting a broad range of *unmodified legacy* applications, managed by unmodified commodity operating systems *[emphasis added]*.

Our thesis, in this paper, is that mechanisms for protection against malicious kernels are better suited to protecting specialized processes whose limited interface with the OS has been carefully considered, rather than unmodified, general-purpose, legacy applications.

Subsequent work by Ports and Garfinkel [22] reconsidered and refined the security properties provided by Overshadow. Ports and Garfinkel proposed extensions to Overshadow that prevent a variety of attacks by a malicious OS on a protected application. For example, they observe that incorrect mapping of process IDs can lead to signal misdelivery. To prevent this attack, Ports and Garfinkel associate a "secure process ID" with each process. This secure process ID, which is independent of the usual process ID managed by the OS, is communicated to the parent process on `fork()` and is used for reliable signal delivery.

The attacks considered and protected against are similar to our Iago attacks. However, Ports and Garfinkel are concerned with maintaining semantic guarantees for OS services (e.g., time, entropy, the filesystem, mutual exclusion from critical sections, reliable interprocess communication) in the face of OS misbehavior. By contrast, we show how a malicious kernel can use system call return values in ways not related to the semantic content of these system calls. In some cases, our attacks can cause a protected process to undertake arbitrary computation.

Threat model We consider a trusted application running on a malicious kernel. We assume that the application is unmodified and linked against unmodified system libraries, though the implementation of specific library functions might be modified by the protection system.

The kernel is kept by the protection system from directly reading or manipulating the application's state. The kernel still handles system calls on behalf of the application, however. We assume that it can provide return values of its choice to system calls made by the application. We focus on scalar return values: for example, the `ssize_t` return value of the `read` system call rather than the buffer filled as a result of the read.

The kernel's goal is to subvert the trusted application into disclosing its secrets or behaving otherwise than intended. In the limit, the kernel's goal is to cause the application to undertake arbitrary computation. Simple denial of service is not in scope, because a malicious kernel could always crash or just refuse to boot.

Costs and benefits of abstraction Our threat model abstracts away the details of how applications are protected from a malicious kernel. The benefits of this abstraction are, first, that our findings may be applicable to more than just one protection mechanism and, second, that we are able to run concrete experiments using an off-the-shelf Linux environment. The cost is that we cannot say with certainty that any attacks we identify will actually apply to a specific protection mechanism: It is possible that special-case handling that we have overlooked makes our attacks impossible on some particular system. (We emphatically *do not* claim that we have broken the Overshadow system.)

We believe that the tradeoffs favor studying the problem in the abstract, as we do. In exhibiting attacks that require no other affordance than the system call API, we focus attention on this API as the crux of security in this setting. That is, even a perfect defense mechanism that makes the kernel an untrusted peer to applications is not, by itself, sufficient to secure these applications from attack.

Note that, while we necessarily abstracted Overshadow's protection mechanisms, the actual attacks we describe and mount are absolutely concrete.

Our contributions We make the following contributions:

1. We introduce Iago attacks — attacks in which a malicious kernel induces a protected process to act against its interests by manipulating system call return values — and give a threat model for them.
2. We implement a platform for experimenting with Iago attacks on Linux systems. We add hooks to the Linux kernel and implement a kernel module which contains the bulk of the attack code.
3. We demonstrate Iago attacks against Linux applications. In many cases, our attacks induce arbitrary computation in the protected program. We validate these attacks using our experimentation platform.

The rest of this paper is organized as follows. We begin with a "warmup" and motivating example, showing how an Iago attack that manipulates `getpid()` return values allows connection replay against Apache mod_ssl. We next describe our architecture for experimenting with Iago attacks. Then, we describe our main technical result, an Iago attack that induces arbitrary code execution in any Linux process that uses the `malloc()` C library function. This is followed by a different Iago attack that targets programs using the OpenSSL library. Finally, we consider what makes such Iago attacks possible, and suggest directions for future research.

2. SSL Replay and getpid()

An important challenge for trusted applications running on untrusted kernels is communicating with the outside world. For communicating with a local user, such an application will require a trusted path to input and output devices. On the other hand, a trusted application that wishes to communicate with a remote user or service faces exactly the traditional network security problem (with the kernel as an active network adversary). Cryptography is well suited for solving this problem; for example, Chen et al. [6] propose the use of the SSL protocol. Implementing an SSL server on an untrusted kernel is not trivial; indeed, as Ports and Garfinkel observe [22], applications use the kernel as their source of cryptographic randomness. Failure by an application to obtain strong randomness from the kernel can have catastrophic results, as with the Debian PRNG bug [29].

Ports and Garfinkel propose that the trusted supervisor intercept application reads from entropy sources such as `/dev/random` to supply randomness to the application. In this section, we observe that preventing cryptographic randomness vulnerabilities in trusted applications is more subtle than just providing a source of strong randomness. In particular, we show that an Iago attack targeting a seemingly innocuous system call — `getpid()` — allows replay attacks on Apache servers with mod_ssl.

Background: SSL and Apache Before explaining our attack, we briefly recall the SSL protocol and the architecture of mod_ssl.

An SSL protocol interaction begins with a handshake. The handshake allows the client and server to pick session parameters; to establish shared cryptographic secrets; and to verify the identities of one or both against the public-key infrastructure. The shared cryptographic secrets are derived from public nonces contributed by both client and server (called the client random and server random) and from a secret value that, in the most common configuration (RSA key exchange without ephemeral Diffie-Hellman), is contributed by the client alone. (For the details of the SSL handshake, see Rescorla [25].)

As a consequence, the only protection that SSL provides a server against session replay is the server random value. If an SSL server can be made to reuse a server random value from some legitimate connection, an attacker can replay the packets of that connection. The SSL server will accept the connection, verify and decrypt the application-protocol packets, and pass their contents on to higher-layer code for processing. If the higher-layer code does not itself defend against replay, this weakness can allow attackers to repeat actions that authorized users intended to occur just once. For example, a single transfer of money using PayPal could turn into several transfers of the same amount.

SSL functionality in the Apache Web server is implemented by the mod_ssl extension, which itself is built on the OpenSSL library. In the usual configuration, The Apache parent process performs all initialization tasks, then forks child processes that will handle incoming requests. Crucially, the OpenSSL entropy pool used by mod_ssl to generate randomness for the SSL protocol is seeded with entropy from the kernel only in the parent process. Every child process inherits an identical entropy pool when forked. The child processes avoid generating the same randomness by stirring into their entropy pools values that are not secret but that should be distinct: the process ID, obtained with `getpid()`, and the system time in seconds, obtained with `time()`.[1] For more details, see Ristenpart and Yilek [26].

The attack Given the facts above, mounting a connection-replay Iago attack is straightforward. The kernel records the packets sent by a client to an Apache child process. It then fakes a network connection to another child process, and replays the recorded packets to the child. When the child makes `getpid()` and `time()` system calls to stir its entropy pool, the kernel responds with the same values with which it responded to the child that handled the legitimate connection. Ristenpart and Yilek have experimentally verified the feasibility of essentially this attack, in the context of virtual machine rewinding vulnerabilities [26].

If the supervisor provides secure time to trusted applications, the kernel will need to perform replay within a one-second window; otherwise, there is no limit on how long replay is possible.

Different randomness will be generated in subsequent connections to a child process, but the kernel can simply crash each child after a connection, causing the Apache parent to fork a replacement child with the same initial entropy pool.

Lessons While the attack described above allows connection replay against the most popular Unix SSL server, it is more interesting for relying on such seemingly innocuous system calls as `getpid()`. Apache mod_ssl is not using the process ID for its semantic value as an identifier for a process (for example for sending it signals); instead, it is using it as a nonrepeating nonce. A supervisor mechanism for ensuring reliable signal delivery will not necessarily address this non-semantic use of `getpid()`. (Indeed, who is to say that a repeating process ID is unreasonable? The kernel could cause a child to crash and, when the parent forks a new child in its place, give that child the same process ID the crashed child had.)

One might argue that this attack could be prevented by having child processes obtain additional strong entropy from the operating system. But the fact is that Apache as written does not do this, and in this paper we are considering systems to protect off-the-shelf applications. In addition, there are good reasons why Apache is written the way that it is: most importantly, child processes may run with restricted privileges, and may not have access to `/dev/random` or other sources of entropy.

3. Iago infrastructure

In this section, we briefly describe our implementation of a malicious kernel. Readers not interested in these details are encouraged to skip to the next section.

To create a malicious kernel to carry out the Iago attacks, we started with Debian revision 35 of version 2.6.32 of the Linux kernel. In order to ease development of the Iago attacks, we modified the kernel as little as possible, pushing most of the implementation of the attacks to a kernel module that could be easily loaded and unloaded at runtime. The separation allows easy development and testing of the attacks.

Changes in the kernel proper consisted of providing hooks for process creation and termination as well as the addition of a new member, `struct shadow_state *ss`, in the `mm_struct` structure — the structure which maintains all of the state for a process's memory map. The `shadow_state` structure contains function pointers for the malicious implementation of the `brk`, `mmap2`, and `munmap` system calls. At process creation time, if the kernel module is loaded and wishes to attack the process, it can set `ss` to point to a particular `shadow_state` instance whose function pointer members are initialized to point to the desired, malicious functionality. To enable the use of the standard, nonmalicious functions in the module, the kernel exports symbols corresponding to the "real" functions which can be called as needed.

The implementation of the three system calls is changed to check if the `ss` member is non-`NULL` and if so if the function pointer corresponding to the system call is non-`NULL`. If both are non-`NULL`, then the function pointed to by the pointer is used; otherwise the real function is called. For example, the complete implementation of the `brk` system call is given in Listing 2. The others are similar. Note the calls to `down_write()` and `up_write()`. These are to lock

[1] In cryptographic terms, this is called domain separation.

Listing 2. New implementation of the `brk` system call.

```
SYSCALL_DEFINE1(brk,
                unsigned long, brk)
{
    unsigned long retvalue;
    struct mm_struct *mm;
    struct shadow_state *ss;
    mm = current->mm;
    down_write(&mm->mmap_sem);
    ss = mm->ss;
    if (unlikely(ss != NULL) &&
        ss->brk != NULL)
        retvalue = (*ss->brk)(brk);
    else
        retvalue = real_brk(brk);
    up_write(&mm->mmap_sem);
    return retvalue;
}
```

Table 1. Lines of code for each component of our malicious kernel. The number for the kernel is the sum of the number of lines added (129) and the number of lines deleted (12). The kernel module is separated into the core — which includes the code for the sysfs interface, as well as the process creation and exit hooks — and the profiles described in Sections 4 and 5.

Component	lines of code
kernel	141
module core	354
malloc profile	111
openssl profile	111

and unlock the read/write semaphore that protects the `mm_struct` structure. In fact, a significant fraction of the implementation is concerned solely with avoiding race conditions and deadlocks, including handling the module being unloaded in the middle of an active Iago attack.

The majority of the Iago attacks is implemented as a kernel module. When the module is loaded, it installs hooks for process creation and exit and exports a simple control interface using the sysfs pseudo file-system. The sysfs interface allows executables on disk to be associated with a *profile*.

A profile is the implementation of a particular attack and consists of a malicious implementation of the system calls the attack requires. When a process is created after the module has been loaded, the process creation hook is called. If the executable on disk has been associated with a profile, then the process's `mm->ss` member is set to an appropriately filled `shadow_state` structure. As the program executes, the relevant system calls are handled by the code for the profile as described above.

The effort to construct a malicious kernel from a nonmalicious kernel is relatively minor. Table 1 shows a breakdown of the amount of code written.

In principle, the `read` (or any other system call) could be handled in the same manner. However, since the *behavior* of `read` does not need to change for our attacks, we rely on normal input redirection or socket behavior to supply the necessary data.

Similarly, one could easily modify the kernel to prevent address space layout randomization (ASLR). A process can inhibit the randomization of its children in Linux by calling the `personality()` function with the `ADDR_NO_RANDOMIZE` bit

Table 2. Standard I/O functions which read files [23].

`fgetc()`	`getchar_unlocked()`
`fgets()`	`getdelim()`
`fread()`	`getline()`
`fscanf()`	`gets()`
`getc()`	`scanf()`
`getc_unlocked()`	`vfscanf()`
`getchar()`	`vscanf()`

of the argument set. Since it is easiest to work with a consistent address space layout including stack location, all of our victim programs are launched via a helper program which sets the arguments and environment to a known state, performs input and output redirection, and disables ASLR.

4. Compromising any program using `malloc()`

In this section, we show how any program which uses `malloc()` — including the 4-line program in Listing 1 — can be induced to perform arbitrary code execution by a malicious kernel that behaves exactly like a normal kernel except for some carefully chosen return values for standard Linux system calls. We describe the attack in stages.

4.1 `mmap()` and `read()`

For the first stage, consider the following code fragment

```
p = mmap(NULL, 1024, prot,
         flags, -1, 0);
read(fd, p, 1024);
```

which memory maps a 1024 byte region of memory via the `mmap2` system call and then reads up to 1024 bytes into it from a file descriptor using the `read` system call. This fragment of code is vulnerable to an Iago attack.

Since the kernel is responsible for memory management, a malicious kernel can return an address that is *not* a newly allocated memory region, but rather is an address on the stack. When the `read` occurs, the stack will be overwritten with up to 1024 bytes of the kernel's choice. At this point, a saved return address on the stack may be overwritten and the program can be coerced into executing a return-oriented program [27].

4.2 Standard I/O

Most programs do not themselves use the `mmap()` and `read()` functions; however, any program that uses standard I/O functions to read from a file — such as those listed in Table 2 — does. In particular, standard I/O functions like `fread()` perform I/O buffering for performance reasons. A buffer sized to hold one file system block, typically 4096 bytes, is allocated by `mmap()` in the EGLIBC internal function `_IO_file_doallocate()` and filled by the `_IO_new_file_underflow()` function which calls `read()`.

As before, the kernel can respond to the `mmap2` call with the address of a saved return address on the stack and then respond to `read` with a return-oriented program. In this way, any program that performs file input using the standard I/O functions is vulnerable.

4.3 Malloc

By carefully responding to `brk` system calls, a malicious kernel can confuse malloc into writing a single word of the kernel's choice into the application's memory. How this is accomplished depends heavily on the specifics of the operation of the malloc implementation and how it interacts with the system call wrappers in the rest of libc. We describe this in detail below.

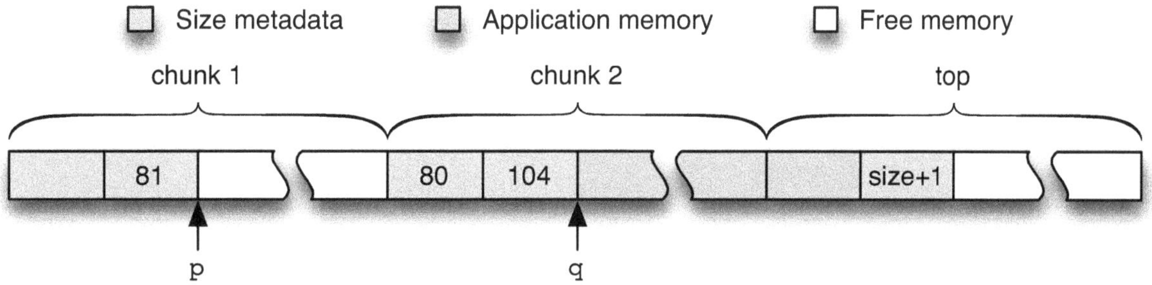

Figure 2. The state of the heap after the following function calls.

```
void *p = malloc(72);
void *q = malloc(100);
free(p);
```

chunk 1 has a size of 80 bytes (72 plus 4 for metadata plus 4 to get an 8 byte alignment) and has the `PREV_INUSE` bit set since it is the first chunk (hence a `size` field of 81 rather than 80).
chunk 2 has a size of 104 bytes (100 plus 4 for metadata) and the `PREV_INUSE` bit is clear, because `p` was freed, so the size of chunk 1 is stored in `prev_size`. Since this chunk is in use, the application memory extends into what would otherwise be the `prev_size` field of the top chunk.
top is the top-most chunk. It is always free and always has the `PREV_INUSE` bit set.
Note that pointers `p` and `q` point 8 bytes after the start of their corresponding chunks.

The version of malloc used in EGLIBC 2.1.2 is a substantially modified version of ptmalloc2 by Wolfram Gloger based on Doug Lea's dlmalloc. EGLIBC's malloc is cleanly separated into upper and lower halves. The upper half is responsible for allocating and freeing regions of memory for the application by requesting a new region of memory from the lower half, splitting and merging free regions, managing a menagerie of free lists, and generally performing the bookkeeping necessary to handle application requests. It implements the public functions specified by the C99 standard [7, Section 7.20.3] including `malloc()` and `free()`. This half is, by now, well studied in the literature [1, 3, 4, 13, 21]. The lower half, by contrast, is tasked with claiming and releasing pages of memory from and to the operating system. It is this half that we are most interested in.

Malloc's view of allocated memory is different from the application programmer's. Every region of allocated memory tracked by malloc is called a *chunk*. Broadly speaking, there are three types of chunks, chunks that are in use by the program, free chunks, and the special "top" chunk which can grow and shrink as malloc's lower half requests memory from and returns memory to the system. Each chunk contains the metadata necessary to free the chunk, place it on free lists, and coalesce it with adjacent chunks. (Having inline metadata is not the only way to structure an allocator, see Novark and Berger for a concise overview of several approaches [19, Section 2].) A chunk is defined as

```
struct malloc_chunk {
     size_t prev_size;
     size_t size;
     /* ... */
};
```

where the elided members are for managing doubly-linked lists of chunks. The least-significant bit of the `size` member is the `PREV_INUSE` bit. If it is set, then the previous chunk is in use (or is not tracked by malloc). Otherwise, it is free and the `prev_size` member contains its size. The second-least-significant bit of `size` is the `IS_MMAPPED` bit and it is set if the chunk was allocated using `mmap()`. (The third-least-significant bit is also metadata other than the size but it is not important here.) After a chunk is created to satisfy an application request, `malloc()` returns the address 8 bytes past the start of the chunk; that is, the address of memory after the `size` member.[2] This is the view of the allocated memory that the programmer has.

The only member that is always needed when a chunk is in use is the `size` member. The `prev_size` member is only needed when the preceding chunk is free. As a result, `prev_size` can share space with the preceding chunk and the members for managing the linked lists can share space with the application memory. Thus, each chunk has only a 4 byte overhead.

Figure 2 shows the three chunks — chunk 1, chunk 2, and top — that result after several calls to `malloc()` and `free()`. First, memory is allocated from the system by the lower half of malloc, described below, to produce top. Then, chunk 1 and chunk 2 are split off from top and pointers to the application region of the chunk is returned to the program. Finally chunk 1 is freed and the `PREV_INUSE` bit and the `prev_size` member of chunk 2 are set resulting in the values in memory shown in the figure.

When malloc's upper half needs more memory, because it cannot satisfy a request from the free chunks, for example, it calls the internal function `sYSMALLOc()`, passing the size of memory it needs to accommodate the `malloc()` request, including 4 bytes for the `size` member, and maintaining 8 byte alignment. If `sYSMALLOc()` can satisfy the request, it will return a pointer to the application memory of a chunk of the requested size as well as potentially modifying the top chunk.

A simplified description of the algorithm used by the internal function `sYSMALLOc()` is given in Algorithm 1. This omits all error handling not essential for our purposes, allocations on threads other than the main thread, and issues of noncontiguous allocations including applications calling `__sbrk()` themselves. The `set_size()` function sets the size member of a chunk; `chunk2mem()` returns the application's view of the chunk, namely, it returns the address 8 bytes past the beginning of the chunk; and `chunk_at_offset(chunk, offset)` treats the memory at address `chunk + offset` as a chunk.

[2] On 64 bit systems, `size_t` is typically 8 bytes so the address returned by `malloc()`, in that case, is 16 bytes past the start of the chunk. For concreteness, we focus on the 32 bit case.

Algorithm 1 A simplified version of the `sYSMALLOc` algorithm.

```
1: function sYSMALLOc(nb)                                ▷ nb is the request size in bytes plus 4 aligned to an 8 byte boundrary
2:   if nb > mmap_threshold then
3:     size ← nb + 4 aligned to a page boundary
4:     p ← mmap(size)
5:     if mmap() call succeeded then
6:       set_size(p, size|IS_MMAPPED)
7:       return chunk2mem(p)
8:   top_size ← the size of the top chunk
9:   size ← nb + top_pad + 8 − top_size aligned to a page boundrary
10:  brk ← __sbrk(size)
11:  if __sbrk() call failed then
12:    Add the size of the current top chunk, top_size, back into size and align to a page boundrary
13:    if size < 1 MB then
14:      size ← 1 MB
15:    brk ← mmap(size)
16:    if mmap() call succeeded then
17:      top ← brk
18:      set_size(top, size|PREV_INUSE)
19:  else
20:    if brk is the end of the top chunk then
21:      set_size(top, (size + top_size)|PREV_INUSE)     ▷ extend the top chunk by size
22:    else                                               ▷ first call to malloc()
23:      let correction be the number of bytes needed to ensure chunk2mem(brk) is 8-byte aligned
24:      if correction > 0 then
25:        brk ← brk + correction
26:      correction ← correction + top_size               ▷ this was subtracted out in line 9
27:      extend correction so that brk + size + correction ends on a page boundrary
28:      snd_brk ← __sbrk(correction)
29:      if __sbrk() call failed then                     ▷ determine where the end of the allocated memory lies
30:        correction ← 0
31:        snd_brk ← __sbrk(0)
32:      top ← brk
33:      set_size(top, (snd_brk − brk + correction)|PREV_INUSE))
34:  p ← top
35:  size ← the size of the top chunk
36:  if size > nb + 8 then
37:    top ← chunk_at_offset(top, nb)
38:    set_size(p, nb|PREV_INUSE)                         ▷ allocate nb bytes
39:    set_size(top, (size − nb)|PREV_INUSE)
40:    return chunk2mem(p)
41:  return NULL
```

Lines 2–7 handle the case where the requested size nb meets the threshold to be allocated directly by `mmap()`. Lines 8–10 attempt to extend the program's data memory using `__sbrk()` far enough to accommodate the request along with some additional padding. If `__sbrk()` fails, then lines 11–18 resort to allocating at least one megabyte of memory using `mmap()` which will become the new top chunk shortly. In the common case, `__sbrk()` will succeed and will furthermore have extended the space previously allocated by an `__sbrk()`. If so, then the size of the top chunk is set to be the old size plus the size of the newly allocated region; line 21. The first time `sYSMALLOc()` is called, there will have been no previous call to `__sbrk()` and thus no space to extend so lines 23–33 will perform the initial setup which consists of ensuring the beginning and ending alignment of the memory is correct. (This code path is also taken in the event the `__sbrk()` on line 10 failed but the `mmap()` succeeded.) Finally, if any of the allocation paths have succeeded in creating a top chunk that is large enough to satisfy the request, then line 37–40 will split an nb-sized chunk off and return a pointer to the application memory region.

The alignment fixup the first time `sYSMALLOc()` is called in lines 23–33 is to ensure that chunks that are split from the top chunk are 8-byte aligned and that the top chunk ends on a page boundary. We can use the interaction of the three calls to `__sbrk()` (lines 10, 28, and 31) to control where malloc thinks the data memory starts and ends. This is integral to confusing it into writing a word of our choice at a memory location also of our choice. To see how we can accomplish this, we need to look at the details of the `__sbrk()` function, the `__brk()` wrapper function, and the `brk` system call.

At the lowest level, the `brk` system call takes as an argument the requested new program break — the end of the process's data memory — and is supposed to return the break that results from the call. In the special case that the argument is 0, `brk` just returns the current break without changing it. The EGLIBC wrapper function `__brk()` takes the requested break as an argument and returns 0 if the break returned by the system call is at least as great as the requested break and -1 otherwise. EGLIBC maintains a global variable `__curbrk` which is initially `NULL` but is updated with

Algorithm 2 Pseudocode for the `__sbrk()` function.

```
function __sbrk(increment)
    if __curbrk = NULL then
        __brk(0)
    if increment = 0 then
        return __curbrk
    oldbrk ← __curbrk
    if oldbrk + increment does not overflow then
        if __brk(oldbrk + increment) = 0 then
            return oldbrk
    return −1
```

the result of the `brk` system call in `__brk()`, even if `__brk()` ultimately returns an error.

By contrast, the `__sbrk()` function takes an amount by which the break should be incremented and returns the previous value of the break if it is able to extend the break by at least that amount, otherwise it returns −1. Algorithm 2 contains the pseudocode for `__sbrk()`.

In order to control where malloc thinks the start and end of the data memory region lie, the kernel only needs to respond appropriately to the `brk` system calls. To see this, assume the kernel wants malloc to think the start of kernel memory is at address S and the end lies at address E and that the first call to `sYSMALLOc()` has argument nb which is less than the threshold for using `mmap()`. Since malloc will ensure that its start of data memory is on an 8-byte boundary, assume that S is also on an 8-byte boundary.

At line 10, `sYSMALLOc()` will call `__sbrk()` passing in some positive increment $size > nb$. Since this is the first time `__sbrk()` has been called, `__curbrk` is `NULL` and so `__brk(0)` is called to set it. At this point, the kernel responds to the `brk` system call with $S - 1$. Since the increment is positive, `__brk()` is called with argument $S - 1 + size$. The kernel responds to the second `brk` system call with $S - 1 + size$, exactly as requested and thus `__sbrk()` returns $S - 1$.

Since the `__sbrk()` call succeeded and this is the first call to `sYSMALLOc()`, it will determine that it needs to increase brk by 1 on line 25 to reach an 8-byte alignment. It will then call `__sbrk()` a second time (line 28) with an additional correction so that the ending address ends on a page boundary. This causes a third and final `brk` system call. The kernel returns E. If E is less than the requested break, which it will be for our use, then `__curbreak` will be set to E and `__sbrk()` will return −1. Finally, `__sbrk()` is called a final time (line 31) to determine the end of memory and `__sbrk()` will return E without consulting the kernel. This process is illustrated in Figure 3.

After the region of data memory is determined, `sYSMALLOc()` sets that as the top chunk and then splits off a chunk of size nb to satisfy the request. In particular, line 39 writes $(E - S - nb)|$`PREV_INUSE` to location $S+nb+4$, see Figure 4. By carefully picking the values of S and E, we can cause `sYSMALLOc()` to write a word we choose to any location in memory that has an address congruent to 4 modulo 8.

In particular, the word in memory we wish to overwrite is a saved instruction pointer from a `call` instruction. Fortunately (for the attacker), gcc ensures that the stack pointer is congruent to 0 modulo 16 before every `call` so that the instruction pointer is saved to an address congruent to 12 modulo 16 and thus congruent to 4 modulo 8. The address we choose to write is that of the `_IO_gets()` function—which is the implementation of the `gets()` function—and we write it over the saved instruction

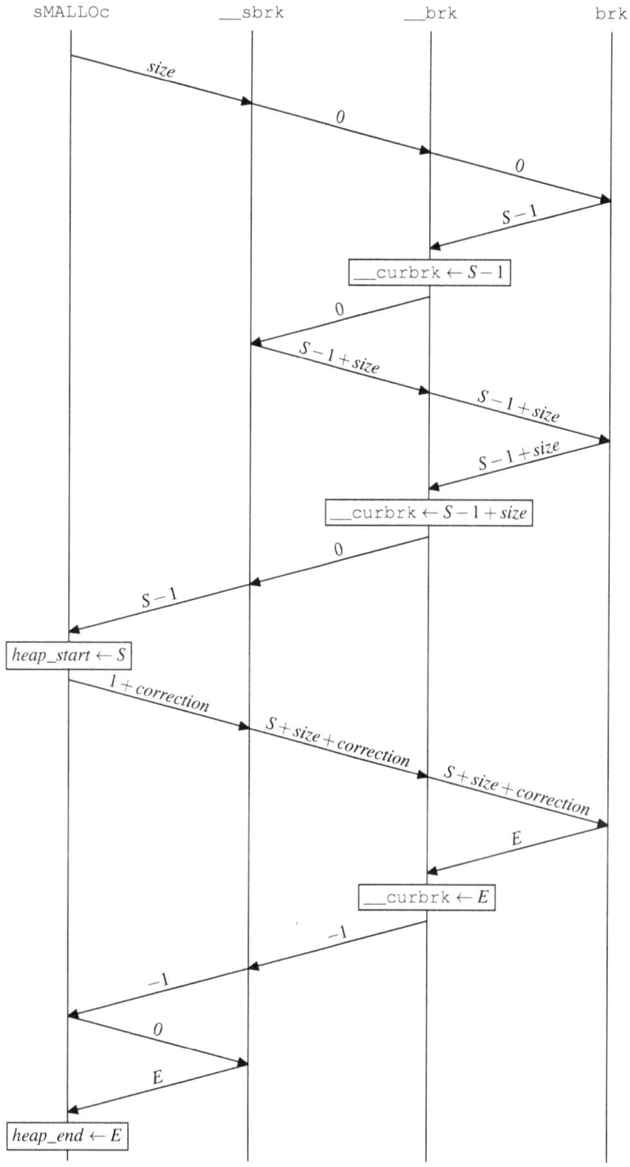

Figure 3. The sequence of function and system calls along with their arguments and the return values used to control which region of memory malloc treats as the heap. Labels on left-facing arrows are arguments; labels on right-facing arrows are return values.

pointer in `_int_malloc()`'s stack frame.[3] In fact, we cannot write the address of `_IO_gets()` because the address is even and ORing `PREV_INUSE` adds one to the address. Fortunately, the first byte in the function is `0x55` which is the opcode for the `push ebp` instruction and can safely be skipped since we will not be returning from this function.

A complete example

As a complete example, consider the program in Listing 1. The request for 100 bytes is increased to 104 bytes for chunk metadata. Since this is already a multiple of 8, $nb = 104$. The `_IO_gets()` function is loaded at address `0xb7ef2010`. The saved instruc-

[3] The code for `sYSMALLOc()` is inlined into `_int_malloc()` which is called by `malloc()`.

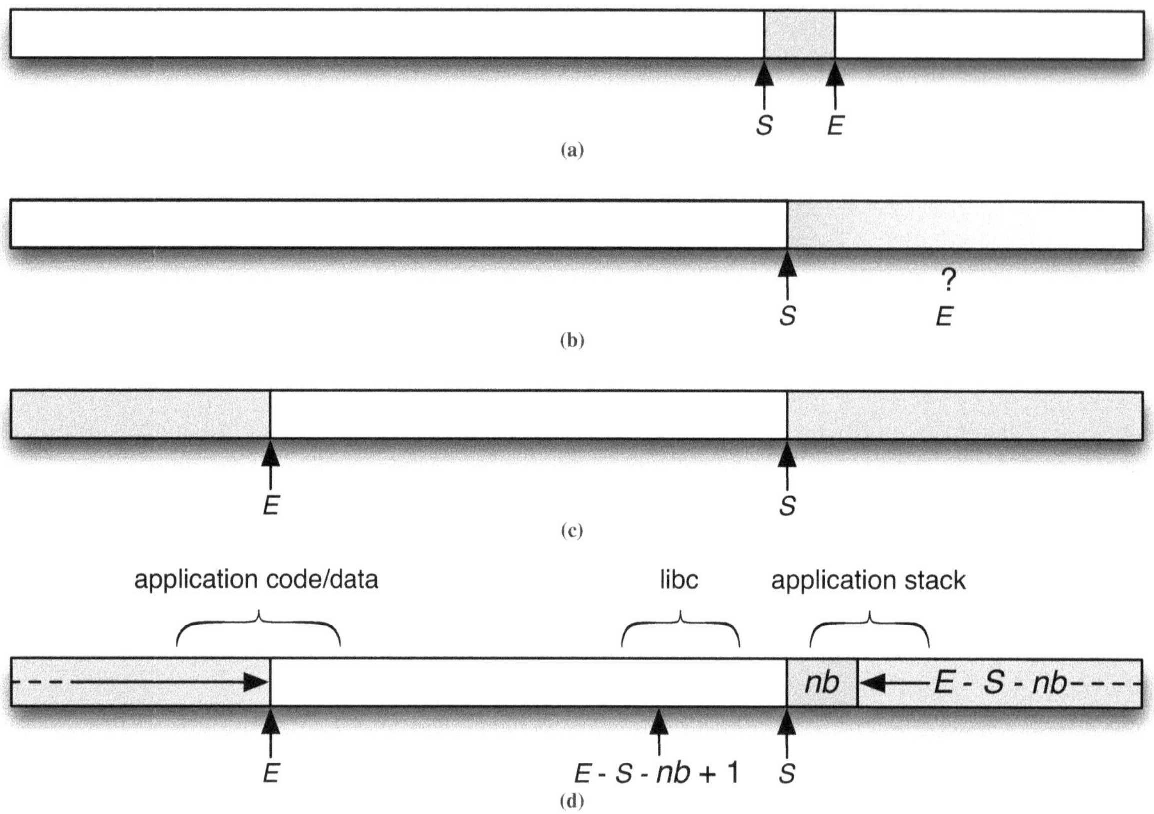

Figure 4. Confusing malloc into overwriting a saved instruction pointer.

During the first call to `sYSMALLOc()`, malloc will request that the break be extended in order to return a chunk of size nb. The first call to `__sbrk()` (line 10) will extend the break and return the old break. At this point, malloc thinks the start of the heap is at location S — the return value from `__sbrk()` and the end of the heap is simply S plus the size it requested the break be extended, as illustrated in (a).

The kernel returns a value that is not 8 byte aligned so malloc increases the start of the heap until it is aligned and requests the break be extended by the corresponding amount using a second call to `__sbrk()` (line 28). The kernel returns a value less than S which causes `__sbrk()` to return a failure. At this point, (b), malloc knows the start of the heap but not the end.

Next, `__sbrk()` is called a third time to determine the end of the heap E, as shown in (c). This happens without calling into the kernel because EGLIBC has recorded the current value of the break from the previous call to `__sbrk()`.

Finally, a chunk of size nb is split off from the heap which causes $E - S - nb + 1$ to be written to address $S + nb + 4$ as shown in (d). By carefully responding to system calls, a saved instruction pointer on the application's stack, at address $S + nb + 4$, can be overwritten with the address of the second byte of a function in libc, namely $E - S - nb + 1$.

tion pointer for `_int_malloc()` is on the stack at location `0xbfffe03c`. Since we want to overwrite the value at that address, we let $S =$ `0xbfffe03c` $- 104 - 4 =$ `0xbfffdfd0`. And thus $E = S +$ `0xb7ef2010` $+ 104 =$ `0x77ef0048`. After responding to the `brk` system calls as described above, `_int_malloc()` returns to second instruction in the `_IO_gets()` function.

The `_IO_gets()` function calls a series of functions including `_IO_default_uflow()`; `_IO_doallocate()`, which allocates a new buffer via the `mmap2` system call; and finally, `_IO_new_file_underflow()`, which fills the buffer using the `read` system call. The kernel responds to the `mmap2` system call with the address of the saved instruction pointer in `_IO_default_uflow()`'s stack frame, `0xbfffe000`. For, `read`, the kernel fills in the buffer with a return-oriented program.

Table 3 shows the relevant system calls used by the program, their arguments, and how the kernel responds. The arguments and return values for `brk` are addresses; the arguments for `mmap2` and `read` are the sizes; and the return value for `mmap2` is the address. The other arguments are unimportant.

Table 3. Modified system call returns.

System call	Argument	Return value
brk	0	bfffdfcf
brk	c001efcf	c001efcf
brk	c001f000	77ef0048
mmap2	1000	bfffe000
read	1000	1e*

* `read` reads the 30 byte exploit into the buffer.

For this example, our exploit is trivial: It is just a chained return-into-libc attack that chains together a return into the `write()` function which returns into the `_exit()` function. When the program is run with the kernel responding to system calls normally, the program immediately exits. When it is run with the malicious kernel, the kernel causes malloc to overwrite its stack with the exploit payload and the `write()` function outputs a line of text on standard out before exiting via `_exit()`:

```
$ ./victim
Hi there!
```

Arbitrary, Turing-complete computation is possible by changing the exploit to be a more complicated return-oriented program.

5. Compromising OpenSSL

The procedure for compromising malloc given in Section 4 is general purpose and applies to any program that directly or indirectly calls `malloc()`. However, it is only applicable for the first call to `malloc()`. After the initial call, the program break has been established by EGLIBC and the break can only be increased beyond what is requested lest `__sbrk()` fail in `sYSMALLOc()` on line 10. In principle, this is no problem since the kernel can take control and coerce the application to launch an arbitrarily complicated return-oriented program which is able to disclose whatever private information was to remain hidden from the kernel. In practice, emulating enough of the legitimate software to perform the desired malicious action can be quite complicated [5] and taking control further into the program's execution can simplify exploits. In this section, we show how to leverage malloc's fallback to `mmap()` to accomplish this in some cases where the allocated buffer is used as the destination of a `read()` call, similar to the code snippet in Section 4.1.

From Section 4.3, we can control the starting and ending addresses of the program's data region by responding to `brk` system calls. There is an additional restriction on where we can place the end of the data region, which is described below, but the idea is to leverage this ability to control where in a program's execution `sYSMALLOc()` is called a subsequent time. That is, the program makes a number of calls to `malloc()` and `free()` and one of the buffers allocated by `malloc()` is passed to `read()`.

By responding appropriately to `brk`, the kernel arranges for the size of the program's data region to be just large enough that when the program attempts to allocate the region of memory which will be passed to `read()`, malloc is forced to call `sYSMALLOc()`. If the allocation is larger than the *mmap_threshold*, the allocation will be memory mapped (lines 2–7) and so the kernel can return the address of the memory it wishes to overwrite. Otherwise, `__sbrk()` will be called. At this point, the kernel can refuse to increase the break in response to the `brk` system call which will cause `__sbrk()` to fail and `sYSMALLOc()` will fall back on `mmap()` (lines 11–18) and again the kernel can provide the address it wants.

There are several caveats with this method. The first is the restriction on ending addresses for the data region. Due to an assertion early in `sYSMALLOc()`, the end of the data region must be aligned on a page boundary.[4] The second is that the chosen end of the data region must be at an address that is less than the requested one to cause the second call to `__sbrk()` to fail. Thus if we want the end to be at a greater address than requested, we must initially set the end at a smaller address and then handle successive `brk` requests normally until we reach the point we wish it to fail. The final caveat is that a program may allocate a great deal of memory initially and then free it such that subsequent allocations come from the free chunks. The upshot of these caveats is that we cannot always arrange for `brk` to fail for exactly the allocation we wish. However, it may be possible to fail several allocations early.

[4] This assertion appears to be a (mostly harmless) bug in EGLIBC. A comment in the code after the second `__sbrk()` (corresponding to line 28) indicates that the third call is to find the end of memory in the hope that the allocation will still be possible. If the end does not lie on a page boundary, then the next call to `sYSMALLOc()` will (erroneously) abort the program rather than attempt `mmap()` or return `NULL`.

Table 4. Modified system call returns for OpenSSL s_server.

System call	Argument	Return value
brk	0	081e4fff
brk	08205fff	08205fff
brk	08206000	081f8000
brk	0821a000	081f8000
mmap2	1000000	bfeff000

A complete example

As an example of the technique of making malloc fall back on `mmap()`, we describe attacking the OpenSSL s_server program. This program (usually started by running the `openssl` binary with the `s_server` option) listens on a specified port for incoming connections and sets up a TLS/SSL connection. Afterward, incoming data is decrypted and written to standard out and data read from standard in is encrypted and sent over the socket. The secret key and certificate used in the TLS/SSL protocol are stored in files on disk.

Under the assumptions of an Overshadow-like system, the kernel would be prevented from reading the contents of the secret key on disk and, of course, it could not read it from `openssl`'s memory during execution. With the help of OpenSSL's s_client program — the companion program to s_server — the kernel will cause s_server to disclose its secret key, in this case, the RSA private exponent.

The first step is to launch OpenSSL s_server.

```
$ openssl s_server -key secret.key \
-cert cert.pem -accept 8080
```

This starts the server listening on port 8080. As before, the kernel responds to the first three `brk` system calls in order to set the length of data memory appropriately as described in Table 4. This causes the top chunk to have `0x13000` bytes of memory, initially.

The next step is to launch OpenSSL s_client with the exploit payload.

```
$ openssl s_client -connect \
localhost:8080 <exploit
```

The client will connect to the server and send the exploit code. After the client connects, the server will allocate `0x4000` bytes of memory for a buffer into which it will read the decrypted data. However, by this point, neither the free chunks nor the top chunk will be large enough to accommodate this allocation, so `sYSMALLOc()` requests more memory via `__sbrk()`. This time, the kernel responds to `brk` by returning the same value as before. This causes `__sbrk()` to return -1 and `sYSMALLOc()` falls back on `mmap()`. The kernel responds to the `mmap2` system call with an address on the stack. The server sets up a TLS connection with the client and then reads the encrypted exploit payload. The payload is decrypted and stored in the buffer which is really part of `SSL_read()`'s stack frame. Rather than returning to the function that called `SSL_read()`, it returns to a simple return-oriented program which calls the `write()` function to write the contents of the private exponent of the secret key to `stderr` and then exits.

6. Discussion and Conclusions

We have introduced Iago attacks: attacks in which a malicious kernel induces a protected process to act against its interests by manipulating system call return values. We have defined a threat model for Iago attacks, implemented a platform for experimenting with Iago attacks, and used this platform to demonstrate Iago attacks against Linux applications, including any application which uses `malloc()`. Some of our attacks induce arbitrary computation in the protected program.

Iago attacks provide a partial answer to an open problem posed by Chen et al.: "The implications of maliciously changing the behavior of seemingly innocuous parts of the system call API, such as those for managing identity and concurrency, are still largely unstudied" [6, Section 2.2].

Iago attacks are evidence that protecting applications from malicious kernels is more difficult than previously realized. We believe that there are several fundamental reasons for this difficulty. First, the system call API was not designed to be an untrusted RPC interface, so unsurprisingly it is a difficult interface to secure. Second, system calls are used at all layers of a program, including the libraries the program links against; securing applications against Iago attacks requires understanding the system calls made at every layer. Third, system calls are frequently used in other ways than for their nominal semantic content; providing a replacement to process IDs for reliable signal delivery does nothing to help OpenSSL's reliance on `getpid()` for entropy stirring.

Ports and Garfinkel [22] suggest that *verifying* that return values are correctly computed is easier than undertaking to compute them, and that a trusted supervisor monitoring the behavior of an untusted kernel can be smaller and simpler than the kernel itself. Our findings do not refute this claim, but they do suggest that the gap between verifying and computing may be smaller than previously realized, at least for the more complex of a kernel's tasks. For some tasks, such as managing virtual memory, verifying return values may require the supervisor to have a complete understanding of a kernel's memory management algorithms and data structures.

Address-space layout randomization makes it hard to exploit memory bugs, but the untrusted kernel is in charge of process creation. How can the supervisor be sure that the kernel isn't placing the process' memory segments in predictable locations?[5] For that matter, what constitutes a reasonable memory layout? At a crucial point, the attack we describe in Section 4.3 overlays an `mmap`ed memory region on the stack, and perhaps this could be noticed and prevented by the supervisor. But there are legitimate reasons that processes would want to map memory on top of an existing mapping. More generally, we believe that variants of our attack are possible without overlapping memory regions. One promising target for such an approach is the stack segment. Oberheide recently demonstrated the possibility of "stack overflow" attacks [20], in which the stack of a program is induced to extend down so far (by means, for example, of a recursive function that parses user input) that it (implicitly) overlaps some other memory segment, leading memory safety guarantees to be violated. Oberheide was able to exhibit stack overflow attacks against real programs run on benign kernels; such attacks would be easier to mount when a malicious kernel decides the layout of the stack and other memory segments in process memory.

Understanding the situations in which verifying return values is easier than computing them, for virtual memory as well as other subsystems represented in the system call API, remains an important open problem. A particularly interesting challenge: Is it always possible to verify a system call return value based on the current state of the system, or are there system call values that can only be provisionally verified and must be checked for consistency with subsequent return values? Put another way, is it or isn't it possible to verify the behavior of a kernel using a constant amount of state as a function of the time a process has been running?

One possibility is that running arbitrary applications on an untrusted kernels is too ambitious a goal. Instead, the technologies developed for such systems can and should be applied to secure custom or special-purpose tasks as part of a larger system, minimizing the trusted computing base required for these tasks. We observe a similar trajectory for system call interposition, which, when introduced, was envisioned as a means for sandboxing arbitrary untrusted applications [10, 11, 24]. Sandboxing complex general-purprose software proved to be difficult [9]; today, system call interposition is used fruitfully for sandboxing special-purpose processes, such as the Chromium renderer [2].

We believe that the software to be run safely on untrusted kernels will need to be designed specifically for that purpose. As we have shown, assumptions about system call behavior can be present at all levels of the software stack, not just in the application code itself. For example, we have shown that any application that calls `malloc` is potentially vulnerable. But even an application whose memory allocation has been rewritten to avoid `malloc` might find that its libraries do; for example, EGLIBC's `printf` implementation does.

If the applications that will run on untrusted kernels are written from scratch, it is no longer necessary to use the legacy Unix system call API. An important question then arises: are there other resource-management APIs that would be easier to secure as untrusted RPC interfaces? We hope to tackle this question in future work. As inspiration, we note that Mach featured a user-space memory manager [12], and that research operating systems such as the Exokernel [8] have radically reimagined the boundary between kernel and application.

[5] One intriguing possibility is that, on process startup, a shim runs that randomizes the runtime environment. But this is no silver bullet; past work has repeatedly shown that attackers are able to adjust to uncertainty about their target's memory layout; see, e.g., Sotirov and Dowd [28].

Acknowledgments

We thank Dan Boneh, Nadia Heninger, David Kohlbrenner, Eric Rescorla, Stefan Savage, and Vitaly Shmatikov for helpful discussions about this work; Michael Bailey, Peter Chen, J. Alex Halderman, Peter Honeyman, Jon Oberheide, and others at the University of Michigan for their comments on an early presentation of this work; the anonymous reviewers for their helpful suggestions; and Katharine Tillman for suggesting a name for the attack.

This material is based upon work supported by National Science Foundation under grant CNS-0831532 (Cyber Trust) and by the MURI program under AFOSR Grant No. FA9550-08-1-0352.

References

[1] Anonymous. Once upon a free()…. *Phrack Magazine*, 57(9), August 2001. http://www.phrack.org/archives/57/p57_0x09_Once%20upon%20a%20free()_by_anonymous%20author.txt.

[2] Adam Barth, Collin Jackson, Charles Reis, and The Google Chrome Team. The security architecture of the Chromium browser. Online: http://seclab.stanford.edu/websec/chromium/, 2008.

[3] blackngel. Malloc des-maleficarum. *Phrack Magazine*, 66(10), November 2009. http://www.phrack.org/archives/66/p66_0x0a_Malloc%20Des-Maleficarum_by_blackngel.txt.

[4] blackngel. ptmalloc v2 & v3: Analysis & corruption. *Phrack Magazine*, 67(8), November 2010. http://www.phrack.org/archives/67/p67_0x08_The%20House%20Of%20Lore:%20Reloaded%20ptmalloc%20v2%20&%20v3:%20Analysis%20&%20Corruption_by_blackngel.txt.

[5] Stephen Checkoway, Ariel J. Feldman, Brian Kantor, J. Alex Halderman, Edward W. Felten, and Hovav Shacham. Can DREs provide

long-lasting security? The case of return-oriented programming and the AVC Advantage. In David Jefferson, Joseph Lorenzo Hall, and Tal Moran, editors, *Proceedings of EVT/WOTE 2009*. USENIX/ACCURATE/IAVoSS, August 2009.

[6] Xiaoxin Chen, Tal Garfinkel, E. Christopher Lewis, Pratap Subrahmanyam, Carl A. Waldspurger, Dan Boneh, Jeffrey Dwoskin, and Dan R.K. Ports. Overshadow: a virtualization-based approach to retrofitting protection in commodity operating systems. In James Larus, editor, *Proceedings of ASPLOS 2008*, pages 2–13. ACM Press, March 2008.

[7] ISO/IEC FDIS 9899:1999 (E). *Programming languages – C*. ISO, 1999.

[8] Dawson R. Engler, M. Frans Kaashoek, and James W. O'Toole. Exokernel: An operating system architecture for application-level resource management,. In Mark Weiser, editor, *Proceedings of SOSP 1995*, pages 251–66. ACM Press, December 1995.

[9] Tal Garfinkel. Traps and pitfalls: Practical problems in system call interposition based security tools. In Virgil Gligor and Mike Reiter, editors, *Proceedings of NDSS 2003*. Internet Society, February 2003.

[10] Tal Garfinkel, Ben Pfaff, and Mendel Rosenblum. Ostia: A delegating architecture for secure system call interposition. In Mike Reiter and Dan Boneh, editors, *Proceedings of NDSS 2004*. Internet Society, February 2004.

[11] Ian Goldberg, David Wagner, Randi Thomas, and Eric A. Brewer. A secure environment for untrusted helper applications. In Greg Rose, editor, *Proceedings of USENIX Security 1996*. USENIX, July 1996.

[12] David B. Golub and Richard P. Draves. Moving the default memory manager out of the mach kernel. In Alan Langerman, editor, *Proceedings of Mach Symposium 1991*, pages 177–88, November, 1991. USENIX.

[13] Michel Kaempf. Vudo malloc tricks. *Phrack Magazine*, 57(8), August 2001.
`http://www.phrack.org/archives/57/p57_0x08_Vudo%20malloc%20tricks_by_MaXX.txt`.

[14] David Lie, Chandramohan Thekkath, and Mark Horowitz. Implementing an untrusted operating system on trusted hardware. In Larry Peterson, editor, *Proceedings of SOSP 2003*, pages 178–92. ACM Press, October 2003.

[15] Jonathan M. McCune, Bryan Parno, Adrian Perrig, Michael K. Reiter, and Arvind Seshadri. Minimal tcb code execution (extended abstract). In Birgit Pfitzmann and Patrick McDaniel, editors, *Proceedings of IEEE Security & Privacy ("Oakland") 2007*, pages 267–72. IEEE Computer Society, May 2007.

[16] Jonathan M. McCune, Bryan Parno, Adrian Perrig, Michael K. Reiter, and Arvind Seshadri. How low can you go? Recommendations for hardware-supported minimal TCB code execution. In James Larus, editor, *Proceedings of ASPLOS 2008*, pages 14–25. ACM Press, March 2008.

[17] Jonathan M. McCune, Bryan Parno, Adrian Perrig, Michael K. Reiter, and Arvind Seshadri. Flicker: An execution infrastructure for TCB minimization. In Steven Hand, editor, *Proceedings of EuroSys 2008*, pages 315–28. ACM Press, March 2008.

[18] Jonathan M. McCune, Adrian Perrig, and Michael K. Reiter. Safe passage for passwords and other sensitive data. In Giovanni Vigna, editor, *Proceedings of NDSS 2009*. The Internet Society, February 2009.

[19] Gene Novark and Emery D. Berger. DieHarder: Securing the heap. In Angelos D. Keromytis and Vitaly Shmatikov, editors, *Proceedings of CCS 2010*. ACM Press, October 2010.

[20] Jon Oberheide. The stack is back. Presented at Infiltrate 2012, January 2012. Presentation. Slides:
`http://jon.oberheide.org/files/infiltrate12-thestackisback.pdf`.

[21] Phantasmal Phantasmagoria. The malloc maleficarum: Glibc malloc exploitation techniques. Bugtraq, October 2005.
`http://seclists.org/bugtraq/2005/Oct/118`.

[22] Dan R.K. Ports and Tal Garfinkel. Towards application security on untrusted operating systems. In Niels Provos, editor, *Proceedings of HotSec 2008*. USENIX, July 2008.

[23] POSIX.1-2008/IEEE Std 1003.1-2008. *The Open Group Base Specifications Issue 7*. IEEE and The Open Group, 2008.

[24] Niels Provos. Improving host security with system call policies. In Vern Paxson, editor, *Proceedings of USENIX Security 2003*. USENIX, August 2003.

[25] Eric Rescorla. *SSL and TLS: Designing and Building Secure Systems*. Addison-Wesley, 2000.

[26] Thomas Ristenpart and Scott Yilek. When good randomness goes bad: Virtual machine reset vulnerabilities and hedging deployed cryptography. In Wenke Lee, editor, *Proceedings of NDSS 2003*. Internet Society, February 2003.

[27] Ryan Roemer, Erik Buchanan, Hovav Shacham, and Stefan Savage. Return-oriented programming: Systems, languages, and applications. *Trans. Info. & Sys. Sec.*, 2012. To appear.

[28] Alexander Sotirov and Mark Dowd. Bypassing browser memory protections in Windows Vista. Presented at Black Hat 2008, August 2008. Online:
`http://www.phreedom.org/research/bypassing-browser-memory-protections/bypassing-browser-memory-protections.pdf`.

[29] Scott Yilek, Eric Rescorla, Hovav Shacham, Brandon Enright, and Stefan Savage. When private keys are public: Results from the 2008 Debian OpenSSL vulnerability. In Anja Feldmann and Laurent Mathy, editors, *Proceedings of IMC 2009*, pages 15–27. ACM Press, November 2009.

InkTag: Secure Applications on an Untrusted Operating System

Owen S. Hofmann Sangman Kim Alan M. Dunn Michael Z. Lee Emmett Witchel
The University of Texas at Austin
{osh, sangmank, adunn, mzlee, witchel}@cs.utexas.edu

Abstract

InkTag is a virtualization-based architecture that gives strong safety guarantees to high-assurance processes even in the presence of a malicious operating system. InkTag advances the state of the art in untrusted operating systems in both the design of its hypervisor and in the ability to run useful applications without trusting the operating system. We introduce *paraverification*, a technique that simplifies the InkTag hypervisor by forcing the untrusted operating system to participate in its own verification. *Attribute-based access control* allows trusted applications to create decentralized access control policies. InkTag is also the first system of its kind to ensure consistency between secure data and metadata, ensuring recoverability in the face of system crashes.

Categories and Subject Descriptors D.4.6 [*Operating Systems*]: Security and Protection—Access controls, Invasive software

General Terms Security, Verification

Keywords Application protection, Virtualization-based security, Paraverification

1. Introduction

Operating systems are a vexing Achilles heel in the security architecture of modern computing systems. The OS is the root of trust, so compromising the OS compromises *every* program on the system. On discretionary access control operating systems like Linux and Windows, controlling any process running as root (administrator) is a kernel compromise because the root user can load code and data into the kernel's address space. If an application could remain safe even if the operating system were compromised, then operating system exploits would no longer have the security emergency status that they have today.

This paper introduces InkTag, a system in which secure, trustworthy programs can **efficiently verify an untrusted, commodity operating system's behavior**, with a small degree of assistance from a small, trusted hypervisor. OS implementations are complex. However, verifying OS behavior is possible without reimplementing OS subsystems in the hypervisor, because OS services often have simple specifications. OS complexity comes from supporting these simple services simultaneously for many different processes. Global behavior and resource management is much more complicated than the specification for an individual process. For instance, swapping and copy-on-write heuristics in Linux require many thousands of lines of code, but auditing an application's page tables and checksumming the page contents requires only a few hundred. Verifying that the OS provides system services correctly allows InkTag to avoid having to reason about the OS's implementation of these services.

Though feasible, efficiently and safely verifying OS behavior remains a significant challenge. The InkTag hypervisor must implement deep introspection into architecture-level primitives, such as page tables, to isolate trusted applications from an untrusted operating system. The range of "normal" operating system behavior is large, making recognition of malicious behavior a challenge. While verifying OS behavior is hard, doing it efficiently is even harder. Modern virtualization hardware improves performance by relieving hypervisor software from having to process many common operations. Unfortunately, it is often those exact operations, e.g., page table updates, that are crucial for verifying OS behavior.

InkTag introduces *paraverification*, which enables verification of OS behavior with limited hypervisor complexity. Most previous systems have attempted to verify unmodified operating systems. InkTag requires the untrusted OS to provide information and resources to both the hypervisor and application that allow them to efficiently verify the operating system's actions. Using paraverification to force the OS to make verification easier and more efficient is similar to the way paravirtualization forces an OS to make virtualization more efficient.

Prior work on untrusted operating systems [11] has focused on simply isolating trusted code and data from the OS, with minimal support for securely using OS features. InkTag addresses important issues in the completeness and usability of untrusted operating systems, such as providing users of an untrusted OS with flexible access control and crash consistency for hypervisor and OS data structures. InkTag advances the design and implementation of OS verification in the following ways:

1. InkTag introduces paraverification, where an untrusted operating system is required to perform extra computation to make verifying its own behavior easier.
2. InkTag is the first system to provide users of an untrusted OS with flexible access control, that allows applications to define access control policies for their own secure files (files with privacy and integrity managed by InkTag). Access control is vital for sharing data between processes with different levels of privilege. Our prototype applies flexible access control to a multi-user wiki application, providing hypervisor-enforced privacy, integrity, and access control for wiki code and data.
3. InkTag is the first system to provide crash consistency between security-critical metadata managed by the hypervisor and data managed by the untrusted OS.
4. InkTag directly addresses *Iago attacks* [8], a new class of attacks against systems providing trusted applications in untrusted operating systems that manipulates the return values

ASPLOS'13, March 16–20, 2013, Houston, Texas, USA.

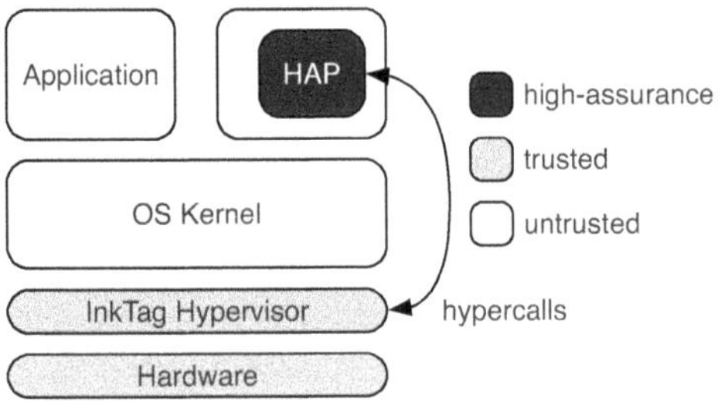

Figure 1. InkTag design overview. In InkTag high-assurance processes (HAPs) make hypercalls to the virtual machine hypervisor to verify the runtime behavior of the operating system. The hypervisor is trusted.

of system calls (e.g., mmap) to cause a trusted application to harm itself.

Section 2 gives an overview of InkTag, while Section 3 explains InkTag's high-level design. Section 4 introduces paraverification. Section 5 describes access control in InkTag, followed by our design for storage (§6), implementation (§7) and evaluation (§8). Section 9 covers related work and Section 10 concludes.

2. Overview

InkTag is a hypervisor-based system that protects trusted applications from an untrusted OS, allowing trusted applications to securely use untrusted OS services. The hypervisor protects application code, data, and control flow from the OS, allowing applications to execute in isolation. Mutually trusting secure applications can securely and privately share data without interference from the OS or other applications. Each secure application coordinates directly with the InkTag hypervisor via hypercalls to detect OS misbehavior.

Figure 1 shows an overview of the InkTag architecture. Trusted application code executes in a **high-assurance process, or HAP**, which is isolated from the OS. Nearly all application-level changes are contained in a small, 2000-line library (libinktag) the use of which is largely encapsulated in the standard C library. InkTag extends a standard hypervisor to monitor the untrusted OS using paravirtualized device drivers and virtualization hardware. InkTag defines new hypercalls for HAPs to verify OS behavior.

InkTag shares its basic threat model and security guarantees with previous work where a trusted hypervisor verifies an untrusted operating system's actions; such as SP^3 [47], and especially Overshadow [11]. We first discuss issues generic to all approaches, then starting with Section 2.4 discuss issues specific to InkTag.

2.1 Threat Model

InkTag assumes that the OS is completely untrusted and can behave in arbitrarily malicious ways. Applications running on the OS have both an untrusted context maintained by the OS used for requesting OS services, and a trusted context used for executing code that must be isolated from the OS. The developer trusts the InkTag hypervisor and the trusted execution context of the application. The trusted application context is isolated from the OS by the hypervisor.

InkTag does not address application-level bugs, and will not stop an application that deliberately divulges secret data (e.g., by putting it in the arguments of a system call that the OS handles).

InkTag cannot guarantee untrusted OS availability, but can detect this class of misbehavior. Trivially, a malicious OS could simply shut down every time it was started, though the InkTag hypervisor will detect such misbehavior. More subtle availability attacks are possible, such as deleting volatile data, which will be detected in a timely manner, but may result in the loss of data between misbehavior and detection.

2.2 Size of trusted computing base (TCB)

The operating system consists of millions of lines of code, so its elimination from the trusted computing base seems, *prima facie*, to increase security. However, the KVM hypervisor includes an entire OS (sometimes called a type 2 hypervisor). Eliminating trust in the guest instance of Linux is of little security value if the hypervisor contains its own instance.

However, simpler hypervisors (type 1) exist, and contain fewer lines of code than a typical operating system. Additionally, the hypervisor interface is a hardware interface, which is far simpler and easier to make secure than the hundreds of semantically complex system calls exported by a general-purpose operating system. For example, from 2010 to 2012, a search of the National Vulnerability Database [31] returns 12 exploits for Xen and 16 exploits for KVM that have an impact worse than denial of service. By contrast, there are 53 such vulnerabilities published for the Linux kernel in 2012, of which only 7 are driver vulnerabilities. These vulnerabilities spanned many different core kernel services such as memory management, file systems, network protocol implementations, and syscalls. The situation is not much better for Windows 7: in 2012, there were 9 privilege escalation and 31 remote code execution bulletins listed [1].

2.3 Security guarantees

Here we summarize the security guarantees provided to an InkTag application. The InkTag hypervisor ensures that a HAP's process context (registers) and address space are isolated from the the operating system. Then, InkTag ensures that a HAP can use a subset of services provided by the untrusted OS to interact with secure files (files with privacy and integrity managed by InkTag through encryption and hashing), and verify that those services were provided correctly. InkTag shares these basic security guarantees, as well as implementation techniques, with previous work such as Overshadow.

In addition to the majority of HAP code that executes in a trusted context, each HAP also contains a small amount of *untrusted trampoline* code that interacts with the operating system (this is similar to Overshadow's *uncloaked shim*). The InkTag hypervisor switches control between secure HAP code and the untrusted trampoline, while the untrusted operating system schedules among the untrusted trampoline and other contexts. This allows the InkTag hypervisor to control switches into and out of a secure context and ensure control flow integrity. Then, the InkTag hypervisor encrypts and hashes HAP pages to ensure privacy and integrity for the HAP's address space: this is analogous to Overshadow's *multi-shadowing* technique.

Control flow integrity As with traditional applications, a HAP running in InkTag may be interrupted at any time by the operating system. InkTag must not allow the operating system to read or modify the application's processor registers. Doing so could leak private data, or allow the operating system to modify the application's control flow or data by changing the instruction pointer, condition flags, or a register value. The InkTag hypervisor interposes on every context switch between a secure HAP and the operating system. On context switches, the hypervisor saves processor registers, and overwrites their values before switching to the OS.

Address space integrity In addition to application registers, the InkTag hypervisor must ensure privacy and integrity for code and data in a HAP's address space. When an untrusted operating system attempts to read application memory, InkTag hashes memory and encrypts it, ensuring that the untrusted operating system cannot read application secrets. When the HAP accesses the memory again, the InkTag hypervisor decrypts it and verifies the hash, to ensure that the memory was not modified by the operating system.

The position and order of pages in an application's virtual address space is also an important integrity property. InkTag ensures that every page of memory is mapped at the virtual address requested by the application, either via information about the HAP's initial state contained in the ELF binary, or via a request to a memory mapping function such as `brk()` or `mmap()`. The problem of synchronizing the mapping information between application and hypervisor motivates our primary contribution, paraverification, described in detail in Section 4.

File I/O To perform useful work, a HAP isolated from an untrusted operating system must still be able to use a subset of OS services. The InkTag hypervisor must ensure that the application can still rely on those services even when running on a malicious OS.

Most importantly, InkTag provides HAPs with the ability to securely interact with files despite the fact that they are read from and written to disk by the untrusted operating system, by guaranteeing integrity for file memory mappings. InkTag applications primarily identify files through a 64-bit *object identifier*, or OID. Most file operations are expressed as operations on OIDs, even though real applications generally expect to use string filenames: mapping string filenames to OIDs is a contribution of InkTag, as discussed later in this section. When an application maps an OID into memory (through a call to `mmap`) and receives an address for the new mapping, InkTag ensures that later references to that address will access the desired file. Privacy and integrity for file data are ensured via InkTag's guarantee of address space privacy and integrity, by hashing and encrypting in-memory file data in response to accesses by the untrusted operating system. To handle file I/O via `read()` and `write()` system calls, our application-level library translates these calls into operations on memory-mapped files.

Process control HAPs may also create new processes through calls to `fork()` and execute binaries in these processes with `exec()`. The InkTag hypervisor ensures that the untrusted operating system executes these operations correctly. In the case of `fork()`, InkTag ensures that the new HAP is a clone of its parent. For `exec()`, InkTag ensures that the new HAP, specified by the identifier of the binary file passed to `exec()` is loaded into memory correctly (i.e., each section in the binary is loaded unmodified into the correct virtual address), based on the information specified by the ELF format binary.

Other OS services Because InkTag guarantees control flow and data integrity for HAPs, a HAP may safely invoke system calls not explicitly secured by InkTag. However, it must consider the results of those system calls as it considers any data provided by an untrusted source. For example, InkTag does not manage network I/O, however it is possible for applications to safely communicate over the network via mechanisms such as transport layer security (TLS [13]), that enable secure communication over an untrusted channel.

2.4 InkTag contributions

InkTag advances work on untrusted operating systems along two axes: the underlying architecture for isolating processes from the operating system, and the set of core OS services that applications may use securely.

Paraverification Isolating an application's address space from an untrusted operating system is a daunting task. Whereas previous work has used unmodified OS kernels, InkTag employs *paraverification*, a technique similar to paravirtualization, in which the untrusted kernel is required to send to the hypervisor information about updates to process state (that the hypervisor then checks for correctness). Paraverification simplifies the design of the InkTag hypervisor by allowing it to directly use high-level information from the kernel, rather than having to deduce that information from low-level updates such as changes to bits on process page tables.

Hardware virtualization The utility of virtualization has prompted the rapid introduction of hardware support for virtualizing processor state, as well as hardware support for virtualizing memory management. Eliminating software from these performance-critical processing paths is a clear advantage, but systems like InkTag require validation of OS updates to HAP page tables. InkTag minimizes the performance impact of validation via a combination of the efficiency afforded by paraverification and a two-level approach to protection. InkTag uses hardware MMU virtualization for coarse-grained separation between secure and insecure data. Then it uses software only when needed, to manage the userspace portions of HAP page tables.

Access control and naming The InkTag hypervisor allows HAPs to specify access control policies on secure files, with privacy and integrity managed by InkTag through encryption and hashing. InkTag's access control mechanism is described in detail in Section 5. Although InkTag applications identify files via an integer OID, most applications and users expect to reference files through a string name. InkTag allows applications to map from string names to OIDs, while maintaining important integrity properties (such as the trusted nature of the `/etc` directory).

Consistency To protect the integrity of file contents, InkTag, like similar systems, must maintain additional metadata in the form of hashes of file data pages. InkTag is the first such system to provide crash consistency between file metadata and data. Consistency is vital in this setting: without consistent data and metadata, the InkTag hypervisor cannot protect file integrity. An application must either discard the inconsistent data, or accept the possibility of tampering by an untrusted OS.

2.5 API

HAPs communicate with the InkTag hypervisor primarily by making hypercalls. InkTag maintains the simplicity of the hypervisor interface by adding only 14 hypervisor calls. Table 1 summarizes InkTag's hypercall interface. It refers to several concepts that will be introduced shortly, but what is clear is that the number of calls is limited and their function is mostly intuitive.

In addition to invoking operations through hypercalls, the InkTag hypervisor shares two data structures with the guest kernel and HAPs First, an InkTag application must describe the layout of its virtual address space. A HAP enters each of its memory mappings into an array of descriptors in its virtual address space, specifying the base address of the array as part of the `INIT` hypercall. Second, the untrusted kernel sends information about updates to process state to the InkTag hypervisor. These updates are communicated through a shared queue, similar to existing paravirtual interfaces.

3. Address space management

Address space management is the foundation for InkTag's security guarantees. We discuss $\mathbb{S}$-pages, InkTag's abstraction for secure address spaces, and how InkTag uses hardware memory management virtualization features that are part of modern virtualization hardware.

3.1 Objects and secure pages

InkTag's basic file abstraction is an *object*. All files, including binary executables, are represented by an InkTag object. Objects are identified by a 64-bit *object identifier* (OID). Section 5.4 discusses translating between human-readable names and OIDs, however OIDs are the main abstraction used by the InkTag hypervisor.

Hypercall	Arguments	Description
Process control		
`INIT`	*control addr*	Starts a new HAP. The HAP passes to the hypervisor the address of a control structure, which specifies which binary the HAP was loaded from, and the base address of the HAP's list of virtual memory mappings.
`EXEC`	*new hap OID*	Start a HAP, ensuring that it is loaded from the binary identified by *OID*.
`CLONE`		Create a new HAP that is a duplicate of the current state of the calling HAP.
`SWITCH_TO_HAP`	*hap id*	Invoked by untrusted trampoline code to switch context back into a HAP.
`SYSCALL`	*new PC*	On any hypercall, a HAP may request a switch out of secure execution to invoke a system call by specifying a program counter value for a service routine in untrusted code. `SYSCALL` is used when invoking a system call is the only desired behavior.
Memory management		
`UNMAP`	*memory range*	Ensure that $\mathbb{S}$-pages within the specified virtual address range are unmapped.
`REMAP`	*old_range, new_range*	Move any $\mathbb{S}$-page mappings from *old_range* to *new_range*.
Files and access control		
`ACCESS`	*OID*	Check if the current HAP has access to *OID*.
`CREATE`	*OID, namespace*	Create a new file within the given namespace.
`SET_LENGTH`	*OID*	Set the length of a file for which the HAP has write permission.
`OID_ACL`	*OID, acl*	Set the ACL on a file.
`ADD_DROP`	*add_attr, drop_attr*	Add and/or drop attributes from a HAP's list of attributes.
Paraverification		
`MMU_REGISTER`	*queue addr*	Invoked by the untrusted kernel to specify a location in memory that contains a queue of updates to HAP address spaces (such as page table updates).
`MMU_FLUSH`		Invoked by the untrusted kernel to notify the InkTag hypervisor that the queue is full, and must be processed.

Table 1. The hypercall interface to the InkTag hypervisor

Throughout the rest of the paper, we use the term OID interchangeably with object.

Objects are comprised of *secure pages ($\mathbb{S}$-pages)*, which are the basic mechanism by which InkTag enforces address space privacy, address space integrity, and access control policy for files. $\mathbb{S}$-pages consist of a block of data (4 KB for most pages on x86 processors), in memory or on disk, with additional metadata. $\mathbb{S}$-pages include a hash of the data contained with the page, as well as information about which resource the page describes, in the form of a $\langle OID, offset\rangle$ pair. An object identifies a set of pages that share a single OID, and may refer to a file on disk or a private memory region created dynamically by an application (e.g., an anonymous mmap).

The InkTag hypervisor encrypts $\mathbb{S}$-pages to ensure privacy, and hashes them to ensure integrity. When a HAP accesses an $\mathbb{S}$-page for which it has read permission, the InkTag hypervisor transparently decrypts the page, allowing the HAP access to cleartext. If an $\mathbb{S}$-page is accessed by the operating system, a regular application, or a HAP without read permission, the InkTag hypervisor detects the access and re-encrypts the page. Even if a malicious operating system can read the data within an $\mathbb{S}$-page, InkTag guarantees privacy because the OS can read only encrypted data.

Similarly, only the hypervisor can update the hash associated with an $\mathbb{S}$-page. When a HAP updates an $\mathbb{S}$-page for which it has write permission, the InkTag hypervisor updates the hash. If the OS modifies the data in the $\mathbb{S}$-page, the InkTag hypervisor will detect the modification, because hashing the modified data will not match the recorded hash.

The untrusted OS views $\mathbb{S}$-pages as standard data pages, and remains responsible for placing $\mathbb{S}$-pages in memory and on disk. The additional metadata attached to $\mathbb{S}$-pages is transparent to the guest OS: the InkTag hypervisor updates and tracks $\mathbb{S}$-page metadata as the operating system or application moves or transforms the data such as by mapping a file in memory or by writing a page to the virtual disk.

Each HAP must provide a description of its address space to the InkTag hypervisor, in the form of a list of memory mappings $[\langle address\_range, OID, offset\rangle, \ldots]$, each of which defines a sequence of $\mathbb{S}$-pages. With a description of the address space, the hypervisor may then validate individual page table updates requested by the untrusted OS. For example, suppose the OS attempts to map virtual address V to physical frame P in a HAP's page tables. The hypervisor examines the HAP's memory map for a range that includes V. If one exists, the hypervisor then verifies that the HAP has access to the specified OID. Finally, the hypervisor checks that frame P actually contains the correct $\mathbb{S}$-page, by checking P's hash against the stored metadata. If all of these checks succeed, the hypervisor now considers P to be a physical frame containing an $\mathbb{S}$-page, and the HAP has a valid mapping of address V to P. Thus, when the HAP attempts to access the $\mathbb{S}$-page, InkTag will decrypt its contents and provide the HAP with cleartext access.

3.2 Nested paging

The InkTag hypervisor is designed to run on modern processors that support hardware assistance for virtualization. Such processors are designed to simplify the task of writing hypervisor software by automatically creating a self-contained environment for the guest OS, without requiring manual intervention by hypervisor software.

One of the primary tasks of any hypervisor (including InkTag), is virtualizing memory management. The hypervisor must ensure that the guest operating system has access only to those pages of memory that represent its virtualized physical address space. For early x86 hypervisors, this required intercepting page table updates made by the guest OS, transforming *guest-physical addresses* (physical addresses from the point of the virtualized guest) into *host-physical addresses* (actual physical addresses of the frames of memory that constitute the guest's virtualized physical memory),

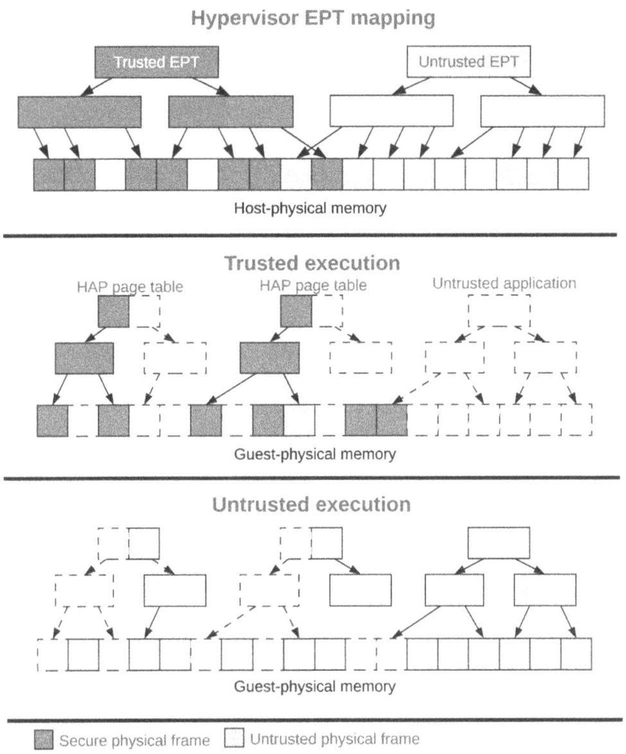

Figure 2. Address space protection using both EPT and management of HAP page tables. The InkTag hypervisor uses two EPTs to divide access between physical frames containing cleartext 𝕊-pages, and those containing untrusted data or encrypted 𝕊-pages. Then, it manages HAP page tables to restrict access within the set of secure frames.

and installing modified page tables for the guest OS that contain the transformed mappings.

Hardware MMU virtualization As might be expected, virtualizing memory in this manner adversely affects both hypervisor complexity and hypervisor performance. In response, more recent x86 processors have supported *nested paging*. With nested paging, guest memory accesses are translated through two separate page tables. First, guest-virtual addresses are translated into guest-physical addresses by traditional page tables managed entirely by the guest OS. Then, guest-physical addresses are translated into host-physical addresses by the *extended page table* (EPT)[1]. The EPT is managed by the hypervisor, but does not need to be updated in response to changes to guest page tables, as it only maps between guest-physical and host-physical address spaces. Meanwhile, the guest OS is free to perform arbitrary modifications to its own page tables, as all accesses will be restricted by EPTs to memory explicitly approved by the hypervisor.

Nested paging is a significant step forward for hypervisors. However, as discussed in section 3.1, the InkTag hypervisor's primary means of enforcing privacy, integrity, and access control is through detailed management of OS page table updates. A key goal for designing the InkTag hypervisor is to retain the necessary control over guest OS page table updates, while still being able to harness the performance benefits of modern virtualization hardware.

Nested isolation InkTag takes advantage of hardware MMU virtualization by using a combination of hardware EPT support and management of individual OS page table updates. Rather than use a single EPT for all of guest execution, the InkTag hypervisor uses two separate EPT trees. The *trusted EPT* is installed during isolated HAP execution, while the *untrusted EPT* is used during execution of the operating system and other applications (Figure 2). The contents of both EPTs are entirely managed by the hypervisor, and are therefore trustworthy. The trusted/untrusted label refers to the contents of the physical frames they map. The trusted EPT primarily maps physical frames that contain cleartext 𝕊-pages, while the untrusted EPT maps all other frames, including encrypted 𝕊-pages, data belonging to the OS, and untrusted applications.

Using separate EPTs for trusted and untrusted contexts allows InkTag to coarsely control access to secure pages. Physical frames holding cleartext 𝕊-pages are not mapped in the untrusted EPT If the OS or an untrusted application accesses a cleartext 𝕊-page frame, the access causes a fault that is handled by the hypervisor. InkTag hashes the contents of the frame, encrypts the frame's contents, maps it in the untrusted EPT, and unmaps it from the trusted EPT. If the trusted HAP accesses the frame again, the hypervisor decrypts the frame, verifies the contents against the hash, maps it in the trusted EPT, and unmaps it from the untrusted EPT.

In addition to the coarse access control provided by EPTs, InkTag must subdivide access to physical frames among executing HAPs. When executing in trusted mode, every HAP can potentially access any physical frame holding a cleartext 𝕊-page. However, not every HAP should have access to all 𝕊-pages. The InkTag hypervisor restricts access for an individual HAP to a subset of physical frames by managing OS page table updates for the HAP address space. Importantly, the InkTag hypervisor is only required to manage HAP page tables, and only for the part of the address space accessible in user mode (the lower half of the address space in the x86-64 architecture). All other page tables (including the kernel address space for HAPs) can be managed by the OS without hypervisor intervention.

By combining the access control for physical frames provided by EPT with management of guest page tables only when necessary, InkTag isolates HAPs from an untrusted operating system while still taking advantage of modern virtualization hardware.

4. Paraverification

The task of managing 𝕊-pages requires that the InkTag hypervisor have deep visibility into low-level OS operations, such as updating page tables. This kind of detailed introspection introduces complexity into the hypervisor that can impede efforts to reason about its correctness. In addition, interposing on low-level operations harms performance with needless traps into the hypervisor.

Previous systems have attempted to remove trust from the operating system in a way that is largely transparent to *both the application and operating system*. This section highlights the significant challenges to application security and system performance presented by this approach.

4.1 Verification challenges

InkTag creates a secure address space for HAPs by managing only the user mode portions of HAP page tables, as described in Section 3.2. Here we explain all the steps necessary for the InkTag hypervisor to detect and interpret a page table update. InkTag must intercept low-level page table updates (*"Set page table entry at address A to x."*), determine their high-level effects (*"Map physical frame P at virtual address V."*), and compare those effects against the address space specified by an application (*"The application wants to map the 𝕊-page S at address V, do the contents of the physical frame have the same hash as S?"*).

[1] EPT is the terminology used for nested paging on Intel processors. Although InkTag was designed for Intel processors, we believe the design to be equally applicable to AMD processors.

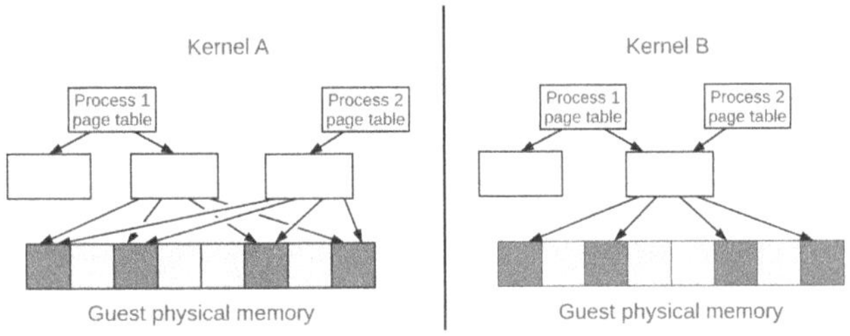

Figure 3. Two kernels mapping the address space of process that share a file. Both are non-malicious, but kernel B confounds efficient verification efforts by sharing page tables between processes.

Interpreting low-level updates Consider the task of placing a memory mapping into an application's page tables. The InkTag hypervisor can protect page table memory so the OS faults into the hypervisor when it attempts to write the page table. However, in order to determine the OS's intent, the hypervisor must then unprotect page table memory, wait for the OS to update the page table, and then retroactively determine what state changed by examining a significant amount of context information, such as saved backups of previous page table state and the role of the modified page in the application's page tables.

To efficiently interpret low-level page table updates, InkTag maintains state that allows it to determine high-level effects without reconstructing the entire address space on each update. For example, InkTag remembers which physical frames are used in application page tables, their position in the page table hierarchy, and the range of virtual addresses that they might map. Then, when the kernel sets a single entry at the leaf of the page table tree, InkTag can determine which virtual address is affected without tracing the page table from its root.

Maintaining state to efficiently verify page table updates requires InkTag to make basic assumptions about the structure of page tables. Recording the address mapped by each page of a page table requires that page tables are arranged in trees, and that separate page tables do not share any pages. A significant challenge for InkTag is that it is possible for an operating system to violate these assumptions, while still correctly managing an application's address space.

Figure 3 shows two applications that both map the same 2MB region of the same file, with both mappings aligned on a 2MB boundary (2MB is the range of virtual addresses mapped by a single leaf of a page table in the x86-64 architecture, which maps 512 4KB pages). An operating system could share a page between the page tables of both applications, while still correctly mapping each application's address space.

Even with an operating system that is both non-malicious and respects assumptions about page table structure, it is possible for the order in which the hypervisor receives updates to create the appearance of malicious or non-standard behavior. The technique of trapping writes to page tables, allowing the OS to make updates, then later examining the (potentially multiple) modified entries means that the hypervisor may not perceive updates in the same order as they were performed by the guest OS. Suppose the OS deallocates a page of file data, and then reuses that page as a page table for a different process. In this order, these updates may be benign. In the other order, it appears that the OS is allowing one application access to another's page tables, a likely violation of address space integrity.

Determining application intent Once a low-level page table update has been interpreted as an operation on a HAP's virtual address space, InkTag must determine if the mapping installed by the operating system is consistent with the application's operations on its address space. The application itself records its address space operations by making a hypercalls for all such operations, such as the `mmap()` system call. The hypervisor must communicate with the application to synchronize this information, and should do so with low overhead. Page faults can be a performance-critical operation, and mechanisms exist in the Linux kernel to quickly query the contents of the address space on a page fault, including balanced trees and caches of recently faulted areas. InkTag should handle faults without significant additional overhead, and also without simply duplicating these performance-oriented structures in both the hypervisor and application.

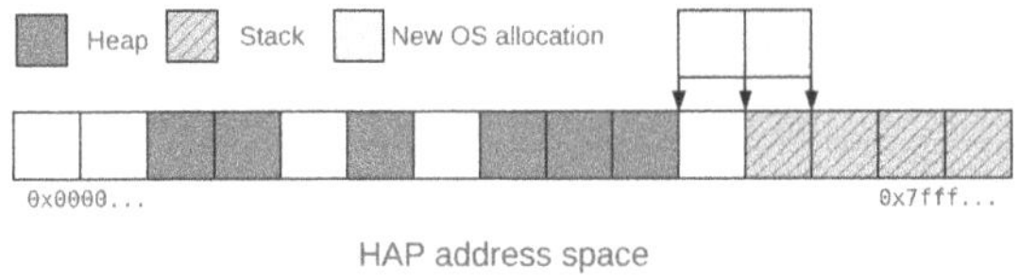

Figure 4. An Iago attack. An application relying on the OS to allocate its address space may be subverted by a malicious OS, if the OS allocates memory regions that are not disjoint.

Protecting applications from OS duplicity Although InkTag can isolate a HAP from the operating system, the application must still interact with the OS in order to use essential services, such as opening files and mapping its address space. Traditionally, through system calls such as `mmap()`, applications allow the operating system to determine where in their address space to map resources. Although `mmap()` allows an application to specify a fixed address for a mapping, this feature is seldom used by application code. Applications' reliance on OS allocation of the address space opens the door to *Iago attacks* [8], a class of attacks against systems with untrusted operating systems.

Iago attacks exploit the fact that existing applications and libraries, most importantly the standard C library, do not expect a malicious operating system. They do not verify that a virtual address returned by the OS in response to `mmap()` corresponds to an existing mapping in the application address space. For example, an application expects to run with its heap and stack in disjoint regions of its virtual address space. If the application requests a new memory mapping, the operating system could return an address that overlaps the application's stack. Writes to the new mapping will overwrite portions of the stack, introducing a vector to a traditional return-to-libc or return-oriented programming attack [43].

4.2 Paraverification

We introduce a new technique called **paraverification** to simplify the hypervisor by requiring the untrusted operating system to participate in verifying its own behavior. Paraverification helps InkTag efficiently address the challenges of verifying address space integrity, drawing inspiration from commonly-used *paravirtualization* techniques [5], which improve performance when an OS is run in a virtual machine. Both paraverification and paravirtualization work by having the OS communicate a high-level description of its intent directly to the hypervisor. Indeed, our paraverification implementation uses the Linux kernel's paravirtualization interface. Before modifying a process's page tables in the example above, the OS must first make a hypercall to correlate the page table update with a high-level application request. The kernel's paravirtualization interface includes a natural hook for this hypercall.

Although the guest operating system participates in verification, it safely remains untrusted because the hypervisor protects resources that it does not trust the OS to modify. Rather than protecting application page tables, detecting faults from the untrusted

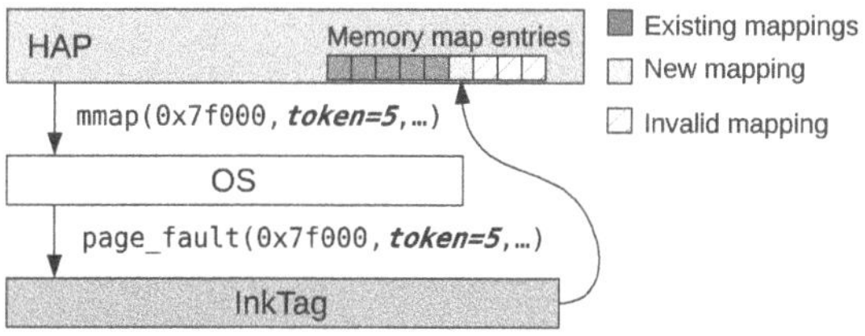

Figure 5. Paraverified isolation. A HAP maintains a list of memory mappings in its secure address space, providing the untrusted OS indices into the list. The untrusted OS must pass the same index to the InkTag hypervisor in order to handle page faults.

OS, and trying to re-verify address space integrity, the InkTag hypervisor protects application page tables and then considers any access to be malicious. The OS cannot update the tables directly, it must use the paravirtual interface, and the hypervisor will respond to unexpected accesses by taking corrective action (such as killing the OS).

4.3 Paraverified isolation

InkTag isolates a HAP's address space using paraverified operations on secure pages. As described in section 4.1, InkTag must validate OS page table updates to ensure that HAP virtual addresses map the correct, unmodified 𝕊-page. To do so, the untrusted operating system must pair each page table update with data proving that the update reflects the application's intent.

When a HAP maps a region of memory to a file, it provides the untrusted OS kernel a secure *token* that describes the mapping. The token is an unforgeable statement from the application to the hypervisor that fully describes the requested mapping. One possibility for a token would be an HMAC on a description of the desired mapping, using a secret key shared between the HAP and the hypervisor. InkTag does not use an HMAC, but a simple integer, which we now explain.

Because InkTag isolates a HAP from the operating system and must manage HAP page tables, it can optimize the communication of tokens from application to the untrusted OS to the hypervisor. All InkTag HAPs maintain a list of the mappings that make up their address space, in the form of a list with nodes allocated from a single array at a known virtual address in the application's address space. The untrusted OS cannot forge or modify entries in the array, as it does not have access to the HAP's address space. Because the hypervisor intercepts all page table updates for the HAP, it can trivially keep a small translation lookaside buffer for just the virtual addresses that map the array of nodes. In InkTag, a token to describe a memory mapping consists of a simple integer index into its list of maps.

On initialization, a HAP invokes a hypercall to inform the hypervisor about the base and limit of its mapping list. When the HAP creates a new memory mapping, it allocates a new entry from its array of nodes, initializes it with information about the mapping: the address range, OID and offset the HAP intends to map, as well as a marker to indicate that this entry is now valid. The HAP then sends the index of the entry to the untrusted OS as a token. When the OS incurs a page fault, it uses its existing structures for indexing memory mappings (already in service to handle the page fault) to locate the token and sends it to the hypervisor along with the remaining information describing the page table update: the address of the page table entry, the updated page table value, and the affected virtual address.

Upon receiving the page table update and token, the hypervisor ensures the token describes a valid index in the HAP's array. If so, it uses its lookaside buffer to translate the virtual address and retrieves the mapping information. If the described address range matches the fault, the hypervisor uses the provided object and offset information to verify the contents of the newly mapped physical frame. If the address range does not match the fault, the index is not contained within the HAP's array, or the index does not specify a valid entry, the hypervisor will not install the new mapping. In the rare event that the virtual address corresponding to the entry is not mapped, the hypervisor does not install the mapping and injects a page fault into the application when it is next scheduled. The page fault, if correctly handled by the untrusted OS, will cause the hypervisor to refill its lookaside buffer, the application retries the original access and faults again, and the hypervisor may now access the entry for the token.

Paraverification for HAP address spaces significantly reduces the complexity of the InkTag hypervisor. Significant OS code is dedicated to efficiently looking up memory ranges during memory management. Without paraverification, InkTag must duplicate this code so that it may efficiently respond to changes in the HAP's page tables. Instead, InkTag leverages the existing OS index structures by requiring that the OS look up the relevant token for a new mapping.

4.4 Verification of address space invariants

An Iago attack subverts application security by violating invariants that the application assumes are true about its address space: that mappings returned by the operating system do not overlap. However, an untrusted OS may violate this invariant at any time. In response, a HAP could take on the responsibility of allocating regions of its address space, only requesting new mappings at fixed addresses, and not accepting any variation from the untrusted OS. However, we wish to avoid importing significant OS functionality into either the hypervisor or application. Alternately, a HAP may verify that each mapping allocated on its behalf by the OS respects necessary invariants. We take this approach with InkTag, while shifting the burden of proving that mappings respect invariants from the HAP to the untrusted operating system.

InkTag HAPs use an array of descriptors to enumerate the contents of their address space. They maintain a linked list of entries, sorted in address order, with integer indices serving as previous and next pointers. When a HAP requests a new mapping from the OS, in addition to returning the newly allocated address, the OS also must return a token to the application: the index of the application's entry in its list of maps that is immediately previous to the new address allocated by the untrusted OS. As a result, the HAP can trivially both validate that the new map does not overlap any existing maps, and insert it into the list in the proper location, without needing to maintain its own sorting structures.

As with page table updates, paraverification for address space invariants allows applications to defend against a duplicitous operating system, while relying on existing indexing structures within the untrusted OS to perform most verification tasks.

5. Access control

Isolation and address space integrity provide the building blocks for secure HAP execution under an untrusted operating system. However, real systems require usable mechanisms for securely sharing data. InkTag is the first system to provide access control under an untrusted OS.

Access control mechanisms in InkTag should meet the following criteria:

- **Efficiency.** Ultimately, the hypervisor will be responsible for enforcing access control, and must do so on performance-critical events, such as updating page tables. In addition, we wish to avoid bloating the trusted computing base by requiring the hypervisor to evaluate complex policy decisions. A good access control mechanism will have a simple and efficient hypervisor implementation.

- **Familiarity.** A wide spectrum of access control mechanisms exist, both in the literature and in practice. However, most systems still rely on, and are well served by, users and groups. InkTag's access control mechanism should map easily onto these familiar primitives.
- **Flexibility.** Although users and groups will ease adoption, we also believe that the security-critical applications that InkTag is designed to support will benefit from the ability to create custom, descriptive access control policies. A shared, omnipotent user such as the Unix "root" creates similar security problems to a shared operating system, so users of InkTag should be able to create policies for their data without the blessing of a system administrator.

Unlike traditional access control systems that define principals (such as users in Unix), InkTag allows new principals, or even new types of principals, to be defined in a decentralized way. For example, an InkTag system might implement decentralized groups, in which any set of users can create a new group and agree to a group administrator. Similarly, an InkTag system can implement decentralized user login: each user must only trust her own personal login program, not a special system binary (§5.3).

5.1 Attributes for access control

Access control in InkTag is based on *attributes*. An attribute is a string, such as $.user.alice$ or $.group.prof$. Each HAP in InkTag carries a list of attributes that is inherited across events such as `fork()` and `exec()`, similar to the way in which Unix processes have an effective user or group id. Each OID has an access control list that specifies the attributes that must be carried by a HAP for that HAP to access the object. OID access control lists are divided into three access modes: read, write, and modify. Each access mode specifies an *attribute formula*, a logical formula that must evaluate to true for a HAP to access the object.

The read and write access modes of an OID specify formulas that must evaluate to true for a principal to read or write the object. For example, $W = .user.alice$ is a simple formula that evaluates to true (allowing write access) if a HAP has the $.user.alice$ attribute. $R = (.user.alice) \vee (.group.prof)$ is a formula that evaluates to true (allowing read access) if a HAP has either the $.user.alice$ or the $.group.prof$ attribute. The modify access mode allows a HAP to modify the attribute formula for any of the access modes in an OID's access control list.

In addition to access control lists on OIDs, attributes themselves also specify access control lists, albeit with only two modes: add and modify. The add access mode allows a HAP that satisfies the associated attribute formula to add the attribute to its own list. Access control lists on attributes are the mechanism by which HAPs in InkTag can take on the role of different principals, analogous to a `setuid` binary in Unix that allows a user to access resources owned by another principal. For example, the $.user.alice$ attribute might have the access mode $A = .apps.login$, which means that any HAP that has the $.apps.login$ attribute can add the $.user.alice$ attribute. A HAP can drop an attribute it owns at any time via a hypercall. As with files, the modify access mode for an attribute allows a HAP to change an attribute's access control list. Modifying attributes is how InkTag HAPs manage their access control credentials.

All attribute formulas are expressed in disjunctive normal form (DNF) without any negations. This makes attribute formulas simple to evaluate in the hypervisor, and also easy for people to understand. Checking attribute formulas requires only 207 lines of code in the InkTag hypervisor.

5.2 Decentralized access control

An important goal for InkTag's attribute system is *decentralization*. An InkTag user should be able to define new principals and policies to control access to her files. Decentralized access control allows high-assurance, multi-user services to define their own access control policies, enforced by the hypervisor, without relying on a system administrator.

InkTag decentralizes attributes with *hierarchically named attributes*. Attributes are named hierarchically, as a list of components separated with a '.' character. If a HAP has attribute X, then the HAP may create new attributes named $X.Y$ for any Y. For example, if user `alice` is represented using the attribute $.user.alice$, she might create the attribute $.user.alice.photos$ for her photo-sharing program. This attribute could be used both to restrict photo access to specific authorized programs, as well as to ensure that a photo-sharing program does not access unrelated files, by running it with only the attribute $.user.alice.photos$, and not the parent attribute $.user.alice$.

5.3 Login and decentralized login

User login provides an instructive case study for access control. First, consider a system that wants to have a single trusted login program. The system must provide a trusted path from that binary to a shell that runs with a user's attribute (e.g., $.user.alice$).

The InkTag hypervisor starts every HAP with a special attribute $.bin.\langle\text{oid}\rangle$, where $\langle\text{oid}\rangle$ is the string representation of the file's OID. The system administrator defines the $.apps.login$ attribute with an add access mode $A = .bin.\langle\text{login oid}\rangle$ where $\langle\text{login oid}\rangle$ identifies the login binary. When the login binary starts, it makes a hypercall to obtain the $.apps.login$ attribute. The $.user.alice$ attribute has an add access mode $A = .apps.login$, allowing the login program to add the $.user.alice$ attribute when presented with the proper credential (such as a password). Users trust the login program to drop the $.apps.login$ attribute, so once Alice has control, the HAP can no longer change users. The login program then `exec`s Alice's shell, which runs with the $.user.alice$ attribute.

With centralized login, all users trust the login binary (and its administrator). With decentralized login, a user need only trust her own login binary, though she still must obtain permission for her user name from an administrator (after all, it is the login process being decentralized, not the add user operation). The user administrator (whoever can run programs that have the $.user$ attribute) establishes the $.user.alice$ attribute with an add access mode $A = .apps.login.alice$. Alice compiles her login program, informs the login administrator (who can run programs that have the $.apps.login$ attribute), to create the $.apps.login.alice$ attribute with add access mode $A = .bin.\langle\text{alice login oid}\rangle$.

To log in, Alice executes her login program, which is given the attribute $.bin.\langle\text{alice login oid}\rangle$ by the hypervisor. The login program obtains the $.apps.login.alice$ attribute, dropping the attribute $.bin.\langle\text{alice login oid}\rangle$. It then checks Alice's credential (e.g., password), and if valid, obtains the $.user.alice$ attribute, dropping the attribute $.apps.login.alice$, and starting a shell.

With decentralized login, a user can completely control how they log in, using whatever credentials and process they desire. There is no single login binary that serves as a target for malicious attacks. A compromised decentralized login binary gives the attacker credentials only for the compromised user. In practice, systems would likely provide a default login binary for users who do not want to create their own.

As part of future work, we plan on investigating the security implications of InkTag's attribute-based access control.

5.4 Naming and integrity

InkTag does not currently support sets of OIDS (i.e., directories). However, the hierarchical layout of traditional file systems does convey an important property that is essential for application security: file integrity. Consider the standard Unix `/etc` directory. Applications rely on the property that only trusted system administrators can create or modify files in `/etc`, because those configuration files can dramatically change application behavior. InkTag must provide some mechanism to convey similar security-essential information.

InkTag provides integrity guarantees for files with specialized attributes called *namespaces*. Namespaces are strings created hierarchically, as attributes, and have access control lists that allow a HAP to add the namespace to its list of attributes. Although we consider attributes for access control and namespaces to be conceptually distinct, they are functionally identical.

Namespaces convey integrity information by acting as gatekeepers to file creation. When an application creates a new file, the InkTag hypervisor must assign the file an OID. Each OID is generated from two components: a namespace and an arbitrary string, similarly to the way in which a file is created within a directory, with a given file name. To generate an OID, the application must carry the desired namespace in its list of attributes. The hypervisor hashes the two components, and uses the result as the new OID. Any HAP that later accesses the file knows that it was created by a HAP that carried the associated namespace.

Note that namespaces do not restrict file access—a HAP may open a file created within a namespace regardless of whether it carries that namespace in its list. Consider a configuration directory similar to `/etc`. In InkTag, there would exist a $.ns.etc$ namespace, with the add access mode $A = .group.sysadmin$. A HAP run by a system administrator (member of the sysadmin group, thus carrying the $.group.sysadmin$ attribute) may create a file by adding the $.ns.etc$ attribute, specifying a name (e.g. "passwd"), and passing both components to the hypervisor, which permits the OID's creation.

A HAP opening the file generates the OID by hashing $.ns.etc$ and "passwd," though it is not required to carry the $.ns.etc$ namespace, only to know of its existence. The HAP can trust that the contents of the file were generated by a system administrator, because only a member of of the sysadmin group could create the file initially (as checked by the hypervisor), and it trusts such principals to correctly manage access control for files they create.

6. Storage and consistency

InkTag stores secure page metadata in memory for any secure pages whose data segments also reside in memory. The untrusted operating system is responsible for placing the data segments of secure pages on the virtual disk. For secure pages to be durable, InkTag must also store secure metadata: the OID and offset corresponding to each block of data, its hash, and the encryption initialization vector (IV) necessary to decrypt the data. This section addresses a number of practical challenges in persistently and transparently storing $\mathbb{S}$-page metadata, including addressing consistency between OS and InkTag storage.

Data layout InkTag must synchronize updates to $\mathbb{S}$-pages and metadata, and should store secure metadata efficiently. When the OS issues a read request for secure page data, the hypervisor should not require significant additional lookup work in order to also read in secure page metadata. Also, storing secure metadata should not confound OS disk scheduling by adding disk seeks to store or retrieve secure metadata.

InkTag addresses these goals by interspersing storage of secure page data and metadata on the physical disk, then presenting the

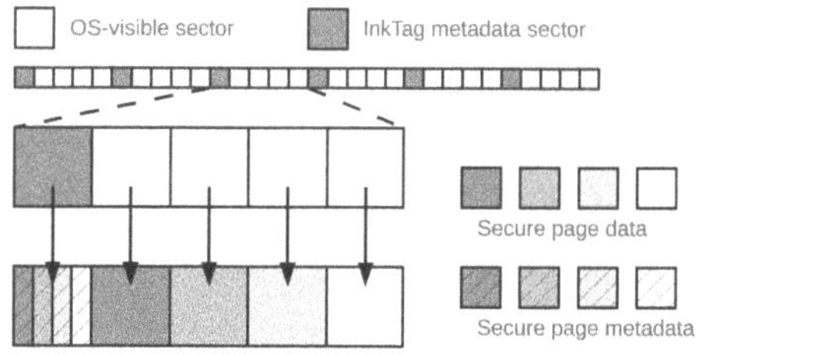

Figure 6. InkTag disk layout. Data and metadata are interleaved to optimize disk scheduling.

data storage to the untrusted OS as a contiguous virtual disk without the sectors employed to store secure metadata. The size of the media, as seen by the untrusted OS, is smaller than the size of the physical drive or backing file. When reading or writing a secure page, the secure InkTag metadata will always reside in the closest metadata storage block, causing limited performance overheads.

Synchronizing storage of secure data and metadata InkTag employs paraverification techniques to properly synchronize storage of secure data and metadata. Before the untrusted OS may write out a page via the virtual disk, it must notify the InkTag hypervisor. If the physical frame being written contains data for an $\mathbb{S}$-page, InkTag ensures that the page is encrypted, and passes the relevant metadata to the backend driver for the virtual disk. The backend consumes this metadata while writing pages to the physical disk, placing each piece of secure metadata in the metadata block closest to disk block containing the data for the $\mathbb{S}$-page.

Providing guarantees on data availability Although InkTag is unable to provide availability guarantees in many cases, the hypervisor can enforce OS deadlines for writing out dirty data. For example, if a reasonable upper bound for dirty data residing in the OS is 30 seconds, InkTag may suspect OS malfeasance if it has not detected a write of a particular secure page after 45 seconds. Although the hypervisor may not be able to retrieve $\mathbb{S}$-pages in memory that the OS has simply erased, it can prevent applications from proceeding under the incorrect assumption that $\mathbb{S}$-pages are safely on disk. Similarly, a HAP may notify the InkTag hypervisor when it explicitly requests that dirty pages be written out (such as when invoking the `msync` system call), and receive confirmation when the writeback actually occurs, or a warning that the OS has not complied.

Preventing deletion or loss of high-assurance data Because filesystem indexing structures vary widely between file systems, it is difficult to verify their correctness at hypervisor level. As a result, a malicious OS could appear to comply with InkTag policy by writing out file data blocks but not updating filesystem metadata, leaving file data blocks inaccessible.

InkTag provides a secure `fsck` mechanism for *conservation of high-assurance data* in the face of this threat. Secure page metadata includes file and offset information, allowing InkTag to reconstruct secure files independently of OS indexing structures. In addition, InkTag may prevent the OS from overwriting a secure page, unless the OS is replacing the page with a newer version of the same secure page, or if a newer version of the page has previously been written elsewhere on disk.

Consistency for secure pages in the face of crashes InkTag is the first system to address consistency requirements for an untrusted operating system. Without proper filesystem consistency, file data may become unavailable, file updates may be lost, and access control changes may not be honored.

When the OS writes an $\mathbb{S}$-page to disk on behalf of a HAP, both the new $\mathbb{S}$-page and its hash must be stored. If the system crashes after only writing the 𝕊-page contents or the hash, valid data could become unavailable, because InkTag would be unable to verify its authenticity. InkTag keeps two versions of each 𝕊-page's hash: the version for the page on disk before the update, and after. Before a data write, InkTag will store the updated hash on disk. Because disk drives write blocks atomically, a hash matching the data will always be on disk, and high-assurance data on the backing store will always be available.

In our current prototype, per-file metadata (such as access control information and the file's length) is stored separately from the guest filesystem, in storage private to the hypervisor. We leave to future work enforcing consistency between per-file and per-page metadata.

7. Implementation

This section describes our prototype implementation of InkTag. InkTag consists of three major components: the InkTag hypervisor, extensions to the untrusted guest OS to support paraverification, and tools to compile user-level applications to run as HAPs.

7.1 InkTag hypervisor

The InkTag hypervisor is built as an extension to the KVM (Kernel Virtual Machine) hypervisor, a standard module included in the Linux kernel. We extend the Linux 2.6.36 kernel and KVM implementation. InkTag is built to support Intel's VMX hardware virtualization support, although we believe its design to be equally applicable to hardware virtualization support in AMD processors.

During execution of the untrusted guest operating system and non-InkTag applications, the hypervisor behaves almost identically to a hypervisor without InkTag support, with most virtualization tasks handled by hardware virtualization extensions present in the processor. The untrusted EPT (§3.2) is used to translate guest-physical addresses during untrusted execution, and most page table operations (except for those on a HAP's address space) occur without hypervisor intervention.

Scheduling Upon scheduling a HAP, InkTag must ensure that the untrusted OS cannot execute any code in a high-assurance context. To protect the HAP from the OS, it disallows automatic vectoring of interrupts and exceptions by the virtualization hardware. If InkTag allowed the hardware to vector interrupts automatically, then the operating system would gain control while still executing in a high-assurance context, with cleartext access to secure pages. Intel processors allow for fine-grained control over enabled virtualization features via bits in the virtual machine control structure (VMCS), the hardware descriptor used to control virtualization. To schedule a HAP, InkTag clears many of the feature bits in the VMCS, installs the trusted EPT, and then transfers control to the HAP.

When an interrupt or exception occurs during HAP execution, InkTag saves and then clears the HAP's register file. The untrusted OS must be prevented from reading or writing HAP registers. InkTag directs the instruction pointer to a small *untrusted trampoline* in a part of the HAP's address space unprotected by InkTag. This trampoline is responsible for interactions between the HAP and the guest OS (such as invoking system calls), and also for rescheduling the HAP when the HAP's process context is rescheduled by the operating system. The HAP receives system call results from the trampoline, but does not trust it — all information is validated as if it came from the untrusted OS.

Page tables Each HAP has two page tables, and shares the system-wide trusted and untrusted EPTs. One page table is written directly by the untrusted kernel, which we refer to as the *OS page table*. It is written directly by the OS (even when using the paravirtualized interface, Linux also updates the page table directly), and its contents are not trusted. The other page table is written only by the InkTag hypervisor in response to calls by the untrusted OS that are successfully verified, which we refer to as the *hypervisor page table*. The hypervisor page table is trusted. For a non-malicious OS, its page table should be a superset of the hypervisor page table.

When a HAP runs in untrusted mode (e.g., just before making a system call), `cr3` points to the OS page table, and when a HAP runs in trusted mode, the hypervisor points `cr3` to the hypervisor page table. In trusted mode, there is a single untrusted mapping, for the pages used to marshal and unmarshal system call arguments. InkTag must guarantee that the OS has not overlapped the mapping of this area with any trusted mapping. In untrusted mode, the process can map any 𝕊-page, but access to that page will be detected by the permission bits in the untrusted EPT, and the hypervisor will encrypt and hash the page before giving the untrusted code access to the page.

Although the untrusted OS cannot access the hypervisor page tables, it is responsible for their allocation. On each page table allocation on behalf of a HAP, the guest OS must also allocate a hypervisor page table page and send both to the InkTag hypervisor in order to successfully add to the page table tree. The hypervisor protects the hypervisor page table page from the guest OS until that part of the page table tree is deallocated, at which point the guest regains access.

7.2 Untrusted OS extensions

We extend the untrusted guest kernel to support paraverification. Information about updates to HAP page tables form the majority of paraverification events, and take advantage of existing paravirtualization callbacks present in the Linux kernel. We install an untrusted module into the guest kernel to handle these callbacks. The kernel module is responsible for receiving tokens from HAPs requesting memory mappings, and passing these tokens to the InkTag hypervisor on page faults.

Although untrusted, the guest kernel module is cooperative when uncompromised, and attempts to minimize the amount of communication with the InkTag hypervisor. Any hypercall causes a VM-exit (a context switch from guest to hypervisor), thus unnecessary communication should be avoided to maximize performance. The untrusted kernel module tracks which processes contain HAPs, and communicates page table information only for those processes. In addition, the kernel module performs extensive batching of page table updates. While the Linux paravirtualization interface supports some batching of address space updates (such as a series of page table updates occurring before a TLB flush), our kernel module extends this buffering significantly, because the InkTag hypervisor can safely wait to process most updates until directly before scheduling a HAP. This allows communication of paraverification information without any additional VM-exits, as scheduling a HAP already requires passing control to the InkTag hypervisor.

7.3 Building HAPs

In our current prototype, InkTag HAPs must be compiled from C source code. C applications are built as HAPs primarily by replacing the standard C library and startup files with InkTag-specific versions. We modify standard C startup files to initialize the current process as a HAP before passing control to the C library. On initialization, the HAP sends the OID of its executable to the InkTag hypervisor, which initializes a HAP context, and adds the $.bin.\langle\mathsf{oid}\rangle$ attribute. Note that any process may invoke initialization claiming to be any executable OID. However, after initialization the InkTag hypervisor will ensure integrity for the process address space. Thus to continue executing as a HAP, the process must construct an address space that is byte-for-byte identical, and thus functionally equivalent, to the originally claimed binary.

	Linux	InkTag	Overhead
null	0.04	2.23	55.80×
open/close	0.87	6.90	7.95×
ctxsw 2p/0k	0.71	1.01	1.41×
File create	5.46	12.92	2.36×
File delete	3.40	7.56	2.23×
mmap	4059.20	40360.00	9.94×
pagefault	0.89	6.68	7.50×
fork	99.00	567.80	5.74×
fork+exec	290.60	882.60	3.04×

Table 2. LMbench latency microbenchmark results (in microseconds.)

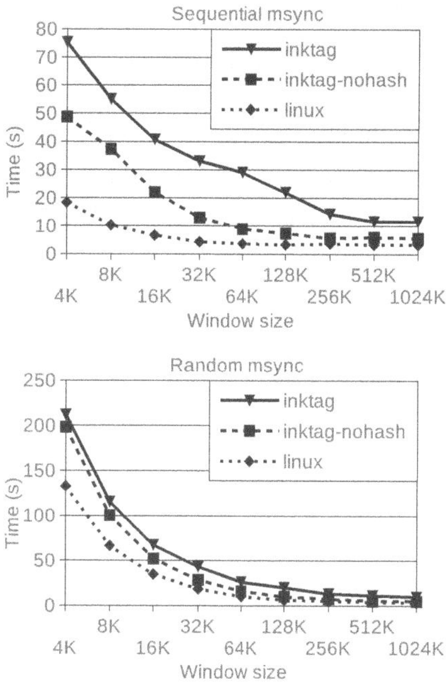

Figure 7. InkTag storage backend performance as measured by sequential or random msync()s on a memory-resident file.

We automate HAP interaction with the InkTag hypervisor by interposing on system calls in the standard C library. For example, when an application calls `mmap()`, the system call is intercepted by our trusted InkTag library. The library performs the system call, validates the result to ensure that the untrusted OS does not violate invariants for the address space (§4.4), and passes a token to the untrusted OS for handling page faults in the newly mapped region (§4.3).

InkTag does not expose information about hashes and encryption keys for 𝕊-pages to applications. Thus HAPs must interact with secure files by mapping them into their address space. We implement `mmap()`-based versions of standard `read()` and `write()` system calls to support applications that rely on those calls for file I/O.

7.4 Block Driver

To implement transparent loading of 𝕊-page metadata, we add a new block driver implementation to the QEMU (the userspace portion of KVM) block driver interface. The new block driver transparently translates read and write requests from the hardware emulation layer. Doing the translation at this level puts us at the lowest layer before the actual hardware allowing us to better adjust and handle the block requests.

Our secure metadata consists of two 32-byte hashes, an OID, and an offset. We place secure page metadata once every 32 pages of normal data. We track which disk sectors contain valid 𝕊-pages using a bitmap. This bitmap is mapped and updated as HAPs execute, and is written to disk only upon shutdown. This policy is safe even in the event of a crash: there will be enough data on disk to be able to recover the bitmap.

8. Evaluation

In this section we evaluate the performance overhead imposed by our InkTag prototype built in the KVM hypervisor. We evaluated InkTag's performance using two different machines: we run latency and SPEC CPU benchmarks on an i7 860 running at 2.80GHz, and InkTag block storage and application benchmarks on an Intel i7 870 at 2.93GHz. Both machines have quad-core processors, 8GB of memory, and run Ubuntu 10.04.4.

We modify the 2.6.36 Linux kernel and QEMU 0.12.5 for InkTag, and run unmodified versions for the baseline. VM guests run with a single virtual CPU, 2GB of memory, and the same kernel as the host. In the InkTag guest, all benchmark binaries run as HAPs.

8.1 Microbenchmarks

Table 2 shows results from the LMBench [30] suite of OS microbenchmarks. LMBench is a series of portable microbenchmarks focused on measuring individual OS operations in isolation. We restrict our evaluation to focus on file operations, memory manipulation, and process creation, as these are the areas that will be affected by running as an InkTag HAP. We modify LMBench only enough to turn its components into HAPs: 68 lines of modifications to the build system and 5 lines of configuration changes.

The null syscall benchmark primarily measures the latency of switching between an application and the OS, and represents the worst case for InkTag. A HAP must context switch from user context, to the virtual machine, then into the operating system, and then return along the opposite path. The high latency for switching between application and OS directly impacts the performance of nearly all of the LMBench microbenchmarks, as they measure interactions between an application and the operating system. Additionally, operations that involve any kind of page table update, such as `mmap`, `fork`, and `fork+exec`, are also affected due to the InkTag hypervisor validating each page table update. These overheads appear large in isolation; however, most applications are significantly less sensitive to system call latency than microbenchmarks. Most of the LMBench benchmarks show a difference in latency that is 10s of microseconds or less.

8.2 Storage

We evaluate InkTag's storage backend with a benchmark that synchronizes regions varying in size from a 256MB secure file cached in memory to the virtual disk. We disable host OS caching for our virtual disk, to best simulate the effect of actual disk scheduling on I/O throughput. Figure 7 shows the performance of syncing varying window sizes, from 4KB to 1MB, either sequentially through the file or in random order. In addition, we show numbers for a version of InkTag in which we have disabled encryption and hashing, in order to isolate the effect of disk scheduling on performance. The encryption and hashing occur when the OS touches 𝕊-pages to sync them to disk. Our InkTag prototype interleaves 𝕊-page data and metadata at an interval of 32 pages (128KB). For window sizes above 128KB, InkTag approaches the performance of a standard block device, as the InkTag block driver can combine a page of metadata with 32 data pages in a single write to the backing device. Beneath that threshold, InkTag's performance suffers, especially for sequential writes. This is due to InkTag's metadata lay-

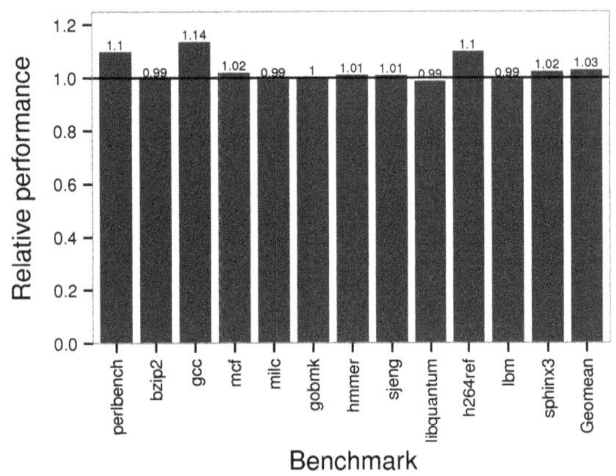

Figure 8. SPEC CPU2006 benchmark performance. "Geomean" indicates the geometric mean of relative performance.

	Linux	InkTag
Apache latency	195 ms	220 ms (1.13×)
Apache throughput	462.42 req/s	453.93 req/s (1.02×)
Dokuwiki throughput	13.6 req/s	8.83 req/s (1.54×)

Table 3. InkTag performance for large applications.

	Apache		DokuWiki	
	Linux	InkTag	Linux	InkTag
Check hash	-	209	-	2,911,649
Check zero hash	-	57	-	2,893,517
Update hash	-	82	-	1,029
EPT fault	689	1,131	10,668	78,055
VM-exit	171,145	1,217,042	138,801	11,216,363

Table 4. Counts of performance-critical events during benchmark execution. We count the number of times InkTag must hash a data page ("Check hash"), hash a data page that should be zero-initialized ("Check zero hash"), encrypt a page and update its hash ("Update hash"), fault on a nested page table ("EPT fault"), and context-switch out of the guest ("VM-exit").

out. For example, sequential writes to each of the 4KB pages in a single cluster of data pages represents a good case for disk scheduling. InkTag, however, must write the metadata page followed by the data page for each of these writes, causing the disk to seek back and forth instead of writing sectors in sequential order.

8.3 Application benchmarks

We measure the overhead imposed by InkTag with three different types of applications: CPU-bound SPEC benchmarks, the Apache web server, and DokuWiki, a complete wiki application converted to use InkTag attributes for authentication.

SPEC With little OS interaction, CPU-bound applications exhibit little performance overhead when running as HAPs. Figure 8 shows results for selected benchmarks from the SPEC 2006 [19] suite (InkTag does not support Fortran). Out of twelve benchmarks, nine benchmarks run within a 3% performance overhead of unmodified KVM, and `gcc` benchmark has the largest overhead of 14%.

Apache Table 3 shows results for our evaluation of the performance of the Apache webserver when compiled as a HAP. We run the standard `ab` benchmarking tool included with Apache on the machine hosting the virtualized guest, providing nearly unlimited bandwidth from the web server to client. We execute 10,000 requests from client to server, at a concurrency level of 100. The Apache web server serves requests with a 13% overhead in latency, and a 2% overhead in throughput relative to normal virtualized execution. Apache represents a relatively good case for InkTag: with several long-lived processes, Apache rarely has to pay the increased costs imposed by InkTag for application initialization and teardown.

DokuWiki In order to demonstrate the ability of InkTag to provide security for realistic workloads, we modified the DokuWiki[2] wiki server to take advantage of InkTag secure files and access control. DokuWiki is a wiki written in PHP that stores wiki pages as files in the server filesystem. We recompiled the PHP CGI binary to work with InkTag and ran DokuWiki as a CGI script. We added an InkTag authentication module to DokuWiki to allow a user to log in with their system credentials (similar to the decentralized login process described in §5.3) and to restrict access to wiki content via InkTag access control.

To test the effect of InkTag on a representative set of modifications to a representative DokuWiki installation, we downloaded a set of 6,430 revisions of 765 pages from the DokuWiki website (which is itself run using DokuWiki) to simulate wiki activity. We evaluate DokuWiki with a 90% read workload, which we believe a reasonable characterization of a wiki workload. Each write replaces a page with the subsequent revision of a page in the downloaded DokuWiki corpus. We measured the total wallclock time for 10 clients to perform a collective 1,000 requests on the wiki. Our wiki client makes use of an XML RPC interface that DokuWiki provides to avoid the need for programmatically interfacing with DokuWiki forms.

As a HAP with InkTag authentication, DokuWiki runs with a 1.54× overhead over a baseline virtualized execution. As a PHP application, DokuWiki maps a large number of scripts (with integrity assured by the InkTag hypervisor) into memory and exercises a significant amount of anonymous temporary memory. As with OS users, InkTag's authentication aligns along process boundaries. Thus, we must run DokuWiki as an inefficient CGI application, not as an Apache module. CGI is a performance worst case for InkTag: each request initializes and destroys an entire application address space.

Virtualization metrics Table 4 shows counts for a number of performance-critical events during the execution of our large application benchmarks. Specific to InkTag execution are the number of times physical frames are hashed, as well the number of times the hash of the associated $\mathbb{S}$-page is updated (this event also counts the number of times an $\mathbb{S}$-page must be encrypted). With a few long-lived processes, most of the address space for the Apache web server remains mapped in the trusted EPT, requiring relatively few hash updates. DokuWiki, which constructs and destroys an address space for each request, has a large number of hash operations.

Of particular note are the number of times InkTag is requested to verify the hash for a page consisting entirely of zeroes. In fact, the vast majority of hash operations are invoked to determine if a page is initialized to zero (2.8 out of 2.9 million hash operations for the DokuWiki benchmark). InkTag optimizes this case: when asked to verify the hash of a physical frame, InkTag compares the hash value with the hash of a zero page. If the page should contain only zero, InkTag simply verifies that property, rather than computing a full digest. As a result, computation of hashes is not a significant factor in InkTag's performance overhead. Similarly, while encryption is necessary for privacy, it does not significantly affect running time: the majority of pages that would otherwise be encrypted due to access by the operating system are in fact anonymous memory regions that have been unmapped by an application. The entire

[2] `http://www.dokuwiki.org`

memory region is being destroyed, so it needs only be erased, not encrypted for privacy and hashed for integrity.

A major factor for InkTag performance is the number of times the processor must switch context between the virtual machine and the host. In the DokuWiki benchmark, for example, InkTag must exit the virtual machine nearly two orders of magnitude more often than a standard execution. We hope to investigate ways to reduce the cost of such context switches as part of future work.

9. Related work

Untrusted operating systems InkTag, XOMOS [26], SP^3 [47], and Overshadow [11, 35] share the goal of minimizing the ability of an untrustworthy system component to tamper with a sensitive application. Previous work focused on isolating high-assurance applications from the system, while InkTag focuses on allowing the application to *use* untrusted system services, providing access control and crash recovery for persistent storage. For example, while Overshadow guarantees that user processes are isolated from the operating system, it does not implement access control for secure data: once an application that has created a secure file terminates, there is no meaningful way for processes to share access to that file.

Just as InkTag allows a trusted process and hypervisor to stop trusting the OS, CloudVisor [49] allows a trusted process, OS, and nested hypervisor to stop trusting the hypervisor and other cloud management software. Another approach, exemplified in Proxos [44], essentially reimplements portions of the OS in the application; this approach does not address shared abstractions between mutually untrusting programs.

Virtual machines The use of virtual machine monitors to help protect operating system and application execution is not a new concept; there have been systems ranging from providing dedicated virtual hardware per secure application [18] to enforcing kernel entry and exit points to provide system integrity [42]. By allowing applications to make use of extensive operating system facilities for sharing data, while still verifying its behavior, InkTag provides a much more flexible solution than heavyweight per-application virtualization. At the other end of the spectrum, simple code integrity is not sufficient to ensure operating system safety [21].

Trusted computing Recent systems, including Flicker [29], TrustVisor [28], and Memoir [33] leverage the TPM to completely isolate sensitive computations, such as encryption and random number generation, from the OS. These systems can protect an application's random number generator's internals from being leaked to the OS, but they cannot protect larger code that requires OS functionality, such as file access.

Benign OS integrity Another related branch of research attempts to prevent malicious inputs from compromising a non-malicious OS, including HookSafe [45], KernelGuard [39], and several others [2, 10, 27, 40]. These systems often prevent specific classes of security problems and are not designed for the strong adversarial model InkTag can defend against.

VM introspection Several systems attempt to enforce security properties on a non-malicious guest OS by interpreting low-level events based on expert information [24, 34, 38, 46], automatic source code extraction [17, 20, 23], or inferred from observing program executions [4, 14]. This interpretation is fragile (called the semantic gap [9]) and, broadly speaking, work in this area assumes a weak adversarial model. InkTag's paraverification avoids the semantic gap and provides fundamentally stronger guarantees.

Sandboxing This work is concerned with assuring the integrity of necessary OS functionality; yet this is easily conflated with the goal of isolating untrusted applications, or sandboxing. Several recent sandboxing architectures have explored techniques that limit OS access [15, 36, 48], or monitor system calls [3, 6, 16, 22, 37] to protect the OS's sharing abstractions from a malicious application.

Hierarchically Named Access Control In recent years, work in the area of hierarchical naming and attribute based access control has landed mostly in the area of distributed systems and grid computing [7, 12]. ABAC [41] and XACML [32] are both projects aimed at bringing attribute based access control to the enterprise world. InkTag differs in scope, whereas these projects try to define attributes on employees, InkTag tries to implement flexible access control at the level of individual processes.

UserFS [25] allows principals to hierarchically manage creation and deletion of sub-principals. The system uses traditional UIDs as a namespace for managing access control of files and resources. UserFS achieves the goals of efficiency and familiarity but has difficultly easily expressing group semantics and even more flexible access control policy since processes can have only one UID or effective UID at a time. InkTag does not depend on the complicated code in the guest operating system, and can achieve more flexible policies through attributes.

10. Conclusion

InkTag represents a significant step forward in verifying the behavior of untrusted operating systems. By removing the burden of attempting to verify a completely unmodified operating system, paraverification enables a simple, high-performance hypervisor implementation. InkTag is the first such system to enable access control for secure data, as well as address essential system issues such as crash consistency between OS-managed data and secure metadata.

Acknowledgments

We thank the anonymous reviewers and Carl Waldspurger for their comments on earlier versions of this paper. This research is supported by NIH R01 LM011028-01, NSF CNS-0905602, and NSF CAREER CNS-0644205.

References

[1] Microsoft security bulletin search, 2012. `http://technet.microsoft.com/security/bulletin`.

[2] Martín Abadi, Mihai Budiu, Úlfar Erlingsson, and Jay Ligatti. Control-flow integrity. In *CCS*, 2005.

[3] Anurag Acharya and Mandar Raje. MAPbox: Using parameterized behavior classes to confine applications. In *USENIX Security*, 2000.

[4] Arati Baliga, Vinod Ganapathy, and Liviu Iftode. Automatic inference and enforcement of kernel data structure invariants. In *ACSAC*, 2008.

[5] Paul Barham, Boris Dragovic, Keir Fraser, Steven Hand, Tim Harris, Alex Ho, Rolf Neugebauer, Ian Pratt, and Andrew Warfield. Xen and the art of virtualization. In *SOSP*, 2003.

[6] Massimo Bernaschi, Emanuele Gabrielli, and Luigi V. Mancini. REMUS: A security-enhanced operating system. *TISSEC*, 5(1), 2002.

[7] Rakesh Bobba, Omid Fatemieh, Fariba Khan, Carl A. Gunter, and Himanshu Khurana. Using attribute-based access control to enable attribute-based messaging. In *ACSAC*, 2006.

[8] Stephen Checkoway and Hovav Shacham. Iago attacks: Why the system call API is a bad untrusted RPC interface. In *ASPLOS*, March 2013.

[9] Peter M. Chen and Brian D. Noble. When virtual is better than real. In *HotOS*, pages 133–, 2001.

[10] Shuo Chen, Jun Xu, Emre C. Sezer, Prachi Gauriar, and Ravishankar K. Iyer. Non-control-data attacks are realistic threats. In *USENIX Security*, 2005.

[11] Xioaxin Chen, Tal Garfinkel, E. Christopher Lewis, Pratap Subrahmanyam, Carl A. Waldspurger, Dan Boneh, Jeffery Dwoskin, and Dan R. K. Ports. Overshadow: A virtualization-based approach to retrofitting protection in commodity operating systems. In *ASPLOS*, May 2008.

[12] Lorenzo Cirio, Isabel F. Cruz, and Roberto Tamassia. A role and attribute based access control system using semantic web technologies. In *OTM*, 2007.
[13] Tim Dierks and Eric Rescorla. RFC 5246: The Transport Layer Security (TLS) Protocol: Version 1.2. http://tools.ietf.org/html/rfc5246, 2008.
[14] Brendan Dolan-Gavitt, Tim Leek, Michael Zhivich, Jonathon Giffin, and Wenke Lee. Virtuoso: Narrowing the semantic gap in virtual machine introspection. In *Oakland*, May 2011.
[15] John R. Douceur, Jeremy Elson, Jon Howell, and Jacob R. Lorch. Leveraging legacy code to deploy desktop applications on the web. In *OSDI*, 2008.
[16] Timothy Fraser, Lee Badger, and Marc Feldman. Hardening COTS software with generic software wrappers. In *Oakland*, 1999.
[17] Timothy Fraser, Matthew R. Evenson, and William A. Arbaugh. VICI—virtual machine introspection for cognitive immunity. In *ACSAC*, pages 87–96, 2008.
[18] Tal Garfinkel, Ben Pfaff, Jim Chow, Mendel Rosenblum, and Dan Boneh. Terra: A virtual machine-based platform for trusted computing. In *SOSP*, October 2003.
[19] John L. Henning. SPEC CPU2006 benchmark descriptions. *ACM SIGARCH Computer Architecture News*, 34(4):1–17, 2006.
[20] Owen S. Hofmann, Alan M. Dunn, Sangman Kim, Indrajit Roy, and Emmett Witchel. Ensuring operating system kernel integrity with OSck. In *ASPLOS*, March 2011.
[21] Ralf Hund, Thorsten Holz, and Felix C. Freiling. Return-oriented rootkits: bypassing kernel code integrity protection mechanisms. In *USENIX Security*, 2009.
[22] Kapil Jain and R. Sekar. User-level infrastructure for system call interposition: A platform for intrusion detection and confinement. In *NDSS*, 2000.
[23] Xuxian Jiang, Xinyuan Wang, and Dongyan Xu. Stealthy malware detection through VMM-based "out-of-the-box" semantic view reconstruction. In *CCS*, pages 128–138, 2007.
[24] Stephen T. Jones, Andrea C. Arpaci-Dusseau, and Remzi H. Arpaci-Dusseau. Antfarm: tracking processes in a virtual machine environment. In *USENIX*, 2006.
[25] Taesoo Kim and Nickolai Zeldovich. Making linux protection mechanisms egalitarian with UserFS. In *USENIX Security*. USENIX Association, 2010.
[26] David Lie, Chandramohan A. Thekkath, and Mark Horowitz. Implementing an untrusted operating system on trusted hardware. In *SOSP*, pages 178–192. ACM Press, 2003.
[27] Peter A. Loscocco, Perry W. Wilson, J. Aaron Pendergrass, and C. Durward McDonell. Linux kernel integrity measurement using contextual inspection. In *STC*, 2007.
[28] Jonathan M. McCune, Yanlin Li, Ning Qu, Zongwei Zhou, Anupam Datta, Virgil Gligor, and Adrian Perrig. TrustVisor: Efficient TCB reduction and attestation. In *Oakland*, May 2010.
[29] Jonathan M. McCune, Bryan Parno, Adrian Perrig, Michael K. Reiter, and Hiroshi Isozaki. Flicker: An execution infrastructure for TCB minimization. In *EuroSys*, April 2008.
[30] Larry McVoy and Carl Staelin. LMbench: portable tools for performance analysis. In *USENIX*, pages 23–23, Berkeley, CA, USA, 1996. USENIX Association.
[31] NIST. National vulnerability database. http://nvd.nist.gov/, 2012.
[32] OASIS. eXtensible access control markup language. https://www.oasis-open.org/committees/tc_home.php?wg_abbrev=xacml, 2012.
[33] Bryan Parno, Jacob R. Lorch, John R. Douceur, James Mickens, and Jonathan M. McCune. Memoir: Practical state continuity for protected modules. In *Oakland*, 2011.
[34] Bryan D. Payne, Martim D. P. de A. Carbone, and Wenke Lee. Secure and flexible monitoring of virtual machines. In *ACSAC*, 2007.
[35] Dan R. K. Ports and Tal Garfinkel. Towards application security on untrusted operating systems. In *HotSec*, San Jose, CA, USA, 2008. USENIX.
[36] Shaya Potter and Jason Nieh. Apiary: Easy-to-use desktop application fault containment on commodity operating systems. In *USENIX*, 2010.
[37] Neils Provos. Improving host security with system call policies. In *USENIX Security*, 2003.
[38] Nguyen Anh Quynh and Yoshiyasu Takefuji. Towards a tamper-resistant kernel rootkit detector. In *SAC*, 2007.
[39] Junghwan Rhee, Ryan Riley, Dongyan Xu, and Xuxian Jiang. Defeating dynamic data kernel rootkit attacks via VMM-based guest-transparent monitoring. In *ARES*, Fukuoka, Japan, March 2009.
[40] Junghwan Rhee and Dongyan Xu. LiveDM: Temporal mapping of dynamic kernel memory for dynamic kernel malware analysis and debugging. Technical report, Purdue University, West Lafayette, IN, February 2010.
[41] Mike Ryan, Ted Faber, Mei-Hui Su, John Wroclawski, and Steve Schwab. A.B←A.C. http://abac.deterlab.net/, 2012.
[42] Arvind Seshadri, Mark Luk, Ning Qu, and Adrian Perrig. SecVisor: A tiny hypervisor to provide lifetime kernel code integrity for commodity OSes. In *SOSP*, pages 335–350, 2007.
[43] Hovav Shacham. The geometry of innocent flesh on the bone: Return-into-libc without function calls (on the x86). In *CCS*, pages 552–61. ACM Press, October 2007.
[44] Richard Ta-min, Lionel Litty, and David Lie. Splitting interfaces: Making trust between applications and operating systems configurable. In *OSDI*, pages 279–292, 2006.
[45] Zhi Wang, Xuxian Jiang, Weidong Cui, and Peng Ning. Countering kernel rootkits with lightweight hook protection. In *CCS*, 2009.
[46] Min Xu, Xuxian Jiang, Ravi Sandhu, and Xinwen Zhang. Towards a VMM-based usage control framework for OS kernel integrity protection. In *SACMAT*, 2007.
[47] Jisoo Yang and Kang G. Shin. Using hypervisor to provide data secrecy for user applications on a per-page basis. In *VEE*, pages 71–80, 2008.
[48] Bennet Yee, David Sehr, Gregory Dardyk, J. Bradley Chen, Robert Muth, Tavis Ormandy, Shiki Okasaka, Neha Narula, and Nicholas Fullagar. Native client: A sandbox for portable, untrusted x86 native code. In *Oakland*, pages 79–93, 2009.
[49] Fengzhe Zhang, Jin Chen, Haibo Chen, and Binyu Zang. CloudVisor: retrofitting protection of virtual machines in multi-tenant cloud with nested virtualization. In *SOSP*, 2011.

Safe and Automatic Live Update for Operating Systems

Cristiano Giuffrida Anton Kuijsten Andrew S. Tanenbaum
Vrije Universiteit, Amsterdam
{giuffrida, akuijst, ast}@cs.vu.nl

Abstract

Increasingly many systems have to run all the time with no downtime allowed. Consider, for example, systems controlling electric power plants and e-banking servers. Nevertheless, security patches and a constant stream of new operating system versions need to be deployed without stopping running programs. These factors naturally lead to a pressing demand for live update—upgrading all or parts of the operating system without rebooting. Unfortunately, existing solutions require significant manual intervention and thus work reliably only for small operating system patches.

In this paper, we describe an automated system for live update that can safely and automatically handle major upgrades without rebooting. We have implemented our ideas in PROTEOS, a new research OS designed with live update in mind. PROTEOS relies on system support and nonintrusive instrumentation to handle even very complex updates with minimal manual effort. The key novelty is the idea of *state quiescence*, which allows updates to happen only in safe and predictable system states. A second novelty is the ability to automatically perform transactional live updates at the *process level*, ensuring a safe and *stable* update process. Unlike prior solutions, PROTEOS supports automated state transfer, state checking, and *hot rollback*. We have evaluated PROTEOS on 50 real updates and on novel live update scenarios. The results show that our techniques can effectively support both simple and complex updates, while outperforming prior solutions in terms of flexibility, security, reliability, and stability of the update process.

Categories and Subject Descriptors D.4.7 [*Operating Systems*]: Organization and Design

General Terms Design, Experimentation, Reliability

Keywords Live update, Automatic updates, State transfer, State checking, Update safety, Operating systems

1. Introduction

Modern operating systems evolve rapidly. Studies on the Linux kernel have shown that its size has more than doubled in the last 10 years, with a growth of more than 6 MLOC and over 300 official versions released [64]. This trend leads to many frequently released updates that implement new features, improve performance, or fix important bugs and security vulnerabilities. With today's pervasive demand for 24/7 operation, however, the traditional patch-install-reboot cycle introduces unacceptable downtime for the operating system (OS) and all the running applications. To mitigate this problem, enterprise users often rely on *"rolling upgrades"* [27]—upgrading one node at a time in a highly replicated software system—which, however, require redundant hardware (or virtualized environments), cannot normally preserve program state across system versions, and may introduce a very large update window with high exposure to mixed version races [29].

Live update (sometimes also called *hot* or *dynamic* update) is a potential solution to this problem, due to its ability to upgrade a running system on the fly with no service interruption. To reach widespread adoption, however, a live update solution should be practical and trustworthy. We found that existing solutions for operating systems [12–14, 20, 56] and generic C programs [10, 21, 55, 55, 59, 60] meet these requirements only for simple updates. Not surprisingly, many live update solutions explicitly target small security patches [10, 12]. While security patches are a critical application for live update—as also demonstrated by the commercial success of solutions like Ksplice [12]—we believe there is a need for solutions that can effectively handle more complex updates, such as upgrading between operating system versions with hundreds or thousands of changes.

We note two key limiting factors in existing solutions. First, they scale poorly with the size and complexity of the update. This limitation stems from the limited system support to ensure update safety and transfer the run-time state from one system version to another. Existing solutions largely delegate these challenging tasks to the programmer. When applied to updates that install a new OS version with major code and data structure changes, this strategy requires an unbearable effort and is inevitably error prone.

Second, they scale poorly with the number of live updates applied to the system. This limitation stems from the update mechanisms employed in existing solutions, which assume a rigid address space layout, and glue code and data changes directly into the running version. This strategy typically leads to an *unstable* live update process, with memory leakage and performance overhead growing linearly over time (§2.3). We found that both limiting factors introduce important reliability and security issues, which inevitably discourage acceptance of live update.

This paper presents PROTEOS, a new research operating system designed to safely and automatically support many classes of live updates. To meet this challenge, PROTEOS introduces several novel techniques. First, it replaces the long-used notion of *function* [12] and *object* [14] *quiescence* with the more general idea of *state quiescence*, allowing programmer-provided *state filters* to specify constraints on the update state. The key intuition is that operating systems quickly transition through many states with different properties. Restricting the update to be installed only in specific states dramatically simplifies reasoning on update safety.

Further, PROTEOS employs transactional *process-level* live updates, which reliably replace entire processes instead of individual objects or functions. To increase the update surface and sup-

ASPLOS'13, March 16–20, 2013, Houston, Texas, USA.

port complex updates, we explore this idea in a design with all the core OS subsystems running as independent event-driven processes on top of a minimal message-passing substrate running in kernel mode. Using processes as updatable units ensures a *stable* update process and eliminates the need for complex patch analysis and preparation tools. In addition, PROTEOS uses hardware-isolated processes to sandbox the state transfer execution in the new process version and support *hot rollback* in case of run-time errors.

Finally, PROTEOS relies on compiler-generated instrumentation to automate state transfer (migrating the state between processes), state checking (checking the state for consistency), and tainted state management (recovering from a corrupted state), with minimal run-time overhead. Our state transfer framework is designed to *automatically* handle common structural state changes (e.g., adding a new field to a `struct`) and recover from particular tainted states (i.e., memory leakage), while supporting a convenient programming model for extensions. As an example, programmers can register their own callbacks to handle corrupted pointers or override the default transfer strategy for state objects of a particular type.

Our current PROTEOS implementation runs on the x86 platform and supports a complete POSIX interface. Our state management framework supports C and assembly code. Its instrumentation component is implemented as a link-time pass using the LLVM compiler framework [50].

We evaluated PROTEOS on 50 real updates (randomly sampled in the course of over 2 years of development) and novel live update scenarios: *online diversification*, *memory leakage reclaiming*, and *update failures* (§6.3). Our results show that: (i) PROTEOS provides an effective and easy-to-use update model for both small and very complex updates. Most live updates required minimal effort to be deployed, compared to the "*tedious engineering effort*" reported in prior work [20]; (ii) PROTEOS is reliable and secure. Our state transfer framework reduces manual effort to the bare minimum and can safely rollback the update when detecting unsafe conditions or run-time errors (e.g., crashes, timeouts, assertion failures). Despite the complexity of some of the 50 updates analyzed, live update required only 265 lines of custom state transfer code in total. (iii) The update techniques used in PROTEOS are *stable* and efficient. The run-time overhead is well isolated in allocator operations and only visible in microbenchmarks (6-130% overhead on allocator operations). The service disruption at update time is minimal (less than 5% macrobenchmark overhead while replacing an OS component every 20s) and the update time modest (3.55s to replace all the OS components). (iv) The update mechanisms used in PROTEOS significantly increase the update surface and enable novel live update scenarios. In our experiments, we were able to update *all* the OS components in a single fault-tolerant transaction and completely *automate* live update of as many as 4,873,735 type transformations throughout the entire operating system (§6.3).

Contribution. This paper makes several contributions. First, we identify the key limitations in existing live update solutions and present practical examples of reliability and security problems. Second, we introduce a new update model based on *state quiescence*, which generalizes existing models but allows updates to be deployed only in predictable system states. Third, we introduce transactional process-level updates, which allow safe *hot rollback* in case of update failures, and present their application to operating systems. Fourth, we introduce a new reliable and secure state transfer framework that automates state transfer, state checking, and tainted state management. Finally, we have implemented and evaluated these ideas in PROTEOS, a new research operating system designed with live update in mind. We believe our work raises several important issues on existing techniques and provides effective solutions that can drive future research in the field.

```
static struct task_struct *copy_process(...) {
  ... (1)
  p = dup_task_struct(current);
  if (!p)
    goto fork_out;
  ... (2) //unsafe update point
  retval = copy_creds(p, clone_flags);
  if (retval < 0)
    goto bad_fork_free;
  ... (3)
}
```

Old version:

```
static struct task_struct
  *dup_task_struct(...) {
  ...
  prepare_creds();
  ...
}
int copy_creds(...) {
  ...

  ...
}
```

New version:

```
static struct task_struct
  *dup_task_struct(...) {
  ...

  ...
}
int copy_creds(...) {
  ...
  prepare_creds();
  ...
}
```

Figure 1. An unsafe live update using function quiescence.

2. Background

Gupta has determined that the validity of a live update applied in an arbitrary state S and using a state transfer function T is undecidable in the general case [37]. Hence, system support and manual intervention are needed. Unfortunately, existing solutions offer both limited control over the update state S and poor support to build the state transfer function T.

2.1 Safe Update State

Prior work has generally focused on an update-agnostic definition of a safe update state. A number of solutions permit both the old and the new version to coexist [20, 21, 56], many others disallow updates to active code [10, 12, 14, 31, 36]. The first approach yields an highly unpredictable update process, making it hard to give strong safety guarantees. The second approach relies on the general notion of *function* (or *object*) *quiescence*, which only allows updates to functions that are not on the call stack of some active thread.

Figure 1 demonstrates that quiescence is a weak requirement for a safe update state. The example proposed (inspired by real code from the Linux `fork` implementation) simply moves the call `prepare_creds()` from the function `dup_task_struct` to the function `copy_creds`. Since `copy_process` is unchanged, function quiescence would allow the update to happen at any of the update points (1, 2, 3). It is easy to show, however, that the update point (2) is unsafe, since it may allow a single invocation of the function `copy_process()` to call (i) the old version of the function `dup_task_struct()` and (ii) the new version of the function `copy_creds()`. Due to the nature of the update, the resulting execution would *incorrectly* call `prepare_creds()` twice—and not once, as expected during normal update-free execution.

To address this problem, prior live update solutions have proposed pre-annotated transactions [61], update points [60], or static analysis [59]. These strategies do not easily scale to complex operating system updates and always expose the programmer to the significant effort of manually verifying update correctness in all the possible system states. PROTEOS addresses this problem using our new notion of *state quiescence*, which generalizes prior update safety mechanisms and allows the programmer to dynamically express update constraints on a per-update basis. In the example, the programmer can simply specify a *state filter* (§4.3) requesting no `fork` to be in progress at update time.

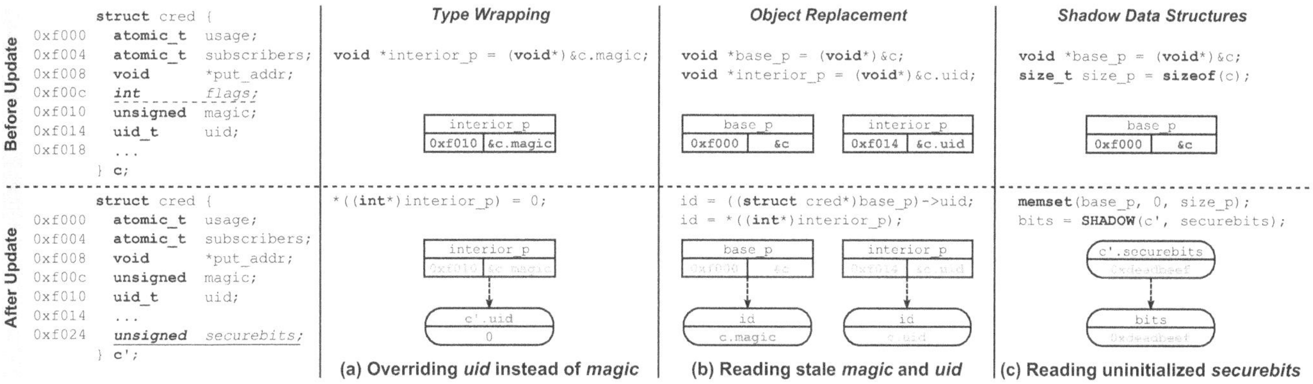

Figure 2. Examples of live update vulnerabilities introduced by unhandled pointers into updated data structures: (a) Type-unsafe memory writes; (b) Misplaced reads of stale object data; (c) Uninitialized reads.

2.2 State Transfer

Prior work has generally focused on supporting data type transformations in a rigid address space organization. Three approaches are dominant: *type wrapping* [59, 60], *object replacement* [14, 20, 21, 55], and *shadow data structures* [12, 56]. Type wrapping instruments data objects with extra padding and performs in-place type transformations. Object replacement dynamically loads the new objects into the address space and transfers the state from the old objects to the new ones. Shadow data structures are similar, but preserve the old objects and only load the new fields of the new objects. While some have automated the generation of type transformers [59, 60], *none* of the existing live update solutions for C provides automated support for transforming pointers and reallocating dynamic objects. Figure 2 demonstrates that failure to properly handle pointers into updated objects can introduce several problems, ranging from subtle logical errors to security vulnerabilities. Type wrapping may introduce type-unsafe memory reads/writes for stale interior pointers into updated objects. This is similar to a typical dangling pointer vulnerability [8], which, in the example, causes the pointer `interior_p` to erroneously write into the field `uid` instead of the field `magic`. Object replacement may introduce similar vulnerabilities for stale base pointers to updated objects. In the example, this causes the pointer `base_p` to erroneously read from the field `magic` in the old object instead of the field `uid` in the new one. It may also introduce misplaced reads/writes for stale interior pointers into updated objects. In the example, this causes the pointer `interior_p` to read the field `uid` from the old object instead of the new one. Finally, shadow data structures may introduce missing read/write errors for nonupdated code accessing updated objects as raw data. This may, for example, lead to uninitialized read vulnerabilities, as shown in the example for the field `securebits`.

Prior solutions have proposed static analysis to identify all these cases correctly [60]. This strategy, however, requires sophisticated program analysis that scales poorly with the size of the program, limits the use of some legal C idioms (e.g., `void*` pointers), and only provides the ability to *disallow* updates as long as there are some live pointers into updated objects. Thus, extensive *manual* effort is still required to locate and transfer all the pointers correctly in the common case of long-lived pointers into updated data structures. In our experience, this effort is unrealistic for nontrivial state changes. PROTEOS addresses this problem by migrating the *entire state* from one process version to another, automating pointer transfer and dynamic object reallocation with none of the limitations above. This is possible using our run-time state introspection strategy implemented on top of LLVM-based instrumentation (§5.2).

2.3 Stability of the update process

We say that a live update process is *stable* if version τ of the system with no live update applied behaves no differently than version $\tau - k$ of the same system after k live updates. This property is crucial for realistic long-term deployment of live update. Unfortunately, the update mechanisms used in existing live update solutions for C repeatedly violate the stability assumption. This is primarily due to the rigid address space organization used, with every update loading new code and data directly into the running version. This *in-place* strategy typically introduces memory leakage (due to the difficulties to reclaim dead code and data) and poorer spatial locality (due to address space fragmentation). For example, prior work on server applications reported 40% memory footprint increase and 29% performance overhead after 10 updates [60]. Further, solutions that redirect execution to the new code via binary rewriting [10, 12, 21, 56] introduce a number of trampolines (and thus overhead) that grows linearly with the number and the size of the updates. Finally, shadow data structures change the code representation and force future updates to track all the changes previously applied to the system, complicating version management over time. PROTEOS' *process-level* updates eliminate all these issues and ensure a *stable* live update process (§5).

3. Overview

Our design adheres to 3 key principles: (i) *security and reliability*: updates are only installed in predictable system states and the update process is safeguarded against errors and unsafe conditions; (ii) *large update surface*: no constraints on the size, complexity, and number of updates applied to the system; (iii) *minimal manual effort*: state filters minimize code inspection effort to ensure safety; automated state transfer minimizes programming effort for the update; process-level updates make deploying live updates as natural as installing a new release, with no need for specialized toolchains or complex patch analysis tools.

3.1 Architecture

Figure 3 shows the overall architecture of PROTEOS. Our design uses a minimalistic approach with a thin kernel only managing the hardware and providing basic IPC functionalities. All the core operating system subsystems are confined into hardware-isolated processes, including drivers, scheduling, process management, memory management, storage, and network stack. The OS processes communicate through message passing and adhere to a

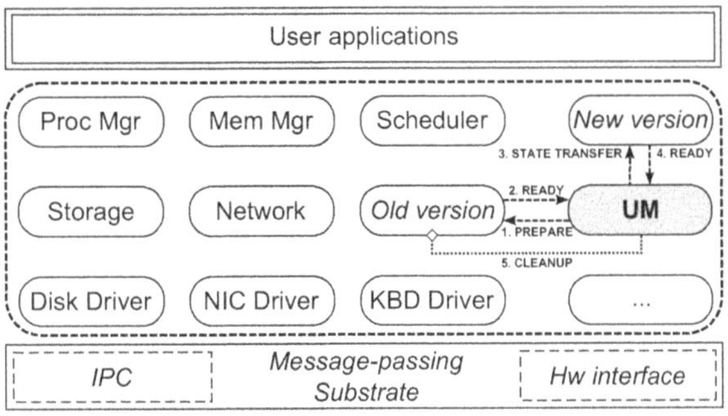

Figure 3. The architecture of PROTEOS.

well-defined event-driven model. This design is advantageous for a number of reasons. First, it introduces clear module boundaries and interfaces to simplify updatability and reasoning on update safety. Second, live updates are installed by replacing entire processes, with a new code and data representation that is no different from a freshly installed version of the system. This strategy fulfills the stability requirement and simplifies deployment of live updates. Third, the MMU-based isolation sandboxes the execution of the *entire* state transfer code in the new version, simplifying detection and isolation of run-time errors and allowing for safe *hot rollback* and no memory leakage. Finally, our event-driven update model facilitates state management and allows the system to actively *cooperate* at update time, a strategy which translates to a much more predictable and controllable live update process [33].

The update process is orchestrated by the *update manager* (UM), which provides the interface to deploy live updates for all the OS processes (including itself). When an update is available, the update manager loads the new process instances in memory and requests all the processes involved in the update to converge to the required update state. When done, every process reports back to UM and blocks. At the end of the *preparation phase*, the update manager *atomically* replaces all the processes with their new counterparts. The new processes perform state transfer and report back to the update manager when done. At the end of the *state transfer phase*, the old processes are cleaned up and the new processes are allowed to resume execution. Synchronization between the update manager and the OS processes is entirely based on message passing. Live updates use atomic transactions: the update manager can safely abort and rollback the update during any stage of the update process, since *no* changes are made to the original process. Figure 3 depicts the steps of the update process for single-component live updates (multicomponent updates are discussed in §4.5).

3.2 Update example

In PROTEOS, building a live update is as simple as recompiling all the updated components using our LLVM compiler plugin. To apply the update, programmers use **prctl**, a simple command-line utility that interfaces directly with the update manager. For example, the following command instructs the update manager to install a new version of the memory manager in the default live update state (*no event in progress*):

```
% prctl update mm /bin/mm.new
```

In our evaluation, we used this update to apply important changes to page fault handling code. An example of a multicomponent update is the following:

```
% prctl mupdate net /bin/net.new \
      -state 'num_pending_writes == 0'
% prctl mupdate e1000 /bin/e1000.new
% prctl mupdate-start
```

In our evaluation, we used this update to change the interface between the network stack and the network drivers. The state filter for the variable **num_pending_writes** is used to ensure that no affected interface interactions are in progress at update time. In our experiments, this change was applied automatically, with no manual effort required. Without the filter, the change would have required several lines of manual and error-prone state transfer code. Since interface changes between versions are common in modern operating systems [62, 63], we consider this an important improvement over the state of the art. While it should be clear that not all the updates can be so smoothly expressed with a simple state filter, this example does show that, when the state is well-captured in the form of global data structures, programmers can much more easily reason on update safety in terms of state quiescence, which frees them from the heroic effort of validating the update in many transient (and potentially unsafe) system states. In our model, identifying a single and well-defined safe update state is sufficient to guarantee a predictable and reliable update process.

3.3 Limitations

The OS design adopted in PROTEOS is not applicable as-is to commodity operating systems. Nonetheless, our end-to-end design can be easily applied to: (i) microkernel architectures used in common embedded OSes, such as L4 [49], Green Hills Integrity [3], and QNX [45]; (ii) research OSes using process-like abstractions, such as Singularity [47]; (iii) commodity OS subsystems running in user space, such as filesystems [2] and user-mode drivers in Windows [57] or Linux [19]; (iv) long-running user-space C programs. We make no claim that our OS design is the *only* possible design for a live update system. PROTEOS merely illustrates one way to implement several novel techniques that enable *truly* safe and automatic live updates. For instance, our single-component live update strategy could be also applied to monolithic OS architectures, using shadow kernel techniques [24] to enable state transfer between versions. The reduced modularity, however, would complicate reasoning on update safety for nontrivial updates. Failure to provide proper process-like isolation for the state transfer code, in turn, would lower the dependability of our hot rollback strategy.

We stress that the individual techniques described in the paper (e.g., state quiescence, automated state transfer, and automated state checking) have general applicability, and we expect existing live update solutions for commodity OSes or user-space programs to directly benefit from their integration. To encourage adoption and retrofit existing OSes and widely deployed applications, we explicitly tailored our techniques to the C programming language.

A practical limitation of our approach is the need for annotations to handle ambiguous pointer transfer scenarios (§5.3). Our experience, however, shows that the impact of these cases is minimal in practice (§6.1). Moreover, we see this as a feature rather than a limitation. Annotations compensate for the effort to manually perform state transfer and readjust all the pointers. Failing to do so leads to the reliability and security problems pointed out earlier.

Finally, a limitation of our current implementation is the inability to live update the message-passing substrate running in kernel mode. Given its small size and relatively stable code base, we felt this was not a feature to particularly prioritize. The techniques presented here, however, are equally applicable to the kernel code itself. We expect extending our current implementation to pose no more challenges than enabling live update for the update manager, which PROTEOS already supports in its current form (§4.5).

```
static int my_init() {
  ... //initialization code
  return 0;
}
int main() {
  event_eh_t my_ehs = {init : my_init};
  sys_startup(&my_ehs);
  while(1) { // event loop
    msg_t m;
    sys_receive(&m);
    process_msg(&m);
  }
  return 0;
}
```

Figure 4. The event-driven programming model.

4. Live Update Support

This section describes the fundamental mechanisms used to implement safe and automatic live update in PROTEOS.

4.1 Programming model

Figure 4 exemplifies the event-driven model used in our OS processes. The structure is similar to a long-running server program, but with special *system events* managed by the run-time system—implemented as a library transparently linked against every OS process as part of our instrumentation strategy. At startup, each process registers any custom *event handlers* and gives control to the runtime (i.e., **sys_startup()**).

At boot time, the runtime transparently invokes the *init* handler (**my_init** in the example) to run regular initialization code. In case of live update, in contrast, the runtime invokes the *state transfer* handler, responsible for initializing the new process from the old state. The default *state transfer* handler (also used in the example) *automatically* transfers all the old state to the new process, following a default state transfer strategy (§5.4). This is done by applying LLVM-based state instrumentation at compile time and automatically migrating data between processes at runtime.

After startup, each process enters an endless *event loop* to process IPC messages. The call **sys_receive()** dispatches regular messages to the loop, while transparently intercepting the special system events part of the update protocol and handling all the interactions with the update manager. The event loop is designed to be short lived, thanks to the extensive use of asynchronous IPC. This ensures scalability and fast convergence to the update state. Fast *state quiescence* is important to replace many OS processes in a single atomic transaction, eliminating the need for unsafe cross-version execution in complex updates. Note that this property does not equally apply to function *quiescence*, given that many OS subsystems never quiesce [56]. In PROTEOS, *all* the nonquiescent subsystems are isolated in *event loops* with well-defined mappings across versions. This makes it possible to update *any* nonquiescent part of the OS with no restriction. The top of the loop is the only possible *update point*, with an update logically transferring control flow from an invocation of **sys_receive()** in the old process to its counterpart in the new process (and back in case of *hot rollback*).

4.2 Virtual IPC endpoints

Two properties make it possible to support transactional process-level updates for the entire OS. First, updates are *transparent* to any nonupdated OS process or user program. Second, updates are *atomic*: only one version at the time is logically visible to the rest of the system. To meet these goals, PROTEOS uses *virtual endpoints* in its IPC implementation. A virtual endpoint is a unique version-agnostic IPC identifier assigned to the *only* active instance of an OS process. At update time, the kernel atomically rebinds all the virtual endpoints to the new instances. The switchover, which occurs at the end of the preparation phase, transparently redirects all the IPC invocations to the new version.

4.3 State filters

Unlike prior solutions, PROTEOS relies on *state quiescence* to detect a safe update state. This property allows updates to be installed only when particular constraints are met by the global state of the system. *State filters* make it possible to specify these constraints on a per-update basis. A state filter is a generic boolean expression written in a C-like language and evaluated at runtime. Our state filter evaluator supports the arithmetic, comparison, and logical operators allowed by C. It can also handle pointers to dynamically allocated objects, compute the value of any global/static variable (and subelements), and invoke read-only functions with a predetermined naming scheme. State filters reflect our belief that specifying a safe update state should be as easy as writing an assertion to check the state for consistency. Our evaluator is implemented as a simple extension to our state management framework (§5), which already provides the ability to perform run-time state introspection.

At the beginning of the preparation phase, every to-be-updated OS process receives a string containing a state filter, which is installed and transparently evaluated at the end of every following event loop iteration. When the process transitions to the required state, the expression evaluates to **true**, causing the process to report back to the update manager and block at the top of the event loop. The default state filter forces the process to block immediately. To support complex state filters that cannot be easily specified in a simple expression, PROTEOS can automatically compile generic state filter functions (written in C) into binary form. This is simply accomplished by generating *intermediate* process versions that only differ from the old ones by a new filter function **sf_custom**. Since the change is semantics-preserving, the intermediate versions can be automatically installed in the default update state before the actual update process takes place. State filter functions give the programmer the flexibility to express complex state constraints using any valid C code. On the other hand, regular state filters, are a simpler and smoother solution for online development and fast prototyping. They are also safer, since the state expression is checked for correctness by our state transfer framework.

4.4 Interface filters

Our short-lived event loop design is not alone sufficient to guarantee convergence to the update state in the general case, especially when the system is under heavy load. To give stronger convergence guarantees in particular scenarios, PROTEOS supports (optional) *interface filters* for every to-be-updated OS process. Each filter is transparently installed into the kernel at the beginning of the preparation phase. Its goal is to monitor the incoming IPC traffic and temporarily block delivery of messages that would otherwise delay state quiescence. Programmers can specify *filtering rules* similar to those used in packet filters [40], to selectively blacklist or whitelist delivery of particular IPC messages by source or type.

4.5 Multicomponent updates

Changes that affect IPC interactions require the system to atomically update multiple processes in a single update transaction. To support multicomponent updates, the update manager orderly runs the preparation protocol with every to-be-updated OS process. The overall preparation phase is strictly *sequential*, namely the process

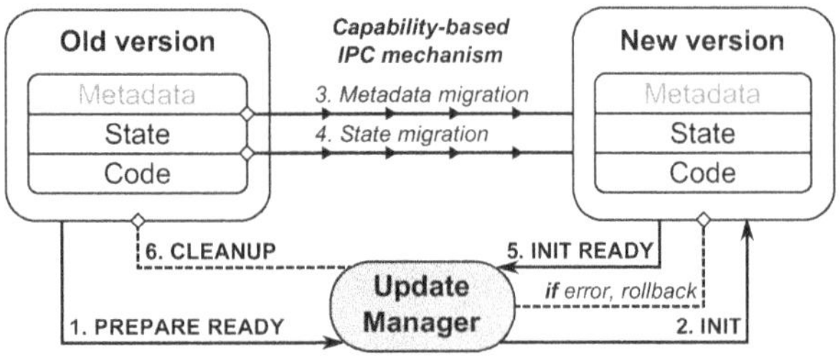

Figure 5. The state transfer process.

i in the update transaction is only requested to start the preparation phase after the process $i-1$ has already reached state quiescence and blocked. The state transfer phase is, in contrast, completely *parallel*. Parallelism is allowed to avoid placing any restrictions on state transfer extensions that require updated processes to initialize some mutual state. Our sequential preparation strategy, in turn, ensures a predictable live update process and gives the programmer full control over the update transaction, while preserving the ability to safely and automatically rollback the update in case of programming errors (i.e., deadlocks or other synchronization issues). Our design introduces a new structured definition of the live update problem: a live update is feasible if it is possible to identify a sequence of state and interface filters able to drive the system into a state with a valid mapping—and state transfer function—in the new version. Our experience shows that this approach is effective and scales to complex updates. For instance, following a top-down update strategy, we were successfully able to implement a *fault-tolerant* update transaction that atomically replaces *all* the OS processes, *including the update manager itself*.

To update the update manager, PROTEOS uses two simple ideas. First, the update manager is constrained to be the last process in the update transaction to obey the semantics of the update process. At the end of the preparation phase, kernel support allows the update manager to block and atomically yield control to its new process version. Second, the new version completes the update process as part of its own state transfer phase. Once the automated state transfer process completes (§5.1), the new manager updates its state to account for its own update and normally waits for the other OS processes to synchronize. This simple strategy added less than 200 lines of code to our original update manager implementation.

4.6 Hot rollback

In case of unexpected errors, *hot rollback* enables the update manager to abort the update process and safely allow the old version to resume execution. Our manager can detect and automatically recover from the following errors: (i) timeouts in the preparation phase (e.g., due to broken dependencies in the update transaction or poorly designed state/interface filters which lead to deadlocks or other synchronization errors); (ii) timeouts in the state transfer phase (e.g:, due to synchronization errors or infinite loops); (iii) fatal errors in the state transfer phase (e.g., due to crashes, panics, or error conditions automatically detected by our state checking framework). The MMU-based protection prevents any run-time errors from propagating back to the old version. Fatal errors are ultimately intercepted by the kernel, which simply notifies the update manager—or its old instance, which is automatically revived by the kernel when the update manager itself is updating—to perform rollback. To atomically rollback the update during the state transfer phase, the update manager simply requests the kernel to freeze all the new instances, rebind all the virtual endpoints to the old instances, and unblock them. The new instances are cleaned up next in *cooperation* with the old version of the system.

5. State Management

To automate process-level updates, PROTEOS needs to automatically migrate the state between the old and the new process. Our migration strategy makes no assumptions about compiler optimizations or number of code or data structures changed between versions. In other words, the two processes are allowed to have *arbitrarily different* memory layouts. This allows us to support arbitrarily complex state changes with no impact on the stability of the update process. To address this challenge, PROTEOS implements *precise* run-time state introspection, which makes it possible to automate pointer transfer and dynamic object reallocation even in face of type changes. Our goal is to require help from the programmers only in the *undecidable* cases, for example, ambiguous pointer scenarios (§5.3), semantic changes that cannot be automatically settled by our state mapping and migration strategy (e.g., an update renumbering the error codes stored in global variables), and changes that also require updating external state (e.g., an update modifying the representation of some on-disk data structures).

5.1 State transfer

To support run-time state introspection, every OS process is instrumented using an LLVM link-time pass, which embeds *state metadata* in a predefined section of the final ELF binary. The metadata contains the relocation and type information required to introspect all the state objects in the process at runtime. The metadata structures use a fixed layout and are located in a randomized location only known to the process and the kernel.

Figure 5 depicts the state transfer process. The migration phase starts with the state transfer framework transferring all the metadata from the old version to the new version (local address space). This is done using a capability-based design, with the kernel granting (only) the new process read-only access to the address space of the old process. At the end of the metadata migration phase, both the old and the new metadata are available locally. This allows the framework to introspect both the old and the new state and remap all the state objects across versions. The mapping relies on a version-agnostic *naming scheme* established at compile time. This enables the framework to unambiguously pair functions, variables, strings, and dynamic objects across versions.

At the end of the pairing phase, all the paired objects are scheduled for transfer by default. Programmers can register extensions to change the pairing rules (e.g., in case of variable renaming) or instruct the framework to avoid transferring particular objects (§5.4).

In the data migration phase, the framework traverses all the old state objects (and their inner pointers) scheduled for transfer and ordinately migrates the data to their counterparts in the new version. Our traversal strategy is similar, in spirit, to a precise garbage collector that relocates objects [67]. There are, however, important differences to point out. First, all the dynamic (and static) objects are reallocated (loaded) in the new process. Second, our event loop design allows no state objects on the stack at update time. This eliminates the need to create dynamic metadata for all the local variables, which would degrade performance. Note that, to encourage adoption of our state transfer framework in other update and execution contexts (e.g., multithreaded server applications), however, our instrumentation can already support dynamic metadata generation for local variables (disabled in PROTEOS), using stack instrumentation strategies similar to those adopted by garbage collectors [67]. Finally, objects are possibly reallocated (or loaded) with a different run-time type. Unlike prior solutions, our framework applies type transformations (for both objects and pointers) on-the-fly, analyzing the type differences between paired objects at runtime. This eliminates the need for complex patch analysis tools and exposes a powerful programming model to state transfer exten-

```
struct s { //old version          struct s { //new version
  int flags;                        int flags;
  char string[3];                   int id;
  short id;                         char string[2];
  union IXFER(my_u) u;              union IXFER(my_u) u;
  void *userdata;                   PXFER(int) addr;
  PXFER(int) addr;                  int newfield;
} my_s;                           } my_s;
short *p = &my_s.id;              int *p = &my_s.id;
```

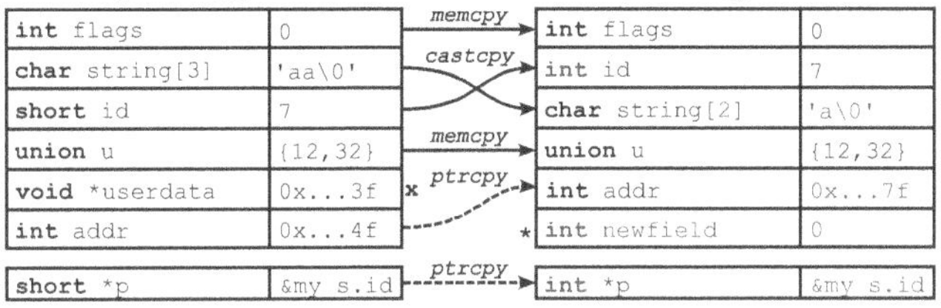

Figure 6. Automating type and pointer transformations.

sions. We clarify this claim with an example. To deploy a live update that added a new field in the middle of the **struct buf_desc** (a core data structure of the buffer cache) in our evaluation, we only had to write a simple type-based state transfer callback (§5.4) that reinitialized the new field in every object in the new version. The latter is a programmer-provided function automatically invoked by the framework on every transferred object of the requested type (e.g., **struct buf_desc**). This allows the programmer to focus on the data transformation logic while the framework automatically performs dynamic object reallocation and updates all the live pointers into the new objects. Since this **struct** was used in complex data structures like hash tables and linked lists (chained together by several base and inner pointers), this is a significant improvement over existing techniques, which would have required extensive and error-prone manual effort to implement state transfer.

5.2 Metadata instrumentation

Our LLVM transformation pass operates at the LLVM IR level and generates metadata for global/static variables (and constants), functions, and strings. Although functions and strings need not be normally transferred to the new version, their metadata is necessary to transfer pointers correctly. For each object, the pass records information on the address, the name, and the type. To create unique and version-coherent identifiers to pair static state objects across versions, our pass uses both *naming* (e.g., global variable name) and *contextual* (e.g., module name for static functions/variables) information derived from debug symbols. Note that this strategy does not prevent debug symbols from being completely stripped with no restriction from the final binary. To create metadata for dynamically allocated objects, in turn, the pass analyzes and instruments each allocation site found in the original code. Our static analysis can automatically identify **malloc/free** and **mmap/munmap** allocator abstractions, which PROTEOS natively supports for every OS process. For each allocation site, the pass records the name (derived from the caller and the allocation variable), the allocator name, and the static type. The name and the allocator name are used to pair (and reallocate) allocation sites across versions. The static type is used to dynamically determine the run-time type of every allocated object. For example, an allocation of the form **ptr = malloc(sizeof(msg_t)*4)** will be associated a static type **msg_t** and a run-time type **[4 x msg_t]**. The pass replaces every allocation/deallocation call with a call to a wrapper function responsible to dynamically create/destroy metadata for every dynamic object. To minimize the performance impact, the wrappers normally use in-band descriptors to store the metadata for the dynamic state objects. The allocators, however, support special flags to let the programmer control the allocation behavior (e.g., use out-of-band metadata for special I/O regions, or remap DMA buffers at state transfer time instead of explicitly reallocating them).

5.3 Pointer transfer

Pointers pose a fundamental challenge to automating state transfer for C programs. To transfer base and interior pointers correctly, our framework implements dynamic *points-to* analysis on top of the precise type information provided by our instrumentation. Our analysis is cast-insensitive and does not forbid or limit the use of any legal C programming idiom (e.g., **void***), a problem in prior work [59, 60]. Our pointer transfer strategy follows 5 steps (an example is presented in Figure 6): (i) locate the target object (and the inner element, for interior pointers); (ii) locate the target object counterpart in the new version according to the output of the pairing phase; (iii) remap the inner element counterpart in case of type changes; (iv) reinitialize the pointer according to the target object (and element) counterpart identified; (v) schedule the target object for transfer. The last step is necessary to preserve the shape of arbitrarily complex data structures. In addition, the traversal allows our framework to structurally prevent any memory leakages (i.e., unreachable dynamic objects) in the old version from propagating to the new version. Note that our pointer traversal strategy relies only on the run-time type of the target object (and element), with no assumptions on the original pointer type. This strategy can seamlessly support generic **void*** pointers and eliminates the need to explicitly deal with pointer casting. Our framework can also automatically handle pointers with special integer values (e.g., **NULL** or **MAP_FAILED** (-1)) and guard pointers that mark buffer boundaries. Uninitialized pointers are structurally prevented in the allocators and dangling pointers disallowed by design. While our pointer analysis can handle all these common scenarios automatically, we have identified practical cases of *pointer ambiguity* that always require (typically one-time) user intervention, pointers stored as integers and **unions** with inner pointers, in particular. Manually handling these cases via annotations or callbacks (§5.4) is necessary to ensure precise pointer analysis. More details on our points-to analysis and our pointer transfer strategy are published elsewhere [32].

5.4 Transfer strategy

Our framework follows a well-defined default state transfer strategy, while allowing programmer-provided extensions to arbitrarily override the default behavior.

Figure 6 shows an example of the transfer strategy followed by our framework for a simple update. All the objects and the pointers are automatically transferred (and reallocated on demand) to the new version in spite of type changes. Our default transfer strategy automates state transfer for many common structural changes, such as: (i) primitive type transformations, (ii) array truncation/expansion, and (iii) addition/deletion/reordering of **struct** fields. Extensions can be used to handle more complex state changes (and cases of pointer ambiguity) with minimal effort. The latter are supported in the form of *type-based* or *object-based* annotations or callbacks, evaluated every time the framework traverses or remaps the intended type (or object). Annotations are implemented at the preprocessor level with no changes in the compiler. Figure 6 shows an example, with the **IXFER** and **PXFER** type-based annotations forcing the framework to **memcpy** the **union u** (without introspecting it) and perform pointer transfer of the integer **addr**.

Programmer-provided state transfer callbacks, in turn, provide a more generic extension mechanism to override the default state transfer behavior during any stage of the state transfer process and

Category	#	Multi	Update LOC Total	Median	90thP	Changes Fun	Var	Ty	Manual effort Ann	SF	ST LOC	Time (ms) Med Upd
Bug fixes	15	4	1593	18	1231	27	2	2	-	2	55	397
Maintenance	12	5	2206	62	872	16	7	8	-	1	16	230
New features	19	6	10122	195	2435	199	45	101	-	1	63	202
Performance	4	1	652	179	291	10	2	7	-	0	131	358
Total	50	16	14573	63	709	252	56	118	14	4	265	272

Table 1. Overview of all the updates analyzed in our evaluation.

at several possible levels of abstraction. For instance, programmers can register object-level callbacks and element-level callbacks—evaluated when the framework performs a particular action on a given object or an element part of an object, respectively. To specify the trigger entity in the most flexible way, callbacks can be registered by object/element storage (e.g., data, heap), object/element name (e.g., `my_var_namespace_*`), and object/element type (e.g., `struct my_struct_s`), or using any combination thereof. To support many possible trigger events, programmers can register object/element pairing callbacks (to override the default name-based pairing strategy adopted by the framework), object/element transfer callbacks (to override the default transfer strategy or selectively schedule individual objects for transfer), and pointer transfer callbacks (to override the default pointer transfer strategy). Note that the callbacks are automatically and logically chained together by the framework. For example, a user-defined element pairing callback that remaps a `struct` field in a nonstandard way in the new version is automatically invoked by the framework when either transferring the original field to the new version or remapping an inner pointer to the field into an updated object. The callbacks all run in the context of the new process version after completing the metadata migration phase, allowing the programmer to seamlessly access objects in the old and the new version (and their metadata information) with no restriction. The callbacks are written directly in C, providing the ability to operate arbitrary transformations in the state transfer code—even changing external state on the disk, for example. In addition, this allows the programmer to remap complex data structures that significantly change their representation across versions (e.g., a hash table transformed into multiple balanced BSTs) and cannot be automatically paired (nor transferred) by our framework. Even in such complex state transformation scenarios, our programming model can provide a generic callback-driven interface to locate and traverse all the objects (and pointers) to transfer, allowing the programmer to select the best level of abstraction to operate and concentrate on data transformations rather than on manual and error-prone state introspection.

5.5 State checking

Our state management framework supports automated state checking using generic *state invariants*. The idea is to detect an invalid state when conservatively defined invariants are violated. *Target-based* invariants are naturally enforced by our *points-to* analysis (i.e., a pointer not pointing to any valid object is invalid). Other invariants are determined by static analysis. We support *value-based* invariants (derived from value set analysis of integer variables) and *type-based* invariants, which verify that a pointer points to a target of a valid type at runtime. This is done by recording metadata on all the valid implicit and explicit pointer casts (i.e., `bitcast` and `inttoptr` LLVM instructions). State checking is performed on the old version before the transfer and on the new version after the transfer. In both cases, the transfer is atomically aborted when invariants violations are found (unless extensions change the default behavior). Checking both the old and the new state allows the framework to detect: (i) a tainted state in the old version (i.e., arbitrary memory corruption) and possibly let extensions recover from it; (ii) corruption in the new state introduced by the state transfer code itself; (iii) violating assumptions in the state transfer process. An example in the latter category is the attempt to transfer a pointer to an old object that no longer exists (or no longer has its address taken) in the new version.

6. Evaluation

We have implemented PROTEOS on the x86 platform. The current PROTEOS implementation is a major rewrite of the original MINIX 3 microkernel-based operating system, which only provided process-based isolation for all the core OS components and restartability support for stateless device drivers [43]. Our current prototype includes 22 OS processes (8 drivers and 14 servers) and supports a complete POSIX interface. The static instrumentation is implemented as an LLVM pass in 6550 LOC [1]. The state management framework is implemented as a static library written in C in 8840 LOC. We evaluated PROTEOS on a workstation equipped with a 12-core 1.3Ghz AMD Opteron processor and 4GB of RAM. For evaluation purposes, we ported the C programs in the SPEC CPU 2006 benchmark suite to PROTEOS. We also put together an *sdtools* macrobenchmark, which emulates a typical syscall-intensive workload with common development operations (compilation, text processing, copy, delete) performed on the entire OS source tree. We repeated all our experiments 21 times and reported the median. Our evaluation focuses on 4 key aspects: (i) *Experience*: Can PROTEOS effectively support both simple and complex updates with minimal effort? (ii) *Performance*: Do our techniques yield low run-time overhead and realistic update times? (iii) *Service disruption*: Do live updates introduce low service disruption? (iv) *Memory footprint*: How much memory do our techniques use?

6.1 Experience

To evaluate the effort in deploying live updates, we randomly sampled 50 real updates produced by the team of core MINIX 3 developers in the course of over 2 years. The live update infrastructure, in turn, was developed independently to ensure a fair and realistic update evaluation. We carefully analyzed each update considered, prepared it for live update, and finally deployed it online during the execution of our SPEC and *sdtools* benchmarks. We successfully deployed all the live updates considered and checked that the system was fully functional before and after each experiment. In 4 cases, our first update attempt failed due to bugs in the state transfer code. The resulting (pointer) errors, however, were immediately detected by our state transfer framework and the update safely rolled back with no consequences for the system. We also

[1] Source lines of code reported by David Wheeler's SLOCCount.

	PROTEOS	Linux
malloc	2.30	1.41
free	1.19	1.09
mmap	1.41	1.77
munmap	1.06	1.42

Table 2. Execution time of instrumented allocator operations normalized against the baseline.

verified that the update process was stable (no performance/space overhead increase over time) and that our live update infrastructure could withstand arbitrary compiler optimization changes between versions (e.g., from `-O1` to `-O3`). Table 1 presents our findings.

The first three grouped columns provide an overview of all the updates analyzed, with the number of updates considered per category and the number of updates that involved multiple OS processes. The *New features* category has the highest number of updates, given that MINIX 3 is under active development. Of the 50 updates considered, 16 involved multiple OS processes. This confirmed the importance of supporting multicomponent live updates. The second group of columns shows the number of lines of code (total, median, 90th percentile) changed across all the updates, with a total of nearly 15,000 LOC. The third group shows the number of functions, variables, and types changed (i.e., added/deleted/modified). For example, *New features* updates introduced 199 function changes, 45 variable changes, and 101 type changes. The fourth group, in turn, shows the manual effort required in terms of annotations, state filters, and lines of code for state transfer extensions. We only had to annotate 14 declarations (using 3 object-based annotations, 10 type-based annotations, and 1 type-based callback) throughout the entire PROTEOS source code. Encouragingly, this was a modest *one-time* effort that required less than 1 man week. The annotations were only necessary for **unions** with inner pointers and special nontransferrable state objects (e.g., allocator variables). Custom state filters, in turn, were only required for 4 updates. We found that, for most updates, our event loop design gave sufficient predictability guarantees in the default update state. In the remaining cases, however, we faced complex interface changes that would have required extensive manual effort without support for custom state filters. From empirical evidence, we also believe that more than half of the updates would have been extremely hard to reason about using only function quiescence. Despite the many variable and type changes, all the updates required only 265 LOC of state transfer extensions. We found that our state transfer framework was able to fully automate most data structure changes (i.e., addition/removal). In addition, our type-based state transfer callbacks minimized the effort to handle cross-cutting type changes. Finally, the last column reports the median update time, with a value of 272ms across all the updates. We also measured a maximum update time of 3550ms for cross-cutting updates that replaced *all* the OS processes (individually or in a single multicomponent and fault-tolerant transaction).

We now compare our results with prior solutions. Before ours, Ksplice was the only OS-level live update solution evaluated with a comprehensive list of updates over a time interval [12]. Compared to ours, however, their evaluation is based on security patches of much smaller size. Their median patch size is less than 5 LOC, and the 90th percentile less than 30 LOC. As Table 1 demonstrates, PROTEOS was evaluated with much more complex updates, while only requiring 265 LOC for state transfer extensions (compared to 132 LOC for Ksplice's 64 small patches [1]). Many other live update solutions for C present only case studies [13, 14, 20, 56] or lack a proper quantitative analysis of the manual effort required [10, 21, 55]. Many researchers, however, have reported "*tedious implementation of the transfer code*" [13], "*tedious engineering efforts*" [20], "*tedious work*" [21], and "*an arduous testing process that spanned several weeks of concentrated work*" [10]. In contrast, we found our techniques to reduce the live update effort to the bare minimum. In particular, our entire update evaluation required only 10 man days. Ginseng [60] and Stump [59] are the only prior solutions for C that provide quantitative measurements for the manual effort. Ginseng (*Stump*) required 140 (*186*) source changes and 336 (*173*) state transfer LOC to apply 30 (*13*) server application updates introducing 21919 (*5817*) new LOC in total. While it is difficult to directly compare their results on server applications with ours, we believe that our techniques applied to the same set of updates would have significantly reduced the effort, avoiding manual inspection or code restructuring to eliminate unsupported C idioms, posing no restriction on the nature of the data structure changes, and assisting the programmer in challenging tasks like heap traversal, pointer transfer, and state checking.

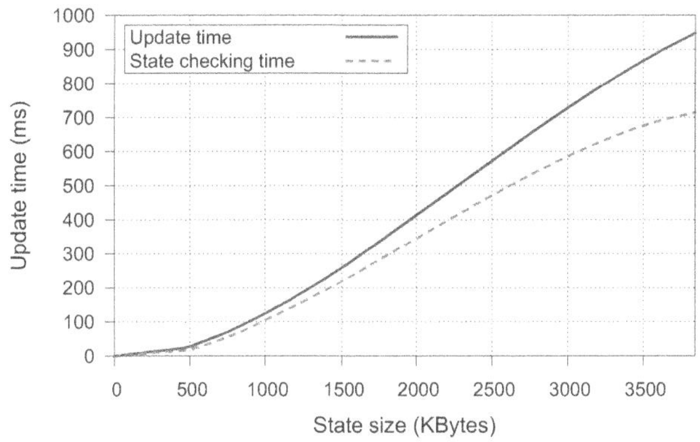

Figure 7. Update time vs. run-time state size.

6.2 Performance

We evaluated the run-time overhead imposed by the update mechanisms used in PROTEOS. Virtual endpoints introduce only update-time costs and no extra run-time overhead on IPC. Transparent interception of special system events introduces only 3 additional cycles per event loop iteration. An important impact comes also from the microkernel-based design itself. Much prior work has been dedicated to improving the performance of IPC [52] and microkernel-based systems in general [39, 53]. Our focus here is on the update techniques rather than on microkernel performance. For instance, our current measurements show that the **gettimeofday**, **open**, **read**, **write**, **close** system calls are 1.05-8.27x slower than on Linux due to our microkernel design. These numbers are, however, pessimistic, given that we have not yet operated many optimizations described in the literature [39, 52, 53].

Much more critical is to assess the cost of our state instrumentation, which directly affects the applicability of our techniques to other OS architectures or user-space applications. To this end, we first ran our SPEC and *sdtools* macrobenchmarks to compare the base PROTEOS implementation with its instrumented version. Our repeated experiments reported no noticeable performance degradation. This is expected since static metadata, used only at update time, is isolated in a separate ELF section with no impact on spatial locality. The use of in-band descriptors to generate dynamic metadata, in turn, minimizes the run-time overhead on allocator operations. To isolate this overhead, we measured the cost of our instrumentation on 10,000 **malloc/free** and **mmap/munmap** repeated allocator operations. We ran the experiments for multiple allocation sizes (0-16MB) and reported the median overhead

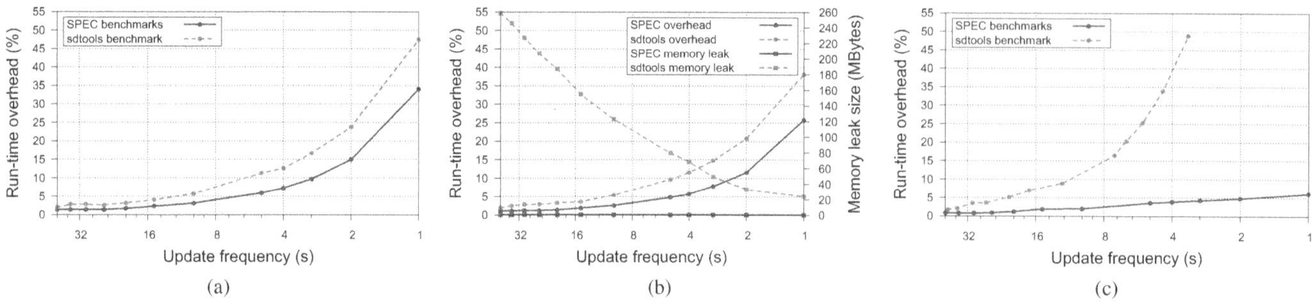

Figure 8. Run-time overhead vs. update frequency. Results are reported for our benchmarks in 3 different live update scenarios: (a) online diversification; (b) memory leakage reclaiming; (c) update failures.

for `malloc/free` (the overhead does not generally depend on the allocation size) and the maximum overhead for `mmap/munmap` (the overhead generally decreases with the allocation size). For comparison, we also ported our instrumentation to Linux user-space programs and ran the same microbenchmarks on Ubuntu 10.04 LTS 32-bit (`libc` allocators). Table 2 depicts our results, with a different (but comparable) impact of our state instrumentation in the two allocator implementations. The highest overheads in PROTEOS and Linux are incurred by `malloc` (130%) and `mmap` (77%), respectively. Note that these results are overly pessimistic, since common allocation patterns typically yield poorer spatial locality, which will likely mask the overhead on allocator operations further.

We now compare our results with prior live update techniques. Live update solutions based on (more intrusive) instrumentation strategies have reported macrobenchmark results with worst-case overheads of 6% [60], 6.71%[59], and 96.4% [55]. Solutions based on binary rewriting, in turn, have reported microbenchmark results with 1%-8% invocation overhead [56] for updated functions. Unlike all the existing techniques, our overhead is well-isolated in allocator operations and never increases with the number and the size of the updates applied to the system (stability assumption).

To assess the impact of live updates on the system, we also analyzed the distribution of the update time in more detail. Figure 7 depicts the update time (the time from the moment the update is signaled to the moment the new version resumes execution) as a function of the run-time state size (total size of all the static and dynamic state objects). These (interpolated) results reflect average measurements obtained during the execution of our macrobenchmarks for all the single-component updates used in our evaluation. The figure shows that the update time grows approximately linearly with the state size. This behavior stems from the fact that the update time is heavily dominated by state transfer and state checking (isolated in the figure). The time to load the new processes in memory and complete the preparation phase is normally marginal. We experimented with many state filters to quiesce all the common OS process interactions and found that the time to reach state quiescence was only a few milliseconds in the worst case. This property makes any overhead associated to evaluating state and interface filters in the preparation phase *marginal*. While our overall update times are generally higher than prior solutions for simple updates (since we replace entire processes instead of individual functions), the resulting impact is still orders of magnitude shorter than any reboot and bearable for most systems.

6.3 Service disruption

To substantiate our last claim, we evaluated the service disruption caused by live update. Figure 8 shows the run-time overhead incurred by our macrobenchmarks when periodically updating OS processes in a round-robin fashion. The overhead increases for shorter update intervals, with more disruption incurred by *sdtools*. The figures present three novel live update scenarios. Figure 8a presents results for an *online diversification* scenario—an idea we have also developed further in [34]. We implemented a source-to-source transformation able to *safely* and automatically change 3872 type definitions (adding/reordering `struct` elements and expanding arrays/primitive types) throughout the entire operating system. The changes were randomized for each generated operating system version, introducing a heavily diversified memory layout across updates. This scenario stressed the capabilities of our state transfer framework, introducing an average of 4,873,735 type transformations at each update cycle and approximating an upper bound for the service disruption. Figure 8b presents a *memory leakage reclaiming* scenario. Updates were performed between identical OS versions (approximating a lower bound for the service disruption), but we deliberately introduced a memory leak bug (similar to one found during development) that caused the virtual filesystem not to free the allocated memory at `exec()` time. Shorter update intervals increase the overhead but allow our state transfer framework to automatically repair leaks more quickly. The tradeoff is evident for *sdtools*, which `exec()`ed several programs during the experiment. Figure 8c presents an *update failures* scenario. We deliberately simulated state transfer crashes or 2-second timeouts (in equal measure) for each update, resulting in more severe service disruption for the syscall-intensive benchmark *sdtools*, but with no system-perceived impact. This scenario stressed the *unique* fault-tolerant capabilities of our live update infrastructure, able to withstand significant update failures and automatically rollback the entire update transaction with no consequences for the operating system and all the running programs. Overall, our experiments reported a negligible overhead for update intervals larger than 20s. Given that updates are relatively rare events, we expect the update-induced service disruption to be minimal in practice.

6.4 Memory footprint

Our metadata instrumentation naturally leads to a larger memory footprint at runtime. Our current implementation required an average of 65 bytes for each type, 27 extra bytes for each variable/constant/string, 38 extra bytes for each function with address taken, 10 extra bytes for each allocation, and 38 bytes for each allocation site. During the execution of our macrobenchmarks, we measured an average state overhead (i.e., metadata size vs. run-time state size) of 18% and an overall memory footprint overhead of 35% across all the operating system processes. While comparable to prior instrumentation-based live update techniques [56, 59, 60], our memory footprint overhead never increases with the number and the size of the updates applied to the system. This is ensured by our stable live update strategy. For comparison, we also ported the Linux ACPI driver to PROTEOS. Despite the very complex code base, adding updatability only required 2 type-based callbacks for 2 `unions`. In this case, the state overhead and the overall memory footprint overhead measured were 41% and 37%, respectively.

7. Related work

Several live update solutions are described in the literature, with techniques targeting operating systems [12–14, 20, 56], C programs [10, 21, 55, 59, 60], object-oriented programs [46, 74], programming languages [11, 26, 73], database systems [18], and distributed systems [6, 7, 9, 16, 17, 27, 28, 48, 76]. We focus here on live update for operating systems and generic C programs, but we refer the interested reader to [5, 35, 44, 68] for more complete surveys.

K42 [13, 14, 72] is a research OS that supports live update functionalities using object-oriented design patterns. To update live objects, K42 relies on system-enforced quiescence, transparently blocking all the threads calling into updated objects. Unfortunately, this strategy leads to a poorly predictable update process, with hidden thread dependencies potentially leading to *unrecoverable* deadlocks. In contrast, PROTEOS gives programmers full control over the update process and can automatically recover from synchronization errors (e.g., deadlocks) introduced by poorly designed update transactions using a predefined timeout. In addition, K42 provides *no* support for automated state transfer. Unlike existing live update techniques for C, however, their object-oriented approach offers a solution to the stability problem. The downside is that their techniques are limited to object-oriented programs. In contrast, the techniques we propose have more general applicability. For instance, state filters and our state management framework can be used to improve existing live update solutions for the Linux kernel [12, 20, 56] and generic C programs [10, 21, 55, 59, 60]. Our framework could be, for example, integrated in existing solutions to automatically track pointers to updated data structures or abort the update in case of unsafe behavior. Our process-level updates, in turn, are an elegant solution to the stability problem for user-level live update solutions. Also note that, while explicitly conceived to simplify state management—no need for explicit update points and stack instrumentation—and minimize manual effort—simpler to reason on update safety and control multicomponent live update transactions—our event-loop design is not strictly required for the applicability of our techniques. For instance, our event-driven model can be easily extended to multithreaded execution using annotated per-thread update points, as previously suggested in [59]. When backward compatibility is not a primary concern, however, we believe our event-driven strategy to offer a superior design for safe and automatic live update. For this reason, we opted for a pure event-driven model for our current PROTEOS implementation.

DynaMOS [56] and LUCOS [20] are two live update solutions for the Linux kernel. They both apply code updates using binary rewriting techniques. To handle data updates, DynaMOS relies on shadow data structures, while LUCOS relies on virtualization to synchronize old and new data structure versions at each write access. Both solutions advocate running the old and the new version in parallel. Unlike ours, their cross-version execution strategy leads to a highly unpredictable update process. In addition, state transfer is delegated entirely to the programmer.

Ksplice [12] is an important step forward over its predecessors. Similar to DynaMOS [56], Ksplice uses binary rewriting and shadow data structures to perform live updates. Unlike all the other live update solutions for C, however, Ksplice prepares live updates at the object code layer. This strategy simplifies patch analysis and does not inhibit any compiler optimizations or language features. Process-level updates used in PROTEOS take these important guarantees one step further. Not only are the two versions allowed to have arbitrarily different code and data layout, but patch analysis and preparation tools are no longer necessary. The new version is compiled and deployed as-is, with changes between versions automatically tracked by our state transfer framework at runtime. Moreover, Ksplice does not support update states other than function quiescence and provides no support for automated state transfer, state checking, or hot rollback.

Related to OS-level live update solutions is also work on extensible operating systems [15, 22, 69, 70] (which only allow predetermined OS extensions), dynamic kernel instrumentation [58, 75] (which is primarily concerned with debugging and performance monitoring), microkernel architectures [23, 42, 49, 71] (which can replace OS subsystems but not without causing service loss [23]), and online maintenance techniques [54, 66] (which require virtualization and domain-specific migration tools).

Similar to OS-level solutions, existing live update techniques for user-space C programs all assume an in-place update model, with code and data changes loaded directly into the running version. Redirection of execution is accomplished with compiler-based techniques [59, 60], binary rewriting [10, 21], or stack reconstruction [55]. Some techniques assume quiescence [10], others rely on predetermined update points [55, 59, 60] or allow unrestricted cross-version execution [21]. Unlike PROTEOS, these solutions offer no support to specify safe update states on a per-update basis, do not attempt to fully automate state transfer or state checking, and fail to ensure a transactional and stable update process.

Recent efforts on user-space C programs by Hayden et al. [41], developed independently from our work, also suggest using entire programs as live updatable units. Unlike our process-level updates, however, their update strategy encapsulates every program version inside a shared library and allows the old and the new version to share the same process address space with no restriction at live update time. This strategy requires every program to be compiled with only position-independent code—which may be particularly inefficient on some architectures—and also fails to properly isolate, detect, and recover from errors in the state transfer code. In addition, their state transfer strategy does not support interior pointers and unrestricted use of `void*` pointers, nor does it attempt to automate pointer transfer for heap-allocated objects with no user intervention. Finally, their system includes xfgen, a tool to generate state transformers using a domain-specific language. While a high-level language may reduce the programming effort, we found much more natural to express state transfer extensions for C programs directly in C, using a convenient and well-defined callback interface.

The techniques used in PROTEOS draw inspiration from prior work in different research areas. Our state filters are inspired by DYMOS [51], an early dynamic modification system that allowed programmers to specify procedures required to be inactive at update time. State filters are more general and easier to use, allowing programmers to specify safe update states in the most natural way. The idea of state transfer between processes was first explored by Gupta [36], but his work assumed a fixed memory layout and delegated state transfer entirely to the programmer. Our state introspection strategy is inspired by garbage collector-style object tracking, a technique also explored in live update solutions for managed languages like Java [74]. Similarly, our update-time memory leakage reclaiming strategy is inspired by prior precise garbage collection techniques for C programs [67]. Finally, state checking is inspired by invariants-based techniques to detect anomalous program behavior [4, 25, 30, 38, 65, 77]. Unlike prior techniques, our state invariants are conservatively derived from static analysis, eliminating false positives that arise from learning *likely* invariants at runtime.

8. Conclusion

In this paper, we presented PROTEOS, a new research OS designed with live update in mind. Unlike existing solutions, the techniques implemented in PROTEOS can efficiently and reliably support several classes of updates with minimal manual effort. State and interface filters allow updates to happen only in predictable system states and give programmers full control over the update process. Process-level updates completely eliminate the need for complex toolchains, enable safe hot rollback, and ensure a stable update process. Our state management framework reduces the state transfer burden to the bare minimum, fully automating state transfer for common structural state changes and exposing a convenient programming model for extensions. Finally, our state checking framework can automatically identify errors in a tainted state and detect violating assumptions in the state transfer process itself.

Acknowledgments

We would like to thank the anonymous reviewers for their comments. This work has been supported by European Research Council under grant ERC Advanced Grant 2008 - R3S3.

References

[1] Ksplice performance record. `http://www.ksplice.com/cve-evaluation`, 2009.

[2] FUSE: Filesystem in userspace. `http://fuse.sourceforge.net/`, 2012.

[3] Green hills integrity. `http://www.ghs.com/products/rtos/integrity.html`, 2012.

[4] S. V. Adve, V. S. Adve, and Y. Zhou. Using likely program invariants to detect hardware errors. In *Proc. of the IEEE Int'l Conf. on Dependable Systems and Networks*, 2008.

[5] S. Ajmani. A review of software upgrade techniques for distributed systems, 2004.

[6] S. Ajmani, B. Liskov, and L. Shrira. Scheduling and simulation: How to upgrade distributed systems. In *Proc. of the Ninth Workshop on Hot Topics in Operating Systems*, volume 9, pages 43–48, 2003.

[7] S. Ajmani, B. Liskov, L. Shrira, and D. Thomas. Modular software upgrades for distributed systems. In *Proc. of the 20th European Conf. on Object-oriented Programming*, pages 452–476, 2006.

[8] P. Akritidis. Cling: A memory allocator to mitigate dangling pointers. In *Proc. of the 19th USENIX Security Symp.*, page 12, 2010.

[9] J. P. A. Almeida, M. v. Sinderen, and L. Nieuwenhuis. Transparent dynamic reconfiguration for CORBA. In *Proc. of the Third Int'l Symp. on Distributed Objects and Applications*, pages 197–207, 2001.

[10] G. Altekar, I. Bagrak, P. Burstein, and A. Schultz. OPUS: Online patches and updates for security. In *Proc. of the 14th USENIX Security Symp.*, volume 14, pages 19–19, 2005.

[11] J. R. Andersen, L. Bak, S. Grarup, K. V. Lund, T. Eskildsen, K. M. Hansen, and M. Torgersen. Design, implementation, and evaluation of the resilient Smalltalk embedded platform. *Comput. Lang. Syst. Struct.*, 31(3-4):127–141, 2005.

[12] J. Arnold and M. F. Kaashoek. Ksplice: Automatic rebootless kernel updates. In *Proc. of the Fourth ACM European Conf. on Computer Systems*, pages 187–198, 2009.

[13] A. Baumann, G. Heiser, J. Appavoo, D. Da Silva, O. Krieger, R. W. Wisniewski, and J. Kerr. Providing dynamic update in an operating system. In *Proc. of the USENIX Annual Tech. Conf.*, page 32, 2005.

[14] A. Baumann, J. Appavoo, R. W. Wisniewski, D. D. Silva, O. Krieger, and G. Heiser. Reboots are for hardware: Challenges and solutions to updating an operating system on the fly. In *Proc. of the USENIX Annual Tech. Conf.*, pages 1–14, 2007.

[15] B. N. Bershad, S. Savage, E. G. Sirer, M. E. Fiuczynski, D. Becker, C. Chambers, and S. Eggers. Extensibility, safety and performance in the SPIN operating system. In *Proc. of the 15th ACM Symp. on Oper. Systems Prin.*, volume 29, pages 267–284, 1995.

[16] T. Bloom. *Dynamic module replacement in a distributed programming system*. PhD thesis, MIT, Cambridge, MA, USA, 1983.

[17] T. Bloom and M. Day. Reconfiguration and module replacement in Argus: Theory and practice. *Software Engineering J.*, 8(2):102–108, 1993.

[18] C. Boyapati, B. Liskov, L. Shrira, C. Moh, and S. Richman. Lazy modular upgrades in persistent object stores. In *Proc. of the 18th ACM Conf. on Object-Oriented Programming, Systems, Languages, and Applications*, pages 403–417, 2003.

[19] S. Boyd-Wickizer and N. Zeldovich. Tolerating malicious device drivers in Linux. In *Proc. of the USENIX Annual Tech. Conf.*, page 9, 2010.

[20] H. Chen, R. Chen, F. Zhang, B. Zang, and P. Yew. Live updating operating systems using virtualization. In *Proc. of the Second Int'l Conf. on Virtual Execution Environments*, pages 35–44, 2006.

[21] H. Chen, J. Yu, R. Chen, B. Zang, and P. Yew. POLUS: A powerful live updating system. In *Proc. of the 29th Int'l Conf. on Software Eng.*, pages 271–281, 2007.

[22] C. Cowan, T. Autrey, C. Krasic, C. Pu, and J. Walpole. Fast concurrent dynamic linking for an adaptive operating system. In *Proc. of the Third Int'l Conf. on Configurable Distributed Systems*, pages 108–115, 1996.

[23] F. M. David, E. M. Chan, J. C. Carlyle, and R. H. Campbell. CuriOS: Improving reliability through operating system structure. In *Proc. of the 8th USENIX Symp. on Operating Systems Design and Implementation*, pages 59–72, 2008.

[24] A. Depoutovitch and M. Stumm. Otherworld: giving applications a chance to survive OS kernel crashes. In *Proc. of the 5th ACM European Conf. on Computer systems*, pages 181–194, 2010.

[25] M. Dimitrov and H. Zhou. Unified architectural support for soft-error protection or software bug detection. In *Proc. of the 16th Int'l Conf. on Parallel Architecture and Compilation Techniques*, pages 73–82, 2007.

[26] D. Duggan. Type-based hot swapping of running modules. In *Proc. of the Sixth ACM SIGPLAN Int'l Conf. on Functional programming*, pages 62–73, 2001.

[27] T. Dumitras and P. Narasimhan. Why do upgrades fail and what can we do about it?: Toward dependable, online upgrades in enterprise system. In *Proc. of the 10th Int'l Conf. on Middleware*, pages 1–20, 2009.

[28] T. Dumitras, J. Tan, Z. Gho, and P. Narasimhan. No more HotDependencies: Toward dependency-agnostic online upgrades in distributed systems. In *Proc. of the Third Workshop on Hot Topics in System Dependability*, page 14, 2007.

[29] T. Dumitras, P. Narasimhan, and E. Tilevich. To upgrade or not to upgrade: impact of online upgrades across multiple administrative domains. In *Proc. of the ACM Conf. on Object-Oriented Programming, Systems, Languages, and Appilcations*, pages 865–876, 2010.

[30] M. D. Ernst, J. Cockrell, W. G. Griswold, and D. Notkin. Dynamically discovering likely program invariants to support program evolution. In *Proc. of the 21st Int'l Conf. on Software Eng.*, pages 213–224, 1999.

[31] O. Frieder and M. E. Segal. On dynamically updating a computer program: From concept to prototype. *J. Syst. Softw.*, 14(2):111–128, 1991.

[32] C. Giuffrida and A. Tanenbaum. Safe and automated state transfer for secure and reliable live update. In *Proc. of the Fourth Int'l Workshop on Hot Topics in Software Upgrades*, pages 16–20, 2012.

[33] C. Giuffrida and A. S. Tanenbaum. Cooperative update: A new model for dependable live update. In *Proc. of the Second Int'l Workshop on Hot Topics in Software Upgrades*, pages 1–6, 2009.

[34] C. Giuffrida, A. Kuijsten, and A. S. Tanenbaum. Enhanced operating system security through efficient and fine-grained address space randomization. In *Proc. of the 21st USENIX Security Symp.*, page 40, 2012.

[35] D. Gupta. *On-line software version change*. PhD thesis, Indian Institute of Technology Kanpur, 1994.

[36] D. Gupta and P. Jalote. On-line software version change using state transfer between processes. *Softw. Pract. and Exper.*, 23(9):949–964, 1993.

[37] D. Gupta, P. Jalote, and G. Barua. A formal framework for on-line software version change. *IEEE Trans. Softw. Eng.*, 22(2):120–131, 1996.

[38] S. Hangal and M. S. Lam. Tracking down software bugs using automatic anomaly detection. In *Proc. of the 24th Int'l Conf. on Software Eng.*, pages 291–301, 2002.

[39] H. Hartig, M. Hohmuth, J. Liedtke, J. Wolter, and S. Schönberg. The performance of microkernel-based systems. In *Proc. of the 16th ACM Symp. on Oper. Systems Prin.*, pages 66–77, 1997.

[40] D. Hartmeier. Design and performance of the OpenBSD stateful packet filter (pf). In *Proc. of the USENIX Annual Tech. Conf.*, pages 171–180, 2002.

[41] C. M. Hayden, E. K. Smith, M. Denchev, M. Hicks, and J. S. Foster. Kitsune: Efficient, general-purpose dynamic software updating for C. In *Proc. of the ACM Conf. on Object-Oriented Programming, Systems, Languages, and Appilcations*, 2012.

[42] J. N. Herder, H. Bos, B. Gras, P. Homburg, and A. S. Tanenbaum. Reorganizing UNIX for reliability. In *Proc. of the 11th Asia-Pacific Conf. on Advances in Computer Systems Architecture*, pages 81–94, 2006.

[43] J. N. Herder, H. Bos, B. Gras, P. Homburg, and A. S. Tanenbaum. Failure resilience for device drivers. In *Proc. of the Int'l Conf. on Dependable Systems and Networks*, pages 41–50, 2007.

[44] M. Hicks. *Dynamic software updating*. PhD thesis, Univ. of Pennsylvania, 2001.

[45] D. Hildebrand. An architectural overview of QNX. In *Proc. of the Workshop on Micro-kernels and Other Kernel Architectures*, pages 113–126, 1992.

[46] G. Hjálmtýsson and R. Gray. Dynamic C++ classes: A lightweight mechanism to update code in a running program. In *Proc. of the USENIX Annual Tech. Conf.*, page 6, 1998.

[47] G. C. Hunt and J. R. Larus. Singularity: Rethinking the software stack. *SIGOPS Oper. Syst. Rev.*, 41(2):37–49, 2007.

[48] J. Kramer and J. Magee. The evolving philosophers problem: Dynamic change management. *IEEE Trans. Softw. Eng.*, 16(11):1293–1306, 1990.

[49] O. K. Labs. OKL4 community site. `http://wiki.ok-labs.com/`, 2012.

[50] C. Lattner and V. Adve. LLVM: A compilation framework for lifelong program analysis & transformation. In *Proc. of the Int'l Symp. on Code Generation and Optimization*, page 75, 2004.

[51] I. Lee. *Dymos: A dynamic modification system*. PhD thesis, Univ. of Wisconsin-Madison, 1983.

[52] J. Liedtke. Improving IPC by kernel design. In *Proc. of the 14th ACM Symp. on Oper. Systems Prin.*, pages 175–188, 1993.

[53] J. Liedtke. On micro-kernel construction. In *Proc. of the 15th ACM Symp. on Oper. Systems Prin.*, pages 237–250, 1995.

[54] D. E. Lowell, Y. Saito, and E. J. Samberg. Devirtualizable virtual machines enabling general, single-node, online maintenance. In *Proc. of the 11th Int'l Conf. on Architectural support for programming languages and operating systems*, volume 39, pages 211–223, 2004.

[55] K. Makris and R. Bazzi. Immediate multi-threaded dynamic software updates using stack reconstruction. In *Proc. of the USENIX Annual Tech. Conf.*, pages 397–410, 2009.

[56] K. Makris and K. D. Ryu. Dynamic and adaptive updates of non-quiescent subsystems in commodity operating system kernels. In *Proc. of the Second ACM European Conf. on Computer Systems*, pages 327–340, 2007.

[57] Microsoft. Windows User-Mode driver framework. `http://msdn.microsoft.com/en-us/windows/hardware/gg463294`, 2010.

[58] R. G. Minnich. A dynamic kernel modifier for Linux. In *Proc. of the LACSI Symposium*, 2002.

[59] I. Neamtiu and M. Hicks. Safe and timely updates to multi-threaded programs. In *Proc. of the ACM SIGPLAN Conf. on Programming Language Design and Implementation*, pages 13–24, 2009.

[60] I. Neamtiu, M. Hicks, G. Stoyle, and M. Oriol. Practical dynamic software updating for C. In *Proc. of the ACM SIGPLAN Conf. on Programming Language Design and Implementation*, pages 72–83, 2006.

[61] I. Neamtiu, M. Hicks, J. S. Foster, and P. Pratikakis. Contextual effects for version-consistent dynamic software updating and safe concurrent programming. In *Proc. of the ACM SIGPLAN Conf. on Programming Language Design and Implementation*, pages 37–49, 2008.

[62] Y. Padioleau, J. L. Lawall, and G. Muller. Understanding collateral evolution in Linux device drivers. In *Proc. of the First ACM European Conf. on Computer Systems*, pages 59–71, 2006.

[63] Y. Padioleau, J. Lawall, R. R. Hansen, and G. Muller. Documenting and automating collateral evolutions in Linux device drivers. In *Proc. of the Third ACM European Conf. on Computer Systems*, pages 247–260, 2008.

[64] N. Palix, G. Thomas, S. Saha, C. Calvès, J. Lawall, and G. Muller. Faults in Linux: Ten years later. In *Proc. of the 16th Int'l Conf. on Architectural support for programming languages and operating systems*, pages 305–318, 2011.

[65] K. Pattabiraman, G. P. Saggese, D. Chen, Z. T. Kalbarczyk, and R. K. Iyer. Automated derivation of application-specific error detectors using dynamic analysis. *IEEE Trans. Dep. Secure Comput.*, 8(5):640–655, 2011.

[66] S. Potter and J. Nieh. Reducing downtime due to system maintenance and upgrades. In *Proc. of the 19th USENIX Systems Administration Conf.*, pages 6–6, 2005.

[67] J. Rafkind, A. Wick, J. Regehr, and M. Flatt. Precise garbage collection for C. In *Proc. of the 2009 Int'l Symp. on Memory management*, pages 39–48, 2009.

[68] M. E. Segal and O. Frieder. On-the-fly program modification: Systems for dynamic updating. *IEEE Softw.*, 10(2):53–65, 1993.

[69] M. Seltzer and C. Small. Self-monitoring and self-adapting operating systems. In *Proc. of the Sixth Workshop on Hot Topics in Operating Systems*, pages 124–129, 1997.

[70] M. I. Seltzer, Y. Endo, C. Small, and K. A. Smith. Dealing with disaster: Surviving misbehaved kernel extensions. In *Proc. of the Second USENIX Symp. on Operating Systems Design and Implementation*, pages 213–227, 1996.

[71] J. S. Shapiro, J. M. Smith, and D. J. Farber. EROS: A fast capability system. In *Proc. of the 17th ACM Symp. on Oper. Systems Prin.*, pages 170–185, 1999.

[72] C. A. N. Soules, D. D. Silva, M. Auslander, G. R. Ganger, and M. Ostrowski. System support for online reconfiguration. In *Proc. of the USENIX Annual Tech. Conf.*, pages 141–154, 2003.

[73] G. Stoyle, M. Hicks, G. Bierman, P. Sewell, and I. Neamtiu. Mutatis mutandis: Safe and predictable dynamic software updating. *ACM Trans. Program. Lang. Syst.*, 29(4), 2007.

[74] S. Subramanian, M. Hicks, and K. S. McKinley. Dynamic software updates: A VM-centric approach. In *Proc. of the ACM SIGPLAN Conf. on Programming Language Design and Implementation*, volume 44, pages 1–12, 2009.

[75] A. Tamches and B. P. Miller. Fine-grained dynamic instrumentation of commodity operating system kernels. In *Proc. of the Third ACM Symp. on Oper. Systems Prin.*, pages 117–130, 1999.

[76] Y. Vandewoude, P. Ebraert, Y. Berbers, and T. D'Hondt. Tranquility: A low disruptive alternative to quiescence for ensuring safe dynamic updates. *IEEE Trans. Softw. Eng.*, 33(12):856–868, 2007.

[77] P. Zhou, W. Liu, L. Fei, S. Lu, F. Qin, Y. Zhou, S. Midkiff, and J. Torrellas. AccMon: Automatically detecting memory-related bugs via program counter-based invariants. In *Proc. of the 37th Annual IEEE/ACM Int'l Symp. on Microarchitecture*, pages 269–280, 2004.

Verifying Security Invariants in ExpressOS

Haohui Mai Edgar Pek Hui Xue
Samuel T. King P. Madhusudan
University of Illinois at Urbana-Champaign
{mai4,pek1,huixue2,kingst,madhu}@illinois.edu

Abstract

Security for applications running on mobile devices is important. In this paper we present ExpressOS, a new OS for enabling high-assurance applications to run on commodity mobile devices securely. Our main contributions are a new OS architecture and our use of formal methods for proving key security invariants about our implementation. In our use of formal methods, we focus solely on proving that our OS implements our security invariants correctly, rather than striving for full functional correctness, requiring significantly less verification effort while still proving the security relevant aspects of our system.

We built ExpressOS, analyzed its security, and tested its performance. Our evaluation shows that the performance of ExpressOS is comparable to an Android-based system. In one test, we ran the same web browser on ExpressOS and on an Android-based system, and found that ExpressOS adds 16% overhead on average to the page load latency time for nine popular web sites.

Categories and Subject Descriptors D.4.6 [*Operating Systems*]: Security and Protection; D.2.4 [*Software Engineering*]: Software/Program Verification

General Terms Security, Verification

Keywords mobile security; microkernel; programming by contracts; automatic theorem proving

1. Introduction

Modern mobile devices have put a wealth of information and ever-increasing opportunities for social interaction at the fingertips of users. At the center of this revolution are smart phones and tablet computers, which give people a nearly constant connection to the Internet. Applications running on these devices provide users with a wide range of functionality, but vulnerabilities and exploits in their software stacks pose a real threat to the security and privacy of modern mobile systems [7, 18].

Current work on secure operating systems has focused on formalizing UNIX implementations [14, 36] and on verifying microkernel abstractions [17, 20]. Although these projects approach or achieve full functional correctness, they require a large verification effort (the seL4 paper claims that it took 20 man-years to build and prove [20]) and detailed knowledge of low-level theorem-proving expertise.

This paper presents ExpressOS, a new OS we designed to provide high assurance security mechanisms for application security policies, and a verified implementation of the mechanisms that ExpressOS uses to enforce security policies. Our design includes an OS architecture for coping with legacy hardware safely, a programming language and run-time system for building our operating system, and a set of proofs on our kernel implementation that provide high assurance that our system can uphold the security invariants we define.

A key novelty of our verification approach is to focus on a set of security invariants of the code *without attempting full-blown functional correctness*. For example, we have verified that the private storage areas for different applications are isolated in ExpressOS. We *do not* derive this security invariant by showing the every aspect of all involved components, like the file systems and the device drivers, is correct. Instead, ExpressOS isolates the above components as untrusted system services. The proofs show that ExpressOS encrypts all private data of applications before sending it out to the system services, and ExpressOS places security checks correctly so that only the application itself can access its private data.

The proofs focus on seven security invariants covering secure storage, memory isolation, user interface (UI) isolation, and secure IPC. By proving these invariants, ExpressOS enables sensitive applications to provably isolate their state (mostly ensuring integrity of state; confidentiality is also ensured to a certain degree, but side-channel attacks are not provably prevented), and run-time events from malicious applications running on the same device.

We achieve the proofs of these invariants by annotating source code with formal specifications written using mathematical abstractions of the properties, using code contracts [23] and BOOGIE-based tools [8, 22], writing ghost-code annotations that track and update these mathematical abstractions according to the code's progress, and by discharging verification using either abstract interpretation or automatic theorem provers (mainly SMT solvers [12]). A thorough verification of the invariants above requires only a modest annotation effort ($\sim 2.8\%$ annotation overhead).

To evaluate the security and the performance of ExpressOS, we have built a prototype system that runs on x86 hardware and exports a subset of the Android/Linux system call interfaces. To evaluate security, we have examined 383 recent vulnerabilities listed in CVE [9]. The ExpressOS architecture successfully prevents 364 of them. To evaluate performance, we have used an ASUS Eee PC and run a web browser on top of ExpressOS. Our experiments show that the performance of ExpressOS is comparable to Android: ExpressOS shows 16% overhead for the web browsing benchmark.

Our contributions are:

- ExpressOS is the first OS architecture that provides verifiable, high-level abstractions for building mobile applications.

ASPLOS'13, March 16–20, 2013, Houston, Texas, USA.

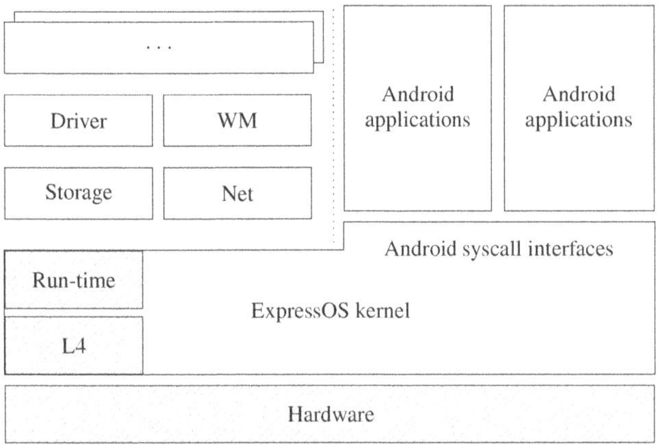

Figure 1: Overall architecture of ExpressOS. Android applications run directly on top of the ExpressOS kernel. Boxes that are left to the vertical dotted line represent the system services in ExpressOS. Shaded regions show the trusted computing base (TCB) of the system.

- ExpressOS shows that verifying security invariants is feasible with the help of new programming languages and sparse source code annotations.
- We have built ExpressOS and our experiments show that this type of OS can be practical and improve the security of software systems running on mobile devices.

2. ExpressOS overview

The primary goal of ExpressOS is to be a practical, high assurance operating system. As such, ExpressOS should support diverse hardware and legacy applications. Also, security invariants of ExpressOS should be formally verified.

This section provides an overview to the architecture, the verification approach, and system components of ExpressOS. Section 5 discusses the security implications of our architecture and the detailed design of the ExpressOS kernel.

2.1 Architecture for verification

Figure 1 describes the architecture of ExpressOS. The architecture includes the ExpressOS kernel, system services, and abstractions for applications.

ExpressOS uses four main techniques to simplify verification effort. First, ExpressOS pushes functionality into microkernel services, just like traditional microkernels, reducing the amount of code that needs to be verified. Second, it deploys end-to-end mechanisms in the kernel to defend against compromised services. For example, the ExpressOS kernel encrypts all data before sending it to the file system service. Third, ExpressOS relies on programming language type-safety to isolate the control and data flows within the kernel. Fourth, ExpressOS makes minor changes to the IPC system-call interface to expose explicitly IPC security policy data to the kernel. By using these techniques, ExpressOS isolates large components of the kernel while still being able to prove security properties about the abstractions they operate on.

Current techniques to isolate components and manage the complexity of a kernel include software-fault isolation [6, 30, 35], isolating application state through virtualization [2, 10, 37], and microkernel architectures [14, 17, 20, 36]. These techniques alone, however, are insufficient for verifying the implementation of a system's security policies – the correctness of the security policies still relies on the correctness of individual components. For example, an isolated but compromised file system might store private data with world-readable permissions, compromising the confidentiality of the data.

2.2 Design principles

In order to meet the overall goal of ExpressOS, three design principles guide our design:

- *Provide high-level, compatible, and verifiable abstractions.* ExpressOS should provide high-level, compatible abstractions (e.g., files) rather than low-level abstractions (e.g., disk blocks), so that existing applications can run on top of ExpressOS, and developers can express their security policies through familiar abstractions. More importantly, the security of these abstractions should be formally verifiable to support secure applications.
- *Reuse existing components.* ExpressOS should be able to reuse existing components to reduce the engineering effort to support production environments. Some of the components might have vulnerabilities. ExpressOS isolates these vulnerabilities to ensure they will not affect the security of the full system.
- *Minimize verification effort.* Fully verifying a practical system requires significant effort, thus the verification of ExpressOS focuses *only on security invariants*. Also, this principle enables combining lightweight techniques like code contracts with heavywieght techniques like Dafny annotations [22] to further reduce verification effort.

2.3 Verification approach

Our modular design limits the scope of verification down to the ExpressOS kernel. The ExpressOS kernel is implemented in C# and Dafny [22], both of which are type-safe languages. Dafny is a research programming language from Microsoft Research that researchers use to teach people about formal methods. Like SPIN [4] and Singularity [17], type-safety ensures that the ExpressOS kernel is free of memory errors, and provides fine-grain isolation between components within the kernel. A static compiler compiles both C# and Dafny programs to object code for native execution.

We verify security invariants in ExpressOS with both code contracts and Dafny annotations. Code contracts are verified using abstract interpretation techniques, which have low annotation overhead but are unable to reason about complicated properties, like properties about linked lists. In contrast, Dafny annotations are verified using logical constraint solvers, which are capable of handling complicated properties, but require a heavy annotation burden and deep expertise in formal methods to use. Based on their charactertics, we verified simpler security invariants using code contracts, and more complex ones (like manipulation of linked lists) in Dafny, where we use ghost variables (i.e., variables that aid verification) to connect the proofs of both techniques. The combination enables high productivity for verification using code contracts, yet still retaining the the full expressive power of Dafny to verify complicated properties needed to prove security invariants.

We verify security invariants that involve asynchronous execution contexts by reducing them into the object invariants of relevant data structures (Please see Section 4 for more about object invariants). Verification in asynchronous execution contexts is challenging due to the separation of the control and data flows. Verifying only the security invariants, however, has a simple solution. In particular, we express security invariants and the object invariants of relevant data structures in terms of ghost variables, and the object invariants imply the original security invariants. The main advantage is that these object invariants can be reasoned about locally; therefore it is easier to verify them rather than reason about asynchronous execution contexts.

2.4 The ExpressOS kernel

The ExpressOS kernel is responsible for managing the underlying hardware resources and providing abstractions to applications running above. The ExpressOS kernel uses L4 to access the underlying hardware. L4 provides abstractions for various hardware-related activities, such as context switching, address space manipulation, and inter-process communication (IPC). L4 resides in the TCB of ExpressOS, although a variant of L4, seL4 [20], has been fully formally verified.

2.5 System services

ExpressOS separates subsystems as system services running on top of the ExpressOS kernel. These services include persistent storage, device drivers, networking protocols, and a window manager for displaying application GUIs and handling input. ExpressOS reuses the existing implementation from L4Android [21] to implement these services.

All these services are untrusted components in ExpressOS. They are isolated from the ExpressOS kernel. The isolation combined with other techniques (discussed in Section 5) ensures that the verified security invariants remain valid even if a system service is compromised.

2.6 Application abstractions

The ExpressOS kernel exports a subset of the Android system call interfaces directly to applications. These abstractions include processes, files, sockets, and IPC. ExpressOS supports unmodified Android applications like a Web Browser to run on top of it directly.

The ExpressOS kernel provides an alternative set of IPC interfaces that is more amenable to formal verification, but still enables applications to perform Android-like IPC operations. First, it exposes all IPC interfaces as system calls rather than using `ioctl` calls. Second, it requires all IPC channels to be annotated with permissions, so that the ExpressOS kernel can perform access control on IPC operations. This design choice enables us to verify IPC operations in ExpressOS.

3. Threat Model

An untrusted Android application runs directly on ExpressOS. Such an application contains arbitrary code and data, along with a manifest listing all its required permissions. The user grants all permissions listed on the manifest to the application once he or she agrees to install it into the system. ExpressOS must be able to confirm that all activities of the application conform to its permissions, and all security invariants defined by ExpressOS (discussed in Section 5) must hold during the lifetime of the system.

ExpressOS should be able to isolate multiple applications. An application must not be able to compromise any security invariants of other applications.

The TCB of ExpressOS includes the hardware, the L4 microkernel, the compilers, and the language run-time. All system services in ExpressOS, however, are untrusted. ExpressOS should be able to maintain its security invariants for all applications even if the system services execute arbitrary code.

This paper focuses only on confidentiality and integrity; availability is out of the scope of this paper.

4. Formal methods background

In this section, we describe a few basic verification related concepts for readers who are not familiar with formal techniques. Experienced readers could skip this section.

The idea of verification is to use a verifier to reason about the implementation of a program: whether its behavior matches programmer's intentions, which are formalized and referred to as the *specification*.

The Floyd-Hoare style approach to verification achieves modular verification by annotating each function/method with pre- and post-conditions, and annotating the rest of the code with appropriate assertions that capture the specification. In this paper we focus on proving *safety properties*, which models properties that fail in finite time (availability is not a safety specification, typically). In particular, a *pre-condition* (*post-condition*) specifies certain assertions that have to hold before (after) executing a function. *Object invariants* refer to assertions that have to hold both before and after executing any methods in the object. Figure 4 shows an example of pre- and post-conditions used in ExpressOS.

Complex specifications, such as the security specifications we prove in our code, cannot always be stated in terms of assertions on the program state that is in scope at the point of assertion. This leads us to use *ghost code* in the verification. Ghost code is code added to the original program to aid formal reasoning during verification but is not needed at run-time. Ghost code changes only the *ghost states* associated with *ghost variables*, which are annotated with the keyword `ghost`. The ghost state can never change the semantics of the original code (for instance, a conditional on a ghost variable followed by an update of a real program variable is disallowed, syntactically). Furthermore, ghost code must always be provably terminating.

Ghost variables can range over mathematical types that are not supported in the programming language, including abstract sets, lists, etc., and can be used for abstracting the data contained in the program using mathematical objects, and thus encode specifications naturally (for example, a ghost sequence variable can track the sequence of keys stored in a linked list and we can then assert that this sequence is sorted). Apart from the ghost code for mathematical abstractions of the specification, the code is also annotated with additional information to prove a property of a correct program (typical examples include updating ghost states to reflect how the code meets the specification, inductive invariants on loops to facilitate automated reasoning for recursion, etc.). One good example of ghost variables in use is the `CurrentState` variable shown in Figure 4, which help maintain information during verification about the current state of the `Page` object.

The verification system (ours are based mostly on the suite of BOOGIE-based verification tools, including Dafny) proceeds to verify the code by taking straight-line fragments flanked by pre- and post-annotations, and derives verification conditions, which capture the semantics of the program, and are purely logical statements whose validity implies correctness of the code segments. These logical statements are, thanks to ghost code, often expressible in quantifier-free first-order theories combining arithmetic, arrays, recursive data-structures, sets, sequences, etc., and can be discharged using automatic constraint solvers, especially the emerging powerful class of SMT solvers.

For some of the simpler specifications, a completely automatic analysis based on *abstract interpretation* is feasible. We use the code contracts framework to achieve this in ExpressOS.

5. Proving security invariants

This section describes that how we apply the techniques described in Section 2 to verify security invariants on the implementation of storage, memory management, user interface, and IPC in ExpressOS.

5.1 Secure storage

The storage system of ExpressOS provides guarantees of access control, confidentiality, and integrity for applications, yet still offers the same sets of storage APIs as Linux. The storage system is implemented as an additional layer on top of the basic storage APIs (e.g., `open()`, `read()`, and `write()`), which are provided by the untrusted storage service.

```
static SecureFSInode Create(Thread current,
                            ByteBufferRef metadata,
                            ...)
{
  ...
  var ret = InitializeAndVerifyMetadata(...);
  ...

  var metadata_verified = ret == 0;
  ...

  var access_permission_checked
    = SecurityManager.CanAccessFile(current, metadata);
  ...

  // Verify both Property 1 and Property 2
  Contract.Assert(metadata_verified
                  && access_permission_checked);

  return ...;
}
```

Figure 2: Relevant code snippets in C# for Property 1 and Property 2.

The first security invariant for secure storage that the ExpressOS kernel enforces is:

SI 1. *An application can access a file only if it has appropriate permissions. The permissions cannot be tampered with by the storage service.*

An application can implement its security policy directly on top of SI 1. For example, an application might restrict the permission of a file so that only the application itself has access to it.

Since other compromised components such as the storage service and device drivers can affect SI 1, the first step of verifying SI 1 is to isolate the effects of these services. The ExpressOS kernel uses the HMAC algorithm [3] to achieve this goal. The ExpressOS kernel prepends several pages to all files managed by the secure storage system. These pages store metadata such as permissions, the size of the file, as well as an HMAC signature of these pages. The ExpressOS kernel checks the HMAC signature to ensure the integrity of the metadata when loading the file into the memory.

Now SI 1 can be reduced to the following two lower level properties:

Property 1 (Integrity-Metadata). *The signature of a file's metadata is always checked before an application can perform any operations on it.*

Property 2 (Access Control). *An application can only access a file when it has appropriate permissions.*

Figure 2 shows relevant code of Property 1 and Property 2. The `Create()` function calls `InitializeAndVerifyMetadata()` to verify the HMAC signature of the metadata. Then it calls `SecurityManager.CanAccessFile()` to determine whether the current process has appropriate permissions to open the file. Finally, the annotation of `Contract.Assert()` instructs the verifier to prove that both the integrity of the metadata, and the access permission of the file have been checked.

The reduction is a trade-off between formal verification and practicality. We argue that pragmatically the conjunction of Property 1 and Property 2 implies SI 1. The reduction captures the important fact that ExpressOS misses no security checks in its access control logic, which is the main point of verifying ExpressOS. It does assume the implementation of relevant libraries like AES / SHA-1, and the one of `InitializeAndVerifyMetadata()` and `SecurityManager.CanAccessFile()` is correct. These components can be verified independently, and a verified implementation can be plugged into the system to further strengthen the proof.[1]

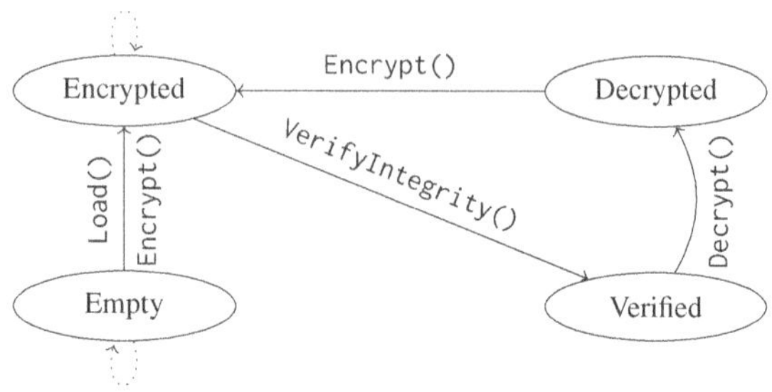

Figure 3: State transition diagram for the Page object. Ellipses represent the states. Solid and dotted arrows represent the successful and failed transitions.

The ExpressOS kernel also enforces integrity and confidentiality of its secure storage system:

SI 2. *Only the application itself can access its private data. Neither other applications nor system services can access or tamper with the data.*

Similar to SI 1, the ExpressOS kernel uses encryption to defend against compromised system services. From a high level, it partitions a file into multiple pages, and then it encrypts each page with AES for confidentiality. To ensure integrity, it signs each encrypted page with the HMAC algorithm, and packs the results to the metadata of the file. The overall implementation is similar to Cryptfs [39].

ExpressOS assigns each application a different private key during installation; therefore SI 2 can be reduced to the following two properties:

Property 3 (Confidentiality). *Every page is encrypted before it is sent to the storage service.*

Property 4 (Integrity). *Each page loaded from the storage service has the appropriate integrity signature.*

The idea behind verifying Property 3 and Property 4 is to use the ghost variable `CurrentState` to record the current state of the page. Figure 3 shows the state transition diagram for a Page object. A page can be in the state of `Empty`, `Verified`, `Decrypted`, and `Encrypted`, meaning that (1) the page is empty, (2) its integrity has been verified, (3) its contents have been decrypted, and (4) its contents have been encrypted. To verify these properties, we specify the valid state transitions as the pre- and post-conditions of the relevant functions. For example, the specifications of `Decrypt()` state that the page should has its integrity verified before entering the function, and its contents are decrypted afterwards.

Figure 4 shows the relevant code snippets. Notice that Property 3 can be specified as a pre-condition of the function `Flush()`: the function can only be called if the page is in the `Encrypted` state.

[1] The `InitializeAndVerifyMetadata()` function parses binary data read from the disk and verifies its integrity, which is easier implemented in C. To demonstrate the feasibility of this approach, we have implemented `InitializeAndVerifyMetadata()` in C, and verified its correctness with VCC [8].

```
class CachePage {
  enum State { Empty, Verified, Decrypted, Encrypted }
  [Ghost] State CurrentState;

  void Encrypt(...) {
    Contract.Requires(CurrentState == State.Empty
                      || CurrentState == State.Decrypted);
    Contract.Ensures(CurrentState == State.Encrypted);
    ...
  }

  void Decrypt(...) {
    Contract.Requires(CurrentState == State.Verified);
    Contract.Ensures(CurrentState == State.Decrypted);
    ...
  }

  // Verify the integrity of the page,
  // Returns true if the page is authentic.
  bool VerifyIntegrity(...) {
    Contract.Requires(CurrentState == State.Encrypted);
    Contract.Ensures(!Contract.Result<bool>()
                     || CurrentState == State.Verified);
    ...
  }

  // Load the content of the page from
  // the storage service.
  bool Load(...) {
    Contract.Requires(CurrentState == State.Empty);
    Contract.Ensures(!Contract.Result<bool>()
                     || CurrentState == State.Encrypted);
    ...
  }

  void Flush(...) {
    Contract.Requires(CurrentState == State.Encrypted);
    ...
  }
}
```

Figure 4: Relevant code snippets in C# for Property 3 and Property 4. `Contract.Requires()` and `Contract.Ensures()` specify the pre- and post-conditions of the functions.

```
static uint HandlePageFault(Process proc,
                            uint faultType,
                            Pointer faultAddress,
                            Pointer faultIP)
{
  Contract.Requires(proc.ObjectInvariant());

  ...
  AddressSpace space = proc.Space;
  var region = space.Regions.Find(faultAddress);

  if (region == null || (faultType & region.Access) == 0)
    return 0;

  ...
  var shared_memory_region = IsSharedRegion(region);
  var ghost_page_from_fresh_memory = false;

  if (shared_memory_region)
  {
    ....
  }
  else
  {
    page = Globals.PageAllocator.AllocPage();
    ghost_page_from_fresh_memory = true;
    ...

    if (region.File != null)
    {
      // Assertion of Property 5
      Contract.Assert(region.File.GhostOwner == proc);
      var r = region.File.Read(...);
      ...
    }
    ...
  }

  Contract.Assert(shared_memory_region
                  ^ ghost_page_from_fresh_memory);
  ...
}
```

Figure 5: Code snippets for the page fault handler.

For compatibility reasons, ExpressOS does allow an application to create unencrypted, public readable files. ExpressOS, however, does not provide additional security invariants for these files.

5.2 Memory isolation

The ExpressOS kernel enforces proper access control and isolation for all memory of the applications:

SI 3. *If a memory page of an application is backed by a file, the pager can map it in if and only if the application has proper access to the file.*

SI 4. *An application cannot access the memory of other applications, unless they explicitly share the memory.*

The challenge of verifying SI 3 is that there is insufficient information available for verification at the point of assertions (i.e., in the pager). This is because the security checks are executed in different contexts, where both the control and data flows are separated in these two contexts.

ExpressOS addresses this challenge by connecting the information indirectly through the *object invariants* of relevant data structures. It strengthens these object invariants to contain information about the security checks, so that the object invariants can derive the desired security invariants.

Figure 5 and Figure 6 show the relevant implementation of the pagers. From a high level, the ExpressOS kernel organizes the virtual memory of a process with a series of `MemoryRegion` objects. A `MemoryRegion` represents a continuous region of the virtual memory, which has information on its access permissions and location. In addition, if the region is mapped to a file, it contains a reference to the mapped file (i.e., the `File` field in the `MemoryRegion` class). Since we have verified that the ExpressOS kernel properly checks access to files in Section 5.1, SI 3 can be reduced to the following property:

Property 5. *When the page fault handler serves a file-backed page for a process, the file has to be opened by the same process.*

The key of verifying Property 5 is to use a ghost variable to record the *ownership* of the relevant objects, and to specify object invariants based on the ownership. For example, the first assertion in Figure 5 specifies Property 5, which gets verified through a series of object invariants.

First, the `AddressSpace` class represents the virtual address space of a process by a sequence of `MemoryRegion` objects. Intuitively the `AddressSpace` object "owns" all `MemoryRegion` objects

```
class MemoryRegion {
  ...
  var File: File;
  var GhostOwner: Process;

  function ObjectInvariant() : bool ... {
    File != null ==> File.GhostOwner == GhostOwner
    ...
  }
}

class Process {
  var space: AddressSpace;

  function ObjectInvariant() : bool ... {
    space != null && space.GhostOwner == this
    ...
  }
}

class AddressSpace {
  var GhostOwner: Process;
  var Head: MemoryRegion;

  // Ghost variable to record the sequence of
  // MemoryRegions owned by this AddressSpace
  ghost var Contents: seq<MemoryRegion>;

  function ObjectInvariant() : bool ... {
    forall x :: x in Contents ==>
      x != null && x.ObjectInvariant()
      && x.GhostOwner == GhostOwner;
    ...
  }

  method Find(address: Pointer) returns (ret: MemoryRegion)
  requires ObjectInvariant();
  ensures ObjectInvariant();
  ensures ret != null ==>
    ret.ObjectInvariant() && ret.GhostOwner == GhostOwner;

  method Insert(r: MemoryRegion)
  requires r != null && r.GhostOwner == GhostOwner;
  requires ObjectInvariant() && r.ObjectInvariant();
  ...
  ensures ObjectInvariant();
}

class File { ... var GhostOwner: Process; }
```

Figure 6: Reduced code snippets in Dafny for the MemoryRegion and the AddressSpace class.

in the sequence, which is specified in the object invariant of the AddressSpace object:

$$\forall x,\ x \in \texttt{Contents} \rightarrow \quad x \neq \texttt{null} \wedge x.\texttt{ObjectInvariant()} \\ \wedge x.\texttt{GhostOwner == GhostOwner}$$

The Find() method looks up and returns the corresponding MemoryRegion object for the virtual address, therefore it only returns MemoryRegion objects that are owned by the AddressSpace object. Combining it with the object invariant above can lead to the post-condition of Find():

$$\texttt{ret != null} \rightarrow \quad \texttt{ret.ObjectInvariant()} \wedge \\ \texttt{ret.GhostOwner == GhostOwner}$$

At the first assertion in Figure 5, this is simplified down to:

```
region.File.GhostOwner  ==  region.GhostOwner
                        ==  space.GhostOwner
```

The object invariant of the proc object ensures that

```
proc.space.GhostOwner == proc
```

This leads to the assertion of Property 5.

Property 5 is strictly weaker than the property that ensures full functional correctness. For example, Property 5 does not enforce that the file used in page fault handler has to be the exact same file that was requested by the user. The property, however, shows that the file must be opened by the same process. It maintains isolation since the access to the file has been properly checked. Moreover, it can be verified through object invariants.

We combine code contracts and Dafny to verify this property. Dafny verifies the MemoryRegion and AddressSpace class, because Dafny is able to reason about the linked lists in their implementation. The verification results from Dafny are expressed as properties of ghost variables (i.e., the GhostOwner fields). These properties are exported to code contracts as ground facts with the Contract.Assume() statements. Using Contarct.Assume() is a simple way let code contracts know about proofs about Dafny code. Additionally, we annotate the GhostOwner fields as read-only fields in C# to ensure soundness.

SI 4 can be expressed in a slightly different way to ease the verification.

Property 6 (Freshness). *The page fault handler maps in a fresh memory page when the page fault happens in non-shared memory.*

The idea is to ensure that the page fault handler always allocates a fresh memory page, i.e., a memory page that is not overlapped with any allocated pages. ExpressOS adopted the verified memory allocator from seL4 [34] for this purpose. ExpressOS dedicates a fixed region to this allocator in order to implement this property. The reduction allows specifying this property as the second assertion in Figure 5.

5.3 UI isolation

The ExpressOS kernel enforces the following UI invariant:

SI 5. *There is at most one currently active (i.e., foreground) application in ExpressOS. An application can write to the screen buffer only if it is currently active.*

To write to the screen, an application requests shared memory from the window manager, and writes screen contents onto the shared memory region. In ExpressOS, this can only be done through an explicit API so that the ExpressOS kernel knows exactly which memory region is the screen buffer.

The ExpressOS kernel enforces SI 5 by explicitly enabling and disabling the write access of screen buffers when changing the currently active application.

The object invariant of UIManager in Figure 7 specifies SI 5. The boolean ghost variable ScreenEnabled (which is not shown in the paper) denotes whether the application has write access to the screen. The initial value of ScreenEnabled is set to false for each application. Since it is the only API to manipulate the screen, the object invariant implies that only the current application has write access to the screen buffer.

5.4 Secure IPC

To simplify verification, ExpressOS provides an alternative, secure IPC (SIPC) interface over the Android's IPC interface. First, SIPC exposes all IPC functionality explicitly through system calls to eliminate the implementation and verification efforts on complex logic in ioctl() of Android's IPC. Second, the ExpressOS kernel enforces proper access controls for SIPC, compared to relying on

```
class UIManager
{
  Process ActiveProcess;

  [ContractInvariantMethod]
  void ObjectInvariantMethod() {
    Contract.Invariant(ActiveProcess == null
                       || ActiveProcess.ScreenEnabled);
  }

  void OnActiveProcessChanged(Process next) {
    Contract.Requires(next != null);
    Contract.Ensures(ActiveProcess == next);
    ...
  }

  void DisableScreen() {
    Contract.Ensures(ActiveProcess == null);
    Contract.Ensures(
      !Contract.OldValue(ActiveProcess).ScreenEnabled);
    ...
  }

  void EnableScreen(Process proc) {
    ...
    Contract.Ensures(ActiveProcess == proc);
    Contract.Ensures(ActiveProcess.ScreenEnabled);
    ...
  }
}
```

Figure 7: Relevant code snippets for SI 5. `[ContractInvariantMethod]` annotates the method that specifies the object invariants.

the receiver of Android's IPC for proper access control. This design moves the access control logic of SIPC into the ExpressOS kernel.

SIPC provides basic functionality to the applications, including creating SIPC channels, connecting to SIPC channels, and sending and receiving messages over the channel. Applications can still perform Android-like IPC operations using the SIPC interface.

The ExpressOS kernel enforces the following security invariants for SIPC:

SI 6. *An application can only connect to SIPC channels when it has appropriate permissions.*

SI 7. *An SIPC message will be sent only to its desired target.*

SI 6 and SI 7 can be verified with similar approaches described above.

SI 6 is an access control invariant, thus the strategy of proving SI 6 is similar to the one of SI 1. We use a ghost variable to indicate whether the process has properly checked the permissions when opening a new SIPC channel.

We follow the proving strategy of Property 5 to verify SI 7. The idea is to create a `SIPCMessage` object for each IPC message, and to introduce a ghost variable `target` to record the target process of the message, which provides sufficient information to verify SI 7.

5.5 Verification experience

Overall, we found the verification effort in terms of annotations practical for the properties that were proven correct. While we developed the system and wrote code, we came up with the relevant security properties at the level of the module we were writing, and formalized it using appropriate annotations. Combining code contracts and Dafny reduced the code to annotation ratio down to about 2.8% (implementing the specification defined by the annotations). There were some instances where the code we wrote was not actually correct, and using the verification tools to prove the property led us to find the error. Equally importantly, formalizing the specification at the level of the code crystallized the vague properties we had in mind, and helped us write better code as well.

One lesson that we had in ExpressOS was to refine the shapes and aliasing information of the objects through redesigning data structures, and implementing ownership using ghost variables. Simpler shapes eased the verification. For example, we have reimplemented the the `MemoryRegion` object as a singly-linked list instead of a doubly-linked one, since verifying the manipulations of the linked list in the latter case requires specifying reachability predicates, which are difficult to reason about within SMT-based frameworks. The verification of heap structure properties in Dafny was achieved sometimes using further ghost annotations in the style of natural proofs [24, 27].

In simpler cases we used ownership to constrain the effect of aliasing. For example, the ghost field `GhostOwner` in the `AddressSpace` object specified which `Process` had created the object. The information was used in proving that each process creates its own `AddressSpace` object, effectively forbidding aliasing between `AddressSpace` objects of different processes.

One potential drawback we found during verification was that the specification using ghost code is sometimes too intimately interleaved with the implementation. Consequently, the specification gets strewn all across the code, and it is our responsibility that this actually is correct. Though the mathematical abstractions do help to some extent to distance the specification from the code, ghost updates to these abstractions are still intimately related. To illustrate this, consider a programmer implementing the code `Encrypt()` in Figure 4, and consider the scenario where the actual encryption fails for some reason, and yet the programmer puts the page into the `Encrypted` state. The verifier will go through even though the implementation is incorrect with respect to what the developer wanted; the onus of writing the correct specification is on the developer.

While we did not encounter any case where we noticed we made errors in inadvertently formulating too weak a specification, we did spend time double-checking that our *specifications* were indeed correct. We think an alternate mechanism for writing specifications that are a bit more independent from the code, resilient to code changes, and yet facilitates automated proving would make the developer's work more robust and productive.

6. Implementing ExpressOS

The implementation of ExpressOS consists of two parts: the ExpressOS kernel and ExpressOS services. The ExpressOS kernel is a single-thread, event-driven kernel built on top of L4::Fiasco. We have implemented the kernel in C# and Dafny, which is compiled to native X86 code using a static compiler.

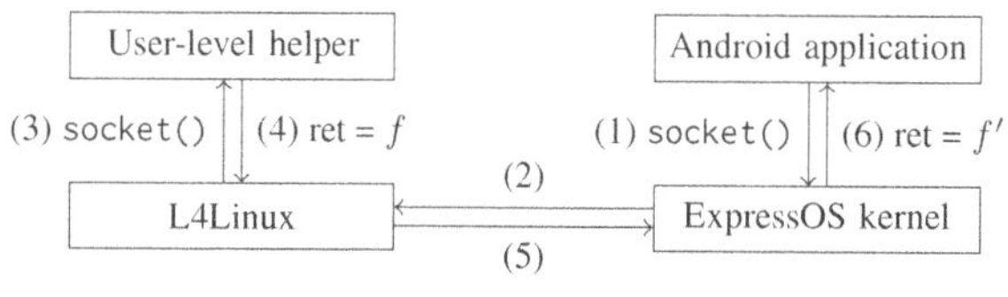

Figure 8: Work flow of handling the `socket()` system call in ExpressOS. The arrows represent the sequences of the work flow.

The implementation of ExpressOS kernel includes processes, threads, synchronization, memory management (e.g. `mmap()`), secure storage, and secure IPC. The kernel also implements a subset of Linux system calls to support Android applications like the Android Web browser. The kernel contains about 15K lines of code. The source code is available at `https://github.com/ExpressOS`.

The ExpressOS kernel delegates the implementation of system calls to ExpressOS services whenever it does not affect the soundness of the verification. These services include file systems, networks, device drivers, as well as Android's user-level services like window manager and service manager. ExpressOS reuses L4Android to implement these services. L4Android is a port of Android to a Linux kernel that runs on top of L4::Fiasco (i.e., L4Linux).

The rest of the section describes (i) how to dispatch a system call to ExpressOS services, (ii) how to bridge Android's binder IPCs between ExpressOS and Android's system services, and (iii) how to support shared memory between an application and ExpressOS services.

Dispatching a system call to ExpressOS services. The ExpressOS kernel forwards system calls with IPC calls to L4Android. Figure 8 shows the workflow of handling the `socket()` system call in the ExpressOS kernel. When (1) the application issues a `socket()` system call to the ExpressOS kernel, (2) the kernel wraps it as an IPC call to the L4Linux kernel. The L4Linux kernel executes the system call (which might involve a user-level helper like the step (3) & (4)), and (5) returns the result back to the ExpressOS kernel. The ExpressOS kernel (6) interprets the result and returns it to the application.

It is important for the ExpressOS kernel to maintain proper mappings between the file descriptors (fd) of the user-level helper and those of the application. In Figure 8, it maps between the fd f and f' so that subsequent calls like `send()` and `recv()` can be handled correctly. This workflow mirrors the implementation of the Coda file system inside Linux [19].

Bridging Android's binder IPC. Android applications communicate to Android system services (e.g., the window manager) through the Android's binder IPC interface. The ExpressOS kernel extends the mechanism in Figure 8 to bridge the binder IPC. The user-level helper in Figure 8 acts as a proxy between the Android application and Android system services. Both the user-level helper and the ExpressOS kernel transparently rewrite the IPC messages to support advanced features like exchanging file descriptors.

Supporting shared memory. To support shared memory between Android applications and Android services, the ExpressOS kernel maps all physical memory of L4Linux into its virtual address space. It maps the corresponding pages to the address space of the application when sharing occurs. We have modified L4Linux to expose its page allocation tables so that the ExpressOS kernel is able to compute the address. Both the ExpressOS kernel and L4Linux use the L4 Runtime Environment (L4Re) to facilitate this process.

7. Evaluation

This section describes our evaluation of ExpressOS. To evaluate to what extent that the ExpressOS architecture can prevent attacks, we examined 383 relevant real-world vulnerabilities to analyze the security of the system. Then, we present the performance measurements of ExpressOS.

7.1 Vulnerability study

To understand to what extent ExpressOS is able to withstand attacks, we studied 742 real-world vulnerabilities (from Jun, 2011 to Jun, 2012) listed in CVE. 383 out of 742 are valid vulnerabilities, and they affect different components used in Android. We manually examined each of them, and classified it into one of the four categories based on its location:

In the core of the kernel. The vulnerability exists in the core of the Linux kernel, which means that the same functionality is implemented in the ExpressOS kernel. The proofs of ExpressOS ensure that such a vulnerability cannot affect any security invariants discussed in Section 5. If the vulnerability is irrelevant to the security invariants, the language run-time ensures it cannot subvert the control flow and data flow integrity to circumvent the proofs.

In the libraries used by applications. The vulnerability exists in the libraries used by the applications, like the Adobe Flash Player and libpng. In the worst case, the attacker can gain full control of applications by exploiting the vulnerability. ExpressOS ensures that the compromised application must adhere to its permissions, which prevents it from accessing other applications' private data, effectively protecting sensitive applications from compromised applications.

In system services. The vulnerability exists in the system services of ExpressOS, including the file system, the networking stack, device drivers, and Android user-level services. ExpressOS combines three techniques to contain the vulnerability.

First, ExpressOS uses end-to-end security mechanisms and the protections provided by the ExpressOS kernel to protect file system and network data. For example, both the confidentiality and integrity of any private data remain intact when the storage service is compromised, because SI 2 ensures that the attacker cannot access or tamper with private data. Similarly, the attacker cannot eavesdrop or tamper with any TLS/SSL/HTTPS connections, even if he or she compromises the networking service.

Second, ExpressOS isolates applications and system services, and restricts updates to the screen (i.e., SI 5) to contain compromises of the window manager service. An attacker with a compromised window manager takes full control of the physical screen. Successful attacks, however, still require information about UI widgets in the targeted application, and the ability to provide timely visual feedback to the user. For example, the attacker might steal the user's input by overlaying a malicious application running in background on top of the targeted application. The isolation mechanism prevents the window manager from accessing the memory of the targeted application to retrieve the exact locations of UI widgets, and SI 5 prevents the malicious application running in background updating the screen to timely react to the user's input.

Third, the L4 layer isolates the system services and the ExpressOS kernel. An attacker can potentially compromise the L4Android kernel with a vulnerability. However, the ExpressOS kernel remains intact because the L4 layer manages allocation of physical memory and the IOMMU, ensuring that the ExpressOS kernel's memory is isolated from all system services.

ExpressOS currently does not prevent compromises where a service acts as a privileged deputy that allows the attacker to use its permissions to attack the system. For example, "the Bluetooth service in Android 2.3 before 2.3.6 allows remote attackers within Bluetooth range to obtain contact data via an AT phone book transfer." (CVE-2011-4276), and "the HTC IQRD service for Android ... does not restrict localhost access to TCP port 2479, which allows remote attackers to send SMS messages." (CVE-2012-2217).

In sensitive applications. If an application is exploited, there is not much that ExpressOS can do for that application. Although we proved our implementation of several security policies in ExpressOS, if an application configures its policy incorrectly or its application logic leads to a security compromise, there is little the ExpressOS kernel can do to protect it.

Figure 9 summarizes our analysis of 383 vulnerabilities. ExpressOS is able to prevent 364 (95%) of them.

Location	Example	Num.	Prevented
The core of the kernel	Logic errors in the futex implementation allow local users to gain privileges.	9	9 (100%)
Libraries of applications	Buffer overflow in libpng 1.5.x allows attackers to execute arbitrary code.	102	102 (100%)
System services	Missing checks in the vold daemon allows local users to execute arbitrary code.	240	226 (93%)
Sensitive applications	The BoA application stores a security question's answer in clear text which allows attackers to obtain the sensitive information.	32	27 (84%)
Total		383	364 (95%)

Figure 9: Categorization on 383 relevant vulnerabilities listed in CVE. It shows the number of vulnerabilities that ExpressOS prevents.

A large portion of vulnerabilities are due to memory errors in application libraries or in the system services. The verified security invariants and the protection from the ExpressOS kernel protect the data of sensitive applications from being compromised.

Out of the 383 vulnerabilities, there are two vulnerabilities related to covert channels. For example, the Linux kernel before 3.1 allows local users to obtain sensitive I/O statistics to discover the length of another user's password (CVE-2011-2494). These types of vulnerabilities are beyond the scope of our verification efforts and something ExpressOS is unable to prevent.

7.2 Performance

We evaluate the performance of ExpressOS by measuring the execution time of a variety set of benchmarks. We compared the performance of benchmarks running on ExpressOS, unmodified L4-Android, and Android-x86. All experiments run on an ASUS Eee PC 1005HA with an Intel Atom N270 CPU running at 1.60 GHz, 1GB of DDR2 memory, and a Seagate ST9160314AS 5,400 RPM, 160G hard drive. Our Eee PC connects to our campus network through its built-in Atheros AR8132 Fast Ethernet NIC.

Both ExpressOS and L4Android run the L4Linux 3.0.0 kernel. The Android-x86 runs on top of Linux 2.6.39. All three systems run the same Android 2.3.7 (Gingerbread) binaries in user spaces.

We evaluate the performance of the Android web browser on real network, and microbenchmarks evaluating different aspects of system performance, including IPC, the file system, the graphics subsystem, and the networking stack. All numbers reported in this section are the mean of five runs.

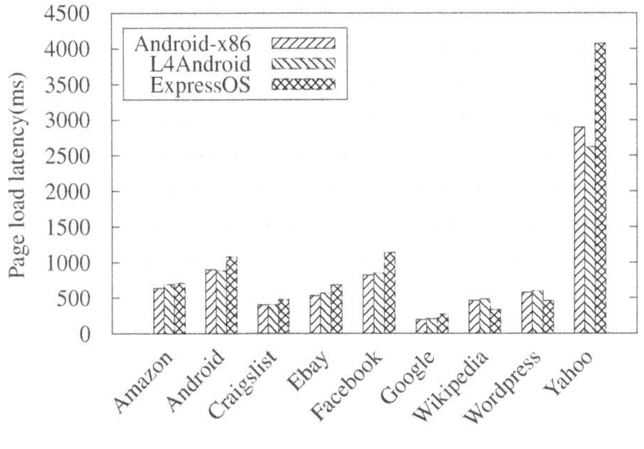

Figure 10: Page load latency in milliseconds for nine web sites for the same browser under Android-x86, L4Android, ExpressOS over a real network connection.

Page load latency in web browsing. We measure the page load latency for nine popular web sites to characterize the overall performance of ExpressOS compared to L4Android and Android-x86. The page load latency for a web site is the latency from initial URL request to the time when the browser fires the DOM `onload` event. The app clears all caches between each run.

Figure 10 shows the page load latency for nine web sites of all three systems. L4Android has 2% overhead on average, suggesting that the microkernel layer added by ExpressOS adds little overhead in real-world web browsing.

ExpressOS shows 14% and 16% overhead on average compared to L4Android and Android-x86.

IPC performance. We uses a simple ping-pong IPC benchmark to compare the performance of the SIPC mechanism in ExpressOS against the Android's Binder IPC mechanism. There are two entities (the server and the client) in this benchmark. For each round, the client sends a fixed-size IPC message to the server. The server receives the message and sends an IPC message back to the client which has the same content. Then the client receives the reply and continues to the next round.

We measured the total execution time for 10,000 rounds of this benchmark on Android-x86, L4Android and ExpressOS. We measured the performance with different message sizes, including four bytes, 1KB, 4KB, 8KB, and 16KB. Figure 11 describes the results of this benchmark. These numbers show that it is possible to implement a verifiable IPC mechanism in the ExpressOS architecture without sacrificing efficiency.

Other microbenchmarks. We further evaluate the performance of ExpressOS with three microbenchmarks, including (1) a SQLite benchmark (SQLite) which creates a new database, then inserts 25,000 records in one transaction, and writes all data back to the disk. (2) A network benchmark (Netcat), which receives a 32M file from local network. (3) A graphics benchmark (Bootanim), showing a PNG image, and adding light effects with OpenGL, which is derived from the boot animation program from Android.

These microbenchmarks help to categorize different aspects of the ExpressOS's performance. First, the SQLite benchmark manipulates the heap heavily, thus it is used to evaluate the performance of memory subsystem. Second, the Netcat benchmark helps quantify the effects of microkernel servers, because ExpressOS delegates all networking operations to L4Android. Finally, the Bootanim benchmark helps quantify the cost of using user-level helpers. Manipulating the screen heavily relies on Android's Binder IPC and shared semaphores, both of which are forwarded back and forth between the ExpressOS kernel and the user-level helpers in L4Android.

Figure 12 describes the results of all three microbenchmarks above. For the SQLite benchmark, both ExpressOS and L4Android are about 10% slower than Android-x86. For the Netcat benchmark, Android-x86, L4Android, and ExpressOS perform almost the same. ExpressOS is about 10% slower than L4Android in the Bootanim benchmark, but surprisingly, Android-x86 performs significantly worse than both L4Android and ExpressOS. We suspect that it might be due to some subtle differences between the kernel of L4Android and Android-x86, since all three systems are using the same user-level binaries.

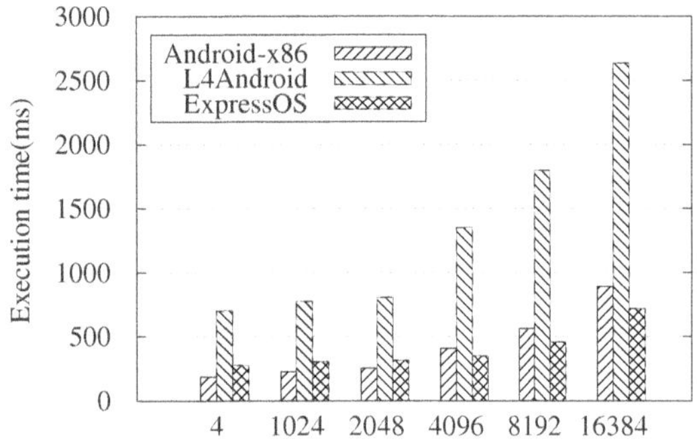

Figure 11: Performance of the ping-pong IPC benchmark of Android-x86, L4Android, and ExpressOS. X axis shows the size of IPC messages, Y axis shows the total execution time of running 10,000 rounds of ping-pong IPC.

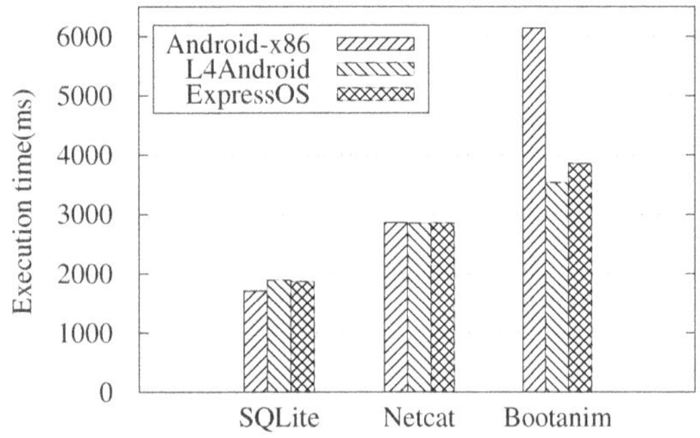

Figure 12: Performance results of the SQLite, Netcat and the Bootanim microbenchmark. X axis shows the type of the benchmark. Y axis shows their total execution time in milliseconds.

8. Related work

Attempts to eliminate defects of operating systems with full formal verification date back to the late 1970s. Dealing with all details of real-world operating systems has been a challenge for heavyweight full formal verification methods. Verifying OSes that provide UNIX abstractions has been cumbersome (e.g., UCLA Secure Unix [36], PSOS [14], and KSOS [26] provide partially verified UNIX abstractions). Hypervisors and microkernels have lower-level abstractions that are more amenable for verification [5, 8, 16, 20, 28], but they provide lower-level abstractions such as IPC, interrupts and context switches, which are not immediately meaningful to applications.

The key difference between ExpressOS and the above work is that the verification of ExpressOS only focuses on security invariants rather than achieving full functional correctness. ExpressOS ensures that defects in unverified parts of the system cannot subvert the security invariants. As a result, ExpressOS provides high-level abstractions (e.g., files) with verified security invariants, and verifying these security invariants requires only $\sim 2.8\%$ annotation overhead.

Alternative approaches to improve security of operating systems include controlling information flows in operating systems [13, 40], separating application state through virtualization [2, 10, 37], intercepting security decisions in reference monitors [1, 29], and exposing browser abstractions at lowest software layer [32]. These techniques reduce the TCB dramatically down to the implementation of themselves. There are two differences between them and ExpressOS. First, ExpressOS does not require the applications to pervasively adopt new APIs, instead it provides Android/Linux system calls so that it can run legacy applications directly. Second, ExpressOS provides formally verified abstractions to the applications, where other techniques trust their implementation.

Implementing OS in safe languages has several benefits, such as avoiding memory errors, and isolating control and data flows in a finer granularity [4, 11, 15, 17, 25]. ExpressOS inherits these benefits, and further verifies that the security invariants in it always hold using code contracts and Dafny.

The current implementation of ExpressOS trusts the language run-time and the L4 microkernel. Verve [38] and seL4 [20] have verified the language run-time and the L4 microkernel. They are complementary to ExpressOS: ExpressOS can plug them in to further reduce the size of TCB. ExpressOS might also benefit from potential hardware support [31, 33].

9. Conclusions

This paper has presented ExpressOS, a new OS architecture that provides formally verified security invariants to mobile applications.

The verified security invariants covers various high-level abstractions, including secure storage, memory isolation, UI isolation, and secure IPC. By proving these invariants, ExpressOS provides a secure foundation for sensitive applications to isolate their state and run-time events from malicious applications running on the same device.

The verification effort on ExpressOS focuses on the most important properties from a system builder's perspective rather than full functional correctness. Also, ExpressOS combines several verification techniques to further reduce the verification effort. The approach is relatively lightweight and has about $\sim 2.8\%$ annotation overhead.

Our evaluation shows that ExpressOS is effective in preventing existing vulnerabilities from different attack surfaces. Besides its strong security guarantees, ExpressOS is a practical system with performance comparable to native Android.

Our experience suggests that the verification technique we pursue is mature enough to be broadly used by systems developers in order to obtain lightweight proofs of safety and security by focusing on a small but crucial subset of properties.

Acknowledgments

We thank Xi Wang, and our anonymous reviewers for their valuable feedback on this paper. We thank Rustan Leino for encouraging us to use Dafny for our verification tasks. We also thank Shuo Tang for implementing an earlier version of the system. This research was funded in part by AFOSR MURI grant FA9550-09-01-0539, ONR grant N000141210552, NSF grant CCF-1018182, and supported by Intel through the ISTC for Secure Computing.

References

[1] J. P. Anderson. Computer security technology planning study. Technical report, HQ Electronic Systems Division (AFSC), Oct. 1972. ESD-TR-73-51.

[2] J. Andrus, C. Dall, A. Van't Hof, O. Laadan, and J. Nieh. Cells: A virtual mobile smartphone architecture. In *Proceedings of the 23rd ACM Symposium on Operating System Principles*, Cascais, Portugal, Oct. 2011.

[3] M. Bellare, R. Canetti, and H. Krawczyk. Keying hash functions for message authentication. In *Proceedings of the 16th Annual International Cryptology Conference on Advances in Cryptology*, Santa Barbara, CA, Aug. 1996.

[4] B. N. Bershad, S. Savage, P. Pardyak, E. G. Sirer, M. E. Fiuczynski, D. Becker, C. Chambers, and S. Eggers. Extensibility safety and performance in the SPIN operating system. In *Proceedings of the 15th ACM Symposium on Operating Systems Principles*, Copper Mountain, CO, Dec. 1995.

[5] W. Bevier. Kit: A study in operating system verification. *IEEE Transactions on Software Engineering*, 15:1382–1396, 1989.

[6] M. Castro, M. Costa, J.-P. Martin, M. Peinado, P. Akritidis, A. Donnelly, P. Barham, and R. Black. Fast byte-granularity software fault isolation. In *Proceedings of the 22nd ACM Symposium on Operating System Principles*, Big Sky, MT, Oct. 2009.

[7] B. X. Chen and N. Bilton. Et tu, google? android apps can also secretly copy photos. `http://bits.blogs.nytimes.com/2012/03/01/android-photos`.

[8] E. Cohen, M. Dahlweid, M. Hillebrand, D. Leinenbach, M. Moskal, T. Santen, W. Schulte, and S. Tobies. VCC: A practical system for verifying concurrent C. In *Proceedings of the 22nd International Conference on Theorem Proving in Higher Order Logics*, Munich, Germany, Aug. 2009.

[9] Common Vulnerabilities and Exposures (CVE). `http://cve.mitre.org`.

[10] R. S. Cox, S. D. Gribble, H. M. Levy, and J. G. Hansen. A safety-oriented platform for web applications. In *Proceedings of the 27th IEEE Symposium on Security and Privacy*, Oakland, CA, May 2006.

[11] J. Criswell, A. Lenharth, D. Dhurjati, and V. Adve. Secure virtual architecture: a safe execution environment for commodity operating systems. In *Proceedings of the 21st ACM Symposium on Operating System Principles*, Stevenson, WA, Oct. 2007.

[12] L. M. de Moura and N. Bjørner. Z3: An efficient SMT solver. In *Proceedings of the 14th International Conference on Tools and Algorithms for Construction and Analysis of Systems*, Budapest, Hungary, Mar. 2008.

[13] W. Enck, P. Gilbert, B.-G. Chun, L. P. Cox, J. Jung, P. McDaniel, and A. N. Sheth. Taintdroid: an information-flow tracking system for realtime privacy monitoring on smartphones. In *Proceedings of the 9th Symposium on Operating Systems Design and Implementation*, Vancouver, BC, Canada, Oct. 2010.

[14] R. J. Feiertag and P. G. Neumann. The foundations of a provably secure operating system (PSOS). In *Proceedings of the 1979 National Computer Conference*, New York City, NY, June 1979.

[15] M. Golm, M. Felser, C. Wawersich, and J. Kleinöder. The JX operating system. In *Proceedings of the USENIX 2002 Annual Technical Conference*, Monterey, CA, June 2002.

[16] M. Hohmuth and H. Tews. The VFiasco approach for a verified operating system. In *Proceedings of the 19th European Conference on Object-Oriented Programming*, Glasgow, UK, July 2005.

[17] G. C. Hunt and J. R. Larus. Singularity: rethinking the software stack. *ACM SIGOPS Operating Systems Review*, 41(2):37–49, Apr. 2007.

[18] G. Keizer. Google pulls 22 more malicious android apps from market. `http://www.computerworld.com/s/article/9222595/Google_pulls_22_more_malicious_Android_apps_from_Market`.

[19] J. J. Kistler and M. Satyanarayanan. Disconnected operation in the Coda file system. *ACM Transactions on Computer Systems*, 10(1):3–25, Feb. 1992.

[20] G. Klein, K. Elphinstone, G. Heiser, J. Andronick, D. Cock, P. Derrin, D. Elkaduwe, K. Engelhardt, R. Kolanski, M. Norrish, T. Sewell, H. Tuch, and S. Winwood. seL4: formal verification of an OS kernel. In *Proceedings of the 22nd ACM Symposium on Operating System Principles*, Big Sky, MT, Oct. 2009.

[21] M. Lange, S. Liebergeld, A. Lackorzynski, A. Warg, and M. Peter. L4Android: a generic operating system framework for secure smartphones. In *Proceedings of the 1st ACM Workshop on Security and Privacy in Smartphones and Mobile devices*, Chicago, IL, Oct. 2011.

[22] K. R. M. Leino. Dafny: an automatic program verifier for functional correctness. In *Proceedings of 16th International Conference on Logic for Programming, Artificial Intelligence, and Reasoning*, Dakar, Senegal, Apr. 2010.

[23] F. Logozzo. Practical verification for the working programmer with codecontracts and abstract interpretation. In *Proceedings of the 12th Conference on Verification, Model Checking and Abstract Interpretation*, Austin, TX, Jan. 2011.

[24] P. Madhusudan, X. Qiu, and A. Stefanescu. Recursive proofs for inductive tree data-structures. In *Proceedings of the 39th ACM SIGPLAN-SIGACT Symposium on Principles of Programming Languages*, Philadelphia, PA, Jan. 2012.

[25] A. C. Myers and B. Liskov. A decentralized model for information flow control. In *Proceedings of the 16th ACM Symposium on Operating System Principles*, Saint Malo, France, Oct. 1997.

[26] T. Perrine, J. Codd, and B. Hardy. An overview of the kernelized secure operating system (KSOS). In *Proceedings of the 7th DoD/NBS Computer Security Initiative Conference*, Gaithersburg, MD, Sept. 1984.

[27] X. Qiu, P. Garg, A. Stefanescu, and P. Madhusudan. Natural proofs for structure, data, and separation. Unpublished manuscript, 2012.

[28] J. S. Shapiro, J. M. Smith, and D. J. Farber. EROS: a fast capability system. In *Proceedings of the 17th ACM Symposium on Operating System Principles*, Charleston, SC, Dec. 1999.

[29] E. G. Sirer, W. de Bruijn, P. Reynolds, A. Shieh, K. Walsh, D. Williams, and F. B. Schneider. Logical attestation: an authorization architecture for trustworthy computing. In *Proceedings of the 23rd ACM Symposium on Operating Systems Principles*, Cascais, Portugal, Oct. 2011.

[30] M. M. Swift, B. N. Bershad, and H. M. Levy. Improving the reliability of commodity operating systems. In *Proceedings of the 19th ACM Symposium on Operating Systems Principles*, Bolton Landing, NY, Oct. 2003.

[31] J. Szefer and R. B. Lee. Architectural support for hypervisor-secure virtualization. In *Proceedings of 17th International Conference on Architectural Support for Programming Languages and Operating Systems*, London, England, UK, Mar. 2012.

[32] S. Tang, H. Mai, and S. T. King. Trust and protection in the Illinois browser operating system. In *Proceedings of the 9th Symposium on Operating Systems Design and Implementation*, Vancouver, BC, Canada, Oct. 2010.

[33] M. Tiwari, J. K. Oberg, X. Li, J. Valamehr, T. Levin, B. Hardekopf, R. Kastner, F. T. Chong, and T. Sherwood. Crafting a usable microkernel, processor, and I/O system with strict and provable information flow security. In *Proceedings of 38th International Symposium on Computer Architecture*, San Jose, CA, June 2011.

[34] H. Tuch, G. Klein, and M. Norrish. Types, bytes, and separation logic. In *Proceedings of the 34th annual ACM SIGPLAN-SIGACT Symposium on Principles of Programming Languages*, Nice, France, Jan. 2007.

[35] R. Wahbe, S. Lucco, T. E. Anderson, and S. L. Graham. Efficient software-based fault isolation. In *Proceedings of the 14th ACM symposium on Operating Systems Principles*, Asheville, NC, Dec. 1993.

[36] B. J. Walker, R. A. Kemmerer, and G. J. Popek. Specification and verification of the UCLA Unix security kernel. *Communications of the ACM*, 23(2):118–131, Feb. 1980.

[37] A. Whitaker, M. Shaw, and S. D. Gribble. Scale and performance in the Denali isolation kernel. In *Proceedings of the 5th Symposium on Operating Systems Design and Implementation*, Boston, MA, Dec. 2002.

[38] J. Yang and C. Hawblitzel. Safe to the last instruction: automated verification of a type-safe operating system. In *Proceedings of ACM SIGPLAN 2010 Conference on Programming Language Design and Implementation*, Toronto, Ontario, Canada, June 2010.

[39] E. Zadok, I. Badulescu, and A. Shender. Cryptfs: A stackable vnode level encryption file system. Technical report, Columbia University, June 1998. CUCS-021-98.

[40] N. Zeldovich, S. Boyd-Wickizer, E. Kohler, and D. Mazières. Making information flow explicit in HiStar. In *Proceedings of the 7th Symposium on Operating Systems Design and Implementation*, Seattle, WA, Nov. 2006.

Stochastic Superoptimization

Eric Schkufza
Stanford University
eschkufz@cs.stanford.edu

Rahul Sharma
Stanford University
sharmar@cs.stanford.edu

Alex Aiken
Stanford University
aiken@cs.stanford.edu

Abstract

We formulate the loop-free binary superoptimization task as a stochastic search problem. The competing constraints of transformation correctness and performance improvement are encoded as terms in a cost function, and a Markov Chain Monte Carlo sampler is used to rapidly explore the space of all possible programs to find one that is an optimization of a given target program. Although our method sacrifices completeness, the scope of programs we are able to consider, and the resulting quality of the programs that we produce, far exceed those of existing superoptimizers. Beginning from binaries compiled by `llvm -O0` for 64-bit x86, our prototype implementation, STOKE, is able to produce programs which either match or outperform the code produced by `gcc -O3`, `icc -O3`, and in some cases, expert handwritten assembly.

Categories and Subject Descriptors D.1.2 [*Automatic Programming*]: Program Synthesis; D.1.2 [*Automatic Programming*]: Program Transformation; D.1.2 [*Automatic Programming*]: Program Verification; D.3.4 [*Processors*]: Optimization

General Terms Performance, Verification

Keywords 64-bit; x86; x86-64; Binary; Markov Chain Monte Carlo; MCMC; Stochastic Search; Superoptimization; SMT

1. Introduction

For many application domains there is considerable value in producing the most performant code possible. Unfortunately, the traditional structure of a compiler's optimization phase is often ill-suited to this task. Attempting to factor the optimization problem into a collection of small subproblems that can be solved independently, although suitable for generating consistently good code, leads to the well-known phase ordering problem. In many cases, the best possible code can only be obtained through the simultaneous consideration of mutually dependent issues such as instruction selection, register allocation, and target-dependent optimization.

Previous approaches to this problem have focused on the exploration of all possibilities within some limited class of programs. In contrast to a traditional compiler, which uses performance constraints to drive the generation of a single program, these systems consider multiple programs and then select the one that is best able to satisfy those constraints. Solutions range from the explicit enumeration of a class of programs that can be formed using a large executable hardware instruction set [2] to implicit enumeration through symbolic theorem proving techniques of programs over some restricted register transaction language [9, 11, 14].

```
[r8:rdi] = rsi * [ecx:edx] + r8 + rdi
```

```
# gcc -O3

.L0:
  movq rsi, r9
  movl ecx, ecx
  shrq 32, rsi
  andl 0xffffffff, r9d
  movq rcx, rax
  movl edx, edx
  imulq r9, rax
  imulq rdx, r9
  imulq rsi, rdx
  imulq rsi, rcx
  addq rdx, rax
  jae .L2
  movabsq 0x100000000, rdx
  addq rdx, rcx
.L2:
  movq rax, rsi
  movq rax, rdx
  shrq 32, rsi
  salq 32, rdx
  addq rsi, rcx
  addq r9, rdx
  adcq 0, rcx
  addq r8, rdx
  adcq 0, rcx
  addq rdi, rdx
  adcq 0, rcx
  movq rcx, r8
  movq rdx, rdi
```

```
# STOKE

.L0:
  shlq 32, rcx
  movl edx, edx
  xorq rdx, rcx
  movq rcx, rax
  mulq rsi
  addq r8, rdi
  adcq 0, rdx
  addq rdi, rax
  adcq 0, rdx
  movq rdx, r8
  movq rax, rdi
```

Figure 1. Montgomery multiplication kernel from the OpenSSL big number library, compiled by `gcc -O3` (left) and STOKE (right). The STOKE code is 16 lines shorter, 1.6x faster, and slightly faster than expert handwritten assembly.

An attractive feature of these systems is completeness: If a program exists that meets the desired constraints, that program will be found. Unfortunately, completeness also places limitations on the space of programs that can realistically be considered. Because of the huge number of programs involved, explicit enumeration-based techniques are limited to programs of up to some fixed length which is currently well below the threshold at which many interesting optimizations take place. Implicit enumeration techniques can overcome this limitation, but at the cost of expert-written rules for shrinking the search space. The resulting optimizations are as good, but no better, than the quality of the rules written by an expert.

ASPLOS'13, March 16–20, 2013, Houston, Texas, USA.

We overcome these limitations by taking a different approach based on incomplete search: the competing requirements of correctness and speed are defined as terms in a cost function over the complex search space of all loop-free executable hardware instruction sequences, and the program optimization task is formulated as a cost minimization problem. Although the resulting search space is highly irregular and not amenable to exact optimization techniques, the common approach of employing a Markov Chain Monte Carlo (MCMC) sampler to explore the function and produce low-cost samples is sufficient for producing high quality programs.

Although our technique sacrifices completeness by trading systematic enumeration for stochastic search, we nonetheless dramatically increase the space of programs that our system is able to consider while simultaneously improving the quality of the resulting code. Consider the example shown in Figure 1, the Montgomery multiplication kernel from the OpenSSL big number library for arbitrary precision integer arithmetic. Beginning from a binary compiled by `llvm -O0` (116 lines, not shown), we produce a code sequence which is 16 lines shorter and 1.6 times faster than the one produced by `gcc -O3`, and even slightly faster than the expert handwritten assembly included in the OpenSSL repository. The performance improvement results primarily from the use of a different assembly level algorithm than the one given in the original code which is beyond the dataflow preserving algebraic transformations of a traditional compiler. The code is both automatically discovered and verified to be equivalent to the original. To the best of our knowledge, it is truly optimal: it is the fastest program for this function written in the 64-bit x86 (x86-64) instruction set.

Our work makes a number of contributions that have not previously been demonstrated. The remainder of this paper explores each in turn. Section 2 summarizes previous work in superoptimization and discusses its limitations. Section 3 presents a mathematical formalism for transforming the program optimization task into a stochastic cost minimization problem. Section 4 discusses how that theory is applied in a system for optimizing the runtime performance of x86-64 binaries, and Section 5 describes our prototype implementation, STOKE. Finally, Section 6 evaluates STOKE on a set of benchmarks drawn from cryptography, linear algebra, and low-level programming, and shows that STOKE is able to produce code that either matches or outperforms the code produced by production compilers.

2. Related Work

Previous approaches to superoptimization have focused on the exploration of all possibilities within some restricted class of programs. Although these systems have been demonstrated to be quite effective within certain domains, their general applicability remains limited. We discuss these limitations in the context of the Montgomery multiplication kernel shown in Figure 1.

The structure of the code is as follows: Two 32-bit values, ecx and edx, are concatenated and multiplied by the 64-bit value rsi to produce a 128-bit product. Two more 64-bit values, rdi and r8 are added to that product, and the result is split between two registers, r8 and rdi. The primary source of optimization is best highlighted by comparison. The code produced by `gcc -O3`, Figure 1 (left), performs the 128-bit multiplication as four 64-bit multiplications and then combines the results; the rewrite produced by STOKE, Figure 1 (right), uses a hardware intrinsic which requires that the inputs first be permuted and then moved to distinguished register locations so that the multiplication may be performed in a single step. The odd looking move on line 5 produces the non-obvious but necessary side effect of zeroing the upper 32 bits of `rdx`.

Massalin's original paper on superoptimization [14] describes a system that explicitly enumerates sequences of code of increasing length and selects the first such code identical to the input program on a set of testcases. Massalin reports being able to optimize instruction sequences of up to length 12. However to do so, it is necessary to restrict the set of enumerable opcodes to between 10 and 15. In contrast, STOKE used a large subset of the nearly 400 x86-64 opcodes, some with over 20 variations, to produce the 11 instruction kernel shown in Figure 1. It is unlikely that Massalin's approach would scale to an instruction set of this magnitude.

Denali [11], and the more recent Equality Saturation technique [18], attempt to gain scalability by only considering programs that are known to be equal to the input program. Candidate programs are explored through successive application of equality preserving transformation axioms. Because these techniques are goal-directed, they dramatically improve both the number of primitive instructions and the length of programs that can realistically be considered. However, both also rely heavily on expert knowledge. It is unclear whether an expert would know a priori to encode an equality axiom defining the multiplication transformation shown in Figure 1, or more generally, whether a set of expert written rules could ever cover the set of all interesting program optimizations. It is nonetheless worth noting that these techniques can to a certain extent deal with loop optimizations, while other techniques, including our own, are limited to loop-free code.

Bansal [2] describes a system that automatically enumerates 32-bit x86 superoptimizations and stores the results in a database for later use. By exploiting symmetries between programs that are equivalent up to register renaming, Bansal is able to scale this method to optimizations that take input code sequences of at most length 6 and produce code sequences of at most length 3. This approach has the dual benefit of hiding the high cost of superoptimization by performing a search once and for all offline and eliminating the dependence on expert knowledge. To some extent, the low cost of performing a database query also allows the system to overcome the low upper bound on instruction length through the repeated application of the optimizer along a sliding code window. However, the multiplication kernel shown in Figure 1 has the interesting property shared by many real world programs that no sequence of short superoptimizations will transform the code produced by `gcc -O3` into the code produced by STOKE. We follow Bansal's approach in overall system architecture by using testcases to help classify programs as promising or not and submitting the most promising candidates to a verification engine to prove or refute their correctness.

Sketching [17] and Brahma [9] address the closely related component-based program synthesis problem. These systems rely on either a declarative program specification, or a user-specified partial program, and operate on statements in bit-vector calculi rather than directly on hardware instructions. Liang [12] considers the task of learning programs from testcases alone, but at a similarly high level of abstraction. Although useful for synthesizing non-trivial programs, the internal representations used by these systems precludes them from reasoning directly about the runtime performance of the code that they produce.

STOKE differs from previous approaches to superoptimization by relying on incomplete stochastic search and making heavy use of MCMC sampling to explore the extremely high dimensional, irregular search space of loop-free assembly programs. For many optimization problems of this form, MCMC sampling is the only known general solution method which is also tractable. Successful applications are many, and include protein alignment [16], code breaking [6], and scene modeling and rendering in computer graphics [5, 19].

3. Cost Minimization

To formulate the program optimization task as a cost minimization problem, we first define a cost function with terms that balance the hard constraints of correctness preservation and the soft constraints of performance improvement. The primary advantage of this approach is that it removes the burden of reasoning directly about the mutually-dependent optimization issues faced by a traditional compiler. For instance, rather than considering the trade-offs between register allocation and instruction selection, we simply define a term which reflects the primary consequence of the decision: expected runtime. We then utilize a cost minimization search procedure to produce a program that balances those trade-offs as effectively as possible. We run the procedure for as long as is feasible, and select the lowest-cost result which satisfies all of the hard constraints.

In formalizing this idea we use the following notation. We refer to an input program as the *target* ($\mathcal{T}$) and a candidate compilation as a *rewrite* ($\mathcal{R}$), we say that a function $f(X;Y)$ takes inputs X and is parameterized by Y, and finally, we define the indicator function for boolean variables:

$$\mathbf{1}\{\phi\} = \begin{cases} 1 & \phi = \text{true} \\ 0 & \phi = \text{false} \end{cases} \tag{1}$$

3.1 Cost Function

At the highest level, a cost function should include both a correctness term $\text{eq}(\cdot)$ and a performance term, $\text{perf}(\cdot)$. An optimization, $\mathcal{R}'$, is any rewrite for which the cost function obtains a minimum value and the correctness term is zero.

$$c(\mathcal{R};\mathcal{T}) = \text{eq}(\mathcal{R};\mathcal{T}) + \text{perf}(\mathcal{R};\mathcal{T}) \tag{2}$$

$$\mathcal{R}' = \arg\min_{r} \Big(\text{perf}(r;\mathcal{T}) \;\Big|\; \text{eq}(r;\mathcal{T}) = 0\Big) \tag{3}$$

The transformation correctness term, $\text{eq}(\cdot)$, measures the similarity of two functions. The term is zero if and only if the two functions are equal. For our purposes, two code sequences are regarded as functions of registers and memory contents, and are equal if for all machine states that agree on the live inputs with the respect to the target, the two codes produce identical side effects on the live outputs with respect to the target. Because program optimization is undefined for ill-formed programs, it is unnecessary that $\text{eq}(\cdot)$ be defined for a target or rewrite that produce some undefined behavior. However nothing prevents us from doing so, and it would be a straightforward extension to produce a definition of $\text{eq}(\cdot)$ which preserved hardware exception behavior as well.

The performance improvement term, $\text{perf}(\cdot)$, quantifies the performance improvement of a rewrite with respect to the target. Depending on the application, this term could reflect code size, expected runtime, number of disk accesses, power consumption, or any other measure of resource usage. Crucially, the extent to which this term accurately reflects the performance improvement of a rewrite directly affects the quality of the results discovered by a search procedure.

3.2 MCMC Sampling

In general, we expect cost functions of the form described above to be highly irregular and not amenable to exact optimization techniques. The common approach to solving this problem is to employ the use of an MCMC sampler. Although a complete discussion of MCMC sampling techniques is beyond the scope of this paper, we summarize the main ideas here.

MCMC sampling is a technique for drawing elements from a probability density function in direct proportion to its value: regions of higher probability are sampled from more often than regions of low probability. When applied to cost minimization, this technique has the attractive property that in the limit the most frequently occuring sample will be taken from the minimum (optimal) value of the function. In practice, well before this limiting behavior is observed, MCMC sampling functions as an intelligent hill climbing method which is robust against irregular functions that are dense with local minima. A common method (described by [8]) for transforming an arbitrary cost function, $c(\cdot)$, into a probability density function is the following, where β is a constant and Z is a partition function that normalizes the distribution:

$$p(\mathcal{R};\mathcal{T}) = \frac{1}{Z}\exp\Big(-\beta \cdot c(\mathcal{R};\mathcal{T})\Big) \tag{4}$$

Although computing Z is in general intractable, the Metropolis-Hastings algorithm for generating Markov chains is designed to explore density functions such as $p(\cdot)$ without the need to compute the partition function [10, 15]. The basic idea is simple. The algorithm maintains a current rewrite $\mathcal{R}$ and proposes a modified rewrite $\mathcal{R}^*$ as the next step in the chain. The *proposal* $\mathcal{R}^*$ is either accepted or rejected. If the proposal is accepted, $\mathcal{R}^*$ becomes the current rewrite. Otherwise another proposal based on $\mathcal{R}$ is generated. The algorithm iterates until its computational budget is exhausted, and so long as the proposals are *ergodic* (capable of transforming any point in the space to any other through some sequence of applications) the algorithm will in the limit produce a sequence of samples with the properties described above (i.e., in proportion to their cost). This global property depends on the local acceptance criteria of a proposal $\mathcal{R} \rightarrow \mathcal{R}^*$, which is governed by the Metropolis-Hastings acceptance probability, where $q(\mathcal{R}^*|\mathcal{R})$ is the proposal distribution from which a new rewrite $\mathcal{R}^*$ is sampled given the current rewrite, $\mathcal{R}$:

$$\alpha(\mathcal{R} \rightarrow \mathcal{R}^*;\mathcal{T}) = \min\left(1, \frac{p(\mathcal{R}^*;\mathcal{T})q(\mathcal{R}|\mathcal{R}^*)}{p(\mathcal{R};\mathcal{T})q(\mathcal{R}^*|\mathcal{R})}\right) \tag{5}$$

This proposal distribution is key to a successful application of the algorithm. Empirically, the best results are obtained by a distribution which makes both local proposals that make minor modifications to $\mathcal{R}$ and global proposals that induce major changes. In the event that the proposal distributions are symmetric, $q(\mathcal{R}^*|\mathcal{R}) = q(\mathcal{R}|\mathcal{R}^*)$, the acceptance probability can be reduced to the much simpler Metropolis ratio, which can be computed directly from $c(\cdot)$:

$$\begin{aligned} \alpha(\mathcal{R} \rightarrow \mathcal{R}^*;\mathcal{T}) &= \min\left(1, \frac{p(\mathcal{R}^*;\mathcal{T})}{p(\mathcal{R};\mathcal{T})}\right) \\ &= \min\left(1, \exp\left(-\beta \cdot \frac{c(\mathcal{R}^*;\mathcal{T})}{c(\mathcal{R};\mathcal{T})}\right)\right) \end{aligned} \tag{6}$$

The important properties of the acceptance criteria are the following: If $\mathcal{R}^*$ is better (has a higher probability/lower cost) than $\mathcal{R}$, the proposal is always accepted. If $\mathcal{R}^*$ is worse (has a lower probability/higher cost) than $\mathcal{R}$, the proposal may still be accepted with a probability that decreases as a function of the ratio in value between $\mathcal{R}^*$ and $\mathcal{R}$. This property prevents the search from becoming trapped in local minima while remaining less likely to accept a move that is much worse than available alternatives.

4. x86-64 Binary Optimization

Having discussed cost minimization in the abstract, we now turn to the practical details of implementing cost minimization for optimizing the runtime performance of x86-64 binaries. As x86-64 is one of the most complex ISAs currently available, we expect that the discussion in this section should generalize well to other architectures.

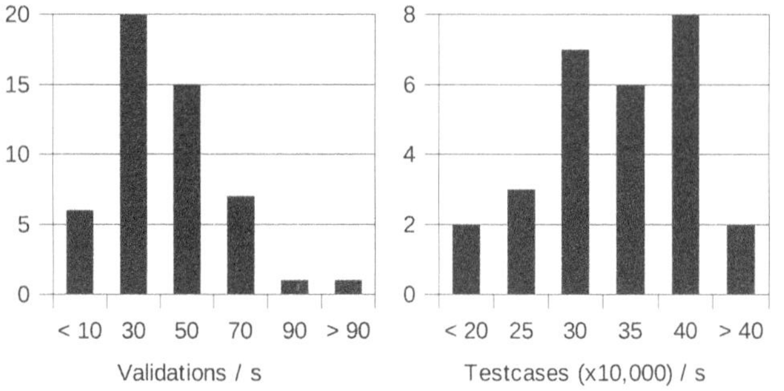

Figure 2. Histograms of validations per second (left), and testcase evaluations per second (right), for the benchmarks discussed in Section 6. The low validation throughput is insufficient for MCMC sampling and motivates an approach based on testcases.

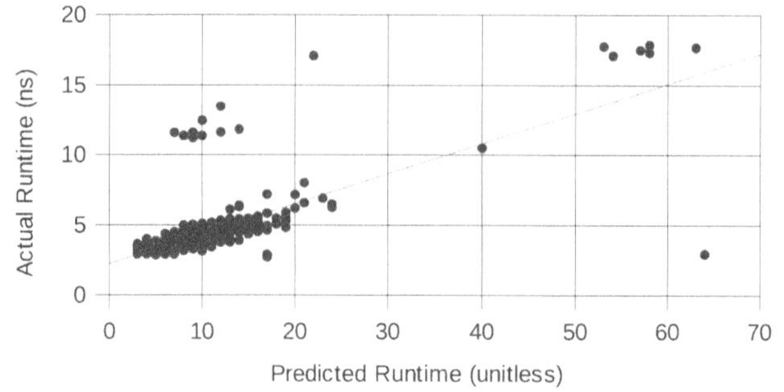

Figure 3. Comparison of predicted and actual runtimes for the benchmarks described in Section 6, along with rewrites generated in the course of our experiments. The points are well correlated but distinguished by outliers characterized by instruction level parallelism and memory traffic at the micro-op level. The approximation is sufficient for the benchmarks we consider.

4.1 Transformation Correctness

For loop-free sequences of x86-64 assembly code, a natural choice for implementing the transformation correctness term is a symbolic validator such as the one used in [4]. For a candidate rewrite, the term may be defined in terms of an invocation of the validator as:

$$\mathrm{eq}(\mathcal{R};\mathcal{T}) = 1 - \Big(\mathbf{1}\{\mathrm{VALIDATE}(\mathcal{T},\mathcal{R})\}\Big) \tag{7}$$

Unfortunately, the total number of validations that can currently be performed per second, even for modestly sized codes, is low. Figure 2 (left) suggests that for the benchmarks discussed in Section 6 the number is well below 100. Because MCMC sampling is effective only insofar as it is able to explore sufficiently large numbers of proposals, the repeated computation of Equation 7 in its inner-most loop would almost certainly drive that number well below a useful threshold.

This observation motivates the definition of an approximation to $\mathrm{eq}(\cdot)$ based on testcases, τ. Intuitively, we execute the proposal $\mathcal{R}^*$ on a set of inputs and measure "how close" the output is to the output of the target on those same inputs. For a given input, we use the number of bits difference in live outputs (i.e., the Hamming distance) to measure correctness. Besides being much faster than using a theorem prover, this approximation of program equivalence has the added advantage of producing a smoother landscape than the 0/1 output of a symbolic equality test; it provides a useful notion of "almost correct" that can help to guide the search.

$$\begin{aligned}\mathrm{eq}'(\mathcal{R};\mathcal{T},\tau) = &\sum_{t\in\tau}\mathrm{reg}(\mathcal{R};\mathcal{T},t) + \mathrm{mem}(\mathcal{R};\mathcal{T},t)\\ &+\sum_{t\in\tau}\mathrm{err}(\mathcal{R};\mathcal{T},t)\end{aligned} \tag{8}$$

In the above formula, $\mathrm{reg}(\cdot)$ compares the side effects, $\mathrm{val}(\cdot)$, that both functions produce on live register outputs, ρ, with respect to the target, and counts the number of bits that the results differ by. These outputs can include general purpose, SSE, and condition registers. $\mathrm{mem}(\cdot)$ is defined analogously for live memory outputs, μ. We use the population count function, $\mathrm{POP}(\cdot)$, to count the number of 1-bits in the 64-bit representation of an integer.

$$\mathrm{reg}(\mathcal{R};\mathcal{T},t) = \sum_{r\in\rho}\mathrm{POP}\Big(\mathrm{val}(\mathcal{T},r)\oplus\mathrm{val}(\mathcal{R},r)\Big) \tag{9}$$

$$\mathrm{mem}(\mathcal{R};\mathcal{T},t) = \sum_{m\in\mu}\mathrm{POP}\Big(\mathrm{val}(\mathcal{T},m)\oplus\mathrm{val}(\mathcal{R},m)\Big) \tag{10}$$

$\mathrm{err}(\cdot)$ is used to distinguish programs which exhibit undefined behavior, by counting and then penalizing the number of segfaults, $\mathrm{sigsegv}(\cdot)$, floating point exceptions, $\mathrm{sigfloat}(\cdot)$, and reads from undefined memory or registers, $\mathrm{undef}(\cdot)$, which occur during execution of a rewrite. Note that $\mathrm{sigsegv}(\cdot)$ is defined in terms of the target, which determines the set of addresses which may be successfully dereferenced by a rewrite for a particular testcase. Rewrites are run in a sandbox to ensure that undefined behavior can be detected safely. The extension to additional exceptional behavior would be straightforward.

$$\begin{aligned}\mathrm{err}(\mathcal{R};\mathcal{T},t) = &\ w_{sf}\cdot\mathrm{sigsegv}(\mathcal{R};\mathcal{T},t)\\ &+ w_{fp}\cdot\mathrm{sigfloat}(\mathcal{R};t)\\ &+ w_{ur}\cdot\mathrm{undef}(\mathcal{R};t)\end{aligned} \tag{11}$$

The evaluation of $\mathrm{eq}'(\cdot)$ may be accomplished either by JIT compilation, or the use of a hardware emulator. In our experiments we have chosen the latter. Figure 2 (right) shows the number of testcase evaluations that our emulator is able to perform per second: just under 500,000. This implementation allows us to define an optimized method for computing $\mathrm{eq}(\cdot)$ which achieves sufficient throughput to be useful for MCMC sampling.

$$\mathrm{eq}^*(\mathcal{R};\mathcal{T},\tau) = \begin{cases}\mathrm{eq}(\mathcal{R};\mathcal{T}) & \mathrm{eq}'(\mathcal{R};\mathcal{T},\tau)=0\\ \mathrm{eq}'(\mathcal{R};\mathcal{T},\tau) & \text{otherwise}\end{cases} \tag{12}$$

In addition to performance, Equation 12 has the following desirable properties. First, failed computations of $\mathrm{eq}(\cdot)$ will produce a counterexample testcase that may be used to refine τ as described in [4]. The careful reader will note that refining τ affects the cost function, $c(\cdot)$, and effectively changes the search space that it defines. However in practice, the number of failed validations that are required to produce a robust set of testcases that accurately predict success is quite low. Second, as discussed above, it smooths the search space by allowing the transformation equality metric to incrementally quantify the difference between two programs.

4.2 Performance Improvement

A straightforward method for computing the performance improvement term is to JIT compile both target and rewrite and compare their runtimes. Unfortunately, as with the transformation correctness term, the amount of time required to both compile a function and execute it sufficiently many times to eliminate transient performance effects is prohibitively expensive to be used in the inner-most loop of MCMC sampling. In our experiments, we adopt a simple heuristic for approximating the runtime performance of a function, which is based on a static approximation of the average latencies of its instructions.

$$\begin{aligned} \mathrm{perf}(\mathcal{R};\mathcal{T}) &= H(\mathcal{R}) - H(\mathcal{T}) \\ H(f) &= \sum_{i \in \mathrm{inst}(f)} \mathrm{LATENCY}(i) \end{aligned} \tag{13}$$

Figure 3 shows a reasonably high correlation between the heuristic and the actual runtimes of the benchmarks described in Section 6, along with rewrites for those benchmarks which were generated in the course of our experiments. Outliers are characterized by disproportionately high instruction level parallelism at the micro-op level and the performance effects of inconsistent memory access times. A more accurate model of the second order performance effects introduced by a modern CISC processor is straightforward if tedious to construct and we expect would be necessary for more complex programs. Nonetheless, the approximation is largely sufficient for the benchmarks that we consider. Whatever errors stem from this imprecision can be addressed by recomputing $\mathrm{perf}(\cdot)$ using the slower JIT compilation method as a postprocessing step. In our experiments we record the top-n lowest cost samples produced by MCMC sampling, rerank each based on their actual runtimes, and return the best result.

4.3 MCMC Sampling

For x86-64 binary optimization, we represent candidate rewrites as finite loop-free sequences of instructions, of length ℓ, where a distinguished token, UNUSED, allows for the representation of programs that contain fewer than ℓ instructions. This simplifying assumption is essential to the formulation of MCMC sampling discussed in Section 3.2, as it places a constant value on the dimensionality of the search space. The interested reader may consult [1] for a thorough treatment of why this is necessary. Our definition of the proposal distribution, $q(\cdot)$, chooses among four possible moves: the first two minor, and the last two major:

Opcode. With probability p_c, an instruction is selected at random, and its opcode is replaced by a random opcode. The new opcode is drawn from an equivalence class of opcodes which require the same number and type of operands as the old opcode. We construct these classes from the set of arithmetic and fixed point SSE opcodes.

Operand. With probability p_o, an instruction is selected at random and one of its operands is replaced by a random operand drawn from an equivalence class of operands with equivalent types to the old operand. If the operand is an immediate, its value is drawn from a set of predefined constants. We construct this set using the range -16 to 16 and all subsequent powers of 2.

Swap. With probability p_s, two lines of code are selected at random and interchanged. Each line may correspond to either an instruction or the UNUSED token.

Instruction. With probability p_i, an instruction is selected at random and replaced either by an unconstrained random instruction or the UNUSED token. A random instruction is constructed by first selecting an opcode at random and then choosing random operands of the appropriate types. The UNUSED token is proposed with probability p_u.

These definitions satisfy the ergodicity property described in Section 3.2. Any program can be transformed into any other through repeated application of Instruction moves. These definitions also satisfy the symmetry property, and thus allow the computation of acceptance probability using Equation 6. To see why, note that the probabilities of performing all four move types are equal to the probabilities of undoing the transformations they produce using a move of the same type. Opcode and operand moves are constrained to sample from identical equivalence classes before and after acceptance. Swap and instruction moves are similarly unconstrained in both directions.

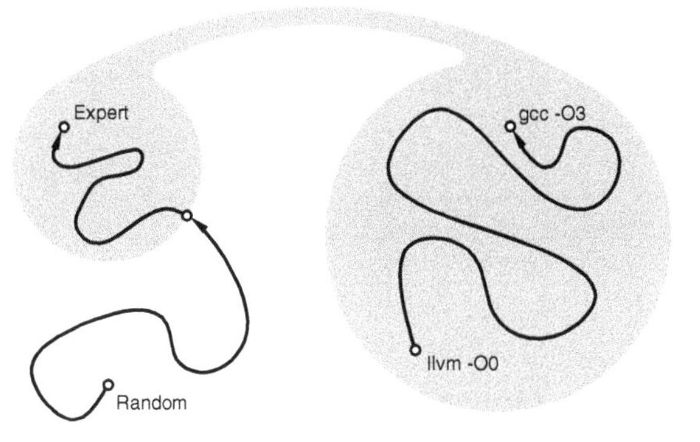

Figure 4. Abstract depiction of the search space for the Montgomery multiplication benchmark. O0 and O3 optimized codes occupy a densely connected part of the space which is easily traversed. Expert code occupies an entirely different region of the space which is reachable only by way of an extremely low probability path.

4.4 Separating Synthesis from Optimization

An early implementation of STOKE based on the above principles, was able to consistently transform `llvm -O0` code into the equivalent of `gcc -O3` code. Unfortunately, it was unable to produce results which were competitive with expert hand-written code. The reason is suggested by Figure 4, which gives an abstract depiction of the search space for the Montgomery multiplication benchmark. For loop-free sequences of code, `llvm -O0` and `gcc -O3` codes differ primarily with respect to efficient use of the stack and choices of individual instructions. Beyond these differences, the resulting codes are algorithmically quite similar. This is because compiler optimizers are generally designed to compose many small local transformations: dead code elimination deletes one instruction, constant propagation changes one register to an immediate, and strength reduction replaces a multiplication with an add. With respect to the search space, such sequences of local optimizations define a region of equivalent programs that are densely connected by very short sequences of moves (often just one) that are easily traversed by a local search method. Beginning from `llvm -O0` code, MCMC sampling will quickly identify local inefficiencies one by one, improve each in turn, and hill climb its way to a `gcc -O3` code.

The expert code discovered by STOKE occupies an entirely different region of the search space. As noted earlier, it has the property that no sequence of small equality preserving transformations connect it to either the `llvm -O0` or the `gcc -O3` code. It represents a completely distinct algorithm for implementing the Montgomery multiplication kernel at the assembly level, one which requires that its input values be permuted and relocated to distinguished register locations to permit the use of hardware intrinsics. The only method we know of for a local search procedure to transform either code into the expert code is to traverse the extremely low probability path that builds the expert code in place next to the original, all the while increasing its cost, only to delete the original code at the very end. Although MCMC sampling is guaranteed to traverse this path in the limit, the likelihood of it doing so in any reasonable amount of time is so low as to be useless in practice.

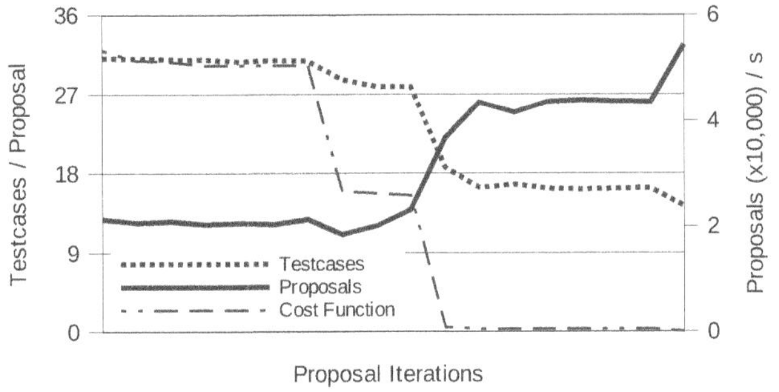

Figure 5. Proposals evaluated per second versus testcases evaluated prior to early termination, during synthesis for the Montgomery multiplication benchmark. Reducing the number of evaluated testcases produces an almost 3x improvement in proposal throughput. Cost function shown unitless for reference.

This observation motivates the division of cost minimization into two phases:

- **Synthesis** A synthesis phase focused solely on correctness, which attempts to locate regions of equivalent programs which are distinct from the region occupied by the target.
- **Optimization** An optimization phase focused on speed, which searches for the fastest program within each of those regions.

The two phases share the same search implementation; only the starting point and the acceptance functions are different. Synthesis begins with a random starting point (a sequence of randomly chosen instructions), while optimization begins with a code sequence known to be equivalent to the target. For proposals, synthesis ignores the performance improvement term altogether and simply uses Equation 12 as its cost function. Optimization uses both terms, which allows it to measure improvement while also allowing it to experiment with "shortcuts" that (temporarily) violate transformation correctness.

4.5 Optimized Acceptance Computation

The optimized method for computing $\mathrm{eq}^*(\cdot)$ given in Equation 12 is sufficiently fast for MCMC sampling. However, its performance can be further improved. As described so far, $\mathrm{eq}^*(\cdot)$ is computed by first running a proposal on testcases, summing the results, noting the ratio in total cost with that of the current rewrite, and then sampling a random variable to decide whether or not to accept the proposal. Instead, by first sampling the random variable p, and then computing the maximum value of the ratio that the algorithm will accept given p, it is possible to terminate the evaluation of testcases as soon as that bound is exceeded.

Specifically, because the formulation of the proposal distribution $q(\cdot)$ is symmetric we may compute the acceptance probability $\alpha(\cdot)$ of a proposal directly from $c(\cdot)$ as shown in Equation 6. By first sampling p we can invert $\alpha(\cdot)$ to solve for the maximum cost rewrite $c(\cdot)$ that the algorithm will accept.

$$
\begin{aligned}
p &< \alpha(\mathcal{R} \to \mathcal{R}^*; \mathcal{T}) \\
&< \min\left(1, \exp\left(-\beta \cdot \frac{c(\mathcal{R}^*; \mathcal{T})}{c(\mathcal{R}; \mathcal{T})}\right)\right) \\
c(\mathcal{R}^*; \mathcal{T}, \tau) &< c(\mathcal{R}; \mathcal{T}, \tau) - \frac{\log(p)}{\beta}
\end{aligned}
\tag{14}
$$

Because the computation of $\mathrm{eq}'(\cdot)$ is based on the iterative evaluation of testcases, it is only necessary to do so for as long as the running sum does not exceed this upper bound. Once it does, we know that the proposal is guaranteed to be rejected, and no further computation is necessary. Figure 5 shows the result of applying this optimization during synthesis for the Montgomery multiplication benchmark. As the value of the cost function decreases, so too do the average number of testcases which must be evaluated prior to early termination. This in turn produces a considerable increase in the number of proposals evaluated per second, which at peak exceeds 50,000.

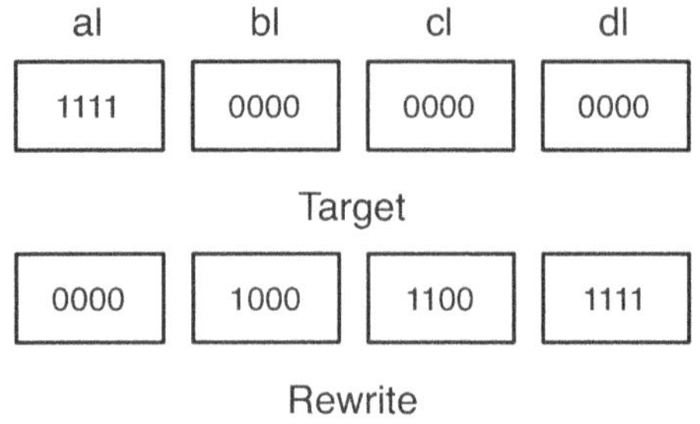

	al	bl	cl	dl
$\mathrm{val}(\mathcal{T}, \mathrm{al}) \oplus \mathrm{val}(\mathcal{R}, \cdot)$	1111	0111	0011	0000
$\mathrm{POP}\big(\mathrm{val}(\mathcal{T}, \mathrm{al}) \oplus \mathrm{val}(\mathcal{R}, \cdot)\big)$	4	3	2	0
$w_m \cdot \mathbf{1}\{\mathrm{al} \neq \cdot\}$	0	1	1	1

$$
\begin{aligned}
\mathrm{reg}(\mathcal{T}, \mathcal{R}, \tau) &= 4 \\
\mathrm{reg}'(\mathcal{T}, \mathcal{R}, \tau) &= \min(4, 3+1, 2+1, 1) \\
&= 1
\end{aligned}
$$

Figure 6. Strict versus improved equality functions for a machine state in which ax is live out. Strict assigns the maximum possible cost to a rewrite which produces the correct value in the wrong location. Improved assigns a cost of almost zero.

4.6 Improved Equality Metric

A second and even more important improvement stems from the observation that the definition of $\mathrm{reg}(\cdot)$ given in Equation 9 is unnecessarily strict. An illustrative example is shown in Figure 6. Consider a simplified machine with four 4-bit registers, and a target function that produces side effects in register al. The final machine states produced by running the target and a candidate rewrite are shown at the top of the figure. Because the rewrite produces the inverse of the desired value in al, it is assigned the maximum possible cost. This is unfortunate however, as the rewrite does produce the correct value, only in the wrong place: dl. A substantial improvement in performance is obtained by rewarding rewrites that produce correct (or nearly correct) values in the wrong locations. The improved cost function examines all registers of equivalent bit-width, $\mathrm{bw}(\cdot)$, selects the one that most closely matches the value of the target register, and assigns an additional small penalty, w_m, if the selected register differs from the original.

$$
\begin{aligned}
\mathrm{reg}'(\mathcal{R}; \mathcal{T}, \tau) &= \sum_{r \in \rho} \min_{r' \in \mathrm{bw}(r)} \mathrm{R}(r, r'; \tau) \\
\mathrm{R}(r, r'; \tau) &= \mathrm{POP}\big(\mathrm{val}(\mathcal{T}, r) \oplus \mathrm{val}(\mathcal{R}, r')\big) \\
&\quad + w_m \cdot \mathbf{1}\{r \neq r'\}
\end{aligned}
\tag{15}
$$

For brevity, we note that it is possible to improve the definition of memory equality analogously. Although we do so in our experiments, the time required to compute this term does grow quadrat-

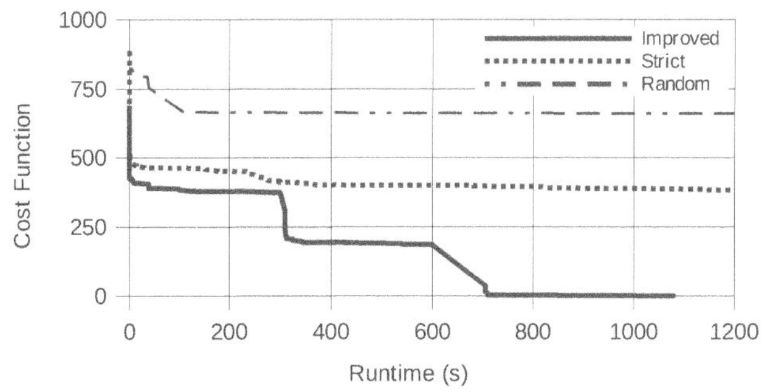

Figure 7. Strict versus improved synthesis cost functions for the Montgomery multiplication benchmark. In the amount of time (s) required for the improved function to converge, the strict function produces a result comparable to that of a purely random search.

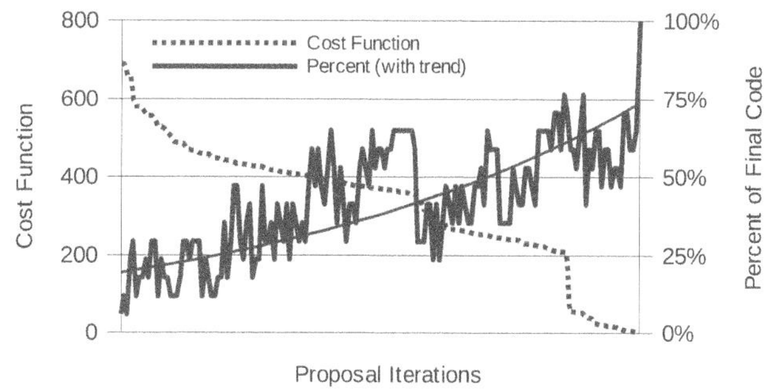

Figure 8. Cost function versus percentage of instructions which appear in the final zero-cost rewrite. Random search is an effective method for performing synthesis insofar as it is able to discover partially correct rewrites incrementally.

ically with the size of the target function's memory footprint. We expect that for more complex programs, an alternate implementation will be necessary.

Figure 7 shows the results of using the improved definitions of register and memory equality during synthesis for the Montgomery multiplication benchmark. In the amount of time required for the improved cost function to converge to a zero-cost rewrite, the strict version obtains a minimum cost which was only slightly superior to that obtained by a purely random search. The dramatic increase in performance can be explained as an implicit parallelization of the search procedure. By allowing a rewrite to place a correct value in an arbitrary location, the improved cost function allows candidates to simultaneously explore up to as many alternate computations as can be fit within an instruction sequence of length ℓ.

4.7 Why and When Synthesis Works

It is not intuitive that a randomized search procedure should synthesize a correct rewrite from such an enormous search space in such a short amount of time. In our experience, the reason why is that synthesis is effective precisely when it is possible to discover portions of a correct rewrite incrementally, as opposed to all at once. Figure 8 plots the current best cost obtained during synthesis against the percentage of instructions appearing in both that rewrite and the final rewrite for the Montgomery multiplication benchmark. As search proceeds, the percentage of correct code increases in inverse proportion to the value of the cost function. While this is very encouraging and there are many programs that can be synthesized in pieces, each of which increases the average number of correct bits in the output, there are certainly interesting programs that do not satisfy this property. In the limit, any code which performs a complex computation that is reduced to a single boolean value poses a problem for our technique. The discovery of partially correct computations is useful as a guide for random search only insofar as it in turn produces a partially correct result, which can be detected by a cost function.

This observation motivates the desire for a cost function which maximizes the signal produced by a partially correct rewrite. We discussed a successful application of this principle in Section 4.6. Nonetheless, there remains room for improvement. Consider a program which rounds its inputs up to the next highest power of two. This program has the interesting property of differing from the program which simply returns zero in just one bit per testcase. The improved cost function discussed above assigns a very low cost to this constant zero function, which although nearly perfect is completely wrong, and exhibits no partially correct computations that can be hill-climbed to a correct rewrite.

Fortunately, we note that even when synthesis fails, optimization is still possible. It must simply proceed only from the region occupied by the target as a starting point.

5. STOKE

STOKE is a prototype implementation of the concepts described above. Its high-level design is shown in Figure 9. A user provides a target binary which is created using a standard compiler (in our experiments, `llvm -O0`); in the event that the target contains loops, STOKE identifies loop-free subsequences of the code which it will attempt to optimize instead. The user also provides an annotated driver in which the target is called in an appropriate context. Based on the user's annotations, STOKE automatically generates random inputs to the target, compiles the driver, and runs the code under instrumentation to produce testcases. The target and testcases are broadcast to a set of synthesis threads which after a fixed amount of time report back validated candidate rewrites. In like fashion, multiple threads perform optimization on both the target and those rewrites. Finally, the set of rewrites with a final cost that is within 20% of the minimum result are re-ranked based on actual runtime, and the best result is returned to the user.

5.1 Test Case Generation and Evaluation

STOKE automatically generates testcases using annotations provided by a user. Because STOKE operates on x86-64 assembly, those inputs are limited to fixed-width bit strings, which unless otherwise specified, are sampled uniformly at random. If the target uses an input to form a memory address, the user must annotate that input with a range of values that guarantee that the resulting addresses are legal given the context in which the target is invoked. The compiled program is executed under instrumentation using Intel's PinTool [13]. As each instruction is executed, the tool records the state of all general purpose, SSE, and condition registers, as well as dereferenced memory. The initial state of the registers, along with the first values dereferenced from each memory address are used to form testcase inputs. Outputs are formed analogously. By default, STOKE generates 32 testcases for each target.

For each testcase, The set of addresses dereferenced by the target are used to define the sandbox in which candidate rewrites are executed. Attempts to dereference invalid addresses are trapped and replaced by instructions which produce a constant zero value. Attempts to read from registers in an undefined state and computations which produce floating point exceptions are handled analogously.

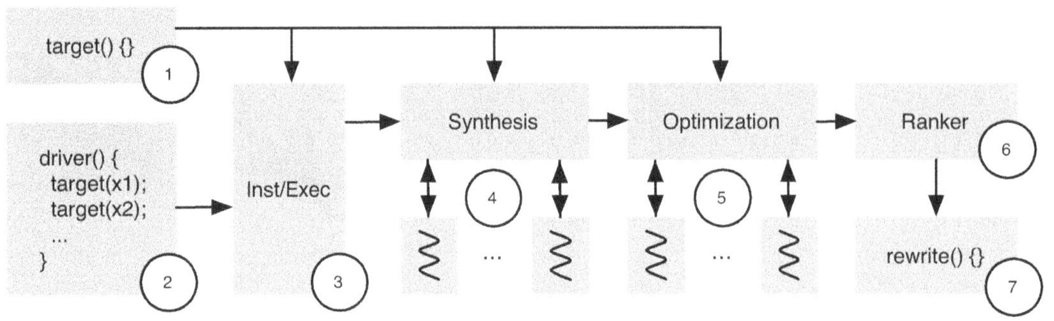

Figure 9. The high-level design of STOKE. A target binary created by a production compiler (1) and driver code (2) are run under instrumentation (3) using automatically generated inputs to produce testcases. Synthesis threads (4) use the target and testcases to generate candidate rewrites, which along with the target are refined by optimization threads (5). The results are ranked (6) and the rewrite with the lowest cost is returned to the user (7).

w_{sf}	1	p_c	0.16	p_u	0.16
w_{fp}	1	p_o	0.5	β	0.1
w_{ur}	2	p_s	0.16	ℓ	50
w_m	3	p_i	0.16		

Figure 10. MCMC sampling parameters used by STOKE during both synthesis and optimization phases.

5.2 Validation

STOKE uses a sound procedure for validating the equality of two sequences of loop-free assembly which is similar to the one described in [2]. Code sequences are converted into SMT formulae in the quantifier free theory of bit-vector arithmetic used by the STP [7] theorem prover, and used to produce a query which asks whether both sequences produce the same side effects on live outputs when executed from the same initial machine state. For our purposes, a machine state consists of general purpose, SSE, and condition registers, and memory. Depending on type, registers are modeled as between 8- and 128-bit vectors. Memory is modeled as two vectors: a 64-bit address and an 8-bit value (x86-64 is byte addressable).

STOKE first asserts the constraint that both sequences agree on the initial machine state of the live inputs with respect to the target. Next, it iterates over the instructions in the target, and for each instruction asserts a constraint which encodes the transformation it produces on the machine state. These constraints are chained together to produce a constraint on the final machine state of the live outputs with respect to the target. Analogous constraints are asserted for the rewrite. Finally, for all pairs of memory accesses at addresses $\texttt{addr}_1$ and $\texttt{addr}_2$, STOKE asserts an additional constraint which relates their values: $\texttt{addr}_1 = \texttt{addr}_2 \Rightarrow \texttt{val}_1 = \texttt{val}_2$. Using these constraints, STOKE performs an STP query which asks whether there does not exist an initial machine state which causes the two sequences to produce different values for the live outputs with respect to the target. If the answer is "yes", then the sequences are determined to be equal. If the answer is "no", then the prover produces a counter example which is used to produce a new testcase.

STOKE makes two simplifying assumptions which are necessary to keep validator runtimes tractable. First, it assumes that stack addresses are represented exclusively as constant offsets from the stack pointer. This allows STOKE to treat stack addresses as nameable locations, and minimizes the number of expensive memory constraints which must be asserted. This is essential for validating against `llvm -O0` code, which exhibits heavy stack traffic. Second, it treats 64-bit multiplication and division as uninterpreted functions by asserting the constraint that the instructions produce identical arbitrary values when executed on identical inputs. This assumption is necessary irrespective of the compiler toolchain used to produce the target. Whereas STP diverges when reasoning explicitly about two or more such operations, our benchmarks contain as many as four per program.

5.3 Parallel Synthesis and Optimization

Synthesis and optimization are executed in parallel on a small cluster consisting of 40 dual-core 1.8 GHz AMD Opterons. Both are allocated computational budgets of 30 minutes. The MCMC sampling parameters used by both phases are summarized in Figure 10.

6. Evaluation

In addition to the Montgomery multiplication kernel discussed previously, STOKE was evaluated on benchmarks drawn both from the literature and real-world high-performance codes. The performance improvements obtained for those kernels are summarized in Figure 11 (top), while corresponding STOKE runtimes are shown in Figure 11 (bottom). Beginning from binaries compiled using `llvm -O0`, STOKE consistently discovers rewrites which match the performance of the code produced by `gcc -O3` and `icc -O3`. In several cases, the performance exceeds both and is comparable to expert handwritten assembly. As we explain below, the improvement often results from the discovery of a completely distinct assembly level algorithm for implementing the target code. We close with a discussion of the benchmarks which highlight STOKE's limitations.

6.1 Hacker's Delight

Hacker's Delight [20], commonly referred to as "the bible of bit-twiddling hacks", is a collection of techniques for encoding otherwise complex algorithms as small loop-free sequences of bit-manipulating instructions. Gulwani [9] notes this as a source of benchmarks for program synthesis and superoptimization, and identifies a 25 program benchmark which ranges in complexity from turning off the right-most bit in a word, to rounding up to the next highest power of 2, or selecting the upper 32 bits from a 64-bit multiplication. Our implementation of the benchmark uses the C code found in the original text. For brevity, we discuss only the programs for which STOKE discovers an algorithmically distinct rewrite.

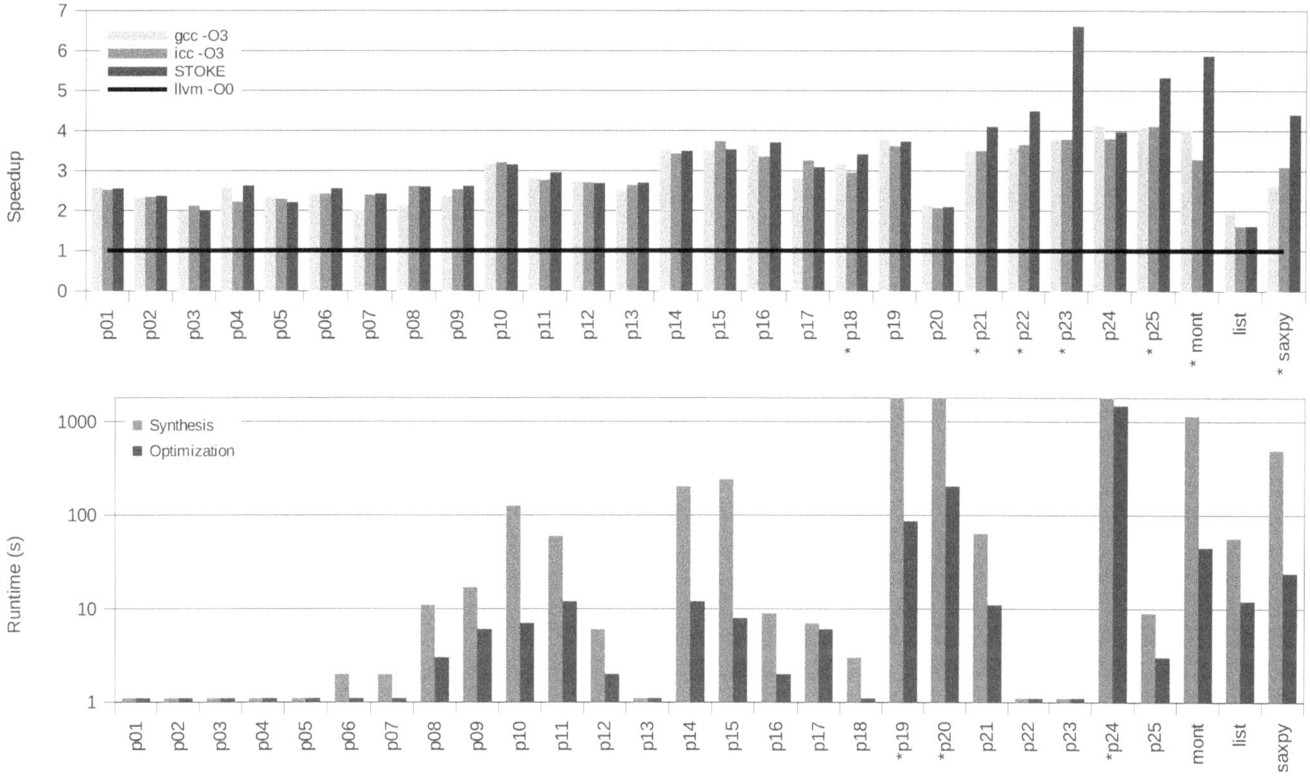

Figure 11. (Top) Average speedup over `llvm -O0` for benchmark kernels. Beginning from code produced by `llvm -O0`, STOKE discovers rewrites which are comparable to code produced by `gcc -O3` and `icc -O3`. In some cases, the rewrite outperforms both, and are comparable to expert handwritten assembly. Kernels for which STOKE discovered an algorithmically distinct rewrite are annotated with a star. (Bottom) Synthesis and optimization runtimes. Kernels for which synthesis timed out are annotated with a star.

Figure 12 shows the "Cycle Through 3 Values" benchmark, which takes an input, x, and transforms it to the next value in the sequence $\langle a, b, c\rangle$: a becomes b, b becomes c, and c becomes a. Hacker's Delight points out that the most natural implementation of this function is a sequence of conditional assignments, but notes that for an ISA without conditional move intrinsics the implementation shown is cheaper than one which uses branch instructions. For x86-64, which has conditional move intrinsics, this is an instance of premature optimization. Unfortunately, neither `gcc` nor `icc` are able to detect this, and are forced to transcribe the code as written. There are no sub-optimal subsequences in the resulting code. Both are simply unable to reason about the semantics of the function as a whole. We expect that equality-preserving superoptimizers would exhibit similar behavior for the same reason. STOKE on the other hand, rediscovers the natural implementation from the 41 line `llvm -O0` compilation. We note that although this rewrite is only five lines long, it remains beyond the reach of superoptimizers based on brute force enumeration.

In similar fashion, for machines without 64-bit instructions, the implementation that Hacker's Delight recommends for the "Compute the Higher Order Half of a 64-bit Product" multiplies two 32-bit inputs in four parts and aggregates the results. The computation resembles the Montgomery multiplication benchmark, and STOKE discovers a rewrite which requires a single multiplication using the appropriate 64-bit intrinsic.

STOKE additionally discovers a number of typical superoptimizer rewrites. These include using the popcnt intrinsic, which counts the number of 1-bits in an integer, as an intermediate step in the "Compute Parity" and "Determine if an Integer is a Power of 2" benchmarks.

6.2 SAXPY

SAXPY (Single-precision Alpha X Plus Y) is a level 1 vector operation in the Basic Linear Algebra Subsystems Library [3]. The function makes heavy use of heap accesses and presents the opportunity for optimization using vector intrinsics. To allow for STOKE to discover this possibility, our implementation is unrolled four times by hand, as shown in Figure 13. Despite heavy annotation to indicate that the arrays pointed to by x and y are aligned and do not alias each other, the production compilers either cannot detect the possibility of a compilation using vector intrinsics, or are precluded from doing so by some internal heuristic.

STOKE on the other hand, when given identical information, is able to discover the natural implementation: the constant a is broadcast four ways from a general purpose register into an SSE register, and then multiplied by and added to the contents of x and y, which are loaded into SSE registers four elements at a time. The four way broadcast does not appear anywhere in either the `gcc -O3` code, or in the original 61 line `llvm -O0` code. As noted above, despite the simplicity, the length of the resulting code is well beyond the reach of existing superoptimizers.

6.3 Limitations

Bansal [2] identifies the Linked List Traversal Benchmark for superoptimizers shown in Figure 14. The code iterates over a list of integers and multiplies each of the elements by two. The code is unique with respect to the benchmarks discussed so far, as it con-

```
int p21(int x, int a, int b, int c) {
  return ((-(x == c)) & (a ^ c)) ^
         ((-(x == a)) & (b ^ c)) ^ c;
}
```

```
# gcc -O3

.L0:
  movl edx, eax
  xorl edx, edx
  xorl ecx, eax
  cmpl esi, edi
  sete dl
  negl edx
  andl edx, eax
  xorl edx, edx
  xorl ecx, eax
  cmpl ecx, edi
  sete dl
  xorl ecx, esi
  negl edx
  andl esi, edx
  xorl edx, eax
```

```
# STOKE

.L0:
  cmpl edi, ecx
  cmovel esi, ecx
  xorl edi, esi
  cmovel edx, ecx
  movq rcx, rax
```

Figure 12. Cycling Through 3 Values benchmark. STOKE sees through the esoteric implementation which `gcc -O3` translates literally (left) and rediscovers the intuitive algorithm using conditional move intrinsics (right).

tains a loop. As a result, STOKE is unable to optimize the function as a whole, but rather only its inner-most loop-free fragment. STOKE discovers the same optimizations as Bansal's superoptimizer, the elimination of stack traffic and a strength reduction from multiplication to bit shifting. However it fails in like fashion to eliminate the instructions which copy the head pointer from and back to the stack on every iteration of the loop. The production compilers on the other hand, are able to eliminate the memory traffic by caching the pointer in a register prior to entering the loop. As a result, the rewrite discovered by STOKE is slower than the code produced by `gcc -O3` (surprisingly, `icc` does not perform strength reduction, and produces code which performs similarly). This shortcoming could be addressed by extending our framework to validate and propose modifications to code containing loops.

As shown in Figure 11 (bottom), STOKE is unable to synthesize a rewrite for three of the Hacker's Delight Benchmarks. All three benchmarks, despite being quite complex, have the interesting property that they produce results which differ by only a single bit from a simple yet completely incorrect alternative. The "Round Up to the Next Highest Power of 2" benchmark is nearly indistinguishable from the function which always returns zero. The same is true of the "Next Highest with Same Number of 1-bits", and a small transformation to the "Exchanging Two Fields" benchmark with respect to the identity function. Nonetheless, for these three benchmarks, using its optimization phase alone STOKE is still able to discover rewrites which perform comparably to the production compiler code, which we believe to be optimal. Unfortunately, in general we do not expect this to be the case. A more sophisticated cost function, as described in section 4.7, is surely necessary.

7. Conclusion and Future Work

We have shown a new approach to the loop-free binary superoptimization task which formulates program optimization as a stochastic search problem. Compared to a traditional compiler, which factors optimization into a sequence of small independently solvable subproblems, our framework is based on cost minimization and considers the competing constraints of transformation correctness and performance improvement simultaneously. We show that an MCMC sampler can be used to rapidly explore cost functions of this form and produce low cost samples which correspond to high quality optimizations. Although our method sacrifices completeness, the scope of programs which we are able to consider, and the quality of the rewrites we produce, far exceed those of existing superoptimizers.

```
void SAXPY(int* x, int* y, int a) {
  x[i]   = a * x[i]   + y[i];
  x[i+1] = a * x[i+1] + y[i+1];
  x[i+2] = a * x[i+2] + y[i+2];
  x[i+3] = a * x[i+3] + y[i+3];
}
```

```
# gcc -O3

.L0:
movslq ecx,rcx
leaq (rsi,rcx,4),r8
leaq 1(rcx),r9
movl (r8),eax
imull edi,eax
addl (rdx,rcx,4),eax
movl eax,(r8)
leaq (rsi,r9,4),r8
movl (r8),eax
imull edi,eax
addl (rdx,r9,4),eax
leaq 2(rcx),r9
addq 3,rcx
movl eax,(r8)
leaq (rsi,r9,4),r8
movl (r8),eax
imull edi,eax
addl (rdx,r9,4),eax
movl eax,(r8)
leaq (rsi,rcx,4),rax
imull (rax),edi
addl (rdx,rcx,4),edi
movl edi,(rax)
```

```
# STOKE

.L0:
movd edi,xmm0
shufps 0,xmm0,xmm0
movups (rsi,rcx,4),xmm1
pmullw xmm1,xmm0
movups (rdx,rcx,4),xmm1
paddw xmm1,xmm0
movups xmm0,(rsi,rcx,4)
```

Figure 13. SAXPY benchmark. Unlike `gcc -O3` (top), STOKE discovers a rewrite which uses SSE vector instructions (bottom).

```
while ( head != 0 ) {
  head->val *= 2;
  head = head->next;
}
```

```
# gcc -O3

  movq -8(rsp), rdi
.L4:
  sall (rdi)
  movq 8(rdi), rdi
.L6:
  testq rdi, rdi
  jne .L4
```

```
# STOKE

.L4:
  movq -8(rsp), rdi
  sall (rdi)
  movq 8(rdi), rdi
  movq rdi, -8(rsp)
.L6:
  movq -8(rsp), rdi
  testq rdi, rdi
  jne .L4
```

Figure 14. Linked List Traversal benchmark. STOKE discovers the same rewrite (right) as Bansal's superoptimizer, but fails to cache the head pointer in a register, as in the `gcc -O3` code (left).

Although our prototype implementation, STOKE, is in many cases able to produce rewrites which are competitive with or outperform the code produced by production compilers, there remains substantial room for improvement. In future work, we intend to pursue both a validation and proposal mechanism for code containing loops and a synthesis cost function which is robust against targets with numerous deceptively attractive, albeit completely incorrect, synthesis alternatives.

Acknowledgments

The authors would like to thank Peter Johnston, Juan Manuel Tamayo, and Kushal Tayal for their assistance in the implementation of STOKE, Ankur Taly and David Ramos for their advice regarding the semantics of x86-64 opcodes and the use of STP, Jake Herczeg for his time spent designing Figure 4, and Martin Rinard for suggesting a technique which focuses more on testcases than validation. This work was supported by NSF grant CCF-0915766 and the Army High Performance Computing Research Center.

References

[1] C. Andrieu, N. de Freitas, A. Doucet, and M. I. Jordan. An introduction to MCMC for machine learning. *Machine Learning*, 50(1-2):5–43, 2003.

[2] S. Bansal and A. Aiken. Automatic generation of peephole superoptimizers. In *ASPLOS*, pages 394–403, 2006.

[3] L. S. Blackford, J. Demmel, J. Dongarra, I. Duff, S. Hammarling, G. Henry, M. Heroux, L. Kaufman, A. Lumsdaine, A. Petitet, R. Pozo, K. Remington, and R. C. Whaley. An updated set of basic linear algebra subprograms (BLAS). *ACM Transactions on Mathematical Software*, 28:135–151, 2001.

[4] C. Cadar, D. Dunbar, and D. R. Engler. Klee: Unassisted and automatic generation of high-coverage tests for complex systems programs. In *OSDI*, pages 209–224, 2008.

[5] S. Chenney and D. A. Forsyth. Sampling plausible solutions to multi-body constraint problems. In *SIGGRAPH*, pages 219–228, 2000.

[6] P. Diaconis. The markov chain monte carlo revolution. *Bulletin of the American Mathematical Society*, 46(2):179–205, Nov. 2008.

[7] V. Ganesh and D. L. Dill. A decision procedure for bit-vectors and arrays. In *CAV*, pages 519–531, 2007.

[8] W. R. Gilks. *Markov Chain Monte Carlo in Practice*. Chapman and Hall/CRC, 1999.

[9] S. Gulwani, S. Jha, A. Tiwari, and R. Venkatesan. Synthesis of loop-free programs. In *PLDI*, pages 62–73, 2011.

[10] W. K. Hastings. Monte carlo sampling methods using markov chains and their applications. *Biometrika*, 57(1):97–109, Apr. 1970.

[11] R. Joshi, G. Nelson, and K. H. Randall. Denali: A goal-directed superoptimizer. In *PLDI*, pages 304–314, 2002.

[12] P. Liang, M. I. Jordan, and D. Klein. Learning programs: A hierarchical bayesian approach. In *ICML*, pages 639–646, 2010.

[13] C.-K. Luk, R. S. Cohn, R. Muth, H. Patil, A. Klauser, P. G. Lowney, S. Wallace, V. J. Reddi, and K. M. Hazelwood. Pin: Building customized program analysis tools with dynamic instrumentation. In *PLDI*, pages 190–200, 2005.

[14] H. Massalin. Superoptimizer - a look at the smallest program. In *ASPLOS*, pages 122–126, 1987.

[15] N. Metropolis, A. W. Rosenbluth, M. N. Rosenbluth, A. H. Teller, and E. Teller. Equation of state calculations by fast computing machines. *The Journal of Chemical Physics*, 21(6):1087–1092, 1953.

[16] A. F. Neuwald, J. S. Liu, D. J. Lipman, and C. E. Lawrence. Extracting protein alignment models from the sequence database. *Nucleic Acids Research*, 25:1665–1677, 1997.

[17] A. Solar-Lezama, L. Tancau, R. Bodík, S. A. Seshia, and V. A. Saraswat. Combinatorial sketching for finite programs. In *ASPLOS*, pages 404–415, 2006.

[18] R. Tate, M. Stepp, Z. Tatlock, and S. Lerner. Equality saturation: a new approach to optimization. In *POPL*, pages 264–276, 2009.

[19] E. Veach and L. J. Guibas. Metropolis light transport. In *SIGGRAPH*, pages 65–76, 1997.

[20] H. S. Warren. *Hacker's Delight*. Addison-Wesley Longman Publishing Co., Inc., Boston, MA, USA, 2002.

Automated Repair of Binary and Assembly Programs for Cooperating Embedded Devices

Eric Schulte* Jonathan DiLorenzo† Westley Weimer† Stephanie Forrest*

* Department of Computer Science
University of New Mexico
Albuquerque, NM 87131-0001
{eschulte,forrest}@cs.unm.edu

† Department of Computer Science
University of Virginia
Charlottesville, VA 22904-4740
{jd9hz,weimer}@cs.virginia.edu

Abstract

We present a method for automatically repairing arbitrary software defects in embedded systems, which have limited memory, disk and CPU capacities, but exist in great numbers. We extend evolutionary computation (EC) algorithms that search for valid repairs at the source code level to assembly and ELF format binaries, compensating for limited system resources with several algorithmic innovations. Our method does not require access to the source code or build toolchain of the software under repair, does not require program instrumentation, specialized execution environments, or virtual machines, or prior knowledge of the bug type.

We repair defects in ARM and x86 assembly as well as ELF binaries, observing decreases of 86% in memory and 95% in disk requirements, with 62% decrease in repair time, compared to similar source-level techniques. These advances allow repairs previously possible only with C source code to be applied to any ARM or x86 assembly or ELF executable. Efficiency gains are achieved by introducing stochastic fault localization, with much lower overhead than comparable deterministic methods, and low-level program representations.

When distributed over multiple devices, our algorithm finds repairs faster than predicted by naïve parallelism. Four devices using our approach are five times more efficient than a single device because of our collaboration model. The algorithm is implemented on Nokia N900 smartphones, with inter-phone communication fitting in 900 bytes sent in 7 SMS text messages per device per repair on average.

Categories and Subject Descriptors D.2.3 [*Software Engineering*]: Coding Tools and Techniques; D.2.5 [*Software Engineering*]: Testing and Debugging; D.3.2 [*Language Classifications*]: Macro and Assembly Languages; I.2.8 [*Artificial Intelligence*]: Heuristic methods

General Terms Experimentation, Languages

Keywords Automated program repair, evolutionary computation, fault localization, assembly code, bytecode, legacy software

ASPLOS'13, March 16–20, 2013, Houston, Texas, USA.

1. Introduction

Automated software repair is an emerging research area in which algorithmic and heuristic approaches are used to search for, generate, and evaluate candidate repairs for software defects. It has received attention in programming languages (e.g., [15]), operating systems (e.g., [26]) and software engineering (e.g., [33, 35]) venues. Automated repair methods have been applied to multiple classes of software engineering and security defects (e.g., [35]) including hard-to-fix concurrency bugs [15], have won human-competitive awards [9], and automatic repairs have been successfully pitted against DARPA Red Teams to demonstrate quality [26]. With bug repair dominating software development costs (90% of the total cost of a typical software project is incurred after delivery [28]) such automated techniques are of increasing importance.

However, few automated repair techniques apply to resource constrained embedded systems, instead targeting desktop client software such as Firefox [15, 26], server software such as MySQL [15] or webservers, or design-by-contract Eiffel programs [33]. Given the tight coupling between embedded software and the unique execution environments in which they operate, desktop testing and repair tools are often insufficient. Current research in this field is increasingly out of step with the needs of industry, in which embedded microprocessors account for more than 98% of all produced microprocessors [4]. One example of a wide-reaching embedded defect was the "Zune bug," in which 30GB Microsoft Zune Media Players froze up on the last day of a leap year [2]. In addition, previous repair techniques that apply to binaries [26] or assembly language [27] have uniformly targeted Intel x86, despite "the widespread dominant use of the ARM processor in mobile and embedded systems" [8].

Evolutionary computation (EC) is a stochastic search method based on Darwinian evolution, which has been applied to the automated repair problem. Like other search methods, EC is relevant when it is easier to evaluate a candidate solution than to predict the form of a correct solution [5].[1] Although EC techniques do not yet synthesize large programs in traditional languages, they can repair a wide variety of real defects at the source-code level in real-world software applications [20].

We propose to repair assembly language and executable binary programs directly using EC across multiple architectures, including embedded and mobile systems. Resource constraints in embedded

[1] In this paper we use the term genetic algorithm (GA) interchangably with evolutionary computation (EC). GAs and Genetic Programming (GP) are two concrete realizations of the general EC framework. GAs are typically defined over linear strings and GP typically refers to tree-based executable representations of programs. Our method uses linear strings that are executable.

and mobile systems preclude the use of existing techniques. For example, it is not feasible to trace all operands that CPU instructions read or write (as in [26, Sec. 2.1.1]) or even to trace all instructions visited (as in [35]). A pre-set, unified locking discipline may not be available (as used by [15]). Source code with debugging information may not be available, so statements and abstract syntax trees cannot be accurately identified to reduce search-space size (as used by [35]), and, formal pre- and post-condition annotations are unlikely to be present (as used by [33]). Finally, most embedded devices do not ship with a complete compiler toolchain, and a deployed device may not have the storage or RAM to support its original mission together with a heavyweight repair framework that uses the GCC toolchain. The closest assembly-level repair work is a preliminary four-page short paper [27] that proposes automated program repair on x86 assembly language, but does not address fault localization, multiple architectures, repairing executables, or distribution across multiple systems.

The main contributions of this paper are as follows:

- An architecture-independent representation and stochastic fault localization algorithm that supports automatic program repair at the assembly and binary levels. We demonstrate applicability to x86 and ARM processors. Although sampling for fault localization is not new, its application and evaluation in the domain of program repair is, and our technique is an order-of-magnitude faster and of comparable accuracy to deterministic methods.
- An empirical demonstration that disk space and memory requirements are 95.22% and 85.71% smaller, respectively, than similar methods, allowing application to mobile and embedded systems.
- An empirical comparison across different levels of program representation with respect to EC's success and efficiency at finding repairs.
- A demonstration that most source-statement-level repairs reported previously [35] can also be carried out at the assembly and binary level with a 62.43% average decrease in the time required to perform a repair between the AST and ELF levels.
- A distributed GA that performs automated program repair across multiple embedded devices. Four devices using our approach are five times faster than a single device for our repair benchmarks.
- Empirical demonstration of the repair method on Nokia N900 smartphones (600 MHz ARM Cortex-A8 CPU, 256 MB memory). Using two phones, the distributed algorithm conducts repairs with just under 900 bytes sent (or 7 SMS messages) per participant per repair.

2. Background

In automated software repair (e.g., [26, 33, 35]), defects are corrected by searching over and evaluating a solution space of possible repairs. The set of repairs (fixes) may be generated from random variations of the instructions in the program, as in GenProg [20]; from formal source code annotations, as in AutoFix-E [33]; or from a pre-defined library, such as the locking changes used by the AFix project [15] or the clamp-variable-to-value operation of Clearview [26].

Our work is based on the EC approach [9, 35, 36]. EC mimics Darwinian evolution in a computational algorithm that searches for candidate solutions to a given problem [14]. In the program repair context, a population of program variants is generated by applying random mutations to the original buggy source code. These variants are then compiled using the program's build toolchain, and the resulting executables are evaluated against the program's test suite. The test suite assesses the goodness, or *fitness*, of each variant, and the fitness value is used to *select* which variants will remain in the population, undergoing additional mutations. In addition to mutation, the algorithm uses *crossover* to exchange instructions between two variants, producing a recombination of partial solutions. The process iterates until a variant passes all test cases and also fixes the bug, or until an upper time limit is reached.

To reduce the size of the search space of possible repairs, mutation and crossover operators are limited to re-organizing statements present in the original program. No new statements are created, and sub-statement program elements, such as expressions, are not changed directly. Fault localization (e.g., [16]) focuses the mutation operators on statement nodes executed on the buggy input. To collect this information, an execution trace is recorded from an instrumented version of the program run against the test suite.

We extend this previous work to run directly on compiled assembly files and linked ELF executables, and we introduce a stochastic method of fault localization appropriate for these lower-level representations. These extensions remove the requirement for source code availability and the need for compilation and linking (for the ELF level) as part of the search process. It is applicable to arbitrary assembly and ELF programs rather than only C-language programs and enables repairs that are not expressible at the C statement level.

3. Technical Approach

Build processes generate intermediate representations, each of which is a possible target for automated repair, and each of which poses unique challenges for the repair method. These challenges include: the form of the representation and mutation operators, the granularity of fault localization information, and the tools required to express a representation as an executable program. The following subsection reviews the repair framework at a high level, which mirrors the AST algorithm [35, 36]. We summarize the technical and algorithmic aspects of ASM and ELF repairs, including the resources required by each level of representation, the effects of representation on mutation operations, and the requirements for expression as executable programs.

3.1 Evolutionary Repair Algorithm

The algorithm shown in Figure 1 applies to source-level ASTs, compiled ASM, and compiled and linked ELF repairs. Section 4.1 reports values for the parameters, such as popsize, used in our experiments. The next subsections present the stochastic fault localization algorithm, ASM and ELF representations, and mutation and crossover operators.

The overall structure in Figure 1 is iterative. Tournament selection selects variants for the next iteration (generation) (Lines 8, 12); retained variants exchange sub-strings to produce offspring (Line 9); all variants are mutated (Line 16), and the process repeats until a solution is found (Line 18).

3.2 Stochastic Fault Localization

In large programs, it is reasonable to assume that most parts of the program are *not* related to a given bug [16], and fault localization methods often target code executed on the bug-inducing input. Accurate fault localization is critical for targeting the repair operators [35, Fig. 5] and is an important factor in running time [36, Fig. 1].

Our earlier work recorded entire sequences, or paths [35], of executed statements using various weighting factors [16], which required expensive program instrumentation or runtime harnesses. A key challenge is obtaining accurate enough information for guiding automated repairs, while maintaining the efficiency required for embedded devices.

```
Input: Program P to be repaired.
Input: Set of positive testcases p ∈ PosT.
Input: Set of negative testcases n ∈ NegT.
Output: Repaired program variant V.
Path_PosT ← ⋃_{p∈PosT} locations visited by P(p)
Path_NegT ← ⋃_{n∈NegT} locations visited by P(n)
Path ← set_weights(Path_NegT, Path_PosT)
Pop ← initial_population(P, pop_size)
repeat
    NewPop ← ∅
    for i = 1 → (pop_size × cross_percent) by 2 do
        V1, V2 ← tournament(Pop), tournament(Pop)
        NewPop ← NewPop ∪ {crossover(V1, V2)}
    end for
    for i = 1 → (pop_size × (1 − cross_percent)) do
        NewPop ← NewPop ∪ {tournament(Pop)}
    end for
    Pop ← ∅
    for all ⟨V, Path_V⟩ ∈ NewPop do
        Pop ← Pop ∪ {fitness(mutate(V, Path_V))}
    end for
until ∃⟨V, Path_V, f_V⟩ ∈ Pop | f_V = max_fitness
return V
```

Figure 1. High-level pseudocode for EC-based automatic program repair, which applies to all levels of representation. Representation-specific subroutines such as fitness(V) and mutate(V, $Path_V$) are described subsequently.

Many traditional code profilers (e.g., `gcov`) are language specific and rely on the insertion of assembly instrumentation consuming unacceptable storage and run-time resources. For example, instrumentation of the `flex` benchmark [35] at the C-language level required storing sequential ordering information from about 443,399 raw statement visits, with program instrumentation increasing the CPU run-time by a factor of 100. Direct extensions [2] such as deterministic sampling of the program counter (e.g., using `ptrace`) performed poorly in our preliminary work.

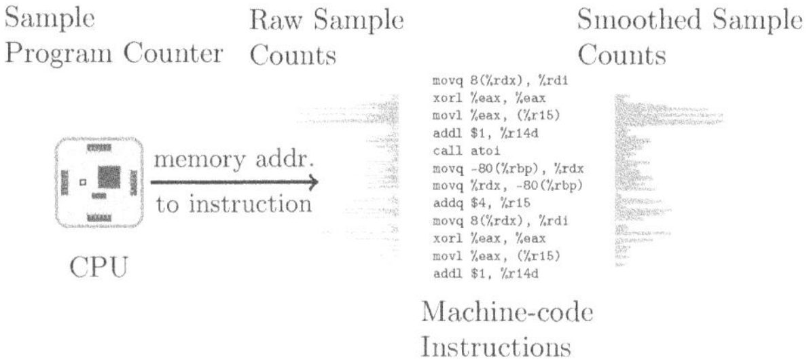

Figure 2. Stochastic Fault Localization (raw and smoothed samples from the `merge-cpp` benchmark).

To address these constraints, we propose a sampling approach to fault localization (Figure 2), which is applicable to arbitrary assembly and ELF programs and dramatically reduces resource requirements compared to earlier work. We sample the program counter (PC) across multiple executions of the program. These sampled memory addresses are then mapped to bytes in the `.text` section of ELF files or to specific instructions in ASM files. The result is a count of the total number of times each instruction in the program was sampled. Stochastic sampling only approximates control flow and is vulnerable to gaps, elided periodic behavior, over-sampled instructions, etc. To overcome these limitations, we apply a 1-D Gaussian convolution to the sampled addresses with a radius of 3 assembly instructions, s.t. the smoothed value of each sample $G(x)$ is a weighted sum of the raw value $F(x)$ of itself and its 6 nearest neighbors.

$$G(x) = \sum_{i=-3}^{3} F(x+i) \times \frac{1}{\sqrt{2\pi}} e^{-\frac{1}{2}i^2}$$

This simple transformation increases the chance that instructions that are executed but not directly sampled will be counted, and it improves the correlation between stochastic and deterministic samples (Section 4.2).

Gaussian convolution is an accepted method of smoothing data to reduce detail and noise in fields such as computer vision [29]. However, to our knowledge it has not previously been applied to fault localization. Section 4.2 compares the fault localization information produced by our stochastic sampling to a fully deterministic program trace.

Samples are collected from multiple runs of each of the program's tests. Despite multiple executions of each test, the CPU time required is less than comparable deterministic techniques (Section 4.4). The union of every instruction included in the fault localization from the positive tests, and the union of every instruction included in the fault localization from the negative tests are collected into the positive and negative fault localization respectively. These sets of are then used to guide program repair.

3.3 ASM and ELF Program Representations

In contrast to the tree-structured (nested) source code representation [35], our assembly and ELF level representations use a linear sequence of instructions e.g., as produced by `gcc -S` or `objdump -d -j .text` respectively. Candidate repairs are generated by swapping, inserting or deleting instructions. Pseudo-operations and directives at the assembly level (e.g., `.section .rodata`), and all elements outside of the `.text` section of the executable at the ELF level, are retained in each variant but never modified by mutation. To reduce search space size, each instruction, together with its operands, is treated atomically, and operands are not mutated independently. Both representations are source language and architecture agnostic.

3.3.1 Genetic Operators

ASM and ELF representations are modified using four operators designed for the linear representations: three mutation types and one crossover type (Figure 3). Instructions appearing in the negative localization are ten times more likely to be mutated than instructions appearing in both.

Linked ELF executables often contain hard-coded memory addresses included as literals in the program `.text`. Since there is no general way to distinguish an integer literal from an address literal, our mutation operators occasionally create invalid addresses (recent work may enable improved treatment of literal addresses [1] in the future).

To minimize disturbance of literal addresses and information outside of the `.text` section, the ELF mutation and crossover operators attempt to maintain the length of the linear instruction array in bytes and minimize changes to the in memory addresses of existing instructions.

Delete: A single instruction selected by weight is removed. At the ELF level, every byte of the deleted instruction is replaced with a `nop` byte.

Insert: A single instruction selected at random is copied to a new location selected by weight. At the ELF level, changes to offsets

[2] Code available at http://github.com/eschulte/tracer.

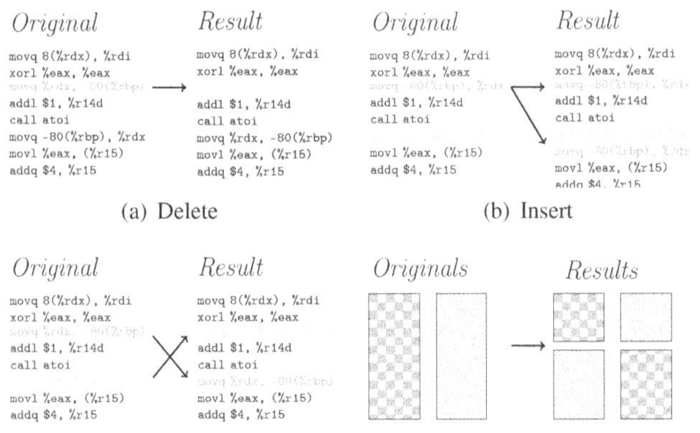

(a) Delete (b) Insert

(c) Swap (d) Crossover

Figure 3. Genetic operators for ASM. ELF mutations have the same form but manipulate bytes instead of text instructions. They also use padding to minimize length changes.

are minimized by removing a number of nearby `nop` instruction equal to the size of the inserted code. In the rare case where there are insufficient `nop` instructions, the size of the `.text` section increases, which usually reduces individual fitness.

Swap: An instruction selected at random is swapped with an instruction selected by weight. This operation is naturally length-preserving and requires no special treatment at the ELF level, although swapping two instructions of different lengths may alter instruction offsets in the short region between those two locations.

Crossover: Given two parent programs (Figure 1, line 11), a single index less than the length of the shorter parent program, is selected at random. Single-point crossover is performed, concatenating the instructions from one parent up to the selected index, and the instructions from the other parent after the selected index. This operation produces two new variant programs. At the ELF level, the index is selected such that the number of bytes before the index is the same in each parent.

3.3.2 Fitness Evaluation

Before fitness evaluation, the variant must be converted to an on-disk executable. Generating an executable from an ASM representation requires writing the array of ASM instructions (and any assembly directives or pseudo-operations) to disk and assembled/linked using instructions taken from the program's original build sequence. The ELF representation is written directly to a binary executable ELF file on disk without any elements of the software project's build toolchain.

The executable is then run against the program's test suite and negative test case. To protect against dangerous behavior by the random variants, a lightweight sandboxing solution was readily constructed from standard Linux utilities (e.g., `ulimit` and `chroot`). All experimental results presented in the paper include the cost of sandboxing. Repairs to kernel-level embedded code that manipulate hardware directly would require different methods. Fitness is assessed by running the executable on all test cases, computing a weighted average score based on the passing test cases, where negative test cases count twice as much as positive ones.

3.4 Motivating Example

Consider the program for exponentiation shown in Figure 4, which illustrates the expressive power of ASM- and ELF-level repairs. It contains a bug in which the two arguments are assigned to the wrong variables.

Buggy Exponentiation Program

```
int main(int argc, char *argv[]) {
  double a,b,c;
  a = atoi(argv[2]); // should be argv[1]
  b = atoi(argv[1]); // should be argv[2]
  c = 1;

  while(b > 0) {
    c = c * a;
    b--;
  }

  printf("%g\n", c);
  return 0;
}
```

Figure 4. Exponentiation with transposed arguments. This program cannot be repaired by simple reorganization of extant C statements.

The repair for this program should assign `atoi(argv[1])` to `a` and `atoi(argv[2])` to `b`. This is not possible using only combinations of extant statements (as in [35]), because each assignment is atomic and subexpressions may not be altered. However, when operating at the lower levels of compiled assembly instructions or linked executables, the repair may be expressed trivially through the transposition of two `mov` instructions. In fact, this program was repaired at the ASM and ELF levels with 3842 and 6453 test executions respectively, but it was not repaired in over 1000 runs of the algorithm at the AST level. In addition to bugs such as this, which are not repairable using combinations of existing atomic source-level statements, other bugs are markedly easier to repair at the ASM and ELF levels (Section 4.3).

3.5 Distributed Genetic Algorithm (DGA)

The methods described in Section 3.2 and Section 3.3 enable automated repair in devices with severely limited disk and memory resources. For example, the Nokia smartphones used in our experiments provide only 256 MB of memory. Also, such devices may not be fast enough to find and evaluate a successful repair in a reasonable amount of time on their own. To address these concerns, we present a distributed genetic algorithm (DGA) that allows multiple devices to collaborate in finding a repair.

As illustration, we consider a group of mutually trusting smartphones cooperating to repair the same bug. The repair may be found more quickly if the search burden can be distributed over many devices. This is a plausible use case given the large number of homogeneous installs of smart phone applications.[3]

The DGA is considered successful, compared to naïve parallelism in which all devices work independently, if the total number of fitness evaluations required to find a repair is reduced, thus reducing time and power costs. A second design goal is to minimize network communication. In the smartphone scenario, we assume that communication occurs via infrequent SMS messages, rather than high-power, high-bandwidth links.

Distributed GAs [17] are based on the insight that separate genetic populations sharing a small amount of data can often outperform a single population of the same total size. Each participating device maintains its own population of variants and periodically shares high-fitness variants with other devices. GAs are known to

[3] In theory, repairs from an untrusted source could be self-certifying (cf. [3]). In this paper we consider only networks of trusted, uncompromised devices.

be more effective when they operate over genetically diverse populations [18], and there is a large literature on the problem of "premature convergence" in GAs (e.g., [10]). Because the search in each sub-population is dominated by local high-fitness variants, diverse sub-populations on each device can explore different parts of the search space in parallel. Performance is thus enhanced by maximizing diversity among the sub-populations stored on each device. We hypothesize this to contribute to our DGA's superlinear reduction in fitness evaluations over naïve parallelism (see Section 4.5).

Two novel aspects of the DGA for software repair are: splitting the fault-localization search space among devices, and diversity-based migration.

3.6 Splitting the Search among Participants

To maximize sub-population diversity, we use fault localization information to constrain the search such that each device explores a different region of the search space. Recall that the repair algorithm modifies only those parts of the program identified by fault localization (Section 3.2) and that positive fault localization instructions are weighted differently from negative instructions with respect to choosing mutation locations. Let S be the ordered list of atomic elements of the program representation (e.g., assembly instructions, or groups of bytes) identified by fault localization over the positive test cases. Given N devices, we assign each device responsibility for two contiguous sub-sequences of S of size $k = \frac{|S|}{N}$, although each device contains the entire program and a list of the statements visited by negative test cases only (Section 3.2). We hypothesize that contiguous statements are likely relevant to the same repair. Formally, if $s_j \in S$ is the jth element of S counting in representation order, then device i of N only modifies elements of S_i where:

$$S_i = \left\{ s_j \in S \,\middle|\, \begin{array}{l} i \bmod N \leq \frac{s_j}{k} < (i+2) \bmod N \\ \vee\ visited\_on\_negative\_tests\_only(s_j) \end{array} \right\}$$

Note that since the insert and swap operators take one operand from the fault localization weighting and one at random, this division does not formally partition the search space, but it does divide the work of searching it into slightly overlapping parcels.

3.7 Diversity-based Migration

Each device periodically communicates a subset of its current population to a subset of the other devices. We hypothesize that search performance is improved if diverse variants are shared. We measure diversity between variants as the number of unique edits in their representations. An iterative calculation identifies the n most diverse variants in a subpopulation. Each variant is assigned one point for each genetic change that is unique across the (initially empty) output set; the candidate with the most points is placed in the output set, with ties broken randomly (this is common in the first generation, when the output set is empty); and the process repeats until the output set contains the desired number of variants.

3.8 Distributed Algorithm Details

Given these methods for dividing the search among different devices, and for identifying diverse variants to share among devices we now formalize the DGA algorithm in Figure 5. The DGA is executed concurrently by N networked nodes, each of which starts with the same information—program to repair, test suite, network topology (for exchanging information), and fault localization. Each node then creates a local initial subpopulation of variants (lines 2–4; Figure 1) and carries out one generation of the repair algorithm.

Each node selects a diverse set of d variants from its subpopulation (Figure 5, line 6). The exact migration topology does not generally affect algorithmic performance [6]. To minimize communication, we use a simple permutation topology, which changes each generation: Each participant passes variants to its "right" neighbor

Algorithm: Distributed Repair
Input: Program P to repair.
Input: Set of positive testcases $p \in PosT$.
Input: Set of negative testcases $n \in NegT$.
Input: Number d of variants per migration.
Input: Number N of networked participants.
1: $Subpop \leftarrow$ initial_population(P, pop_size)
2: **for** $generation = 1 \rightarrow$ gen **do**
3: $Id \leftarrow$ temporary device specific network identifier
4: $Subpop \leftarrow$ run($Subpop, PosT, NegT$) (Fig. 1, 6–17)
5: $Migrants \leftarrow$ div_select($Subpop, d$) (Sec. 3.7)
6: send($succ(Id), Migrants$)
7: $Migrants \leftarrow$ receive($pred(Id)$)
8: $Subpop \leftarrow Subpop \cup Migrants$
9: **end for**

Figure 5. Distributed genetic algorithm (DGA) for program repair. The search is distributed among participants that share information (diverse high-fitness program variants) after each generation.

(line 6) in the permutation, receiving a similar set from its "left" neighbor (line 7). The incoming variants are added to each node's subpopulation and are subject to selection in the next generation. The process then repeats. When participant finds a repair, the repair is sent in an out-of-band message, and the process terminates early (not shown).

The number of variants exchanged is at most $N \times d \times$ gen. Since d is chosen to be small, and the number of generations is small, communication cost is effectively linear in the number of participants. Because all variants share a common ancestor in the original program, only the edit history needs to be communicated (cf. [20, Sec. III-B]). For example, a variant created by deleting instruction 3 and then swapping instructions 1 and 2, can be serialized in a form such as "d(3)s(1,2)". In practice, we encode the operation (delete, insert, or swap) in one byte and operation-specific operands in one or two 16-bit integers. Fitness is included as a final byte. This encoding assumes self-contained compact descriptions of edits, and thus does not admit crossover.

4. Experimental Results

This section presents empirical results evaluating the ASM and ELF representations and the DGA. The results show the following:

1. Stochastic fault localization closely approximates the deterministic approach (Section 4.2).
2. Repair success at the ASM and ELF representation levels is similar to that reported previously for ASTs (Section 4.3).
3. The ASM and ELF representations, together with stochastic fault localization, have small resource footprints, suitable for running on embedded devices (Section 4.4).
4. The DGA increases success rates while reducing total fitness evaluations required to find a repair (Section 4.5).

4.1 Experimental Setup

Table 1 lists the benchmark defective programs evaluated in this paper. For ease of comparison they are taken from earlier work [35] with two additions. `merge` sort was added to evaluate the stochastic fault localization algorithm on a test suite with full assembly statement coverage, and `merge-cpp` was added to demonstrate a language other than C. Each program comes with a regression test suite, used to validate candidate repairs, and at least one test case indicating a defect. These programs have on average 3.69× more assembly instructions and 9.55× more bytes in the `.text` section of ELF files than lines of source code.

Program	C LOC	ASM LOC	ELF Bytes	Program Description	Defect
atris	9578	39153	131756	graphical tetris game	local stack buffer exploit
ccrypt	4249	15261	18716	encryption utility	segfault
deroff	1467	6330	17692	document processing	segfault
flex	8779	37119	73452	lexical analyzer generator	segfault
indent	5952	15462	49384	source code processing	infinite loop
look-s	205	516	1628	dictionary lookup	infinite loop
look-u	205	541	1784	dictionary lookup	infinite loop
merge	72	219	1384	merge sort	improper sorting of duplicate inputs
merge-cpp	71	421	1540	merge sort (in C++)	improper sorting of duplicate inputs
s3	594	767	1804	sendmail utility	buffer overflow
uniq	143	421	1288	duplicate text processing	segfault
units	496	1364	3196	metric conversion	segfault
zune	51	108	664	embedded media player	infinite loop
total	31862	117682	304288		

Table 1. Benchmark programs used in experiments, taken from Weimer *et al.* [35] with the addition of `merge`. Program size is reported as follows: Lines of code (LOC) in the original C source, LOC in the assembly files (x86, as produced by `gcc -S`), and size (in bytes) of the `.text` sections of the x86 ELF files. Each program has a regression test suite and a failing test case indicating a fault.

We used the following GA parameters: population size popsize $=$ 1000; maximum number of fitness evaluations in a trial evals $=$ 5000, mutation rate mut $=$ 1.0 per individual per generation and crossover rate cross $=$ 0.5 crossovers per indivdiual per generation.

Most experiments were run on a machine with 2.2 GHz AMD Opteron processors and 120 GB of memory. The wall-clock evaluation of the DGA was conducted on a single server-class machine, with 3.0 GHz Intel Xeon CPUs and 15.6 GB of memory. Cell phone experiments were conducted on Nokia N900 smartphones, each of which features a 600 MHz ARM Cortex-A8 CPU and 256 MB of mobile DDR memory.

4.2 Fault Localization Evaluation

We collected program counter samples using `oprofile` [21], a system-wide profiler for Linux systems, which doesn't alter the profiled program, runs on embedded devices, and when appropriately configured, has minimal impact on system-wide performance.

We process the samples as described in Section 3.2, explicitly comparing to deterministic approaches (below) and evaluating utility in the context of program repair in Section 4.3. The direct comparison used `merge` sort, which is small and exhaustively tested with 100% statement and branch coverage, as well as `deroff`, which is larger and has less-complete test coverage. The stochastic and deterministic traces taken from the failing test cases of both programs are shown in Figure 6. Inputs for the failing test case exercise the bugs described in Table 1.

Ten stochastic samples and one deterministic sample were collected for both programs. We find high correlations of 0.96 (merge) and 0.65 (deroff) among the stochastic samples, indicating consistency across samples. We find lower correlations of 0.61 (merge) and 0.38 (deroff) between the naïve stochastic (no Gaussian convolution) and deterministic samples, which increase to 0.71 (merge) and 0.48 (deroff) after Gaussian convolution, indicating that smoothing provides significant improvement.

4.3 ASM and ELF Repair Success

Table 2 compares ASM and ELF to AST, averaging over 100 trials of the standard (non-DGA) algorithm for each tested configuration. Memory usage, which varies insignificantly across runs, was calculated from a single run.

Our Nokia smartphones have 256+768 MB of RAM plus swap. In that environment, only 8 of 13 programs can be repaired at the AST level (i.e., memory is exhausted or the repair fails) compared to 10 at the ASM level and 11 at the ELF level.

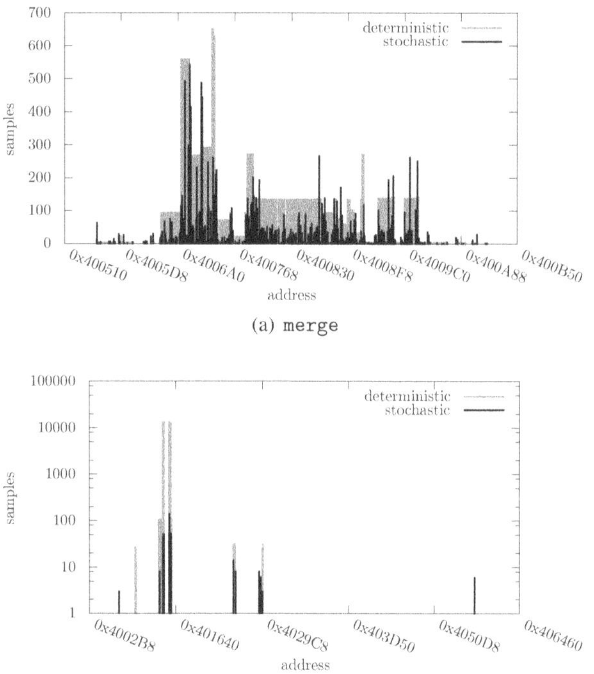

Figure 6. Fault localization in program address space. Results for stochastic sampling shown in *black* identify program regions similar to those found deterministically, shown in *gray*.

We expected the repair process to be much less efficient, especially at the ELF level, both in terms of success rate and time to first repair. Generally, EC searches are more challenging in larger search spaces—more locations to choose for a mutation and more possible instructions to choose from when performing an insertion. However, differences among the average percentage of successful repairs across representations are not large, with values of 65.83%, 70.75% and 78.17% for ELF, ASM and AST respectively. Using Fisher's Exact test to compare success rates we find no significant

	Memory (MB)			Runtime (s)			% Success			Expected Fitness Evaluations		
Program	AST	ASM	ELF	AST	ASM	ELF	AST	ASM	ELF	AST	ASM	ELF
`atris`	2384*	2384*	496	22.87	†	385.63	83	0	5	27.44	†	48806.00
`ccrypt`	6437*	3338*	334	39.15	342.23	21.58	100	100	100	7.00	673.00	25.00
`deroff`	1907*	811	453	37.33	1366.61	292.88	100	98	100	48.00	50.00	454.00
`flex`	691	381	162	1948.84	1125.44	†	6	1	0	78340.50	496255.00	†
`indent`	3242*	1669*	572	3301.88	3852.47	†	4	41	0	62737.25	13517.48	†
`look-s`	420	62	29	747.59	353.81	6.00	100	100	100	41.00	71.00	3.00
`look-u`	430	52	62	12.68	6.38	3.66	100	100	100	90.00	16.00	19.00
`merge`	152	45	57	842.74	100.93	161.35	54	100	84	4456.85	621.00	1008.19
`merge-cpp`	†	50	60	†	121.87	90.56		100	79	†	314.00	2135.2658
`s3`	152	76	43	14.43	23.46	28.02	100	96	50	4.00	4.00	95.00
`uniq`	358	72	72	105.18	3.46	7.18	100	100	100	8.00	46.00	8.00
`units`	572	162	95	1075.16	18778.70	501.54	91	13	51	930.23	57374.63	8538.47
`zune`	76	17	29	36.93	28.79	71.49	100	100	100	17.00	26.00	45.00
average	1402	756	200	323.47	2333.82	121.52	78.17	70.75	65.83	622.45	6542.40	1132.85
w/o `units`	1242	559	135	229.50	278.20	74.02	77.00	76.00	67.18	583.98	188.38	207.15

Table 2. Resource comparison of abstract syntax tree (AST) assembly source (ASM) and ELF binary (ELF) repair representations. "Memory" reports the average max memory required for a repair (as reported by the Unix `top` utility). "Runtime" reports the average time per successful repair in seconds. "% Success" gives the percentage of random seeds for which a valid repair is found within 5000 runs of the full test suite. "Expected Fitness Evaluations" counts the expected number of evaluations per repair (Equation 1). † Indicates that there were no successful repairs in 5000 fitness evaluations. Rows with † are excluded when calculating "Memory", "Runtime" and "Expected Fitness Evaluations" averages. * Indicates memory requirements in excess of the 1024 available on the Nokia smartphones.

difference between AST and either ASM or ELF with p-values of 1 (between AST and ASM), and 0.294 (between AST and ELF). This suggests that automated repair at the ASM and ELF levels is a practical alternative to source-level repair.

Some bugs are more amenable to repair at particular levels of representation. For example, `atris` and `units` are repaired most easily at the AST level, `indent` at the ASM level, and `merge` sort at the ASM and ELF levels.

The `atris` repair involves deleting a call to `getenv`. At the AST level this requires a single deletion, while at the ASM level, three contiguous instructions must be deleted and the repair was not found. The repair was found at the ELF level, and all of the five repairs found were unique, each involving from 3 to 7 accumulated mutation operations.

The `merge` repair involves replacing an `if` statement with its `else` branch. At the AST level this requires swapping exactly those two statements, which is 1 of 4900 possible swap mutations. At the ASM and ELF levels, modification of a single comparison instruction suffices to repair the program. This is one of only 218 such changes possible and is much more easily found by our technique.

The "*Expected Fitness Evaluations*" column reports the expected number of fitness evaluations per repair.

$$\begin{aligned} expected &= fit_s + (runs_s - 1) \times fit_f \text{ where} \quad (1) \\ fit_s &= \text{average evaluations per successful run} \\ fit_f &= \text{average evaluations per failed run} \\ runs_s &= \text{average runs per success} \end{aligned}$$

Given that repair time is dominated by fitness evaluation, which includes compilation and linking at the AST level, and linking at the ASM level, and that for all programs but `units` (an outlier in this regard) the expected number of evaluations is roughly equivalent between levels of representation, we conclude that, when repairs are possible, the repair process is usually more efficient at the ASM and ELF levels than at the AST level.

4.4 Resource Requirements

We desire a repair algorithm that can run within the resource constraints of mobile and embedded devices. We consider three key constraints: CPU usage and runtime, memory requirements, and disk space requirements. Section 4.5 also evaluates network communication for the DGA.

CPU Usage. Runtime costs associated with GA bookkeeping (e.g., sorting variants by fitness, choosing random numbers, etc.) are typically dwarfed by the cost of evaluating fitness. For example, on an average run of `deroff`, bookkeeping accounted for only 13.5% of the runtime. The primary costs are computing fault localization information and fitness evaluation (including compilation and linking depending upon the representation used).

Stochastic fault localization requires from 50 to 5000 runs of the original unmodified program. Importantly, the absolute running time determines the number of required executions, so slow programs require fewer executions and only quickly terminating programs require more than 50 executions. By contrast, AST-level repairs require compilation of an instrumented program with a 100× slowdown per run (Section 3.2). Related executable-level approaches introduce a 300× slowdown to compute fault localization information [26, Sec 4.4], and `ptrace` full deterministic tracing incurs a 1200× slowdown. Our fault localization approach is an order-of-magnitude faster than these previous approaches.

After fault localization is complete, both ASM and ELF representations have lower fitness evaluation costs than the AST-level because compilation and linking are not required. However, the search problem for ASM and ELF is potentially much larger than for AST (compare the size columns in Table 1), suggesting they may need more fitness evaluations to find a repair. If the time to conduct a repair at the AST level is normalized to 1.0, on average ASM repairs take 7.22× and ELF repairs take 0.38×. Using a Mann-Whitney U-test the runtime difference between ELF and AST is a significant improvement, with a p-value of 0.055. While the ASM-level repair is slower, this can be mitigated through collaboration across multiple devices (Section 4.5).

Memory. Memory utilization is important for mobile and embedded devices. The earlier work was conducted on server machines with 8 GB [26] to 16 GB of RAM [35]. By contrast, the Nokia N900 smartphones we consider as indicative use cases have 256 MB Mobile DDR—an order of magnitude less.

Table 2 reports the memory used (in MB) for repairs at the AST, ASM and ELF representations, showing that ASM requires only about 53.91% of the memory of a source-based representation, while ELF is significantly smaller, requiring only 14.29% of the memory. We attribute the low requirements for ELF to the ELF parser we used, which stores only the `.text` section of ELF binaries in memory.

Disk space. Beyond the subject program and its test suite, disk usage is composed of two main elements: the repair tool and the build suite of the program to be repaired. The size of these elements varies greatly with representation level of the repair. For example, repairs at the ELF level do not require the build tool-chain of the original program, enabling repair of embedded programs that are cross-compiled and cannot be built locally. We next discuss the disk space requirements at all three levels.

AST requires the source code and build tool chain of the original program. Our baseline comparison, GenProg, takes 23 MB on disk (including the tool itself, the `gcc` compiler and header files, the `gas` assembler, and the `ld` linker).

ASM requires only the assembly code, assembler, and linker. This is a significantly lighter build requirement. Our ASM implementation is currently incorporated into the AST repair framework [35] to ensure a controlled environment for comparison. It requires 12 MB on disk (including the tool itself, the `gas` assembler, and the `ld` linker).

ELF requires only a compiled executable. Like ASM, our prototype is a modification of the AST-level repair framework, replacing the source-code parser with an ELF parser. It requires only 1.10 MB on disk, an order of magnitude decrease compared to AST.

As one concrete example of the resource limitations of embedded devices, the Nokia N900 smartphone ships with 256 MB of NAND flash storage (holding the Maemo Linux kernel and bootloader, etc., with about 100 MB free), and a 32 GB eMMC store holding a 2GB `ext3` partition, 768 MB of swap, and about 27 GB of free space in a `vfat` partition. The `vfat` partition is unmounted and exported whenever a USB cable is attached to the device, making it unsuitable for a deployed system repair tool. Linux packages install to the NAND flash by default, quickly exhausting space. Repartitioning is possible but uncommon for casual users. Thus, even though the device claims 32 GB of storage, significantly less is available for a stable repair tool. Although these are merely implementation details, we argue that such conditions and the need to minimize the on-disk footprint are indicative of many embedded devices.

4.5 Distributed and Embedded Repair Results

Table 3 summarizes the performance of the DGA with the number of nodes ranging from one to four. The "% Success" column lists the fraction of trials for which a successful repair is found, normalized so that a single non-networked participant has 1.0. Overall success rate improves by 13% from one to four participants because they share diverse variants and collaborate on the search by exploring different portions of the program space.

In most instances, the time to find the first repair is critical. The "Expected Fitness Evals" column measures that effort in a machine-independent manner (Section 4.3). In practice, fitness evaluations (which require repeatedly running the program test suite) account for the majority of algorithmic runtime. The number of fitness evaluations required to find a repair drops by a factor of 5 and the average standard deviation by 62%. Each fitness evaluation includes the time to run the test suite of the subject program.

	% Success				Expected Fitness Evals			
	$\rightarrow$ #nodes $\rightarrow$				$\rightarrow$ #nodes $\rightarrow$			
Program	1	2	3	4	1	2	3	4
`atris`	1	1.00	1.00	1.00	1	0.53	0.40	0.27
`ccrypt`	1	1.00	1.00	1.00	1	0.62	0.27	0.24
`deroff`	1	1.00	1.00	1.00	1	0.58	0.44	0.32
`flex`	1	1.13	1.87	2.07	1	0.87	0.46	0.40
`indent`	1	1.04	1.04	1.04	1	0.25	0.16	0.10
`look-s`	1	1.00	1.00	1.00	1	0.50	0.55	0.29
`look-u`	1	1.00	1.00	1.00	1	0.76	0.37	0.32
`merge`	1	1.69	2.14	2.31	1	0.43	0.22	0.18
`s3`	1	1.00	1.00	1.00	1	0.47	0.31	0.24
`uniq`	1	1.00	1.00	1.00	1	0.49	0.46	0.31
`units`	1	1.27	1.33	1.33	1	0.32	0.11	0.07
`zune`	1	1.00	1.00	1.00	1	0.47	0.36	0.27
h.mean	1	1.07	1.12	1.13	1	0.47	0.28	0.20

Table 3. Distributed repair results as a function of the number of participant nodes. "Success Rate" gives the percentage of random trials that produce a repair, normalized to 1.0 for 1 node. "Expected Fitness Evals" approximates the time and effort required by the first machine to find a repair and is defined in Section 4.3; it is normalized to 1.0 at 1 node. As the number of participants grows from 1 to 4, repairs are found 13% more often and the number of fitness evaluations required decreases by a factor of 5 (harmonic mean of all benchmarks). The results listed in this table are from runs at the AST level and thus `merge-cpp` is not included.

As a baseline, we also measured the performance of naïve parallelism (i.e., using two Nokia cell phones to run two separate copies of the repair algorithm and stopping when the first repair is found) to demonstrate that the distributed algorithm is responsible for the performance gains. For a meaningful comparison, we focused on benchmarks that take more than one generation to repair (i.e., `flex`, `indent`, `merge` and `units`) and thus reached the distributed portion of the DGA algorithm described in Figure 5. Over 100 trials, two nodes running DGA use only 442 total fitness evaluations per repair compared to 848 for naïve parallelism (not counting evaluations performed after the first repair is found). On two nodes, DGA thus requires 48% fewer fitness evaluations than naïve parallelism.

Finally, we calculate the network bandwidth consumed by DGA. Recall that at the end of each generation, each machine sends $d = \mathsf{popsize}/20 = 50$ diverse variants to a neighbor. After the first generation, each variant has one edit in its history (`mutp` $= 1.0$). One third of all mutations are deletions, which can be represented by four bytes (the opcode and the operand and the fitness). Insertions and swaps require six bytes (the opcode, two operands, and the fitness). The expected data size sent from one participant to another after the first generation is thus $50 \times (4 \times \frac{1}{3} + 6 \times \frac{2}{3}) = 267$ bytes. After the second generation, each of the d variants sent will typically have two edit operations in its history, follow the same distribution (and thus require twice as much bandwidth to communicate). Since each of the N networked participants send one batch of variants after every generation, the expected cumulative total network bandwidth used, as a function of the number of generations G before the repair is found, is estimated as:

$$\mathsf{bytes\_sent}(G) \simeq \sum_{i=1}^{G} N \times d \times i \times (4 \times \frac{1}{3} + 6 \times \frac{2}{3})$$

With our default parameters, this estimate implies 801 bytes sent per participant (spread over two network sends or six SMS messages per participant) by the end of the second generation. Empirically, we find that our measured results match this model to within 10%. For example, over eight random trials to repair `merge` with two participants averaging 2.4 generations, DGA sent a total of 7000 bytes in such a way that 51 SMS text messages were required. This implies that just under 875 bytes (or 6.4 SMS text messages) were required per node per trial. We claim that this low communication cost is well within what would be considered reasonable for the task of program repair across embedded or mobile systems.

To measure the impact of communication on run time we next evaluated wall-clock times for the DGA, the original serial algorithm, and an ideal naïve parallel adaptation of the original algorithm with no inter-node communication, all at the AST source code level. These runs were performed on a single server-class machine, with 4 3.0 GHz Intel Xeon CPUs and 15.6 GB of memory using TCP over Ethernet. The DGA incurs a cost from inter-node communication, but the results in Table 4 show that this cost is more than offset by the increased algorithmic efficiency of search space splitting and migration of high-fitness variants among the nodes.

Table 4 shows the mean wall clock time in seconds to find a repair for the DGA and a naïve parallel version of the original serial algorithm. We report results for one to four participating repair nodes (in practice all nodes were run in parallel on a single multicore). The naïve algorithm running on a single node is exactly the original serial algorithm.

Table 4. Mean wall clock time in seconds to find a successful repair at the AST source code level. Communication in the DGA is bulk synchronous. The column "Rounds" gives the number of communication rounds. Results are averaged over 10 attempted repairs of the `units` program. The other three programs that require multiple generations to repair show the same trend with from 1 to 4 nodes, and using DGA or naïve parallel repair algorithm.

	DGA		Naïve Parallel
# Nodes	Seconds	Rounds	Seconds
1			205.531
2	173.868	43.2	195.821
3	135.17	28.2	201.346
4	115.566	14.5	211.989

At each level of parallelization, the distributed algorithm finds repairs faster than the ideal naïve parallelization of the original algorithm. Judging the significance of these differences using the Kolomogorov-Smirnov test (used instead of a T-test because these distributions are not normal given the large differences between runs which do or do not find a repair) yields a value of 0.5 with $p = 0.000214$. The wall clock performance gained by using the distributed algorithm over a naïve parallel algorithm is statistically significant.

5. Related Work

Genetic Algorithms and Evolution of Machine Code. Previous work can be divided into two broad categories. One designs mutation operators to preserve the validity of the programs they manipulate, both over CISC instruction sets [23] running on hardware and more recently over Java byte code [13, 25] running on the Java virtual machine. An alternative is to use generic mutation operators, relying on safety mechanisms built into the CPU and operating system to catch and terminate invalid individuals [19].

Our work follows the second approach, using general operators that can be applied across both CISC x86 and RISC Arm architectures. Given the low cost of linking ASM individuals and writing ELF individuals to disk, we favor using the CPU to check validity, finding that it is adequate.

"Evolvability" analysis [24] has led some to declare x86 assembly code an unfit medium for evolutionary computation [31]. Based on this belief, translations between x86 and more evolvable intermediate languages have been proposed, both to construct evolvable malware [7] and to distribute binary patches [1]. Our results provide a counterexample, showing that EC at the ASM and ELF level can efficiently generate viable program variants. By operating on whole instructions, the negative effects of "argumented instructions" [24] are minimized. Similarly, through the use of `nop` padding in ELF level mutation, changes in the absolute offset are minimized, thus reducing the impact of direct addressing.

Assembly Program Repair. Schulte *et al.* provide the closest instance of related work proposing automated program repair for assembly programs [27]. This preliminary short paper describes EC-generated program repairs to x86 assembly programs, focusing only on x86 assembly as a lowest common denominator for high-level languages (such as C and Haskell). Here, we extended that work to target both ASM and ELF representations, multiple assembly languages (x86 and ARM), propose stochastic fault localization, demonstrate that our technique scales to embedded devices, and propose and demonstrate a novel distributed repair algorithm.

Executable Program Repair. The closest instance of related work that automatically repairs binary executables is the Clearview system [26], which patches errors in deployed Windows x86 binaries. Clearview uses a split-phase learning-and-monitoring approach—program instrumentation is used to learn invariants, and later monitoring notices violations in deployed programs. If a violation occurs, Clearview considers possible patches, evaluating them against an indicative workload of test cases. Clearview focuses on specific error types and prespecifies a set of repair templates (e.g., breaking out of a loop, clamping a variable to a value, etc.). It is therefore less general than our method, although it has obtained impressive results in its domain, patching nine out of twelve historical Firefox vulnerabilities, even in the face of a DARPA Red Team. However, the Clearview approach seems heavy weight; they report experiments involving rack-mount server machines with 16 GB of RAM, VMware virtualization, and a 300× slowdown during the learning phase [26, Sec. 4.4]. By contrast, our work targets resource-constrained embedded environments and uses stochastic sampling to reduce the cost of fault localization, which does not require program instrumentation.

A distributed repair technique has also been described for Clearview which protects application communities, but that work did not report performance results [26]. Their distributed algorithm amortizes the cost of learning invariants (i.e., of computing fault localization information), and ignores the time to find a candidate repair. By contrast we demonstrate a distributed algorithm that finds repairs more quickly.

Distributed Evolutionary Algorithms. The large literature on distributed and parallel genetic algorithms dates back to Grosso [11], who explored the idea of subdividing a GA population into smaller subpopulations with occasional exchanges of fit individuals among the populations. More recent work ranges from implementations tailored to particular hardware configurations [12, 22] to a wide variety of algorithms in which the population is partitioned and individuals are shared among the partitions according to different schemes, e.g., [22]. Parameter tuning (population size, migration rate, etc.) is a concern, with recommendations available for several problem types [6]. Perhaps most relevant to the current work is a Doctoral Colloquium describing a distributed genetic programming implementation on a wireless sensor network [32], although that work is still quite preliminary.

6. Discussion

Compared to automated program repair over C statements, an assembly representation operates over a finite alphabet of elements. A typical assembly instruction consists of an opcode and two or three operands, while C statements may be of arbitrary size and complexity (e.g., `x = 1 + 1 + ...`). In addition, there are typically at least three times more assembly instructions than C statements. These combined facts give an assembly representation limited to permutations of elements of the original program much higher sample rates in the space of possible programs. In a system where the linking of an assembly file does not introduce new instructions or arguments, the alphabet and expressive power of the ASM and ELF representations are equivalent.

We see the effects of this increased coverage in Section 3.4 in which the program is only repaired at the ASM and ELF levels, and in Section 4.3 in which some repairs are much more easily expressed at the ASM and ELF levels.

While introducing new bugs is a possibility, We typically find very small changes which address only the buggy behavior. Specifically we reviewed the repairs presented here and found no evidence of introduced bugs.

While moving from the tree AST representation to the vector ASM and ELF representations may seem minor, the EC community has two separate sub-fields, GP and GA, dedicated to the study of tree- and vector-based representations respectively, each with their own research challenges (e.g., bloat in GP), application domains, best practices, journals and conferences.

There were several technical challenges in the implementation, particularly regarding the manipulation of ELF files. Existing tools such as the GNU ELF tool suite (`libfd`) and its BSD equivalent (`libelf`) do not support changes to the contents of existing ELF files. We thus developed our own libraries for manipulating ELF files, including support for the automated updates to ELF file metadata in response to an altered `.text` section[4].

Although ELF files do support symbolic addressing through symbol names and run-time linkers, direct addresses pose a significant problem for the randomly changing raw binary code sections. This is mitigated by mutation operators that minimize disruption to the location of compiled code.

It is sometimes useful to consider the total number of unique repairs produced. For example, additional candidate repairs help developers create high-quality final patches [34]. Because our DGA explicitly manages diversity across sub-populations, we hypothesize that it might produce a wider variety of distinct repairs. We measured uniqueness in terms of changes made to the code: Two repairs are distinct if they use edit operations, treated as unordered sets, that are not identical. With four participants, our DGA found 20% more unique repairs than with one participant. If we consider only the challenging `flex`, `indent`, `merge` and `units` repairs, the the number of discovered unique repairs increases to 73%.

Some may argue that it is aesthetically unappealing to modify code at all, particularly with a stochastic algorithm such as EC. We believe that distributed automated repair methods will be necessary in the future, as embedded devices become ubiquitous and are deployed in a wide range of environments. As the computational power of distributed embedded devices eclipses that of centralized servers, timely centralized testing and repair becomes infeasible (cf. already 28–29 day lag times are reported in recent surveys for centralized repairs [30]).

There are several areas of potential future work. For example, we expect that variations of this technique could be used to optimize performance of programs for specific environments. A second area is proactive diversity to disrupt software monocultures. In security settings, randomization is often inserted into compiled programs to prevent malicious attacks. Assembly code evolution could be used to add diversity to deployed software.

[4] Code available at: http://github.com/eschulte/rw-elf and http://github.com/eschulte/elf.

6.1 Limitations and Caveats

The fine granularity of repairs at the ASM and ELF levels may be a poor match for conventional test suites. For example, we have observed ASM-level repairs that change the calling convention of one particular function. Such a repair has no direct representation at the C source level, and a test suite designed to maximize statement coverage (for example) may not speak to the validity of such a repair. Producing efficient test suites that give confidence that an implementation adheres to its specification remains an open problem in software engineering. Our work shares this general weakness with all other approaches that use test suites or workloads to validate candidate repairs (e.g., Clearview [26] and GenProg [35]). In this regard, sandboxing is crucial: we have observed ASM variants that subvert the testing framework by deleting key test files, leading to perfect fitness for all subsequent variants until the test framework is repaired.

Benchmark selection is a threat to the external validity of our experiments. We used benchmarks taken from published papers to admit direct comparison; to mitigate this threat we augmented the benchmark set with very high test coverage and non C-language examples.

Our DGA uses a self-contained compact encoding of each variant, to facilitate communication among nodes via SMS. This encoding precluded the use of crossover because it would not be meaningful to exchange information between two variants under the encoding, even though crossover is an important feature of many GAs. This restriction implies that our results might not generalize to other GAs. Since crossover can improve search time and success rates, it is possible that our results would be improved with a DGA implementation that supports crossover. This could be tested using a recently published *patch* representation [20] that supports a concise encoding of crossover.

7. Summary and Conclusion

This paper extends previous work on automated program repair at the AST level to compiled (ASM) and linked (ELF) programs. The new representations allow repairs when source code cannot be parsed into ASTs (e.g., due to unavailable source files, complex build procedures or non-C source languages). They also reduce memory and disk requirements sufficiently to enable repairs on resource constrained devices. We also introduce a stochastic fault localization technique, which is applicable to these representations and devices, and present a distributed repair algorithm that allows costly repair processes to be split across multiple devices.

Importantly for embedded devices, our techniques reduce memory requirements by up to 85%, disk space requirements by up to 95% (Section 4.4), and repair generation time up to 62% (Section 4.4), which enables application to resource-constrained environments. We demonstrate our technique on Nokia N900 smartphones whose resource constraints which serve as a practical proxy for future low power computing systems.

Our fault localization algorithm is based on stochastic sampling and Gaussian convolution. It provides the instruction- and byte-level precision required by the ASM and ELF representations, while retaining sufficient accuracy to guide automated repair. In addition, it is ten times faster than previous approaches and more suited to devices where direct instrumentation is infeasible.

We take advantage of these reduced resource requirements in a distributed repair algorithm in which multiple cell phones communicate via SMS messages to find repairs more quickly. Sections 3.8 and 4.5 detail the algorithm. Using four devices we increase success rates by 13% and reduce fitness evaluation burdens by a factor of five—a superlinear improvement over naïve parallelism. The distributed algorithm's use of multiple populations could also be used to speed up serial repair on a single device. Communication costs are low: two phones require under 900 bytes (or 7 SMS messages) per participant per repair on our benchmarks.

Taken together, these techniques constitute the first general automated method of program repair applicable to binary executables, and are a first step in the application of automated software repair to the growing field of mobile and embedded devices.

7.1 Acknowledgments

C. Le Goues, N. Holtschulte, R. Bodik, and the anonymous reviewers provided helpful comments on the manuscript. The work was supported by DARPA (P-1070-113237), DOE (DE-AC02-05CH11231), NSF (SHF-0905236, SHF-0905373, CCF-0954024) and the Santa Fe Institute.

References

[1] S. Adams. Google software updates: Courgette (design documents). `http://dev.chromium.org/developers/design-documents/software-updates-courgette`, 2011.

[2] BBC News. Microsoft zune affected by 'bug'. In *http://news.bbc.co.uk/2/hi/technology/7806683.stm*, Dec. 2008.

[3] M. Costa, J. Crowcroft, M. Castro, A. Rowstron, L. Zhou, L. Zhang, and P. Barham. Vigilante: End-to-end containment of internet worm epidemics. *ACM Trans. Comput. Syst.*, 26(4):1–68, 2008. ISSN 0734-2071. doi: http://doi.acm.org/10.1145/1455258.1455259.

[4] C. Ebert and C. Jones. Embedded software: Facts, figures, and future. *Computer*, 42(4):42–52, 2009.

[5] A. Eiben and J. Smith. *Introduction to Evolutionary Computing*. Springer, 2003.

[6] F. Fernández, M. Tomassini, and L. Vanneschi. An empirical study of multipopulation genetic programming. *Genetic Programming and Evolvable Machines*, 4(1):21–51, 2003.

[7] P. Ferrie. Malware analysis: Flibi night. *Virus Bulletin*, pages 4–5, March 2011.

[8] J. Fitzpatrick. An interview with Steve Furber. *Commun. ACM*, 54: 34–39, May 2011. doi: http://doi.acm.org/10.1145/1941487.1941501. URL `http://doi.acm.org/10.1145/1941487.1941501`.

[9] S. Forrest, W. Weimer, T. Nguyen, and C. Le Goues. A genetic programming approach to automated software repair. In *Genetic and Evolutionary Computing Conference*, 2009.

[10] J. J. Grefenstette. Optimization of control parameters for genetic algorithms. *IEEE Transactions on Systems, Man and Cybernetics*, 16 (1):122–128, 1986.

[11] P. B. Grosso. *Computer Simulations of Genetic Adaptation: Parallel Subcomponent Interaction in a Multilocus Model*. PhD thesis, The University of Michigan, Ann Arbor, MI, 1985.

[12] S. Harding. Genetic programming on graphics processing units bibliography. Memorial Univeristy, Canada, Feb. 9, 2010. `http://www.gpgpgpu.com`.

[13] B. Harvey, J. A. Foster, and D. A. Frincke. Towards byte code genetic programming. In *Genetic and evolutionary computing conference*, page 1234, 1999.

[14] J. H. Holland. *Adaptation in Natural and Artificial Systems*. MIT Press, Cambridge, MA, 1992. Second edition.

[15] G. Jin, L. Song, W. Zhang, S. Lu, and B. Liblit. Automated atomicity-violation fixing. In *Programming Language Design and Implementation*, pages 389–400, 2011.

[16] J. A. Jones and M. J. Harrold. Empirical evaluation of the tarantula automatic fault-localization technique. In *Automated Software Engineering*, pages 273–282, 2005. ISBN 1-59593-993-4. doi: http://doi.acm.org/10.1145/1101908.1101949.

[17] Z. Konfrst. Parallel genetic algorithms: Advances, computing trends, applications and perspectives. In *Parallel and Distributed Processing Symposium*. IEEE, 2004.

[18] J. R. Koza. *Genetic Programming: On the Programming of Computers by Means of Natural Selection*. MIT Press, 1992.

[19] F. Kühling, K. Wolff, and P. Nordin. Brute-force approach to automatic induction of machine code on CISC architectures. In *European Conference on Genetic Programming*, pages 288–297, 2002. ISBN 3-540-43378-3.

[20] C. Le Goues, M. Dewey-Vogt, S. Forrest, and W. Weimer. A systematic study of automated program repair: Fixing 55 out of 105 bugs for $8 each. In *International Conference on Software Engineering*, 2012.

[21] J. Levon. *OProfile Manual*. Victoria University of Manchester, 2004.

[22] A. Munawar, M. Wahib, M. Munetomo, and K. Akama. A survey: Genetic algorithms and the fast evolving world of parallel computing. In *High Performance Computing and Communications*, pages 897–902, 2008. ISBN 978-0-7695-3352-0. doi: http://doi.ieeecomputersociety.org/10.1109/HPCC.2008.77.

[23] P. Nordin, W. Banzhaf, and F. D. Francone. Efficient evolution of machine code for CISC architectures using instruction blocks and homologous crossover. In *Advances in Genetic Programming 3*, pages 275–299. June 1999. ISBN 0-262-19423-6. URL `http://www.aimlearning.com/aigp31.pdf`.

[24] C. Ofria, C. Adami, and T. C. Collier. Design of evolvable computer languages. *IEEE Transactions on Evolutionary Computation*, 6:420–424, 2002.

[25] M. Orlov and M. Sipper. Genetic programming in the wild: evolving unrestricted bytecode. In *Genetic and evolutionary computation*, pages 1043–1050, 2009. ISBN 978-1-60558-325-9.

[26] J. H. Perkins, S. Kim, S. Larsen, S. Amarasinghe, J. Bachrach, M. Carbin, C. Pacheco, F. Sherwood, S. Sidiroglou, G. Sullivan, W.-F. Wong, Y. Zibin, M. D. Ernst, and M. Rinard. Automatically patching errors in deployed software. In *Symposium on Operating Systems Principles*, pages 87–102, October 2009.

[27] E. Schulte, S. Forrest, and W. Weimer. Automated program repair through the evolution of assembly code. In *Automated Software Engineering*, pages 313–316, 2010.

[28] R. C. Seacord, D. Plakosh, and G. A. Lewis. *Modernizing Legacy Systems: Software Technologies, Engineering Process and Business Practices*. Addison-Wesley, 2003. ISBN 0321118847.

[29] L. G. Shapiro, G. C. Stockman, L. G. Shapiro, and G. Stockman. *Computer Vision*. Prentice Hall, 2001. ISBN 0130307963.

[30] Symantec. Internet security threat report. Technical report, `http://eval.symantec.com/mktginfo/enterprise/white_papers/ent-whitepaper_symantec_internet_security_threat_report_x_09_2006.en-us.pdf`, Sept. 2006.

[31] S. Thomas. Taking the redpill: Artificial evolution in native x86 systems. `http://spth.vxheavens.com/ArtEvol.html`, October 2010.

[32] P. Valencia. In situ genetic programming for wireless sensor networks. In *SenSys Doctoral Colloquium*, 2007.

[33] Y. Wei, Y. Pei, C. A. Furia, L. S. Silva, S. Buchholz, B. Meyer, and A. Zeller. Automated fixing of programs with contracts. In *International Symposium on Software Testing and Analysis*, pages 61–72, 2010.

[34] W. Weimer. Patches as better bug reports. In *Generative Programming and Component Engineering*, 2006.

[35] W. Weimer, T. Nguyen, C. Le Goues, and S. Forrest. Automatically finding patches using genetic programming. In *International Conference on Software Engineering*, pages 364–367, 2009.

[36] W. Weimer, S. Forrest, C. L. Goues, and T. Nguyen. Automatic program repair with evolutionary computation. *Commun. ACM*, 53 (5):109–116, 2010.

Verifying Systems Rules Using Rule-Directed Symbolic Execution

Heming Cui * Gang Hu * Jingyue Wu Junfeng Yang
{heming,ganghu,jingyue,junfeng}@cs.columbia.edu
Columbia University

Abstract

Systems code must obey many rules, such as "opened files must be closed." One approach to verifying rules is static analysis, but this technique cannot infer precise runtime effects of code, often emitting many false positives. An alternative is symbolic execution, a technique that verifies program paths over all inputs up to a bounded size. However, when applied to verify rules, existing symbolic execution systems often blindly explore many redundant program paths while missing relevant ones that may contain bugs.

Our key insight is that only a small portion of paths are relevant to rules, and the rest (majority) of paths are irrelevant and do not need to be verified. Based on this insight, we create WOODPECKER, a new symbolic execution system for effectively checking rules on systems programs. It provides a set of builtin checkers for common rules, and an interface for users to easily check new rules. It directs symbolic execution toward the program paths relevant to a checked rule, and soundly prunes redundant paths, exponentially speeding up symbolic execution. It is designed to be heuristic-agnostic, enabling users to leverage existing powerful search heuristics.

Evaluation on 136 systems programs totaling 545K lines of code, including some of the most widely used programs, shows that, with a time limit of typically just one hour for each verification run, WOODPECKER effectively verifies 28.7% of the program and rule combinations over bounded input, whereas an existing symbolic execution system KLEE verifies only 8.5%. For the remaining combinations, WOODPECKER verifies 4.6 times as many relevant paths as KLEE. With a longer time limit, WOODPECKER verifies much more paths than KLEE, *e.g.*, 17 times as many with a four-hour limit. WOODPECKER detects 113 rule violations, including 10 serious data loss errors with 2 most serious ones already confirmed by the corresponding developers.

Categories and Subject Descriptors D.2.4 [*Software Engineering*]: Software/Program Verification; D.2.5 [*Software Engineering*]: Testing and Debugging; D.4.5 [*Operating Systems*]: Reliability

General Terms Algorithms, Experimentation, Reliability, Verification

* These authors contributed equally to this work.

ASPLOS'13, March 16–20, 2013, Houston, Texas, USA.

Keywords Symbolic execution, Path Slicing, Verification, Error Detection, Systems Rules

1. Introduction

Systems code must obey a variety of rules. For instance, assertions must succeed, allocated memory must be freed, opened files must be closed, file read or write must be done on opened files, and atomic `rename` must be used correctly [55, 63]. Violating these rules may easily lead to critical failures such as program crashes, resource leaks, data losses, and security breaches.

One approach to verifying rules is static analysis [25, 26, 61]. This technique has high coverage because it analyzes all code a compiler can see. However, without running code, it has difficulties inferring precise runtime effects of code, such as whether two pointers point to the same memory location or two branch conditions are equivalent. For soundness, it has to conservatively assume the worst, often emitting numerous false positives which require costly manual inspection. Although previous work [26] reduced false positives with heuristics, it aggressively traded off soundness. It may thus miss many errors and cannot be applied to verification.

An appealing alternative to verifying rules is *symbolic execution* [11, 12, 33, 42], a powerful technique that systematically explores program paths for errors. Instead of running a program on concrete input consisting of zeros and ones, it runs the program on *symbolic* input initially allowed to have any value. When the execution branches based on symbolic input, this technique explores both branches by conceptually forking two executions, each maintaining constraints on symbolic input required for the program to proceed down the given path. By systematically exploring paths, this technique achieves higher statement coverage than manual or random testing [12]. By actually running code, it sees the precise runtime effects of code and eliminates false positives (barring limitations of constraint solving).

Symbolic execution has been applied to detect serious errors in systems code [12, 13, 64] and generate high-coverage tests [12]. Moreover, it has been applied to *verify* program paths and code [12, 18, 39, 52]. At each dangerous operation such as an assertion on symbolic input, it checks if any input value may fail the operation. If it finds no such inputs for a path, it effectively verifies the path over the symbolic input. If it verifies all paths, it effectively verifies the entire program over the symbolic input. This verification approach is a form of *bounded verification* [17]. Researchers have argued and experimentally shown that checking all inputs within a small scope can effectively detect a high portion of bugs and achieve high statement and branch coverage [5, 12, 19, 38].

Although it is tempting to verify systems rules using symbolic execution, this technique faces another difficult challenge of *path explosion*: it can rarely explore all paths of a typical program simply because of the sheer number of paths.

Our key insight is that although the number of program paths is enormous, only a small portion of the paths are relevant to a checked rule, and the rest (majority) of the paths are irrelevant and do not need to be checked. Specifically, a typical rule involves only a small number of instructions, or *events*, during execution. For instance, the rule "opened files must be closed" involves only the events that open and close files, such as `fopen()` and `fclose()` calls. From a verification perspective, paths leading to the same event sequence are equivalent, and only one of them need be checked. (See §2 for an example.) Unfortunately, existing symbolic execution systems are not designed to check rules; they often blindly explore many redundant paths while missing relevant ones that may contain bugs.

Based on our key insight, we create WOODPECKER,[1] a symbolic execution system for effectively checking rules on systems programs. Similar to most previous symbolic execution systems, WOODPECKER emits no false positives, and can record and replay the program path leading to each error it detects. In addition, WOODPECKER allows users to easily check rules by writing custom checkers, and provides a set of builtin checkers to help users bootstrap the checking process. Given a rule, it performs *rule-directed symbolic execution*: instead of blindly exploring all paths, it first statically "peeks" into the paths and then symbolically executes only the paths relevant to the rule, greatly speeding up symbolic execution for both verification and bug detection.

To effectively direct symbolic execution toward a rule, WOODPECKER faces three key algorithmic challenges. First, given a rule, how can WOODPECKER determine what paths are redundant? Second, how can WOODPECKER work with different rules? It would be impractical if each rule requires a different symbolic execution algorithm. Third, how can WOODPECKER integrate with the clever search heuristics in existing symbolic execution systems? These heuristics absorb much dedicated research efforts and can steer checking toward interesting paths (*e.g.*, those more likely to have bugs) when verifying all is not feasible. They have been shown to effectively increase statement coverage and detect errors [12, 13].

WOODPECKER solves these challenges using two ideas: a simple but expressive checker interface and a sound, checker- and heuristic-agnostic search algorithm. A checker implementing the interface provides methods to inform WOODPECKER (1) which executed instructions are events and (2) which static instructions may be events regarding a rule. These methods abstract away the checker details, enabling WOODPECKER's search algorithm to be checker-agnostic.

Once WOODPECKER finishes exploring a path, it uses the checker-provided methods to determine which branches off the path should be pruned. Specifically, if an off-the-path branch cannot (1) affect any event executed in the path or (2) reach any new event not in the path, then it cannot lead to a different event sequence, so WOODPECKER prunes this branch without missing errors. This pruning is heuristic-agnostic because it is done only at the end of a path and does not interfere with the search heuristics otherwise. By pruning irrelevant branches, WOODPECKER can speed up symbolic execution *exponentially* because each pruned branch in principle halves the number of paths to explore.

We have implemented WOODPECKER on top of the LLVM compiler framework [1]. To leverage the powerful search heuristics in existing symbolic execution systems, we carefully integrate WOODPECKER with KLEE [12]. To prune branches, we leverage a modified version of *path slicing* [40] that computes a *slice* of a path containing instructions key for reaching an event sequence [23].

[1] We name our system after the woodpecker bird because this bird finds bugs similarly: it uses its acute hearing to locate wood-boring bugs before hammering into the wood [8].

We also create five checkers, including the *assertion*, *memory leak*, *open-close*, *file access*, and *data loss* checkers, to check the five rules mentioned in the first paragraph of this paper.

We evaluated WOODPECKER on 136 systems programs, totaling 545K lines, including some of the most widely used programs such as file, shell, and text utilities in GNU `coreutils`, user and group management utilities in `shadow`, `tar`, `sed`, `CVS`, and `git`. Our results show that

1. With a time limit of typically just one hour for each verification run, WOODPECKER effectively verifies 111 out of 387 (28.7%) program and rule combinations over bounded input. These verification processes often finish within tens of minutes. In contrast, KLEE verifies only 33 out of 387 (8.5%) combinations.
2. For the remaining combinations, WOODPECKER verifies 4.6 times as many relevant paths as KLEE. This speedup is unsurprising as 86.8% of the paths KLEE explores are redundant.
3. With a longer time limit, WOODPECKER verifies even more relevant paths than KLEE. For instance, WOODPECKER verifies 17 times as many paths as KLEE for `coreutils` within 4 hours.
4. WOODPECKER detects total 113 rule violations. It detects 10 serious data loss errors. Nine of these errors may corrupt source code repositories and the other one may cause new user accounts to have wrong (security) settings. The 2 most serious ones have been confirmed by the corresponding developers.

This paper makes three main contributions. Our first contribution is the rule-directed symbolic execution approach which checks systems rules and uses them to direct symbolic execution. Our second contribution is the WOODPECKER system with a simple yet expressive checker interface, a set of builtin checkers, and a sound, checker- and heuristic-agnostic search algorithm that leverages path slicing to prune redundant paths and speed up symbolic execution. Our last contribution is our experimental evaluation that verifies rules on real-world programs and detects serious errors.

The remainder of this paper is organized as follows. We first show an example (§2) and overview (§3) of WOODPECKER. We describe its checker interface (§4), search algorithm (§5), and builtin checkers (§6). We present its implementation (§7) and evaluation (§8). We finally discuss related work (§9) and conclude (§10).

2. An Example

To illustrate how WOODPECKER works and its key benefits, we show an example in Figure 1. Although simple, this program implements the core functionality of `cat` in GNU `coreutils`. It iterates through the command line arguments, opens each argument as a file, and prints the file to the standard output. If an argument is "`-`" or no argument is present, it reads from the standard input. It converts non-printable characters before printing them (lines 15–17), emulating what "`cat -v`" does.

2.1 Difficulties in Existing Approaches

Suppose we want to automatically verify the open-close rule on this program, *i.e.*, `fopen()` at line 9 and `fclose()` at line 22 always pair up. If this rule is violated, each iteration of the outer loop (lines 5–23) leaks a file pointer, so this program may exhaust all file descriptors on a long list of input files. Fortunately, this rule holds because the true branch of line 21 is taken if and only if the true branch of line 8 is taken. However, automatically verifying this fact using existing approaches can be quite challenging.

Static analysis is not good at computing precise constraints on values, so it may have difficulties computing that the conditions at lines 8 and 21 are, despite their syntactic differences, semantically equivalent. It is not good at precisely tracking where pointers point to either, so it may even have difficulties determining that variable `infile` must point to the same element of `argv` at lines 8 and 21 in the same iteration of the outer loop. Alias analysis is the standard

```
1 : int main(int argc, char **argv) {
2 :   FILE *input_desc;
3 :   int argind = 1;
4 :   const char *infile = "-";
5 :   do { // iterate over input files and print one by one
6 :     if(argind < argc)
7 :       infile = argv[argind];
8 :     if(strcmp(infile, "-")) // input is a file
9 :       input_desc = fopen(infile, "r");
10:     else // input is stdin
11:       input_desc = stdin;
12:     if(!input_desc) continue;
13:     int c;
14:     while((c = fgetc(input_desc)) != EOF) {
15:       if(c < 32 && c != '\n') { // non-printable char
16:         putchar('^');
17:         putchar(c + 64);
18:       } else // printable char
19:         putchar(c);
20:     }
21:     if(infile[0] != '-' || infile[1] != 0)
22:       fclose(input_desc); // input is a file
23:   } while (++argind < argc);
24:   return 0;
25: }
```

Figure 1: *A simple program based on* `cat` *from* `coreutils`.

method to compute whether two pointers point to the same location, but it often collapses results from multiple loop iterations into one, especially when the loop bound cannot be statically determined, such as this outer loop. It may thus imprecisely compute that `infile` may point to different locations at lines 8 and 21. Due to these difficulties, static analysis may conservatively consider lines 8, 9, 21, and 23 a feasible path fragment and lines 8, 11, 21, and 22 another one, emitting false positives that require manual inspection.

Symbolic execution avoids false positives by exploring only feasible paths, but it faces another difficult challenge of path explosion. Consider the program in Figure 1. Although simple, it may still have too many paths for symbolic execution to completely explore, even if we bound the input to be small. In particular, the symbolic branch instruction at line 15 doubles the number of paths for each input byte.

We ran KLEE on this program with a small input bound: three command line arguments, each with two bytes, and two files, each with eight bytes. Although KLEE explored 698,116 paths[2] in an hour, it unsurprisingly did not explore all paths. Worse, of all the paths it explored, 99.84% are redundant regarding the rule. For instance, all paths forked at lines 14 and 15 are redundant to each other because they affect neither `fopen` nor `fclose` operations, so only one of them need be checked.

2.2 Bounded Verification with WOODPECKER

Since WOODPECKER already comes with an open-close checker, users simply specify this checker to check the rule. To check new rules, users can write their own checkers. To prepare the program in Figure 1, users compile it to *bitcode*, the well-defined, easy-to-analyze RISC-like LLVM assembly code [1]. Users then specify the symbolic input and start checking. For instance, they can mark command line arguments and input files symbolic, and specify their maximum sizes.

[2] Since KLEE works on LLVM assembly programs with `Libc` linked in, it sees much more paths than static analysis.

```
3:        argind = 1;
4:        infile = "-";
6:true    argind < argc
7:        infile = argv[argind];
8:true    strcmp(infile, "-")
9:        input_desc = fopen(infile);
12:       if(input_desk) continue;
14:true   (c=fgetc(input_desc)) != EOF
15:false  c<32 && c!= '\n'
19:       putchar(c);
14:false  (c=fgetc(input_desc)) != EOF
21:true   infile[0]!='-' || infile[1] != 0
22:       fclose(input_desc);
23:false  ++argind < argc
24:       return 0;
```

Figure 2: *A path explored by* WOODPECKER *and its pruning results.* Each executed instruction is tagged with its static line number. Branch instructions are also tagged with their outcome (true or false). Events (green) concerning the rule are the `fopen()` and `fclose()` calls tagged with 9 and 22. Crossed-out (gray) instructions are elided from the slice, so their off-the-path branches are not explored by WOODPECKER. Only the off-the-path branches of lines 6, 8, and 23 (italic, blue), are explored by WOODPECKER.

To explore paths, WOODPECKER conceptually forks executions upon a symbolic branch instruction with both branches allowed by the current constraints. For instance, it forks executions when it first executes lines 6, 8, 14, 15, and 23. It does not fork at line 21 because the constraints collected from line 8 makes only one branch of line 21 feasible. By exploring only feasible paths, WOODPECKER avoids emitting false positives.

Given all forked paths, WOODPECKER can prioritize how they are explored using various heuristics. To leverage existing heuristics, we have carefully integrated it with KLEE. We will describe this integration and WOODPECKER's search algorithm in §5; in the remainder of this section we illustrate how WOODPECKER prunes redundant paths using our example.[3]

WOODPECKER prunes redundant paths when it finishes exploring a path. Suppose it explores a path as shown in Figure 2. (The paths explored depend on the heuristic used.) As discussed in the previous subsection, without directing symbolic execution with the rule, KLEE would have to explore the off-the-path branches at lines 14 and 15. Fortunately, WOODPECKER prunes these branches because it determines that they have no effect on the event sequence (lines 9 and 22) in this path.

To do so, WOODPECKER leverages a previous *path slicing* algorithm that computes a *slice* that captures instructions key to reach the exact event sequence in a path [23]. The resultant slice contains the instructions not crossed out in Figure 2. It includes the events (9 and 22) and all instructions that the events transitively control- or data-depend upon. For instance, it includes 8:true because if the false branch is taken, the execution will not reach 9; it includes 7, 6:true, 4, and 3 because they set the `infile` used by 8:true. It includes 23:false because if the true branch is taken, the execution will reach new instances of `fopen()` and `fclose()` calls. It excludes all instructions in the inner loop (lines 14–20) and the return instruction (line 24) because they do not affect the event sequence. WOODPECKER then explores only the off-the-path branches included in the slice, and prunes the other ones, *i.e.*, those at lines 14 and 15.

[3] For clarity, this paper presents WOODPECKER's algorithm at the source level, instead of the bitcode level.

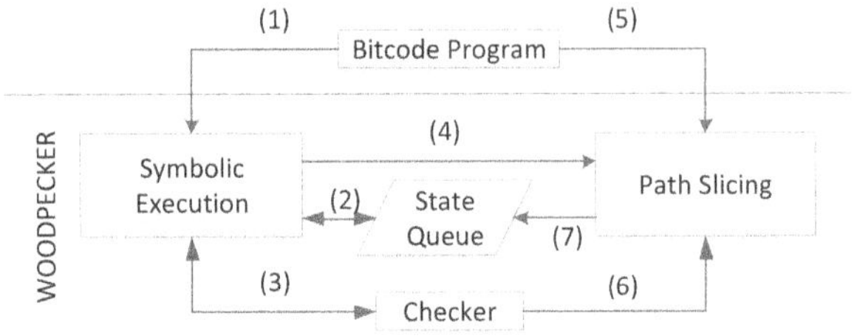

Figure 3: WOODPECKER *architecture.*

We ran WOODPECKER on this example with the same input bound as KLEE. WOODPECKER completely explored all 1,802 paths that may lead to different event sequences, verifying that our example has no open-close errors over the bounded input. This verification process took only 212.7 seconds. We observed similar benefits of WOODPECKER on the real programs evaluated (§8).

3. WOODPECKER Overview

Figure 3 shows WOODPECKER's architecture. We explain this architecture as well as how the components interact; the numbered labels in the figure correspond to the numbers in the list below

(1) WOODPECKER checks programs in bitcode, the LLVM assembly language [1]. Given a bitcode program, WOODPECKER invokes KLEE to execute (more precisely, interpret) bitcode instructions.
(2) If executing one instruction (*e.g.*, a symbolic branch instruction) on a program state leads to new states, WOODPECKER adds them to the *state queue* for future exploration.
(3) It passes the executed instruction and its operands to the checker for errors.
(4) If the instruction executed is at the end of a path, WOODPECKER applies path slicing to compute redundant branches that do not affect the event sequence in the path.
(5) As part of the computation to determine if a branch is redundant, WOODPECKER statically visits the off-the-path instructions a branch may reach.
(6) For each instruction visited, it queries the checker to determine whether the instruction may be an event.
(7) Given the redundant branches, it searches a *branch tree* (§5) to find the corresponding states forked from the branches, and removes the states from the queue.

WOODPECKER then removes a state from the state queue and repeats these steps until it explores all paths or reaches a given time limit. This process essentially implements WOODPECKER's search algorithm (§5) with steps (3) and (6) invoking the checker through the checker interface (§4).

Assumptions. WOODPECKER often effectively prunes paths for rules involving a small number of events. Most systems rules, including all the rules we check, have this property. If a rule involves many instructions such as all load instructions, WOODPECKER may not be as effective.

WOODPECKER's effectiveness may also depend on specific search heuristics and programs. For instance, if all program paths are of the same length, depth-first search may work better because it reaches the end of a path and triggers pruning sooner. If some program paths are very short, breadth-first search may work better because it reaches the end of a short path sooner. We explicitly designed WOODPECKER to give users flexibility to choose heuristics.

Our current design of WOODPECKER checks one rule at a time because our anecdotal experience with statically checking system rules is that developers often prefer to focus on one type of bug before context-switching to a different type. WOODPECKER can be extended to check multiple rules simultaneously, to further amortize the cost of symbolic execution. However, WOODPECKER's path slicing needs to be modified so that events from different rules are analyzed separately. We leave this for future work.

```
class Checker {
  // Clones internal checker state.
  Checker *Clone();

  // Called by WOODPECKER after it executes instruction ki.
  // struct KInstruction contains instruction operands.
  // Returns false if an error is detected, and true otherwise.
  // s is program state after ki is executed.
  // evmask outputs whether the instruction is an event and,
  // if so, what operands matter.
  bool OnExecution(const ExecutionState *s,
                   const KInstruction *ki, Bitmask& evmask);

  // Called by WOODPECKER to check
  // whether a static instruction may be an event.
  bool MayBeEvent(const Instruction *i);
};
```

Figure 4: *The* WOODPECKER *checker interface.*

At the implementation level, WOODPECKER requires bitcode or source (so we can compile it to bitcode) programs. WOODPECKER aborts a path upon inline x86 assembly or a call to an external function it does not know. For soundness, developers have to lift x86 assembly to bitcode and provide summaries for external functions. (The external function problem is alleviated because KLEE links in a `Libc` implementation.) Moreover, the underlying components that WOODPECKER leverages make assumptions as well. For instance, KLEE requires constraint solving, which can be quite expensive and sometimes intractable. Path slicing requires alias analysis, and the one used in WOODPECKER makes several assumptions [6]; a "sounder" alias analysis [35] would remove these assumptions. Our slicing is conservative: it never marks a relevant branch as redundant, but it may mark redundant branches as relevant [23].

Although WOODPECKER is similarly limited by its underlying components such as KLEE, the general ideas in WOODPECKER can benefit other symbolic execution systems. For instance, it can be combined with systems such as S2E [13] and its search techniques [9, 43] to soundly reduce the number of paths to explore.

4. Checker Interface

Figure 4 shows WOODPECKER's checker interface. It consists of three key methods. The `Clone` method clones a checker's internal state. Whenever WOODPECKER clones a program state for later exploration, it also clones the checker state, so that the program and checker states are always consistent.

WOODPECKER calls `OnExecution` after executing each instruction. This method does three things. First, it updates the internal state of the checker. For instance, if the instruction is a call `fp = fopen()`, the open-close checker updates its internal state to map file pointer `fp` to the opened state. Second, this method detects whether the executed instruction causes an error. If so, it returns false, so WOODPECKER can invoke KLEE to generate a testcase that reproduces the error. Lastly, this method outputs variable `evmask`, which indicates whether the executed instruction is an event. This information helps WOODPECKER compute relevant branches (§5).

Variable `evmask` is a bitmask instead of a boolean flag because `OnExecution` also uses it to indicate which operands matter to the checked rule. If an operand does not matter, WOODPECKER does not include instructions affecting it in the slice. For instance,

Algorithm 1: WOODPECKER's search algorithm

```
  Input : program prog, initial state s0, checker checker
  Global: state queue q, branch tree brtree
  RuleDirectedSE(prog, s0, checker)
      q.add(⟨s0, prog.entry⟩)
      while q not empty and time limit not reached do
          ⟨s, i⟩ ← q.remove()
          if i is not a symbolic branch statement or only one branch
          is feasible then
              ⟨s′, i′⟩ ← run(s, i)
              HandleNewState(s, i, s′, i′, checker)
          else // fork states and add constraints
              s_true ← s + {i.cond = true}
              s_false ← s + {i.cond = false}
*             brtree.add(i, s_true, s_false)
              HandleNewState(s, i, s_true, i.true_br, checker)
              HandleNewState(s, i, s_false, i.false_br, checker)
  HandleNewState(s, i, s′, i′, checker) // Note: s′ is updated
*     if not checker.OnExecution(s, i, evmask) then
*         return // error detected!
*     s′.path.push_back(i)
*     if evmask ≠ 0 then
*         s′.events.push_back(⟨i, evmask⟩)
      if s′ is not end of path then q.add(⟨s′, i′⟩)
*     else Prune(s′, checker) // s′ is end of path
  Prune(s, checker)
      slice ← Slice(s.path, s.events, checker)
      foreach symbolic branch i in s.path but not in slice do
          br ← branch of i not executed in s.path
          pruned ← brtree.find_states(br)
          q.remove(pruned)
      brtree.remove(s)  // because s is end of path
  Slice(path, events, checker)
      slice ← empty sequence
      for i ∈ reverse(path) do
          if any e ∈ events transitively depends on i then
              slice.push_front(i)
          else if i is a branch instruction then
              for j ∈ instructions i reaches off path do
                  if checker.MayBeEvent(j) then
                      slice.push_front(i)
                      break
      return slice
```

consider the open-close checker. The arguments to `fopen()` do not matter, whereas the argument to `fclose()` does. Implementation-wise, the most significant bit of `evmask` indicates whether the instruction is an event, and the ith bit indicates whether the ith operand matters. (We show an example on how WOODPECKER uses `evmask` in §5.)

WOODPECKER calls `MayBeEvent` to check whether a static instruction, if executed, may be an event of the checked rule. WOODPECKER uses this information to compute which branches may lead to new events (§5).

5. Search Algorithm

This section describes WOODPECKER's checker- and heuristic-agnostic search algorithm (Algorithm 1) and how it integrates with existing search heuristics.

Functions `RuleDirectedSE` and `HandleNewState` together without the starred lines implement a typical search process in existing symbolic execution systems and model checkers. This search process maintains a queue of program state and instruction-to-execute pairs, initialized to contain the initial state and the program entry. It removes a state and instruction pair from the queue, executes the instruction on the state, adds the resultant states to the queue, and repeats until the state queue is empty or a time limit is reached. Different search heuristics can be implemented by varying the order in which states are added to or removed from the queue. For instance, depth-first search would remove the state last added, and breadth-first search would remove the state first added.

The starred lines and the additional functions `Prune` and `Slice` together give WOODPECKER the power of checking rules and pruning redundant paths without restricting search heuristics. This additional code does four things. First, in `HandleNewState`, it calls the checker's `OnExecution` to check for rule violations and set `evmask` (§4).

Second, it maintains a program path and an event sequence in the resultant state s', later used by `Prune` to prune redundant states. Specifically, it appends each executed instruction to the `path` field of s'. It appends the instruction to the `events` field of s' if `evmask` is nonzero, *i.e.*, the instruction is an event.

Third, whenever WOODPECKER reaches the end of a program path, it calls `Prune` to remove redundant states from the queue. `Prune` first calls `Slice` to compute from the current path a *slice* that, if preserved, guarantees the same event sequence. If a symbolic branch instruction is in the path but not the slice, taking either of its branches should lead to the same event sequence, so WOODPECKER prunes the states reached from the off-the-path branch.

Fourth, to find the states reached from a branch, WOODPECKER uses a *branch tree* to track forked branches and states on the queue. The leaf nodes of this tree are all states to explore, and the internal nodes are all branch instructions. At each fork, WOODPECKER replaces the node representing the current state with a node representing the branch instruction, and adds the two forked states as two child nodes. At the end of a path, WOODPECKER removes the node representing the current state from the tree, as well as its parents if they become childless. To find states given a branch *br*, function `find_states` simply returns the leaf nodes in the subtree rooted from *br*. The subtree rooted from *br* may have more than one states because the search heuristic may first probe *br* and its child states without reaching the end of a path, and then switch to explore *br*'s sibling branch to the end of a path.

Function `Slice` implements an improved version of *path slicing* [40]. Given a trace of instructions and a target instruction in the trace, path slicing traverses the trace backwards and computes a slice capturing the instructions sufficient for the execution to reach the target. Intuitively, these instructions include "branches whose outcome matters" to reach the target and "mutations that affect the outcome of those branches" [21]. For instance, it takes a branch instruction into the slice if the instruction's off-the-path branch may cause the execution not to reach the target. The resultant slice includes all instructions that the target transitively control- and data-depends upon.

`Slice` improves the original version of path slicing in two ways. First, it slices toward a sequence of instructions, not just one instruction, to capture instructions that guarantee the same event sequence. Operationally, `Slice` captures a branch instruction into the slice if the off-the-path branch of this instruction may reach new events and thus alter the event sequence. (See our previous work [23] for more details.) Second, `Slice` uses the `evmask` values returned by `OnExecution` (§4) to compute a more precise slice. To illustrate, consider the code snippet below:

```
char *filename;
if(*)
    filename = "A";
else
    filename = "B";
FILE *fp = fopen(filename, "r");
```

Suppose fopen is an event and we are given a path 2:true, 3, and 6. If at line 6, the returned evmask indicates that no operands of fopen are important, then Slice does not take any instructions between lines 1–5. However, if evmask indicates that operand filename is also important, Slice takes 2:true and 3.

Discussion. Algorithm 1 is checker-agnostic because all checker details are abstracted behind the checker interface. It is also heuristic-agnostic because it prunes states only at the end of a program path, and does not dictate how states should be added to or removed from the queue. Thus, this algorithm enables WOODPECKER to work with any checker and any heuristic. Moreover, this algorithm is sound because it never prunes a branch that may lead to a different event sequence, guaranteed by Slice.

6. Checkers

WOODPECKER's checking interface enables users to write their own checkers. To bootstrap checking, WOODPECKER also provides a set of builtin checkers, described in this section.

The *assertion checker* is the simplest builtin checker. It checks that the assert() statements never fail. Although existing symbolic execution systems such as KLEE can already check assertions, WOODPECKER can use them to direct checking toward only the paths that may trigger the assertions, thus enjoying large speedup (§8). Implementing this checker is extremely easy because assert is macro-expanded down to an if-statement and a call to assert_failed(), so this checker considers only assert_failed() calls events.

The *memory leak checker* checks that (1) every heap-allocated object is freed and (2) freed memory is not freed again. It tracks memory allocators malloc, calloc, realloc, strdup, strndup, and getline, and deallocators free and realloc. Function getline allocates memory if its first argument points to NULL. Function realloc allocates memory if its pointer argument is NULL and its size argument is greater than 0; it frees memory if its pointer argument is not NULL and its size argument is 0; or it both allocates and frees memory otherwise from this checker's perspective. Tracking these nuances is made easy because WOODPECKER does run code.[4]

The *open-close checker* checks that (1) an opened file is always closed and (2) a closed file is not closed again. It tracks fopen, fopen64, and fdopen for opening and fclose for closing files.

The *file access checker* checks that (1) file read or write operations are done on opened files and (2) no file read or write operations are done on a file with errors (after ferror() returns nonzero). In addition to the open and close file operations, it also tracks nine file access operations, such as fread, fwrite, fgets, and fputs and two error-checking operations ferror() and ferror_unlocked().

The *data loss checker* checks for problematic sequences of file operations that may cause data loss. Although a POSIX-conforming rename guarantees atomic replacement of the destination link despite failures, it does not guarantee anything about file data. Thus, the source must be flushed and synced before the rename so that a crash would not make the destination point to incomplete data [55, 63]. Moreover, prior to this rename, the destination should not be unlinked or renamed so that a crash would not lose the destination link. Figure 5 illustrates these rules. The rename checker tracks 19 file system operations, such as the ones shown in Figure 5. Specifically, it checks that (1) a file is properly flushed (via fflush) and synced (via fsync, sync, or fdatasync) before it is renamed (via rename) to a destination link; (2) the destination link is not unlinked (via unlink, rmdir, or rename) before the rename; and (3) a file descriptor is not closed via close if it is associated with a FILE object.[5]

```
fp = fopen("src", "w");
fwrite(fp, ...)
fflush(fp); // must flush data from Libc to OS
fd = fileno(fp);
fsync(fd); // must sync data from OS to disk
fclose(fd);
// unlink("dst"); ERROR! shouldn't remove dst
// rename("dst", "bak"); ERROR! shouldn't remove dst
rename("src", "dst");
```

Figure 5: *How to atomically rename a file to avoid data loss.*

Additional support for checkers. WOODPECKER provides three additional mechanisms to help user write checkers. First, it provides an alias analysis (§7) for checkers to resolve function pointers in MayBeEvent. If an instruction passed to MayBeEvent is an indirect call, MayBeEvent can use this analysis to resolve possible call targets. This mechanism is used in all our checkers.

Second, WOODPECKER provides a default mechanism to suppress redundant error reports. The same error may occur along multiple program paths, leading to redundant reports. Given a sequence of events in an error report, WOODPECKER hashes all these events and their call stacks, and filters future reports with an identical hash, improving diagnosis experience. This mechanism is used in our memory leak and open-close checkers because they often emit many reports.

Third, WOODPECKER allows a checker to concretize symbolic data. The instruction operands passed to OnExecution may be symbolic. For instance, the data loss checker may see symbolic file names in rename. Although a checker can track the checker-relevant status of symbolic data, the implementation would be quite complex because it has to track advanced constraints. Instead, WOODPECKER allows a checker to selectively concretize symbolic data into a constant allowed by the constraints. A checker should do so only on the operands it cares about. This mechanism is used only by the data loss checker on the rename operands.

7. Implementation

We have implemented WOODPECKER on top of the LLVM compiler [1] and the KLEE symbolic execution system [12]. We reimplemented a previous path slicing algorithm [23]. Our implementation consists of 10,328 lines of code, including 2,968 lines of modifications to KLEE, 5,771 lines of code for path slicing, and 1,589 lines of code for the builtin checkers. The lines of code for each individual checker are show in Table 1.

In the remainder of this section, we discuss several implementation issues, two on modeling the environment for symbolic execution and three on improving the precision and speed of path slicing.

7.1 Modeling the File System

Most of the systems programs we check need to interact with the file system. Although KLEE already comes with a symbolic file system implementation that supports fake in-memory files with symbolic data, this file system has three limitations, preventing us from checking some rules and programs. First, KLEE does not track

[4] An alternative leak checker implementation is to modify KLEE because it already tracks memory objects, but these modifications must (1) track whether each memory object is allocated by the application or library code because we want to report only application leaks; and (2) maintain diagnosis information such as the call stacks. We rejected this design because these modifications are too checker-specific.

[5] Libc function fileno allows developers to get the file descriptor from a FILE object as illustrated in Figure 5.

the modifications to the real files with concrete data on disk. Thus, when it restores a program state to explore, it may see the old on-disk file system state, inconsistent with the restored program state. Second, KLEE supports only a small set of file operations with its symbolic file system; operations such as `link`, `rename`, and `chdir` are not supported. Lastly, a relative minor issue is that KLEE restricts the names of symbolic files to be A, B, ..., and Z, and no other files can be symbolic.

WOODPECKER solves these issues with a new in-memory file system layer that implements copy-on-write on a real file system, similar to `unionfs` [51]. If a concrete file is never written along a program path, WOODPECKER directs all reads to the file on disk. If the file is ever written, WOODPECKER creates an in-memory copy of the file private to the current program state, and directs all future reads and writes to this private copy. This file system supports more operations than KLEE's, such as `link`, `rename`, and `chdir`. It also allows users to mark arbitrary files as symbolic if the file names match user-given patterns. For instance, users can mark all `git` internal files as symbolic with the "`.git/*`" pattern.

7.2 Modeling `mmap`

Several programs we check allocate memory or read file data by calling `mmap`, which KLEE does not handle: it simply returns `EPERM` on `mmap`. One solution is to pass `mmap` calls to the underlying operating system, but this solution is still problematic because the memory allocated by the operating system's `mmap` is not saved and restored with the program state. WOODPECKER solves this problem by re-implementing `mmap` to allocate memory using KLEE's `malloc`. Our implementation currently handles two `mmap` modes: `MAP_PRIVATE` and `MAP_ANONYMOUS` because the other two modes, `MAP_SHARED` and `MAP_FIXED`, are not used in the programs we check. (Adding them is easy.)

7.3 Summarizing Functions

Users can improve WOODPECKER by providing two types of function summaries. First, to track data dependencies, path slicing needs to know what memory locations an external function may read or write. For instance, given a branch instruction that matters to reach an event, if its outcome depends on a value written by an external function, then the corresponding call must be included in the slice. For speed, we also summarize several popular `Libc` functions already linked in by KLEE, such as `memcpy`. These functions are frequently called, and their execution may contain a large number of instructions, so iterating over all these instructions for slicing may take long. In total, we summarize 22 `Libc` or external functions.

Second, to track dependencies between instructions, our slicing algorithm frequently queries alias analysis. The particular one we used is `bddbddb` [6, 58, 59]. For better alias results, `bddbddb` needs to know custom memory allocators, deallocators, and copiers such as `memcpy`. In total, we summarize 43 such functions.

7.4 Limiting Context Sensitivity

For precision, `bddbddb`'s alias analysis distinguishes alias results for different call graph paths, or *contexts*. In programming language terms, this analysis is *context-sensitive*. To gain context sensitivity, `bddbddb` conceptually creates a unique function clone for each possible context to the function. To efficiently store these function clones and contexts, `bddbddb` uses an advanced data structure called the binary decision diagrams [46], which often store large data sets compactly. Despite so, this cloning may explode for large programs with complex call graphs, such as `git`. Moreover, when there are many contexts, computing the alias results also takes long.

We worked around context explosion using two techniques. First, we modified `bddbddb` to limit the maximum number of function clones. If this limit is ever reached, our modified `bddbddb` stops creating function clones. Although in theory this approach may cause some precision loss because results of some contexts are merged together, in practice the maximum number of function clones is already large enough to yield precise results. We used this workaround only for `git`. Second, we replaced a few indirect calls in the evaluated programs with direct calls. If a function pointer has many call sites and may point to several functions, it may explode the contexts because each call site and possible function target combination leads to a function clone. In many cases, though, the function pointer has only one target, but `bddbddb` cannot infer this fact. We thus modified 23 lines in `shadow`, 10 in `tar`, and 17 in `git` to replace frequent indirect calls with direct calls.

7.5 Caching Analysis Results

For speed, WOODPECKER caches static analysis results extensively. For instance, it caches alias results. It also caches the results from a checker's `MayBeEvent` because whether a static instruction is an event does not change during symbolic execution.

8. Evaluation

We evaluated WOODPECKER on total 136 widely used systems programs, including 96 programs in GNU `coreutils` version 8.12, a basic file, shell, and text manipulation utilities suite [20]; 30 programs in `shadow` 4.1.5, a user and group management utilities suite [54]; `tar` 1.26, an archival program [56]; `sed` 4.2.1, a text stream transformation program [31]; `CVS` 1.11.23, a version control program [24]; and seven programs from `git` 1.7.9.4, another version control program [30]. We chose the latest stable version of each program at the time of experiment. We excluded `printf`, `md5sum`, and `date` from `coreutils` and `sulogin`, `chfn`, and `gpasswd` from `shadow` because they caused aborts either in WOODPECKER, KLEE, or STP (KLEE's underlying constraint solver [2, 28]). For example, a floating point constraint generated by `printf` likely caused STP to crash.

We compiled all programs to LLVM bitcode using LLVM `gcc`-2.7 with `-O2` or `-O3`. We ran all experiments on four 2.8 Ghz dual-socket hexa-core Intel Xeon X5660 machines with 64 GB memory and Linux 2.6.38. To fully use the available cores, we ran roughly ten experiments concurrently on each machine. We observed little interference between concurrent experiments because symbolic execution is mostly CPU bound.

In addition to measuring WOODPECKER's verification results, we also compared it with KLEE, a state of the art symbolic execution system. For both WOODPECKER and KLEE experiments, we used the same settings as the ones used by the KLEE authors [12] whenever applicable. Some settings were removed from the open source version of KLEE, so we reimplemented them with the help from a KLEE author [10]. We adjusted some settings because some programs we evaluated are different, sometimes much larger.

Specifically, we used up to three two-byte symbolic command line arguments for `coreutils` and `shadow`, and four eight-byte arguments for other programs. We added a concrete username argument for most programs in `shadow` to match their expectations. We used five 200-byte symbolic files for `tar` because it requires large file headers, and two eight-byte files for all the other programs. We also marked the configuration files symbolic for `CVS` and `git` because these version control programs run different paths based on different configurations. Since exploring all paths may take forever, we bounded each experiment for one hour for `coreutils` and `shadow`, three hours for `git`, and twelve hours for all other programs. In many experiments, WOODPECKER verified all paths within minutes; see §8.1. Since the results may depend on search heuristics, we chose the same heuristics that yielded the best results for KLEE [12]. (We also experimented with depth-first search but it

Checkers	Lines of Code	Programs Checked	Programs Verified		Relevant Paths Verified		Redundant Paths	
			WOODPECKER	KLEE	WOODPECKER	KLEE	WOODPECKER	KLEE
Assertion	102	57	13	3	195,268	45,763	69,795	195,178
Memory leak	399	103	32	7	1,024,676	176,475	451,836	1,657,721
Open-close	211	72	19	4	528,676	82,883	203,407	512,439
File access	344	120	40	12	1,694,393	377,181	496,651	2,141,111
Data loss	533	35	7	7	132,136	89,779	22,996	117,225
Total	1,589	387	111	33	3,575,149	772,081	1,244,685	4,623,674

Table 1: *Summary of verification results.*

caused KLEE to cover much fewer statements. Thus, we exclude depth-first search results from this section.)

The following subsections focus on

§8.1: Can WOODPECKER effectively verify many or all relevant paths over bounded input? Can it outperform KLEE significantly in this regard?

§8.2: Can WOODPECKER effectively detect rule violations? WOODPECKER can also be used as an error detector in addition to a verifier.

§8.3: Is it costly to compute what branches to prune? This cost must be smaller than the time it takes to actually explore the branches.

8.1 Verification Results

Table 1 summarizes the verification results. The number of programs checked by each checker is smaller than the total number of programs evaluated because we excluded trivially verifiable programs, *i.e.*, those with no events regarding a rule. The table shows the number of programs verified over bounded input for both WOODPECKER and KLEE. WOODPECKER verifies 111 out of 387 (28.7%) program and rule combinations over bounded input. KLEE verifies only 33 (8.5%) combinations. WOODPECKER's verification experiments often finished quickly, within tens of minutes (not shown in the table).

For the other 276 programs, Table 1 shows the number of relevant paths verified. Overall, WOODPECKER verifies 4.6 times as many relevant paths as KLEE. This speedup is unsurprising because 86.8% of the paths KLEE explores are redundant (see detailed results below). The table also shows the number of redundant paths pruned by WOODPECKER or explored by KLEE. Although WOODPECKER prunes redundant paths, they are already forked, which means that WOODPECKER has already queried the constraint solver to determine whether the corresponding branches are feasible. Since constraint solving is the most costly for WOODPECKER (and likely any symbolic execution system), we count the number of pruned paths as wasted work done by WOODPECKER. The real benefit of pruning is that it prevents future forks from the pruned paths. As shown in the table, KLEE explores 3.7 times as many redundant paths as WOODPECKER prunes. Note that it hugely favors KLEE to compare the amount of wasted work by the number of redundant paths because KLEE fully explores them whereas WOODPECKER does not.

We observed that, with a longer time limit, WOODPECKER verified much more paths than KLEE's. The reason is that initially

Time Limit	Programs Verified			Paths Verified		
	W	K	W- K	W	K	W/K
1 hour	73	7	67	2,776,499	532,222	5.2
2 hours	104	31	73	6,933,817	662,558	10.5
4 hours	112	39	73	14,437,294	847,621	17.0

Table 2: *With a longer time limit,* WOODPECKER *verified much more paths than* KLEE. W represents WOODPECKER's results and K KLEE's, both obtained from `coreutils`.

KLEE may hit some relevant paths by chance, but over time it gets stuck exploring redundant paths nearby. Table 2 shows the results with the time limit set to one, two, and four hours for **`coreutils`**. With a one-hour limit, WOODPECKER verified 5.2 times as many paths as KLEE. With a four-hour limit, WOODPECKER verified 17.0 times as many. This big increase is unsurprising because WOODPECKER exponentially speeds up symbolic execution. We observed similar results (not shown) with a larger input bound.

To evaluate how directed WOODPECKER is, we define *search efficiency* as the percentage of relevant paths explored over all paths ever forked. We use this metric only on the programs with a subset of paths verified because WOODPECKER finished quickly on the verified programs. From the data in Table 1, we can compute that WOODPECKER's average search efficiency is 64.9% whereas KLEE's is 29.2%, a 35.7% difference.

This difference is even larger on each individual program. Figure 6–10 show the search efficiency for each program and checker. The top subfigure show results for WOODPECKER, and the bottom KLEE. The solid or hatched portion of each bar shows the search efficiency, with solid meaning all relevant paths verified. The white portion shows roughly the amount of wasted work. The more solid bars in a figure, the more programs are verified. The larger the solid or hatched portion and the smaller the white portion in a bar, the less work is wasted. We identified whether a path KLEE explored was relevant or redundant by running WOODPECKER's search algorithm together with KLEE without actually pruning paths. Over all programs and checkers, WOODPECKER's median search efficiency is 62.9% whereas KLEE's is 16.7%, a 46.2% difference.

8.2 Rule Violations Detected

Table 3 shows the rule violations detected, broken down by checkers and programs. WOODPECKER detected many memory leaks and unclosed file pointers in the checked programs. A common pattern is that these programs allocate memory or open files, but exit without freeing these resources if some failure occurs. This pattern is considered bad programming practice at least. Worse, they may also have security implications because previous work [15, 16] has shown that leaked memory or file pointers may needlessly extend sensitive data lifetime, posing privacy risks. Some of the detected errors are already fixed in the latest version of the program, illustrating developers' concerns over these errors. (To avoid inflating our bug counts, we did not include these fixed errors in the table.)

Programs	mem leak	open-close	data loss
`coreutils`	40	13	0
`shadow`	11	5	1
`tar`	4	0	0
`sed`	3	0	0
`CVS`	3	1	2
`git`	19	4	7
Total	80	23	10

Table 3: *Number of rule violations detected.* The assertion and file access checkers are not listed because they detected no violations.

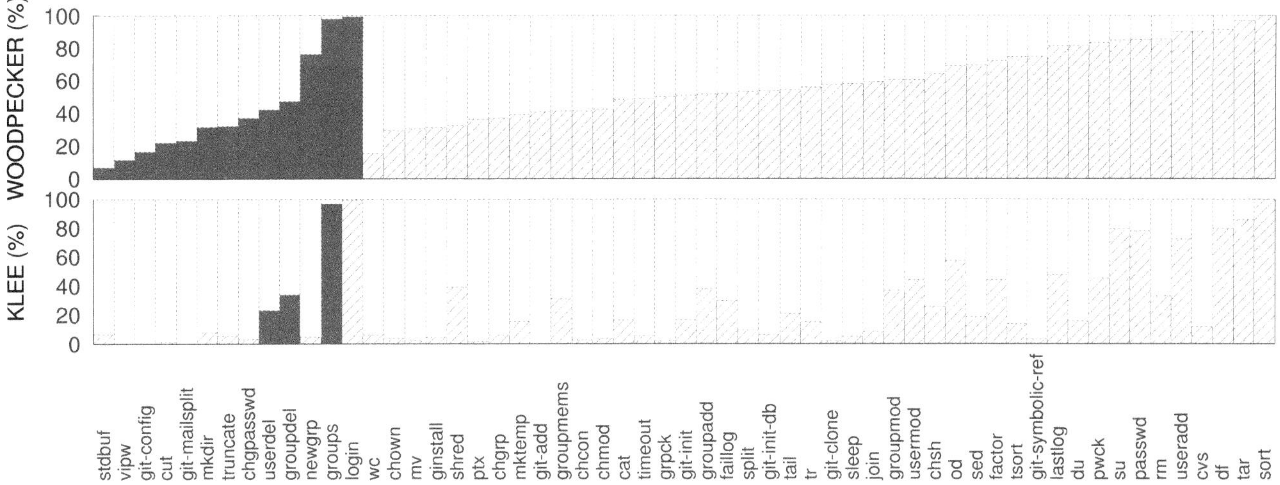

Figure 6: *Search efficiency with the assertion checker.* The top subfigure show results for WOODPECKER, and the bottom KLEE. The solid or hatched portion of each bar shows the search efficiency, with solid meaning all relevant paths verified. The white portion shows the amount of wasted work. The more solid bars in a figure, the more programs are verified. The larger the solid or hatched portion and the smaller the white portion in a bar, the less work is wasted. WOODPECKER's median search efficiency of the hatched bars is 56.8%, whereas KLEE's is only 16.2%.

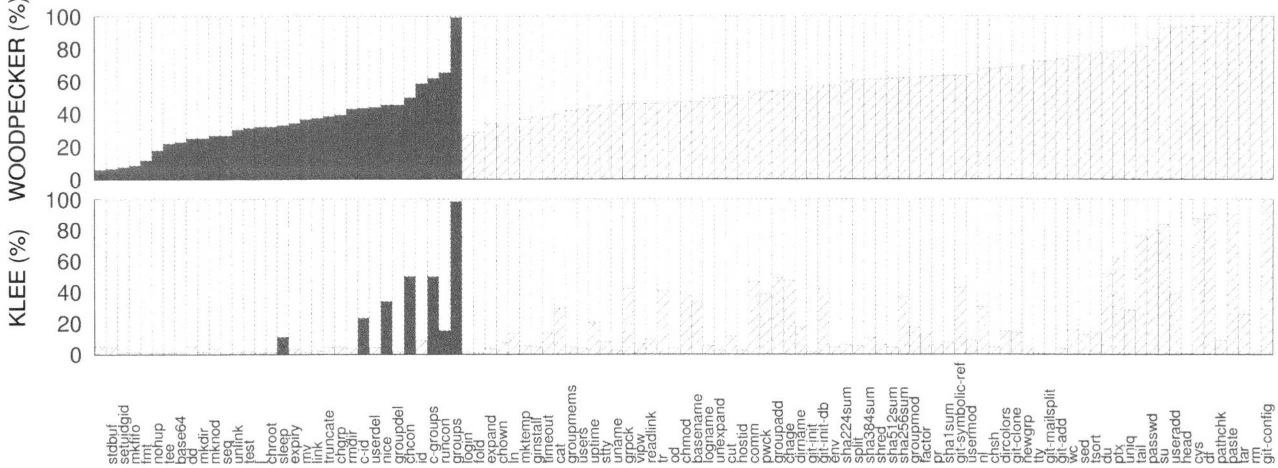

Figure 7: *Search efficiency with the memory leak checker.* WOODPECKER's median search efficiency of the hatched bars is 61.3%, whereas KLEE's is 12.7%.

There are two more-serious open-close errors detected in `git` and `CVS`. The `git mailsplit` command iterates through a list of mbox files and splits each into individual email files. Its `split_mbox` function opens a mbox file, but does not close the file if it reaches the end of the file before a newline. Thus, file descriptors may be exhausted with a long list of such files. The `CVS` function `parse_config` returns without closing a configuration file if there is any syntax error. This function is also called for each authentication or `Root` request in `CVS` server mode, potentially exhausting file descriptors.

WOODPECKER also detected ten serious data loss errors, seven in `git`, two in `CVS`, and one in `shadow`. These programs often deal with crucial files such as source code or `/etc` configurations, so they are extremely careful with file writes. They do not update files in place because a crash may leave a partially updated file. Instead, they create temporary files, and then sync and atomically rename them. Despite so, WOODPECKER still finds serious errors in them.

The seven `git` errors may all corrupt source repositories. They share the same pattern. To commit changes, users first run a series of "`git add`" to add the new or modified files to an *index*, and then commit the index. This index is stored in file `.git/index`. When "`git add`" is called, `git` carefully creates a temporary file `.git/index.lock` to store the new index, and then renames it to `.git/index`. Unfortunately, `git` does not call `fsync` on the temporary file, so a crash can still corrupt the index, which further corrupts the repository if committed. This error pattern has been confirmed by the `git` developers. The two `CVS` errors are similar.

The `shadow` data loss error WOODPECKER detected may cause new user accounts to have wrong settings such as wrong home directory locations, account expiration dates, and maximum numbers of inactive days. The defaults of these settings are stored in `/etc/default/useradd`, which `useradd` in `shadow` updates. However, when updating this file, `useradd` first renames `/etc/default/useradd` to a backup file, before renaming the

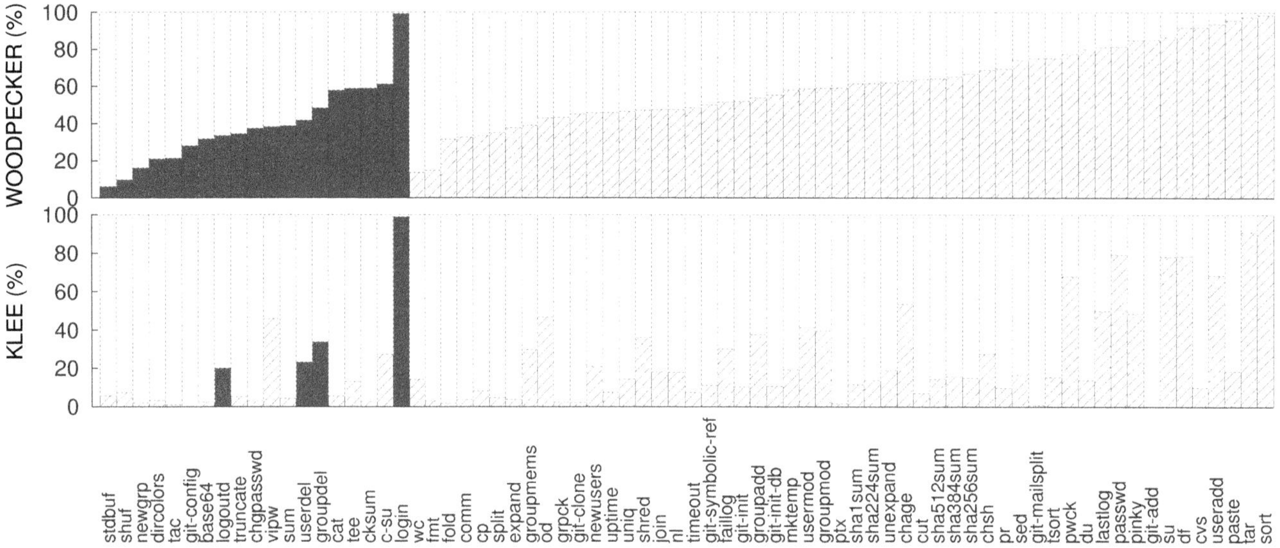

Figure 8: *Search efficiency with the open-close checker.* WOODPECKER's median search efficiency of the hatched bars is 59.2%, whereas KLEE's is 15.3%.

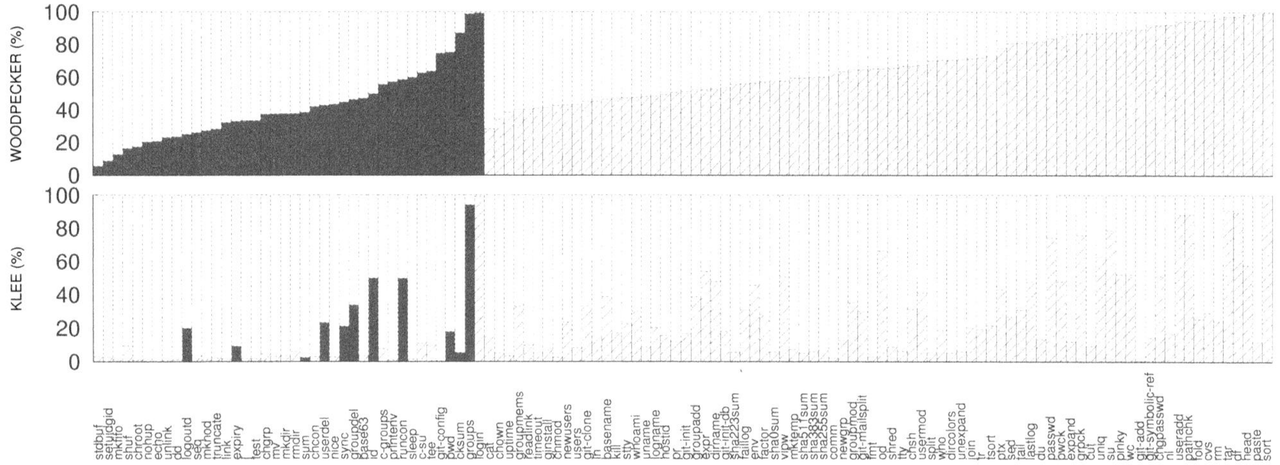

Figure 9: *Search efficiency with the file access checker.* WOODPECKER's median search efficiency of the hatched bars is 65.4%, whereas KLEE's is 20.9%.

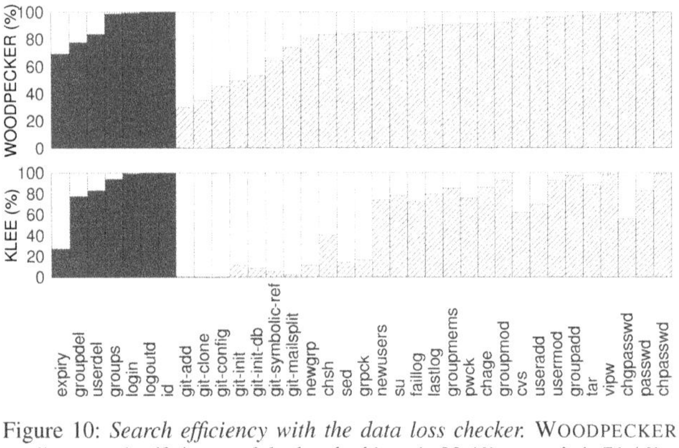

Figure 10: *Search efficiency with the data loss checker.* WOODPECKER's median search efficiency of the hatched bars is 89.4%; KLEE's is 71.1%.

temporary file to `/etc/default/useradd`. If a crash occurs between the two rename operations, the `/etc/default/useradd` link would be lost. When new users are created, `useradd` would use wrong defaults, potentially causing security issues. This error has been confirmed and fixed by the `shadow` developers.

Programs	Pruning (%)	Alias (%)
coreutils	0.82	0.49
shadow	1.98	0.11
tar	4.59	5.87
sed	0.69	0.50
CVS	4.36	4.64
git	8.99	11.71

Table 4: *Analysis overhead over total verification time.*

Detecting these data loss errors requires much precision. For instance, one of the `git` errors involves file operations spanning five levels of call stack with hundreds of function calls between them. Static analysis would likely get lost facing this complexity.

8.3 Overhead of Pruning

When WOODPECKER prunes branches, it needs to slice out irrelevant instructions from a path. In addition, it also needs to compute alias results needed by path slicing. Both pruning and alias analysis may take time. If the combined overhead is larger than the time it takes to actually explore the pruned paths, pruning would not be worthwhile. Table 4 shows the relative overhead of pruning and analysis analysis. Both analyses have low overhead for simple programs, and moderately increased overhead for complex programs such as `git`. Note that `bddbddb` saves alias results on disk, so we can run it only once for a program and reuse the results over all checking sessions. We plan to implement this optimization in future work.

9. Related Work

This section compares WOODPECKER to automated checking or verification techniques.

Static analysis. Several static analysis systems can also check rules. Meta Compilation [26, 27, 36, 61] provides a simple state machine language with pattern matching support for describing rules. It checks the rules on (potentially infeasible) program paths. It aggressively traded off soundness for low false positive rates, so while it can effectively detect thousands of errors [14], it cannot be used for verification. ESP is a static verifier [25] that also abstracts rules into state machines and verifies them on program paths. Although it has been applied to verify that the `gcc` from SPEC95 benchmark does not print to unopened files, this version of `gcc` uses only simple boolean flags to control whether to open files, and opens only up to a statically determined number (15) of files in a compilation pass [25]. Without inferring precise runtime effects of code, ESP is likely to emit false positives on many programs such as the simple one in Figure 1.

Symbolic execution. Symbolic execution, or more precisely the recent development of this technique characterized by the mixture of concrete and symbolic executions [11, 12, 33, 42, 45, 48, 49, 53], has gained much traction. Researchers have used this technique to detect serious errors [12, 13, 64], generate high-coverage tests [12], reuse thread schedules on different inputs [22, 23], (re)produce a buggy execution [4, 44, 66], verify paths or programs over bounded input [52], *etc.* WOODPECKER is complementary to much of the previous work. Its rule-directed approach may benefit many of these systems and, as discussed earlier, its carefully designed search algorithm can leverage the powerful search heuristics in existing systems. Below we discuss five related systems.

The S2E system [13] symbolically executes binary programs by dynamically translating x86 assembly to LLVM bitcode using QEMU [50]. It allows users to specify what code to symbolically explore paths for, and treats other code as the "environment" that runs concretely. It categorizes a set of heuristics with variable soundness and performance to handle the transitions between symbolic and concrete executions. It can also use a cluster to provide linear speedup of symbolic execution [9]. Recently, a state merging technique [43] has been proposed within S2E. This technique reduces the number of paths to explore by merging several into one. Doing so may actually slow down symbolic execution, so this technique employs heuristics to estimate the cost and benefit of state merging. S2E's goals are very different from WOODPECKER's. S2E is not designed to check rules. Nor does it automatically direct symbolic execution given a rule implemented using its interface. Its heuristics may remove paths unsoundly, inappropriate for verification. Its state merging technique is purely dynamic, whereas WOODPECKER leverages static analysis to prune paths before they are executed. Nonetheless, many ideas in WOODPECKER are orthogonal to those in S2E. For instance, WOODPECKER may use S2E to merge paths and provide linear speedup of symbolic execution on a cluster; S2E may use WOODPECKER to guide symbolic execution toward the rules users want to check and soundly prune irrelevant paths.

To reproduce a buggy execution, two systems attempt to compute a feasible program path reaching a given line of code using symbolic execution [44, 66]. They do so using a combination of symbolic execution and static analysis. DyTa [29] appears to share the same goal except it starts from statically detected errors. DyTa was briefly described in a 3-page paper [29] in the demonstration track of ICSE '11, and we could not find a full paper describing its implementation. Another system focuses symbolic execution on the patch between two versions of a program [47]. Again, these systems do not check rules. Nor do they attempt to explore all paths relevant to the rules for verification. At a technical level, these systems separate their static analysis and symbolic execution: they statically analyze a program's data- and control-dependencies to compute a potentially feasible path, then use symbolic execution to validate whether the path is feasible. This clear separation is different from how WOODPECKER combines static analysis and symbolic execution: WOODPECKER uses symbolic execution to explore paths and, for each explored path, it applies static analysis on the off-the-path branches to compute whether they are relevant. Previous work has shown that the information provided by a path significantly improves static analysis precision [40], a key advantage of path slicing over program slicing.

Bouncer [21] computes filters to block malicious input by combining static analysis and symbolic execution. Bouncer can be viewed as an application of path slicing [40], with precision improvements to the original path slicing algorithm in [40]. WOODPECKER applies path slicing for a different goal: speeding up symbolic exploration of paths. One path slicing improvement in WOODPECKER is that WOODPECKER slices toward an event sequence, instead of a single event.

Program Slicing. Program slicing [57] can remove irrelevant static statements from a program. It can aid debugging and optimization. Dynamic program slicing [3, 67] produces more accurate slicing results than static program slicing, but may unsoundly remove relevant branches. Path slicing [40] soundly removes irrelevant statements from a program path, and is more precise than program slicing. WOODPECKER greatly benefits from path slicing and can be viewed as an application of path slicing to speeding up symbolic execution.

Other techniques. Testing is lightweight and can address some limitations of static analysis, but previous work shows that manual or random testing tends to have low coverage [12]. As Jhala and Majumdar [40] pointed out in their path slicing paper, counterexample-guided program analyses [7, 37**? ?**] can leverage path slicing to compute shorter counterexamples and better refine their abstractions. These analyses are purely static, unlike the symbolic execution WOODPECKER targets. Recent work on explicit-state software model checking [32, 34, 41, 60, 62, 63, 65] has yielded many serious errors in real systems. This technique excels at exploring nondeterministic choices in the environment such as whether a disk `read` fails, thus it is complementary to symbolic execution that explores feasible program paths over unconstrained input, such as the input data `read` reads. Some of these systems can also soundly reduce the number of executions to explore. However, their reduction is purely dynamic and they do not leverage static analysis to guide the exploration.

10. Conclusion

We have presented WOODPECKER, a symbolic execution system designed to verify systems rules over bounded input. Leveraging the insight that only a small portion of paths are relevant to a checked rule, WOODPECKER soundly removes redundant paths and drives symbolic execution to effectively verify rules. It comes with a set of builtin checkers for common rules, and an interface for users to check custom rules. Given a rule, WOODPECKER uses a sound, checker- and heuristic-agnostic search algorithm to direct symbolic execution toward the paths relevant to the rule. Evaluation on 136 widely used programs totaling 545K lines of code shows that WOODPECKER can effectively verify rules on programs and paths over bounded input and detect serious errors.

Acknowledgments

Roxana Geambasu, Ying Xu, and the anonymous reviewers provided many helpful comments, which have substantially improved the content and presentation of this paper. This work was supported in part by AFRL FA8650-11-C-7190, FA8650-10-C-7024, and FA8750-10-2-0253; ONR N00014-12-1-0166; NSF CCF-1162021, CNS-1117805, CNS-1054906 (CAREER award), and CNS-0905246; an AFOSR YIP award; and a Sloan Research Fellowship.

References

[1] The LLVM compiler framework. `http://llvm.org`.

[2] STP Constraint Solver. `https://sites.google.com/site/stpfastprover/`.

[3] H. Agrawal and J. R. Horgan. Dynamic program slicing. In *Proceedings of the ACM SIGPLAN '90 Conference on Programming Language Design and Implementation (PLDI '90)*, pages 246–256, 1990.

[4] G. Altekar and I. Stoica. ODR: output-deterministic replay for multicore debugging. In *Proceedings of the 22nd ACM Symposium on Operating Systems Principles (SOSP '09)*, pages 193–206, Oct. 2009.

[5] A. Andoni, D. Daniliuc, S. Khurshid, and D. Marinov. Evaluating the "small scope hypothesis". Technical report, MIT CSAIL, 2002.

[6] D. Avots, M. Dalton, V. B. Livshits, and M. S. Lam. Improving software security with a C pointer analysis. In *Proceedings of the 27th International Conference on Software Engineering (ICSE '05)*, pages 332–341, May 2005.

[7] T. Ball and S. K. Rajamani. Automatically validating temporal safety properties of interfaces. In *Proceedings of the Eighth International SPIN Workshop on Model Checking of Software (SPIN '01)*, pages 103–122, May 2001.

[8] BBC. The life of birds documentary.

[9] S. Bucur, V. Ureche, C. Zamfir, and G. Candea. Parallel symbolic execution for automated real-world software testing. In *Proceedings of the 6th ACM European Conference on Computer Systems (EUROSYS '11)*, pages 183–198, 2011.

[10] C. Cadar. Private email communication, Mar. 2012.

[11] C. Cadar, V. Ganesh, P. M. Pawlowski, D. L. Dill, and D. R. Engler. EXE: automatically generating inputs of death. In *Proceedings of the 13th ACM conference on Computer and communications security (CCS '06)*, pages 322–335, Oct.–Nov. 2006.

[12] C. Cadar, D. Dunbar, and D. Engler. KLEE: unassisted and automatic generation of high-coverage tests for complex systems programs. In *Proceedings of the Eighth Symposium on Operating Systems Design and Implementation (OSDI '08)*, pages 209–224, Dec. 2008.

[13] V. Chipounov, V. Kuznetsov, and G. Candea. S2E: a platform for in-vivo multi-path analysis of software systems. In *Sixteenth International Conference on Architecture Support for Programming Languages and Operating Systems (ASPLOS '11)*, pages 265–278, 2011.

[14] A. Chou, J. Yang, B. Chelf, S. Hallem, and D. Engler. An empirical study of operating systems errors. In *Proceedings of the 18th ACM Symposium on Operating Systems Principles (SOSP '01)*, pages 73–88, Nov. 2001.

[15] J. Chow, B. Pfaff, T. Garfinkel, K. Christopher, and M. Rosenblum. Understanding Data Lifetime via Whole System Simulation. In *Proceedings of the 13th USENIX Security Symposium*, 2004.

[16] J. Chow, B. Pfaff, T. Garfinkel, and M. Rosenblum. Shredding Your Garbage: Reducing Data Lifetime Through Secure Deallocation. In *Proceedings of the 14th USENIX Security Symposium*, 2005.

[17] E. Clarke and D. Kroening. Hardware verification using ANSI-C programs as a reference. In *Proceedings of ASP-DAC 2003*, pages 308–311, January 2003.

[18] A. Coen-Porisini, G. Denaro, C. Ghezzi, and M. Pezzé. Using symbolic execution for verifying safety-critical systems. In *Proceedings of the Eighth European Software Engineering Conference held jointly with the Ninth ACM SIGSOFT International Symposium on Foundations of Software Engineering (ESEC/FSE-9)*, pages 142–151, 2001.

[19] P. Collingbourne, C. Cadar, and P. H. Kelly. Symbolic crosschecking of floating-point and SIMD code. In *Proceedings of the 6th ACM European Conference on Computer Systems (EUROSYS '11)*, pages 315–328, Apr. 2011.

[20] Coreutils - GNU core utilities. `http://www.gnu.org/software/coreutils`.

[21] M. Costa, M. Castro, L. Zhou, L. Zhang, and M. Peinado. Bouncer: securing software by blocking bad input. In *Proceedings of the 21st ACM Symposium on Operating Systems Principles (SOSP '07)*, pages 117–130, Oct. 2007.

[22] H. Cui, J. Wu, C.-C. Tsai, and J. Yang. Stable deterministic multithreading through schedule memoization. In *Proceedings of the Ninth Symposium on Operating Systems Design and Implementation (OSDI '10)*, Oct. 2010.

[23] H. Cui, J. Wu, J. Gallagher, H. Guo, and J. Yang. Efficient deterministic multithreading through schedule relaxation. In *Proceedings of the 23rd ACM Symposium on Operating Systems Principles (SOSP '11)*, Oct. 2011.

[24] CVS. `http://www.cvshome.org`.

[25] M. Das, S. Lerner, and M. Seigle. Esp: path-sensitive program verification in polynomial time. In *Proceedings of the ACM SIGPLAN 2002 Conference on Programming Language Design and Implementation (PLDI '02)*, pages 57–68, June 2002.

[26] D. Engler, B. Chelf, A. Chou, and S. Hallem. Checking system rules using system-specific, programmer-written compiler extensions. In *Proceedings of the Fourth Symposium on Operating Systems Design and Implementation (OSDI '00)*, Sept. 2000.

[27] D. Engler, D. Yu Chen, S. Hallem, A. Chou, and B. Chelf. Bugs as deviant behavior: A general approach to inferring errors in systems code. In *Proceedings of the 18th ACM Symposium on Operating Systems Principles (SOSP '01)*, 2001.

[28] V. Ganesh and D. L. Dill. A decision procedure for bit-vectors and arrays. In *Proceedings of the 19th International Conference On Computer Aided Verification (CAV' 07)*, pages 519–531, 2007.

[29] X. Ge, K. Taneja, T. Xie, and N. Tillmann. Dyta: dynamic symbolic execution guided with static verification results. In *Proceedings of the 33rd International Conference on Software Engineering*, ICSE '11, pages 992–994, 2011.

[30] Git. `http://git-scm.com/`.

[31] GNU sed. `http://www.gnu.org/software/sed`.

[32] P. Godefroid. Model Checking for Programming Languages using VeriSoft. In *Proceedings of the 24th Annual Symposium on Principles of Programming Languages (POPL '97)*, pages 174–186, Jan. 1997.

[33] P. Godefroid, N. Klarlund, and K. Sen. Dart: Directed automated random testing. In *Proceedings of the ACM SIGPLAN 2005 Conference on Programming Language Design and Implementation (PLDI '05)*, pages 213–223, June 2005.

[34] H. Guo, M. Wu, L. Zhou, G. Hu, J. Yang, and L. Zhang. Practical software model checking via dynamic interface reduction. In *Proceedings of the 23rd ACM Symposium on Operating Systems Principles (SOSP '11)*, Oct. 2011.

[35] B. Hackett and A. Aiken. How is aliasing used in systems software? In *Proceedings of the 14th ACM SIGSOFT International Symposium on Foundations of Software Engineering (SIGSOFT '06/FSE-14)*, pages 69–80, Nov. 2006.

[36] S. Hallem, B. Chelf, Y. Xie, and D. Engler. A system and language for building system-specific, static analyses. In *Proceedings of the ACM*

SIGPLAN 2002 Conference on Programming Language Design and Implementation (PLDI '02), 2002.

[37] T. A. Henzinger, R. Jhala, R. Majumdar, , and G. Sutre. Lazy abstraction. In *Proceedings of the 29th Annual Symposium on Principles of Programming Languages*, pages pp. 58–70, 2002.

[38] D. Jackson and C. A. Damon. Elements of style: Analyzing a software design feature with a counterexample detector. *IEEE Trans. Softw. Eng.*, 22(7):484–495, July 1996.

[39] J. Jaffar, V. Murali, J. A. Navas, and A. E. Santosa. Tracer: A symbolic execution tool for verification. In *Proceedings of the 24th international conference on Computer aided verification*, CAV'12, July 2012.

[40] R. Jhala and R. Majumdar. Path slicing. In *Proceedings of the ACM SIGPLAN 2005 Conference on Programming Language Design and Implementation (PLDI '05)*, pages 38–47, 2005.

[41] C. Killian, J. W. Anderson, R. Jhala, and A. Vahdat. Life, death, and the critical transition: Finding liveness bugs in systems code. In *Proceedings of the Fourth Symposium on Networked Systems Design and Implementation (NSDI '07)*, pages 243–256, April 2007.

[42] J. C. King. A new approach to program testing. In *Proceedings of the international conference on Reliable software*, pages 228–233, 1975.

[43] V. Kuznetsov, J. Kinder, S. Bucur, and G. Candea. Efficient state merging in symbolic execution. In *Proceedings of the ACM SIGPLAN 2012 Conference on Programming Language Design and Implementation (PLDI '12)*, pages 193–204, 2012.

[44] K.-K. Ma, Y. P. Khoo, J. S. Foster, and M. Hicks. Directed symbolic execution. In *The 18th International Static Analysis Symposium*, SAS '11, Sept. 2011.

[45] R. Majumdar and R.-G. Xu. Directed test generation using symbolic grammars. In *Proceedings of the Seventh European Software Engineering Conference held jointly with the Seventh ACM SIGSOFT International Symposium on Foundations of Software Engineering (ESEC/FSE-7)*, pages 553–556, 2007.

[46] J. S. Metos and J. V. Oldfield. Binary decision diagrams: From abstract representations to physical implementations. In *DAC '83: Proceedings of the 20th conference on Design automation*, pages 567–570, 1983.

[47] S. Person, G. Yang, N. Rungta, and S. Khurshid. Directed incremental symbolic execution. In *Proceedings of the 32nd ACM SIGPLAN conference on Programming language design and implementation*, PLDI '11, pages 504–515, 2011.

[48] C. S. Păsăreanu and N. Rungta. Symbolic pathfinder: symbolic execution of java bytecode. In *Proceedings of the IEEE/ACM international conference on Automated software engineering*, ASE '10, pages 179–180, 2010.

[49] C. S. Păsăreanu, N. Rungta, and W. Visser. Symbolic execution with mixed concrete-symbolic solving. In *Proceedings of the 2011 International Symposium on Software Testing and Analysis*, ISSTA '11, pages 34–44, 2011.

[50] QEMU. `http://www.qemu.org`.

[51] D. P. Quigley, J. Sipek, C. P. Wright, and E. Zadok. UnionFS: User- and Community-oriented Development of a Unification Filesystem. In *Proceedings of the 2006 Linux Symposium*, volume 2, pages 349–362, Ottawa, Canada, July 2006.

[52] D. A. Ramos and D. R. Engler. Practical, low-effort equivalence verification of real code. In *Proceedings of the 23rd international conference on Computer aided verification*, CAV'11, pages 669–685, 2011.

[53] K. Sen, D. Marinov, and G. Agha. CUTE: A concolic unit testing engine for C. In *Proceedings of the 10th European Software Engineering Conference held jointly with the 13th ACM SIGSOFT International Symposium on Foundations of Software Engineering (ESEC/FSE-13)*, pages 263–272, Sept. 2005.

[54] shadow. `http://pkg-shadow.alioth.debian.org/`.

[55] S. Smith. Eat my data: How everybody gets file io wrong. In *OSCON 2008*, July 2008.

[56] tar. `http://www.gnu.org/software/tar/`.

[57] M. Weiser. Program slicing. In *Fifth International Conference on Software Engineering*, pages 439–449, 1981.

[58] J. Whaley. bddbddb Project. `http://bddbddb.sourceforge.net`.

[59] J. Whaley and M. S. Lam. Cloning-based context-sensitive pointer alias analysis using binary decision diagrams. In *Proceedings of the ACM SIGPLAN 2004 Conference on Programming Language Design and Implementation (PLDI '04)*, pages 131–144, June 2004.

[60] M. Yabandeh, N. Knezevic, D. Kostic, and V. Kuncak. CrystalBall: Predicting and preventing inconsistencies in deployed distributed systems. In *Proceedings of the Sixth Symposium on Networked Systems Design and Implementation (NSDI '09)*, Apr. 2009.

[61] J. Yang, T. Kremenek, Y. Xie, and D. Engler. MECA: an extensible, expressive system and language for statically checking security properties. In *Proceedings of the 10th ACM conference on Computer and communications security (CCS '03)*, pages 321–334, Oct. 2003.

[62] J. Yang, P. Twohey, D. Engler, and M. Musuvathi. Using model checking to find serious file system errors. In *Proceedings of the Sixth Symposium on Operating Systems Design and Implementation (OSDI '04)*, pages 273–288, Dec. 2004.

[63] J. Yang, C. Sar, and D. Engler. Explode: a lightweight, general system for finding serious storage system errors. In *Proceedings of the Seventh Symposium on Operating Systems Design and Implementation (OSDI '06)*, pages 131–146, Nov. 2006.

[64] J. Yang, C. Sar, P. Twohey, C. Cadar, and D. Engler. Automatically generating malicious disks using symbolic execution. In *Proceedings of the 2006 IEEE Symposium on Security and Privacy (SP '06)*, pages 243–257, May 2006.

[65] J. Yang, T. Chen, M. Wu, Z. Xu, X. Liu, H. Lin, M. Yang, F. Long, L. Zhang, and L. Zhou. MODIST: Transparent model checking of unmodified distributed systems. In *Proceedings of the Sixth Symposium on Networked Systems Design and Implementation (NSDI '09)*, pages 213–228, Apr. 2009.

[66] C. Zamfir and G. Candea. Execution synthesis: a technique for automated software debugging. In *Proceedings of the 5th ACM European Conference on Computer Systems (EUROSYS '10)*, pages 321–334, Apr. 2010.

[67] X. Zhang and R. Gupta. Cost effective dynamic program slicing. In *Proceedings of the ACM SIGPLAN 2004 Conference on Programming Language Design and Implementation (PLDI '04)*, pages 94–106, 2004.

HOTL: A Higher Order Theory of Locality

Xiaoya Xiang Chen Ding Hao Luo
Department of Computer Science
University of Rochester
{xiang, cding, hluo}@cs.rochester.edu

Bin Bao *
Adobe Systems Incorporated
bbao@adobe.com

Abstract

The locality metrics are many, for example, miss ratio to test performance, data footprint to manage cache sharing, and reuse distance to analyze and optimize a program. It is unclear how different metrics are related, whether one subsumes another, and what combination may represent locality completely.

This paper first derives a set of formulas to convert between five locality metrics and gives the condition for correctness. The transformation is analogous to differentiation and integration. As a result, these metrics can be assigned an order and organized into a hierarchy.

Using the new theory, the paper then develops two techniques: one measures the locality in real time without special hardware support, and the other predicts multicore cache interference without parallel testing. The paper evaluates them using sequential and parallel programs as well as for a parallel mix of sequential programs.

Categories and Subject Descriptors C.4 [*Performance of Systems*]: Modeling Techniques

Keywords Locality metrics, Locality modeling

1. Introduction

The memory system of a computer is organized as a hierarchy. Locality metrics are used in software and hardware to manage and optimize the use of the memory hierarchy. For locality analysis, the basic unit of information is a data access, and the basic relation is a data reuse. The theory of locality is concerned with the fundamental properties of data accesses and reuses, just as the graph theory is with nodes and their links.

An influential theory developed over the past four decades is the working-set locality theory (WSLT) [14]. In this paper, we develop a similar theory for cache locality (CLT). Cache locality metrics are many and varied. To quantify performance, we use the miss rate. To manage sharing, we use the footprint. To analyze and optimize a program, we use the reuse distance. Some metrics are hardware dependent, useful for evaluating a specific machine and managing it at run time. Others are hardware independent, useful for optimizing a program for all cache sizes. The two types of metrics are converging in multicore caching, where the total cache size is fixed but the available portion for each program varies.

In this paper we consider five locality metrics, with a short description here and the precise definitions in the next section.

- *Footprint*: the expected amount of data a program accesses in a given length window.
- *Inter-miss time*: the average time between two cache misses in a given size cache.
- *Volume fill time*: the average time for the program to access a given volume of data.
- *Miss ratio*: the fraction of references that cause cache misses.
- *Reuse distance*: for each data access, the amount of data accessed between this and the previous access to the same datum.

To denote them collectively, we insert 'et' between the last two, take the initial letters (except for the fill time from which we take one 'l'), and produce the acronym "Filmer".

We present a theory showing that the five Filmer metrics can be mutually derived from each other. The conversion involves taking the difference in one direction and the sum in the reverse direction. The theoretical relation is analogous to differentiation and integration. Hence we call it a *higher order theory* of locality (HOTL).

Similar conversions have been part of the working set theory, making it the first HOTL theory (Section 2.8). The working set theory was developed to analyze locality in the main memory. The new theory we develop is for cache memory. It endows each of the five cache locality metrics the collective strength of all its Filmer peers:

- *Efficiency*. If we can measure one Filmer metric on-line, we can calculate all the others at the same time.
- *Composability*. The miss rate does not compose in that when a group of programs are run together, the number of misses is not the sum of the misses of each member running alone. If another Filmer metric is composable, then we can compose the miss rate indirectly.
- *Hardware sensitivity*. If we can measure the effect of cache associativity and other hardware parameters on the miss rate, we can compute their impact on the other metrics.

The conversion methods we describe are not always accurate. The correctness depends on whether the footprint statistics in reuse windows is similar to the footprint in general windows, in other words, whether the reuse windows are representative of general windows. We call the condition the *reuse-window hypothesis*. The Filmer metrics capture different aspects of an execution: the reuse distance is per access, the footprint is per window, while the miss-ratio has the characteristics of both. Their conversion creates con-

* The work was done when Bin Bao was a graduate student at the University of Rochester.

ASPLOS'13, March 16–20, 2013, Houston, Texas, USA.

flicts, and the reuse-window hypothesis is the condition for reconciliation.

Our recent work shows that one of the Filmer metrics, the average data footprint, can be computed efficiently [46]. In this work, we further improve the efficiency through sampling. More importantly, we apply the HOTL theory to convert it to reuse distance and predict the miss ratio. The purpose of the miss-ratio prediction is twofold: to validate the theory and to show a practical value. The main results are:

- *Real-time locality measurement.* The HOTL-enabled technique predicts the miss ratio for thousands of cache sizes with a negligible overhead. When tested on SPEC 2006 and PARSEC parallel benchmarks, the prediction matches the actual miss ratio measured using the hardware counters. Without sampling, the analysis is 39% faster than simulating a single cache size. With sampling, the end-to-end slowdown is less than 0.5% on average with only three programs over 1%.
- *Cache interference prediction.* The HOTL-enabled technique predicts the effect of cache sharing without parallel testing. For pair interference, the result can be characterized as half-and-half (Section 4.5).

Knowing the miss rate does not mean knowing the memory performance. The actual effect of a cache miss depends significantly on data prefetching, memory-bus arbitration, and other factors either in the CPU above the cache hierarchy or the main memory below. In this paper, we limit our scope to the models of data and cache usage and to methods that measure and reduce the number of cache misses.

2. The Higher Order Theory of Cache Locality

The theory includes a series of conversion methods and their correctness condition. We will refer to these methods collectively as the HOTL conversion for the Filmer metrics.

2.1 Locality Metrics

The working set theory defines the locality metrics to measure the intrinsic demand of a process [13]. The actual performance is the hardware response to the program demand. By defining locality metrics independent of their specific uses, the approach combines clarity and concision on the one hand and usefulness and flexibility on the other. We follow the same approach and say that a locality metric is *program intrinsic* if it uses only the information from the data access trace of a program. Throughout the paper, we use n to denote the length of the trace and m the total amount of data accessed in the trace.

A footprint is defined on a time window, and the miss ratio for a cache size. Since we do not know a priori in which window or cache the metrics may be used, we define the footprint and miss ratio metrics to include all windows and all cache sizes — they are functions over a parameter range.

The five metrics we consider are program intrinsic functions defined on a sequential data access trace. The time is logical and counted by the number of data accesses from the start of the execution. The cache is fully associative and uses the LRU replacement, with a fixed cache-block size. We will consider the physical time and set associative cache when we apply the basic theory. We use the term miss ratio if the time is logical and miss rate if it is physical.

2.2 Average Footprint

A footprint is the amount of data accessed in a time window. A performance tool often measures it for some execution window, i.e. taking a snapshot. A complete measure should consider *all* execution windows. For each length l, the average footprint $fp(l)$ is the average footprint size in all windows of length l.

Let W be the set of all length-l windows in a length-n trace. Each window w has a footprint fp_w. The average footprint $fp(l)$ is the total footprint in these windows divided by $n - l + 1$, the number of the length-l windows.

$$fp(l) = \frac{\sum_{all\ w\ of\ length\ l} fp_w}{n - l + 1}$$

For example, the trace "abbb" has 3 windows of length 2: "ab", "bb", and "bb". The size of the 3 footprints is 2, 1, and 1, so $fp(2) = (2 + 1 + 1)/3 = 4/3$.

The footprint is composable in that the combined footprint of two programs is the sum of their individual footprints (assuming no data sharing). We have used this property when developing efficient models of cache sharing [45, 46]. Another useful property, which we will explore in Section 3, is that the footprint is amenable to sampling.

The working set theory defined the average number of pages accessed in a time window as the working set size and gave a linear-time method to estimate the size [13]. A number of other approximate solutions followed [9, 27, 36, 39]. Our recent work gave two algorithms to measure the footprints in all execution windows and compute either the distribution [45] or the average [46] of the footprints for windows of the same length. The average footprint, e.g. the one in the preceding example, can be computed precisely in linear time. We use the average footprint in this work. Our measurement algorithm [46] will play a critical role in the new theory in Section 2.7.

2.3 Volume Fill Time

Intuitively, we may consider the cache as a reservoir and the data access of a program a stream feeding into the reservoir with new content. Having a fixed capacity, the reservoir discharges (evicts) previous volumes as it receives the new flows. The key concept in this analogy is the volume fill time, the time taken for a stream to fill the reservoir.

The volume fill time is the time a program takes to access a given amount of data, or symbolically, $vt(v)$ for volume v. The metric is program intrinsic. To model hardware, we simplify and assume that the cache is fully associative LRU. Under the assumption, the volume fill time $vt(c)$ is the time for a program to fill the cache of size c. Whether the cache is empty or not, after $vt(c)$, the cache is populated with the data (and only the data) accessed in the last $vt(c)$ time. In the cold-start cache, all data will be brought in by cache misses. In the warm cache, the fraction of the data already in the cache will stay, and the rest will be brought in by cache misses. We call the volume fill time interchangeably as the *cache fill time*.

The fill time can be defined in two different ways. First, we define it as the inverse of the footprint function:

$$vt(c) = \begin{cases} fp^{-1}(c) & \text{if } 0 \le c \le m \\ \infty & \text{if } c > m \end{cases}$$

where m is the total amount of program data. Within the range $0 \le c \le m$, the invariant $fp(vt(c)) = fp(fp^{-1}(c)) = c$ symbolizes the conversion that when the footprint is the cache size, the footprint window is the fill time. The conversion is shown visually in Figure 1. From the average footprint curve, we find the cache size c on the y-axis and draw a level line to the right. At the point the line meets the curve, the x-axis value is the fill time $vt(c)$.

A careful reader may question the uniqueness of the fill time. For example for the trace "xx...x", it is unclear what should be the fill time $vt(1)$. When defined as the inverse function fp^{-1}, the same problem happens if there are x_1, x_2 such that $fp(x_1) =$

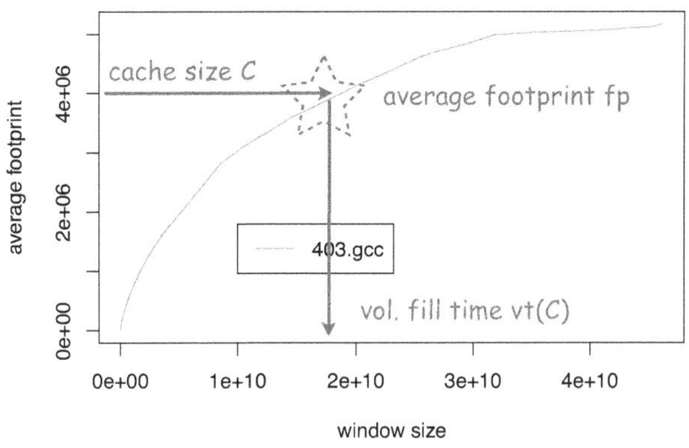

Figure 1: Defining the volume fill time using the footprint.

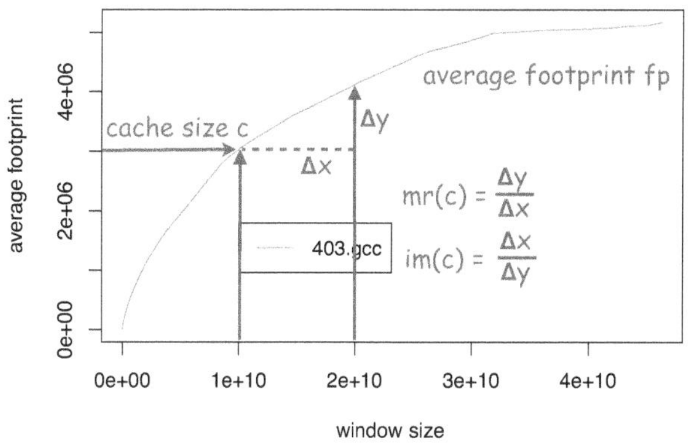

Figure 2: Equivalent conversions of the footprint to the miss ratio and the fill time to the inter-miss time.

$fp(x_2)$. However, this problem does not occur using the footprint-based definition. We will prove later in Section 2.7 that the average footprint is a concave function. As a result, it is strictly increasing, and as its inverse, vt is a proper function and strictly increasing as well. We call the footprint-based definition the *Filmer fill time*.

Alternatively, we can define the fill time in a different way. For the volume v, we find all windows in which the program accesses v amount of data. The average window length is then the fill time. We refer to the second definition the *direct fill time*, since it is defined directly, not through function inversion.

Consider another example trace "abbc". The Filmer fill time is $vt_{Filmer}(1) = 1$, since all single-element windows access one datum. The direct fill time takes the 5 windows with the unit-size data access: "a", "b","b", "bb", and "c" and computes the average $vt_{direct}(1) = (1+1+1+2+1)/5 = 6/5$. The Filmer definition uses the windows of the same length. The direct definition uses the windows of possibly different lengths.

The cache fill time is related to the residence time in the working set theory [14]. Once a program accesses in a data block but stops using it afterwards, its residence time in cache is the time it stays in cache before being evicted.

In Appendix A, we give an algorithm to measure the direct fill time. In Section 4.4, we show that the direct definition has serious flaws and is unusable in practice. Unless explicitly specified in the rest of the paper, by fill time we mean the Filmer fill time.

2.4 Inter-miss Time and Miss Ratio

We derive the inter-miss time for fully associative LRU cache of size c. Starting at a random spot in an execution, run for time $vt(c)$, the program accesses c amount of data and populates the cache of size c. It continues to run and use the data in the cache until the time $vt(c+1)$, when a new data block is accessed, triggering a capacity or a compulsory miss [24]. The time interval, $vt(c+1) - vt(c)$, is the miss-free period when the program uses only the data in cache. We use this interval as the average inter-miss time $im(c)$[1]. The reciprocal of $im(c)$ is the miss ratio $mr(c)$.

$$im(c) = \begin{cases} vt(c+1) - vt(c) & \text{if } 0 \le c < m \\ \frac{n}{m} & \text{if } c \ge m \end{cases}$$

Since the fill time is the inverse function of the footprint, we can compute the miss ratio from the footprint directly. The direct conversion is simpler and more efficient. In practice, we measure the footprint not for all window sizes but only those in a logarithmic series. Let x and $x + \Delta x$ be two consecutive window sizes we measure, we then compute the miss ratio for cache size $c = fp(x)$:

$$mr(c) = mr(fp(x)) = \frac{fp(x+\Delta x) - fp(x)}{\Delta x}$$

Being a simpler and more general formula, we will use it in the theoretical analysis and empirical evaluation. To cover all cache sizes in practice, we use it as the miss ratio for all cache sizes $c \in [fp(x), fp(x+\Delta x))$.

The fill time (vt) conversion and the footprint (fp) conversion are equivalent. Figure 2 shows the two visually. For the same two data points on the footprint curve, let $\Delta x = x_2 - x_1$ be the difference in the window length and $\Delta y = y_2 - y_1$ be the difference in the amount of data access. The fill time conversion computes the inter-miss time $im(y_1) = \frac{vt(y_2)-vt(y_1)}{y_2-y_1} = \frac{\Delta x}{\Delta y}$, and the footprint conversion computes the miss ratio $mr(fp(x_1)) = mr(y_1) = \frac{fp(x_2)-fp(x_1)}{x_2-x_1} = \frac{\Delta y}{\Delta x}$.

For associative cache, Smith showed that cache conflicts can be estimated based on the reuse distance [37]. Hill and Smith evaluated how closely such estimate matched with the result of cache simulation [25]. We next derive the reuse distance. Once derived, we can use it and the Smith formula to estimate the effect of cache conflicts and refine the miss ratio prediction.

2.5 Reuse Distance

For each memory access, the *reuse distance*, or *LRU stack distance*, is the number of distinct data used between this and the previous access to the same datum [31]. The reuse distance includes the datum itself, so it is at least 1. The probability function $P(rd = c)$ gives the fraction of data accesses that have the reuse distance c. The capacity miss ratio, $mr(c)$, is the total fraction of reuse distances greater than the cache size c, i.e. $mr(c) = P(rd > c)$. Consequently,

$$P(rd = c) = mr(c-1) - mr(c)$$

The reuse distance has extensive uses in program analysis and locality optimization. Any transformation that shortens a long reuse distance reduces the chance of a cache miss. At the program level, reuse distance analysis extends dependence analysis, which identifies reuses of program data [1], to count the volume of the intervening data [4, 8, 10]. At the trace level, the analysis can correlate the change in locality in different runs to derive program-level patterns and complement static analysis [21, 30, 49].

[1] In the working-set theory, the corresponding metric is the time between page faults and known as the lifetime.

To review the conversion formulas, let's consider the example trace "xyzxyz...". Assuming it infinitely repeating, we have $m = 3$ and $n = \infty$. The following table shows the discrete values of the Filmer metrics computed according to the HOTL conversion.

t	$fp(t)$	c	$vt(c)$	$im(c)$	$mr(c)$	P(rd=c)
1	1	1	1	1	1	0
2	2	2	2	1	1	0
3	3	3	3	∞	0	1
4	3	4	∞	∞	0	0

2.6 The Higher Order Relations

In algebra, the term order may refer to the degree of a polynomial. Through differentiation, a higher order function can derive a lower order function. If we use the concept liberally on locality functions (over the discrete integer domain), we see a higher order locality theory, as shown in a metrics hierarchy in Figure 3.

locality metrics	formal property	useful characteristics
3rd order: footprint, volume fill time	concave/ convex	linear-time, amenable to sampling, composable (dynamic locality)
2nd order: miss ratio, inter-miss time	monotone	machine specific, e.g. cache size/associativity (cache locality)
1st order: reuse distance	non-negative	decomposable by code units and data structures (program locality)

Figure 3: The hierarchy of cache locality metrics. The five locality metrics are mutually derivable by either taking the difference of the metrics when moving down the hierarchy or taking the sum of the metrics when moving up.

In the preceding sections, we have shown the series of conversions from the third order metric, the footprint, to the first order metric, the reuse distance. To compute a lower order metric, the HOTL conversion takes the difference of the function of a higher order metric. The inter-miss time is the difference of the fill times, and the reuse distance is the difference of the miss ratios.

The conversion formulas are all reversible. We can calculate a higher order metric by integrating the function of a lower order metric. For example, the miss ratio is the sum of the reuse distances greater than the cache size. The fill time is the sum of the inter-miss times up to the cache size.

The mathematical property is different depending on the order of the locality metric, as shown in the second column in Figure 3. Going bottom up, the reuse distance is a distribution, so the range is non-negative. For just compulsory and capacity misses, the miss ratio is monotone and non-increasing, i.e. the stack property [31]. The footprint has been shown to be monotone [46]. Later we will prove a stronger property.

Although the phrase higher order was not used, the working set theory was about the higher order relations between the working set size, the miss rate, and the reuse-time interval. In Section 2.8, we will compare the two higher order theories.

2.7 The Correctness Condition

The conversion from the footprint to the miss ratio is not always correct. To understand correctness, consider the reuse distance and the footprint both as window statistics. The reuse distance is the footprint of a reuse window. A reuse window starts and finishes with two accesses to the same datum with no intervening reuses. For a program with n accesses to m data, there are $n - m$ finite-length reuse windows. They are a subset of all windows. The number of all windows is n choose 2 or $\frac{n(n+1)}{2}$. We define the average footprint over all reuse windows as $rfp(l)$, the same way we define $fp(l)$ over all windows.

In this section, we show the correctness condition: for the HOTL conversions to be correct, the two functions, $fp(l)$ and $rfp(l)$, must be equal.

To show this result, we introduce a different formula for predicting the miss ratio. To estimate whether an access is a miss for cache size c, we take the reuse window length l, find the average footprint $fp(l)$, and predict it a cache miss if and only if $fp(l) > c$. We call this method the *reuse-time conversion*. Let $P(rt = t)$ be the density function of the reuse time, that is, the fraction of reuse windows with the length t. The miss ratio predicted by the reuse-time conversion is as follows. We label the result mr_{rt} to indicate that the prediction is based on the reuse time. The first access to a datum has the reuse time of ∞.

$$mr_{rt}(fp(l)) = P(rt > l) = \sum_{t=l+1}^{\infty} P(rt = t)$$

If we re-label $fp(l)$ as the working set size, the formula is identical to that of Denning and Schwartz (Section 2.8). However, the use of $fp(l)$ is an important difference. The reuse-time conversion is a modified version of Denning and Schwartz. We may call it an augmented Denning-Schwartz conversion.

Take the example trace "xxyxxz". Two of the average footprints are $fp(3) = 2$ and $fp(4) = \frac{7}{3}$. The reuse times, i.e. the length of the reuse windows, are $\infty, 2, \infty, 3, 2, \infty$. The reuse-time conversion is $mr_{rt}(2) = mr_{rt}(fp(3)) = \sum_{t=4}^{\infty} P(rt = t) = 50\%$. The Filmer conversion is based on the footprint. We call it mr_{fp} and have $mr_{fp}(2) = fp(4) - fp(3) = 33\%$. In general for small traces, the reuse-time conversion is more accurate, as is the case in this example.

Next we prove that for large traces, the miss ratio prediction is the same whether using the reuse time or using the footprint. Then we will show the correctness condition of the entire HOTL theory as a corollary.

From the view of the locality-metrics hierarchy, the reuse-time conversion is bottom up from a first-order metric to a second-order metric. The footprint conversion is top-down from a third-order metric to the same second-order metric. If they meet and produce the same result, we have the equivalence relation across the entire hierarchy.

To prove the equivalence, we need the recently published formula that computes the average footprint from the reuse-time distribution [46].

Lemma 2.1 (Xiang formula [46]).

$$\begin{aligned} fp(w) &= m - \frac{1}{n-w+1}\Big(\sum_{i=1}^{m}(f_i - w)I(f_i > w) \\ &\quad + \sum_{i=1}^{m}(l_i - w)I(l_i > w) \\ &\quad + n\sum_{t=w+1}^{n-1}(t - w)P(rt = t)\Big) \end{aligned} \tag{1}$$

The symbols are defined as:

- f_i: the first access time of the i-th datum.

- l_i: the *reverse* last access time of the i-th datum. If the last access is at position x, $l_i = n + 1 - x$, that is, the first access time in the reverse trace.
- $P(rt = t)$: the fraction of accesses with a reuse time t.
- $I(p)$: the predicate function equals to 1 if p is true; otherwise 0.

If we assume $n \gg w$, the equation can be simplified to

$$fp(w) \approx m - \sum_{t=w+1}^{n-1} (t - w)P(rt = t)$$

Theorem 2.2 (Footprint and reuse-time conversion equivalence). *For long executions ($n \gg w$), the footprint conversion and the reuse-time conversion produce equivalent miss-ratio predictions.*

Proof Let the cache size be c and l and $l + x$ be two consecutive window sizes such that $c \in [fp(l), fp(l + x))$. The miss ratio by the footprint conversion is $\frac{fp(l+x)-fp(l)}{x}$.

Expand the numerator $fp(l + x) - fp(l)$ using the approximate equation from Lemma 2.1:

$$\begin{aligned}
&fp(l + x) - fp(l) \\
\approx& m - \sum_{t=l+x+1}^{n-1} (t - l - x)P(rt = t) - m + \sum_{t=l+1}^{n-1} (t - l)P(rt = t) \\
=& \sum_{t=l+1}^{n-1} (t - l)P(rt = t) - \sum_{t=l+x+1}^{n-1} (t - l - x)P(rt = t) \\
=& \sum_{t=l+1}^{l+x} (t - l)P(rt = t) + \sum_{t=l+x+1}^{n-1} (t - l)P(rt = t) \\
&- \sum_{t=l+x+1}^{n-1} (t - l - x)P(rt = t) \\
=& \sum_{t=l+1}^{l+x} (t - l)P(rt = t) + x \sum_{t=l+x+1}^{n-1} P(rt = t) \\
\approx& \sum_{t=l+1}^{l+x} xP(rt = t) + x \sum_{t=l+x+1}^{n-1} P(rt = t) \\
=& x \sum_{t=l+1}^{n-1} P(rt = t) \\
\approx& x \sum_{t=l+1}^{\infty} P(rt = t)
\end{aligned}$$

The miss ratio, $\frac{fp(l+x)-fp(l)}{x}$, is approximately $\sum_{t=l+1}^{\infty} P(rt = t)$, which is the result of the reuse-time conversion. Note that the equation is approximately true also because of the earlier simplifications made to the Xiang formula. ∎

The two predictions being the same does not mean that they are correct. They may be both wrong. Since the correct calculation can be done using reuse distance, the correctness would follow if from the reuse time, we can produce reuse distance. In other words, the correctness depends on whether the all-window footprint used by the reuse time conversion is indeed the reuse distance. We can phrase the correctness condition as follows:

COROLLARY 2.3 (Correctness). *The footprint-based conversions are accurate if the footprints in all reuse windows have the same distribution as the footprints in all windows, for every reuse window length l.*

When the two are equal, using the all-window footprint is the same as using the reuse distance. We posit as a hypothesis that the condition holds in practice, so the HOTL conversion is accurate. We call it the *reuse-window hypothesis*.

Consider the following two traces. The second trace has a smaller difference between the all-window footprint fp and the reuse-window footprint rfp. The smaller difference leads to more accurate miss ratio prediction by HOTL. The hypothesis does not hold in either trace, so the prediction is not completely accurate. As to real applications, we will show an empirical evaluation for the full suite of SPEC CPU2006 benchmark programs [23] and a number of PARSEC parallel programs [6].

trace	$fp(2)$	$rfp(2)$	mr(1) *pred*	mr(1) *real*	error $\lvert pred - real \rvert$
wwwx	4/3	1	1/3	2/4	17%
wwwwx	5/4	1	1/4	2/5	5%

Finally, we show another consequence of Theorem 2.2.

COROLLARY 2.4 (Concavity). *The average footprint $fp(x)$ is a concave function.*

Since $\frac{fp(l+x)-fp(l)}{x} \approx \sum_{t=l+1}^{\infty} P(rt = t)$, $fp(l)$ always increases but increases at a slower rate for a larger l. The function is obviously concave. In the higher order relation, the concavity guarantees that the miss ratio predicted by HOTL is non-increasing with the cache size (as expected from the inclusion property [31]).

2.8 Comparison with Working Set Theory

The first higher-order locality theory is the working set theory, pioneered in Peter Denning's thesis work [13]. His 1968 paper established the relation between the working set size, the miss rate, and the inter-reference interval (iri). The last one is the same as reuse time. The notion of reuse distance or the LRU stack distance was not formalized until 1970 [31]. Figure 4 shows the parallels between the working set locality theory (WSLT) and the new cache locality theory of this paper (CLT).

HOTL hierarchy	working set locality theory (WSLT)	cache locality theory (CLT)
data volume (3rd order)	mean WS size s(T)	mean footprint fp(T), mean fill time vt(c)
miss rate (2nd order)	time-window miss rate m(T), lifetime L(T)=1/m(T)	LRU miss rate mr(c), inter-miss time im(c)=1/mr(c)
reference behavior (1st order)	inter-reference interval (reuse time) distribution P(iri=x)	reuse distance distribution P(rd=x)

Figure 4: Comparison between two higher order locality theories: the working set locality theory (WSLT) for dynamic partitioned primary memory and the cache locality theory (CLT) for cache memory.

WSLT computes the metrics bottom up. The base metric, $P(iri = x)$, is the histogram of the inter-reference intervals (reuse time), measured in linear time in a single pass of the address trace. The time-window miss ratio $m(T)$ is the sum of reuse time. The mean working set size $s(T)$ is the sum of $m(T)$.

$$m(T) = P(rt > T)$$
$$s(T+1) = s(T) + m(T)$$

Taking together, the working set size $s(T)$ is the second order sum of the reuse frequency.

The $s(T)$ formula was first proved by Denning and Schwartz in 1972 [15]. The formulation assumes an infinitely long execution with a "stationary" state ("the stochastic mechanism ... is stationary"). The working set, $w(t, T)$, is the number of distinct pages accessed between time $t - T + 1$ and t. The average working set size, $s(T)$, is the limit value when taking the average of $w(t, T)$ for all t. The proof is based on the fact that only recurrent pages with an infinite number of accesses contribute to the mean working set size.

In 1978, Denning and Slutz defined the generalized working set (GWS) as a time-space product [16]. The product, denoted here as $st(T)$, is defined for finite-length execution traces, variable-size memory segments, all cache replacement policies that observe the stack property. Interestingly, they found the same recursive relation. The GWS formula is as follows, where the last term is the extra correction to take into account the finite trace length.

$$st(T+1) = st(T) + Tm(T) - a(T)$$

Dividing both sides by T, we have the last term vanishing for large T and see the same recursive relation for GWS in finite-length traces as $s(T)$ in infinitely long traces.

In the present paper, the same recurrence emerges in Section 2.7 as an outcome of Theorem 2.2. For the average footprint, we have effectively

$$fp(T+1) = fp(T) + m(T)$$

If we view the following three as different definitions of the working set: the limit value in 1972 [15], the time-space product in 1978 [16], and the average footprint in 2011 [46], we see an identical equation which Denning envisioned more than four decades ago (before the first proof in 1972). We state it as a law of locality and name it after its inventor:

Denning's Law of Locality *The working set is the second-order sum of the reuse frequency, and conversely, the reuse frequency is the second-order difference of the working set.*

As the relativity theory gives the relation between space and time, Denning's law gives the relation between memory and computation: the working set is the working memory, and the reuse frequency is a summary of program actions (time transformed into frequency and a spectrogram of time). The law states that the relation is higher order.

Our work augments Denning's law in two ways. First, it is the final step to conclusively prove Denning's Law — that it holds for the footprint working set in finite-length program executions. The 1972 proof depends on the idealized condition in infinite-length executions. Subsequent research has shown that the working set theory is accurate and effective in managing physical memory for real applications [14]. The new proof subsumes the infinitely long case and makes Denning's law a logical conclusion for all (long enough) executions. It gives a theoretical explanation to the long observed effectiveness of the working set theory in practice.

Second, we extend HOTL to include cache memory. For main memory, the locality is parameterized in time: the working set of a program in a time quantum. For cache, the primary constraint is space: the miss ratio for a given cache size. Denning et al. named them the "time-window miss ratio" and the "LRU miss ratio" and noted that the two are not necessarily equal [15, 16]. The following formulas show the two miss ratios:

working set	$m(T) = P(rt > T)$
cache locality	$mr(fp(T)) = P(rt > T)$

In the above juxtaposition, the only difference is the parameter to the miss rate function. In $m(T)$, the parameter is the time window length. In $mr(fp(T))$, the parameter is the cache size. Through the second formula, this work connects the cache size and the reuse frequency. In Section 2.4, we show how the time-centric and the space-centric views have different derivations but the same miss ratio. Then in Section 2.7, we give the reuse-window hypothesis as the condition for correctness, which implies the equality between the time-window miss ratio and the LRU miss ratio.

3. Sampling-based Locality Analysis

The footprint can be analyzed through sampling, e.g. by tracing a window of program execution periodically. Sampling has two benefits. First, by reducing the sampling frequency, the cost can be arbitrarily reduced. Second, sampling may better track a program that has significant phase behavior.

Uniform sampling We implement footprint sampling using a technique pioneered by shadow profiling [32] and SuperPin [42]. When a program starts, we set the system timer to interrupt at some preset interval. The interrupt handler is shown in Figure 5. It forks a sampling task and attaches the binary rewriting tool Pin [29]. The Pin tool instruments the sampling process to collect its data access trace, measures all-window footprints using the Xiang formula [46]. In the meanwhile, the base program runs normally until the next interrupt.

Require: This handler is called whenever a program receives the timer interrupt
1: $pid \leftarrow fork()$
2: **if** $pid = 0$ **then**
3: Attach the Pin tool and begin sampling until seeing c distinct memory accesses
4: Exit
5: **else**
6: Reset the timer to interrupt in k seconds
7: Return
8: **end if**

Figure 5: The timer-interrupt handler for footprint sampling

Footprint Sampling Footprint by definition is amenable to sampling. We can start a sample at any point in an execution and continue until the sample execution accesses enough data to fill the largest cache size of interest. We can sample multiple windows independently, which means they can be parallelized. It does not matter whether the sample windows are disjoint or overlapping, as long as the choice of samples is random and unbiased.

The Associative Cache A program execution produces a series of m samples at regular intervals, $x_1, x_2, \ldots, x_m$. We use them in the following way:

1. For each sample x_i, with trace length n_i, predict the miss ratio function $mr(x_i, c)$ for each cache size c by the following:
   (a) Use the analysis of Xiang et al. [46] to compute the average footprint function fp.
   (b) Use the footprint conversion to compute the capacity miss ratio for cache size c.

(c) Use the miss-ratio conversion to compute the reuse distance distribution and the Smith formula [37] to estimate the number of conflict misses for cache size c.

2. For all x_i, take the weighted average and compute the miss ratio for all cache sizes for the program $mr(c) = \frac{\sum_{i=1}^{m} mr(x_i,c)*n_i}{\sum_{i=1}^{m} n_i}$.

The Phase Effect The preceding design assumes phase behavior. Since different samples may come from different phases, combining their footprints would lose the phase distinction. To validate the conjecture, we will compare the phase-sensitive sampling with phase-insensitive sampling. The former, as just described, computes the miss ratio for each sample and then takes the average. The next design combines the footprint from all the samples and then computes the miss ratio. Specifically, the second design is as follows:

1. For each sample x_i, with trace length n_i,
   - Use the analysis of Xiang et al. [46] to compute the average footprint function fp.
2. For all samples x_i, take the weighted average and compute the fp function for the program $fp = \frac{\sum_{i=1}^{m} fp(x_i)*n_i}{\sum_{i=1}^{m} n_i}$.
3. Use the footprint and miss-ratio conversions and the Smith formula [37] to estimate the number of cache misses.

Comparison with Reuse Distance Sampling To be statistically sound, reuse distance sampling must evenly sample reuse windows. After picking an access, it needs to trace the subsequent program accesses until the next data reuse. When a reuse window is long, it does not know a priori how long to monitor, so it has to keep analyzing until seeing the next reuse or until the reuse distance exceeds the largest cache size of interest. The cut-off strategy is also used in footprint sampling.

Beneath this similarity lies two important differences. The reuse distance measures the locality by examining reuses. The footprint measures the locality by examining data accesses. Footprint sampling computes the distribution of all reuse distances from a single sample window using the HOTL conversion. The footprint analysis and conversion take linear time. In comparison, each reuse window sample produces just one reuse distance. It takes asymptotically higher time cost to measure the reuse distance in the sample (than it takes HOTL conversion to compute all reuse distances from the same sample). Hence the advantage of footprint sampling is algorithmic and computational, and this strength comes from the HOTL theory.

4. Evaluation

4.1 Experimental Setup

We have tested the full set of 29 benchmarks from SPEC 2006 and 8 from the PARSEC v2.1 suite. All programs are instrumented by Pin [29] and profiled on a Linux cluster where each node has two Intel Xeon 3.2GHz processors. PARSEC is run on a machine with two Intel Xeon E5649 processors. In simulation, we simulate a single-level cache, which is shared in the case of parallel code. On a real machine, the baseline is the program run time without instrumentation or any analysis.

For SPEC 2006, we use the first reference input provided by the benchmark suite. Table 1 shows for each SPEC 2006 program the length of trace n, the size of data m and the time of the unmodified program execution. The length of SPEC 2006 traces ranges from 20 billion in *403.gcc* to 2.1 trillion in *436.cactusADM*. The amount of data ranges from 3MB in *416.gamess* to 1.7GB in *429.mcf*. For PARSEC, we test programs using the three provided input sizes: simsmall, simmedium and simlarge. We run each with 4 threads, a commonly used configuration.

benchname	n (10^{11})	m ($10^7 bytes$)	T (sec)
400.perlbench	4.2	24.4	457
401.bzip2	1.7	39.3	263
403.gcc	0.2	40.4	72
410.bwaves	14.4	98.2	1664
416.gamess	4.8	0.3	444
429.mcf	1.2	175.7	1172
433.milc	3.8	74.2	1077
434.zeusmp	5.7	51.9	1555
435.gromacs	9.8	1.4	1272
436.cactusADM	20.6	65.5	3411
437.leslie3d	6.8	12.9	1212
444.namd	6.8	4.7	915
445.gobmk	0.9	2.7	173
447.dealII	7.3	88.5	773
450.soplex	1.0	16.2	604
453.povray	4.8	0.3	493
454.calculix	9.5	16.4	1512
456.hmmer	4.9	4.2	303
458.sjeng	7.0	18.2	1356
459.GemsFDTD	8.6	86.9	1397
462.libquantum	3.0	16.8	1391
464.h264ref	2.6	2.7	143
465.tonto	10.0	5.2	1312
470.lbm	3.3	42.9	1491
471.omnetpp	2.3	17.6	1048
473.astar	1.4	29.5	512
481.wrf	9.7	76.8	1895
482.sphinx3	8.9	5.1	1765
483.xalancbmk	3.6	43.8	778

Table 1: The SPEC2006 integer and floating-point benchmarks. For each benchmark, n is the memory trace length of whole execution, m is the number of distinct data blocks (size in bytes) accessed during the execution, and T is the execution time without any instrumentation or analysis.

Locality sampling is implemented using fork, as described in Section 3. The implementation does not yet recognize system calls, so sampling handles only 22 of the 29 sequential programs. Nor does the sampling implementation handle multi-threaded code. We evaluate miss-ratio prediction using the full trace of the 8 parallel programs.

3073 Cache Sizes In the analysis, the footprint and reuse distance numbers are bin-ed using logarithmic ranges as follows. For each (large enough) power-of-two range, we sub-divide it into (up to) 256 equal-size increments. As a result, we can predict the miss ratio not just for power-of-two cache sizes, but 3073 cache sizes between 16KB and 64MB.

4.2 Miss-Ratio Prediction

We first evaluate the accuracy and the speed of miss-ratio prediction, made by the Filmer conversion and locality sampling, tested on sequential and parallel programs, and verified through simulation and hardware counters.

4.2.1 Sequential Programs

We first use cache simulation to evaluate the accuracy of Filmer-based miss ratio prediction. Instead of evaluating each of the 29

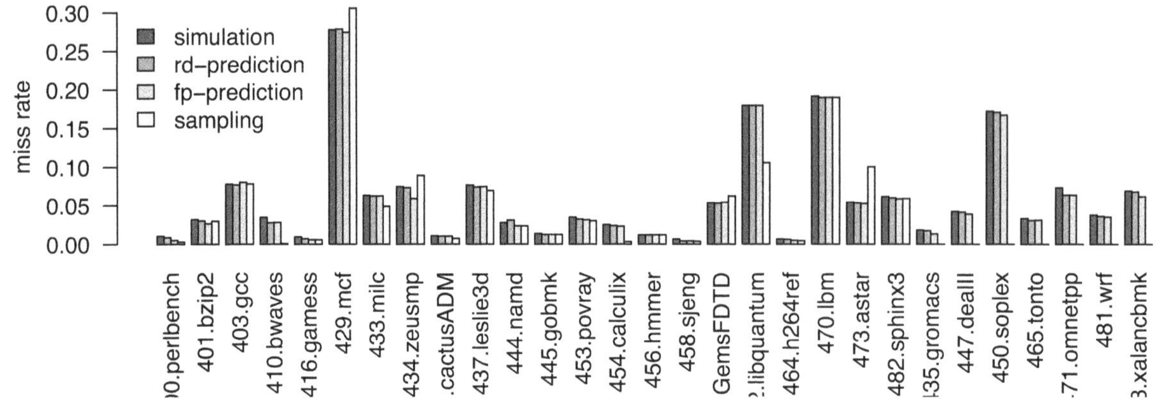

(a) 8-way, 32KB cache

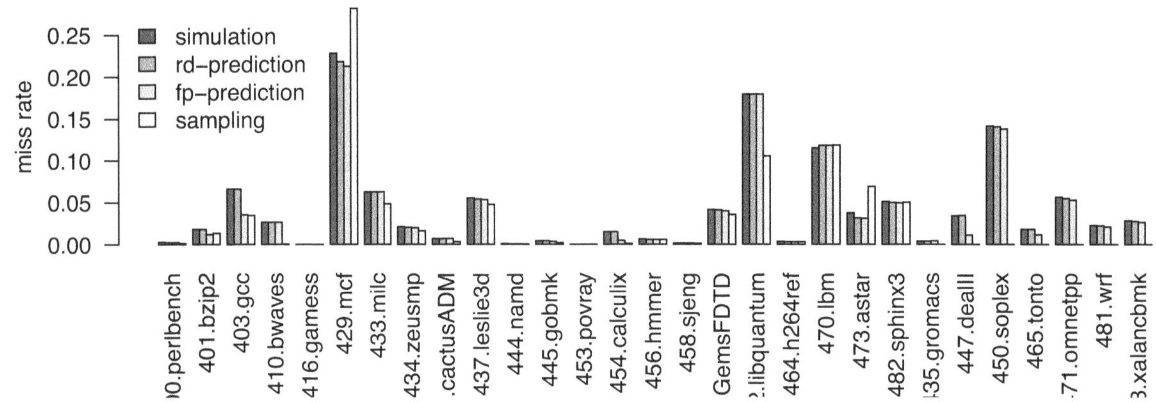

(b) 8-way, 256KB cache

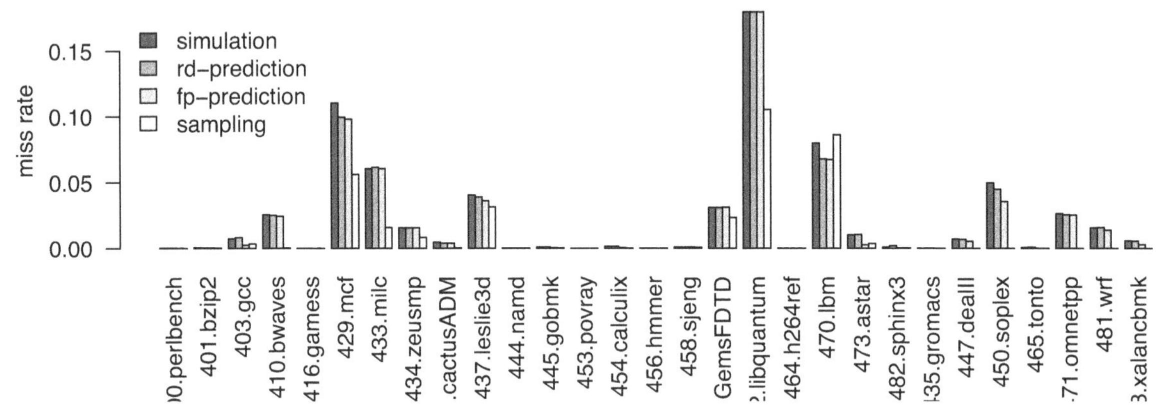

(c) 16-way, 8MB cache

Figure 6: Accuracy of the miss-ratio prediction by reuse distance, footprint (HOTL conversion in Section 2.4), and footprint sampling (Section 3) for 29 SPEC 2006 benchmarks, each on 3 (of the 3073) cache configurations, compared with cache simulation. (a) 8-way, 32KB cache. (b) 8-way, 256KB cache. (c) 16-way, 8MB cache. The sampling results are for 22 out of 29 programs (not the last 7). The average time cost of sampling is 0.5% (Table 2).

programs on 3073 cache sizes, we show results for 3 configurations: 32KB, 8-way associative L1D; 256KB, 8-way associative L2; and 8MB, 16-way associative L3. They are the cache configurations on our test machine. We will compare our prediction to the performance counter result later. The cache-block size is 64 bytes in all cases. The accuracy for the other 3070 cache sizes looks similar.

Figure 6 plots the measured and predicted miss ratios. The *rd-prediction*, which uses the measured reuse distance, is the most accurate. The other two, *fp-prediction* and *sampling* measure the footprint and then use the HOTL conversion in Section 2.4. The HOTL conversion *fp-prediction* closely matches the reuse-distance analysis *rd-prediction* in almost all cases, showing that the footprint-converted reuse distance is almost identical to the measured reuse distance—hence the validity of the reuse-window hypothesis.

The Phase Effect The reuse distances of a program, when added together regardless of phases, predict the (capacity) miss ratio accurately, because an access is a cache capacity miss if and only if its reuse distance is greater than the cache size. On the other hand, the footprint should be affected by phases. As the footprint changes from phase to phase, it is possible that taking the global average might lose critical information.

A consistent result from the theory and the experiments is that the two are largely equivalent, as far as computing the miss ratio is concerned. The theory gives the conversion procedure from the footprint to the reuse distance. The experiments show, by the close match between *rd-prediction* and *fp-prediction* in Figure 6, the conversion is accurate for most programs. This suggests that reuse windows are representative of all windows, and this is why the prediction is accurate in spite of the phase effect.

Another evidence, for which we do not include the results in the paper, is that the two sampling designs in Section 3, phase sensitive and insensitive, produce almost identical predictions.

Analysis Speed Table 2 compares the cost of four analysis methods: the simulation sim, the reuse distance rd [49], the footprint fp [46], and the footprint sampling sp. For simulation we could use the algorithm of Smith and Hill [25] to simulate all three configurations in one pass. For speed comparison, we ran the simplest simulator once for each configuration. The simulation cost in table 2 is the average of the three runs.

The cost for reuse distance analysis ranges from 52 times to 426 times with an average of 153 times. The footprint analysis costs about 7 times less, with slowdowns between 6 and 66 times and on average 23 times. Simulation for a single configuration has slowdowns from 14 to 80 times, with an average of 38 times.

Comparing the average, we see that measuring the footprint, the third order Filmer metric that can compute the second order metric miss ratio for all cache sizes, is 39% faster than simulating for a single cache size, before we use footprint sampling.

4.2.2 Locality Sampling

For this experiment, we choose somewhat arbitrarily the frequency of one sample every 10 seconds. The sample length is the volume fill time for the cache size. Sampling analysis is not always accurate. Visible errors are seen in *mcf*, *libquantum* and *astar* in Figure 6. The reason, as shown by the last column of Table 2, is that it covers less than 1% of the execution. The coverage is computed by the ratio of the number of sampled instructions to the total number of instructions (counted by our full trace profiling). The coverage is as low as 0.006% in *lbm*. The low coverage does not mean low accuracy. The prediction of *lbm* is 99% accurate for the 32KB cache, 97% for the 256KB cache, and 92% for the 8MB cache.

In Table 2, we show the slowdown in the end-to-end run time by the column marked $samp$. It ranges from 0% to 2.14%. Three programs have a visible cost of over 1%. They are *bwaves* 2.1%, *GemsFDTD* 1.3% and *milc* 1.5%. The reason for the relatively high cost may be the non-trivial interference between the sampling task and the parent task. Across all programs, the average visible overhead is below a half percent. If we measure the total CPU time, sampling takes between 0% and 80% of the original run time. The average cost is 19%, of which over 18% is hidden by shadow profiling.

$benchname$	sim	rd	fp	$samp$	cov
400.perlbench	49	219	34	0.24%	3.1%
401.bzip2	34	139	24	0.73%	1.5%
403.gcc	24	88	15	0.55%	0.1%
410.bwaves	57	196	35	2.14%	0.5%
416.gamess	62	286	40	0.29%	2.9%
429.mcf	10	56	6	0.14%	0.03%
433.milc	21	74	9	1.53%	0.04%
434.zeusmp	25	102	14	0.81%	0.06%
435.gromacs	40	142	19	-	-
436.cactusADM	40	167	21	0.00%	1.1%
437.leslie3d	42	131	23	0.00%	0.01%
444.namd	44	155	24	0.00%	2.2%
445.gobmk	35	130	23	0.22%	1.1%
447.dealII	54	209	34	-	-
450.soplex	13	52	7	-	-
453.povray	51	220	33	0.00%	1.8%
454.calculix	39	127	19	0.11%	1.8%
456.hmmer	80	426	59	0.00%	0.8%
458.sjeng	34	152	23	0.82%	0.4%
459.GemsFDTD	42	181	21	1.28%	0.01%
462.libquantum	17	48	9	0.00%	0.01%
464.h264ref	101	424	66	0.00%	1.2%
465.tonto	52	168	30	-	-
470.lbm	14	76	6	0.00%	0.01%
471.omnetpp	17	69	10	-	-
473.astar	15	73	11	0.80%	0.9%
481.wrf	33	113	19	-	-
482.sphinx3	30	117	16	0.59%	1.2%
483.xalancbmk	31	99	21	-	-
average	38	153	23	0.47%	0.9%

Table 2: Time comparison between different profiling methods and cache simulation for SPEC 2006. The baseline is the execution time without any instrumentation or analysis. The middle four columns show the slowdown compared to the baseline: sim for simulating one cache size, rd for reuse distance profiling, fp for footprint profiling, and $samp$ for footprint sampling. The last column cov gives the sampling coverage.

4.2.3 Parallel Programs

Figure 7 shows that for 3 of the 3073 cache configurations and across the 3 input sizes, the predicted miss ratio matches closely with the simulated miss ratio, similar to the results we saw in the sequential programs. The accuracy shows that the reuse-window hypothesis holds for these threaded applications.

The last column of table 3 shows the slowdowns of footprint profiling, which ranges from 14 times to 159 times with an average of 113 times. We did not profile reuse distance for PARSEC because it took too long. We note that the footprint analysis shows 5 times as much overhead in 4-threaded tests as in sequential programs (159 times in PARSEC vs. 23 times in SPEC 2006). The reason is that our data analysis is still serial, so the overhead is proportional to the total amount of work. We plan to parallelize the footprint analysis in the future, building on recent work in parallelizing the reuse-distance analysis [12, 22, 33].

4.3 Validation on a Real Machine

In Figure 8, we compare the simulation result with the miss ratio measured by the hardware counters on our test machine. To measure the actual misses, we use Intel's VTune tool to record three hardware counter events named

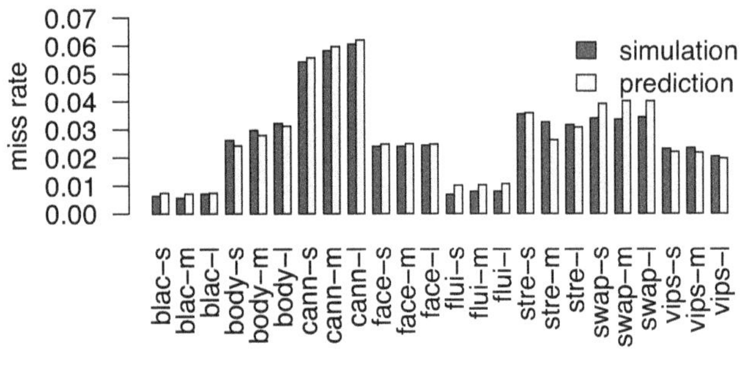

(a) 8-way, 32KB cache

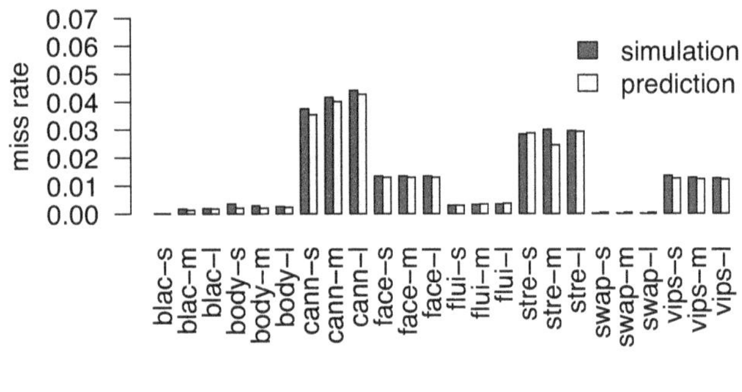

(b) 8-way, 256KB cache

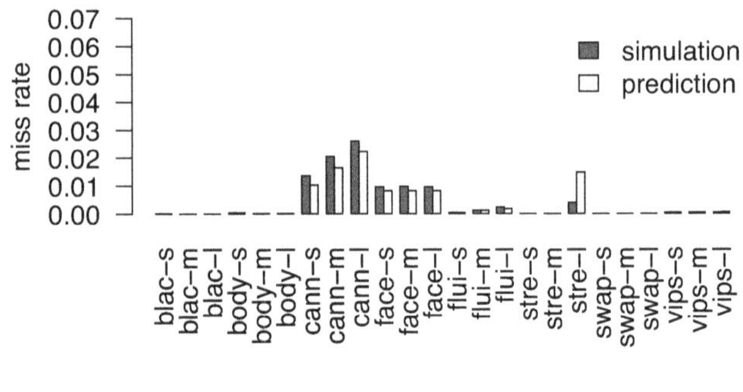

(c) 16-way, 8MB cache

Figure 7: Accuracy of the miss-ratio prediction for 3 (of the 3073) cache configurations and 3 input sizes, compared with cache simulation. (a) 8-way, 32KB cache. (b) 8-way, 256KB cache. (c) 16-way, 8MB cache.

```
OFFCORE_RESPONSE_0.DATA_IN.LOCAL_DRAM
MEM_INST_RETIRED.LOADS
MEM_INST_RETIRED.STORES
```

The measured miss ratio is the first count divided by the sum of the last two counts.

The figure shows a significant difference in *gcc*. The reason is that the simulation considers only data accesses but the hardware counter counts instruction misses in the data cache, which we believe are significant in *gcc*.

4.4 Direct Fill Time vs. Filmer Fill Time

The measurement of the direct fill time, definition in Section 2.3 and algorithm in Section A, takes so long that the only programs we could finish are 10 of the 11 SPEC 2000 integer benchmark programs. Table 4 compares the average time for these programs.

bench name	*input size*	n (10^9)	m $(10^6 bytes)$	T (sec)	slow-down
black -scholes	S	0.1	0.4	0.093	129
	M	0.4	1.2	0.384	91
	L	1.6	4.4	1.542	88
body -track	S	0.3	8.1	0.285	129
	M	1.1	11.1	0.948	155
	L	4.0	14.8	3.35	111
canneal	S	0.6	43.0	1.525	19
	M	1.3	84.3	3.859	15
	L	2.7	164.9	8.804	14
facesim	S	12.7	344.2	7.448	139
	M	12.7	344.2	7.306	131
	L	12.7	344.2	7.86	116
fluid -animate	S	0.5	10.5	0.429	114
	M	1.3	20.6	0.983	145
	L	3.9	57.6	2.9	124
stream -cluster	S	0.5	1.2	0.722	87
	M	2.6	2.9	1.641	138
	L	9.6	9.5	6.951	173
swapt -ions	S	3.6	0.9	2.349	134
	M	1.4	1.2	0.935	114
	L	5.7	1.9	3.766	132
vips	S	1.0	13.5	0.748	159
	M	3.1	26.9	2.228	140
	L	8.6	15.7	7.332	103

Table 3: The PARSEC parallel benchmarks. For each benchmark, n is the memory trace length of whole execution, m is the size of program data (in bytes) accessed during the execution, and T is the execution time without any instrumentation or analysis. The last column is the slowdown of the footprint analysis.

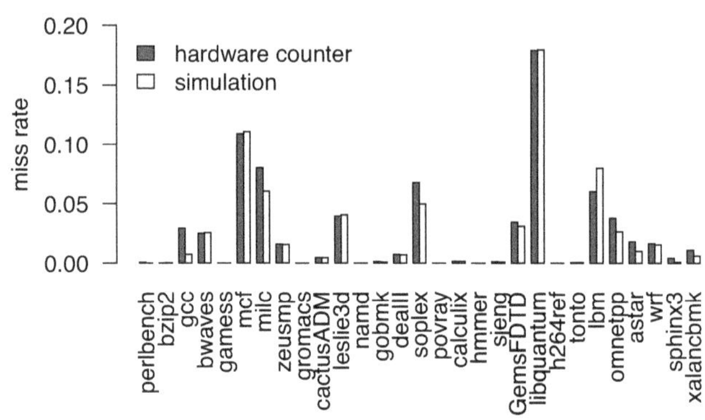

Figure 8: Comparison between hardware counter measured L3 cache miss ratio and the simulation result.

An unmodified SPEC 2000 program runs for 3 minutes on average, the direct fill time analysis takes over 22 hours. The average overhead is more than 7 hours for each minute. In comparison, the per minute overhead is an hour and a half for reuse distance and 7 minutes if we first compute footprint and then derive the Filmer fill time.

More problematic is that with the direct fill time, the predicted miss ratio is not monotone. Worse, the miss ratio may be negative. Consider an example trace with 100 a's followed by 11 b's, 1 c, 20 d's, 15 e's, 1 f and 320 g's. The average time to fill a 4-element cache, $vt(4)$, is 161.5, is longer than the average time to fill a 5-element cache, $vt(5)$, which is 149.5. Since the direct fill time

analysis	avg. time	avg. slowdown
direct fill time (Section A)	22h12m11s	446x
reuse distance	3h57m36s	84x
Filmer fill time (Section 2.3)	22m4s	8x

Table 4: Speed comparison for 10 SPEC 2000 integer benchmarks. The average trace length n is 47 billion, data size m is 73MB, and baseline run time is 3 minutes and 16 seconds.

decreases when the cache size v increases, the predicted miss ratio is negative!

The preceding example was constructed based on an analysis of real traces. During experimentation, we found that the miss ratios of some cache sizes were negative. While most of the 3000 or so sizes had positive predictions, the negatives were fairly frequent and happened in most test programs. It seemed contradictory that it could take a program longer to fill a smaller cache. The reason is subtle. To compute the direct fill time, we find windows with the same footprint and take the average length. As we increase the footprint by 1, the length of these windows will increase but the number of such windows may increase more, leading to a lower average, as happened in the preceding example.

In contrast, the Filmer fill time is a positive, concave function (Corollary 2.4). Its miss-ratio prediction is monotone and can be measured in near real time (Section 4.2.2).

4.5 Predicting Cache Interference

A complete 2-program co-run test for the 29 SPEC 2006 benchmarks would include $\binom{29}{2} = 406$ program pairs. To reduce the clutter in the graphs we show, we choose 20 programs. To avoid bias, we pick programs with the smallest benchmark ids. Since we profile data accesses only, we exclude perlbench and gcc because their large code size may cause significant instruction misses in the data cache. After the removal, we have 20 SPEC benchmark programs from 401.bzip2 to 464.h264ref. The trimming reduces the number of pair-run tests to $\binom{20}{2} = 190$.

Cache interference models were pioneered by Thiebaut and Stone [41], Suh et al. [39] and Chandra et al. [9], who computed the cache interference by the impact of the peer footprint on the self locality.[2] The footprint is measured for a single window length [41] and approximated for multiple lengths [9, 39]. Our subsequent work found a way to measure all-window footprints precisely and efficiently [17, 45, 46]. The self locality is measured by the reuse distance. As the measurement problem for the footprint is solved, the speed of reuse-distance analysis becomes the bottleneck. We found that by profiling up to two days for each program, the reuse distance analyzer by Zhong et al. [49] could finish only 8 SPEC 2006 programs [46]. The total modeling time was over 106 CPU hours, 94% of which was spent on the reuse-distance analysis. In this study, we have measured reuse distance for all benchmarks (see Table 2 for measurement costs). Some programs took over 4 days.

Based on the new theory, we compute the reuse distance from the footprint and predict the co-run interference. Figure 9 compares the measured and predicted miss ratios. There are 190 pair runs for a total of 380 executions. The x-axis orders these executions by the measured miss ratios from the lowest to the highest. For easy viewing, we connect the points into a line. The measured curve is necessarily monotone. The prediction is to match the measurement.

[2] Chandra et al. also gave a model that used only the reuse distance [9]. Zhuravlev et al. used it and two other such models and found that in task scheduling, they did not significantly outperform a simple model that used only the miss rate [51].

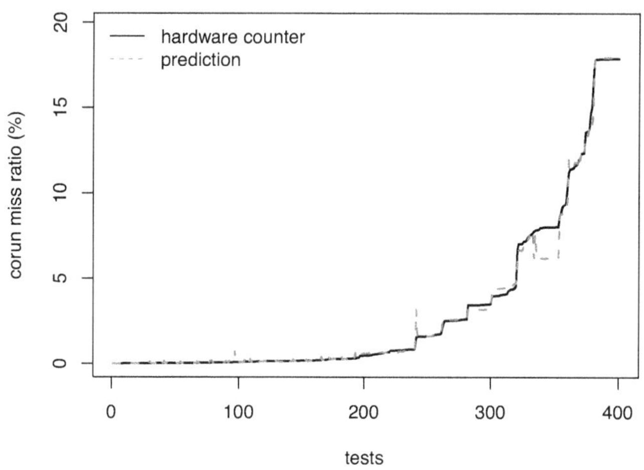

(a) linear scale miss ratios

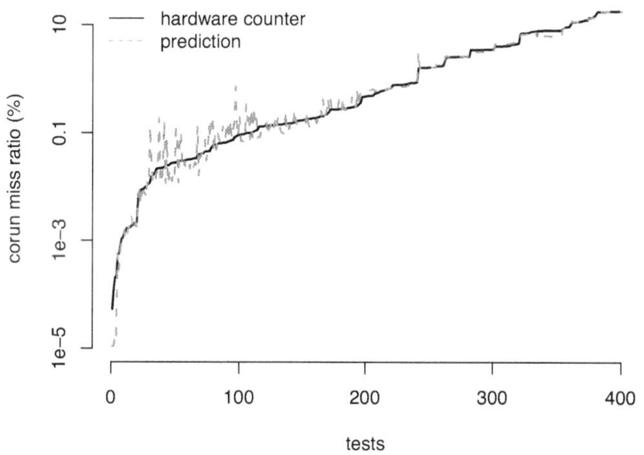

(b) logarithmic scale miss ratios

Figure 9: The predicted and measured miss ratios of the 380 executions in 190 pair runs. The executions are ordered by the ascending miss ratio as measured by the hardware counters in exhaustive testing. For each execution, the solid (black) line shows the hardware counter result, and the dotted (red) line shows the prediction. The prediction takes about a *half* percent of the time of exhaustive testing. Just two executions have a significant error in both graphs, which are a *half* percent of all executions.

Figure 9 has two graphs, showing the miss ratio in the linear scale in the upper graph and the logarithmic scale in the lower graph. The prediction is mostly accurate. The errors happen but for different executions in the two graphs. If an error is visible in the linear scale but not in the logarithmic scale, the error is significant in absolute terms but not in relative terms. Similarly, we have errors significant relatively but not absolutely. The two graphs show just two errors that are significant in both scales. In the other 378 (99.5%) executions, the prediction is either accurate or the error insignificant. From visual inspection, the error is significant in just 0.5% of all executions.

To make the prediction, the analysis needs 1 hour 4 minutes CPU time for sampling, almost as fast as we can run the 20 programs without analysis. In comparison, the exhaustive testing takes over 9 days (estimated) of CPU time. The cost saving is 99.5%.

To see interference in 3-program co-runs, the exhaustive testing has to re-test and collect results anew, but the modeling needs no additional testing. Indeed, the new model has been used in an on-line system to regroup eight programs to run on two quad-core processors (to have a higher performance or at least a more repeatable performance) [47]. The exhaustive testing of the 4-program co-runs in our 20-program suite would need 19 thousand test executions and have taken months of time.

To summarize the pair interference experiment, we can say that the result is half and half: the modeling takes half percent of the time and has a significant error in a half percent of executions.

5. Related Work

The concept of locality has evolved from an observation that a program does not use all the data at all times, to quantitative metrics that we can evaluate and compare but for which we must solve the dual problems of speed and precision.

Locality sampling A publicly available system for locality sampling is the SLO tool developed by Beyls and D'Hollander [5]. SLO instruments a program to skip every k accesses and take the next address as a sample. A bounded number of samples are kept in a sample reservoir. To track reuse windows, it checks each access to see if it is an access to some sampled datum. The instrumentation code is carefully engineered in GCC to have just two conditional statements for each memory access (one for address and the other for counter checking). Reservoir sampling reduces the time overhead from 1000-fold slow-down to only a factor of 5 and the space overhead to within 250MB extra memory. The sampling accuracy is 90% with 95% confidence. The accuracy is measured in the reuse time, not the reuse distance or the miss ratio.

To accurately measure reuse distance, a record must be kept to count the number of distinct data appeared in a reuse window. Zhong and Chang developed the bursty reuse distance sampling, which divides a program execution into sampling and hibernation periods [48]. In the sampling period, the counting uses a tree structure and costs $O(\log \log M)$ per access. If a reuse window extends beyond a sampling period into the subsequent hibernation period, the counting uses a hash-table, which reduces the cost to $O(1)$ per access. Multicore reuse distance analysis uses a similar scheme for analyzing multi-threaded code [35]. Its fast mode improves over hibernation by omitting the hash-table access at times when no samples are being tracked. Both methods compute the reuse distance accurately.

StatCache is based on unbiased uniform sampling [3]. After a data sample is selected, StatCache puts the page under the OS protection to capture the next access to the same datum. It uses the hardware counters to measure the time distance till the reuse. OS protection is limited by the page granularity. Two other systems, developed by Cascaval et al. [7] and Tam et al. [40], used the special support on IBM processors to trap accesses to specified data addresses. To reduce the cost, these methods used a small number of samples. Cascaval et al. used the Hellinger Affinity Kernel to infer the accuracy of sampling [7]. Tam et al. predicted the miss rate curves in real time [40].

Locality measurement Reuse distance is a shorter name for the LRU stack distance defined by Mattson et al. [31]. The fastest precise method takes $O(n \log m)$ time, where n is the length of the trace and m is the size of data [34]. A variation of the algorithm powered the Cheetah cache simulator [38], widely distributed as part of the SimpleScalar tool set. By approximating long-distance reuses (with a guaranteed precision e.g. 99%), the cost can be reduced to $O(n \log \log m)$ [49]. This $n \log \log m$ algorithm is used in the two most recent sampling studies [35, 48]. In our experiments, the cost is several hundred times slowdown. The average cost reported in another study is as high as several thousand times slowdown (although with a different implementation) [35]. Zhong et al. gave a lower bound result indicating that the (asymptotic) cost cannot be further reduced for full reuse distance analysis [49]. Recent studies found efficient algorithms to parallelize the reuse distance analysis to run on MPI [33] or GPU [12, 22].

Time-based conversion [27, 36] and StatStack [19, 20] each gave a statistical formula to convert the reuse time distribution to miss rate, so did the working set theory [15]. These methods were not guaranteed to be correct or have a bounded error. This work gives a different conversion method based on the footprint formula and the correctness condition for the conversion.

If the cost of measuring $O(n)$ reuse windows was high, the cost of measuring $O(n^2)$ footprint windows was prohibitively high. In 2008, a sub-quadratic cost $O(n \log m)$ solution was proposed [17]. Later, the algorithm was implemented and made 70 times faster [45]. These two methods measure the full distribution, including for example, the maximum and the minimum sizes. Instead of the full distribution, Xiang et al. showed that the average footprint can be measured in linear time $O(n)$, and it is a monotone function [46]. Based on the HOTL theory in this paper, we have reduced the analysis cost to a negligible level using sampling and proved that the footprint function is concave.

Program sampling Arnold and Ryder pioneered a general framework to sample Java code, i.e. the first few invocations of a function or the beginning iterations of a loop [2]. It has been adopted for hot-stream prefetching in C/C++ in bursty sampling [11] and extended to sample both static and dynamic bursts for calling context profiling [50]. Shadow profiling pauses a program at preset intervals and forks a separate process to profile in parallel with the base program [32, 42]. Before the new theory, the reuse distance analysis is not a good target for these techniques because of the uncertain length of the reuse windows. With the new theory, locality sampling becomes a similar task as frequency profiling. Like frequency profiling, the cost can be adjusted by simply changing the sampling rate.

Filmer metrics in multi-threaded code The locality metrics in particular the footprint and the reuse distance have been extended to multi-threaded code by a number of studies, including composable modeling of shared footprint [18], statistical modeling in concurrent reuse distance [27], and direct measurement by multi-core reuse distance [35]. In a concurrent program, the reuse distance is affected by data sharing, thread interleaving and composition. These studies solved the problems by characterizing the relation between the private reuse distance (PRD) and the concurrent reuse distance (CRD). For loop-based code, Wu and Yeung gave a scaling model to predict how the reuse distance changes when the work is divided by a different number of threads [43]. These modeling techniques have found uses in co-scheduling [26] and multicore cache hierarchy design [44]. In this paper, we use footprint sampling and HOTL conversion in multi-threaded code and show the result that the reuse-window hypothesis holds there as it does in sequential code.

6. Summary

In this paper, we have compiled five Filmer metrics— the footprint, the inter-miss time, the volume fill time, the miss ratio curve and the reuse distance—and shown that they are mutually derivable. The derivations form a higher order relation. We prove that two of the miss-ratio derivations, by the footprint and by the reuse time, are mathematically equivalent. As a result, the correctness of the conversion depends on the reuse-window hypothesis. In addition, we prove that the average footprint is a concave function. We also give a direct definition of the fill time and show it to be unusable in practice. When comparing with the working set theory, we show the recurring theoretical result which we call Denning's law of locality. We show how the new theory complements and extends the previous theory.

Based on the new theory, we have developed a novel technique of locality sampling and used it to predict the miss ratio. When tested on the full suite of the SPEC 2006 benchmarks, the HOTL conversion predicts the miss ratio for over 3000 cache sizes at a speed 39% faster than cache simulation for a single cache size. The prediction is accurate compared to simulation and hardware counter results. Locality sampling obtains a similar accuracy by examining 0.9% of the execution and incurring a cost of less than 0.5% of the time of the unmodified code. When used to predict cache interference, the new technique takes 0.5% of the time of the exhaustive testing and predicts the interference accurately for 99.5% of the executions.

In summary, we have shown that the Filmer metrics can be measured in real time, and they are easy to compose and convert. We expect that the higher order theory and the sample technique will provide a new foundation for developing future techniques of locality analysis and optimization.

Acknowledgments

The comparison with the working set theory was done in collaboration with Peter Denning. It was a rare privilege to discuss the field defining ideas with their creator. He was also the first to use the acronyms HOTL, WSLT and CLT when commenting on our paper and suggested the comparative view in Figure 4. Kim Hazelwood, Ramesh Peri and Tipp Moseley answered our questions about Pin and shadow profiling. We also thank Jacob Brock, Xipeng Shen, Donald Yeung, other colleagues, the reviewers of ASPLOS and the program committee especially P. Sadayappan for the careful review and constructive critiques, which are invaluable in improving the presentation of both the theory and the evaluation.

References

[1] R. Allen and K. Kennedy. *Optimizing Compilers for Modern Architectures: A Dependence-based Approach*. Morgan Kaufmann Publishers, Oct. 2001.

[2] M. Arnold and B. G. Ryder. A framework for reducing the cost of instrumented code. In *Proceedings of PLDI*, pages 168–179, Snowbird, Utah, June 2001.

[3] E. Berg and E. Hagersten. Fast data-locality profiling of native execution. In *Proceedings of SIGMETRICS*, pages 169–180, 2005.

[4] K. Beyls and E. D'Hollander. Generating cache hints for improved program efficiency. *Journal of Systems Architecture*, 51(4):223–250, 2005.

[5] K. Beyls and E. D'Hollander. Discovery of locality-improving refactoring by reuse path analysis. In *Proceedings of HPCC. Springer. Lecture Notes in Computer Science Vol. 4208*, pages 220–229, 2006.

[6] C. Bienia, S. Kumar, J. P. Singh, and K. Li. The PARSEC benchmark suite: characterization and architectural implications. In *Proceedings of PACT*, pages 72–81, 2008.

[7] C. Cascaval, E. Duesterwald, P. F. Sweeney, and R. W. Wisniewski. Multiple page size modeling and optimization. In *Proceedings of PACT*, pages 339–349, 2005.

[8] C. Cascaval and D. A. Padua. Estimating cache misses and locality using stack distances. In *Proceedings of ICS*, pages 150–159, 2003.

[9] D. Chandra, F. Guo, S. Kim, and Y. Solihin. Predicting inter-thread cache contention on a chip multi-processor architecture. In *Proceedings of HPCA*, pages 340–351, 2005.

[10] A. Chauhan and C.-Y. Shei. Static reuse distances for locality-based optimizations in MATLAB. In *Proceedings of ICS*, pages 295–304, 2010.

[11] T. M. Chilimbi and M. Hirzel. Dynamic hot data stream prefetching for general-purpose programs. In *Proceedings of PLDI*, Berlin, Germany, June 2002.

[12] H. Cui, Q. Yi, J. Xue, L. Wang, Y. Yang, and X. Feng. A highly parallel reuse distance analysis algorithm on gpus. In *Proceedings of IPDPS*, 2012.

[13] P. J. Denning. The working set model for program behaviour. *Communications of ACM*, 11(5):323–333, 1968.

[14] P. J. Denning. Working sets past and present. *IEEE Transactions on Software Engineering*, SE-6(1), Jan. 1980.

[15] P. J. Denning and S. C. Schwartz. Properties of the working set model. *Communications of ACM*, 15(3):191–198, 1972.

[16] P. J. Denning and D. R. Slutz. Generalized working sets for segment reference strings. *Communications of ACM*, 21(9):750–759, 1978.

[17] C. Ding and T. Chilimbi. All-window profiling of concurrent executions. In *Proceedings of PPoPP*, 2008. *poster paper*.

[18] C. Ding and T. Chilimbi. A composable model for analyzing locality of multi-threaded programs. Technical Report MSR-TR-2009-107, Microsoft Research, August 2009.

[19] D. Eklov, D. Black-Schaffer, and E. Hagersten. Fast modeling of shared caches in multicore systems. In *Proceedings of HiPEAC*, pages 147–157, 2011. *best paper*.

[20] D. Eklov and E. Hagersten. StatStack: Efficient modeling of LRU caches. In *Proceedings of ISPASS*, pages 55–65, 2010.

[21] C. Fang, S. Carr, S. Önder, and Z. Wang. Path-based reuse distance analysis. In *Proceedings of CC*, pages 32–46, 2006.

[22] S. Gupta, P. Xiang, Y. Yang, and H. Zhou. Locality principle revisited: A probability-based quantitative approach. In *Proceedings of IPDPS*, 2012.

[23] J. L. Henning. Spec cpu2006 benchmark descriptions. *SIGARCH Computer Architecture News*, 34(4):1–17, 2006.

[24] M. D. Hill. *Aspects of cache memory and instruction buffer performance*. PhD thesis, University of California, Berkeley, Nov. 1987.

[25] M. D. Hill and A. J. Smith. Evaluating associativity in CPU caches. *IEEE Transactions on Computers*, 38(12):1612–1630, 1989.

[26] Y. Jiang, K. Tian, and X. Shen. Combining locality analysis with online proactive job co-scheduling in chip multiprocessors. In *Proceedings of HiPEAC*, pages 201–215, 2010.

[27] Y. Jiang, E. Z. Zhang, K. Tian, and X. Shen. Is reuse distance applicable to data locality analysis on chip multiprocessors? In *Proceedings of CC*, pages 264–282, 2010.

[28] S. F. Kaplan, Y. Smaragdakis, and P. R. Wilson. Flexible reference trace reduction for VM simulations. *ACM Transactions on Modeling and Computer Simulation*, 13(1):1–38, 2003.

[29] C.-K. Luk, R. S. Cohn, R. Muth, H. Patil, A. Klauser, P. G. Lowney, S. Wallace, V. J. Reddi, and K. M. Hazelwood. Pin: building customized program analysis tools with dynamic instrumentation. In *Proceedings of PLDI*, pages 190–200, 2005.

[30] G. Marin and J. Mellor-Crummey. Cross architecture performance predictions for scientific applications using parameterized models. In *Proceedings of SIGMETRICS*, pages 2–13, 2004.

[31] R. L. Mattson, J. Gecsei, D. Slutz, and I. L. Traiger. Evaluation techniques for storage hierarchies. *IBM System Journal*, 9(2):78–117, 1970.

[32] T. Moseley, A. Shye, V. J. Reddi, D. Grunwald, and R. Peri. Shadow profiling: Hiding instrumentation costs with parallelism. In *Proceedings of CGO*, pages 198–208, 2007.

[33] Q. Niu, J. Dinan, Q. Lu, and P. Sadayappan. PARDA: A fast parallel reuse distance analysis algorithm. In *Proceedings of IPDPS*, 2012.

[34] F. Olken. Efficient methods for calculating the success function of fixed space replacement policies. Technical Report LBL-12370, Lawrence Berkeley Laboratory, 1981.

[35] D. L. Schuff, M. Kulkarni, and V. S. Pai. Accelerating multicore reuse distance analysis with sampling and parallelization. In *Proceedings of PACT*, pages 53–64, 2010.

[36] X. Shen, J. Shaw, B. Meeker, and C. Ding. Locality approximation using time. In *Proceedings of POPL*, pages 55–61, 2007.

[37] A. J. Smith. On the effectiveness of set associative page mapping and its applications in main memory management. In *Proceedings of ICSE*, 1976.

[38] R. A. Sugumar and S. G. Abraham. Efficient simulation of caches under optimal replacement with applications to miss characterization. In *Proceedings of SIGMETRICS*, Santa Clara, CA, May 1993.

[39] G. E. Suh, S. Devadas, and L. Rudolph. Analytical cache models with applications to cache partitioning. In *Proceedings of ICS*, pages 1–12, 2001.

[40] D. K. Tam, R. Azimi, L. Soares, and M. Stumm. RapidMRC: approximating L2 miss rate curves on commodity systems for online optimizations. In *Proceedings of ASPLOS*, pages 121–132, 2009.

[41] D. Thiébaut and H. S. Stone. Footprints in the cache. *ACM Transactions on Computer Systems*, 5(4):305–329, 1987.

[42] S. Wallace and K. Hazelwood. Superpin: Parallelizing dynamic instrumentation for real-time performance. In *Proceedings of CGO*, pages 209–220, 2007.

[43] M.-J. Wu and D. Yeung. Coherent profiles: Enabling efficient reuse distance analysis of multicore scaling for loop-based parallel programs. In *Proceedings of PACT*, pages 264–275, 2011.

[44] M.-J. Wu and D. Yeung. Identifying optimal multicore cache hierarchies for loop-based parallel programs via reuse distance analysis. In *Proceedings of the ACM SIGPLAN Workshop on Memory System Performance and Correctness*, pages 2–11, 2012.

[45] X. Xiang, B. Bao, T. Bai, C. Ding, and T. M. Chilimbi. All-window profiling and composable models of cache sharing. In *Proceedings of PPoPP*, pages 91–102, 2011.

[46] X. Xiang, B. Bao, C. Ding, and Y. Gao. Linear-time modeling of program working set in shared cache. In *Proceedings of PACT*, pages 350–360, 2011.

[47] X. Xiang, B. Bao, C. Ding, and K. Shen. Cache conscious task regrouping on multicore processors. In *Proceedings of CCGrid*, pages 603–611, 2012.

[48] Y. Zhong and W. Chang. Sampling-based program locality approximation. In *Proceedings of ISMM*, pages 91–100, 2008.

[49] Y. Zhong, X. Shen, and C. Ding. Program locality analysis using reuse distance. *ACM Transactions on Programming Languages and Systems*, 31(6):1–39, Aug. 2009.

[50] X. Zhuang, M. J. Serrano, H. W. Cain, and J.-D. Choi. Accurate, efficient, and adaptive calling context profiling. In *Proceedings of PLDI*, pages 263–271, 2006.

[51] S. Zhuravlev, S. Blagodurov, and A. Fedorova. Addressing shared resource contention in multicore processors via scheduling. In *Proceedings of ASPLOS*, pages 129–142, 2010.

A. Measuring the Direct Fill Time

As defined in Section 2.3, the direct fill time is the average length of all windows that have the same-size footprint. For a trace of n accesses to m data, the fill time algorithm counts all $O(n^2)$ windows but reduces the quadratic cost of counting in three ways. The solution is similar in design to all-window footprint measurement [17, 45].

Counting by footprint size rather than window length The footprint size in a window is up to m, the size of data. Although there are up to n windows ending at each element, there are at most m different footprint sizes. By counting m footprint sizes rather than n windows, the algorithm reduces the counting cost from $O(n^2)$ to $O(nm)$.

Consider the example in Figure 10. Take the trace till the second access of b (before $|$). It is the 6th access, so there are 6 windows ending there. Only 3 distinct elements are accessed, so the 6 windows have at most 3 different footprint sizes. From small to large, the 6 windows have a length 1 to 6 and footprints 1,2,3,3,3,3 respectively.

aabacb | acadaadeedab

Windows ending at the second *b*
b, cb, acb, bacb, abacb, aabacb

Figure 10: There are 3 different footprints for the 6 windows ending at the second b, so the 6 windows can be counted in 3 (instead of 6) steps.

Relative precision footprint size By measuring data sizes with a relative precision, for example, 99% or 99.9%, the number of different footprint sizes becomes $O(\log m)$ instead of m. The cost of the algorithm becomes $O(n \log m)$.

Trace compression A user sets a positive threshold c. The trace is divided into a series of k intervals. Each interval has c distinct elements (except for the last interval, which may have fewer than c distinct elements). This is known as trace compression [28]. The algorithm traverses the trace interval by interval rather than element by element. The length of the trace is reduced from n to k, and the cost becomes $O(ck \log m)$.

The algorithm computes the full distribution of the fill time $VT(v)$, from which we can compute the average fill time $vt(v)$. As far as we know, this is the first algorithm that computes the direct fill time with a guaranteed precision. We have implemented it and shown the results in the evaluation section.

To Hardware Prefetch or Not to Prefetch?

A Virtualized Environment Study and Core Binding Approach

Hui Kang Jennifer L. Wong

Department of Computer Science
Stony Brook University
{hkang,jwong}@cs.stonybrook.edu

Abstract

Most hardware and software venders suggest disabling hardware prefetching in virtualized environments. They claim that prefetching is detrimental to application performance due to inaccurate prediction caused by workload diversity and VM interference on shared cache. However, no comprehensive or quantitative measurements to support this belief have been performed.

This paper is the first to systematically measure the influence of hardware prefetching in virtualized environments. We examine a wide variety of benchmarks on three types of chip-multiprocessors (CMPs) to analyze the hardware prefetching performance. We conduct extensive experiments by taking into account a number of important virtualization factors. We find that hardware prefetching has minimal destructive influence under most configurations. Only with certain application combinations does prefetching influence the overall performance.

To leverage these findings and make hardware prefetching effective across a diversity of virtualized environments, we propose a dynamic prefetching-aware VCPU-core binding approach (PAVCB), which includes two phases - classifying and binding. The workload of each VM is classified into different cache sharing constraint categories based upon its cache access characteristics, considering both prefetch requests and demand requests. Then following heuristic rules, the VCPUs of each VM are scheduled onto appropriate cores subject to cache sharing constraints. We show that the proposed approach can improve performance by 12% on average over the default scheduler and 46% over manual system administrator bindings across different workload combinations in the presence of hardware prefetching.

Categories and Subject Descriptors D.4.1 [*Operating Systems*]: Scheduling; B.3.2 [*Design Styles*]: Cache memories

General Terms Measurement, Performance, Algorithms

Keywords Prefetching, Virtualization, Shared Cache

1. Introduction

Virtualization has been adopted in both large enterprise infrastructures and thin desktop clients. The overall success of consolidating a diversity of applications on such platforms depends on the efficiency of virtualization. Significant efforts have been placed towards understanding, measuring, and optimizing the impact of different layers on application performance in virtualized environments. The main directions include both software and hardware components from programming language [24], operating systems and virtual machine monitors (aka., VMM or hypervisor) [1, 17, 26], to memory paging [29, 39] and shared processor cache [10]. One particular type of hardware architecture support widely implemented in modern multi-core and multi-socket chip-multiprocessor systems (CMPs) is hardware prefetching. The influence of this mechanism on virtualization is yet to be fully understood.

Hardware prefetching is a commonly employed optimization approach to mitigate the lag of main memory speed behind processor speed. Application programs can also explicitly take advantage of hardware prefetching to improve the performance [28]. Hardware prefetching, however, can severely degrade the system performance, when excessive prefetching requests contend for limited memory bandwidth and cache resources shared by different cores of a CMP. Since virtualization further complicates the cache sharing by consolidating multiple virtual machines (VMs) on a single CMP, the effectiveness of hardware prefetching can be unclear. If we can understand how hardware prefetching influences such consolidated applications in VMs, we can not only determine whether hardware prefetching should be enabled or disabled, but also design a better scheduler to enforce appropriate last-level cache (LLC) sharing among VMs.

In the first half of the paper, we study the impact of hardware prefetching on consolidated applications on three typical CMP architectures: Intel core-based Xeon, Intel Nehalem-based Xeon, and AMD Phenom. The application benchmarks are selected from traditional server workloads such as database (OLTP) and file server (Filebench), as well as emerging shared memory programs for CMPs (PARSEC suite). We compare the benchmark performance of hardware prefetching under different system configurations, the variations that cover important consolidation factors – number of VCPUs and VMs, VCPU-core binding, and workload interference between VMs. Conventional wisdom is that hardware prefetching is harmful to multi-core systems due to workload diversity [13], and thus many virtualization benchmark results are done with prefetching disabled for performance best practice [11, 12, 14, 37, 38]. However, we find that hardware prefetching has insignificant influence on the performance of OLTP, Filebench, and the applications in PARSEC. Only under a few particular benchmark combinations does prefetching degrade the overall system and application performance significantly.

These findings motivate us to derive a scheduling approach that makes hardware prefetching effective across a diversity of virtualized environments by preventing those destructive cases via appropriate VCPU-core binding. When VMs are consolidated on the

ASPLOS'13, March 16–20, 2013, Houston, Texas, USA.

same cache, the workload characteristics run in each VM determines whether the compound effect of hardware prefetching and cache sharing improves or degrades the system performance. Prior research considering cache related characteristics as the deterministic factors [35] ignored the influence of hardware prefetching, when determining optimal cache sharing via VCPU-core binding. We predict the cache performance of consolidated workloads via three important cache access characteristics of individual workloads. These characteristics consist of metrics that measure cache demand requests, as well as prefetching requests. Based upon the profiled characteristics of each VM, we design a heuristic-based VCPU-core binding algorithm. Results show that in the presence of hardware prefetching, the proposed VCPU-core binding strategy improves the overall consolidated performance by 12% on average compared to the default VM scheduler and always performs better than other manual VM placements.

In summary, the major contributions of this paper are as follows:

- We provide a comprehensive study of the influence of hardware prefetching in virtualized environments, running PARSEC, OLTP, and Filebench on top of three types of CMP architectures. To the best of our knowledge, this work is the first performance evaluation of hardware prefetching in virtualization environments.
- We propose an application classification scheme based on three important cache access characteristics. The classification scheme predicts the effect of cache sharing between different co-located workloads in the presence of hardware prefetching. It aims to reduce the cache contention due to VM interference, as well as aggressive prefetching requests.
- We develop a prefetching-aware VCPU-core binding approach, which not only allows the consolidated workloads to receive performance improvement through hardware prefetching, but also limits any negative impact of hardware prefetching.

The rest of the paper is organized as follows. Section 2 presents the methodology for evaluating the influence of hardware prefetching and reports the measurement results. In Section 3, we describe the cause to destructive impact of hardware prefetching by characterizing three cache access metrics of each workload and present a prefetching-aware VCPU-core binding algorithm. Section 4 evaluates the proposed algorithm on different CMP architectures. We summarize the related work in Section 5 before concluding.

2. Is Prefetching Harmful?

In this section, we first investigate the influence of hardware prefetching on cache performance. Experiments show that the cache miss rate is not a deterministic factor to application performance in the presence of hardware prefetching. In the rest of this section, we experimentally analyze the application performance, of the systems with and without hardware prefetching.

2.1 Motivations

When hardware prefetching is enabled, the cache controller prefetches the data from main memory before the actual reference in order to avoid the memory access lag behind processor speeds. While prefetching can hide the memory access latency and improve system performance, there are associated costs, such as polluting the cache lines due to inaccurate prefetch requests and wasting memory bandwidth which leads to severe performance degradation. In addition, both operating systems and applications are oblivious of the specific hardware prefetching algorithm, so the prefetching influence is uncontrollable and unpredictable. Therefore, in the virtualized environment the conventional wisdom is that applications running in the VM that otherwise receive benefits through prefetching significantly, can also lose system performance due to

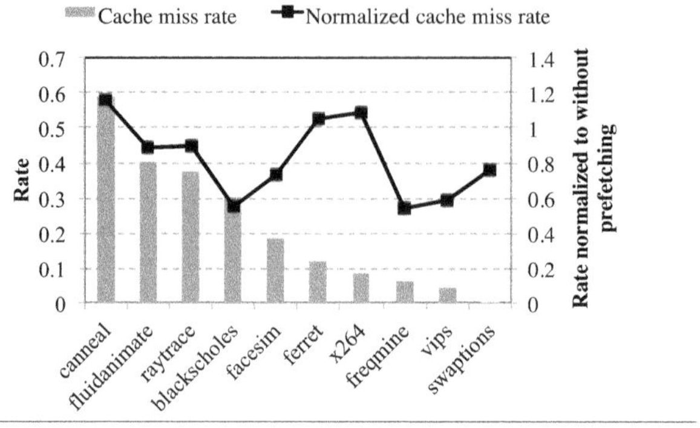

Figure 1. Cache miss rate with hardware prefetching (left axis) and normalized to without prefetching (right axis).

the consolidated workloads from co-located VMs. Since VMs sharing cores and LLC are isolated in their memory address spaces, cache lines inserted by prefetch requests from one VM have a high chance to conflict with cache access requests from other VMs, an undesirable event that will increase the cache miss rate.

To understand the effects of hardware prefetching on cache performance in the virtualized environment, we evaluate the cache miss rate in the presence and absence of hardware prefetching respectively. In this experiment, two VMs run the same benchmark on a physical host. In Figure 1, the bars show the cache miss rates for each benchmark in decreasing order, when hardware prefetching is enabled. Without loss of generality, all cache misses measured throughout the paper are LLC misses. The x-axis represents the benchmarks selected from a diverse set of applications. The LLC cache miss rates vary from $< 5\%$ to $> 40\%$ across the 11 benchmarks. The details of the experimental setup are presented in Section 2.2. From the cache access perspective, when hardware prefetching is enabled the VM running cache intensive workloads will induce more cache misses, leading to the inference that prefetching degrades system performance. Additionally, hardware prefetching is assumed to have insignificant influence, neither positive nor negative, on applications that are not cache intensive.

However, given the uncontrollable and unclear nature of hardware prefetching mechanisms, determining cache performance directly from cache miss rates only provides a limited perspective of prefetching influence. The line in Figure 1 compares cache miss rate for each benchmark with and without hardware prefetching. The right y-axis represents the LLC cache miss rate relative to the miss rate without hardware prefetching. Based on these results we find two interesting behaviors. Firstly, only three out of the 11 benchmarks experience degraded cache performance; they are canneal, ferret, and x264. The average degradation is around 9.5%, while the average improvement for the remaining 8 benchmarks is 27%. This indicates that hardware prefetching actually has minimal negative influence on most benchmarks run in the virtualized environment in terms of the cache miss rate of the whole system. Secondly, we observe that no matter the overall cache miss rate of the benchmark is, hardware prefetching has minimal negative influence. For example, the cache intensive benchmarks fluidanimate, raytrace, blackscholes, and facesim receive 10-46% improvement of their cache miss rates in the presence of hardware prefetching. However, hardware prefetching increases the cache miss rates of ferret and x264 by 4.6% and 8.4%, which are less cache intensive.

In addition, although the cache miss rate measures the influence of hardware prefetching on data installed in cache lines, the benchmark performance depends on other factors such as CPU, I/O, or application behavior. Therefore, more comprehensive information needs to be obtained from the application performance perspective (e.g., running time, throughput) before judging prefetching influence. We conducted a series of experiments systematically to show that the benefits of prefetching outweigh the harmfulness on most benchmarks under different system configurations and hardware prefetching mechanisms. The next two subsections describe the experimental setup used in all experiments throughout the paper and our findings.

2.2 Experimental Methodology

In this subsection, we present our methodology to evaluate the hardware prefetching influence in the virtualized environment. This methodology is adapted from Zhang [42]. We first give an overview of the specifications of processor and cache hierarchy of our testbed. These processors vary in the microarchitecture and are typical CMPs on the market. We then introduce the benchmark application suites. Finally, we describe a set of VM configuration parameters that may affect the influence of hardware prefetching. Overall, these experiments cover various important factors on the level of programs (types of workloads, working set sizes), VM configurations (VCPU-core binding), sharing level (number of VMs or VCPUs per LLC), and architectures (number of cores and LLC cache size). As the focus of this study is on the influence of hardware prefetching, we compare the benchmark performance with and without hardware prefetching.

2.2.1 Processor and Cache Hierarchies

CMPs with different core architectures and cache hierarchies have different implementations of hardware prefetching. We select three representative CMP architectures on the market: Intel Core-based Xeon, Nehalem-based Xeon, and AMD Phenom II. These processors vary widely in the number of cores, the cache levels, and geometry of the caches on the chip. Table 1 summarizes the processor specifications we use to evaluate the effect of hardware prefetching. Note that only one processor socket per machine is used for experimentation, unless explicitly stated. For each architecture, hardware prefetching can be enabled/disabled either by programmatically setting the bit of the related model-specific register (MSR) or through the BIOS. For example, Intel processors expose the hardware prefetching option on BIOS, while `MSRC001_1022` is the related MSR for AMD processors [2]. To verify that prefetching is enabled/disabled, we use OProfile [27] to read the corresponding events from the hardware performance counter.

2.2.2 Application Benchmarks

The experimental workloads comprise of 11 applications from PARSEC 2.1 benchmark suite [5], the OLTP benchmark of SysBench [33], and the fileserver mode of Filebench [9] (Table 2). These benchmarks are selected to represent typical workloads run on virtualized desktops and server environments, as well as to represent a wide diversity of cache access behaviors. All selected benchmarks are modern multi-thread applications programmed for use on multi-core systems. Next, we describe each benchmark and the corresponding performance metric.

PARSEC 2.1 is a recently released benchmark suite, offering a wide variety of current and emerging applications for CMP design research in both industry and academia. The design of algorithms in PARSEC applications takes into account of the many cores on a single socket, each with access to shared caches. PARSEC benchmarks exhibit different memory access behaviors, different data sharing pattern, and different working set sizes. PARSEC is widely used in research [3, 4, 8, 42]. Table 2 lists the selected benchmarks from PARSEC used throughout this paper. Each benchmark is experimented with its native input data set and runs a specific number of threads, which is equal to the number of VCPUs configured for the VM. The performance metric for these benchmarks is the execution time.

Table 2. Benchmarks

Application name	Working set size (byte)	Feature
PARSEC 2.1		
raytrace	512M	data parallel
freqmine	1G	data-parallel
ferret	128M	pipeline
blackscholes	2M	data-parallel
canneal	2G	unstructured
bodytrack	8M	data-parallel
facesim	256M	data-parallel
vips	16M	data-parallel
fluidanimate	128M	data-parallel
swaptions	512K	data-parallel
x264	16M	pipeline
OLTP		
MySQL	> 1G	data-parallel
Filebench		
Fileserver	> 1G	I/O parallel

Online Transaction Processing (OLTP) is an important benchmark for evaluating architecture and system design and has been studied for decades [23]. Many small businesses have been outsourcing their in-house database to virtualized cloud environment, and therefore it is imperative for us to evaluate the prefetching influence on such applications. In this work, we use MySQL to create a database and drive the workloads using SysBench [33]. We create a 10GB size database, which is significantly larger than the VM memory size. The client machine launches 16 threads; each is connected to the database VM and performs transactions on the database tables. A transaction can include several statements such as range queries, column updates, insertion, and deletion. Each benchmark run includes 30, 000 transactions. The performance metric for the OLTP benchmark is the execution time.

Filebench is a file system and storage benchmark framework. It emulates the I/O behaviors of the applications, e.g., mail server, web server, database server. We experiment with file server mode. In this mode, by default the benchmark generates 100 threads to produce a sequence of open, read, and close operations on multiple files in a directory tree with a log file append. The performance metric for Filebench is the throughput, i.e., number of I/O operations per second.

2.2.3 VM Configurations

The influence of hardware prefetching can be affected by how co-located VMs interfere with each other when accessing the shared cache. Since the interaction between VMs on the shared cache is determined by the workload consolidation and the placement of VCPUs, we consider the following factors that are specific to virtualized environments: number of VCPUs and VMs consolidated on the host, the VCPU-core binding, and workload combination.

Number of VCPUs and VMs. In a virtualized system, when the LLC is shared by VCPUs of different VMs, VMs contend the cache resource by evicting the cache blocks belonging to others. Both the number of VCPUs and the number of VMs impact the sharing of the LLC, resulting in different effects on hardware prefetching. The conventional suggestion to disable hardware prefetching is mainly based upon the intuition that data prefetched to the cache induce prefetching pollution between the co-running VMs. Thus, it is important to evaluate the effect of hardware prefetching under different consolidation levels (number of VMs per physical host). We experiment with two and three VMs on a LLC. In addition, we vary the number of VCPUs for each VM such that the multi-thread benchmarks are able to make use of the multiple VCPUs to achieve parallelism. The number of VCPU for each VM is 1, 2, or 4.

Table 1. Experimental testbed: processor specifications

–	Intel Core-based Xeon	Intel Nehalem-based Xeon	AMD Phenom II
CPU model	Harpertown, X5460	Westmere, X5650	X4 955
# cores on socket	4	6	4
Frequency (GHz)	3.16	2.67	3.2
L1 size	32KB	32KB	64KB
L2 size	2 x 6MB, each shared by 2cores	6 x 256KB, Private	4 x 512 KB, private
L3 size	None	12MB, shared by all	6MB, shared by all
Main memory	8GB	24GB	6GB

VCPU-core binding. The binding between VCPUs and cores determines the cache a VM can access. Workloads running inside the VM have different preference to the VCPU-core binding types. Certain applications obtain benefits from running on a single LLC due to the large portion of shared memory of the application working set. On the other hand, when an application has a larger working set size than a single LLC, access to more caches will boost its performance. Since prefetching requests are treated the same as demand requests in cache insertion, the extent of the prefetching effects depends on the exact VCPU-core binding as well. We experiment with different VCPU-core binding to cover different scenarios. In general, we investigate three types of VCPU-core bindings described as follows:

- INDIVIDUAL_DEDICATED – This binding type assigns each VM an individual LLC to avoid inter-VM cache interference and binds each VCPU to a dedicated core. To satisfy this binding type, there are two conditions: (1) the number of LLCs should be equal to the number of VM, or greater, and (2) the number of cores in each LLC should be equal to the number of VM's VCPUs, or greater. Otherwise, this binding type is not available for the VM configuration. For example, in the case of two VMs each with two VCPUs on the Intel X5460 processor, we have two LLCs for each VM and the total number of VCPUs is equal to the number of available cores. Thus, we assign VCPU0 of VM1 to core 0 and VCPU1 of VM1 to core 4, and VCPU0 of VM2 to core 2 and VCPU1 of VM2 to core 6 [1]. Figure 2(a) illustrates the INDIVIDUAL_DEDICATED binding for this case. For certain type of processor with only one shared LLC (i.e., Intel X5650), VCPUs of different VMs must share the LLC, so we equally share the LLC among these VMs.
- SHARING_DEDICATED – This type allows cache sharing between VMs, and binds VCPUs to dedicated cores. Since the cache accesses to the LLC are interfered between VMs, this binding type allows us to understand hardware prefetching influence due to VM consolidation. Exhaustively permuting all combinations of VCPU-core bindings is not only time consuming, but unnecessary; we experiment with the most straightforward bindings. For example, in the case of two VMs each with 2 VCPUs on Intel X5460 processor, we assign each VCPU to a dedicated core as shown in Figure 2(b).
- SHARING_ALL – The difference between this binding type and the previous is that when VCPUs are assigned to the LLC, they are allowed to run on more than one core, instead of a dedicated core. The motivation is to explore the potential effects from the hypervisor scheduling. As VCPUs of different VMs share the same LLC and are scheduled to appropriate cores, this binding type may exhibit the impact of the hypervisor scheduler on how hardware prefetching influences the system performance. Figure 2(c) shows the SHARING_ALL binding for two VMs each with two VCPUs. Each VCPU is allowed to run on two cores, while each LLC is shared by two VMs.

[1] Note the core numbering is consistent with the architecture numbering.

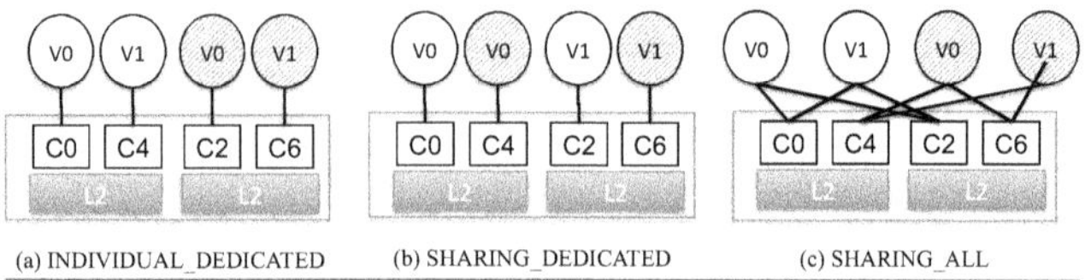

Figure 2. Illustration of VCPU-core binding types for 2 VMs each with 2 VCPUs on Intel Core-based X5460

Workload interference. Due to the wide range of workload variations to be consolidated in the virtualized environments, we additionally study combinations of different workloads and their effect on prefetching. Since the benchmarks have large variability in cache access patterns, the impacts of hardware prefetching on each benchmark are different. It is important to understand whether the combination of two benchmarks with positive prefetching influence individually can still obtain benefit from hardware prefetching, and vice versa for other kinds of combinations.

2.3 Measurements and Observations

Based on the methodology in the previous subsection, we are able to measure the benchmark performance to determine whether hardware prefetching degrades application performance in the virtualized environment. We compare the benchmark performance with and without hardware prefetching following a series of VM configurations as described in Section 2.2.3. Section 2.3.1 presents the results of running the same benchmark in each VM with various number of VCPUs and VMs sharing the LLC. We then run combinations of different workloads in Section 2.3.2. Finally, in Section 2.3.3 we examine the effect of various VCPU-core binding types. For all experiments, we report the results with hardware prefetching normalized to without prefetching [2].

We experiment with both Xen-4.0.1 and KVM within Linux 2.6.34 as the hypervisor for all the experiments. The performance results are of the same magnitude and demonstrate similar patterns. Due to space limitations, we only include the results for the Xen hypervisor. All benchmarks are installed in the Fedora 14 VMs. Each VM is allocated 1536MB memory.

2.3.1 Varying Number of VCPUs and VMs

In the first set of experiments, we study the influence of hardware prefetching by varying the number of VCPUs for each VM. We setup two VMs, running the same benchmark. For each VM, we configure its number of the VCPUs as 1, 2, and 4. Figure 3 illustrates the benchmark performance in the presence of hardware prefetching normalized to without prefetching across all three types of processors. The VCPU-core binding type is SHARING_ALL.

[2] To be consistent with other benchmarks, we convert the throughput metric of Filebench to its reciprocal.

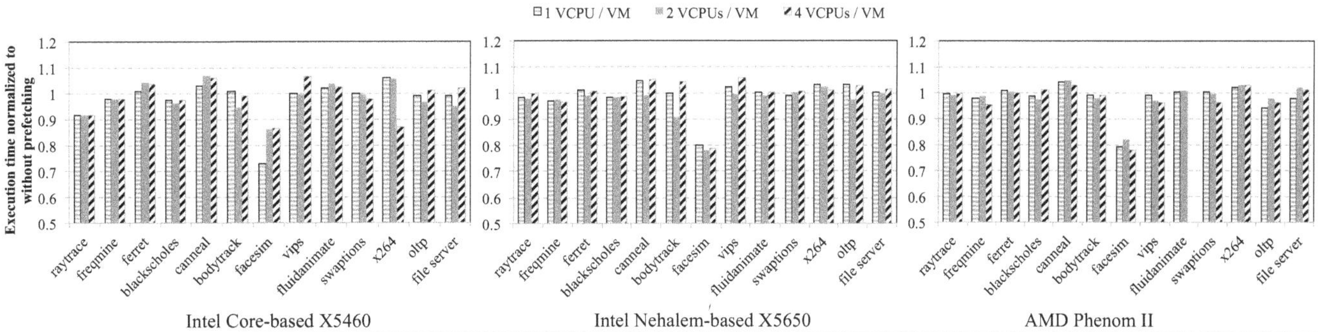

Figure 3. Normalized performance: varying the number of VCPUs per VM under SHARING_ALL (lower is better).

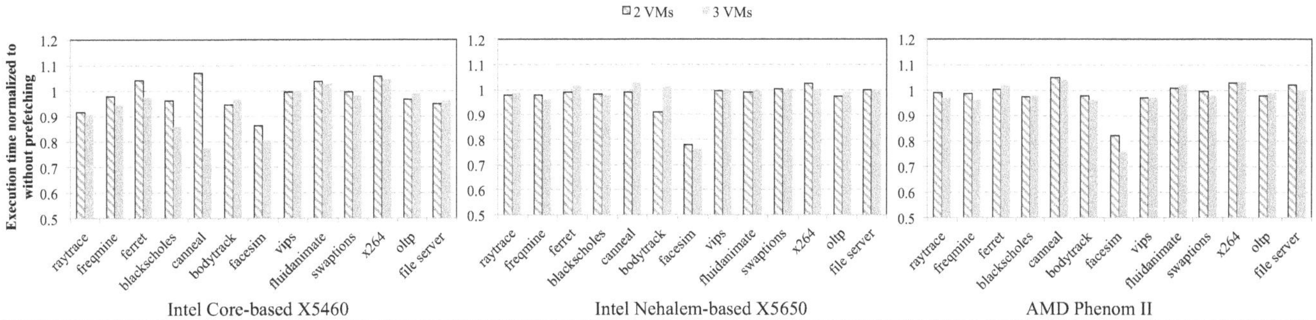

Figure 4. Normalized performance: varying the number of VMs under SHARING_ALL (lower is better).

Intuitively, as the number of VCPUs sharing the same LLC increases, hardware prefetching may insert more cache lines inducing conflicts among these VCPUs. However, as Figure 3 shows, hardware prefetching overall has minimal harmful influence on the benchmarks across all processors, regardless to the number of VCPUs per VM. Most benchmarks in the PARSEC suite have improved performance from prefetching by a variety from $> 20\%$ (for facesim) to 3% (for freqmine). In contrast, only ferret, canneal, and x264 experience performance loss due to prefetching on all three CMPs. The average degradations are minimal ($3.8\%, 2.3\%, 1.7\%$) on each CMP. In addition, the effect of prefetching does not matter to the performance of OLTP and file server benchmark; the performance variation is within $\pm 5\%$ over all VCPU configurations and CMP types. These two benchmarks have significantly larger working set size than the LLC and unpredicted access patterns, so the prefetching controller issues less prefetching requests compared to other benchmarks.

The second set of experiments regarding the consolidation level is to increase the number of VMs on the physical host. Figure 4 shows the results of running two and three VMs on each processor. The normalized performance generally has similar patterns as in the VCPU experiments: the increase of VMs does not affect the prefetching influence on the benchmark performance. Most benchmarks have performance improvement. The average degradations are only $4.5\%, 1.6\%, 2.1\%$ across two and three VMs experiments under each CMP types. Overall, regardless of the number of VMs or VCPUs on the processor, the harmful influence of hardware prefetching is minimal on all CMP types.

2.3.2 Varying Workload Combinations

The previous subsection shows that hardware prefetching has minimal negative influence on all the benchmarks under SHARING_ALL binding when VMs run the same types of workloads. However, certain applications such as canneal and ferret perform better without prefetching, while facesim consistently receives performance improvement from hardware prefetching. The question that then arises is "Do two VMs running different applications adversely affect each other due to prefetching or does prefetching improve the performance of both VMs?"

In this subsection, we study the performance impact of hardware prefetching when the co-located VMs run combinations of different applications. For this purpose, we run two different benchmarks in two VMs and exhaust all possible combinations of benchmarks. Due to space constraints, we focus on the results of canneal and facesim, two benchmarks that show distinct performance variations in the presence of prefetching as shown in Section 2.3.1. We present the results of pairing canneal and facesim with all the other applications from PARSEC on the Intel X5460 processor.

Figure 5(a) and (b) show the performance of running canneal and all other applications under all three binding types, normalized to without hardware prefetching. Figure 5(a) is the normalized performance for canneal and Figure 5(b) for the co-running applications. The first set of bars in Figure 5(a) is canneal's performance when the co-running application is canneal. We observe that no matter what the co-running application is, hardware prefetching degrades canneal's performance. For example, canneal's performance degradations of running with facesim ($\sim 20\%$) and ferret ($\sim 10\%$) are more severe than with others. Figure 5(b) shows the performance impact on the co-located applications follows their behvaoir when running with itself as in the previous subsection. For example, facesim still benefits from hardware prefetching when running with canneal, while ferret does not. Further, the impact of hardware prefetching also depends on how the two VMs share the LLC (i.e., the VCPU-binding types).

The results of running facesim with other benchmarks are shown in Figure 5(c) and (d). The performance of facesim is consistently improved by hardware prefetching despite the co-running application. For the co-running applications, ferret, canneal, and x264's performance are degraded with prefetching as they are when the co-running application is the same, while the other co-running applications do not have significant destructive influence. These

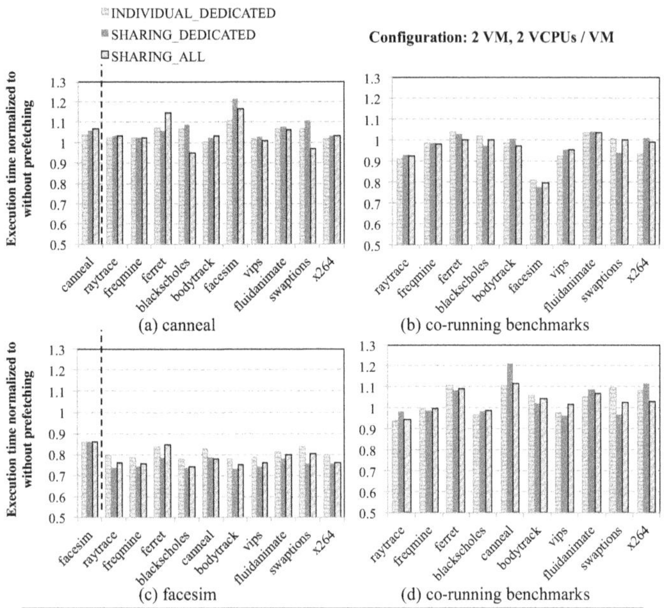

Figure 5. Performance of paired workload combinations of canneal (a, b) and facesim (c, d) with other benchmarks on Intel X5460

observations follow the same trend as in the workload combinations with canneal.

In summary, these experiments show that sharing the cache between inappropriate applications can exacerbate the performance loss due to hardware prefetching. However, this set of experiments differ from those in Section 2.3.1 in that the performance variation could depend on either the VCPU-core binding types or application combinations. To further distinguish inappropriate combination from inappropriate VCPU-core binding as the major cause of the performance degradation in those cases, it is necessary for us to study the influence of VCPU-core binding types when two VMs run the same applications, which is followed in the next subsection.

2.3.3 Varying VCPU-core Bindings

Section 2.3.2 shows that for certain applications (e.g., canneal), the performance degradation due to prefetching is more severe when running with another type of application than with the same type. In this subsection we use the same experimental setup as in Section 2.3.1, but explore the performance influence under different VCPU-core bindings.

We evaluate the benchmark performance with and without prefetching under three types of VCPU-core bindings whenever possible. To compare with the results in Section 2.3.2, we only present the results on the Intel X5460 processor. The three binding types are INDIVIDUAL_DEDICATED, SHARING_DEDICATED, and SHARING_ALL as described in Section 2.2.3. All three binding types are available for the two VMs each with two VCPUs. For the cases of two VMs each with 4 VCPUs and 3 VMs, we did not experiment with the binding type of INDIVIDUAL_DEDICATED because in these cases either the number of VCPUs of one VM exceeds the available cores on the LLC or the number of VMs is greater than the available LLCs. Configuring VMs with a number of VCPUs greater than the cores will severely degrade its performance, a configuration not recommended by most virtualization solutions.

Figure 6 presents the performance results of different VCPU and VM configurations under three VCPU-core binding types. The results show that the negative impact of hardware prefetching is insignificant regardless to the VCPU-core binding types, when two VMs run the same type of applications. For example in the case of two VM each with two VCPUs (Figure 6(a)), the worst performance degradation for canneal is up to 6.8% under SHARING_ALL. In contrast the degradation for canneal is 16.7% and 14.6% when co-running with facesim and ferret respectively as shown in Figure 5(a). For the other two cases (Figure 6(b) and (c)), the performance loss only appears occasionally, and the degradation is insignificant.

2.4 Summary

Overall the experimental study illustrates hardware prefetching has minimal impact on consolidated application performance in virtualized environments despite popular belief. However, when co-located VMs are run in particular application combinations, the performance degradation due to hardware prefetching is considerable. In addition, we determine that cache miss rate alone is not a deterministic factor to the impact of hardware prefetching. These results indicate that it is important to characterize the application combinations where the negative impact is significant, as this helps to determine improved VM sharing of the LLCs.

3. Prefetching and Cache Sharing

We have shown that hardware prefetching is not detrimental to application performance under most virtualization configurations and therefore can be enabled. However, we did observe several cases with significant performance degradations due to prefetching: when VMs run particular combinations of applications (e.g., canneal and facesim). There are two ways of eliminating this drawback – enabling/disabling the hardware prefetching manually per system or dynamically assigning VMs to the appropriate cache via VCPU-core binding. The former method is undesirable because it relies on a system administrator's domain knowledge to manually configure the hardware prefetching for each system.

We propose a dynamic heuristic-based VCPU-core binding approach to determine appropriate cache sharing between VMs. Our strategy has two goals: (1) if an application does not benefit from hardware prefetching, we should limit its negative impact on the co-located VMs; (2) if the prefetching can benefit performance, we select the VCPU-binding type to maximize the overall performance enhancement. We motivate these two goals based upon the fact as shown in Section 2.3, i.e., the influence of hardware prefetching depends on the applications in co-located VMs sharing the cache. For example, in Figure 5(a) the performance degradation of canneal varies from 2% to 21% depending on the co-running applications.

The proposed approach is comprised of an application classification scheme and a heuristic VCPU-core binding algorithm. In Section 3.1, we identify three important cache access properties that characterize the effect of both prefetching requests and demand requests on application combinations: *self-prefetching influence*, *Ratio of Prefetching miss rate to total Cache miss rate (RPC)*, and *cache miss rate*. These characteristics are used to categorize applications into different cache sharing constraint classes (Section 3.2). In Section 3.3, we describe how the heuristic algorithm determines the VCPU-core binding based upon the cache sharing constraints of the co-located applications and the CMP topology.

3.1 Cache Access Characteristics

In this subsection, we analyze the cache access characteristics of individual applications in the VM to predict the cache interference when co-located with another VM. Unlike CPU, memory, or I/O bandwidth, the cache resource is hard to be isolated between VMs. As a result, VMs contend for cache completely oblivious to each other. The interference between VMs on the LLC depends on

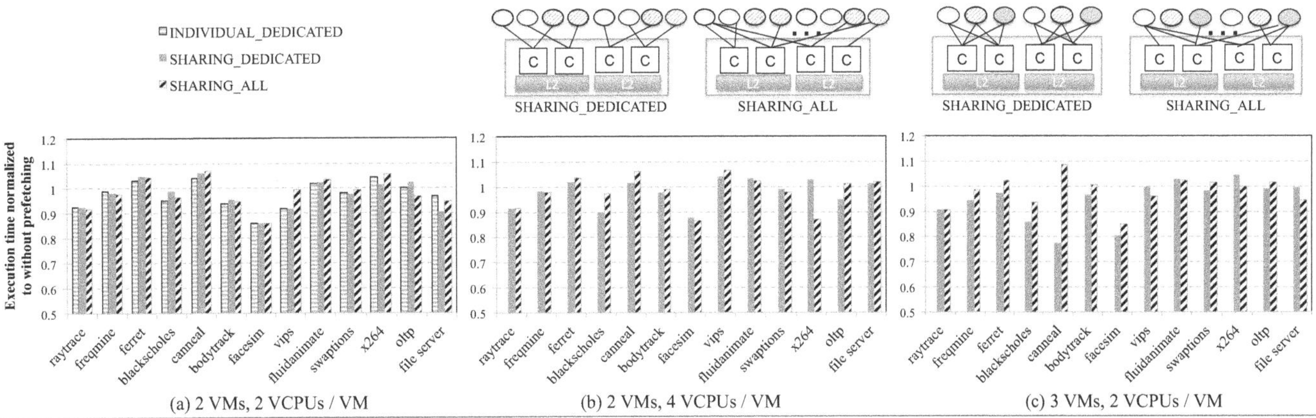

Figure 6. Performance in the presence of hardware prefetching under different VCPU-core binding types on Intel core-based X5460. Refer to Figure 2 for the illustration of binding types for (a).

the workload types, as well as VCPU-core binding types. When making a decision to schedule VCPUs on the appropriate cores and LLCs, we need to know not only the impact of cache sharing on workloads in each VM, but its effect to the co-located VMs. For example, if a VM runs an application that benefits from shared cache access, its VCPUs should be placed together on a single LLC rather than separate LLCs. On the other hand, a VM aggressively issuing demand and prefetching requests should be placed on a separate LLC to avoid influencing any other VMs.

The three cache access characteristics determine the variations of application performance when sharing cache with another VM. Self-prefetching influence measures whether hardware prefetching would improve or degrade the application performance when consolidated with the same workload in another VM. RPC measures the benefit to the application performance caused by hardware prefetching. Cache miss rate is used to estimate the cache footprint of the application.

Self-prefetching influence is defined as the performance influence of hardware prefetching when co-located VMs run the same workload; its effect could be either positive or negative. If the self-prefetching influence is positive, the benchmark receives performance improvement due to prefetching. On the other hand, a negative influence means that hardware prefetching degrades the application performance. For example, the results in Figure 3 show that the self-prefetching influence for canneal is negative, while it is positive for facesim. In addition, prefetching degrades canneal's performance when it shares the LLC with the other types of applications (Figure 5(a)), while facesim benefits from prefetching with others (Figure 5(c)) whether the LLC is shared or not. As applications with positive and negative self-prefetching influence have such distinct behaviors, we believe that self-prefetching influence is an important factor for determining whether an application should be sharing an LLC with other VMs.

A negative self-prefetching application should be prevented from sharing the cache with another VM. When two VMs run the same benchmark, the cache access behaviors are supposed to be the similar. Therefore, if both co-located VMs run the applications with negative self-prefetching influence, the cache lines inserted by the prefetching controller will pollute the cache by conflicting with demand data. Further, when a VM running a negative self-prefetching influence workload shares the LLC with VMs running different workloads, the prefetching request can be more aggressive. The more aggressive prefetching degrades the application performance because of the increased cache pollution and wasted memory bandwidth.

For example, Table 3 shows the statistics of prefetching requests under all three VCPU-core binding types when we run combinations of canneal with canneal, facesim with facesim, and canneal with facesim. We use CC (canneal, canneal), FF (facesim, facesim), and CF (canneal, facesim) to represent the three combinations respectively. The numbers for (canneal, canneal) and (facesim, facesim) are the measurements of one VM in these combinations because the two VMs run the same workload type. The tuple for (canneal, facesim) is the measurement of each VM in the combination. Since self-prefetching influence of canneal (negative) and facesim (positive) is different, the statistics show that applications with different self-prefetching influence have distinct patterns in prefetching effect.

In the second column, the percentage of prefetching miss in the total LLC miss (PPL) reflects the proportion of missed cache accesses which are attributed to prefetching miss. The higher PPL is, the worse prefetching performs. We observe that the PPLs for (canneal, canneal) are very similar ($\sim$ 0.4) despite the binding types, while in (canneal, facesim) the PPLs for the canneal VM vary from 0.38 to 0.54. This difference mainly comes from the two binding types sharing the LLC. Under the two binding types of sharing LLC, the VM running canneal of (canneal, facesim) has half of the LLC misses due to prefetching misses (i.e., 0.47 and 0.54). In addition, when comparing canneal in (canneal, canneal) and (canneal, facesim) of the SHARING_$*$ types, we find that its PPL increases from 0.41/0.37 to 0.54/47. The increased PPL infers that the prefetching controller degrades the cache performance for canneal when sharing LLC with VMs running different workload types. On the other hand, the PPLs of facesim in (canneal, facesim) do not change too much compared with (facesim, facesim). Instead of increasing the PPL, the two binding types of sharing the LLC actually reduce the PPL for facesim in (canneal, facesim) from 0.35 to 0.30/0.29. Thus, facesim does not suffer from sharing the LLC with other VMs in the presence of hardware prefetching.

Further, the third column shows that sharing LLC between two VMs in (canneal, facesim) increases the number of prefetching requests from 3×10^9 of INDIVIDUAL_DEDICATED to more than 7×10^9 and 5.5×10^9 under SHARING_DEDICATED and SHARING_ALL respectively for canneal. On the contrary, the number of prefetching requests is reduced for facesim.

From both statistics, we know that canneal suffers from prefetching when sharing the LLC with VMs running a different workloads, while the effect is insignificant for facesim. This is consistent with the normalized application performance as shown in Figure 7. The sharing of LLC degrades the performance of canneal in (canneal,

Table 3. LLC prefetching statistics for the VMs in combinations of CC, FF, and CF

VCPU-core binding type	PPL			# of prefetching requests ($\times 10^9$)		
	CC	FF	CF	CC	FF	CF
INDIVIDUAL_DEDICATED	0.38	0.35	(0.38, 0.35)	3.0	29.4	(2.9, 24.9)
SHARING_DEDICATED	0.41	0.37	(0.54, 0.30)	3.2	31.3	(7.0, 16.7)
SHARING_ALL	0.37	0.36	(0.47, 0.29)	3.4	29.7	(5.5, 17.9)

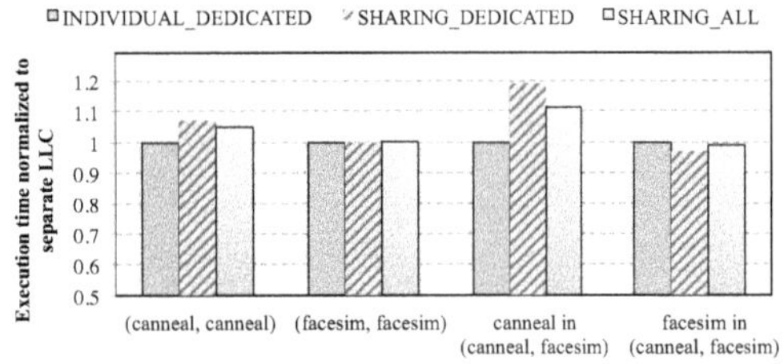

Figure 7. Execution time normalized to INDIVIDUAL_DEDICATED for VMs in combinations of (canneal, canneal), (facesim, facesim), and (canneal, facesim).

facesim) by 20% and 10% relative to having a dedicated LLC, while facesim benefits from sharing the LLC although the improvement is insignificant.

Therefore, it is preferable to assign a dedicated LLC to the VM running negative self-prefetching influence workloads, while it does not matter to positive self-prefetching influence workloads. These results demonstrate that self-prefetching influence is an important characteristic to determine the cache sharing among VMs.

RPC expressed as P_m/L_m, where P_m is the prefetching miss rate and L_m is the total LLC miss rate, reflects how much benefit an application can receive from prefetching. Hardware prefetching can improve the system performance if and only if the prefetching controller predicts data access accurately and inserts data into the cache timely. In this case, missed prefetching requests will account for a large portion of total missed requests. However, not all prefetching requests contribute to the performance improvement: some missed requests make wrong predictions and some are repeated. To avoid overestimating the contribution of missed prefetching requests, we should consider both the prefetching miss rate and the total cache miss rate. In other words, we prefer a binding type that generates a high prefetching miss rate and relative low total cache miss rate. For example, the prefetching miss rate and total LLC miss rate for an application are 50% and 20% using binding type A, while they are 20% and 20% using binding type B. Based upon these numbers we can infer that binding type A uses more prefetching requests to populate the LLC than type B. As they run the same application and have similar total LLC miss rates, binding type A performs better than B because more prefetched data hides the memory latency of the memory access on demand request.

In addition, the estimated benefit should be normalized because the benefit is approximately proportional to the total percentage of prefetching requests over the total LLC requests. The final expression of RPC is $(w * P_m/L_m)$, where the weight w is the percentage of prefetching requests in the total LLC requests. Among different VCPU-core binding types, we prefer a higher RPC.

To decide whether a VM could share the LLC with another VM, we need to know how much an application will suffer from cache contention in the presence of hardware prefetching. The challenge is that pairing every two applications would be too expensive to use online. Instead of brute-force testing all the possibilities of running with other applications, we propose a simple approach to predict the performance impacts of sharing the cache with the co-located VM using the RPC of individual VMs. Because most CMP

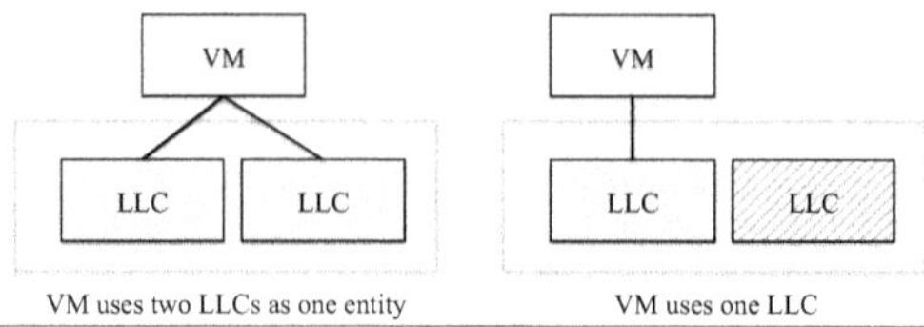

Figure 8. Illustration of prefetching cache behavior of VM contention using two LLCs

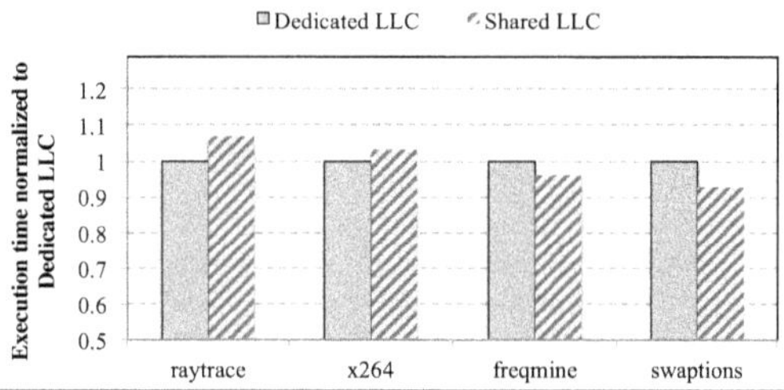

Figure 9. Execution time normalized to dedicated LLC (using two LLCs) for each benchmark in Table 4 when running with facesim.

machines have more than one LLC, we can compare the RPC of each VM using two LLCs and one LLC by binding its VCPUs to selected cores. The reduced size by half from two LLCs to one emulates the situation of losing cache space due to contention as shown in Figure 8. Therefore, a higher RPC under two LLCs indicates that the VM uses more prefetched data with a dedicated LLC than sharing the LLC with another VM. On the contrary, a higher RPC under one LLC implies a performance improvement by placing VCPUs on a single LLC or minimal cache contention with other VMs.

We select four benchmarks with a wide variety of cache miss rates based on Figure 1 to illustrate using the RPC to determine the cache sharing preference of each application. We evaluate the RPC for raytrace, x264, freqmine, and swaptions with one LLC and two LLCs when the VM run alone on Intel X5460 processor. Table 4 presents the RPC and the preferred cache sharing type of each application. At the column of preferred type, we indicate the proper sharing type for the higher RPC. Raytrace and x264 have higher RPC under two LLCs, while freqmine and swaptions under one LLC. Since the two LLCs are considered as a single cache entity, using a dedicated cache improves the performance for raytrace and x264. One LLC represents the cache performance when half of the cache is taken away due to contention. Sharing a LLC with other VMs has insignificant influence on freqmine and swations. To validate these observations, we plot the performance of these applications when running with facesim in Figure 9 (Recall that facesim has positive self-prefetching influence and is not harmful to the co-located applications). We find that raytrace and x264 have better performance using separated LLCs, while sharing LLC improves the performance for freqmine and swaptions. These results are consistent with the preferred types derived from the RPC of each application in Table 4.

Cache miss rate. In addition to the above two characteristics, cache contention depends on the working set size of the VM. When the working set size of the VM is less then the LLC size, cache

Table 4. Preferred sharing type for individual applications based upon RPC

# of LLCs used	raytrace		x264		freqmine		swaptions	
	RPC	Preferred type	RPC	Preferred type	RPC	Preferred type	RPC	Preferred type
One LLC	0.47	–	0.38	–	1.06	shared	0.33	shared
Two LLCs	0.67	dedicated	0.5	dedicated	0.7	–	0.2	–

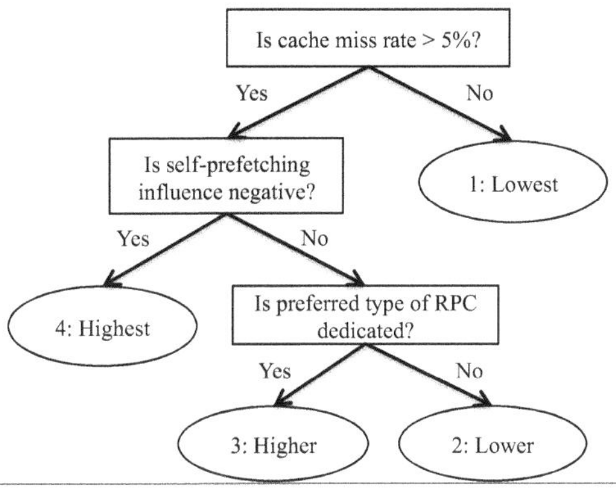

Figure 10. Sharing constraint decision tree classifier

Table 5. Constraint classification for PARSEC benchmarks.

Class	Benchmarks
4: Highest	canneal, ferret
3: Higher	raytrace, blackscholes, fluidanimate, x264
2: Lower	facesim, freqmine
1: Lowest	swaptions, bodytrack, vips

contention is not a crucial factor to the application performance. As a result, sharing LLC with a small working set VM does not degrade the performance of co-located VM, even if prefetching is beneficial to the workload. If the cache miss rate is low ($< 5\%$), the application is free to share the resources with any other workload.

3.2 Cache Sharing Constraint Classification

We use the three cache access characteristics to categorize the applications into cache sharing constraint classes, which guide whether VMs can share a cache or not. Figure 10 illustrates the classification decision tree. For constraint classification, the decision tree applies a sequence of test on the three cache access characteristics. The constraint category can be determined by following the path in the tree which leads to the leaf. The higher cache sharing constraint the application is, the higher priority it has to be limited to a dedicated cache. For example, we categorize the benchmarks in PARSEC in the order of cache sharing constraint, as shown in Table 5 based on the experimental results in Section 2.3 and 3.1.

3.3 Prefetching-Aware Binding Approach

Based on the above memory access characteristics, we propose a heuristic-based approach to predict an efficient VCPU and core binding for scheduling co-located VMs on appropriate cores and caches in the presence of hardware prefetching. The two principles behind the proposed approach are that when determining which VMs can share a cache, we should limit the negative impact of hardware prefetching on certain workloads, and we should maximize the benefit of hardware prefetching in a shared cache environment. Moreover, in such consolidated systems, we need to consider other resources than the shared cache.

So far we have assumed cache resources are the major bottleneck for all the workloads. However, application performance

Algorithm 1: Pseudo-code of PAVCB algorithm

```
1  Input: V: number of VMs, L: number of LLCs with
   associated cores, C: classification of the VMs, R_V: CPU
   running time vector under default scheduler ;
2  Output: VM and core bindings ;
3  rebalance := 0 ;
4  B_{V,L} := Partition (R_V) ;
5  if B_{V,L} is unbalanced then
6      rebalance := 1 ;
7  B̄_{V,L} := Binding(B_{V,L}, C) ;
8  if rebalance is 1 then
9      if B̄_{V,L} is unbalanced then
10         Adjust the high cache constraint VMs to balance the
           CPU load across LLCs ;
```

also depends on other system resources such as CPU. When VMs run together, the hypervisor may prioritize certain workloads over others. Considering the consolidated workloads consisting of one cache intensive workload and one non-intensive one, we can assign the two VMs a shared cache because the interference between these two VMs could be low, leaving the CPUs on other caches under-utilized. This unbalanced utilization across the CPUs creates a bottleneck, degrading the application performance. Alternatively, a better strategy is to spread these two VMs across two caches. Thus, the binding approach should distribute VMs across caches such that the CPU resource utilizations are distributed as evenly as possible. The integration of CPU sharing illustrates how these cache access characteristics can be used to complement other factors in scheduling VCPUs. The proposed approach can also integrate balancing I/O resource between VMs, which we consider as a future work.

Algorithm 1 presents the pseudo-code of the *P*refetching-*A*ware *V*CPU-*C*ore *B*inding (PAVCB) algorithm. The algorithm returns the VCPU-core bindings for the given VMs (V) and the set of LLCs (L). We assume a profiling program has identified the three cache access characteristics of each application in the VMs and has classified them into the cache sharing constraint categories denoted by C in the algorithm. The profiling phase can be implemented as an online software tool using the hardware performance counters [30] or micro-architectural cache miss estimator [7, 32]. In addition, we run these VMs using the default scheduler, i.e., without any binding, to obtain the average running time for each VM as another input (R_V).

PAVCB first splits the VMs into L (the number of LLCs) groups with similar aggregated running time based on the running time vector R_V (line 4) [3]. We denote the partitioned groups as $B_{V,L}$. Each group is assigned to a single LLC. The balanced partitioning ensures that no core will have higher utilization than another. This eliminates any CPU bottleneck as much as possible, allowing a more informative view of cache contention. If we fail to divide the

[3] The partition problem by itself is NP-complete. Since the number of VMs and LLCs are typically small, we can use some greedy algorithm to solve it in polynomial time.

Algorithm 2: Binding – Heuristic core binding

```
Input: B_{V,L}: partitioned VM groups for each LLC, C:
    classification of the VMs ;
Output: VM and core bindings ;
for each LLC d in the C LLCs do
    for each VM v in the LLC d do
        if v's cache sharing constrain ≥ 3 then
            Bind v's VCPUs to d ;
        else
            Bind v's VCPUs to all cores on the processor ;
```

VMs into balanced groups (e.g., 3 VMs with similar CPU running time), we set the `rebalance` flag (line 5-6). Then PAVCB uses the partition $B_{V,L}$ and the classification C as the inputs to the Binding function (line 7).

The Binding function, as shown in Algorithm 2, determines whether a VM should be limited to a single cache or allowed to use more shared caches. The high cache constraint VMs (i.e., belong to category 3 or 4) can only use their original assigned LLC to avoid negative effect of the cache contention with hardware prefetching, while the less cache constrained VMs (i.e., belong to category 1 or 2) can be scheduled on more cores in addition to its original assignment. Although the less constrained VM can be scheduled on more shared caches, this does not create more contentions than using the assigned cache. Either the VM only occupies a small portion of the shared cache due to a small cache footprint (category 1) or the VM prefers a shared cache (category 2). In addition, since such VM can be scheduled to more physical cores, the chance of contending with any other VM decreases. As a result, enabling more VCPUs to these VMs can improve the performance by increasing its scheduled times.

On return from the Binding function (line 7 of Algorithm 1), $\overline{B}_{V,L}$ is the new VCPU-core binding. Finally, if the `rebalance` flag is set or $\overline{B}_{V,L}$ is unbalanced, we need to rebalance the VM partition by adjusting the high cache constraint VMs (line 9-11). This can be done by binding them onto more cores to distribute the CPU time across LLCs. In the extreme case, the final result will be identical to the default scheduler.

4. Experimental Evalution

In order to evaluate the effectiveness of our approach, we implemented the PAVCB algorithm as a user-space scheduler in the host OS, i.e., domain0 on Xen or Linux with KVM. We enforce the VCPU-core binding decision via Xen's hypercalls or Linux's process affinity system calls. All experiments are run on two machines: one with two Intel X5460 processors and the other with two Intel X5650 processors. We did not experiment on the AMD X4 architecture as our machine has only one such processor with a single shared LLC and therefore no interesting core binding options.

We evaluate the proposed approach under 9 workloads of benchmark combinations, as shown in Table 6. The workload combinations are formed from the benchmarks selected from the PARSEC suite based on their cache sharing constraints (Table 5). Each workload consists of benchmarks of both high and low cache sharing constraint categories, and the number of benchmarks from each category is varied. For every workload combination, one VM runs one benchmark application.

We compare the performance of PAVCB to the default hypervisor scheduler (i.e., the credit scheduler of Xen), and other possible manual bindings. The default scheduler allocates the CPU time fairly among all the VMs, but the default scheduler has minimal

Table 6. Workloads (WL) with PARSEC benchmarks

# of VMs / host	WL	Benchmark set
3	1	canneal, facesim, vips
	2	canneal, facesim, facesim
	3	ferret, x264, swaptions
4	4	canneal, ferret, fluidanimate, facesim
	5	ferret, raytrace, fluidanimate, freqmine
	6	canneal, x264, freqmine, swaptions
5	7	canneal, ferret, fluidanimate, facesim, bodytrack
	8	canneal, x264, facesim, bodytrack, vips
	9	ferret, blackscholes, freqmine, facesim, swaptions

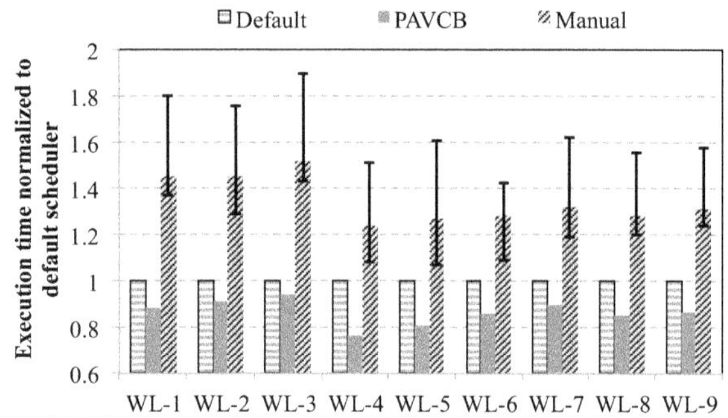

Figure 11. Performance comparison between default scheduler, PAVCB, and manual bindings on Intel X5460 (lower is better).

consideration of the cache contention when determining the VM placement. For the manual VCPU-core bindings, we assume that the system administrator tries to balance the number of VMs across the LLCs. For example, there are three possible bindings to allocate 4 VMs on two LLCs, if each LLC should have two VMs. If the number of VMs across the LLCs can not be balanced (e.g., 3-VM and 5-VM workloads), we allow one LLC to have one more VM than the other LLC. We experiment with all the possible combinations of balanced manual bindings under this rationale. Note that this does not include all feasible combinations. The output of the PAVCB schedules the VCPUs of a VM to the cores of the selected LLC. For example, for workload 4 (WL-4), PAVCB will schedule canneal on the cores of one LLC, ferret and fluidanimate on the cores of the other LLC, and facesim on all cores.

Figure 11 shows the workload performance on the machine with two Intel X5460 processors. We calculate the aggregated completion time of each benchmark in the workload combination and normalize the results to the default scheduler. For the manual bindings, we present the normalized worst and best performance characterization along with the median. In all cases, we observe that PAVCB has better performance than the default scheduler and all manual binding combinations.

For example, WL-1 through WL-3 are for 3-VM workloads. The bindings determined by PAVCB are always as balanced as the best among the manual possibilities, because PAVCB will evenly distribute the CPU contention onto all the cores. The performance of 3-VM workloads under the default scheduler and PAVCB is significantly better than the worst manual binding by $> 70\%$. The worst case occurs when the two LLCs have unbalanced VM placement, i.e., two VMs on one LLC and one VM on one LLC. The placement of the high cache constrained VM and low cache constrained VM (e.g., canneal and facesim) on the same LLC further exacerbates the performance degradation. Although both the default scheduler and PAVCB can balance workload stress across the LLCs, PAVCB improves the performance over the default by $\sim 10\%$. This is because PAVCB prevents high cache sharing con-

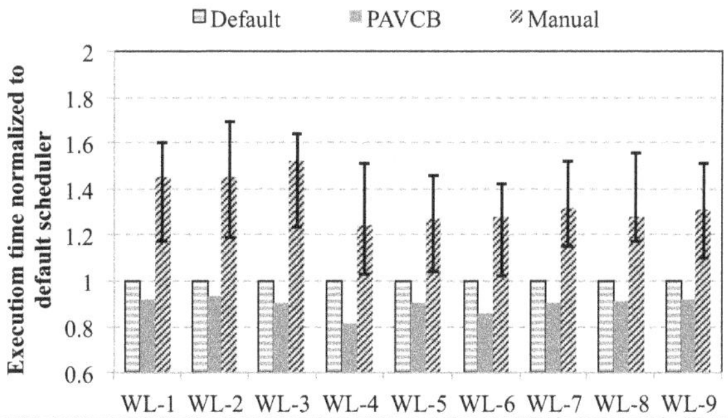

Figure 12. Performance comparison between default scheduler, PAVCB, and manual bindings on Intel X5650 (lower is better).

strained VMs from contending for the cache resources with other VMs by isolating them.

For 4-VM workloads (WL-4 to WL-6) and 5-VM workloads (WL-7 to WL-9), the performance degradation of the worst manual binding is reduced. However, since all LLCs are fully loaded under these workloads, cache sharing contributes more to the performance difference than the unbalanced load on LLCs. The results show that PAVCB performs on average better than the default scheduler by 19% and 13% under 4-VM and 5-VM workloads respectively. We conclude that in each case PAVCB schedules VMs onto appropriate cores and LLCs, achieving better performance than the default scheduler and other possible manual bindings.

Figure 12 shows the results on the machine with two Intel X5650 processors. The results show that PAVCB improves the performance over the default scheduler by 11% on average and consistently outperforms other manual bindings by 45% on average.

5. Related Work

We survey related research along two main lines: hardware prefetching optimization and shared cache management.

Hardware Prefetching. The primary costs of inaccurate hardware prefetching are increased off-chip memory bandwidth contention and cache pollution. Two main categories of approaches have been proposed to improve the effectiveness of hardware prefetching: prefetching controller optimization and cache management.

With prefetching controller optimization, a subset of the work focuses on utilizing a throttling technique to reduce useless prefetching requests. Examples include feedback-directed prefetching [32], dynamically coordinating the aggressiveness of multicore prefetching controllers [6], prefetching-aware memory controllers [19, 20], and hybrid prefetching controllers for linked data structure and streamed-based data structure [7, 36]. Other approaches aim for better allocation of the bandwidth among the cores. Inappropriate allocation of the limited bandwidth will degrade both system performance and individual applications, especially when multi-programmed applications running on multiple cores interfere with each other [21, 25]. The bandwidth contention is exemplified with prefetching. Liu and Yan [22] studied the interaction between hardware prefetching and bandwidth partitioning and its impact on CMP system performance. They presented an analytic model to decide whether prefetching should be applied with the presence of bandwidth partitioning.

The second category is to improve the cache management policy in the presence of hardware prefetching. Recent cache management policies fail to achieve expected performance improvement when ignoring the effects of hardware prefetching [16, 18, 40]. Wu and Jaleel proposed a prefetching-aware cache replacement policy, which distinguishes between prefetching requests and demand requests because the cache lines inserted into the LLC by demand requests are more like to be performance-critical than by prefetching requests [40]. Srinath proposed to use a dedicated cache buffer for prefetched data [32].

The main challenge and disadvantage of all of the above approaches is the requirement of a new cache architecture in real machines and migrating the entire software stack to it. The approach presented in this work is a software-only solution via hardware performance counters, and implementable in existing CMPs. Moreover, since these related hardware solutions are orthogonal to our proposed approach, combining both may offer additional prefetching benefits on future processors.

Shared cache management. CMPs concurrently run a number of applications with a wide variety of cache access characteristic on the multiple cores. When these applications use one or more shared caches, application performance is typically determined by how well the shared cache is managed. One line of work is to use hardware performance counters (HPC) to profile the cache related metrics and partition the shared cache at the OS-level [43]. For example, the cache miss rate is considered as an important factor when mapping the application threads to physical cores [44]. A miss rate curve (MRC) is proposed in [34] to predict performance as a function of L2 cache size. The predicted results guide how to partitioning the shared cache in a multi-programmed environment. Additionally, ROCS [30] characterizes the application cache behavior in page-granularity and dynamically maps cache unfriendly pages to a particular region of the LLC via memory address translation. As described in Section 3, the proposed PAVCB algorithm uses the HPCs to collect cache access characteristics.

Other approaches enhance the sharing-oblivious LRU cache replacement policy to handle requests from different threads or cores sharing the cache. Srikantaiah [31] differentiated cache misses between intra-core and inter-core to identify a few hot blocks, which will be stored in a small region of the LLC by individual cores. Alternatively, PIPP [41] implicitly partitions the shared cache by targeted insertion and promotion. Cruise [15], a hardware/software co-designed approach, uses both the knowledge of underlying cache replacement policy and application cache utility information to determine optimal thread-core scheduling.

Since the above shared cache management solutions are designed for dedicated machines, the effectiveness of these approaches is unclear in virtualized environments. For example, the additional address translation from guest physical address to host physical address complicates the system-level solutions in both time and space complexity. Cache insertion and eviction decisions based upon per process/thread could be wrong if these processes/threads belong to a single VM.

The work of Cuanta [10] is the most related to the presented PAVCB approach. It estimates the cache usages of co-located VMs and selects an efficient VM placement by predicting the performance degradation due to cache interference. A critical distinction between Cuanta and PAVCB is that Cuanta requires a synthetic loader to control the cache usage for certain applications in order to predict the application performance under different interference. In contrast, PAVCB is completely self-contained and considers only hardware prefetching behavior.

6. Conclusion

We present a comprehensive study of hardware prefetching in virtualized environments. The experiments cover a wide spectrum of important factors, including application benchmarks, VM configurations, and processor architectures. We have found that despite conventional belief, the negative influence of hardware prefetching is minimal on consolidated applications. Only under a few particular benchmark combinations does prefetching have an influence on application performance. By recognizing these combinations, we can avoid sharing cache between these applications in the presence of hardware prefetching.

We identify three cache access characteristics to categorize the applications into cache sharing constraint classes. Based upon the profiled characteristics of each VM, the proposed PAVCB algorithm determines appropriate LLC sharing via VCPU-core binding with hardware prefetching. On different CMPs, the PAVCB always delivers performance improvement of 12% on average over the default scheduler and 46% over other manual bindings.

References

[1] ADAMS, K., AND AGESEN, O. A comparison of software and hardware techniques for x86 virtualization. In *ASPLOS* (2006), pp. 2–13.

[2] AMD. BIOS and kernel developer's guide for AMD family 10h processors. White Paper, 2010.

[3] BARROW-WILLIAMS, N., FENSCH, C., AND MOORE, S. A communication characterisation of Splash-2 and Parsec. In *IISWC* (2009), pp. 86–97.

[4] BHATTACHARJEE, A., AND MARTONOSI, M. Characterizing the TLB behavior of emerging parallel workloads on chip multiprocessors. In *PACT* (2009), pp. 29–40.

[5] BIENIA, C. *Benchmarking Modern Multiprocessors*. PhD thesis, Princeton University, January 2011.

[6] EBRAHIMI, E., MUTLU, O., LEE, C. J., AND PATT, Y. N. Coordinated control of multiple prefetchers in multi-core systems. In *Micro* (2009), pp. 316–326.

[7] EBRAHIMI, E., MUTLU, O., AND PATT, Y. N. Techniques for bandwidth-efficient prefetching of linked data structures in hybrid prefetching systems. In *HPCA* (2009), pp. 7 - 17.

[8] FERDMAN, M., ADILEH, A., KOCBERBER, O., VOLOS, S., ALISAFAEE, M., JEVDJIC, D., KAYNAK, C., POPESCU, A. D., AILAMAKI, A., AND FALSAFI, B. Clearing the clouds: a study of emerging scale-out workloads on modern hardware. In *ASPLOS* (2012), pp. 37–48.

[9] FILEBENCH. Filebench. `http://sourceforge.net/apps/mediawiki/filebench`.

[10] GOVINDAN, S., LIU, J., KANSAL, A., AND SIVASUBRAMANIAM, A. Cuanta: quantifying effects of shared on-chip resource interference for consolidated virtual machines. In *SoCC* (2011), pp. 22:1–22:14.

[11] IBM. IBM eServer xSeries 366 tuning tips. Technical Report, 2005.

[12] IBM. Virtualization on the IBM system x3950 server. Technical Report, 2006.

[13] IBM. Tuning IBM system x servers for performance. Technical Report, 2007.

[14] INTEL. Achieving fast, scalable I/O for virtualized servers. White Paper, 2009.

[15] JALEEL, A., NAJAF-ABADI, H. H., SUBRAMANIAM, S., STEELY, S. C., AND EMER, J. CRUISE: cache replacement and utility-aware scheduling. In *ASPLOS* (2012), pp. 249–260.

[16] JALEEL, A., THEOBALD, K. B., STEELY, JR., S. C., AND EMER, J. High performance cache replacement using re-reference interval prediction (RRIP). In *ISCA* (2010), pp. 60–71.

[17] JONES, S. T., ARPACI-DUSSEAU, A. C., AND ARPACI-DUSSEAU, R. H. Geiger: monitoring the buffer cache in a virtual machine environment. In *ASPLOS* (2006), pp. 14–24.

[18] KHAN, S. M., TIAN, Y., AND JIMENEZ, D. A. Sampling dead block prediction for last-level caches. In *Micro* (2010), pp. 175–186.

[19] LEE, C. J., MUTLU, O., NARASIMAN, V., AND PATT, Y. N. Prefetch-Aware DRAM controllers. In *Micro* (2008), pp. 200–209.

[20] LEE, C. J., MUTLU, O., NARASIMAN, V., AND PATT, Y. N. Prefetch-aware shared resource management for multi-core systems. In *ISCA* (2011), pp. 141–152.

[21] LIU, F., JIANG, X., AND SOLIHIN, Y. Understanding how off-chip memory bandwidth partitioning in chip multiprocessors affects system performance. In *HPCA* (2010), pp. 1–12.

[22] LIU, F., AND SOLIHIN, Y. Studying the impact of hardware prefetching and bandwidth partitioning in chip-multiprocessors. In *SIGMETRICS* (2011), pp. 37–48.

[23] LO, J., BARROSO, L. A., EGGERS, S. J., GHARACHORLOO, K., LEVY, H. M., AND PAREKH, S. S. An analysis of database workload performance on simultaneous multithreaded processors. In *ISCA* (1998), pp. 39–50.

[24] MA, Z., SHENG, Z., GU, L., WEN, L., AND ZHANG, G. DVM: towards a datacenter-scale virtual machine. In *VEE* (2012), pp. 39–50.

[25] MURALIDHARA, S. P., SUBRAMANIAN, L., MUTLU, O., KANDEMIR, M., AND MOSCIBRODA, T. Reducing memory interference in multicore systems via application-aware memory channel partitioning. In *Micro* (2011), pp. 374–385.

[26] ONGARO, D., COX, A. L., AND RIXNER, S. Scheduling I/O in virtual machine monitors. In *VEE* (2008), pp. 14–24.

[27] OPROFILE. A system profiler for Linux. `http://http://oprofile.sourceforge.net`.

[28] PAN, S., CHERNG, C., DICK, K., AND LADNER, R. E. Algorithms to take advantage of hardware prefetching. In *ALENEX* (2007).

[29] SINGH, B. Page/slab cache control in a virtualized environment. In *Linux Symposium* (2010), pp. 252–262.

[30] SOARES, L., TAM, D., AND STUMM, M. Reducing the harmful effects of last-level cache polluters with an os-level, software-only pollute buffer. In *MICRO* (2008), pp. 258–269.

[31] SRIKANTAIAH, S., KANDEMIR, M., AND IRWIN, M. J. Adaptive set pinning: managing shared caches in chip multiprocessors. In *ASPLOS* (2008), pp. 135–144.

[32] SRINATH, S., MUTLU, O., KIM, H., AND PATT, Y. N. Feedback directed prefetching: Improving the performance and bandwidth-efficiency of hardware prefetchers. In *HPCA* (2007), pp. 63–74.

[33] SYSBENCH. Sysbench: a system performance benchmark. `http://sysbench.sourceforge.net`.

[34] TAM, D., AZIMI, R., SOARES, L., AND STUMM, M. Managing shared L2 caches on multicore systems in software. In *WIOSCA* (2007).

[35] TANG, L., MARS, J., VACHHARAJANI, N., HUNDT, R., AND SOFFA, M. L. The impact of memory subsystem resource sharing on datacenter applications. In *ISCA* (2011), pp. 283–294.

[36] VERMA, S., KOPPELMAN, D. M., AND PENG, L. Efficient prefetching with hybrid schemes and use of program feedback to adjust prefetcher aggressiveness. *Journal of Instruction-Level Parallelism*, 13 (2011), 1–14.

[37] VMWARE. VMware VMmark v1.0.0 Results - Dell PowerEdge R900. Technical Report, 2008.

[38] VMWARE. Performance best practices for VMware vSphere 5.0. Technical Report, 2011.

[39] WALDSPURGER, C. A. Memory resource management in vmware esx server. In *SIGOPS Oper. Syst. Rev.* (2002), pp. 181–194.

[40] WU, C.-J., JALEEL, A., MARTONOSI, M., STEELY, JR., S. C., AND EMER, J. PACMan: prefetch-aware cache management for high performance caching. In *Micro* (2011), pp. 442–453.

[41] XIE, Y., AND LOH, G. H. PIPP: promotion/insertion pseudo-partitioning of multi-core shared caches. In *ISCA* (2009), pp. 174–183.

[42] ZHANG, E., JIANG, Y., AND SHEN, X. Does cache sharing on modern CMP matter to the performance of contemporary multithreaded programs? In *PPoPP* (2010), pp. 203–212.

[43] ZHANG, X., DWARKADAS, S., AND SHEN, K. Towards practical page coloring-based multicore cache management. In *Eurosys* (2009), pp. 89–102.

[44] ZHURAVLEV, S., BLAGODUROV, S., AND FEDOROVA, A. Addressing shared resource contention in multicore processors via scheduling. In *ASPLOS* (2010), pp. 129–142.

Demand-Based Coordinated Scheduling for SMP VMs

Hwanju Kim[†], Sangwook Kim[§], Jinkyu Jeong[†], Joonwon Lee[§], Seungryoul Maeng[†]

[†]Computer Science Department, Korea Advanced Institute of Science and Technology (KAIST), Daejeon, Korea
[§]College of Information and Communication Engineering, Sungkyunkwan University, Suwon, Korea

hjukim@calab.kaist.ac.kr, swkim@csl.skku.edu, jinkyu@calab.kaist.ac.kr, joonwon@skku.edu, maeng@kaist.ac.kr

Abstract

As processor architectures have been enhancing their computing capacity by increasing core counts, independent workloads can be consolidated on a single node for the sake of high resource efficiency in data centers. With the prevalence of virtualization technology, each individual workload can be hosted on a virtual machine for strong isolation between co-located workloads. Along with this trend, hosted applications have increasingly been multithreaded to take advantage of improved hardware parallelism. Although the performance of many multithreaded applications highly depends on communication (or synchronization) latency, existing schemes of virtual machine scheduling do not explicitly coordinate virtual CPUs based on their communication behaviors.

This paper presents a demand-based coordinated scheduling scheme for consolidated virtual machines that host multithreaded workloads. To this end, we propose communication-driven scheduling that controls time-sharing in response to inter-processor interrupts (IPIs) between virtual CPUs. On the basis of in-depth analysis on the relationship between IPI communications and coordination demands, we devise IPI-driven coscheduling and delayed preemption schemes, which effectively reduce synchronization latency and unnecessary CPU consumption. In addition, we introduce a load-conscious CPU allocation policy in order to address load imbalance in heterogeneously consolidated environments. The proposed schemes are evaluated with respect to various scenarios of mixed workloads using the PARSEC multithreaded applications. In the evaluation, our scheme improves the overall performance of consolidated workloads, especially communication-intensive applications, by reducing inefficient synchronization latency.

Categories and Subject Descriptors D.4.1 [*OPERATING SYSTEMS*]: Process Management—Scheduling

General Terms Algorithms, Experimentation, Performance

Keywords Virtualization, Synchronization, Coscheduling

1. Introduction

Ever-evolving hardware parallelism and virtualization have been enabler technologies for consolidation of independent workloads on a single powerful node. With the prevalence of virtualization technology, an individual workload can be hosted in an isolated container, a virtual machine (VM), in which a user can control entire software stack. As processor architectures have been enhancing their computing capacity by adding more cores, multiple independent VMs can be consolidated in a single machine in order to improve resource utilization. In this environment, efficient management of shared resources is crucial for the performance of consolidated workloads.

On the software side, many applications have been increasing thread-level parallelism in order to take advantage of improved hardware parallelism. Emerging multithreaded workloads such as RMS (recognition, mining and synthesis) applications [6] are continuously evolving their algorithms to make the best use of available cores. The thread-level parallelization, however, typically requires synchronization with respect to the resources shared by multiple threads. Firstly, all threads in a single process share an address space whereby a page table update requires synchronization of corresponding hardware structures such as translation lookaside buffer (TLB). Secondly, multiple threads can share a memory region via shared variables whose updates must be safely serialized by using synchronization primitives. Such synchronization should be efficiently handled because it is a dominant factor affecting the scalability of multithreaded applications.

In the case where a multithreaded workload is hosted on an SMP VM, the synchronization performance could be degraded by uncoordinated scheduling of virtual CPUs (vCPUs). Since multiple vCPUs can time-share a physical CPU (pCPU), their executions are dictated by a hypervisor scheduler. If the scheduler is oblivious to synchronization demands of vCPUs, it could delay the execution of a critical vCPU upon which other ones depend to make progress, thereby aggravating contention for shared resources. Many researchers have addressed this issue by proposing coordinated scheduling such as relaxed coscheduling [26], balance scheduling [24], spinlock-aware schemes [13, 17, 25, 28], and hybrid coscheduling [27, 30]. The previous schemes, however, did not explicitly coordinate vCPUs in the event of synchronization-related communication between vCPUs that host multithreaded workloads.

This paper presents a demand-based coordinated scheduling scheme for consolidated SMP VMs that host multithreaded workloads. Inspired by traditional demand-based coscheduling for workstation clusters [3, 4, 9, 22, 23], we introduce communication-driven scheduling that dynamically coordinates communicating vCPUs in the event of inter-vCPU synchronization, while managing the other ones in an uncoordinated fashion. Such demand-based coordination can effectively reduce synchronization latency without sacrificing the throughput of non-communicating vCPUs. We take inter-processor interrupt (IPI) into account as inter-vCPU communication signal, which is virtualized and therefore can be unobtrusively recognized by the hypervisor. In order to correlate a certain type of IPI with coordination demand, we investigate synchronization behaviors that involve IPI communication in ker-

ASPLOS'13, March 16–20, 2013, Houston, Texas, USA.

nel and user spaces based on the experimental analysis of various multithreaded workloads hosted in SMP VMs.

Our findings on the basis of the analysis are summarized as follows: Firstly, uncoordinated scheduling of vCPUs that synchronize TLB states could incur significant performance degradation of applications that intensively manipulate their shared address spaces. Secondly, contention on user-level synchronization primitives can lead to kernel-level spinlock contention, which could result in lock-holder preemption (LHP) by uncoordinated scheduling. Thirdly, such LHPs derived from user-level contention are closely connected with IPI communication for thread wake-up operations. Finally, IPI communication for thread wake-up can guide the hypervisor to coordination of vCPUs that host coscheduling-friendly workloads.

Based on the findings, we propose IPI-driven coscheduling and delayed preemption as communication-driven scheduling schemes. The IPI-driven coscheduling allows a vCPU that receives an urgent IPI to be preemptively scheduled in order to reduce synchronization latency. The IPI-driven delayed preemption enables a vCPU that initiates a thread wake-up IPI to urgently request additional time slice in order to safely release a spinlock, which is likely held for user-level synchronization, thereby being protected from LHP. For these IPI-driven scheduling schemes, we devise *urgent vCPU first scheduling*, which makes a preemption decision in response to an urgent IPI while cooperating with a proportional-share scheduler for inter-VM fairness. Finally, in conjunction with the communication-driven scheduling, we introduce load-conscious balance scheduling that assigns sibling vCPUs, which belong to the same VM, onto different pCPUs in a best-effort manner while avoiding negative effect of load imbalance.

Our proposed scheme was implemented based on Linux Completely Fair Scheduler (CFS) [18] and the Kernel Virtual Machine (KVM) hypervisor [15]. We evaluated our scheme for various mixes of multithreaded and sequential workloads. For the evaluation, we chose the *PARSEC* benchmark suite [6], which includes 13 emerging multithreaded applications with diverse characteristics. From the results, the demand-based coordinated scheduling improves overall performance compared to the uncoordinated and the balance scheduling [24], especially for synchronization-intensive applications. In addition, the load-conscious balance scheduling improves the performance on imbalanced pCPU loads arising when parallel and sequential workloads are consolidated.

The remainder of this paper is organized as follows: Section 2 describes related work on previous coordinated scheduling and contention management schemes for non-virtualized and virtualized environments, and presents our motivation. Section 3 introduces the design and implementation of our proposed scheme based on experimental analysis. In Section 4, we present our evaluation results and analysis with various scenarios of consolidation. Finally, Section 5 discusses alternative approaches complementary to our scheme and Section 6 concludes our work and presents future direction.

2. Related Work and Motivation

2.1 Uncoordinated vs. Coordinated Scheduling

Uncoordinated scheduling, also called local scheduling, allows each per-CPU scheduler to make its own decision on time-sharing among its assigned threads without any coordination with threads on other CPUs. This type of scheduling maximizes CPU utilization while managing local threads with priority-based or proportional share-based policies. For effective utilization of global CPU resources, a load balancer strives to evenly distribute threads onto available CPUs. In this manner, the uncoordinated scheduling achieves high throughput with low overheads due to the independent scheduling decisions. Since this scheme can effectively handle general workloads with simple implementation, it has been widely employed in most commodity OSes [18, 21] and hypervisors [5, 15].

The uncoordinated scheduling, however, has been known to be ineffective for communicating workloads such as multithreaded and parallel applications [20]. The performance of such workloads highly depends on communication (or synchronization) latency between cooperative threads. Since uncoordinated scheduling is oblivious to dependency between threads on different CPUs, it could increase communication latency by preempting a thread on which cooperative ones depend to make progress. Accordingly, a communication-sensitive application needs the underlying scheduler to coordinate its threads in order to minimize communication latency. A large volume of research on coordinated scheduling has been conducted in traditional multiprocessor and cluster environments [3, 4, 9, 10, 20, 22, 23, 29].

Coscheduling [20] is a representative scheme of coordinated scheduling that allows cooperative threads to be synchronously scheduled and descheduled. Such strictly coordinated scheduling gives an illusion that cooperative threads run on a dedicated machine without communication latency. Despite its effectiveness in minimizing communication latency, the strict requirement of synchronous progress can cause CPU fragmentation, since cooperative threads cannot be scheduled until their required CPUs are all available. Many researchers have claimed that the CPU fragmentation problem becomes serious leading to ineffective CPU utilization in an environment where parallel applications are concurrently hosted with sequential workloads [3, 4, 9, 16, 22, 23, 29].

An alternative solution to this problem is demand-based (dynamic [22, 23] or implicit [3, 4, 9]) coscheduling, which dynamically initiates coscheduling only for communicating threads, whereas non-communicating ones are managed in an uncoordinated fashion. The rationale behind this scheme is that communication is a tangible signal of coordination demand for most parallel workloads. In this regard, it can reduce the communication latency of cooperative threads on demand, while retaining high CPU utilization by relaxing strict coscheduling requirement. Many studies showed that demand-based coscheduling achieves higher overall performance, compared to uncoordinated scheduling and strict coscheduling, in network-of-workstation (NOW) environments where various workloads are generally mixed [2–4, 9].

2.2 Coordination Issues on SMP VMs

Coordinated scheduling is also a compelling issue on SMP VMs as data centers have increasingly been virtualized today. Since commodity OSes have been meant to be running on bare-metal CPUs, they typically make liberal use of spin-based synchronization primitives (e.g., spinlocks) to protect short critical sections. Once the OSes are virtualized, however, a spinlock-protected critical section can be suspended by an underlying hypervisor scheduler. In particular, preempting a vCPU that holds a contended spinlock (i.e., LHP) could increase synchronization latency while forcing contending vCPUs to unnecessarily consume CPU cycles [11, 24, 25]. Accordingly, uncoordinated scheduling can lead to significant scalability bottleneck in consolidating SMP VMs.

In order to address this problem, coordinated scheduling schemes [7, 13, 17, 24–28, 30] have been proposed for SMP VMs to reduce inter-vCPU synchronization latency. As with traditional job scheduling, most proposals have aimed at loosely coordinated scheduling to avoid the inefficiency of strict coscheduling. The VMware ESX server introduced the *relaxed coscheduling* [26], which enables sibling vCPUs to make progress at similar rates by preventing their runtime from being largely skewed. The *balance scheduling* [24] is a probabilistic coscheduling scheme, which increases the likelihood of coscheduling sibling vCPUs by assigning them to different pCPUs. Those two schemes proactively balance pCPU resources on sibling vCPUs without considering any specific coordination demand.

Dynamically coordinated scheduling for SMP VMs has been mainly focused on alleviating excessive busy-waiting on preempted spinlocks of guest OS kernels. Most schemes selectively manipulate scheduling policies for VMs that involve spinlocks based on explicit (user- or OS-informed) [25, 27, 28, 30] or implicit information [7, 25]. Dynamic adaptive scheduling [28] implemented demand-based coscheduling by regarding OS-informed excessive wait time on spinlocks as an indicator of coordination demand, while hybrid schemes [27, 30] selectively coschedule the vCPUs of a concurrent VM specified by a user. Other than coscheduling, some approaches dynamically adjust preemption policy [25] and the length of time slice [7] in order to minimize the synchronization latency on spinlocks. Uhlig *et al.* [25] proposed *delayed preemption* that defers involuntary context switching of a lock-holder vCPU to minimize synchronization latency. In order to identify a lock-holder vCPU, they proposed an OS-informed approach and an inference technique based on the fact that a spinlock is held only in the kernel mode.

Alternative approaches are helping locks [11] and hardware-assisted contention management [1, 12]. Both approaches have the same purpose that avoids busy-waiting on a likely preempted spinlock. The helping lock approach replaces OS spinlocks with spin-then-block based ones, which allow a vCPU that spins on a lock over a threshold period to sleep until the lock is eventually available [11]. The hardware-assisted scheme enables a pCPU to detect excessive spinning by monitoring PAUSE instruction, which is used within a busy-wait loop; Intel and AMD provide Pause Loop Exiting (PLE) [12] and Pause Filter [1], respectively. Once excessive pause-loop is detected based on spin threshold empirically set, a pCPU raises an exception, which causes the transition into the hypervisor (i.e., VMEXIT), so that the hypervisor can handle the contention. On this exception, the hypervisor scheduler allows a corresponding vCPU to yield its pCPU to another one. Although the helping locks and the hardware-assisted scheme effectively reduce the amount of unnecessary busy-waiting, they are reactive approaches triggered once contention occurs after spinning, albeit short.

2.3 Motivation

As with traditional NOW environments [2], virtualized data centers can embrace diverse workloads including parallel, sequential, and interactive applications. With the emergence of Infrastructure-as-a-Service (IaaS) clouds and virtual desktop infrastructure (VDI), such heterogeneity becomes more general. In addition, as modern architectures have been increasing their computing capacity, high consolidation density of SMP VMs can be realized. In order to efficiently support dynamic and diverse thread-level parallelism of consolidated applications, a hypervisor scheduler should carefully coordinate vCPUs based on their workload characteristics.

Considering heterogeneity of consolidated workloads, demand-based coordinated scheduling is an effective approach for SMP VMs to achieve high overall performance of communicating and non-communicating workloads. Although coordination demand can take place for various purposes in user and kernel layers in a VM, prior work on demand-based coscheduling [28] coordinates vCPUs based only on kernel-level spinlock synchronization by means of an OS-assisted technique. Inspired by traditional demand-based coscheduling in NOW environments [3, 23], we investigate that inter-vCPU communication can be a useful signal for coordination demands from the broad viewpoint of kernel-level and user-level synchronization.

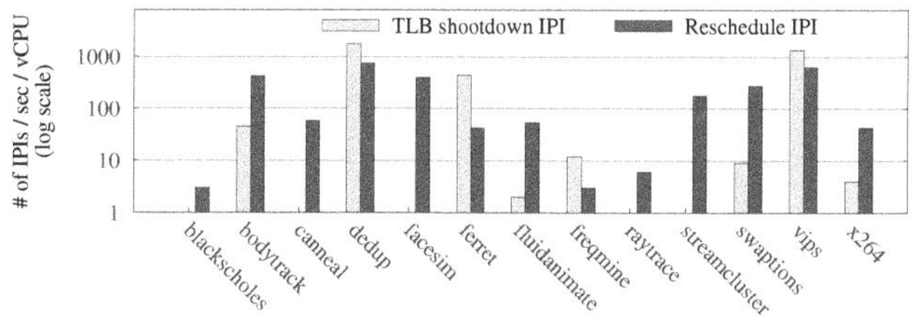

Figure 1. The number of IPIs per second per vCPU of the PARSEC applications: In the case of Linux, TLB shootdown and reschedule IPIs are dominantly used, whereas the other types of IPIs such as function-call IPIs are rarely generated.

3. Demand-Based Coordinated Scheduling

This section presents the design and implementation of the proposed demand-based coordinated scheduling. Fundamentally, our scheme aims at non-intrusive design without collaboration of specific guest-side software (e.g., kernel, user-level applications, and libraries). In addition, our communication-driven coordination manipulates only time-sharing decisions while vCPU-to-pCPU assignment is carried out independently. We present the experimental analysis and implementation for our communication-driven scheduling and the load-conscious balance scheduling for adaptive vCPU-to-pCPU assignment in the following subsections.

3.1 Communication-Driven Scheduling

As mentioned, our hypothesis is that inter-vCPU communication can be used as an indicator of coordination demand. For non-intrusive design, we take IPIs into account as inter-vCPU communication signals, which can be unobtrusively observed by the hypervisor. In order to investigate the implications of IPIs for consolidated multithreaded workloads, we conducted experimental analysis with the PARSEC 2.1 benchmark suite [6], which is comprised of various types of emerging multithreaded applications. Using *native input*, each application ran with eight threads in an 8-vCPU VM, which is consolidated on two quad core processors; the detailed environment is explained in Section 4. Figure 1 shows IPI rates (the number of IPIs per second per vCPU) observed by the KVM hypervisor while each PARSEC application is solely running inside a VM. As shown in the figure, the applications have diverse characteristics in terms of the rates and types of IPIs. The following subsections explain the role of each IPI type and addresses how those low-level signals are related to the demands of kernel- and user-level coordination.

3.1.1 Kernel-Level Coordination Demands

We investigate kernel-level coordination demands and how they are correlated with inter-vCPU communication. In order to identify kernel-level coordination demands, we examine how much the ratio of CPU time spent in the kernel is affected by contention between VMs under uncoordinated scheduling. If the kernel time ratio is largely amplified compared to that without contention, we can figure out that kernel-level contention is not properly resolved by uncoordinated scheduling. We used the Linux CFS scheduler as an uncoordinated scheduler and *streamcluster*, which consumes considerable CPU with heavy communication, as a contending workload. To measure the amplification, we compare the two cases: *solorun* (without contention) and *corun* (with contention).

Figure 2 shows that the ratio of CPU time consumed in kernel and user spaces for each application. As shown in the figure, the ratio of kernel-level CPU time in the corun case is largely amplified by up to 30× compared to the solorun. Interestingly, such amplifi-

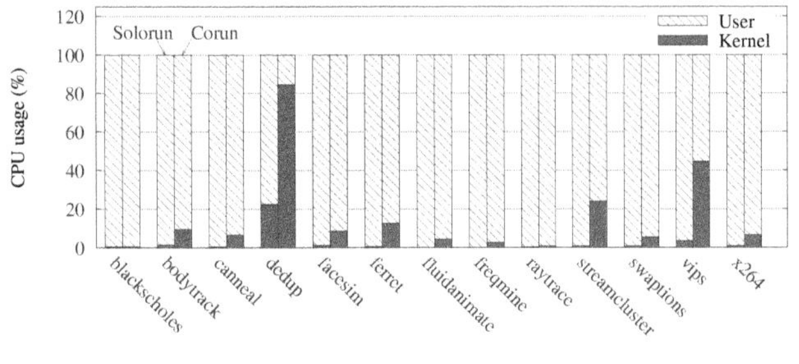

Figure 2. The amplification of kernel time ratio for PARSEC applications in the case of corun with *streamcluster*.

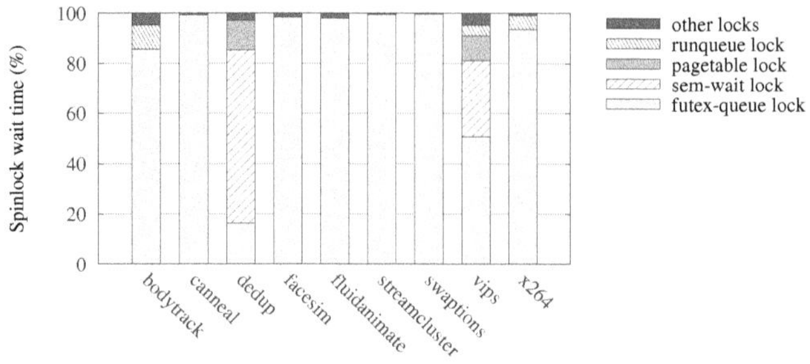

Figure 3. The breakdown of spinlock wait time for the applications where lock spinning time is largely amplified in the case of corun with *streamcluster*.

Application	Function			
	TLB shootdown		Lock spinning	
	% for total CPU usage	% for kernel CPU usage	% for total CPU usage	% for kernel CPU usage
bodytrack	1.96	24.75	**4.56**	**57.58**
canneal	0.02	0.42	**4.02**	**85.17**
dedup	**42.55**	**51.44**	**35.82**	**43.30**
facesim	0.02	0.35	**4.33**	**75.57**
ferret	**8.5**	**75.9**	1.97	17.81
fluidanimate	0.02	0.60	**3.11**	**92.56**
streamcluster	0.02	0.18	**10.35**	**91.11**
swaptions	0.81	13.11	**5.24**	**84.79**
vips	**41.35**	**87.74**	4.32	9.17
x264	0.08	1.03	**6.98**	**89.72**

Table 1. The function-level profiling of CPU usage with respect to the applications whose kernel time ratio is largely amplified in the case of corun with *streamcluster*: The kernel CPU cycles are dominantly consumed for TLB shootdown and lock spinning (bold numbers represent significant amplification for each function).

cation takes place even in the applications that spend most of their time in user space in the case of solorun. In addition, the applications that show largely amplified kernel time are communication-intensive workloads: all applications except *blackscholes*, *freqmine*, and *raytrace* (refer to their IPI rates in Figure 1). This result implies that kernel-level coordination is required for communication-intensive applications even though they are not inherently kernel-intensive. In order to identify the cause of the amplification, we conducted function-level profiling of CPU cycles consumed in the guest kernel by using *perf*. As shown in Table 1, amplified kernel CPU time is mostly spent on two synchronization functions: 1) TLB shootdown and 2) lock spinning.

TLB shootdown is a kernel-level operation for TLB synchronization via inter-CPU (inter-vCPU) communication. In native systems, the kernel ensures that a TLB entry invalidated on one CPU is synchronized with the corresponding entries on the other CPUs for the coherent view of a shared address space. To this end, commodity OSes such as Linux and Windows use an IPI to notify a remote CPU of TLB invalidation. A CPU that initiates TLB shootdown starts busy-waiting until its all recipient CPUs acknowledge IPIs for the sake of TLB consistency. The busy-waiting is efficient in native systems due to the low latency of hardware-based IPIs and high-priority IPI handlers.

Once virtualized, however, a busy-waiting vCPU could consume excessive CPU cycles if one of the recipient vCPUs is not immediately scheduled. This problem becomes serious, as multithreaded applications typically multicast (or broadcast) TLB shootdown IPIs to the vCPUs associated with a shared address space. Note that the applications that show large amplification of TLB shootdown time involve a considerable traffic of TLB shootdown IPIs; *dedup*, *ferret*, and *vips* pressure their shared address spaces with intensive TLB shootdown operations at the rate of 1761, 443, and 1350 IPIs/sec/vCPU, respectively. Therefore, a TLB shootdown IPI is regarded as a performance-critical signal of inter-vCPU communication that needs to be urgently handled for reducing unnecessary busy-waiting.

Next, the excessive lock spinning, which is another source of kernel time amplification, has been well known as inefficient kernel-level synchronization arising from uncoordinated scheduling. This phenomenon typically stems from the LHP problem where a vCPU that is holding a spinlock is involuntarily descheduled before releasing it. Unlike TLB shootdown, unfortunately, spinlock-based synchronization itself does not entail an explicit signal of inter-vCPU communication. It is important to note, however, that excessive lock spinning happens in the workloads with a large traffic of inter-vCPU communication, especially reschedule IPIs (see Figure 1). A reschedule IPI is used to notify a remote CPU of the availability of a thread newly awakened by a local CPU. Based on this observation, we analyze which type of locks lead to pathological spinning and why this situation likely occurs in reschedule-IPI-intensive applications.

In order to pinpoint where excessive lock spinning occurs, we used *lockstat* [1], which reports holding and waiting time statistics for kernel synchronization primitives. Figure 3 shows the ratio of spinlock wait times for the applications that show considerable amplification of lock spinning time. As shown in the result, a *futex-queue* spinlock mostly results in problematic waiting time; the average wait time of the futex-queue spinlock is 192–13687μs, which is abnormal considering that spinlock-protected critical sections generally last for a few microseconds [25]. The futex is the kernel-level support to provide user-level applications with synchronization primitives such as mutex, conditional variable, and barrier. A futex-queue spinlock is used to protect a wait queue associated with a user-level synchronization object. Accordingly, synchronization-intensive applications lead to contention on the futex-queue lock by requesting aggressive queueing operations.

We take a closer look at the futex-queue lock contention from the perspective of inter-vCPU communication. Figure 4 depicts a typical procedure of how a user-level application interacts with the kernel-level futex support for synchronization. Once a thread exits a critical section, it releases a mutex and notifies, if any, a waiting thread that the lock is available through a futex system call. Then the kernel locates the futex queue associated with the mutex and tries to acquire the queue's spinlock (i.e., futex-queue

[1] The current lockstat in the Linux kernel replaces the default spinlock, *ticket spinlock*, with the old unfair lock by the lock debugging feature. We modified the lock debugging feature to use the ticket spinlock for consistent analysis.

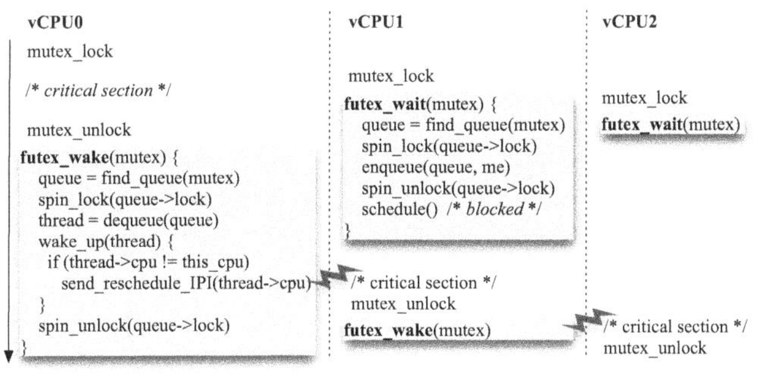

Figure 4. The interaction between user-level synchronization and the kernel support (futex): a gray region represents kernel context and a lightening mark is a reschedule IPI sent from left to right.

lock) to safely dequeue and wake up a thread waiting on the queue. If the thread is decided to be scheduled on a remote CPU by the scheduler, a reschedule IPI is triggered in order to inform the CPU of the newly runnable thread. Note here that the reschedule IPI is sent with the futex-queue lock held. At this point, futex-queue LHP can happen if the waking vCPU is preempted right after sending a reschedule IPI before releasing the lock by either its recipient or another one.

From the analysis, a reschedule IPI can give the hypervisor scheduler a hint that its initiating vCPU likely holds a spinlock. Although the explained procedure is related to a futex-queue lock, our finding is generalized to the relationship between a wait-queue lock and reschedule IPI. Most OSes provide wait-queue APIs for thread-level communication and synchronization [18, 21]. In the Linux kernel, for example, general wake-up functions, prefixed with *__wake_up*, traverse a wait-queue and wake up one or more threads blocked in the queue with its corresponding lock held. In addition, block-based synchronization primitives in the kernel such as *mutex* and *semaphore* maintain their own wait-queues and wake up a waiting thread while holding a spinlock. Note that *dedup* and *vips*, which put significant pressure on their shared address spaces, suffer from excessive spinning on the wait-queue lock (*sem-wait lock*) of *mm*'s semaphore, which is used to protect a shared address space.

Given this hint, the hypervisor can delay the preemption of a vCPU that initiates a reschedule IPI when another vCPU makes a preemption attempt. The amount of delay should be appropriately chosen to allow a vCPU to safely release a likely held spinlock. Since a spinlock-protected critical section is generally short [11, 25], the delay can be empirically determined. However, a critical section that entails IPI transmission, which causes VMEXIT, could be prolonged by hypervisor intervention. To figure out a suitable delay, we conducted sensitivity analysis in Section 4.1.1. Although a sufficiently large value helps avoid LHP, it may prolong the execution of other urgent vCPUs, for example a recipient of a TLB shootdown IPI. A previous delayed preemption scheme that is triggered wherever in kernel space [25] has a larger time window of preemption delay, which may degrade the performance of other urgent vCPUs.

Finally, a wait-queue lock can also be held in a wait procedure other than wake-up operations. As shown in Figure 4, however, a critical section in the wait procedure (*futex_wait*) is extremely short without being interposed by any VMEXIT. Hence, we suppose that wait-queue LHP is unlikely to happen in a wait procedure. With our kernel instrumentation that informs the hypervisor of lock-holding locations, described in Section 4.1.1, we notice that negligible LHPs (near zero) occur in the futex wait function while each PARSEC application is running with *streamcluster*; almost all

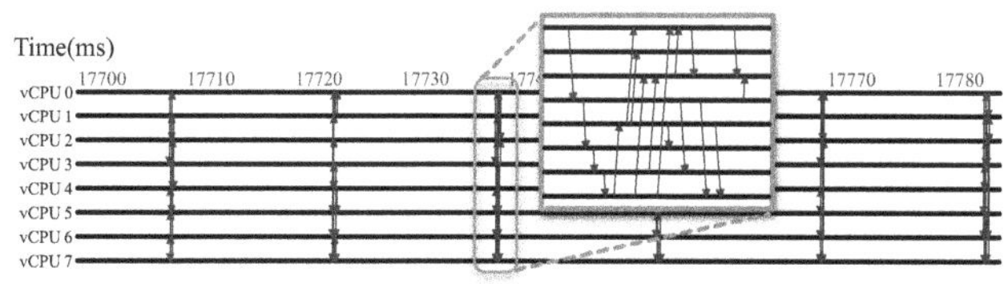

Figure 5. A synchronization behavior of *streamcluster* identified as reschedule IPI transmissions (vertical arrows) for about 80ms.

LHPs happen in *futex_wake* and *futex_requeue*, both of which entail reschedule IPI transmission within a critical section.

3.1.2 User-Level Coordination Demands

Traditional demand-based coscheduling in workstation clusters [3, 4, 9, 22, 23] had dealt with the coordination for user-level applications in which multiple threads heavily communicate with each other. When a thread sends its counterpart a message in order to synchronize a part of parallel computation, the kernel scheduler boosts the priority of the recipient thread so that the communicating threads are coscheduled. The implicit coscheduling [3, 4, 9] takes advantage of an underlying priority-based scheduler, which typically raises the priority of a blocked thread when waking it up. Such demand-based coscheduling was implemented in messaging libraries and firmware of network interface cards for special types of parallel workloads such as bulk synchronous parallel programs.

In virtualized environments, the hypervisor cannot be aware of the actual semantic of user-level communication without the support of threading or messaging libraries. From the viewpoint of the hypervisor, instead, user-level communication could accompany a reschedule IPI if a blocked thread is woken up immediately by a communication message. Since user-level synchronization typically employs block or spin-then-block based primitives, communication between threads can be recognized as reschedule IPIs by the hypervisor. Hence, the hypervisor scheduler can make use of reschedule IPIs to coordinate user-level communication.

Figure 5 depicts a trace of reschedule IPIs obtained by the hypervisor while *streamcluster* is running inside an 8-vCPU VM. The *streamcluster* application makes heavy use of barrier-based synchronization where each thread locally computes its job until a synchronization point, at which all the threads wait for the next stage. This type of application shows no communication during local computation, but involves bulk synchronization at a barrier. As shown in the figure, this behavior is captured via reschedule IPI communication; two to four barrier synchronizations occur at a time within 1ms in a fine-grained manner. If vCPUs are coscheduled in response to reschedule IPIs, all the threads can initiate their computations simultaneously on the coscheduled vCPUs.

The performance impact of coscheduling driven by a reschedule IPI depends on how a hosted application manages contention for its parallel computation. Firstly, a parallel application could involve less efficient synchronization when its hosting vCPUs are not coscheduled. For example, in the event of contention, a spin-then-block synchronization primitive allows a thread to busy-wait for a short period of time until blocked. If the contention is resolved during the spinning, it can avoid a blocking operation, which is expensive due to OS and hypervisor involvements. When such an application runs on coscheduled vCPUs, contention is likely resolved in spin phase without expensive blocking operations. Secondly, depending on algorithms to coordinate parallel computation, additional synchronizations can be induced when threads run on uncoordinated vCPUs. If a scheduler delays the execution of a vCPU that hosts a thread on which other ones depend to make progress, more threads can be blocked with additional contention.

Coscheduling reduces such execution delay so that the number of unnecessary contentions can be effectively curtailed.

The reschedule-IPI-driven coscheduling, however, may not affect the performance of the workloads whose contention management is insensitive to coscheduling. Since a reschedule IPI is generally used for thread scheduling while not confined to the use of synchronization, coscheduling driven by every reschedule IPI cannot improve the performance involving context switch overheads unless a hosted workload is coscheduling-friendly. For efficiency, reschedule-IPI-driven coscheduling can be selectively applied to the VMs that run coscheduling-friendly workloads, while the other scheduling schemes that resolve kernel-level contention are globally enabled. To this end, we enable the hypervisor to expose a knob to selectively enable each feature of the IPI-driven scheduling a per-VM basis. In this work, we use a priori information about coscheduling-friendly characteristics such as spin-then-block synchronization and leave hypervisor-level estimation as future work; the feasibility of hypervisor-level estimation is discussed in Section 4.2.

3.1.3 Urgent vCPU First Scheduling

Our analysis shows that IPIs are the communication signals that enable a hypervisor scheduler to coordinate communicating vCPUs for reducing unnecessary contention. Firstly, when a TLB shootdown IPI is initiated, its recipient vCPU can be urgently scheduled to reduce the amount of busy-waiting of a sender vCPU. Secondly, when a reschedule IPI is initiated, its sender vCPU, which is currently running, can be protected from preemption by another vCPU to reduce the amount of lock spinning due to wait-queue LHP. In addition, its recipient vCPU can be coscheduled to alleviate inefficient or unnecessary user-level contention. In order to handle these coordination demands, we introduce urgent vCPU first (UVF) scheduling, which performs preemptive scheduling and delayed preemption in response to corresponding IPI signals, called *urgent IPIs*.

The UVF scheduling does not replace but complements the proportional-share scheduler in order for its scheduling decision to comply with inter-VM fairness. To this end, per-pCPU FIFO queue, named *urgent queue*, is added over the primary runqueue of the proportional-share scheduler. When a vCPU requests to enter urgent state in response to an IPI, it is inserted into an urgent queue while being included in the primary runqueue; a currently running vCPU can also request to enter urgent state. When a scheduler picks a next vCPU, before inspecting the primary runqueue, it firstly checks whether a vCPU is waiting on the urgent queue and is eligible to run immediately without violating inter-VM fairness by consulting the proportional-share scheduler. If so, the urgent vCPU is preemptively scheduled so that its urgent operation can be promptly handled. Otherwise, a next vCPU is selected from the primary runqueue by the proportional-share scheduler.

In response to an urgent IPI, a corresponding vCPU can request to enter urgent state in two ways: 1) event-based and 2) time-based requests. Firstly, the event-based request is used for a vCPU to be retained in urgent state until pending urgent events are all acknowledged. A TLB shootdown IPI uses the event-based request to keep its recipient vCPU in urgent state until acknowledged in the event of end-of-interrupt (EOI) for its corresponding vector; an EOI signal is triggered right after a requested TLB entry is invalidated. Secondly, the time-based request allows an IPI to specify a time during which a corresponding vCPU can run in urgent state. A reschedule IPI uses the time-based request to preserve its sender vCPU in urgent state until its requested time is taken to release a wait-queue lock. In addition, a recipient vCPU of a reschedule IPI can also be urgently scheduled during a requested time for user-level coordination by means of the time-based request.

The UVF scheduling employs its own time slice, named *urgent tslice*, for urgent vCPUs to expedite pending requests. Since multiple VMs can involve urgent IPIs concurrently, the urgent tslice should be a short time period to improve overall responsiveness. The vCPUs waiting on an urgent queue are served in a round-robin manner with the urgent tslice, during which an urgently running vCPU is protected by preemption. If an urgent vCPU cannot handle all requests during the time slice, it is requeued at the tail of an urgent queue retaining urgent state. Although extremely short urgent tslice improves overall turnaround time, it needs to be long enough for an urgent vCPU to handle at least one urgent request for useful work in the time slice. For example, the urgent tslice can be preferably set greater than or equal to the preemption delay requested by a reschedule IPI sender.

The UVF scheduling introduces an additional knob, called *urgent allowance*, for a vCPU to borrow an urgent tslice from its future CPU allocation by trading short-term fairness for overall efficiency. This mechanism is similar to the Borrowed-Virtual-Time scheduling [8] and Partial Boosting [14] in that a latency-sensitive vCPU (i.e., urgent vCPU) is given dispatch preference while not disrupting long-term CPU fairness. For example in the CFS scheduler, vCPU execution time is monitored in *virtual runtime*, which proceeds at a rate inversely proportional to a given share. If the virtual runtime of a vCPU is larger than that of the currently running one, it cannot be preemptively scheduled while waiting until its virtual runtime becomes minimum in the runqueue [18]. This strict short-term fairness inhibits efficiency by increasing unnecessary busy-waiting due to the prolonged scheduling latency of urgent vCPUs. In order to address this issue, an urgent vCPU is allowed to preemptively run by borrowing the urgent tslice from its future CPU time, only if its time is greater than that of the currently running one within a urgent allowance. In the case of CFS, the urgent allowance is represented in the form of virtual time; in the *Xen Credit scheduler*, it can be specified as *credit*. With a short urgent tslice under one millisecond, the urgent allowance can improve efficiency with a little time lag.

3.2 Load-Conscious Balance Scheduling

In our scheme, vCPU-to-pCPU assignment is separately carried out being decoupled from the communication-driven scheduling. This subsection describes how load imbalance typically happens in heterogeneous workloads and presents our load-conscious balance scheduling scheme for adaptive vCPU-to-pCPU assignment.

3.2.1 Load Imbalance in Consolidated Workloads

In uncoordinated or loosely coordinated scheduling, a load balancer distributes the loads imposed by runnable vCPUs onto available pCPUs as evenly as possible. The load balancing minimizes idle CPU fragmentation so that high CPU throughput and responsiveness can be achieved. Since frequent vCPU migration leads to inefficient use of warm hardware state such as CPU caches, most schemes adopt lazy algorithms to balance global loads. Firstly, once a pCPU goes idle, it tries to steal a waiting vCPU from a busier pCPU like a work-stealing mechanism. In the case where all pCPUs are busy, secondly, waiting vCPUs are periodically migrated onto less loaded pCPUs. Since the load balancing operations are loosely triggered, pCPU loads could be temporarily imbalanced between the invocations of the load balancer.

In addition to the transient load imbalance, pCPU loads can be biased in a situation where VMs are consolidated with different or dynamic loads on their vCPUs. Independent VM instances can have different numbers of vCPUs while holding fair shares. Given the equal shares, a vCPU of a single-core VM has twice shares (i.e., load) than that of a dual-core VM. Although all VMs have the same number of vCPUs with fair shares, each vCPU

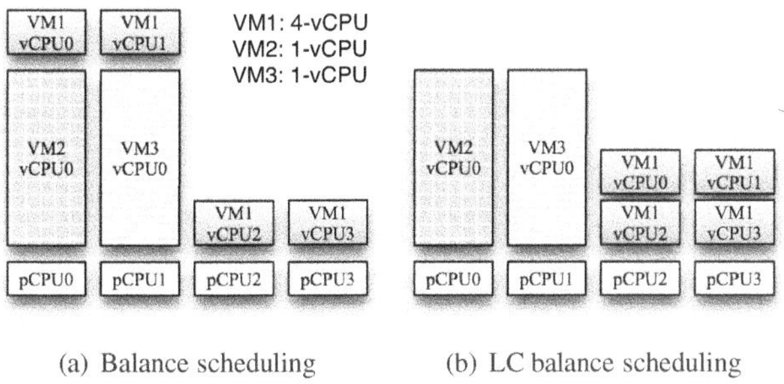

Figure 6. The vCPU-to-pCPU assignment of the balance and LC balance scheduling on four pCPUs whose loads are imbalanced by one 4-vCPU VM and two 1-vCPU VMs: All VMs are given fair shares and the size of each vCPU represents the amount of shares. The vCPU of 1-vCPU VM has shares four times more than that of 4-vCPU VM.

could be given different shares depending on the number of active vCPUs. Proportional-share schedulers for SMP VMs (e.g., CFS group scheduler and Xen Credit scheduler) monitor recent idleness of existing vCPUs in order to distribute a VM's shares only to its active vCPUs. For example, if shares, `S`, are given to a 4-vCPU VM that runs only a sequential workload on a vCPU while idling the others, the active vCPU is allotted whole amount of the shares, `S`. Once the workload enters a parallel phase busying all vCPUs, `S/4` is evenly distributed to each vCPU. This adaptive allocation reduces ineffective shares wasted by inactive vCPUs, but can increase the extent of load imbalance by different amounts of vCPU shares.

3.2.2 Load-Conscious Balance Scheduling

A simple and effective algorithm of vCPU-to-pCPU assignment is the balance scheduling [24], which assigns sibling vCPUs onto different pCPUs in order to prevent them from time-sharing (contending for) a pCPU; the time-sharing of sibling vCPUs is so-called *vCPU stacking* in [24]. Avoiding vCPU stacking can increase the likelihood of coscheduling sibling vCPUs, compared to uncoordinated scheduling, so that negative effect on synchronization latency can be relieved. To this end, this scheme restricts the pCPU affinity of an awakened vCPU to the set of pCPUs to which no sibling vCPU is assigned, while letting the underlying scheduler choose an appropriate pCPU (e.g., least-loaded pCPU) in the specified affinity.

The balance scheduling, however, could degrade synchronization latency if pCPU loads are imbalanced at the moment of assignment. In this case, since the algorithm does not allow vCPU stacking without considering global loads, a vCPU can be assigned to an overloaded pCPU when underloaded ones are all occupied by its sibling vCPUs. Figure 6(a) shows the situation in which the four vCPUs of VM1 are assigned to different pCPUs while loads are imbalanced by the vCPUs with larger shares of two 1-vCPU VMs; all VMs are given fair shares and the size of each vCPU represents the amount of shares. As shown in the figure, although pCPU2 and pCPU3 are sufficiently underloaded, vCPU0 and vCPU1 of VM1 are confined to the overloaded pCPUs (pCPU0 and pCPU1) in order to avoid vCPU stacking. As a result, synchronization latency can be prolonged due to high scheduling latency on the overloaded pCPUs. Moreover, the balance scheduling of VM1 can hurt the performance of 1-vCPU VMs (VM2 and VM3) by contending for the overloaded pCPUs; in this example, each 1-vCPU VM is entitled to monopolize a pCPU without interference for inter-VM fairness.

We propose load-conscious (LC) balance scheduling, which is an adaptive assignment policy based on the balance scheduling and load balancing. In order to avoid ineffective assignment on imbalanced pCPU loads, this scheme selectively allows vCPU stacking in the case where the balance scheduling can aggravate load imbalance. When a vCPU is woken up, the algorithm obtains a set of candidate pCPUs to which no sibling vCPUs are assigned. Then, it decides whether each candidate pCPU is overloaded by checking if the load of each pCPU is higher than the average load of all pCPUs. If at least one underloaded pCPU exists in the set, the set is determined as the pCPU affinity of the vCPU as the balance scheduling does. Otherwise (i.e., all the candidates are overloaded), the affinity is set to all pCPUs without any restriction so that the vCPU can be assigned to an underloaded pCPU. Finally, vCPU stacking is also allowed when the load balancer tries to migrate the vCPU to an underloaded pCPU to which its sibling vCPU has been assigned. Figure 6(b) shows the assignment by the LC balance scheduling where vCPU stacking is allowed on skewed loads.

Although the LC balance scheduling allows vCPU stacking only on underloaded pCPUs, synchronization latency can be adversely affected by contention between sibling vCPUs that communicate with each other. For example, when a vCPU receives a reschedule IPI and is woken up on the pCPU where its sender vCPU is running, wake-queue LHP can happen if the woken vCPU immediately preempts the sender. Therefore, in conjunction with the LC balance scheduling, our communication-driven scheduling is essential to alleviate such negative effect of vCPU stacking by coordinating communicating vCPUs as described in Section 3.1.3; this impact is evaluated in Section 4.1.2.

4. Evaluation

We implemented our proposed scheme based on the Linux CFS scheduler and the KVM hypervisor [15] in the Linux kernel 3.2.0. For proportional sharing for VMs, we used the CFS group scheduling, which proportionally distributes given shares to each VM. All per-VM threads including vCPUs are grouped together via *cgroup* interface [19]. For fair sharing of pCPUs, equal shares are given to each VM (group); the shares were set to default shares (1024) multiplied by the number of pCPUs. The prototype was installed on Dell PowerEdge R610, equipped with two quad-core Intel Xeon X5550 2.67GHz processors and 24GB RAM; eight physical cores are available with hyperthreading disabled. We used Ubuntu 11.04 Linux with the kernel version 3.2.0 as a guest OS.

In order to show the impact of each proposed scheme, we conducted experiments for the following UVF scheduling policies:

- `Resched-DP`: In response to a reschedule IPI, its initiating vCPU enters urgent state for delayed preemption using a time-based request.
- `TLB-Co`: In response to a TLB shootdown IPI, its recipient vCPU enters urgent state for coscheduling using an event-based request.
- `Resched-Co`: In response to a reschedule IPI, its recipient vCPU enters urgent state for coscheduling using a time-based request.

As mentioned, the first two schemes coordinate kernel-level contention, while the last one is for the coordination of user-level contention. For vCPU-to-pCPU assignment, the LC balance scheduling (`LC Balance`) was used with the UVF scheduling schemes. We used the default CFS scheduler (denoted as `Baseline`) as an uncoordinated scheduler. In addition, the balance scheduling (denoted as `Balance`), which implements probabilistic coscheduling, was also compared with our schemes. We ran each mixed workload repeatedly (at least three times) in order to fully overlap their executions. We disabled the dynamic tick feature in the host kernel (i.e., hyper-

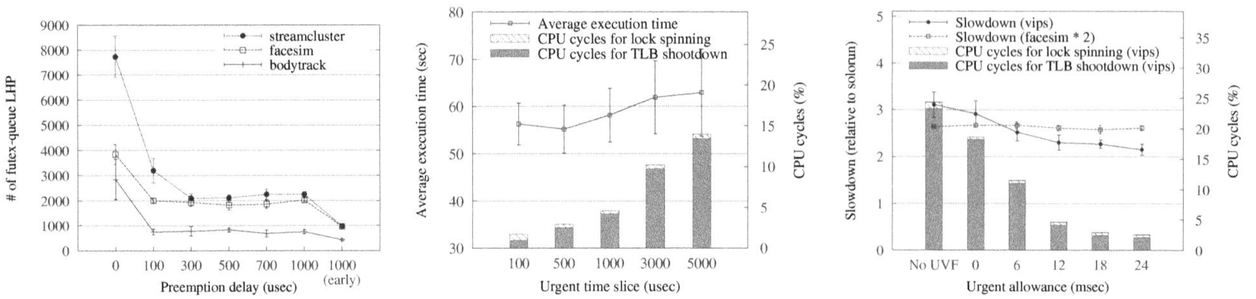

(a) Preemption delay (b) Urgent time slice (c) Urgent allowance

Figure 7. Parameter sensitivity of the UVF scheduling

visor), since this energy-related feature affects the performance of several applications in the case of solorun.

4.1 Coordination for Kernel-Level Contention

4.1.1 Parameter Sensitivity

As described in Section 3.1.3, the UVF scheduling uses three parameters: 1) preemption delay, 2) urgent tslice, and 3) urgent allowance. Firstly, preemption delay specifies a time during which a vCPU that initiates a reschedule IPI is allowed to release a wait-queue lock before being preempted. Secondly, urgent tslice decides the turnaround time of multiple urgent vCPUs waiting on a pCPU. Finally, urgent allowance determines how much short-term fairness is traded for overall efficiency by allowing an urgent vCPU to borrow its future time slice. This subsection presents sensitivity analysis on these parameters; for every analysis, an 8-vCPU VM with 4GB memory was used to host a parallel application and the LC balance scheduling was used for vCPU-to-pCPU assignment.

Firstly, with respect to the preemption delay, we chose three communication-intensive applications (*streamcluster*, *facesim*, and *bodytrack*) in which futex-queue locks are dominantly contended with considerable reschedule IPIs. The *dedup* application was used as a corunning workload to generate intensive preemptions, since it induces significant thread wake-ups by fine-grained communication. `Resched-DP` was applied only to a main workload while a corunning one is not affected by delay parameters for consistent interference; all UVF features but `Resched-DP` are disabled. We measured the number of LHPs by enabling the hypervisor to identify which spinlock is held at the time when a vCPU is preempted. To this end, we instrumented the Linux spinlock functions to record an instruction pointer where a spinlock is acquired in a per-vCPU variable shared with the hypervisor; the variable maintains multiple instruction pointers for nested lock acquisitions.

Figure 7(a) shows the number of futex-queue LHPs averaged on five runs as the amount of preemption delay increases. As shown in the figure, the number of LHPs is significantly reduced by `Resched-DP` (up to 75%). With the delay parameters larger than 300μs, the numbers of LHPs become stable without further noticeable reduction. One thing to note is that there still remain LHPs even though the delay is increased up to 1ms. In order to find the source of the remaining LHPs, we also obtained an instruction pointer at the time of preemption. From the analysis, many remaining LHPs happened during the preparation for reschedule IPI transmission. Such preparation involves multiple APIC (Advanced Programmable Interrupt Controller) accesses, which cause transitions to the hypervisor via VMEXIT. By multiple hypervisor interventions during the preparation, a critical section that includes IPI transmission is prolonged and thus likely to be suspended by preemption before firing an IPI. To verify this, we applied *early delayed preemption*, which is triggered on the first access to the APIC register for IPI transmission (i.e., ICR read in x86 APIC). As shown in the figure, the early delayed preemption further reduces the remaining LHPs.

Secondly, we analyzed the impact of urgent tslice by using a TLB-shootdown-intensive application, *vips*, since TLB shootdown latency is sensitive to urgent tslice when multiple recipient vCPUs concurrently request urgent scheduling on a pCPU. In order for multiple vCPUs to contend in an urgent queue, we ran three *vips* VMs with `TLB-Co` and `Resched-DP` (with 500μs preemption delay) enabled. Figure 7(b) shows the execution time and CPU cycles averaged on ten runs as urgent tslice is increased. As expected, a larger time slice increases the scheduling latency of TLB-IPI-recipient vCPUs leading to a larger amount of CPU cycles consumed for TLB shootdown. Although a short time slice, 100μs, results in the lowest consumption of CPU cycles for TLB shootdown, the performance is less than that for 500μs due to the overheads caused by frequent context switches.

Finally, we investigated the effectiveness of urgent allowance considering the dependency on the proportional-share scheduler. In the CFS scheduler, urgent allowance is represented as virtual time. It allows a vCPU whose virtual runtime is greater than that of the currently running one within an urgent allowance to preemptively run during an urgent tslice, which is borrowed from its future CPU time. For evaluation, we chose *vips* and *facesim* as main and corunning workloads, respectively. The reason we select *facesim* as a corunner is that it can impede the urgent scheduling of the *vips* VM by repeated sleep and wake-up of its worker threads. We coran two *facesim* VMs with `TLB-Co` and `Resched-DP` enabled; preemption delay and urgent tslice were set to 500μs.

Figure 7(c) shows the slowdown relative to solorun of both workloads and the CPU cycles of the *vips* VM. As shown in the result, larger urgent allowance improves the performance of *vips* while not sacrificing that of *facesim*. The CFS scheduler places an awakened vCPU before the minimum virtual runtime by a half of *sched_latency*, which is 24ms in our default configuration. Accordingly, the awakened vCPUs of the *facesim* VMs are frequently placed 12ms before those of the *vips* VM. Considering this policy, an urgent allowance value larger than 12ms helps an urgent vCPU effectively borrow future time slice to preemptively handle urgent IPIs.

On the basis of the analysis, we chose 500μs as preemption delay and urgent tslice, and 18ms as urgent allowance in the remaining evaluations. In addition, we did not apply the early delayed preemption to `Resched-DP`. Since the type of an IPI to be sent cannot be identified at the first ICR read access, early delayed preemption is performed at every type of IPI transmission. In order to evaluate the impact of delayed preemption specifically for reschedule IPI transmission, we excluded this optimization from `Resched-DP`.

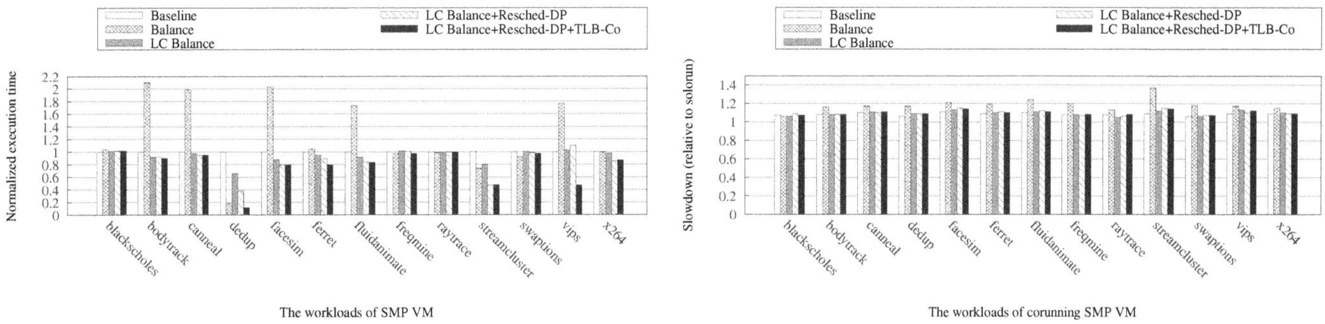

(a) Normalized execution time of SMP VM's workloads

(b) Slowdown relative to solorun of *x264* in a UP VM

Figure 8. The performance for the mix of an SMP (8-vCPU) VM for parallel workloads and four UP VMs for sequential workloads.

4.1.2 Mix of Parallel and Sequential Workloads

We evaluated our proposed scheme in the environment where sequential and parallel workloads are consolidated. This environment represents typical consolidation scenarios in data centers that embrace heterogeneous workloads (e.g., IaaS clouds and VDI). For this type of mixed workloads, we ran an 8-vCPU VM for a parallel workload from the PARSEC suite, while corunning four 1-vCPU VMs (called UP VMs), each of which hosted a sequential workload, *x264* single-threaded version. As mentioned in Section 3.2.1, the mix of sequential and parallel workloads intrinsically incurs load imbalance. Although a UP VM was used in this evaluation, an SMP VM that runs a sequential workload can cause similar load imbalance by activeness-based share distribution.

Figure 8(a) shows the normalized execution time of each parallel workload running in an 8-vCPU VM. The first thing to note is that the balance scheduling degrades the performance compared to the baseline in some cases: *bodytrack*, *canneal*, *facesim*, *ferret*, *fluidanimate*, and *vips*. As mentioned in Section 3.2.2, this result is caused by ineffective vCPU-to-pCPU assignment of the balance scheduling in the case where pCPU loads are imbalanced; a vCPU of the 8-vCPU VM can be assigned to an overloaded pCPU where a UP VM's vCPU with larger shares (up to 8×) is running. Nevertheless, the baseline case does not always outperform the balance scheduling due to vCPU stacking by uncoordinated scheduling.

The LC balance scheduling resolves the problem of ineffective vCPU-to-pCPU assignment of the balance scheduling by preventing a vCPU from being assigned to an overloaded pCPU. Since the LC balance scheduling, however, allows vCPU stacking on imbalanced pCPU loads, unnecessary busy-waiting can happen due to the contention between sibling vCPUs. In the case of *dedup* and *streamcluster*, the LC balance scheduling shows lower performance than the balance scheduling, since the negative effect of vCPU stacking outweighs the benefit from avoiding load imbalance.

As shown in the figure, the UVF scheduling improves the performance (by -1–89% compared to the baseline and 0–83% compared to the LC balance scheduling) by effectively coordinating sibling vCPUs that contend with each other. In more detail, `Resched-DP` improves the performance of the applications that highly contend for wait-queue locks (*dedup*, *facesim*, *ferret*, *fluidanimate*, *streamcluster*, and *x264*), while `TLB-Co` contributes the performance improvement of TLB-shootdown-intensive applications (*dedup*, *ferret*, and *vips*). As a result, the UVF scheduling along with the LC balance scheduling achieves the best performance among all the scheduling schemes.

We also evaluated the slowdown relative to solorun of the *x264* single-threaded applications in four UP VMs. In this experiment where eight pCPUs are fairly shared by five VMs, the workload of a UP VM is unlikely to suffer slowdown, since each UP VM is entitled to monopolize a single pCPU without time-sharing; in practice, despite a dedicated pCPU, slowdown could exist by contentions for other types of resources such as shared caches and memory bandwidth. Figure 8(b) shows the average slowdown of *x264* in the UP VMs depending on the mixed parallel workloads (on the X-axis) and scheduling schemes. As shown in the figure, the balance scheduling results in noticeable slowdown of UP VMs by up to 1.37×, while the baseline and our schemes show a little slowdown close to one. As mentioned in Section 3.2.2, the balance scheduling can degrade the performance of UP VMs by assigning some vCPUs of the SMP VM to the pCPUs where those of UP VMs are running. Such nontrivial slowdown implies that the load-oblivious assignment of the balance scheduling can compromise inter-VM fairness.

4.1.3 Mix of Parallel Workloads

We also evaluated the mix of parallel workloads, each of which ran in an 8-vCPU VM. In this type of mix, every pCPU can be time-shared by vCPUs of different VMs. We chose two corunning applications with different characteristics: *freqmine* and *dedup*. The *freqmine* application is CPU-saturated with a little communication between threads. Accordingly, this workload consumes high pCPU bandwidth, but infrequently preempts the currently running vCPUs. The *dedup*, on the other hand, has varying CPU consumption with a significant amount of communication between threads, thereby inducing intensive preemptions.

Figure 9 shows the weighted speedup of corunning workloads. The weighted speedup is the sum of the speedups relative to solorun of each workload (i.e., $\Sigma(Time_{solorun}/Time_{corun})$). As shown in Figure 9(a), communication-intensive applications suffer from unfair performance degradation while running with the CPU-bound *freqmine* application under uncoordinated scheduling (i.e., baseline). The balance scheduling mostly resolves such degradation, since the communication-intensive workloads are likely to be coscheduled by preempting the CPU-bound *freqmine* on balanced loads, where the LC balance scheduling takes similar effect. The UVF scheduling contributes to more performance improvement especially for TLB-shootdown-intensive applications (*dedup*, *ferret*, and *vips*). `Resched-DP` shows little effect because of infrequent preemptions of *freqmine*.

In Figure 9(b), the performance of *dedup* (corunner), which is sensitive to TLB-shootdown latency with heavy communication traffic, drops significantly in the case of the baseline. Similarly, the balance scheduling alleviates such large performance degradation by spreading sibling vCPUs. LC balance scheduling achieves higher performance of both workloads than the balance scheduling, since loads are frequently imbalanced by the varying loads of *dedup*. Furthermore, the UVF scheduling shows the best overall

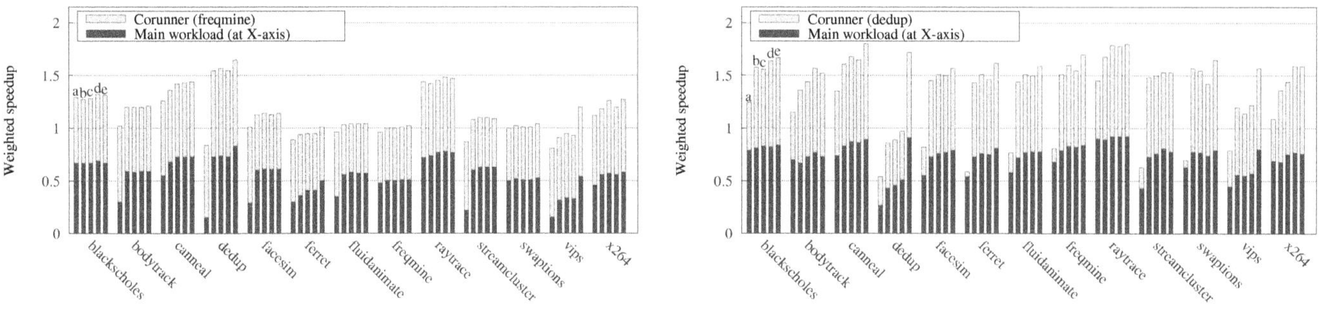

(a) Corun with *freqmine* (b) Corun with *dedup*

Figure 9. The weighted speedup of two parallel workloads (a: `Baseline`, b: `Balance`, c: `LC Balance`, d: `LC Balance+Resched-DP`, e: `LC Balance+Resched-DP+TLB-Co`).

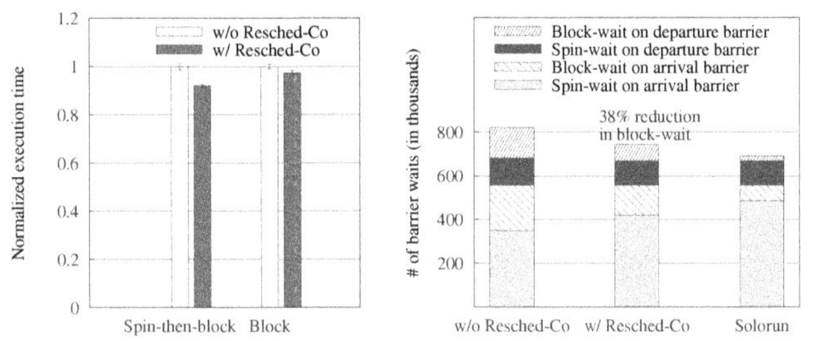

(a) Performance (b) The number of barrier waits

Figure 10. The performance impact of Resched-Co and the breakdown of spin-then-block barrier waits of *streamcluster* that coruns with *bodytrack*.

performance along with the LC balance scheduling. Some drops in weighted speedup in the case of `Resched-DP` alone stems from the performance degradation of *dedup*, since the delayed preemption of a main workload defers the TLB-shootdown of *dedup*. This problem is resolved in the case where `TLB-Co` is applied.

4.2 Coordination for User-Level Contention

As mentioned in Section 3.1.2, inter-thread communication in a synchronization-intensive application can be recognized as bulk traffic of reschedule IPIs. For this type of synchronization-intensive applications, user-level contention can be reduced by coscheduling vCPUs in response to their reschedule IPIs. For the evaluation, we chose *streamcluster*, which intensively uses its in-house barrier, from the PARSEC suite. The *streamcluster* application is coscheduling-friendly, since it adopts a spin-then-block synchronization in its in-house barrier designed for the fine-grained synchronization. Using this primitive, when a thread reaches a barrier, it firstly spins for a short period (approximately 0.1ms) and is then blocked if all threads have not arrived at the barrier yet. If all the threads are coscheduled and their computation loads are not skewed, more barrier waits avoid blocking, which induces context switch and VMEXIT, at the smaller expense of spinning. We coran *bodytrack*, by which *streamcluster* suffers larger interference than any other mixes. For `Resched-Co`, when a reschedule IPI is initiated, its recipient vCPU enters urgent state for 500μs, which is the same as the urgent tslice.

Figure 10(a) shows the performance improvement of *streamcluster* to which `Resched-Co` is applied; `Resched-DP` and `TLB-Co` were enabled in both cases. As shown in the figure, `Resched-Co` improves the performance by 8% in the case of spin-then-block barrier while the performance of *bodytrack* is not affected (the result for *bodytrack* is omitted from the graph for brevity). As expected, this improvement is higher than that of block-based barrier (2.7%). This result demonstrates that spin-then-block synchronization is more coscheduling-friendly. In order to identify the effect of coscheduling, we obtained the information of barrier waits with regard to how many waits are resolved in spin phase and whether additional contentions occur. Figure 10(b) shows the breakdown of barrier waits in *streamcluster*.

The in-house barrier internally uses a *pthread* conditional variable in two ways. Firstly, an arrival barrier is used for all threads to wait for synchronously proceeding to a next stage. Secondly, a departure barrier is used to make sure all threads to entirely depart from a previous stage before starting a next arrival phase. The number of arrival barrier waits is deterministic in the program, whereas departure barrier waits can be increased if the execution of an awakened thread on the arrival barrier is delayed until another thread arrives at the barrier after completing the current stage. Accordingly, the number of departure barrier waits could be increased by the skewed execution of threads. As shown in the figure, block-waits are reduced by 38% due to the parallel executions on coscheduled vCPUs by `Resched-Co`. In addition, the number of departure barrier waits is also reduced by 29%, since the progress of threads is less likely biased by coscheduling. As a result, the wait behavior of coscheduling is close to the solorun, compared to that without coscheduling.

The reduction in blocking operations leads to less reschedule IPIs required for synchronization because a reschedule IPI is triggered to wake up a blocked thread. In this experiment, `Resched-Co` decreases the number of reschedule IPIs for *streamcluster* by 21%. Such IPI reduction alleviates the cost of hypervisor interventions for IPI communication (e.g., VMEXIT and APIC virtualization). Furthermore, the association between the reduction in reschedule IPIs and the benefit from coscheduling can allow the hypervisor to infer coscheduling-friendly workloads. If the bulk traffic of reschedule IPIs is reduced once vCPUs are coscheduled by `Resched-Co`, the hypervisor can infer that the coscheduling has a positive effect on the applied workload.

4.3 Effectiveness with Hardware-Assisted Contention Management

We evaluated our scheme on Intel PLE-enabled processors [12], which support hardware-assisted contention management described in Section 2.2. For this experiment, our prototype was installed on Dell PowerEdge R710 equipped with two quad-core Intel Xeon E5607 2.27GHz processors. For the processors to detect busy-

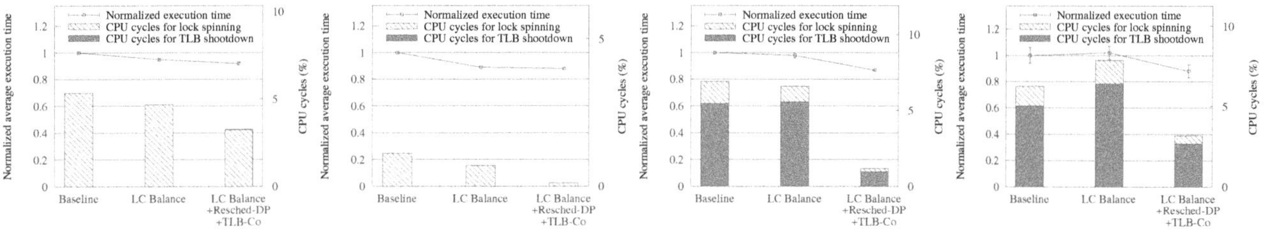

(a) streamcluster (b) facesim (c) ferret (d) vips

Figure 11. Normalized execution time and CPU cycles of parallel workloads in an SMP VM mixed with four UP VMs running *x264* on PLE-enabled processors.

Application	streamcluster	facesim	ferret	vips
Reduction in pause-loop exits (%)	44.5	97.7	74.0	37.9

Table 2. Reduction in pause-loop exits by the UVF scheduling compared to the baseline.

waiting, PLE_Gap and PLE_Window [12] were set to 128 and 4096, respectively; these values are used in KVM and Xen by default. In PLE-enabled processors, the UVF scheduling cancels urgent state once a pause-loop exit occurs, since this exit indicates that the urgent vCPU starts unnecessary busy-waiting. We evaluated the mix of a parallel and four sequential workloads as in Section 4.1.2 with two futex-intensive applications (*streamcluster* and *facesim*) and two TLB-shootdown-intensive applications (*ferret* and *vips*) as parallel workloads.

Figure 11 shows the average execution time normalized to the baseline and CPU cycles for lock spinning and TLB shootdown. As shown in the result, the performance is improved by 8–13% in our scheme (LC balance scheduling with `Resched-DP` and `TLB-Co`). It is because our scheme proactively alleviates the number of busy-waits, whereas the hardware-assisted scheme reactively resolves contention by yielding a pCPU once busy-waiting is detected. Note that our proactive coordination significantly reduces the CPU cycles for lock spinning and TLB shootdown. Alleviating the number of busy-waits, furthermore, leads to the reduction in pause-loop exits. As shown in Table 2, the number of pause-loop exits is reduced by 37.9–97.7%, which means much lower overheads of hypervisor intervention.

Nevertheless, the hardware support to notify the hypervisor of prolonged busy-waiting is an essential fallback, since scheduling-oriented schemes cannot completely eliminate all the excessive busy-waiting in guest OSes. Although `Resched-DP` is effective for communication-intensive applications, it cannot resolve the LHPs that happen in the kernel without reschedule IPI communication. Other than lock spinning, furthermore, busy-waiting has been prevalently used in the kernel for performance optimization based on the assumption that CPUs are physically dedicated. In this regard, the hardware-assisted scheme is complementary to our coordinated scheduling for efficient contention management.

In addition, the current yielding scheme on a pause-loop exit can be refined with the aid of the UVF scheduling. Currently, at every pause-loop exit, a vCPU tries to yield the pCPU to another regardless of the type of busy-waiting. The UVF scheduling, however, can allow a vCPU that sends a TLB shootdown IPI to busy-wait for more time favorably without yielding the pCPU if its recipient vCPUs can be urgently scheduled. Since the hypervisor can identify if the current busy-waiting is for TLB synchronization by checking the transmission of TLB shootdown IPIs, it can determine whether a vCPU yields its pCPU or busy-waits for additional time slice based on the urgent scheduling of recipient vCPUs.

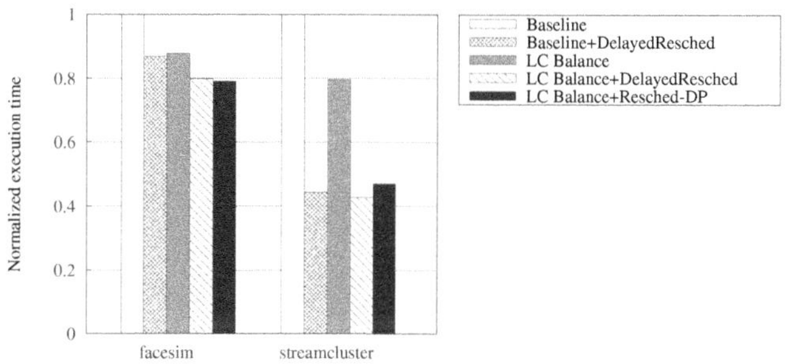

Figure 12. The performance impact of the delayed transmission of reschedule IPIs (denoted as `DelayedResched`) by means of OS modification.

5. Discussion

With regard to wait-queue LHP, OS re-engineering is a possible approach to eliminate the root cause of the problem. As explained, most wait-queue LHPs arise from reschedule IPI transmission inside a spinlock-protected critical section, since the IPI transmission can break the critical section by expensive VMEXITs while involving vCPU wake-up. In order to avoid this problem, the kernel can delay the IPI transmission until exiting the critical section. Since a reschedule IPI is not mandated to be tightly coupled with thread wake-up, it can be safely deferred right after the end of a spinlock-protected critical section, which is generally short and non-preemptable. The engineering cost, however, is nontrivial because every critical section within which thread wake-up is invoked should be modified. We simply modified futex-related wake-up procedures (*futex_wake* and *futex_requeue*), which are hot spots of wait-queue LHP, to use the delayed reschedule IPIs.

Figure 12 shows the performance of *streamcluster* and *facesim*, which are futex-intensive, in the same consolidation scenario as Section 4.1.2 (mix of a parallel and four sequential workloads). The delayed transmission of reschedule IPIs is denoted as `DelayedResched`. As expected, `DelayedResched` improves the performance of the baseline and the LC balance scheduling by excluding reschedule IPIs from critical sections protected by futex-queue spinlocks. The performance improvement is comparable to the case of our scheduling-based solution, `Resched-DP`. Based on the result, we believe that the likelihood of LHP due to IPI transmissions and VMEXITs can be effectively curtailed by virtualization-friendly OS re-engineering.

In addition, virtualization-friendly spinlocks are compelling OS re-engineering. The default spinlock implementation of the Linux kernel is *ticket spinlock*, which enforces FIFO-based lock acquisitions for fairness. The ticket spinlock does not fit for virtualized OSes, since a vCPU can excessively busy-wait for not only a preempted lock-holder, but also preempted lock-waiters that precede the vCPU in FIFO order. For this reason, traditional unfair spinlocks are considered to be efficient for virtualized OSes by allowing lock acquisitions regardless of wait order. Furthermore, as mentioned in Section 2.2, helping locks such as spin-then-block locks are more virtualization-friendly by reducing the amount of unnecessary spinning; those locks have analogous effect to hardware-assisted contention management. Although OS modification would be nontrivial task, compact and well-designed re-engineering has become highly advocated along with hypervisor-level solutions.

6. Conclusions and Future Work

This paper proposes a demand-based coordinated scheduling, which dynamically manipulates time-sharing for coscheduling and delayed preemption in response to inter-vCPU communication, IPIs. On the basis of in-depth analysis on the relationship between synchronization behaviors and IPI communications for consolidated multithreaded workloads, we argue that IPIs are effective signals for the hypervisor to coordinate vCPUs. A TLB shootdown IPI can notify the hypervisor of urgent scheduling demand of a recipient vCPU, while a reschedule IPI implies that an initiating vCPU likely holds a wait-queue spinlock, and that a recipient one possibly involves user-level synchronization. These coordination demands related to IPIs are dominantly found in emerging multithreaded applications. In addition, our load-conscious balance scheduling is essential in the situations where global loads are transiently or intrinsically imbalanced. We believe that such load imbalance could frequently happen in heterogeneously consolidated environments such as IaaS clouds and VDI.

We plan to extend our coordinated scheduling to support automatic detection of user-level synchronization demands and expand the coverage of inferring lock-holder vCPUs. Currently, we rely on a priori information about coscheduling-friendly applications with regard to user-level synchronization. We can enable the hypervisor to monitor the rate of reschedule IPIs for the inference about coscheduling-friendly workloads. In addition, as can be seen in the early preemption delay, there are more chances to infer a lock-holder vCPU that involves hypervisor intervention. We will reinforce the delayed preemption by increasing the coverage that infers lock-holder vCPUs. Finally, we are exploring cooperation with paravirtualized approaches and hardware-assisted contention management.

Acknowledgments

The authors would like to thank the anonymous reviewers for their feedback and suggestions. This work was partly supported by the National Research Foundation of Korea(NRF) grant funded by the Korea government(MEST) (No. 2012-0000148), and by the IT R&D program of MKE/KEIT [10041244, Smart TV 2.0 Software Platform].

References

[1] AMD. Amd64 architecture programmer's manual volume 2: System programming, 2010.

[2] R. H. Arpaci, A. C. Dusseau, A. M. Vahdat, L. T. Liu, T. E. Anderson, and D. A. Patterson. The interaction of parallel and sequential workloads on a network of workstations. In *Proc. SIGMETRICS*, 1995.

[3] A. C. Arpaci-Dusseau. Implicit coscheduling: coordinated scheduling with implicit information in distributed systems. *ACM TOCS*, 19(3): 283–331, 2001.

[4] A. C. Arpaci-Dusseau, D. E. Culler, and A. M. Mainwaring. Scheduling with implicit information in distributed systems. In *Proc. SIGMETRICS*, 1998.

[5] P. Barham, B. Dragovic, K. Fraser, S. Hand, T. Harris, A. Ho, R. Neugebauer, I. Pratt, and A. Warfield. Xen and the art of virtualization. In *Proc. SOSP*, 2003.

[6] C. Bienia, S. Kumar, J. P. Singh, and K. Li. The PARSEC benchmark suite: characterization and architectural implications. In *Proc. PACT*, 2008.

[7] H. Chen, H. Jin, K. Hu, and J. Huang. Scheduling overcommitted VM: Behavior monitoring and dynamic switching-frequency scaling. *FGCS*, 2011.

[8] K. J. Duda and D. R. Cheriton. Borrowed-virtual-time (BVT) scheduling: supporting latency-sensitive threads in a general-purpose scheduler. In *Proc. SOSP*, 1999.

[9] A. C. Dusseau, R. H. Arpaci, and D. E. Culler. Effective distributed scheduling of parallel workloads. In *Proc. SIGMETRICS*, 1996.

[10] D. Feitelson. Gang scheduling performance benefits for fine-grain synchronization. *JPDC*, 16(4):306–318, 1992.

[11] T. Friebel and S. Biemueller. How to deal with lock holder preemption. In *Xen Summit*, 2008.

[12] Intel. Intel 64 and ia-32 architectures software developer's manual. volume 3b: System programming guide, part 2, 2010.

[13] W. Jiang, Y. Zhou, Y. Cui, W. Feng, Y. Chen, Y. Shi, and Q. Wu. CFS optimizations to KVM threads on multi-core environment. In *Proc. ICPADS*, 2009.

[14] H. Kim, H. Lim, J. Jeong, H. Jo, and J. Lee. Task-aware virtual machine scheduling for I/O performance. In *Proc. VEE*, 2009.

[15] A. Kivity, U. Lublin, and A. Liguori. KVM: the Linux virtual machine monitor. In *Proc. OLS*, 2007.

[16] W. Lee, M. Frank, V. Lee, K. Mackenzie, and L. Rudolph. Implications of I/O for gang scheduled workloads. In *Proc. IPPS*, 1997.

[17] Y. Lee, W. Son, S. Park, G. Lee, D. Howard, and D. Slezak. Design and implementation of a locking-aware scheduler for multiprocessor environments. *Convergence and Hybrid Information Technology*, 6935: 384–390, 2011.

[18] W. Mauerer. *Professional Linux Kernel Architecture*. Wrox Press Ltd., 2008.

[19] P. B. Menage. Adding generic process containers to the Linux kernel. In *Proc. OLS*, 2007.

[20] J. Ousterhout. Scheduling Techniques for Concurrent Systems. In *Proc. ICDCS*, 1982.

[21] M. Russinovich and D. A. Solomon. *Windows Internals: Including Windows Server 2008 and Windows Vista, Fifth Edition*. Microsoft Press, 5th edition, 2009.

[22] P. Sobalvarro, S. Pakin, W. Weihl, and A. Chien. Dynamic coscheduling on workstation clusters. In *Proc. IPPS*, 1998.

[23] P. G. Sobalvarro and W. E. Weihl. Demand-based coscheduling of parallel jobs on multiprogrammed multiprocessors. In *Proc. IPPS*, 1995.

[24] O. Sukwong and H. S. Kim. Is co-scheduling too expensive for SMP VMs? In *Proc. EuroSys*, 2011.

[25] V. Uhlig, J. LeVasseur, E. Skoglund, and U. Dannowski. Towards scalable multiprocessor virtual machines. In *Proc. VM*, 2004.

[26] VMWare. VMware, Inc. VMware vSphere 4: The CPU scheduler in VMware ESX 4.1. Technical report, 2010.

[27] C. Weng, Z. Wang, M. Li, and X. Lu. The hybrid scheduling framework for virtual machine systems. In *Proc. VEE*, 2009.

[28] C. Weng, Q. Liu, L. Yu, and M. Li. Dynamic adaptive scheduling for virtual machines. In *Proc. HPDC*, 2011.

[29] Y. Wiseman and D. G. Feitelson. Paired gang scheduling. *IEEE TPDS*, 14(6):581–592, 2003.

[30] Y. Yu, Y. Wang, H. Guo, and X. He. Hybrid co-scheduling optimizations for concurrent applications in virtualized environments. In *Proc. ICNAS*, 2011.

Traffic Management: A Holistic Approach to Memory Placement on NUMA Systems

Mohammad Dashti
Simon Fraser University
mdashti@sfu.ca

Alexandra Fedorova
Simon Fraser University
fedorova@sfu.ca

Justin Funston
Simon Fraser University
jfunston@sfu.ca

Fabien Gaud
Simon Fraser University
fgaud@sfu.ca

Renaud Lachaize
UJF
renaud.lachaize@imag.fr

Baptiste Lepers
CNRS
baptiste.lepers@imag.fr

Vivien Quéma
Grenoble INP
vivien.quema@imag.fr

Mark Roth
Simon Fraser University
mroth@sfu.ca

Abstract

NUMA systems are characterized by Non-Uniform Memory Access times, where accessing data in a remote node takes longer than a local access. NUMA hardware has been built since the late 80's, and the operating systems designed for it were optimized for access locality. They co-located memory pages with the threads that accessed them, so as to avoid the cost of remote accesses. Contrary to older systems, modern NUMA hardware has much smaller remote wire delays, and so remote access costs *per se* are not the main concern for performance, as we discovered in this work. Instead, *congestion on memory controllers and interconnects*, caused by memory traffic from data-intensive applications, hurts performance a lot more. Because of that, memory placement algorithms must be redesigned to target traffic congestion. This requires an arsenal of techniques that go beyond optimizing locality. In this paper we describe *Carrefour*, an algorithm that addresses this goal. We implemented *Carrefour* in Linux and obtained performance improvements of up to 3.6× relative to the default kernel, as well as significant improvements compared to NUMA-aware patchsets available for Linux. *Carrefour* never hurts performance by more than 4% when memory placement cannot be improved. We present the design of *Carrefour*, the challenges of implementing it on modern hardware, and draw insights about hardware support that would help optimize system software on future NUMA systems.

Categories and Subject Descriptors D.4.1 [*OPERATING SYSTEMS*]: Process Management—scheduling

Keywords NUMA, operating systems, multicore, scheduling

ASPLOS'13, March 16–20, 2013, Houston, Texas, USA.

1. Introduction

Modern servers are built from several *processor nodes*, each containing a multicore CPU and a local DRAM serviced by one or more memory controllers (see Figure 1). The nodes are connected into a single cache-coherent system by a high-speed *interconnect*. Physical address space is globally shared, so all cores can transparently access memory in all nodes. Accesses to a local node go through a local memory controller; accesses to remote nodes must traverse the interconnect and access a remote controller. Remote accesses typically take longer than local ones, giving these systems a property of *N*on-*U*niform *M*emory *A*ccess time (NUMA).

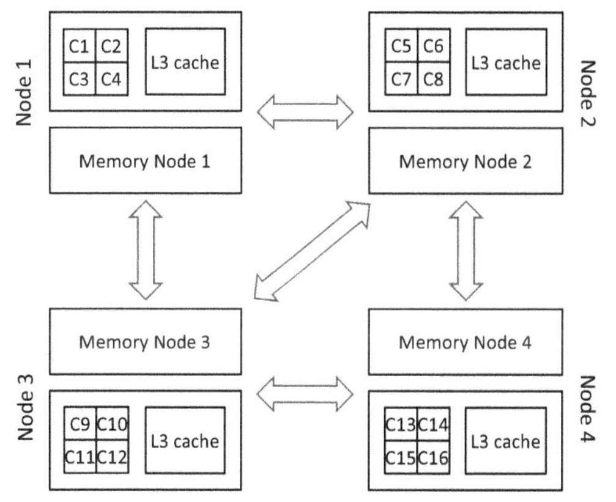

Figure 1. A modern NUMA system, with four nodes and four cores per node. At the time of the writing, NUMA systems are built with up to 8 nodes and 10 cores per node.

It is well understood that optimal performance on NUMA systems can be achieved only if we place threads and their memory in consideration of the system's physical layout. For instance, previous work on NUMA-aware memory placement focused on maximizing locality of accesses, that is, placing memory pages such that data accesses are satisfied from a local node whenever possible. That was done to avoid very high costs of remote memory accesses. Contrary to insights from previous work, we discover that on modern NUMA systems remote wire delays, that is, delays resulting from traversing a greater physical distance to reach a remote node, are *not* the most important source of performance overhead. On the other hand, *congestion on interconnect links and in memory controllers*, which results from high volume of data flowing across the system, can dramatically hurt performance. This motivates the design of new NUMA-aware memory placement policies.

To make these statements concrete, consider the following facts. On NUMA systems circa 1990s, the time to access data from a remote node took 4-10 times longer than from a local node [31]. On NUMA systems that are built today, remote wire delays add at most 30% to the cost of a memory access [7]. For most programs, this latency differential alone would not have a substantial impact on performance. However, fast modern CPUs are able to generate memory requests at very high rates. Massive data traffic creates congestion in memory controller queues and on interconnects. When this happens, memory access latencies can become as large as 1000 cycles, from a normal latency of only around 200. Such a dramatic increase in latencies can slow down data-intensive applications by more than a factor of three. Fortunately, high latencies can be avoided or substantially reduced if we carefully place memory pages on nodes so as to avoid traffic congestion.

In response to the changes in hardware bottlenecks, we approach the problem of thread and memory placement on NUMA systems from an entirely new perspective. We look at it as the problem of *traffic management*. Our algorithm, called *Carrefour*[1], places threads and memory so as to avoid traffic hotspots and prevent congestion in memory controllers and on interconnect links. This is akin to traffic management in the context of city planning: popular residential and business hubs must be placed so as to avoid congestion on the roads leading to these destinations.

The mechanisms used in our algorithm: e.g., migration and replication of memory pages, are well understood, but the algorithm itself is new. Our algorithm makes decisions based on global observations of traffic congestion. Previous algorithms optimized for locality, and relied on local information, e.g., access pattern of individual pages. We found that in order to effectively manage congestion on modern systems we need an arsenal of techniques that go beyond optimizing locality. While locality plays a role in managing congestion (when we reduce remote accesses, we reduce interconnect traffic), alone it is not sufficient to achieve the best performance. The challenge in designing *Carrefour* was to understand how to combine different mechanisms in an effective solution for modern hardware.

Implementing an effective NUMA-aware algorithm on modern systems presents several challenges. Modern systems do not have the same performance monitoring hardware that was present (or assumed) on earlier systems. Existing instruction sampling hardware cannot gather the profiling data needed for the algorithm with the desired accuracy and speed. We had to navigate around this problem in our design. Furthermore, the memory latencies that we are optimizing are lower than on older systems, so we can tolerate less overhead in the algorithm.

We implemented *Carrefour* in Linux and evaluated it with several data-centric applications: k-means clustering, face recognition, map/reduce, and others. *Carrefour* improves performance of these applications, with the largest gain of 3.6× speedup. When memory placement cannot be improved *Carrefour* never hurts performance by more than 4%. Existing NUMA-aware patches for the Linux kernel perform less reliably and in general fall short of improvements achieved with *Carrefour*.

[1] *Carrefour*– (French) intersection, crossroads.

2. Traffic congestion on modern NUMA systems

In this section, we demonstrate that the effects of traffic congestion are more substantial than those of wire delays, and motivate why memory placement algorithms must be redesigned. To that end, we report data from two sets of experiments. In the first set, our goal is to measure the effects of wire delays only. We run applications in two configurations: *local-memory* and *remote-memory*. Under *local-memory*, the thread and its data are co-located on the same NUMA node; under *remote-memory*, the thread runs on a different node than its data. To ensure that wire delay is the dominant performance factor, we had to avoid congestion on memory controllers and interconnects, so we run one application at a time and use only one thread in each application. We do not include applications with CPU utilization less than 30%, because memory performance is not their main bottleneck. The experiments are run on a system described in Section 4 (Machine A – illustrated in Figure 1). We use applications from the NAS, PARSEC and map/reduce Metis suites, also described in Section 4.

Figure 2(a) shows relative completion time under *remote-memory* vs. *local-memory* configuration. The performance degrades by at most 20% under *remote-memory*, which is consistent with at most 30% difference in local-vs-remote memory latencies measured in microbenchmarks [7].

In the second set of experiments, we want to observe traffic congestion, so we run each application with as many threads as there are cores. We demonstrate how performance varies under two memory placement policies on Linux, as they induce different degrees of traffic congestion. The first policy is *First-touch* (F) - the default policy where the memory pages are placed on the node where they are first accessed. The second policy is *Interleaving* (I) - where memory pages are spread evenly across all nodes. Although these are not the only possible and not necessarily the best policies, comparing them illustrates the salient effects of traffic congestion.

Figure 2(b) shows the absolute difference in completion time achieved under *first-touch* and *interleaving*. The policy that performed the best is indicated in parenthesis next to the application name; a "-" is shown when the application performs equally well with either policy. We observe that the differences are often much larger than what we can expect from wire delays alone. For Streamcluster, a k-means clustering application from PARSEC, the performance varies by a factor of two depending on the memory placement policy!

To illustrate that these differences are due to traffic congestion, we show in Table 1 some supporting data for the two applications, *Streamcluster* and *PCA* (a map/reduce application)[2]. ***Local access ratio*** is the percent of all memory accesses sourced from a local node; ***Memory latency*** is the average number of cycles to satisfy a memory request from any node; ***Memory controller imbalance*** is the standard deviation of the load across all memory controllers, expressed as percent of the mean. Load is measured as the number of requests per time unit; ***Average interconnect (IC) usage*** shows the utilized interconnect bandwidth as percent of total, averaged across all links, the ***imbalance*** shows the standard deviation of utilization across the links as percent of mean utilization; ***L3MPKI*** is the number of last-level (L3) cache misses per thousand instructions; ***IPC*** is the number of instructions per cycle.

The data in Table 1 leads to several curious observations. First, we see that locality of memory accesses either does not change regardless of the memory management policy, or *decreases* under the better performing policy. For *Streamcluster*, most of the memory pages happen to be placed on a single node under *first-touch* (be-

[2] We are unable to present the same data for all applications due to space constraints, but the conclusions reached from their measurements are qualitatively similar.

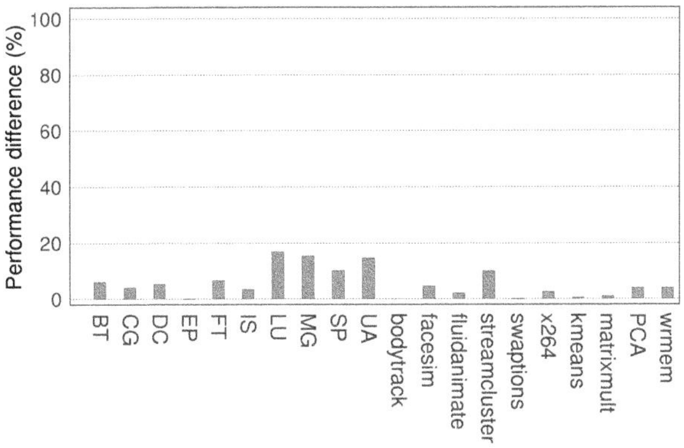

(a) Perf. difference for single-thread versions of applications between local and remote memory configurations.

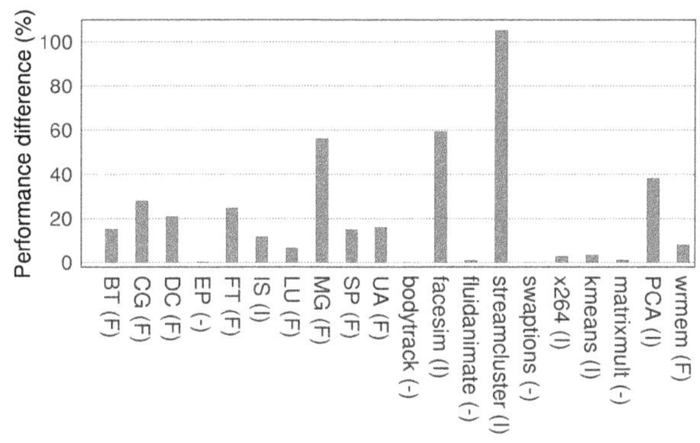

(b) Absolute perf. difference for multi-thread versions of applications between First-touch (F) and interleaving (I).

Figure 2. Performance difference of applications depending on the thread and memory configuration.

	Streamcluster		*PCA*	
	Best (I)	Worst (F)	Best (I)	Worst (F)
Local access ratio	25%	25%	25%	33%
Memory latency	476	**1197**	465	**660**
Mem-ctrl. imbalance	8%	**170%**	5%	**130%**
IC: imbalance, (avg)	22% (59%)	**85%** (33%)	20% (48%)	**68%** (31%)
L3MPKI	16.85	16.89	7.35	7.4
IPC	0.29	**0.15**	0.52	**0.36**

Table 1. Traffic congestion effects

cause a single thread initializes them at the beginning of the program). Under *interleaving* the pages are spread across all nodes, but since the threads access data from all four nodes, the overall access ratio is about the same in both configurations. For *PCA*, interleaving decreases the local access ratio and yet *increases* performance. So the first surprising conclusion is that ***better locality does not necessarily improve performance***!

And yet, the IPC substantially improves (2× for *Streamcluster* and 41% for *PCA*), while the L3 miss rate, as well as L1 and L2 miss rates, remain unchanged. The explanation emerges if we look at the memory latency. Under interleaving, the memory latency reduces by a factor of 2.48 for *Streamcluster* and 1.39 for *PCA*. This effect is entirely responsible for performance improvement under the better policy. The question is, *what is responsible for memory latency improvements*? It turns out that interleaving *dramatically reduces memory controller and interconnect congestion* by alleviating the load imbalance and mitigating traffic hotspots. Rows 5, 6 in Table 1 show significant reductions in imbalance under interleaving, and Figure 3 illustrates these effects visually for *Streamcluster*. So even without improving locality (we even *reduce* it for *PCA*), we are able to substantially improve performance. And yet, existing NUMA-aware algorithms disregarded traffic congestion, optimizing for locality only. Our work addresses this shortcoming.

Although the two selected applications performed significantly better under interleaving, this does not mean that interleaving is the only desired policy on modern NUMA hardware. In fact, as Figure 2(b) shows, many NAS applications fared a lot worse with interleaving. In the process of designing the algorithm we learned that a range of techniques – interleaving, page replication and co-location – must be judiciously applied to different parts of the address space depending on global traffic conditions and page access patterns. So the challenge in designing a good algorithm is understanding when to apply each technique, while navigating around the challenges of obtaining accurate performance data and limiting the overhead.

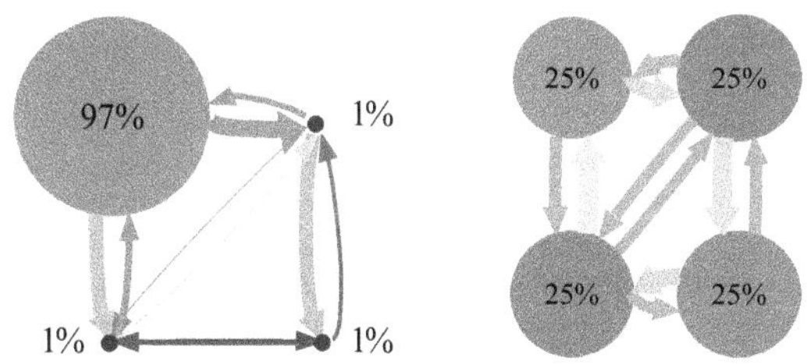

Figure 3. Traffic imbalance under first-touch (left) and interleaving (right) for *Streamcluster*. Nodes and links bearing the majority of the traffic are shown proportionately larger in size and in brighter colours. The percentage values show the fraction of memory requests destined for each node. The figure is drawn to scale.

3. Design and Implementation

We begin by describing the mechanisms composing the algorithm: *page co-location*, *interleaving*, *replication* and *thread clustering*. Then we explain how they fit together.

3.1 The mechanisms

Page co-location is when we re-locate the physical page to the same node as the thread that accesses it. Co-location works well for pages that are accessed by a single thread or by threads co-located on the same node.

Page interleaving is about evenly distributing physical pages across nodes. Interleaving is useful when we have imbalance on memory controllers and interconnect links, and when pages are accessed by many threads. Operating systems usually provide an interleaving allocation policy, but only give an option to enable or disable it globally for the entire application. We found that interleaving works best when judiciously applied to parts of the address space that will benefit from it.

Page replication is about placing a copy of a page on several memory nodes. Replication distributes the pressure across memory controllers, alleviating traffic hotspots. An added bonus is eliminat-

Global statistics	
MC-IMB	Memory controller imbalance (as defined in Section 2)
LAR	Local access ratio (as defined in Section 2)
MAPTU	Memory (DRAM) accesses per time unit (microsecond)
Per-application statistics	
MRR	Memory read ratio. Fraction of DRAM accesses that are reads
CPU%	Percent CPU utilization
Per-page statistics	
Number of accesses	The number of sampled data loads that fell in that page
Access type	Read-only or read-write

Table 2. Statistics collected for the algorithm.

ing remote accesses on replicated pages. When done right, replication can bring very large performance improvements. Unfortunately, replication also has costs. Since we keep multiple copies of the same page, we must synchronize their contents, which is like running a cache coherency protocol in software. The costs can be very significant if there is a lot of fine-grained read/write sharing. Another potential source of overhead is the synchronization of page tables. Since modern hardware walks page tables automatically, page tables themselves must be replicated across nodes and kept in sync. Finally, replication increases the memory footprint. We should avoid it for workloads with large memory footprints for fear of increasing the rate of hard page faults.

Thread clustering is about co-locating threads that share data on the same node, to the extent possible[3]. Examination of prior work on the subject revealed two thread clustering algorithms most relevant for our project [15, 30]. Tam's algorithm [30] always co-located on the same node threads that shared data. Kamali's algorithm [15] balanced between increased contention and the benefits of co-operative sharing. It only co-located data-sharing threads, provided that these threads would not aggressively compete for the node's shared resources. We confirmed the importance of balancing the two goals in our experiments, so our algorithm assumes the Kamali's variant of thread clustering. Since thread clustering is well documented and understood, we did not evaluate it in our implementation.

3.2 The Algorithm

Our memory management algorithm has three components: *measurement*, *global decisions* and *page-local decisions*. The measurement component continuously gathers various metrics (Table 2) that later drive page placement decisions. Global and per-application metrics are collected using hardware counters with very low overhead. Per-page statistics are collected via instruction-based sampling (IBS) [12], which can introduce significant overheads at high sampling rates. Section 3.3 describes how we keep the overheads at bay. Global decisions are based on system-wide traffic congestion and workload properties which determine what mechanisms to use. Page-local decisions examine access patterns of individual pages to decide their fate.

3.2.1 Global Decisions

The global decision-making process is outlined in Figure 4.

Step 1: we decide whether to enable *Carrefour*. We only want to run *Carrefour* for applications that generate substantial memory traffic. Other applications would not be affected by memory placement policies, so there is no reason to subject them to sampling overhead. This decision is driven by the application's memory access rate (MAPTU – see Table 2). *Carrefour* is enabled for applications with the MAPTU above a certain threshold. The MAPTU threshold is to be determined experimentally and the right setting may vary from system to system. We found the threshold of 50 MAPTU worked well on all hardware we evaluated, and the performance was not very sensitive to its choice. To determine the right MAPTU threshold on a system very different from ours, we recommend running a benchmark suite under different NUMA policies, noting which applications are affected and using the lowest observed MAPTU from those experiments.

Once we decided whether there is sufficient memory traffic to justify running *Carrefour*, we need to decide which of the available mechanisms, replication, interleaving and co-location, should be enabled for each application given its memory access patterns. The goal here is to choose the most beneficial techniques and avoid any associated overhead. The next three steps take care of this decision.

Step 2: we decide whether it is worthwhile to use replication. Replication risks introducing significant overheads if it forces us to run out of RAM (and causes additional hard page faults) or requires frequent synchronization of pages across nodes (see more discussion in Section 3.3.2). To avoid the first peril, we conservatively enable replication only if there is sufficient free RAM to replicate the entire resident set. That is, the fraction of free RAM must be at least $1 - \frac{1}{NUM\_NODES}$. This is a conservative threshold, because not all pages will be replicated, and not all resident pages will be accessed frequently enough to generate significant page fault overhead if evicted. Evaluating the trade-off between replication benefit and potentially increased page-fault rate was outside the scope of the work. This requires workloads that both benefit from replication and have very large memory-resident sets, which we did not encounter in our experiments.

To avoid the overhead associated with the synchronization of page content across nodes, we do not replicate pages that are frequently written. An application must have the memory read ratio (MRR) of at least 95% in order for its memory pages to be considered for replication[4]. The setting of this parameter can have a very significant effect on performance. While we found that the performance was not sensitive when we varied the parameter in the range of 90-99%, it is always safe to err on the high side.

Step 3: we decide whether to use interleaving. Interleaving improves performance if we have large memory controller imbalance. We enable interleaving if memory controller imbalance is above 35%, but found that the performance was not highly sensitive to this parameter. Applications that benefit from interleaving usually begin with a very large imbalance.

Step 4: we decide whether or not to enable co-location. Co-location will be triggered only for pages that are accessed from a single node, and so it will not exacerbate the imbalance if memory-intensive threads are evenly spread across nodes, which is ensured by thread clustering. Therefore, we enable co-location if the local access rate is slightly less than ideal (LAR $<$ 80%). Performance is not highly sensitive to this parameter; we observed that if this parameter is completely eliminated from the algorithm, the largest performance impact is only a few percent.

Although we expect that optimal settings for the parameters used in the algorithm would vary from one system to another, we found that we did not need to adjust the settings when we moved between the two experimental systems used in our evaluation. Although our systems had the same number of nodes and both used

[3] We never want to sacrifice CPU load balance in favour of clustering.

[4] MRR is approximated as fraction of L1 refills from DRAM in modified state, because there is no a hardware counter that provides this quantity precisely per core, as opposed to per-node. Similarly, due to hardware counter limitations described in Section 3.3.2, it is very difficult to measure the MRR per page. That is why we use the MRR for the entire application.

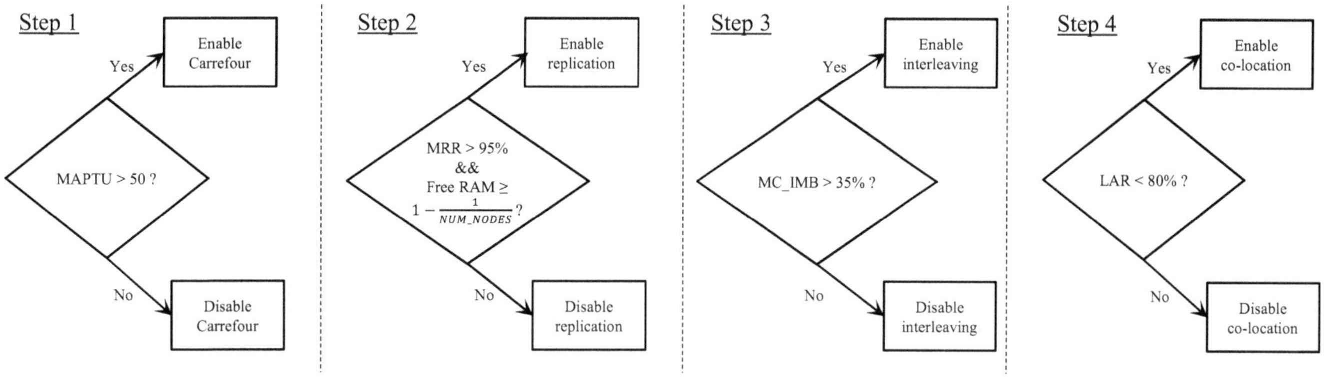

Figure 4. Global decisions in *Carrefour*.

AMD CPUs, they differed in the number of cores per node, the cache-coherency protocol (broadcast vs. directory-based), and one had a higher interconnect throughput than the other. Therefore, it is possible that the algorithm parameters settings are rather stable across all but drastically different systems.

3.2.2 Page-local Decisions

Carrefour makes page-local decisions depending on the mechanisms enabled: e.g., pages are only considered for replication if replication is enabled for that application. The following explanation assumes that all three mechanisms are enabled.

To decide the fate of each page, we need at least two memory-access samples for that page. If the page was accessed from only a single node we migrate it to that node. We do not migrate the thread, because we assume that thread clustering, performed before memory placement, already made good thread placement decisions. If the page is accessed from two or more nodes, it is a candidate for either interleaving or replication. If the accesses are read-only, the page is replicated. Otherwise it is marked for interleaving. To decide where to place a page marked for interleaving, we use two probabilities: $P_{migrate}$ and P_{node}. $P_{migrate}$ determines the likelihood of migrating the page away from the current node. $P_{migrate}$ is the MAPTU of the current node as the fraction of MAPTU on all nodes, so the higher the load on the current node relative to others, the higher the chance that we will migrate a page. P_{node} gives us the probability of migrating a page to a particular node, and it is the complement of $P_{migrate}$ for that node, so *Carrefour* will migrate the page to the least loaded node.

3.3 Implementation

We implemented *Carrefour* in the Linux kernel 3.6.0. *Carrefour* runs measures the selected performance indicators, and with periodicity of one second makes decisions regarding page placement and resets statistic counters. To a large extent, *Carrefour* relies on well-understood mechanisms in the Linux kernel, such as physical page migration. The non-trivial aspects of the implementation were understanding how to accomplish fast and accurate sampling of memory accesses and navigating around the overheads of replication. We describe how we overcame these challenges in the two sections that follow.

3.3.1 Fast and accurate memory access sampling

A crucial goal of the algorithm is to quickly and accurately detect memory pages that cause the most DRAM accesses, and accurately estimate the read/write ratio of those pages. To that end, we used Instruction-Based Sampling (IBS) – hardware-supported sampling of instructions available in AMD processors. Intel processors support similar functionality in the form of PEBS: Precise Event-Based Sampling. IBS can be configured to deliver instruction samples at a desired interval, e.g., after expiration of a certain number of cycles or micro-ops. Each sample contains detailed information about the sampled instruction, such as the address of the accessed data (if the instruction is a load or a store), whether or not it missed in the cache and how long it took to fetch the data. Unfortunately, every delivered sample generates an interrupt, so processing samples at a high rate becomes very costly. Other systems that relied on IBS performed off-line profiling [17, 27], so they could tolerate much higher overhead than what would be acceptable in our online algorithm.

After experimenting with IBS on our systems, we found that for most applications the sampling interval of 130,000 cycles incurs a reasonable overhead of less than 5%. The desired sampling rate can be trivially derived for new systems: it amounts to experimenting with different sampling rates and settling for the one that generates acceptable runtime overhead.

Our initial decision was to filter out all the samples that did not generate a DRAM access. However, we found that the resulting number of samples was extremely low. Even very memory-intensive workloads access DRAM only a few times for every thousand instructions. That, combined with a low IBS sampling frequency, gave us the sampling rate of less than one hundred thousandth of a percent, and made it very difficult to generate a sufficient number of samples. Furthermore, filtering samples that did not access DRAM caused us to miss the accesses generated by the hardware prefetcher. These accesses are not part of any instruction so they will not be tagged by IBS. For prefetch-intensive applications, we obtain a very small number of samples and a very distorted read-write ratio.

To address this problem, we used two solutions. First, is the adaptive sampling rate. When the program begins to run, we sample it at a relatively high rate of 1/65,000 cycles. If after this measurement phase we take fewer than ten actions in the algorithm (an action is any change in page placement) we switch to a much lower rate of 1/260,000 cycles. Otherwise we continue sampling at the high rate.

The second solution was, when filtering IBS samples, to retain not just the data samples that accessed the DRAM, but those that hit in the first-level cache as well. First-level cache loads include accesses to prefetched data, so we avoid prefetcher-related inaccuracy. On the one hand, considering cache accesses can introduce "noise" in the data, because we could be sampling pages that never access DRAM. On the other hand, *Carrefour* is only activated for memory-intensive applications, and for them there is a higher correlation between the accesses that hit in the cache and those that access DRAM.

With these two solutions combined, we were able to successfully identify the pages that are worth replicating, while this was nearly impossible prior to introducing these solutions. For example, for *Streamcluster* we used to be able to detect only a few percent of the pages that are worth replicating, but with these solutions in place, we were able to identify 100% of them[5].

However, even though performance became much better (we were able to speed up *Streamcluster* by 26% relative to the default kernel), we were still far from the "ideal" manual replication, which sped it up by more than 2.5×. To approach ideal performance, we had to mitigate the overheads of replication, which we describe next.

3.3.2 Replication

Replication has overhead from the following three sources. First, there is the initial set-up cost and slightly more expensive page faults. Modern hardware walks page tables automatically, so a separate copy of a page table must be created for each node. Page faults become slightly more costly, because a new page table entry must be installed on every node. To avoid these costs when we are not likely to benefit from replication, we avoid replication unless the applications has at least a few hundred pages marked for replication[6].

The second source of overhead comes from additional hard page faults if we exceed the physical RAM capacity by replicating pages. As explained earlier, we avoided this overhead by conservatively setting the free memory threshold when enabling replication.

The final and most significant source of overhead stems from the need to synchronize the contents of replicated pages when they are written. This involves a physical page copy and is very costly. Before explaining how we avoid this overhead we provide a brief overview of our implementation of replication.

In Linux, a process address space is represented by a `mm_struct`, which keeps track of valid address space segments and holds a pointer to the page table, which is stored as a hierarchical array. Since modern hardware walks page tables automatically, we cannot modify the structure of the page table to point to several physical locations (one for each node) for a given virtual page. Instead, we must maintain a separate copy of the page table for each node and synchronize the page tables when they are modified, even for virtual pages that are not replicated. Linux dictates that the page table entry (PTE) be locked when it is being modified. We do not make any changes to this locking protocol. The only difference is that we designate one copy of the page table as the *master copy*, and only lock the PTE in the master copy while installing the corresponding PTEs into all other replicas.

When a page is replicated, we create a physical copy on every memory node that runs threads from the corresponding application. We install a different virtual-to-physical translation in each node's page table. We write-protect the replicated page, so when any node writes that page we receive a page protection fault. To handle this fault, we read-protect the page on all nodes except the faulting one, and enable writing on the faulting node. If another node accesses that page, we must copy the new version of the page to that node, enable the page for reading and protect it from writing.

We refer to all the actions needed to keep the pages synchronized as *page collapses*. Collapses are extremely costly, and would occur if we replicate a page that is write-shared. Even with very infrequent writes (e.g., one in 1000 accesses), the collapse overhead could be prohibitively high. With limited capabilities of IBS, we are unable to detect read/write ratio on individual pages with sufficient accuracy. That is why we use the application-wide MRR and disable replication for the entire application if the MRR is low. Furthermore, we monitor collapse statistics of individual pages and disable replication for any page that generated more than five collapses.

With these optimizations, as well as those described in Section 3.3.1, we were able to avoid replication costs for the applications we tested and approached within 10% the performance of manual replication for *Streamcluster*.

4. Evaluation

In this section, we study the performance of *Carrefour* on a set of benchmarks. The main questions that we address are the following:

1. *How does Carrefour impact the performance of applications, including those that cannot benefit from its heuristics?*
2. *How does Carrefour compare against existing heuristics for modern NUMA hardware?*
3. *How well does Carrefour leverage the different memory placement mechanisms?*
4. *What is the overhead of Carrefour?*

To assess the performance of *Carrefour*, we compare it against three other configurations: *Linux* – a standard Linux kernel with the default first-touch memory allocation policy, *Manual interleaving* – a standard Linux kernel with the interleaving policy manually enabled for the application, and *AutoNUMA* – a recent Linux patchset [2] considered as the best thread and memory management algorithm available for Linux.

The rest of the section is organized as follows: we first describe our experimental testbed. Next, we study single-application scenarios, followed by workloads with multiple co-scheduled applications. We then detail the overhead of *Carrefour* and conclude with a discussion on additional hardware support that would improve *Carrefour*'s operation.

4.1 Testbed

We used two different machines for the experiments:

Machine A has four 2.3GHz AMD Opteron 8385 processors with 4 cores in each (16 cores in total) and 64GB of RAM. It features 4 nodes (i.e., 4 cores and 16GB of RAM per node) interconnected with HyperTransport 1.0 links.

Machine B has four 2.6GHz AMD Opteron 8435 processors with 6 cores in each (24 cores in total) and 64GB of RAM. It features 4 nodes (i.e., 6 cores and 16GB of RAM per node) interconnected with HyperTransport 3.0 links.

All experiments were performed on both machines. We present the main performance results for both machines. However, due to space constraints, we only show the detailed profiling measurements for machine A (the results obtained on machine B are qualitatively similar).

We used Linux kernel v3.6 for all experiments. For the AutoNUMA configuration, we used AutoNUMA v27 and disabled PMD scan because we it decreases performance on all applications we measured[7].

We used the following set of applications: the PARSEC benchmark suite v2.1 [26], the FaceRec facial recognition engine

[5] *Streamcluster* holds shared data in a single large array, so it is trivial to detect which data is worth replicating and implement a manual solution to use as the performance upper-bound.

[6] We use the threshold of at least 500 pages. Performance is not highly sensitive to this parameter.

[7] We also tested AutoNUMA v28. The performance results are very similar. However, we observed a significantly higher standard deviation (up to 18% on machine A and 23% on machine B) which makes profiling very difficult.

v5.0 [10], the Metis MapReduce benchmark suite [22] and the NAS parallel benchmark suite v3.3 [24]. PARSEC applications run with the native workload. From the available workloads in NAS we chose those with the running time of at least ten seconds. We excluded applications whose CPU utilization was below 33%, because they were not affected by memory management policies. We also excluded applications using shared memory across processes (as opposed to threads) or memory-mapped files, because our replication mechanism does not yet support this behaviour. For *FaceRec*, we used two kinds of workloads: a short-running one and a long running one (named *FaceRecLong* in the remainder of the paper). The reason why we present two different workloads is to show that *Carrefour* is able to successfully handle very short workloads (less than 4s on machine B when running with *Carrefour*). Each experiment was run ten times. Overall, we observed a standard deviation between 1% and 2% for the *Linux*, *Manual interleaving* and *Carrefour* configurations. *AutoNUMA* has a more significant standard deviation (up to 9% on machine A and 13% on machine B).

4.2 Single-application workloads

Performance comparison. Figures 5 and 6 show the performance improvement relative to default Linux obtained under all configurations for machine A and machine B. Performance improvement is computed as:

$$\frac{DefaultLinux_{time} - System_{time}}{System_{time}} * 100\%,$$

where $System$ can be either *Carrefour*, Manual interleaving or AutoNUMA.

We can make two main observations. First, *Carrefour* almost systematically outperforms default Linux, AutoNUMA, and Manual interleaving, sometimes quite substantially. For instance, when running *Streamcluster* or *FaceRecLong*, we observe that *Carrefour* is up to 58% faster than Manual interleaving, up to 165% faster than AutoNUMA, and up to 263% faster than default Linux on machine B. Second, we observe that, unlike other techniques, *Carrefour* never performs significantly worse than default Linux: the maximum performance degradation over Linux is below 4%. In contrast, AutoNUMA and Manual interleaving cause performance degradations of up to 25% and 38% respectively. Besides, we notice that Manual Interleaving has a very irregular impact on performance. While it does fairly well for PARSEC, NAS applications suffer significant performance degradation (up to 38%) when run with manual interleaving.

IS is an exception among the NAS benchmarks: Manual interleaving improves its performance, while *Carrefour* does no better than default Linux. That is because IS suffers from very short imbalance bursts that we are not able to correct due to limited sampling accuracy achievable with low overhead using existing hardware counters. Section 4.6 discusses hardware counter support that would help us address this problem.

In order to understand the reasons for the performance impact of the different policies, we study in detail a set of applications whose performance is improved the most by *Carrefour*. To that end, we present several metrics: the load imbalance on memory controllers (Figure 7(a)), the load imbalance on interconnect links (Figure 7(b)), the average memory latency (Figure 8(a)) and the local access ratio (Figure 8(b)).

We draw the following observations. First, *Carrefour* much better balances the load on both memory controllers and interconnect links than Linux and AutoNUMA. Not surprisingly, Manual interleaving is also very good at balancing the load. Nevertheless, we observe in Figure 8(a) that *Carrefour* induces lower average memory latencies than Manual interleaving, which explains its better performance. To understand why *Carrefour* reduces memory latencies we refer to Figure 8(b), which shows that *Carrefour* not only balances the load on memory controllers and interconnect links, but also often induces a much higher ratio of local memory accesses than other techniques. This is a consequence of *Carrefour*'s judiciously applying the right techniques (interleaving, replication or co-location) in places where they are beneficial. Interleaving mostly balances the load; replication and co-location in addition to balancing the load improve the local access ratio. Better locality improves latencies in two ways: it avoids remote wire delays and, most importantly, decreases congestion on the interconnect links.

We also study MG as a representative example of the NAS applications, for which *Carrefour* does not bring significant improvements over default Linux (but still performs better than AutoNUMA and Manual interleaving in most cases). MG has a low imbalance and a very good local access ratio to begin with. That is why Manual interleaving has a very bad impact on such workloads, significantly decreasing the local access ratio and as a result stressing the interconnect.

Looking inside *Carrefour*. To better understand the behavior of *Carrefour*, we show in Table 3 the number of replicated pages, the number of interleaved pages, and the number of co-located pages for the chosen benchmarks. These numbers provide a better insight into how *Carrefour* manages the memory. We observe that *all* three memory placement mechanisms are in use, and that most applications rely on two or three techniques. As discussed previously, MG does not suffer from traffic congestion, so *Carrefour* does not enable any technique for this application.

A legitimate question we can ask is whether *Carrefour* always selects the best technique. In Table 4, we report the performance improvement over Linux obtained when running a full-fledged *Carrefour* and when running a reduced version of *Carrefour* enabling only one technique at a time. We observe that *Carrefour* systematically selects the best technique. It is also interesting to remark how different techniques work together and how the numbers provided here echo those in Table 3. We notice that, for all the studied applications except MG and SP, the combination of several techniques employed by *Carrefour* outperforms any single technique, even when a given technique has a dominant impact (e.g., for Streamcluster). The slight performance degradation for MG corresponds to the monitoring overhead of *Carrefour*.

4.3 Multi-application workloads

In this section, we study how *Carrefour* behaves in the context of workloads with multiple applications that are co-scheduled on the same machine. The goal is to assess that *Carrefour* is able to work on complex access patterns and to make the distinction between the diverse requirements of different applications. We consider several scenarios based on some of the applications previously studied in Section 4.2:

(i) *MG + Streamcluster*, (ii) *PCA + Streamcluster*, (iii) *FaceRecLong + Streamcluster*. We chose these scenarios because they exhibit interesting patterns, which require combining several memory placement techniques in order to achieve good performance.

Each application is run with half as many threads as the number of cores (i.e., 8 threads on machine A, 12 on machine B). With two applications, the workload occupies all the available cores. The threads of each application are clustered on the same node, so each application uses all the cores on two of the four nodes on a machine.

Figure 9 shows, for each workload, the performance improvement with respect to Linux for AutoNUMA, Manual interleaving and *Carrefour* on machine A and machine B. We observe that *Carrefour* always outperforms AutoNUMA and Manual interleaving, by up to 62% and 36% respectively. Besides, *Carrefour* also out-

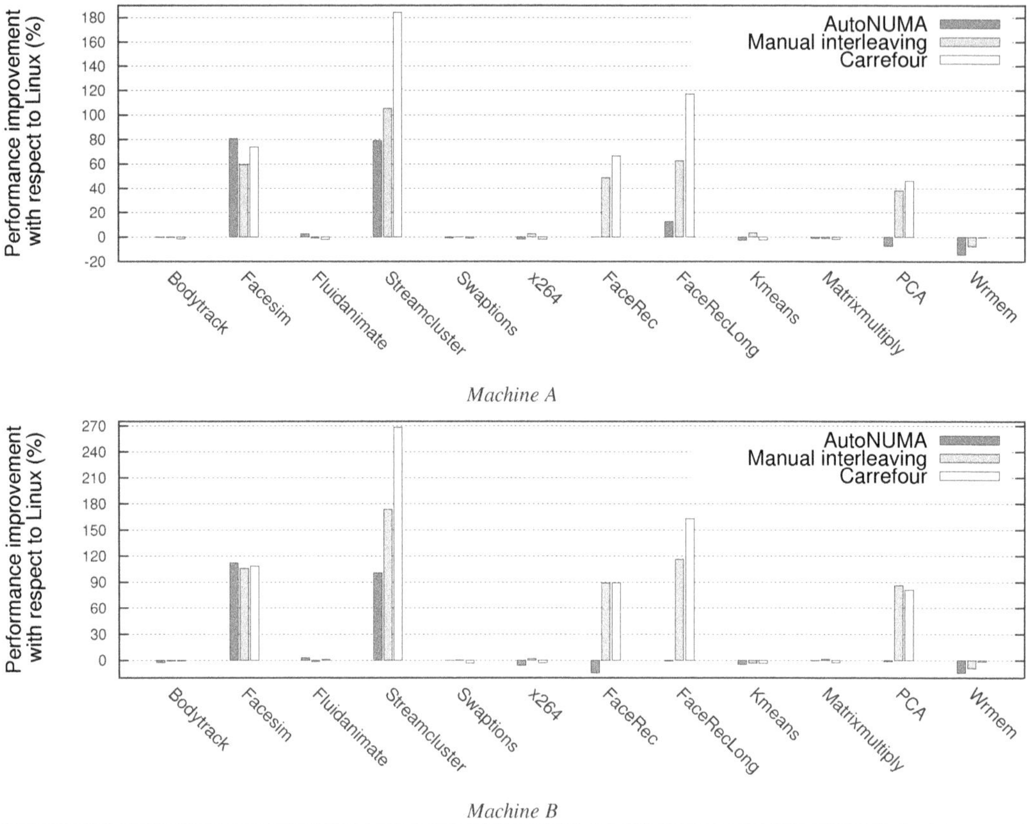

Figure 5. PARSEC/Metis: AutoNUMA, Manual interleaving and *Carrefour* vs.Default Linux.

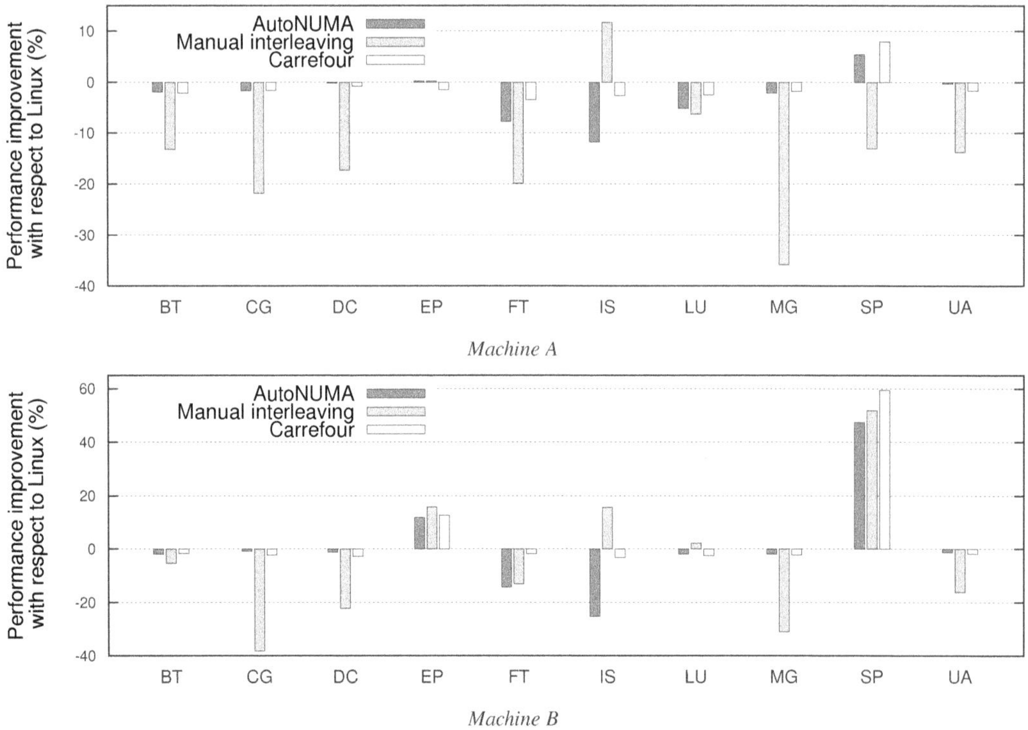

Figure 6. NAS: AutoNUMA, Manual interleaving and *Carrefour* vs. Default Linux.

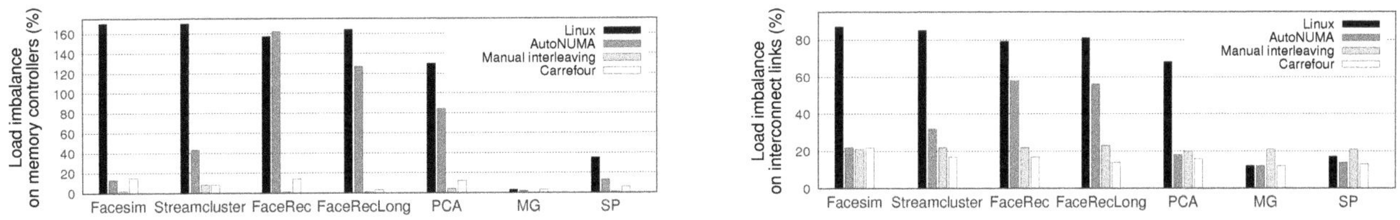

(a) memory controllers

(b) interconnect links

Figure 7. Load imbalance for selected single-application benchmarks (machine A).

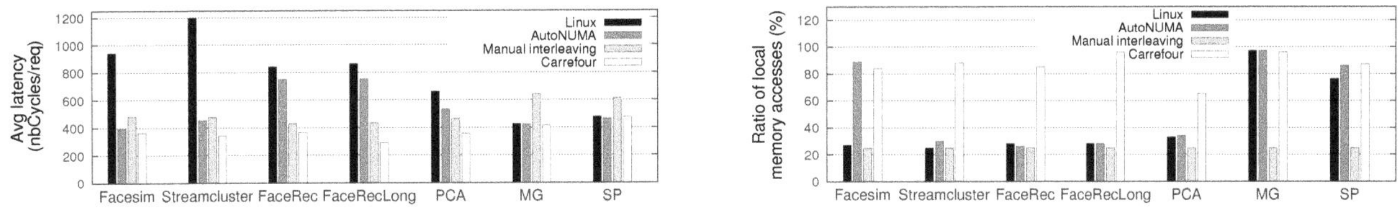

(a) Average memory latency

(b) Local memory access ratio

Figure 8. DRAM latency and locality for selected single-application benchmarks (machine A).

	Nb replicated pages	Nb interleaved pages	Nb migrated pages
Facesim	0	431	10.1k
Streamcluster	25.4k	14.5	858
FaceRec	4k	3	1.3k
FaceRecLong	4.1k	5	1.4k
PCA	31k	33	41.3k
MG	0	0	1
SP	0	305	1.7k

Table 3. Number of memory pages that are replicated, interleaved and co-located on single-application workloads (machine A).

	Carrefour	Replication	Interleaving	Co-location
Facesim	74%	-4%	0%	65%
Streamcluster	184%	176%	94%	51%
FaceRec	66%	61%	32%	1%
FaceRecLong	117%	113%	51%	1%
PCA	46%	45%	29%	24%
MG	-2%	-2%	-2%	-2%
SP	8%	-1%	-7%	8%

Table 4. Performance improvement over Linux when running *Carrefour* and the three different techniques individually on single-application workloads (machine A).

performs default Linux, while Manual interleaving hurts MG with a -25% slowdown. Overall, the results obtained with Manual interleaving are closer to the ones of *Carrefour* compared to the other setups.

The reason why Manual interleaving performs relatively well in these scenarios is because, with each application using two domains, there is a lot less cross-domain traffic than in the single-application case. Hence there are fewer "problems" that need to be fixed and there is a smaller discrepancy between the performance of different memory management algorithms.

To explain the results, we show the same detailed metrics as in Section 4.2: load imbalance on memory controllers, load imbalance on interconnect links, average DRAM latency and ratio of local DRAM accesses in Figures 10, 11, 12 and 13 respectively. The metrics are aggregated for the two applications of each workload. As was the case with the single-application workloads, we see that *Carrefour* systematically improves the latency of the studied workloads for two reasons: a more balanced load on memory controllers and interconnect links as well as an improved locality for DRAM accesses. Note that, for each workload, the depicted latencies are averaged over the two applications. This explains the small latency variations between Linux, AutoNUMA and Manual Interleaving in the case of MG + Streamcluster.

Finally, we show in Table 5 the performance improvement for each application when the effects of only one of the techniques are enabled. We observe that the multi-applications workloads perform as well or better with an arsenal of techniques used in *Carrefour* rather than with any single technique alone (especially for PCA + Streamcluster).

4.4 Overhead

Carrefour incurs CPU and memory overhead. The first source of CPU overhead is the periodic IBS profiling. To measure CPU overhead, we compared performance of *Carrefour* with Linux on those applications where *Carrefour* does not yield any performance benefits. We observed the overhead between 0.2% and 3.2%. Adaptive sampling rate in *Carrefour* is crucial to keeping this overhead low. A second and potentially significant source of CPU overhead is replication, if we perform a lot of collapses. A single collapse costs a few hundred microseconds when it occurs in isolation. Parallel

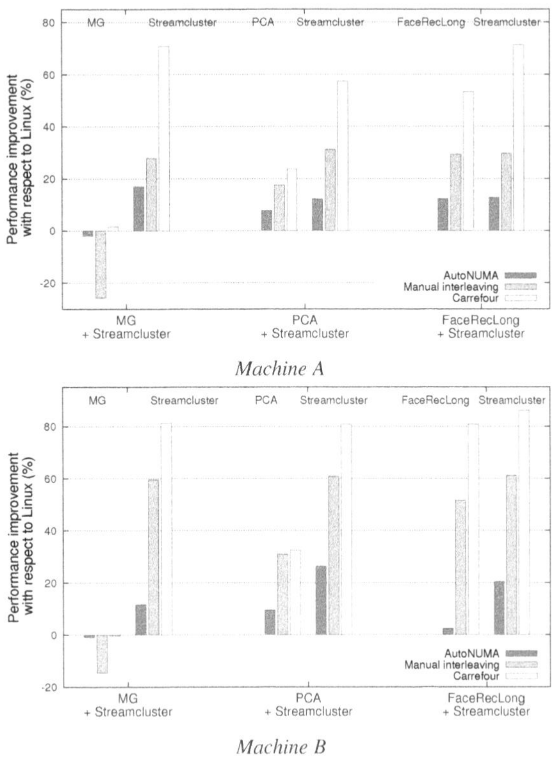

Figure 9. Multi-application workloads: AutoNUMA, Manual interleaving and *Carrefour* vs. Default Linux.

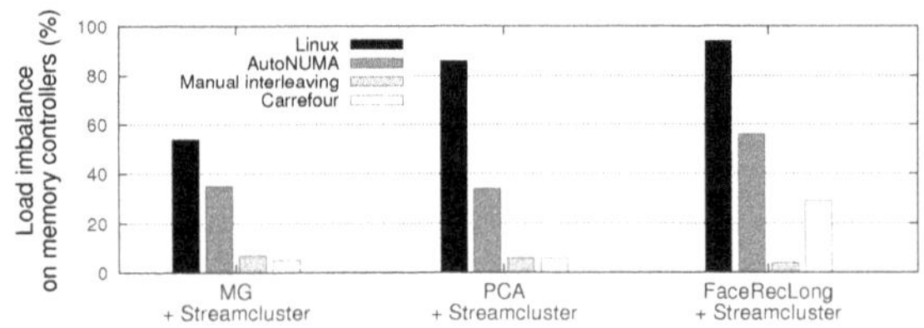

Figure 10. Multi-application workloads: load imbalance on memory controllers (machine A).

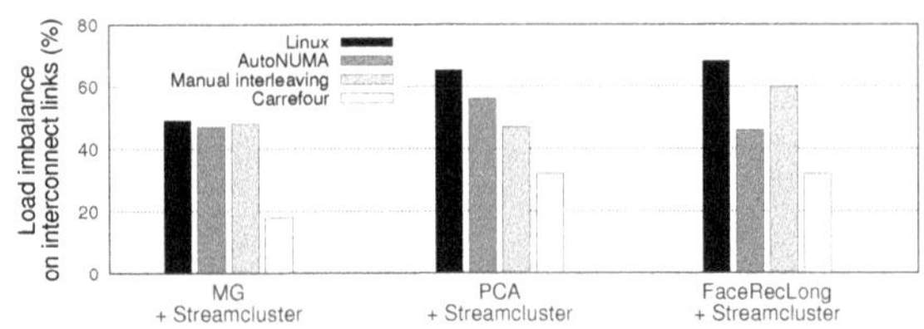

Figure 11. Multi-application workloads: load imbalance on interconnect links (machine A).

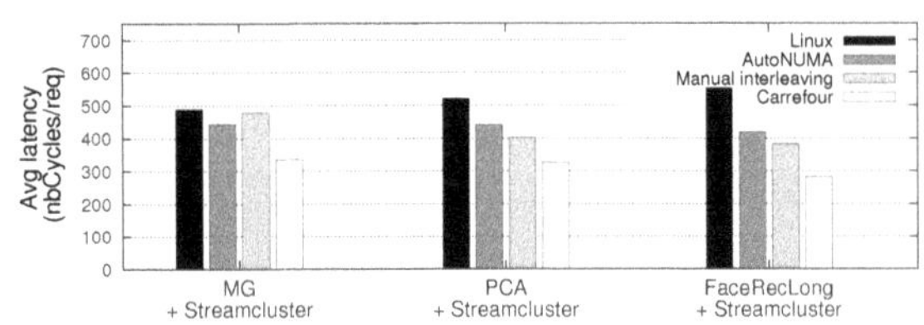

Figure 12. Multi-application workloads: average memory latency (machine A).

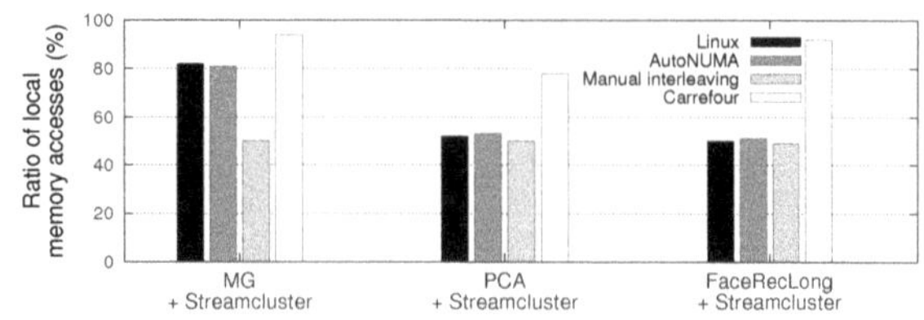

Figure 13. Multi-application workloads: local memory access ratio (machine A).

	Carrefour	Replication	Interleaving	Co-location
MG + Streamcluster	2% / 71%	2% / 73%	-5% / 17%	-1% / 6%
PCA + Streamcluster	24% / 57%	18% / 57%	8% / 5%	14% / 1%
FaceRecLong + Streamcluster	53% / 71%	53% / 71%	12% / 9%	12% / 4%

Table 5. Multi-application workloads: performance improvement over Linux when running *Carrefour* and the three different techniques individually (machine A).

collapses can take a few milliseconds because of lock contention. That is why it is crucial to avoid collapses and other synchronization events by disabling replication for write-intensive workloads, as is done in *Carrefour*.

The first source of memory overhead is the allocation of data structures to keep track of profiling data. This overhead is negligible: e.g., 5MB on Machine A with 64GB of RAM. *Carrefour*'s data structures are pre-allocated on startup to avoid memory allocation during the runtime. We limit the number of profiled pages to 30,000 to avoid the cost of managing dynamically sized structures. The second source of memory overhead is memory replication. When enabled, replication introduces a memory footprint overhead of 400MB (353%), 60MB (210%), 60MB (126%) and 614MB (5%) for Streamcluster, FaceRec, FacerecLong and PCA respectively.

4.5 Impact on energy consumption

It was observed that remote memory accesses require significantly more energy than local ones [11]. Since *Carrefour* may both decrease and increase the number of remote memory accesses, we were interested in evaluating its impact on energy consumption[8]. We show the results for selected applications from single-application workloads on Machine A. We report the increase in energy consumption as well as the increase in completion time of all configurations compared to default Linux in Figure 14. Completion time increase is computed here as:

$$\frac{System_{time} - DefaultLinux_{time}}{DefaultLinux_{time}} * 100\%.$$

We observe that there is a strong relationship between the completion time and the energy consumption: if the completion time is decreased, the energy consumption is also decreased proportionally. As a result, *Carrefour* saves up to 58% of energy. When no traffic management is needed, *Carrefour* on its own has a low impact on energy consumption (e.g., 2% on MG).

More generally, we found that the increase of remote memory accesses has little or no impact on the global energy consumption of the machine. For example, Manual interleaving drops the local access ratio of MG from 97% to 25% and thus proportion-

[8] We used IPMI which gives access to the current global power consumption on our servers.

ally increases the number of remote accesses. However, the energy consumption increase is slightly lower that the completion time increase, which indicates that the extra energy overhead of remote memory accesses have no strong impact on overall energy consumption.

4.6 Discussion: hardware support

We have shown that a traffic management system like *Carrefour* can bring significant performance benefits. However, the challenge in building *Carrefour* was the need to navigate around the limitations of the performance monitoring units of our hardware as well as the costs of replicating pages. In this section, we draw some insights on the features that could be integrated into future machines in order to further mitigate the overhead and improve accuracy, efficiency and performance of traffic management algorithms.

First, *Carrefour* would benefit from hardware profiling mechanisms that sample memory accesses with high precision and low overhead. For instance, it would be useful to have a profiling mechanism that accumulates and aggregates page access statistics in an internal buffer before triggering an interrupt. In this regard, the AMD Lightweight Profiling [1] facility seems a promising evolution of profiling hardware[9], but we believe the hardware should go even further, and not only accumulate the samples but be configured to aggregate them according to user needs, to reduce the number of interrupts even further.

Second, *Carrefour* would benefit from dedicated hardware support for memory replication. We believe that there should be interfaces allowing the operating system to indicate to the processor which pages to replicate. The processor would then be in charge of replicating the pages on the nodes accessing it and maintaining consistency between the various replicas (in the same way as it maintains consistency for cache lines). Given that maintaining consistency between frequently written pages is costly, we believe that such processors should also be able to trigger an interrupt when a page is written too frequently. The OS would then decide to keep the page replicated or to revert the replication decision.

This hardware support can be made a lot more scalable than cache coherency protocols, because it is not automatic, but controlled by the OS, which, armed with better hardware profiling, will only invoke it for pages that perform very little write sharing. So the actual synchronization protocol would be triggered infrequently.

5. Related Work

In this section, we explain how *Carrefour* relates to different works on multicore systems. First, we review systems aimed at maximizing data locality. Second, we contrast *Carrefour* with previous contention-aware systems. Third, we consider application-level techniques to mitigate contention on data-sharing applications. Finally, we discuss traffic characterization observations for modern NUMA systems.

Locality-driven optimizations NUMA-aware thread and memory management policies were proposed for earlier research systems [6, 9, 18, 31] as well as in commercial OS. Their main difference from our work is that their goal was to optimize *locality*. However, on modern systems, the main performance problems are due to traffic congestion. Our algorithm is the first one that meets the goal of mitigating traffic congestion. Among the above-mentioned works, the one most related to Carrefour is the system by Verghese et al. [31] for early cache-coherent NUMA machines, which leverages page replication and migration mechanisms. Their system relies on assumptions about hardware support that do not hold on currently available machines (e.g., precise per-page access statistics). Thus, *Carrefour*'s logic is more involved, as it is more difficult to amortize the costs of the monitoring and memory page placement mechanisms. The authors noticed that locality-driven optimizations could, as a side effect, reduce the overall contention in the system. However, their system does not systematically address contention issues. For instance, shared written pages are not taken into account, whereas *Carrefour* uses memory interleaving techniques when there is contention on such pages. Moreover, the load on memory controllers is ignored when making page replication/migration decisions.

Similarly to earlier NUMA-aware policies, Solaris and Linux focus primarily on co-location of threads and data, but to the disadvantage of data-sharing workloads, replication is not supported. Linux provides the option to interleave parts of the address space across all memory nodes, but the decision when to invoke the interleaving is left to the programmer or the administrator. Solaris supports the notion of a home load group, such that the thread's memory is always allocated in its home group and the thread is preferentially scheduled in its home group. This, again, favours locality, but does not necessarily address traffic congestion.

The recent AutoNUMA patches for Linux also implement locality-driven optimizations, along two main heuristics. First, threads migrate toward nodes holding the majority of the pages accessed by these threads. Memory residence is determined by page fault statistics. Second, pages are periodically unmapped from a process address space and, upon the next page fault, migrated to the requesting node. As shown in the evaluation section, this approach yields irregular results. We attribute this limitation to the following sources of overhead: local thread/page migration decisions that do not take data sharing patterns nor access frequencies into account (thus leading to page bouncing or useless migrations) nor MC/interconnect load (thus leading to memory load imbalance/congestion), continuous overhead due to the scanning/unmapping of page-table entries and the corresponding soft page faults. In contrast, *Carrefour* makes global data placement decisions based on precise traffic patterns and adjusts the monitoring overhead based on the observed contention level.

Locality-driven optimizations for data-sharing applications were addressed in a study that dynamically identified data-sharing thread groups and co-located them on the same node [30]. However, that solution was for a system with a centralized (UMA) memory architecture. Thus, it only studied the benefits of thread placement for improved cache locality and did not address the placement of memory pages on multiple memory nodes.

Zhou and Demsky [32] investigated how to distribute memory pages to caches on a many-core Tilera processor, in order to implement an efficient garbage collector. The authors tried various policies but found that maximizing locality was the best approach for their system. This is in contrast to the systems *Carrefour* is targeting, where reducing congestion is more important than just improving locality. Also, the authors used a very different method for monitoring page access patterns that relies on software-serviced TLB misses, which is not possible on x86.

Contention management techniques Several recent studies addressed contention issues in the memory hierarchy. Some of these works were designed for UMA systems [16, 21, 33] and are inefficient on NUMA systems because they fail to address or even accentuate issues such as remote access latencies and contention on memory controllers and on the interconnect links [5]. Other works have been specifically designed for NUMA systems but only partially address contention issues. The N-Mass thread placement algorithm [19] attempts to achieve good DRAM locality while avoid-

[9] Unfortunately, Lightweight Profiling is only available on recent AMD processors (AMD Bulldozer) and we were not able to evaluate it in this work. We plan to study it in the future.

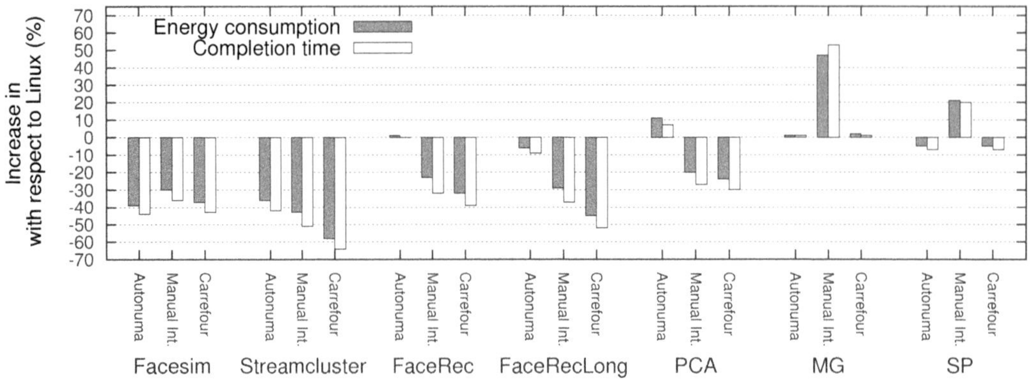

Figure 14. Increase in completion time and energy consumption for selected single-application benchmarks with respect to Linux (machine A). Lower is better.

ing cache contention. However, it does not address contention issues at the level of memory controllers and interconnect links. Two studies [3, 20] have shown the importance of taking memory controller congestion into account for data placement decisions, but they did not provide a complete solution to address multilevel resource contention. The most comprehensive work to date on NUMA-aware contention management is the DINO scheduler [5], which spreads memory intensive threads across memory domains and accordingly migrates the corresponding memory pages. However, DINO does not address workloads with data sharing between threads or processes, which require identifying per-page memory access patterns and making the appropriate data placement decisions.

No-sharing application design principle When introducing a new resource-management policy in the OS, it is worth asking whether a similar or better effect could be achieved by restructuring the application. In our context, it is important to consider the so-called *no-sharing* principle of application design. The key idea behind no-sharing is that the data must be partitioned or replicated between memory nodes, and a thread needing to access data in a different domain than its own either migrates to the target domain or asks the thread running in that domain to perform the work on its behalf, instead of fetching the data over the memory channels [4, 8, 14, 23, 25, 28, 29]. While the no-sharing architecture was primarily motivated by the need to avoid locking, it could similarly help reduce the amount of traffic sent across the interconnect, and thus alleviate the traffic congestion problem.

Unfortunately, no-sharing architectures are not a universal remedy. First of all, they trade-off data accesses for messages or thread migration; the trade-off is only worth making if the size of the data used in a single operation is much larger than the size of the message or the state of the migrated thread [8]. Second, adopting a no-sharing architecture often requires very significant changes to the application (and to the OS, if the application is OS-intensive). A good illustration of the potential challenges can be gleaned from two studies that converted a database system to the no-sharing design. The first study took the path of least resistance and simply replicated and/or partitioned the database among domains, adding a message-routing layer on top [28]. While this worked well for small read-mostly workloads, for large workloads replication had very significant memory overhead (unacceptable because of increased paging), and partitioning required *a priori* knowledge of query-to-data mapping, which is not a reasonable assumption in a general case. A solution that overcame these limitations, DORA [25], required a very significant restructuring of the database system, which could easily amount to millions of dollars in development costs for a commercial database.

Our goal was to address scenarios where adopting a no-sharing architecture is not feasible either for technical reasons or for practical considerations. Providing an OS-level, rather than an application-level, solution allows us to address many applications at once. Understanding the limitations of the OS-level solution and determining what optimizations can be done only at the level of an application is an open research question. Although we did provide some comparison of *Carrefour* with application-level techniques, a deeper analysis of this problem would be worthwhile.

Traffic characterization on modern systems A recent study characterized the performance of emerging "scale-out" workloads on modern hardware [13]. The authors observed that there is little inter-thread data sharing, and the utilization of the off-chip memory bandwidth is low. As a result, they argue that memory bandwidth on existing processors is unnecessarily high. Our findings do not agree with this observation. Although it is also true that the workloads we consider perform very little fine-grained data sharing, they still stress the cross-chip interconnect, because they access a large working set, which is spread across the entire NUMA memory space. The authors of the scale-out study reported a very low bandwidth utilization ($<10\%$), even for database workloads. In contrast, our measurements show a utilization as low as 45% in some cases. These differences could be because the authors of [13] used a system with only two chips and 12 cores in their experiments. On larger systems, more threads are making requests to remote memories and so there is greater pressure on bandwidth. Further, we found that low bandwidth utilization is not necessarily a healthy symptom. In our experiments, performance dropped steeply even as bandwidth utilization went from 10% to 30%. The interconnect became the bottleneck even at a fraction of the total available bandwidth! The reason is that memory requests are not spread evenly in time; they are bursty. Burstiness causes requests to clash on the link even if the overall bandwidth is not exceeded. In summary, we conclude that contrary to the suggestion made in [13], it is too early to reduce the bandwidth of cross-chip interconnects on large multicore systems, especially if they are used for running large data-centric workloads.

6. Conclusion

We presented *Carrefour*, a new memory management algorithm for NUMA systems that manages traffic on memory controllers and interconnects. Earlier NUMA-aware memory management policies aimed to mitigate the cost of remote wire delays, which is no longer the main bottleneck on modern systems. *Carrefour*'s design was motivated by the evolution of modern NUMA hardware, where traffic congestion plays a much larger role in performance than wire delays.

System design principles embodied in *Carrefour* are important not only for today's systems, but also for future hardware. The amount of memory bandwidth per core is projected to decrease in the future [8], so managing traffic congestion will be as crucial as ever.

7. Code availability

The source code for *Carrefour* will be made available at https://github.com/Carrefour.

8. Acknowledgments

We thank Oracle Labs and the British Columbia Innovation Council for funding this work.

References

[1] AMD64 Technology Lightweight Profiling Specification, Aug. 2010. `http://support.amd.com/us/Processor_TechDocs/43724.pdf`.

[2] AutoNUMA: the other approach to NUMA scheduling. LWN.net, Mar. 2012. `http://lwn.net/Articles/488709/`.

[3] M. Awasthi, D. Nellans, K. Sudan, R. Balasubramonian, and A. Davis. Handling the problems and opportunities posed by multiple on-chip memory controllers. In *PACT*, 2010.

[4] A. Baumann, P. Barham, P.-E. Dagand, T. Harris, R. Isaacs, S. Peter, T. Roscoe, A. Schüpbach, and A. Singhania. The Multikernel: A New OS Architecture for Scalable Multicore Systems. In *SOSP*, 2009.

[5] S. Blagodurov, S. Zhuravlev, M. Dashti, and A. Fedorova. A Case for NUMA-aware Contention Management on Multicore Systems. In *USENIX ATC*, 2011.

[6] W. Bolosky, R. Fitzgerald, and M. Scott. Simple but Effective Techniques for NUMA Memory Management. In *SOSP*, 1989.

[7] S. Boyd-Wickizer, H. Chen, R. Chen, Y. Mao, F. Kaashoek, R. Morris, A. Pesterev, L. Stein, M. Wu, Y. Dai, Y. Zhang, and Z. Zhang. Corey: an operating system for many cores. In *OSDI*, 2008.

[8] S. Boyd-Wickizer, M. F. Kaashoek, R. Morris, and N. Zeldovich. A software approach to unifying multicore caches. Technical Report MIT-CSAIL-TR-2011-032, 2011.

[9] T. Brecht. On the Importance of Parallel Application Placement in NUMA Multiprocessors. In *USENIX SEDMS*, 1993.

[10] CSU Face Identification Evaluation System. `http://www.cs.colostate.edu/evalfacerec/index10.php`.

[11] B. Dally. Power, programmability, and granularity: The challenges of exascale computing. `http://techtalks.tv/talks/54110`.

[12] P. Drongowski and B. Center. Instruction-based sampling: A new performance analysis technique for amd family 10h processors. 2007.

[13] M. Ferdman, A. Adileh, O. Kocberber, S. Volos, M. Alisafaee, D. Jevdjic, C. Kaynak, A. D. Popescu, A. Ailamaki, and B. Falsafi. Clearing the clouds: A study of emerging scale-out workloads on modern hardware. In *ASPLOS*, 2012.

[14] B. Gamsa, O. Krieger, and M. Stumm. Tornado: Maximizing Locality and Concurrency in a Shared Memory Multiprocessor Operating System. In *OSDI*, 1999.

[15] A. Kamali. Sharing aware scheduling on multicore systems. In *MSc Thesis, Simon Fraser Univ.*, 2010.

[16] R. Knauerhase, P. Brett, B. Hohlt, T. Li, and S. Hahn. Using OS Observations to Improve Performance in Multicore Systems. *IEEE Micro*, 28(3):pp. 54–66, 2008.

[17] R. Lachaize, B. Lepers, and V. Quéma. MemProf: A Memory Profiler for NUMA Multicore Systems. In *USENIX ATC*, 2012.

[18] R. P. LaRowe, Jr., C. S. Ellis, and M. A. Holliday. Evaluation of NUMA Memory Management Through Modeling and Measurements. *IEEE TPDS*, 3:686–701, 1991.

[19] Z. Majo and T. R. Gross. Memory management in numa multicore systems: Trapped between cache contention and interconnect overhead. In *ISMM*, 2011.

[20] Z. Majo and T. R. Gross. Memory System Performance in a NUMA Multicore Multiprocessor. In *SYSTOR*, 2011.

[21] A. Merkel, J. Stoess, and F. Bellosa. Resource-Conscious Scheduling for Energy Efficiency on Multicore Processors. In *EuroSys*, 2010.

[22] Metis MapReduce Library. `http://pdos.csail.mit.edu/metis/`.

[23] Z. Metreveli, N. Zeldovich, and F. Kaashoek. Cphash: a cache-partitioned hash table. In *PPoPP*, 2012.

[24] NAS Parallel Benchmarks. `http://www.nas.nasa.gov/publications/npb.html`.

[25] I. Pandis, R. Johnson, N. Hardavellas, and A. Ailamaki. Data-oriented transaction execution. *Proc. VLDB Endow.*, 3:928–939, September 2010. ISSN 2150-8097.

[26] PARSEC Benchmark Suite. `http://parsec.cs.princeton.edu/`.

[27] A. Pesterev, N. Zeldovich, and R. T. Morris. Locating cache performance bottlenecks using data profiling. In *EuroSys*, 2010.

[28] T.-I. Salomie, I. E. Subasu, J. Giceva, and G. Alonso. Database engines on multicores, why parallelize when you can distribute? In *EuroSys*, 2011.

[29] X. Song, H. Chen, R. Chen, Y. Wang, and B. Zang. A case for scaling applications to many-core with OS clustering. In *EuroSys*, 2011.

[30] D. Tam, R. Azimi, and M. Stumm. Thread Clustering: Sharing-Aware Scheduling on SMP-CMP-SMT Multiprocessors. In *EuroSys*, 2007.

[31] B. Verghese, S. Devine, A. Gupta, and M. Rosenblum. Operating system support for improving data locality on CC-NUMA compute servers. In *ASPLOS*, 1996.

[32] J. Zhou and B. Demsky. Memory management for many-core processors with software configurable locality policies. In *ISMM*, 2012.

[33] S. Zhuravlev, S. Blagodurov, and A. Fedorova. Addressing Contention on Multicore Processors via Scheduling. In *ASPLOS*, 2010.

OWL: Cooperative Thread Array Aware Scheduling Techniques for Improving GPGPU Performance

Adwait Jog† Onur Kayiran† Nachiappan Chidambaram Nachiappan† Asit K. Mishra§
Mahmut T. Kandemir† Onur Mutlu* Ravishankar Iyer§ Chita R. Das†

The Pennsylvania State University†
University Park, PA 16802
(adwait, onur, nachi, kandemir, das)@cse.psu.edu

Carnegie Mellon University*
Pittsburgh, PA 15213
onur@cmu.edu

Intel Labs §
Hillsboro, OR 97124
(asit.k.mishra, ravishankar.iyer)@intel.com

Abstract

Emerging GPGPU architectures, along with programming models like CUDA and OpenCL, offer a cost-effective platform for many applications by providing high thread level parallelism at lower energy budgets. Unfortunately, for many general-purpose applications, available hardware resources of a GPGPU are not efficiently utilized, leading to lost opportunity in improving performance. A major cause of this is the inefficiency of current warp scheduling policies in tolerating long memory latencies.

In this paper, we identify that the scheduling decisions made by such policies are agnostic to thread-block, or cooperative thread array (CTA), behavior, and as a result inefficient. We present a coordinated CTA-aware scheduling policy that utilizes four schemes to minimize the impact of long memory latencies. The first two schemes, CTA-aware two-level warp scheduling and locality aware warp scheduling, enhance per-core performance by effectively reducing cache contention and improving latency hiding capability. The third scheme, bank-level parallelism aware warp scheduling, improves overall GPGPU performance by enhancing DRAM bank-level parallelism. The fourth scheme employs opportunistic memory-side prefetching to further enhance performance by taking advantage of open DRAM rows. Evaluations on a 28-core GPGPU platform with highly memory-intensive applications indicate that our proposed mechanism can provide 33% average performance improvement compared to the commonly-employed round-robin warp scheduling policy.

Categories and Subject Descriptors C.1.4 [*Computer Systems Organization*]: Processor Architectures—Parallel Architectures; D.1.3 [*Software*]: Programming Techniques—Concurrent Programming

General Terms Design, Performance

Keywords GPGPUs; Scheduling; Prefetching; Latency Tolerance

1. Introduction

General Purpose Graphics Processing Units (GPGPUs) have recently emerged as a cost-effective computing platform for a wide range of applications due to their immense computing power compared to CPUs [1, 6, 7, 25, 28, 48]. GPGPUs are characterized by numerous programmable computational cores and thousands of simultaneously active fine-grained threads. To facilitate ease of programming on these systems, programming models like CUDA [46] and OpenCL [39] have been developed. GPGPU applications are typically divided into several kernels, where each kernel is capable of spawning many threads. The threads are usually grouped together into *thread blocks*, also known as *cooperative thread arrays (CTAs)*. When an application starts its execution on a GPGPU, the CTA scheduler initiates scheduling of CTAs onto the available GPGPU cores. All the threads within a CTA are executed on the same core typically in groups of 32 threads. This collection of threads is referred to as a warp and all the threads within a warp typically share the same instruction stream, which forms the basis for the term *single instruction multiple threads*, SIMT [7, 8, 37].

In spite of the high theoretically achievable thread-level parallelism (TLP) (for example, GPGPUs are capable of simultaneously executing more than 1024 threads per core [48]), GPGPU cores suffer from high periods of inactive times resulting in underutilization of hardware resources [24, 44]. Three critical reasons for this are: 1) on-chip memory and register files are limiting factors on parallelism, 2) high control flow divergence, and 3) inefficient scheduling mechanisms. First, GPGPUs offer a limited amount of programmer-managed memory (shared memory) and registers. If the per-CTA requirements for these resources are high, then the effective number of CTAs that can be scheduled simultaneously will be small, leading to lower core utilization [5, 28]. Second, when threads within a warp take different control flow paths, the number of threads that can continue execution in parallel reduces. Recent works that have tackled this problem include [14, 15, 44, 49]. Third, the inefficiency of the commonly-used round-robin (RR) scheduling policy [5, 15, 44] to hide long memory fetch latencies, primarily caused by limited off-chip DRAM bandwidth, contributes substantially to the under-utilization of GPGPU cores.

With the RR scheduling policy, both the CTAs assigned to a core and all the warps inside a CTA are given equal priority, and are executed in a round-robin fashion. Due to this scheduling policy, most of the warps arrive at long latency memory operations roughly at the same time [44]. As a result, the GPGPU core becomes *inactive* because there may be no warps that are *not* stalling due to a memory operation, which significantly reduces the capability of hiding long memory latencies. Such inactive periods are especially prominent in memory-intensive applications. We observe that out of 38 applications covering various benchmarks suites, 19 applications suffer from *very high* core inactive times (on average 62% of total cycles are spent with no warps executing). The primary

ASPLOS'13, March 16–20, 2013, Houston, Texas, USA.

cause of the high core inactivity is the large amount of on-chip and off-chip traffic caused by the burst of long-latency memory operations coming from all warps, leading to high round-trip fetch latencies. This in turn is mainly attributed to limited off-chip DRAM bandwidth available in GPGPUs. It is anticipated that this problem will be aggravated in emerging heterogeneous architectures, where the main memory is unified and shared by both CPU and GPGPU cores [3, 29–31]. This problem also becomes more severe with core scaling and the increase in the number of simultaneously executing threads [24], in a way that is similar to the memory bandwidth problem in multi-core systems [38, 42].

The goal of this paper is to tackle the under-utilization of cores for improving the overall GPGPU performance. In this context, we propose the *c(O)operative thread array a(W)are warp schedu(L)ing policy*, called OWL[1]. OWL is based on the concept of *focused* CTA-aware scheduling, which attempts to mitigate the various components that contribute to long memory fetch latencies by *focusing* on a selected subset of CTAs scheduled on a core (by *always* prioritizing them over others until they finish). The proposed OWL policy is a four-pronged concerted approach:

First, we propose a CTA-aware two-level warp scheduler that exploits the architecture and application interplay to intelligently schedule CTAs onto the cores. This scheme groups all the available CTAs (N CTAs) on a core into smaller groups (of n CTAs) and schedules all *groups* in a round-robin fashion. As a result, it performs better than the commonly-used baseline RR warp scheduler because 1) it allows a smaller group of warps/threads to access the L1 cache in a particular interval of time, thereby reducing cache contention, 2) improves latency hiding capability and reduces inactive periods as not all warps reach long latency operations around the same time. This technique improves the average L1 cache hit rate by 8% over RR for 19 highly memory intensive applications, providing a 14% improvement in IPC performance.

Second, we propose a locality aware warp scheduler to improve upon the CTA-aware two-level warp scheduler, by further reducing L1 cache contention. This is achieved by *always* prioritizing a group of CTAs (n CTAs) in a core over the rest of the CTAs (until they finish). Hence, unlike the base scheme, where each group of CTAs (consisting of n CTAs) is executed one after another and thus, does not utilize the caches effectively, this scheme always prioritizes one group of CTAs over the rest whenever a particular group of CTA is ready for execution. The major goal is to take advantage of the locality between nearby threads and warps (associated with the same CTA) [21]. With this scheme, average L1 cache hit rate is further improved by 10% over the CTA-aware two-level warp scheduler, leading to an 11% improvement in IPC performance.

Third, the first two schemes are aware of different CTAs but do not exploit any properties common among different CTAs. Across 38 GPGPU applications, we observe that there is significant DRAM page locality between consecutive CTAs. On average, the same DRAM page is accessed by consecutive CTAs 64% of the time. Hence, if two *consecutive* CTA groups are scheduled on two different cores and are *always* prioritized according to the locality aware warp scheduling, they would access a *small* set of DRAM banks more frequently. This increases the queuing time at the banks and reduces memory bank level parallelism (BLP) [41]. On the other hand, if non-consecutive CTA groups are scheduled and *always* prioritized on two different cores, as we propose, they would concurrently access a larger number of banks. This reduces the contention at the banks and improves BLP. This proposed scheme (called the bank-level parallelism aware warp scheduler), increases average BLP by 11% compared to the locality aware warp scheduler, providing a 6% improvement in IPC performance.

Fourth, a drawback of the previous scheme is that it reduces DRAM row locality. This is because rows opened by a CTA cannot be completely utilized by its consecutive CTAs since consecutive CTAs are not scheduled simultaneously any more. To recover the loss in DRAM row locality, we develop an opportunistic prefetching mechanism, in which some of the data from the opened row is brought to the nearest on-chip L2 cache partition. The mechanism is opportunistic because the degree of prefetching depends upon the number of pending demand requests at the memory controller.

We evaluate the performance of the OWL scheduling policy, consisting of the four components integrated together, on a 28-core GPGPU platform simulated via GPGPU-Sim [5] and a set of 19 highly memory intensive applications. Our results show that OWL improves GPGPU performance by 33% over the baseline RR warp scheduling policy. OWL also outperforms the recently-proposed two-level scheduling policy [44] by 19%.

2. Background and Experimental Methodology

This section provides a brief description of GPGPU architecture, typical scheduling strategies, main memory layouts of CTAs, application suite and evaluation metrics.

2.1 Background

Our Baseline GPGPU Architecture: A GPGPU consists of many simple cores (streaming multiprocessors), with each core typically having a SIMT width of 8 to 32 (NVIDIA's Fermi series has 16 streaming multiprocessors with a SIMT width of 32 [48] and AMD's ATI 5870 Evergreen architecture has 20 cores with a SIMT width of 16 [2]). Our target architecture (shown in Figure 1 (A)) consists of 28 shader cores each with a SIMT width of 8, and 8 memory controllers. This configuration is similar to the ones studied in recent works [4, 5]. Each core is associated with a private L1 data cache and read-only texture and constant caches along with a low latency shared memory (scratchpad memory). Every memory controller is associated with a slice of the shared L2 cache for faster access to the cached data. We assume write-back polices for both L1 and L2 caches and optimistic performance model for atomic instructions [5, 16]. The minimum L2 miss latency is assumed to be 120 compute core cycles [56]. The actual miss latency could be higher because of queuing at the memory controllers and variable DRAM latencies. Cores and memory controllers are connected via a two-dimensional mesh. We use a 2D mesh topology, as it

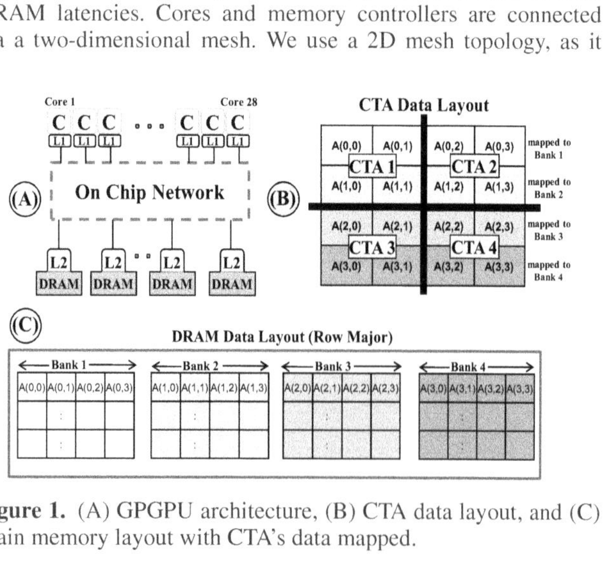

Figure 1. (A) GPGPU architecture, (B) CTA data layout, and (C) Main memory layout with CTA's data mapped.

[1] Owl is a bird known for exceptional *vision* and *focus* while it hunts for food. Our proposed scheduling policy also follows an owl's philosophy. It intelligently selects (*visualizes*) a subset of CTAs (out of many CTAs launched on a core) and *focuses* on them to achieve performance benefits.

is scalable, simple, and regular [4, 5, 43]. A detailed baseline platform configuration is described in Table 1, which is simulated on GPGPU-Sim 2.1.2b, a cycle-accurate GPGPU simulator [5].

Canonical GPGPU Application Design: A typical CUDA application consists of many kernels (or grids) as shown in Figure 2 (A). These kernels implement specific modules of an application. Each kernel is divided into groups of threads, called cooperative thread arrays (CTAs) (Figure 2 (B)). A CTA is an abstraction which encapsulates all synchronization and barrier primitives among a group of threads [28]. Having such an abstraction allows the underlying hardware to relax the execution order of the CTAs to maximize parallelism. The underlying architecture in turn, sub-divides each CTA into groups of threads (called warps) (Figure 2 (C) and (D)). This sub-division is transparent to the application programmer and is an architectural abstraction.

CTA, Warp, and Thread Scheduling: Execution on GPGPUs starts with the launch of a kernel. In this work, we assume sequential execution of kernels, which means only one kernel is executed at a time. After a kernel is launched, the CTA scheduler schedules available CTAs associated with the kernel in a round-robin and load balanced fashion on all the cores [5]. For example, CTA 1 is assigned to core 1, CTA 2 is assigned to core 2 and so on. After assigning at least one CTA to each core (provided that enough CTAs are available), if there are still unassigned CTAs, more CTAs can be assigned to the same core in a similar fashion. The maximum number of CTAs per core (N) is limited by core resources (number of threads, size of shared memory, register file size, etc. [5, 28]). Given a baseline architecture, N may vary across kernels depending on how much resources are needed by a CTA of a particular kernel. If a CTA of a particular kernel needs more resources, N will be smaller compared to that of another kernel whose CTAs need fewer resources. For example, if a CTA of kernel X needs 16KB of shared memory and the baseline architecture has 32KB of shared memory available, a maximum of 2 CTAs of kernel X can be executed simultaneously.

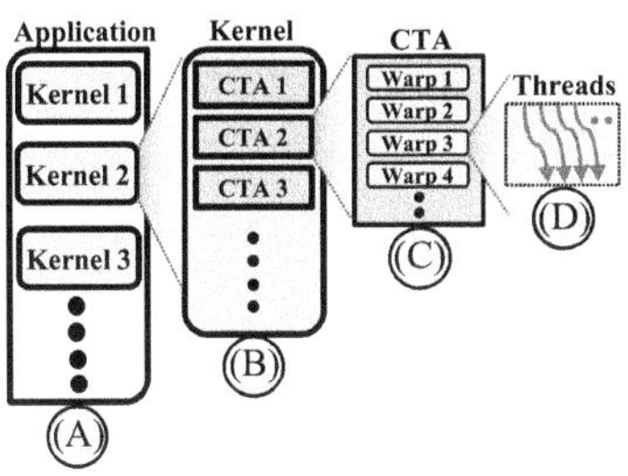

Figure 2. GPGPU application hierarchy.

The above CTA assignment policy is followed by per-core GPGPU warp scheduling. Warps associated with CTAs are scheduled in a round-robin (RR) fashion on the assigned cores [5, 44] and get *equal* priority. Every 4 cycles, a warp ready for execution is selected in a round-robin fashion and fed to the 8-way SIMT pipeline of a GPGPU core. At the memory stage of the core pipeline, if a warp gets blocked on a long latency memory operation, the entire warp (32 threads) is scheduled out of the pipeline and moved to the pending queue. At a later instant, when the data for the warp arrives, it proceeds to the write-back stage, and then fetches new instructions.

CTA Data Layout: Current GPU chips support ~10× higher memory bandwidth compared to CPU chips [25]. In order to take full advantage of the available DRAM bandwidth and to reduce the number of requests to DRAM, a kernel must arrange its data accesses so that each request to the DRAM is for a large number of consecutive DRAM locations. With the SIMT execution model, when all threads in a warp execute a memory operation, the hardware typically detects if the threads are accessing consecutive memory locations; if they are, the hardware coalesces all these accesses into a single consolidated access to DRAM that requests all consecutive locations at once. To understand how data blocks used by CTAs are placed in the DRAM main memory, consider Figure 1 (B). This figure shows that all locations in the DRAM main memory form a single, consecutive address space. The matrix elements that are used by CTAs are placed into the linearly addressed locations according to the row major convention as shown in Figure 1 (B). That is, the elements of row 0 of a matrix are first placed in order into consecutive locations (see Figure 1 (C)). The subsequent row is placed in another DRAM bank. Note that, this example is simplified for illustrative purposes only. The data layout may vary across applications (our evaluations take into account different data layouts of applications).

Table 1. Baseline configuration

Shader Core Config.	1300MHz, 5-Stage Pipeline, SIMT width = 8
Resources / Core	Max. 1024 Threads, 32KB Shared memory, 32684 Registers
Caches / Core	32KB 8-way L1 Data cache, 8KB 4-way Texture cache 8KB 4-way Constant cache, 64B line size
L2 Cache	16-way 512 KB/Memory channel, 64B line size
Scheduling	Round-robin warp scheduling, (among ready warps), Load balanced CTA scheduling
Features	Memory coalescing enabled, 32 MSHRs/core, Immediate post dominator based branch divergence handling
Interconnect	2D Mesh (6 × 6; 28 cores + 8 Memory controllers), 650MHz, 32B channel width
DRAM Model	FR-FCFS (Maximum 128 requests/MC), 8MCs, 4 DRAM banks/MC, 2KB row size
GDDR3 Timing	800MHz, t_{CL} = 10, t_{RP} = 10, t_{RC} = 35, t_{RAS} = 25 t_{RCD} = 12, t_{RRD} = 8, t_{CDLR} = 6, t_{WR} = 11

2.2 Workloads and Metrics

Application Suite: There is increasing interest in executing various general-purpose applications on GPGPUs in addition to the traditional graphics rendering applications [5, 32]. In this spirit, we consider a wide range of emerging GPGPU applications implemented in CUDA, which include NVIDIA SDK [47], Rodinia [10], Parboil [53], MapReduce [19], and a few third party applications. In total, we study 38 applications. While Rodinia applications are mainly targeted for heterogeneous platforms, Parboil benchmarks primarily stress throughput computing focused architectures. Data-intensive MapReduce and third party applications are included for diversity. We execute these applications on GPGPU-Sim, which simulates the baseline architecture described in Table 1. The applications are run until completion or for 1 billion instructions (whichever comes first), except for `IIX` where we execute only 400 million instructions because of infrastructure limitations.

Evaluation Metrics: In addition to using *instructions per cycle (IPC)* as the primary performance metric for evaluation, we also consider auxiliary metrics like bank level parallelism and row buffer locality. Bank level parallelism (BLP) is defined as the number of average memory banks that are accessed when there is at least one outstanding memory request at any of the banks [26, 27, 41, 42]. Improving BLP enables better utilization of DRAM bandwidth. Row-buffer locality (RBL) is defined as the average hit-rate of the row buffer across all memory banks [27]. Improving RBL increases the memory service rate and hence also enables better DRAM bandwidth utilization.

3. Motivation and Workload Analysis

Round robin (RR) scheduling of warps causes almost all warps to execute the same long latency memory operation (with different addresses) at roughly the same time, as previous work has shown [44]. For the computation to resume in the warps and the core to become active again, these long-latency memory accesses need to be completed. This inefficiency of RR scheduling hampers the latency hiding capability of GPGPUs. To understand it further, let us consider 8 CTAs that need to be assigned to 2 cores (4 CTAs per core). According to the load-balanced CTA assignment policy described in Section 2.1, CTAs 1, 3, 5, 7 are assigned to core 1 and CTAs 2, 4, 6, 8 are assigned to core 2. With RR, warps associated with CTAs 1, 3, 5 and 7 are executed with equal priority on core 1 and are executed in a round-robin fashion. This execution continues until all the warps are blocked (when they need data from main memory). At this point, there may be no ready warps that can be scheduled, making core 1 inactive. Typically, this inactive time is very significant in memory intensive applications, as multiple requests are sent to the memory subsystem by many cores in a short period of time. This increases network and DRAM contention, which in turn increases queuing delays, leading to very high core inactive times.

To evaluate the impact of RR scheduling on GPGPU applications, we first characterize our application set. We quantify how much IPC improvement each application gains if *all* memory requests magically hit in the L1 cache. This improvement, called PMEM, is depicted in Table 2, where the 38 applications are sorted in descending order of PMEM. Applications that have high PMEM ($>= 1.4\times$) are classified as Type-1, and the rest as Type-2. We have observed that the warps of highly memory intensive applications (Type-1) wait longer for their data to come back than warps of Type-2 applications. If this wait is eliminated, the performance of `SAD`, `PVC`, and `SSC` would improve by 639%, 499% and 460%, respectively (as shown by the PMEM values for these applications).

Across Type-1 applications, average core inactive time (CINV) is 62% of the total execution cycles of all cores (Table 2). During this inactive time, no threads are being executed in the core. The primary reason behind this high core inactivity is what we call *MemoryBlockCycles*, which is defined as the number of cycles during which all the warps in the core are stalled waiting for their memory requests to come back from L2 cache/DRAM (i.e., there are warps on the core but they are all waiting for memory). Figure 3 shows the fraction of *MemoryBlockCycles* of all the cores out of the total number of cycles taken to execute each application. Across all 38 applications, *MemoryBlockCycles* constitute 32% of the total execution cycles, i.e., 70% of the total inactive cycles. These results clearly highlight the importance of reducing the *MemoryBlockCycles* to improve the utilization of cores, and thus GPGPU performance.

Another major constituent of inactive cycles is *NoWarpCycles*, which is defined as number of cycles during which a core has *no warps* to execute, but an application has *not* completed its execution as some other cores are still executing warps. This might happen due to two reasons: (1) availability of a small number of CTAs within an application (due to an inherently small amount of parallelism) [24] or (2) the CTA load imbalance phenomenon [5], where some of the cores finish their assigned CTAs earlier than the others. We find that *NoWarpCycles* is prominent in `LUD` and `NQU`, which are Type-2 applications. From Table 2, we see that although core inactive time is very high in `LUD` and `NQU` (64% and 95%, respectively), *MemoryBlockCycles* is very low (Figure 3). We leave

Table 2. GPGPU application characteristics: *(A) PMEM*: IPC improvement with perfect memory (All memory requests are satisfied in L1 caches), Legend: H = High ($>= 1.4$x) , L = Low (< 1.4x); *(B) CINV*: The ratio of inactive cycles to the total execution cycles of all the cores.

#	App. Suite	**Type-1 Applications**	Abbr.	PMEM	CINV	#	App. Suite	**Type-2 Applications**	Abbr.	PMEM	CINV
1	Parboil	Sum of Abs. Differences	SAD	H (6.39x)	91%	20	CUDA SDK	Separable Convolution	CON	L (1.23x)	20%
2	MapReduce	PageViewCount	PVC	H (4.99x)	93%	21	CUDA SDK	AES Cryptography	AES	L (1.23x)	51%
3	MapReduce	SimilarityScore	SSC	H (4.60x)	85%	22	Rodinia	SRAD1	SD1	L (1.17x)	20%
4	CUDA SDK	Breadth First Search	BFS	H (2.77x)	81%	23	CUDA SDK	Blackscholes	BLK	L (1.16x)	17%
5	CUDA SDK	MUMerGPU	MUM	H (2.66x)	72%	24	Rodinia	HotSpot	HS	L (1.15x)	21%
6	Rodinia	CFD Solver	CFD	H (2.46x)	66%	25	CUDA SDK	Scan of Large Arrays	SLA	L (1.13x)	17%
7	Rodinia	Kmeans Clustering	KMN	H (2.43x)	65%	26	3rd Party	Denoise	DN	L (1.12x)	22%
8	CUDA SDK	Scalar Product	SCP	H (2.37x)	58%	27	CUDA SDK	3D Laplace Solver	LPS	L (1.10x)	12%
9	CUDA SDK	Fast Walsh Transform	FWT	H (2.29x)	58%	28	CUDA SDK	Neural Network	NN	L (1.10x)	13%
10	MapReduce	InvertedIndex	IIX	H (2.29x)	65%	29	Rodinia	Particle Filter (Native)	PFN	L (1.08x)	10%
11	Parboil	Sparse-Matrix-Mul.	SPMV	H (2.19x)	65%	30	Rodinia	Leukocyte	LYTE	L (1.08x)	15%
12	3rd Party	JPEG Decoding	JPEG	H (2.12x)	54%	31	Rodinia	LU Decomposition	LUD	L (1.05x)	64%
13	Rodinia	Breadth First Search	BFSR	H (2.09x)	64%	32	Parboil	Matrix Multiplication	MM	L (1.04x)	4%
14	Rodinia	Streamcluster	SC	H (1.94x)	52%	33	CUDA SDK	StoreGPU	STO	L (1.02x)	3%
15	Parboil	FFT Algorithm	FFT	H (1.56x)	37%	34	CUDA SDK	Coulombic Potential	CP	L (1.01x)	4%
16	Rodinia	SRAD2	SD2	H (1.53x)	36%	35	CUDA SDK	N-Queens Solver	NQU	L (1.01x)	95%
17	CUDA SDK	Weather Prediction	WP	H (1.50x)	54%	36	Parboil	Distance-Cutoff CP	CUTP	L (1.01x)	2%
18	MapReduce	PageViewRank	PVR	H (1.41x)	46%	37	Rodinia	Heartwall	HW	L (1.01x)	9%
19	Rodinia	Backpropogation	BP	H (1.40x)	33%	38	Parboil	Angular Correlation	TPAF	L (1.01x)	6%

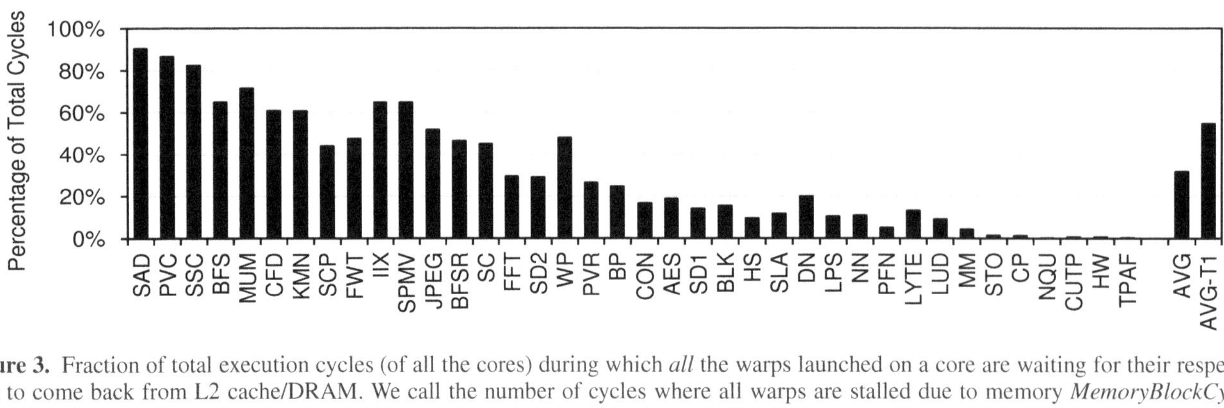

Figure 3. Fraction of total execution cycles (of all the cores) during which *all* the warps launched on a core are waiting for their respective data to come back from L2 cache/DRAM. We call the number of cycles where all warps are stalled due to memory *MemoryBlockCycles*. AVG-T1 is the average (arithmetic mean) value across all Type-1 applications. AVG is the average value across all 38 applications.

improving the performance of Type-2 applications for future work, and focus on improving the performance of Type-1 applications where the main cause of core idleness is waiting on memory.

Note that Type-1 applications are present across all modern workload suites like MapReduce, Parboil, Rodinia, and CUDA SDK, indicating that memory stalls are a fundamental bottleneck in improving the performance of these applications. We have found that Type-1 applications are most affected by limited off-chip DRAM bandwidth, which leads to long memory stall times. Our goal is to devise new warp scheduling mechanisms to both reduce and tolerate long memory stall times in GPGPUs.

4. The Proposed OWL Scheduler

In this section, we describe OWL, c(O)operative thread array a(W)are warp schedu(L)ing policy, which consists of four schemes: CTA-aware two-level warp scheduling, locality aware warp scheduling, bank-level parallelism aware warp scheduling, and opportunistic prefetching, where each scheme builds on top of the previous.

4.1 *CTA-Aware*: CTA-aware two-level warp scheduling

To address the problem posed by RR scheduling, we propose a CTA-aware two-level warp scheduler, where all the available CTAs launched on a core (N CTAs) are divided into smaller *groups* of n CTAs. Assume that the size of each CTA is k warps (which is pre-determined for an application kernel). This corresponds to each group having $n \times k$ warps. *CTA-Aware* selects a single group (having n CTAs) and prioritizes the associated warps ($n \times k$) for execution over the remaining warps ($(N - n) \times k$) associated with the other group(s). Warps within the same group have equal priority and are executed in a round-robin fashion. Once all the warps associated with the first selected group are blocked due to the unavailability of data, a group switch occurs giving opportunity to the next CTA group for execution (and this process continues in a round-robin fashion among all the CTA groups). This is an effective way to hide long memory latencies, as now, a core can execute the group(s) of warps that are not waiting for memory while waiting for the data for the other group(s).

How to choose n: A group with n CTAs should have enough warps to keep the core pipeline busy in the absence of long latency operations [44]. Based on the GPU core's scheduling model described in Section 2, we set the minimum number of warps in a group to the number of pipeline stages (5 in our case). It means that, the minimum value of $n \times k$ should be 5. Since k depends on the GPGPU application kernel, the group size can vary for different application kernels. As each group can only have integral number of CTAs (n), we start with $n = 1$. If $n \times k$ is still smaller than the minimum number of warps in a group, we increase n by 1 until we have enough warps in the group for a particular application kernel. After the first group is formed, remaining groups are also formed in a similar fashion. For example, assume that the total number of CTAs launched on a core is $N = 10$. Also, assume that the number of pipeline stages is 5, and the number of warps in a CTA (k) is 2. In this case, the size of the first group (n) will be set to 3 CTAs, as now, a group will have 6 (3×2) warps, satisfying the minimum requirement of 5 (number of pipeline stages). The second group will follow the same method and have 3 CTAs. Now, note that the third group will have 4 CTAs to include the remaining CTAs. The third group cannot have only 3 CTAs ($n = 3$), because that will push the last CTA (10th CTA) to become the fourth group by itself, violating the minimum group size (in warps) requirement for the fourth group. We call this scheme CTA-aware two-level scheduling (*CTA-Aware*), as the groups are formed taking CTA boundaries into consideration and a two-level scheduling policy is employed, where scheduling within a group (level 1) and switching among different groups (level 2) are both done in a round-robin fashion.

The need to be CTA-aware: Two types of data locality are primarily present in GPGPU applications [21, 44, 51]: (1) Intra-warp data locality, and (2) Intra-CTA (inter-warp) data locality. Intra-warp locality is due to the threads in a warp that share contiguous elements of an array, which are typically coalesced to the same cache line. This locality is exploited by keeping the threads of a warp together. Intra-CTA locality results from warps within the same thread-block sharing blocks or rows of data. Typically, data associated with one CTA is first moved to the on-chip memories and is followed by the computation on it. Finally, the results are written back to the main global memory. Since the difference between access latencies of on-chip and off-chip memories is very high [5], it is critical to optimally utilize the data brought on-chip and maximize reuse opportunities. Prioritizing some group of warps agnostic to the CTA boundaries may not utilize the data brought on-chip to the full extent (because it may cause eviction of data that is reused across different warps in the same CTA). Thus, it is important to be CTA-aware when forming groups.

4.2 *CTA-Aware-Locality*: Locality aware warp scheduling

Although *CTA-Aware* scheduling we just described is effective in hiding the long memory fetch latencies, it does not effectively utilize the private L1 cache capacity associated with every core. Given the fact that L1 data caches of the state-of-the art GPGPU architectures are in the 16-64 KB range [48] (as well as in CMPs [22]), in most cases, the data brought by a *large number* of CTAs executing simultaneously does not fit into the cache (this is true for a majority of the memory-intensive applications). This hampers the opportunity of reusing the data brought by warps, eventually leading to a high number of L1 misses. In fact, this problem is more severe with the RR scheduling policy, where the number of simultaneously executing CTAs taking advantage of the caches in a given interval of time is more than that with our CTA-Aware scheduling policy. In many-core and SMT architectures, others [11, 55] also observed a similar phenomenon, where many simultaneously executing threads (which share the same cache) cause cache contention, leading to increased cache misses. One might argue that, this situation can be addressed by increasing the size of L1 caches, but that would lead to (1) higher cache access latency, and (2) reduced hardware resources dedicated for computation, thereby hampering parallelism and the ability of the architecture to hide memory latency further.

Problem: In order to understand the problem with *CTA-Aware* scheme, consider Figure 4 (A). Without the loss of generality, let us assume that the group size is equal to 1. Further, assume that at core 1, CTA 1 belongs to group 1, CTA 3 belongs to group 2, etc., and each CTA has enough warps to keep the core pipeline busy ($1 \times k \geq$ number of pipeline stages). According to *CTA-Aware*, the warps of group 1 are prioritized until they are blocked waiting for memory. At this point, the warps of CTA 3 are executed. If the warps of CTA 1 become ready to execute (because their data

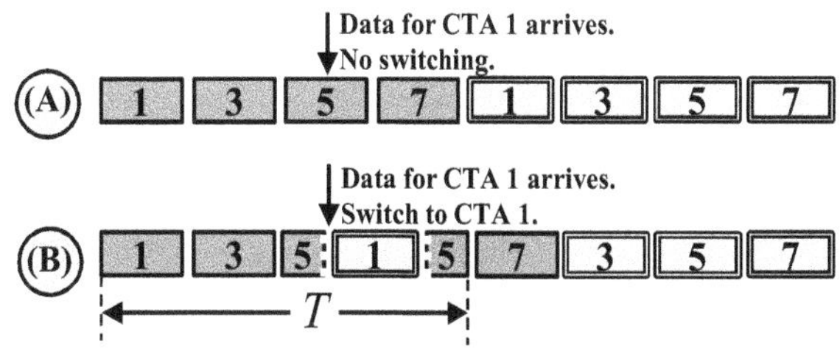

Figure 4. An illustrative example showing the working of (A) CTA-aware two-level warp scheduling (*CTA-Aware*) (B) Locality aware warp scheduling (*CTA-Aware-Locality*). Label in each box refers to the corresponding CTA number.

Table 3. Reduction in combined L1 miss rates (texture, constant, data) with our warp scheduling mechanisms over baseline RR scheduling.

#	App.	*CTA-Aware*	*CTA-Aware-Locality*	#	App.	*CTA-Aware*	*CTA-Aware-Locality*	#	App.	*CTA-Aware*	*CTA-Aware-Locality*
1	SAD	6%	42%	7	KMN	27%	49%	14	SC	0%	0%
2	PVC	89%	90%	8	SCP	0%	0%	15	FFT	1%	1%
3	SSC	1%	8%	9	FWT	0%	0%	16	SD2	0%	0%
4	BFS	1%	17%	10	IIX	27%	96%	17	WP	0%	0%
5	MUM	1%	2%	11	SPMV	0%	8%	18	PVR	1%	2%
6	CFD	1%	2%	12	JPEG	0%	0%	19	BP	0%	0%
				13	BFSR	2%	16%		**AVG-T1**	**8%**	**18%**

arrives from memory) when the core is executing warps of CTA 5 (Figure 4 (A)), *CTA-Aware* will keep executing the warps of CTA 5 (and will continue to CTA 7 after that). It will not choose the warps from CTA 1 even though they are ready because it follows a strict round-robin policy among different CTAs. Thus, the data brought by the warps of CTA 1 early on (before they were stalled) becomes more likely to get evicted by other CTAs' data as the core keeps on executing the CTAs in a round-robin fashion. This strict round robin scheduling scheme allows larger number of threads to bring data to the relatively small L1 caches, thereby increasing cache contention due to the differences in the data sets of different CTAs and hampering the effective reuse of data in the caches. Although *CTA-Aware* performs better in utilizing L1 caches compared to RR (because it restricts the number of warps sharing the L1 cache simultaneously), it is far from optimal.

Solution: To achieve better L1 hit rates, we strive to reduce the number of simultaneously executing CTAs taking advantage of L1 caches in a particular time interval. Out of N CTAs launched on a core, the goal is to *always* prioritize only one of the CTA groups of size n. n is chosen by the method described in Section 4.1. In general, on a particular core, *CTA-Aware-Locality* starts scheduling warps from group 1. If warps associated with group 1 (whose size is n CTAs) are blocked due to unavailability of data, the scheduler can schedule warps from group 2. This is essential to keep the core pipeline busy. However, as soon as any warps from group 1 are ready (i.e., their requested data has arrived), *CTA-Aware-Locality again* prioritizes these group 1 warps. If all warps belonging to group 1 have completed their execution, the next group (group 2) is chosen and is *always* prioritized. This process continues until all the launched CTAs finish their execution.

The primary motivation of using this scheme is that, in a particular time interval, only n CTAs are given higher priority to keep their data in the private caches such that they get the opportunity to reuse it. Since this scheme reduces contention and increases reuse in the L1 cache, we call it locality aware warp scheduling (*CTA-Aware-Locality*). Note that, as n is closer to N, *CTA-Aware-Locality* degenerates into RR, as there can be only one group with N CTAs.

Typically, a GPGPU application kernel does not require fairness among the completion of different CTAs. CTAs can execute and finish in any order. The only important metric from the application's point of view is the total execution time of the kernel. A fair version of *CTA-Aware-Locality* can also be devised, where the CTA group with highest priority is changed (and accordingly, priorities of all groups will change) in a round-robin fashion (among all the groups) after a fixed interval of time. We leave the design of such schemes to future work.

Figure 4 (B) shows how *CTA-Aware-Locality* works. Again, without loss of generality, let us assume that the group size is equal to 1. We show that, *CTA-Aware-Locality* starts choosing warps belonging to CTA 1 (belonging to group 1) once they become ready, unlike *CTA-Aware*, where scheduler keeps on choosing warps from CTA 5 (group 3), 7 (group 4) and so on. In other words, we *always* prioritize a small group of CTAs (in this case, group 1 with $n = 1$) and shift the priority to the next CTA only after CTA 1 completes its execution. During time interval T, we observe that only 3 CTAs are executing and taking advantage of the private caches, contrary to 4 CTAs in the baseline system (Figure 4 (A)). This implies that a smaller number of CTAs gets the opportunity to use the L1 caches concurrently, increasing L1 hit rates and reducing cache contention.

Discussion: *CTA-Aware-Locality* aims to reduce the L1 cache misses. Table 3 shows the reduction in L1 miss rates (over baseline RR) when *CTA-Aware* and *CTA-Aware-Locality* schemes are incorporated. On average, for Type-1 applications, *CTA-Aware* reduces the overall miss rate by 8%. *CTA-Aware-Locality* is further able to reduce the overall miss rate (by 10%) by scheduling warps as soon as the data arrives for them, rather than waiting for their turn, thereby reducing the number of CTAs currently taking advantage of the L1 caches. With *CTA-Aware-Locality*, we observe maximum benefits with Map-Reduce applications `PVC` and `IIX`, where the reduction in L1 miss rates is 90% and 96%, respectively, leading to significant IPC improvements (see Section 5). Since these applications are very memory intensive (highly ranked among Type-1 applications in Table 2) and exhibit good L1 data reuse within CTAs, they significantly benefit from *CTA-Aware-Locality*. Interestingly, we find that 8 out of 19 Type-1 applications show negligible reduction in L1 miss rates with both *CTA-Aware* and *CTA-Aware-Locality*. Detailed analysis shows that these applications do not exhibit significant cache sensitivity, thus, do not provide sufficient L1 data reuse opportunities. In `WP`, because of resource limitations posed by the baseline architecture (Section 2), there are only 6 warps that can be simultaneously executed. This restriction eliminates the possibility of getting benefits from *CTA-Aware-Locality*, as only one group (with 6 warps) can be formed, and no group switching/prioritization occurs.

4.3 *CTA-Aware-Locality-BLP*: BLP aware warp scheduling

In the previous section, we discussed how *CTA-Aware-Locality* helps in hiding memory latency along with reducing L1 miss rates. In this section, we propose *CTA-Aware-Locality-BLP*, which not only incorporates the benefits of *CTA-Aware-Locality*, but also improves DRAM bank-level parallelism (BLP) [41].

Problem: In our study of 38 applications, we observe that the same DRAM row is accessed (shared) by consecutive CTAs 64% of the time. Table 4 shows these row sharing percentages for all the Type-1 applications. This metric is determined by calculating the average fraction of consecutive CTAs (out of total CTAs) accessing the same DRAM row, averaged across all rows. For example, if a row is accessed by CTAs 1, 2, 3, and 7, its consecutive CTA row sharing percentage is deemed to be 75% (as CTAs 1, 2, 3 are consecutive). We observe that for many GPGPU applications, the consecutive CTA row sharing percentages are very high (up to 99% in `JPEG`). For example, in Figure 1 (B), we observe that the row sharing percentage is 100%, as CTA 1 opens 2 rows in Bank 1 (A(0,0) and A(0,1)) and Bank 2 (A(1,0) and A(1,1)); and, CTA 2 opens the same rows again as the data needed by it to execute is also mapped to the same rows. These high consecutive CTA row sharing percentages are not surprising, as CUDA programmers are encouraged to form CTAs such that the data required by the consecutive CTAs is mapped to the same DRAM row for high DRAM row locality, improving DRAM bandwidth utilization [28]. Also, many data layout optimizations are proposed to make CTA conform to the DRAM layout [54] to get the maximum performance.

Table 4. GPGPU application characteristics: *Consecutive CTA row sharing*: Fraction of consecutive CTAs (out of all CTAs) accessing the same DRAM row. *CTAs/Row*: Average number of CTAs accessing the same DRAM row.

#	App.	Cons. CTA row sharing	CTAs/Row	#	App.	Cons. CTA row sharing	CTAs/Row	#	App.	Cons. CTA row sharing	CTAs/Row
1	SAD	42%	32	7	KMN	66%	2	14	SC	1%	2
2	PVC	36%	2	8	SCP	0%	1	15	FFT	14%	5
3	SSC	20%	2	9	FWT	85%	2	16	SD2	98%	35
4	BFS	23%	5	10	IIX	36%	2	17	WP	93%	7
5	MUM	17%	32	11	SPMV	98%	6	18	PVR	38%	2
6	CFD	81%	10	12	JPEG	99%	16	19	BP	99%	4
				13	BFSR	71%	8		**AVG**	**64%**	**15**

In Section 4.2, we proposed *CTA-Aware-Locality* where a subset of CTAs (one group) is *always* prioritized over others. Although this scheme is effective at reducing cache contention and improving per-core performance, it takes decisions agnostic to inter-CTA row sharing properties. Consider a scenario where two consecutive CTA groups are scheduled on two different cores and are being *always* prioritized according to *CTA-Aware-Locality*. Given that the consecutive CTAs (in turn warps) share DRAM rows, the CTA groups access a *small* set of DRAM banks more frequently. This increases the queuing time at the banks and reduces the bank level parallelism (BLP). To understand this problem in-depth, let us revisit Figure 1 (C), which shows the row-major data layout of CTAs in DRAM [28]. The elements in row 0 of the matrix in Figure 1 (B) are mapped to a single row in bank 1, elements in row 1 are mapped to bank 2, and so on. To maximize row locality, it is important that the row that is loaded to a row buffer in a bank is utilized to the maximum, as row buffer hit latency (10 DRAM cycles (t_{CL})) is almost twice cheaper than row closed latency (22 DRAM cycles (t_{RCD} + t_{CL})), and almost three times cheaper than row conflict latency (32 DRAM cycles ($t_{RP} + t_{RCD} + t_{CL}$)) [41]. *CTA-Aware-Locality* prioritizes CTA 1 (group 1) at core 1 and CTA 2 (also, group 1) at core 2. When both the groups are blocked, their memory requests access the same row in both bank 1 and bank 2, as CTA 1 and CTA 2 share the same rows (row sharing = 100%).

Figure 5 (A) depicts this phenomenon pictorially. Since consecutive CTAs (CTAs 1 and 2) share the same rows, prioritizing them in different cores enables them to access these same rows concurrently, thereby providing high row buffer hit rate. Unfortunately, for the exact same reason, prioritizing consecutive CTAs in different cores leads to low BLP because all DRAM banks are not utilized as consecutive CTAs access the same banks (In Figure 5 (A), two banks stay idle). Our goal is to develop a series of techniques that achieve both high BLP and high row buffer hit rate. First, we describe a bank-level parallelism aware warp scheduling mechanism, *CTA-Aware-Locality-BLP*, which improves BLP at the expense of row locality.

Solution: To address the above problem, we propose *CTA-Aware-Locality-BLP*, which not only inherits the positive aspects of *CTA-Aware-Locality* (better L1 hit rates), but also improves DRAM bank level parallelism. The key idea is to still *always* prioritize one CTA group in each core, but to ensure that *non-consecutive CTAs* (i.e., CTAs that do not share rows) are *always* prioritized in different cores. This improves the likelihood that the executing CTA groups (warps) in different cores access different banks, thereby improving bank level parallelism.

Figure 5 (B) depicts the working of *CTA-Aware-Locality-BLP* pictorially with an example. Instead of prioritizing consecutive CTAs (CTAs 1 and 2) in the two cores, *CTA-Aware-Locality-BLP* prioritizes non-consecutive ones (CTAs 1 and 4). This enables all four banks to be utilized concurrently, instead of two banks staying idle, which was the case with *CTA-Aware-Locality* (depicted in Figure 5 (A)). Hence, prioritizing non-consecutive CTAs in different cores leads to improved BLP. Note that this comes at the expense of row buffer locality, which we will restore with our next proposal, *Opportunistic Prefetching* (Section 4.4).

One way to implement the key idea of *CTA-Aware-Locality-BLP* is to prioritize different-numbered CTA groups in consecutive cores concurrently, instead of prioritizing the same-numbered CTA groups in each core concurrently. In other words, the warp scheduler in each core prioritizes, for example, the first CTA group in core 1, the second CTA group in core 2, the third CTA group in core 3, and so on. Since different-numbered CTA groups are unlikely to share DRAM rows, this technique is likely to maximize parallelism. Algorithm 1 more formally depicts the group formation and group priority assignment strategies for the three schemes we have proposed so far.

Discussion: Figure 6 shows the change in BLP and row buffer hit rate with *CTA-Aware-Locality-BLP* compared to *CTA-Aware-Locality*. Across Type-1 applications, there is an 11% average increase in BLP (AVG-T1), which not only reduces the DRAM queuing latency by 12%, but also reduces overall memory fetch latency by 22%. In `JPEG`, the BLP improvement is 46%. When *CTA-Aware-Locality-BLP* is incorporated, we observe 14% average reduction in row locality among all Type-1 applications. We note that, even though there is a significant increase in BLP, the decrease in row locality (e.g., in `JPEG`, `SD2`) is a concern, because reduced row

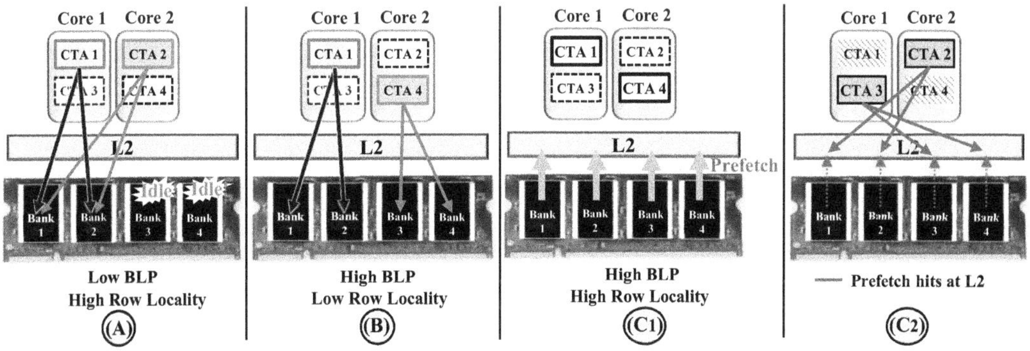

Figure 5. An example illustrating (A) the under-utilization of DRAM banks with *CTA-Aware-Locality*, (B) improved bank-level parallelism with *CTA-Aware-Locality-BLP*, (C1, C2) the positive effects of *Opportunistic Prefetching*.

Algorithm 1 Group formation and priority assignment

▷ k is the number of warps in a CTA
▷ N is the number of CTAs scheduled on a core
▷ n is the minimum number of CTAs in a group
▷ g_size is the minimum number of warps in a group
▷ g_core is the number of groups scheduled on a core
▷ num_cores is the total number of cores in GPGPU
▷ $group\_size[i]$ is the group size (in number of CTAs) of the ith group
▷ $g\_pri[i][j]$ is the group priority of the ith group scheduled on the jth core.
▷ The lower the $g\_pri[i][j]$, the higher the scheduling priority. Once a group is chosen, the scheduler cannot choose warps from different group(s) unless all warps of the already-chosen group are blocked because of unavailability of data.

procedure FORM_GROUPS
  $n \leftarrow 1$
  while $(n \times k) < g\_size$ **do**
    $n \leftarrow n + 1$
  $g\_core \leftarrow \lfloor N/n \rfloor$
  for $g\_num = 0 \rightarrow (g\_core - 1)$ **do**
    $group\_size[g\_num] \leftarrow n$
  if $(N \bmod n) \neq 0$ **then**
    $group\_size[g\_core - 1] \leftarrow group\_size[g\_core - 1] + (N \bmod n)$

procedure CTA-AWARE
  FORM_GROUPS
  for $core\_ID = 0 \rightarrow (num\_cores - 1)$ **do**
    for $g\_num = 0 \rightarrow (g\_core - 1)$ **do**
      $g\_pri[g\_num][core\_ID] \leftarrow 0$
▷ All groups have equal priority and executed in RR fashion.

procedure CTA-AWARE-LOCALITY
  FORM_GROUPS
  for $core\_ID = 0 \rightarrow (num\_cores - 1)$ **do**
    for $g\_num = 0 \rightarrow (g\_core - 1)$ **do**
      $g\_pri[g\_num][core\_ID] \leftarrow g\_num$

procedure CTA-AWARE-LOCALITY-BLP
  FORM_GROUPS
  for $core\_ID = 0 \rightarrow (num\_cores - 1)$ **do**
    for $g\_num = 0 \rightarrow (g\_core - 1)$ **do**
      $g\_pri[g\_num][core\_ID] \leftarrow (g\_num - core\_ID) \bmod g\_core$

locality adversely affects DRAM bandwidth utilization. To address this problem, we propose our final scheme, memory-side *Opportunistic Prefetching*.

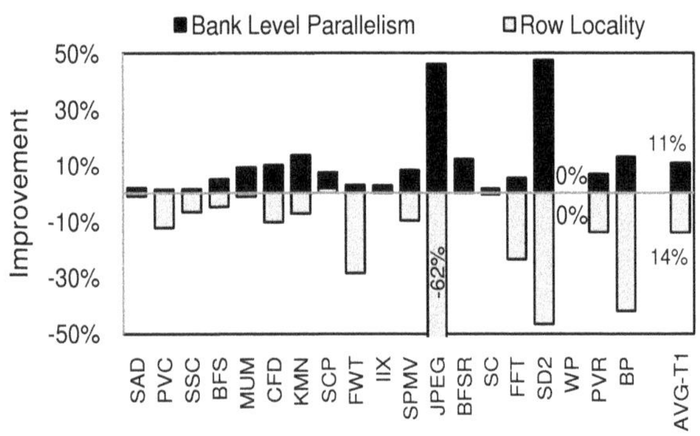

Figure 6. Effect of *CTA-Aware-Locality-BLP* on DRAM bank-level parallelism and row locality, compared to *CTA-Aware-Locality*.

4.4 Opportunistic Prefetching

In the previous section, we discussed how *CTA-Aware-Locality-BLP* improves bank-level parallelism, but this comes at the cost of row locality. Our evaluations show that, on average, 15 CTAs access the same DRAM row (shown under CTAs/row in Table 4). If these CTAs do not access the row when the row is fetched into the row buffer the first time, data in the row buffer will not be efficiently utilized. In fact, since *CTA-Aware-Locality-BLP* tries to schedule different CTAs that access the same row at *different times* to improve BLP, these different CTAs will need to re-open the row over and over before accessing it. Hence, large losses in row locality are possible (and we have observed these, as shown in Figure 6), which can hinder performance. Our goal is to restore row buffer locality (and hence efficiently utilize an open row as much as possible) while keeping the benefits of improved BLP.

Solution: We observe that prefetching cache blocks of an *already open row* can achieve this goal: if the prefetched cache blocks are later needed by other CTAs, these CTAs will find the prefetched data in the cache and hence do not need to access DRAM. As such, in the best case, even though CTAs that access the same row get scheduled at different times, they would not re-open the row over and over because opportunistic prefetching would prefetch all the needed data into the caches.

The key idea of *opportunistic prefetching* is to prefetch the so-far-unfetched cache lines in an already open row into the L2 caches, just before the row is closed (i.e., after all the demand requests to the row in the memory request buffer are served). We call this *opportunistic* because the prefetcher, sitting in the memory controller, takes advantage of a row that was already opened by a demand request, in an opportunistic way. The prefetched lines can be useful for both currently executing CTAs, as well as, CTAs that will be launched later. Figure 5 (C1, C2) depicts the potential benefit of this scheme. In Figure 5 (C1), during the execution of CTAs 1 and 4, our proposal prefetches the data from the open rows that could potentially be useful for other CTAs (CTAs 2 and 3 in this example). If the prefetched lines are useful (Figure 5 (C2)), when CTAs 2 and 3 execute and require data from the same row, their requests will hit in the L2 cache and hence they will not need to access DRAM for the same row.

Implementation: There are two key design decisions in our opportunistic prefetcher: *what cache lines to prefetch* and *when to stop prefetching*. In this paper, we explore simple mechanisms to provide an initial study. However, any previously proposed prefetching method can be employed (as long as they generate requests to the same row that is open) – we leave the exploration of such sophisticated techniques to future work.

What to prefetch? The prefetcher we evaluate starts prefetching when there are no more demand requests to an open row. It sequentially prefetches the cache lines that were *not* accessed by demand requests (after the row was opened the last time) from the row to the L2 cache slice associated with the memory controller.

When to stop opportunistic prefetching? We study two possible schemes, although there are many design choices possible. In the first scheme, the prefetcher stops immediately after a demand request to a *different* row arrives. The intuition is that a demand request is more critical than a prefetch, so it should be served immediately. However, this intuition may not hold true because servicing useful row-hit prefetch requests before row-conflict demand requests can eliminate future row conflicts, thereby improving performance (also shown by Lee et al. [34]). In addition, additional latency incurred by the demand request if prefetches were continued to be issued to the open row even after the demand arrives can be hidden in GPGPUs due to the existence of a large number of warps. Hence, it may be worthwhile to keep prefetching even after a demand to a different row arrives. Therefore, our second scheme prefetches at least a minimum number of cache lines (C) regardless of whether or not a demand arrives. The value of C is set to a value *lower* initially. The prefetcher continuously monitors the number of demand requests at the memory controller queue. If that number is less than a *threshold*, the value of C is set to a value *higher*. The idea is that if there are few demand requests waiting, it could be beneficial to keep prefetching. In our baseline implementation, we set *lower* to 8, *higher* to 16, and *threshold* to the average number of pending requests at the memory controller. Section 5.1 explores sensitivity to these parameters. More sophisticated mechanisms are left as part of future work.

4.5 Hardware Overheads

CTA-aware scheduling: The nVIDIA warp scheduler has low warp-switching overhead [37] and warps can be scheduled according to their pre-determined priorities. We take advantage of such priority-based warp scheduler implementations already available in existing GPGPUs. Extra hardware is needed to dynamically calculate the priorities of the warps using our schemes (Algorithm 1). In addition, every core should have a group formation mechanism similar to Narasiman et al.'s proposal [44]. We synthesized the RTL design of the hardware required for our warp scheduler using the 65nm TSMC libraries in the Synopsys Design Compiler. For a 28-core system, the power overhead is 57 mW and the area overhead is 0.18 mm^2, which is less than 0.05% of the nVIDIA GeForce GTX 285 area.

Opportunistic prefetching: Opportunistic prefetching requires the prefetcher to know which cache lines in a row were already sent to the L2. To keep track of this for the currently-open row in a bank, we add n bits to the memory controller, corresponding to n cache lines in the row. When the row is opened, the n bits are reset. When a cache block is sent to the L2 cache from a row, its corresponding bit is set. For 4 MCs, each controlling 4 banks, with a row size of 32 cache blocks (assuming column size of 64B), the hardware overhead is 512 bits ($4 \times 4 \times 32$ bits). The second prefetching mechanism we propose also requires extra hardware to keep track of the average number of pending requests at the memory controller. This range of this register is 0-127 and its value is computed approximately with the aid of shift registers.

5. Experimental Results

In this section, we evaluate our proposed scheduling and memory-side prefetching schemes with 19 Type-1 applications, where main memory is the main cause of core idleness.

5.1 Performance Results

We start with evaluating the performance impact of our scheduling schemes (in the order of their appearance in the paper) against the *Perfect-L2* case, where all memory requests are L2 cache hits. We also show results with Perfect-L1 (PMEM), which is the ultimate upper bound of our optimizations. Recall that each scheme builds on top of the previous.

Effect of *CTA-Aware*: We discussed in Section 4.1 that this scheme not only helps in hiding memory latency, but also partially reduces cache contention. Figure 7 shows the IPC improvements of Type-1 applications (normalized to RR). Figure 8 shows the impact of our scheduling schemes on *MemoryBlockCycles* as described in Section 3. On average (arithmetic mean), *CTA-Aware* provides 14% (9% harmonic mean (hmean), 11% geometric mean (gmean)) IPC improvement, with 9% reduction in memory waiting time (*MemoryBlockCycles*) over RR. The primary advantage comes from the reduction in L1 miss rates and improvement in memory latency hiding capability due to CTA grouping. We observe significant IPC improvements in `PVC` (2.5×) and `IIX` (1.22×) applications, as the miss rate drastically reduces by 89% and 27%, respectively. As expected, we do not observe significant performance improvements in `SD2`, `WP`, and `SPMV` as there is no reduction in miss rate compared to RR. We see improvements in `JPEG` (6%) and `SCP` (19%), even though there is no reduction in miss-rates (see Table 3). Most of the benefits in these benchmarks are due to the better hiding of memory latency, which comes inherently from the CTA-aware two-level scheduling. We further observe (not shown) that *CTA-Aware* achieves similar performance benefits compared to the recently proposed two-level warp scheduling [44]. In contrast to [44], by introducing awareness of CTAs, our *CTA-Aware* warp scheduling mechanism provides a strong foundation for the remaining three schemes we develop.

Effect of *CTA-Aware-Locality*: The main advantage of this scheme is further reduced L1 miss rates. We observe 11% average IPC improvement (6% decrease in *MemoryBlockCycles*) over *CTA-Aware*, and 25% (17% hmean, 21% gmean) over RR. We observe 81% IPC improvement in `IIX`, primarily because of 69% in L1 miss rates. Because of the row locality and BLP trade-off (this scheme sacrifices BLP for increased row locality), we observe that some applications may not attain optimal benefit from *CTA-Aware-Locality*. For example, in `SC`, IPC decreases by 4% and *MemoryBlockCycles* increases by 3% compared to *CTA-Aware*, due to a 26% reduction in BLP (7% increase in row locality). We also observe similar results in `MUM`: 1% increase in row locality, 10% reduction in BLP, which causes 3% reduction in performance compared to *CTA-Aware*. In `SD2`, we observe a 7% IPC improvement over *CTA-Aware* on account of a 14% increase in row-locality, with a 21% reduction in BLP. Nevertheless, the primary advantage of *CTA-Aware-Locality* is the reduced number of memory requests due to better cache utilization (Section 4.2), and as a result of this, we also observe an improvement in DRAM bandwidth utilization due to reduced contention in DRAM banks.

Effect of *CTA-Aware-Locality-BLP*: In this scheme, we strive to achieve better BLP at the cost of row locality. Using this scheme, on average, we observe 6% IPC (4% hmean, 4% gmean) improvement, and 3% decrease in *MemoryBlockCycles* over *CTA-Aware-Locality*. BLP increases by 11%, which also helps in the observed 22% reduction in overall memory fetch latency (12% reduction

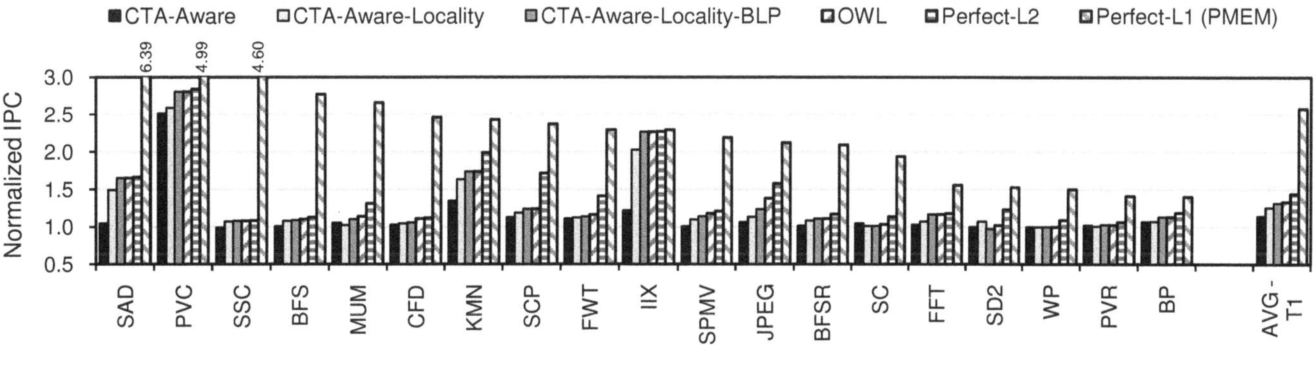

Figure 7. Performance impact of our schemes on Type-1 applications. Results are normalized to RR.

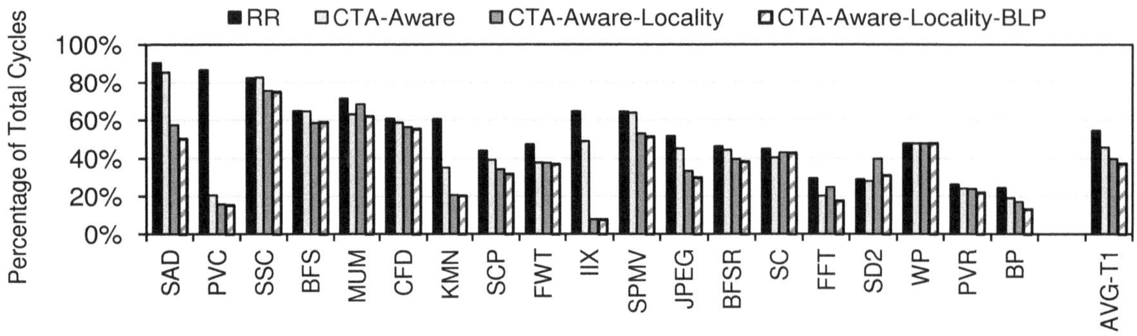

Figure 8. Impact of different scheduling schemes on *MemoryBlockCycles* for Type-1 applications. Results are normalized to the total execution cycles with baseline RR scheduling.

in queuing latency). In SD2, we see a significant increase in BLP (48%) over *CTA-Aware-Locality*, but performance still reduces (by 10%) compared to *CTA-Aware-Locality*, due to a 46% reduction in row locality. In contrast, in JPEG, the effects of the 62% reduction in row locality is outweighed by the 46% increase in BLP, yielding a 10% IPC improvement over *CTA-Aware-Locality*. This shows that both row locality and BLP are important for GPGPU performance.

Combined Effect of OWL (Integration of *CTA-Aware-Locality-BLP* and opportunistic prefetching): The fourth bar from the left in Figure 7 shows the performance of the system with OWL. We can draw four main conclusions from this graph. First, using opportunistic prefetching on top of *CTA-Aware-Locality-BLP* consistently either improves performance or has no effect. Second, on average, even a simple prefetching scheme like ours can provide an IPC improvement of 2% over *CTA-Aware-Locality-BLP*, which is due to a 12% improvement in L2 cache hit rate. Overall, OWL achieves 19% (14% hmean, 17% gmean) IPC improvement over *CTA-Aware* and 33% (23% hmean, 28% gmean) IPC improvement over RR. Third, a few applications, such as JPEG, gain significantly (up to 15% in IPC) due to opportunistic prefetching, while others, such as FWT, SPMV, and SD2, gain only moderately (around 5%), and some do not have any noticeable gains, e.g., SAD, PVC, and WP. The variation seen in improvements across different applications can be attributed to their different memory latency hiding capabilities and memory access patterns. It is interesting to note that, in SCP, FWT, and KMN, some rows are accessed by only one or two CTAs. The required data in these rows are demanded when they are opened for the first time. In these situations, even if we prefetch all the remaining lines, we do not observe significant improvements. Fourth, we find that the scope of improvement available for opportunistic prefetching over *CTA-Aware-Locality-BLP* is limited: *Perfect-L2* can provide only 13% improvement over *CTA-Aware-Locality-BLP*. This is mainly because if an application inherently has a large number of warps ready to execute, the application will also be able to efficiently hide the long memory access latency. We observe that prefetching might not be beneficial in these applications even if the prefetch-accuracy is 100%.

We conclude that the proposed schemes are effective at improving GPGPU performance by making memory less of a bottleneck. As a result, OWL enables the evaluated GPGPU to have performance within 11% of a hypothetical GPGPU with a perfect L2.

5.2 Sensitivity Studies

In this section, we describe the critical sensitivity studies we performed related to group size, DRAM configuration and opportunistic prefetching.

Sensitivity to group size: In Section 4.1, we mentioned that the minimum number of warps in a group should be at least equal to the number of pipeline stages. Narasiman et al. [44] advocated that, if the group size is too small, the data fetched in DRAM row buffers is not completely utilized, as fewer warps are prioritized together. If the group size is too large, the benefits of two-level scheduling diminishes. Figure 9 shows the effect of the group size on performance. The results are normalized to RR and averaged across all Type-1 applications. We observe that when minimum group size is 8 warps, we get the best IPC improvements (14% for *CTA-Aware*, 25% for *CTA-Aware-Locality* and 31% for *CTA-Aware-Locality-BLP* over RR), and thus, throughout our work, we have used a minimum group size of 8, instead of 5 (which is the number of pipeline stages).

Sensitivity to the number of DRAM banks: Figure 10 shows the change in performance of *CTA-Aware-Locality-BLP* with the number of DRAM banks per MC. We observe that as the number of banks increases, the effectiveness of *CTA-Aware-Locality-BLP* increases. This is because having additional banks enables more benefits from exposing higher levels of BLP via our proposed techniques. As a result, the performance improvement of our proposal is 2% higher with 8 banks per MC than with 4 banks per MC (our baseline system). We conclude that our techniques are likely to become more effective in future systems with more banks.

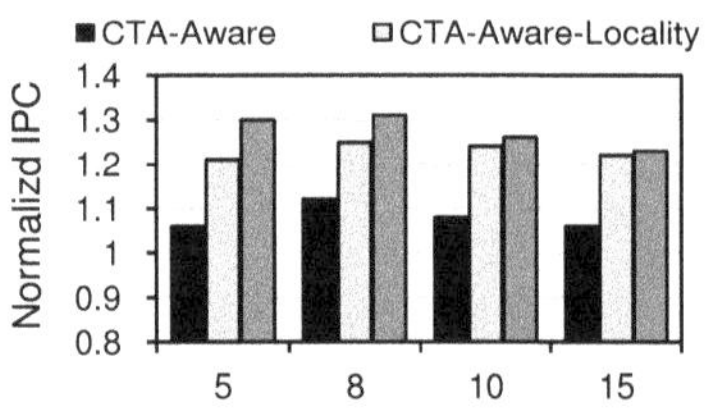

Figure 9. Sensitivity of IPC to group size (normalized to RR).

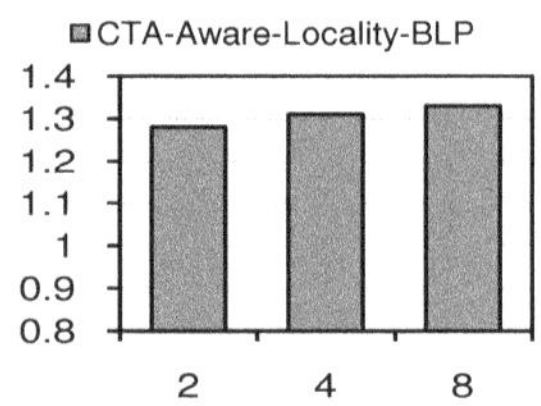

Figure 10. Sensitivity of IPC to the number of banks (normalized to RR).

Sensitivity to Opportunistic Prefetching Parameters: We experimented with all combinations of *lower* and *upper* values for the prefetch degree in the range of 0 (no-prefetching) to 32 (prefetching all the columns in a row) with a step size of 8. The value of *threshold* is also varied similarly, along with the case when it is equal to the average memory controller queue length. Figure 11 shows the best case values achieved across all evaluated combinations (*Best OWL*). We find that the average performance improvement achievable by tuning these parameter values is only 1% (compare *Best OWL* vs. OWL). This can possibly be achieved by implementing a sophisticated prefetcher that can dynamically adjust its parameters based on the running application's characteristics, which comes at

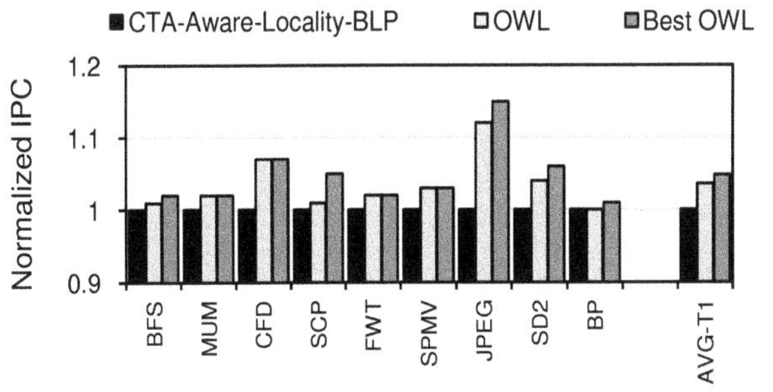

Figure 11. Prefetch degree and throttling threshold sensitivity.

the cost of increased hardware complexity. We leave the design of such application-aware memory-side prefetchers as a part of the future work, along with more sophisticated techniques to determine what parts of a row to prefetch.

6. Related Work

To our knowledge, this is the first paper in the context of GPGPUs to propose (1) *CTA-aware* warp scheduling techniques to improve both cache hit rates and DRAM bank-level parallelism, and (2) memory-side prefetching mechanisms to improve overall GPGPU performance by taking advantage of open DRAM row buffers. We briefly describe the closely related works in this section.

Scheduling in GPGPUs: The two-level warp scheduling mechanism proposed by Narasiman et al. [44] increases the core utilization by creating larger warps and employing a two-level warp scheduling scheme. This mechanism is not aware of CTA boundaries. In our work, we propose CTA-aware warp scheduling policies, which improve not only L1 hit rates, but also DRAM bandwidth utilization. We find that the combination of all of our techniques, OWL, provides approximately 19% higher performance than two-level warp scheduling. Gebhart et al. [17] also proposed a two-level warp scheduling technique. Energy reduction is the primary purpose of their approach. Even though we do not evaluate it, OWL is also likely to provide energy benefits as reduced execution time (with low hardware overhead) is likely to translate into reduced energy consumption. Concurrent work by Rogers et al. [51] proposed a cache-conscious warp scheduling policy. Their work improves L1 hit rates for cache-sensitive applications. OWL not only reduces cache contention, but also improves DRAM bandwidth utilization for a wide range of applications. Recent work from Kayiran et al. [24] dynamically estimates the amount of thread-level parallelism that would improve GPGPU performance by reducing cache and DRAM contention. Our approach is orthogonal to theirs as our CTA-aware scheduling techniques improve cache and DRAM utilization for a *given* amount of thread-level parallelism.

BLP and Row Locality: Bank-level parallelism and row buffer locality are two important characteristics of DRAM performance. Several memory request scheduling [3, 12, 26, 27, 33–35, 41, 50, 58, 59] and data partitioning [20, 40, 57] techniques have been proposed to improve one or both within the context of multi-core, GPGPU, and heterogeneous CPU-GPU systems [3]. Our work can be combined with these approaches. Mutlu and Moscibroda [41] describe parallelism-aware batch scheduling, which aims to preserve each thread's BLP in a multi-core system. Hassan et al. [18] suggest that optimizing BLP is more important than improving row buffer hits, even though there is a trade-off. Our work uses this observation to focus on enhancing BLP, while restoring the lost row locality by memory-side prefetching. This is important because, in some GPGPU applications, we observe that both BLP and row locality are important. Similar to our proposal, Jeong et al. [20] observe that both BLP and row locality are important for maximizing benefits in multi-core systems. The memory access scheduling proposed by Yuan et al. [58] restores the lost row access locality caused by the in-order DRAM scheduler, by incorporating an arbitration mechanism in the interconnection network. The staged memory scheduler of Ausavarungnirun et al. [3] batches memory requests going to the same row to improve row locality while also employing simple in-order request scheduling at the DRAM banks. Lakshminarayana et al. [33] propose a potential function that models the DRAM behavior in GPGPU architectures and a SJF DRAM scheduling policy. The scheduling policy essentially chooses between SJF and FR-FCFS at run-time based on the number of requests from each thread and their potential of generating a row buffer hit. In our work, we propose low-overhead *warp scheduling and prefetching* schemes to improve *both* row locality and BLP. Exploration of the combination of our warp scheduling techniques with memory request scheduling and data partitioning techniques is a promising area of future work.

Data Prefetching: To our knowledge, OWL is the first work that uses a memory-side prefetcher in GPUs. Our opportunistic prefetcher complements the CTA-aware scheduling schemes by taking advantage of open DRAM rows. The most relevant work on hardware prefetching in GPUs is the L1 prefetcher proposed by Lee et al. [36]. Carter et al. [9] present one of the earliest works done in the area of memory-side prefetching in the CPU domain. Many other prefetching mechanisms (e.g., [13, 23, 45, 52]) have been proposed within the context of CPU systems. Our contribution in this work is a specific prefetching algorithm (in fact, our proposal can potentially use the algorithms proposed in literature), but to employ the idea prefetching in conjunction with new BLP-aware warp scheduling techniques to restore row buffer locality and improve L1 hit rates in GPGPUs.

7. Conclusion

This paper proposes a new warp scheduling policy, OWL, to enhance GPGPU performance by overcoming the resource under-utilization problem caused by long latency memory operations. The key idea in OWL is to take advantage of characteristics of cooperative thread arrays (CTAs) to concurrently improve cache hit rate, latency hiding capability, and DRAM bank parallelism in GPGPUs. OWL achieves these benefits by 1) selecting and prioritizing a group of CTAs scheduled on a core, thereby improving both L1 cache hit rates and latency tolerance, 2) scheduling CTA groups that likely do not access the same memory banks on different cores, thereby improving DRAM bank parallelism, and 3) employing opportunistic memory-side prefetching to take advantage of already-open DRAM rows, thereby improving both DRAM row locality and cache hit rates. Our experimental evaluations on a 28-core GPGPU platform demonstrate that OWL is effective in improving GPGPU performance for memory-intensive applications: it leads to 33% IPC performance improvement over the commonly-employed baseline round-robin warp scheduler, which is not aware of CTAs. We conclude that incorporating CTA awareness into GPGPU warp scheduling policies can be an effective way of enhancing GPGPU performance by reducing resource under-utilization.

Acknowledgments

We thank the anonymous reviewers, Rachata Ausavarungnirun, Kevin Kai-Wei Chang, Mahshid Sedghi, and Bikash Sharma for their feedback on earlier drafts of this paper. This research is supported in part by NSF grants #1213052, #1152479, #1147388, #1139023, #1017882, #0963839, #0811687, #0953246 and grants from Intel and nVIDIA.

References

[1] AMD. Radeon and FirePro Graphics Cards, Nov. 2011.

[2] AMD. Heterogeneous Computing: OpenCL and the ATI Radeon HD 5870 (Evergreen) Architecture, Oct. 2012.

[3] R. Ausavarungnirun, K. K.-W. Chang, L. Subramanian, G. H. Loh, and O. Mutlu. Staged Memory Scheduling: Achieving High Performance and Scalability in Heterogeneous Systems. In *ISCA*, 2012.

[4] A. Bakhoda, J. Kim, and T. Aamodt. Throughput-effective On-chip Networks for Manycore Accelerators. In *MICRO*, 2010.

[5] A. Bakhoda, G. Yuan, W. Fung, H. Wong, and T. Aamodt. Analyzing CUDA Workloads Using a Detailed GPU Simulator. In *ISPASS*, 2009.

[6] M. M. Baskaran, U. Bondhugula, S. Krishnamoorthy, J. Ramanujam, A. Rountev, and P. Sadayappan. A Compiler Framework for Optimization of Affine Loop Nests for GPGPUs. In *ICS 2008*.

[7] M. M. Baskaran, J. Ramanujam, and P. Sadayappan. Automatic C-to-CUDA Code Generation for Affine Programs. In *CC/ETAPS 2010*.

[8] M. Bauer, H. Cook, and B. Khailany. CudaDMA: Optimizing GPU Memory Bandwidth via Warp Specialization. In *SC*, 2011.

[9] J. Carter, W. Hsieh, L. Stoller, M. Swanson, L. Zhang, E. Brunvand, A. Davis, C.-C. Kuo, R. Kuramkote, M. Parker, L. Schaelicke, and T. Tateyama. Impulse: Building a Smarter Memory Controller. In *HPCA*, 1999.

[10] S. Che, M. Boyer, J. Meng, D. Tarjan, J. Sheaffer, S.-H. Lee, and K. Skadron. Rodinia: A Benchmark Suite for Heterogeneous Computing. In *IISWC*, 2009.

[11] X. E. Chen and T. Aamodt. Modeling Cache Contention and Throughput of Multiprogrammed Manycore Processors. *IEEE Trans. Comput.*, 2012.

[12] E. Ebrahimi, R. Miftakhutdinov, C. Fallin, C. J. Lee, J. A. Joao, O. Mutlu, and Y. N. Patt. Parallel Application Memory Scheduling. *MICRO*, 2011.

[13] E. Ebrahimi, O. Mutlu, and Y. N. Patt. Techniques for Bandwidth-Efficient Prefetching of Linked Data Structures in Hybrid Prefetching Systems. In *HPCA*, 2009.

[14] W. Fung, I. Sham, G. Yuan, and T. Aamodt. Dynamic Warp Formation and Scheduling for Efficient GPU Control Flow. In *MICRO*, 2007.

[15] W. W. L. Fung and T. M. Aamodt. Thread Block Compaction for Efficient SIMT Control Flow. In *HPCA*, 2011.

[16] W. W. L. Fung, I. Singh, A. Brownsword, and T. M. Aamodt. Hardware Transactional Memory for GPU Architectures. In *MICRO*, 2011.

[17] M. Gebhart, D. R. Johnson, D. Tarjan, S. W. Keckler, W. J. Dally, E. Lindholm, and K. Skadron. Energy-efficient Mechanisms for Managing Thread Context in Throughput Processors. In *ISCA*, 2011.

[18] S. Hassan, D. Choudhary, M. Rasquinha, and S. Yalamanchili. Regulating Locality vs. Parallelism Tradeoffs in Multiple Memory Controller Environments. In *PACT*, 2011.

[19] B. He, W. Fang, Q. Luo, N. K. Govindaraju, and T. Wang. Mars: A MapReduce Framework on Graphics Processors. In *PACT*, 2008.

[20] M. K. Jeong, D. H. Yoon, D. Sunwoo, M. Sullivan, I. Lee, and M. Erez. Balancing DRAM Locality and Parallelism in Shared Memory CMP Systems . In *HPCA*, 2012.

[21] W. Jia, K. A. Shaw, and M. Martonosi. Characterizing and Improving the Use of Demand-fetched Caches in GPUs. In *ICS*, 2012.

[22] A. Jog, A. K. Mishra, C. Xu, Y. Xie, V. Narayanan, R. Iyer, and C. R. Das. Cache Revive: Architecting Volatile STT-RAM Caches for Enhanced Performance in CMPs. In *DAC*, 2012.

[23] D. Joseph and D. Grunwald. Prefetching Using Markov Predictors. *IEEE Trans. Comput.*, 1999.

[24] O. Kayiran, A. Jog, M. T. Kandemir, and C. R. Das. Neither More Nor Less: Optimizing Thread-Level Parallelism for GPGPUs. In *CSE Penn State Tech Report, TR-CSE-2012-006*, 2012.

[25] S. Keckler, W. Dally, B. Khailany, M. Garland, and D. Glasco. GPUs and the Future of Parallel Computing. *IEEE Micro*, 2011.

[26] Y. Kim, D. Han, O. Mutlu, and M. Harchol-Balter. ATLAS: A Scalable and High-performance Scheduling Algorithm for Multiple Memory Controllers. In *HPCA*, 2010.

[27] Y. Kim, M. Papamichael, O. Mutlu, and M. Harchol-Balter. Thread Cluster Memory Scheduling: Exploiting Differences in Memory Access Behavior. In *MICRO*, 2010.

[28] D. Kirk and Wen-mei. W. Hwu. Programming Massively Parallel Processors. 2010.

[29] K. Krewell. Amd's Fusion Finally Arrives. *MPR*, 2011.

[30] K. Krewell. Ivy Bridge Improves Graphics. *MPR*, 2011.

[31] K. Krewell. Most Significant Bits. *MPR*, 2011.

[32] K. Krewell. Nvidia Lowers the Heat on Kepler. *MPR*, 2012.

[33] N. B. Lakshminarayana, J. Lee, H. Kim, and J. Shin. DRAM Scheduling Policy for GPGPU Architectures Based on a Potential Function. *Computer Architecture Letters*, 2012.

[34] C. J. Lee, O. Mutlu, V. Narasiman, and Y. N. Patt. Prefetch-Aware DRAM Controllers. In *MICRO*, 2008.

[35] C. J. Lee, V. Narasiman, O. Mutlu, and Y. N. Patt. Improving Memory Bank-Level Parallelism in the Presence of Prefetching. In *MICRO*, 2009.

[36] J. Lee, N. Lakshminarayana, H. Kim, and R. Vuduc. Many-thread Aware Prefetching Mechanisms for GPGPU Applications. In *MICRO*, 2010.

[37] E. Lindholm, J. Nickolls, S. Oberman, and J. Montrym. NVIDIA Tesla: A Unified Graphics and Computing Architecture. *IEEE Micro*, 2008.

[38] T. Moscibroda and O. Mutlu. Memory Performance Attacks: Denial of Memory Service in Multi-Core Systems. In *USENIX SECURITY*, 2007.

[39] A. Munshi. The OpenCL Specification, June 2011.

[40] S. P. Muralidhara, L. Subramanian, O. Mutlu, M. Kandemir, and T. Moscibroda. Reducing Memory Interference in Multicore Systems via Application-Aware Memory Channel Partitioning". In *MICRO*, 2011.

[41] O. Mutlu and T. Moscibroda. Parallelism-Aware Batch Scheduling: Enhancing both Performance and Fairness of Shared DRAM Systems. In *ISCA*, 2008.

[42] O. Mutlu and T. Moscibroda. Stall-Time Fair Memory Access Scheduling for Chip Multiprocessors. In *MICRO*, 2007.

[43] N. Chidambaram Nachiappan, A. K. Mishra, M. Kandemir, A. Sivasubramaniam, O. Mutlu, and C. R. Das. Application-aware Prefetch Prioritization in On-chip Networks. In *PACT*, 2012.

[44] V. Narasiman, M. Shebanow, C. J. Lee, R. Miftakhutdinov, O. Mutlu, and Y. N. Patt. Improving GPU Performance Via Large Warps and Two-level Warp Scheduling. In *MICRO*, 2011.

[45] K. J. Nesbit, and J. E. Smith. Data Cache Prefetching Using a Global History Buffer. In *HPCA*, 2004.

[46] NVIDIA. CUDA C Programming Guide, Oct. 2010.

[47] NVIDIA. CUDA C/C++ SDK code samples, 2011.

[48] NVIDIA. Fermi: NVIDIA's Next Generation CUDA Compute Architecture, Nov. 2011.

[49] M. Rhu and M. Erez. CAPRI: Prediction of Compaction-Adequacy for Handling Control-Divergence in GPGPU Architectures. In *ISCA 2012*.

[50] S. Rixner, W. J. Dally, U. J. Kapasi, P. R. Mattson, and J. D. Owens. Memory Access Scheduling. In *ISCA*, 2000.

[51] T. G. Rogers, M. O'Connor, and T. M. Aamodt. Cache-conscious Wavefront Scheduling. In *MICRO*, 2012.

[52] S. Srinath, O. Mutlu, H. Kim, and Y. N. Patt. Feedback Directed Prefetching: Improving the Performance and Bandwidth-Efficiency of Hardware Prefetchers. In *HPCA*, 2007.

[53] J. A. Stratton et al. Parboil: A Revised Benchmark Suite for Scientific and Commercial Throughput Computing. 2012.

[54] I. J. Sung, J. A. Stratton, and W.-M. W. Hwu. Data Layout Transformation Exploiting Memory-level Parallelism in Structured Grid Many-core Applications. In *PACT*, 2010.

[55] R. Thekkath, and S. J. Eggers. The Effectiveness of Multiple Hardware Contexts. In *ASPLOS*, 1994.

[56] H. Wong, M.-M. Papadopoulou, M. Sadooghi-Alvandi, and A. Moshovos. Demystifying GPU Microarchitecture Through Microbenchmarking. In *ISPASS*, 2010.

[57] H. Yoon, J. Meza, R. Ausavarungnirun, R. Harding, and O. Mutlu. Row Buffer Locality Aware Caching Policies for Hybrid Memories. In *ICCD*, 2012.

[58] G. Yuan, A. Bakhoda, and T. Aamodt. Complexity Effective Memory Access Scheduling for Many-core Accelerator Architectures. In *MICRO*, 2009.

[59] W. K. Zuravleff and T. Robinson. Controller for a Synchronous DRAM that Maximizes Throughput by Allowing Memory Requests and Commands to Be Issued Out of Order. *U.S. Patent Number 5,630,096*, 1997.

Improving GPGPU Concurrency with Elastic Kernels

Sreepathi Pai Matthew J. Thazhuthaveetil R. Govindarajan

Supercomputer Education and Research Centre,
Indian Institute of Science, Bangalore, India
sree@hpc.serc.iisc.ernet.in, mjt@serc.iisc.in, govind@serc.iisc.in

Abstract

Each new generation of GPUs vastly increases the resources available to GPGPU programs. GPU programming models (like CUDA) were designed to scale to use these resources. However, we find that CUDA programs actually do not scale to utilize all available resources, with over 30% of resources going unused on average for programs of the Parboil2 suite that we used in our work. Current GPUs therefore allow concurrent execution of kernels to improve utilization. In this work, we study concurrent execution of GPU kernels using multiprogram workloads on current NVIDIA Fermi GPUs. On two-program workloads from the Parboil2 benchmark suite we find concurrent execution is often no better than serialized execution. We identify that the lack of control over resource allocation to kernels is a major serialization bottleneck. We propose transformations that convert CUDA kernels into *elastic kernels* which permit fine-grained control over their resource usage. We then propose several elastic-kernel aware concurrency policies that offer significantly better performance and concurrency compared to the current CUDA policy. We evaluate our proposals on real hardware using multiprogrammed workloads constructed from benchmarks in the Parboil 2 suite. On average, our proposals increase system throughput (STP) by 1.21x and improve the average normalized turnaround time (ANTT) by 3.73x for two-program workloads when compared to the current CUDA concurrency implementation.

Categories and Subject Descriptors D.3.3 [*Programming Languages*]: Language Constructs and Features; C.1.2 [*Processor Architectures*]: Multiple Data Stream Architectures (Multiprocessors)

Keywords GPGPU, CUDA, Concurrent Kernels

1. Introduction

Graphics Processing Units (GPUs) have evolved from hardware-accelerated fixed-function pipelines to multicore data parallel computation engines. Increasingly general purpose in nature, many are now used exclusively for *General Purpose GPU (GPGPU)* code (i.e. non-graphical or computational code), especially as components of some of the world's fastest supercomputers [19].

Each new GPU generation incorporates features that expand their ability to tackle larger and more complex computational problems. The architectural resources available to GPU programs also increase with each new GPU generation. We observe that from the NVIDIA Tesla [9] to the NVIDIA Kepler [13], shared memory has trebled, registers have quadrupled, and the number of hardware threads has doubled (Table 1). GPU programming models like CUDA and OpenCL have been designed to allow older programs to take advantage of these increased resources without any programmer intervention. Programs written in CUDA for the Tesla scale to use the increased resources available on the Kepler because CUDA requires parallelism to be made explicit and performs resource allocation at runtime.

Resource	Tesla (1.3)	Fermi (2.0)	Kepler (3.0)
Registers	16384	32768 (2x)	65536 (2x)
Shared Memory	16384	49152 (3x)	49152
Threads	1024	1536 (1.5x)	2048 (1.33x)
Resident Blocks	8	8	16 (2x)

Table 1. Resources per Streaming Multiprocessor across three NVIDIA GPU generations. Multipliers in parentheses indicate change over preceding generation.

In reality, however, we find that CUDA programs are unable to effectively utilize these additional resources. Programs from the Parboil2 benchmark suite, for example, utilize only 20–70% of resources on average (Section 2). Ironically, we find that the *grid*[1], a GPU programming construct that was designed to achieve scalability, also leads to under-utilization of those same resources. A grid is the runtime instance of a GPU kernel, and consists of *thread blocks*. By allowing the programmer to create a large number of thread blocks – more than the resources available in the hardware – CUDA grids can scale up to newer hardware by simply increasing the number of thread blocks that run concurrently. This is possible because in the CUDA programming model, each thread block in the grid is an independent unit of parallelism and can execute independently of other thread blocks in the grid. Each thread block, in turn, consists of threads which ultimately consume resources and execute on the hardware. The number of threads in a thread block and the number of thread blocks in a grid are decided by the programmer, who divides the work to be performed among the thread blocks. Apart from work distribution and scalability, thread blocks are also used to allocate resources for a grid which leads to under-utilization of resources.

Figure 1 illustrates how resource allocation at the thread block level leads to wastage. Each thread block occupies a fixed amount of the GPU's resources – registers, threads and shared memory – which it occupies exclusively until it finishes. A GPU runs as many thread blocks concurrently as possible until limitations due to *any* of (i) number of registers, (ii) threads, (iii) shared memory or

[1] Although these constructs are common to all GPU programming models, we use CUDA terminology in this paper for consistency.

ASPLOS'13, March 16–20, 2013, Houston, Texas, USA.

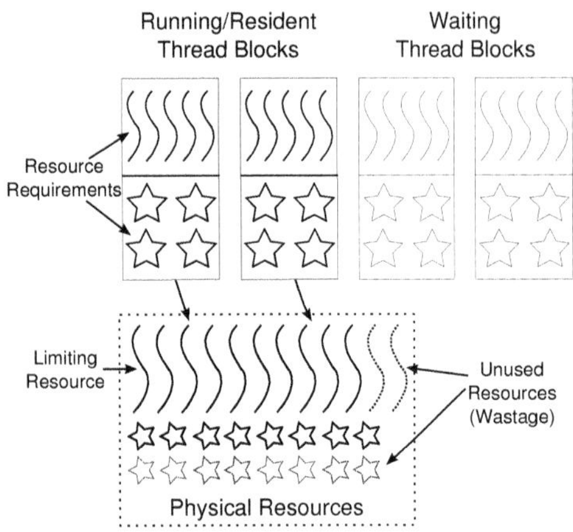

Figure 1. Resource wastage due to allocation at Thread Block granularity.

(iv) maximum number of resident blocks is reached. It is possible, and in our experience quite common, for thread blocks to exhaust only one of these resources (the *limiting resource*), while leaving the others underutilized. For example, on the Fermi, a thread block that uses 16 registers per thread and contains 128 threads per thread block is limited by the maximum number of resident blocks (8) and not by the number of registers or threads. The unused resources obviously cannot accommodate another thread block from the same grid and are therefore wasted.

If the hardware were able to modify grid and thread block sizes, it could choose sizes that would optimize the utilization of hardware resources. Unfortunately, grids are specified at the programming model level and provide the basis for work distribution. Most programmers size grids and thread blocks on the amount of work available, and not for optimal utilization of hardware resources.

The only way to utilize these wasted resources, then, is to allow concurrent execution of other *independent* grids whose thread blocks could possibly utilize these wasted resources. Such independent grids may be obtained from other concurrently executing GPGPU programs or from other *streams* (Section 3.1) in the same program. As a consequence, current GPUs have begun supporting concurrent execution of independent grids. Policies vary, but in general, after thread blocks from a grid have been dispatched to hardware limits, any leftover resources are distributed to the next independent grid. Under this "LEFTOVER" policy, concurrent execution is not guaranteed – it is still possible for running (or resident) thread blocks from one grid to consume too many resources, preventing other grids from executing concurrently. In practice, we find this is actually a serious problem – 50% of the kernels from the Parboil2 benchmark consume too many resources and prevent concurrent execution of other Parboil2 kernels (Section 2).

Past work [1, 7, 8, 14] has motivated GPU concurrency as a method to improve GPU throughput. Adriaens et al. [1] propose the use of GPU concurrency for mobile GPUs, Ravi et al. [14] look at GPGPU applications in the cloud and Guevara et al. [8] and Gregg et al. [7] demonstrate throughput improvements due to concurrency. Although these works partition GPU resources among concurrent kernels, the granularity of their techniques is either too coarse, operating at the level of a thread block [1, 7, 8], or their techniques are not general enough to apply to all kernels [14]. We show in this work that they either underutilize resources significantly or do not perform as well as our policies.

We make the following contributions:

- We identify major inhibitors of GPGPU concurrency in the CUDA execution model where long running kernels and memory transfers act as serialization bottlenecks. We propose a technique to time-slice kernel execution and memory transfers to mitigate this serialization.
- We find that the current CUDA Streams API and its hardware implementation lead to a high degree of "false serialization", and we build a replacement *Non-serializing Streams* API to work around these limitations in the existing API and hardware.
- We identify a lack of mechanisms to control the resource usage of a grid which leads to poor utilization and poor concurrency and therefore propose and describe the use of *elastic kernels*, a mechanism to control resource allocation for grids during runtime.
- We propose and study elastic-kernel-aware concurrency policies that perform significantly better than the default LEFTOVER policy, achieving a higher degree of concurrency as well as performance.
- Finally, we evaluate our proposals on real hardware using multiprogram workloads constructed from the Parboil2 benchmark suite. Averaged across the workloads, our best elastic policy improves system throughput (STP) by 1.21x and average normalized turnaround time (ANTT) by 3.73x over CUDA execution. Our time-slicing technique improves geomean STP by 7.8% and geomean ANTT by 1.55x where applicable. Our policies improve the average number of concurrent kernels by 1.53x over CUDA, and reduce kernel waiting time by up to three orders of magnitude.

This paper is organized as follows. Section 2 describes the motivation for GPGPU concurrency and how current concurrency policies are ineffective. Section 3 identifies other factors that inhibit GPGPU concurrency. Elastic kernels and elastic-kernel aware concurrency policies are presented in Section 4. Our Non-Serializing Streams API is described in Section 5. Section 6 contains the evaluation of our proposals and presents performance results.

2. Motivation

The NVIDIA Fermi is the only GPU available (as of Q2, 2012) with the software and hardware ability to run multiple GPU grids concurrently. Therefore, we use it in our examination of GPGPU concurrency mechanisms and policies.

Table 2 presents the resources used by the grids of all 18 kernels of the Parboil2 benchmark suite when executed on the NVIDIA Fermi GPU. Observe that no grid from any kernel utilizes 100% of all resources. The vast majority of grids exhaust only a single resource. On the Fermi, this is either registers or resident blocks. Overall, over 40% of threads and blocks, 30% of registers and 80% of shared memory are not used on average. When we examine the benchmarks in the Rodinia 2 suite [3], we arrive at similar conclusions: 35% of threads, 47% of registers, 88% of shared memory and 52% of blocks are not utilized on average.

Since these wasted resources cannot be utilized by thread blocks from the same grid, the Fermi GPU supports concurrent execution of up to 16 grids. Independent grids must be identified and the programs modified in order to convey dependency information to CUDA. None of the programs in the Parboil2 or Rodinia 2 benchmarks currently executes multiple grids in parallel; support for GPU concurrency is relatively new. So, in this work, we use multiprogrammed workloads which are a convenient source of independent grids. Therefore, in this paper, the term "GPU concurrency" exclusively refers to the concurrent execution of independent grids from multiprogrammed workloads.

The Fermi's concurrency policy is not publicly documented. Our experiments using microbenchmarks of concurrently executing synthetic kernels suggest that the Fermi uses the LEFTOVER policy. Under this policy, a grid begins concurrent execution only if there are enough resources to allow execution of at least one of its thread blocks. This is a fairly conservative policy and seems di-

Program	Kernel	TB	TPB	T%	R%	S%	B%
bfs	BFS_in_GPU	1	512	2	2	2	1
	BFS_multi_blk...	14	512	33	31	26	12
mri-q	ComputePhiMag...	4	512	10	5	0	4
	ComputeQ_GPU	1024	256	83	94	0	62
fft	GPU_FFT_Global	1024	128	67	62	0	100
stencil	block2D_hybrid...	512	256	67	94	17	50
cutcp	cuda_cutoff...	121	128	67	75	69	100
tpacf	gen_hists	201	256	50	70	81	38
histo	histo_final	42	512	100	94	0	38
	histo_intermediates	65	498	100	75	0	38
	histo_main	84	768	100	94	100	25
	histo_prescan	64	512	100	75	25	38
sad	larger_sad_calc_16	99	32	15	33	0	88
	larger_sad_calc_8	99	128	59	66	0	88
	mb_sad_calc	1584	61	33	50	38	100
mm	mysgemmNT	528	128	50	94	6	75
lbm	performStream...	13000	100	58	98	0	88
spmv	spmv_jds_texture	112	192	88	98	0	88
	Average			60	67	20	57

Table 2. Resource usage of Parboil2 kernels on the Fermi GPU. Legend: TB=Thread Blocks,TPB=Threads per Thread Block, T=Threads used, R=Registers used, S=Shared Memory used, B=Thread Blocks used. All usage is expressed as percentage of total GPU resources.

Program	Kernel	CP	KT (ms)	Calls	FPT (%)
bfs	BFS_in_GPU	16	14.41	2	37
	BFS_multi_blk...	15	49.57	1	63
mri-q	ComputePhiMag...	16	0.002	1	0.002
	ComputeQ_GPU	2	44.91	2	99.998
fft	GPU_FFT_Global	0	0.11	8	100
stencil	block2D_hybrid...	2	2.70	100	100
cutcp	cuda_cutoff...	0	2.86	11	100
tpacf	gen_hists	13	840.40	1	100
histo	histo_final	0	0.07	100	6
	histo_intermediates	0	0.18	100	16
	histo_main	0	0.85	100	75
	histo_prescan	0	0.03	100	3
sad	larger_sad_calc_16	15	0.04	1	4
	larger_sad_calc_8	15	0.19	1	19
	mb_sad_calc	0	0.80	1	77
mm	mysgemmNT	2	5.51	1	100
lbm	performStream...	0	23.69	100	100
spmv	spmv_jds_texture	0	0.13	1	100

Table 3. Concurrent Execution possible on Fermi (LEFTOVER policy) for Parboil2 kernels. Legend: CP=Concurrent Pairs with kernel starting first (0–17), KT=Average Kernel Time, FPT=Fraction of GPU Program Time.

rected at improving resource utilization whenever possible. It is a poor policy for concurrency, however, because it cannot guarantee that two independent grids will always execute concurrently. If a grid consumes all thread blocks, for example, no other independent grid can execute concurrently with it. Thus, for concurrent execution under this policy, the programmer must ensure that each independent grid will not consume too many resources. Table 3 shows that 9 of the 18 Parboil2 kernels do not form concurrent pairs at all (i.e. zero concurrent pairs) under this policy. Similarly, in the Rodinia 2 [3] benchmark suite, 22 kernels (of the total 38) do not form concurrent pairs under this policy. The LEFTOVER policy also makes concurrent execution of grids a function of GPU resources, which keeps changing over GPU generations.

An alternative policy, *spatial partitioning*, is suggested by Adriaens et al. [1]. Under this policy, the streaming multiprocessors (SM) of a GPU are partitioned among thread blocks of concurrently executing grids. While independent pairs of grids can therefore always execute concurrently, albeit with fewer resources, their work does not consider the wastage due to the GPU's resource allocation mechanisms. Each partition wastes the same percentage of resources as when the grids were executing alone. Thus, this policy does not improve GPU resource utilization.

In this work, we show that the grid's resource allocation considerations can be separated from the programming model considerations by the use of what we term "elastic kernels". Since elastic kernels provide finer control over GPU resources, we can design concurrency policies that improve concurrency *and* resource utilization. These policies can then attempt to achieve both high system throughput and low turnaround time when compared to current policies that only try to achieve maximum concurrency or maximum resource utilization.

3. Limiters of GPU Concurrency

The performance benefits of GPU concurrency are governed by Amdahl's Law – speedup is limited by the extent of serialization. Serialization due to dependences demanded by program semantics is unavoidable, but serialization which arises as artifacts of the GPU execution model decreases potential GPU concurrency. In this section, we identify a number of serialization factors, all of which must be tackled to reduce the extent of serialization. Before we describe these causes of serialization, we first review how concurrency is expressed in GPU programs.

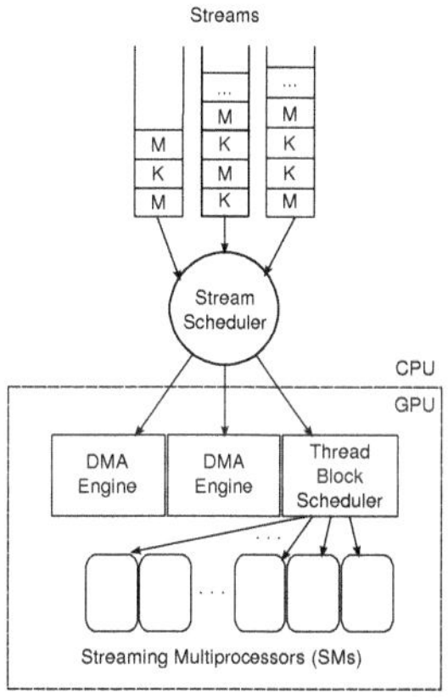

Figure 2. Components that affect concurrency on the Fermi GPU. Streams contain Memory (M) or Kernel (K) commands. A DMA engine performs unidirectional data transfers. With two DMA engines on the Fermi, two memory transfers may run concurrently with kernel execution.

3.1 Task-level Concurrency in GPU programs

The tasks in a GPU program can be divided broadly into memory operations (memory allocations, memory transfers, memsets, etc.) and kernel executions. Task-level concurrency in a GPU program therefore involves exploiting concurrency between memory operations and kernels. CUDA uses a mechanism called *Streams* [12, 15] to expose task-level concurrency in a GPGPU program. Each stream is a queue-like structure into which the CPU program inserts *commands*. Each command is either a memory operation or a kernel execution. Commands placed in the same stream execute in order, but those from different streams can execute concurrently subject to resource availability.

Figure 2 presents a simplified view of the various components that play a role in the concurrent execution of GPU tasks: (i) *Streams*, which contain commands to be sent to the GPU, (ii) the *Stream Scheduler*, which dispatches commands from each stream to the hardware units, sending memory transfer commands to one of the two DMA engines depending on the direction of the transfer, and sending kernel execution commands to the *Thread Block*

Scheduler, (iii) The *Thread Block Scheduler* which instantiates a grid for the kernel as specified by the programmer and then dispatches thread blocks from the grid to the *Streaming Multiprocessors* as described in Section 1. The Fermi Thread Block Scheduler can dispatch thread blocks from up to 16 concurrently executing grids.

In the following sections, we describe how each component of the above GPU execution model can contribute to unnecessary serialization.

3.2 Serialization due to Lack of Resources

A GPU consists of a number of Stream Multiprocessors (SM). Each SM has a fixed amount of resources in terms of thread blocks, registers, threads and shared memory. For a kernel to begin execution on an SM, resources for the execution of at least one of its thread block must be available. Under the current LEFTOVER policy, two grids cannot execute concurrently if the one scheduled first consumes too many resources to allow the other to begin execution. Since the resources consumed are specified by the programmer, the Thread Block Scheduler is forced to serialize the execution of such grids.

One way to guarantee concurrent execution and prevent serialization is to partition the SMs among the different grids [1]. This guarantees that each grid will always have resources to execute and multiple grids can execute across different SMs. However, as noted in Section 2, it does not address the problem of under-utilization of resources. Hence, in this paper, we explore an alternative technique that seeks instead to control the amount of resources occupied by a grid to allow concurrent execution. This will also allow multiple grids to share the same SM. In Section 4, we show that support for kernels which we term *elastic kernels* can allow control of SM resources by permitting modification of their grid and thread block dimensions. This allows us to design resource allocation policies that can guarantee resources for grids to varying degrees and thus allow concurrent execution, preventing serialization due to lack of resources.

3.3 Serialization due to Inter-stream Scheduling

The LEFTOVER concurrency policy renders the concurrency relation non-commutative, making the order in which grids are dispatched to the Thread Block Scheduler important. Figure 3 illustrates this by an example using grids from cutcp, bfs and fft. From Table 2, we know that the grids from cutcp and fft consume 100% of resident blocks. Thus, grids starting after them will not have resident blocks or threads to run and will have to wait. However, neither grid from bfs consumes all of the resources, so it is possible for other grids to execute with them. Assume now that `GPU_FFT_Global` from fft is already running. Now, the grids from cutcp and bfs arrive, in that order, and must wait for `GPU_FFT_Global` to complete. After `GPU_FFT_Global` finishes execution, the scheduler must decide which grid from cutcp or bfs must execute first. A FIFO scheduler would execute the kernel from cutcp first, thus serializing bfs's grid, while a concurrency-aware scheduler would first dispatch bfs, leading to concurrent execution with cutcp. Thus, to avoid serialization, we either need to reorder grids to maximize concurrency or we need to ensure that order of arrival does not matter. The latter can be achieved by controlling resource allocation so that no one grid blocks the execution of another. In Section 4.3, we describe several resource-limiting policies using elastic kernels to allow kernels to execute regardless of dispatch order.

3.4 Serialization due to Kernel Execution

A long-running grid can serialize the execution of grids from *other* programs if it consumes too many resources, preventing other grids

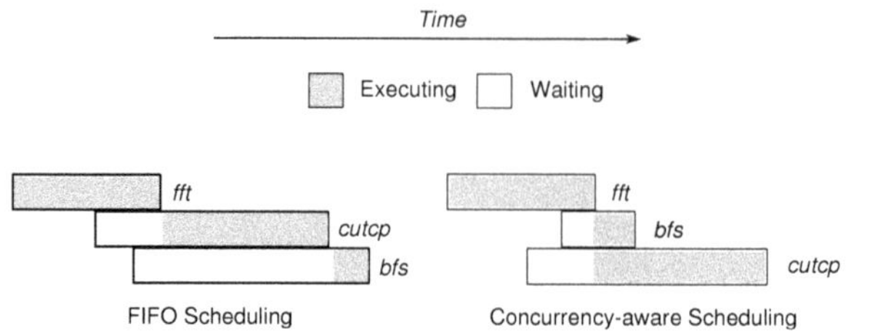

Figure 3. Execution of kernels from bfs, cutcp and fft with a FIFO scheduler and a Concurrency-aware scheduler. Note: Timeline is not to scale.

from executing concurrently with it. Even if it allows concurrent execution, the resources it occupies will be unavailable to other kernels for the duration of its execution, possibly slowing them down. The ability to time slice such long running kernels can help improve not only turnaround time, but also throughput and resource utilization. Grid execution is not pre-empted in current CUDA implementations. The large amount of state involved (also noted by [1]) make pre-emption prohibitively expensive. However, this is true only if we want the ability to stop and restore a grid at any arbitrary point of execution. Instead, we propose to use the discrete nature of grid execution to identify points where little or no state will need to be preserved. Completion of a thread block is an example of one such point. The thread block is the unit of state in a grid and there is no state to save after it completes. Therefore the thread block scheduler can switch from kernel K_1 to K_2 by simply: (i) halting the dispatch of ready thread blocks from K_1's grid, allowing current thread blocks to complete, and (ii) starting the dispatch of ready thread blocks from K_2's grid.

While this still means that we cannot pre-empt a running block, in practice this scheme enables concurrency, and requires no additional state to be preserved. The Thread Block Scheduler already maintains state on which blocks have completed and therefore can restart a grid where it left off. We describe our implementation for time-slicing of GPU grids in Section 4.4.

3.5 Serialization due to Memory Transfers

Current NVIDIA GPUs have two DMA engines. One performs memory transfers to the GPU and the other performs memory transfers from the GPU. Thus, the GPU can sustain two memory transfers at the same time. Further, memory transfers can execute in parallel with kernel execution. However, since only one transfer can be active in a given direction, memory transfers can cause serialization similar to that caused by long-running grids. A large memory transfer in one program can stall progress in other concurrently executing programs as they wait for the DMA engine to become free. Increasing the number of DMA engines is not a solution, since PCIe bandwidth is the actual limiting factor. But increasing the number of memory transfers that can be active and time-slicing between them can reduce waiting time. Figure 4 uses lbm and bfs to illustrate the problem and how timeslicing memory transfers can help. Initially, a 100MB memory transfer in lbm prevents execution of bfs's memory transfer, which in turn causes bfs's kernels to serialize behind lbm's kernel. By timeslicing the large memory transfer, bfs's memory transfer finishes early, and its kernel can execute in parallel with lbm's memory transfer. In our implementation, we break up a long-running memory transfer into smaller chunks and interleave them with chunks of other active memory transfers, thus achieving memory transfer timeslicing.

3.6 Serialization in the CUDA API

The CUDA API contains several functions that *implicitly synchronize* commands from different streams [12], i.e. they act as

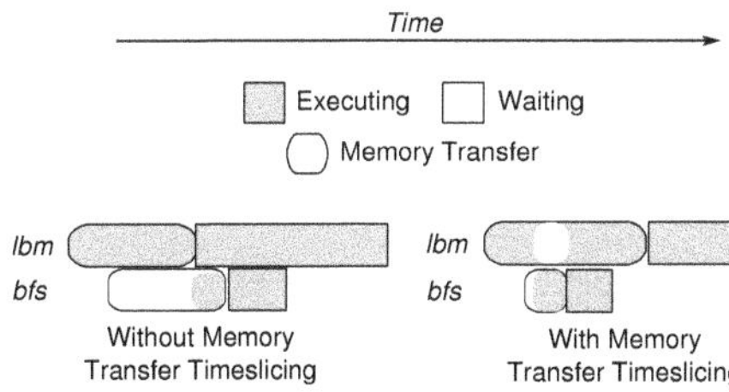

Figure 4. Memory transfers can stall progress across programs, but time-slicing them can reduce waiting times. Note: Timeline is not to scale.

program-wide barriers for GPGPU functionality. For example, device memory allocation functions `cudaMalloc` and `cudaFree` will wait for all currently executing commands to complete before executing, and will prevent later commands from beginning execution until they complete. The effects of this barrier-like behaviour can be severe – if a `cudaFree` is issued when the GPU is executing a kernel, it will wait as long as the kernel takes to finish execution while stalling progress across the rest of the program. The `cudaMemset` function is another source of serialization, but one that seems unnecessarily so since it can be associated with a stream [12], unlike `cudaFree` which is global in nature. It is difficult for us to comment on the difficulty of implementing non-serializing API functions without concrete low-level details of the driver and hardware, but we observe in our experiments that serializing functions can lower throughput drastically.

3.7 Serialization in the Implementation

Finally, we note a source of serialization that is specific to the implementation on the Fermi. To maintain ordering of commands in a single stream, the Fermi uses "signals" [15] between the kernel and memory transfer hardware queues. These signals act as barriers and prevent Kernel–Memory Transfer, Memory Transfer–Kernel, Memory Transfer–Memory Transfer, and Kernel–Kernel dependencies (abbreviated as *K–M*, *M–K*, *M–M* and *K–K* respectively) from being violated in a stream. Unfortunately, in the current implementation, these signals act as a barrier between commands of *all* streams. Thus, a K–M (or M–K) dependency in one program imposes a barrier between commands from all concurrently executing GPU programs. The CUDA Programming Guide calls this an "implicit synchronization caused due to a dependency check" [12].

This *false serialization* can severely restrict the ability of programs to exploit concurrency. For our evaluation, therefore, we developed a replacement for the default CUDA streams implementation that does not suffer from this problem. Our "Non-Serializing Streams" (NSS) implementation provides CUDA-like Streams behaviour but uses alternate methods that do not induce serialization to enforce intra-stream dependencies. Section 5 describes our NSS implementation.

4. Elastic Kernels

Elastic kernels decouple physical hardware resource allocation for thread blocks from logical program-level grid and thread block identity. In Section 4.1, we first describe how an ordinary CUDA kernel can be transformed into an elastic kernel by source-to-source transformations. These transformations are necessary because we currently implement elastic kernels in software. The resulting elastic kernel can run using physical grid and thread block dimensions that are different from programmer specified grid and thread block dimensions. Then, the algorithm presented in Section 4.2 uses this ability to control the resource usage of an elastic kernel. Given resource constraints, the algorithm computes physical grid and thread block dimensions such that the elastic kernel's grid will satisfy those constraints. Next, in Section 4.3, we describe several elastic-kernel aware concurrency policies which improve concurrency by controlling the resources allocated to an elastic kernel. Finally, we describe how elastic kernels are used to implement time-slicing of kernels in Section 4.4.

4.1 Elastic Kernel Transformations

Currently, the hardware maps logical thread blocks and threads to physical thread blocks and threads using a $1 : 1$ logical-to-physical mapping scheme. If we could implement an $N : 1$ logical-to-physical mapping scheme while preserving CUDA semantics, we can achieve fine-grained resource allocation for GPU grids.

The idea of an $N : 1$ mapping for CUDA grids has been explored by Stratton et al. in their MCUDA [17, 18] work which executes CUDA grids efficiently on multicore CPUs. They developed a technique called *iterative wrapping* (similar to *chunked iteration* [16]) to efficiently run the large number of CUDA threads on the comparatively fewer threads available on the CPU. Iterative wrapping executes N CUDA thread blocks using a single CPU thread by inserting an enclosing iterative loop. However, it does not change the number of thread blocks or threads. Our work uses a similar $N : 1$ mapping scheme, but performs a GPU-to-GPU transformation and also allows modification of the number of threads and thread blocks. Changing the number of threads or thread blocks will change thread identities which, in turn, will affect any work distribution based on identity being used by the kernel. Therefore, our transformations also preserve the original identity of each thread block and thread. Essentially, the elastic kernel uses whatever physical grid it was launched with to execute the original logical grid.

We note that some kernels (e.g. `histo_main_kernel` in histo) can run with changed thread blocks or threads even without our transformations. To identify such kernels, we performed a test where the number of blocks and threads was varied for each kernel and their results compared to that obtained by the kernel running with the original number of blocks and threads.[2] Only 4 kernels of the 18 among the Parboil2 benchmarks passed the test. These kernels can run with different grid and thread block dimensions because they compute a *global* thread identifier and use it as a basis for work distribution. While we do not need to transform such kernels, in this work we apply our transformations to all kernels.

Our $N : 1$ mapping scheme takes a 2D logical grid and a 3D logical thread block and executes them using a 1D grid and 1D thread blocks. Listing 1 shows the code for a physical thread block that implements our mapping scheme. This code is placed around the original kernel code and implements a general transformation from physical grid identities to logical grid identities while looping over the original kernel code. To preserve program semantics with respect to identities, we also replace any references to physical dimension variables (`gridDim`, `blockDim`) and physical identity variables (`blockIdx`, `threadIdx`) in the original kernel code with their logical equivalents (`gd`, `bd`, `bi` and `ti` respectively). The code is now an elastic kernel that can execute the original logical grid faithfully with any number of physical thread blocks as well as any physical thread block dimension.

Although the code of Listing 1 allows us to change thread block dimensions, we do not do so for kernels that use shared memory or synchronization instructions. In general, doing so could split a logical thread block across two physical thread blocks. This would violate CUDA semantics for shared memory accesses and behaviour of synchronization instructions. Essentially, shared memory accesses

[2] This test only identifies kernels which *cannot* handle different grid and thread block dimensions. We still need to examine the code for those that pass to verify that the kernels can indeed display elastic kernel behaviour.

```
// find global thread id in physical grid
// note: physical grid and thread blocks are 1D
int tid = threadIdx.x + blockIdx.x * blockDim.x;

// iterate over threads in logical grid
for(int gtid = tid;
    gtid < (gdX * gdY * bdX * bdY * bdZ);
    gtid += blockDim.x * gridDim.x)
  {
    // linearized identities in logical grid
    int block_id = gtid / (bdX * bdY * bdZ);
    int thread_id = gtid % (bdX * bdY * bdZ);

    // logical block identities
    int biX = block_id % gdX;
    int biY = block_id / gdX;

    // logical thread identities
    int tiX = (thread_id % (bdX * bdY)) % (bdX);
    int tiY = (thread_id % (bdX * bdY * bdZ)) / (bdX * bdY);
    int tiZ = thread_id / (bdX * bdY * bdZ);

    // original kernel code follows
    // ...
  }
```

Listing 1. Code in each physical thread block to execute logical thread blocks according to our mapping scheme. The values `gdX`, `gdY`, `bdX`, `bdY`, and `bdZ` are logical grid and thread block dimensions as set by the programmer.

are tied to physical thread blocks and not logical thread blocks and such a split would lead to incorrect execution. Similarly, it is not currently possible to synchronize threads across different physical thread blocks without using slow global synchronization primitives. Therefore, in this work, we do not apply thread block resizing to kernels that use shared memory or synchronization instructions, i.e. 9 of the 18 kernels in the Parboil2 benchmarks.

Our software implementation suffers from two performance issues. Firstly, we are forced to use ordinary variables to store logical identities and dimensions. This increases register usage of the kernel and can cause a potential drop in throughput because the number of threads that can be resident could reduce. Dedicated hardware registers for logical identities and dimensions would solve this problem. The second performance issue arises from the use of the division and modulus operations in our transformed kernels which are not supported natively by the Fermi hardware. Their use increases the runtime of elastic kernels compared to the original kernels. Note that a hardware implementation of elastic kernels would not have these issues and would also be completely transparent to the programmer.

4.2 Resource Control with Elastic Kernels

In this section, we present an algorithm to limit physical resource usage for grids of elastic kernels. To control physical resource usage, we manipulate the elastic kernel's physical grid and thread block dimensions. By changing the number of physical thread blocks, we can control the utilization of threads and registers. For thread block-level resources like shared memory and resident blocks, grid dimensions must be modified. For thread-level resources likes threads and registers, either grid dimensions or thread block dimensions can be modified.

Given resource constraints ($Limits$), Algorithm 1 determines the physical grid and thread block dimensions for an elastic kernel that satisfies those constraints. The input to the algorithm is the number of logical thread blocks, the number of logical threads per thread block and resource constraints on the four resources – resident thread blocks, shared memory, threads and registers. The algorithm first obtains the current resource usage of each thread block using BLOCKUSAGE, a routine derived from the CUDA Occupancy Calculator [11], which calculates the number of registers, threads, shared memory and thread blocks that the kernel currently occupies. Then, the algorithm sets the number of physical thread blocks to the maximum number of concurrent thread blocks that can be accommodated on the GPU (i.e. $MaxResident$) since all blocks in excess of $MaxResident$ have to wait to execute and, on the NVIDIA Fermi, also prevent blocks of later concurrent grids from beginning execution. The algorithm then reduces the number of thread blocks further to meet constraints on the maximum number of resident blocks. As thread blocks and threads are coupled, reducing thread blocks will also reduce the total number of threads ($ChangeInThreads$). If the kernel supports thread block resizing, we compensate by increasing the number of threads per thread block. Finally, for each resource constraint on shared memory, threads, or registers, the algorithm reduces the number of blocks to satisfy the constraint. The number of blocks and threads computed by this algorithm are the physical grid and thread block dimensions respectively and can be used to run the elastic kernel under the specified resource constraints.

Algorithm 1 Algorithm GETPHYGRID

function GETPHYGRID($Kernel, Blocks, Threads, Limits$)
  $Usage \leftarrow$ BLOCKUSAGE($Kernel$)
  $MaxResident \leftarrow Usage.SMBlocks * GPU.SMCount$

  $Blocks \leftarrow$ MIN($Blocks, MaxResident, Limits.Blocks$)
  if THREADSPERBLOCKCANCHANGE($Kernel$) **then**
    $Incr \leftarrow \lfloor (ChangeInThreads/Blocks) \rfloor$
    $Threads \leftarrow Threads + Incr$
  end if

  REDUCEBLOCKS($Limits.ShMem, Usage.ShMem$)
  REDUCEBLOCKS($Limits.Threads, Usage.Threads$)
  REDUCEBLOCKS($Limits.Registers, Usage.Registers$)

  return ($Blocks, Threads$)
end function

procedure REDUCEBLOCKS($RLimit, PerBlockUsage$)
  // $Blocks$ refers to the value in GETPHYGRID
  $CurUsage \leftarrow Blocks * PerBlockUsage$
  if $CurUsage > RLimit$ **then**
    $Deficit \leftarrow CurUsage - RLimit$
    $ReduceBlocks \leftarrow \lceil Deficit/PerBlockUsage \rceil$
    $Blocks \leftarrow Blocks - ReduceBlocks$
  end if
end procedure

4.3 Elastic Kernel Aware Concurrency Policies

With mechanisms to elasticize a CUDA kernel and control its resource usage available, we now present policies that impose resource constraints on elastic kernels in order to improve concurrency. These policies are implemented at the Stream Scheduler level and apply their resource constraints during the launch of a kernel.

4.3.1 MEDIAN

The MEDIAN policy uses profile-based information to reserve resources for a hypothetical *median* kernel. Using the data in Table 2 about the programs in Parboil2, we compute this median kernel's resources to be 224 threads, 6144 registers and 256 bytes of shared memory per thread block. These numbers are the medians for those resources among the Parboil2 kernels. The MEDIAN policy limits the resource usage of actual kernels to ensure that each streaming multiprocessor will have resources leftover to run one block of this median kernel.

4.3.2 MPMAX

The multiprogram maximum or MPMAX policy also uses profile information to reserve resources. For each program, the MPMAX policy constructs a largest kernel based on the maximum resource usage of its kernels. This largest kernel need not correspond to an actual kernel of the program – it may have the register usage of one kernel and the shared memory usage of another. Then, for each program, it computes the othersLargest kernel by repeating a similar procedure using the largest kernels of other concurrently executing programs. Thus, the othersLargest kernel is different for each of the programs executing concurrently. Then, like MEDIAN, the resources of each actual kernel in a program are restricted so that one thread block of the othersLargest kernel will always have enough resources to run.

4.3.3 EQUAL

The EQUAL policy partitions GPU resources equally among all concurrently running programs. For two program workloads, for example, it limits each grid's resource usage to 50% of GPU resources. It is based on the Even SM partitioning heuristic of Adriaens et al. [1]. It is thus a form of spatial partitioning though our implementation does not prevent multiple grids from executing concurrently on the same SM. Thus, this policy dedicates resources for each concurrently executing grid, but without incurring the per-SM wastage noted in Section 2.

4.3.4 QUEUEMOLD

The QUEUEMOLD policy is based on the GetAffinityByMolding algorithm of Ravi et al. [14]. This policy examines all kernels waiting to be launched and modifies the resources requested by them if they make excessive use of: (i) shared memory or (ii) threads. In our implementation, the policy examines kernels waiting in the NSS scheduler queues. If the sum total of shared memory of a newly arrived kernel and a kernel waiting in the queue exceeds the total shared memory available, the number of thread blocks of the waiting kernel is reduced. Similarly, if the thread usage of a waiting kernel exceeds 512 threads, the number of thread blocks (or the number of threads per block) is reduced. The original implementation also uses a notion of *affinity* in order to distribute kernels across multiple GPUs. Since we do not use multiple GPUs in our evaluation, we do not use any affinity values. Note that this policy only modifies the resources used by a kernel if another kernel arrives in the queue before it is launched.

4.4 Implementing Timeslicing of Grid Execution

We implement timeslicing using elastic kernels. By default, elastic kernels iterate over all the thread blocks of the original grid in a single launch. We modify them to accept *offset* and *limit* parameters, so as to restrict execution to only a certain range of thread blocks of the original grid. As each range completes, we simply relaunch the kernel with the next range. The per-invocation ranges for each kernel are currently chosen offline to ensure that the runtime of each range is nearly equal to 1ms whenever possible. The thread block scheduler would, of course, be able to do this online.

5. Non-Serializing Streams Implementation

To avoid false serialization on the NVIDIA Fermi due to dependency checks inserted by the CUDA Streams implementation as described in Section 3.7, we develop a CUDA-like streams implementation called "Non-Serializing Streams" (NSS) that does not introduce false serialization. NSS is also used to implement our elastic policies, and can timeslice kernel execution and memory transfers. It also reorders items in the queues so as to avoid the issues caused by inter-stream scheduling (Section 3.3).

NSS prevents false serialization by avoiding any action that would insert or perform a dependency check in a CUDA stream. In general, submitting each command in the NSS stream to a different

```
if(threadIdx.x == 0
   && threadIdx.y == 0
   && threadIdx.z == 0) {

  int blocks_done = atomicAdd(blocks_done_d, 1);

  if(blocks_done == (gridDim.x * gridDim.y - 1) {
      blocks_done_d = 0;
      blocks_done_h = 1;
    }
}
```

Listing 2. Kernel completion notification code that is inserted onto every exit path of a kernel to notify the CPU that the kernel has completed.

CUDA stream prevents dependency checks from being inserted since no dependency checks are inserted between commands of different CUDA streams. However, this does not mean that we need a new CUDA stream for each command. Since we are only concerned with the serializing behaviour of the *M–K* and *K–M* dependency checks, we only need two CUDA streams. One of these is used for all memory operations, and the other is used for kernel execution. The use of different and exclusive streams for memory and kernel commands prevents CUDA from inserting *M–K* and *K–M* dependency checks. However, NSS must enforce these dependencies.

To enforce *M–K* dependencies in NSS, we note that in the current API, memory transfers that involve pageable memory are synchronous. So a memory transfer is nearly complete when the function call returns. NSS can thus enforce *M–K* dependencies by simply waiting for the `cudaMemcpy` call to complete. This does not present a performance limitation in our studies because none of the applications in Parboil2 use asynchronous memory transfers.

Enforcing *K–M* and *K–K* dependencies is harder since kernel launches are always asynchronous and CUDA provides no way to check if a kernel has completed without introducing a dependency check. We therefore improvise a kernel completion notification mechanism as follows. On every exit path of a kernel, we add the code snippet in Listing 2. This code counts the thread blocks that have finished executing so far in the GPU-side `blocks_done_d` variable. Once all thread blocks have finished, the CPU/GPU shared (host-memory mapped) `blocks_done_h` is set, alerting a polling routine on the CPU of the completion of this kernel.

Like our elastic kernel transformations, the addition of this code also changes the original kernel. Firstly, the number of registers used by the kernel may increase. This affects the number of resident threads and throughput. Secondly, atomic operations have low throughput, causing a performance loss when compared to the original kernel.

The NVIDIA Kepler K20 based on the GK110 GPU is advertised to contain a *Hyper-Q* feature [13] that provides one hardware queue per CUDA stream and prevents this form of serialization. So, on the GK110, NSS may be able to use hardware dependency checks without incurring the overheads of false serialization.

6. Evaluation

6.1 Workload Construction

We evaluate our policies using multiprogrammed workloads since all of the Parboil2 benchmarks are single-threaded serial CUDA programs. However, since CUDA does not execute grids from different programs concurrently [12], we cannot obtain a multiprogrammed workload execution by simply running the programs together. To work around this limitation, we study multithreaded CUDA programs whose individual threads execute traces of the

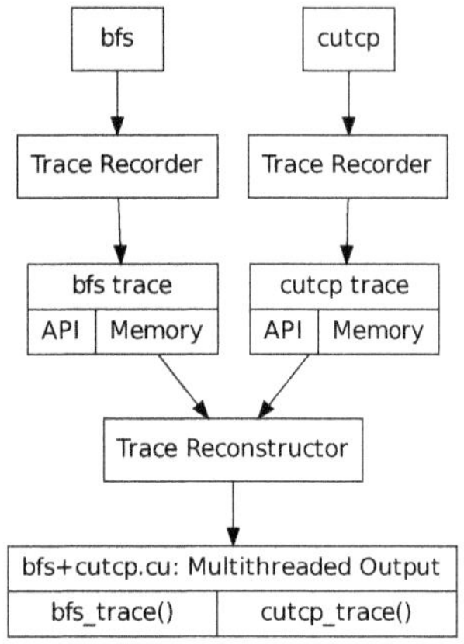

Figure 5. Construction example of a multithreaded concurrent CUDA workload from traces of individual programs bfs and cutcp.

original Parboil2 programs. Figure 5 illustrates the procedure we use to construct such a multithreaded "multiprogrammed" workload. We run each program in Parboil2 individually and obtain traces of its CUDA API calls using `ltrace`. Simultaneously, we obtain the memory and argument values passed to those API calls using a library interposer we have developed for the CUDA Runtime API. These traces are input to our trace reconstructor which outputs a C program that replays the traced API calls. To obtain an n-program workload, we reconstruct the n original programs as separate threads of a new n-threaded program. Each thread represents an individual program of the workload and consists of three distinct parts: (i) an initialization part to load the CUDA modules, functions and textures, (ii) a "replay" part to re-execute the program's kernel launches and memory transfers using values from the stored trace, and (iii) a cleanup part to release any resources obtained. Since the original programs do not use streams, our trace reconstructor also translates the original non-stream CUDA API calls (e.g. `cudaMemcpy`) to their functionally equivalent CUDA Streams API (e.g. `cudaMemcpyAsync`) or the corresponding NSS replacement to obtain concurrent execution. Thus, we essentially obtain a re-execution of the CUDA portions of the original programs as a concurrent workload.

6.2 Methodology

We evaluate workloads consisting of two programs. Each workload has four variants that are all generated from the same trace. The first variant single uses CUDA API calls and runs each trace of the workload one after the other, so that each trace executes alone with the full resources of the GPU at its disposal. The second variant cuda uses CUDA API calls and runs each trace concurrently with a separate CUDA stream for each trace, establishing the baseline for CUDA concurrency. The third variant nss replaces the use of CUDA Streams API by our Non-Serializing Streams implementation (Section 5) to work around the false serialization encountered by the cuda variant. Finally, the fourth variant elastic builds on nss and allows the resources assigned to a grid to be varied by the policies of Section 4.3. This variant also has kernel timeslicing enabled. All variants execute the same kernel source code to mitigate the performance issues of our software implementation as described in Section 4.1 and to provide a fair comparison.

There are a total of 55 two-program workloads, of which we evaluate 54. The bfs+lbm workload was not evaluated because it experiences CUDA launch timeouts. The implementation of bfs in the Parboil2 benchmarks uses a global atomic barrier which requires that all its thread blocks be resident concurrently. However, CUDA does not guarantee that all thread blocks will be resident concurrently. While the standalone execution of bfs is not affected, the execution with lbm causes the global atomic barrier to deadlock.

The workloads are run on a Fermi-equipped NVIDIA Tesla C2070 with CUDA driver 295.41 and CUDA runtime 4.2, the latest available at the time of writing. The host machine is a quad-core Intel Xeon W3550 CPU with 16GB of RAM and runs the 64-bit version of Debian Linux 6.0.

We report the performance of each workload using the *System Throughput (STP)* and the *Average Normalized Turnaround Time (ANTT)* metrics [6]. In our results, we substitute runtime for cycles in the equations for STP and ANTT. We record the runtime for each individual program as the time spent in the replay portion of the thread but subtract all time spent in performing trace I/O, which is an artifact of our workload construction technique. To account for interleaving effects, we use Tuck and Tullsen's methodology [20] – the replay part runs until all of the programs in the workload have been replayed at least 7 times. The last runtime of each program in the workload is discarded to avoid counting non-overlapping executions. For each program in the workload, the execution times of its replays are averaged and used in the equations for STP and ANTT as the multiprogram mode time. The single variant provides the single-program mode execution time for a program.

We use the log files generated by the NVIDIA Compute Command Line Profiler [10] to compute other metrics such as utilization and waiting time. Utilization is estimated from the start and end times of kernels because the profiler does not report starting and ending times of each individual thread block. We define waiting time as the time from API call (e.g. `cuLaunchKernel`) to actual execution as reported in the profiler log. This measures waiting time in the GPU's hardware queues and does not contain time spent in NSS queues (which is accounted for in the total program time). Since the CPU and GPU use different clocks, we use the `TIMESTAMPFACTOR` value stored in the log by the CUDA Profiler to correlate the two timestamps. We use the Linux User Space Tracing Toolkit [4] to record API calls on the CPU side.

In our initial experiments, CUDA memory allocation functions limit achievable STP to that of nss (Section 3.6). To mitigate this, we built a custom GPU memory allocator based on the CPU memory allocator `jemalloc` 3.2.0 [5] and use it for all the variants. Although our custom allocator uses the CUDA allocation functions internally, by allocating memory in bulk and recycling allocations, it calls them less frequently than the original program. Another possibility would be to ignore `cudaMalloc` and `cudaFree` from the second and first run onwards respectively. In such experiments, the average STP improves by about 5% and the ANTT improves by 10% over those reported in our evaluation. We also replace `cudaMemset` with a custom, non-serializing implementation in all variants.

6.3 Analyzing Runtime Behaviour of Kernels in Concurrent Workloads

Kernel execution dominates the runtime of workloads. In concurrent workloads, a kernel's execution time is affected by the presence of other concurrently executing kernels. To better understand the effect of other concurrent kernels on execution time, we classify each instance of a kernel into one of four *overlap categories* (Figure 6). For each kernel instance we identify its set of *co-runners*, i.e. other kernels whose instances overlap with it in time. Four overlap categories can then be defined as:

- EXCLUSIVE: If the set of co-runners is empty, the kernel instance is classified as EXCLUSIVE, i.e. it ran alone.
- SHARED/FULL: If the set of co-runners is not empty, but the kernel instance being classified started before all co-runners, we classify it as SHARED/FULL. In this case, the instance started

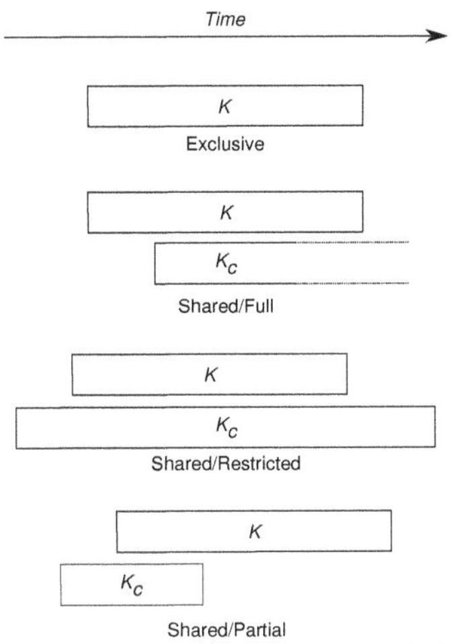

Figure 6. Overlap Categories: Categorization of a kernel instance K based on its overlap with other kernels.

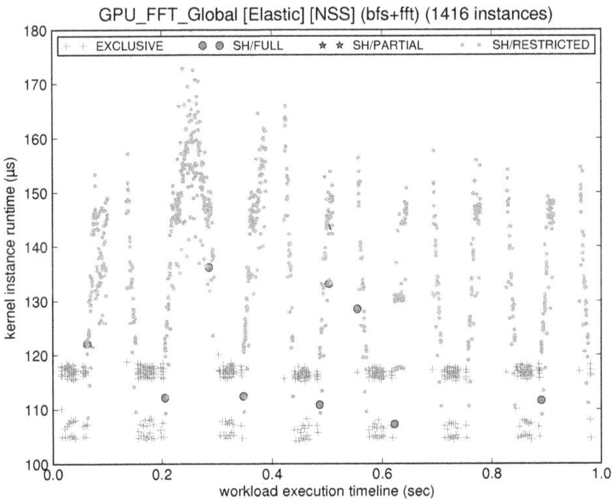

Figure 7. Runtimes of GPU_FFT_Global instances from one run of the bfs+fft workload under the MEDIAN elastic policy with each instance categorized into one of the four overlap categories.

alone, but will share some of its runtime with concurrently executing kernels.

- SHARED/RESTRICTED: If the kernel instance started after any of its co-runners then it will run with restricted resources. If none of the earlier co-runners terminated before this kernel, we classify it as SHARED/RESTRICTED.
- SHARED/PARTIAL: If, however, some earlier co-runner terminated before this kernel did, possibly making its resources available to this kernel, we classify the instance as SHARED/PARTIAL.

We expect the runtime for an EXCLUSIVE kernel instance in a concurrent workload to be similar to when the kernel runs alone. For all of the SHARED categories, however, we expect the runtime to vary depending on the degree of overlap with other kernels. Additionally, for SHARED/PARTIAL and SHARED/RESTRICTED, we expect the runtime to further vary based on the resources allocated to the kernel by the GPU.

To illustrate this categorization, Figure 7 portrays the execution of the GPU_FFT_Global kernel from the fft benchmark during its execution as part of the bfs+fft two-program workload. In the figure, the y-axis shows the runtime of each GPU_FFT_Global kernel instance, while the x-axis denotes the start time of the corresponding instance along the workload execution timeline. Using information from CUDA profiler log files, each instance has been categorized into one of the four overlap categories, indicated by different markers in the figure. Initially, during transfers of data by bfs, GPU_FFT_Global kernel instances run in EXCLUSIVE mode. When the kernels of bfs begin execution, the instances of GPU_FFT_Global transition to running mostly in SHARED/RESTRICTED mode because both the kernels of bfs take much longer to complete (see Table 3). A few SHARED/PARTIAL and SHARED/FULL instances can be observed during the transitions from one bfs kernel to another. The runtimes of each GPU_FFT_Global instance demonstrate the trends we have described in the previous paragraph.

Variant(+Policy)	STP		ANTT	
	geomean	best	geomean	worst
cuda	1.03	1.24	6.71	194.93
nss	1.18	1.81	3.05	69.07
elastic+mpmax	1.25	2.08	1.80	19.23
elastic+median	1.24	1.95	1.86	16.83
elastic+equal	1.18	1.83	1.91	30.70
elastic+queuemold	1.18	1.79	2.08	17.94

Table 4. Overall STP and ANTT results for two-program workloads. Note: ANTT is a lower-is-better metric.

Variant(+Policy)	Improvement		MTSpeedup
	STP	ANTT	
cuda	1.00	1.00	1.00
nss	1.15	2.20	1.20
elastic+mpmax	1.21	3.73	1.28
elastic+median	1.20	3.62	1.24
elastic+equal	1.14	3.51	1.15
elastic+queuemold	1.15	3.22	1.17

Table 5. Improvements in STP and ANTT and Multithreaded Speedup (MTSpeedup) for two-program workloads over the cuda variant. For MTSpeedup, a workload's execution time is taken as the maximum execution time of the programs in that workload.

6.4 Results

We evaluate all possible two-programmed workloads (except for bfs+lbm as noted) of the 11 programs from Parboil2 (Table 2) with the elastic policies MPMAX, MEDIAN, EQUAL and QUEUEMOLD.

6.4.1 Overall Results

Table 4 shows the average STP and ANTT across the workloads. All elastic policies improve throughput and turnaround time compared to cuda and nss. The elastic policies have the best STP values compared to all the variants. Similarly, their worst ANTT values are considerably lower than both cuda and nss, indicating that they have better turnaround times. Table 5 shows that compared to cuda, on average the elastic policy MPMAX improves system throughput by 1.21x and turnaround time by 3.73x. Viewing the workload as a multithreaded workload, on average the elastic policy MPMAX obtains a 1.28x speedup (Table 5) over cuda. The nss variant also improves on cuda's STP by 15%, and its ANTT is significantly better by 2.20x. On average, although the elastic polices EQUAL and QUEUEMOLD perform better than cuda, they do not do as well as our elastic policies, for reasons explained in the following sections.

In experiments with four-program workloads (excluding bfs), we find that the average STP value is 1.21 for the elastic policy MEDIAN. The average ANTT for four-program workloads is 6.61 for MPMAX, which is 8.9x better than that of cuda. The multithreaded speedup for four-program workloads also increases to

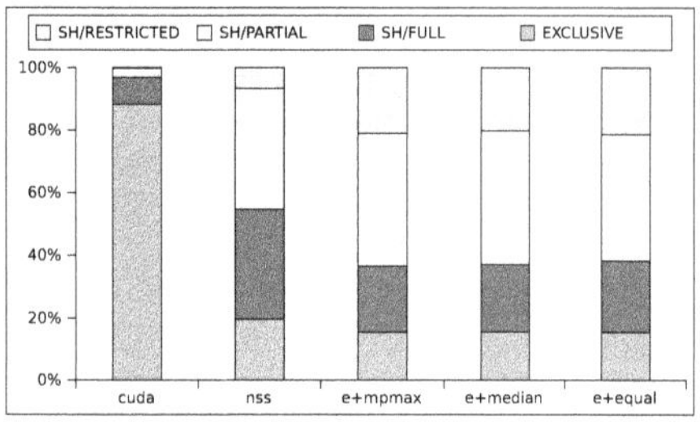

Figure 8. Fraction of execution time of kernels spent in different overlap categories per variant and per policy.

1.47 as compared to cuda. Due to lack of space, we do not elaborate on our results for four-program workloads in this paper.

6.4.2 Effect of Elastic Policies on Kernel Runtime Behaviour

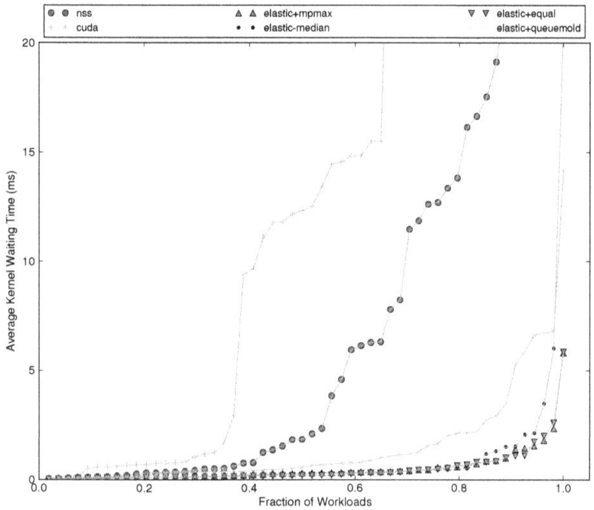

Figure 9. Average Kernel Waiting Time for two-program workloads. Lower is better.

Figure 8 shows the breakup of execution timing across kernel using the categories of Section 6.3. While the cuda kernels largely run in EXCLUSIVE mode about 90% of the time, the elastic policies tend to spread execution over the four categories.

Although EXCLUSIVE mode implies high performance on a per-kernel instance basis, in the case of cuda, this comes at the cost of waiting time. Figure 9 shows the distribution of average waiting time for a kernel for each workload under each variant. Kernel waiting times under cuda are higher than those under any of the other variants. The mean waiting times under cuda (130.5ms) and nss (11.21ms) are significantly higher than those for the elastic policies – MPMAX (0.53ms), MEDIAN (0.96ms), EQUAL (0.51ms) and QUEUEMOLD (1.57ms). The cuda kernels thus have to wait up to three orders of magnitude more time to execute compared to any of the elastic policies. This delay can largely be attributed to false serialization introduced by the CUDA implementation. The nss variant shows a 11.6x reduction in average kernel waiting time by eliminating false serialization, but still suffers a mean waiting time of 11.21ms due to lack of resources. The elastic policies reduce waiting times even further by preventing serialization due to lack of resources.

6.4.3 Effect of Elastic Policies on STP and ANTT

Figure 10 shows the distribution of STP values for all workloads. The elastic policy MPMAX has the highest STP values for nearly

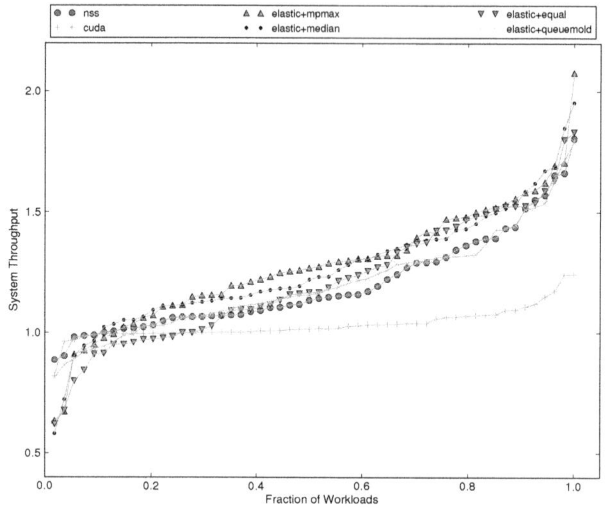

Figure 10. System throughput for each two-program workload, higher is better.

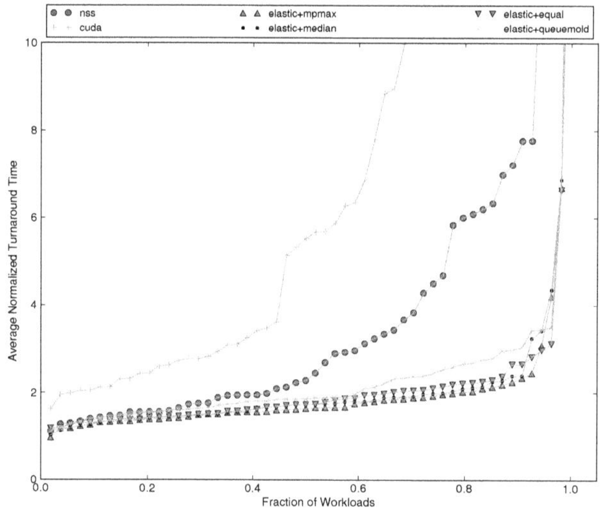

Figure 11. Average Normalized Turnaround Time for each two-program workload, lower is better.

40% of the workloads. For the remaining 60%, it behaves similarly to elastic policy MEDIAN. Both these policies offer significantly better performance than non-resource aware nss and cuda. The performance of the third elastic policy EQUAL is not quite as straightforward. For about 30% of the workloads, it performs poorly, even worse than nss. It shadows but is lower than MEDIAN and MPMAX for about 35% of the workloads. Then, for the remaining 35% of the workloads, its performance is like that of MPMAX. Finally, the elastic QUEUEMOLD exhibits performance that is only marginally better than nss.

The performance variation in STP exhibited by these policies is determined by their resource-limiting decisions. Both the MEDIAN and EQUAL elastic policies set aside a fixed amount of GPU resources regardless of the workload. By design, the MEDIAN policy does not take away too many resources from a running kernel in about half of the workloads. (This will be borne out later in the next section while examining utilization.) For the remainder, the reserved resources are not enough to improve concurrency, causing the drop in performance. The EQUAL elastic policy, takes away too many resources in the worst performing 30% of the workloads. At

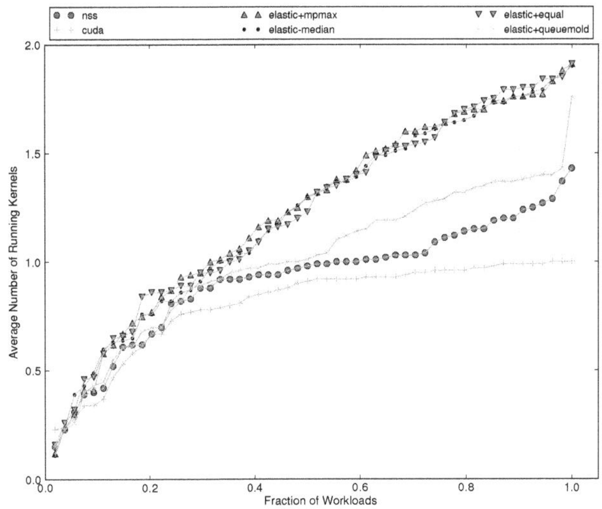

Figure 12. Average number of Running Kernels for each two-program workload.

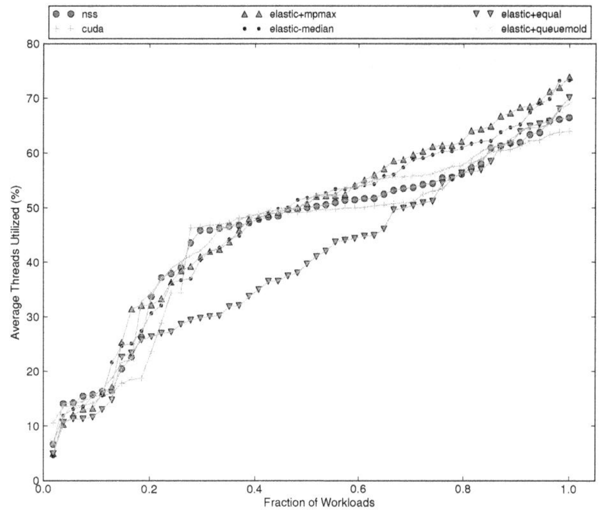

Figure 13. Average utilization of threads for each two-program workload.

the other end, the reserved half of resources is adequate to provide the rapid execution in the best performing 35% of the workloads. Our evaluation of the performance of QUEUEMOLD shows that it gets few opportunities to reduce the resources of individual kernels; given the wide disparity in kernel execution times (Table 3), the NSS queues rarely contain two or more kernels. Therefore, under QUEUEMOLD, most of the kernels execute with full resources like in nss. The elastic policy MPMAX differs from EQUAL and MEDIAN in that the GPU resources reserved vary *per program and per workload*. Thus, MPMAX avoids overcommitting resources and achieves a balance that delivers good concurrency and good performance. We conclude that for two program workloads, a policy that adapts to co-executing programs delivers the best performance.

Figure 11 shows the distribution of ANTT values across workloads. The elastic policies other than QUEUEMOLD display similar behaviour. The QUEUEMOLD shows lower ANTT values than nss but 60% of the values are clearly higher than the other elastic policies. Section 6.4.5 will show that the kernel timeslicing implemented for all elastic policies leads to reduction in ANTT compared to nss. For cuda the high degree of serialization leads to very high values of ANTT. This is corroborated by Figure 9 which shows that average waiting time for kernel execution is much higher for these variants as compared to the elastic variants, indicating a high degree of serialization.

6.4.4 Effects of Policies on Utilization

Figure 12 shows the average number of concurrent kernels for each variant and the different elastic policies. All elastic policies except for QUEUEMOLD behave similarly, with the average number of concurrent kernels ranging from 1.23 for MPMAX to 1.22 for EQUAL. This is 1.53x better than cuda, which averages 0.81 concurrently running kernels and also 1.34x better than the nss variant which averages 0.92 concurrently running kernels.

However, a higher average number of concurrent kernels alone does not necessarily translate into higher utilization of GPU resources. The average number of threads utilized (Figure 13) is high even for nss and cuda because these variants do not limit resource usage. However, the EQUAL policy, which enforces large fixed limits, shows much lower thread utilization. For performance, thread utilization as well as number of concurrent kernels should be high.

6.4.5 Effects of Time-slicing

In all our experiments so far, timeslicing of kernels has been enabled for long running grids from the following benchmarks (in order of grid running time): mm, lbm, mri-q and tpacf, i.e. 33 of the 54 workloads. To quantify the impact of timeslicing, we performed additional measurements with kernel timeslicing turned off. For the timeslicing-enabled subset of workloads, time-slicing of kernels with a timeslice value of approximately 1ms produces an overall improvement of 7.8% in geomean STP and improves geomean ANTT by 1.55x over elastic policies that do not have timeslicing enabled (evaluated using the MPMAX elastic policy). For all 54 workloads, time-slicing of kernels produces improvements of 3.3% geomean STP and 1.28x improvements in geomean ANTT over elastic policies that do not perform timeslicing.

Next we evaluate the effect of memory transfer slicing with a 4MB chunk size. Our experiments reveal no significant effect on geomean STP or geomean ANTT. The 4MB memory chunk size used means that only transfers from the following programs will be time-sliced (size of transfers in parentheses): mm (4.1M), tpacf (4.7M), bfs (7.6M, 45M), stencil (64M) and lbm (105M), i.e. 40 pairs. However, over 97% of dynamic transfers in our workloads are less than 1MB in size. Hence, memory transfers do not seem to be a significant serialization bottleneck in practice yet.

7. Related Work

To the best of our knowledge, our work is the first to examine an actual implementation of GPGPU concurrency and to identify and address issues of poor resource utilization and poor concurrency. We have also identified many serialization factors in the CUDA execution model, the CUDA API and hardware implementation that inhibit GPGPU concurrency and have proposed solutions for all of them. We now list works that have examined GPU concurrency and resource allocation for concurrent execution of GPGPU kernels.

Guevara et al. [8] present the first work on GPU concurrency that predates the NVIDIA Fermi GPU. The GPUs they use do not support hardware concurrency, so they resort to combining the source of two kernels into a single kernel at compile-time to execute them concurrently, a technique they call "thread interleaving". Their technique only merges kernels together and does not change resource allocation for each kernel.

Gregg et al. [7] introduce the *KernelMerge* runtime framework to investigate GPGPU concurrency for OpenCL programs. This framework uses a technique similar to thread interleaving to merge kernels into a single kernel, but does so at runtime. However, each thread block of this merged kernel can choose to execute thread blocks of any of the merged kernels under the control of a scheduler. Thus, different scheduling algorithms can achieve different partitioning of resources at the thread block level.

G. Wang et al. [21] propose the use of *kernel fusion* to achieve power efficiency on the GPU. Again, they use a technique similar to thread interleaving to merge kernels. All of these works demonstrate significant improvements in throughput and power efficiency through the use of GPU concurrency. Also, their merging technique does not require hardware support for concurrency. However, merging kernels into one large kernel leads to wastage of resources because GPU resources cannot be reclaimed until both component kernels finish. In our work, we have used hardware support available on the NVIDIA Fermi to achieve concurrency.

L. Wang et al. [22] propose *context funneling* to execute kernels from different GPU contexts concurrently. Their technique allows kernels from different operating system threads (which before CUDA 4 used different contexts) or kernels from different programs to execute concurrently.

Adriaens et al. [1] propose that GPU streaming multiprocessors be *spatially partitioned* for GPU concurrency. They partition the set of streaming multiprocessors (SMs) among concurrently executing programs using different SM partitioning heuristics and evaluate their policies using the GPGPU-Sim [2] simulator. In this paper, we base our EQUAL policy on their Even SM spatial partitioning heuristic which distributes SMs evenly among concurrent applications. We have evaluated EQUAL in this paper and shown that it significantly underutilizes resources compared to our policies.

The work closest to our own is the work by Ravi et al. [14] which uses GPU concurrency to improve GPU throughput for applications in the cloud. A key feature of their work is the ability to change the resources assigned to a kernel by varying grid and thread block dimensions, a technique they call *molding*. However, they only claim to support molding for kernels which are already written to run with any number of threads. As we have shown, there are only 4 such kernels among the 18 in the Parboil2 benchmark suite. Our work proposes a transformation (Section 4.1) to convert any kernel to an elastic kernel. We base our QUEUEMOLD policy on their GetAffinityByMolding resource allocation algorithm and evaluate it in our paper. We find that given the wide disparity in execution times of GPU kernels (Table 3), this policy rarely finds the opportunity to limit resources of kernels and does not perform as well as our policies.

8. Conclusion

In this paper, we looked at concurrent execution of GPGPU workloads. We showed that the current grid programming model of the GPU leads to wastage that can be reduced by concurrent execution of GPGPU workloads. However, we found that the current implementation of concurrency on the GPU suffers from a wide variety of serialization issues that prevent concurrent execution of GPGPU workloads. To the best of our knowledge, this is the first work that raises these issues. Prominent among these issues are serialization due to lack of resources, and serialization due to exclusive execution of long-running kernels and memory transfers. To tackle serialization due to lack of resources, we proposed *elastic kernels*, a mechanism that allows fine grain control over the amount of resources allocated to a GPU kernel. We used this ability to build elastic kernel-aware concurrency policies that significantly improve concurrency for GPGPU workloads. To tackle serialization due to long-running kernels, we also presented a simple and effective technique to timeslice kernel execution using elastic kernels. We have also identified several other implementation issues in the CUDA hardware and API that inhibit GPGPU concurrency, and have suggested solutions for all of them.

Our proposals improve average system throughput (STP) by 1.21x and average normalized turnaround time (ANTT) by 3.73x for two-program workloads compared to CUDA on real hardware. They also increase the number of concurrent kernels by 1.53x and reduce waiting times for kernels by three orders of magnitude. Our policies also achieve higher throughput, lower turnaround times and better resource utilization when compared to a static partitioning scheme and a runtime resource allocation scheme. Finally, our proposal for time-slicing of kernels improves STP by 7.8% and ANTT by 1.55x for programs with long running kernels.

Acknowledgments

We thank Sanjiv Satoor and Dibyapran Sanyal of NVIDIA for assistance with the CUDA Profiler. We thank our anonymous reviewers and our shepherd, Rodric Rabbah, for their feedback which has significantly improved this work. We acknowledge partial funding from Microsoft Corporation towards this work.

References

[1] J. Adriaens et al. The case for GPGPU spatial multitasking. In *HPCA*, 2012.

[2] A. Bakhoda et al. Analyzing CUDA Workloads Using a Detailed GPU Simulator. In *ISPASS*, 2009.

[3] S. Che et al. Rodinia: A benchmark suite for heterogeneous computing. In *IISWC*, 2009.

[4] M. Desnoyers et al. LTTng-UST User Space Tracer.

[5] J. Evans. A Scalable Concurrent malloc(3) Implementation for FreeBSD. In *BSDcan*, 2006.

[6] S. Eyerman and L. Eeckhout. System-level Performance Metrics for Multiprogram Workloads. *IEEE Micro*, 28(3), 2008.

[7] C. Gregg et al. Fine-grained resource sharing for concurrent GPGPU kernels. In *HotPar*, 2012.

[8] M. Guevara et al. Enabling task parallelism in the CUDA scheduler. In *Workshop on Programming Models for Emerging Architectures (PMEA)*, 2009.

[9] E. Lindholm et al. NVIDIA Tesla: A unified graphics and computing architecture. *IEEE Micro*, 28(2):39–55, 2008.

[10] NVIDIA. Compute Command Line Profiler: User Guide.

[11] NVIDIA. CUDA Occupancy Calculator.

[12] NVIDIA. NVIDIA CUDA C Programming Guide (version 4.2).

[13] NVIDIA. NVIDIA's Next Generation CUDA Compute Architecture: Kepler GK110.

[14] V. T. Ravi et al. Supporting GPU sharing in cloud environments with a transparent runtime consolidation framework. In *HPDC*, 2011.

[15] S. Rennich. CUDA C/C++ Streams and Concurrency.

[16] J. Shirako et al. Chunking parallel loops in the presence of synchronization. In *ICS*, 2009.

[17] J. A. Stratton et al. Efficient compilation of fine-grained SPMD-threaded programs for multicore CPUs. In *CGO*, 2010.

[18] J. A. Stratton, S. S. Stone, and W. mei W. Hwu. MCUDA: An efficient implementation of CUDA kernels for multi-core CPUs. In *LCPC*, 2008.

[19] TOP500.org. The Top 500.

[20] N. Tuck and D. M. Tullsen. Initial Observations of the Simultaneous Multithreading Pentium 4 Processor. In *PACT*, 2003.

[21] G. Wang, Y. Lin, and W. Yi. Kernel fusion: An effective method for better power efficiency on multithreaded GPU. In *Proceedings of the 2010 IEEE/ACM Int'l Conference on Green Computing and Communications & Int'l Conference on Cyber, Physical and Social Computing*, GREENCOM-CPSCOM '10, 2010.

[22] L. Wang, M. Huang, and T. El-Ghazawi. Exploiting concurrent kernel execution on graphic processing units. In *HPCS*, 2011.

Practical Automatic Loop Specialization

Taewook Oh Hanjun Kim Nick P. Johnson Jae W. Lee† David I. August

Princeton University, Princeton, NJ
{twoh, hanjunk, npjohnso, august}@princeton.edu

†Sungkyunkwan University, Suwon, Korea
jaewlee@skku.edu

Abstract

Program specialization optimizes a program with respect to program invariants, including known, fixed inputs. These invariants can be used to enable optimizations that are otherwise unsound. In many applications, a program input induces predictable patterns of values across loop iterations, yet existing specializers cannot fully capitalize on this opportunity. To address this limitation, we present Invariant-induced Pattern based Loop Specialization (IPLS), the first fully-automatic specialization technique designed for everyday use on real applications. Using dynamic information-flow tracking, IPLS profiles the values of instructions that depend solely on invariants and recognizes repeating patterns across multiple iterations of hot loops. IPLS then specializes these loops, using those patterns to predict values across a large window of loop iterations. This enables aggressive optimization of the loop; conceptually, this optimization reconstructs recurring patterns induced by the input as concrete loops in the specialized binary. IPLS specializes real-world programs that prior techniques fail to specialize without requiring hints from the user. Experiments demonstrate a geomean speedup of 14.1% with a maximum speedup of 138% over the original codes when evaluated on three script interpreters and eleven scripts each.

Categories and Subject Descriptors D.3.4 [*Programming Languages*]: Processors—Code generation, Compilers, Optimization

General Terms Design, Languages, Performance

Keywords Loop specialization, Partial evaluation, Profile based optimization, Program specialization

1. Introduction

Conventional compilers apply optimizations with guarantees of correctness for all valid program inputs [1]. Even if the program input is known at compile-time, the compiler cannot take full advantage of optimization opportunities specific to the program input. Program specialization exploits these opportunities by optimizing a program with respect to a *static input* that is fixed across all invocations of the program. *Static instructions*—those which depend solely on static input or program invariants—always produce the same values across multiple program executions. A compiler generates a specialized program by replacing static instructions with the precomputed values and by residualizing *dynamic instructions*—those which may depend on some non-static inputs. By evaluating static instructions at compile-time, a specialized program generally runs faster than the program generated by the input-unaware compiler.

In many cases, values computed by the static instructions induce repeating patterns across loop iterations. Script interpreters exemplify this property: most script interpreters include an instruction that maintains the program counter of the script. Using this instruction, the interpreter main loop determines the next instruction in the script to dispatch. Since most scripts have loops, a value trace of the program counter exhibits repeating patterns. When these patterns are generated by static instructions, the pattern can be reliably predicted across program runs, since no aspect of the dynamic input will affect those patterns. The interpreter's main loop can be specialized for this pattern by first unrolling the main loop by the length of the pattern and then optimizing each unrolled iteration with respect to the corresponding value.

Many program specializers fail to automatically generate a specialized program that reflects the repetition inherent in the known input. Compile-time analysis to discriminate static and dynamic instructions is too imprecise, thus limiting the specializer's ability to search for repeating patterns among static instructions and in turn limiting application speedup. Existing specializers resort to user annotations to identify those instructions which depend solely on known input [2, 8, 12, 18].

Some specializers [3, 25] do not need user annotations. Instead, they use dynamic information to identify constant or hot values and perform specialization at runtime. However, the cost of dynamic code generation is high. Shankar et al. create multiple specialized instances of the loop for frequently-observed values and apply partial unrolling [25]. This approach introduces dispatch conditions to the hot loop which grow with the number of hot values. To conquer large specialized regions, the number of dispatch conditions grows so large as to limit application speedup.

To overcome these problems, this paper presents Invariant-induced Pattern based Loop Specialization (IPLS). IPLS is the **first fully-automatic program specialization** technique that is applicable to **several complex and widely-deployed script interpreters**. By specializing a program at the granularity of patterns, IPLS enables aggressive optimization across a large window of loop iterations. The choice of patterns over hot values reduces the dispatch overhead.

IPLS is composed of three stages: profiling, pattern detection, and code generation. IPLS profiler identifies static instructions in the program using dynamic information flow tracking and traces the values computed by static instructions. IPLS pattern detector looks for repeating patterns across different iterations in the value trace, which are characteristics of the static instructions. IPLS code generator specializes the program with respect to the detected pattern by unrolling the loop by the length of the pattern and special-

ASPLOS'13, March 16–20, 2013, Houston, Texas, USA.

izing each unrolled iteration to the corresponding value from the pattern.

The performance of IPLS is evaluated using the following set of open-source C programs: the Lua script interpreter [17], the Perl script interpreter [22], and the Python script interpreter [23]. These programs are non-trivial and widely deployed. IPLS automatically specializes these applications and achieves a geomean speedup of 14.1% while increasing program size only by 7.0%. To the best of our knowledge, IPLS is the first program specialization technique that profitably specializes all of these script interpreters.

The primary contributions of this work are:

- The first fully-automatic technique powerful and robust enough to specialize complex applications such as the Perl, Python and Lua interpreters;
- Profiling and analysis to identify fixed input-driven patterns across loop iterations; and,
- Implementation and evaluation on real-world applications.

2. Motivation

Compilers conservatively optimize programs for all valid inputs to guarantee correctness, even though some inputs are effectively invariant. To achieve greater optimization, program specialization allows a compiler to optimize a target program against a specific static input. Here, the *target program* is the program for a specializer to optimize, and *static inputs* are the inputs that are unchanged across program invocations. *Dynamic inputs* are all other inputs; the specializer assumes that dynamic inputs may change across invocations.

2.1 Example: Script Interpretation

Script interpretation is a key application domain for program specialization [14]. A script interpreter executes the same script multiple times with different inputs. Since the script is an input to the interpreter, and it is often reused without a change, the interpreter and the script can be considered as a target program and a static input. The inputs to the script are dynamic inputs. If the script is repeatedly executed, program specialization can optimize the interpreter against the script creating an interpreter which performs better on that script. This accelerates future runs of the script.

Figure 1 illustrates how a script interpreter is specialized for a script. The interpreter has a main loop that reads, parses and executes instructions such as ADD and FOR. The script has a loop that accumulates values from zero to the dynamic input value. Due to the loop in the script, the main loop of the interpreter iterates over the same sequence of values (i.e. instructions from the script) multiple times. As shown in Figure 1(b), the same code blocks are executed repeatedly to create an input-driven loop.

A program specializer can specialize the interpreter for the input-driven loop of the repeated operations. As Figure 1(c) illustrates, the specializer detects the repeated pattern induced by the static input, and creates a customized loop optimized for the repeating values in OPC (i.e. FOR and ADD). By stitching several iterations into a sequence, many bookkeeping instructions become unnecessary and can be removed by later optimization. The final specialized interpreter is shown in Figure 1(d), and the new specialized program reflects the loop structure within the script.

2.2 Benefits of Pattern based Loop Specialization

Existing fully-automatic program specializers fail to effectively specialize programs with input-driven loops. For example, the specializer proposed by Bala et al. [3] creates only one specialized loop for each hot loop of the program and does not optimize the loop across iteration boundaries. If their specializer is used for the

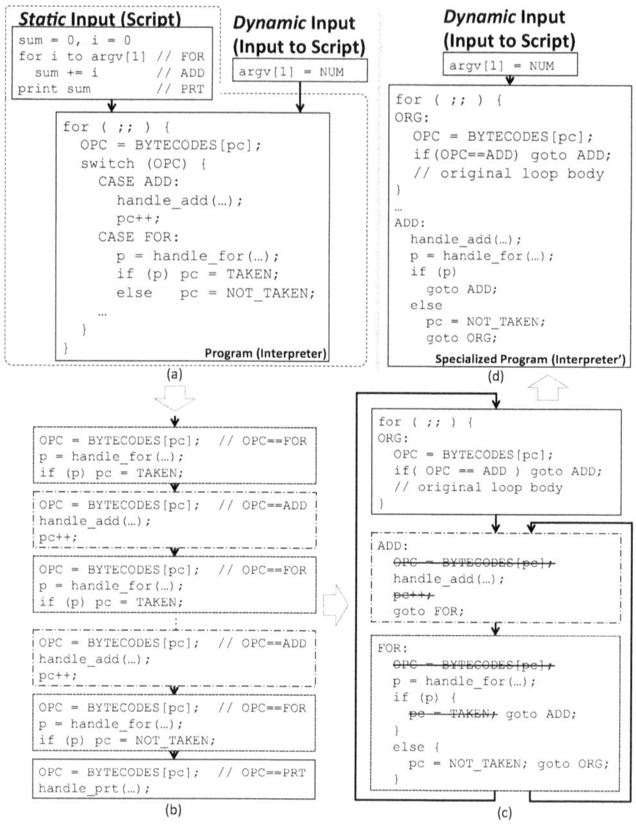

Figure 1. A static input script induces a repeating pattern in variable OPC. The interpreter can be specialized with respect to the input script by exploiting this repetition: (a) program, static and dynamic inputs, (b) trace of recurring values across loop iterations, (c) loop iterations stitched into a specialized loop, (d) final specialized code.

example program in Figure 1, it would create a specialized loop for the case of either OPC==ADD or OPC==FOR, but not both.

Shankar et al. overcome this limitation by creating a specialized loop for each of the hot values observed in the original loop [25]. When applied to the program in Figure 1, they create two specialized loops: for both OPC==ADD and OPC==FOR. However, this approach suffers from dispatching overhead proportional to the length of the input-driven loop. Although the input-driven loop in the script in Figure 1(c) has a length of only two (with ADD and FOR), it can be much longer in general. Inserting dispatch instructions for each of the repeating values can incur significant control-flow overhead. A specializer may impose an upper bound on the maximum number of the input-driven loop to limit the control-flow overhead, but only at the cost of lost specialization opportunities. Unlike these approaches, IPLS streamlines the execution of multiple iterations in the original loop associated with a pattern by maintaining one dispatch condition for each specialized pattern.

Another issue with the previous approaches is frequent exits from specialized codes. Figure 2 shows a script with skewed execution paths. The path with {FOR, IF, SUB} will be taken more frequently than that with {FOR, IF, ADD}. A hot-value based specializer may classify FOR, IF, and SUB as hot, but not ADD. Since it does not generate a specialized loop for OPC==ADD, it jumps back to the original dispatch routine when the next OPC value is ADD. In the next iteration it will jump back to the special-

```
sum = 0, i = 0
for i to argv[1]         // FOR
  if rand() % 4 == 1     // IF
    sum += i             // ADD
  else
    sum -= i             // SUB
print sum                // PRT
```

Figure 2. An input script featuring biased control flow.

ized loop for `OPC==FOR`. As a result, the specializer introduces unnecessary back-and-forth transfers of program control between the specialized loop and the original loop. IPLS avoids this problem by capturing the pattern of {`FOR`, `IF`, `ADD|SUB`} using a loop detection algorithm and generating specialized codes with respect to this pattern. Specializing less-frequently-taken paths in an input-driven loop may increase the code size, but our evaluation shows that increase in binary size is moderate.

3. Overview of IPLS

This section describes IPLS using a simple script interpreter and an input script as an example. Figure 3(c) shows the control flow graph (CFG) representation of the main loop of the interpreter for a simple script language and Figure 3(b) is an input script to that interpreter. The input script is transformed into a sequence of opcodes: `FOR`, `ADD`, and `PRT`. The interpreter's main loop fetches an opcode, branches to the corresponding opcode handler, and repeats. If the input script executes many times, specializing the interpreter with respect to the input script will be highly beneficial.

In Figure 3(c), basic blocks `A`, `B`, `C`, `D`, `ADD`, `MUL`, `FOR` and `PRT` compose the main loop while `PRE` is a preheader block. Individual instructions of the basic blocks are expressed in a medium-level compiler intermediate representation. In the loop header block `A`, `OP` loads the next opcode from address `ADDR`. The next opcode is fetched into `OP` and the interpreter branches to the basic block corresponding to the opcode: if the value of `OP` is `FOR`, the interpreter jumps to the basic block `FOR`, and so on. The value of `ADDR` comes either from the loop preheader `PRE` when the loop is invoked, or from basic block `D` through the loop backedge.

The workflow of IPLS consists of three stages as depicted in Figure 3(a): profiling, pattern detection and code generation. The rest of this section will provide a high-level overview of these three stages using the example interpreter and script. Figures 3(d) through (f) show the output of each stage while IPLS specializes the interpreter.

3.1 Profiling

The first stage of IPLS is profiling. The profiler instruments the target program and runs the instrumented program with the static input. The values of the static input propagate along the data flow of the program to identify some instructions as static. A static instruction always produces the same value since it depends only on program invariants including the static input, hence can be precomputed at compile-time.

The goal of the profiling stage is to identify static instructions and the values they compute, thus enabling aggressive constant propagation and control flow optimization in the later stages. Towards this goal the profiled executable collects the following information:

- Values computed by the static instructions for each iteration of the loop;
- Address-value pairs for static load instructions (a load instruction is static if the result of the load is computed from a static instruction);
- A set of distinct control-flow paths through each iteration of the loop;
- The number of instructions affected by each static instruction in an iteration; and
- Addresses of all basic blocks within the loop and all functions within the program.

To find static instructions within the program precisely without user annotations and/or heroic static analysis, IPLS employs Dynamic Information Flow Tracking (DIFT) [26]. The only information required from the user is *which* program inputs IPLS may assume fixed across different executions. For example, a user simply directs a script is a fixed input to the interpreter, but inputs to the script are not. This information is propagated along the data flow of the program by instrumented instructions, hence it is possible to decide whether each instruction depends only on static input. Implementation details will be discussed in Section 4.

Figure 3(d) depicts the results of profiling for the example program in Figure 3(c). Since `ADDR` points to an opcode derived from the static input script throughout execution, both `ADDR` and `OP` are classified as static. Therefore, the values of `ADDR` and `OP` are traced every iteration. The basic blocks executed in each iteration are also traced as represented by black boxes in Figure 3(d). The values of `ADDR` and `OP` constitute an address-value pair of the static load instruction for each iteration. For example, during the first iteration, the address-value pair is `<P, ADD>` since the value of `ADDR` equals to `P` and the value of `OP` to `ADD`.

3.2 Pattern Detection

The pattern detection stage interprets profiling results to identify repeating patterns of values computed by static instructions. Such a repeating pattern suggests the existence of an input-driven loop. One can customize this input-driven loop via constant propagation and control flow optimization to generate a specialized loop that efficiently executes those iterations covered by the pattern.

Since there are multiple static instructions within the loop, the patterns they generate may suggest multiple ways to specialize the loop. In Figure 3(d), two static instructions generate two patterns (`ADDR = [P, P+1]` and `OP = [FOR, ADD]`). These two patterns are of the same length, and produce the same control flow pattern, though this is generally not the case. The specializer frequently must select among several specialization strategies using heuristics described in Section 5.

The pattern detector's choice of pattern for specialization determines the *dispatching instruction*, i.e. the static instruction whose value will control the path taken during each iteration. While executing the loop, if the dispatching instruction computes the value at the beginning of the pattern, specialized code blocks are dispatched. In the example, `ADDR =` ϕ`(PRE, D)` is the dispatching instruction and the pattern is `ADDR = [P, P+1]`. The dispatch condition compares `ADDR` to `P`, and if equal, dispatches into specialized code.

A detected pattern can be represented as a graph called *Meta-Level Loop*. Each value in the pattern, which is produced by the dispatching instruction, corresponds to a node in the graph. The graph has an edge if the values corresponding to the nodes are generated from the adjacent iterations of the loop. By representing the pattern as a graph, it is possible to capture more complex patterns than a repeating sequence of values.

In addition, the pattern detection stage also outputs information about heap constants by analyzing the address-value pairs of static

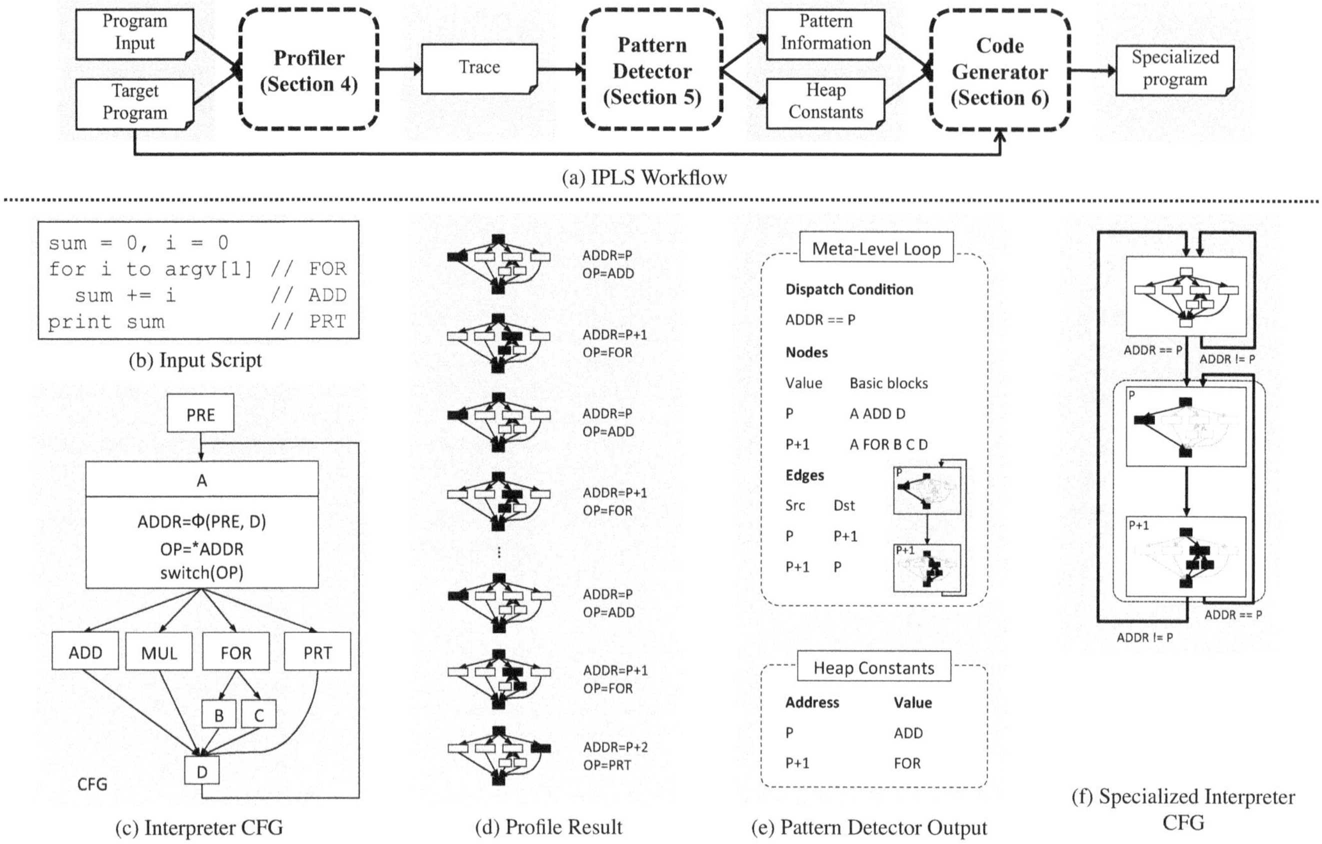

Figure 3. IPLS Specialization: (a) the high-level structure of IPLS, (b) a fixed, static input script, (c) CFG of a script interpreter, (d) result of profiling, including a pattern of static values and their associated iteration control traces, (e) result of pattern detection, and (f) the loop produced by code generation.

load instructions taken in the profiling stage. IPLS assumes that, if the value v corresponding to the address a is identical across the all address-value pairs and the pair of $\langle a, v \rangle$ appeared more than twice, address a holds a constant value v. The code generator specializes a program using this information about heap constants. For example, the static load instruction `OP=*ADDR` in Figure 3(d) always loads `ADD` at address `P` and `FOR` at address `P+1`, so the two heap constants are passed to the code generator.

Figure 3(e) shows the output of the pattern detection stage. A meta-level loop describes the pattern induced by the instruction `ADDR = Φ(PRE, D)`, with two nodes `P, P+1` and two edges `(P, P+1), (P+1, P)`. The code specialized with respect to this meta-level loop will be dispatched if the value of `ADDR` becomes `P`. Each node contains a set of basic blocks which are invoked while tracing the node. If different iterations generating the same value invoke different basic blocks, basic block information stored in the meta-level loop takes a union of them. For example, in Figure 3(d), two iterations generating value `P+1` invoke basic blocks {`A, FOR, B, D`}, while the other invokes {`A, FOR, C, D`}. Therefore, a union of those two is reported as basic blocks corresponding to the value `P+1` in the meta-level loop. The code generator uses this basic block information when creating code blocks specialized for the corresponding value.

3.3 Code Generation

The code generation stage creates specialized codes for each meta-level loop identified in the pattern detection stage. It duplicates the original loop for each node in the meta-level loop and specializes the duplicated loop with respect to the value corresponding to the meta-level node. The code generator also inserts instructions to dispatch the specialized codes.

IPLS specializes a loop by first creating a special version for each iteration (meta-level node). When IPLS duplicates and specializes a loop iteration, it duplicates only those basic blocks listed in the meta-level node. This not only serves to minimize code growth caused by specialization, but also simplifies the control flow of the specialized loop. These simplifications enable more instruction level parallelism in a meta-level node.

The code generator then inserts branch instructions to link multiple specialized iterations into a specialized meta-level loop. In the example, it adds branches from the end of the specialized loop for `ADDR == P` to the head of the specialized loop for `ADDR == P+1` and vice versa, reflecting the two meta-level loop edges `(P, P+1)` and `(P+1, P)`.

These branches are *unconditional* if both of the following conditions are met. First, the next iteration must execute. Second, the value computed by the dispatching instruction of this meta-level loop is equal to the value that the next meta-level loop node is specialized for. For example, a branch from the specialized loop for node `P` to node `P+1` will be an unconditional jump, if it is guaranteed at the end of the specialized loop for node `P` that the loop executes at least one more iteration and that the value of `ADDR` will be `P+1` at the following iteration.

If these conditions cannot be guaranteed at specialization time, the branch must be *conditional*. For example, at the end of the specialized loop for node P+1, if the value of ADDR for the next instruction is only known at runtime, a conditional branch instruction whose predicate value is ADDR == P will be inserted to reflect the meta-level loop backedge from node P+1 to node P.

The code generator also exploits heap constants to perform specialization across load instructions. For example, when specializing the duplicated loop with respect to the value P of ADDR in Figure 3, no further specialization is possible without the information that address ADDR holds a heap constant value ADD. Since information about heap constants is acquired by profiling, IPLS inserts instructions to verify the assumed constant value against actually loaded values into the specialized code. This information breaks dependences between the load instruction and its users, hence exposing additional instruction-level parallelism.

Together with address information about basic blocks and functions provided by the profiler, information about heap constants is used to specialize indirect branches and indirect function calls. If a branch/function call target address is derived solely from a heap constant and the address matches the starting address of a basic block or function in the program, an indirect branch/function call can be replaced by a direct branch/function call to the target address. This replaced branch/function call is guarded by a comparison instruction to confirm the heap constant value. This transformation potentially reduces pipeline stalls by simplifying the program's control flow.

Figure 3(f) depicts the structure of the final optimized code after specialization guided by the meta-level CFG and heap constants in Figure 3(e). The main loop of the original interpreter (top white box) dispatches the specialized meta-level loop when the value of ADDR is equal to P. Specialized codes (round dotted box) are created by duplicating the original main loop twice for each meta-level loop node and specializing each of them using information about meta-level CFG and heap constants. Only necessary basic blocks (colored black) are duplicated during specialization. Under the assumption that the value of ADDR of next iteration is guaranteed to be P+1 at the end of the specialized loop for node P, the branch from node P to P+1 is unconditional. However, branch from node P+1 to P is conditional because the value of the ADDR for the next iteration cannot be determined statically at the end of the specialized loop for node P+1.

4. Profiling

The profiling stage of IPLS collects information to enable the compiler to specialize the program with respect to a given static input. As described in Section 3.1, the IPLS profiler performs a variation of value profiling, load profiling, and path profiling.

Two optimizations distinguish the IPLS profilers from related techniques: (i) the IPLS profiler restricts its observations to static instructions, and (ii) it restricts the scope of value profiling to operations within the header of the target loop. These restrictions limit profiling results to safe specialization assumptions, yet provide information strong enough to support aggressive program specialization. The insight that allows these optimizations is that a specializer may only transform according to *static* program values, and that the dispatch condition (Section 5) must be computable at the start of *every iteration*.

Before profiling, the user marks some portion of the program input as static, such as the input script of an interpreter. We say an instruction is *static* if all of its operands (including values read from memory) are static values. If an instruction is static, then the sequence of values which that instruction generates during program execution is invariant across program executions. This property makes static instructions good candidates for program specialization. The IPLS profiler only collects information pertaining to *static* inputs. By employing DIFT, IPLS collects information related only to the *static* input, obviating the need for heroic static analysis.

```
FILE* fp = fopen(argv[1], 'r');
metadata_fp = metadata_argv[1];
...
fread(buf, 1, size, fp);
metadata_fread = metadata_size & metadata_fp;
memset(metadata_buf, metadata_fread, size*1);
...
```

(a) Instrumented code that reads input

```
OP = *ADDR;
metadata_op = *(metadata_addr);
if (metadata_op == 1)
  printLoadTrace(...);
switch (OP) {
  ...
}
```

(b) Instrumented code that uses input

Figure 4. Instrumentation added by the IPLS profiler to achieve dynamic information-flow tracking.

DIFT tags each intermediate value in the program as either *static* or *dynamic*. Profiling instrumentation propagates these tags along the original data flow of the program. To improve DIFT precision, the profiler tracks information flows along register or memory data dependences, but *optimistically* ignores information flows which potentially occur along control dependences. As a consequence, our implementation may report an instruction as static when a conservative implementation would report that values as dynamic (whether or not it actually is dynamic). This improved precision is desirable, since it allows IPLS to perform value profiling on instructions which are *likely* to be static, thus increasing applicability in difficult benchmarks. The trade-off is the risk that specialization will attempt to predict a dynamic value, with no guarantee that the its sequences of values are invariant across program executions.

Incorrectly tagged values have no effect on overall correctness of the specialization procedure, and in practice have minimal effect on IPLS' ability to correctly predict value sequences. There are a few reasons for this. First, IPLS code generation inserts pattern prediction routines at the position of the original hot loop. By virtue of this position, IPLS pattern prediction only executes in cases where the control precondition of the original hot loop is satisfied. This control precondition implies many of the control preconditions of dynamic values in the program, making them effectively static with respect to that position in the program. In the worst case, code generation guarantees safety by falling through to the general loop when all dispatch conditions fail. Mispredictions prevent the general loop from dispatching into the specialized loop, resulting in a lost optimization opportunity (Section 6). Experimental results indicate that sequence prediction is robust and that sequence misprediction has negligible effect on the performance of specialized applications (Section 7).

To support the pattern detector (Section 5), the IPLS profiler performs value profiling on candidate dispatch conditions. The value profiler only observes static instructions *in the loop header*. The dispatch condition must be computable during every iteration of the loop, and all static operations within the loop header satisfy this constraint. This restriction greatly reduces the amount of data

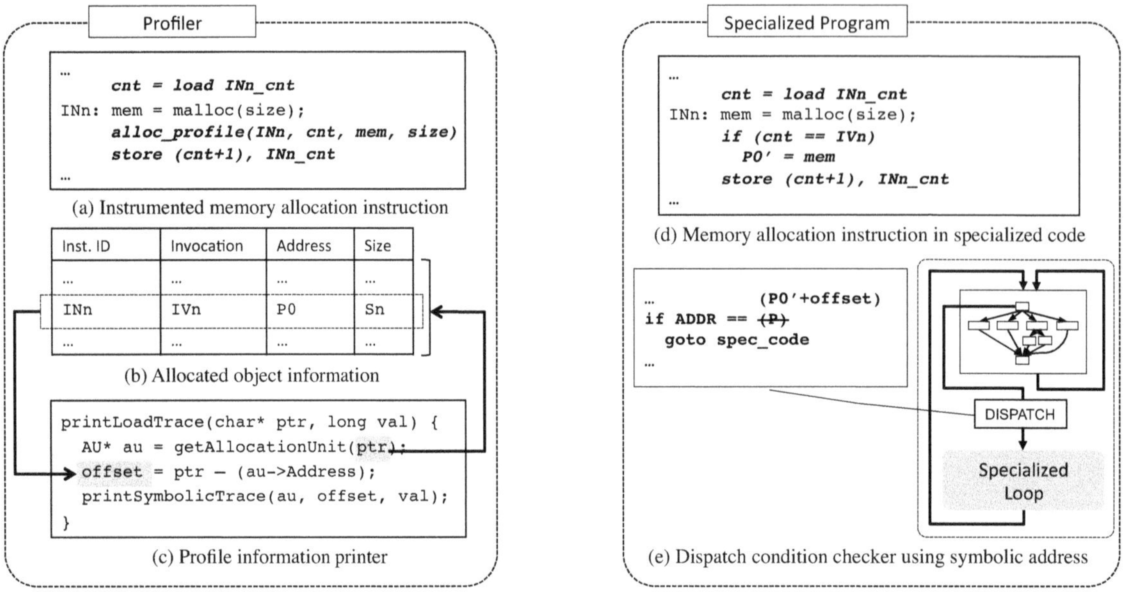

Figure 5. IPLS uses object-relative memory profiling to generate repeatable, symbolic names for relocatable addresses. Variable *INn_cnt* maintains the invocation count of the instruction *INn*.

collected, and in turn reduces the processing overhead of the pattern detector. As a corollary, later analysis of profiling results is insensitive to limited profile coverage, since it ignores operations which do not execute at least once per loop iteration. Note, however, that load profiling is still performed on all static loads within the loop, not only those from the header.

Figure 4 shows the instrumentation to track dynamic information flow. Figure 4(a) is the part of the program which reads the input file specified by the first command line argument. Figure 4(b) is the part which uses the input. `ADDR` in Figure 4(b) points to each element of `buf` in Figure 4(a) through its execution, hence `OP` loads the value read from the input file. Bold and italicized lines are the instructions automatically instrumented by the compiler for tracing metadata and printing profile information.

The code snippet shows that metadata of `argv[1]` is propagated to the metadata of `OP`, through the instrumented instructions. The profiler reports the information related to `OP` only if its metadata set to `1` meaning the value is *static*, which is true only when the metadata of `argv[1]` is `1`. Metadata of command line inputs, which indicates whether the input is static or not, is given by the user.

Since instrumentation is added at an intermediate representation level, instrumentation is not possible of functions whose source code is not available at specialization time. For this reason, tracing the flow of metadata across standard library calls are handled exceptionally via custom information flow tracking instructions. For example, Figure 4(a) shows custom tracking instructions for calls to `fopen` and `fread`.

Another issue of the IPLS profiler is profiling of pointer values. Recall the example in Figure 3 that the dispatch condition of the specialized code was `ADDR == P`. However, the value `P` is a memory address, and there is no guarantee that the absolute pointer value `P` is consistent across across multiple executions of the specialized program. To address this problem, IPLS performs a variation of object-relative memory profiling [27] to derive consistent symbolic names for such pointers.

The IPLS profiler uses symbolic addresses instead of absolute numbers. A symbolic address is a tuple of (instruction ID, invocation counter, offset). *Instruction ID* is an unique static ID of the memory allocation instruction that allocates the object pointed by the address, and *invocation counter* means the number of invocations of the instruction with instruction ID when the object is allocated. *offset* refers to the offset from the base of the object.

Figure 5 describes how the object-relative memory profiling is performed in IPLS. During the execution, the IPLS profiler traces every memory allocation instructions. Figure 5(a) shows the instrumentation to trace memory allocation in bold and italic. For every invocation of memory allocation instruction, `alloc_profile` function call is followed to trace the unique instruction ID of the memory allocation instruction, its invocation counter, start address and size of the allocated object. Traced information is maintained as a table shown in Figure 5(b).

When the profiler outputs the information related to a pointer, it prints the symbolic address tuple instead of absolute number by referring the table. For example, to trace the pointer `P`, which is in range of $[P0, P0 + Sn)$, the profiler finds the corresponding instruction ID and the invocation counter for the object pointed by `P` using the table (`INn` and `IVn` for the example in the figure), calculates the *offset*, and prints those numbers as described in Figure 5(c).

Figure 5(e) shows the use of symbolic address on the specialized program side. Instead of using the absolute value of pointer `P` to check the dispatch condition of the specialized loop, it uses a value `P0′ + offset` which is generated from the symbolic address: `P0′` comes from the `IVn`-th invocation of instruction with ID `INn`, and value `offset` directly comes from the output of the profile. In order to get the value of `P0′` while executing the specialized program, instrumentation is added to the memory allocation instruction `INn`, as shown in Figure 5(d).

5. Pattern Detection

The IPLS pattern detector analyzes profiling information to identify specialization opportunities. The output of this stage includes meta-level loops which represent repeating patterns within the traced values computed by static instructions, and possible heap constants extracted from the trace of static load instructions.

In addition to the meta-level loop, the pattern detector uses the *meta-level trace* to represent the repeating patterns in the program. While the meta-level loop represents patterns across multiple iterations of a single invocation of a loop, the meta-level trace represents patterns across multiple invocations of the loop. Figure 6(a) shows a summarized trace of values generated by a static instruction in a loop across multiple invocations. For the first and second invocations of the loop, the loop iterates for 8 times before it terminates, and for the third invocation it runs for only four iterations. Across first and second invocation of the loop, the static instruction computes exactly the same sequence of values. Therefore, the specializer can exploit patterns which emerge across the *invocations* along with the patterns detected across the *iterations* of a single invocation.

In order to find a meta-level loop or meta-level trace from a given trace of values, the pattern detector first transforms the sequence of trace values into a graph: each traced value becomes a node of the graph, and edges are added between two values adjacent in the trace. Figure 6(b) depicts a graph generated from the trace in Figure 6(a).

To detect a meta-level loop, IPLS runs a natural loop detection algorithm on the graph built from the trace. In the example of Figure 6(b), an edge from node `d` to node `b` forms a backedge because its destination node dominates its source node, and a meta-level loop including nodes `b`, `c`, `e`, and `d` can be detected. The dispatch condition for the specialized loop for the meta-level loop is met if the computed value of the static instruction whose profiled values induce the meta-level loop matches the value of the loop header.

Meta-level traces are created by merging all iteration traces that share the same value for the first iteration. The dispatch condition for the specialized codes for a meta-level trace is determined by the common value from the first iterations. Since the traces of the three invocations shown in Figure 6(a) share the same value `a` generated from the first iteration, Figure 6(b) can be a meta-level trace. However, if the value diverges after the first iteration for different invocations, and some of them appear with a very low probability across invocations, specialized loops for those values will merely increase the program size without much benefit. To prevent this case, only the trace of invocations which share an identical iteration trace are included in the meta-level trace. In Figure 6(a), traces of the first and second invocations are identical, hence are combined in the meta-level trace, yet the trace of the third invocation is excluded because there is no common trace.

At this point the pattern detector may have found several patterns in the trace data. However, the loop can only be specialized according to one pattern. To find the right pattern for specialization, IPLS uses a heuristic based on two measures: (1) coverage of the pattern and (2) number of the instructions affected by the static instruction generating the pattern. IPLS chooses the pattern for which the product of these measures is greatest.

The *coverage* of the pattern is calculated by taking a ratio of the number of iterations covered by the pattern to the total number of iterations in the trace. This measure is related to the benefit of specialization since a higher coverage means that the specialized code likely accelerates a greater portion of the total iterations. The profiler measures the invocation count of the instructions affected by the static instruction s. This number is related to the benefit since a higher number implies more computation to be optimized away via precomputation. In the example of Figure 3(d), the pattern of `ADDR = [P, P+1]` and the pattern of `OP = [FOR, ADD]` have the same coverage. While the instruction computing `ADDR` affects two instructions (i.e., `OP=*ADDR` and `switch(OP)`), the instruction `OP=*ADDR` affects only one instruction (`switch(OP)`). Therefore, IPLS chooses to optimize the loop with respect to the pattern of `ADDR = [P, P+1]`. If the coverage of the pattern is less than 0.01, IPLS discards the pattern.

	Invocation		
	0	1	2
Iter 0	a	a	a
Iter 1	b	b	g
Iter 2	c	c	i
Iter 3	d	d	h
Iter 4	b	b	
Iter 5	e	e	
Iter 6	d	d	
Iter 7	f	f	

(a) Example trace

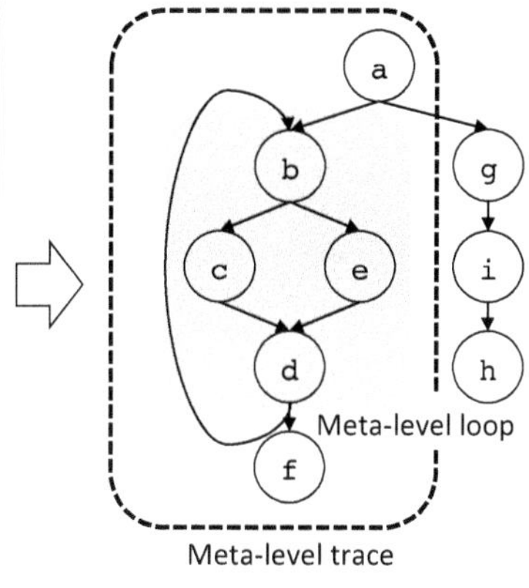

(b) Meta-level loop/trace detected from example trace (a)

Figure 6. Meta-level loops/traces detection extracts a graph which resembles a control-flow graph in which loops are identified.

6. Code Generation

Code generation takes advantage of meta-level loop/trace information and possible heap constant information passed by the pattern detector to specialize codes. Specialized codes are expected to have less computation than the corresponding original codes and be better structured to exploit instruction-level parallelism.

Figure 7 describes how the program represented as a control flow graph in Figure 7(a), which is taken from Figure 3(c), is specialized step by step using the information in Figure 3(e). Throughout this section the code generation process will be explained by walking through the figure.

Step 1: Splitting header and latch block First, IPLS splits the original loop header block and loop latch blocks (blocks which are the source of a loop backedge). As of now, IPLS targets only natural loops for specialization. Natural loops can be canonicalized to have only one backedge and only one latch block. Dispatch instructions for specialized codes are added to the new header block, and the new latch block becomes a point where the control flow merged after the execution of specialized codes. Figure 7(b) shows a new control flow graph after splitting the header and latch blocks.

As shown in the figure, ϕ-nodes placed in the original loop header are moved to new header after splitting. If the dispatch instructions of the specialized codes depend on ϕ-nodes, no other modifications are required. However, if dispatch instructions depend on some other instructions, the instruction and instructions upon which it depends must be cloned into the new header block.

Step 2: Cloning basic blocks To create versions of the loop iteration corresponding to observed traces, the compiler clones basic blocks in the nodes in a meta-level loop/trace. As described in Section 3.3, basic blocks to be cloned for each meta-level node are provided by the pattern detector, which is based on profiling. For a branch instruction in a cloned block, if the original branch target block is also cloned then the instruction is fixed to branch to the corresponding cloned block. If not, the branch jumps to the target block in the original loop. Figure 7(c) depicts the control flow graph after cloning of basic blocks and adjusting branches.

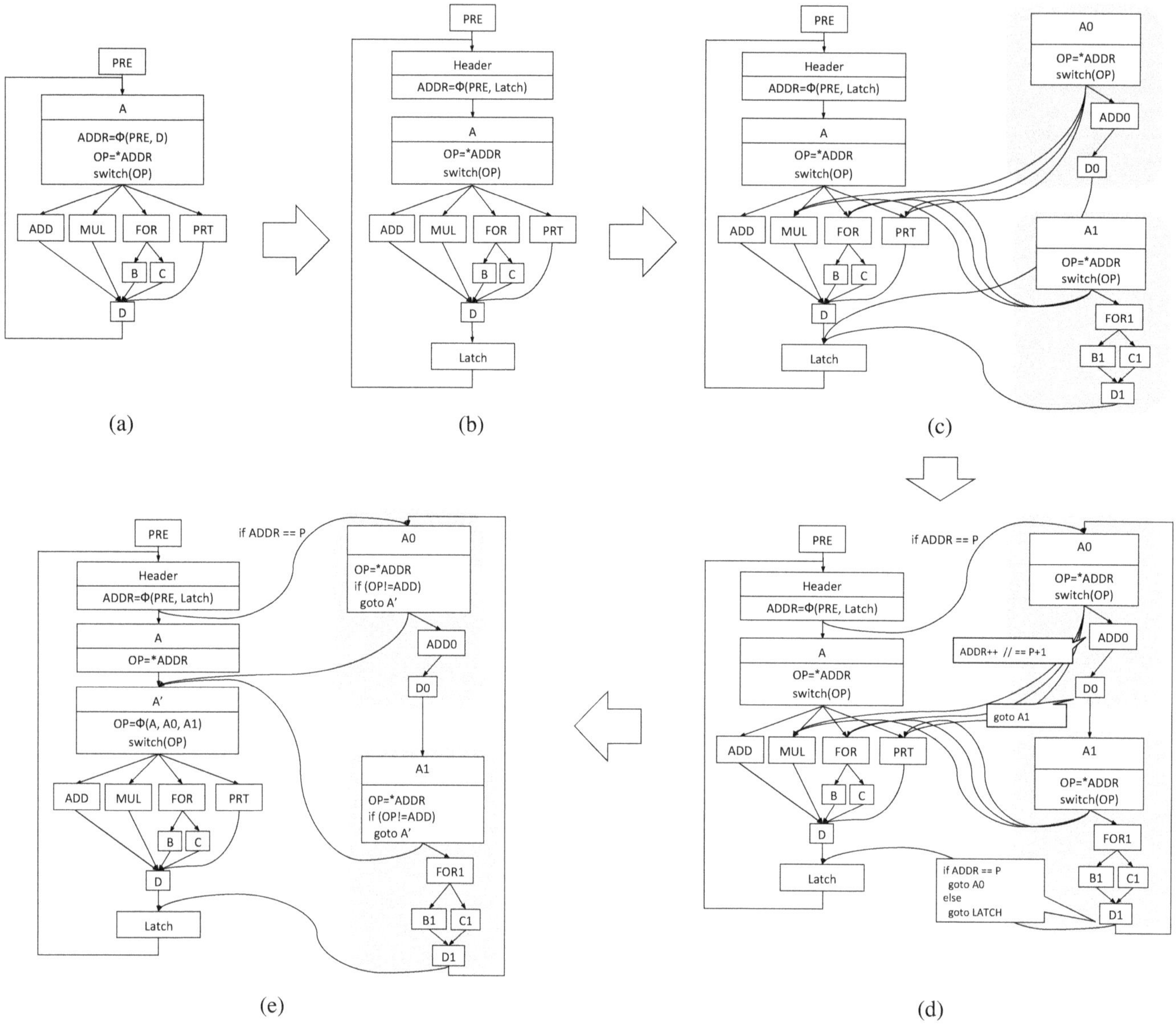

Figure 7. The code generation process: (a) original loop, (b) splitting the loop header and latch, (c) cloning and specializing iterations from a pattern, (d) adding dispatch conditions and stitching specialized iterations into a loop, and (e) adding unexpected exit conditions.

Instead of cloning basic blocks invoked in each node during profiling, one alternative can be analyzing executable basic blocks for each meta-level node and cloning all executable blocks, to minimize the number of returns back to the unspecialized loop. This happens when a branch jumps to a basic block that is never executed during profiling. This approach makes sense because cloned blocks for each meta-level node are specialized for a specific value of the instruction inducing meta-level loop/trace, and specialization may mark a large portion of basic blocks within the loop as unreachable. In practice, the analysis marks every basic block to be executable for non-negligible cases, especially if the specialized loop contains an inner loop. Since cloning the entire loop may lead to code size explosion, IPLS clones the profiled basic blocks only.

Step 3: Adding dispatch instruction and meta-level edges After cloning basic blocks for each meta-level node, dispatch instructions are inserted at the loop header created in Step 1 to invoke the specialized loops. The pattern detector informs the code generator of a dispatch condition for each meta-level loop and trace. Figure 7(d) depicts the control flow edge inserted to dispatch the specialized loop, which is taken when the value of `ADDR` becomes `P` (Actually, the value acquired by the symbolic representation of value `P` is used in dispatch instructions, as described in Section 4, but we use the absolute value `P` here to simplify explanation).

Branches for meta-level edges are also added in this step. The branches are conditioned on the dynamic value of dispatch condition. The branch at the end of block `D1` in Figure 7(d) shows this. The branch checks whether the value of `ADDR` will actually be `P` on the next iteration. If it matches, it jumps to the specialized loop corresponding to the value of `ADDR` being `P`, or returns to the original loop otherwise. If a meta-level node has multiple outgoing edges, IPLS uses a switch statement instead of a branch.

Sometimes a simplified control flow between cloned basic blocks makes branches for meta-level edges unconditional. The branch added at the end of block `D0` in Figure 7(d) is the case. Since blocks `A0` through `D0` have a straightened control flow, and block `ADD0` contains the instruction that increases the value of `ADDR` by one, so the value of `ADDR` for the next iteration is guaranteed to be `P+1` at the end of `D0`. Therefore, without checking, the loop specialized for the condition of `ADDR == P+1` is invoked after the execution of `D0`. Such simplification of the control flow opens opportunities to exploit instruction-level parallelism across different iterations.

Step 4: Exploiting possible heap constants As the last step of code generation, IPLS exploits possible heap constant information.

Figures 7(d) and (e) differ in block `A0`, where the switch instruction has been replaced with a conditional branch. This replacement is possible because the specializer knows (i) `ADDR` must point to `P` and (ii) the pattern detector reports that the memory at `P` holds a heap constant value `ADD`. However, the switch cannot be simply replaced by an unconditional branch. The heap constant information is derived via profiling, which must be verified at runtime; instructions to check the validity of possible heap constant information must remain.

Though it seems that there is no benefit by using heap constant information in block `A0`, performance is improved by replacing switch instructions (often lowered to a jump table in assembly) with conditional branches, which improve the performance of branch prediction. Particularly, the branch prediction is nearly perfect for such cases since the heap constant information is generally true. Although it is not clear in this example, heap constant information also breaks dependences between load instruction and its uses, because the loaded value can be safely assumed to be the expected heap constant after the checking instruction. Breaking dependences creates more optimization opportunities, including better chances for instruction level parallelism.

As an alternative to checking heap constants and branching, speculation assumes all possible heap constants. Also, instead of inserting a comparison between the expected and actual values, it simply logs the comparison result. Then the program occasionally checks the logged value at runtime to see if a *misspeculation* has occurred, and if so, the program *rolls back* to the previous checkpoint of the program, where the program maintains correct state. By removing conditional branches speculative execution opens additional opportunities to exploit instruction level parallelism. However, the overhead of logging and periodic checking of comparison results may negate the benefit coming from more instruction level parallelism. In this paper, we do not use speculative techniques and leave them for future work.

7. Evaluation

A prototype for IPLS is implemented in the LLVM compiler framework [16]. We evaluate it against the following open source C programs: a Lua script interpreter (Lua-5.2.0), a Perl script interpreter (Perl-5.14.2), and a Python script interpreter (Python-2.7.2). All script interpreters first translate the given scripts into an internal intermediate representation and then execute these translated versions. Each interpreter includes a hot loop that performs fetch-execute cycle on the IR. IPLS specialized the fetch-execute loop in each interpreter. All programs are compiled with maximum optimization (`-O3`) using clang compiler version 3.2.

IPLS specializes these C programs against eleven inputs. Each input is a script that is interpreted by the C program. The eleven input programs are selected from the Computer Language Benchmarks Game [7], which are commonly available for all three interpreters and single-threaded (IPLS does not support specialization of multi-threaded programs yet). All evaluations are measured on an Intel Xeon X7460 64-bit processor running at 2.66GHz.

Input	Script (Lines of code)	Iteration coverage(%)	Meta-level-loops/traces
Lua-5.2.0 (19,832 LOC)			
	binary-trees (50)	78.01%	5
	fannkuch-redux (48)	74.75%	6
	fasta (98)	42.63%	5
	k-nucleotide (66)	98.50%	2
	mandelbrot (27)	99.99%	4
	meteor (223)	0.76%	7
	nbody (121)	97.57%	4
	pidigits (104)	99.61%	9
	regex-dna (46)	2.93%	5
	reverse-complement (40)	0.00%	2
	spectral-norm (43)	88.90%	5
Perl-5.14.2 (201,786 LOC)			
	binary-trees (47)	99.99%	4
	fannkuch-redux (55)	99.99%	4
	fasta (122)	98.99%	11
	k-nucleotide (29)	99.93%	2
	mandelbrot (77)	99.90%	4
	meteor (235)	99.90%	10
	nbody (107)	99.90%	10
	pidigits (47)	95.06%	11
	regex-dna (49)	99.92%	3
	reverse-complement (29)	99.99%	4
	spectral-norm (49)	99.99%	4
Python-2.7.2 (314,921 LOC))			
	binary-trees (70)	9.36%	2
	fannkuch-redux (56)	35.02%	3
	fasta (118)	3.03%	4
	k-nucleotide (57)	5.15%	1
	mandelbrot (55)	52.09%	1
	meteor (205)	2.06%	5
	nbody (116)	76.48%	6
	pidigits (40)	1.15%	3
	regex-dna (44)	11.23%	8
	reverse-complement (37)	64.83%	10
	spectral-norm (56)	48.77%	5

Table 1. Execution characteristics of each interpreter and each static input: *Iteration coverage* denotes the fraction of hot loop iterations which are executed in specialized code. *Meta-level loops/-traces* denotes the number of identified patterns for each of which a specialized loop is generated.

Figure 8 shows whole program speedup for the programs specialized with IPLS over original program execution. Figure 9 depicts the program size increase after specialization. As shown, IPLS achieves a geomean speedup of 14.1% in program execution with 7.0% of program size increase.

7.1 Lua-5.2.0

For Lua-5.2.0, speedup of the specialized program correlates to the fraction of iterations executed in the specialized loop. Table 1 shows this trend: *Iteration coverage* column shows the fraction of all iterations of the main loop which execute within specialized code. There is a clear distinction between cases where iteration coverage is less than 3% and cases where iteration coverage is greater than 70%. In the latter case, specialization yields 7.4%–138% speedups, while in the former case, specialization yields a performance degradation.

Low iteration coverage is caused by two factors: unexpected exits due to the limited coverage of path profiling, and value mispredictions which prevent dispatch into the specialized loop.

Input script	Ratio of dynamic instruction counts
binary-trees	1.11
fannkuch-redux	1.13
fasta	1.01
k-nucleotide	1.16
mandelbrot	2.28
meteor	0.99
nbody	1.55
pidigits	1.58
regex-dna	1.00
reverse-complement	1.00
spectral-norm	1.65

Table 2. Ratio of dynamic instruction count of the original program to that of the specialized program for Lua-5.2.0. Larger numbers indicate a greater reduction in dynamic instructions.

Input script	Lua (%)	Perl (%)	Python (%)
binary-trees	19.46	0.00	20.10
fannkuch-redux	2.13	0.00	3.32
fasta	12.50	0.00	0.99
k-nucleotide	0.00	0.00	46.90
mandelbrot	0.00	0.00	1.10
meteor	4.22	0.00	8.67
nbody	0.00	0.00	0.30
pidigits	0.03	0.00	46.83
regex-dna	9.71	0.00	1.66
reverse-complement	0.57	0.00	0.00
spectral-norm	1.25	0.00	8.33

Table 3. Unexpected exits from the specialized loop as a fraction of the number of iterations running in a specialized loop.

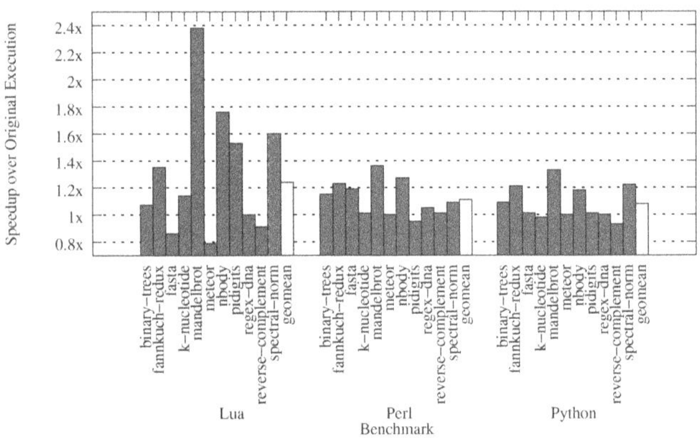

Figure 8. Whole-program speedup with three interpreters: Lua, Perl, and Python, and 11 input scripts for each.

Profile coverage may be limited when a path does not occur during training. Since IPLS generates specialized loops according to path profiling, the program may take an unexpected path within an iteration of its hot loop. To guarantee correctness, the code generator inserts tests which detect this case, and conservatively branches to the unspecialized code. We call such exits *unexpected.* Since the dispatch condition may only enter the specialized loop at the beginning of a pattern, if a specialized loop experiences an unexpected exit the remainder of that pattern must execute in non-specialized code before there is an opportunity to re-enter specialized code. The occurrence of unexpected exits among the total number of iterations is shown in Table 3.

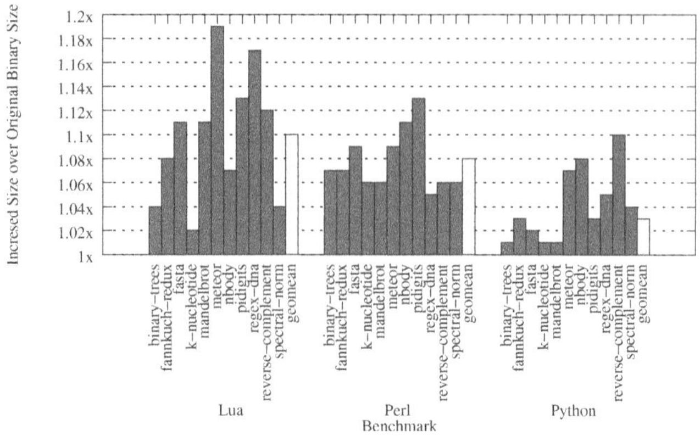

Figure 9. Code size increase after specialization for three interpreters: Lua, Perl, and Python, and 11 input scripts for each.

Additionally, value misprediction may prevent the main loop from dispatching into the specialized loop. This occurs for some input scripts in which control dependences carry information from dynamic input to the dispatch condition. In other words, our optimistic implementation of DIFT occasionally misclassifies a dynamic value as static. As a result, the specialized program may experience a pattern that did not occur during profiling. In such cases, the main loop does not dispatch to the specialized code, decreasing iteration coverage. For example, the hottest loop in `reverse-complement` includes an `if` statement which is predicated on a dynamic input. This induces two different control paths in the script and foils IPLS value prediction.

`Fasta` experiences performance degradation even though the program has good iteration coverage. Difference in dynamic instruction counts after specialization, shown in Table 2, explains this. The numbers in the table show the ratio of dynamic instruction count of the original program to specialized program. Therefore, larger numbers in the table mean that fewer dynamic instructions were executed in the specialized program than the original. Unlike other programs with high iteration coverage, the number is moderate for `Fasta`. This implies that for `Fasta` specialization was not able to find enough precomputable static instructions to amortize the dispatch overhead introduced in the original loop.

7.2 Perl-5.14.2

Table 1 shows that Perl executes more than 99% of its main loop iterations in specialized code for almost all inputs. This suggests that the detected patterns are good predictors of the values. This high predictability stems from the unique implementation of the Perl interpreter's intermediate representation. For instance, `reverse-complement` is implemented using Perl's `split` operation instead of a syntactic `if` statement. Since the Perl interpreter implements large operations such as `split` as a single opcode, the control flow in Perl scripts are typically less dependent on dynamic input.

The Perl interpreter's main loop is structured differently than others. While other interpreters load the opcode, parse it, and branch to the appropriate handler, each handler in the Perl interpreter returns a function pointer that serves as a continuation to the next operation. Hence, the Perl interpreter repeatedly performs indirect calls. This is beneficial for IPLS since there can be no unexpected exits. On the other hand, it limits IPLS since there are fewer opportunities to optimize precomputable instructions.

This suggests that most performance improvements for Perl are caused by increased instruction-level parallelism exposed by unrolling the loop, and by better branch prediction caused by replacing indirect function call with conditional branch and direct function call. The ratio of dynamic instructions before and after specialization for Perl ranges from 0.96 to 1.02, except 0.90 in `pidigits`, which shows no benefit from precomputation.

`Pidigits` is the only Perl input which experienced slow down. For `pidigits`, IPLS selects a dispatch condition for 11 specialized meta-level loop/trace. This dispatch condition is generated as 11 load-and-conditional-branch sequences which execute upon every iteration of the main loop. The simple structure of Perl's main loop features such a low fetch-execute overhead that the IPLS dispatch condition is comparably heavy. The benefits of specialization does not overcome the high dispatch overheads and low iteration coverage in the case of `pidigits`.

7.3 Python-2.7.2

Like the Lua interpreter, application speedup for Python generally follows iteration coverage. As shown in Table 1, among the 5 scripts whose iteration coverage is greater than 30%, 4 showed better speedup with Python than other scripts: `fannkuch-redux`, `mandelbrot`, `nbody`, and `spectralnorm`.

Python `reverse-complement`, experiences a slow down despite high iteration coverage. The hottest loop in `reverse-complement` consists of a single meta-level node. Specialization of a singleton meta-level loop has negligible benefit since there are no opportunities for optimization over multiple iterations.

As shown in Table 3, the rate of unexpected exit is generally low, but is significant for three benchmarks: `binary-tree`, `k-nucleotide` and `pidigits`. These unexpected exits have a detrimental effect on iteration coverage and, in turn, on application speedup. Unexpected exits are caused by coverage limitations during path profiling. The Python interpreter's main loop has complicated control flow which is not determined by the current opcode. For example, Python performs reference counting within the main loop and counts the number of operations for preemptive switching among user-threads (although IPLS does not support multi-threaded script, we did not disable the multi-threading features of the interpreter). These rare behaviors are dynamic in the sense that they don't depend on the static input script. Since IPLS uses a natural loop detection algorithm to recognize meta-level loops, not all nodes included in the meta-level loop need to be hot. For the meta-level nodes not frequently observed during profiling, yet which are included in the meta-level loop, their path profile information may lack coverage of complex control flow within the main loop, causing unexpected exits.

8. Related Work

Compile-time Specialization Program specialization requires binding-time information, which classifies all instructions in the target program as either static or dynamic. To obtain the binding-time information, C-Mix [2, 18] and Tempo [8, 9] rely on compile-time analysis and user annotations. Unlike C-Mix and Tempo, IPLS exploits profiling information to obtain the binding-time information, so IPLS is complementary to these previous works.

Berlin et al. [4, 5] propose a specializer that optimizes scientific programs written in high-level languages such as LISP. Since control flows in scientific programs are not affected by input values, they unroll loops to expose parallelism inherent in the underlying numerical computation. However, the loop unrolling may cause a code explosion, so they explicitly exclude loops with high iteration counts from unrolling. Although the authors propose a heuristic to stop unrolling beyond a certain threshold, the heuristic is not evaluated. C-Mix [2, 18] and Tempo [8, 9] also suffer from code explosion, and rely on user annotation to avoid the problem. Since IPLS uses pattern based loop unrolling, this work neither has a code explosion problem, nor requires any user annotation.

JSpec [24] specializes Java using C as an intermediate language and uses Tempo for binding-time analysis. Kleinrubatscher et al. [15] propose a specializer for a subset of FORTRAN using abstract interpretation to gather binding-time information.

Run-time Specialization Run-time specialization [3, 10–13, 19, 25] has an advantage over compile-time specialization because it can exploit run-time constants that are not available at compile-time. However, run-time specialization suffers from high overhead of dynamic code generation. Tempo [10] supports both compile-time and run-time specialization sharing binding-time analysis together, but run-time specialization of Tempo achieves about 80% of the speedup of compile-time specialization, due to the run-time overheads [21]. It shows that specializing the program statically as much as possible can maximize the potential performance of specialized programs. Exploiting profiling results at compile-time, IPLS avoids the run-time overheads.

DyC [12, 13] is a run-time specializer, primarily focused on reducing run-time overheads from dynamic code generation and optimization. DyC requires user annotations to direct optimization policy and improve the precision of binding time information given by compile-time analysis. Although Calpa [20] automatically generates the annotations for DyC with profile information, it is limited to annotations about optimization policy only. Therefore, without programmers hint, Calpa's final result is still limited by compile-time analysis. Unlike DyC, IPLS is a fully-automatic specializer that does not require any user annotation.

Bala et al. [3] and Shankar et al. [25] propose run-time specializers that, like IPLS, do not require any user annotation. The specializers automatically find and optimize frequently executed traces by exploiting the information available at run-time only. Since they detect hot values to find traces, multiple traces in hot code regions can be generated increasing dispatching overheads. However, IPLS detect patterns before specializing codes, so IPLS can reduce dispatching overheads. In addition, while Shankar et al. [25] rely on strong type systems of Java to optimize program with possible heap constants, IPLS can specialize programs written in C language without type system supports.

Bolz et al. and Yermolovich et al. propose Just-In-Time compilers which are optimized to the specific requirements of extracting performance benefits from script interpreters [6, 28]. Script interpreters cannot benefit from tracing-JIT techniques [11, 29] which do not trace across multiple iterations. That is because each iteration in main loops of interpreters has diverse control flow due to different instructions in the script. Addressing the problem, these compilers find frequently executed traces in the scripts that stretch over multiple iterations of the interpreter main loops, and specialize the interpreters for the traces. This approach is similar to IPLS, but the JIT compilers require user annotations to the interpreter program at branch instruction handlers to find boundaries of loops in the scripts, and at data structures to find static values.

9. Conclusion

This paper proposes Invariant-induced Pattern based Loop Specialization (IPLS), the first fully-automatic specialization technique that exploits input-driven patterns across loops. IPLS profiles programs to specialize, and traces how invariants are propagated using information-flow tracking. With the profiling results, IPLS finds repeating patterns across multiple iterations of hot loops, and then specializes the loops predicting values in the loops. Without any user annotation, IPLS specializes three real-world script interpreters and eleven scripts each, yielding a geomean speedup of

14.1% over the original codes yet causing only 7% program size growth.

Acknowledgments

We thank the entire Liberty Research Group for their support and feedback during this work. We also thank the anonymous reviewers for their insightful comments and suggestions. This material is based on work supported by National Science Foundation Grants 0964328 and 1047879, and DARPA contract FA8750-10-2-0253. Jae W. Lee was partly supported by the Korean IT R&D program of MKE/KEIT KI001810041244. All opinions, findings, conclusions, and recommendations expressed throughout this work are those of the authors and do not necessarily reflect the views of the aforementioned funding agencies.

References

[1] R. Allen and K. Kennedy. *Optimizing compilers for modern architectures: a dependence-based approach*. Morgan Kaufmann Publishers Inc., 2002.

[2] L. O. Andersen. *Program Analysis and Specialization for the C Programming Language*. PhD thesis, DIKU, University of Copenhagen, May 1994.

[3] V. Bala, E. Duesterwald, and S. Banerjia. Dynamo: A transparent dynamic optimization system. In *Proceedings of the ACM SIGPLAN '00 Conference on Programming Language Design and Implementation*, pages 1–12, June 2000.

[4] A. Berlin. Partial evaluation applied to numerical computation. In *Proceedings of the 1990 ACM conference on LISP and functional programming*, pages 139–150, 1990.

[5] A. Berlin and D. Weise. Compiling scientific code using partial evaluation. *IEEE Computer*, 23:25–37, December 1990.

[6] C. F. Bolz, A. Cuni, M. Fijalkowski, and A. Rigo. Tracing the meta-level: PyPy's tracing JIT compiler. In *Proceedings of the 4th workshop on the Implementation, Compilation, Optimization of Object-Oriented Languages and Programming Systems*, pages 18–25, 2009.

[7] Computer Language Benchmarks Game. http://shootout.alioth.debian.org/.

[8] C. Consel, L. Hornof, F. Noël, J. Noyé, and N. Volansche. A uniform approach for compile-time and run-time specialization. In *Selected Papers from the International Seminar on Partial Evaluation*, pages 54–72, 1996.

[9] C. Consel, J. L. Lawall, and A.-F. Le Meur. A tour of Tempo: a program specializer for the C language. *Science of Computer Programming*, 52:341–370, August 2004.

[10] C. Consel and F. Noel. A general approach for run-time specialization and its application to C. In *Proceedings of the ACM Symposium on Principles of Programming Languages*, pages 145–156, January 1996.

[11] A. Gal, B. Eich, M. Shaver, D. Anderson, D. Mandelin, M. R. Haghighat, B. Kaplan, G. Hoare, B. Zbarsky, J. Orendorff, J. Ruderman, E. W. Smith, R. Reitmaier, M. Bebenita, M. Chang, and M. Franz. Trace-based just-in-time type specialization for dynamic languages. In *Proceedings of the 2009 ACM SIGPLAN conference on Programming language design and implementation*, pages 465–478, 2009.

[12] B. Grant, M. Mock, M. Philipose, C. Chambers, and S. Eggers. Annotation-directed run-time specialization in C. In *Proceedings of the ACM SIGPLAN Symposium on Partial Evaluation and Semantics-Based Program Manipulation (PEPM)*, pages 163–178, June 1997.

[13] B. Grant, M. Philipose, M. Mock, C. Chambers, and S. Eggers. An evaluation of staged run-time optimizations in DyC. In *Proceedings of the ACM SIGPLAN Symposium on Programming Language Design and Implementation*, pages 293–304, May 1999.

[14] N. D. Jones, P. Sestoft, and H. Søndergaard. An experiment in partial evaluation: the generation of a compiler generator. *ACM SIGPLAN Notices*, 20:82–87, August 1985.

[15] P. Kleinrubatscher, A. Kriegshaber, R. Zöchling, and R. Glück. FORTRAN program specialization. *ACM SIGPLAN Notices*, 30:61–70, April 1995.

[16] C. Lattner and V. Adve. LLVM: A compilation framework for lifelong program analysis & transformation. In *CGO '04: Proceedings of the International Symposium on Code Generation and Optimization*, page 75, 2004.

[17] Lua. http://www.lua.org/.

[18] H. Makholm. Specializing C — an introduction to the principles behind C-Mix/II. Technical report, University of Copenhagen, Department of Computer Science, 1999.

[19] H. Masuhara and A. Yonezawa. Run-time bytecode specialization. In *Proceedings of the Second Symposium on Programs as Data Objects*, pages 138–154, 2001.

[20] M. Mock, M. Berryman, C. Chambers, and S. Eggers. Calpa: A tool for automating dynamic compilation. In *Proceedings of the Second Workshop on Feedback-Directed Optimization*, pages 100–109, November 1999.

[21] F. Noel, L. Hornof, C. Consel, and J. L. Lawall. Automatic, template-based run-time specialization: Implementation and experimental study. In *Proceedings of the 1998 International Conference on Computer Languages*, 1998.

[22] Perl. http://www.perl.org/.

[23] Python. http://www.python.org/.

[24] U. P. Schultz, J. L. Lawall, and C. Consel. Automatic program specialization for Java. *ACM Transactions on Programming Languages and Systems*, 25:452–499, July 2003.

[25] A. Shankar, S. S. Sastry, R. Bodík, and J. E. Smith. Runtime specialization with optimistic heap analysis. In *Proceedings of the 20th annual ACM SIGPLAN conference on Object-oriented programming, systems, languages, and applications*, pages 327–343, 2005.

[26] G. E. Suh, J. W. Lee, D. Zhang, and S. Devadas. Secure program execution via dynamic information flow tracking. In *Proceedings of the 11th international conference on Architectural support for programming languages and operating systems*, pages 85–96, 2004.

[27] Q. Wu, A. Pyatakov, A. N. Spiridonov, E. Raman, D. W. Clark, and D. I. August. Exposing memory access regularities using object-relative memory profiling. In *Proceedings of the International Symposium on Code Generation and Optimization*, 2004.

[28] A. Yermolovich, C. Wimmer, and M. Franz. Optimization of dynamic languages using hierarchical layering of virtual machines. In *Proceedings of the 5th symposium on Dynamic languages*, pages 79–88, 2009.

[29] M. Zaleski, A. D. Brown, and K. Stoodley. YETI: a graduallY extensible trace interpreter. In *Proceedings of the 3rd international conference on Virtual execution environments*, pages 83–93, 2007.

Portable Performance on Heterogeneous Architectures

Phitchaya Mangpo Phothilimthana Jason Ansel Jonathan Ragan-Kelley Saman Amarasinghe

Computer Science and Artificial Intelligence Laboratory
Massachusetts Institute of Technology
{mangpo, jansel, jrk, saman}@csail.mit.edu

Abstract

Trends in both consumer and high performance computing are bringing not only more cores, but also increased heterogeneity among the computational resources within a single machine. In many machines, one of the greatest computational resources is now their graphics coprocessors (GPUs), not just their primary CPUs. But GPU programming and memory models differ dramatically from conventional CPUs, and the relative performance characteristics of the different processors vary widely between machines. Different processors within a system often perform best with different algorithms and memory usage patterns, and achieving the best overall performance may require mapping portions of programs across all types of resources in the machine.

To address the problem of efficiently programming machines with increasingly heterogeneous computational resources, we propose a programming model in which the best mapping of programs to processors and memories is determined empirically. Programs define *choices* in how their individual algorithms may work, and the compiler generates further choices in how they can map to CPU and GPU processors and memory systems. These choices are given to an empirical autotuning framework that allows the space of possible implementations to be searched at installation time. The rich choice space allows the autotuner to construct poly-algorithms that combine many different algorithmic techniques, using both the CPU and the GPU, to obtain better performance than any one technique alone. Experimental results show that algorithmic changes, and the varied use of both CPUs and GPUs, are necessary to obtain up to a 16.5x speedup over using a single program configuration for all architectures.

Categories and Subject Descriptors I.2.5 [*Artificial Intelligence*]: Programming Languages and Software; D.3.4 [*Programming Languages*]: Processors—Compilers

General Terms Experimentation, Languages, Performance

Keywords Autotuning, Compilers, GPGPU, Heterogeneous

ASPLOS'13, March 16–20, 2013, Houston, Texas, USA.

1. Introduction

The past decade has seen an explosion in processor parallelism, with the move to multicores. The next major architectural trend is the move from symmetric multiprocessors to *heterogeneous* systems, with multiple *different* processors and memories.

A major source of heterogeneity today is the widespread availability graphics coprocessors (GPUs), which can now be used for general purpose computation. GPUs can offer large speedups, thanks to high processor density and high memory bandwidth. Conventional wisdom often holds that, if a program can be mapped into GPU execution, it should be, since it will benefit from the immense computational resources. Instead, our results show that the choices in mapping to heterogeneous machines are much more complex.

A major challenge in utilizing heterogeneous resources is the diversity of devices on different machines, which provide widely varying performance characteristics. A program optimized for one coprocessor may not run as well on the next generation of processors or on a device from a different vendor, and a program optimized for GPU execution is often very different from one optimized for CPU execution. The relative performance of the CPUs and GPUs also varies between machines. On one machine, a specific portion of a computation may run best on the CPU, while on another machine it may run best on the GPU. There is also a scheduling problem: even if a specific kernel may perform better on the GPU, if the GPU is overloaded and the CPU is idle, it may be best to balance the workload between the two, or it may be best to place computation somewhere it runs more slowly but nearer to where its output will be used.

For many applications, mapping across all of a machine's resources—in different ways per-machine, and per-program—is essential to achieving high performance. In our SVD benchmark, the best performing programs used both the CPU and GPU concurrently for a significant subset of total work on some machines but not on the others.

Researchers are proposing even more asymmetric heterogeneous architectures with varied types of cores on a single chip [16]. But even on symmetric multicore systems without a GPU, the model of a multicore as simply a collection of identical independent cores does not hold in practice. Many modern processors dynamically scale up the frequency of a core when the cores around it are idle and share different amounts of resources between pairs of cores, making the performance of one core highly dependent on the workload of its neighbors [7]. While these techniques improve performance for many workloads, it implies that naively allocating a program more threads is not the optimal strategy for every algorithm on every system.

The traditional goal of a compiler is to map a program to a specific piece of hardware. Most compiler optimizations reason about program transformations using a simplified model of a specific processor target. This simple model of the performance of the machine is often implied by the heuristics that guide optimization. In heterogeneous machines, there are now multiple processors, with wildly different features and performance characteristics. It is extremely difficult for a single, comprehensible model to capture behavior across many processors and memory subsystems on which code may run, in order to reason about mapping a program to a heterogeneous machine. Compiling a program for a heterogeneous machine requires complex, interdependent choices of *algorithm:* which algorithm to use; *placement:* on which resources to place computations and data; and *mapping:* how much parallelism to exploit and how to use specialized memories.

We present a solution to the problem of efficiently programming diverse heterogeneous systems based on empirical autotuning. At installation time, a search space of possible program implementations is explored using an evolutionary autotuner that tests performance on representative inputs. This search space includes not only when to use different coprocessors, cores, and memory subsystems, but also how to use them. The autotuner is able to switch between entirely different algorithmic techniques encoded in the program, and between multiple strategies for mapping them to heterogeneous computational resources, and to combine the different techniques encoded in the program into a large search space of poly-algorithms.

Our work extends the PetaBricks language and compiler [3], which allows the programmer to specify algorithmic choices at the language level. Using this mechanism, PetaBricks programs define not only a single algorithm, but a search space of possible algorithms. The extensions to PetaBricks presented in this paper include:

- Compiler passes and static analyses to automatically convert subsets of existing PetaBricks programs into OpenCL kernels that can be run on a variety of architectural backends, and coexist as choices available to the autotuner. This includes static analyses to help efficiently manage the memory of these coprocessing devices, and reduce data movement between kernel executions.
- A GPU management runtime that allows coprocessor devices to be efficiently utilized in the PetaBricks workstealing runtime without requiring the calling CPU thread to block on GPU operations, providing automatic memory management, and allowing efficient overlapping of computation and communication.
- Autotuning enhancements to search different divisions of GPU and CPU work, and to allow the exploration of choices on the GPU, such as choices of in which of the many memory spaces to place different data, and choices of how much data to run on the GPU.

We show experimentally how different heterogeneous systems require different algorithmic choices for optimal performance. We show that, even when migrating between two architectures with modern GPUs, one can obtain up to a 16.5x speedup by retraining for each architecture. We show how diverse architectures perform best with differing divisions of work between the GPU and the CPU on each machine. The different configurations found are often non-obvious, and suggest that empirical tuning techniques are required to get the best performance on modern machines.

1.1 Contributions

We believe this is the first system which automatically determines the best mapping of programs in a high level language across a heterogeneous mix of parallel processing units, including placement of computation, choice of algorithm, and optimization for specialized memory hierarchies. With this, a high-level, architecture independent language can obtain comparable performance to architecture specific, hand-coded programs.

To realize this system,

- we integrate choices of devices, memories, and execution parameters into the PetaBricks autotuning compiler;
- we automate both the OpenCL code generation and selection process for a traditionally hand-written scratchpad memory optimization that requires significant memory access rewriting and the generation of multi-phase cooperative loads and stores;
- we introduce a runtime system that incorporates the use of a GPU coprocessor into a work-stealing system without the need to block on copies and GPU operations;
- we introduce a compiler analysis to identify when to use no copy, lazy copy, and eager copy memory management techniques.

This paper focuses not on the impact of individual optimizations, but on how to integrate many techniques together to automate the process of generating code and to achieve good performance on any heterogeneous machine.

In evaluating our system across a range of applications and architectures, we show that algorithmic choices are required to get optimal performance across machines with different processor mixes, and the optimal algorithm is different in different architectures. Unlike prior work, we add the additional axis of algorithmic choice and global learning to our search space. We paint a complex picture of the search space where the best device(s) to use depends on the algorithm being run, the context it is being called from, and the underlying hardware being used. We show that the choice of how and when to use the GPU is complex with no simple answer. The best mapping of a program to devices depends not only on the execution times of different pieces of the program but also data location and existing tasks in the queues. Finally, we demonstrate that splitting work to run concurrently both on the GPU and the CPU can significantly outperform using either processor alone.

2. PetaBricks Language Background

The PetaBricks language provides a framework for the programmer to describe multiple ways of solving a problem while allowing the autotuner to determine which of those ways is best for the user's situation [3]. It provides both algorithmic flexibility (multiple algorithmic choices) as well as coarse-grained code generation flexibility (synthesized outer control flow).

At the highest level, the programmer can specify a *transform*, which takes some number of inputs (the `from` keyword) and produces some number of outputs (the `to` keyword). In this respect, the PetaBricks transform is like a function call in a procedural language. The major difference is that it allows the programmer to specify multiple pathways to convert the inputs to the outputs for each transform. Pathways are specified in a dataflow manner using a number of smaller building blocks called *rules*, which encode both the data dependencies of the rule and C++-like code that converts the rule's inputs to outputs.

Dependencies are specified by naming the inputs and outputs of each rule, but unlike in a traditionally dataflow programming model, more than one rule can be defined to output the same data. Thus, the input dependences of a rule can be satisfied by the output of one or more rules. The PetaBricks compiler and autotuner decide which rules to use to satisfy such dependencies by determining which are most computationally efficient for a given architecture and input. For example, on architectures with multiple processors, the autotuner may find that it is preferable to use rules that minimize

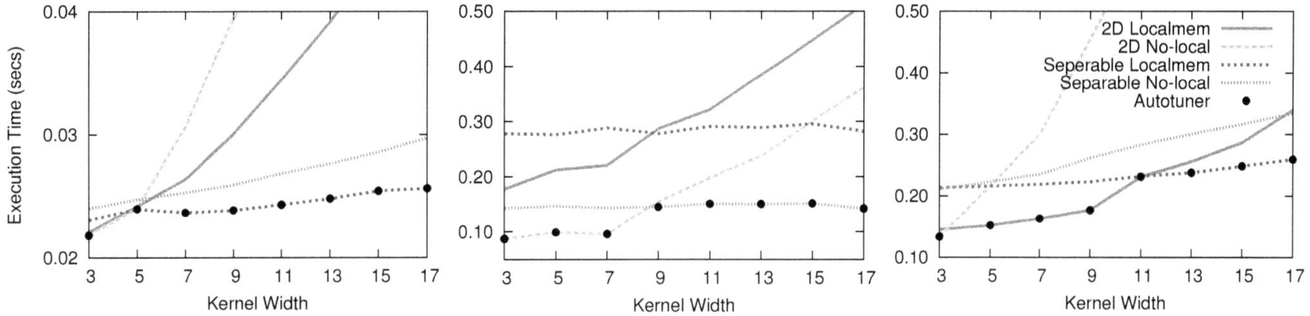

(a) Desktop (b) Server (c) Laptop

Figure 2. Execution time (lower is better) of different possible mappings of `SeparableConvolution` to OpenCL with varying kernel widths on three test systems when the input size is 3520×3520. The three test systems are described in Section 6.1. Our autotuner (described in Section 5) always discovers the best configuration for each system and width. Note that each mapping is optimal for at least one machine and kernel width. In handwritten OpenCL, these would correspond to four distinct programs the programmer would need to write.

the critical path of the transform, while on sequential architectures, rules with the lowest computational complexity may be a better choice.

2.1 Convolution in PetaBricks

Figure 1 shows `SeparableConvolution`, an example PetaBricks program. This program computes the convolution of a 2D matrix with a separable 2D kernel. The main transform (starting on line 1) maps from input matrix `In` to output matrix `Out` by convolving the input with the given `Kernel`. It does this using one of two rules:

- *Choice 1* maps from `In` to `Out` in a single pass, by directly applying the `Convolve2D` transform.
- *Choice 2* maps from `In` to `Out` in two passes, by first performing the `ConvolveRows` transform, storing its result in `buffer`, and then performing the `ConvolveColumns` transform on this intermediate result.

The three `Convolve*` transforms are each defined in terms of a single data parallel rule which, for each point in `Out`, computes a sum of the points in the corresponding `KWIDTH`-sized region of `In` weighted by the corresponding points in the `Kernel`. `ConvolveRows` and `ConvolveColumns` apply only in the horizontal and vertical directions, respectively, while `Convolve2D` applies both dimensions simultaneously, iterating over a 2D window of `In` for each output point. Based on the experimental data, the autotuner chooses which rules to run (a choice of algorithm), and how to map them onto the machine, including runtime scheduling strategy, parallelism, data placement, and the choice of processors on which to run.

2.2 The Choice Space for SeparableConvolution

The top-level `SeparableConvolution` transform compiles into two simple rules, each of which computes the entire `Out` matrix from the entire `In` matrix. Internally, these rules apply the `Convolve*` transforms which are defined elementwise, without sequential dependencies, and so can be executed in a data parallel fashion over the entire output space. As one choice, these data parallel rules can be compiled directly into equivalent OpenCL kernels, with each *work-item* computing a single cell of `Out`.

Because of its simple data parallel pattern, this example runs most efficiently when all `Convolve*` transform are executed entirely in the OpenCL runtime, but the ideal choices of *algorithm* and *mapping to the memory system* vary across machines, and for each machine across different kernel sizes. However, even though not optimal for this benchmark, the choice to run some fraction of the computation on the CPU is also available to the autotuner.

Intuitively, when blur size (kernel's width) is large, implementing the separable convolution as a pair of 1D passes over the data, first in the horizontal and then in the vertical direction, performs asymptotically less work than a single 2D convolution pass. Starting each block of work with an extra phase which prefetches a block of `In` into scratchpad memory shared by all processors in the block saves memory bandwidth compared to separately loading many overlapping inputs through the (slower) main memory hierarchy. But when the kernel size is small, the overhead (in bandwidth for intermediate results, and in kernel invocations) of multiple passes overtakes the computational complexity advantage of separable computation, making a single 2D pass faster, and the overhead of explicit prefetching into OpenCL local memory cannot be offset by the smaller number of redundant loads saved across a block of work. Where these tradeoffs dominate varies between machines. And the underlying machines vary further: on an OpenCL target where the shared memory maps to the same caches and buses used for all loads and stores, the explicit prefetch phase nearly always represents wasted work.

Figure 2 shows the running times of four distinct OpenCL choices (2D Convolution and Separable Convolution, each with and without local memory prefetching) generated by PetaBricks for `SeparableConvolution`, on three different machines (described in Section 6.1), over kernel sizes from 3-17. The ideal choice (the lowest line at a given point) varies among the four choices, depending on both the targeted machine and the kernel size. As expected, the execution times of the single-pass 2D algorithms increase faster than those of the two-pass separable algorithms as the kernel size increases, and the use of scratchpad memory helps little when the kernel size is small and worsens the performance on the CPU OpenCL runtime. But how exactly these effects interact, and the relative behavior of each choice, varies substantially across machines.

In short, simply mapping this program to the OpenCL runtime is not sufficient. *How* it is mapped (whether or not to prefetch shared inputs into scratchpad memory), and *which algorithms* to use, is a complex choice, highly dependent on the specific workload and target architecture.

The choices we make in automatically mapping to OpenCL are described further in the next section, while more detailed empirical evaluation and discussion of the best choices for this and other benchmarks on a diverse set of heterogeneous machines is given in Section 6.

```
transform SeparableConvolution
from In[w, h], Kernel[KWIDTH]
to Out[w−KWIDTH+1, h−KWIDTH+1]
{
  // Choice 1: single pass 2D convolution
  to(Out out) from(In in, Kernel kernel) {
    Convolve2D(out, in, kernel);
  }

  // Choice 2: two−pass separable convolution
  to(Out out) from(In in, Kernel kernel)
  using(buffer[w−KWIDTH+1, h]) {
    ConvolveRows(buffer, in, kernel);
    ConvolveColumns(out, buffer, kernel);
  }
}

transform Convolve2D
from In[w, h], Kernel[KWIDTH]
to Out[w−KWIDTH+1, h−KWIDTH+1]
{
  Out.cell(x,y)
  from(In.region(x, y, x+KWIDTH+1, y+KWIDTH+1) in, Kernel kernel)
  {
    ElementT sum = 0;
    for(int x = 0; x < KWIDTH; x++)
      for(int y = 0; y < KWIDTH; y++)
        sum += in.cell(x,y) ∗ kernel.cell(x) ∗ kernel.cell(y);
    return sum;
  }
}

transform ConvolveRows
from In[w, h], Kernel[KWIDTH]
to Out[w−KWIDTH+1, h]
{
  Out.cell(x,y)
  from(In.region(x, y, x+KWIDTH, y+1) in, Kernel kernel)
  {
    ElementT sum = 0;
    for(int i = 0; i < KWIDTH; i++)
      sum += in.cell(i,0) ∗ kernel.cell(i);
    return sum;
  }
}

transform ConvolveColumns
from In[w, h], Kernel[KWIDTH]
to Out[w, h−KWIDTH+1]
{
  Out.cell(x,y)
  from(In.region(x, y, x+1, y+KWIDTH) in, Kernel kernel)
  {
    ElementT sum = 0;
    for(int i = 0; i < KWIDTH; i++)
      sum += in.cell(0,i) ∗ kernel.cell(i);
    return sum;
  }
}
```

Figure 1. PetaBricks code for `SeparableConvolution`. The top-level transform computes `Out` from `In` and `Kernel` by *either* computing a single-pass 2D convolution, *or* computing two separate 1D convolutions and storing intermediate results in `buffer`. Our compiler maps this program to multiple different executables which perform different *algorithms* (separable vs. 2D blur), and map to the GPU in different ways.

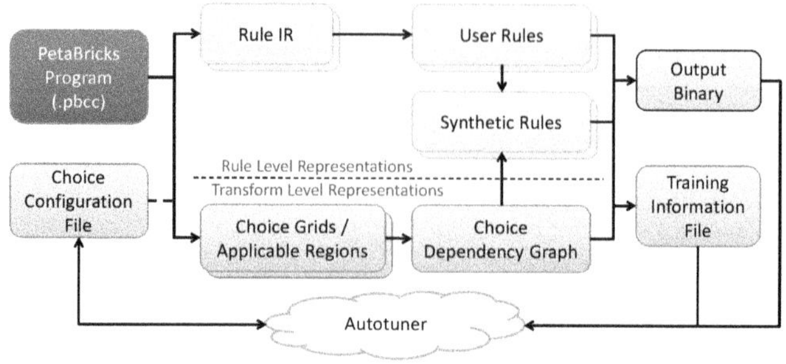

Figure 3. Flow for the compilation of a PetaBricks program with a *single* transform. (Additional transforms would cause the center part of the diagram to be duplicated.)

3. Compiling PetaBricks for Heterogeneous Machines

Figure 3 displays the general flow for the compilation of a PetaBricks transform. Compilation is split into two representations. The first representation operates at the rule level, and is similar to a traditional high level sequential intermediate representation. The second representation operates at the transform level, and is responsible for managing choices and for code synthesis.

The main transform level representation is the *choice dependency graph*, which is the primary way that choices are represented in PetaBricks. At a high level, the information contained in the choice dependency graph is similar to a familiar data dependency graph, however, the data is represented as an "inverse" of that graph: data dependencies are represented by vertices, while rules are represented by graph hyperedges. Additionally, data may be split into multiple vertices in the choice dependency graph if the transform contains rules that operate on just subregions of that data. The PetaBricks compiler uses this graph to manage code choices and to synthesize the outer control flow of the rules.

The final phase of compilation generates an *output binary* and a *training information file* containing static analysis information. These two outputs are used by the autotuner (described in Section 5), to search the space of possible algorithmic choices and other parameters. Autotuning creates a *choice configuration file*, which can either be used by the output binary to run directly or can be fed back into the compiler to allow additional optimizations.

3.1 OpenCL Kernel Generation

Since the PetaBricks language is more general (and supports calling arbitrary C/C++ code), only a subset of a PetaBricks program can be converted into OpenCL kernels. The process of generating additional choices for OpenCL execution is done early in the compilation process, before scheduling. The conversion process consists of three phases that are applied to each original user defined rule to inject equivalent synthetic OpenCL rules when possible.

In the first phase, a dependency analysis is performed to determine if the execution pattern of the rule fits into the OpenCL execution model. Sequential dependency patterns and data parallel dependency patterns can both be mapped to OpenCL kernels, but more complex parallel patterns, such as wavefront parallelism, can not be in our current implementation. It is possible that some sets of algorithmic choices will permit a mapping while others will not. The choice dependency graph is analyzed to determine if a rule can be mapped to OpenCL. The analysis looks at direction of the computed dependency for the strongly connected component associated with each of the rule's outputs. If there is no dependency, or the dependency is eliminated by selecting the rule choice under consideration, then the outer dependency pattern of the rule can be mapped to OpenCL.

If a rule passes the first phase, it goes to the second phase where the body of the transform is converted into OpenCL code. This phase includes a number of syntactic conversions. It is also responsible for rewriting data accesses to use GPU global memory, detecting a number of language constructs, such as calls to external libraries, that can not be mapped to OpenCL, and disqualifying a rule from being converted to OpenCL. This phase can also detect some language constructs (such as inline native code), which can not be supported by OpenCL. The majority of these constructs are detected statically; however, there are a few more subtle requirements, sometimes OpenCL-implementation specific, which we detect by attempting to compile the resulting transform and rejecting synthetic OpenCL rules that do not compile.

The third phase attempts to optimize the *basic* version of OpenCL codes generated from the second phase by utilizing GPU local memory, known as OpenCL local memory or CUDA shared memory. For a subset of the mapped OpenCL rules, the *local memory* version can be generated. To do so, we analyze input data access pattern. A *bounding box* is a rectangular region of an input matrix that is used for computing an entry of the output matrix. If the size of the bounding box is a constant greater than one, then the local memory version of the GPU code is created; if the size of the bounding box is one, there is no need to copy the data into local memory because threads that share the same local memory never access the same data. The local memory version consists of two parts. First, all work-items on the GPU cooperate to load the data into local memory that will be accessed by the work-group they belong to. The second part is the actual computation derived from the basic version by replacing global memory accesses with local memory accesses. This local memory version is presented as a choice to the autotuner.

3.2 Data Movement Analysis

A second group of OpenCL analyses are performed at scheduling time in the compiler for determining how data is copied in and out of GPU memory. The PetaBricks compiler generates a unique schedule for each assignment of choices in a transform. These schedules represent parallelism as dependency trees that are given to the workstealing runtime. After each schedule is generated, it is analyzed for GPU data movement requirements. This analysis looks at preceding rule applications in the schedule and classifies applicable output regions generated on the GPU into three states:

- *must copy-out* regions are those that are immediately followed by a rule that executes on the CPU in the current schedule. For these regions, data is copied eagerly.
- *reused* regions are those immediately followed by another rule on the GPU. For these regions the data is left in GPU memory between rule applications.
- *may copy-out* are regions followed by dynamic control flow which we cannot analyze statically. For these regions, we employ a lazy copy-out strategy. A check is inserted before any code that may consume one of these regions to ensure that the required data is in CPU memory. If it is not, then the copy-out is performed when the data is requested.

Depending on the result of this analysis, tasks to prepare, copy-in, execute, and check copy-out status are inserted into the schedule by the compiler.

4. Runtime System

This section describes the runtime tasks, the *workstealing* model for CPU tasks, the *work-pushing* model for GPU tasks, and the integration of the two models. Figure 4 presents an overview of the different parts of the system that will be described in this section.

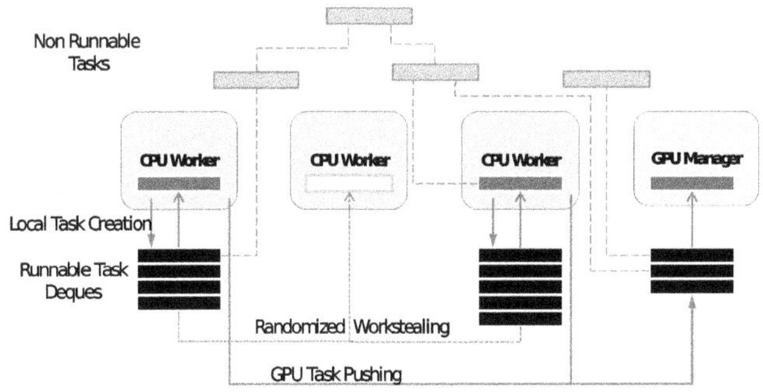

Figure 4. Overview of the runtime system. Worker threads use workstealing among themselves, and the GPU management thread only receives works that are pushed by the workers. Tasks exist in both a *runnable* and *non-runnable* state. Runnable tasks exist in deques of different threads, while non-runnable tasks are accessible only through dependency pointers in other tasks.

4.1 PetaBricks Workstealing Task Model

The PetaBricks runtime uses a workstealing mechanism similar to the one introduced in Cilk [11]. Instead of a stack, each thread has a THE-protocol [11] deque of tasks. Each thread continually pops tasks off the *top* of its deque and executes them, when tasks are created they are pushed onto the *top* of the local deque of the thread creating the task. When a thread is out of work, it choses a random victim thread and attempts to steal work off the *bottom* of that thread's deque. When starting a transform, much of the scheduling work is deferred in a continuation task that can be stolen by another thread.

Unlike Cilk, the PetaBricks task model supports arbitrary (non-cyclic) dependency graphs between tasks. To support this, dynamic dependency pointers are maintained from each incomplete task to those tasks that depend on it. When a task completes, it may return a continuation task to which all of its dependents are forwarded. Since task dependencies for dependent tasks are created in parallel to a task being executed, some care must be taken when managing tasks. Each task has a state, a count of dependencies, and a list of pointers to dependent tasks. A task can be in one of 5 states:

- *new task* is the initial state for a task. Dependencies may only be added to a task while it is in the new state, and those tasks that the new task depends on have to be tasks not already in the *complete* state. Adding a dependency to a task atomically increments the task's dependency count and adds the task to the appropriate dependents lists, following any needed continuation pointers. When dependency creation is finished, the task transitions to a *runnable task* if its dependency count is zero, otherwise to a *non-runnable task*.
- *non-runnable task* is the state for tasks whose dependency count is greater than zero. These tasks are waiting for other tasks to complete. Non-runnable tasks are stored only in the dependents lists of other tasks and are not stored in any central or thread-specific location. The task completion that eventually decrements the dependency count from one to zero is responsible for enqueuing the task in its thread-local deque.
- *runnable task* is the state for tasks that have zero dependencies and can be executed. These tasks are either being executed or are in exactly one thread-local deque of tasks. Runable tasks can be stolen. When executed, if the task returns a continuation task,

it transitions into the *continued* state, otherwise, it transitions to the *complete* state.

- *complete task* is the state for tasks that have already been executed and did not result in a continuation task. When a task becomes complete, it decrements the dependency count of each of its dependents and enqueues any dependent that becomes runnable. The dependents list is then cleared. Any subsequent attempt to depend on this task results in a no-op.
- *continued task* is the state for tasks that have been executed and returned a continuation. When a task enters the continued state a pointer is stored to the continuation task and the dependents list is transferred to the continuation task. Subsequent attempts to depend on this task instead depend on the continuation task (and possibly, recursively, a continuation of the continuation task).

4.2 GPU Management Thread and GPU Tasks

In this highly decentralized model, managing a GPU accelerator presents some challenges. First, for performance, it is important to overlap data transfer operations with computation. Second, one does not want to have many worker threads blocking and waiting for GPU operations to complete.

To address these challenges, we add a dedicated GPU management thread that is responsible for keeping track of all data that resides in GPU memory and schedule operations on the GPU. It operates using the same task representation as CPU threads', allowing dependencies between GPU and CPU tasks. A tasks is marked as either GPU or CPU task. We use workstealing scheme to manage CPU tasks, but work-pushing scheme to handle GPU tasks. CPU worker threads' deques can only contain CPU tasks, and the GPU management thread's FIFO queue can only contain GPU tasks.

Figure 5 depicts what happens when a task becomes runnable in different scenarios. We define the term *cause* as follow. Task A *causes* task B to become runnable when task A satisfies the last dependency of task B; more precisely, task A decrements the dependency count of task B to zero. When a GPU task becomes runnable, it is pushed to the bottom of the GPU management thread's queue as shown in Figure 5(a). When a GPU task causes a CPU task to become runnable, the GPU management thread chooses a random CPU worker and pushes the task to the bottom of that thread's deque as shown in Figure 5(b). When a CPU task causes another CPU task to become runnable, the CPU worker that runs the former task pushes the newly runnable task to the top of its own local deque as shown in Figure 5(c).

There are four classes of GPU tasks that are run by the GPU management thread. For each execution of a GPU kernel, there are one *prepare* task, zero or more *copy-in* tasks, one *execute* task, and zero or more *copy-out completion* tasks.

- *Prepare* tasks allocate buffers on the GPU, and update metadata for GPU execution.
- *Copy-in* tasks copy the required input data to the GPU. One copy-in task is responsible for one input. This task performs a non-blocking write to a GPU buffer and becomes a *complete* immediately after the call, so the GPU manager thread does not have to wait and can execute the next task in its queue right away.
- *Execute* tasks initiate the asynchronous execution of the kernel, perform non-blocking reads from GPU buffers to must copy-out regions, and put may copy-out regions into *pending storage*.
- *Copy-out completion* tasks check the status of the non-blocking reads called by the execute task. If the status of a read is complete, the copy-out completion task corresponding to that output data transitions to the *complete* state. If the read is not complete, the GPU manager thread pushes the task back to the end of its queue.

There is no dependency between GPU tasks because the GPU management thread only runs one task at a time; the GPU tasks associated to one GPU kernel execution only need to be enqueued by following order: prepare, copy-in, execute, and copy-out completion, to ensure the correctness. However, CPU tasks may depend on GPU copy-out completion tasks.

4.3 Memory Management

GPU memory is allocated and managed by the GPU management thread. The GPU management thread keeps a table of information about data stored in the GPU. Each region stored on the GPU can either be a copy of a region of a matrix in main memory or an output buffer for newly computed data that must eventually be copied back to main memory. The GPU management thread is responsible for releasing buffers that become stale because the copy in main memory has been written to and for copying data back to main memory when the data is needed or when it has been flagged for eager copy-out.

The memory management process includes various optimizations to minimize data transfer between the GPU and the CPU. Before we further explain our implementation, the term *matrix* and *region* should be clarified. A matrix is an input or an output of a transform, and is an n-dimensional dense array of elements. A region is a part of a matrix, defined by a start coordinate and size that is an input or an output of a rule.

Copy-in Management Before the GPU management thread executes a *copy-in* task, it will check whether the data is already on the GPU. It can already be on the GPU either if it was copied in for another task execution or if it was the output of another task on the GPU. If all data that will be copied in by the task is already on the GPU, then the GPU management thread will change the status of that *copy-in* task to *complete* without actually executing the task, otherwise it will perform the required copy.

Copy-out Management A single output matrix might be generated by multiple rules in a transform. For example, one task might generate the interior elements of a matrix and other tasks will generate the edges and corners. Instead of creating multiple small buffers on the GPU for these multiple rule outputs, it is often more efficient to create one big buffer for the entire matrix and have the individual tasks output to regions of this buffer. Creating one buffer will take less time than creating multiple buffers because there is an overhead associated with each read from GPU memory, and copying out multiple regions individually requires extra copying to consolidate the data back to the original buffer. It is also possible that some regions of a matrix will be generated on the CPU while others will be generated on the GPU. Our code generation and memory management needs to handle these more complex cases to keep track of which regions of a matrix have been written.

In order to apply this optimization, we use a static analysis for each possible schedule to determine which regions of the matrix are generated on the GPU. The GPU management thread will wait until all of the individual regions have been computed to change the state of the larger matrix.

CPU-GPU Work Balancing If a rule can be run on GPU, choices of how much data should be computed on the GPU are presented to our autotuner. At the extremes, the entire rule could computed on the GPU, or the entire rule could be computed on the CPU. We implement the CPU-GPU work balancing feature by having the autotuner pick a CPU/GPU ratio that defines how much of the data should be computed on each device. This ratio can be set in fixed 1/8th increments. The GPU-CPU ratio shared among all the

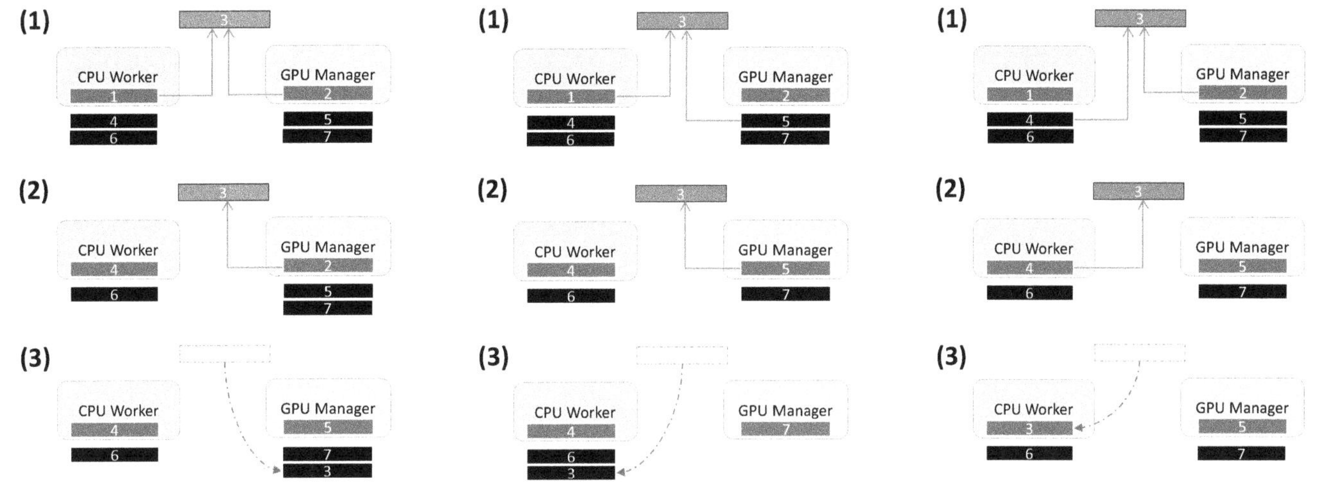

(a) A GPU task is always pushed to the bottom of the GPU management thread's queue.

(b) The GPU management thread pushes a CPU task to the bottom of a random CPU worker's deque.

(c) A CPU worker pushes a CPU task to the top of its own deque.

Figure 5. Three different cases when a task become runnable. The events progress from (1) to (3). Green tasks are GPU non-runnable tasks. Grey tasks are CPU non-runnable tasks.

rules in the same transform because they compute the same matrix but different regions. The system divides the matrix so that the first part is on GPU and the second part is on CPU.

5. Autotuner

This section describes the PetaBricks autotuner representation, the evolutionary autotuning algorithm, and how the synthesized OpenCL choices are represented to the tuner.

5.1 Autotuning Representation

Choices are represented in a configuration file that contains three types of structures. The first type is selectors which allow the autotuner to make algorithmic choices. Selectors can make different decisions when called with different input sizes dynamically. Using this mechanism, selectors can be used by the autotuner to construct poly-algorithms that dynamically switch algorithms at recursive call sites. Formally, a selector s consists of $\vec{C_s} = [c_{s,1}, \ldots, c_{s,m-1}] \cup \vec{A_s} = [\alpha_{s,1}, \ldots, \alpha_{s,m}]$ where $\vec{C_s}$ are input size cutoffs associated with algorithms $\vec{A_s}$. During program execution the runtime function $SELECT$ chooses an algorithm depending on the current input size by referencing the selector as follows:

$$SELECT(input, s) = \alpha_{s,i} \text{ s.t. } c_{s,i} > size(input) \geq c_{s,i-1}$$

where $c_{s,0} = 0$ and $c_{s,m} = \infty$. The components of $\vec{A_s}$ are indices into a discrete set of applicable algorithmic choices available to s, which we denote $Algorithms_s$.

In addition to these algorithmic choice selectors, the configuration file contains many other discrete tunable parameters. These tunable parameters include number of OpenCL work-items in the work-group, sequential/parallel cutoffs, and user defined parameters. Each tunable parameter is an integer with a positive bounded range.

5.2 Autotuning Algorithm

The autotuner uses an evolutionary algorithm to search through the available choice space. It maintains a population of candidate algorithms which it continually expands using a set of mutators and prunes by performance in order to allow the population to evolve more optimal algorithms. The input sizes used for testing during this process grow exponentially, which naturally exploits any optimal substructure inherent to most programs.

A key aspect of the autotuning algorithm is the mutation process. The mutation process is asexual, in that there is only a single parent algorithm for each newly created candidate. Additionally, newly created algorithms are only added to the population if they outperform the parent algorithm they were created from. Mutators are functions that create a new algorithm configuration by changing an existing configuration. The set of mutator functions is different for each program, and is generated fully automatically with the static analysis information extracted by the PetaBicks compiler.

There are different types of mutation operators that operate on specific parts of the program configuration. *Selector manipulation mutators* either add, remove, or change a level in a specific selector represented in the choice configuration file. *Synthetic function manipulation mutators* apply a change to a range of the underlying parameters based on the current input size being tested. Finally, *tunable manipulation mutators* randomly change a tunable value. Values that are compared to an input size, such as cutoffs, are scaled randomly by a value taken from a lognormal distribution. This means that small changes are more likely than large changes and a value is equally likely be halved as it is to be doubled. Values choosing from a set of choices, such as an algorithm, are chosen uniform randomly when mutated.

5.3 GPU Choice Representation to Autotuner

The compiler exposes four classes of GPU choices to the autotuner. First, there is the decision of if and when to use the GPU. This is encoded as an algorithmic choice in the selectors constructed by the autotuner. The autotuner can construct selectors that use the GPU for some input sizes and not others. The autotuner can also construct poly-algorithms that run some parts of the computation on the GPU and other parts on the CPU.

The second type of choice is memory mapping from PetaBricks

code to OpenCL. The choice indicates whether or not to use the local memory of the device when possible. This choice exists only if the OpenCL kernel with local memory version of a rule is generated. This is also mapped to an algorithmic choice using a selector constructed by to autotuner.

The third type is the number of work-items in the work-groups (or so called local work size) of each OpenCL kernel, since assigning the right local work size is a common optimization for GPU computing. These parameters are mapped to tunable values that the autotuner can explore independently of algorithmic choices.

The final one is GPU-CPU workload ratio of each transform, which defines what percentage of a region should be computed on the GPU. To limit the search space size, the possible ratios restricted to multiples of $1/8$.

In a big picture, every transform provides 12 levels of algorithmic choices for 12 different ranges of input sizes. Note that all levels of the same transform have the same number of algorithmic choices. For example, in SeparableConvolution configuration, each level of each `Convolve*` transform has three possible choices: using CPU backend, using OpenCL backend with global memory only, and using OpenCL backend with local memory optimization. Each `Convolve*` has two OpenCL kernels, so each of them has its own tunable parameters for local work size and GPU-CPU workload ratio. Apart from OpenCL related parameters, the configuration also includes other parameters such as split size for CPU work-stealing model, number of execution threads on CPU, and a sequential/parallel cutoff.

5.4 Challenges with Runtime Kernel Compilation

The PetaBricks autotuning approach runs large numbers of tests on small input sizes in order to quickly explore the choice space and seed exploration for larger input sizes. With only the CPU, these tests on small input sizes are very cheap and greatly improve convergence time. However, with our OpenCL backend these small tests take a much larger amount of time, because OpenCL kernels are compiled dynamically at runtime. These kernel compiles represent a fixed startup cost, often on the order of a few seconds, that dominate execution time for small input sizes. This factor increases autotuning time.

To address this problem we use two techniques. First, we cache the intermediate representation (IR) used by the OpenCL compiler. The first time we run a program, we store the OpenCL runtime-specific IR for each compiled kernel with the hash of the source for that kernel. This IR is reused in subsequent executions in order to skip the parsing and optimization phases of kernel compilation. Second, we adjusted the parameters of the autotuner so that it runs fewer tests at small input sizes. This involved both skipping extremely small input sizes entirely and running fewer tests on the smaller input sizes we do use. The result of these optimizations reduced typical training times from many days for some benchmarks to an average of 5.2 hours. This training time is still heavily influenced by architecture-specific JITing, which OpenCL does not allow to be cached. Full binary caching, as allowed by other languages such as CUDA, would further reduce training times.

6. Experimental Results

Our experimental results explore the extent to which different heterogeneous systems require different configurations to obtain optimal performance. To this end, our experiments test how configurations tuned for one heterogeneous system perform when run on a different system. We examine these differences both by testing relative performance and by examining the configurations and algorithmic choices of these tuned configurations.

Name	# Possible Configs	Generated OpenCL Kernels	Mean Autotuning Time	Testing Input Size
Black-Sholes	10^{130}	1	3.09 hours	500000
Poisson2D SOR	10^{1358}	25	15.37 hours	2048^2
SeparableConv.	10^{1358}	9	3.82 hours	3520^2
Sort	10^{920}	7	3.56 hours	2^{20}
Strassen	10^{1509}	9	3.05 hours	1024^2
SVD	10^{2435}	8	1.79 hours	256^2
Tridiagonal Solver	10^{1040}	8	5.56 hours	1024^2

Figure 8. Properties of the benchmarks. The number of configurations are calculated from the parameters described in Section 5.3.

6.1 Methodology

Figure 9 lists the representative test systems used in our experiments and assigns code names that will be used in the remainder of the section. We chose these machines to represent three diverse systems a program may run on. Desktop represents a high-end gaming system with a powerful processor and a graphics card. Server represents a large throughput-oriented multicore system one might find in a data center. It does not have a graphics card, we instead use a CPU OpenCL runtime that creates optimized parallel SSE code from OpenCL kernels. Laptop represents a laptop (it is actually a Mac Mini), with a low-power mobile processor and a graphics card. Together, our test systems cover graphics cards from both AMD and NVIDIA, use three different OpenCL runtimes, have two different operating systems, and range in cores from 2 to 32.

In our experiments we first create three program configurations by autotuning: *Desktop Config* is the configuration tuned on Desktop; *Server Config* is the configuration tuned on Server; and *Laptop Config* is the configuration tuned on Laptop.

Next, we run each of these three configurations on each of our three machines. Since we are migrating configurations between machines with different numbers of processors, for fairness, we remove the thread count parameter from the search space and set the number of threads equal to the number of processors on the current machine being tested. (On Server, the number of threads is set to 16 which provides better performance on every benchmark.)

Finally, for some benchmarks, we also include baseline results for comparison. We do this either by writing a PetaBricks program configuration by hand, by running OpenCL programs included as sample code in the NVIDIA OpenCL SDK, or by running CUDPP applications. We use the label *Hand-coded OpenCL* to indicate the performance of a standalone OpenCL program not using our system. These baselines are described in detail for each benchmark.

Figure 8 lists properties of each of our benchmarks from the PetaBricks benchmark suite. The configuration space is large, ranging from 10^{130} to 10^{2435}. Our system automatically creates up to 25 OpenCL kernels per benchmark. Average autotuning time was 5.2 hours. This training time is larger as a result of overheads from OpenCL kernel compilation, which dominate tuning time for many benchmarks. Individual benchmarks are described in more detail in the following section.

6.2 Benchmark Results and Analysis

Figure 6 summarizes the auto tuned configurations for each benchmark and Figure 7 shows the performance of each of these configurations on each system. Detailed analysis for each benchmark is provided in this section, and a more high level overview is provided in the next section.

	Desktop Config	Server Config	Laptop Config
Black-Sholes	100% on GPU	100% on OpenCL	Concurrently 25% on CPU and 75% on GPU
Poisson2D SOR	Split on CPU followed by compute on GPU	Split some parts on OpenCL followed by compute on CPU	Split on CPU followed by compute on GPU
SeparableConv.	1D kernel+local memory on GPU	1D kernel on OpenCL	2D kernel+local memory on GPU
Sort	Polyalgorithm: above 174762 2MS (PM), then QS until 64294, then 4MS until 341, then IS on CPU[1]	Polyalgorithm: above 7622 4MS, then 2MS until 2730, then IS on CPU[1]	Polyalgorithm: above 76830 4MS (PM), then 2MS until 8801 (above 34266 PM), then MS4 until 226, then IS on CPU[1]
Strassen	Data parallel on GPU	8-way parallel recursive decomposition on CPU, call LAPACK when $< 682 \times 682$	Directly call LAPACK on CPU
SVD	First phase: task parallism between CPU/GPU; matrix multiply: 8-way parallel recursive decomposition on CPU, call LAPACK when $< 42 \times 42$	First phase: all on CPU; matrix multiply: 8-way parallel recursive decomposition on CPU, call LAPACK when $< 170 \times 170$	First phase: all on CPU; matrix multiply: 4-way parallel recursive decomposition on CPU, call LAPACK when $< 85 \times 85$
Tridiagonal Solver	Cyclic reduction on GPU	Direct solve on CPU	Direct solve on CPU

Figure 6. Summary of the different autotuned configurations for each benchmark, focusing on the primary differences between the configurations. [1]For sort we use the abbreviations: IS = insertion sort, 2MS = 2-way mergesort, 4MS = 4-way mergesort, QS = quicksort, PM = with parallel merge.

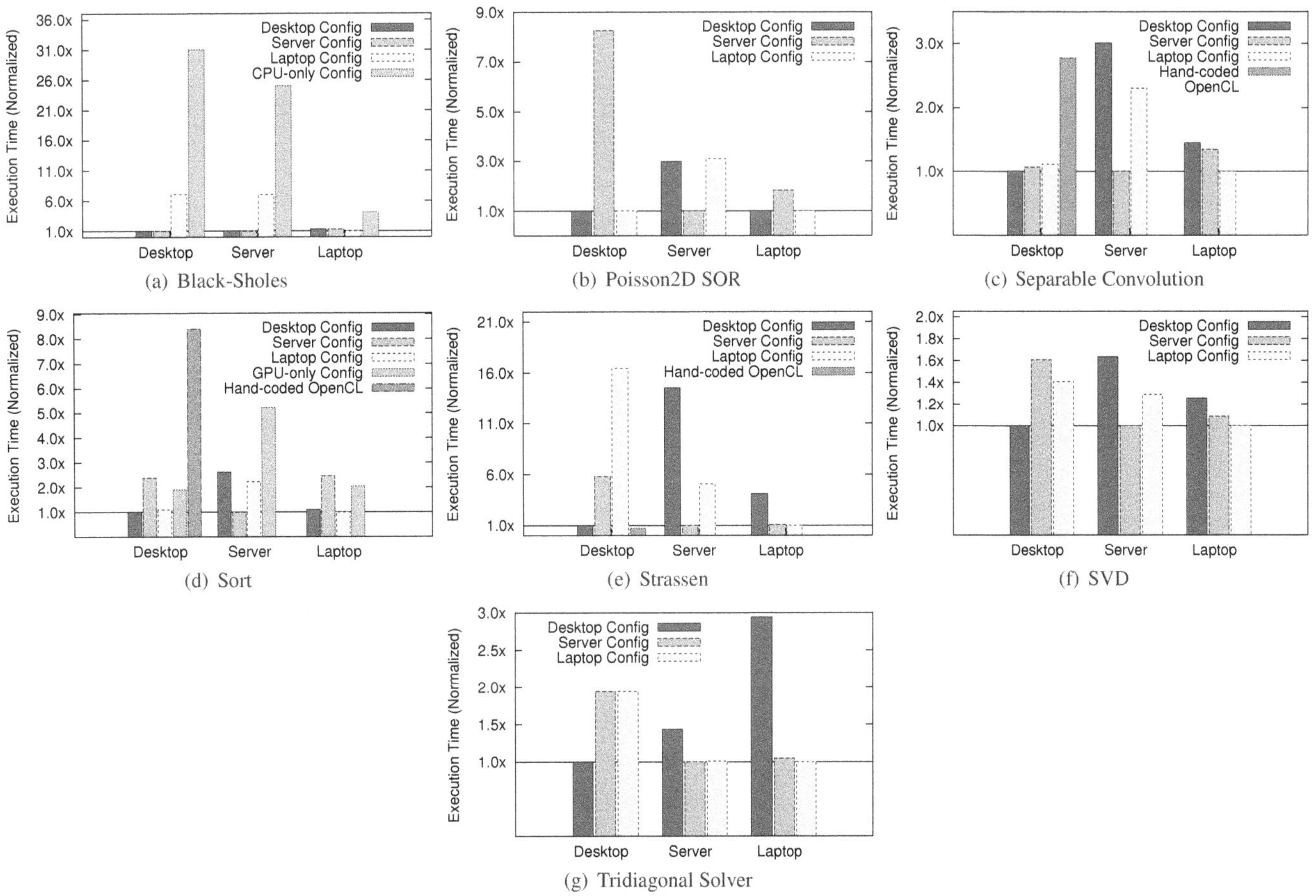

(a) Black-Sholes
(b) Poisson2D SOR
(c) Separable Convolution
(d) Sort
(e) Strassen
(f) SVD
(g) Tridiagonal Solver

Figure 7. Benchmark performance when varying the machine and the program configuration. Execution time on each machine is normalized to the natively autotuned configuration. Lower is better. 7(c), 7(d), and 7(e) include *Hand-coded OpenCL* as a baseline taken from the NVIDIA SDK sample code. This baseline uses NVIDIA-specific constructs and only runs on our Desktop system. These hand-coded OpenCL baselines implement 1D separable convolution, radix sort, and matrix multiply respectively. As additional baselines, 7(b) includes a *CPU-only Config* which uses a configuration autotuned with OpenCL choices disabled and 7(d) includes *GPU-only Config* which uses PetaBricks bitonic sort on the GPU.

Codename	CPU(s)	Cores	GPU	OS	OpenCL Runtime
Desktop	Core i7 920 @2.67GHz	4	NVIDIA Tesla C2070	Debian 5.0 GNU/Linux	CUDA Toolkit 4.2[1]
Server	4× Xeon X7550 @2GHz	32	None	Debian 5.0 GNU/Linux	AMD Accelerated Parallel Processing SDK 2.5[2]
Laptop	Core i5 2520M @2.5GHz	2	AMD Radeon HD 6630M	Mac OS X Lion (10.7.2)	Xcode 4.2[1]

Figure 9. Properties of the representative test systems and the code names used to identify them in results. The OpenCL runtimes marked [1] targets the GPUs of the machines, while [2] targets the CPU by generating optimized SSE code.

Black-Sholes The Black-Scholes benchmark results (Figure 7(a)) show that on some machines it is fastest to divide the data and compute part of the output on the CPU and another part concurrently on the GPU. Black-Scholes implements a mathematical model of a financial market to solve for the price of European options. Each entry of the output matrix can be computed from the input matrix by applying the Black-Scholes formula.

The autotuned Black-Scholes configurations on the Desktop and Server both perform all computation using the GPU/OpenCL backend, while the configuration on the Laptop divides the work such that 25% of the computation is performed on the CPU, and 75% is performed on the GPU. This 25/75 split provides a 1.3x speedup over using only the GPU on the Laptop, while such a split produces a 7x slowdown on the other two systems.

The reason why these configurations perform this way is the OpenCL performance for Black-Sholes is an order of magnitude better than the CPU performance on the Desktop and Server. However, on the laptop the relative performance of the GPU is only about 4x the performance of the CPU. This can be seen in the *CPU-only Config* bar in Figure 7(a), which is a baseline configuration that does not use the GPU/OpenCL backend. On the laptop, where the relative performance of the two processors is close, exploiting heterogeneous parallelism between the CPU and the GPU results in performance gains.

Poisson2D SOR The Poisson2D SOR benchmark (Figure 7(b)) shows that the choice of which backend is best for each phase of the computation can change between machines. This benchmark solves Poisson's equation using Red-Black Successive Over-Relaxation (SOR). Before main iteration, the algorithm splits the input matrix into separate buffers of red and black cells for cache efficiency.

In the Desktop and Laptop tuned configuration, this splitting is performed on the CPU and then actual iterations are performed using the OpenCL GPU backed. In the Server configuration, nearly the opposite happens; the OpenCL backend is used for splitting a large area of the matrix, and the CPU backend is used for the main iterations. The reason for this switch is the very different performance profiles of the OpenCL backends. The Desktop and Laptop utilize actual GPUs while the Server OpenCL backend shares the CPU.

Separable Convolution The Separable Convolution benchmark (Figure 7(c)) highights the effect of algorithmic choices on the GPU. Three configurations, all using only OpenCL for computation, provide very different performance on each machine. This benchmark is used as a driving example in Section 2.1, which describes the choices benchmark in more detail. At width 7, shown here, Desktop performs best using 1D separable convolution on the GPU with the GPU local memory. Laptop, with the less powerful GPU, performs best using local memory but with the single-pass 2D convolution algorithm, because the overhead of synchronization and creating an extra buffer to store the intermediate results between the two passes dominates the computational savings of the separable algorithm. The best configuration on Server uses the OpenCL version of separable convolution, but without local memory prefetching, since the CPUs' caches perform best here without explicit prefetches.

The results also show 2.3x better performance than OpenCL baseline implementation taken from the OpenCL samples in the NVIDIA SDK (Figure 7(c)). Our implementation differs from this sample code in that in our generated code each work-item computes exactly one entry of the output, while in the sample code each work-item computes multiple entries of the output. This optimization in the sample code not only increases code complexity, but also results in worse performance than our PetaBricks implementation on the Tesla C2070. Performance on these machines is complex and unpredictable, making hard-coded choices often lose to our automatically inferred results.

Sort The Sort benchmark (Figure 7(d)) shows that for some tasks it makes sense to run on the CPU. The benchmark includes 7 sorting algorithms: merge sort, parallel merge sort, quick sort, insertion sort, selection sort, radix sort, and bitonic sort; in addition, merge sort and parallel merge sort have choices of dividing a region into two or four subregions. The configuration defines a poly-algorithm that combines these sort building blocks together into a hybrid sorting algorithm

None of the tuned configurations choose to use OpenCL in the main sorting routine (although some helper functions, such as copy, are mapped to OpenCL). The choices in CPU code are complex, and result in up to a 2.6x difference in performance between autotuned configurations. Each configuration is a poly-algorithm that dynamically changes techniques at recursive call sites. Desktop uses 2-way merge sort with parallel merge at the top level, switches to quick sort when sizes of sub-arrays are smaller, switches to 4-way merge sort with sequential merge when sizes are even smaller, and finally ends with insertion sort as a base case when size is less than 341. Server uses 4-way merge sort with sequential merge, switches to 2-way merge sort when sizes are smaller, and finally switches to insertion sort when size is less than 2730. Laptop alternatively switches between 4-way and 2-way merge sort, uses parallel merge until size is less than 34266, and switches to insertion sort when size is less than 226.

For comparison, we wrote a configuration by hand that uses bitonic sort in OpenCL using our system (*GPU-only Config* in Figure 7(d)). This configuration is between 1.9 and 5.2x slower than the native autotuned configuration. Interestingly, this configuration does beat the Server configuration on both of the other machines that have GPUs. This means that, if one had the Server configuration, using the GPU instead would give a speedup, but not as much of a speedup as re-tuning on the CPU.

As a second baseline, we include the radix sort sample program from the NVIDIA SDK (*Hand-coded OpenCL* in Figure 7(d)). This OpenCL implementation of Sort performs 8.4x worse than our autotuned configuration and 4.4x worse than our bitonic sort configuration. The poor performance of both of these GPU Sort baselines, relative to our autotuned Sort, speak to the difficulty writing a high performance Sort on the GPU. Researchers have developed faster methods for GPU sorting, however, these methods require both an autotuning system and heroic programmer effort [?], and their performance generally does not account for overhead in copying data to and from the GPU, which our benchmarks do.

Strassen The Strassen benchmark (Figure 7(e)) shows that choosing the right configuration for each architecture results in very large performance gains. The Strassen benchmark performs a dense matrix-matrix multiplication. The choices include: transposing any combination of the inputs; four different recursive decompositions, including Strassen's algorithm; various blocking methods; naive matrix multiplication; and calling the LAPACK external library.

Figure 7(e) shows the performance of our Strassen benchmark with different configurations. Laptop configuration gives a 16.5x slowdown on Desktop. OpenCL is used in the Desktop configuration, and C++/Fortran (through a call to LAPACK) is used in the Server and Laptop configurations. The large computation to communication ratio in matrix multiplication stresses the difference in relative CPU/GPU computational power between Desktop, with a high performance graphics card, and Laptop, with a mobile graphics card. This results in the Desktop GPU producing a speedup compared to its CPU, and the Laptop GPU producing a slowdown.

Altough Server and Laptop both use CPUs, their optimal configurations are different. On Server, the best algorithm is to recursively decompose the matrices in 8-way parallel fashion until the regions are smaller than a certain size, call LAPACK on the small regions, and finally combine the data. On Laptop, the best algorithm is to make a direct call to LAPACK without any decomposition.

As a baseline, we include the matrix multiplication OpenCL sample from the NVIDIA SDK (*Hand-coded OpenCL* in Figure 7(e)). This baseline runs 1.4x faster than our autotuned configuration on Desktop. The reason for this difference is the hand-coded OpenCL uses a number complex manual local memory optimizations that accumulate partially computed outputs in local memory shared between work-items. We have not implemented a similar optimization in our system; however, it would be possible to automatically perform a similar optimization.

Singular Value Decomposition (SVD) The results for SVD (Figure 7(f)) are particularly interesting because on some systems the autotuner constructs a poly-algorithm with task parallel divisions between the GPU and the CPU, and the complexity of the benchmark provides a large number of choices in the search space. This benchmark approximates a matrix through a factorization that consumes less space. SVD is a variable accuracy benchmark where many of the choices available to the autotuner, such as how many eigenvalues to use, impact the quality of of the approximation. The autotuner must produce an algorithm which meets a given accuracy target. These variable accuracy features are described in more detail in [4].

On Desktop, the autotuned configuration divides the work by using the GPU to compute one matrix and the CPU to concurrently compute another matrix. Since the computations of the two matrices are very similar, and the CPU and the GPU have relatively similar performance for these computations on Desktop, overall throughput is increased by dividing the work in this way.

This benchmark also demonstrates that the best configurations of a sub-program might be different when the sub-program is a part of different applications even running on the same machine. The SVD benchmark uses the Strassen code to perform matrix multiplication. However SVD uses matrix multiply on sub-regions of multiple larger arrays (resulting in different data locality) and possibly making multiple calls concurrently. Due to the different data-accessing patterns, the cache behaviors are not the same on the CPU, the bank conflicts on GPU memory vary, and the interactions between subsystems change. This makes the best configurations differ for Strassen inside SVD and in isolation. While the best matrix multiplication configuration on Desktop for Strassen in isolation always uses the GPU, the best one for this benchmark is 8-way parallel recursive decomposition and then calling LAPACK. The autotuned configurations on Server and Laptop for this benchmark are also different from Strassen in isolation.

Tridiagonal Solver The Tridiagonal Solver benchmark (Figure 7(g)) shows that often algorithmic changes are required to utilize the GPU. The benchmark solves a system of a equations where the matrix contains non-zero elements only on cells neighboring and on the diagonal and includes a variety of techniques including polyalgorithms. We implement a subset of the algorithmic choices described in [9, 30].

Similar to the Strassen benchmark, the GPU is only used on the Desktop machine; however, in order to utilize the GPU, an algorithmic change is required. Cyclic reduction is the best algorithm for Desktop when using the GPU. If a machine does not use OpenCL, it is better to run the sequential algorithm as demonstrated used on Server and Laptop.

Our best configuration on Desktop is 3.5x slower than CUDPP[30] on input size 512. Some of this slowdown is a result of OpenCL being generally slower than CUDA when using the NVIDIA toolchain. Additionally, our automatically generated OpenCL kernel is not as highly optimized as CUDPP's kernel, which guarantees the efficient use of shared memory without bank conflicts.

6.3 Results Summary

In all of our benchmarks, algorithmic choices—which traditional languages and compilers do not expose—play a large role in performance on heterogeneous systems since the best algorithms vary not only between machines but also between processors within a machine. Ultimately, the complex and interdependent space of best mapping choices seen in these benchmarks would be very difficult to predict from first principles, alone, but our empirical exploration effectively and automatically accounts for many interacting effects on actual machine performance, in each program on each system.

Taken together, these seven benchmarks demonstrate even more of the complexity in mapping programs to heterogeneous machines than any one benchmark alone.

- *Strassen* shows that choosing the right configuration for each specific architecture can provide a huge performance improvement. In this benchmark, choosing to use a data parallel accelerator can yield large speedups (16.5x) on some machines, and large slowdowns (4.1x) on others, for the same problem, depending on the exact characteristics of all heterogeneous processors in the system.
- *Poisson 2D SOR* further supports the previous argument by showing that the optimal placement of computations across the processors in one system is almost the opposite of another.
- *Tridiagonal Solver* demonstrates that not only where computations run, but also which algorithms to use on that particular resource, can dramatically affect performance.
- *Separable Convolution* shows that, even when a program is best run entirely on the data-parallel compute resources, the best algorithm to use and the best strategy for mapping to the complex heterogeneous memory hierarchy vary widely both across machines and across program parameters (kernel size).
- *Sort*, on the other hand, shows that even parallel problems may not always be best solved by data parallel accelerators, and that complex machine-specific algorithmic choice is still essential to performance on a smaller array of conventional processors.
- *SVD* shows that the best performance can require mapping por-

tions of a program across all different processor types available, and together with Strassen, it shows that the best configurations of the same sub-program in different applications vary on the same system.

- Finally, while SVD confirms that sometimes it is best to run different portions of a program on different subsystems concurrently, *Black-Scholes* illustrates that sometimes it is best to run the same portion of the program but different regions of data across multiple heterogeneous subsystems simultaneously; therefore, considering the workload balance between processor types is important to achieve the optimal performance on a heterogeneous system.

7. Related Work

A number of offline empirical autotuning frameworks have been developed for building efficient, portable libraries in specific domains. ATLAS [27] utilizes empirical autotuning to produce a cache-contained matrix multiply, which is then used in larger matrix computations in BLAS and LAPACK. FFTW [10] uses empirical autotuning to combine solvers for FFTs. Other autotuning systems include SPARSITY [14] for sparse matrix computations, SPIRAL [23] for digital signal processing, and OSKI [26] for sparse matrix kernels.

The area of iterative compilation contains many projects that use different machine learning techniques to optimize lower level compiler optimizations [1, 2, 12, 22]. These projects change both the order that compiler passes are applied and the types of passes that are applied. However, these projects do not explore the type of algorithmic choices that the PetaBricks language exposes, and these systems create only compile time, not runtime choices.

The use of autotuning techniques is even more commonplace when optimizing GPGPU programs. Autotuning is typically applied in a program or domain-specific fashion. Such systems use autotuners to construct poly-algorithms for solving large tridiagonal systems [9], for tuning GPU sorting algorithms [?], autotuning 3D FFT with a focus on padding and bandwidth optimizations [21], autotuning sparse matrix-vector multiply by building performance models [8], and to tune dense linear algebra with a mix of model-driven and empirical techniques [25]. These techniques are often specific to a problem or class of problems.

Besides problem-specific techniques, there is a high-level directive-based GPU programming that uses HMPP workbench to automatically generate CUDA/OpenCL code, and auto-tunes on the optimization space on the generated GPU kernels [13]. However, this technique and the previous ones only point towards autotuning as a necessity in order to get the best performance on modern GPUs; they do not address how to utilize all available resources together to achieve the best performance on a heterogeneous system.

Several methods to efficiently distribute workload between different devices have been studied. StarPU applies work-stealing framework to balance work among subsystems [5]. However, StarPU requires the programmer to write separate CPU and GPU code, and relies entirely on dynamic work-stealing guided by automatic hints to distribute tasks. CnC-HC automatically generates CPU, GPU, and FPGA code and uses a work-stealing scheduler to distribute work among different devices guided by manual hints only [24]. Qilin, automatically generates code and uses *adaptive mapping* for performance tuning [20]. During the training run, Qilin executes the program on different input sizes on CPUs and GPUs separately, and uses the result to determine workload partitions between the CPUs and the GPUs. However, the mapping of these systems may not be ideal. Our system automates the entire process, both translating kernels to different targets, and empirically determining where they should run in our hybrid work-stealing/work-pushing runtime. For real applications, the ideal mapping is globally non-linearly inter-dependent with all other choices, and our global optimization captures this during autotuning. Our results demonstrate the importance of global learning.

CGCM [15] uses a technique for automatic management of GPU/CPU memory communication. This technique is similar to our analysis for determining when lazy or eager copy-outs are used. Their technique uses a conservative reachability analysis to determine where to insert calls into a runtime that dynamically tracks and maps data to different memories. They focus on a number of optimizations to this technique to reduce runtime overhead. While CGCM manages data movement automatically, it requires some programmer help when managing parallelism.

A number of other programming languages attempt to make programming for GPGPU devices easier. CUDA-lite [29], automates some of the parallelization and memory management tasks in writing CUDA. JCUDA [28] alleviates many of the difficulties in using the GPU from Java code. There have also been efforts to map subsets of C to the GPU [6, 19]. These techniques put affine data access restrictions on the program. There have been other efforts to map OpenMP to the GPU [17]. While these efforts make running code on the GPU easier, they will produce the same code for each heterogeneous system and do not allow algorithmic choice, or empirically infer the best mapping for each machine.

Researchers have also studied the relative throughput of the CPU and the GPU and discovered contradictory findings with some studies showing 100x performance differences and others just 2.5x [18]. Our work sheds more light on this debate, showing that both claims can be correct. The best device to use is highly dependant both on the architecture and algorithmic choices and cannot be determined by simple relative performance numbers. We also show cases where the best throughput is obtained by using both the CPU and the GPU in parallel.

8. Conclusions

Programmers and compilers collaborate to map problems into precise machine instructions. There are many choices in how to map a given problem onto a particular machine. The programmer typically makes the higher-level choices (e.g. which algorithms to use), while a compiler will make the lower-level choices in how to map to a specific machine (e.g. register allocation, instruction selection, loop transformations). Both the programmer's and the compiler's decisions are often based on heuristic models of machine performance. Simplistic models of machine performance are assumed when the programmer performs O analysis or cache blocking, or when the compiler uses heuristics like minimizing instructions executed or stack spills.

It is increasingly difficult for a single model to accurately represent the complex heterogeneous machines in widespread use today. Further, on these machines, high-level algorithmic and scheduling choices, and low-level machine mapping choices, interact in complex ways to influence actual machine performance. We have found, and our results show, that simultaneous empirical exploration of algorithmic and machine mapping choices can effectively compile an array of programs to efficient execution on modern heterogeneous parallel machines, including both multicore CPUs and GPUs. The best choices for each heterogeneous machine are often complex, and map portions of different algorithms in multiple ways across all processors and memories in the machine. Our results further show that this full choice space is important to consider, since the best algorithms and mapping strategies on one heterogeneous system are often not the same as on another.

Models are still useful in some situations. The search space of all possible choices in algorithm and machine mapping is enormous, and many individual choices have optimal substructure, so reducing the empirical search space with model-driven choices can be both essential and effective, even when autotuning. Most of all, models aid human comprehension, which can be essential to creating new algorithms and optimizations, and new architectures on which to run them. But compilers should not be wedded to models and heuristics alone when faced with programs and machines of ever-increasing complexity.

Acknowledgments

We would like to thank the anonymous reviewers for their constructive feedback, David Garcia for many suggestions on OpenCL related problems on the Khronos forum, and NVIDIA for donating a graphics card used to conduct experiments. This work is partially supported by DOE award DE-SC0005288, DOD DARPA award HR0011-10-9-0009 and NSF award CCF-0632997.

References

[1] F. Agakov, E. Bonilla, J. Cavazos, B. Franke, G. Fursin, M. F. P. O'boyle, J. Thomson, M. Toussaint, and C. K. I. Williams. Using machine learning to focus iterative optimization. In *Symposium on Code Generation and Optimization*, 2006.

[2] L. Almagor, Keith D. Cooper, Alexander Grosul, Timothy J. Harvey, Steven W. Reeves, Devika Subramanian, Linda Torczon, and Todd Waterman. Finding effective compilation sequences. In *Conference on Languages, Compilers, and Tools for Embedded Systems*, New York, NY, USA, 2004.

[3] Jason Ansel, Cy Chan, Yee Lok Wong, Marek Olszewski, Qin Zhao, Alan Edelman, and Saman Amarasinghe. Petabricks: A language and compiler for algorithmic choice. In *Programming Language Design and Implementation*, Dublin, Ireland, Jun 2009.

[4] Jason Ansel, Yee Lok Wong, Cy Chan, Marek Olszewski, Alan Edelman, and Saman Amarasinghe. Language and compiler support for auto-tuning variable-accuracy algorithms. In *Symposium on Code Generation and Optimization*, Chamonix, France, Apr 2011.

[5] Cédric Augonnet, Samuel Thibault, Raymond Namyst, and Pierre-André Wacrenier. StarPU: a unified platform for task scheduling on heterogeneous multicore architectures. *Concurrency and Computation: Practice and Experience*, 23(2), 2011.

[6] Muthu Baskaran, J. Ramanujam, and P. Sadayappan. Automatic c-to-CUDA code generation for affine programs. In Rajiv Gupta, editor, *Compiler Construction*, volume 6011. Springer Berlin / Heidelberg, 2010.

[7] J. Charles, P. Jassi, N.S. Ananth, A. Sadat, and A. Fedorova. Evaluation of the Intel Core i7 Turbo Boost feature. In *Symposium on Workload Characterization*, Oct 2009.

[8] Jee W. Choi, Amik Singh, and Richard W. Vuduc. Model-driven autotuning of sparse matrix-vector multiply on GPUs. In *Symposium on Principles and Practice of Parallel Programming*, New York, NY, USA, 2010.

[9] Andrew Davidson, Yao Zhang, and John D. Owens. An auto-tuned method for solving large tridiagonal systems on the GPU. In *Parallel and Distributed Processing Symposium*. IEEE, May 2011.

[10] Matteo Frigo and Steven G. Johnson. The design and implementation of FFTW3. *Proceedings of the IEEE*, 93(2), February 2005.

[11] Matteo Frigo, Charles E. Leiserson, and Keith H. Randall. The implementation of the cilk-5 multithreaded language. In *Programming language design and implementation*, New York, NY, USA, 1998.

[12] Grigori Fursin, Cupertino Miranda, Olivier Temam, Mircea Namolaru, Elad Yom-Tov, Ayal Zaks, Bilha Mendelson, Edwin Bonilla, John Thomson, Hugh Leather, Chris Williams, Michael O'Boyle, Phil Barnard, Elton Ashton, Eric Courtois, and Francois Bodin. MILEPOST GCC: machine learning based research compiler. In *GCC Developers' Summit*, Jul 2008.

[13] Scott Grauer-Gray, Lifan Xu, Robert Ayalasomayajula, and John Cavazos. Auto-tuning a high-level language targeted to GPU codes. In *Innovative Parallel Computing Conference*. IEEE, May 2012.

[14] Eun-jin Im and Katherine Yelick. Optimizing sparse matrix computations for register reuse in SPARSITY. In *Computational Science*. Springer, 2001.

[15] Thomas B. Jablin, Prakash Prabhu, James A. Jablin, Nick P. Johnson, Stephen R. Beard, and David I. August. Automatic CPU-GPU communication management and optimization. In *Programming language design and implementation*, New York, NY, USA, 2011.

[16] Rakesh Kumar, Dean M. Tullsen, Norman P. Jouppi, and Parthasarathy Ranganathan. Heterogeneous chip multiprocessors. *Computer*, 38(11), November 2005.

[17] Seyong Lee, Seung-Jai Min, and Rudolf Eigenmann. OpenMP to GPGPU: a compiler framework for automatic translation and optimization. *SIGPLAN Not.*, 44, February 2009.

[18] Victor W. Lee, Changkyu Kim, Jatin Chhugani, Michael Deisher, Daehyun Kim, Anthony D. Nguyen, Nadathur Satish, Mikhail Smelyanskiy, Srinivas Chennupaty, Per Hammarlund, Ronak Singhal, and Pradeep Dubey. Debunking the 100X GPU vs. CPU myth: an evaluation of throughput computing on CPU and GPU. In *international symposium on Computer architecture*, New York, NY, USA, 2010.

[19] Allen Leung, Nicolas Vasilache, Benoit Meister, Muthu Baskaran, David Wohlford, Cedric Bastoul, and Richard Lethin. A mapping path for multi-GPGPU accelerated computers from a portable high level programming abstraction. In *Workshop on General-Purpose Computation on Graphics Processing Units*, New York, NY, USA, 2010.

[20] Chi-Keung Luk, Sunpyo Hong, and Hyesoon Kim. Qilin: exploiting parallelism on heterogeneous multiprocessors with adaptive mapping. In *International Symposium on Microarchitecture*, New York, NY, USA, 2009.

[21] Akira Nukada and Satoshi Matsuoka. Auto-tuning 3-d FFT library for CUDA GPUs. In *High Performance Computing Networking, Storage and Analysis*, New York, NY, USA, 2009.

[22] Eunjung Park, L.-N. Pouche, J. Cavazos, A. Cohen, and P. Sadayappan. Predictive modeling in a polyhedral optimization space. In *Symposium on Code Generation and Optimization*, April 2011.

[23] Markus Puschel, Jose M. F. Moura, Jeremy R. Johnson, David Padua, Manuela M. Veloso, Bryan W. Singer, Jianxin Xiong, Franz Franchetti, Aca Gacic, Yevgen Voronenko, Kang Chen, Robbert W. Johnson, and Nicholas Rizzolo. SPIRAL: Code generation for DSP transforms. In *Proceedings of the IEEE*, volume 93. IEEE, Feb 2005.

[24] Alina Sbîrlea, Yi Zou, Zoran Budimlíc, Jason Cong, and Vivek Sarkar. Mapping a data-flow programming model onto heterogeneous platforms. In *International Conference on Languages, Compilers, Tools and Theory for Embedded Systems*, New York, NY, USA, 2012.

[25] V. Volkov and J.W. Demmel. Benchmarking GPUs to tune dense linear algebra. In *Supercomputing*, November 2008.

[26] Richard Vuduc, James W. Demmel, and Katherine A. Yelick. OSKI: A library of automatically tuned sparse matrix kernels. In *Scientific Discovery through Advanced Computing Conference*, San Francisco, CA, USA, June 2005.

[27] Richard Clint Whaley and Jack J. Dongarra. Automatically tuned linear algebra software. In *ACM/IEEE Conference on Supercomputing*, Washington, DC, USA, 1998.

[28] Yonghong Yan, Max Grossman, and Vivek Sarkar. JCUDA: A programmer-friendly interface for accelerating Java programs with CUDA. In Henk Sips, Dick Epema, and Hai-Xiang Lin, editors, *Euro-Par 2009 Parallel Processing*, volume 5704. Springer Berlin / Heidelberg, 2009.

[29] Sain zee Ueng, Melvin Lathara, Sara S. Baghsorkhi, and Wen mei W. Hwu. CUDA-Lite: Reducing GPU programming complexity. In *Workshops on Languages and Compilers for Parallel Computing*. Springer, 2008.

[30] Yao Zhang, Jonathan Cohen, and John D. Owens. Fast tridiagonal solvers on the GPU. In *Symposium on Principles and Practice of Parallel Programming*, January 2010.

Efficient Virtualization on Embedded Power Architecture® Platforms

Aashish Mittal Dushyant Bansal
Sorav Bansal
Indian Institute of Technology Delhi

Varun Sethi
Freescale Semiconductor India

Abstract

Power Architecture® processors are popular and widespread on embedded systems, and such platforms are increasingly being used to run virtual machines [11, 22]. While the Power Architecture meets the Popek-and-Goldberg virtualization requirements for traditional trap-and-emulate style virtualization, the performance overhead of virtualization remains high. For example, workloads exhibiting a large amount of kernel activity typically show 3-5x slowdowns over bare-metal.

Recent additions to the Linux kernel contain guest and host side paravirtual extensions for Power Architecture platforms. While these extensions improve performance significantly, they are guest-specific, guest-intrusive, and cover only a subset of all possible virtualization optimizations.

We present a set of host-side optimizations that achieve comparable performance to the aforementioned paravirtual extensions, on an unmodified guest. Our optimizations are based on adaptive in-place binary translation. Unlike the paravirtual approach, our solution is guest neutral. We implement our ideas in a prototype based on Qemu/KVM. After our modifications, KVM can boot an unmodified Linux guest around 2.5x faster. We contrast our optimization approach with previous similar binary translation based approaches for the x86 architecture [4]; in our experience, each architecture presents a unique set of challenges and optimization opportunities.

Categories and Subject Descriptors C.0 [*General*]: Hardware/software interface; C.4 [*Performance of systems*]: Performance attributes; D.4.7 [*Operating Systems*]: Organization and Design

General Terms Performance, Design

Keywords Virtualization, Virtual Machine Monitor, Dynamic Binary Translation, Power Architecture Platforms, Architecture Design, Code Patching, TLB, In-place Binary Translation, Read/write Tracing, Adaptive Page Resizing, Adaptive Data Mirroring

1. Introduction

Embedded devices based on Power Architecture processors are dominant for their favourable power/performance characteristics. Virtualization on these platforms is compelling for several applications including high availability (active/standby configuration without additional hardware), in-service upgrade, resource isolation, and many more [11, 22]. While newer Power Architecture platforms have explicit support for efficient virtualization [2, 3], a majority of prevalent embedded devices run on older Power Architecture platforms that use traditional trap-and-emulate style virtualization [19]. These older platforms have power and cost advantages and are expected to remain relevant for at least many more years. Several systems based on these platforms are being actively manufactured (e.g., P1020 and P2020 series [16, 17], BSC9131 and BSC9132 [1], etc.) with applications in wireless (e.g., Femtocell solutions for LTE), high-speed networking, and more. Efficient virtualization is highly desirable on these platforms.

The current virtualization approach on Power Architecture platforms uses traditional trap-and-emulate. The guest operating system is run unprivileged, causing each execution of a privileged operation to exit into the hypervisor. For guest workloads executing a large number of privileged instructions, these VM exits are a major source of performance overhead. Table 1 lists the performance of vanilla Linux/KVM on a few common workloads, comparing them with bare-metal performance. For example, a guest Linux boot takes almost 5x longer when run virtualized.

The poor performance of simple trap-and-emulate style virtualization has led to the inclusion of paravirtual extensions in the Linux kernel on both guest and host sides for Power Architecture platform [18]. The paravirtual extension in the guest rewrites the guest (binary) kernel code at startup time to replace most privileged instructions with hypervisor-aware unprivileged counterparts. At guest startup, the guest creates a shared address space with the host through a *hypercall*. This shared address space is used by the hypervisor to store guest state information, which is accessible to the guest without incurring a trap. Table 1 lists KVM performance after enabling paravirtual extensions in the guest and the host. While paravirtual extensions improve performance significantly over unmodified KVM, this approach has obvious shortcomings related to requirements of being able to access and modify guest source code, inability to optimize dynamically loaded code (e.g., loadable modules), etc. These constraints make this approach ineffective and/or impractical in many real-world and commercial settings.

We propose a host-side adaptive in-place binary translation mechanism to optimize guest privileged instructions at runtime, and improve the performance of unmodified (and untrusted) guests. Our approach is more general than the paravirtualization approach; we can optimize dynamically generated/loaded code, and can gracefully handle self-referential and self-modifying code in the guest. The second-last column in Table 1 summarizes the performance results of our host-side binary translation approach.

S.No.	Benchmark	Description	Bare-metal	KVM	KVM-PV	KVM-BT	Speedup
			Running Time in sec (lower is better)				
1	`linux-boot`	Boots a Linux 3.0 guest	6.5	30.03	11.79	12.39	2.4x
2	`echo-spawn`	Spawns 1000 echo processes	1.4	21.34	6.5	6.85	3.1x
3	`find`	Executes `'find / -name temp'`	0.39	1.89	0.67	0.83	2.3x
4	`lame`	MP3 encoder	0.44	0.56	0.49	0.50	1.1x
`lmbench` microbenchmarks			Latency in $msec$ (lower is better)				
5	`syscall`	Writes one word to /dev/null	0.0002	0.020	0.003	0.003	6.7x
6	`stat`	Invokes the stat system call	0.003	0.033	0.006	0.007	4.7x
7	`fstat`	Invokes fstat system call on an open file	0.001	0.021	0.004	0.004	5.3x
8	`open/close`	Opens a temporary file for reading and closes it immediately	0.006	0.067	0.013	0.023	2.9x
9	`sig-hndl`	Installs a signal handler	0.001	0.024	0.004	0.004	6x
10	`pipe`	Passes a word from process A to process B and back to A and measures round-trip time	0.003	0.066	0.033	0.041	1.6x
11	`fork`	Calls `fork` and `exit`	1.084	6.641	1.640	1.679	3.9x
12	`exec`	Calls `fork`, `exec` and `exit`	3.065	20.543	6.254	6.681	3.1x
13	`sh`	Calls `fork`, `exec sh -c` and `exit`	6.645	45.164	13.842	14.719	3.1x
`Unixbench` microbenchmarks			Raw Score in 10 seconds (higher is better)				
15	`dhrystone2`	Focuses on string handling	49697211	48110141	49014236	48957180	1.02x
16	`syscall`	Calls the getpid system call	7863359	124854	818940	652829	5.2x
17	`cswitch`	Spawns a child process with which it carries on a bi-directional pipe conversation	420968	60746	307136	240653	4.0x
18	`proc-create`	Forks and reaps a child that immediately exits.	44667	2470	9432	8714	3.5x
19	`pipe`	Writes 512 bytes to a pipe and read them back	3324145	188208	1111797	923218	4.9x
20	`hanoi`	Calls compute-intensive hanoi program	8853023	8689401	8846663	8836219	1.02x
`Unixbench Filesystem` microbenchmarks			Throughput in KBps with 256 bufsize and 2000 max blocks (higher is better)				
21	`file-read`	Read from a file	182340	11524	58647	49830	4.3x
22	`file-write`	Write to a file	99850	10500	39500	38200	3.6x
23	`file-copy`	Transfers data from one file to another	59612	5432	22225	20070	3.7x

Table 1. Performance comparison of bare-metal, unmodified KVM, KVM-paravirtual, and our (KVM-BT) approach. The details of the benchmarks, our test system, and the various KVM variants is discussed in Section 5. The last column computes the speedup of `KVM-BT` over `KVM`.

Our host-side virtualization optimizations are based on adaptive in-place binary translation. On observing a large number of VM exits by a guest instruction, we translate that instruction *in-place* to directly execute the corresponding VMM logic (thus avoiding an exit). In doing so, we directly modify the guest's address space. This is in contrast to a *full* binary translation approach that translates the entire guest code (e.g., VMware's x86-based binary translator [4]). We compare the two approaches in more detail later in this section and also in Section 6.1.

Modifying the guest's address space has obvious pitfalls. Firstly, we must ensure correctness in presence of arbitrary branches in the code. For example, it would be incorrect if the guest could potentially jump to the middle of our translated code. To ensure correctness, we replace a privileged guest instruction by at most one translated instruction in the guest's address space. Because instructions are fixed length and word aligned on Power Architecture platform, this ensures that there can never be a branch to the middle of our translated code. Any branch could only reach either the beginning or the end of our replacement instruction.

Not all guest privileged instructions can be emulated by just one replacement instruction. Such instructions are instead replaced with a branch to a code fragment in a host-managed translation cache. This branch is implemented as a single instruction in the guest's address space, and the translation cache is allocated in guest virtual address space such that it always remains accessible to this instruction. Finding, allocating, and protecting appropriate space for the translation cache was our second challenge. Branch instructions using direct-addressing on Power Architecture platforms can only address $\pm$32MB relative/absolute offsets in the guest virtual address space, and this places constraints on the placement of the translation cache. It is possible for the guest to be already using all such virtual address space that satisfies the required placement constraints. We present a scheme to *steal* data pages from guest's address space to place the translation cache. To protect against guest accesses, we mark the pages in the stolen space *execute-only*. This causes the hardware to trap into the VMM on any guest read/write access to this space. We call this mechanism *read/write tracing*. Read/write tracing is also used to maintain safety against in-place guest modification, in presence of self-referential and self-modifying code.

Finally, read/write tracing can cause a large number of page faults, especially due to false sharing. The problem is exacerbated on embedded Power Architecture platform, where OS typically uses huge pages to reduce TLB pressure. We found that such page faults can significantly reduce performance. We implement two important optimizations to address this problem, namely *adaptive page resizing* and *adaptive data mirroring*.

Our work differs from previous x86-based binary translation work by VMware [4] in many ways, with most differences stemming from differences in the two architectures. First, unlike VMware's binary translator, our approach translates in-place. As we discuss later, this approach requires certain architectural features but has advantages in design simplicity and performance. Second, VMware's translator places its translation cache and other data structures at the top of the guest virtual address space and relies on x86 segmentation hardware to protect them from guest access. As we discuss later, these design choices are not suited to Power Architecture platforms, due to Power Architecture ISA addressing constraints and lack of segmentation hardware. We create space for our translation cache by stealing data pages from guest address space and protect it using read/write tracing. Further, address space manipulation on embedded Power Architecture platforms present unique challenges due to constraints on page sizes, alignments, and TLB cache sizes. These challenges are unique to embedded architectures, and have not been observed in previous work on x86 virtualization. We address these challenges using our adaptive page resizing algorithm. Finally, we present and evaluate an important optimization to reduce read/write tracing overhead, namely adaptive data mirroring. In this optimization, we make a copy of the traced pages in another unused part of the guest address space and adaptively translate read/write accesses to this data such that they do not trap.

In summary, this paper presents an efficient host-side optimization solution for Power Architecture virtualization. Our approach, based on in-place binary translation (also called in-place BT in the rest of the paper), significantly improves the performance of an unmodified guest. We present novel solutions to deal with challenges like address space allocation for the translation cache and optimizing read/write tracing overhead for small software-managed TLB caches. We study an interesting three-way tradeoff on the embedded platform between the number of VM exits due to privileged instructions, the number of tracing page faults, and the number of TLB misses due to TLB pressure, and offer an optimization solution. The paper is organized as follows. Section 2 characterizes the performance of KVM on Power Architecture platform and discusses the typical sources of overhead. Section 3 discusses our in-place binary translation approach. We discuss read/write tracing and the associated optimizations in Section 4. Section 5 presents our experiments and results, and finally Sections 6-7 conclude.

2. Performance Characterization of KVM on Power Architecture Platforms

We first characterize KVM's performance on embedded Power Architecture platforms. We perform our experiments on Linux/KVM running on Freescale P2020 embedded Power Architecture platform. On our test platform, the virtualization overheads of trap-and-emulate style virtualization can be up to 15x for compute-intensive workloads executing a large number of privileged instructions (Table 1). The primary source of overhead are VM-exits due to guest privileged instructions. Table 2 lists the most executed privileged opcodes and briefly explains their semantics. Figure 1 shows the percentage of exits caused due to each opcode. Only five distinct opcodes result in more than 80% of exits on all four benchmarks. Table 3 presents the frequency profile of VM exits on the Linux boot benchmark in more detail (similar profiles are seen on other benchmarks too).

We next profile the number of distinct program counter (PC) values that cause exits. Figure 2 shows a histogram on the number of distinct PC values and the frequency of exits on them. Table 4 presents the exit profile of different PCs in more detail for the Linux boot benchmark. For example, around 92% of all exits are caused by only 93 distinct PCs for guest Linux boot. Other benchmarks also show similar locality for VM exits. These measurements con-

Opcode	Description
`mfmsr`	Move from machine state register
`mtmsr`	Move to machine state register
`mfspr`	Move from special purpose register
`mtspr`	Move to special purpose register
`wrtee(i)`	Write MSR External Enable
`rfi`	Return from Interrupt
`tlbwe`	Writes a TLB entry in hardware
Exception	**Description**
`dtlbmiss`	Page fault on data due to TLB not present
`itlbmiss`	Page fault on instruction due to TLB not present
`dsi`	Page fault due to insufficient privilege

Table 2. Sources of VM Exits: Opcodes and Exceptions

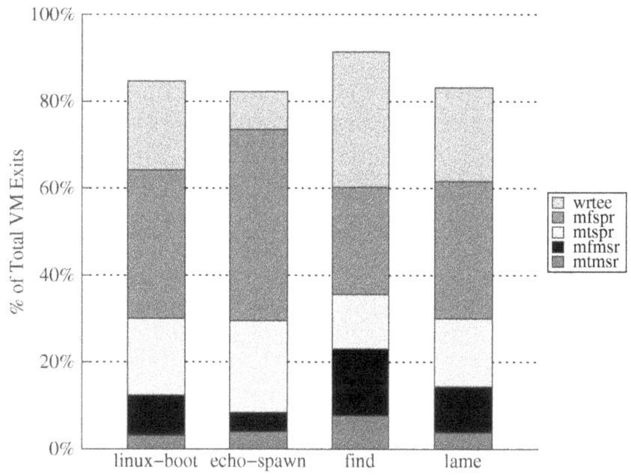

Figure 1. Main sources of VM exits

Instruction class	Exit count	% of total exits
`mfspr`	4484245	33.8
`wrtee`	2792109	21.1
`mtspr`	2307647	17.4
`mfmsr`	575302	9.5
`rfi`	413847	4.3
`mtmsr`	391813	3.1
`dtlbmiss`	198239	1.5
`itlbmiss`	192046	1.4

Table 3. Main sources of VM exits and their frequency on guest Linux boot (refer Table 2 for semantics of these opcodes)

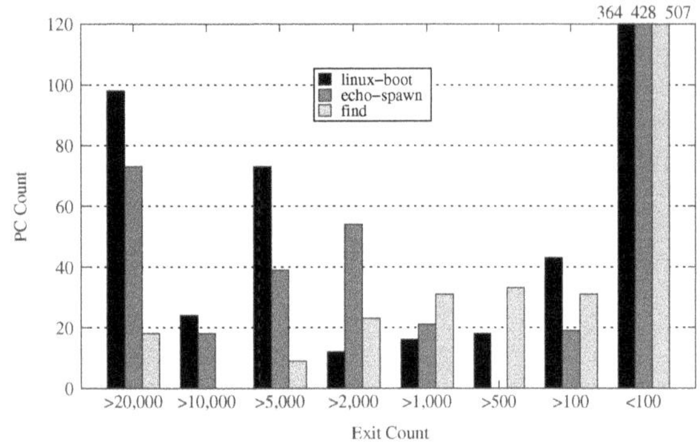

Figure 2. Histograms representing the number of distinct exit-causing PCs and their corresponding exit frequency. For example, 93 distinct PCs result in >20,000 exits each during Linux boot.

Exit count	PC count	% of total exits
>20000	93	91.9
>10000	23	3.1
>5000	68	4.2
>2000	12	0.3
>1000	17	0.2
<1000	420	0.2

Table 4. Exit frequency information for distinct PC values. For example, 93 distinct PCS result in >20,000 exits each, accounting for 91.9% of total VM exits.

firm that binary translating only the most frequently executed opcodes/PCs is likely to produce large improvements.

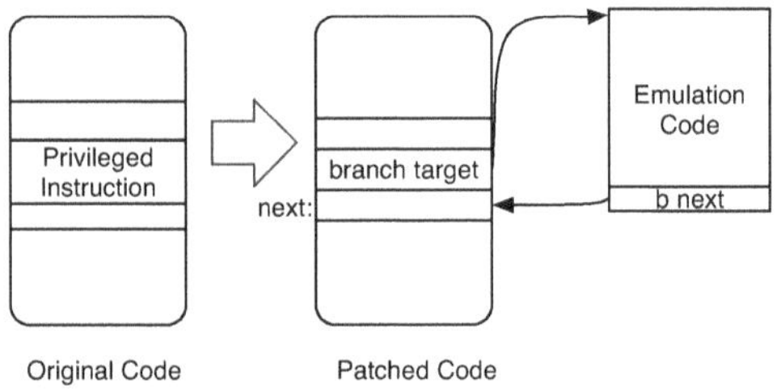

Figure 3. Figure showing patching of multiple instructions with `branch` instruction.

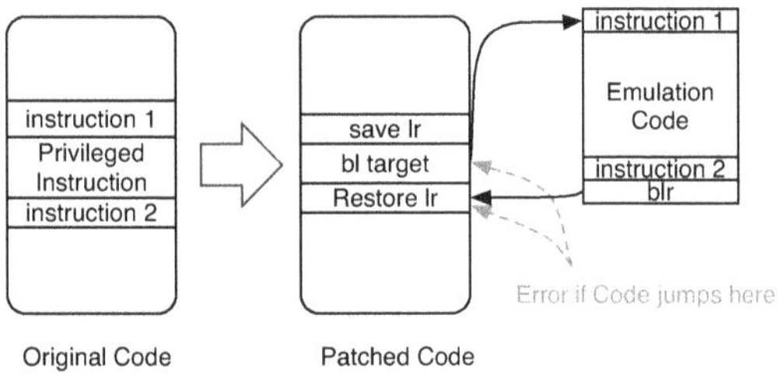

Figure 4. Figure showing patching of multiple instructions using `bl` instruction. This approach fails in presence of arbitrary guest jumps.

3. In-place Binary Translation

We monitor PCs causing a large number of VM exits and binary translate them to avoid these exits. We translate guest instructions in-place. Some privileged instructions can be emulated by single-instruction translations. For example, `mfmsr` is translated to a `load` instruction to the address of the emulated `msr` register. Other opcodes which can be translated to single instructions are `mfspr` and `mtspr` (refer Table 2 for semantics of these opcodes). These opcodes requiring single-instruction translations cause the bulk of privileged exits in common workloads (refer Figure 1). We call the privileged instruction that was patched, the *patch-site*.

Other privileged opcodes require translation to multiple instructions. For such opcodes, we store the emulation code in the translation cache, and patch the original instruction with a `branch` instruction to jump to its emulation code. The emulation code in the translation cache is terminated with another branch *back* to the instruction following the patch-site (see Figure 3). Because each patch-site requires a different terminating branch instruction, a new translation is generated for each patch-site.

The translated code needs to access either the emulated guest state or the translation cache. Both these data structures need to be allocated in the guest virtual address (VA) space for efficient virtualization. We now discuss the resulting placement constraints on these data structures.

Single-instruction translations access the emulated state using `load` and `store` instructions. To avoid any register overwrites, these memory access instructions must encode the address within the opcode. Power Architecture ISA allows the specification of a signed 16-bit displacement. This implies that the emulated state must lie either in the top or bottom 32KB of the guest address space. For many present-day operating systems, the top 32KB of virtual address (VA) space is often unused and can be used to store the emulated state. If such address space is not available, single-instruction translations can be converted to multiple-instruction translations to allow more placement flexibility, as we discuss next.

For multiple-instruction translations, we replace the privileged instruction with a branch to the translation cache. Branch instructions are of two types: direct and indirect. On Power Architecture, direct branches specify a signed 26-bit absolute or PC-relative (relative to current program counter) offset (`branch <addr>` or `branch <pc+addr>`), while indirect branches specify a 32-bit register operand (e.g., `blr`). Further, a branch instruction could choose to save the PC in the link register (e.g., `bl <addr>`). For example, `bl` (branch and save return address in link register) is typically used for function calls, and `blr` (branch to the address saved in link register) for function returns.

Hence, for multiple-instruction translations, the address of the translated code (in the translation cache) must be accessible through the 26-bit offset specified in the `bl` instruction. The 26-bit offset could either be PC-relative or absolute. A PC-relative 26-bit offset constrains the translated code to lie within ±32MB of the patch-site. This is usually not possible because such address space is already occupied by the guest and/or its applications. An absolute 26-bit offset constrains the translated code to lie either in the top 32MB (0xfe000000-0xffffffff) or in the bottom 32MB (0x0-0x2000000) of the virtual address (VA) space. Most present-day operating systems reserve the top VA space for the kernel. In such systems, it is possible to use the top 32MB for storing the translation cache, provided the kernel is not already using those addresses. However, a branch back to the instruction following the patch-site will still require a 32-bit offset specification. We discuss two of the many approaches we tried to solve this problem:

1. Using `bl` and `blr`: We placed the translation cache in the top 32MB of the VA space and replaced the patch-site with a `bl` instruction (with absolute addressing) that saves the address of the following instruction in the link register. The translated code is then terminated with a `blr`.

2. Using branch: We placed the translation cache within ±32MB of the patch-site and used the branch instruction to jump to it. The translated code is terminated with a branch back to the address following the patch-site. Because the patch-site is within ±32MB of the patch-site, the branch back can be implemented using the branch opcode.

The first approach (using bl and blr) clobbers the link register, and there is no way to save and restore the link register without replacing multiple guest instructions. As we discussed earlier, it is dangerous to replace multiple guest instructions for a single patch-site as a guest could potentially jump to the middle of our replacement code (as shown in Figure 4). Hence, we abandoned this approach.

We used the second approach of placing the translation cache within ±32MB of the patch-site and using the branch opcode to jump to it and back. Finding unused space for the translation cache within ±32MB of the patch-site is usually not possible because the guest is typically already using these addresses. In this case, we *steal* a contiguous address space from the data sections of the guest. The data sections of the guest are identified by parsing the kernel header (embedded system bootloaders typically work by having access to guest kernel images in standard formats, e.g., ELF). The original data at the stolen guest addresses is copied into hypervisor space, and is replaced by our translation cache contents. All instructions accessing the stolen address space are made to trap (using read/write tracing) and the hypervisor supplies the correct value. If no space in any of the guest's data sections satisfies our ±32MB placement constraints, we simply forego that optimization opportunity.

To store the emulated guest register state (which will be accessed by our translated code), we search for *unused* guest VA space. We assume that the guest maps its kernel at the top of its VA space (e.g., Linux maps the kernel starting at 0xc0000000), and that if a page table mapping does not exist there, the corresponding VA space is unused. We allocate this unused VA space for storing the emulated guest state. If the guest later uses this VA space (by creating a mapping for it in the TLB), we move our guest emulated state to another location after invalidating all current translations. We assume that the guest kernel will not access a kernel virtual address without a priori mapping it in its VA space (e.g., it will not use demand paging for the kernel pages). Violation of this assumption by a guest could cause incorrect guest behaviour. Almost all commercial and open operating systems available today for embedded Power Architecture platforms conform with this assumption. We expect the user to disable our host-side optimizations (using a flag to the Qemu/KVM command line invocation for example) if he expects the guest to behave in a non-conforming manner. He could also choose to install a kernel module in the guest (similar to the "tools" mechanism used in popular virtualization software) to allocate unused guest virtual address space for the host. For a Linux guest, we simply use the top 64 KB of the VA space to store our emulated guest registers; this space is never used by Linux. We call this the *shared space*, as it is shared between the guest and the host. As we discuss later, we also use the shared space for storing the data cache for adaptive data mirroring.

Compared to full binary translation, in-place binary translation is simpler and results in higher performance. Full binary translation incurs an overhead of a potentially extra terminating jump after every basic block because typically, code layout in the translation cache is different from guest's code layout. More importantly, full binary translation approaches incur significant overhead for indirect jumps (e.g., the call/ret microbenchmark in [4] incurs a 400% overhead). VMware hides this overhead by only translating kernel code and running user applications *directly* on hardware, by observing that translation is not required for safe execution of most user code on most guest operating systems. A fully secure BT implementation, however, will require translation of all user code, and will show significant overhead due to indirect branches for user-level compute-intensive workloads (like SPECInt). Also, VMware's full binary translator will always show significant overhead for compute-intensive kernel-level workload involving indirect branches. Our in-place binary translation approach avoids these overheads.

On the other hand, in-place BT requires certain architectural features. In our implementation, we rely on Power Architecture ISA's fixed-length aligned nature of instructions and its support for separate user and kernel rwx page protection bits to safely implement in-place BT. These features are not available on x86, perhaps making in-place BT a misfit for x86. Our work highlights that subtle architectural variations result in widely different optimization solutions. Further, in-place BT has its own challenges regarding translation cache placement, dealing with self-referential and self-modifying code, and optimizing TLB utilization. Our work provides solutions to these challenges.

4. Read/Write Tracing and Associated Optimizations

Read/write tracing is required to emulate access to space stolen for the translation cache and to protect against read/write accesses to the privileged instructions that were translated in-place. Embedded Power Architecture platforms use software-managed TLBs, and all TLB manipulation instructions are privileged. Hence, the hypervisor traps all guest TLB accesses and has full control on all address space manipulation activity by the guest. We use hardware page-protection bits to implement read/write tracing. Embedded Power Architecture platforms provide orthogonal rwx protection bits per page for both user/supervisor privilege levels. Using these bits, we can mark a guest page containing a patch-site execute-only in user mode. This allows the execution of an instruction on this page to proceed uninterrupted (necessary for execution of both patched instruction and translation code), but any read or write access causes a page fault (and a VM exit). On a page fault, the hypervisor emulates the faulting instruction in software. We call this method memory read/write tracing (similar to VMware's memory write tracing on x86 [4]).

We implement software emulations of memory instructions in KVM to handle the resulting page faults. There are 36 different memory opcodes in Power Architecture ISA that need to be emulated. For read instructions, we simply return the original contents of the memory address in the appropriate destination operand. The original contents may be obtained either from the present guest page (if the address does not intersect with a patch-site), or from a hypervisor table storing the original contents (if the address matches a patch-site or if the address belongs to the stolen translation cache address space), or both. A similar strategy is used for write instructions.

Read/write tracing results in extra traps (tracing page faults) into the hypervisor. Most of these traps are either due to accesses to stolen space for translation cache or due to false sharing (i.e., access to unpatched guest data lying on the same page as the patch-site). The false sharing problem is aggravated by the huge page sizes used on embedded architectures to reduce TLB pressure. We also observe a number of traps due to read/write accesses to the patch-sites themselves, especially at guest boot time (for Linux guest). We found that Linux scans (and potentially modifies) its own code sections at boot time on Power Architecture platforms, and could get confused if it observes an incorrect value (due to in-place BT). Also, the kernel (or modules) could potentially read/write its own code even after booting. These extra traps could degrade guest performance.

We implement two optimizations to reduce tracing page faults. Our first optimization adaptively resizes guest pages to reduce false sharing. Our second optimization adaptively mirrors guest data (which is causing a large number of faults) to reduce the number of tracing page faults. For the second optimization, we also translate the faulting instruction to access the mirrored data. We next discuss both these optimizations.

4.1 Adaptive Page Resizing

Most embedded operating systems use huge pages (Linux uses a 256MB page) for the kernel on Power Architecture platforms to reduce TLB pressure. Typical TLB sizes on embedded Power Architecture processors are small. For example, the software-managed TLB on our test system is a combination of a 16-entry fully-associative cache of variable-sized page table entries and a 512-entry 4-way set-associative fixed-size (4KB) page table entries. The latter is used mostly for user pages. A faster L1 TLB lookup cache is implemented in hardware, and all invalidations to maintain consistency with the software-programmed L2 TLB are done automatically. The variable-pagesize TLB cache supports 11 different page sizes: 4K, 16K, 64K, 256K, 1M, 4M, 16M, 64M, 256M, 1G, and 4G. Further a page of size S must be S-byte aligned in physical and virtual address spaces.

The hypervisor traps guest accesses to the TLB, and creates appropriate *shadow TLB entries* that are loaded into hardware while the guest is running (similar to the hardware-managed shadow page tables used in x86 [4]). The guest cannot directly access the shadow TLB entries, as guest's accesses to the TLB entries are trapped and emulated by the hypervisor. This allows the hypervisor full flexibility in choosing the size and privileges of its shadow TLB entries. For example, the hypervisor can setup multiple shadow TLB entries, to shadow a single guest TLB entry representing a larger page. To minimize TLB pressure, the hypervisor typically uses one shadow TLB entry per guest TLB entry. For example, if the guest uses 4MB pages, then the shadow TLB will also have corresponding entries for 4MB pages. We implement read/write tracing by disabling read/write privileges in the shadow TLB entry. Disabling read/write privileges on a TLB entry representing a large page predictably causes an unacceptably large number of tracing page faults (every kernel data access becomes a page fault on Linux if we disable read/write privileges on the 256MB kernel page). Similarly, always using 4KB pages for the shadow TLB causes an unacceptably large number of TLB misses. We evaluate both these schemes in our experiments.

A more intelligent strategy is required to size the guest shadow TLB entries to balance the tradeoff between tracing page faults due to false sharing and TLB misses. The adaptive page resizing algorithm resizes shadow TLB entries dynamically and adaptively. After patching a privileged guest instruction, if we notice a high number of tracing page faults on that page, we *break* the page into smaller fragments (and the corresponding TLB entry into smaller TLB entries). After breaking, we only mark the TLB entry containing the patch-site execute-only, and leave the remaining unmodified. To minimize false sharing, we keep the size of the page containing the patch-site as small as possible, without adversely affecting performance. All other pages created by this fragmentation are sized as large as possible, to minimize the overall number of TLB entries. While smaller pages reduce false sharing, they also result in increased TLB pressure.

After fragmentation of a large page, if we still notice a high number of page faults on the smaller page (which we do not want to break further to avoid TLB pressure), we remove all patch-sites on that page and re-instate read/write privileges on it. The decision on whether to remove the patch-sites on a page, depends on the tradeoff between the number of privileged-instruction exits and the number of tracing page faults on that page.

Breaking a large page potentially creates many smaller pages due to alignment restrictions. For example, if the kernel has mapped itself using a 256MB page at virtual address (0xc0000000,0xcfffffff), and a patch is to be applied at address 0xc0801234, and we have decided to break the patch-site page into a 4MB page, the new set of TLB entries will be for addresses
(0xc0000000,0xc03fffff);(0xc0400000,0xc07fffff);
(0xc0800000,0xc0bfffff);(0xc0c00000,0xc0ffffff);
(0xc1000000,0xc1ffffff);(0xc2000000,0xc2ffffff);
(0xc3000000,0xc3ffffff);(0xc4000000,0xc7ffffff);
(0xc8000000,0xcbffffff);(0xcc000000,0xcfffffff). Notice that each page of size S is S-byte aligned and S is always one of the values supported by the architecture.

We use two policies to determine the size of the smaller pages, depending on the nature of the page faults. We found that typically tracing page faults occur either in bursts (a large number of faults occur on a small set of closely-located addresses on a single large page) or in scans (faults are spread over a large region with a small number of faults per address). For bursts, the ideal configuration is to resize the pages such that all faulting addresses belong to one small page (which can be untraced). Hence, on observing a burst, we try and break that page such that all patch-sites on that page belong to the "shortest" page. We discuss the tradeoffs involved in choosing the size of the shortest page in our experiments. If we observe that the number of faults on the shortest page is still greater than threshold T, we untrace it by removing all its patch-sites. For scans, where the tracing page faults are distributed across a large address range, the page is broken into two halves and the half with larger number of tracing page faults is untraced. We do this only if the number of tracing page faults is greater than threshold T (this threshold is the same as that used for bursts).

For both bursts and scans, if we find that neighbouring pages have identical `rwx` privileges as a result of untracing, we opportunistically merge them into a larger page to reduce TLB pressure. These checks for opportunistic merging are performed every 100ms.

The threshold T is determined dynamically, as it depends on the tradeoff between the number of privileged instruction exits and tracing page faults on that page. On tracing a page, we record the number of privileged instruction exits that this page was experiencing, before it got patched and traced. This serves as our threshold T for that page. If in future, the number of tracing page faults we are experiencing on this page is greater than T, we untrace it by removing all its patches. On each tracing or untracing event on a page, the threshold T is updated and is used to determine whether to again trace or untrace the page during future execution. Hence, after a page is untraced, T is also used to determine whether to retrace it or not (we retrace if the number of privileged instruction exits $> T$). Our dynamic thresholding mechanism relies on the assumption that the expected number of privileged instruction exits (or page faults) after untracing (or after retracing) will be similar to what had been observed previously. To avoid long-term effects of transient guest behaviour, we implement graceful aging by decreasing T linearly with time.

The adaptive page resizing algorithm automatically sizes (and resizes) the pages containing both the stolen address space for the translation cache and the patch-sites. The algorithm also untraces and retraces pages dynamically to minimize VM exits. Our algorithm aims to effectively handle the tradeoff between privileged-instruction exits, tracing page faults, and TLB misses. We evaluate the effectiveness of our algorithm in our experiments.

4.2 Adaptive Data Mirroring

After implementing adaptive page resizing, we still observed up to 50% performance overhead due to tracing page faults. One source for this overhead are the tracing page faults on the data region stolen for the translation cache. We found that another major source of this overhead were tracing page faults due to accesses to function dispatch tables and exception handler tables which were co-located with kernel code. Often these tables share the same 4KB region as the privileged kernel code accessing them, rendering our adaptive page resizing algorithm ineffective on these accesses.

We avoid these faults by dynamically monitoring such page faults, adaptively copying the data being accessed to the shared space (mirroring), and translating the instructions accessing this data to read/write from the new location. This optimization prevents future page faults on this data. The mirrored data is maintained as a cache of word-sized values in the shared space. The translation code for the faulting instruction checks the cache to see if the data has been mirrored. If the check succeeds, a value is returned-from/updated-in (for read/write respectively) the cache, else the read/write operation is executed on the original address (potentially resulting in a trap and emulate). These translations of memory access instructions are also stored in the translation cache.

To maintain guest correctness, the pages containing patches for faulting instructions (due to tracing) need to be read/write traced too. This can potentially result in a chain-effect: tracing of these new pages can cause more tracing page faults, resulting in more pages to be patched and traced, resulting in more tracing page faults, and so on.... Fortunately, we do not see this chain effect in practice. The faulting instructions that are patched typically reside on a page that is already being traced, causing this cycle to converge on the first iteration. Intuitively, kernel code which causes privileged VM-exits or tracing page faults is likely to be spatially close, and will eventually lead to a small set of traced pages. We observed this behaviour in all our experiments with Linux guests. Even if the read/write tracing chain becomes long, we rely on our adaptive page resizing algorithm to break this chain by removing the trace on a page (and all the associated patch-sites) if that page experiences a large number of page faults.

5. Experimental Results

We implemented our optimizations in Linux/KVM version 3.0, which has paravirtual extensions for Power. To measure performance of *unmodified* KVM and KVM with our optimizations, we disabled the paravirtual extensions. We perform our experiments on Freescale QorIQ P2020 platform, which is optimized for single-threaded performance per watt for networking and telecom applications. Our system has a 1.2GHz processor with 32KB L1 cache and 512 KB L2 cache. We use RAMdisk for our experiments to eliminate I/O overheads.

Our benchmarks are described in Table 1. We use four macrobenchmarks, namely `linux-boot`, `echo-spawn`, `find` and `lame`. These benchmarks have also been used in a previous performance study [13]. The others are microbenchmarks from the widely-used `lmbench` [14] and `Unixbench` [10] toolsets. These toolsets are routinely used for system benchmarking. `linux-boot` and `echo-spawn` execute a large number of privileged instructions, while `find` executes relatively fewer privileged instructions. `lame` is largely computation-bound with mostly user-level unprivileged computation and some I/O. Hence, `lame` seldom exits to the hypervisor and shows virtualized performance close to baremetal. We do not report performance comparisons on purely user-level compute-intensive workloads because they exhibit near baremetal performance for all cases. We also do not report performance comparisons on device-bound (e.g., network-bound or disk-bound) workloads because they are limited by the performance of the emulated device. In this work, we focus on CPU virtualization and do not study optimizations for I/O virtualization.

We implement the following optimizations in Linux/KVM:

- In-place binary translation, stealing address space for translation cache, and read/write tracing (`In-place-BT`)
- Adaptive page resizing (`Adapt-PR`)
- Adaptive data mirroring and translation of faulting instructions (`Adapt-DM`). `Adapt-DM` includes `Adapt-PR`.

Table 5 summarizes our performance results before and after these optimizations. Different workloads show different improvements. The improvement primarily depends on the three-way tradeoff between the number of VM exits due to privileged instructions, the number of tracing page faults, and the number of page faults due to increased TLB pressure (TLB misses). Figures 5 and 6 show the reduction in VM exits and page faults due to all these three reasons for each workload, before and after our optimizations (the full raw data is also available on the last page). The exits due to access violation faults (`Acc. Viol.`) are primarily due to tracing page faults, but may also include certain access violations due to the guest itself. We call exits due to execution of privileged instructions in user mode privileged exits. We do not report exit statistics for `lmbench` microbenchmarks because the `lmbench` suite is configured to run a variable number of iterations in each run, making it difficult to compare the number of exits across different optimizations. Similarly, we do not report exit statistics for `Unixbench Filesystem` microbenchmarks because the number of exits on these benchmarks depends on the throughput achieved in that run, which makes it difficult to compare them across different optimizations. We also show the reduction in exits for the paravirtual solution (`KVM-PV`) for comparison. The number of exits in `KVM-PV` can be considered as a lower-bound on the number of exits achievable by a host-side binary translation solution.

Just using `In-place-BT` does not improve performance for a Linux guest. In fact, we find that read/write tracing severely impairs performance because the guest uses a huge 256MB page to map the kernel's code and data. If we trace the entire 256MB page, a Linux guest does not boot even after hours. Even if we break the guest kernel page uniformly into large fragments of size 16MB each (and trace only those fragments which contain patch-sites), it takes multiple hours to boot a Linux guest. On the other hand, if we uniformly break all guest kernel pages into small 4KB fragments, we observe a slowdown of 370% (over base KVM) for `linux-boot`, due to increased TLB pressure resulting in a large number of TLB misses. Similar performance degradation is seen on other benchmarks too (e.g., 300% on `echo-spawn`).

The second column in Table 5 shows the performance of KVM with Optimizations `In-place-BT + Adapt-PR`. Because `Adapt-PR` localizes the trace to a small page and adaptively untraces and retraces pages, we observe a significant runtime improvement on all benchmarks. We first discuss the microbenchmarks. The average improvement in running time in `lmbench`, `Unixbench`, and `Unixbench Filesystem` microbenchmarks is 263%, 217%, and 160% respectively. The correlation between the performance improvement and reduction in the total number of VM exits (Figures 5, 6) is evident. Different microbenchmarks execute different number of privileged instructions and show different corresponding reductions. On macrobenchmarks, we observe an average runtime improvement of 168%, with the maximum improvement seen in `echo-spawn`, which also shows a corresponding reduction (89%) in total number of VM exits. For both microbenchmarks and macrobenchmarks, we notice an increase in the number

Benchmark	KVM	Adapt-PR	Adapt-DM
	Running Time in *sec* (lower is better)		
`linux-boot`	30.03	14.39	12.39
`echo-spawn`	21.34	8.9	6.85
`find`	1.89	1.67	0.83
`lame`	0.56	0.51	0.50
`lmbench`	Latency in *msec* (lower is better)		
`syscall`	0.020	0.003	0.003
`stat`	0.033	0.023	0.007
`fstat`	0.021	0.006	0.004
`open/close`	0.067	0.040	0.023
`sig-hndl`	0.024	0.004	0.004
`pipe`	0.066	0.068	0.041
`fork`	6.641	2.221	1.679
`exec`	20.543	8.971	6.681
`sh`	45.164	19.265	14.719
`Unixbench`	Raw Score (higher is better)		
`dhrystone2`	48110141	48988135	48957180
`syscall`	124854	748931	652829
`cswitch`	60746	148344	240653
`proc-create`	2470	6378	8714
`pipe`	188208	411186	923218
`hanoi`	8689401	8839987	8836219
`Unixbench Filesystem`	Throughput in KBps (higher is better)		
`file-read`	11524	26286	49830
`file-write`	10500	16400	38200
`file-copy`	5432	9783	20070

Table 5. Performance Improvements obtained by Adaptive Page Resizing (`Adapt-PR`) and Adaptive Data Mirroring (`Adapt-DM`) optimizations.

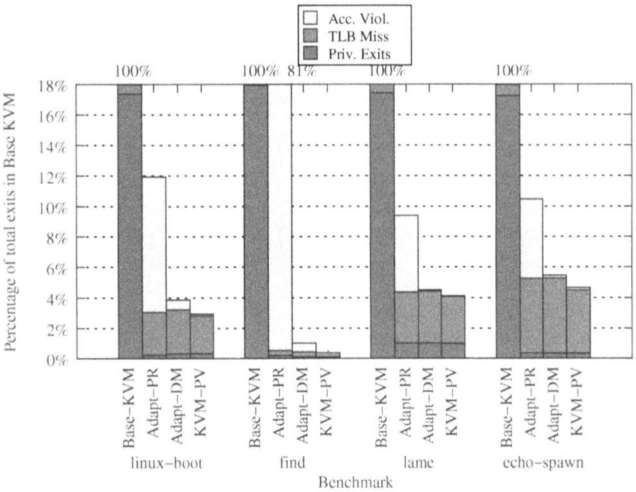

Figure 5. Percentage reduction in VM exits for macrobenchmarks.

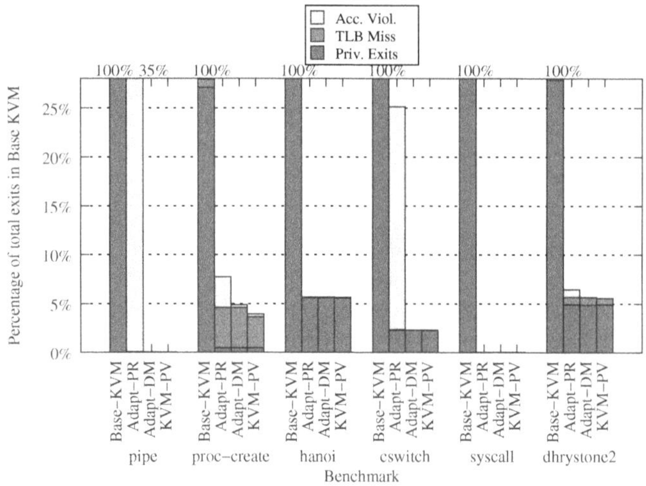

Figure 6. Percentage reduction in VM exits for Unixbench microbenchmarks.

of TLB misses and access violations (due to tracing page faults) on average. The net effect however remains largely positive.

We analyze `Adapt-PR` in more detail. We use three algorithm parameters for our implementation: a burst is detected if we observe more than 5000 faults in a 100ms interval; the dynamic threshold T (to decide whether to untrace/retrace a page) decreases linearly with time at the rate of 500 exits per 100ms; and on a split due to a burst of tracing page faults, the shortest page size is set to 64KB. We found through experimentation that the performance of our algorithm is largely insensitive to the first two parameters, i.e., differences in performance are seen only at large changes to these parameters. For the last parameter dictating the shortest page size on a TLB split due to bursty tracing page faults, we tried a few different values. Figure 7 shows our results. We found that if the shortest page is configured to 4KB (the shortest possible), the number of TLB misses increases significantly due to increased TLB pressure. If the shortest page is too large (e.g., 256KB), the number of privileged exits remains high (large number of tracing page-faults due to false sharing causes the page to get untraced resulting in a large number of privileged exits). We found a shortest-page limit of 64KB to work best, and hence use that for our algorithm. Figure 8 also shows the TLB configuration over time (as decided by our `Adapt-PR` algorithm) for `linux-boot`.

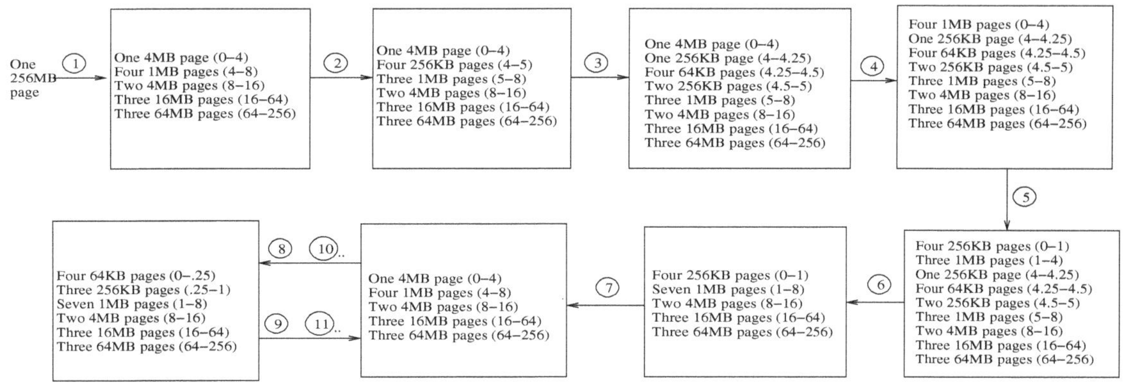

Figure 8. TLB configurations over time (as dictated by `Adapt-PR` algorithm) during `linux-boot`. The numbers in brackets represent address ranges in MB. KVM starts with one 256MB TLB entry, which is broken into thirteen different TLB entries (1). Steps (2), (3), (4), (5) are page splits due to scan pattern of tracing page faults. Steps (6) and (7) merge small fragments into larger ones opportunistically. Steps (1) through (7) finish in the first 1-2 seconds of bootup time. The configuration then shuttles between the last two configurations (8), (9), (10), (11), ..., splitting on observing bursty tracing page faults and merging opportunistically. Most of the time during this workload is spent in the second last configuration (thirteen different TLB entries).

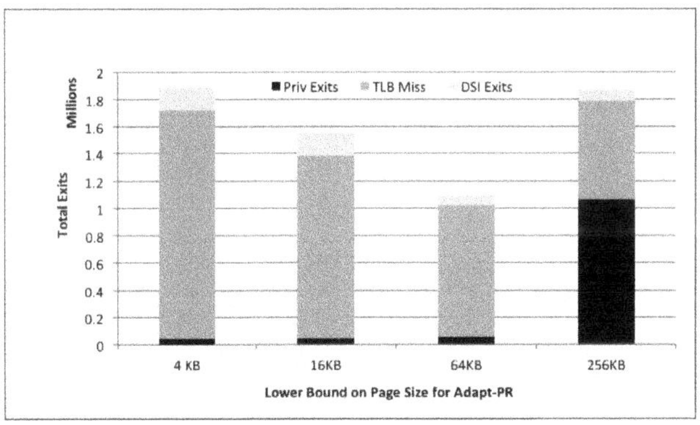

Figure 7. Exit profile of Linux boot for different lower bounds on the shortest-page in `Adapt-PR`.

Our next optimization, `Adapt-DM`, further reduces tracing page faults, resulting in further average runtime improvement of 157%, 112%, and 209% in `lmbench`, `Unixbench`, and `Unixbench Filesystem` microbenchmarks respectively, and 137% in macrobenchmarks. For this optimization, we allocated a 512B cache of mirrored values (mirror cache) in the shared space. We separately allocated 60KB of space to mirror the contents of the space stolen for the translation cache. We allocated the latter separately from the mirror cache to reduce checking overhead in the `Adapt-DM` translation code for accesses to the translation cache space (which is the common case). The value 60KB was chosen (instead of the full 64KB of the stolen space) to allow this space to reside in the 64KB page already reserved for the shared space, hence reducing the number of extra TLB entries (see Figure 9). Improvements due to `Adapt-DM` are seen in almost all our benchmarks with the highest improvement of 201% recorded on `find` among the macrobenchmarks. The only exception is `Unixbench syscall` where `Adapt-DM` surprisingly causes a 12% slowdown over `Adapt-PR`. On further analysis, we found that this happened because of a large number of evictions in the mirror cache. `syscall` is a synthetic microbenchmark and incidentally shows an exceptionally large number of accesses to the last 4KB of the 64KB space stolen for the translation cache. Because this 4KB region is mirrored in the mirror cache, this causes cache pressure and evictions. We do not expect such behavior in real workloads. There is a clear correlation between the runtime improvement and the reduction in the number of tracing page faults (Figures 5,6). The average reduction in the number of tracing page faults is greater than 99% on `Unixbench` microbenchmarks and 96% on macrobenchmarks.

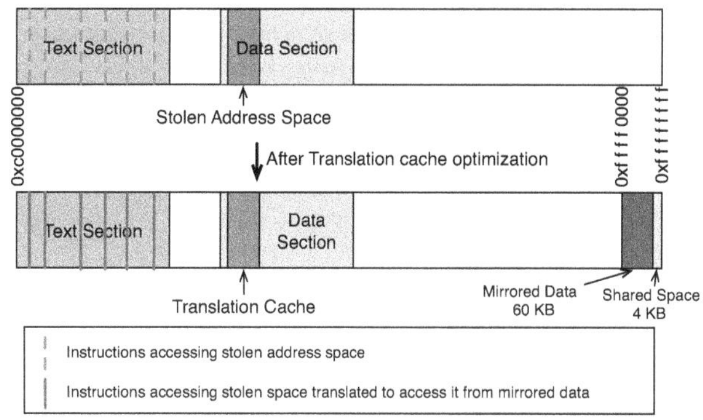

Figure 9. Address space layout before and after `Adapt-DM`

`Adapt-DM` optimization also reduces the number of privileged-instruction exits and TLB misses on many of our benchmarks. This happens due to an interesting indirect effect. Without `Adapt-DM`, certain guest code pages are adaptively broken into smaller pages and privileged-instruction patches on some of these smaller pages are removed to reduce tracing page faults. With `Adapt-DM`, the number of tracing page faults decreases. This allows `Adapt-PR` to not have to kick in, allowing pages to remain unbroken and privileged-instructions to remain patched. This reduces both TLB misses and number of privileged instruction exits. We observe this effect in almost all our benchmarks. We notice up to 33% decrease in the number of TLB misses (for `Unixbench cswitch`), and up to 52% decrease in the number of privileged-instruction exits (for `Unixbench pipe`). Finally, we note that both `Adapt-PR` and `Adapt-DM` work together for our optimization solution. As we have already seen, `Adapt-PR` alone is unable to provide the best achievable performance. Similarly, `Adapt-DM` alone (without

Adapt-PR) causes mirroring of data in large pages causing high pressure on our mirror cache resulting in significant performance degradation.

Overall, the three optimizations together provide performance comparable to paravirtualization, without having to modify the Linux guest. When compared to bare-metal, the virtualization overhead is still significant. Much of this overhead is due to extra host-side processing required for memory management. For example, all TLB access instructions in the guest need to exit to hypervisor. Similarly, all instructions that switch supervisor/user privilege levels in guest need to also switch their shadow TLB entries, thus requiring an exit to the hypervisor. Because almost all our benchmarks focus intensely on virtualization-sensitive operations, they all execute many such privileged instructions that require VM exits, resulting in low performance relative to bare-metal. These overheads also existed in VMware's software and hardware virtualization approaches before the introduction of hardware nested page tables [8]. For example, the `forkwait` benchmark in [4] is similar to our `echo-spawn` and takes 36.9 seconds on VMware's software virtualization platform and 106.4 seconds on VMware's hardware virtualization platform, compared to 6.0 seconds on bare-metal. i.e., 6x and 18x slowdowns on software and hardware virtualization platforms respectively. The 6x slowdown for `forkwait` on x86 software virtualization platform is comparable to the 5x slowdown seen on our system for `echo-spawn`. The introduction of hardware nested page tables on newer x86 platforms allows workloads like `forkwait` to execute with very few VM exits, thus eliminating these large overheads. These qualitative comparisons with x86 virtualization lead us to believe that our optimizations achieve close to the best possible performance for Power Architecture platforms achievable with software-only techniques. Newer Power Architecture processors optimize memory management for virtualization [20] and could potentially further bridge this gap between virtualized and bare-metal performance. Our optimizations target the older Power Architecture processors, which are also expected to remain highly relevant for many more years for their popularity due to power and cost advantages.

We next measure the overhead and effectiveness of our adaptive page resizing algorithm. We statically configured the shadow TLB to the best observed configuration for Linux boot benchmark. In this configuration, we loaded the shadow TLB with 13 entries: one entry of size 4MB (`0xc0000000-0xc03fffff`), four entries of size 1MB each (covering `0xc0400000-0xc07fffff`), two entries of size 4MB each (covering `0xc0800000-0xc0ffffff`), three entries of size 16MB each (covering `0xc1000000-0xc3ffffff`), and three entries of size 64MB each (covering `0xc4000000-0xcfffffff`). Of these 13 entries, the first two entries were marked execute-only (kernel code is nearly 5MB long) and the rest remained unmodified. We compared the performance of this configuration with our adaptive page resizing algorithm. We disabled Adapt-DM optimization for this experiment. Also, to avoid effects due to the placement of the translation cache on Adapt-PR algorithm, we allocated the translation cache in the guest explicitly (using our custom "tools" module installed in the guest) for this experiment. To distinguish this configuration from that used in previous experiments on Adapt-PR, we call it Adapt-PR+. Table 6 summarizes our results. Figures 10 and 11 show the corresponding reduction in VM exits and page faults. Identical configurations were used for both Static-TLB and Adapt-PR in this experiment. For Linux boot benchmark, we observe that our resizing algorithm performs within 1-2% of the statically optimal solution. For other benchmarks, our resizing algorithm performs within 18% of the static configuration, sometimes outperforming it by up to 15%. In all cases where Adapt-PR+ shows overhead over Static-TLB, we notice that our adaptive algorithm first breaks the guest into a large number of smaller pages, and then merges them back. This overhead of splitting and merging and the resulting extra VM exits is reflected in the runtime comparison. These programs (esp. microbenchmarks) run for a short time; the overhead of Adapt-PR+ becomes smaller as the programs run longer. We also studied the programs where Adapt-PR+ outperforms Static-TLB (e.g., `lmbench sh`). In these cases, the static TLB configuration was not the optimal choice and our page resizing algorithm resulted in better performance.

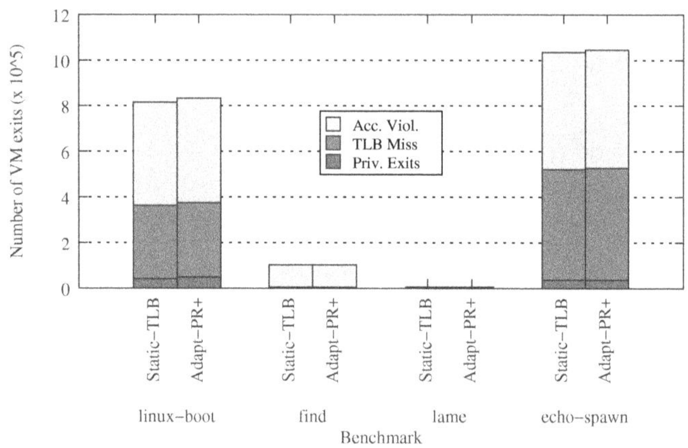

Figure 10. Comparison of VM exits for macrobenchmarks (Static-TLB vs. Adapt-PR+)

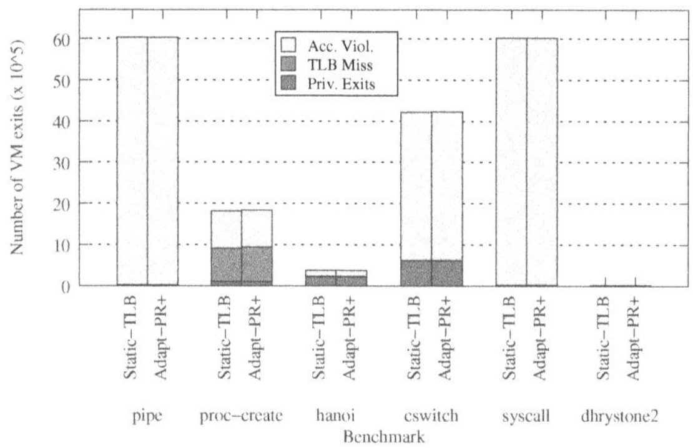

Figure 11. Comparison of VM exits for Unixbench microbenchmarks (Static-TLB vs. Adapt-PR+)

6. Discussion

6.1 Comparison with Full Binary Translation

We call a binary translator which translates all guest instructions a *full* binary translator. VMware's x86-based binary translator [4] is an example of such a system. A full binary translator translates all guest code, and not just the privileged instructions (as done in our system). The advantage of our approach is its simplicity and often higher performance (e.g., indirect branches perform poorly on a full binary translator). The disadvantage of our approach is that we change the guest's address space directly and have to thus monitor guest's accesses to our modified regions (which we do using read/write tracing). As we demonstrate in this work, it is possible to do this correctly and efficiently using our proposed optimizations for embedded Power Architecture platforms.

Our in-place binary translation approach relies on the fixed-length word-aligned nature of Power Architecture instructions. We

Benchmark	Static-TLB	Adapt-PR+
	Running Time in *sec* (lower is better)	
linux-boot	12.98	13.02
echo-spawn	8.0	7.80
find	0.90	0.98
lame	0.51	0.51
lmbench	Latency in *msec* (lower is better)	
syscall	0.007	0.009
stat	0.011	0.012
fstat	0.008	0.009
open/close	0.022	0.026
sig-hndl	0.008	0.009
pipe	0.053	0.062
fork	2.068	2.020
exec	7.792	7.457
sh	17.076	16.565
Unixbench	Raw Score (higher is better)	
dhrystone2	48833854	48904947
syscall	344877	286057
cswitch	160575	159256
proc-create	7101	7679
pipe	557045	469538
hanoi	8835343	8690019
Unixbench Filesystem	Throughput in KBps (higher is better)	
file-read	28346	24151
file-write	22450	19050
file-copy	12201	10408

Table 6. Measuring the overhead and performance of adaptive page resizing (`Adapt-PR+`) algorithm, in comparison to a statically configured TLB (`Static-TLB`). The static TLB configuration was setup such that it provides the best performance for the Linux boot benchmark. We disable `Adapt-DM` optimization and allocate translation cache explicitly from the guest (using guest tools) for this experiment.

ensure that a guest cannot possibly jump to the middle of our translation by relying on this property. Because the x86 architecture has variable-sized non-aligned instructions, in-place binary translation is much harder (or perhaps impossible) to implement correctly on x86.

We also rely on the ability to read/write trace guest pages by marking them `execute-only`. This is possible on embedded Power Architecture platform due to the availability of separate `read-write-execute` page protection bits. In contrast, the x86 architecture provides only `read-only` and `no-execute` (NX) bits, which are less powerful, and insufficient to implement `execute-only` privileges at page granularity.

Subtle differences in architectures greatly impact VMM design. We believe that our approach is perhaps a misfit for the x86 architecture for reasons outlined above. Similarly, a full binary translator is perhaps an overkill for embedded Power Architecture virtualization, given that our lightweight adaptive in-place binary translator can achieve the same (or better) effect with less engineering effort. The interplay of full binary translation with small TLB sizes also remains to be studied.

6.2 Fidelity Limitations

While our virtualization solution provides *near-complete* architectural fidelity to the guest, there remain two corner-case fidelity limitations:

1. We steal space from the guest OS's data section to store our translation cache. As we protect the translation cache only against read/write access (and not execute access), fidelity could get violated if the guest OS branches to an address in its data section. Such behaviour is not expected of a "well-behaved" OS.
2. The second fidelity violation is due to storage of emulated guest register state in unused guest VA space. As discussed in Section 3, fidelity could get violated if the guest accesses this unused VA space *without* first creating a corresponding TLB mapping.

Despite these corner-case fidelity limitations, we guarantee correctness by relying on known behaviour of the guest OS. Similar limitations also exist in VMware's x86-based virtualization solution which combines direct execution with binary translation [4].

6.3 Relevance to Other Architectures

Our work provides an interesting contrast to previous work on x86 virtualization [4], and brings forth interesting implications of seemingly innocuous architectural differences. These differences are: x86 platforms have segmentation, embedded Power Architecture platforms have software-loaded TLB, variable page sizes, and orthogonal `rwx` protection bits; Power Architecture platforms have fixed length aligned instructions, x86 platforms have variable length instructions. Embedded Power Architecture platforms share some of these features with other architectures (e.g., MIPS, SPARC, ARM) and some of our techniques are relevant in these contexts. However, in our experience, reaching the "optimal" solution for any architecture typically requires a separate detailed study of its features and limitations.

Our techniques are also relevant to the newer generation of Power Architecture processors which have hardware virtualization support. A combination of software and hardware techniques can provide better performance than plain hardware virtualization [5]. Although our implementation and experiments are based on a 32-bit Power Architecture processor, our solution is also relevant to 64-bit Power Architecture platforms.

6.4 Other Related Work

Binary translation has been previously used in various contexts, namely cross-ISA portability [7, 21], hardware-based performance acceleration [12], dynamic runtime compiler optimizations [6], program shepherding [9], testing and debugging [15]. Binary translation was first used for efficient virtualization on the x86 architecture by VMware [4], and our work is perhaps closest to their approach. The difference is in the translator's design, as previously discussed in Section 6.1.

The recent extension to the Linux kernel for Power Architecture paravirtualization contrasts with our approach. While the paravirtual modifications require extensive changes to the Linux kernel, our approach can achieve comparable performance with only host-side optimizations. Unlike the paravirtual approach, we can optimize dynamically generated/loaded code and ensure correct behaviour in presence of self-referential and self-modifying guest code. We also do not require a trusted guest. The host-guest shared spaces are guest-specific and do not grant a guest any more privileges than it already has. An untrusted guest can at most crash itself.

We present our experiments and results on a uniprocessor guest but our ideas are equally relevant to a multiprocessor guest. For a multiprocessor guest, these optimizations must be implemented for each virtual CPU (VCPU). To reduce synchronization overheads, separate translation and data caches need to be maintained for each VCPU. This minimizes synchronization overheads at the potential cost of marginally higher space overheads. We expect our optimizations to show equivalent performance improvements on a multiprocessor.

7. Conclusion

We discuss the design and implementation of an efficient host-side virtualization solution for embedded Power Architecture processors. We propose and validate a set of host-side optimizations, namely *in-place binary translation* (including stealing of address space for translation cache and read/write tracing), *adaptive page resizing*, and *adaptive data mirroring*. Of these, in-place binary translation and adaptive page resizing are new techniques, not previously used for x86-based software virtualization, highlighting that different architectures offer different opportunities and challenges, and thus require different optimization solutions. The Linux/KVM-based prototype system developed on our ideas shows significant performance improvements on common workloads, and compares favourably to previously-proposed paravirtual approaches. We hope our techniques add to the "optimization toolset" for efficient virtualization on other (newer) instruction set architectures in future.

Acknowledgments

We thank Stuart Yoder for helpful technical discussions on embedded Power Architecture processors. We also thank Sudhanshu Mittal for facilitating the logistics of this collaboration between I.I.T. Delhi and Freescale Semiconductor India Pvt. Ltd. Finally, a special thanks to the anonymous ASPLOS reviewers for suggestions that substantially improved the paper.

References

[1] QorIQ Qonverge BSC 9131 RDB for Femtocell base station development. `http://www.freescale.com/webapp/sps/site/prod_summary.jsp?code=BSC9131RDB` (as on Jan 10, 2013).

[2] Freescale Semiconductor. Hardware and software assists in virtualization, Rev 0, Aug. 2009.

[3] Freescale Semiconductor. Freescale's embedded hypervisor for QorIQTM. P4 Series Communications Platform, Rev 1, Oct. 2008.

[4] K. Adams and O. Agesen. A comparison of software and hardware techniques for x86 virtualization. In *ASPLOS '06*.

[5] O. Agesen, J. Mattson, R. Rugina, and J. Sheldon. Software techniques for avoiding hardware virtualization exits. In *USENIX ATC '12*.

[6] V. Bala, E. Duesterwald, and S. Banerjia. Dynamo: a transparent dynamic optimization system. *ACM SIGPLAN Notices*, 35(5):1–12, 2000.

[7] S. Bansal and A. Aiken. Binary translation using peephole superoptimizers. In *OSDI '08*.

[8] R. Bhargava, B. Serebrin, F. Spadini, and S. Manne. Accelerating two-dimensional page walks for virtualized systems. In *ASPLOS '08*.

[9] D. Bruening. *Efficient, Transparent and Comprehensive Runtime Code Manipulation*. PhD thesis, Massachusetts Institute of Technology, 2004.

[10] byte-unixbench: A Unix benchmark suite. byte-unixbench: A Unix benchmark suite. `http://code.google.com/p/byte-unixbench` (as on Jan 10, 2013).

[11] G. Heiser. The role of virtualization in embedded systems. 2008.

[12] A. Klaiber. The technology behind Crusoe processors. Technical report, Transmeta Corp., January 2000. URL `http://www.transmeta.com`.

[13] KVM PowerPC: About exit timing. KVM PowerPC: About exit timing. `http:///www.linux-kvm.org/page/PowerPC_Exittimings` (as on Jan 10, 2013).

[14] L. McVoy and C. Staelin. lmbench: portable tools for performance analysis. In *USENIX ATC '96*.

[15] N. Nethercote and J. Seward. Valgrind: a framework for heavyweight dynamic binary instrumentation. *SIGPLAN Not.*, 42(6):89–100, June 2007.

[16] P1010 and P1014 low-power communication processors. P1010 and p1014 low-power communication processors. `http://cache.freescale.com/files/32bit/doc/fact_sheet/QP1010FS.pdf` (as on Jan 10, 2013).

[17] P1023 Product Summary. P1023 product summary. `http://www.freescale.com/webapp/sps/site/prod_summary.jsp?code=P1023` (as on Jan 10, 2013).

[18] Paravirtual Extensions to Linux for Power Architecture Virtualization. Paravirtual extensions to Linux for Power Architecture virtualization. `http://svn.dd-wrt.com/browser/src/linux/pb42/linux-3.2/Documentation/virtual/kvm/ppc-pv.txt?rev=18112` (as on Jan 10, 2013).

[19] G. J. Popek and R. P. Goldberg. Formal requirements for virtualizable third generation architectures. *Commun. ACM*, 17(7):412–421, 1974. ISSN 0001-0782.

[20] Power ISA Version 2.06 Revision B. Power ISA Version 2.06 Revision B. `http://www.power.org/resources/downloads/PowerISA_V2.06_PUBLIC.pdf` (as on Jan 10, 2013).

[21] Qemu: open source processor emulator. Qemu: open source processor emulator. `http://fabrice.bellard.free.fr/qemu/` (as on Jan 10, 2013).

[22] S. Yoder. KVM on Embedded Power Architecture Platforms. `http://www.linux-kvm.org/wiki/images/c/c2/2011-forum-embedded-power.pdf` (as on Jan 10, 2013).

Raw Data on Exit Count

Unmodified KVM

	Priv. Exits	TLB misses	Acc. Viol.
linux-boot	11509859	402274	13823
echo-spawn	9829128	419191	18005
find	802777	2486	46
lame	60312	1932	23
unix-dhrystone2	154460	973	40
unix-syscall	22541901	953	41
unix-cswitch	26459239	1102	49
unix-proc-create	41882	621658	60036
unix-pipe	28714485	979	41
unix-hanoi	4005414	914	40

Static-TLB

	Priv. Exits	TLB misses	Acc. Viol.
linux-boot	41770	320941	452482
echo-spawn	35929	485870	513294
find	908	2676	98113
lame	637	2052	3124
unix-dhrystone2	7663	1197	6158
unix-syscall	12791	1135	6006963
unix-cswitch	614104	1260	3608524
unix-proc-create	101427	815074	897920
unix-pipe	15742	1144	6008821
unix-hanoi	224929	1116	151104

In-place-BT + Adapt-PR

	Priv. Exits	TLB misses	Acc. Viol.
linux-boot	27537	334458	1062541
echo-spawn	36464	503341	536993
find	1487	2889	650758
lame	636	2085	3126
unix-dhrystone2	7663	1186	1224
unix-syscall	5752	1140	1158
unix-cswitch	616643	8288	6020365
unix-proc-create	102315	845228	640888
unix-pipe	19102	1221	10012062
unix-hanoi	224709	1158	2032

Adapt-PR+

	Priv. Exits	TLB misses	Acc. Viol.
linux-boot	48560	326825	460001
echo-spawn	35823	492129	518255
find	965	2655	98145
lame	636	2085	3126
unix-dhrystone2	7656	1127	6132
unix-syscall	15105	1130	6008149
unix-cswitch	616684	7702	3609690
unix-proc-create	100796	835408	897302
unix-pipe	18762	1113	6010468
unix-hanoi	225211	1088	151308

In-place-BT + Adapt-PR + Adapt-DM

	Priv. Exits	TLB misses	Acc. Viol.
linux-boot	38367	345035	77467
echo-spawn	35014	506295	18624
find	851	2782	4701
lame	644	2114	46
unix-dhrystone2	7648	1140	38
unix-syscall	6324	1159	40
unix-cswitch	610986	5567	49
unix-proc-create	99081	846053	60026
unix-pipe	9185	1165	75
unix-hanoi	224970	1169	876

KVM-PV

	Priv. Exits	TLB misses	Acc. Viol.
linux-boot	40451	295672	14181
echo-spawn	34602	427351	17011
find	719	2392	46
lame	625	1916	24
unix-dhrystone2	7667	1001	40
unix-syscall	5197	948	41
unix-cswitch	608549	1059	49
unix-proc-create	98569	652042	60034
unix-pipe	7648	968	42
unix-hanoi	224660	943	41

Research Directions for 21st Century Computer Systems

ASPLOS 2013 Panel

Mark D. Hill

Computer Sciences Department
University of Wisconsin-Madison
markhill@cs.wisc.edu

Abstract

Four recent efforts call out architectural challenges and opportunities up and down the software/hardware stack. This panel will discuss, *"What should the community do to facilitate, transcend, or refute these partially overlapping visions?"* The panel is chaired by Mark D. Hill with other panel members not finalized for the ASPLOS'13 proceedings.

Categories and Subject Descriptors C. [Computer Systems Organization], D. [Software].

General Terms Algorithms, Measurement, Performance, Design, Economics, Reliability, Security, Languages, Verification.

Keywords computer systems, architecture, programming methods, performance, energy, new technology.

1. Four Studies

This panel will discuss four recent studies.

1.1 NAS Report "The Future of Computing Performance: Game Over or Next Level?"

Fuller led software and hardware researchers Barroso, Colwell, Dally, Dobberpuhl, Dubey, Hill, Horowitz, Kirk, Lam, McKinley, Moore, and Yelick to a 2011 report [1]. It found that: (a) Computer hardware has transitioned to multicore, (b) Dennard scaling of CMOS has broken down, (c) Parallelism and locality must be exploited by software, and (d) Chip power will soon limit multicore scaling. It recommended enhanced research investment in:

- Algorithms to exploit parallel processing,
- Programming methods to enable efficient use of parallel systems,
- Long-term efforts on rethinking of the canonical computing "stack,"
- Parallel architectures driven by applications,
- Making computer systems more power efficient,
- Cooperation & innovation of open interfaces for parallel programming,
- Tools and methods to transform legacy apps to parallel systems, and
- Increased emphasis on parallelism in computer science education.

1.2 CCC Workshops "Advancing Computer Architecture Research (ACAR)"

Oskin and Torrellas led two two-day 2010 workshops with dozen participants. *ACAR-1 Failure is not an Option: Popular Parallel Programming* [2] advocated research advancing:

- Data centers and large-scale systems,
- Architectures to enhance programmability,
- Hardware-software co-design and asymmetry, and
- Domain specific languages.

ACAR-2 Laying a New Foundation for IT: Computer Architecture for 2025 and Beyond [3] advocated:

- Revisiting the boundary between hardware and software,
- Adding new capabilities for computer architectures, especially for security and reliability, and
- Exploitation of emerging technologies.

1.3 ISAT Workshop "Advancing Computer Systems without Technology Progress"

Hill and Kozyrakis led 48 software and hardware researchers in a two-day 2012 workshop [4] whose premises were that (a) CMOS transistors will soon stop getting "better," (b) Post-CMOS technologies are not ready, and (c) Computer system superiority is central to US security, government, education, commerce, etc. The workshop participants were asked, "How to advance computer systems without (significant) technology progress?" and found:

- Even with stalling technology progress, two decades of Moore's Law-like performance per unit energy gains (~1000x) are possible
- By wringing out inefficiencies used to harvest Moore's Law,
- Including via (a) hardware and software specialization and co-design, (b) reducing software bloat, and (c) ex-ploitation of lower-precision or approximate computing.

ASPLOS'13, March 16–20, 2013, Houston, Texas, USA.
ACM 978-1-4503-1870-9/13/03.

1.4 CCC White Paper "21st Century Computer Architecture"

Hill led Adve, Ceze, Irwin, Kaeli, Martonosi, Torrellas, Wenisch, Wood, Yelick and others in a 2012 community white paper [5]. It found that: (a) Semiconductor technology and computer architecture (writ broadly) were key—intentionally invisible—enablers for past information and communication technology (ICT) innovations. (b) Semiconductor technology is facing significant challenges, as new smaller transistors are not necessarily "better" due to power, reliability, interconnect and one-time engineering costs and concerns. (c) Compelling future ICT visions exist—e.g., personalized medicine, terrorist network analysis, and telepresence—that often require processing "big data" using distributed designs, working within form-factor constraints, and reconciling rapid deployment with efficient operation. It recommended that computer systems architecture to enable 21st Century ICT innovation:

- *Architecture as Infrastructure: From Sensors to Clouds.* With computers as a pillar of societal infrastructure, research must examine computation and communication in context—from sensors to data centers—considering human-centric design goals including improved programmability, privacy, security, and availability.
- *Energy First.* More energy-efficient systems—to make up for stalled transistor energy improvement—will re-quire 100x parallelism, specialization (beyond GPUs), and cross-layer design to manage communication even with big data.
- *New Technologies.* Emerging technologies provide challenges and opportunities: Flash and phase change memory for storage, photonic and 3D chip stacking for communication, and near-threshold CMOS and exotic technologies in computation.
- *Cross-cutting.* ICT researchers must develop richer inter-layer interfaces to empower change via further ab-stracting parallelism, heterogeneity, communication, security, reliability, etc.

References

[1] S. Fuller and L. Millett, "The Future of Computing Performance: Game Over or Next Level?," The National Academy Press, 2011 (http://books.nap.edu/openbook.php?record_id=12980&page=R1).

[2] J. Torrellas and M. Oskin, "Failure is not an Option: Popular Parallel Programming," Workshop on Advancing Computer Architecture Research, August 2010 (http://www.cra.org/ccc/docs/ACAR_Report_Popular-Parallel-Programming.pdf).

[3] M. Oskin and J. Torrellas, "Laying a New Foundation for IT: Computer Architecture for 2025 and Beyond," Workshop on Advancing Computer Architecture Research, September 2010 (http://www.cra.org/ccc/docs/ACAR2-Report.pdf).

[4] M. Hill and C. Kozyrakis, "Advancing Computer Systems without Technology Progress," ISAT Outbrief, April 17-18, 2012, of DARPA/ISAT Workshop, March 26-27, 2012 (http://www.cs.wisc.edu/~markhill/papers/isat2012_ACSWTP.pdf).

[5] A community white paper, "21st Century Computer Architecture," Computing Community Consortium, May 25, 2012 (http://cra.org/ccc/docs/init/21stcenturyarchitecturewhitepaper.pdf).

Unikernels: Library Operating Systems for the Cloud

Anil Madhavapeddy, Richard Mortier[1], Charalampos Rotsos, David Scott[2], Balraj Singh,
Thomas Gazagnaire[3], Steven Smith, Steven Hand and Jon Crowcroft

University of Cambridge, University of Nottingham[1], Citrix Systems Ltd[2], OCamlPro SAS[3]
first.last@cl.cam.ac.uk, first.last@nottingham.ac.uk, dave.scott@citrix.com, first@ocamlpro.com

Abstract

We present *unikernels*, a new approach to deploying cloud services via applications written in high-level source code. Unikernels are single-purpose appliances that are compile-time specialised into standalone kernels, and sealed against modification when deployed to a cloud platform. In return they offer significant reduction in image sizes, improved efficiency and security, and should reduce operational costs. Our Mirage prototype compiles OCaml code into unikernels that run on commodity clouds and offer an order of magnitude reduction in code size without significant performance penalty. The architecture combines static type-safety with a single address-space layout that can be made immutable via a hypervisor extension. Mirage contributes a suite of type-safe protocol libraries, and our results demonstrate that the hypervisor is a platform that overcomes the hardware compatibility issues that have made past library operating systems impractical to deploy in the real-world.

Categories and Subject Descriptors D.4 [*Operating Systems*]: Organization and Design; D.1 [*Programming Techniques*]: Applicative (Functional) Programming

Keywords microkernels, virtualization, type-safety

1. Introduction

Operating system virtualization has revolutionised the economics of large-scale computing by providing a platform on which customers rent resources to host virtual machines (VMs). Each VM presents as a self-contained computer, booting a standard OS kernel and running unmodified application processes. Each VM is usually specialised to a particular role, e.g., a database, a webserver, and scaling out involves cloning VMs from a template image.

Despite this shift from applications running on multi-user operating systems to provisioning many instances of single-purpose VMs, there is little actual specialisation that occurs in the image that is deployed to the cloud. We take an extreme position on specialisation, treating the final VM image as a single-purpose appliance rather than a general-purpose system by stripping away functionality at compile-time. Specifically, our contributions are: (*i*) the *unikernel* approach to providing sealed single-purpose appliances, particularly suitable for providing cloud services; (*ii*) evaluation of a complete implementation of these techniques using a functional programming language (OCaml), showing that the benefits of type-safety need not damage performance; and (*iii*) libraries and language extensions supporting systems programming in OCaml.

ASPLOS'13, March 16–20, 2013, Houston, Texas, USA.

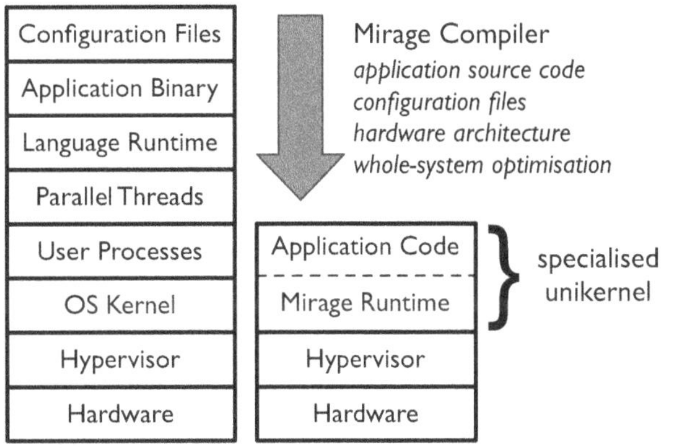

Figure 1: Contrasting software layers in existing VM appliances *vs.* unikernel's standalone kernel compilation approach.

The unikernel approach builds on past work in library OSs [1–3]. The entire software stack of system libraries, language runtime, and applications is compiled into a single bootable VM image that runs directly on a standard hypervisor (Figure 1). By targeting a standard hypervisor, unikernels avoid the hardware compatibility problems encountered by traditional library OSs such as Exokernel [1] and Nemesis [2]. By eschewing backward compatibility, in contrast to Drawbridge [3], unikernels address cloud services rather than desktop applications. By targeting the commodity cloud with a library OS, unikernels can provide greater performance and improved security compared to Singularity [4]. Finally, in contrast to Libra [5] which provides a libOS abstraction for the JVM over Xen but relies on a separate Linux VM instance to provide networking and storage, unikernels are more highly-specialised single-purpose appliance VMs that directly integrate communication protocols.

We describe a complete unikernel prototype in the form of our OCaml-based Mirage implementation (§3). We evaluate it via micro-benchmarks and appliances providing DNS, OpenFlow, and HTTP (§4). We find sacrificing source-level backward compatibility allows us to increase performance while significantly improving the security of external-facing cloud services. We retain compatibility with external systems via standard network protocols such as TCP/IP, rather than attempting to support POSIX or other conventional standards for application construction. For example, the Mirage DNS server outperforms both BIND 9 (by 45%) and the high-performance NSD server (§4.2), while using very much smaller VM images: our unikernel appliance image was just 200 kB while the BIND appliance was over 400 MB. We conclude by discussing our experiences building Mirage and its position within the state of the art (§5), and concluding (§6).

2. Architecture of an Appliance

Virtualisation is the enabling technology for the cloud, widely deployed via hypervisors such as Xen [6]. VM appliances are built to provide a small, fixed set of services. Thus, datacenter appliances typically consist of a Linux or Windows VM booted over Xen with loosely-coupled components: a guest OS kernel hosting a primary application (e.g., MySQL, Apache) with other services (e.g., cron, NTP) running in parallel; and typically attaching an external storage device with configuration files and data.

Our key insight is that the hypervisor provides a virtual hardware abstraction that can be scaled dynamically – both vertically by adding memory and vCPUs, and horizontally by spawning more VMs. This provides an excellent target for *library operating systems* (libOSs), an old idea [1, 2] recently revisited to break up monolithic OSs [3]. LibOSs have never been widely deployed due to the difficulty of supporting a sufficient range of real-world hardware, but deploying on a hypervisor such as Xen allows us to bypass this issue by using the hypervisor's device drivers, affording the opportunity to build a practical, clean-slate libOS that runs natively on cloud computing infrastructure.

We dub these VMs *unikernels*: specialised, sealed, single-purpose libOS VMs that run directly on the hypervisor. A libOS is structured very differently from a conventional OS: all services, from the scheduler to the device drivers to the network stack, are implemented as libraries linked directly with the application. Coupled with the choice of a modern statically type-safe language for implementation, this affords configuration, performance and security benefits to unikernels.

2.1 Configuration and Deployment

Configuration is a considerable overhead in managing the deployment of a large cloud-hosted service. Although there are (multiple) standards for location and format of configuration files on Linux, and Windows has the Registry and Active Directory, there are no standards for many aspects of application configuration. To address this, for example, Linux distributions typically resort to extensive shell scripting to glue packages together.

Unikernels take a different approach, by integrating configuration into the compilation process. Rather than treating the database, web server, etc., as independent applications which must be connected together by configuration files, unikernels treat them as libraries within a single application, allowing the application developer to configure them using either simple library calls for dynamic parameters, or build system tools for static parameters. This has the useful effect of making configuration decisions explicit and programmable in a host language rather than manipulating many ad-hoc text files, and hence benefiting from static analysis tools and the compiler's type-checker. The end result is a big reduction in the effort needed to configure complex multi-service application VMs.

2.2 Compactness and Optimisation

Resources in the cloud are rented, and minimising their use reduces costs. At the same time, multi-tenant services suffer from high variability in load that incentivises rapid scaling of deployments to meet current demand without wasting money. Unikernels link libraries that would normally be provided by the host OS, allowing the Unikernel tools to produce highly compact binaries via the normal linking mechanism. Features that are not used in a particular compilation are not included and whole-system optimization techniques can be used. In the most specialised mode, all configuration files are statically evaluated, enabling extensive dead-code elimination at the cost of having to recompile to reconfigure the service. The small binary size (on the order of kilobytes in many cases) makes deployment to remote datacenters across the Internet much smoother.

2.3 Unikernel Threat Model and Implications

Before considering the security implications of the unikernel abstraction, we first state our context and threat model. We are concerned with software that provides network-facing services in multi-tenant datacenters. Customers of a cloud provider typically must trust the provider not to be malicious. However, software running in such an environment is under constant threat of attack, from both other tenants and Internet-connected hosts more generally.

Unikernels run above a hypervisor layer and treat it and the control domain as part of the trusted computing base (for now, see §5.3). However, rather than adopt a multi-user access control mechanism that is inordinately complex for a specialised appliance, unikernels use the hypervisor as the sole unit of isolation and let applications trust external entities via protocol libraries such as SSL or SSH. Internally, unikernels adopt a defence in depth approach: firstly by compile-time specialisation, then by pervasive type-safety in the running code, and finally via hypervisor and toolchain extensions to protect against unforseen compiler or runtime bugs.

2.3.1 Single Image Appliances

The usual need for backwards compatibility with existing applications, e.g., the POSIX API, the OS kernel and the many userspace binaries involved mean that even the simplest appliance VM contains several hundred thousand, if not millions of, lines of active code that must be executed every time it boots (§4.5). Even widely deployed codebases such as Samba and OpenSSL still contain remote code execution exploits published as recently as April 2012 [7, 8], and serious data leaks have become all too commonplace in modern Internet services. A particularly insidious problem is that misconfiguring an image can leave unnecessary services running that can significantly increase the remote attack surface.

A unikernel toolchain performs as much compile-time work as possible to eliminate unnecessary features from the final VM. All network services are available as libraries, so only modules explicitly referenced in configuration files are linked in the output. The module dependency graph can be easily statically verified to only contain the desired services. While there are some Linux package managers that take this approach [9], they are ultimately constrained by having to support dynamic POSIX applications.

The trade-off with using too many static configuration directives that are compiled into the image is that VMs can no longer be cloned by taking a copy-on-write snapshot of an existing image. If this is required, a dynamic configuration directive can be used (e.g., DHCP instead of a static IP). Our prototype Mirage unikernels contain substantially fewer lines of code than the Linux equivalent, and the resulting images are significantly smaller (§4.5).

2.3.2 Pervasive Type-Safety

The requirement to be robust against remote attack strongly motivates use of a type-safe language. An important decision is whether to support multiple languages within the same unikernel. An argument for multiple languages is to improve backwards compatibility with existing code, but at the cost of increasing the complexity of a single-image system and dealing with interoperability between multiple language runtimes.

The alternative is to eschew source-level compatibility and rewrite system components entirely in one language and specialise that toolchain as best as possible. Although it is a daunting engineering challenge to rewrite protocols such as TCP, this is possible for an experimental system such as our Mirage prototype. In choosing this path, we support interoperability at the *network protocol* level: components communicate using type-safe, efficient implementations of standard network protocols. The advantage of running on a hypervisor is that the reverse is also possible: existing non-OCaml code can be encapsulated in separate VMs and communicated with via message-passing, analogous to processes in a conventional OS (§5.2). Likewise, access control within the appliance no longer requires userspace processes, instead depending on the language's type-safety to enforce restrictions. the virtual address space can be simplified into a single-address space model.

Mirage's single-language focus eases the integration of security techniques to protect the remaining non-type-safe components of the system (notably, the garbage collector) and to provide defence-in-depth in case a compiler bug allows the type-safety property to be violated. Some of these, such as stack canaries and guard pages, are straightforward translations of standard techniques and so we do not discuss them further. However, two depend on the unique properties of the unikernel environment and we describe these next.

2.3.3 Sealing and VM Privilege Dropping

As unikernels are single-image and single-address space, they exercise fewer aspects of the VM interface and can be sealed [10] at runtime to further defend against bugs in the runtime or compiler. This means that any code not present in the unikernel at compile time will never be run, completely preventing code injection attacks. Implementing this policy is very simple: as part of its start-of-day initialisation, the unikernel establishes a set of page tables in which no page is both writable and executable and then issues a special *seal* hypercall which prevents further page table modifications. The memory access policy in effect when the VM is sealed will be preserved until it terminates. The hypervisor changes necessary to implement the sealing operation are themselves very simple;[1] by contrast, implementing an equivalent *Write Xor Execute* [11] policy in a conventional operating system requires extensive modifications to libraries, runtimes, and the OS kernel itself.

This approach does mean that a running VM cannot expand its heap, but must instead pre-allocate all the memory it needs at startup (allocation *within* the heap is unaffected, and the hypervisor can still overcommit memory between VMs). This is a reasonable constraint on cloud infrastructures, where the memory allocated to the VM has already been purchased. The prohibition on page table modification does not apply to I/O mappings, provided that they are themselves non-executable and do not replace any existing data, code, or guard pages. This means that I/O is unaffected by sealing a VM, and does not inherently invalidate the memory access policy.

This optional facility is the only element of unikernels that requires a patch to the hypervisor instead of running purely in the guest. The privilege dropping patch is very simple and would benefit any other single-address space operating system, and so it is being upstreamed to the main Xen distribution. Note that Mirage can run on unmodified versions of Xen without this patch, albeit losing this layer of the defence-in-depth security protections.

2.3.4 Compile-Time Address Space Randomization

While VM sealing prevents an attacker from introducing attack code, it does not prevent them from executing code which is already present. Although use of whole-system optimization can eliminate many targets for such an attack, enough might be left to assemble a viable exploit using return-oriented programming style techniques. Conventionally, these would be protected against using runtime address space randomization, but this requires runtime linker code that would introduce significant complexity into the running unikernel. Fortunately, it is also unnecessary. The unikernel model means that reconfiguring an appliance means recompiling it, potentially for every deployment. We can thus perform address space randomisation at compile time using a freshly generated linker script, without impeding any compiler optimisations and without adding any runtime complexity.

[1] Including the API definition, our patch to Xen 4.1 added fewer than 50 lines of code in total.

3. Mirage Unikernels

Our Mirage prototype produces unikernels by compiling and linking OCaml code into a bootable Xen VM image. We implement all but the lowest-level features in OCaml and, to assist developers testing and debugging their code, provide the ability to produce POSIX binaries that run Mirage services on UNIX, as well as Xen VM images. We now discuss some of the key design decisions and components of Mirage: use of OCaml (§3.1), the PVBoot library that initialises a basic environment (§3.2), a modified language runtime library for heap management and concurrency (§3.3), and its type-safe device drivers (§3.4) and I/O stack (§3.5).

3.1 Why OCaml?

We chose to implement Mirage in OCaml for four key reasons. First, OCaml is a full-fledged systems programming language [12] with a flexible programming model that supports functional, imperative and object-oriented programming, and its brevity reduces lines-of-code (LoC) counts that are often considered correlated with attack surface. Second, OCaml has a simple yet high-performance runtime making it an ideal platform for experimenting with the unikernel abstraction that interfaces the runtime with Xen. Third, its implementation of static typing eliminates type information at compile-time while retaining all the benefits of type-safety, another example of specialisation. Finally, the open-source Xen Cloud Platform [12] and critical system components [13, 14] are implemented in OCaml, making integration straightforward.

However, this choice does impose tradeoffs. OCaml is still a relatively esoteric language compared with other systems languages such as C/C++. Using OCaml also necessitated a significant engineering effort to rebuild system components, particularly the storage and networking stacks. Given the other benefits of OCaml, we do not feel either of these are significant impediments for a research prototype. One early decision decision we took is to adopt the multikernel [15] philosophy of running a VM per core, and the single-threaded OCaml runtime has fast sequential performance that is ideal for this need. Each Mirage unikernel runs over Xen using a single virtual CPU, and multicore is supported via multiple communicating unikernels over a single instance of Xen.

We did explore applying unikernel techniques in the traditional systems language, C, linking application code with Xen MiniOS, a cut-down libc, OpenBSD versions of libm and printf, and the lwIP user-space network stack. However, we found that a DNS appliance constructed in this way from the high performance NSD DNS server performed considerably worse than the Mirage DNS server, even after several rounds of optimisation (Figure 10). It seems likely that producing even a similarly performing prototype in C would still require very significant engineering effort and would not achieve any of the type-safety benefits.

3.2 PVBoot Library

PVBoot provides start-of-day support to initialise a VM with one virtual CPU and Xen event channels, and jump to an entry function. Unlike a conventional OS, multiple processes and preemptive threading are not supported, and instead a single 64-bit address space is laid out for the language runtime to use. PVBoot provides two memory page allocators, one slab and one extent. The slab allocator is used to support the C code in the runtime; as most code is in OCaml it is not heavily used. The extent allocator reserves a contiguous area of virtual memory which it manipulates in 2MB chunks, permitting the mapping of x86_64 superpages. Memory regions are statically assigned roles, e.g., the garbage collected heap or I/O data pages. PVBoot also has a domainpoll function that blocks the VM on a set of event channels and a timeout.

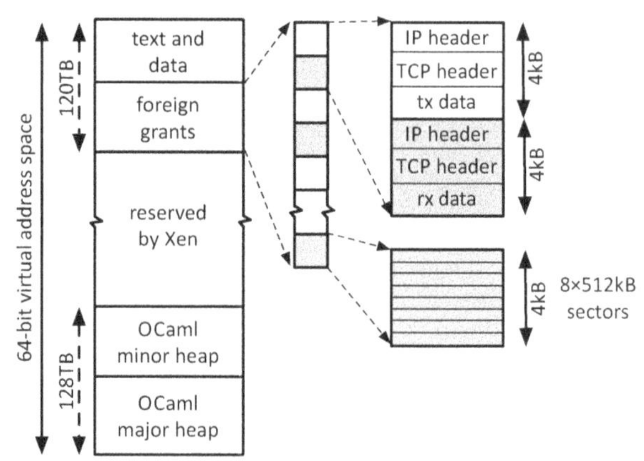

Figure 2: Specialised virtual memory layout of a 64-bit Mirage unikernel running on Xen.

PVBoot provides minimal support for an asynchronous, event-driven VM that sleeps until I/O is available or times out. Device drivers are *all* provided outside PVBoot in type-safe OCaml (§3.4).

3.3 Language Runtime

Mirage executes OCaml code over a specialised language runtime modified in two key areas: memory management and concurrency. Figure 2 shows the memory layout of a Mirage unikernel, divided into three regions: text and data; external I/O pages; and the OCaml heaps. The text and data segments contain the OCaml runtime, linked against PVBoot. This is the only address space available in the kernel. The application's main thread is launched immediately after boot and the VM shuts down when it returns.

The OCaml garbage collector splits the heap into two regions: a fast minor heap for short-lived values, and a large major heap to which longer-lived values are promoted on each minor heap collection. These areas are allocated below the low virtual address space reserved by Xen: the minor heap has a single 2 MB extent that grows in 4 kB chunks, and the major heap has the remainder of virtual memory, growing in 2 MB superpage chunks using the extent allocator. Memory mapping large contiguous areas is usually discouraged to allow Address Space Randomization (ASR) to protect against buffer overflows [16], and so a normal userspace garbage collector maintains a page table to track allocated heap chunks. Mirage unikernels avoid ASR at runtime in favour of a more specialised security model (§2.3), and guarantee a contiguous virtual address space, simplifying runtime memory management.

VMs communicate directly by having the local VM grant memory page access rights to the remote VM via the hypervisor [17]. PVBoot allocates external memory pages from a reserved area of virtual memory, and allocates a small proxy value in the small, fast OCaml minor heap. Mirage provides a library to reference that data from OCaml without requiring a data copy (§3.4). Specialising memory layout to distinguish I/O pages in this way significantly reduces the amount of data that the garbage collector has to scan. This reduced garbage collector pressure is one of two key factors that let the Mirage network stack exhibit predictable performance; the other is pervasive library support for zero-copy I/O (§3.4.1).

To provide concurrency beyond PVBoot's simple domainpoll function, Mirage integrates the Lwt cooperative threading library [18]. This internally evaluates blocking functions into event descriptors to provide straight-line control flow for the developer. Written in pure OCaml, Lwt threads are heap-allocated values, with only the thread main loop requiring a C binding to poll for external

```
cstruct ring_hdr {          || auto-generates these functions:
  uint32_t req_prod;        || set_req_prod : buf → uint32 → unit
  uint32_t req_event;       || get_req_prod : buf → uint32
  uint32_t rsp_prod;        || ...
  uint32_t rsp_event;       || set_stuff : buf → uint64 → unit
  uint64_t stuff            || get_stuff : buf → uint64
} as little_endian          ||
```

Figure 3: Syntax extension mapping C structs *(left)* to OCaml values by autogenerating efficient accessor functions *(right)*.

events. Mirage provides an evaluator that uses domainpoll to listen for events and wake up lightweight threads. The VM is thus either executing OCaml code or blocked, with no internal preemption or asynchronous interrupts. The main thread repeatedly executes until it completes or throws an exception, and the domain subsequently shuts down with the VM exit code matching the thread return value.

A useful consequence is that most scheduling and thread logic is contained in an application library, and can thus be modified by the developer as they see fit. For example, threads can be tagged with local keys for debugging, statistics or prioritisation, depending on application needs. Thread scheduling is platform-independent with timers stored in a heap-allocated OCaml priority queue, and can be overridden by the application (e.g. we have previously demonstrated the benefit of custom scheduling for the Sqlite library database in an earlier prototype [19]). Only the run-loop is Xen-specific, to interface with PVBoot.

3.4 Device Drivers

Mirage drivers interface to the device abstraction provided by Xen. Xen devices consist of a *frontend* driver in the guest VM, and a *backend* driver that multiplexes frontend requests, typically to a real physical device [20]. These are connected by an event channel to signal the other side, and a single memory page divided into fixed-size request slots tracked by producer/consumer pointers. Responses are written into the same slots as the requests, with the frontend implementing flow control to avoid overflowing the ring. Xen device classes using this model include Ethernet, block storage, virtual framebuffer, USB and PCI.

Manipulating these shared memory rings is the base abstraction for all I/O throughout Mirage. The shared page is mapped into OCaml using the built-in Bigarray module, which wraps externally allocated memory safely into the OCaml heap and makes it available as an array. Reading and writing into the shared page must precisely match the C semantics, and is a relatively slow operation in OCaml since fixed-size integers are boxed values that are heap-allocated before being copied into the shared page.[2] We used `camlp4` to add a new cstruct keyword to OCaml to directly map C structures (Figure 3). Declaring a cstruct generates accessor functions for directly manipulating the external memory array. The extension also handles endian conversion, and is used extensively through the network stack for header parsing [22].

This approach permits Mirage drivers to be implemented as pure OCaml libraries relying on just two extra intrinsics: inline assembly providing read and write memory barriers. The Ring module implements the base protocol and adds an asynchronous threading interface to push requests and wait for responses. Higher-level modules such as Netif and Blkif implement networking and block drivers, and interoperate with unmodified Xen hosts. A beneficial side-effect of our re-implementation of these protocols was to fuzz-test the existing code, and we discovered and reported several edge-case bugs in Linux/Xen as a result, including an important security issue (XSA-39).

[2] The FoxNet network stack also reported this issue in SML [21].

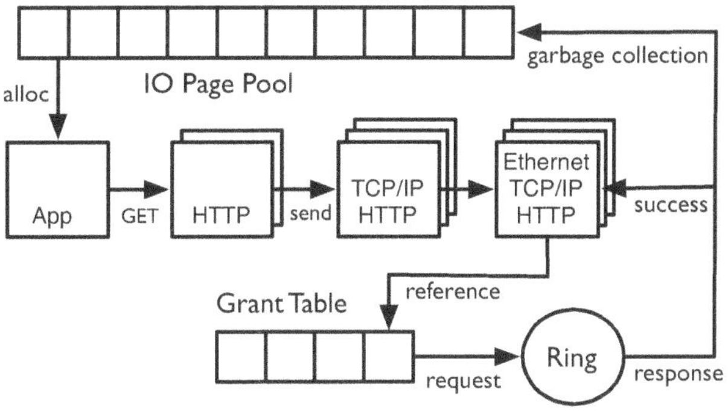

Figure 4: Example zero-copy write for an HTTP GET. The application writes its request into an I/O page, and the network stack segments it into fragments to write to the device ring. When a response arrives the pages are collected and the write thread notified.

3.4.1 Zero-Copy Device I/O

The Xen device protocol does not write data directly into the shared memory page, but rather uses it to coordinate passing 4 kB memory pages by reference. Two communicating VMs share a *grant table* that maps pages to an integer offset (called a *grant*) in this table, with updates checked and enforced by the hypervisor. The grant is exchanged over the device driver shared ring, and looked up by the remote VM to map or copy that page into its own address space. Once within the remote (non-Mirage) VM, the data must be transferred into the application. As POSIX APIs do not support zero-copy sockets, this usually entails a second copy from the receiving VM's kernel into the appropriate userspace process.

Mirage unikernels do not have a userspace, so received pages are passed directly to the application without requiring copying. The cstruct library avoids incurring copying overhead by slicing the underlying array into smaller views; once views are all garbage-collected, the array is returned to the free page pool. The network stack can thus safely re-use fragments of incoming network traffic and proxy it directly into another device (e.g., an HTTP proxy) while avoiding having to manage the page manually.

However, there are still a few resources that must be manually tracked and freed, e.g., the contents of the shared grant table between VMs. Mirage uses the OCaml type system to enforce invariants that ensure resources are correctly freed, via higher-order functions that wrap any use of a given resource such as a grant reference. When the function terminates, whether normally via timeout or an unknown exception, the grant reference is freed. As well as preventing resource leaks, particularly on error paths, this allows the scheduler to free resources by cancelling light-weight threads. These composable higher-order functions, also known as *combinators*, are used throughout Mirage to safely expose system resources. Note that these combinators do not entirely eliminate resource leaks, since references that are held in data structures and never removed will remain forever, but the OCaml programming style encourages the use of many small data structures and reusable utility libraries that help prevent such problems.

3.5 Type-Safe Protocol I/O

Mirage implements protocol libraries in OCaml to ensure that *all* external I/O handling is type-safe, making unikernels robust against memory overflows. Protocols are structured as non-blocking parsing libraries with separate client/server logic that spawns lightweight threads. Libraries are accessed via preemptive state handles, enabling multiple protocol stacks within the same unikernel. Table 1 lists the protocols currently implemented in Mirage, sufficient to self-host our website[3] infrastructure, including wiki, blog and DNS servers on the Amazon EC2 public cloud.

Subsystem	*Implemented Protocols*
Core	Lwt, Cstruct, Regexp, UTF8, Cryptokit
Network	Ethernet, ARP, DHCP, IPv4, ICMP, UDP, TCP, OpenFlow
Storage	Simple key-value, FAT-32, Append B-Tree, Memcache
Application	DNS, SSH, HTTP, XMPP, SMTP
Formats	JSON, XML, CSS, S-Expressions

Table 1: System facilities provided as Mirage libraries.

Data arrives to both the network and storage stacks as a stream of discrete packets. Mirage bridges the gap between packets and streams by using channel iteratees [23] that map functions over infinite streams of packets to produce a typed stream. Iterators eliminate many of the fixed-size buffers that are often used in a less tightly coupled conventional kernel/userspace. Chained iterators route traffic directly to the relevant application thread, blocking on intermediate system events if necessary. We now describe the specifics of networking (§3.5.1) and storage (§3.5.2).

3.5.1 Network Processing

The Mirage network stack emphasises application-level control over strict modularity, exposing most details of the underlying protocol to application control. It provides two communication methods: a fast on-host inter-VM vchan transport, and an Ethernet transport for external communication. vchan is a fast shared memory interconnect through which data is tracked via producer/consumer pointers. It allocates multiple contiguous pages for the ring to ensure it has a reasonable buffer and once connected, communicating VMs can exchange data directly via shared memory without further intervention from the hypervisor other than interrupt notifications.[4] vchan is present in upstream Linux 3.3.0 onwards, enabling easy interaction between Mirage unikernels and Linux VMs.

Internet connectivity is more complex: an application links to a protocol library such as HTTP, which links with a TCP/IP network stack, which in turns links to the network device driver. The application reads and writes I/O pages with the protocol library so they can be transmitted directly. When reading packets, the network stack splits out headers and data using cstruct subviews (§3.4.1). Writing data requires more processing as the stack must prepend variable-length protocol headers for TCP, IP and Ethernet before the data payload, and sometimes segment large payloads into smaller fragments for transmission. This is solved via scatter-gather I/O: the network stack allocates a header page for every write, and the network libraries rearrange incoming payloads into sub-views as needed, before writing all the fragments into the device ring as one packet. Figure 4 illustrates this write path.

3.5.2 Storage

Traditional OS kernels layer filesystems over block devices accessed via POSIX sockets or mmap, and coalesce writes into a kernel buffer cache [24]. Applications needing precise control over when a write is actually persisted must either invoke the fsync syscall or explicitly request non-buffered direct access and issue sector-aligned requests. Modern Linux kernels provide libaio for asynchronous block requests only, forcing applications to use different APIs for networking and storage.

In contrast, Mirage block devices share the same Ring abstraction as network devices, using the same I/O pages to provide effi-

[3] http://openmirage.org/

[4] When data is continuously flowing between VMs, each side checks for outstanding data before blocking, reducing the number of hypervisor calls.

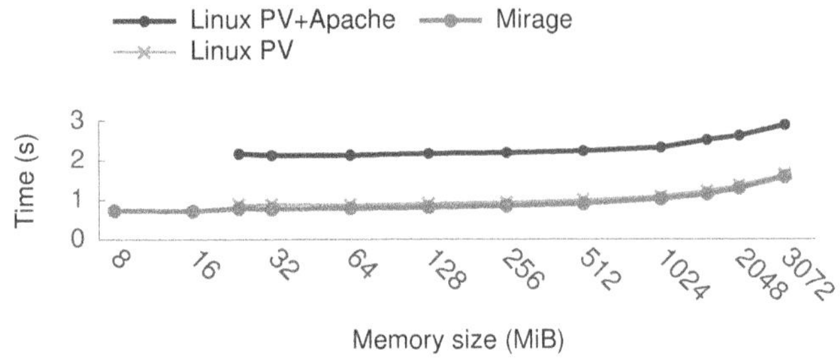

Figure 5: Domain boot time comparison.

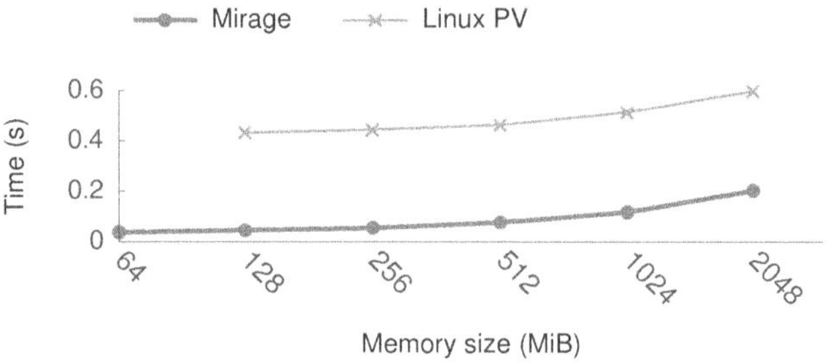

Figure 6: Boot time using an asynchronous Xen toolstack.

cient block-level access, with filesystems and caching provided as OCaml libraries. This gives control to the application over caching policy rather than providing only one default cache policy. Different caching policies can be provided as libraries (OCaml modules) to be linked at build time, with the only built-in policy being that all writes are guaranteed to be direct.

For example, we ported a third-party copy-on-write binary tree storage library[5] to Mirage. This can be used as a storage backend by applications, with caching policy and buffer management being explicitly managed within in the library. Our FAT-32 storage library also implements its own buffer management policy where data reads are returned as iterators supplying one sector at a time. This avoids building large lists in the heap while permitting internal buffering within the library by having it request larger sector extents from the block driver. Finally, we found that our DNS server gained a dramatic speed increase by applying a memoization library to *network* responses (§4); this technique could also be used to implement persistent self-paging of very large datasets [25].

4. Evaluation

As Mirage is a clean-slate implementation of many OS components, we evaluate it against more conventional deployments in stages. We first examine micro-benchmarks (§4.1) to establish baseline performance of key components, followed by more realistic appliances: a DNS server, showing performance of our safe network stack (§4.2); an OpenFlow controller appliance (§4.3); and an integrated web server and database, combining storage and networking (§4.4). Finally, we examine the differences in active LoC and binaries in these appliances, and the impact of dead-code elimination (§4.5).

4.1 Microbenchmarks

These microbenchmarks demonstrate the *potential* benefits of unikernel specialisation by examining performance in simple, controlled scenarios. Evaluations are composed of identical OCaml code executing in different hosting environments: *linux-native*, a Linux kernel running directly on the bare metal with an ELF binary version of the application; *linux-pv*, a Linux kernel running as a paravirtualised Xen domU with an ELF binary version of the application; and *xen-direct*, the application built as a type-safe unikernel, running directly over Xen. We verified that CPU-bound applications are unaffected by unikernel compilation as expected, as the hypervisor architecture only affects memory and I/O.

4.1.1 Boot Time

Unikernels are compact enough to boot and respond to network traffic in real-time.

Mirage generates compact VMs which boot very quickly. Figure 5 compares boot times for a Mirage webserver against a minimal Linux kernel, and a more realistic *linux-pv* Debian Linux running Apache2. Time is measured from startup to the point where boot is complete, signalled by the VM sending a special UDP packet to the control domain. The minimal Linux kernel measures this "time-to-userspace" via an `initrd` that calls the `ifconfig` ioctls directly to bring up a network interface before explicitly transmitting a single UDP packet. The more realistic Debian Linux running Apache2 uses the standard Debian boot scripts and measures time-to-userspace by waiting until Apache2 startup returns before transmitting the single UDP packet. The Mirage unikernel transmits the UDP packet as soon as the network interface is ready. As the memory size increases, the proportion of Mirage boot time due to building the domain also increases to approximately 60% for memory size 3072 MiB. Mirage matches the minimal Linux kernel, booting in slightly under half the time of the Debian Linux.

It is difficult to distinguish between the minimal Linux VM and Mirage in Figure 5. The boot time is skewed by the Xen control stack synchronously building domains, since latency isn't normally a prime concern for VM construction. We modified the Xen toolstack to support parallel domain construction, and isolate the VM startup time in Figure 6. This clearly distinguishes the differences between the Mirage unikernel and Linux: Mirage boots in *under 50 milliseconds*. Such fast reboot times mitigate the concern that redeployment by reconfiguration is too heavyweight, as well as opening up the possibility of regular micro-reboots [14].

4.1.2 Threading

Garbage collected heap management is more efficient in a single address-space environment. Thread latency can be reduced by eliminating multiple levels of scheduling.

Figure 7a benchmarks thread construction time, showing the time to construct millions of threads in parallel where each thread sleeps for between 0.5–1.5 seconds and then terminates. The *linux-pv* userspace target, which most closely mirrors a conventional cloud application, is slowest with the same binary running on native Linux coming in next. The two *xen-* targets using the different memory allocators perform notably better due to the test being limited by the GC speed: thread construction occurs on the OCaml heap so creating millions of threads triggers regular compaction and scanning. The *xen-* runtime is faster due to the specialised address space layout described earlier (§2). There is little extra benefit to using superpages (*xen-extent* cf. *xen-malloc*), as the heap grows once to its maximum size and never subsequently shrinks.

We also evaluated the precision of thread timers: a thread records the domain wallclock time, sleeps for 1–4 seconds and records the difference between the wallclock time and its expected wakeup time. Figure 7b plots the CDF of the jitter, and shows that the unikernel target provides both lower and more predictable latency when waking up millions of parallel threads. This is due simply to the lack of userspace/kernel boundary eliding Linux's syscall overhead.

[5] `https://github.com/Incubaid/baardskeerder`

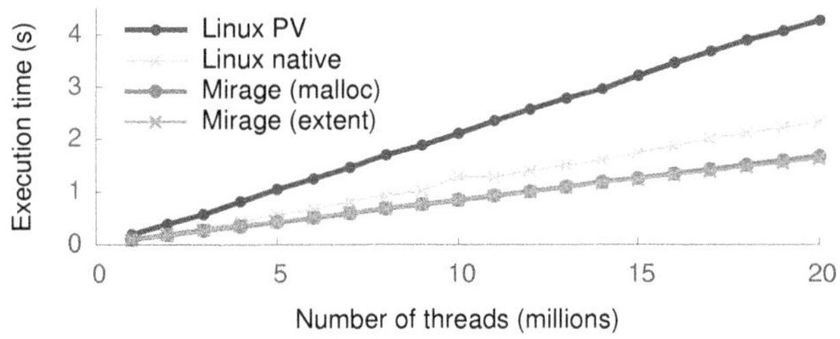

(a) Creation times.

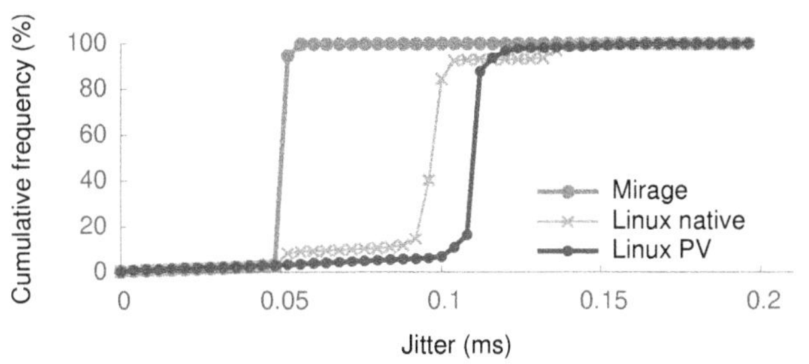

(b) Jitter for 10^6 parallel threads sleeping and waking after a fixed period.

Figure 7: Mirage thread performance.

4.1.3 Networking and Storage

Unikernel low-level networking performs competitively to conventional OSs, despite being fully type-safe. Library-based block management performs on par with a conventional layered storage stack.

As a simple latency test against the Linux stack we flooded 10^6 pings from the Linux *ping* client running in its own VM to two targets: a standard Linux VM, and a Mirage unikernel with the Ethernet, ARP, IPv4 and ICMP libraries. This stress tests pure header parsing without introducing any userspace element for Linux. As expected, Mirage suffered a small (4–10%) increase in latency compared to Linux due to the slight overhead of type-safety, but both survived a 72-hour flood ping test.

We compared the performance of Mirage's TCPv4 stack, implementing the full connection lifecycle, fast retransmit and recovery, New Reno congestion control, and window scaling, against the Linux 3.7 TCPv4 stack using `iperf`. All hardware offload was disabled to provide the most stringent test of Mirage: the naturally higher overheads of implementing low-level operations in OCaml rather than C mean that hardware offload (particularly TCP segmentation) disproportionately improves Mirage's performance compared to Linux. Performance is on par with Linux: Mirage's receive throughput is slightly higher due to the lack of a userspace copy, while its transmit performance is lower due to higher CPU usage. Both Linux and Mirage can saturate a gigabit network connection, and we expect that adding transmit hardware offload support will allow even our experimental TCP stack to 10 Gb/s performance.

Configuration	*Throughput [std. dev.] (Mbps)* 1 flow		10 flows	
Linux to Linux	1590	[9.1]	1534	[74.2]
Linux to Mirage	1742	[18.2]	1710	[15.1]
Mirage to Linux	975	[7.0]	952	[16.8]

Figure 8: Comparative TCP throughput performance with all hardware offload disabled.

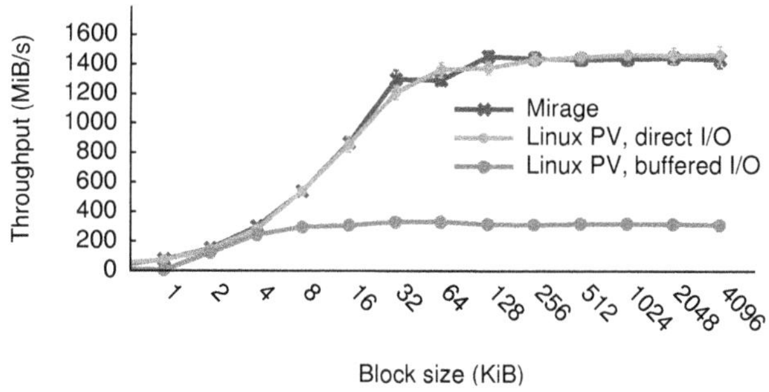

Figure 9: Random block read throughput, +/- 1 std. dev.

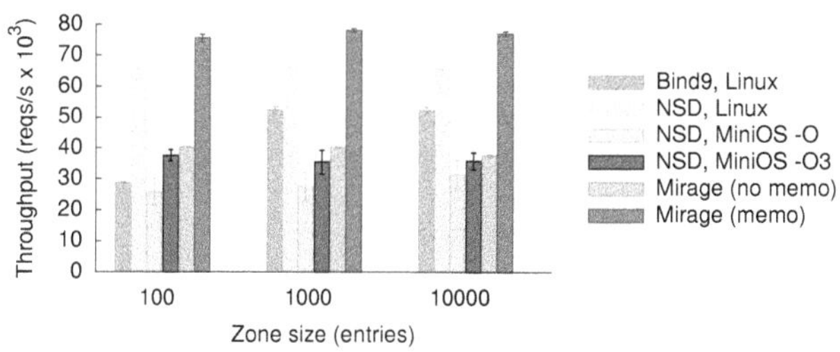

Figure 10: DNS performance with increasing zone size.

Figure 9 shows a simple random read throughput test using *fio* of a fast PCI-express SSD storage device, comparing a Mirage *xen-direct* appliance against a Linux RHEL5 kernel (2.6.18) using buffered and direct I/O. Again, as expected, the Linux direct I/O and Mirage lines are effectively the same: both use direct I/O and so impose very little overhead on the raw hardware performance. However, the performance impact of the Linux buffer cache *is* notable: it causes performance to plateau at around 300 MB/s in contrast to the 1.6 GB/s achieved if the buffer cache is avoided. The lack of a buffer cache is not significant for the appliances we target: such applications already manage their own storage.

4.2 DNS Server Appliance

The Mirage DNS Server appliance contains the core libraries, the Ethernet, ARP, IP, DHCP and UDP libraries from the network stack, and a simple in-memory filesystem storing the zone in standard Bind9 format. Figure 10 compares the throughput of the Mirage appliance on Xen against two best-of-breed nameservers: Bind 9.9.0, a mature and widely used DNS server; and NSD 3.2.10, a recent high performance implementation.

Bind achieves 55 kqueries/s for reasonable zone file sizes.[6] As a more recent rewrite focused on performance, NSD does better, achieving around 70 kqueries/s. The Mirage appliance initially performed very poorly, but dramatically improved when we introduced memoization of responses to avoid repeated computation. A simple 20 line patch, this increased performance from around 40 kqueries/s to 75–80 kqueries/s. Errorbars indicate unbiased estimates of $\mu \pm \sigma$ across 10 runs.

There is other evidence [26] that algorithmic performance improvements substantially exceed those due only to machine-level optimization, and Mirage's use of functional programming provides an effective platform for further experimentation in this regard. A further example is DNS label compression, notoriously

[6] We were unable to determine the cause of Bind's poor performance with small zone sizes, but the results are consistently reproducible.

tricky to get right as previously seen label fragments must be carefully tracked. Our initial implementation used a naive mutable hashtable, which we then replaced with a functional map using a customised ordering function that first tests the size of the labels before comparing their contents. This gave around a 20% speedup, as well as securing against the denial-of-service attack where clients deliberately cause hash collisions.

DNS also provides a good example where Mirage type-safety should bring significant security benefits. For example, in the last 10 years the Internet Systems Consortium has reported 40 vulnerabilities in the Bind software.[7] Of these, 25% were due to memory management errors, 15% to poor handling of exceptional data states, and 10% to faulty packet parsing code, *all* of which would be mitigated by Mirage's type-safety.

Finally, the other main benefit of Mirage is shown by comparing the size of the Linux and Mirage appliances: the Mirage appliance is 183.5 kB in size compared with 462 MB in-use for the Linux VM image. While some of this difference can be accounted to the fact that our libraries do not implement the complete feature-set of BIND9 or NSD, we do include all features required by the *queryperf* test suite and the Mirage appliance is sufficient to self-host the project infrastructure online.

We also tested both NSD and BIND compiled in libOS mode with the *newlib-1.16* embedded libc, the lwIP-1.3.0 network stack and the standard Xen-4.1 MiniOS device drivers. Performance was significantly lower than expected with further benchmarking revealing that this is due to unexpected interactions between MiniOS `select(2)` scheduling and the `netfront` driver. Our experiences with the C libOS libraries reinforced our notion that such programming is rather fragile – using embedded systems libraries often means giving up performance (e.g., optimised libc assembly is replaced by common calls) – and a more fruitful approach would be to break the Linux kernel into a libOS as Drawbridge does for Windows 7 [3].

4.3 OpenFlow Controller Appliance

OpenFlow is a software-defined networking standard for Ethernet switches [27]. It defines an architecture and a protocol by which the *controller* can manipulate *flow tables* in Ethernet switches, termed *datapaths*. Mirage provides libraries implementing an OpenFlow protocol parser, controller, and switch. By linking against the controller library, appliances can exercise direct control over hardware and software OpenFlow switches, subject to any network administration policies in place. Conversely, by linking against the switch library, an appliance can be controlled as if it were an OpenFlow switch, useful in scenarios where the appliance provides network layer functionality, e.g., acts as a router, switch, firewall, proxy or other middlebox. As software implementations, these libraries can be extended according to specific appliance needs, e.g., to enable flows to be identified by the DNS domain of either endpoint, or defined in terms of HTTP URLs.

We benchmark our OpenFlow implementation using the OFlops platform [28]. For the controller benchmark we use *cbench* to emulate 16 switches concurrently connected to the controller, each serving 100 distinct MAC addresses. Experiments run on a 16-core AMD server with 40 GB RAM, and each controller is configured to use a single thread. We measure throughput in requests processed per second in response to a stream of *packet-in* messages produced by each emulated switch under two scenarios: *batch*, where each switch maintains a full 64 kB buffer of outgoing *packet-in* messages; and *single*, where only one *packet-in* message is in flight from each switch. The first measures the absolute throughput when servicing requests, and the second measures throughput of the controller when serving connected switches fairly.

[7] `http://www.isc.org/advisories/bind`

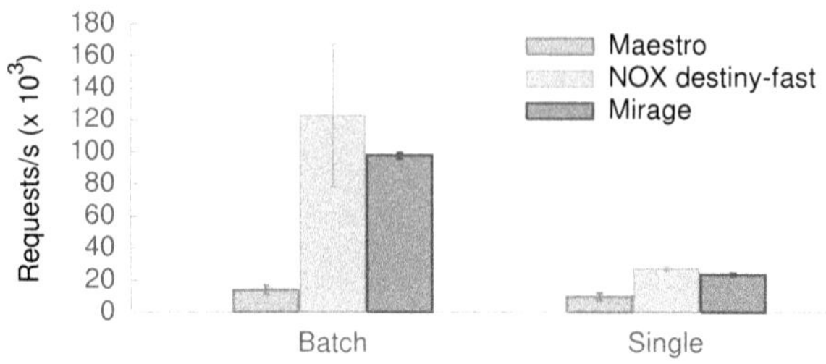

Figure 11: OpenFlow controller performance ($\mu \pm \sigma$).

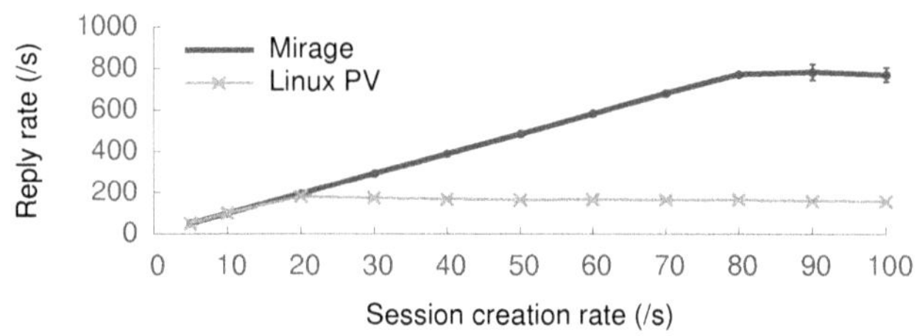

Figure 12: Simple dynamic web appliance performance.

Figure 11 compares the *xen-direct* Mirage controller against two existing OpenFlow controllers: Maestro [29], an optimised Java-based controller; and the optimised C++ *destiny-fast* branch of NOX [30], one of the earliest and most mature publicly available OpenFlow controllers. Unsurprisingly, the optimised NOX branch has the highest performance in both experiments, although it does exhibit extreme short-term unfairness in the batch test. Maestro is fairer but suffers significantly reduced performance, particularly on the "single" test, presumably due to JVM overheads. Performance of the Mirage appliance falls between NOX and Maestro, showing that Mirage manages to achieve most of the performance benefits of optimised C++ which retaining the high-level language features such as type-safety.

4.4 Dynamic Web Server Appliance

Our final appliance implements a simple "Twitter-like" service. It maintains an in-memory database of tweets and is exercised through two API calls: one to `GET` the last 100 tweets for an individual, and the other to `POST` a tweet to an individual. The Mirage implementation integrates the third-party Baardskeerder B-tree storage library, ported to Mirage with only a small patch to use the `Block` APIs instead of UNIX I/O. We compare the Mirage unikernel implementation against a Linux-based appliance running *nginx*, *fastCGI* and *web.py*. We used the *httperf* benchmark tool as a client on the same physical box with separate dedicated cores, connecting over the local bridge to avoid the possibility of the Ethernet becoming the bottleneck. Each *httperf session* issues 10 requests: 1 tweet and 9 'get last 100 tweets'.

Figure 12 shows the results. The unikernel implementation clearly scales much better: scaling is linear up to around 80 sessions (800 requests – each session consists of 10 HTTP requests, 9 GETs and 1 POST) before it becomes CPU bound. In contrast, Linux VM performance is much worse, reaching its limit at around 20 sessions. For comparison, the same Linux VM serving two clients just a single static page via *nginx* achieves up to 5,000 requests/s before hitting CPU and *fd* limits. Although substantially higher than the (unoptimised) Mirage implementation, there are other benefits to Mirage discussed earlier: smaller memory footprint (32 MB against 256 MB), type-safety and security.

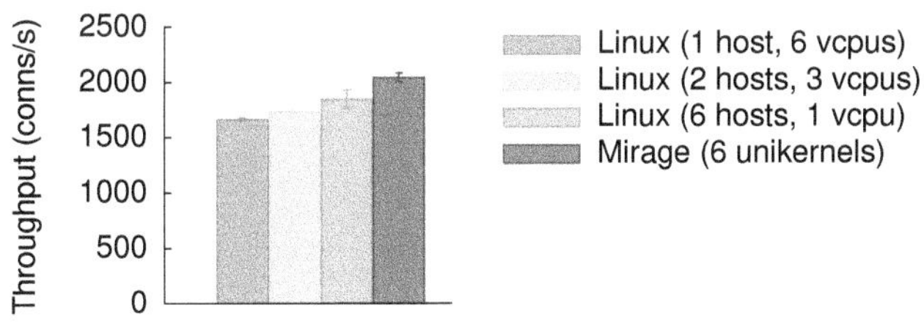

Figure 13: Static page serving performance, comparing Mirage and Apache2 running on Linux.

Figure 13 compares performance of the Mirage web appliance against a standard Linux VM running Apache2 using the mpm-worker backend with the number of workers sized to the number of vCPUs, serving a single static page. The Linux VM was run in three configurations: a single VM given 6 vCPUs, two VMs each given 3 vCPUs and finally 6 VMs each given a single vCPU. As Mirage unikernels do not support multi-core, only one configuration was run of 6 unikernels each with a single vCPU. The results show first, that scaling out appears to improve the Apache2 appliance performance more than having multiple cores and second, that the Mirage unikernels exceed the Apache2 appliance in all cases.

4.5 Code and Binary Size

Direct comparison of lines-of-code (LoC) is rarely meaningful due to factors including widespread use of conditional compilation and complex build systems. We attempt to control for these effects by configuring according to reasonable defaults, and then pre-processing to remove unused macros, comments and whitespace. In addition, to attempt a fair comparison against the 7 million LoC left in the Linux tree after pre-processing, we ignore kernel code associated with components for which we have no analogue, e.g., the many architectures, network protocols, and filesystems that Linux supports. As we are concerned with network-facing guest VMs that share the underlying hypervisor, we do not include LoC for Xen and its management domains; these can be separately disaggregated as desired [14, 31].

Figure 14a shows LoC for several popular server components, computed by the *cloc* utility. Even after removing irrelevant code, a Linux appliance involves at least 4–5x more LoC than a Mirage appliance. Note that, although the Mirage libraries are not yet as feature-rich as the industry-standard C applications, their library structure ensures that unused dependencies can be shed at compile-time even as features continue to be added. For example, if no filesystem is used, then the entire set of block drivers are automatically elided. Performing such dependency analysis across the kernel and userspace is non-trivial in a Linux distribution.

Compiled binary size is another effective illustration of this, and Table 2 gives binary sizes for the benchmark appliances. The first column used the default OCaml dead-code elimination which drops unused modules, and the second uses ocamlclean,[8] a more extensive custom tool which performs dataflow analysis to drop unused functions *within* a module if not otherwise referenced; this is safe due to the lack of dynamic linking in Mirage [32]. Either way, all Mirage kernels are significantly more compact than even a cut-down embedded Linux distribution, without requiring any work on the part of the programmer beyond using the Mirage APIs to build their application.

[8] `http://github.com/avsm/ocamlclean`

Appliance	*Binary size (MB)*	
	Standard build	Dead code elimination
DNS	0.449	0.184
Web Server	0.673	0.172
OpenFlow switch	0.393	0.164
OpenFlow controller	0.392	0.168

Table 2: Sizes of Mirage unikernels, before and after dead-code elimination. Configuration and data are compiled directly into the unikernel.

5. Discussion & Related Work

We next discuss the relationship of both unikernels and Mirage to the previous work on which they build, from fields such as type-safety, library OSs and security.

5.1 Type-safe and library OSs

The desire to apply type-safety in the OS is not new: type-safe OSs have been built in a range of languages including Haskell [33, 34], Java [35], Standard ML [21], C#/.Net [4], and Modula-3 [36]. The last of these, SPIN [36], is perhaps the closest in nature to Mirage: SPIN is an extensible OS that relies on Modula-3 type-safety to dynamically link extensions into the kernel. More recently, Singularity [4] restructured the OS to sit above the Common Language Runtime, achieving many similar type-safety benefits. The unikernel approach is somewhat orthogonal: it proposes a restructuring of the OS to specifically target services hosted on the public cloud, which benefits from but does not mandate type-safety. The particular implementation presented here, Mirage, also uses an extremely portable functional language which means the Mirage core and network stack can even be compiled to JavaScript for execution on *node.js*;[9] and ports to ARM and a FreeBSD kernel module are functional in an alpha state.

Restructuring the OS into a set of libraries that are linked into the application has been explored extensively. Exokernel [1], Nemesis [2], and Scout [37] all pursued this approach with considerable success. Indeed, the specific technique of page re-use for efficient network I/O (§3.5.1) is directly inspired by the high-performance Cheetah web server for the Exokernel [38]. More recently, Drawbridge [3] adapts Windows to be a library operating system where applications communicate via networking protocols, showing that this approach scales to real commercial operating systems. However, previous library OSs suffered from poor hardware support with device drivers either needing to be written from scratch or wrapped in a compatibility layer [39]. Unikernels use similar libOS techniques but targets the cloud as a deployment platform, with our Mirage implementation using the Xen hypervisor as a low-level common hardware interface.

Finally, Libra [5] adapts the JVM to sit directly above Xen, targeting Java workloads specifically. In particular, Libra uses a gateway server running in a standard Linux VM to provide access to standard OS services such as a networking stack and filesystem IO. Application-hosting VMs access these services by communicating with the other VM via the gateway process. In contrast, Unikernels are more highly-specialised but also more complete, providing single-purpose appliance VMs that directly support standard network and filesystem protocols.

5.2 Legacy Support

Perhaps the most obvious potential problem with the unikernel approach is how best to support legacy systems. The extreme position we take does appear to require a great deal of re-implementation,

[9] Admittedly without a specific purpose in mind, though it is useful for educational purposes and ensuring portability.

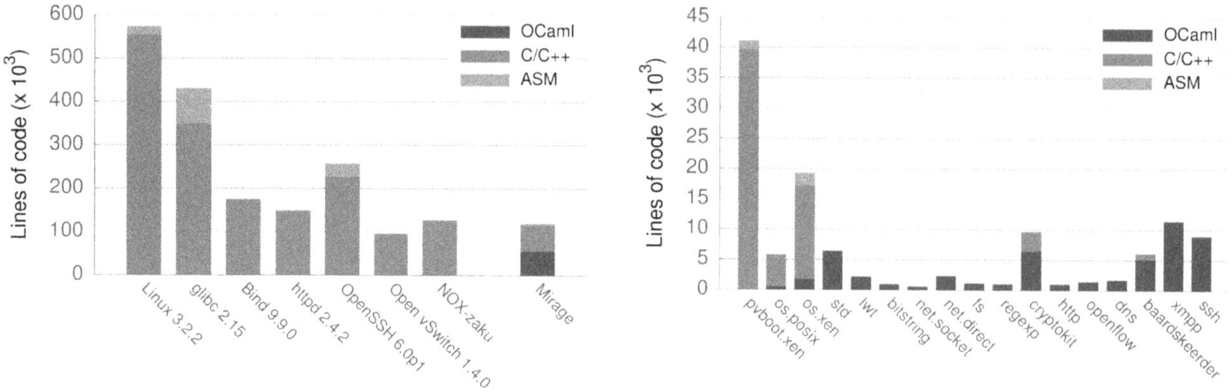

(a) Key cloud components *vs.* the Mirage unikernel codebase.

(b) Key components of the Mirage unikernel.

Figure 14: Comparison of lines-of-active-code counts.

possibly in an unfamiliar language if using our Mirage prototype. Consider for example the standard implementation of the SSL protocol in the OpenSSL [40] library, or storage formats such as *ext2* that are only properly documented in their standard implementation's code: a complete rewrite of such key components cannot be lightly undertaken! On the other hand, these security-critical libraries currently present complex APIs that often lead to serious vulnerabilities [41], and higher-level functional interfaces would be very valuable alternatives to existing C implementations.

Alternative approaches retrofit type-safety to existing codebases, using, e.g., tools like CIL or CCured [42, 43]. Unfortunately, it turns out to be considerable work to implement specialisation techniques for the particular underlying platforms, and it would be hard to integrate the results of these into a unikernel. At the other end of the spectrum, recent tools such as HipHop [44] take steps toward the unikernel approach, translating PHP code into C++ and then compiling a single binary containing the entire PHP application. One can envisage further specialising such binaries into unikernels, though the benefits of static type-safety would not accrue with PHP.

We take an approach pioneered by the Flux OSKit [39], which encapsulated existing code to port it into the new system. Flux did so by targeting the multiboot bootloader standard and then wrapping device drivers from systems such as Linux to fit within it, and encapsulation is a very promising technique to apply to larger cloud components. For example, 'big data' processing systems, such as Map-Reduce, Hadoop, and Dryad [45–47] are typically structured as a set of intercommunicating processes, farmed out within a datacenter. Each of these processes could be encapsulated as a single VM and message-passing between VMs implemented via Vchan. This approach is similar to UNIX privilege separation [48], and provides an incremental deployment path, ensuring existing reliably engineered components can continue to be used and that multiple, new, untested components need not be introduced all at once.

5.3 Deeper, Higher, Broader

One shortcoming of the Mirage unikernel implementation is that it still relies on a great deal of unsafe code, notably the Xen hypervisor and management domain, *dom0*. This raises the question, can we push the unikernel further down? This would require either re-implementing the hypervisor itself or, for more resource constrained platforms, forgoing it completely, focusing instead on a single encapsulated application. In both cases, much of the current approach – such as the I/O stack – would carry over, but native support for many-core hardware would require additional work. One

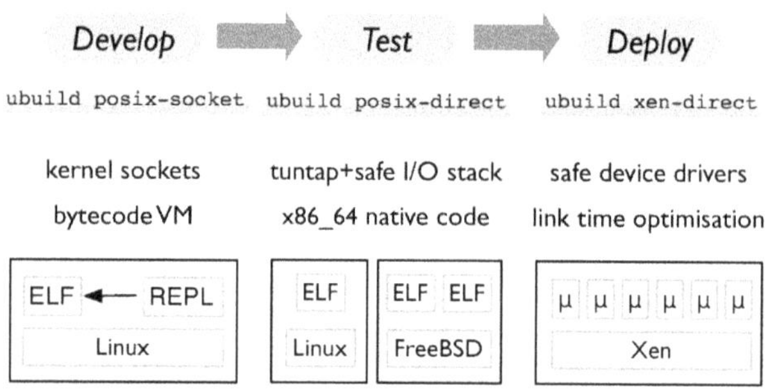

Figure 15: Specialising a Mirage application through recompilation alone, from interactive UNIX Read-Eval-Print Loop, to reduced dependency on the host kernel, and finally a unikernel VM.

interesting possibility is to build on the Barrelfish [15] software. Existing cloud orchestration layers such as OpenStack or Eucalyptus [49] exhibit high latency when manipulating small VMs, when compared to processes running with a single OS. Unikernels depend on running multiple VMs for parallelization, and so improvements will be needed in this space. Finally, the use of cooperative threading does require some form of broader management system, as a single bug can completely deadlock an entire appliance.

In tandem, the question arises as to how high the level of abstraction can be raised. Internet protocols are relatively straightforward to implement due to the comprehensive and reasonably accurate RFC specifications. However higher level services (e.g., filesystems, cryptographic libraries and middleware) are often only informally specified at best. Fortunately, tools to specify correct implementations are being developed by the community [50, 51], and some theorem provers can extract OCaml code from these specifications [52]. Work exploring application of verification techniques to key system components, notably the compiler backend and an OS microkernel [53, 54] is also promising.

Finally, thinking more broadly, development for and deployment to the cloud raise questions concerning workflow and orchestration. Real-world cloud computing deployments already have increasingly sophisticated orchestration systems to manage the remote deployment of VMs, and we have designed Mirage to take advantage of this (e.g. with small deployment binary sizes). Figure 15 illustrates how Mirage code is locally developed and tested on a UNIX-like system before compilation into a unikernel for deployment to the cloud. The developer first builds the posix-socket target, which links in the bytecode interpreter, makes use of the host kernel's networking stack, and maps keys in the k/v store to local files. This provides a familiar development environment in which to debug and profile application logic. Next, the developer applies the first specialisation step, building for the `posix-direct` target. This removes dependency on the standard OS sockets implementation, instead linking in the unikernel network stack (§3.5), and generating a native-code binary that uses `tuntap` to handle Ethernet traffic, and compile configuration files directly into the binary. The result is that I/O processing is performed within the application, albeit inefficiently due to the data copying induced by `tuntap`. This allows testing of the unikernel locally using UNIX development tools rather than the sparse facilities available when debugging microkernels, facilitating isolation of bugs in application logic, Mirage libraries, or due to interactions between the two.

Finally, the developer further specialises via the `xen-direct` target, generating a standalone unikernel. Application code is cross-compiled and linked with the safe Mirage device drivers, and dead-code elimination: if the application doesn't use a component, e.g., TCP, it will not be compiled in. The result is a VM image bootable on Xen locally or via a public cloud service.[10] The image is much smaller than an equivalent Linux-based distribution (Figure 14), and crucially, *all* I/O traffic is processed by type-safe code, with the performance and security benefits of the specialised runtime.

6. Conclusions

We presented the unikernel approach to significantly improving the safety and efficiency of building and deploying appliances for the cloud. Building on earlier work in library operating systems, we contribute the design and evaluation of a statically type-safe OCaml prototype for a libOS, including a complete clean-slate set of protocol libraries which ensure that deployed unikernels are memory-safe from the ground-up. Our approach also optionally extends the hypervisor with special support for such dedicated VMs to improve runtime security and boot latency.

Through our experimental implementation, we showed how security and efficiency benefits can be achieved by relaxing source-level backwards compatibility requirements by switching to novel programming styles such as those afforded by OCaml. Our evaluation showed that these benefits come at little to no cost to performance in all cases, and can actually improve performance in some. Overall we have demonstrated that the marriage of commodity cloud computing platforms with modern language runtimes is fruitful. Unikernels can serve as a platform for a range of future research exploring how to better take advantage of plentiful cloud computing resources, particularly for distributed applications that benefit from horizontal scaling across cores and hosts. Code for the Mirage prototype and our experiment scripts are open-source, available for download under a BSD-style license from `http://openmirage.org`.

Acknowledgments

We thank Pierre Chambart and Fabrice Le Fessant for contributing OCaml compiler optimizations, and Raphael Proust and Gabor Pali for the Javascript and kFreeBSD targets. Malte Schwarzkopf, Derek Murray, Robert Watson, Jonathan Ludlam, Derek McAuley, Peter G. Neumann, Ewan Mellor, Fernando Ramos, Tim Harris, Peter Sewell, Andrew Moore, Tom Kelly, David Chisnall, Jon Howell, Stephen Kell, Yaron Minsky, Marius A. Eriksen, Tim Deegan, Alex Ho and the anonymous ASPLOS reviewers all contributed valuable feedback. This work was primarily supported by Horizon Digital Economy Research, RCUK grant EP/G065802/1, and a portion was sponsored by the Defense Advanced Research Projects Agency (DARPA) and the Air Force Research Laboratory (AFRL), under contract FA8750-11-C-0249. The views, opinions, and/or findings contained in this report are those of the authors and should not be interpreted as representing the official views or policies, either expressed or implied, of the Defense Advanced Research Projects Agency or the Department of Defense.

[10] Mirage currently automates this process for Amazon EC2, wrapping custom kernels in a block device and registering them as AMIs.

References

[1] D. R. Engler, M. F. Kaashoek, and J. O'Toole, Jr. Exokernel: an operating system architecture for application-level resource management. In *Proc. 15th ACM Symposium on Operating Systems Principles (SOSP)*, pages 251–266, Copper Mountain, CO, USA, December 3–6 1995.

[2] Ian M. Leslie, Derek McAuley, Richard Black, Timothy Roscoe, Paul T. Barham, David Evers, Robin Fairbairns, and Eoin Hyden. The design and implementation of an operating system to support distributed multimedia applications. *IEEE Journal of Selected Areas in Communications*, 14(7):1280–1297, 1996.

[3] Donald E. Porter, Silas Boyd-Wickizer, Jon Howell, Reuben Olinsky, and Galen C. Hunt. Rethinking the library OS from the top down. In *Proc. 16th International Conference on Architectural Support for Programming Languages and Operating Systems (ASPLOS)*, pages 291–304, Newport Beach, CA, USA, March 5–11 2011.

[4] Galen C. Hunt and James R. Larus. Singularity: rethinking the software stack. *SIGOPS Operating Systems Review*, 41(2):37–49, 2007.

[5] Glenn Ammons, Jonathan Appavoo, Maria Butrico, Dilma Da Silva, David Grove, Kiyokuni Kawachiya, Orran Krieger, Bryan Rosenburg, Eric Van Hensbergen, and Robert W. Wisniewski. Libra: a library operating system for a JVM in a virtualized execution environment. In *Proc. 3rd International Conf. on Virtual Execution Environments (VEE)*, pages 44–54, San Diego, CA, USA, June 13–15 2007. ACM.

[6] Paul Barham, Boris Dragovic, Keir Fraser, Steven Hand, Tim Harris, Alex Ho, Rolf Neugebauer, Ian Pratt, and Andrew Warfield. Xen and the Art of Virtualization. In *Proc. 19th ACM Symposium on Operating Systems Principles (SOSP)*, pages 164–177, Bolton Landing, NY, USA, October 19–22 2003.

[7] US-CERT/NIST. CVE-2012-1182, February 2012.

[8] US-CERT/NIST. CVE-2012-2110, April 2012.

[9] Eelco Dolstra, Andres LÖh, and Nicolas Pierron. Nixos: A purely functional Linux distribution. *J. Funct. Program.*, 20(5-6):577–615, November 2010.

[10] Galen Hunt, Mark Aiken, Manuel Fähndrich, Chris Hawblitzel, Orion Hodson, James Larus, Steven Levi, Bjarne Steensgaard, David Tarditi, and Ted Wobber. Sealing OS processes to improve dependability and safety. *SIGOPS Operating Systems Review*, 41(3):341–354, March 2007.

[11] Theo De Raadt. Exploit mitigation techniques. `http://www.openbsd.org/papers/auug04`, 2004.

[12] David Scott, Richard Sharp, Thomas Gazagnaire, and Anil Madhavapeddy. Using functional programming within an industrial product group: perspectives and perceptions. In *Proc. 15th ACM SIGPLAN International Conference on Functional Programming (ICFP)*, pages 87–92, Baltimore, Maryland, USA, September 27–29 2010.

[13] Thomas Gazagnaire and Vincent Hanquez. Oxenstored: an efficient hierarchical and transactional database using functional programming with reference cell comparisons. *SIGPLAN Notices*, 44(9):203–214, August 2009.

[14] Patrick Colp, Mihir Nanavati, Jun Zhu, William Aiello, George Coker, Tim Deegan, Peter Loscocco, and Andrew Warfield. Breaking up is hard to do: security and functionality in a commodity hypervisor. In *Proc. 23rd ACM Symposium on Operating Systems Principles (SOSP)*, pages 189–202, Cascais, Portugal, October 23-26 2011.

[15] A. Baumann, P. Barham, P. Dagand, T. Harris, R. Isaacs, S. Peter, T. Roscoe, A. Schüpbach, and A. Singhania. The multikernel: a new OS architecture for scalable multicore systems. In *Proc. 22nd ACM Symposium on Operating Systems Principles (SOSP)*, pages 29–44, Big Sky, MT, USA, October 11–14 2009.

[16] Hovav Shacham, Matthew Page, Ben Pfaff, Eu-Jin Goh, Nagendra Modadugu, and Dan Boneh. On the effectiveness of address-space randomization. In *Proc. 11th ACM Conference on Computer and Communications Security (CCS)*, pages 298–307, Washington DC, USA, October 25–29 2004.

[17] Keir Fraser, Steven Hand, Rolf Neugebauer, Ian Pratt, Andrew Warfield, and Mark Williamson. Safe hardware access with the Xen virtual machine monitor. In *Proc. 1st Workshop on Operating System and Architectural Support for the on demand IT InfraStructure (OASIS)*, Boston, MA, USA, October 7–13 2004.

[18] Jérôme Vouillon. Lwt: a cooperative thread library. In *Proc. 2008 ACM SIGPLAN workshop on ML*, pages 3–12, Victoria, BC, Canada, September 21 2008.

[19] Anil Madhavapeddy, Richard Mortier, Ripduman Sohan, Thomas Gazagnaire, Steven Hand, Tim Deegan, Derek McAuley, and Jon Crowcroft. Turning down the LAMP: Software specialisation for the cloud. In *2nd USENIX Workshop on Hot Topics in Cloud Computing*, June 2010.

[20] Andrew Warfield, Keir Fraser, Steven Hand, and Tim Deegan. Facilitating the development of soft devices. In *Proc. USENIX Annual Technical Conference*, pages 379–382, April 10–15 2005.

[21] Edoardo Biagioni. A Structured TCP in Standard ML. In *Proc. ACM SIGCOMM*, pages 36–45, London, UK, Aug. 31–Sep. 02 1994.

[22] Anil Madhavapeddy, Alex Ho, Tim Deegan, David Scott, and Ripduman Sohan. Melange: creating a "functional" Internet. *SIGOPS Operating Systems Review*, 41(3):101–114, 2007.

[23] Oleg Kiselyov. Iteratee IO: safe, practical, declarative input processing. `http://okmij.org/ftp/Streams.html`, 2008.

[24] Chuck Silvers. UBC: an efficient unified I/O and memory caching subsystem for NetBSD. In *Proc. USENIX Annual Technical Conference*, pages 285–290, San Diego, CA, USA, June 18–23 2000.

[25] Steven M. Hand. Self-paging in the Nemesis operating system. In *Proc. 3rd USENIX Symposium on Operating Systems Design and Implementation (OSDI)*, pages 73–86, February 22–25 1999.

[26] President's Council of Advisors on Science and Technology. Report to the President and Congress: Designing a Digital Future: Federally Funded R&D in Networking and IT, December 2010.

[27] OpenFlow Consortium. OpenFlow. `http://openflow.org/`.

[28] Charalampos Rotsos, Nadi Sarrar, Steve Uhlig, Rob Sherwood, and Andrew W. Moore. OFLOPS: An open framework for OpenFlow switch evaluation. In *Proc. Passive and Active Measurements Conference (PAM)*, Vienna, Austria, March 12–14 2012.

[29] Zheng Cai, Alan L. Cox, and T. S. Eugene Ng. Maestro: A system for scalable OpenFlow control. Technical Report TR-10-11, Rice University.

[30] N. Gude, T. Koponen, J. Pettit, B. Pfaff, M. Casado, N. McKeown, and S. Shenker. NOX: towards an operating system for networks. *SIGCOMM Computer Communications Review*, 38:105–110, July 2008.

[31] Derek Gordon Murray, Grzegorz Milos, and Steven Hand. Improving Xen security through disaggregation. In *Proc. 4th ACM SIGPLAN/SIGOPS International Conference on Virtual Execution Environments (VEE)*, pages 151–160, Seattle, WA, USA, March 5–7 2008.

[32] B. Vaugon, Philippe Wang, and Emmanuel Chailloux. Les microcontrôleurs pic programmés en Objective Caml. In *Vingt-deuxièmes Journées Francophones des Langages Applicatifs (JFLA 2011)*, volume Studia Informatica Universalis, pages 177–207. Hermann, 2011.

[33] T. Hallgren, M. P. Jones, R. Leslie, and A. Tolmach. A Principled Approach to Operating System construction in Haskell. *SIGPLAN Notices*, 40(9):116–128, 2005.

[34] Galois Inc. HalVM. `http://halvm.org/`.

[35] Oracle. GuestVM. `http://labs.oracle.com/projects/guestvm/shared/guestvm/guestvm/index.html`.

[36] B. N. Bershad, S. Savage, P. Pardyak, E. G. Sirer, M. E. Fiuczynski, D. Becker, C. Chambers, and S. Eggers. Extensibility, safety and performance in the SPIN operating system. *SIGOPS Operating Systems Review*, 29(5):267–283, December 1995.

[37] David Mosberger and Larry L. Peterson. Making paths explicit in the Scout operating system. In *Proc. 2nd USENIX Symposium on Operating Systems Design and Implementation (OSDI)*, pages 153–167, Seattle, WA, United States, October 28–31 1996.

[38] F. Kaashoek, D. Engler, G. Ganger, H. Brice no, R. Hunt, D. Mazières, T. Pinckney, R. Grimm, J. Jannotti, and K. Mackenzie. Application performance and flexibility on exokernel systems. In *Proc. 16th ACM Symposium on Operating Systems Principles (SOSP)*, pages 52–65, Saint Malo, France, October 5–8 1997.

[39] Bryan Ford, Godmar Back, Greg Benson, Jay Lepreau, Albert Lin, and Olin Shivers. The Flux OSKit: a substrate for kernel and language research. In *Proc. 16th ACM Symposium on Operating Systems Principles (SOSP)*, pages 38–51, Saint Malo, France, October 5–8 1997.

[40] The OpenSSL Project. OpenSSL. `http://openssl.org/`.

[41] Martin Georgiev, Subodh Iyengar, Suman Jana, Rishita Anubhai, Dan Boneh, and Vitaly Shmatikov. The most dangerous code in the world: validating SSL certificates in non-browser software. In *Proc. 19th ACM Conference on Computer and Communications Security (CCS)*, pages 38–49, Raleigh, NC, USA, October 16–18 2012.

[42] George C. Necula, Scott McPeak, Shree Prakash Rahul, and Westley Weimer. CIL: Intermediate language and tools for analysis and transformation of C programs. In *Proc. 11th International Conference on Compiler Construction (CC)*, LNCS 2304, pages 213–228, Grenoble, France, April 8–12 2002.

[43] George C. Necula, Scott McPeak, and Westley Weimer. Ccured: type-safe retrofitting of legacy code. In *Proc. 29th ACM SIGPLAN-SIGACT Symposium on Principles of Programming Languages (POPL)*, pages 128–139, January 16–18 2002.

[44] Facebook. HipHop for PHP. `https://github.com/facebook/hiphop-php/wiki/`, February 2010.

[45] Jeffrey Dean and Sanjay Ghemawat. MapReduce: simplified data processing on large clusters. In *Proc. 6th USENIX Symposium on Operating Systems Design & Implementation (OSDI)*, pages 137–150, San Francisco, CA, USA, December 6–8 2004.

[46] Apache. Hadoop. `http://hadoop.apache.org`, April 2012.

[47] Michael Isard, Mihai Budiu, Yuan Yu, Andrew Birrell, and Dennis Fetterly. Dryad: distributed data-parallel programs from sequential building blocks. In *Proc. 2nd ACM SIGOPS/EuroSys European Conference on Computer Systems (EuroSys)*, pages 59–72, Lisbon, Portugal, March 21–23 2007.

[48] Niels Provos, Markus Friedl, and Peter Honeyman. Preventing privilege escalation. In *Proc. 12th USENIX Security Symposium (SSYM)*, pages 231–242, Washington DC, USA, August 4–8 2003.

[49] Bill Childers. Build your own cloud with Eucalyptus. *Linux J.*, 2010(195), July 2010.

[50] Jeff Lewis. Cryptol: specification, implementation and verification of high-grade cryptographic applications. In *Proc. ACM Workshop on Formal Methods in Security Engineering (FMSE)*, page 41, Fairfax, Virginia, USA, November 2 2007.

[51] Reynald Affeldt, David Nowak, and Yutaka Oiwa. Formal network packet processing with minimal fuss: invertible syntax descriptions at work. In *Proc. 6th Workshop on Programming Languages meets Program Verification (PLPV)*, pages 27–36, January 24 2012.

[52] Nicolas Oury. Observational equivalence and program extraction in the Coq proof assistant. In *Proc. 6th International Conference on Typed Lambda Calculi and Applications (TLCA)*, LNCS 2701, pages 271–285, Valencia, Spain, June 10–12 2003.

[53] Xavier Leroy. Formal certification of a compiler back-end, or: programming a compiler with a proof assistant. In *Proc. 33rd ACM Symposium on Principles of Programming Languages (POPL)*, pages 42–54, Charleston, SC, USA, January 11–13 2006.

[54] G. Klein, K. Elphinstone, G. Heiser, J. Andronick, D. Cock, P. Derrin, D. Elkaduwe, K. Engelhardt, R. Kolanski, M. Norrish, T. Sewell, H. Tuch, and S. Winwood. seL4: formal verification of an OS kernel. In *Proc. 22nd ACM Symposium on Operating Systems Principles (SOSP)*, pages 207–220, Big Sky, MT, USA, October 11–14 2009.

Fine-Grained Fault Tolerance using Device Checkpoints

Asim Kadav, Matthew J. Renzelmann, Michael M. Swift
Computer Sciences Department, University of Wisconsin-Madison
{kadav, mjr, swift} @cs.wisc.edu

Abstract

Recovering faults in drivers is difficult compared to other code because their state is spread across both memory and a device. Existing driver fault-tolerance mechanisms either restart the driver and discard its state, which can break applications, or require an extensive logging mechanism to replay requests and recreate driver state. Even logging may be insufficient, though, if the semantics of requests are ambiguous. In addition, these systems either require large subsystems that must be kept up-to-date as the kernel changes, or require substantial rewriting of drivers.

We present a new driver fault-tolerance mechanism that provides fine-grained control over the code protected. Fine-Grained Fault Tolerance (FGFT) isolates driver code at the granularity of a single entry point. It executes driver code as a transaction, allowing roll back if the driver fails. We develop a novel checkpointing mechanism to save and restore device state using existing power-management code. Unlike past systems, FGFT can be incrementally deployed in a single driver without the need for a large kernel subsystem, but at the cost of small modifications to the driver.

In the evaluation, we show that FGFT can have almost zero runtime cost in many cases, and that checkpoint-based recovery can reduce the duration of a failure by 79% compared to restarting the driver. Finally, we show that applying FGFT to a driver requires little effort, and the majority of drivers in common classes already contain the power-management code needed for checkpoint/restore.

Categories and Subject Descriptors D.4.5 [*Operating Systems*]: Reliability

General Terms Design, Reliability

Keywords Device Drivers, Checkpoints

1. Introduction

In most commodity operating systems, third-party driver code executes in privileged mode. Faulty device drivers cause many reliability issues in these systems [8, 37]. Hence, there has been significant research to tolerate driver failures using programming-language and hardware-protection techniques [3, 6, 15, 16, 23, 26, 46]. These systems execute the entire driver as a single isolated component. However, much of this work focuses on *detecting* failures and *isolating* drivers from the rest of the system. Few of these systems address how to *restore* driver functionality beyond simply reloading the driver, which may leave applications non-functioning.

Most driver-reliability systems do not try to restore device state and instead completely restart failed drivers [17, 42, 48], effectively resetting device state to a known-good configuration. The state-of-the-art mechanism for restoring driver functionality, shadow drivers [41], logs state-changing operations at the driver/kernel interface. Following a failure, shadow drivers restart the driver and replay the log in order to restore internal driver and device state. This resets the driver and device to a state functionally equivalent to its pre-failure state. This approach, complete driver isolation and logging for recovery, poses four problems:

1. *Too hard:* Shadow drivers must be written for every class of driver and must be updated when the interface changes. This adds a large body of code to the kernel requiring constant maintenance, which is a high barrier to adoption. Other systems require substantially rewriting drivers, which is also a barrier.
2. *Not enough:* Shadow drivers must encode the semantics of the kernel/driver interface. However, many drivers have proprietary commands that cannot be captured by a shadow driver common to an entire class, leading to incomplete recovery. Recent work showed that up to 44% of drivers have non-class behavior [21].
3. *Too expensive:* Shadow drivers must interpose on and log *all* invocations of a driver. Continuous monitoring imposes a performance cost, particularly on high-performance devices such as SSDs and NICs even when the critical I/O path is bug-free.
4. *Too slow:* Restarting a driver, the first step of log replay, can be slow (multiple seconds) due to complex initialization code and therefore may not be useful in latency-sensitive environments.

A key source of these problems is that prior systems seek *completeness*: applying to *all* driver code at *all* times. While this reduces the per-driver cost, it pushes up both development and runtime costs.

We developed a new driver fault tolerance mechanism to address these shortcomings called *Fine-grained Fault Tolerance* (FGFT). Rather than isolating and recovering from the failure of an entire driver, FGFT executes a driver *entry point* as a transaction and uses software fault isolation to prevent corruption and detect failures. On entry to a driver, a stub copies parameters to the driver code. Only if the driver executes correctly are the results copied back. If the call faults, FGFT destroys the copy to roll back driver state and fails the call.

In order to restore device state modified by a driver before faulting, we developed a novel *device state checkpointing* mechanism that can capture the device state. The stub captures a checkpoint before invoking the driver, and restores the checkpoint on failure. This mechanism leverages existing power-management code present in most drivers, which greatly reduces the development cost of adopting FGFT.

ASPLOS'13, March 16–20, 2013, Houston, Texas, USA.

FGFT shifts the cost of driver fault tolerance to the faulty code. While shadow drivers and whole-driver isolation require up-front code for any instance of a class of drivers, FGFT instead requires small changes to the driver itself to support isolation and implement checkpointing. Where past isolation mechanisms interpose on *all* driver code and reduce its performance uniformly, FGFT *only* imposes a cost on entry points selected for isolation. Thus, the cost of executing a single call with fault tolerance may be higher with FGFT than other systems, but when applied only to code off the critical path it has much *lower* overhead because the critical code is left unchanged. Thus, one possible use for FGFT is to apply it selectively to vulnerable code suspected or known to have bugs.

The contributions of our work are:

- We describe Fine-Grained Fault Tolerance, a system consisting of a static analysis and code generation tool that provides isolation by executing each driver request on a minimal copy of required driver state. Our system can be used to isolate specific requests and we show from a study of published bugs that fine-grained isolation is practical since bugs only affect 14% of all entry points in buggy drivers.
- We demonstrate a *novel* mechanism to create device checkpoints on a running system. In a study of six drivers, we show that taking a checkpoint is fast, averaging only 20 μs.
- We show how to use checkpoints and transactional execution of driver code to provide fast recovery and remove the permanent overhead of monitoring *all* requests.
- We show that the implementation effort of FGFT is small: we added 38 lines of code to the kernel to trap processor exceptions, and found that device checkpoint code can be constructed with little effort from power-management code present in 76% of drivers in common driver classes.

We begin with an overview of the FGFT design.

2. Design Overview

FGFT is a system to tolerate faults in drivers using a *pay-as-you-go* model based on checkpoints for recovery. This system protects code from faults at the granularity of a single thread executing a single entry point. FGFT recovers from any failures that occur during the function. This can greatly reduce the cost of isolating and tolerating faults because far less code is affected.

We list four goals of providing fine-grained fault tolerance:

1. *Class independent.* Isolation and recovery should be independent of the driver-kernel interface and should be able to recover driver actions from proprietary commands.
2. *Low infrastructure.* Little new code should be added to the kernel in support of FGFT.
3. *Pay-as-you-go.* FGFT should not have a fixed minimum overhead of isolation or monitoring driver behavior. Furthermore, programmer effort should only be required when fault tolerance is desired.
4. *Fast recovery.* FGFT should restore driver functions quickly after a failure without affecting other threads concurrently executing in the driver.

The first goal enables FGFT to apply to a broad range of drivers, and the second reduces the adoption cost for an operating system. Pay-as-you-go ensures that for high-performance drivers, tolerating faults in code off the critical path has little cost. Fast recovery enables its use in latency-sensitive environments.

The two major components of FGFT are an isolation mechanism to prevent a faulty driver from corrupting the OS and to detect failures, and a recovery mechanism to restore the driver to a functioning state after a failure. We begin a discussion of our fault model to motivate our design choices.

2.1 Fault Model

A driver entry point is a driver function invoked by the kernel or applications to access specific driver functionality. Each driver registers a set of functions as entry points, such as to initialize the device or transmit a packet. Driver entry points can be invoked by applications multiple times in arbitrary order. Hence, drivers should not make assumptions about the order or past history of these invocations. FGFT provides fault tolerance at the granularity of a single entry point into a driver. In contrast, past systems treat the entire driver as a component with internal state.

As the driver executes, the FGFT isolation mechanism enforces fine-grained memory safety. It ensures that the driver entry point is only allowed to access data passed to the driver and its stack; access to anything else will be treated as a fault. FGFT detects faults in driver entry points in three ways. First, FGFT detects memory failures (such as null pointer dereferences) and reading/writing unintended kernel and driver structures. Second, FGFT uses marshaling to copy data in and out of the driver. Type errors and malformed structures that cause the marshaling to fail will be detected, although errors with compatible types (such as treating an array of bytes as an array of longs), will not be. FGFT on its own does not provide any semantic checks to enforce driver invariants. Hence, driver faults must be detected within the entry point where they occur. Otherwise, failures that that are triggered when one entry point improperly sets a flag that another read and faults cannot be tolerated. Third, FGFT catches processor exceptions such as NULL pointer exception, general protection fault, alignment fault, divide error (divide by zero), missing segments, and stack faults. It triggers recovery if an exception arises within an isolated driver entry point.

We design for an open-source environment, and therefore trust the compiler to produce code that correctly accesses the stack. We also assume that the driver is unable to hang or damage the device, although it may misconfigure the device.

A key benefit of FGFT is that by operating on specific entry points it can be selective about what code should be hardened against faults. We call the entry points to be isolated *suspect*. The suspect code can execute in isolation while the remainder of the driver executes in the kernel at full speed. Hence, FGFT is useful when specific driver code is known to have problems, such as just-patched code or code with known but un-patched vulnerabilities. We identify at least three cases where a fine-grained model is useful:

1. *Untested code*: Device drivers often contain untested code such as chipset-specific code or recovery code that can be invoked safely using FGFT.
2. *Statically found bugs*: Often static analysis tools identify hard to find/trigger driver bugs with substantial false positive rates. FGFT can be integrated with existing static analysis tools until a fix is issued, which often takes considerable time. This approach limits the overhead to just the buggy code, just when it contains known bugs.
3. *Runtime monitoring tools*: Runtime monitoring tools flag incoming requests based on their parameters, such as a specific `ioctl` command code, or are enabled at run time through module parameters [24] or security tools [32]. FGFT can dynamically decide whether to execute code in isolation or unsafely at full speed.

In our evaluation we analyze a list of bugs and find that they only affect 14% of all driver entry points. Hence, limiting the cost of fault tolerance to affected entry points can be useful. We now describe the two major components of FGFT: isolation and recovery.

2.2 Fine-Grained Isolation

FGFT provides isolation by forcing suspect code to operate on a *copy* of driver and kernel data. This ensures that anything the entry point does will not be seen by other threads or the kernel until it successfully completes, and allows quick recovery after a failure by deleting the copy. Thus, FGFT creates a clean copy of data needed for a driver entry point on every invocation, which consists of all data referenced by the entry point: parameters, global driver variables, and global kernel variables.

We use entry points as the granularity of isolation because it closely matches internal driver structure: they provide a natural boundary for returning errors after a fault, and drivers already synchronize concurrent invocation of entry points. If two driver threads cannot run concurrently in the driver, then driver synchronization ensures that one of them blocks until the other successfully completes. Thus, FGFT reuses existing synchronization mechanisms to ensure that when suspect code runs, no other threads are active in the driver. This ensures that any changes to device state will not be seen until the entry point completes successfully or it fails and recovery completes.

FGFT provides entry-point isolation with a copy-in/out model of driver and kernel state when suspicious entry-points are invoked. FGFT uses static analysis and code-generation to generate another kernel module that contains suspect entry points instrumented for memory safety. FGFT also generates communication code containing marshaling routines to copy driver and kernel state necessary for executing these entry points in isolation. Since the static analysis to marshal the data structures required by the isolated copy can be imprecise, FGFT requires a programmer to annotate ambiguous data types in the driver code. In order to provide even finer control over when to provide fault tolerance, FGFT automatically inserts taps, which are predicates that can decide at runtime whether to invoke the normal or fault-tolerant version of an entry point.

FGFT detects faults through run-time memory safety checks that detect access to unreachable addresses – memory not passed as a parameter or allocated by the entry point. Since, FGFT generates the code for copy-in/out, it is able to provide fine-grained memory safety (base and bound validation [28]). Furthermore, for failure detection, FGFT interposes on kernel trap handlers and detects if the faults originate from the suspicious entry-points and accordingly triggers recovery.

2.3 Checkpoint based Recovery

FGFT relies on checkpoints prior to a driver entry point for recovery. Unlike log-based recovery, which requires knowing how to replay requests, checkpoints can restore state independent of how a function modifies driver state. For example, a checkpoint of a device prior to an `ioctl` call allows its state to be recovered no matter what the call does.

Log-based recovery is also slow enough that the technique may not be useful in latency-sensitive environments. The primary delay comes from probing the device all over again which cold boots the device and performs the initialization steps as shown in Figure 1. For example, during initialization a network driver probes for the device, verifies EEPROM contents, tests the device, and registers the device with the kernel.

The checkpoint of the driver's state in memory is captured automatically through the copy-in/out model of invocation. Suspect code always executes on a copy of the driver state, so the original

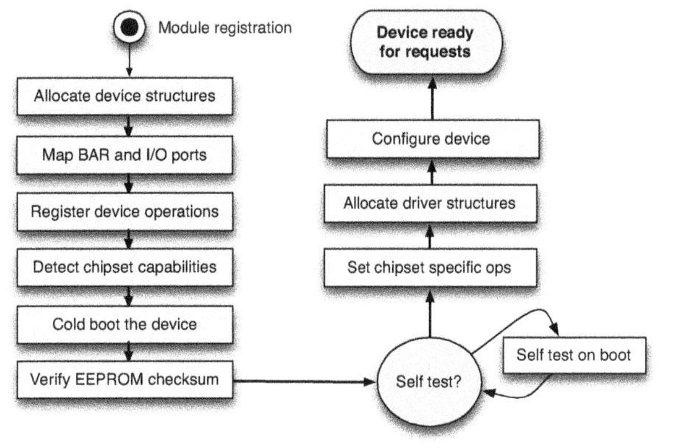

Figure 1. Modern devices perform many operations during initialization such as setting up kernel and device structures based on chipset and device features, checksumming device ROM data, various device tests followed by driver initialization and configuration.

data is unmodified and need not be restored. The major challenge, though, is the *device state*, which may be modified unpredictably by the driver. We therefore require that drivers provide a facility for capturing and restoring device state. Prior to invoking suspect code, FGFT can take a checkpoint, and following a failure, it can restore the checkpoint.

An appealing approach is to treat devices like memory and copy memory-mapped I/O regions. However, reading registers may have side effects such as clearing counters. In addition, some devices overlay two logical registers, one for read and one for write, at the same address. Instead, we take inspiration from code *already present* in many drivers that must perform *nearly the same* task as checkpoint/restore: power management.

The functionality provided by power management, to suspend a device before entering a low power mode and restoring it when transitioning to high power mode is similar to what is required to support device checkpoints. We reuse the suspend/resume code by separating code that supports saving state to memory from the code that actually suspends the device. Similarly, we identify code required for restoring this state. In Section 4, we describe in detail how power management code can be re-factored to support checkpoint/restore in device drivers and how existing driver synchronization can be used to arbitrate device access.

2.4 Design Summary

FGFT improves the state of art in driver recovery and meets its goals. FGFT provides class-independent driver recovery with checkpoints as opposed to restarting the driver. Hence, FGFT discards failed requests and retains proprietary driver state such as *ioctls* that were issued before the failure.

FGFT requires very little kernel code, as the code for isolation is generated automatically and the recovery code requires only small modifications to existing driver code. The annotation cost for isolation and recovery is only required when a driver needs fault tolerance. Only when a suspicious request executes does FGFT execute it in isolation, thus limiting isolation overhead to these requests. Compared to FGFT, Nooks [42] and SUD [3] require a new kernel subsystem and writing and maintaining wrappers around the driver-kernel interface.

There is also no recovery overhead of monitoring correctly executing requests at *all* times since driver recovery is based on checkpoints. Finally, FGFT provides fast recovery since it does not restart the driver and re-execute the complicated device probe routines. The device state is restored from a checkpoint, so recovery is an order of magnitude faster as we demonstrate in our evaluation in Section 5.

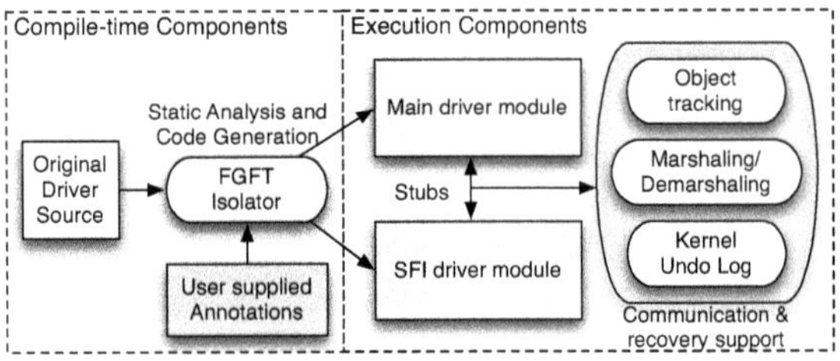

Figure 2. FGFT replicates driver entry points into a normal driver and an *SFI driver module*. A runtime support module provides communication and recovery support.

3. Fine-Grained Isolation

Isolation ensures that the driver and kernel state changes made by a request are not propagated if the request fails. We need the following properties from an isolation mechanism:

1. *Transactional execution*: We need to execute the driver entry points in a transactional fashion to keep a clean copy of all data modified by the driver.
2. *Memory safety and fault detection*: We need to ensure a driver cannot corrupt the kernel or other threads in the driver and provide mechanisms that detect when a driver has failed.
3. *Synchronization*: Threads executing in the driver need to synchronize with other threads to ensure they do not corrupt shared state in the kernel, driver, or device.

To achieve these goals, we rely on well-understood compile-time software fault isolation (SFI) [45]. As a driver entry point operates on data shared with the rest of the driver, the SFI mechanism must allow access to such data but prevent its corruption. FGFT therefore executes isolated code on a *minimal copy* of the driver and kernel, which is a copy of data referenced from an entry point but not entire structures. For example, when a network driver issues an ioctl to update its transmit ring parameters, FGFT uses points-to analysis and pre-determines the fields an entry point can access, such as `netdev→priv→tx_ring` and `netdev→priv→rx_ring`, and will only generate marshaling code to copy in/out only these fields to reduce the generated code and the unnecessary copying of unused fields. If the entry point does not fail, FGFT merges the copy back into the real driver and kernel structures. On a failure, the copy is discarded. In effect, FGFT executes the suspect entry point as a transaction using lazy version management [22].

However, not all data can be copied. Structures shared with the device, such as network transmit and receive rings, cannot be copied because the device will not share the copied structure. Instead, FGFT grants suspect code direct read and/or write access to these structures and relies on device-state checkpointing to restore these structures following a failure. Furthermore, driver code used for recovery cannot be isolated and must be trusted.

We implemented FGFT for the Linux 2.6.29 kernel. Figure 2 shows the components of FGFT. We describe how FGFT provides isolation, communicates with isolated code, and detects failures.

3.1 Software Fault Isolation

As FGFT targets open-source Linux device drivers, we implement SFI using a source-code rewriting tool called *FGFT Isolator* written using CIL [31]. It generates isolation code into the driver and produces communication code, described below, for communicating with the isolated code.

Isolator generates an additional driver module called the *SFI module* that contains a copy of all suspect entry points and all driver functions transitively called from those functions, instrumented for SFI. In addition, Isolator generates a new version of the driver that invokes the SFI module entry points. At the top of the existing entry points, Isolator inserts a test to see whether to execute normally or in isolation, and if so invokes the SFI module.

The decision to invoke a given entry point in isolation can be made in one of three ways. First, a developer can use the attribute `__attribute__((isolate))` to manually specify which functions to isolate. This causes the function to always execute with isolation. Second, FGFT can *automatically* use any static analysis tool to identify buggy code and which entry points are affected. These entry points are then always executed with isolation. Finally, the decision can be made at run time. A fault management system, such as the Solaris Fault management Daemon [39], can call into the SFI module and specify which functions to execute with isolation. Furthermore, it can register a function pointer at run time that takes the same arguments as the suspicious function and returns a decision of whether to isolate or not.

In addition to producing the SFI driver code, Isolator produces communication code that invokes the SFI driver and copies in the minimal driver and kernel state needed by the suspect entry points, copies out any changes made by the SFI driver, and initiates recovery following a detected failure. Isolator manages resource allocation, synchronization and I/O across the two copies. Isolator only detects memory failures. For other failures, such as arithmetic exceptions, we trap processor exceptions and check if they originate from SFI module.

Isolator uses CIL's memory tracking module [31] to instrument all memory references in the driver. It inserts a call to our `memcheck` function that verifies the target of a load/store is valid. If not, it detects a failure and invokes the recovery mechanism. The `memcheck` routine consults a *range table* to verify memory references and provide fine-grained memory protection by only allowing access to driver and kernel data as identified at compile time. This table contains the addresses and lengths of copied data structures and buffers shared with the device. The range table is created on every invocation of a suspect entry point and flushed on return.

We do not add all local variables to the range table because we trust the compiler to generate correct code for moving variables between registers and the stack. However, if the driver ever takes the address of a local variable, or creates an array as a local variable, then Isolator adds a call in the instrumented SFI driver to add the variable's address and length to the range table and remove it from the range table when the variable goes out of scope. Similarly, we trust the compiler to produce valid control transfers and do not instrument branch or call instructions.

3.1.1 Communication Code for Entry Points

FGFT Isolator generates *stub code* to invoke suspect entry points that copies data into and out of the driver. Similar to RPC stubs, these stubs create a copy of the parameters passed to the suspect code, but also copy any driver or kernel global variables it uses. When the suspect entry point completes, stub code copies modified data structures and return values back to the regular driver and kernel in the current thread. An alternative approach would be to rely on transactional-memory techniques to dynamically create a copy of data as it is referenced, which may have lower copying costs but higher run-time costs [2].

Isolator automatically identifies the minimal data needed for an entry point through static analysis. This data includes the structure fields from parameters referenced by the entry point or functions it calls plus fields of global variables referenced. As they copy data, stubs update the range table with the address and length of each object. For objects that cannot be copied (such as those shared with the device), stubs fill in the existing address of the field, its length, and whether the entry point needs read, write, or read/write access.

If suspect code invokes the kernel, Isolator generates stubs for kernel functions that copy parameters to the kernel and copies kernel return values back to suspect code. The SFI driver may pass in fields from its parameters to the kernel as arguments. To avoid creating a new copy of these fields, as would be done by RPC, FGFT maintains an *object tracker* that maps the address of kernel and regular driver objects to the address of objects in the SFI driver. Stub code consults the object tracker when calling into the kernel to determine whether arguments refer to a new or existing object. If an object exists, stubs copy the argument back to the existing object and otherwise temporarily allocate a new object. To support recovery, stubs may generate a *compensation entry* in a *kernel undo log*. This log records operations that must be reversed on failure, such as freeing memory allocations.

The stub code must know the layout of data structures and whether data is shared with the driver in order to correctly copy data. As driver code often contains ambiguous data structures such as `void *` pointers or list pointers (*e.g.*, `struct list_head`), we rely on programmer-provided annotations to disambiguate such code [48]. These annotations also declare which structure fields or parameters are shared with the device and should not be copied. In Section 5, we evaluate the difficulty of providing annotations.

Some driver functions trigger synchronous callbacks. For example, the `pci_register_driver` function causes a callback on the same thread to the driver's `probe` function. FGFT treats the callback as a *nested transaction*: it causes another isolated call operating on a second copy of the data.

3.1.2 Resource Access from SFI module

Some resources cannot be copied into the driver because they attach additional semantics or behavior to memory.

I/O memory. Driver entry points may communicate with the device by writing to I/O memory. Stubs grant the SFI driver read/write access to memory-mapped I/O regions and memory shared with the device via `dma_alloc_coherent`. Isolator identifies these regions with annotations and creates stubs that grant drivers direct read/write access.

Locks. Drivers synchronize with other threads using driver spin locks and mutexes. Hence, SFI grants read access to driver locks and calls the locking API to acquire/release the locks. The stub code for kernel locking routines add a compensation entry to the kernel undo log to release the lock after a failure. To ensure that changes made by suspect code are not seen by the rest of the kernel, the lock stubs defer releasing driver locks until after the entry point returns to the kernel. Apart from driver locks, drivers may acquire kernel-defined locks indirectly through kernel calls. FGFT does not expand the scope of these locks and releases them upon failure through compensation entries in the kernel undo log. Drivers can also directly manipulate kernel data structures while holding kernel-defined locks. FGFT will not recover correctly for such entry points. However, this is increasingly rare in Linux and there is an effort to ensure that kernel data structures are not directly exposed to drivers.

The above mechanism protects shared structures across driver threads. However, the suspicious thread can also block waiting for data to arrive on shared structures that have been copied over from other driver threads. Fortunately, resynchronization across driver threads is uncommon. Using static analysis, we measure how often driver threads wait for other threads using the Linux's `completion` family of functions or by polling in a loop.

Overall, we find driver resynchronization occurs in 2.7% of drivers and 1.4% of all entry points. Most re-synchronizations occur during communication with the device: drivers wait for a device operation to finish and a callback sets the completion structure. In most cases, only the completion structure responsible for device notifications needs to be annotated. However, complex drivers that communicate with devices using a layered interface, such as SCSI or WIFI, may wait for lower layers to communicate with device and update the appropriate drivers structures with the result of the operation. In such cases, annotations are required for completion structures and shared device structures for the driver to work correctly. Finally, driver threads also sleep inside loops waiting for other threads to finish by polling reference counts or driver structures. If these threads modify state across threads, then FGFT will not recover correctly for this fraction of drivers/entrypoints.

Memory allocation. Stubs for allocators invoke the kernel allocator, add the returned memory region to the range table and generate a compensation entry to free the memory on failure. The newly allocated memory is not copied into the driver because its contents do not need to be preserved. For kernel callbacks that implicitly allocate memory an appropriate compensation entry is generated.

3.2 Failure Detection

In addition to protecting the kernel and regular driver code from corruption, isolation provides the primary means to detect failures. FGFT's SFI mechanism implements *spatial memory safety* [28]: every memory reference must be within an object made accessible during the copy process. Thus, references outside the range table indicate a failure.

Stubs can detect additional failures when copying data back to the kernel. For example, if the driver writes an invalid address into a data structure, the copying code will dereference that address and generate an exception. We also modified the Linux kernel exception handlers to detect unexpected traps from the SFI driver as failures. If one occurs, the trap handler sets the instruction pointer to the recovery routine. This is the only change to the Linux kernel, and required 38 lines of code.

The detection mechanisms may miss several categories of failures. First, if the driver violates its own data structure invariants, stubs may not detect the problem. Recent work on identifying and verifying data structure invariants could detect these faults [5]. For example, if a suspect entry point sets a flag indicating that a field is valid but does not set the field, then corruption will leak out of the SFI driver. Second, the driver does not provide strong type safety, so the driver may assign a structure field to the wrong type of data. While this may be detected when the stub copies data, it is not guaranteed. Finally, FGFT does not enforce kernel restrictions on the range of scalar values, such as valid packet lengths.

4. Checkpoint-based recovery

FGFT is built around checkpoint-based recovery. While checkpointing and restoring memory state is simple using techniques such as transactional memory or copy-on-write, it has not previously been possible to capture the state of a device. Without this, restoring memory state will lead to a driver that is inconsistent with respect to its device, believing incorrectly that it has performed an action or is operating in a different mode. We first describe device state checkpointing, which is the basis of FGFT's recovery mechanism. We then describe how FGFT uses device checkpoints to recover in case of a failure.

4.1 Device state checkpointing

To be useful, a device checkpoint mechanism should fulfill the following goals:

1. *Lightweight.* There should be no continuous monitoring or long-latency operations.

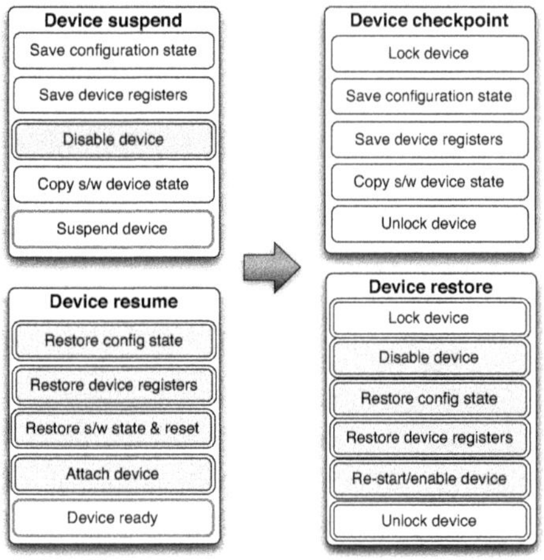

(a)

```
int rtl8139_checkpoint ( ... )

spin_lock_irqsave
      (&tp->lock, flags);

/* save PCI config state */
pci_save_state (pdev);

/* Copy out device state. */
dev->stats.rx_missed_errors +=
    RTL_R32 (RxMissed);


spin_unlock_irqrestore
      (&tp->lock, flags);
```

(b)

```
int rtl8139_restore (...)

spin_lock_irqsave
        (&tp->lock, flags);

/* disable device */
netif_device_detach (dev);

/* restore bus state */
pci_restore_state (pdev);

/* restart device */
if (!netif_running (dev))
    return 0;
rtl8139_init_ring (dev);
rtl8139_hw_start (dev);

RTL_W32 (RxMissed, 0);

/* re-enable device */
netif_device_attach (dev);
spin_unlock_irqrestore
        (&tp->lock, flags);
```

(c)

Figure 3. Our device state checkpointing mechanism refactors code from existing suspend-resume routines to create checkpoint and restore for drivers as shown in Figure (a). The checkpoint routine only stores a consistent device snapshot to memory while the restore loads the saved state and re-initializes the device. Figures (b) and (c) show checkpoint and restore routines in the rtl8139 driver.

2. *Broad.* The mechanism must work with a wide range of devices/drivers, including those with unique behavior.
3. *Consistent.* Drivers are often invoked on multiple threads, and checkpoints must be a consistent view of device state.

We identified the suspend/resume code already present in many drivers as having much of the functionality needed to implement checkpoint and restore. We next describe how power management for drivers works, and then describe how to reuse the functionality for driver recovery with checkpoints.

4.1.1 Suspend/Resume Background

Modern operating systems can dynamically reduce their power consumption to provide a hot *standby* mode, also called *suspend to RAM*, which disables processors and devices but leaves state in memory. One major component of reducing power is to disable devices. Thus, operating systems direct devices to switch to a low-power state when the system goes into standby mode. The behavior of devices is specified by the ACPI specification for the platform and by buses, such as PCI and USB.

In order to transition quickly between standby and full-power mode, drivers implement a power-management interface to save device state before entering standby mode, and to restore device state when leaving standby mode [12, 13]. These operations must be quick to allow fast transitions. The system-wide suspend-to-RAM mechanism saves the memory state of the driver, and the driver is responsible for saving and restoring any volatile device state. Drivers implement a power management interface with methods to save and restore state. For example, Linux PCI devices implement these two methods:

```
int (*suspend) (struct pci_dev *dev,
     pm_message_t state);
int (*resume) (struct pci_dev *dev);
```

When saving device state to memory, the driver may invoke the bus to save bus configuration data, as well as explicitly save the contents of select device registers that are not captured by the configuration state. The driver then instructs the device to suspend itself. Simple devices that have no state simply disable the device.

Upon resume, drivers wake the device, optionally perform a soft reset, restore their saved state. Since the latency of a system to respond post-resume is critical, the initialization is lightweight compared to restarting the driver, as it assumes the device has not changed. Similar to suspend, simple devices may just re-enable the device without restoring state.

For a system to support standby mode, all drivers must support power management. While not all drivers do (Linux is notorious for incomplete support [27]), it is widely implemented by Windows and MacOS drivers, and support in Linux drivers is improving.

The functionality provided by driver power management is very similar to what is needed for device state checkpointing. First, it provides the ability to save device state to memory in a way that allows applications to continue functioning. Second, even though the device may continue to receive power, the soft reset that occurs when re-enabling a device ensures that any previous state is replaced by the restored state. Finally, power management is implemented by most commonly used drivers. However, it is not directly usable for checkpointing: power management routines lack the ability to continue executing after suspending a device because the device has been disabled.

4.1.2 Checkpoint

Device state checkpointing is constructed from a subset of the device suspend support already present in drivers. A device may have many distinct forms of state, each of which require a different mechanism for checkpoint:

1. Device configuration information published through the bus configuration space.
2. Device registers with configuration data specific to the device.
3. Counters and statistics exported by the device and aggregated by the driver.
4. Addresses of memory buffers shared with the driver, such as the DMA ring buffers used by network drivers to send or receive packets.

We note that a checkpoint may not actually contain the full state of the device. Rather, it must contain *enough* information that functionality can later be restored without affecting applications. Thus, device state that can be recreated or recomputed need not be saved. Furthermore, the checkpoint only contains the device state. To be restored properly, it requires a consistent copy of the driver state taken at the same time. Thus, it must be paired with mechanisms such as transactional memory or copy-on-write to save the driver's state.

The configuration state is the easiest to save. Most buses provide a method to save configuration information. For example, PCI drivers in Linux use `pci_save_state`, that saves a set of standard registers and the base address registers (BARs) to memory. Each driver, though, must handle the remaining state, separately.

The driver explicitly saves register contents and counters in an internal driver structure. The difference between registers and counters arises during recovery, described below, because counter values cannot be written back to the device.

Memory buffers shared with the device can be recreated. As a result, most device drivers do not include the address of these buffers in a checkpoint. Instead, they free buffers during suspend and re-allocate them during resume.

Figure 3(a) diagrams the tasks performed by suspend and resume, and shows how that code is shuffled to create checkpoint and restore functionality. Of the suspend code, checkpointing reuses all the functionality except detaching the device with the kernel and suspending the device. As an example, Figure 3(b) shows the code to checkpoint the 8139too driver.

It may be necessary to checkpoint a driver while it is in use. Existing suspend routines assume the device is quiescent when the device state is saved. Checkpoint, though, may be called at any time. Thus, it must be synchronized with other threads using the driver. Because device state checkpointing must be coordinated with other mechanisms for capturing driver state, we do not put our own synchronization code in the checkpoint routine but reuse existing device locks in the driver. Device locks protect against conflicting configuration operations, or operations like resetting the device when I/O operations are in progress. This ensures that we do not corrupt device state assumed by another thread in progress when we reset device state in case of a failure.

4.1.3 Restore

The restore operation can be constructed from a mix of suspend and resume code. Normally the resume function is invoked when the device returns to full power and needs to be reconfigured. In the case of a checkpoint, though, the device is already running at full power. Thus, resume invokes the bottom half of the suspend routine to disable the device before restoring state.

The restore operation proceeds in four steps:

1. Disable the device to put it in a quiescent, known state.
2. Restore bus configuration state.
3. Re-enable the device.
4. Restore device-specific state.

Figure 3(c) shows the code to restore state for a simple network driver. Of the four categories of driver state, only configuration state and saved device registers can be reloaded. Counters, which cannot be written back to the device, are restored by adjusting the driver's version of the counter. Typically, the driver will read the device counter and update a copy in memory, and reset the device's counter. To restore the device's counter state, the driver only resets the device's counter; the in-memory copy of the counter must be saved as part of the driver's memory state.

To restore shared buffers, the driver releases existing shared buffers after disabling the device. As part of re-enabling the device, it recreates shared buffers and notifies the device of their new addresses. While this slows restore, it makes checkpoint very efficient because only irretrievable state is saved.

Unlike suspend-resume, it may be useful to use device state checkpointing from interrupt contexts where sleeping is not allowed. As a result, checkpoint and restore code must convert sleeps

Fault Tolerance
Device recovery: Current recovery mechanisms require writing wrappers to track all device state and full device restart results in long latency.
OS functionality
Fast reboot: Restarting the OS requires probing all bus and device drivers.
NVM operating systems: Providing persistent state of a running system requires ability to checkpoint a running device.
I/O Virtualization
Device consolidation: Re-assignment of passthrough devices across different VMs needs to wait for device initialization.
Live migration: Live migration of pass-through devices converts the millisecond latency of migrations to multiple seconds due to device initialization.
Clone VMs: Ability to launch many cloned VMs very quickly is limited by device initialization.

Table 1. Other uses for fast device state checkpointing.

to busy waits (`udelay` in Linux) and use memory allocation flags safe for interrupt context (`GFP_ATOMIC` in Linux).

Compared to full-driver restart, resume improves performance because it does not re-invoke device probe, often the lengthiest part of starting a device normally. Furthermore, drivers for newer buses such as USB and IEEE1394 do not restart the device because the bus handles this operation. This further reduces restore times. For PCI devices, a further optimization is to avoid changing the power mode of the device. However, we observed that many drivers do not require actually powering down the device before performing restore. For these drivers, restore can be sped up by skipping these unnecessary power mode changes.

4.1.4 Discussion

Device state checkpointing provides several benefits compared with a logging approach to capturing driver/device state. First, it can be invoked at any time and has no cost until invoked. Thus, it has no overhead for infrequent uses. Second, it handles state unique to a device, such as configuration options. Correct standby operation demands that devices remain correctly configured across standby, and hence drivers must already save and restore any required state. However, device state checkpointing relies on power management code, which may not be present in all devices. It also requires a programmer to implement checkpoint/restore for every driver. We evaluate these concerns in Section 5.

Limitations. There is a risk in utilizing a mechanism for an unintended purpose: the driver continues running following a checkpoint and may thus further modify the device state. In contrast, devices are normally idle between suspend and resume. Thus, it is possible that the state saved is insufficient to fully restore the device to correct operation. However, the power management specifications require drivers to fully capture device state in software since devices can transition to an even lower power state where the device is powered off. In such cases, drivers must be able to be restore their original state, following a full reset. Thus, suspend must store enough information to restore from any state.

FGFT does not work with devices with persistent internal state, such as disks and other storage devices, since restore will only restore the transient device state and not the persistent state, such as the contents of files. As a result, use of checkpoints must be coordinated with higher-level recovery mechanisms, such as Membrane [40], to keep persistent data consistent.

Other uses for device state checkpointing. In addition to fault tolerance, device state checkpoints have other uses. Table 1 lists five possible uses. Within an operating system, checkpoints support fast reboot after upgrading system software by restoring device state from a checkpoint rather than reinitializing the driver.

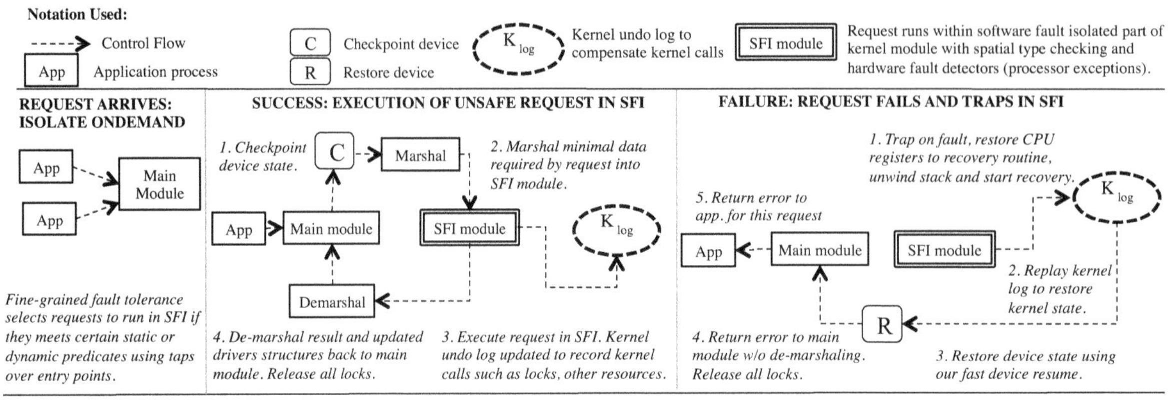

Figure 4. FGFT behavior during successful and failed entry point executions.

Similarly, operating systems using non-volatile memory to survive power failures [1, 30] can restart drivers from a checkpoint rather than reinitializing the device. In virtualized settings, pass-through and virtualization-aware devices [33] allow drivers in guest operating systems to interact with physical hardware. Device state checkpoints enable virtual-machine checkpoints to a pass-through device [25] and live migration, because the device state from the source can be extracted and restored on identical hardware at the destination. With virtual devices, the latency of live migration can be as low as 60ms [10], so a 2 second delay to initialize a pass-through device adds significant downtime [20]. Finally, device state checkpointing enables dynamic fault tolerance at fine granularity as demonstrated by FGFT.

4.2 Recovery with checkpoints

We now describe how FGFT uses isolation and device checkpoints to perform recovery from failures. When a failure is detected, communication stubs call a recovery routine that is responsible for restoring correct driver operation.

Failure anticipation. To prepare for an eventual recovery, generated stubs create a device checkpoint before invoking a suspect entry point. They invoke the `checkpoint` routine. In addition, stubs for kernel functions log compensation entries to undo their effects in the kernel undo log. Driver state is not explicitly checkpointed; instead, suspect code operates on a copy of driver state as described in Section 3. In addition, the stub saves its processor register state, allowing a jump right into the stub if the driver fails.

Recovery steps. In case a failure is detected by SFI or processor exceptions originating from a suspect module, the recovery routine restores driver operation through a sequence of steps as shown in Figure 4:

1. *Unwind thread.* If not already in the stub, the instruction pointer is set to the address of the recovery code in the entry point's stub, which reloads the saved registers. Nested calls to drivers are logically handled as separate transactions, so there is no need to unwind the thread to the outermost entry point.
2. *Restore device state checkpoint.* The stub recovery code calls the driver's `restore` routine to restore the device state.
3. *Free call state.* All temporary structures created for the suspect entry point call such as the range table, object tracker, and copies of kernel/driver structures are released.
4. *Release locks.* Any locks acquired before or during the call to the SFI driver are released, allowing other threads to execute.

If a driver entry point fails, the stub returns an appropriate error indicator, such as a NULL pointer or an error code, and relies on higher-level code to handle the failure. As only the single entry point fails, this failure has little impact on applications. All application state relating to the device, such as open handles, remain valid. Furthermore, other threads in the driver continue to run as soon as the recovery process completes and releases all acquired locks.

Compared to other driver isolation systems, the recovery process is much simpler because only one thread is affected, so other threads are not unwound. In addition, the driver state is left unmodified, so it is not saved and restored. Finally, device state is restored quickly from a checkpoint rather than by replaying a log. Hence, we see that checkpointing device state results in quicker and simpler recovery semantics for driver recovery.

4.3 Implementation effort

A key goal for FGFT is to reduce the implementation effort to isolate a driver. FGFT consists of minimal modifications to the kernel exception handlers (38 lines of code), a kernel module containing the object tracker, range table, and recovery support, and the Isolator tool in OCaml. The module is 1,200 lines of C code, and Isolator is 9700 lines of OCaml that implement: SFI isolation (400 lines), stub generation (7,800 lines), and static analysis of references to parameter fields (1,500 lines). In comparison, Nooks adds 23,000 lines of *kernel code* (85x more than FGFT) to isolate and reload device drivers and shadow drivers add another 1,100 lines of code for recovery. FGFT also does not require any wrappers around the driver interface. Nooks required 14,000 lines of manually written wrappers, which are hard to maintain as the kernel interface changes. FGFT's isolator tool automatically generates similar code for stubs.

5. Evaluation

We implemented device state checkpoint and fine-grained fault tolerance for the Linux 2.6.29 kernel for six drivers across three buses. The evaluation examines the following aspects of FGFT:

1. *Fault Resilience.* What failures can fine-grained fault tolerance handle? We evaluate FGFT using a series of fault injection experiments and report our results.
2. *Performance.* What is the performance loss of fine-grained fault tolerance on steady-state operation? We report the performance cost for applying FGFT on support and core I/O routines.
3. *Recovery Time.* What is the downtime caused by a driver failure? We compare the time taken by FGFT to restore the device and cleanup the failed driver thread state with the time taken to unload and reload a driver.

Fault Type	Description of fault
Corrupt pointers	Dynamic: Corrupt all pointers referenced in a function to random values.
Corrupt stack	Dynamic: corrupt execution stack by copying large chunks of data over stack variable addresses.
Corrupt expressions	Static: corrupt arithmetic instructions by adding invalid operations (like divide by zero).
Skip assignment	Static: remove assignment operations in a function.
Skip parameters	Dynamic: zero incoming parameters in a function.

Table 2. Faults injected to test failure resilience represent runtime and programming errors. Dynamic faults are invoked using `ioctls`, and static faults are inserted with an additional compiler pass.

Driver	Injected Faults	Benign Faults	Native crashes	FGFT crashes
8139too	43	0	43	NONE
e1000	47	0	47	NONE
ens1371	36	0	36	NONE
pegasus	34	1	33	NONE
psmouse	22	1	21	NONE
r8169	46	0	46	NONE
Total	**258**	**2**	**256**	**NONE**

Table 3. Fault injection table with number of unique faults injected per driver. FGFT is able to correctly restore the driver and device state in each case.

4. *Usefulness of FGFT.* Is selectively isolating entry points useful? We evaluate whether suspect entry points can be identified in drivers and whether they reduce the amount of code isolated.

5. *Device Checkpoint Support.* Is re-using existing power management functionality reasonable? We examine the frequency of power management support in existing drivers that facilitates device checkpoints.

6. *Developer Effort.* What is the overhead to the developer to enforce isolation in the system? We measure the effort needed to annotate a driver for isolation and to add checkpointing code.

Unless otherwise specified, we compare FGFT against unmodified drivers running on an unmodified 2.6.29 Linux kernel.

5.1 Fault Resilience

We first evaluate how well FGFT can handle driver bugs using a combination of dynamic and static fault injection over six drivers. These tests evaluate both the ability of fine-grained fault tolerance to isolate and recover driver state as well as the ability of device state checkpointing to restore device functionality. Table 2 describes the types of faults inserted in the SFI module. Static fault injection modifies the driver source code to emulate programming bugs, while dynamic fault injection modifies driver data while running to emulate run time errors. We perform a sequence of trials that test each fault site separately.

During each experiment, we run applications that use the driver to detect whether a driver failure causes the application to fail. For network, we use `ssh`, and `netperf`, and for sound we use `aplay` and `arecord` from the ALSA suite. We tested the mouse by scrolling the device manually as we performed the fault injection experiments. After each injection experiment, we determine if there is an OS/driver crash or the application malfunctions. We re-invoke the failed entry point without the fault to ensure that it continues to work, and that resources such as locks have been released.

We injected a total of 258 unique faults in the native and FGFT drivers. Table 3 shows the number of faults injected for every driver and the outcome. For the native driver, all but two faults crashed the driver or resulted in kernel panics. The two benign faults were missing assignments.

In contrast, when we injected faults into driver entry points protected by FGFT, the driver and the OS remain available for every single fault. Furthermore, in every case, applications continue to execute correctly following the fault. For example, the sound application `aplay` skips for a few milliseconds during driver recovery but continued to play normally. The shell notes this disruption with the message "`ALSA buffer underrun`."

We also verify that internal driver and device state is correctly recovered using the `ethtool` interface for network drivers. We find that when failures happen while changing configuration settings, re-reading settings after a crash always returns correct values.

Finally, we verify that changes to drivers made using non-class interfaces, such as the `proc` and `sys` file systems, before injecting failures and present following recovery. In contrast, shadow drivers cannot replay these actions since they cannot capture non-class driver interactions.

5.2 Performance

The primary cost of using FGFT is the time spent copying data in and out of the SFI module and creating device checkpoints. We measure performance with a gigabit Ethernet driver, as it may send or receive receive more than 75,000 packets per second. Thus, the overhead of FGFT will show up more clearly than on low-bandwidth devices. We evaluate the runtime costs of using FGFT and regular versions of drivers in six configurations:

1. *Native:* Unmodified e1000 driver.
2. $FGFT_{static}$: Statically isolate 75% of code (all off I/O-path).
3. $FGFT_{dyn\text{-}1/2}$: Dynamically isolate every other packet in I/O path.
4. $FGFT_{dyn\text{-}all}$: Dynamically isolate every packet in I/O path.

The *dynamic* experiment measures the additional cost of choosing at runtime whether to invoke the regular or SFI version of a function. Finally, the *dyn-all* test represents the worst case of invoking the SFI module on the I/O path for a high-bandwidth device.

Our test machine consists of a 2.5 GHz Intel Core 2 Quad system congured with 4 GB DDR2 DRAM and an Intel 82541PI gigabit NIC running FGFT. We measure performance with netperf [18] by connecting our test machine to another machine with 1.2 GHz Intel Celeron processor and a Belkin NIC with a crossover cable. Table 4 reports the average of 5 runs.

In the *static* test where code off the I/O-path code is isolated, performance and CPU utilization are unaffected. These results demonstrate that FGFT achieves the goal of only imposing a cost on isolated code.

For the *dyn-1/2* test that isolates at runtime, entry points on the I/O path (the packet send routine) for every other packet, bandwidth dropped 4% and CPU utilization increased 0.5%. Thus, selectively applying isolation, even on critical I/O paths, has a small impact.

The performance drops further when we isolate critical path code on every request since we copy shared driver and kernel data across modules for *each* packet being transmitted. We find a 7.5% performance drop and 1% higher CPU utilization. FGFT is designed to limit isolation costs to specific requests and hence pays a cost of isolation because it needs to setup isolation (create copies) as each packet requests isolation. Overall, these results show that FGFT can be applied at no cost to high bandwidth devices off the I/O path and at marginal cost on the I/O path.

Device Locking: We run netperf using multiple threads to measure the overhead from device locks introduced at isolated entry points. We find that bandwidth drops an additional 2.6% and 4.6%

Single Threaded		
System	**Throughput**	**CPU**
Native	843.6 Mb/s	2.5%
FGFT $_{static}$	843.6 Mb/s	2.5%
FGFT $_{dyn-1/2}$	811.5 Mb/s	2.9%
FGFT $_{dyn-all}$	784.4 Mb/s	3.4%

Multiple Threads			
Threads	**System**	**Throughput**	**CPU**
10	Native	847.7 Mb/s	3.0%
	FGFT $_{dyn-all}$	791.4 Mb/s	4.2%
100	Native	941.7 Mb/s	4.2%
	FGFT $_{dyn-all}$	860.2 Mb/s	10.8%

Table 4. TCP streaming send performance with netperf for regular and FGFT drivers with checkpoint based recovery.

Driver	Class	Bus	Restart recovery	FGFT recovery	Speedup
8139too	net	PCI	0.31s	70μs	4400
e1000	net	PCI	1.80s	295ms	6
r8169	net	PCI	0.12s	40μs	3000
pegasus	net	USB	0.15s	5ms	30
ens1371	sound	PCI	1.03s	115ms	9
psmouse	input	serio	0.68s	410ms	1.65

Table 5. FGFT and restart based recovery times. Restart-based recovery requires additional time to replay logs running over the lifetime of the driver. FGFT does not affect other threads in the driver.

Driver	Class	Bus	Checkpoint times	Restore times
8139too	net	PCI	33μs	62μs
e1000	net	PCI	32μs	280ms
r8169	net	PCI	26μs	30μs
pegasus	net	USB	0μs	4ms
ens1371	sound	PCI	33μs	111ms
psmouse	input	serio	0μs	390ms

Table 6. Latency for device state checkpoint/restore.

with 10 and 100 threads respectively, as compared to FGFT running in a single thread. We also test the `ens1371` sound driver and find that playing multiple overlapping sound files does not result in any lags or distortions. These results show that FGFT introduces low overhead with high bandwidth devices running multiple threads.

5.3 Recovery Time

A major benefit of checkpoint-based recovery is the speed of restoring service. Table 5 lists the time taken by the driver to recover using FGFT and by unloading and reloading the driver. We measure recovery times by recording the time from detection of failure to completion of the restore routine. Overall, FGFT is between 1.6 and 4,400 times faster than restart recovery, and between 145ms and 1.5s faster. The drivers with the largest speedup have complicated probe routines that are avoided by restoring from a checkpoint. Hence, FGFT provides low-latency recovery and frequently offers an order-of-magnitude lower recovery latencies.

Checkpoint/restore latency. We examine the device checkpoint latencies to understand the source of our recovery performance in the previous section. Table 6 shows the latency of a checkpoint or restore for the same six drivers. Checkpointing is very fast, taking only 20μs on average and 33μs at worst. Thus, it is fast enough to be called frequently, such as before the invocation of most driver entry points. Restore times are longer, with a range from 30μs for the r8169 network driver to 390ms for psmouse. USB drivers store less state because the USB bus controller stores configuration information instead of the driver. Thus, during a normal resume, the bus restores configuration state before calling the driver to resume. The psmouse driver represents a legacy device and does not support suspend/resume. Instead, we re-use existing driver code to reset the mouse.

Class	Bus	Drivers reviewed	Drivers with PM	
net	PCI	104	68	65%
net	USB	32	27	84%
net	PCMCIA	4	4	100%
sound	PCI	72	63	88%
sound	USB	3	1	33%
sound	PCMCIA	2	2	100%
ATA	PCI	61	45	74%
SCSI	USB	1	1	100%
SCSI	PCMCIA	5	5	100%
Total	**-**	**284**	**216**	**76%**

Table 7. Drivers with and without power management as measured with static analysis tools. USB drivers (audio and storage) support hundreds of devices with a common driver, and support suspend/resume.

5.4 Utility of Fine Granularity

We evaluate whether selectively isolating specific entry points is useful by looking for evidence that driver bugs are confined to one or a few entry points. If the functions with bugs are reachable through a large number of entry points, then full driver isolation is more useful than per-entry point isolation. For example, if a bug occurs in a low level read routine, then the bug will affect a large number of entry points.

In order to have a large data set, we use a published list of hardware dependence bugs [19] that represent one of the larger number of unfixed bugs in the drivers [11]. We were able to map these bugs in 210 drivers (541 total bugs) to our kernel under analysis. For each driver, we calculate the number of entry points and the fraction of code in the driver that must be isolated.

We find that the bugs are reachable through 643 entry points, for an average of 3 per driver. As a comparison, these drivers have a total of 4,460 entry points (21 per driver), so only 14% of entry points must be isolated. The code reachable from these entry points comprises only 18% of the code in these drivers. These results indicate that at least some classes of driver bugs are confined to a single entry point, and therefore FGFT can reduce the cost of fault tolerance as compared to isolating the entire driver.

5.5 Device Checkpoint Support

Device state checkpointing relies on existing power-management code. We measure how broadly it applies to Linux drivers by counting the number of drivers with power-management support. While modern ACPI-compliant systems require that all devices support power management, many legacy drivers do not.

We perform a simple static analysis over all network, sound, and storage drivers using the PCI, USB, and PCMCIA bus in Linux 2.6.37.6. The analysis scans driver entry points and identifies power management callbacks. Table 7 shows the number of drivers scanned by class and bus and the number that support power management. Overall, we found that 76% of the drivers support power management. Of the drivers that do not support power management, most were either very old, from before Linux supported power management, or worked with very simple devices. Only two modern devices, both Intel 10gb Ethernet cards, did not provide suspend/resume. Thus, we find that nearly all modern devices support power management and can therefore support device state checkpointing.

5.6 Developer effort

The primary development cost in using FGFT is adding annotations, which describe how to copy data between the kernel and the

Driver	Driver LoC	Isolation annotations	
		Driver Annotations	Kernel Annotations
8139too	1,904	15	20
e1000	13,973	32	
r8169	2,993	10	
pegasus	1,541	26	12
ens1371	2,110	23	66
psmouse	2,448	11	19

Table 8. Annotations required by FGFT isolation mechanisms for correct marshaling. Kernel annotations are common to a class, and driver annotations are specific to a single driver.

Driver	Recovery additions	
	LOC Moved	LOC Added
8139too	26	4
e1000	32	10
r8169	17	5
pegasus	22	4
ens1371	16	6
psmouse	19	6

Table 9. Developer effort for checkpoint/restore driver callbacks.

SFI module. Table 8 shows the number of annotations needed to apply FGFT to every function in each of the tested drivers. We separate annotations into *driver annotations*, which are made to the driver code, and *kernel-header annotations*, which are a one-time effort common to all drivers in the class. These annotations are the incremental cost of making a driver fault tolerant, and the implementation effort of Isolator and the kernel code described in Section 4 are the up-front cost.

Overall, drivers averaged 20 annotations, with more annotations for drivers with more complex data structures. Most driver classes required 20 or fewer kernel-header annotations except for sound drivers, which have a more complex interface and required 66 annotations. Thus, the effort to annotate a driver is only modest, as annotations touch only a small fraction of driver code. In comparison, SafeDrive [48] changed 260 lines of code in the e1000 driver for isolation and another 270 lines for recovery. Nooks [42] required 23,000 lines of code to isolate and reload drivers. Thus, these small annotations to drivers may be much simpler than adding a large new subsystem to the kernel.

Checkpointing implementation. We evaluated the ease of implementing device state checkpointing by adding support to the six drivers listed in Table 9. For each driver we show the amount of code we copied from suspend/resume to create checkpoint/restore as well as the number of new lines added. On average, we moved 22 lines of code and added six lines. The new code adds support for checkpoint/restore in interrupt contexts and avoids nested locks when the routines are invoked with a lock held. Even though device state checkpointing requires adding new code, the effort is mostly moving existing code. In comparison, implementing a shadow driver requires (i) building a model of driver behavior and (ii) writing a wrapper for every function in the driver/kernel interface to log state changes.

6. Related work

FGFT draws inspiration from past projects on driver reliability, program partitioning and software fault isolation systems.

Device driver recovery. Prior driver-recovery systems, including Nooks [42], Shadow drivers [41], SafeDrive [48] and Minix 3 [17] all unload and restart a failed driver. In contrast, FGFT takes a checkpoint prior to invoking the driver, and then rolls back to the most recent checkpoint, which is much faster. CuriOS provides transparent recovery and further ensures that client session state can be recovered [14]. However, CuriOS is a new operating system and requires specially written code to take advantage of its recovery system, while FGFT works with existing driver code in existing operating systems. ReViveI/O [29], and similar systems [35] provide whole-system checkpoint/restore by buffering I/O and only letting it reach the device after the next memory checkpoint. However, this approach does not work with polling, where I/O operations cannot be buffered and applied later.

Driver isolation systems. Driver isolation systems rely on hardware protection (Nooks [42] and Xen [15]) or strong in-situ detection mechanisms (BGI [6], LXFI [26], Mondrix [47] and XFI [43]) to detect failures in driver execution. However, in latter systems if the failure is detected *after* any state shared with the kernel has been modified then these systems cannot rollback to a last good state. Other driver isolation systems such as SUD [3] and Linux user-mode drivers [23], require writing class-specific wrappers in the kernel that are hard to maintain as the kernel evolves. FGFT differs from existing isolation systems by providing transactional semantics and limits the runtime overheads only to suspect code.

Software fault tolerance. Existing SFI techniques use programmer annotations (SafeDrive [48]) or API contracts (LXFI [26]) to provide type safety. XFI [43] transforms code binaries to provide inline software guards and stack protection. In contrast, FGFT operates on source code and allows drivers to operate on a copy of shared data. FGFT marshals the minimum required data and uses a range hash to provide spatial safety.

Transactional kernels. FGFT executes drivers as a transaction by buffering their state changes until they complete. VINO [38] similarly encapsulated extensions with SFI and used a compensation log to undo kernel changes. However, VINO applied to an entire extension and did not address recovering device state. In addition, it terminated faulty extensions, while most users want to continue using devices following a failure. FGFT is complementary to other transactional systems, such as TxOS [34], that provide transactional semantics for system calls. These techniques could be applied to driver calls into the kernel instead of using a kernel undo log of compensation records. Currently, these systems do not perform device I/O transactionally and either rely on higher-level atomicity techniques (TxOS [34] and xCalls [44]) or serialize transactions with a lock (TxLinux [36]).

Program Partitioning Program partitioning has been used for security [4, 7] and remote code execution [9]. Existing program partitioning tools statically partition user mode code or move driver code to user mode [16]. FGFT is the first system to partition programs within the kernel and is hence able to provide partitioning benefits to kernel specific components such as interrupt delivery and critical I/O path code. Furthermore, instead of partitioning code in any one domain, FGFT replicates its entry points and decides on a runtime basis whether a particular thread should run in isolation.

7. Conclusions

The performance and development costs of existing driver fault-tolerance mechanisms have restricted their adoption. In this paper, we presented fine-grained fault tolerance, a *pay-as-you-go* model for tolerating driver failures that can be dynamically invoked for specific requests. Fine-grained fault tolerance is made possible due to device checkpoints. This functionality is often considered to require a significant re-engineering of device drivers. However, we demonstrate that checkpoint functionality is already provided by existing suspend/resume code. While we only applied checkpoints to fault tolerance, there are more opportunities to use device checkpoint/restore, such as OS migration, fast reboot, and persistent operating systems that should be explored.

Acknowledgments

This work is supported by National Science Foundation (NSF) grants CNS 0745517 and CNS 0915363 and by a gift from Google. We would like to thank our shepherd Emmett Witchel for useful feedback. Swift has a financial interest in Microsoft Corp.

References

[1] K. Bailey, L. Ceze, S. D. Gribble, and H. M. Levy. Operating system implications of fast, cheap, non-volatile memory. In *Proc. of the 13th HOTOS*, 2011.

[2] A. Birgisson, U. E. Mohan Dhawan, V. Ganapathy, and L. Iftode. Enforcing authorization policies using transactional memory introspection. In *Proc. of the 15th ACM CCS*, Oct. 2008.

[3] S. Boyd-Wickizer and N. Zeldovich. Tolerating malicious device drivers in linux. In *USENIX ATC*, 2010.

[4] D. Brumley and D. Song. Privtrans: Automatically partitioning programs for privilege separation. In *Proc. of the 13th USENIX Security Symposium*, 2004.

[5] S. Butt, V. Ganapathy, M. Swift, and C.-C. Chang. Protecting commodity OS kernels from vulnerable device drivers. In *Proc. of 25th ACSAC*, Dec. 2009.

[6] M. Castro, M. Costa, J.-P. Martin, M. Peinado, P. Akritidis, A. Donnelly, P. Barham, and R. Black. Fast byte-granularity software fault isolation. In *Proc. of the 22nd ACM SOSP*, 2009.

[7] S. Chong et. al. Secure web applications via automatic partitioning. In *Proc. of the 21st ACM SOSP*, 2007.

[8] A. Chou, J. Yang, B. Chelf, S. Hallem, and D. Engler. An empirical study of operating system errors. In *Proc. of the 18th ACM SOSP*, 2001.

[9] B. Chun and P. Maniatis. Augmented smartphone applications through clone cloud execution. In *Proc. of the 12th USENIX HotOS*. USENIX Association, 2009.

[10] C. Clark et. al. Live migration of virtual machines. In *Proc of the 2nd USENIX NSDI*, 2005.

[11] J. Corbet. Trusting the hardware too much. `http://lwn.net/Articles/479653/`. LWN February 2012.

[12] J. Corbet, A. Rubini, and G. Kroah-Hartman. *Linux Device Drivers, 3rd Edition*. O'Reilly Associates, Feb. 2005.

[13] M. Corp. Power management and ACPI - architecture and driver support. `msdn.microsoft.com/en-us/windows/hardware/gg463220`.

[14] F. M. David, E. M. Chan, J. C. Carlyle, and R. H. Campbell. CuriOS: Improving reliability through operating system structure. In *Proc. of the 8th USENIX OSDI*, December 2008.

[15] K. Fraser, S. Hand, R. Neugebauer, I. Pratt, A. Warfield, and M. Williamson. Safe hardware access with the Xen virtual machine monitor. In *OASIS Workhop*, 2004.

[16] V. Ganapathy, M. J. Renzelmann, A. Balakrishnan, M. M. Swift, and S. Jha. The design and implementation of microdrivers. In *Proc. of the 13th ACM ASPLOS*, Mar. 2008.

[17] J. N. Herder, H. Bos, B. Gras, P. Homburg, and A. S. Tanenbaum. Failure resilience for device drivers. In *Proc. of the 2007 IEEE DSN*, June 2007.

[18] R. Jones. Netperf: A network performance benchmark, version 2.1, 1995. Available at `http://www.netperf.org`.

[19] A. Kadav, M. J. Renzelmann, and M. M. Swift. Tolerating hardware device failures in software. In *Proc. of the 22nd ACM SOSP*, 2009.

[20] A. Kadav and M. M. Swift. Live migration of direct-access devices. *SIGOPS Operating Systems Review, 43:95–104*, 2009.

[21] A. Kadav and M. M. Swift. Understanding modern device drivers. In *Proc. of 17th ACM ASPLOS*, 2012.

[22] J. R. Larus and R. Rajwar. *Transactional Memory*. Morgan & Claypool Publishers, 2007.

[23] B. Leslie et. al. User-level device drivers: Achieved performance. *Jour. Comp. Sci. and Tech.*, 20(5), 2005.

[24] B. Liblit, M. Naik, A. X. Zheng, A. Aiken, and M. I. Jordan. Scalable statistical bug isolation. In *Proc of the 26th ACM PLDI*, 2005.

[25] M. Mahalingam and R. Brunner. I/O Virtualization (IOV) For Dummies. `labs.vmware.com/download/80/`. VMworld 2007.

[26] Y. Mao, H. Chen, D. Zhou, X. Wang, N. Zeldovich, and M. Kaashoek. Software fault isolation with api integrity and multi-principal modules. In *Proc. of the 23rd ACM SOSP*, 2011.

[27] P. Mochel. The Linux power management summit. `http://lwn.net/Articles/181888/`, 2006.

[28] S. Nagarakatte, J. Zhao, M. M. Martin, and S. Zdancewic. Softbound: highly compatible and complete spatial memory safety for c. In *Proc. of the 30th ACM PLDI*, 2009.

[29] J. Nakano, P. Montesinos, K. Gharachorloo, and J. Torrellas. ReViveI/O: Efficient handling of i/o in highly-available rollback-recovery servers. In *Proc. of the 12th HPCA, 2006*.

[30] D. Narayanan and O. Hodson. Whole-system persistence. In *Proc. of the 17th ACM ASPLOS*, March 2012.

[31] G. C. Necula, S. Mcpeak, S. P. Rahul, and W. Weimer. CIL: Intermediate language and tools for analysis and transformation of C programs. In *Proc. of the 11th CC*, 2002.

[32] V. Paxson. Bro: a system for detecting network intruders in real-time. In *Proc. of the 7th USENIX Security Symposium*, 1998.

[33] PCI-SIG. I/O virtualization. `http://www.pcisig.com/specifications/iov/`, 2007.

[34] D. E. Porter, O. S. Hofmann, C. J. Rossbach, A. Benn, and E. Witchel. Operating systems transactions. In *Proc. of the 22nd ACM SOSP*, 2009.

[35] P. Ramachandran. *Detecting and Recovering from In-Core Hardware Faults Through Software Anomaly Treatment*. PhD thesis, University of Illinois, Urbana-Champaign, 2011.

[36] C. J. Rossbach et. al. TxLinux: Using and managing hardware transactional memory in an operating system. In *Proc. of the 21st ACM SOSP*, 2007.

[37] L. Ryzhyk, P. Chubb, I. Kuz, and G. Heiser. Dingo: Taming device drivers. In *Proc. of the 4th ACM Eurosys*, Apr. 2009.

[38] M. Seltzer, Y. Endo, C. Small, and K. Smith. Dealing with disaster: Surviving misbehaved kernel extensions. *SIGOPS Operating Systems Review*, 30:213–228, 1996.

[39] Sun Microsystems. Opensolaris community: Fault management. `http://opensolaris.org/os/community/fm/`.

[40] S. Sundararaman et. al. Membrane: Operating system support for restartable file systems. In *Proc. of the 8th USENIX FAST*, 2010.

[41] M. M. Swift, M. Annamalai, B. N. Bershad, and H. M. Levy. Recovering device drivers. In *Proc. of the 6th USENIX OSDI*, 2004.

[42] M. M. Swift, B. N. Bershad, and H. M. Levy. Improving the reliability of commodity operating systems. In *Proc. of the 19th ACM SOSP*, Oct. 2003.

[43] Úlfar Erlingsson, M. Abadi, M. Vrable, M. Budiu, and G. C. Necula. Xfi: software guards for system address spaces. In *Proc. of the 7th USENIX OSDI*, 2006.

[44] H. Volos, A. Tack, N. Goyal, M. Swift, and A. Welc. xcalls: safe i/o in memory transactions. In *Proc of the 4th ACM Eurosys*. ACM, 2009.

[45] R. Wahbe, S. Lucco, T. E. Anderson, and S. L. Graham. Efficient software-based fault isolation. In *Proc. of the 14th ACM SOSP*, Dec. 1993.

[46] D. Williams, P. Reynolds, K. Walsh, E. G. Sirer, and F. B. Schneider. Device driver safety through a reference validation mechanism. In *Proc. of the 8th USENIX OSDI*, 2008.

[47] E. Witchel, J. Rhee, and K. Asanovic. Mondrix: Memory isolation for Linux using Mondriaan memory protection. In *Proc. of the 20th ACM SOSP*, 2005.

[48] F. Zhou et. al. SafeDrive: Safe and recoverable extensions using language-based techniques. In *Proc. of the 7th USENIX OSDI*, 2006.

GPUfs: Integrating a File System with GPUs

Mark Silberstein
University of Texas at Austin
marks@cs.utexas.edu

Bryan Ford
Yale University
bryan.ford@yale.edu

Idit Keidar
Technion – Israel Institute of Technology
idish@ee.technion.ac.il

Emmett Witchel
University of Texas at Austin
witchel@cs.utexas.edu

As GPU hardware becomes increasingly general-purpose, it is quickly outgrowing the traditional, constrained GPU-as-coprocessor programming model. To make GPUs easier to program and improve their integration with operating systems, we propose making the host's file system directly accessible to GPU code. GPUfs provides a POSIX-like API for GPU programs, exploits GPU parallelism for efficiency, and optimizes GPU file access by extending the host CPU's buffer cache into GPU memory. Our experiments, based on a set of real benchmarks adapted to use our file system, demonstrate the feasibility and benefits of the GPUfs approach. For example, a self-contained GPU program that searches for a set of strings throughout the Linux kernel source tree runs over seven times faster than on an eight-core CPU.

Categories and Subject Descriptors D.4.7 [*Operating Systems*]: Organization and Design; I.3.1 [*Hardware Architecture*]: Graphics processors

Keywords Operating Systems Design, GPGPUs, File Systems, accelerators

1. Introduction

The file system is a successful, proven operating system abstraction, which benefits developer productivity by decoupling the application's logical view of storage from low-level details of the location and type of devices on which data physically resides. Modern file systems have buffer caches enabling the system to optimize data access locality across cooperating processes or modules, e.g., by keeping frequently-accessed data or intermediate results in memory to minimize the cost of accesses to slow storage devices.

Unlike CPU applications, programs running on graphical processing units (GPUs) currently have no direct access to files on the host OS file system. Although the power, functionality, and utility of today's GPUs now extend far beyond graphics processing, the coprocessor-style GPU programming model still requires developers to manage movement of data explicitly between its "home" in the CPU's main memory and the GPU's local memory. Managing data transfers between CPU and GPU increases the design complexity and code size of even simple GPU programs requiring file access. While programmers can explicitly optimize data movement, this performance is often not portable to new generations of hardware. Over time, application code to transfer and reuse recently computed data becomes entwined with program logic, making it hard to maintain functionality and performance.

Drawing an analogy to pre-virtual memory days, applications often managed their own address spaces efficiently using manual overlays, but this complex and fragile overlay programming ultimately proved not worth the effort. GPUs are quickly evolving toward general high-performance processors useful for a wide variety of massively parallel, throughput-oriented tasks, and we believe GPU programming should reap the same benefits from the file system abstraction enjoyed by CPU programmers for decades.

We propose **GPUfs** , an infrastructure that exposes the file system API to GPU programs, bringing the convenience and power of file systems to GPU developers. GPUfs offers compute-intensive applications a convenience well-established in the CPU context: to be largely oblivious to where data is located—whether on disk, in main memory, in a GPU's local memory, or replicated across several GPUs or other coprocessors. Further, GPUfs lets the OS optimize data access locality across independently-developed GPU compute modules, using application-transparent caching and data replication, much like a traditional OS's buffer cache optimizes access locality across multi-process computation pipelines. A unified file API interface abstracts away the low-level details of different GPU hardware architectures and their complex inter-device memory consistency models, improving code and performance portability. GPUfs expands the appeal of GPU programming by offering familiar, well-established data manipulation interfaces instead of proprietary GPU APIs. Finally, GPUfs allows GPU code to be self-sufficient, by simplifying or eliminating the complex CPU support code traditionally required to feed data to GPU computations.

As a simple example, consider multiplying a matrix by a vector. GPUs excel at such computational tasks, but most GPU programs will assume that the matrix fits in GPU memory. If the input matrix becomes larger than GPU memory, the program must be invasively modified and its complexity increases sharply—for example, the input must be split into chunks, each chunk processed separately, and data transfers must be overlapped with computation for good performance. File systems traditionally excel at insulating the developer from such low-level data movement details. File systems also excel as a communication substrate for composing different programs. Currently, GPUs are more often used for stand-alone monolithic applications, because the complexity of integrating a

ASPLOS'13, March 16–20, 2013, Houston, Texas, USA.

GPU program into a complex processing pipeline is too high. Data movement is a major source of this complexity.

With GPU hardware changing so rapidly, a key design challenge for GPUfs is to focus on properties likely to be essential to the performance of future as well as current GPUs. Some properties of current GPUs, such as particular memory consistency models, may continue changing rapidly and unpredictably. We believe, however, that two key characteristics—data parallelism and dependence on access locality—will persist as GPU architectures evolve, and GPUfs must address these concerns in order to succeed.

GPUs are designed to optimize for massive data parallelism, by sharing a limited set of "control plane" logic—for instruction fetch, memory management, etc.—among far more numerous "data plane" resources such as vector ALUs. As a result, GPUs are efficient when thousands of lightweight threads run similar or identical code, with little control-flow variation. The traditional file system API was not built with such an execution environment in mind. In GPUfs, therefore, both the API semantics and the file system implementation must be designed to support such massive parallelism, efficiently allowing thousands of GPU hardware threads to invoke `open`, `close`, `read`, or `write` calls simultaneously.

Second, memory locality is vital for performance, due to the variety in memory system speeds and interconnect topologies. Our work currently focuses on discrete GPUs, which today provide higher performance than GPUs integrated with CPUs on the same die. Discrete GPUs have high-bandwidth DRAM, but connect to the host via a peripheral interconnect bus, typically PCIe. These buses are high latency and low bandwidth relative to DRAM buses, effectively 6GB/s for PCIe 2.0. Future multi-GPU systems with both integrated and discrete GPUs will further increase variance in hardware speeds and topologies. The only way for GPUfs to perform well in such systems is with comprehensive OS management of the memory system. The OS must have a global policy to manage data placement and data reuse across CPU and GPU memories based on dynamic access patterns. GPUfs's buffer cache is distributed across all system memories to enable such policies.

We evaluate a prototype implementation of GPUfs on an x86 PC with four NVIDIA GPUs, using several microbenchmarks and two realistic I/O intensive applications. All the presented GPUfs workloads are implemented entirely in the GPU kernel without CPU-side application code. In sequential file access benchmarks, a trivial 16 line GPU kernel using GPUfs outperforms a simple GPU implementation with manual data transfer by up to 40%, and comes within 5% of a hand-optimized double-buffering implementation. A matrix multiply benchmark illustrates how GPUfs easily enables access to datasets larger than the GPU's physical memory, performs from 5% to $4\times$ faster than the manual double-buffering typical in current GPU code, and is about $2\times$ smaller in code size. Two parallel data analysis applications, prioritized image matching and string search, highlight the ability of GPUfs to support irregular workloads in which parallel threads open and access dynamically-selected files of varying size and composition.

This paper makes the following main contributions.

1. The first POSIX-like file system API we are aware of for GPU programs, with semantics modified to be appropriate for the data-parallel GPU programming environment.
2. A design and implementation of a generic software-only buffer cache mechanism for GPUs, employing a lock-free traversal algorithm for data parallel efficiency.
3. A proof-of-concept implementation of GPUfs on NVIDIA FERMI GPUs [21], supporting multi-GPU systems.
4. A quantitative evaluation of a GPU file system that identifies sensitive performance parameters such as page size, and evaluates efficiency relative to hand-coded solutions.

The next section provides an overview of the GPU architecture. We then explain and justify the design choices that we made while building GPUfs, followed by the implementation details of GPUfs on NVIDIA FERMI GPUs. We evaluate the GPUfs prototype implementation in Section 5, and conclude with related work.

2. GPU architecture overview

This section provides a brief, simplified overview of the GPU software/hardware model, highlighting the properties that are particularly relevant to GPUfs. We use NVIDIA CUDA terminology because we implement GPUfs on NVIDIA cards; for more details we refer the reader to the CUDA reference [20].

GPUs are multicore processors. Each core, called *multiprocessor* or *MP*, features a wide SIMD vector unit, which a hardware scheduler multiplexes between multiple execution contexts.

A GPU's basic sequential unit of execution is a *thread*. GPU hardware groups a number of threads (32 in NVIDIA GPUs) into *warps*, and executes all threads in a warp concurrently in lockstep on a single hardware vector unit. Each MP multiplexes many warps onto the same SIMD unit to maximize hardware utilization, executing one warp while another is blocked on a memory access for example. Several warps (up to 32) form a *threadblock*. Threads in a threadblock are always executed on a single MP. Multiple threadblocks form a single complete GPU program, often termed a *kernel* (unrelated to an OS kernel).

A CPU application using the GPU enqueues all threadblocks comprising a kernel into a single global hardware queue. The hardware scheduler dispatches threadblocks onto MPs while assigning unique IDs to each threadblock and each thread in the block. The scheduler strives to maximize the number of warps concurrently scheduled on an MP without exceeding MP hardware resources such as available registers. Given sufficient hardware resources the scheduler can schedule multiple independent kernels at once.

Challenges for GPUfs. There are two characteristics of the GPU execution model that are particularly important in designing system abstractions such as a file system API on a GPU. First, once invoked, warps run to completion *without preemption*. This implies, for example, that using spinlocks to synchronize between running threads in the same kernel may lead to a deadlock. Second, the hardware schedules threadblocks for execution in *a non-deterministic order*, driven solely by the goal of maximizing hardware utilization. This behavior creates challenges in implementing reference-count based parallel versions of `open` and `close` file calls, for example, as described later (§ 4).

3. Design

This section outlines the GPUfs API and file system semantics, focusing on the similarities and differences from the POSIX API, and the properties of GPUs that motivate these design choices. We believe that our design reflects several key properties of data parallel architectures that will apply to future as well as current GPUs and hybrid processors. This section focuses on the high-level aspects of the design and API that are visible to applications using GPUfs, deferring lower-level implementation considerations largely invisible to applications to § 4.

Figure 1 illustrates the architecture of GPUfs. CPU programs are unchanged, but GPU programs can access the host's file system, via a GPUfs library linked into the application's GPU code. The GPUfs library works with the host OS on the CPU to coordinate the file system's namespace and data, caching file data in both CPU and GPU memory largely transparently to the application.

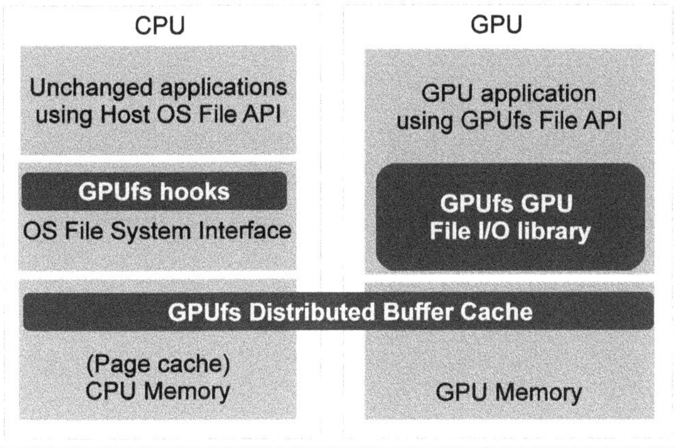

Figure 1. GPUfs architecture

3.1 GPUfs design principles

Two key principles underly the design of GPUfs and the ways in which it deviates from traditional POSIX semantics: making common API operations efficient when executed in data parallel fashion, and choosing consistency and data movement semantics that maximizes file data access locality and minimizes expensive global transfers between GPU and host memory.

API design for structured data parallelism. As we summarized in § 2, GPU hardware offers parallelism at multiple granularities, which combine to achieve high throughput. At finer granularities, the hardware achieves efficiency by sharing control logic across all threads comprising a warp. Processing is efficient when these threads follow the same code paths in lockstep, but highly inefficient if the threads follow divergent paths: *all* the threads in a warp must explore *all* possible divergent paths together, merely masking instructions applicable only to some threads.

Because of these hardware characteristics, a key semantic design decision for any GPU-accessible library or system API is the granularity at which API calls are to be invoked. Operations affecting globally shared file system state, such as `open` and `close` calls, involve control-flow heavy operations and require serialization. Even basic `read` and `write` API calls require updates to the file system's buffer cache data structures. If GPUfs allowed each application to invoke these operations at thread granularity—e.g., each thread opening different files or reading different blocks—these threads would quickly encounter divergent control paths within GPUfs, entailing hardware serialization and inefficiency. Moreover, hardware provides the highest memory throughput when the accesses of all threads in a warp are aligned and can be coalesced into one memory transaction.

For these reasons, GPUfs follows common GPU programming practices by requiring all threads in a warp to cooperate to perform the same operation, and requires applications to invoke the file system API at warp—rather than thread—granularity.

Thus, all application threads in a warp must invoke the same GPUfs call, with the same arguments, at the same point in application code. These lockstep calls together comprise one logical GPUfs operation. For example, GPUfs does not allow an application to open one file *per thread* in parallel, but only one file *per warp*. On the other hand, this warp-granularity API allows the GPUfs *implementation* to parallelize the handling of API calls across threads in the invoking warp—parallelizing file table search operations or data movement, for example. Our prototype currently makes use of this capability only in a few performance-critical cases, highlighting this principle by accelerating memory transfers between the user and system buffers in read/write calls.

As detailed below, considerations of data parallelism also motivated several other design decisions we made in GPUfs: to minimize per-open file state by eliminating seek pointers, decouple the synchronizing side-effects traditionally bound into API calls such as `close`, and constrain `mmap` semantics to avoid the need for complex memory management on critical data parallel paths.

Locality-optimized file consistency model. GPU memory systems have pronounced NUMA characteristics, offering far more bandwidth—over 30× in current systems—and lower latencies to access local GPU memory than to main CPU memory or to that of other discrete GPUs. Performance therefore critically depends on minimizing file data movement between the GPU and CPU, or between GPUs. To enable each GPU to access locally cached file data as independently as possible, GPUfs implements a weak consistency model similar to the *private workspace* model in Determinator [1], and to distributed file systems such as LOCUS [26] or AFS [10]. Once a file page is accessed and cached on a GPU, its threads can read and write to that page locally without further communication with the host—even if the host and/or other GPUs may concurrently read and/or modify that file. GPUfs guarantees that local file modifications propagate to main CPU memory only when the application explicitly *synchronizes* the file or individual pages with backing store, thereby persisting its content. These modifications become visible to other GPUs when they re-open the file.

Concurrent non-overlapping writes to the same file. In the potentially common situation in which a parallel task is executing on several GPUs and CPUs in one system, the same file may be write-shared among all executing processors. Concurrent tasks typically write into different parts of the file: i.e., to the particular range each is assigned to produce. Workspace consistency allows multiple writers without causing memory page thrashing between different GPUs, as a single-writer MESI protocol would exhibit. An important challenge, however, is that GPUfs must be able to handle false sharing of buffer cache pages among different GPUs. As a result, it has to determine which specific portions of a given page were modified on a given GPU when propagating those modifications to the host, to avoid accidentally reverting other portions of the same page that have been modified concurrently by other GPUs. In general, for files opened for *writing*, GPUfs must maintain *two* copies of each cached block per GPU: a working copy to which local writes are performed, and a *pristine* copy preserved when the page is first read. GPUfs "diffs" the working and the pristine copies at the next synchronization point to determine which bytes have been modified and should be written back.

An important common case is *write-once* file access, where GPU application threads produce a new output file without ever reading it or overwriting already-written data. To avoid the costs of both making and storing two copies of file blocks in this case, GPUfs attaches special semantics to files an application opens in a new (`O_GWRONCE`) open mode. GPUfs *never* reads pages of such files from the host into the GPU cache, and instead implicitly assumes the pristine copy of any file block is all zeros—even if the host or some other GPUs may in fact have already written to parts of that page in the underlying file. As a result, when the GPU propagates locally written pages back to the host, determining which bytes have been modified locally reduces to a trivial "diff against zeros." These semantics imply that one GPU's threads will typically never observe writes from other processors while the file is opened for writing, and that multiple GPUs' concurrent writes are guaranteed to merge correctly only if threads write *only once* to *disjoint* file areas. We believe these constraints are consistent with common practices in file-producing data parallel applications, and thus place reasonable semantic demands on applications in order to enable important data movement optimizations.

API	Explanation
gread/gwrite	Reads and writes always supply explicit file offsets, to avoid the file seek pointer becoming a sequential bottleneck.
gopen/gclose	Open and close files in the namespace of a single threadblock. Multiple concurrent open requests to open or close the same file are coalesced into one open/close. The precise semantics are further discussed in the text.
gfsync	Synchronously write back to the host all dirty file pages that are currently neither memory-mapped nor being accessed concurrently via gread or gwrite calls.
gmmap/gmunmap	A relaxed form of mmap that avoids double copies in gread/gwrite. Imposes API constraints discussed in the text.
gmsync	Write back a specific dirty page to the host. The application must coordinate calls to gmsync with updates by other threadblocks.
gunlink	Remove a file. Files unlinked on the GPU have their local buffer space reclaimed immediately.
gfstat	Retrieve file metadata. File size reflects file size at the time of the first gopen call that opened this file on the host.
gftruncate	Truncate a file to a given size, and reclaim any relevant pages from the buffer cache.

Table 1. GPUfs API, and discussion of relaxed file system semantics for GPUfs.

3.2 GPUfs API

Guided by the above principles, we now explore their implications on specific parts of the GPUfs API. GPUfs attempts to preserve the POSIX API's familiar semantics when practical, while diverging as needed for efficiency in GPU environments. Table 1 summarizes the API and its deviations from from POSIX semantics. We prepend a 'g' to GPUfs' API function names to emphasize that their semantics deviates from strict POSIX.

Open and file descriptors. Traditionally, if several POSIX threads concurrently open the same file, each thread obtains a fresh file descriptor in a process-global file table, each descriptor containing a separate seek pointer and other file-open state. For GPU kernels we expect it to be commonplace to open the same file in parallel across hundreds of concurrently running warps, for example when each warp is assigned a given chunk of a given file. Preserving POSIX semantics would in such cases require these gopen calls to coordinate the efficient simultaneous allocation and initialization of large "batches" of file descriptors at once, a complex and likely inefficient file descriptor management task. In GPUfs, therefore, "file descriptors" do not represent individual *file opens* but merely correspond directly to *files*, so that all GPU threads opening the same file obtain a single shared file descriptor. GPUfs forwards the first gopen call on a given file to the CPU to open the file on the underlying host file system. GPUfs then reference counts these open files, so a gopen on an already-open file just increments the file's open count without requiring CPU communication.

Besides the standard open flags, gopen introduces two new flags enabling useful performance optimizations.

- O_GWRONCE: Creates a new write-only file, in which the application will write each byte *at most once*. If data is overwritten, partial updates may occur. This flag eliminates fetching of file content from the CPU before writing, as described above in §3.1.
- O_NOSYNC: Creates a temporary file to be used only by the GPU opening it. GPUfs never writes the file's data to disk on close, and never writes it at all except to reclaim GPU buffer cache space.

Read and write. Because GPUfs dispenses with most per-open state, its file descriptors have no seek pointers. As a result, gread and gwrite correspond to POSIX's pread and pwrite—taking file offsets explicitly as arguments—instead of the traditional streaming read and write. This convention matches common practice in parallel workloads anyway [14], and application threads can maintain their own explicit seek pointers if required, as we demonstrate in our experiments (§5.2.2).

Close and synchronization. POSIX semantics require the contents of a file to be synchronized to stable storage (e.g., disk) after each close. In the common-case sequence of gopen, gwrite, gclose, executed by many GPU threads, POSIX close semantics cause many costly write-backs due to the nondeterministic GPU scheduler. Even if we reference count files, it is common for several threadblocks to open, write, then close the file, sending its reference count temporarily to zero before other threadblocks are scheduled that open the file again. In our experience this situation can be common, and synchronizing files each time the reference count drops to zero results in many unnecessary writes.

GPUfs therefore decouples the file "close" and "synchronize" operations. In particular, gclose does not propagate locally written data back to the CPU, or to other GPUs, until the application explicitly synchronizes file data, by calling gfsync to synchronize either an entire file or a specific offset range.

File mapping. GPUfs allows GPU threads to map portions of files directly into local GPU memory via gmmap/gmunmap. As with traditional mmap, file mapping offers two benefits: the convenience to applications of not having to allocate a buffer and separately read data into it, and opportunities for the system to improve performance by avoiding unnecessary data copying.

Full-featured memory mapping functionality requires user-programmable hardware virtual memory, which current GPUs lack. Even in future GPUs that may offer such control, we expect performance considerations to render traditional mmap semantics impractical in data parallel contexts. GPU hardware shares control plane logic, including memory management, across compute units running hundreds or thousands of threads at once. Thus, any translation change has global impact, likely requiring synchronization too expensive for fine-grained use within individual threads.

GPUfs therefore offers a more relaxed alternative to mmap, permitting more efficient implementation in a data parallel context by avoiding frequent translation updates. There is no guarantee that gmmap will map the entire file region the application requests—instead it may map only a prefix of the requested region, and return the size of the successfully mapped prefix. Further, gmmap is not guaranteed ever to succeed when the application requests a mapping at a particular address: i.e., MMAP_FIXED may not work. Finally, gmmap does not guarantee that the mapping will have *only* the requested permissions: mapping a read-only file may return a pointer to read/write memory, and GPUfs trusts the application not to modify that memory. Improper updates to such "quasi-read-only" pages are never propagated back to the host CPU, so GPUfs ensures host file system integrity despite less stringent page-level access enforcement on data resident in local GPU memory.

These looser semantics ultimately increase efficiency by allowing GPUfs to give the application pointers directly into GPU-local buffer cache pages, residing in the same address space (and protection domain) as the application's GPU code.

3.3 Buffer cache

An essential component of a file system layer is a buffer cache. In CPUs, the buffer cache minimizes disk accesses, which can be a thousand times slower than memory. The GPU page cache extends this principle to GPU file accesses, caching file data in fast local GPU memory to minimize transfers across the relatively slow and bandwidth-constrained peripheral interconnect.

The role of the buffer cache extends beyond simple caching. As on a CPU, a GPU buffer cache enables further performance optimizations such as read-ahead, data transfer scheduling, and asynchronous writes. In multi-processor, multi-GPU systems the buffer cache spans multiple GPUs and serves as an abstraction hiding the low-level details of the shared I/O subsystem.

Due to limitations in the software interfaces available to today's GPU hardware, GPUfs currently implements a private GPU buffer cache for each host CPU process: buffer cache pages are not shared across host applications, as in the OS-maintained buffer cache on the host CPU. Programmable memory protection interfaces on future GPUs could eliminate this limitation, enabling a true cross-user, cross-application GPU buffer cache.[1] On the other hand, multiple kernels launched by the same process can share data via the buffer cache, and we use that feature in our experiments (§5.1.3).

Replacement policies. A GPU file system allows the OS to coordinate file system replacement policies across all hardware in the system. For example, if the GPU is idle, the OS could use GPU memory as a staging area for data before writing it to disk. As GPU computations evolve to become part of heterogeneous processing pipelines, OS management of file system data will enable significant performance optimizations.

Whether standard LRU replacement policies for CPUs will be appropriate for the GPU buffer cache is not yet clear. Typical file access patterns in GPU applications remain to be seen, but we already observe accesses to be fairly chaotic even in workloads with logically sequential accesses, due to the non-deterministic scheduling of threadblocks in the GPU execution model.

Failure semantics. GPUfs has failure semantics similar to the CPU page cache: on failure, file updates not yet committed to disk may be lost. From the application's perspective, successful completion of `gfsync` or `gmsync` ensures that data has been written to the host page cache. The API also allows forcing writes to stable storage, equivalent to `fsync` or `msync` on CPUs.

Unfortunately, GPU failures are more frequent and have severe implications. In existing systems, a GPU program failure—such as an invalid memory access or assertion failure [20]—may require restarting the GPU card, thus losing the GPU's entire memory state. As GPUs continue to become more general-purpose, we expect GPU hardware to gain more resilience to such software failures.

3.4 Resource contention with GPU programs

Operating systems are known to compete with user programs for hardware resources such as caches [23], and are often blamed for decreased performance in high performance computing environments. GPUfs is less intrusive than a complete OS because it has no active, continuously running components. It necessarily adds some overheads, however, in the form of memory consumption, increased program instruction footprint, and the use of GPU hardware registers. We expect the relative effect of these overheads on performance to decrease with future hardware generations, which will provide larger memory, larger register files, and larger instruction caches. And despite these additional costs, we find GPUfs to have good performance in useful application scenarios (§5).

GPUfs by design imposes no overhead on GPU kernels that use no file system functionality. We deliberately avoided design alternatives involving "daemon" threads: i.e., persistent GPU threads dedicated to file system management, such as paging or CPU-GPU synchronization. While enabling more efficient implementation of the file system layer, such threads would violate the "pay-as-you-go" design principle to be discussed further in §4.2

[1] A cross-application buffer cache could potentially be implemented already using the new IPC feature in CUDA 5.0, but this interface still lacks the programmable memory protection that would be necessary to protect a shared GPUfs buffer cache from errant host processes or GPU kernels.

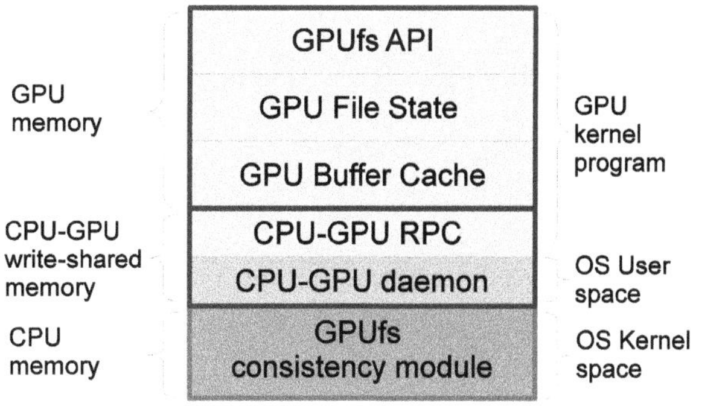

Figure 2. Main GPUfs software layers and their location in the software stack and physical memory.

4. Implementation

This section describes our GPUfs prototype for NVIDIA FERMI GPUs. We first outline the prototype's structure and how it implements the above API, then explore implementation details and challenges. We cover buffer cache management, GPU-CPU communication, file consistency management, and limitations of the current prototype. Some of these implementation choices are likely to be affected by future GPU evolution, but we feel that most considerations discussed here will remain relevant. For simplicity, our current implementation supports parallel invocation of the GPUfs API only at threadblock and not warp granularity. GPUfs calls represent an implicit synchronization barrier, and must be called at the same point with the same parameters from all threads in a threadblock.

Most of GPUfs is a GPU-side library linked with application code. The CPU-side portion runs as a user-level thread in the host application, giving it access the application's CUDA context.

Figure 2 shows the three main software layers comprising GPUfs, their location in the overall software stack shown on the right and indicated by different colors, and the type of memory the relevant data structures are located in shown on the left.

The top layer is the core of GPUfs, which runs in the context of the application's GPU kernels and maintains its data structures in GPU memory. This layer implements the GPUfs API, tracks open file state, and implements the buffer cache and paging.

The communication layer manages GPU-CPU communications, and naturally spans the CPU and GPU components. Data structures shared between the GPU and CPU are stored in write-shared CPU memory accessible to both devices. This layer implements a GPU-CPU Remote Procedure Call (RPC) infrastructure, to be detailed in Section 4.3.

Finally, the GPUfs consistency layer is an OS kernel module running on the host CPU, which manages consistency between the host OS's CPU buffer cache and the GPU buffer caches, according to the file consistency model described above in §3.

The GPUfs file system is inspired by the Linux file system and buffer cache. We now examine its function in more detail.

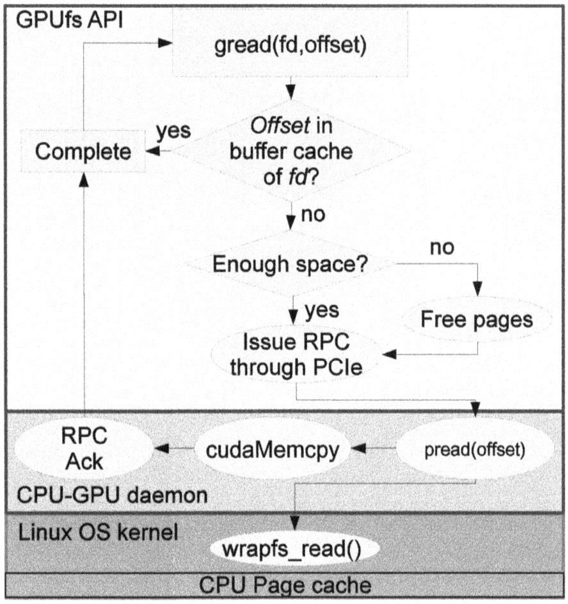

Figure 3. Functional diagram of a call to `gread`. Color scheme is the same as Figure 2.

4.1 File system operations

Open and close. GPUfs keeps track of open and recently closed files in several tables. Each open file has an entry in the *open file table*. This table holds a pointer to a radix tree indexing the file's pages. For each file, the table stores several file parameters, including the pathname and the CPU file descriptor used for data requests handled by the CPU. Finally, each entry stores a reference count of the number of threadblocks holding the file open.

When a file is closed its pages are retained in GPU memory until they are reclaimed for caching other data. The *closed file table* maintains pointers to the caches of closed files, and is a hash table indexed by file inode number in the CPU file system. Because of GPU hardware thread scheduling, files can appear to be closed while still in use by threadblocks that have yet to be scheduled (§3.2). To optimize for this case and to support data reuse in and across kernels, `gopen` checks the closed file table first, and moves the file cache back to the open file table.

Reads and writes. Reads and writes work as expected, first checking the cache for the relevant block, and forwarding requests to the CPU and allocating cache space as necessary. Figure 3 shows a functional summary of `gread`'s operation. Reads and writes exploit the GPU's fine-grain parallelism by using many threads to copy data or initialize pages to zero collaboratively. Reference counts protect pages during memory transfers.

When `gwrite` completes, each thread issues a memory fence to ensure that updates reach GPU memory, in case the GPU buffer cache needs to write the page back to the CPU. Otherwise, due to the GPU's weak memory consistency model, the data paged back via a DMA from the GPU memory might be left inconsistent because the writes might remain buffered in the GPU's L1 cache.

File management operations. File management operations such as `gunlink` and `gftruncate` each generate an RPC to the CPU to request the respective operation on the host. They also reclaim the file page cache on the GPU if necessary.

4.2 GPU buffer cache

Pages, page frames and page table. GPUfs manages file content at the granularity of a buffer cache *page*. This page size is configurable, though performance considerations typically dictate page sizes larger than OS-managed pages on the host CPU—e.g., 256KB, since GPU code often parallelizes the processing of a page across many threads in a threadblock (on the order of 256 threads). The ideal page size depends on empirical considerations explored further in §5. For efficiency, GPUfs pre-allocates pages in a large contiguous memory array, which we call the *raw data array*.

As in Linux, each page has an associated *pframe* structure holding metadata for that page, e.g., the size of the actual data in the page, dirty status, and others. Unlike Linux, pframes contain some file-related information, such as a unique file identifier used for lock-free traversal, and the page's offset in the file, because in GPUfs all pages are backed by a host OS file.

Pframes are allocated in an array separate from the pages themselves, but the ith pframe in this array holds metadata for the ith page in the raw data array, making it easy to translate in both directions, as needed in operations such as `gmunmap` and `gmsync`.

Per-file buffer cache. The buffer cache keeps replicas of previously accessed file content for later reuse. For simplicity the GPUfs buffer cache is per-file, not per-block device as in Linux, but future GPU support for direct access to storage devices may motivate reconsideration of this decision.

A dynamic radix tree indexes each file's buffer cache, enabling efficient page lookups given a file offset. Last-level nodes in the tree hold an array of *fpage* structures, each with a reference to a corresponding pframe. The fpages manage concurrent access to the respective pframes: each holds a read/write reference count and a spinlock, together preventing concurrent access by mutually exclusive operations such as initialization, read/write access, and paging out. The fpages are allocated not by reference, but by value within radix tree nodes. We use in-place data structures to avoid pointer traversal and minimize memory allocations, even though all dynamic memory is managed by GPUfs via special allocators.

Buffer cache management. CPUs handle buffer cache management tasks in a daemon thread, keeping costly activities such as flushing dirty pages out of an application's performance path. GPUs unfortunately have a scheduling-related weakness that makes daemon threads inefficient, affecting the performance of all GPU applications including those not using GPUfs. GPU threadblocks are non-preemptive, so a daemon would require its own threadblock. This dedicated threadblock could be either an independent, constantly running GPU kernel, or it could be part of each GPU application. The former approach reduces performance by permanently consuming a portion of GPU hardware resources, whereas the latter breaks the correctness of GPU applications that rely on the availability of a specific number of threadblocks for execution. Alternatively, offloading GPU cache management to a CPU daemon is impractical on existing hardware due to the lack of atomic operations over a PCIe bus, as explained later in §4.3.

Organizing the file system to avoid asynchronous GPU-initiated activity has important design consequences, such as the need to optimize the paging algorithm for speed. GPUfs performs paging as a part of regular file operations such as `gwrite`, with the GPUfs code hijacking the calling thread to perform paging. To keep paging fast, GPUfs does not use replacement policies that perform a variable amount of work, such as the clock algorithm [5].

GPUfs implements a FIFO-like policy by tracking allocation of last-level radix tree nodes. Newly allocated nodes are placed at the head of a doubly-linked list. When a thread needs to evict pages back to the CPU, it performs a lock-free traversal of this list to reclaim a desired number of pages from a particular file.

To choose the file whose pages will be reclaimed, GPUfs uses a policy similar to Linux's. GPUfs first looks at closed files, which are not in use so their content can be evicted with lower performance penalty for the running application. Furthermore, their pages are clean, so they can be reclaimed without GPU-CPU communication.[2] GPUfs then looks for pages from read-only open files, and as a last resort chooses pages from writable open files.

Lock-free buffer cache access. The buffer cache radix tree is a major contention point among threads accessing the same file. These accesses must be synchronized to avoid data races, such as concurrent attempts to initialize pages belonging to the same intermediate node, or node deletion due to page reclamation, which may be performed concurrently with page lookup.

GPUfs uses lock-free reads and locked updates, similar to Linux's seqlocks [9]. Updates maintain the radix-tree invariants used by readers, and all fields are initialized before a new node becomes visible to readers. Reads can fail, in which case they retry. GPUfs retries once without locking, then locks on its third attempt. To check that the page found is correct, GPUfs assigns a unique identifier to each radix tree during initialization, then propagates this identifier to every page referenced by the tree. This identifier, combined with the page offset, uniquely identifies the page.

The paging algorithm also uses lock-free reads on a doubly linked list used as a FIFO queue.

4.3 GPU-CPU Remote Procedure Call

GPUfs implements an RPC protocol to coordinate data transfers between the CPU and GPU. The GPU serves as a client that issues requests to a file server running on the host CPU. This GPU-as-client design contrasts with the traditional GPU-as-coprocessor programming model, reversing the roles of CPU and GPU.

The challenge of implementing an efficient RPC protocol lies in the CPU/GPU memory consistency model. GPU consistency models are tailored to the bulk-synchronous GPU programming model, where GPU-CPU communications traditionally occur only at kernel invocation boundaries and not while the kernel is running. Except at these points, CPU/GPU consistency is not guaranteed. Our RPC system is thus not currently portable to all GPUs, but relies on hardware providing the following consistency features.

1. **GPU-CPU memory fences.** GPU file read and write requests must be delivered to the CPU while the GPU kernel is running. This is only possible if consistent updates of the CPU-GPU write-shared memory can be enforced in both directions.
2. **GPU cache bypass.** To allow consistent reads of GPU memory from the running GPU kernel, after this memory has been updated by CPU-initiated DMA transfers, GPU reads must either invalidate or bypass the GPU's L1 and L2 caches.

The OpenCL [7] standard, and consequently AMD's discrete GPUs, currently do not support these features. Hybrid AMD GPUs are adding support for the first feature, but are not yet available. Only NVIDIA GPUs currently satisfy all of our requirements.

Challenges due to hardware constraints. RPC implementation is complicated by the lack of atomic operations over the PCIe bus. The new PCIe-III standard includes atomics, but implementation is optional and we know of no hardware currently supporting it.

This limitation precludes the use of efficient one-side communication protocols. A CPU cannot reliably lock and copy a page from GPU memory, for example, without GPU code being involved in acknowledging that the page has been locked. Consequently, the current implementation must resort to a less efficient message-passing protocol for synchronization.

[2] For clarity we omit some technical details on handling dirty files on close.

Today's GPUs also lack a signal-like mechanism accessible to applications, to notify a host CPU process of events originating on the GPU. The current API offers the CPU only coarse-grained notifications when entire GPU kernels or memory transfers complete, and do not allow code *within* a GPU kernel to send notifications. The CPU must therefore poll the GPU-CPU shared memory region continuously to detect RPC requests from the GPU.

RPC protocol implementation. GPU-CPU communications in GPUfs follow a synchronous, stateless client-server protocol, where the GPU sends requests to the CPU and waits for the CPU to acknowledge the request's completion. The RPC request channel is a FIFO queue in write-shared memory, which the CPU polls for requests. Each GPU in the system has a separate RPC request queue, managed exclusively by the GPU that owns that queue.

The GPU uses its request queue only to send commands: when the GPU issues a bulk transfer request such as a bulk data read or write, the CPU initiates a DMA-based bulk data transfer directly to or from the respective GPU buffer cache pages, using source or destination pointers supplied by GPU code. The CPU then notifies the GPU when the transfer completes.

The RPC queue usually contains multiple concurrent requests that, in principle, CPU code could handle in parallel. Our implementation uses a single-threaded, event-based design on the host to restrict the GPU-related CPU load to one CPU, simplify synchronization, and to avoid overwhelming the disk subsystem with concurrent requests. Our implementation thus currently orders file accesses, but data transfers to and from the GPU use multiple asynchronous CPU-GPU channels to utilize full-duplex DMA and overlap GPU-CPU transfers with disk accesses.

4.4 File consistency management

The current prototype implements the locality-optimized file consistency model described in Section 3, though currently only for the common cases of files opened in either read-only (`O_RDONLY`) or write-once mode (`O_GWRONCE`, see §3.2). The GPUfs prototype does not yet implement the diff-and-merge protocol required to support general write-sharing, and thus currently supports only one writer at a time.

If a GPU is caching the contents of a closed file, this cache must be invalidated if the file is opened for write or unlinked by another GPU or CPU. GPUfs propagates such invalidations lazily, if and when the GPU caching this stale data later reopens the file. We call this strategy lazy because closing a file on one GPU or CPU does not actively push an invalidation to other GPUs caching the file. The GPUfs API currently offers no direct way to push changes made on one GPU to another GPU, except when the latter reopens the file. Supporting such invalidations without PCI atomics would require GPUs to run daemon threads waiting for such an invalidation signal, an overhead we wish to avoid (see §4.2).

GPUfs uses WRAPFS [28], a stackable passthru file system, on the CPU to implement file consistency. WRAPFS is a Linux module that introduces a thin software layer on top of any file system, enabling interposition on calls to the underlying file system. We modified WRAPFS to implement our consistency protocol, enabling seamless integration of GPUfs with unmodified CPU programs. The CPU-side GPUfs daemon communicates with this modified WRAPFS module via a special character device. This device is used solely to update and query file state to implement file consistency, and provides no access to actual file content, thereby leaving the host OS's file access policies uncompromised. We do not currently protect against denial-of-service by misbehaved applications via buffer cache invalidation, however.

4.5 Implementation limitations

GPUs contain hardware translation and protection mechanisms that prevent GPU kernels launched by one CPU process from accessing the GPU memory of kernels launched by other processes. Today's GPUs do not offer software interfaces to control this memory protection hardware, however. A GPUfs instance can therefore serve only a single CPU process, and GPUfs cannot share state across GPU invocations by different host processes. For the same reason, GPUfs cannot protect the contents of its GPU buffer caches from corruption by the application it serves. Such features may become feasible once GPU vendors offer appropriate interfaces.

GPUfs does preserve file access protection at the host OS level, however. The host OS prevents a GPUfs application from opening host files the application doesn't have permission to access, and it denies writes of dirty blocks back to the host file system if the GPUfs application has opened the file read-only.

5. Evaluation

We evaluate GPUfs on a SuperMicro server system featuring two 4-core Intel Xeon L5630 CPUs at 2.13GHz with 12MB L3 cache per CPU, and four NVIDIA TESLA C2075 GPUs, each with 6 GB of GDDR5 memory. We run Ubuntu Linux kernel 3.0.0-27, with CUDA SDK 5.0, GPU driver 304.54. GPUfs is mounted atop a regular disk partition; the disk is a 500GB WDC WD5003, 7200RPM. The performance as reported by '`hdparm -t -T`' is 6,600MB/s and 132MB/s for cached and disk reads respectively.

We evaluate the system's performance and utility with several microbenchmarks, and also present two more realistic applications. For every data point we report the arithmetic mean of 5 executions after one warm up, unless stated otherwise. In all experiments we found the standard deviation of the results to be less than 1%.

One important property shared by all the test workloads is that their GPUfs implementation required almost no CPU code: they were entirely implemented in the GPU kernel. For all the workloads, the CPU code is identical, save the name of the GPU kernel to invoke. This is a remarkable contrast with standard GPU development, which always requires substantial CPU programming effort. From our experience we found it significantly easier to develop self-contained GPU programs, and believe that self-contained GPU programming will enable broader adoption of GPUs.

5.1 Microbenchmarks

The microbenchmarks below examine basic system performance and its sensitivity to several important configuration parameters.

5.1.1 Sequential file read

We first evaluate the effect of page size on sequential read performance. The benchmark transfers a single 1.8 GB file, in three ways: (a) reading data from the GPU kernel via GPUfs, (b) using the CUDA memory transfer API in chunks the same size as a GPUfs page (CUDA pipeline), and (c) reading the whole file in one chunk and transferring it to the GPU in one CUDA API call.

The GPU file reading kernel runs with 28 threadblocks (twice the number of active multiprocessors in the GPU), where each threadblock maps pages from a contiguous range in the file. Each threadblock maps one page at a time, until the total 64MB of data is mapped. The number of map requests depends on the page size. The data itself is not accessed, but the pages are fetched from the CPU page cache into the GPU buffer cache. The threadblock then closes the file and exits. GPU file access is not strictly sequential because the order of reads by different threadblock is non-deterministic. We do not anticipate any measurable effect from these non-sequential reads, however, because the file data is cached in CPU memory and fits in the GPU page cache.

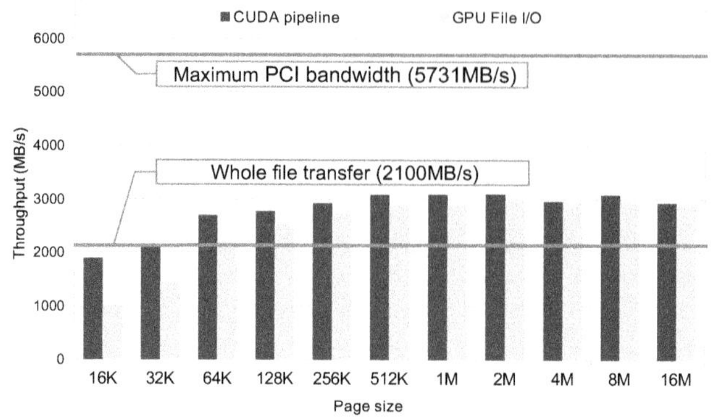

Figure 4. Sequential read performance as a function of the page size. The red line is the maximum achievable PCI bandwidth on this hardware configuration. Higher is better.

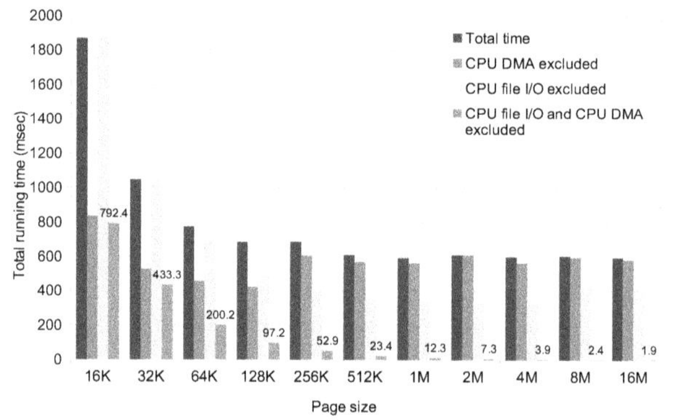

Figure 5. Contribution of different factors to the file I/O performance as a function of the page size. Lower is better.

The CPU code uses `pread` to read each chunk of the file into pinned CPU memory allocated with `cudaHostMalloc`, then issues an asynchronous `cudaMemcpy` to enqueue a DMA transfer request for that chunk, then proceeds to the next chunk (except in the whole file transfer case in which there is only one big chunk). Dividing the file into chunks overlaps file access latency with DMA data transfers to the GPU. An alternative implementation, which copies file content directly from the CPU page cache exposed via `mmap`, performs worse because it prevents CUDA from optimizing DMA transactions and forces `cudaMemcpy` to be synchronous.

The graph in Figure 4 shows read bandwidth for different page sizes. As expected, small GPUfs pages (less than 64KB) result in low performance, and increasing page size increases performance, with diminishing returns after 512 KB. Reading entire files, a common practice among GPU programmers expecting larger transfers to amortize data transfer overheads most effectively, is in fact less efficient than breaking reads into chunks, as chunks allow overlap of `pread` from the CPU page cache with PCI data transfer. The CUDA pipeline implementation appears to achieve the maximum possible file-to-GPU transfer performance on this machine.

GPUfs outperforms simple CUDA whole file reads at 64 KB pages and higher, and achieves on average within 5% of the bandwidth of the hand-pipelined version, a cost we consider to be a reasonable tradeoff for the convenience GPUfs offers.

Figure 5 breaks down the timing of the microbenchmark, by eliminating PCI data transfer time while leaving only the RPC

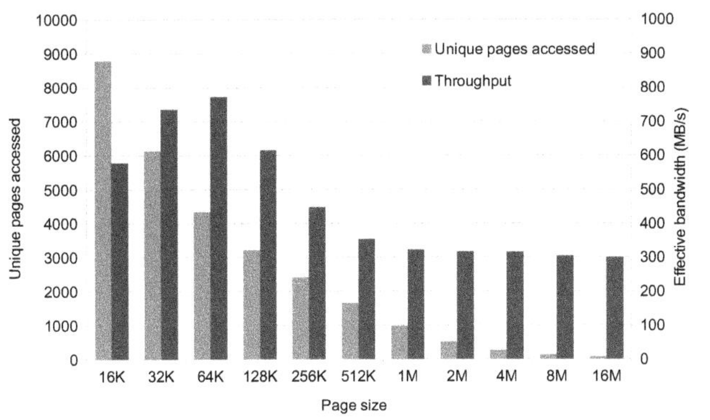

Figure 6. Random read/write performance as a function of page size. Higher is better.

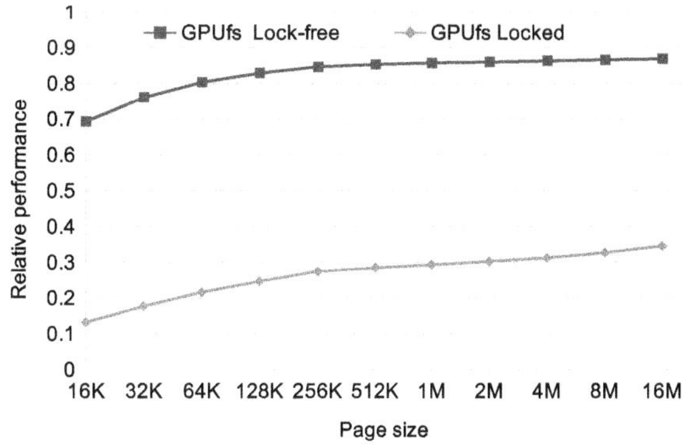

Figure 7. Buffer cache access performance with and without lock-free radix tree traversal, normalized by the raw memory access time.

traffic, eliminating CPU file reads, and eliminating both. The graph shows latency, where lower is better.

Execution time with small pages is dominated by the DMA transfers, which copy too little data per transaction, and by GPUfs API costs. I/O operations become fully overlapped with GPUfs buffer cache code execution for pages larger than 64KB. We see that total page cache access overhead (the rightmost labeled column) diminishes proportionally to page size. This is because the total amount of memory mapped by each threadblock is fixed while the page size changes, so the number of map requests performed by each threadblock is reduced as the page size grows. For pages larger than 128K the CPU page cache becomes the main bottleneck.

5.1.2 Random file read

This experiment shows the performance of random file access for different page sizes. This kernel is invoked with 112 threadblocks, where each threadblock reads 32 32KB data blocks from random offsets in a 1GB file, for a total of 112 MB read. The kernel uses `gread` to read the data into a 32KB array allocated in the GPU on-die scratchpad memory. Unlike `gmmap`, `gread` is not constrained in size to a single cache page, hence it is more appropriate for accessing file data at random offsets. Occasionally, different threadblocks may access the same page and fetch it from the GPU buffer cache. Time measurements are an average over 8 runs.

Figure 6 shows that as with sequential reads, small pages lead to bad performance, but now large pages also lead to bad performance. Small pages fail to amortize transfer costs, while large pages transfer too much data that is not actually read by the application. 64KB achieves the best performance in this test.

We calculate effective throughput in this experiment assuming an ideal case of exactly 112MB of data transferred. To support random accesses from GPU code without GPUfs, a GPU program would typically transfer the whole 1GB and perform the random accesses in GPU memory. Assuming the maximum observed throughput of 3100MB/s (see Figure 4), using only one tenth of the total 1GB of transferred data results in an effective random-access throughput of only 310 MB/s, comparable to GPUfs's worst performance using very large pages. Further, without GPUfs, random access to files whose size exceeds the GPU's physical memory is complex and inefficient in hand-coded GPU programs, often requiring frequent, brief kernel invocations between each random access. GPUfs eliminates from the application the design and implementation complexity required to handle such cases efficiently.

In the above experiments, a 128KB page size achieves a reasonable balance between sequential and random access performance. The optimal page size in general depends on application access pattern, however. In the current implementation, in which GPUfs is deployed on a per-application basis, page size may easily be tailored to the particular application's access patterns if necessary.

5.1.3 Buffer cache access performance

As the "GPUfs-lock-free" case in Figure 7 shows, GPUfs achieves 85–88% of raw memory access performance when accessing files in the GPU buffer cache, for 128KB pages or larger. In this experiment we invoke 112 threadblocks, each reading 64MB of data into the GPU's on-die scratchpad memory in chunks of 16KB. The baseline implementation reads data directly from the GPU's main memory, without using the GPUfs API. The GPUfs implementation reads data from the cached file via `gread`, passing to `gread` a direct pointer to the destination buffer in scratchpad memory. The file is fully prefetched into the GPU page cache by another previously invoked kernel, excluding PCI transfer time from the measurements. We randomized the memory accesses so that every 16KB chunk is read from a different file location, to cause non-trivial contention on the buffer cache data structure.

This workload mimics the behavior of linear algebra kernels, for example, which perform tiled operations on large matrices, prefetching data to be processed into scratchpad memory.

We ran this experiment with a locked traversal of the buffer cache's radix trees, for comparison against our default lock-free implementation. As described in §4.2, we normally use the lock-free traversal to access each page, resorting to locking only in cases of high contention. When file data is fully resident in the buffer cache, GPUfs locks the tree rarely, as confirmed later in Table 2. As a result, Figure 7 shows that the lock-free protocol performs nearly 3× better than the locked protocol across various page sizes.

5.1.4 Matrix-vector product

We run a simple single-precision matrix-vector product kernel to highlight two key benefits of the file system API: automatic data transfer pipelining and code simplification.

This test reads an input matrix and vector from files, and writes the result to an output file. We compare three implementations: one using GPUfs, one that explicitly implements double buffering to overlap the PCI data transfer and the kernel execution (CUDA naïve in Figure 8), and an optimized version of the latter (CUDA optimized). The GPUfs implementation does not call the CUDA host-side API, employing `gmmap` to read the data in the kernel, `gftruncate` to truncate the output file at the start, `gwrite` to write the output, and finally `gfsync` to synchronize the data to disk. The GPUfs buffer cache is sized to 2 GB, with 2MB pages. The "naïve" version implements a simple pipeline, splitting the file

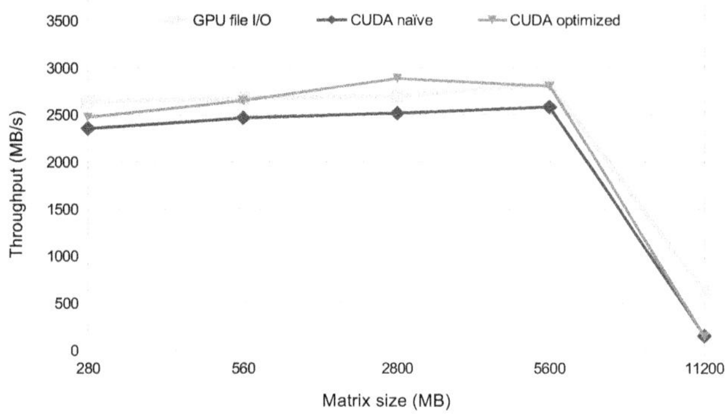

Figure 8. Matrix-vector product for large matrices

into four chunks and processing each chunk independently, overlapping the file read, data transfer and kernel execution between them. Note that the chunk size depends on the size of the input, which is convenient because every GPU kernel invocation may use the same number of threads. The optimized version is similar, but the chunk size is fixed at 70 MB and there are 16 independently processed chunks. Similarly to the CUDA naïve version, each chunk is processed separately, and the file read, data transfer and kernel execution are overlapped between the chunks. Both implementations run the same code for computing the inner-product.

We fix the input vector length to 128K elements, and vary the matrix size from a few megabytes up to 11GB. The largest input does not fit in the GPU's memory, and barely fits into the CPU's RAM. The GPUfs version requires no special treatment for this case, however. While this workload is entirely limited by the PCIe bus bandwidth, and for the largest inputs by the disk bandwidth, it is representative of many kernels that need to read data from disk as part of a large processing pipeline.

Figure 8 shows that the GPUfs based implementation outperforms the double-buffering implementation, achieving maximum PCI bandwidth equivalent to reading sequential files (see Figure 4). The main reason for the performance benefit is that the non-GPUfs code reads the input in large chunks (1GB each), which sometimes causes slowdowns due spurious paging of the CPU buffer cache, stalling the CPU-GPU transfer pipeline. GPUfs performs many shorter reads, due to the 2MB page size in this experiment, and the performance irregularities are smoothed by the fine-grained pipelining performed under the hood by the CPU's RPC daemon.

When file size exceeds available CPU buffer cache (the last data point in the graph), performance falls as the workload becomes disk bound. In this performance regime, GPUfs outperforms both CUDA versions by a factor of 4. The pinned memory allocated for large transfer buffers for the CUDA implementations competes with the CPU buffer cache, slowing it down significantly.

On the other hand, we observe no slowdown for inputs exceeding the size of the GPU buffer cache (larger than 2GB). The FIFO-like replacement policy employed by GPUfs appears to offer adequate efficiency for such streaming workloads.

5.2 Application benchmarks

We now consider two more realistic I/O intensive workloads: image search, and a "grep"-like search of text files. Both applications have highly data-dependent, unbounded working sets that dynamically change during computations. Such dynamic data dependencies are challenging to handle in GPU programs without GPUfs.

Buffer cache size	Time (s)	Pages reclaimed	Lock-free accesses	Locked accesses
2G	53	0	1,088,838	21,516
1G	69	11,509	547,819	574,463
0.5G	99	38,317	176,758	1,351,903

Table 2. Impact of the buffer cache size on the running time and locking behavior for the image search workload. Locked access count also includes unlocked retries.

5.2.1 Finding approximately matching images

The first application's input is a set of query images and several image databases containing many small images. The goal is to find which databases contain images matching the query images, where a match is defined by a threshold on a similarity metric, in our case Euclidian distance. While each image may be present in several databases, the databases must be scanned in a predefined order and only the first match output for a given query image. This process is representative of large-scale image registration tasks, e.g., when processing aerial photographs while attempting to find a matching image in a specific region first.

We can easily parallelize this problem by dynamically or statically splitting the input images between the threadblocks. The databases or/and the input set may not fit in GPU memory, however. Thus, the decision of which database to load and when must be done at runtime depending on the outcome of prior matching attempts. For example, if all the matching images are located at the beginning of the first database, the amount of data to be transferred is much lower than simply transferring all of the databases at once.

Without GPU access to the file system, the CPU must transfer the databases to the GPU first. To avoid redundant PCI transfers, the CPU is likely to split the databases into chunks, small enough so that the amount of redundant data transferred would be negligible, but large enough to amortize the overheads of GPU invocation on each chunk. This heuristic is not only suboptimal and introduces additional overheads, but significantly complicates the code. Furthermore, before starting the kernel to process the next chunk, all previously matched images must be removed from the input set, requiring additional program logic to compact the input array.

GPUfs streamlines this task, making the implementation almost trivial and closely following the design for CPU code. Both the OpenMP parallel CPU and GPUfs-based versions of the program are about 130 ± 10 LOC, counting semicolons.[3] The associated CPU code for the GPU version is only a single line—the GPU kernel invocation.

In our synthetic workload, the images in the input and the databases are randomly generated. Each image is represented as a 4K-element vector. The input contains 2,016 images, amounting to 31.5MB of raw data. We use 3 database files, of sizes 383, 357 and 400 MB, containing about 25,000 images each. The images from the input are injected at random locations in the databases. We invoke the kernel with 28 threadblocks, 512 threads per threadblock.

We measure raw performance using a query set containing only images with no matches in the databases, forcing all databases to be read completely. We flush the OS page cache before each experiment. We set the GPU buffer cache size to 2GB, enough to keep all databases in GPU memory. The GPU throughput achieved is 18GFLOP/s, twice as fast as an 8-core CPU run using OpenMP.

Changing the buffer cache size. We examine the effect of the buffer cache size on program performance in Table 2. Observe that as the amount of available memory decreases, the ratio between lock-free and locked accesses drops due to the paging algorithm's

[3] We tried David Wheeler's SLOCCount but it fails to parse CUDA code.

Input	CPUx8	#GPUs			
		1	2	3	4
No match	119s	53s	27s (2.0×)	18s (2.9×)	13s (4.1×)
Exact match	100s	40s	21s (1.9×)	14s (2.9×)	11s (3.6×)

Table 3. Approximate image matching performance. Speedup for multi-GPU runs relative to a single GPU are given in parentheses.

Input	CPUx8	GPU-GPUfs	GPU-vanilla
Linux source	6.07h	53m (6.8×)	50m (7.2×)
Shakespeare	292s	40s (7.3×)	40s (7.3×)
LOC (semicolon)	80	140 (+52)	178

Table 4. GPU exact string match "grep -w" performance.

attempts to free pages being used. Each threadblock runs independently of the others, and may follow different execution paths, for example accessing the databases relevant to the set of input images it is processing. File access patterns among different threadblocks quickly desynchronizes, a well known effect in large-scale parallel environments, requiring careful implementation and possibly redundant work to avoid.

Finally, we evaluate our implementation's scalability by splitting the query list equally among up to 4 GPUs. We do not evaluate the diff-and-merge algorithm for write-sharing, but the system interaction with the WRAPFS-based consistency daemon is included (as is the case for all experiments presented in this section).

This set of experiments is performed with preliminary warmup in order to prefetch the data into the CPU buffer cache and highlight the scaling capabilities of the system. As confirmed in the experiments in Table 3, GPUfs shows near linear scaling with increasing GPU count because of the lightweight consistency protocol. The first run ("No match") shows the performance of the more regular workload, for which GPUfs shows ideal scaling. The second run is irregular because the number of exact matches per processor is different, and static input partitioning does not scale as well in either the GPUfs or CPU versions. All 4 GPUs together outperform a single CPU execution by about a factor of 9.

The benefits of dynamic database loading becomes apparent as we relax the matching threshold, allowing searches to terminate earlier, and occasionally eliminating the need to accesses lower-priority databases altogether. Runtime decreases as expected; in the degenerate case where images always match the first entry in the first database, runtime falls by 400×—from 53 seconds to a minimum of 130ms—leaving only the costs of initialization, invocation, and matching the query list with the first database page.

5.2.2 Exact string matching in text files

The last experiment is an implementation of a constrained version of grep on a GPU. Given a dictionary and a set of text files, for each word in the dictionary, the program determines how many times and in which files it appears.

This application is conceptually similar to image matching, but with two key differences. The parallelization strategy is different because words are typically short (up to 32 symbols), so each GPU thread is assigned one word, instead of one image per threadblock in the previous case. Second, the output buffer becomes unbounded, so we need to write the output frequently to flush the per-threadblock internal buffer.

This experiment counts the frequencies of modern English words in two datasets: the works of William Shakespeare, and the Linux kernel source code. We search for a specific dictionary of 58,000 modern English words[4], within the complete works of Shakespeare as a single 6MB text file[5], and within the Linux 3.3.1 kernel source containing about 33,000 files for 524MB in total. To simplify the parsing of the dictionary file by a GPU, we reformat the dictionary to align every word on a 32 byte boundary; none of the words in the dictionary exceed that length. The list of input files is itself specified in a file.

Each threadblock opens one file at a time, then each thread searches for a subset of the dictionary that it is allocated to match. Matched words are printed out together with the file name and match count into an internal per-threadblock output buffer, which is then periodically flushed into a global output file. Various text parsing and formatted output tasks required us to implement limited GPU versions of the `sprintf`, `strtok`, `strlen`, `strcat` functions not normally available to GPU code.

This workload puts extremely high pressure on GPUfs because most of the files are fairly small (few kilobytes on average), leading to frequent calls to `gopen` and `gclose`. Since the progress of each threadblock depends on the actual number of matching words in its input subset, the number of concurrently open files eventually reaches the number of concurrently running threadblocks.

As a point of reference we compared two other implementations: a simple CPU program performing the same task on 8 cores (using OpenMP), and a "vanilla" GPU version implemented without GPUfs. Both implementations prefetch the contents of the input files into a large memory buffer first, then do not read from the file system during the matching phase.

The vanilla GPU version pre-allocates a large output buffer in the GPU memory (5GB—all remaining GPU memory), but if it overflows, the GPU kernel crashes. In general, our vanilla GPU version is more limited than the one using GPUfs because it conservatively assumes that the inputs and outputs fit in the GPU's physical memory. Large file support would substantially complicate the implementation, whereas the GPUfs-based version automatically supports arbitrarily large input files.

We present the results (no warmup) in Table 4. Even for such a file-system intensive workload, a single GPU outperforms the 8-core CPU by 6.8×. The GPUfs version is only 9% slower than the vanilla GPU implementation on the Linux kernel input, but the two versions perform similarly on one large input file. The GPUfs-based code is shorter than the vanilla version if we exclude string parsing and formatted output functions (52 lines of code), which are not used in the vanilla version because they are executed on a CPU as a part of a post-processing phase.

We emphasize, however, that no serious effort has been made to optimize either the GPU or CPU version. The main point of this exercise is to highlight the utility of the file system API on GPUs, which opens up new ways to explore the computing power of these massively parallel processors.

6. Related work

To our knowledge GPUfs is the first extension of the file system abstraction to modern GPU architectures. This work touches on many areas from classic OS design and efficient lock-free synchronization to GPU architectures and programming techniques.

General-purpose GPU computing. The research community has focused considerable effort on the problem of providing a general-purpose programming interface to the specialized hardware supported by GPUs (GPGPU). GPGPU computing frameworks such as CUDA [20], OpenCL [7], and others [3, 4, 8, 17, 25] provide

[4] http://www.mieliestronk.com/wordlist.html

[5] http://www.gutenberg.org/ebooks/100

an expressive platform, but none provide any way for GPUs to use host OS services in general, or file system access in particular.

I/O for GPUs. GPUDirect from NVIDIA allows GPUs to access certain storage and network devices without the mediation of the host OS. This technology is exposed via proprietary, low-level hardware-specific interfaces, and does not provide higher-level abstractions, such as a file system API.

Other hardware architectures. The Cell processor [12] pioneered the integration of parallel accelerators into the OS, allowing system calls and file accesses from its Synergistic Processor Elements (SPEs). The SPEs share the same die as the main processor, offering a high bandwidth channel with memory performance more like multicore SMPs than today's discrete GPUs. Also, we are unaware of any published work analyzing file system design tradeoffs or I/O intensive data parallel applications, the focus of this paper.

Intel's Xeon-Phi [11] is a PCIe-attached accelerator sharing the NUMA characteristics of discrete GPUs, but built of more traditional CPU cores that can run a full OS such as Linux. To our knowledge Xeon-Phi does not expose the host's file system to software on the accelerator. We expect many aspects of GPUfs to be relevant to Xeon-Phi systems, particularly the NUMA-driven need to maximize file cache locality. Matuso et al [15] presented a file system layer for Xeon-phi, providing access to the host file system from the card. This design does not explore file I/O in fine-grain data-parallel workloads, however, one of the main foci of our work.

Host OS support for GPU programming. Stuart [24] prototyped CPU-GPU communication via RPC, enabling GPU software to make host system calls. GPUfs includes such a mechanism, but focuses on coping with data parallelism and locality at design level via its GPU buffer cache, to avoid redundant data transfers and GPU-CPU interaction.

Hydra [27] and PTask [22] explore dataflow frameworks for GPU programming, offering host CPU software an API with which to compose GPU modules. GPUfs in contrast focuses on the complementary goal of enhancing the API available to GPU code.

Kato [13] introduces a host OS driver for GPUs that facilitates the OS-managed sharing of GPU resources, allowing different CPU processes to share GPU memory for example. We hope to leverage this complementary functionality to enable future cross-application file system support in GPUfs.

Simplifying data management in GPUs. The complexity of data management in discrete GPUs is well recognized. Gelado [6] suggested ADSM, an asymmetric, CPU-centric shared memory [6]. ADSM emulates a unified address space between CPUs and GPUs, alleviating management problems. Unlike GPUfs, ADSM does not support communications with a running kernel, and also introduces new accelerator-specific abstractions, which GPUfs avoids.

Heterogeneous and multi-core OS design. A number of researchers considered the general problem of building OSes for heterogeneous architectures. The Helios operating system [19] targets heterogeneous systems with multiple programmable devices. However, Helios requires the processors to expose interfaces to three basic hardware primitives: a timer, an interrupt controller, and the ability to catch exceptions. These services are currently not available on most GPUs, making Helios inapplicable to such architectures. Furthermore, Helios does not account for the specifics of massively parallel SIMD architectures, as GPUfs does.

The Barrelfish OS [2] treats the hardware as a network of independent, heterogeneous cores communicating via RPC. Again, it is not clear if a GPU could run Barrelfish directly. Philosophically, Barrelfish argues for a ground-up OS redesign based on message passing. GPUfs takes a more pragmatic view of applications interacting through the file system, keeping the host OS largely intact.

Lock-free algorithms. Lock-free algorithms are a well known technique in parallel programming [16]. Our algorithm was inspired by seqlocks [9] and read-copy update (RCU) [18]. We are unaware of any prior radix tree designs with lock-free traversal available for GPUs.

7. Conclusions

This paper describes the design and implementation of GPUfs, a file system API and implementation allowing data parallel GPU software to access host files directly. GPUfs extends the constrained GPU-as-coprocessor programming model, turning GPUs into first-class computing devices with full file I/O support. GPUfs exploits fine-grained parallelism and memory locality to offer a familiar and efficient file system for GPU programs, and simplifies GPU programming by hiding the complexities of low-level data movement between GPUs and CPUs and among GPUs. Our prototype shows that file system access for GPU kernels enables good performance and ease of development for applications that have not typically been considered suitable for GPU processing. GPUfs achieves good performance on today's architecture, and is likely to benefit from future hardware architecture advances.

Acknowledgments

This research was supported in part by NSF grants CNS-1017785 and CNS-1017206, by the Andrew and Erna Fince Viterbi Fellowship, and by a 2010 NVIDIA research award.

References

[1] Amittai Aviram, Shu-Chun Weng, Sen Hu, and Bryan Ford. Efficient system-enforced deterministic parallelism. In *Proceedings of the 9th USENIX Symposium on Operating Systems Design and Implementation*, October 2010.

[2] Andrew Baumann, Paul Barham, Pierre-Evariste Dagand, Tim Harris, Rebecca Isaacs, Simon Peter, Timothy Roscoe, Adrian Schüpbach, and Akhilesh Singhania. The Multikernel: A new OS architecture for scalable multicore systems. In *Proceedings of the ACM SIGOPS 22nd symposium on Operating Systems Principles*, pages 29–44, New York, NY, USA, 2009.

[3] Amr Bayoumi, Michael Chu, Yasser Hanafy, Patricia Harrell, and Gamal Refai-Ahmed. Scientific and Engineering Computing Using ATI Stream Technology. *Computing in Science and Engineering*, 11(6):92–97, 2009.

[4] Ian Buck, Tim Foley, Daniel Horn, Jeremy Sugerman, Kayvon Fatahalian, Mike Houston, and Pat Hanrahan. Brook for GPUs: Stream Computing on Graphics Hardware. *ACM Transactions on Graphics*, 23(3), August 2004.

[5] Wolfgang Effelsberg and Theo Haerder. Principles of database buffer management. *ACM Transactions on Database Systems*, 9(4):560–595, December 1984.

[6] Isaac Gelado, John E. Stone, Javier Cabezas, Sanjay Patel, Nacho Navarro, and Wen-mei W. Hwu. An asymmetric distributed shared memory model for heterogeneous parallel systems. In *Proceedings of the 15th International Conference on Architectural Support for Programming Languages and Operating Systems*, pages 347–358, New York, NY, USA, 2010.

[7] Khronos Group. *OpenCL - the open standard for parallel programming of heterogeneous systems.* `http://www.khronos.org/opencl`.

[8] Tianyi David Han and Tarek S. Abdelrahman. *hi*CUDA: a high-level directive-based language for GPU programming. In *Proceedings of the 2nd Workshop on General Purpose Processing on Graphics Processing Units (GPGPU-2)*, March 2009.

[9] Stephen Hemminger. fast reader/writer lock for gettimeofday 2.5.30, 2002. `http://lwn.net/Articles/7388/`.

[10] John H. Howard, Michael L. Kazar, Sherri G. Menees, David A. Nichols, M. Satyanarayanan, Robert N. Sidebotham, and Michael J. West. Scale and performance in a distributed file system. *ACM Transactions on Computing Systems*, 6(1), February 1988.

[11] *Intel Xeon-Phi Coprocessor: System Software Developers Guide*, November 2012. `http://www.intel.com/content/www/us/en/processors/xeon/xeon-phi-coprocessor-system-software-developers-guide.html`.

[12] J. A. Kahle, M. N. Day, H. P. Hofstee, C. R. Johns, T. R. Maeurer, and D. Shippy. Introduction to the Cell multiprocessor. *IBM Journal of Research and Development*, 49:589–604, July 2005.

[13] S. Kato, M. McThrow, C. Maltzahn, and S. Brandt. Gdev: First-class GPU resource management in the operating system. In *USENIX Annual Technical Conference*, June 2012.

[14] Walt Ligon and Rob Ross. Parallel i/o and the parallel virtual file system. In William Gropp, Ewing Lusk, and Thomas Sterling, editors, *Beowulf Cluster Computing with Linux*, pages 493–535. MIT Press, 2003.

[15] Yuki Matsuo, Taku Shimosawa, and Yutaka Ishikawa. A file I/O system for many-core based clusters. In *Proceedings of the 2nd International Workshop on Runtime and Operating Systems for Supercomputers*, pages 3:1–3:8, New York, NY, USA, 2012.

[16] Maurice Herlihy and Nir Shavit. *The Art of Multiprocessor Programming*. Morgan Kaufmann, 2008.

[17] Michael D. McCool and Bruce D'Amora. Programming using RapidMind on the Cell BE. In *SC '06: Proceedings of the 2006 ACM/IEEE conference on Supercomputing*, page 222, New York, NY, USA, 2006. ACM.

[18] Paul E. McKenney, Dipankar Sarma, Andrea Arcangeli, Andi Kleen, Orran Krieger, and Rusty Russell. Read-copy update. In *Ottawa Linux Symposium*, pages 338–367, June 2002.

[19] Edmund B. Nightingale, Orion Hodson, Ross McIlroy, Chris Hawblitzel, and Galen Hunt. Helios: heterogeneous multiprocessing with satellite kernels. In *SOSP '09: Proceedings of the 22nd ACM symposium on Operating systems principles*, 2009.

[20] *NVIDIA CUDA 4.2 Developer Guide*. `http://developer.nvidia.com/category/zone/cuda-zone`.

[21] NVIDIA's Next Generation CUDA Compute Architecture: Fermi, 2011. `http://www.nvidia.com/content/PDF/fermi_white_papers/NVIDIA_Fermi_Compute_Architecture_Whitepaper.pdf`.

[22] Christopher J. Rossbach, Jon Currey, Mark Silberstein, Baishakhi Ray, and Emmett Witchel. PTask: operating system abstractions to manage GPUs as compute devices. In *Proceedings of the Twenty-Third ACM Symposium on Operating Systems Principles*, pages 233–248, 2011.

[23] Livio Soares and Michael Stumm. FlexSC: flexible system call scheduling with exception-less system calls. In *Proceedings of the 9th USENIX conference on Operating systems design and implementation*, pages 1–8, Berkeley, CA, USA, 2010.

[24] Jeff A. Stuart, Michael Cox, and John D. Owens. GPU-to-CPU callbacks. In *Third Workshop on UnConventional High Performance Computing (UCHPC 2010)*, August 2010.

[25] Sain-Zee Ueng, Melvin Lathara, Sara S. Baghsorkhi, and Wen-Mei W. Hwu. CUDA-Lite: Reducing GPU Programming Complexity. In *LCPC 2008, 21th Annual Workshop on Languages and Compilers for Parallel Computing*, 2008.

[26] Bruce Walker, Gerald Popek, Robert English, Charles Kline, and Greg Thiel. The LOCUS distributed operating system. In *Proceedings of the ninth ACM symposium on Operating systems principles*, pages 49–70, New York, NY, USA, 1983.

[27] Yaron Weinsberg, Danny Dolev, Tal Anker, Muli Ben-Yehuda, and Pete Wyckoff. Tapping into the fountain of CPUs: on operating system support for programmable devices. In *13th International Conference on Architectural Support for Programming Languages and Operating Systems (ASPLOS '08)*, March 2008.

[28] E. Zadok and I. Bădulescu. A stackable file system interface for Linux. In *LinuxExpo Conference Proceedings*, pages 141–151, Raleigh, NC, May 1999.

DDOS: Taming Nondeterminism in Distributed Systems

Nicholas Hunt, Tom Bergan, Luis Ceze, Steven D. Gribble
Computer Science and Engineering, University of Washington
{nhunt,tbergan,luisceze,gribble}@cs.washington.edu

Abstract

Nondeterminism complicates the development and management of distributed systems, and arises from two main sources: the local behavior of each individual node as well as the behavior of the network connecting them. Taming nondeterminism effectively requires dealing with both sources.

This paper proposes DDOS, a system that leverages prior work on deterministic multithreading to offer: 1) space-efficient record/replay of distributed systems; and 2) fully deterministic distributed behavior. Leveraging deterministic behavior at each node makes outgoing messages strictly a function of explicit inputs. This allows us to record the system by logging just message's arrival time, not the contents. Going further, we propose and implement an algorithm that makes all communication between nodes deterministic by scheduling communication onto a global logical timeline.

We implement both algorithms in a system called DDOS and evaluate our system with parallel scientific applications, an HTTP/memcached system and a distributed microbenchmark with a high volume of peer-to-peer communication. Our results show up to two orders of magnitude reduction in log size of record/replay, and that distributed systems can be made deterministic with an order of magnitude of overhead.

Categories and Subject Descriptors C.2.4 [*Computer Communication Networks*]: Network Protocols and Distributed Systems; D.4.1 [*Operating Systems*]: Process Management; D.4.5 [*Operating Systems*]: Reliability

Keywords Distributed Systems, Reliability, Determinism, Record-and-Replay

1. Introduction

Nondeterminism makes the development of distributed systems difficult. Without the ability to precisely reproduce a buggy execution, it is challenging for developers of distributed applications to track down the root cause of a bug. Further, replicating distributed systems for fault tolerance is hard since nondeterminism can cause the replicas' executions to diverge. Ideally, the behavior of distributed systems would be solely a function of well-defined inputs.

However, nondeterminism is pervasive in distributed systems. Not only does each individual node encounter nondeterminism locally due to timing variations in the operating system and hardware, but the network connecting the nodes is also a major contributor: arbitrary messages can be lost or reordered. Without mechanisms to control both sources, it is exceptionally challenging to replicate distributed systems and to reproduce buggy distributed executions.

There are two main approaches to handling nondeterminism. The first is to *record* and later *replay* the nondeterminism, simplifying debugging by making executions repeatable. The second approach eliminates nondeterminism altogether by executing the program *deterministically* with respect to its explicitly specified inputs. This approach simplifies both debugging and fault-tolerant replication.

This paper describes DDOS, a system we built to explore the trade-offs between record/replay and determinism in distributed systems. In record/replay mode, DDOS generates space-efficient replay logs that can be used to replay an entire distributed system. In deterministic execution mode, the *entire distributed system is executed deterministically* with respect to inputs from outside the distributed system, such as external network packets and user input. To our knowledge, this is the first proposal for fully deterministic execution of arbitrary distributed systems.

Both implementations exploit local-node determinism as provided by prior work in dOS [4]. For record/replay, we observe that given local-node determinism, it is sufficient to record just the arrival time of internal node-to-node messages, and not the message's contents; local determinism guarantees that message contents will be regenerated deterministically during replay. For distributed determinism, we propose an algorithm for delivering internal node-to-node messages deterministically. When combined with local-node determinism, this algorithm guarantees deterministic distributed execution.

DDOS advances prior work in two ways. First, existing record/replay systems [10, 14, 18] often produce prohibitively large logs (multiple gigabytes per hour) because they work at the boundary of each local-node and thus need to record the contents and delivery times of internal network messages. DDOS generates space-efficient logs by exploiting local-node determinism to eliminate the need to log the contents of internal messages. DDOS leverages observations similar to those made by DejaVu [18], but because DejaVu is a full record/replay system, it is not able to achieve the considerable log size reductions that DDOS achieves by exploiting local-node determinism.

Second, existing deterministic execution systems have focused on multithreaded programs. These systems either support single-node determinism only [4, 5, 8] or support distributed systems with a limited communication model [1]. As part of DDOS, we propose and implement an algorithm to make inter-node communication fully deterministic and for arbitrary applications and communication patterns.

Our DDOS implementation supports *arbitrary* distributed POSIX-compatible applications—including applications with data races—without requiring changes to application binaries. Our evaluation shows that our record/replay mechanism can reduce the required

ASPLOS'13, March 16–20, 2013, Houston, Texas, USA.

log sizes by up to 70%, and that our deterministic execution mode imposes up to an order of magnitude overhead relative to nondeterministic execution—these overheads vary wildly with frequency and pattern of communication.

Finally, our evaluation demonstrates the following trade-off between record/replay and deterministic execution: the record/replay mechanisms in DDOS impose a lower performance overhead at the expense of larger logs, whereas the deterministic execution mechanisms lessens the space requirements for logs at the expense of performance.

1.1 Use Cases for Distributed Replay

Debugging. Debugging distributed systems is a daunting task. In addition to tracking down bugs that occur locally within a single node of the system, bugs in distributed systems can be dependent on deep communication chains involving a large number of nodes across the network. Local-node record/replay can help with the first class of bugs, but requires logging all communication between nodes, which can be prohibitive for some applications. Further, local-node record/replay does little to help find bugs of the second class because the root causes of these bugs are visible only when the entire distributed system is replayed as a unit. The space-efficient, full-system record/replay mode provided by DDOS makes this debugging technique more practical.

1.2 Use Cases for Distributed Determinism

Debugging. Determinism helps with debugging by making execution repeatable. For debugging, main difference between determinism and record/replay is that a deterministic system enforces a particular communication schedule between nodes, obviating the need to actually log this communication. The user can observe buggy behavior again by simply re-running the application with the same inputs.

Replication. A second application for distributed determinism is to enable replication of an *entire distributed system* for fault-tolerance. By instantiating multiple copies of a distributed system and replicating the inputs to all copies, distributed determinism guarantees that each replica evolves identically. Prior work on replicating distributed databases has shown that deterministic execution can remove the need for expensive cross-replica two-phase commit protocols, simplifying code and potentially improving performance [30].

1.3 Outline

The rest of this paper is organized as follows. Section 2 overviews the DDOS architecture and provides some background on dOS, which is used by the DDOS implementation. Sections 3 and 4 describe our high-level algorithms for distributed record/replay and deterministic execution. Section 5 describes implementation details of these algorithms. Section 6 offers a evaluation of our system, Section 7 summarizes related work, and Section 8 concludes.

2. DDOS Architecture

DDOS builds on dOS [4], which is an operating system that provides deterministic execution of single-node, multiprocess, multithreaded programs. The basic abstraction provided by dOS is a deterministic process group (DPG), which is a group of local threads and processes that execute as a single deterministic unit. In DDOS, each node of the distributed system executes within its own DPG, and the set of DPGs is collectively referred to as a *distributed DPG* (DDPG).

Sections 3 and 4 detail how we leverage the single-node determinism provided by DPGs. In the rest of this section, we summarize the semantics of DPGs, and then describe how DPGs are combined to form a DDPG.

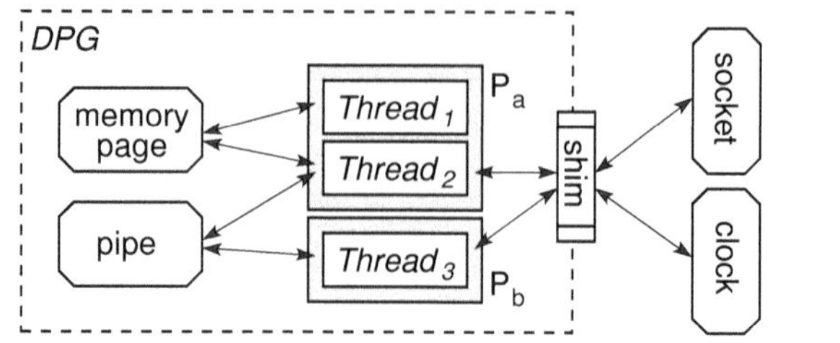

Figure 1. A Deterministic Process Group (from [4])

2.1 Deterministic Process Groups

A DPG is an abstraction that allows a group of multithreaded processes to execute deterministically on a single node. Specifically, DPGs provide a mechanism to partition the sources of nondeterminism that can affect a process into *internal* sources and *external* sources: internal sources of nondeterminism are eliminated from DPGs, but external sources of nondeterminism are fundamentally nondeterministic and cannot be eliminated. Examples of internal sources of nondeterminism include thread scheduling, hardware timing variations, and communication between threads involving pipes, shared-memory, local files, and so on. External sources of nondeterminism include reading physical clocks and communicating with processes outside of a DPG.

Additionally, dOS defines a *shim layer* API that allowed programmers to interpose on all external nondeterminism. Any time a DPG receives input from a nondeterministic external source, dOS funnels that event through the shim layer, allowing the shim programmer to control how that nondeterminism is introduced. For example, a shim may implement the record half of a record/replay mechanism by creating a log entry on every nondeterministic event.

Figure 1 shows an example of a DPG containing two processes and three threads communicating with each other using shared-memory and a pipe. DPGs guarantee this communication happens deterministically. Reading a physical clock or communicating over the network occurs outside of the DPG and is therefore nondeterministic, so this communication must first pass through the shim layer. To enable deterministic execution, dOS schedules a DPG's execution onto a deterministic logical timeline. The scheduling algorithm is described in [4]. dOS performs this scheduling in the operating system kernel, transparently to applications, allowing it to execute arbitrary, unmodified POSIX-compatible applications inside of a DPG.

2.2 Distributed DPGs

DDOS defines a distributed system as a set of deterministic process groups which may be distributed across many different physical machines. Hence, we call this set of DPGs a distributed DPG (DDPG). Each DPG can itself contain one or more multithreaded processes participating in the distributed system. Many DPGs can execute on the same physical machine, and processes not in any DPG can execute alongside DPGs on the same machine. In a DDPG, the network is partitioned into an *internal* network that connects all deterministic process groups in the DDPG, and an *external* network that connects the DDPG to external processes and machines.

Figure 2 shows an example of a DDPG. The DDPG shown is composed of three deterministic process groups executing on two different machines. All communication between DPGs 1, 2, and 3 will occur on the internal network. DDOS controls the internal network to implement either space-efficient record/replay (Section 3) or distributed determinism (Section 4). Communication with Process F, which is outside of the DDPG, occurs on the nondetermin-

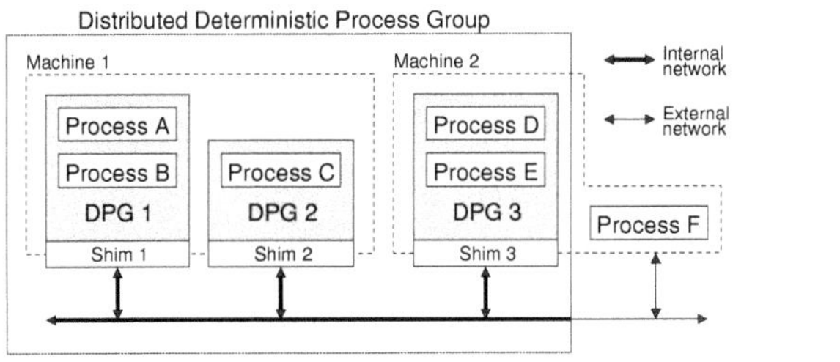

Figure 2. A Distributed DPG

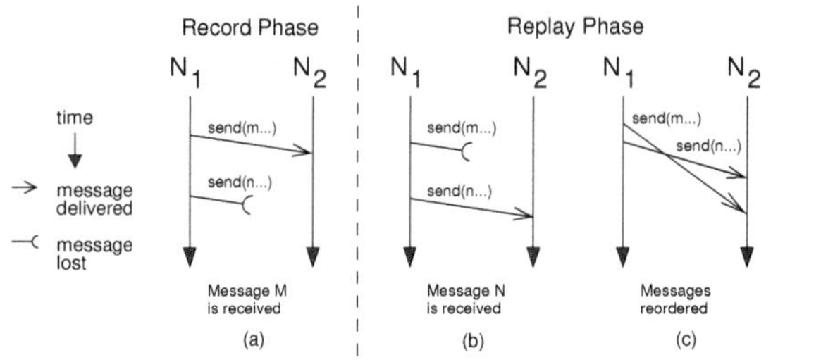

Figure 3. When messages are regenerated during replay, different UDP messages can be lost or reordered

istic external network. All messages received from the external network are considered nondeterministic input.

DDOS exposes the same POSIX-compatible sockets API that Linux provides. Distributed applications can run inside DDPGs without modification: record/replay and distributed determinism are both provided transparently by DDOS.

3. Record/Replay with DDPGs

This section describes our algorithm for space-efficient record/replay of DDPGs. To help understand the trade-offs, we first discuss how a traditional record/replay system would be implemented, and then describe our algorithm in comparison to the traditional approach.

3.1 Single-Node Record/Replay

A traditional approach to record/replay for distributed systems would record each node in the distributed system independently. To reproduce a buggy execution, the node on which the bug manifested would be replayed *in isolation* using the generated log to reproduce the nondeterminism encountered in the original run.

While replaying the failed nodes independently may be convenient, this approach suffers from two drawbacks. First, to ensure accurate replay, *all* network communication between nodes in the distributed system must be recorded. For some applications, the amount of internal communication is so large that this approach becomes infeasible. Second, some distributed system bugs can be understood only after looking at chains of communication between multiple nodes. This information is lost by single-node replay, making these multi-node bugs significantly more difficult to debug.

3.2 Distributed Record/Replay

DDOS records each node independently but replays the entire distributed system as a unit. In this approach, messages between nodes in the distributed system need not be recorded since they will be regenerated during replay. Instead, we record just two sources of nondeterminism at each node: 1) the logical arrival time of internal messages; and 2) all external inputs that any traditional record/replay system would record, including external network packets, clocks, and user input. During replay, we replace these sources of nondeterminism exactly as specified in the log.

To understand why replay is deterministic, recall that all nodes execute in DPGs. Thus, each node's execution evolves deterministically and therefore the network messages generated by each application will be deterministic: as long as internal messages and external input are delivered at the same logical time during replay, messages sent by a DPG will occur at a deterministic logical time and contain deterministic contents.

Reliable Channels. For reliable transport protocols such as TCP, messages sent by one endpoint will be received completely and in-order on the remote side; packet loss is handled transparently by the underlying protocol. During the record phase, a process that consumes data from the network can simply record the number of bytes read and the logical time the data was consumed. Replay looks at the recorded timestamp and waits for that logical time to arrive before receiving exactly the recorded number of bytes from the network.

Unreliable Channels. For unreliable datagram protocols such as UDP, message loss and reordering are exposed to the application. As a result, the network may drop or reorder a different set of datagrams during the record and replay phases, as shown in Figure 3. We handle this by appending a unique sequence number to all UDP messages during the record phase. This sequence number is stripped by the remote node on reception and written to the replay log. We then perform replay with a reliable connection and simulate dropped (or reordered) packets during replay by dropping (or buffering) unexpected messages on the receiving end.

Connection Management. Similar issues arise when establishing TCP connections during replay. Connections to internal addresses need to be reestablished during replay if they were successfully completed in the record phase. However, connection requests that succeeded in the original execution may be dropped during replay. We handle this by retrying connections during replay until they succeed.

Further, connection requests can be reordered by the network, causing them to be accepted in a different order in the record and replay phases. We avoid this by buffering new connections at the accepting node during replay to ensure that new connections are delivered to the application in the same order they were accepted during the record phase.

Dealing With Failures. Node failures due to program bugs are replayed deterministically. Node failures due to hardware crashes are also easily replayed: the node hits the end-of-log during replay, and stalls.

Hardware failures during replay are also possible. Although our approach drastically reduces the required log size for many applications, it requires replaying all nodes in a distributed system at once, increasing the possibility that some node will fail unexpectedly during replay (e.g., due to a hardware failure). Our system assumes no failures during replay: if a node fails during replay, the system must be restarted. We believe this is a reasonable assumptions because the typical use for record/replay is to observe a short segment of execution in a debugging setting. Another feasible solution would detect node failure during replay and then restart that node from a checkpoint, as discussed later in Section 4.3.

Reconfigurable Systems. Because all recording operations are local to a node (there is no global coordination), we naturally support *reconfigurable* systems in which nodes may dynamically enter or leave. This requires no changes to the above protocols: a node enters a system by establishing connections, as described above, and leaves by closing all open connections.

4. Deterministic Execution with DDPGs

Beyond record/replay, DDOS also implements a deterministic distributed execution algorithm. Our algorithm operates at the socket layer, and its job is to ensure that messages on the internal network of a DDPG are delivered deterministically. We first explain the guarantees we desire from this algorithm, and then we describe the algorithm itself.

4.1 Deterministic Guarantee of DDPGs

Our deterministic guarantee is that the entire DDPG executes as a single deterministic unit, relative to input received from clocks, users, the external network, and other sources of external nondeterminism. Our guarantee can be specified in two parts. The first is *local* determinism, provided by DPGs, which ensures that each node of the distributed system executes deterministically relative to its own local inputs. The second part is *global* determinism, provided by DDPGs, which ensures that all messages sent on the internal network are received at a deterministic logical time and have deterministic contents.

Our algorithm guarantees that messages sent on the internal network of a DDPG are delivered deterministically. Specifically, we ensure that network receive operations complete at a deterministic logical time and return a deterministic number of bytes, with deterministic message contents. Further, we ensure that internal listening sockets accept connections in a deterministic order. These guarantees apply to both TCP and UDP channels.

Processes in a DDPG can also communicate via network messages with processes outside of the DDPG. However, messages exchanged with these processes are transferred on the external network, so they are delivered nondeterministically. Record/replay techniques are needed to later reproduce these inputs.

4.2 Deterministic Network Protocol

The basic idea is depicted in Figure 4. We begin by observing that communication occurs when a node *receives* a message from a remote node, not when the message is sent. To ensure deterministic communication, we need to ensure only that nodes consume messages from remote nodes at deterministic points in their logical time; DPGs will guarantee the sends will occur at a deterministic time by construction.

We ensure deterministic message delivery by dividing execution of the DDPG into global *quanta*. Conceptually, messages sent along internal channels are buffered until the end of the global quantum in which they were sent, and are delivered to the receiving node before the next quantum begins. Global quanta end once every node has signaled that it is ready to start the next global quantum; this happens once the local node's DPG has executed some deterministic number of logical time steps. The number of time steps need not be fixed and need not be the same for each node, as long as it is chosen deterministically. The mapping of local logical time to global quanta is illustrated in Figure 4.

A naïve implementation of this algorithm might use a global barrier to stall nodes at the end of every global quantum until all buffered messages have been delivered. However, this is not necessary. Global quanta can be propagated *lazily*. We do this by having each node push an end-of-quantum marker down its internal network channels every time it reaches the end of a global quantum. Remote nodes buffer data as it arrives and are allowed to consume data only up to the end-of-quantum marker of the *previous* quantum. This ensures that remote nodes consume data only if that data was sent in a prior global quantum.

Figure 5 illustrates this lazy protocol. In this figure, DPG_A is currently executing in global quantum 3, and is communicating with three other DPGs over network channels which are shown as queues. DPG_1 and DPG_2 are currently executing in global

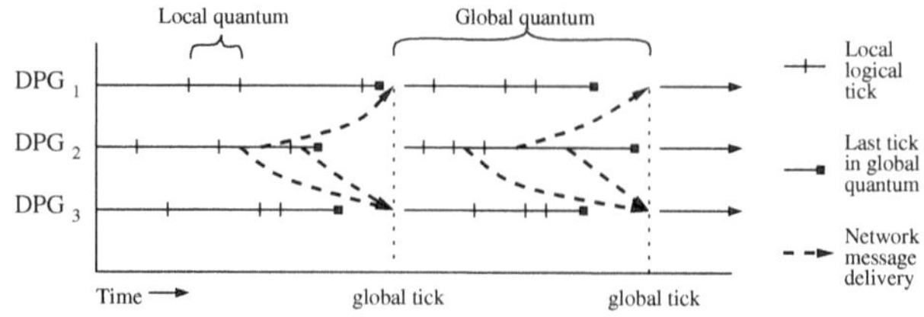

Figure 4. Conceptual view of deterministic communication. Messages are buffered until the end of the current global quantum before being delivered. Global quanta are formed from deterministic numbers of logical time steps in the local DPGs.

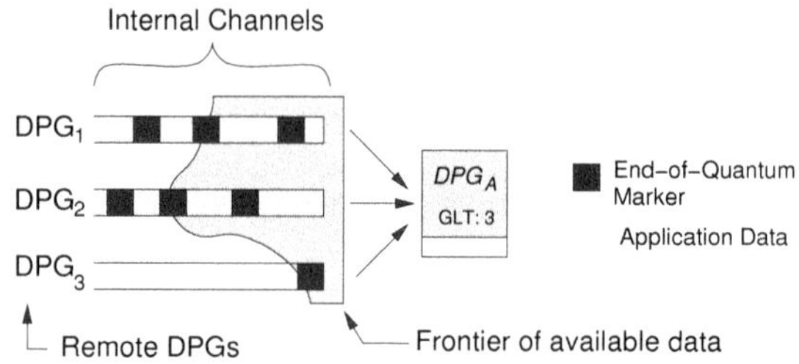

Figure 5. Deterministic communication with lazy barriers. The tokens in each network channel define the *frontier* of data that a DPG can safely consume while preserving determinism.

quantum 4, so they have sent three end-of-quantum markers down their network channels, while DPG_3 is executing in global quantum 2, so it has sent just one marker. The darker shaded region in this figure shows the portion of data that is currently available for DPG_A to read: since DPG_A is executing in the third global quantum, only data sent from the first two global quanta are available. Further, note that DPG_3 is currently executing behind DPG_A and has not yet sent any data, other than the end-of-quantum marker. If DPG_A attempts a `recv` operation on the connection with DPG_3, that `recv` cannot complete until DPG_3 has either sent another end-of-quantum marker or pushed enough data onto the channel to satisfy the request.

Figure 5 also illustrates how we allow each node's notion of current global time to drift from the other nodes, as long as the basic communication constraints are enforced: threads can only consume data from the internal network that was sent in an earlier global quantum. This relaxation can be a significant optimization when compared to a naïve protocol using global barriers. In the limit, when the nodes do not communicate, each node can advance its own view of global time arbitrarily, without waiting for the other nodes to catch up. Only when a node receives data from a remote node must it potentially synchronize with that node.

Promiscuous Operations. Some network operations—such as accepting connections, polling for data with `poll`, or promiscuous receives on UDP sockets—can receive data from multiple remote nodes in a single call. These operations require that the caller waits for *all* nodes it *could* communicate with to catch up in global time before the operation can complete. Once all such nodes have caught up, we deliver incoming data from one sending node at a time, after ordering sending nodes in some deterministic order. For example, a `accept` operation first waits until it has received an end-of-quantum marker for the prior quantum from all other nodes. It then gathers all connection requests, orders them, and finally delivers the connection requests in that order to ensure they are processed deterministically.

In the worst case, where all nodes call globally promiscuous operations such as `accept` in every global quantum, every node will be forced to wait for every other node at the end of every quantum, degrading the relaxed protocol to the naïve protocol that uses global barriers.

Unreliable Channels. Messages sent over UDP channels can be arbitrarily dropped or reordered by the network. We must guarantee in-order lossless message delivery to ensure determinism. Thus, in deterministic execution mode, DDPGs tunnel all UDP connections over a reliable TCP connection.

Reconfigurable Systems. Nodes may leave a DDPG via exiting: this is already deterministic because of the local determinism provided by dOS. Joining a DDPG, however, represents a fundamental source of external nondeterminism in the time at which a node joins. For this reason, we do not consider joins to be useful operations in deterministic execution mode, and we do not support them. (We do support joins in record/replay mode; see Section 3.2.) If desired, `join(N,DDPG)` could be implemented by adding a two-phase commit protocol, to allow all nodes to agree on the quantum at which `N` joins the DDPG, and by logging that quantum for use during further replays.

4.3 Dealing With Failures

Failures in large distributed systems occur frequently, so it is important to understand how these failures affect DDOS. When one DPG attempts to receive data from another DPG along an internal channel, that node needs to wait until the correct end-of-quantum marker is received before data can be returned. If the sender of the data (and thus the marker) fails, the receiver can not continue. This sender/receiver synchronization constrains communication onto a deterministic *logically synchronous network*.

An initial strategy for coping with failure might be as follows: detect a failed node, restore the node from a checkpoint, replay its inputs up to the current state of the system, and finally resume distributed execution. However, distinguishing a failed node from a slow node is difficult, and further, when a node fails, all other nodes in the system must agree on the exact logical time at which that node failed. Detecting failures with this degree of accuracy is a consensus problem which is impossible to solve on asynchronous physical networks given an arbitrary failure model [13].

Thus, a side-effect of the logically synchronous network model is that DDOS cannot guarantee forward progress while preserving determinism without making assumptions about the failure rate of the distributed system. If these assumptions are broken, DDOS must give up either determinism or forward progress. As a further consequence of consensus impossibility, DDOS cannot detect with complete certainty when these assumptions are broken. Therefore, our deterministic guarantees are at best probabilistic, even though these probabilities may be quite high in practice.

One simple way to deal with this problem is to implement a physical timeout mechanism that triggers when a node has not received an end-of-quantum marker from a remote node in some predefined amount of physical time. If the node is blocked on an operation waiting for an end-of-quantum marker to arrive and the timeout triggers, the blocked node can use this timeout to detect a *possible* failure, and alert the system. A user could then decide to restart the node, to continue to wait, or to continue without waiting and sacrifice determinism from that point forward. This might even be incorporated into a larger consensus protocol, such as Paxos [22]. We have not yet implemented this mechanism or investigated it further.

Finally, we note that the problem of failures is common to all systems for deterministic execution, not just DDOS. The fact that DDOS deals with distributed systems simply exacerbates the problem. For example, even in a hardware implementation of determinism, such as DMP [8], determinism could be lost as the result of an alpha particle causing a random bit flip in memory.

```
tom   5000 t:80,u:512 web-serve
jerry 6000 t:10000 memcached
```

Figure 6. An example of a manifest file specifying a two-node DDPG

5. Implementation

DDOS is implemented on top of dOS [4] as a distributed shim program. It uses dOS's shim API to interpose on all socket-related system calls made by a DPG. Depending on the mode of the DDPG (either record/replay or deterministic execution), the shim will either record the results of these system calls to a log, replay the results of the system call from a log, or execute the system call in a deterministic way.

Implementing DDOS as a dOS shim means the physical network is outside of DDOS's control. In other words, the DDOS shims replay or make communication deterministic at the system call layer, but an eavesdropper watching the packets in transit between physical machines could see either imprecise replay or nondeterminism. The shims at either side of the connection, however, ensure that communication observed by the applications is properly controlled.

5.1 Creating a DDPG

A DDPG consists of a set DPGs executing on physical machines, along with a specification that partitions the network into *internal* and *external* channels. To construct a DDPG, the developer writes a *manifest file*. The manifest contains an entry for each of the DPGs, specifying the command to execute, the node to execute the DPG on, as well as the set of TCP and UDP ports on that node that are considered internal to the DDPG. When used for deterministic execution, the manifest also indicates which port the DPG should use for *control channel* connections (Section 5.3). Note that internal channels can only be used to communicate with DPGs: if a port will ever be used by both DPGs and processes outside of a DPG, the port cannot be marked as internal.

Figure 6 shows an example of a manifest file specifying a two-node DDPG. `web-serve` will be run within a DPG on the host `tom`, and connections to TCP port 80 and UDP port 512 will be treated as *internal*; all other connections will be treated as *external*. Similarly, `memcached` will run within a DPG on host `jerry` with a single internal TCP port.

5.2 Record/Replay

The DDOS record/replay shim is implemented as an extension to the single-node record/replay shim originally implemented for dOS. Most of the implementation effort was tedious but straightforward, following prior work on record/replay. Our record shim emits an execution log that can be read by the replay shim. The log files are not compressed, and thus further reduction in log size is likely possible if compression was included.

UDP Sequence Numbers. As described in Section 3.2, UDP messages are tagged with a unique sequence number before being sent. Each thread in a DPG maintains a count of the number of UDP messages it has sent. The sequence number assigned to each outgoing UDP message is a tuple of the sending DPG's id, the sending thread's id, and the current UDP message count of that thread. Because the DPG ids, thread ids, and the UDP message count are all deterministic, these sequence numbers are deterministic as well and can be used to replay UDP communication.

Establishing Connections. If a connection on the internal network was successfully completed during recording, the connection must be successfully completed during replay. However, due to timing variations (Section 3.2), a connection that succeeded during record may fail during replay (for example, the connector may call `connect` before the remote node has had a chance to invoke `listen`). To ensure the same behavior during replay, the replay shim may pause the DDPG execution until the connection can be reestablished and will retry the connection attempt until it succeeds.

Replaying Connection Order. Similarly, DDPGs must ensure that incoming internal network connections are accepted during replay in the same order observed during the record phase. To replay the correct order, the DDOS shims buffer all incoming connection requests during replay; when a process calls `accept`, the buffered connections are checked against the log see if the expected connection has already arrived. If so, the connection is returned to the caller and the DPG that initiated the connection is notified. If the expected connection is not already buffered, the call to `accept` blocks until the anticipated connection is received.

Log Durability. Our current implementation writes log entries to disk asynchronously, as synchronous writes would be prohibitively expensive. This may introduce a window of record loss during a hardware failure. More advanced storage systems [27] or upcoming new hardware [24] may make synchronous writes more viable.

5.3 Deterministic Execution

DDOS implements our deterministic message delivery algorithm with a distributed shim program. This shim program interposes on all socket-layer operations performed by applications to ensure that internal network communication happens deterministically.

Upon startup, the DPGs enter a brief initialization phase where the manifest file is read, pairwise control channels are established between DPGs, and DDPG configuration values—such as the size of a global quantum—are exchanged. Each DPG is assigned a unique id derived from its position in the manifest file. After the initialization phase, the DPGs begin executing their respective programs.

Control channels are used by the DDOS shims to coordinate their execution. Messages sent on the control channel have one of four types, described in Table 1. `CMT_ENDQ` messages broadcast by a DPG at the end of every global quantum. `CMT_CONNREQ` and `CMT_CONNRESP` messages are used to establish virtual network connections between the applications. `CMT_DATA` messages are used to transfer application-level data along a virtual connection.

Control channel are reliable, in-order network connections. All internal network connections between two nodes are multiplexed on to the single control channel connecting the nodes, and both application-level data and the DDOS protocol are transferred along this connection. Because the control channels are in-order, when a DPG sees a `CMT_ENDQ` message from a particular node for quantum n, it is guaranteed to have already seen all other messages sent by that same node in quantum n.

Connection Management. To establish an internal network connection, the local DPG sends a `CMT_CONNREQ` message to the remote DPG containing the target port number, as well as the local port number it's connecting from. Because Linux randomly assigns port numbers to sockets, the port numbers used in DDOS are *virtual port numbers*, assigned deterministically by the DDOS shims.

The remote DPG buffers all connection requests in a sorted queue for the target listening socket. Each request is tagged with a tuple consisting of the global quantum in which the request was sent, the unique id of the connecting node, and the port number the request originated from. The queue is sorted based on this tuple. Requests from prior global quanta are satisfied from the queue in sorted order, while requests from future quanta are kept buffered. Once a connection is accepted (or if the connection request is denied because a listening socket does not exist on the target port), the remote DPG responds with a `CMT_CONNRESP` message.

Type	Description
`CMT_ENDQ`	Broadcast by a node at end of global quantum
`CMT_CONNREQ`	Connection request sent from one DPG to another
`CMT_CONNRESP`	Response for a connection request, indicating connection success or failure
`CMT_DATA`	Contains application-level data being sent between process in a DDPG

Table 1. Control channel message types

Communicating on Internal Channels. Sending data on an internal channel creates a new `CMT_DATA` message containing the length of the message and the data being sent. The message is sent along the control channel to the receiving node. Upon reception of a `CMT_DATA` message, a receiving node reads the entirety of the message and buffers the message in a queue representing the virtual port of the receiving socket. Each message is tagged with the global quantum in which it was sent. Messages from prior global quanta are delivered from the queue in-order, while requests from future quanta are kept buffered. For promiscuous UDP channels, messages are additionally tagged and sorted in the same way that connection requests are tagged and sorted.

Poll/Select Optimization. As mentioned previously in Section 4.2, promiscuous network operations such as `poll` and `select` can potentially add significant overheads to deterministic execution due to the high cost of synchronizing logical timelines across nodes, but this synchronization can sometimes be avoided. For example, when performing a `poll` operation on a set of file descriptors, synchronization with remote nodes can be avoided if either: 1) the remote node's view of global logical time is later than the node's performing the `poll`; or 2) the remote node's view of global logical time is earlier than the caller's, but *all* file descriptors being examined by `poll` from that node have *some* amount of data already available.

In the first condition, the remote node is operating in the future relative to the caller's notion of global logical time. Thus, any data sent by the remote node has already been received by the caller, and no additional synchronization is needed to satisfy the `poll` request.

The second condition exploits the fact that the `poll` family of functions return only a Boolean result indicating whether or not data is available to read—not how much data is available. As long as all file descriptors associated with a remote node have some data that is currently available from a logical time earlier than the caller's notion of global logical time, `poll` can deterministically return a true result without first synchronizing; synchronization can be delayed until the two nodes communicate with a `recv` operation.

Resource Exhaustion. System limits on resource usage, such as limits on open file descriptors, can pose difficulties for correct deterministic behavior. To understand why, consider running a DDPG twice, where no other processes are run on the system during the first execution, but a nondeterministic background process runs during the second execution. If that background process in the second execution opens a large number of file descriptors, the DDPG might be unable to open all of the descriptors it needs to complete, possibly causing the two executions to behave differently. This scenario could be dealt with in two ways: 1) pause the execution of the DDPG until the request can be completed (for example, by waiting for the other process to close some of its descriptors), or 2) report the error to the user and abort execution of the DDPG. For simplicity, our system implements the second approach, leaving implementation of the first method to future work.

6. Evaluation

This section evaluates DDOS. The goal of our evaluation is to answer the following three questions: 1) What are the performance overheads of using DDOS for record/replay and for deterministic execution, relative to nondeterministic execution outside of DDOS? 2) How effective is our space-efficient record/replay mechanism at reducing the size of replay logs? 3) Where do the runtime overheads come from? A more qualitative goal of this evaluation is to demonstrate that we can support real-world applications.

6.1 Applications

We evaluated DDOS with three different types of distributed applications: a microbenchmark with frequent peer-to-peer traffic, a reactive web application with a remote file server, and a distributed scientific application based on the OpenMPI libraries. The distributed scientific application comes from the NAS Parallel Benchmark suite [25].

Peer-to-peer Microbenchmark. The peer-to-peer microbenchmark is a custom program adapted from the `racey` deterministic stress test [15] that we call `racey-dist`. `racey-dist` is a distributed application with single-threaded nodes. The nodes in `racey-dist` form a completely connected graph and send and receive data to the other nodes in the system with high frequency; the data sent and received is combined by each node to compute a signature that is highly sensitive to the pattern of communication, including both the order and content of messages.

Reactive Webserver. The reactive webserver is composed of two applications: a multithreaded server that handles web requests from clients, and a multithreaded instance of `memcached` that serves the files to the webserver from an in-memory database. For our evaluation, each application was run on a separate evaluation node, and a third computer external to the DDPG was used to generate web requests. We used the `ab` benchmarking utility from Apache to generate the workload. Both the webserver and the `memcached` server were configured to run with 8 threads.

OpenMPI Scientific Application. From the NAS OpenMPI parallel benchmarks, we ran `is`, a large-scale integer sorting kernel. We vary the number of MPI processes from 2 to 16, with the threads evenly divided amongst the nodes. Because OpenMPI uses the ssh protocol to remotely spawn tasks, we also ran a separate `dropbear` ssh daemon inside each of the DPGs to accept these connections.

6.2 Correctness

We ran `racey-dist` in a deterministic DDPG 20 times and verified that all executions produced the same signature. For comparison, 20 nondeterministic runs of `racey-dist` produced 20 different signatures.

`racey-dist` stresses the connection management and end-to-end communication of our implementation, so we believe these components are correct. This benchmark also stresses the lazy barrier implementation by buffering connection requests and message contents until global barriers. Our selection of other applications provide an indirect demonstration that the remaining operations—such as promiscuous communication, UDP transmissions, `poll` and `select`, etc.—likely behave properly. The NAS benchmark in particular exercises complex connection management and relies heavily on promiscuous socket operations. We have released the source code [1] and encourage readers to independently test our implementation.

[1] Source code is available at `http://sampa.cs.washington.edu`.

Benchmark	Execution Time			Log Sizes (MB)	
	Nondet	DPGs	DDOS	DPGs	DDOS
`racey-dist`					
2 threads	3 ms	236 ms	135 ms	0.27	0.15
3 threads	22 ms	349 ms	176 ms	0.41	0.23
4 threads	7 ms	307 ms	168 ms	0.54	0.30
`www`					
8 threads	2.5k r/s	188 r/s	217 r/s	599	146
`is`					
2 threads	1.53 s	2.09 s	1.59 s	180	4
4 threads	1.11 s	1.73 s	1.19 s	272	7
8 threads	1.00 s	29.48 s	26.63 s	374	107
16 threads	1.23 s	49.05 s	40.79 s	443	168

Table 2. Execution time of the recorded execution and the resulting log sizes. Nondet is nondeterministic execution; DPGs is each node performing a local record; and DDOS is a DDPG record, where nodes only record communication external to the DDPG.

6.3 Methodology

The evaluation was performed on a five node cluster, each running a dOS-enabled 2.6.24.7 Linux kernel. Four of the machines have 2 Intel Xeon X5550 quad-core processors and 24GB of RAM; the fifth node has 2 Intel Xeon E5520 quad-core processors and 10GB of RAM. Each of the experiments below was executed three times, and the average measure of performance is reported.

We use an application-specific measure of performance for each application. For the `racey-dist` and MPI benchmark, we measure the wall-clock time required to complete the workload. For the webserver benchmark, we use the number of requests handled per second.

6.4 Record/Replay

Table 2 shows the runtime of the recorded executions and the resulting log sizes in MB. For `www`, requests per second is used instead of execution time to report performance in a more meaningful way. Each row contains the results for a single application run with the specified number of threads.

Column 2 shows performance when the distributed system is run nondeterministically, without the use of DPGs or DDPGs. Column 3 shows the results when each node is its own DPG, performing local node recording with the record/replay shim developed in [4]. This column demonstrates the overhead of using a traditional record/replay mechanism as described in Section 3.1, which does not exploit the deterministic properties of DDPGs when logging network communication. Column 5 provides the log sizes produced with this local recording strategy. Finally, Column 4 provides the execution times when DDPGs are used to reduce the logging of network traffic to only that which is external to the DDPG, as described in Section 3, with Column 6 giving the resulting log sizes.

A comparison of Columns 2 and 3 shows that the overhead of dOS's deterministic scheduler plus the overhead of logging local-node inputs results in a 1-2 order of magnitude slowdown in performance. The logs in these executions vary between 200 MB and 600 MB in size.

A comparison of Columns 5 and 6 shows that not logging the internal traffic of a DDPG results in a significant reduction in log size (about 70% in some cases). We also observe that when executing within a DDPG with internal sockets, the application always recovered some performance compared to separate DPGs with record/replay shims. Some of this performance likely comes from not needing to write as much data to disk.

For the `is` benchmark with 8–16 threads, both the log size and performance overheads grew significantly from the execution with 4 threads. In these cases, we observed a large increase in the invocations of `poll` and the `rdtsc` instruction (an x86 instruction that reads a hardware timer) by the application. We suspect this behavior is due to a mechanism in OpenMPI that is enabled when more than one MPI task is executed on a single node. In these cases, over 95% of the entries in record log were for these two operations, and likely contributed to the higher performance overhead as well. This is an example of a case where OS-level record/replay isn't the most efficient solution: a record/replay mechanism at the MPI layer would not be exposed to the `poll` system call and `rdtsc` instruction, and so would probably not see the same performance and logging penalty at the higher thread counts.

Although the record shim does not currently compress the logs during execution, manually compressing the logs after the execution shows that a 50-60% reduction in log size for these applications is possible.

6.5 Deterministic Execution

To evaluate the overheads of deterministic distributed execution, we ran each benchmark in four different modes. Table 3 reports these results. Column 2 shows the application-specific performance measurement when the benchmark is run nondeterministically, without the use of DPGs or DDPGs. Column 3 shows the performance when each node is run as a separate DPG, *without* an encompassing DDPG. In other words, each node runs dOS, but network communication between the nodes is still nondeterministic. Column 4 shows the performance metric when the distributed system is executed within a *fake* DDPG; the fake DDPG does not actually enforce deterministic network communication, but allows us to measure the overhead of just constructing the DDPG and interposing on all socket-layer operations. Finally, Column 5 shows the performance metric when the application is run within a deterministic DDPG, enforcing deterministic network communication between the nodes.

The difference in performance between Columns 2 and 3 is the overhead directly attributable to dOS. In theory, this represents the best performance that DDOS could achieve. In general, we see that the performance tends to be worse for higher thread counts. This is due to serialization of threads by the dOS scheduling algorithm due to resource sharing between the threads in the DPGs (for instance, shared-memory locations or the kernel's file descriptor table). A more complete evaluation and characterization of dOS's performance is available in [4]. dOS does not use a state-of-the-art deterministic scheduler; the addition of more advanced algorithms, such as those in [9], could contribute a substantial performance improvement. Most importantly, in this paper, we are primarily concerned with the overhead added by our algorithm for deterministic network communication, not with the overhead of local-node determinism.

Column 4 adds the cost of creating the DDPG, multiplexing network communication over a control channel, and sending end-of-quantum tokens between the nodes. In this mode, communication remains nondeterministic. We see that this additional communication imposes almost no additional overhead for `racey-dist`, and between 30% to 50% for `www` and `is`. Some results in this column, such as the 3 and 4 thread runs of `racey-dist`, show better performance than the corresponding value in Column 3. We would expect that the results for Fake DDPG would always be worse than DPG executions and believe these non-intuitive results are within measurement error for these experiments.

Finally, column 5 shows the performance when all communication between nodes occurs deterministically. The sources of the additional overheads include nodes waiting for remote nodes to catch up in logical time, and a small amount of additional coordination between the nodes. We see that for `racey-dist`, where communication occurs very frequently and with many nodes, the overheads of deterministic communication are the highest, with a roughly two order of magnitude slowdown. This is attributable to the frequent synchronization of logical clocks, where one node must pause its execution waiting for the other node to catch up. For `www`, we observe a 16x slowdown compared to nondeterministic execution. We characterize the sources of overhead in more detail in the next section.

Benchmark	Nondet	DPGs	Fake DDOS	DDOS
`racey-dist`				
2 threads	<0.01 s	0.46 s	0.48 s	5.33 s
3 threads	0.02 s	0.47 s	0.44 s	1.77 s
4 threads	0.01 s	0.49 s	0.48 s	3.82 s
`www`				
8 threads	2.5k r/s	331 r/s	225 r/s	155 r/s
`is`				
2 threads	1.53 s	1.91 s	1.52 s	10.85 s
4 threads	1.11 s	2.70 s	1.13 s	11.34 s
8 threads	1.00 s	2.64 s	2.41 s	40.17 s
16 threads	1.23 s	4.77 s	6.15 s	55.35 s

Table 3. Execution times for the deterministic execution evaluation. Nondet is nondeterministic execution; DPGs is local determinism only; Fake DDOS sends end-of-quantum markers but doesn't enforce deterministic communication; and DDOS is fully deterministic distributed execution.

6.5.1 Record/Replay and Deterministic Execution Trade-offs

We briefly mentioned the trade-offs between the record/replay mechanism and the deterministic execution mechanisms in Section 1. The above evaluation demonstrates this trade-off empirically.

Consider, for example, the `racey-dist` benchmark. Executing in the record/replay mode of DDOS, `racey-dist` was able to finish its execution in less than a second for all of the configurations evaluated. However, it needed to record about 150 KB - 300 KB to do so. The deterministic executions all required over a second to finish, but did so with minimal logs. This same trade-off can be observed in the results for the other two applications as well.

6.5.2 Overhead Characterization

Reasons For Waiting. Our algorithm might introduce slowdown whenever it forces a node to wait for an end-of-quantum marker from a remote node. Table 4 partitions the total time DDPGs spend waiting into three categories: *promisc* shows the percentage of wait time due to the promiscuous `select` or `poll` operations; *connect* shows the percentage of wait time spent establishing connections with `connect` and `accept`; and *data* shows time spent waiting for data to become available on a deterministic socket (a blocking `recv`, for example).

Consider the `www` benchmark. `memcached` and `www` communicate constantly with one another to satisfy incoming web requests. As a result, a majority of wait time is due to nodes synchronizing their logical clocks while communicating: 91% of wait time is due to this synchronization. A small percentage of the time is attributable to connection setup and tear-down between the webserver and `memcached` at the beginning and end of the execution.

The `is` benchmark does more computation than communication, demonstrated by the fact that only 10% of its wait time occurs during data transmission. Surprisingly, the remaining 90% of the wait time is due to synchronization in the `poll` family of functions. These functions, due to their promiscuous nature, can be extremely expensive, in the worst case requiring the caller to synchronize logical time with all nodes in the system. In this application it was the `dropbear` ssh daemon running in each of the DPGs that was responsible for these promiscuous operations, rather than the actual `is` MPI tasks. This suggests that removing `dropbear` from DPG

Benchmark	Reason for Waiting		
	Promisc.	Connect	Data
racey-dist	18%	21%	61%
www	<1%	9%	91%
is	90%	0%	10%

Table 4. Percentage of time spent blocked waiting for promiscuous operations, connection requests/responses, or data

after the initial MPI tasks have been spawned could lead to a significant performance improvement.

Finally, for the `racey-dist` microbenchmark, the time spent waiting for connection setup is higher that other benchmarks, likely due to its relatively shorter running time.

Quantum Drift. We also measured quantum *drift* to evaluate to what degree distributed execution was synchronous; high values of drift suggest that lazy quantum barriers had a significantly positive effect on performance. We define quantum drift between node A and remote node B to be the difference between node A's current global quantum and the most recent end-of-quantum marker that node A has received from node B.

We instrumented DDOS to compute the maximum quantum drift at every quantum boundary and capture the summary as a histogram. All three benchmarks exhibited a similar trend: the quantum drift was mostly either 0 or 1 quantum, meaning the nodes executed mostly synchronously, but all benchmarks had a long tail of larger drifts, in some cases extending to hundreds of quanta. For `racey-dist`, 86% of drifts were either 0 or 1 quantum, with a tail spread evenly out to 16 quanta. For `www`, these numbers were 99% with a tail to 220 quanta, and for `is`, 98% with a tail to 580 quanta.

7. Related Work

Record/Replay. There have been many proposals for software-based implementations of record/replay. These include systems that provide record/replay of local nondeterminism only, as well as systems that provide record/replay for an entire distributed application.

Of the single-node systems, some record nondeterminism at the system call layer only [29], making replay of multithreaded applications impossible. Others record nondeterministic thread schedules to support multithreaded programs. These include systems that assume uniprocessor execution and record only scheduling decisions [7], as well as systems that support multiprocessors and either record all shared-memory accesses [11, 19, 23] or just synchronization operations [28, 32]. Nondeterminism arising from local sources is eliminated by DPGs, so DDOS never needs to record it.

Other systems provide record/replay for entire distributed systems. `liblog` [14] provides consistent distributed system replay, but is implemented as a userspace library and thus does not support multithreaded execution at the nodes (multithreaded applications are supported, but execution of the threads is serialized). It uses techniques similar to Jockey [29] to record local nondeterminism introduced through `libc` library calls, and additionally tags network messages sent between nodes in the system with Lamport clocks to coordinate replay. All messages received over the network by `liblog` are logged to disk, along with the time they were received.

DejaVu [18] provides record/replay for distributed Java applications and is implemented in a custom JVM. Cooperative ReVirt [2] provides record/replay for arbitrary distributed applications. DejaVu, Cooperative ReVirt and DDOS all make the same observation: internal network messages can be regenerated during replay to save log space. Unlike DDOS, however, both DejaVu and Cooperative ReVirt must record all local-node nondeterminism–including shared-memory access interleavings–so they are not able to achieve the same log size reduction that DDOS achieves by exploiting local-node determinism.

Deterministic Execution. Prior systems for deterministic execution have focused on single-node multithreaded programs. These systems eliminate the nondeterminism due to thread scheduling and shared-memory access interleavings. Some systems require custom hardware support [8, 9, 16] while others work purely in software [1, 3–5, 26]. A common approach divides execution into *quanta*, where communication is prevented for the majority of a quantum and then allowed to happen in a deterministic way when the quantum completes. The deterministic algorithm we proposed for DDOS is most similar to the buffering algorithm proposed by CoreDet [3]: both buffer communication during the quantum, then release communication at the quantum boundary. However, CoreDet's algorithm does not support message queues, and further does not include the lazy-barrier optimization, which is vital for performance on networks that have much higher latency than shared-memory.

Kahn networks [17] are a deterministic model of network communication where processes communicate through unbounded point-to-point queues. It is difficult to schedule arbitrary programs onto Kahn networks without introducing deadlock [12]. Determinator [1] supports multi-node deterministic distributed execution through a limited tree-based communication model that is a restricted form of Kahn network. This limited communication model is mostly used to implement a deterministic distributed shared-memory system. Like all Kahn networks, Determinator does not support many-to-one operations such as a promiscuous UDP `recv`.

Distributed Systems. Our algorithm for deterministic execution is a vector clock [20] algorithm: a node's current vector clock is defined by its current global quantum combined with the end-of-quantum markers it has received from remote nodes. Consequently, our algorithm bears resemblance to other distributed systems algorithms, most notably those for taking distributed snapshots [21], which broadcast local time coordinates in similar ways to our algorithm.

Virtual synchrony [6, 31] provides an atomic multicast primitive. Processes can join one or more *process groups*, and messages can be sent by processes to these groups. A process does not need to be a member of a group to send that group a message. Virtual synchrony ensures that all nodes in the receiving process group receive the same set of messages and in the same order, even if those messages were sent from multiple processes. Virtual synchrony does nothing to address the nondeterminism at the nodes in the system. DDOS's implementation of a logically synchronous network, however, has one important difference: it guarantees *deterministic* communication, rather than simply guaranteeing a consistent order of message delivery.

8. Conclusions

The goal of our work is to understand and explore the role of determinism in distributed systems. We leverage prior work on deterministic multithreading to: 1) significantly reduce log sizes when recording execution of distributed applications; and 2) deterministically execute entire distributed applications from the ground up. We proposed the first algorithm and system for deterministic execution of arbitrary distributed applications and prototyped it in a system we call DDOS.

We have shown that our record/replay mechanism significantly reduces log-sizes, resulting in log savings of 70% in some cases, although at a cost of an order-of-magnitude slowdown in application performance. We also evaluated our deterministic execution algorithm and showed that we can completely eliminate the log of communication between the nodes of a distributed system, although the cost of doing so is usually higher.

Acknowledgements

We thank the members of the UW Sampa and systems research groups for their feedback and fruitful discussions. We also thank our anonymous reviewers and our shepherd, Bhuvan Urgaonkar, for their guidance. This work was supported in part by the National Science Foundation CAREER award 0846004, NSF grants CNS-1016477 and CNS-1217597, a Google PhD fellowship awarded to Tom Bergan, and a Microsoft Faculty Fellowship.

References

[1] A. Aviram, S.-C. Weng, S. Hu, and B. Ford. Efficient System-Enforced Deterministic Parallelism. In *OSDI*, 2010.

[2] M. Basrai and P. M. Chen. Cooperative revirt: Adapting message logging for intrusion analysis. Technical Report CSE-TR-504-04, University of Michigan, 2004.

[3] T. Bergan, O. Anderson, J. Devietti, L. Ceze, and D. Grossman. CoreDet: A Compiler and Runtime System for Deterministic Multithreaded Execution. In *ASPLOS*, 2010.

[4] T. Bergan, N. Hunt, L. Ceze, and S. D. Gribble. Deterministic Process Groups in dOS. In *OSDI*, 2010.

[5] E. Berger, T. Yang, T. Liu, and G. Novark. Grace: Safe and Efficient Concurrent Programming. In *OOPSLA*, 2009.

[6] K. P. Birman. The Process Group Approach to Reliable Distributed Computing. *Communications of the ACM*, 36(12), December 1993.

[7] J. Choi and H. Srinivasan. Deterministic Replay of Java Multithreaded Applications. In *SIGMETRICS SPDT*, 1998.

[8] J. Devietti, B. Lucia, L. Ceze, and M. Oskin. DMP: Deterministic Shared Memory Multiprocessing. In *ASPLOS*, 2009.

[9] J. Devietti, J. Nelson, T. Bergan, L. Ceze, and D. Grossman. RCDC: A Relaxed Consistency Deterministic Computer. In *ASPLOS*, 2011.

[10] G. Dunlap, S. King, S. Cinar, M. Basrai, and P. Chen. ReVirt: Enabling Intrusion Analysis Through Virtual-Machine Logging and Replay. In *OSDI*, 2002.

[11] G. Dunlap, D. Lucchetti, M. Fetterman, and P. Chen. Execution replay of multiprocessor virtual machines. In *VEE*, 2008.

[12] S. A. Edwards and O. Tardieu. SHIM: A Deterministic Model for Heterogeneous Embedded Systems. In *EMSOFT*, 2005.

[13] M. J. Fischer, N. A. Lynch, and M. S. Paterson. Impossibility of distributed consensus with one faulty process. *Journal of the ACM*, 32:374–382, April 1985.

[14] D. Geels, G. Altekar, S. Shenker, and I. Stoica. Abstract replay debugging for distributed applications. In *USENIX Annual Technical Conference*, 2009.

[15] M. Hill and M. Xu. Racey: A Stress Test for Deterministic Execution. `http://www.cs.wisc.edu/~markhill/racey.html`.

[16] D. Hower, P. Dudnik, D. Wood, and M. Hill. Calvin: Deterministic or Not? Free Will to Choose. In *HPCA*, 2011.

[17] G. Kahn. The Semantics of a Simple Language for Parallel Programming. *Information Processing*, pages 471–475, 1974.

[18] R. Konuru. Deterministic replay of distributed java applications. In *In Proceedings of the 14th IEEE International Parallel and Distributed Processing Symposium*, pages 219–228, 2000.

[19] O. Laadan, N. Viennot, and J. Nieh. Transparent, Lightweight Application Execution Replay on Commodity Multiprocessor Operating Systems. In *SIGMETRICS*, 2010.

[20] L. Lamport. Time, Clocks, and the Ordering of Events in a Distributed System. *Communications of the ACM*, 21(7), July 1978.

[21] L. Lamport. Distributed Snapshots: Determining Global States of Distributed Systems. *ACM TOCS*, 3(1), 1985.

[22] L. Lamport. The Part-Time Parliament. *ACM TOCS*, 16(2), 1998.

[23] T. J. LeBlanc and J. M. Mellor-Crummey. Debugging Parallel Programs with Instant Replay. *IEEE TC*, 36(4), 1987.

[24] B. C. Lee, E. Ipek, O. Mutlu, and D. Burger. Architecting Phase Change Memory as a Scalable DRAM Alternative. In *ISCA*, 2009.

[25] NASA Advanced Supercomputing Division. The NAS Parallel Benchmarks. `http://www.nas.nasa.gov/Resources/Software/npb.html`.

[26] M. Olszewski, J. Ansel, and S. Amarasinghe. Kendo: Efficient Deterministic Multithreading in Software. In *ASPLOS*, 2009.

[27] D. Ongaro, S. M. Rumble, R. Stutsman, J. Ousterhout, and M. Rosenblum. Fast Crash Recovery in RAMCloud. In *SOSP*, 2011.

[28] M. Ronsse and K. D. Bosschere. RecPlay: A Fully Integrated Practical Record/Replay System. *ACM TOCS*, 17(2), 1999.

[29] Y. Saito. Jockey: A User-Space Library for Record-Replay Debugging. In *International Symposium on Automated Analysis-driven Debugging*, 2005.

[30] A. Thomson and D. J. Abadi. The case for determinism in database systems. In *VLDB*, 2010.

[31] R. Van Renesse, K. Birman, and S. Maffeis. Horus: A Flexible Group Communication System. *Communications of the ACM*, 39(4), April 1996.

[32] K. Veeraraghavan, D. Lee, B. Wester, J. Ouyang, P. M. Chen, J. Flinn, and S. Narayanasamy. DoublePlay: Parallelizing Sequential Logging and Replay. In *ASPLOS*, 2011.

TSO_ATOMICITY: Efficient Hardware Primitive for TSO-Preserving Region Optimizations

Cheng Wang Youfeng Wu

Programming Systems Lab
Microprocessor and Programming Research / Intel Labs
{cheng.c.wang, youfeng.wu}@intel.com

Abstract

Program optimizations based on data dependences may not preserve the memory consistency in the programs. Previous works leverage a hardware *ATOMICITY* primitive to restrict the thread interleaving for preserving *sequential consistency* in region optimizations. However, ATOMICITY primitive is over restrictive on the thread interleaving for optimizing real-world applications developed with the popular *Total-Store-Ordering* (TSO) memory consistency, which is weaker than sequential consistency. In this paper, we present a novel hardware *TSO_ATOMICITY* primitive, which has less restriction on the thread interleaving than ATOMICITY primitive to permit more efficient program execution than ATOMICITY primitive, but can still preserve TSO memory consistency in all region optimizations. Furthermore, TSO_ATOMICITY primitive requires similar architecture support as ATOMICITY primitive and can be implemented with only slight change to the existing ATOMICITY primitive implementation. Our experimental results show that in a start-of-art dynamic binary optimization system on a large set of workloads, ATOMICITY primitive can only improve the performance by 4% on average. TSO_ATOMICITY primitive can reduce the overhead associated with ATOMICITY primitive and improve the performance by 12% on average.

Categories and Subject Descriptors D.3.3 [**Programming Languages**]: Processors – code generation, optimization.

General Terms: Performance

Keywords: Atomicity; Dynamic Optimization; Memory Consistency

1. Introduction

Program optimizations must preserve the program memory consistency. Traditional optimizations based on data dependences may not preserve the memory consistency in the programs. For example, in the program example shown in Figure 1 (a), *Sequential Consistency* (SC) [22] requires memory operations in a thread to execute in the order specified by its program order. So if load m_1 executes after m_4 (i.e. the result $r1 == 1$), as shown by the arrow, then m_2 must execute after m_3 (i.e. the result $r2 == 1$). Therefore, the result $r1 == 1$ and $r2 == 0$ should never be produced by the program. Programs under SC can use that causality property for synchronization between threads (e.g. in spinlocks) such that the condition $r1 == 1$ will guarantee that load m_2 in Thread 1 reads the store data of m_3 in Thread 2. However, since there is no data dependence between m_1 and m_2, optimizations on Thread 1 based on data dependences may reorder them to Thread 1', (e.g. vectorization optimizations may need that reordering to merge load m_2 with a previous load for vector load). As the result, the program in Figure 1 (b) can produce the result, $r1 == 1$ and $r2 == 0$, with the execution order shown by the arrows in the figure, which may result in incorrect synchronizations (i.e. the optimization in Figure 1 (b) is a *non-SC-preserving optimization*).

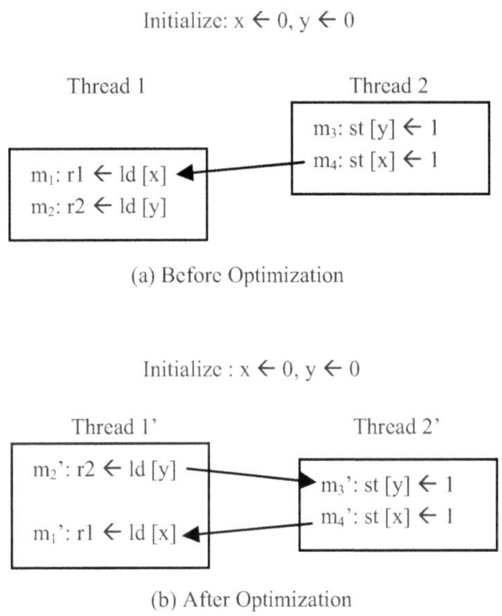

Figure 1: An Non-SC-Preserving and Non-TSO-Preserving Optimization Example

Previous works [2][14][27][30] show that we can leverage the hardware *ATOMICITY primitive* [3][19][21][26][31] to restrict the thread interleaving for preserving SC in region optimizations. For example, we can group m_1 and m_2 in Thread 1 of Figure 1 (a) into a *region* with ATOMICITY primitive such that the hardware will always execute the whole region atomically. Then after optimizing thread 1 to thread 1', the thread interleaving shown in

Figure 1 (b) cannot happen (i.e. the execution of thread 2' cannot interleave between the atomic execution of m_2' and m_1'), and thus SC is preserved in optimizations within the region (i.e. the optimization in Figure 1 (b) becomes an *SC-preserving region optimization* with ATOMICITY primitive).

SC is inefficient for program execution, and is not adopted in practical processor designs. Popular processors like X86 and SPARC deployed a relaxed *Total-Store-Ordering* (TSO) [28][37] memory consistency, which can achieve significantly more efficient program execution than SC. Previous works [13][36] show that majority optimizations, including the one shown in Figure 1, cannot preserve TSO. By restricting the optimizations to be TSO-preserving, 60% of the memory optimization benefit will be lost on average [36]. So in this paper, we study the efficient hardware primitive for preserving the popularly deployed TSO in region optimizations.

We can leverage the existing hardware ATOMICITY primitive to restrict the thread interleaving for preserving TSO in region optimizations. However, TSO has weaker consistency than SC such that ATOMICITY primitive for preserving SC is over-restrictive than necessary for preserving TSO, which leads to less efficient program execution. For example, TSO allows later loads to pass earlier stores in the execution, which is not allowed by SC. So the optimization of reordering m_1 and m_2 in Figure 2 preserves TSO, but not SC. Executing the optimized code region in Thread 1' of Figure 2 (b) atomically (under ATOMICITY primitive) would unnecessarily prevent the thread interleaving shown by the arrows in the figure.

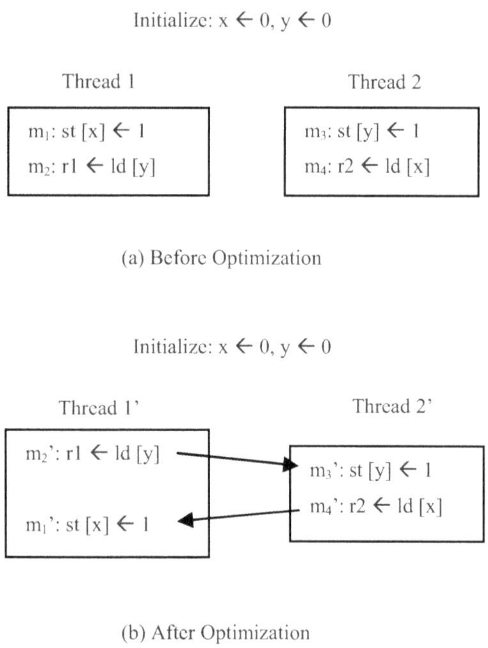

Figure 2: A TSO-Preserving but Non-SC-Preserving Optimization Example

In this paper, we present a novel hardware *TSO_ATOMICITY* primitive, which has weaker restriction on the thread interleaving than ATOMICITY primitive to permit more efficient program execution than ATOMICITY primitive, but can still preserve TSO memory consistency in all region optimizations. For clarity, we refer to the existing ATOMICITY primitive for preserving SC *SC_ATOMICITY* primitive in the rest of the paper. We can use Figure 3 to illustrate the relationship between the memory consistency and the restriction on the thread interleaving for preserving the memory consistency in region optimizations. The stronger memory consistency requires stronger restriction on the thread interleaving for preserving the memory consistency in region optimizations. So the dark area in Figure 3 covers the points that can preserve the memory consistency in region optimizations. For SC, SC_ATOMICITY (short name SC_A) can preserve the memory consistency in region optimizations (i.e. the intersection of SC and SC_A, denoted SC+SC_A, falls in the dark area). For TSO, a weaker restriction on the thread interleaving, TSO_ATOMICITY (short name TSO_A), is enough to preserve the memory consistency in region optimizations (i.e. the intersection of TSO and TSO_A, denoted TSO+TSO_A, falls in the dark area). SC_A can also preserve TSO in region optimizations (i.e. the intersection of TSO and SC_A, denoted TSO+SC_A, falls in the dark area), but is over-restrictive (thus less efficient). TSO_A is too weak to preserve SC in region optimizations (i.e. the intersection of SC and TSO_A, denoted SC+TSO_A, stays out of the dark area).

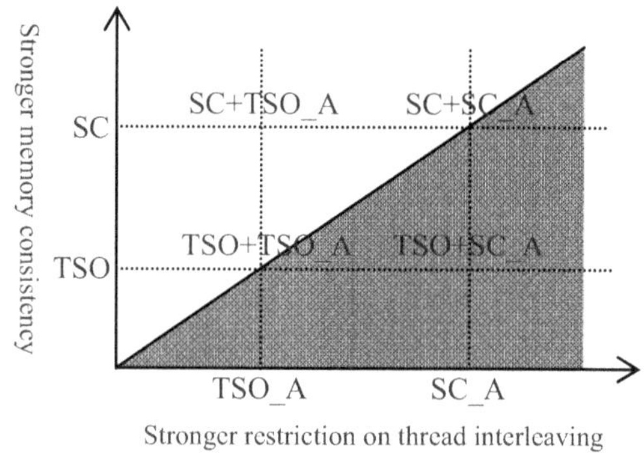

Figure 3: Relationship between Memory Consistency and the Restriction on the Thread Interleaving for Preserving the Memory Consistency in Region Optimizations

We show that TSO_ATOMICITY primitive requires similar architecture support as SC_ATOMICITY primitive and can be implemented with only slight change to the existing SC_ATOMICITY primitive implementation. Our experimental results show that in a state-of-art dynamic binary optimization system with a large set of industrial strength workloads, SC_ATOMICITY primitive can only improve the performance by 4%. TSO_ATOMICITY primitive can reduce the overhead associated with SC_ATOMICITY primitive and improve the performance by 12%.

2. Backgrounds on Memory Consistency Models

2.1 Sequential Consistency

Lamport [22] defines *Sequential Consistency* (SC) as follows. "A system is sequentially consistent if the result of any execution is the same as if the operations of all the processors were executed in some sequential order, and the operations of each individual processor appear in this sequence in the order specified by its program". In this paper, we formally model SC and define:

[Definition 1] A *program* is a set of *memory operations* (i.e. *stores* and *loads*) with a partial *program order*, which partitions all the memory operations into *threads* such that the program order is a total order for memory operations within a thread and there is no program order for memory operations across threads.

We use s to denote a store, l to denote a load and m to denote a load or a store. We use $loc(s)$ and $loc(l)$ to denote the memory location of a store s and a load l respectively. We use L to denote the set of loads in a program and S to denote the set of stores in a program. We use $m_1 <_P m_2$ to denote that m_1 precedes m_2 in the program order $<_P$. As an example, Figure 1 (a) shows a program with thread 1: $\{ m_1, m_2 \}$ and thread 2: $\{ m_3, m_4 \}$ such that $m_1 <_P m_2$ and $m_3 <_P m_4$. We model the execution order of memory operations by a memory order and define:

[Definition 2] A *memory order* is a partial order of the memory operations.

We use $m_1 <_M m_2$ to denote that m_1 precedes m_2 in the memory order $<_M$. So formally we get:

[SC-Memory-Order] A memory order under SC is constrained to be a *total order* satisfying: $m_1 <_P m_2 \Rightarrow m_1 <_M m_2$.

As examples, for the program shown in Figure 1 (a), $m_3 <_M m_4 <_M m_1 <_M m_2$ is a memory order under SC, but $m_2 <_M m_3 <_M m_4 <_M m_1$ is not a memory order under SC, as it violates $m_1 <_P m_2 \Rightarrow m_1 <_M m_2$.

We model the program execution result by a program execution witness and define:

[Definition 3] A *program execution witness* (or in short a *witness*) is a mapping $W: L \rightarrow S \cup \{\perp\}$ such that $W(l) = s$ means that load l reads the data of store s and $W(l) = \perp$ means that load l reads the initial memory data at the entry of the program execution.

In order for the program execution witness to also model the final memory data at the exit of the program execution, we assume that there are loads at the exit of the program execution that read all the memory data. So the final memory data at the exit of the program execution will be witnessed.

A program may have different memory orders in different runs. Different memory orders may get different program execution witnesses. Under SC, each load will witness the most recent store in the memory order. So the program execution witness under SC can be derived from the memory order with the following formula:

[SC-Witness-Formula] $W(l) = latest{<_M} \{ s \mid (loc(s) = loc(l)) \wedge (s <_M l) \}$, where $latest{<_M}$ gets the latest store in the memory order $<_M$ on a set of stores with $latest{<_M} \varnothing = \perp$.

As an example in Figure 1 (b), we can derive the witness, $W(m_2') = \perp$ (i.e. $r2 == 0$) and $W(m_1') = m_4'$ (i.e. $r1 == 1$), from the memory order $m_2' <_M m_3' <_M m_4' <_M m_1'$.

2.2 Total-Store-Ordering

Although SC makes it easy for verifying program correctness with SC-Memory-Order and SC-Witness-Formula, it is inefficient for the program execution, as memory operations from the same thread cannot be reordered in a memory order. Specifically, an earlier store that misses the cache may unnecessarily stall a later load execution, even if there is no data dependence between them. Figure 4 (a) shows an example execution trace under SC. Store m_3 misses the cache, which cannot write the data to the cache to become globally visible through the cache coherence protocol until the cache miss is resolved. All the later memory operations are stalled until the cache miss is resolved, which can take significant amount of time in modern processor executions. It is possible to reduce the pipeline stalls due to the cache miss through hardware speculation techniques [17][32]. But that increases hardware cost, complexity and power consumption.

Popular processors like X86 and SPARC deployed the relaxed *Total-Store-Ordering* (TSO) memory consistency, which is more efficient for the program execution. Figure 4 (b) shows an example execution trace under TSO. Store m_3 can write the store data into an internal *store-queue* waiting for the store miss to be resolved and then write to the cache. Later store m_4 can also append the store data into the store-queue and write to the cache after store m_3. However, later loads m_5 and m_6 can execute without waiting for the cache miss of store m_3 to be resolved. As the result, the execution shown in Figure 4 (b) will have the memory order, $m_1 <_P m_2 <_P m_5 <_P m_6 <_P m_3 <_P m_4$, in which later loads m_5 and m_6 execute before earlier stores m_3 and m_4 write to cache. Note that load m_5 reads the same memory location as store m_3. However, load m_5 can still execute by getting the forwarded data of store m_3 from the store-queue without waiting for the cache miss of store m_3 to be resolved. Compared to the program execution under SC, the program execution under TSO clearly is much more efficient (faster).

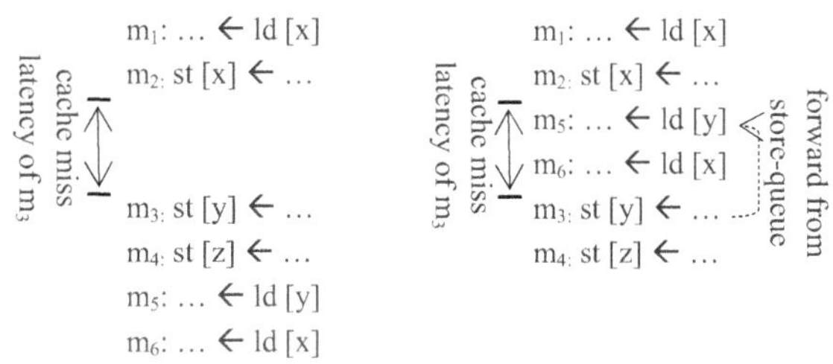

(a) SC (b) TSO

Figure 4: Example Execution Trace in SC and TSO

Except for the reordering between earlier stores and later loads, no other reordering is allowed by TSO. So formally we get:

[TSO-Memory-Order] A memory order under TSO is constrained to be a *total order on all stores* in the program satisfying:

(1) $l_1 <_P l_2 \Rightarrow l_1 <_M l_2$
(2) $s_1 <_P s_2 \Rightarrow s_1 <_M s_2$
(3) $l <_P s \Rightarrow l <_M s$

Due to the store forwarding, a load under TSO will witness the most recent store in the memory order *or in the program order* (i.e. the forwarded data). So the program execution witness under TSO can be derived from the memory order with the following formula:

[TSO-Witness-Formula] $W(l) = latest{<_M} \{ s \mid (loc(s) = loc(l)) \wedge ((s <_M l) \vee (s <_P l))$

As an example, load m_5 in Figure 4 (b) will witness store m_3, which precedes load m_5 in the program order, even though store m_3 does not precede load m_5 in the memory order.

We should note that under SC-Memory-Order, SC-Witness-Formula is mathematically equivalent to TSO-Witness-Formula, as the stores that precede a load in the program order must precede the load in the memory order. So in the rest paper, we simply treat SC and TSO as using the same TSO-Witness-Formula to derive the witness.

2.3 SC_ATOMICITY

There are many existing works [3][19][21][26][31] on hardware transactional memory, which provides an *ATOMICITY* primitive (called *SC_ATOMICITY* primitive in this paper) for a region execution. Formally, we define:

[Definition 4] A *region R* is a set of memory operations in a thread consecutive in the program order. Formally: $m_1 \subseteq R$, $m_2 \subseteq R$, $m_1 <_P m <_P m_2 \Rightarrow m \in R$.

In the figures used in the paper, we simply use a rectangle to represent a region. As an example, Thread 1 in Figure 1 (b) contains a region $\{ m_2', m_1' \}$.

When SC_ATOMICITY primitive is applied on a region, e.g. enclosing the region with a *begin_atomic* marker and an *end_atomic* marker, the hardware will always execute all memory operations in the region atomically. So formally, SC_ATOMICITY primitive enforces the following memory order constraint on a region:

[SC_ATOMICITY-Constraint] $m_1 \subseteq R$, $m_2 \subseteq R$, $m_1 <_M m <_M m_2 \Rightarrow m \in R$

SC_ATOMICITY-Constraint restricts that no memory operation outside a region *R* (including both memory operations in other threads, and memory operations in the same thread but not in region *R*) can interleave in the memory order between any two memory operations in region *R*. Depending on the memory consistency in the program, SC or TSO, the program with SC_ATOMICITY primitive (short name SC_A) on regions can have two corresponding memory consistency models: SC+SC_A and TSO+SC_A. The memory order under SC+SC_A will satisfy SC-Memory-Order in addition to SC_ATOMICITY-Constraint on regions. Similarly, memory order under TSO+SC_A will satisfy TSO-Memory-Order in addition to SC_ATOMICITY-Constraint on regions. As an example, for the program shown in Figure 1 (b), $m_2' <_M m_3' <_M m_4' <_M m_1'$ is a memory order under SC and TSO, but not a memory order under SC+SC_A or TSO+SC_A. As the result, $W(m_2') = \perp$ (i.e. $r2 == 0$) and $W(m_1') = m_4'$ (i.e. $r1 == 1$) is a witness under SC and TSO, but not a witness under SC+SC_A or TSO+SC_A.

For efficiency, existing hardware transactional memory techniques [3][19][21][26][31] implement SC_ATOMICITY primitive optimistically by speculatively executing the region with atomicity violation detection via the snooping mechanism in the cache coherence protocol. For atomicity violation detection, cache lines are extended with speculative read bits and speculative write bits (i.e. a speculative cache) to mark the loads and stores executed in a region respectively. From TSO-Witness-Formula, only the memory order between *conflicted* memory operations (i.e. two memory operations that access the same memory location and at least one of them is a store) will affect the program execution witness. If during the region execution, there is no memory access from other concurrent threads conflicted with the loads and stores in the region as detected by the snooping on read bits and write bits, the region will be witnessed to execute atomically and can be committed at the end of the region execution by atomically clearing all the read bits and write bits in the speculative cache. Otherwise, the execution is rolled back to a checkpoint at the entry of the region and re-executed.

Due to SC_ATOMICITY-Constraint, TSO with SC_ATOMICITY primitive (i.e. TSO+SC_A) suffers certain inefficiency as SC as it restricts any reordering across the region boundary. For example in Figure 5, store m_3 in region *R1* misses the cache and region *R1* cannot commit until the cache miss is resolved. Then the execution of memory operations after region *R1* has to be stalled until region *R1* commits, which has the same inefficiency as SC in Figure 4 (a).

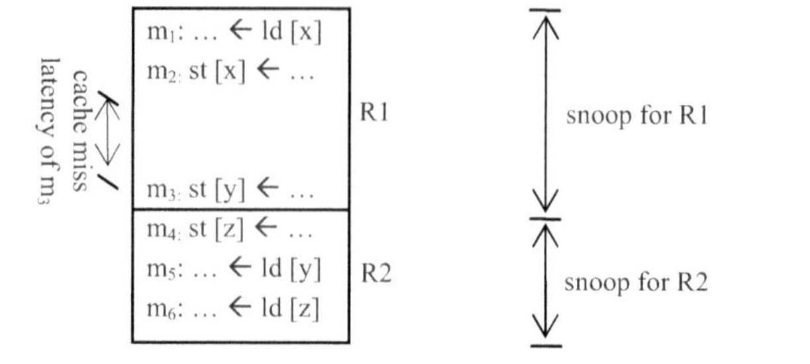

(a) Execution Trace (b) Snooping Period

Figure 5: TSO Execution with SC_ATOMICITY Primitive

Existing hardware speculation techniques [17] may alleviate the performance impact of TSO+SC_A. For example, out-of-order processors may execute loads after region *R1* speculatively within an instruction scheduling window without waiting for region *R1* to be committed (i.e. in-window load speculation). However, this increases the power consumption and is not adopted for power-efficient processors (such as Atom [39]). Moreover, even with in-window load speculation, the retirement of loads after *R1* still needs to be stalled until region *R1* commits. As we show in our experiments later on a dynamic binary optimization system, the stall of retirement due to SC_ATOMICITY primitive can impact 8% performance on average. More aggressive hardware speculation techniques such as multi-version speculative cache [14] may further reduce the stalls on retirement, but that would significantly increase the hardware complexity and power.

3. TSO_ATOMICITY

Instead of improving performance of TSO+SC_A through more aggressive speculations, we relax the constraints of SC_ATOMICITY primitive and develop a novel TSO_ATOMICITY primitive. Formally, TSO_ATOMICITY primitive enforces the following memory order constraints on a region:

[TSO_ATOMICITY-Constraint]

(1) $l_1 \subseteq R$, $l_2 \subseteq R$, $l_1 <_M m <_M l_2 \Rightarrow m \in R$
(2) $s_1 \subseteq R$, $s_2 \subseteq R$, $s_1 <_M m <_M s_2 \Rightarrow m \in R$
(3) $s \subseteq R$, $l \subseteq R$, $s <_M m <_M l \Rightarrow m \in R$

So unlike SC_ATOMICITY which enforces atomic memory order among all memory operations in a region, TSO_ATOMICITY *does not constraint the atomic memory order between earlier loads and later stores in a region.* Depending on the memory consistency in the program, SC or TSO, the program with TSO_ATOMICITY primitive (short name TSO_A) on regions can have two corresponding memory consistency models, SC+TSO_A and TSO+TSO_A, which satisfy SC-Memory-Order and TSO-Memory-Order respectively in addition to TSO_ATOMICITY-Constraint on regions. As an example, for the program shown in Figure 2 (b), $m_2' <_M m_3' <_M m_4' <_M m_1'$ is not a memory order under SC+SC_A or TSO+SC_A, but is a memory order under SC+TSO_A and TSO+TSO_A. Consequently, $W(m_2') = \perp$ (i.e. $r1 == 0$) and $W(m_4') = \perp$ (i.e. $r2$

$== 0$) is not a witness under SC+SC_A or TSO+SC_A, but is a witness under SC+TSO_A and TSO+TSO_A.

TSO+TSO_A can be implemented with only slight change to the existing implementation for TSO+SC_A and can achieve the efficient overlapped region execution as shown in Figure 6 (a). Store m_3 and m_4 in region *R1* write the store data into the store-queue waiting for the cache miss of store m_3 to be resolved, just like regular TSO implementation. TSO_ATOMICITY primitive allows loads after region *R1* to execute without waiting for the cache miss of store m_3 to be resolved. TSO_ATOMICITY primitive also separates the snooping on read bits from that on write bits. Figure 6 (b) shows the snooping periods for TSO_ATOMICITY primitive. Before the execution of instructions after *R1*, we stop the snooping on read bits of region *R1* by atomically clearing all the read bits in the speculative cache such that they can be used to mark loads executed in region *R2* for snooping. However, we still keep the snooping on write bits of *R1* until the cache miss for store m_3 is resolved. This will not affect the overlapped execution of *R2* because stores in *R2* will be appended into the store-queue waiting for the cache miss of store m_3 to be resolved (see TSO implementation in section 2.2), and stores in store-queue will not need to set write bits until the store data is written from the store-queue to the cache, which becomes globally visible. We also keep the register checkpoint for region *R1* until the end of the snooping on write bits of *R1* in case that the snooping may detect conflicts and roll back region *R1*. After all the store data of region *R1* are written from the store-queue to the speculative cache, we commit region *R1* by atomically clearing all the write bits in the speculative cache. Since read bits are cleared earlier before the region commits, TSO_ATOMICITY primitive not only reduces stalls across region boundary to achieve the same efficiency as the regular TSO execution in Figure 4 (b), but also reduces the potential rollback due to the conflicts on read bits (i.e. the case that the thread interleaving is allowed by TSO_ATOMICITY primitive but not by SC_ATOMICITY primitive as shown in Figure 2 (b)).

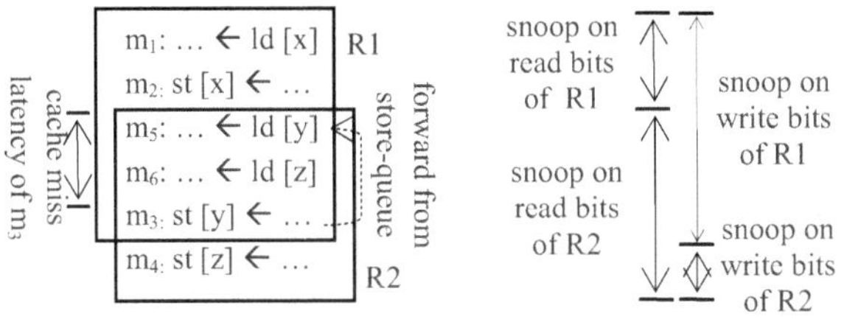

(a) Execution Trace (b) Snooping Period

Figure 6: TSO Execution with TSO_ATOMICITY Primitive

Since TSO_ATOMICITY primitive atomically clear all the read bits after all the loads in the region are executed and atomically clear all the write bits after all the stores in the region are written to the cache and become globally visible, all the loads in the region will be witnessed to execute atomically (i.e. TSO_ATOMICITY-Constraint (1)) and all the stores in the region will witnessed to execute atomically (i.e. TSO_ATOMICITY-Constraint (2)). Since TSO_ATOMICITY primitive always clear write bits later than read bits, TSO_ATOMICITY primitive will only constraint atomic memory order between earlier stores and later loads in a region (i.e. TSO_ATOMICITY-Constraint (3)), but not between earlier loads and later stores in a region.

4. Semantic Comparison

We next compare semantics of different memory consistencies by their program execution witnesses, and define:

[Definition 5] Memory consistency *X* is *equal or stronger* than memory consistency *Y*, if for any program, a program execution witness under consistency *X* is a program execution witness under consistency *Y*.

We use $X \subseteq Y$ to denote that memory consistency *X* is equal or stronger than memory consistency *Y*. Since all the consistencies discussed in previous sections use the same TSO-Witness-Formula to derive the witness from the memory order, we can compare memory consistencies by comparing their memory order constraints. So by definitions, we can get the relationship between different memory consistencies shown in Figure 7.

SC+SC_A	$\subseteq$	SC+TSO_A	$\subseteq$	SC
$\cap$ |		$\cap$ |		$\cap$ |
TSO+SC_A	$\subseteq$	TSO+TSO_A	$\subseteq$	TSO

Figure 7: Relationship between Different Memory Consistencies

4.1 Comparison with Database Isolations

SC_ATOMICITY has been used in database systems to achieve different isolations for transactions [6]. Considering a program composed of regions and treat each region as a transaction, SC+SC_A can achieve the serializable isolation. Many database systems also implemented the more efficient snapshot isolation [6], which only guarantees the following two conditions:

Condition 1: All reads made in a transaction will see a consistent snapshot of the database.

Condition 2: The transaction will successfully commit only if no updates it has made conflict with any concurrent updates made since that snapshot (i.e. no lost update).

Just like that TSO+TSO_A is more efficient for program execution than SC+SC_A, snapshot isolation is more efficient for transaction execution in database system than serializable isolation. So, similar to TSO+TSO_A, the snapshot isolation allows program in Figure 2 (a) to produce the result $r1 == 0$ and $r2 == 0$, which is not allowed by serializable isolation. However, TSO+TSO_A can only guarantee condition 1 of snapshot isolation, but not condition 2. So TSO+TSO_A is even weaker (thus potentially more efficient) than snapshot isolation. As an example, for the program shown in Figure 8, TSO+TSO_A allows the program to produce the result $x == 1$ (with memory order $m_1 <_M m_3 <_M m_2 <_M m_4$), i.e. one of the updates to x is lost, which is not allowed by snapshot isolation.

Initialize: x ← 0

Thread 1	Thread 2
m_1: r1 ← ld [x]	m_3: r2 ← ld [x]
m_2: st [x] ← r1 + 1	m_4: st [x] ← r2 + 1

Figure 8: A Program Example for Comparing TSO+TSO_A with Snapshot Isolation

5. Preserve Memory Consistency in Optimization

We now show that, even though TSO_ATOMICITY primitive relaxes SC_ATOMICITY primitive, it can still preserve TSO in all program optimizations. Similar to [36], we model a program optimization as a transformation from the original program to the optimized program such that the optimized program represents the original program for execution, as shown in Figure 9. Each load l in the original program is mapped to a load l' in the optimized program by OPT_L such that l' represents l to read data. Each store s' in the optimized program is mapped to a store s in the original program by OPT_S such that store s' represents s to write data. We also denote $OPT_S(\perp)=\perp$ so that the optimized program has the same initial data at the entry of the program as the original program. As the results, a program execution witness W' of the optimized program will represent a program execution witness W of the original program such that $W = OPT_S \circ W' \circ OPT_L$. As an example, by reordering m_1 and m_2 in thread 1 of Figure 1 (a) to thread 1' of Figure 1 (b), we get an optimization such that OPT_L maps m_1 and m_2 to m_1' and m_2' respectively, and OPT_S maps m_3' and m_4' to m_3 and m_4 respectively. Then the execution witness of the optimized program $W'(m_1')= m_4'$ (i.e. $r1 == 1$) and $W'(m_2')= \perp$ (i.e. $r2 == 0$) will represent the execution witness of the original program $W(m_1)= m_4$ (i.e. $r1 == 1$) and $W(m_2)= \perp$ (i.e. $r2 == 0$).

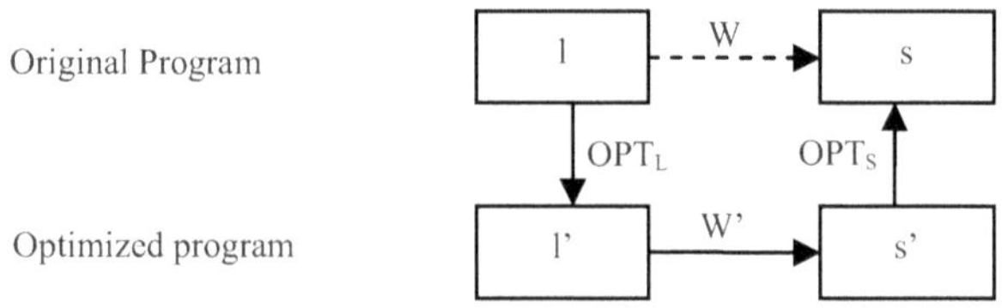

Figure 9: Modeling Optimization

Formally, we define:

[Definition 6] An *optimization* is a transformation from an original program with store set S and load set L to the optimized program with store set S' and load set L' through two mappings: OPT_L: $L \rightarrow L'$ and OPT_S: $S' \rightarrow S$ with $OPT_S(\perp)=\perp$.

OPT_L and OPT_S can model not only memory reordering, but also general optimizations. For example, the redundant load elimination shown in Figure 10 can be modeled as the optimization with $OPT_L(m_1) = OPT_L(m_2) = m_3$.

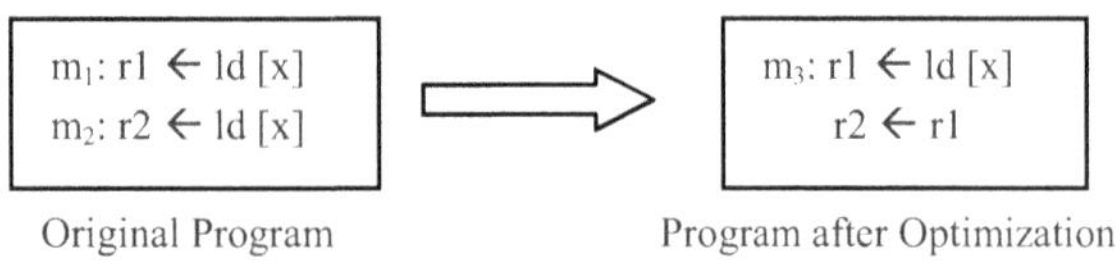

Figure 10: Redundant Load Elimination Example

To preserve the memory consistency, each witness of the optimized program must represent a witness of the original program. So formally, we define:

[Definition 7] An optimization *preserves program execution witness under memory consistency X (*or in short*, preserves memory consistency X*), if for each witness W' of the optimized program under consistency X, there is a witness W of the original program under consistency X such that $W = OPT_S \circ W' \circ OPT_L$.

As an example optimization that do not preserve the memory consistency, the memory order of the program execution in Figure 1 (b) will produce the witness $W'(m_1')= m_4'$ (i.e. $r1 == 1$) and $W'(m_2')= \perp$ (i.e. $r2 == 0$) under SC and TSO. However, no memory order of the original program in Figure 1 (a) would produce the witness $W(m_1) = m_4$ (i.e. $r1 == 1$) and $W(m_2) = \perp$ (i.e. $r2 == 0$) under SC or TSO. So the reordering of m_1 and m_2 in thread 1 of Figure 1 (a) to thread 1' of Figure 1 (b) does not preserve either SC or TSO.

Running the same program under different consistencies may have different memory orders and different memory orders may produce different program execution witnesses. However, we can prove:

[Single-Thread-Witness] Given a single-thread program, the program execution witnesses under all the memory consistencies discussed in previous sections are unique and same, which can be derived with formula: $W(l) = latest{<_P} \{ s \mid (loc(s) = loc(l)) \wedge (s <_P l) \}$, where $latest{<_P}$ gets the latest store in the program order $<_P$ on a set of stores with $latest{<_P} \varnothing = \perp$.

Since all the other memory consistencies discussed in previous sections are equal or stronger than TSO, we can prove Single-Thread-Witness by simply verifying that for a single-thread program, TSO-Witness-Formula with TSO-Memory-Order is mathematically equivalent to the formula in Single-Thread-Witness.

So the program execution witness for a single-thread program is independent of the memory consistency. Optimizations on a single-thread program only need to preserve Single-Thread-Witness based on data dependences for preserving the memory consistency. For multi-thread program, however, this may not be true, as shown by the optimization example in Figure 1. But we can prove:

[Optimization-Theorem] Under SC+SC_A, TSO+SC_A or TSO+TSO_A, an optimization within a region preserves the respective memory consistency, if by treating the region as a single-thread program, the optimization preserves Single-Thread-Witness.

Optimization-Theorem allows us to apply all the traditional data-dependence based optimizations within the region boundary while still preserve the memory consistency under SC+SC_A, TSO+SC_A and TSO+TSO_A. So to optimize a region and preserve SC, we can mark the region with SC_ATOMICITY primitive. The resulting optimized program will preserve SC+SC_A (i.e. preserve SC because SC+SC_A is stronger than SC). Similarly, both SC_ATOMICITY primitive and TSO_ATOMICITY primitive can be applied on a region to preserve TSO in the region optimizations. However, TSO_ATOMICITY primitive cannot be used on a region to preserve SC in the region optimizations, as Optimization-Theorem does not cover SC+TSO_A. Figure 2 shows an example such that an optimization on a region with TSO_ATOMICITY primitive does not preserve SC, as the result $r1 == 0, r2 == 0$ is allowed by the optimized program under SC+TSO_A, but not allowed by the original program under SC.

To prove Optimization-Theorem under SC+SC_A, we only need to show that given any memory order $<'_M$ of the optimized program under SC+SC_A with witness W', we can find a memory order $<_M$ of the original program under SC+SC_A with witness W such that $W = OPT_S \circ W' \circ OPT_L$. To achieve that, we construct the memory order $<_M$ from $<'_M$ such that within threads it is consistent with the program order of the original program, and across threads it is consistent with $<'_M$ under the mapping of

OPT_L and OPT_S. As an example, take a look at the optimization from the program in Figure 2 (a) to the program in Figure 11. Assume the execution of the optimized program gives the memory order $m_3' <'_M m_4' <'_M m_2' <'_M m_1'$ with witness $W'(m_2') = m_3'$ (i.e. r1 == 1) and $W'(m_4') = \perp$ (i.e. r2 == 0), as shown in Figure 11. For the original program, we first construct the memory order $m_1 <_M m_2$ and $m_3 <_M m_4$ to be consistent with the program order $m_1 <_P m_2$ and $m_3 <_P m_4$ within threads. Across threads, we construct the memory order $m_3 <_M m_2$, $m_4 <_M m_2$, $m_3 <_M m_1$ and $m_4 <_M m_1$ to be consistent with the memory order $m_3' <'_M m_2'$, $m_4' <'_M m_2'$, $m_3' <'_M m_1'$ and $m_4' <'_M m_1'$ under the mapping: $m_1 = OPT_S(m_1')$, $m_2' = OPT_L(m_2)$, $m_3 = OPT_S(m_3')$ and $m_4' = OPT_L(m_4)$. The resulting memory order $m_3 <_M m_4 <_M m_1 <_M m_2$ is a memory order of the original program under SC+SC_A with the witness $W(m_2) = m_3$ (i.e. r1 == 1) and $W(m_4) = \perp$ (i.e. r2 == 0). We can verify that, for any memory $<'_M$ of the optimized program under SC+SC_A, the memory order $<_M$ constructed in this way must be a memory order of the original program under SC+SC_A due to SC_ATOMICITY-Constraint. Moreover, the witness W produced by the constructed memory order $<_M$ must satisfy $W = OPT_S \circ W' \circ OPT_L$. This is because within the threads, the optimization preserves Single-Thread-Witness and across threads, $<_M$ is consistent with $<'_M$ under the mapping of OPT_L and OPT_S. Note that as discussed in section 2.1, the program execution witness models the final memory data at the exit of the program execution. So by treating the region as a single thread program, the optimization that preserves Single-Thread-Witness will ensure the correct region live-out stores.

Without SC_ATOMICITY-Constraint of $<'_M$, we may not be able to construct the memory order $<_M$. For example, in the optimization from Figure 2 (a) to Figure 2 (b), the memory order $m_2' <'_M m_3' <'_M m_4' <'_M m_1'$ in Figure 2 (b) violates SC_ATOMICITY-Constraint. Given $<'_M$, if we construct $m_1 <_M m_2$ and $m_3 <_M m_4$ to be consistent with the program order within threads, and across threads $m_2 <_M m_3$, $m_2 <_M m_4$, $m_3 <_M m_1$ and $m_4 <_M m_1$ to be consistent with $<'_M$. The resulting $<_M$ will contain a cycle $m_1 <_M m_2 <_M m_3 <_M m_4 <_M m_1$, which is not a valid memory order.

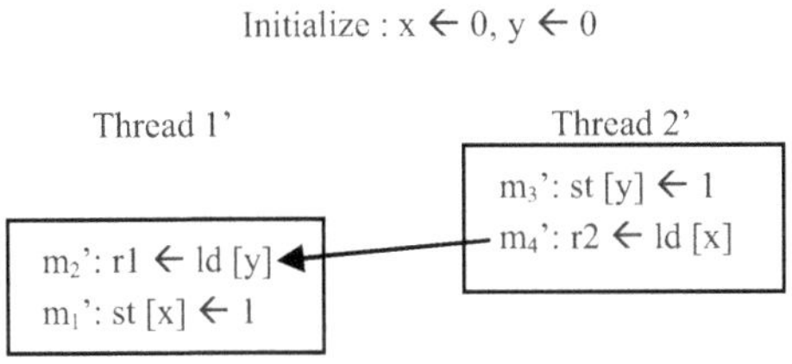

Figure 11: After Optimization

The Optimization-Theorem under TSO+SC_A can be proved in the same way. The Optimization-Theorem under TSO+TSO_A can be proved similarly except that within threads we do not construct memory order $<_M$ *between an earlier store and a later load* to be consistent with the program order, which is not required by TSO-Memory-Order. As an example, for the optimization from Figure 2 (a) to Figure 2 (b), given the memory order $<'_M$ under TSO+TSO_A with witness $W'(m_2') = \perp$ and $W'(m_4') = \perp$, as shown in Figure 2 (b), we will only construct the memory order: $m_2 <_M m_3$, $m_2 <_M m_4$, $m_3 <_M m_1$ and $m_4 <_M m_1$ (note no $m_1 <_M m_2$ or $m_3 <_M m_4$) with witness $W(m_2) = \perp$ and $W(m_4) = \perp$. Then there is no memory order cycle as shown in the previous paragraph, even though TSO_ATOMICITY does not constraint atomic memory order between earlier loads and later stores in a region. We can verify that the memory order $<_M$ constructed in this way must always be a memory order under TSO+TSO_A with the witness W satisfying $W = OPT_S \circ W' \circ OPT_L$.

We should note that in all above discussions, we do not consider branches in the region. By enumerating all paths, it is straightforward to extend the above discussions to regions with branches but without loops. There is an issue to group codes with loops into a region with SC_ATOMICITY primitive or TSO_ATOMCITY primitive, as it may introduce deadlocks due to rollbacks [7], which do not exist in the original program without SC_ATOMICITY primitive or TSO_ATOMCITY primitive. So in loop region optimizations with SC_ATOMICITY primitive or TSO_ATOMICITY primitive, we only speculatively group the code into regions for the optimizations. In case of region rollback, we will discard the optimizations on the region and run the original non-optimized code without SC_ATOMICITY primitive or TSO_ATOMICITY primitive.

6. Experiments

6.1 Hardware Implementation

To evaluate and compare SC_ATOMICITY primitive and TSO_ATOMICITY primitive, we implemented them on a cycle-accurate in-house simulator that faithfully models an out-of-order processor for IA32 microarchitecture. Table 1 shows the microarchitecture parameters for the processor.

Table 1: Simulator Parameters

Components	*Configurations*
Issue Width	4 way
Scheduling Window	54 entries
ROB	168 entries
Load Queue	64 entries
Store Queue	40 entries
L1 I-cache	32K, 4 way, 64 byte line, 1 cycle hit latency
L1 D-cache	32K, 8 way, 64 byte line, 4 cycles hit latency
L2 Unified Cache	256K, 8 way, 64 byte line, 12 cycles hit latency
L3 Uncore Cache	4M, 16 way
Memory Latency	200 Cycles
Core	4

Our out-of-order processor implements TSO. Stores can retire with store data in a store-queue waiting for in-order write-back to the cache (i.e. senior stores). Later instructions can retire with earlier store data in the store-queue. The processor also implements in-window load speculation [17] such that loads can be executed speculatively out-of-order within an instruction schedule window. To maintain the memory order on loads, the speculatively executed loads keep snooping for conflicts in a load queue until loads retire.

To support SC_ATOMICITY primitive or TSO_ATOMICITY primitive, L1 D-cache is extended with speculative read bits and speculative write bits. Loads in a region will set the read bits at load retirement and stores in a region will set write bits at write-back from store-queue to the cache. After all the instructions in a region retire, SC_ATOMICITY primitive cannot commit the region until all the data in the store-queue are drained and written back to cache. That stalls the instructions after the region from retiring, potentially for many cycles if stores miss the last level cache. TSO_ATOMICITY primitive does not stall the instructions after the region from retiring. Instead, it just clears all the read bits and then later instructions can retire normally. When the last store data of the region is written back to cache, the whole region can commit by clearing all the write bits and releasing the register checkpoint for the region.

The register check-pointing for SC_ATOMICITY primitive and TSO_ATOMICITY primitive is implemented lazily through a Copy-On-Write (COW) mechanism at the instruction retirement using a COW queue with 144 entries. We support overlapped execution of at most four regions in TSO_ATOMICITY primitive.

6.2 Dynamic Binary Optimization

To evaluate the optimization benefit with SC_ATOMICITY primitive and TSO_ATOMICITY primitive, we implemented a dynamic binary optimization system in the simulator that takes a program compiled for the IA32 architecture and generates micro-operation (uop) code. The dynamic optimizer dynamically profiles the execution and constructs frames as regions for optimization. A frame is a superblock with all internal branches converted to asserts [30]. Frame regions are widely used in dynamic binary optimization [29][30][33] due to their low runtime optimization overheads. Table 2 lists the optimizations used in the experiments.

Table 2: List of Optimizations

Non-Memory Optimizations	Memory Optimizations
Register-Forward-Propagation	Redundant-Load-Elimination
Register-Backward-Propagation	Store-Load-Forwarding
Identical-Logic-Operation	Dead-Load-Elimination
Condition-Propagation	Dead-Store-Elimination
Assert-Elimination	Store-Fusion
Redundant-Operation-Elimination	Load-Fusion
Dead-Code-Elimination	
Constant-Folding-Propagation	
ALU-Fusion	

Dynamic binary optimization on IA32 micro-operations must preserve TSO for all the programs as the optimizer has no source-level memory consistency information. The optimizer also has no knowledge on whether the optimized code is running in a single-thread application or a multi-thread application. Due to that, we apply SC_ATOMICITY primitive or TSO_ATOMICITY primitive for all the optimized regions.

The benefit of TSO_ATOMICITY primitive over SC_ATOMICITY primitive comes from two facts. First, TSO_ATOMICITY primitive does not stall the retirement of instructions in later regions waiting for the store miss of instructions in earlier regions to be resolved. Second, TSO_ATOMICITY primitive clears read bits earlier to reduce region rollbacks. The stall of retirement across region boundary has high performance impact on small regions due to their frequent crossing of region boundary. The region rollback has high performance impact on large regions due to their high possibility of conflict and large rollback overhead. Frame regions typically have small region sizes (average ~20 instructions, as compared to the ROB size 168). So we focus on evaluating the performance impact of the stall of retirement across region boundary in this paper. The performance impact of region rollback (or squash) due to thread interleaving is negligible in our experiments (Note that our dynamic binary optimization does not optimize regions across the locked instructions so there is no region rollback due to the synchronization through locked instructions).

The stall of retirement across region boundary impacts both single-thread executions and multi-thread executions. The concurrent multi-thread executions make it unstable to evaluate the performance impact due to the non-determinism in the thread synchronizations. So we collect performance data only on single-thread executions. This methodology is similar to other studies on region optimizations with SC_ATOMICITY primitive [27].

We collect performance data on around 400 snippets from about 200 programs in nine categories, as shown in Table 3. Some applications that are represented by other programs are omitted (e.g. tonto in SPEC2006 FP is omitted since it behaves similar to some other programs). This wide range of application coverage is essential to properly evaluate the proposed mechanisms under the complex interaction among original code, the dynamic optimizing compiler, uop code, and out-of-order processors.

Table 3: Applications Used for Evaluation

Application Categories	# of Applications (and examples)	# of snippet
SERVER	14 (e.g. specweb, google_query, oracle_kernel, tpce)	46
WORKSTATION	39 (e.g. eclipse, autocad, verilog, bioinformatics, fluent)	82
MULTIMEDIA	34 (e.g. adobe, sysmark, mobilemark, renderman, cinebench)	73
CONSUMER ELECTRONIC (CE)	26 (e.g. pcmark, h264, mpeg2, real_video, mp3)	44
GAME	20 (e.g. doom3, quake4, battlefield2, splintercell3, ut2004)	31
OFFICE	15 (e.g. excel, access, word, outlook, powerpoint, flash)	34
PRODUCTIVITY TOOL (TOOL)	22 (e.g. xml-parser, winzip, virus-scan, winrar, openssl)	33
SPEC CPU2006 INT (ISPEC06)	9 (all except gobmk, sjeng, xalancbmk)	25
SPEC CPU2006 FP (FSPEC06)	16 (all except tonto)	33

6.3 Performance Evaluation

Figure 12 shows the performance gain from frame optimizations. The baseline performance is for the run without binary optimization. The left bar (non-mem-opt) shows the speedup from binary optimization with only non-memory optimizations listed in the first column of Table 2. Since non-memory optimizations never affect the memory consistency, we do not need SC_ATOMICITY primitive or TSO_ATOMICITY primitive support. Overall, we get about 6.7% performance improvements with the non-memory optimizations. The middle bar (opt with SC_ATOMICITY) shows the speedup with SC_ATOMICITY primitive support to preserve memory consistency for optimizing frames. So all the optimizations listed in Table 2 are applied to the frames. Due to the stall overheads of SC_ATOMICITY primitive across the region boundary, we get only 4% performance improvement over the baseline, even with the additional memory optimizations. The right bar (opt with TSO-ATOMICITY) shows the speedup with TSO-ATOMICITY primitive support. Overall, we get 12% performance improvement over the baseline without dynamic binary optimization, an 8% better than the performance with SC_ATOMICITY primitive support. For certain categories (e.g. CE), the performance difference between SC_ATOMICITY primitive and TSO_ATOMICITY primitive can be as high as 15%. Due to the high stall overhead associated with

SC_ATOMICITY primitives, many prior works do not rely on SC_ATOMICITY to preserve memory consistency during binary optimization. They either work only on single core [20] or restrict certain memory optimizations (e.g. no optimization of stores) [33].

It may be interesting to note that the average performance with SC_ATOMICITY is actually a little lower than that with only non-memory optimizations without SC_ATOMICITY support. The main reasons are 1) SC_ATOMICITY delays the retirements of instructions after the regions, and 2) the regions (frames) is relative small, and the optimization benefit under SC_ATOMICITY cannot fully amortize the overhead at region boundary. We report more detailed data on the impacts of region size and the delay at region boundary in the next subsections.

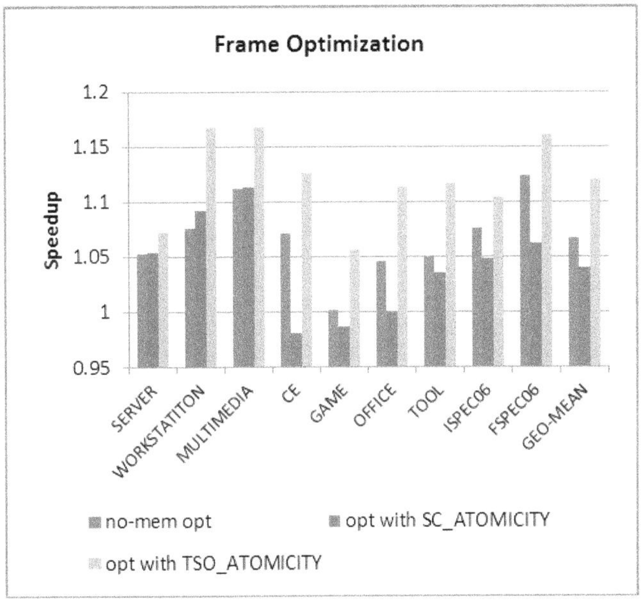

Figure 12: Speedup in Frame Optimization

6.4 Sensitivity to Region Size

Since the performance impact of SC_ATOMICITY primitive and TSO_ATOMICITY primitive is sensitive to the region/frame size, for evaluating the performance impact of larger regions, we extended the dynamic binary optimizer to aggressively build multi-frame regions (including DAG and Loop regions) by connecting paths between frames. Figure 13 shows the average dynamic region sizes of single-frame regions (~20 instructions) and multi-frame regions (~70 instructions). Supporting atomic regions beyond frames has associated HW and SW costs. For example, [11] recommends a two-level atomicity scheme which requires both gated store buffer and speculative cache support, [10] proposes a conditional commit extension to dynamically extend atomic scope, and [1] further elects to make L2 cache, rather than L1 cache, speculative in order to accommodate large atomic regions. So our general multi-frame region really stretches the performance evaluation for large regions than practically deployed.

Figure 14 shows the performance gain from our multi-frame region optimization. Due to the larger region and relatively lower across region overheads, we get more optimization benefit. Overall, we get 15.9% and 20.4% performance improve from SC_ATOMICITY primitive and TSO_ATOMICITY primitive supports, respectively. So even with the large regions, TSO_ATOMICITY primitive still can perform 4.5% better than SC_ATOMICITY primitive.

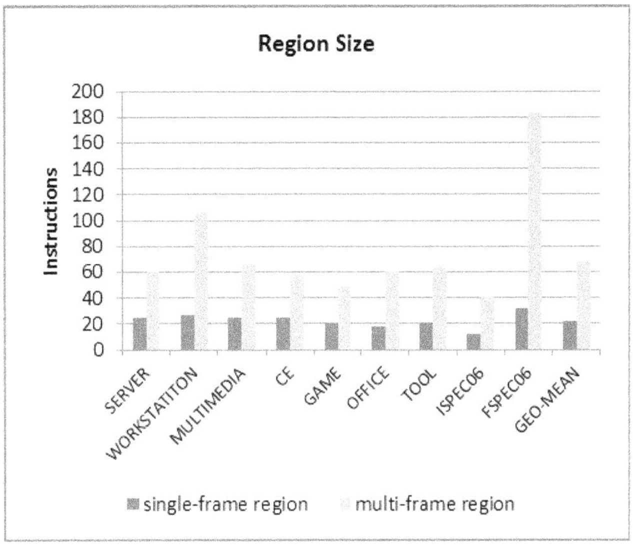

Figure 13: Dynamic Region Instruction Count

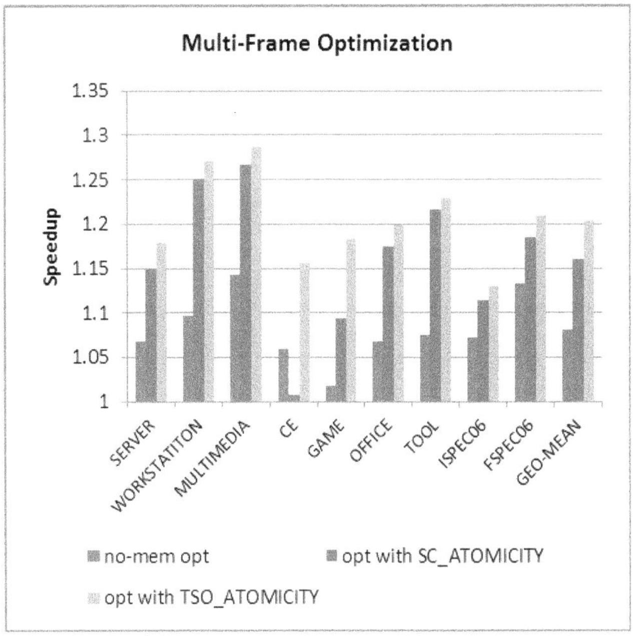

Figure 14: Speedup in Multi-Frame Optimization

Figure 15 shows the average stall cycles per region commit with SC_ATOMICITY primitive for multi-frame regions. Among all the categories, CE and GAME have long stall cycles at region commit, which lead to the big performance differences between TSO_ATOMICITY primitive and SC_ATOMICITY primitive (see Figure 14). FSPEC06 also has long stall cycles. But its larger region size (see Figure 13) amortizes most of the overhead. Note that, for the out-of-order processor, even when the retirement stage is stalled, later instructions can still flow from fetch stage to the reorder buffer and be dispatched for execution. So many stall cycles can be hidden by the out-of-order execution, until the reorder buffer is full. If we were modeling an in-order processor (e.g. an in-order Atom or ARM processor), we would expect the 7 cycles of average stall at region commit to cause more serious performance loss than that shown in Figure 14.

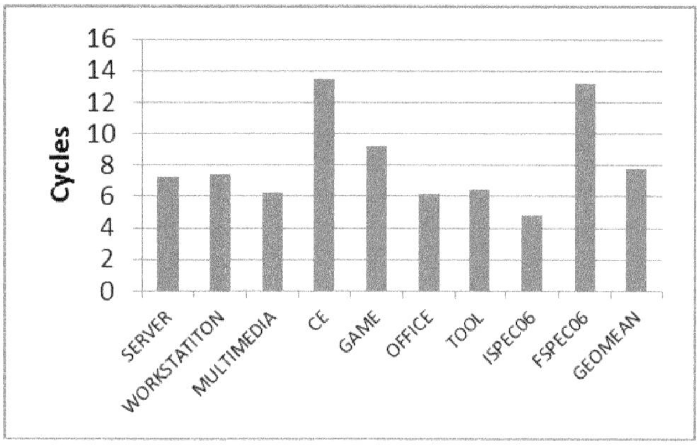

Figure 15: Stall Cycles per Region Commit

7. Related Works

SC_ATOMICITY primitive has been widely studied in transactional memory techniques [3][19][21][26][31] to synchronize threads without locks. Recently, Intel announced a SC_ATOMICITY primitive (called TSX for Transactional Synchronization Extension) for the new Haswell microarchitecture [40]. Recent research work [2] shows that SC_ATOMICITY primitive can be used to preserve sequential consistency in program optimization. Architectural techniques [8][38] also leverage SC_ATOMICITY primitive to reorder memory operations for performance improvement. Our result suggests that TSX won't be able to efficiently support dynamic binary optimizations of frame or superblocks [20], unless TSX is extended to support TSO_ATOMICITY.

Previous works [12][25][36] show that SC and TSO impose considerable memory consistency constraints to the program optimization. Recent work [34] shows that it requires thread-local and shared read-only information in the program in order to achieve efficient SC implementation. Due to that, high-level program language like C [9] and Java [24] typically adopt the relaxed memory consistency models [16][18] to avoid the restrictions on the program optimization. Without high-level language memory consistency information, binary optimization, however, has to obey the processor memory consistency.

There are many research papers and systems on dynamic binary translation (DBT), e.g. Dynamo [4], IA32-EL [5], DynamoRIO [12], Transmeta [20], DAISY [15], Pin [23], Replay[29], Parrot [33], HDTrans [35]. All these works show performance improvement through dynamic binary optimization with little touch on the issues of preserving memory consistency in optimization.

8. Conclusion and Future Works

In this paper, we introduce a novel TSO_ATOMICITY primitive, which can preserve TSO memory consistency in region optimizations efficiently. Our experimental results show that TSO_ATOMICITY primitive can significantly improve the performance over the existing SC_ATOMICITY primitive.

TSO_ATOMICITY primitive introduced in this paper can support not only binary program optimization, but also microarchitecture optimizations. For example, due to the store order constraint, current microarchitecture implementing TSO cannot combine two stores to the same cache line across other stores to reduce the store port pressure. We may leverage TSO_ATOMICITY primitive to combine stores in the store-queue. Furthermore, we believe that additional variances of atomicity primitives can be introduced to efficiently preserve other memory consistencies, e.g. PSO [37], in region optimization.

References

[1] R. Agarwal, J. Torrellas, "FlexBulk: intelligently forming atomic blocks in blocked-execution multiprocessors to minimize squashes", ISCA 2011

[2] W. Ahn, S. Qi, M. Nicolaides, J. Torrellas, J. Lee, X. Fang, S. Midkiff, S and D. Wong, "BulkCompiler: high-performance sequential consistency through cooperative compiler and hardware support", MICRO 2009.

[3] C. S. Ananian and K. Asanovic and B. C. Kuszmaul, C. E. Leiserson and S. Lie, "Unbounded Transactional Memory", HPCA 2005.

[4] V. Bala, E. Duesterwald and S. Banerjia, "Dynamo: A transparent runtime optimization system", PLDI 2000.

[5] L. Baraz, T. Devor, O. Etzion, S. Goldenberg, A. Skalesky, Y. Wang and Y. Zemach, "IA-32 Execution Layer: A Two Phase Dynamic Translator Designed to Support IA-32 Applications on Itanium®-based Systems", MICRO 2003.

[6] H. Berenson, P. Bernstein, J. Gray, J. Melton, E. O'Neil and P. O'Neil, "A Critique of ANSI SQL Isolation Levels", *Proceedings of the 1995 ACM SIGMOD International Conference on Management of Data.*

[7] C. Blundell, E. C. Levwis and M. K. Martin, "Deconstructing Transactions: The Subtleties of ATOMICITY", WDDD 2005.

[8] C. Blundell, M. M. Martin and T. F. Wenisch, "InvisiFence: performance-transparent memory ordering in conventional multiprocessors". ISCA 2009.

[9] H. Boehm and S. V. Adve, "Foundations of the C++ concurrency memory model", PLDI 2008.

[10] E. Borin, Y. Wu, M. Breternitz Jr., C. Wang, "LAR-CC: Large atomic regions with conditional commits," CGO 2011.

[11] E. Borin, Y. Wu, C. Wang, W. Liu, M. -Breternitz, S. Hu, E. Natanzon, S. Rotem and R. Rosner, "TAO: two-level atomicity for dynamic binary optimizations", CGO 2010.

[12] D. Bruening, T. Garnett and S. Amarasinghe, "An infrastructure for adaptive Dynamic Optimization", CGO 2003.

[13] S. Burckhardt, M. Musuvathi and V. Singh. "Verifying local transformations on relaxed memory models", CC 2010.

[14] L. Ceze, J. Tuck, P. Montesinos and J. Torrellas, "BulkSC: bulk enforcement of sequential consistency", ISCA 2007.

[15] K. Ebcioglu , E. R. Altman, "DAISY: dynamic compilation for 100% architectural compatibility", ISCA 1997.

[16] G. Gao, V. Sarkar, "Location Consistency-A New Memory Model and Cache Consistency Protocol", IEEE Trans. Computers, 2000.

[17] K. Gharachorloo, A. Gupta and J. Hennessy, "Two Techniques to Enhance the Performance of Memory Consistency Models", ICPP 1991.

[18] K. Gharachorloo , D. Lenoski , J. Laudon , P. Gibbons , A. Gupta and J. Hennessy, "Memory Consistency and Event Ordering in Scalable Shared-Memory Multiprocessors", ISCA 1990.

[19] L. Hammond, V. Wong, M. Chen. B.D. Carlstrom, J.D. Davis, B. Hertzberg, M.K. Prabhu, H. Wijaya; C. Kozyrakis and K. Olukotun, "Transactional Memory Coherence and Consistency", ISCA 2004.

[20] K. Krewell, "Transmeta Gets More Efficeon", *Microprocessor report*. v.17, October, 2003.

[21] M. Herlihy and J. E. B. Moss, "Transactional memory: Architectural support for lock-free data structures", In Proceedings of *the 20th annual International Symposium on Computer Architecture* (ISCA) 1993.

[22] L. Lamport, "How to Make a Multiprocessor Compute That Correctly Executes Multiprocess Programs", *IEEE Transactions on Computers,* 1979.

[23] C. Luk, R. Cohn, R. Muth, H. Patil, A. Klauser, G. Lowney, S. Wallace, V. Reddi and K. Hazelwood, "Pin: Building Customized Program Analysis Tools with Dynamic Instrumentation", PLDI 2005.

[24] J. Manson, W. Pugh , S. V. Adve, "The Java memory model", POPL 2005.

[25] D. Marino, A. Singh, T. Millstein, M. Musuvathi and S. Narayanasamy, "A Case for SC-Preserving Compiler", PLDI 2011.

[26] K. E. Moore and J. Bobba and M. J. Moravan and M. D. Hill and D. A. Wood, "LogTM: Log-based Transactional Memory", HPCA 2006.

[27] N. Neelakantam, R. Rajwar, S. Srinivas, U. Srinivasan and C. Zilles, "Hardware atomicity for reliable software speculation", ISCA 2007.

[28] S. Owens, S. Sarkar and P. Sewell, "A Better X86 Memory Model: X86-TSO", *Theorem Proving in Higher Order Logics,* (TPHOLs), 2009.

[29] S. Patel and S. Lumetta, "rePLay: A Hardware Framework for Dynamic Optimization". *IEEE Transactions on Computers.*50, 6 (Jun. 2001), 590-608.

[30] S. Patel, T. Tung, S. Bose and M. Crum, "Increasing the size of atomic instruction blocks using control flow assertions", MICRO 2000.

[31] R. Rajwar and M. Herlihy and K. Lai, "Virtualizing Transactional Memory", ISCA 2005.

[32] P. Ranganathan, V. Pai and S. Adve, "Using Speculative Retirement and Larger Instruction Windows to Narrow the Performance Gap between Memory Consistency Models", SPAA 1997.

[33] R. Rosner, Y. Almog, Y, M. Moffie, N. Schwartz and A. Mendelson, "Power Awareness through Selective Dynamically Optimized Frames", ISCA 2004.

[34] A. Singh, S. Narayanasamy, D. Marino, T. Millstein, M. Musuvathi, "End-to-End Sequential Consistency", ISCA 2012.

[35] S. Sridhar, J. S. Shapiro, E. Northup and P. Bungale, "HDTrans: An Open Source, Low-Level Dynamic Instrumentation System", VEE 2006.

[36] C. Wang, Y. Wu, "Modeling and Performance Evaluation of TSO-Preserving Binary Optimization", PACT 2011.

[37] D. L. Weaver and T. Germond, editors, "The SPARC architecture Manual (Version 9)", Prentice-Hall, 1994.

[38] T. F. Wenisch, A. Ailamaki, B. Falsafi and A. Moshovos. "Mechanisms for store-wait-free multiprocessors", ISCA 2007.

[39] "Intel® 64 and IA-32 Architectures Software Developer's Manual Volume 3A", Order Number: 253668032US.

[40] "Intel® Architecture Instruction Set Extensions Programming Reference", February 2012

Wait-n-GoTM: Improving HTM Performance by Serializing Cyclic Dependencies

Syed Ali Raza Jafri*, Gwendolyn Voskuilen*, and T. N. Vijaykumar (* both primary student authors)

School of Electrical and Computer Engineering, Purdue University
{sjafri,geinfeld,vijay}@ecn.purdue.edu

Abstract

Transactional memory (TM) has been proposed to alleviate some key programmability problems in chip multiprocessors. Most TMs optimistically allow concurrent transactions, detecting read-write or write-write conflicts. Upon conflicts, existing hardware TMs (HTMs) use one of three conflict-resolution policies: (1) *always-abort*, (2) *always-wait* for some conflicting transactions to complete, or (3) *always-go* past conflicts and resolve acyclic conflicts at commit or abort upon cyclic dependencies. While each policy has advantages, the policies degrade performance under contention by limiting concurrency (always-abort, always-wait) or incurring late aborts due to cyclic dependencies (always-go). Thus, while always-go avoids acyclic aborts, no policy avoids cyclic aborts. We propose *Wait-n-GoTM* (*WnGTM*) to increase concurrency while avoiding cyclic aborts. We observe that most cyclic dependencies are caused by threads interleaving multiple accesses to a few heavily-read-write-shared delinquent data cache blocks. These accesses occur in code sections called *cycle inducer sections* (*CISTs*). Accordingly, we propose *Wait-n-Go* (*WnG*) conflict-resolution to avoid many cyclic aborts by predicting and serializing the CISTs. To support the WnG policy, we extend previous HTMs to (1) allow multiple readers and writers, (2) scalably identify dependencies, and (3) detect cyclic dependencies via new mechanisms, namely, conflict transactional state, order-capture, and hardware timestamps, respectively. In 16-core simulations of STAMP, WnGTM achieves average speedups of 46% for higher-contention benchmarks and 28% for all benchmarks over always-abort (TokenTM) with low-contention benchmarks remaining unchanged, compared to always-go (DATM) and always-wait (LogTM-SE), which perform worse than and 6% better than TokenTM, respectively.

Categories and Subject Descriptors C.1.4 **[Processor Architectures]:** Parallel Architectures

General Terms Design, Performance

Keywords transactional memory; transactional conflicts; cyclic dependencies; serializing transactions

1. Introduction

Multicores offer significant advantages in terms of power dissipation and performance as compared to uniprocessors. Traditionally, multicores have been programmed using locks. To alleviate some key programmability problems with locks, researchers have proposed transactional memory (TM). TM allows programmers to express atomic regions, or transactions, without using locks. TM implementations ensure atomicity and isolation of transactions. Several hardware TM (HTM) [3,6,8,11,17,18,23,25,28,33], software TM (STM) [1,27], and hybrid TM [4,22,15] implementations have been proposed. Most TMs optimistically allow concurrent transactions, detecting conflicts when a transaction attempts to read or write a data block written by another concurrent transaction. While STMs use software to detect conflicts, HTMs piggyback conflict detection on cache coherence and hence are faster. Therefore, we focus on HTMs though our ideas are applicable to STMs.

Upon detecting a conflict, current HTM proposals employ one of three conflict-resolution policies: (1) *Always-abort:* abort one or more of the conflicting transactions (e.g., [3,8,11,25,28]). (2) *Always-wait:* force one or more of the conflicting transactions to wait for the other(s) to commit or abort, without (e.g., [23,33]) or with (e.g., [5]) thread pre-emption. (3) *Always-go:* allow the conflicting transactions to proceed by forcing commits in the conflict-induced dependence order (e.g., DATM [26]) or by re-executing the backward slice of the conflicting accesses to repair corrupted memory state (e.g., RETCON [7]). Because such repair is hard in the general case, RETCON is limited to simple cases such as counter increments. Another always-go variation, lazy conflict resolution, delays conflict detection until commit, and hence allows transactions to proceed past as-yet-unknown conflicts (e.g., [17]). In general, both always-wait and always-go may incur cyclic waiting and dependencies, respectively, which are resolved via aborts.

While each conflict resolution policy has advantages, they all degrade performance in the presence of contention. Always-abort incurs many aborts even for acyclic dependencies which can be resolved by committing in the dependence order (i.e., producer before consumer). Always-wait aborts less often but incurs long waiting for conflicts to disappear via commits or aborts, disallowing producer-consumer concurrency for acyclic dependencies. Always-go suffers fewer aborts and less waiting for acyclic dependencies. However, the policy incurs late aborts due to cyclic dependencies formed after proceeding past many conflicts, resulting in much lost work. Further, frequent aborts are expensive as TMs typically use randomized back-off to reduce the chances of future conflicts. Improving TM performance is important given that many companies have built or considered building HTM support into their products, including IBM [32], Intel [14], AMD [12], Oracle [16], and Azul [13].

We propose *Wait-n-GoTM (WnGTM)* to address the above performance problems: (1) *always-abort* and *always-wait* limit concurrency while *always-go* incurs late aborts; and (2) none of the existing policies avoid aborts upon cyclic dependencies. WnGTM is based on the guiding principle that to achieve high performance, conflict resolution policies should increase concurrency while avoiding cyclic aborts. Our primary contribution is a new conflict resolution policy, called *Wait-n-Go (WnG)*, which achieves high performance by serializing in-flight, cyclically-conflicting transactions for the right amount of time to avoid many cyclic aborts and then allowing the transactions to proceed past conflicts to increase concurrency. For acyclic dependencies, WnG defaults to always-go to avoid aborts and waiting.

We make the key observation that most cyclic dependencies, and hence aborts, are caused by a few, heavily-read-write-shared data cache blocks. Multiple accesses to one or more such *delin-*

ASPLOS'13, March 16-20, 2013, Houston, Texas, USA.

quent blocks in one transaction are cyclically interleaved with accesses from another transaction, resulting in dependence cycles. We call the section of transactional code comprising all the accesses to a particular delinquent block a *cycle inducer section (CIST)*. (Transactions accessing multiple delinquent blocks have multiple CISTs.) We also observe that CISTs predictably repeat due to systematic program patterns, such as simple operations like enqueue and dequeue of a work queue and update of auxiliary, book-keeping counters, as well as complex computations like general graph insertion and deletion. Such systematic patterns expose the lack of robustness of previous approaches, and result in performance degradation. We specifically note that while lazy conflict resolution implicitly employs always-go and naturally avoids some aborts upon acyclic dependencies, lazy resolution cannot avoid late aborts due to CISTs, just as always-go with eager resolution (e.g., DATM) cannot.

WnG avoids cycles by serializing the CISTs of conflicting transactions. To this end, we propose a hardware CIST predictor that *predicts when a transaction needs to be serialized and for how long to avoid aborts*. The predictor flags the beginning of a CIST so that the (successor) transaction waits for predecessor transactions to exit the CIST (the "wait" in WnG). A successor waiting until the predecessors commit would result in extra waiting (similar to always-wait). Instead, the predictor flags the end of the CIST so that a predecessor can signal the waiting successors to proceed even if the predecessor has not yet committed (the "go" in WnG). Our predictor can handle CISTs with arbitrary control and data flow. Because only a few blocks are delinquent, small prediction tables suffice (e.g., 32 entries per core); and because the delinquent blocks are highly predictable, WnG's waiting is accurate. Conflicting transactions are serialized only through the CISTs, and execute concurrently both before and after the CISTs. Consequently, WnGTM orders commits in the predecessor-successor order to maintain serializability, similar to DATM. This execution schedule satisfies our goal of increasing concurrency while avoiding cyclic aborts. Unlike RETCON [7], WnG can handle CISTs comprising arbitrary computation. Thus, WnG achieves good performance despite systematic cyclic dependencies, and exhibits robustness.

Serializing in-flight, conflicting transactions, as WnG does, is inevitably involved. We manage this complexity by dividing the labor between hardware and software, both for the WnG policy and the mechanisms for waiting at and proceeding past conflicts. On the policy side, we use the hardware solely for the simpler task of CIST prediction and push to software exception handlers the burdensome parts of serialization. On the mechanism side, the hardware handles the simple cases of events that are captured by coherence while the software handles the more difficult remaining cases. Specifically, we extend previous HTMs with three mechanisms. First, we generalize the multi-reader, single-writer abstraction (i.e., multiple reader transactions or a single writer transaction per cache block) which does not order transactions, as used by many previous HTMs, to a multi-reader multi-writer paradigm (i.e., multiple transactions reading and writing the same block concurrently) like DATM which orders transactions. To achieve this ordering, we use a transactional (not coherence) state, *conflict-state*, to identify blocks involved in one or more conflicts. Second, we propose *order-capture* which captures the predecessor-successor ordering in hardware in the simple, common case of conflicts through the L1 cache and in software in the more difficult, uncommon case of conflicts through the L2. Finally, we adapt a hardware *timestamp scheme* from [30] to detect cyclic dependencies and waiting, without relying on broadcasts and degrading scalability like DATM. Our timestamp scheme is independent of the WnG policy ensuring policy-mechanism separation. A key aspect of our mechanisms is that they avoid changing coherence by leveraging TokenTM [8].

In summary, the contributions of this paper are:

- Wait-n-Go conflict resolution policy which increases concurrency while avoiding many cyclic aborts by making conflicting transactions wait for the right amount of time before proceeding even if predecessor transactions have not yet committed;
- Hardware CIST predictor to serialize only the CISTs while allowing concurrent execution before and after the CISTs;
- Three mechanisms extending previous HTMs to enable a multi-reader, multi-writer paradigm, namely, *conflict-state* to identify transactional blocks involved in conflicts, *order-capture* to determine predecessor-successor ordering, and a hardware *timestamp* adaptation to detect cyclic ordering.
- In 16-core simulations of STAMP, WnGTM achieves, on average, 46% and 28% speedups over always-abort (TokenTM) for the higher-contention benchmarks and all the benchmarks, respectively, with low-contention benchmarks remaining unchanged, compared to always-go (DATM) and always-wait (LogTM-SE [33]), which perform worse than and 6% better than TokenTM, respectively.

The rest of the paper is organized as follows. Section 2 describes our Wait-n-Go policy and Section 3 describes Wait-n-GoTM's mechanisms. We discuss related work in Section 4. We describe our experimental methodology in Section 5 and present our results in Section 6. We conclude the paper in Section 7.

2. Wait-n-Go Conflict Resolution

Because the WnG policy is applicable to any TM, we present the policy in this section without referring to any specific TM. Figure 1 illustrates eager always-go (a) and WnG (b) for both acyclic and cyclic conflicts. In the acyclic conflict via non-delinquent data cache block *A*, transaction *T2* writes *A* after *T1* has read *A* (time grows downwards). This conflict causes always-abort to abort and always-wait to wait, while always-go (shown on the left) proceeds past the conflict. WnG defaults to always-go for acyclic conflicts and also proceeds past the conflict (on the right). In the cyclic conflict via delinquent cache block *B*, *T1* reads *B*, *T2* reads and writes to *B*, and then *T1* writes to *B*. This cyclic access pattern causes an abort under both always-abort and always-go (on the left). If not for the initial acyclic conflict, which causes *T2* under always-wait to wait (excessively) for *T1* to commit, the cyclic accesses would also cause always-wait to abort due to cyclic waiting. However, with WnG, on the right, *T2* waits until *T1* completes *B*'s CIST and then *T2* enters the CIST and executes in parallel with the remainder of *T1*. Thus, *T2* avoids aborts, lost work, and time spent in back-off, while achieving concurrency with *T1*.

Figure 1 depicts always-go for eager systems. We clarify that lazy conflict resolution, which implicitly uses always-go, avoids some but not all aborts due to acyclic dependencies. Because lazy resolution implies lazy version management (eager versioning is not possible), acyclic dependencies do not restrict commit order and may cause aborts. For example, in a simple, acyclic write-to-read conflict between two transactions, the reader obtains the old value before the write due to lazy versioning. If the reader reaches commit before the writer (by chance), there is no abort; but if the writer reaches first then the reader has read a stale value and must abort. In contrast, always-go with eager conflict resolution (e.g., DATM) forces the commit order to be in dependence order (either reader first or writer first) and no abort occurs. In addition to such acyclic aborts, lazy resolution cannot avoid cyclic aborts due to CISTs such as the one in Figure 1.

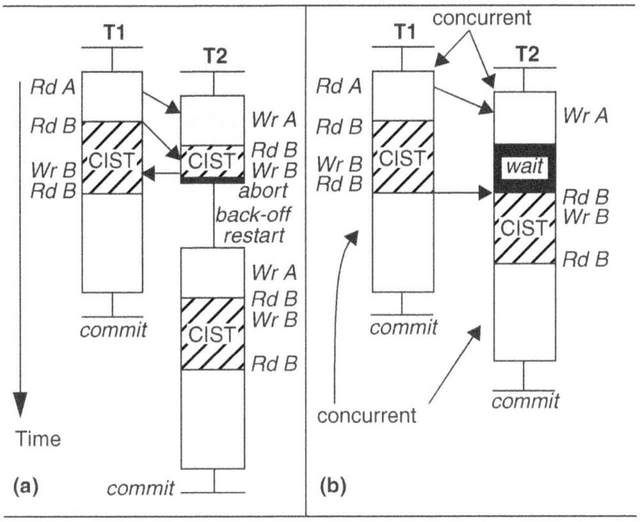

Figure 1. Execution of a CIST for delinquent data cache block *B* (a) with always-go and (b) with WnG

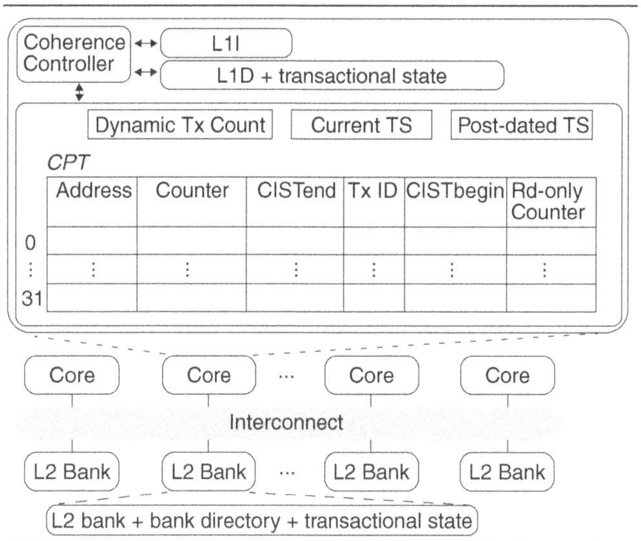

Figure 2. WnGTM hardware

The *WnG* policy consists of two components: (1) a CIST predictor to learn delinquent blocks and CIST boundaries, and (2) using the predicted CIST information to serialize the CISTs.

2.1 Learning the CISTs

To serialize CISTs, the CIST predictor must learn (1) the identities of delinquent blocks, and (2) the boundaries (i.e., start and end) of the corresponding CISTs. For identities, we leverage the fact that only a few delinquent blocks cause the majority of cyclic aborts (e.g., 3 blocks cause 95% of aborts in *intruder*). Thus, block addresses causing aborts are recorded in a per-core hardware *CIST prediction table (CPT)*. We identify repeat offenders as delinquent by incrementing a per table-entry saturating counter whenever the corresponding address triggers an abort. Figure 2 illustrates the CPT. Incrementing the counters upon conflicts rather than aborts would lead to excessive waiting due to many blocks being labeled as delinquent. Because a few blocks cause most aborts, the CPT is small and can be searched in parallel with the L1 cache (e.g., 32 entries per core). As in other hardware prediction schemes, CIST learning occurs throughout execution.

To avoid cycles, a CIST must include *all* accesses to a delinquent block within a transaction (e.g., the CISTS in *T1* and *T2* in Figure 1). Otherwise, a delinquent block might correspond to multiple CISTs, and those CISTs could be arbitrarily interleaved across threads. Thus, by construction (i.e., not a program property), there is a one-to-one correspondence between delinquent blocks and CISTs. To determine CIST boundaries, we assume that a CIST starts at a transaction's first dynamic access to a delinquent block and ends at the last access to the block. While the first access can be determined with 100% accuracy, the last access requires determining when a transaction will no longer access a particular block. We observe that last accesses in previous dynamic instances of a transaction predict the last access in subsequent instances and record the instruction count (from transaction begin) at which the last access occurred, called *CISTend*, in the CPT (see Figure 2). To account for variations across instances, we conservatively use the maximum of the instruction counts among instances, called *max-count*. Thus, hardware updates the CISTend whenever a delinquent block is accessed beyond its current CISTend. In the appendix, we show a real CIST in one of our benchmarks. The CIST includes, as is typical, fairly complex data-access and control-flow structures.

Alternative CISTend metrics, such as PC and the difference between successive delinquent block accesses, tend to be inaccurate due to varied control flow. While max-count could cause excessive waiting due a to large count in an infrequent control-flow path, our results show that max-count is accurate (Section 6.2). Still, incorrect CISTends and slow learning of delinquent blocks may occur and lead to cyclic dependencies which are detected by our timestamps (TS in Figure 2) and result in aborts (Section 3).

Because blocks may cease to be delinquent over time due to lack of accesses, WnG unlearns by decrementing a block's counter at commit when the block associated with a transaction is not accessed in the transaction (aborts do not decrement as an abort may occur before the block is accessed). To capture this association, each CPT entry also holds a unique static transaction identifier assigned by the programmer or compiler (*TxID* in Figure 2).

Further, although a CIST starts at a transaction's first access matching an address in the CPT, WnG records the predicted CIST start instruction, *CISTbegin,* for the separate purpose of handling overlapping CISTs (Section 2.2.2). Analogous to CISTend, CISTbegin uses the minimum instruction count. We will discuss the remaining CPT field (read-only counter) and other state in Figure 2 — L1/L2 transactional state, timestamps (TS), and dynamic transaction (Tx) count — later in Section 2.2.5 and Section 3.

Finally, we accelerate delinquent block and CISTend learning via an aggressive gossip mechanism. Conflicting transactions use gossip to, whenever possible, force immediate saturation of the conflicted block's CPT counter if the block is delinquent for even one of the transactions. Additionally, transactions with the same static identifier exchange CISTends and set the matching CPT entry's CISTend to the largest value. A block's delinquency affects all accessing transactions, irrespective of static identifier, so saturation is gossiped among all conflicting transactions. However, CISTend is static transaction specific and is therefore gossiped only to same-static-identifier transactions. Because conflicting accesses usually generate coherence traffic among the conflicting transactions (conflicts involve writes), gossip information can be piggybacked on coherence. Conflicts via evicted blocks do not generate coherence messages among conflicting transactions so gossip does not occur. Finally, while normal delinquent block learning occurs only upon aborts (for precise learning), gossip occurs upon conflicts as well (to rapidly disseminate learned information).

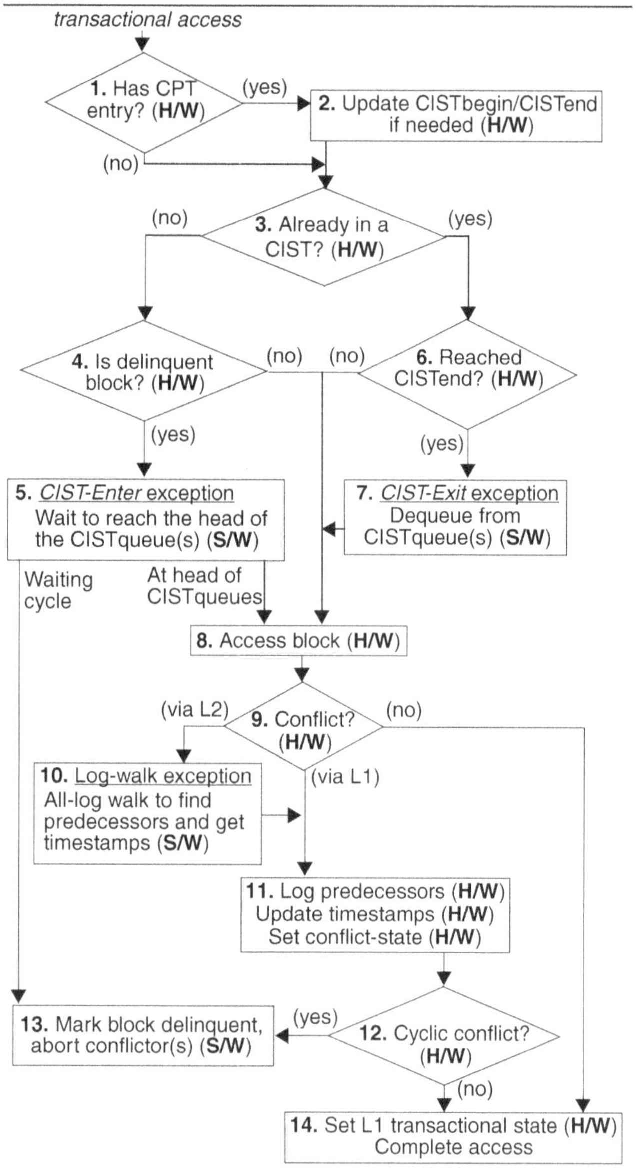

Figure 3. WnGTM access flowchart

2.2 Serializing the CISTs

The WnG conflict resolution policy serializes CISTs. We first cover the simple case of serializing non-overlapping CISTs and then cover fully- or partially-overlapping CISTs. Finally, we describe a few optimizations for our serialization policy.

2.2.1 Non-overlapping CISTs

WnG defaults to an always-go policy (similar to DATM). Accesses to non-delinquent blocks (i.e., the block's address is not in the CPT or the block's counter is not saturated) proceed even if they cause conflicts. This choice causes a few delinquent block aborts which help to bootstrap learning, and allows non-delinquent blocks to form acyclic dependencies which do not cause aborts. Timestamps detect any cycles via non-delinquent blocks, similar to those caused by CISTend mispredictions (Section 2.1).

Figure 3 gives the flowchart of an access in WnGTM. Every transactional access searches the CPT (Figure 3, step 1) and updates the table as necessary (Figure 3, step 2). Recall that accessing a delinquent block (Figure 3, step 4) is synonymous with entering a CIST. (Step 3 pertains to overlapping CISTs and is discussed in the following section.) If the delinquent block access causes a cycle (typically when CIST learning is incomplete), the transaction aborts and increments the block's CPT counter as described in Section 2.1 (Figure 3, step 13); otherwise the access triggers a *CIST-Enter* exception (Figure 3, step 5). We show the precise steps taken during a CIST-Enter exception in Figure 4. The exception serializes threads attempting to enter the CIST by enqueuing the threads in their timestamp order in a per-block *CISTqueue* (Figure 4, steps 1, 2). Though timestamp-ordered enqueueing increases the computation overhead, the ordering avoids cyclic dependencies and, hence, expensive aborts. The thread at the head of the CISTqueue executes the CIST (Figure 4, step 4) and threads are removed as they exit the CIST. Each thread's exception handler simply waits to reach the head of the queue (i.e., the waiting is in software and does not require coherence changes). Figure 5 shows the CIST serialization between two transactions *T1* and *T2*. Upon accessing delinquent block *A*, *T1* raises a CIST-Enter exception and is placed in block *A*'s CISTqueue (back to Figure 3, step 5). When *T2* accesses *A*, *T2* raises a CIST-Enter exception and waits in *A*'s CISTqueue until *T1* exits. To flag CIST exit, upon reaching the CISTend instruction count for the CIST, the thread executing the CIST (*T1*) raises a *CIST-Exit* exception (Section 2.1) and is dequeued from *A*'s CISTqueue (Figure 3, steps 6, 7). Because transactions raise exceptions at both CIST entry and exit, the exception overhead may be high for short transactions. An option would be to serialize the entire transaction instead of only the CIST. Then, serialization would occur as part of transaction begin, which can be a function call instead of an exception. However, we tried this optimization and did not see any benefits. Finally, the remaining steps, 8 - 12 and 14, refer to WnGTM's mechanisms and are explained in Section 3.

Because CISTqueues are per-block, CISTs corresponding to different delinquent blocks may be executed concurrently, improving performance. While dependence cycles may occur if threads' transactions execute multiple CISTs in different orders, most transactions have a single CIST or a single set of overlapping CISTs (covered in the next section) and do not face this issue. For the remaining cases, our timestamp-ordered enqueuing increases the likelihood of (but does not guarantee) the same order for all the CISTs. Finally, because waiting induces a dependence between the waiting thread and the thread being waited for, cyclic waiting is possible. Our timestamp scheme detects these waiting cycles, as shown in Figure 4, steps 2-3, and aborts the transaction (Figure 3, step 13), just as for data dependence cycles.

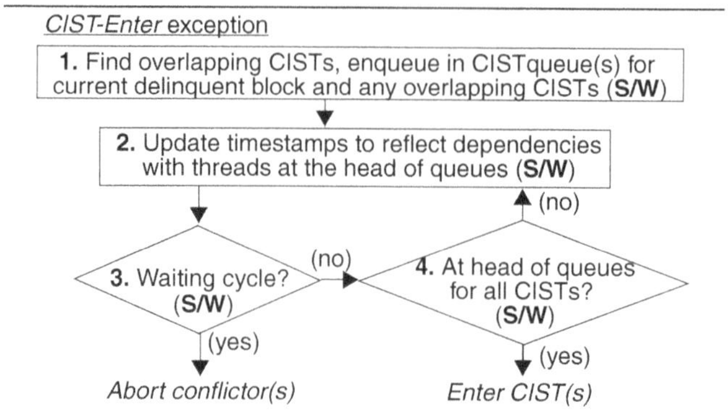

Figure 4. CIST-Enter exception

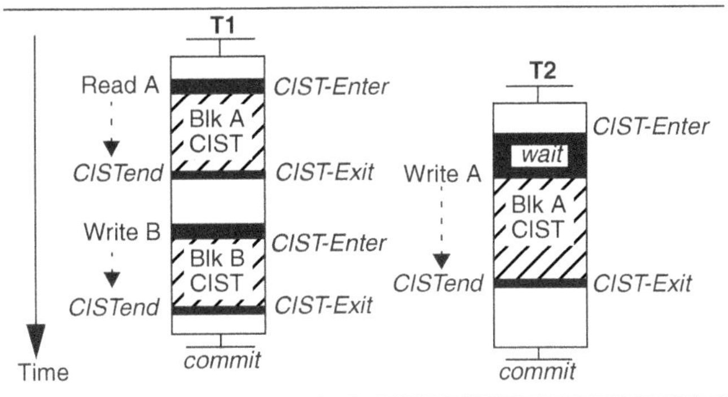

Figure 5. Non-overlapping CISTs

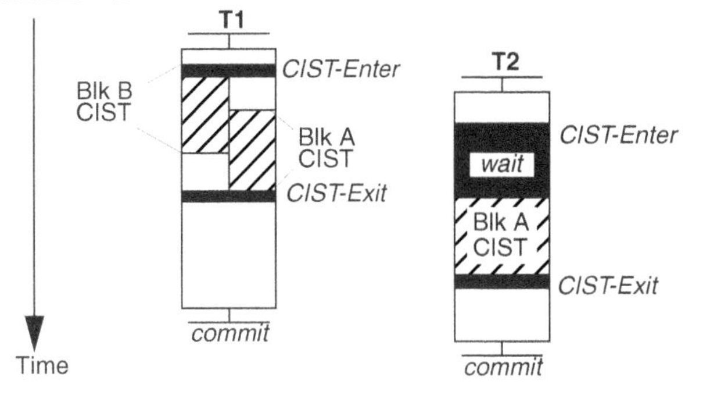

Figure 6. Overlapping CISTs

2.2.2 Overlapping CISTs

Overlapping CISTs occur when a transaction executing a CIST for a delinquent block accesses a different delinquent block before exiting the first CIST. If these overlapping CISTs were treated like non-overlapping CISTs, with each causing a CIST-Enter and CIST-Exit exception, the first CIST would incur a long delay due to the exceptions; we observe overlapping CISTs are not infrequent (e.g., in *intruder*, 27% of transactions have overlapping CISTs). Collapsing overlapping CISTs into a single CIST does not solve the problem because the collapsed CIST would be associated with the earliest accessed delinquent block. This block may differ among threads, causing threads to wait at different CISTqueues for the overlapping CISTs (analogous to acquiring different locks in different threads). Consequently, threads would not wait for each other and would incur cyclic dependencies. For example, in Figure 6, transaction *T1* would wait in block *B*'s CISTqueue while *T2* would wait in block *A*'s CISTqueue.

To avoid the above issues, we force a thread to wait simultaneously for *all* overlapping CISTs and allow a thread to enter the CISTs only when the thread is at the head of the queue for *all* such CISTs (analogous to acquiring all locks together). To identify overlapping CISTs, when a thread raises a CIST-Enter exception at the first delinquent block access, the exception handler walks the CPT and uses the CISTbegin and CISTend fields to determine which other CISTs may overlap with the accessed block's CIST. (We track CISTbegin for this purpose as stated in Section 2.1.) The handler then enqueues the thread in timestamp order in the CIST-queues for each of the overlapping CISTs (Figure 4, steps 1, 2). Note that CIST-Enter exception (Figure 4) is identical for both the non-overlapping and overlapping case, except that in the overlapping case, a thread waits in multiple CISTqueues. As with non-overlapping CISTs, the handler uses timestamps to detect any cycles in the CISTqueues and aborts. Because it is serialized up front, the transaction does not raise further CIST-Enter exceptions upon encountering overlapping CISTs (Figure 3, step 3). Thus, in Figure 6, *T1* raises a single CIST-Enter exception to access the overlapping CISTs for blocks *A* and *B*. To exit overlapping CISTs, a transaction raises a CIST-Exit exception upon reaching the latest of the overlapping CISTs' CISTends, hence, in Figure 6, *T2* must wait for *T1* to finish executing both *A*'s and *B*'s CIST before *T2* may enter *A*'s CIST.

2.2.3 Cycles through multiple acyclic conflicts

Thus far we have discussed cycles formed by multiple accesses to one block (i.e., a CIST) and our CIST prediction targets this case. However, we observe that it is also possible for cycles to form due to acyclic conflicts on multiple blocks, each accessed in different orders in different transactions. If such cycles were systematic, the acyclically conflicting blocks would be learned as delinquent using WnG's learning but serializing the acyclically conflicting blocks' non-overlapping CISTs would not avoid the cycle. To handle this case, CIST prediction could be extended to merge accesses to multiple delinquent blocks into a single CIST, similar to how overlapping CISTs are handled. However, we did not see this behavior in STAMP and therefore our CIST prediction and serialization does not address this case.

2.2.4 Other details

A few other details remain. First, because multiple threads may concurrently execute CIST exceptions, the exception handlers are synchronized in software to ensure proper serialization. Second, because both going past non-delinquent block conflicts and CISTs create acyclic dependencies among threads (i.e., a thread enters a CIST before an exiting thread commits), threads must commit in dependence order. Order-capture (Section 3) ensures correct commit order. Third, in the few cases that a transaction commits before reaching a CIST's CISTend, the commit raises the CIST-Exit exception, releasing any waiting transaction. Fourth, by going past conflicts, transactions may read speculative data and incur faults (e.g., address fault) [26]. We delay handling of such faults until the transaction's predecessors have committed, like DATM [26]. Fifth, non-transactional accesses do not access the CPT and therefore, ignore delinquency. Finally, while WnG does not pre-empt threads waiting at CISTs, pre-emption could be added, similar to lock libraries or always-wait with pre-emption [5].

2.2.5 Other optimizations

We propose two optimizations: (1) to address read-only delinquent blocks and (2) to address unstable delinquent block sets.

First, we address delinquent blocks which are only read by some transactions but read and written by others. To increase concurrency, we wish to serialize read-write and read-only CISTs with respect to each other while allowing multiple concurrent read-only CISTs. To this end, a read-only saturating counter is added to each CPT entry (Figure 2); the counter is incremented at commit if a transaction only read the delinquent block and is decremented immediately upon a write. To serialize, while waiting read-write CISTs proceed one by one, all waiting read-only CISTs, irrespective of queue position, proceed when any read-only thread enters the CIST. Because read-only nature is specific to each transaction, WnG does not gossip read-only information (Section 2.1).

The second optimization targets transactions with unstable delinquent block sets, where soon after a block is learned to be delinquent, the block ceases to be accessed and is unlearned (Section 2.1). In this case, serializing CISTs is ineffective and

WnG's default of always-go for conflicts on non-delinquent blocks (Section 2.2.1) causes many late aborts. We detect such instability by monitoring the per-commit number of prediction counter decrements for any delinquent block. After a few commits, if this number exceeds an *instability-threshold*, the unstable transaction's future instances (i.e., same TxID) irreversibly switch to always-wait and gossip the switch to same-TxID transactions in other threads (Section 2.1). Transactions with other TxIDs continue to use the WnG policy.

3. HTM Mechanisms for Wait-n-Go

Wait-n-GoTM (WnGTM) allows transactions to proceed past conflicts after waiting appropriately (i.e., transactions execute concurrently outside CISTs). Therefore, WnGTM must adopt a *multi-reader, multi-writer* paradigm to ensure serializability among co-existing readers and writers. Accordingly, we generalize previous TMs' *multi-reader single-writer* invariant and unordered transactions, to a multi-reader multi-writer paradigm with ordered transactions like DATM. To this end, WnGTM adds three extensions to previous TMs: a transactional *conflict-state* to detect conflicts (Section 3.2), *order-capture* to identify and track dependencies (Section 3.3), and a *timestamp* scheme adapted from Timetraveler [30] to detect cycles via both data dependencies and waiting (Section 3.4). While the WnG policy can be applied to any STM or HTM, we describe one implementation here. To illustrate that WnG need not alter the coherence protocol, we select TokenTM, which does not change coherence, as our baseline. Previous schemes change coherence for waiting (e.g., LogTM-SE [33]) and conflict detection (e.g., DATM), and degrade scalability by broadcasting dependencies (e.g., DATM). In contrast, these extensions build on TokenTM to avoid coherence changes and on Timetraveler to avoid broadcasts.

3.1 TokenTM: Background

TokenTM avoids coherence changes by allowing transactional state to move with blocks upon conflicts, piggybacked on coherence messages. TokenTM resolves conflicts via L1-resident blocks in hardware and resorts to software all-log walks for the rare conflicts via L1-evicted blocks where hardware cannot identify all the conflicting transactions. TokenTM denotes transactionally accessed blocks using per-block read (*R*) and write (*W*) bits in the private L1s and, to ensure evicted blocks' transactional state is not lost, pushes a summary of this transactional state to all memory levels. To commit in TokenTM, transactions that have conflicted or evicted blocks release transactional state in software (slow commit), while transactions with all L1-resident blocks release transactional state in hardware via a flash clear of the L1 *R* and *W* bits (fast commit). To facilitate these software slow commits and also aborts, TokenTM logs all transactional accesses and old write values. Upon a conflict via an L1-evicted block, the identity of conflictors may not be known (i.e., TokenTM's state in the L2/memory contains only a summary and not the conflictors' identities). In these cases, TokenTM triggers an all-log walk (of all live transactions) to determine the conflictors' identities.

3.2 Conflict-state: Detecting conflicts in WnGTM

Following TokenTM, WnGTM (1) avoids coherence changes and resolves conflicts in the same manner; (2) WnGTM also pushes its transactional state to all memory levels, as we describe in this section; and (3) WnGTM adopts both fast and slow commits as well as all-log walks to manage transactional state.

To detect conflicts under the *multi-reader, multi-writer* paradigm, WnGTM employs a new transactional (not coherence) state,

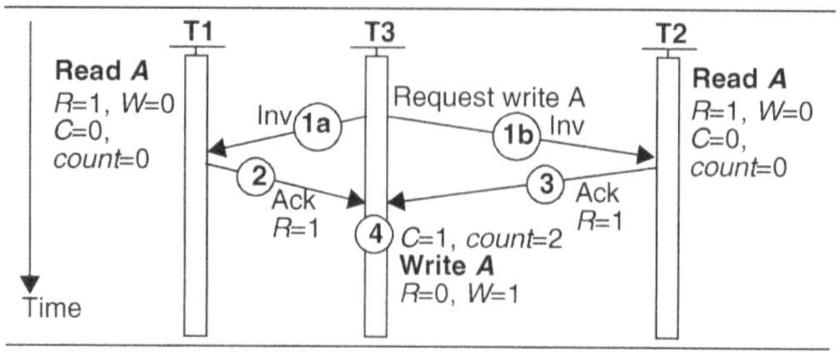

Figure 7. Conflict-state

conflict-state, which avoids coherence changes by moving with the blocks upon a conflicting access. The conflict-state consists of a per-block conflict bit, *C*, signifying that any future access will conflict (i.e., at least one transactional writer exists), and a *count* of the block's current readers and writers. Non-conflicting reads and writes yield non-conflicted (*C=0*) and transactionally clean (*C=0, count=0*) blocks, respectively. In this case a transaction denotes its access by setting the block's L1 *R* or *W* bit, as in TokenTM.

For conflicting accesses, we begin with how the conflict-state detects L1-resident block conflicts and then address conflicts via evicted blocks. In Figure 7, transaction *T3* (writer) conflicts with existing readers *T1* and *T2* on block *A*. As part of invalidation (steps 1a and 1b), *T1* and *T2* piggyback their *R* bits on coherence to *T3* (steps 2 and 3). Finally, in step 4, *T3* adds the bits to the block's *count* and sets the block's *C* bit (denoting a conflict) and local L1 *W* bit (denoting *T3*'s write). Another transaction's future access to block *A* will move *A* to the corresponding thread's L1 where *T3*'s *W* bit will be added to *count* (so that count will equal 3). Thus the *C* bit and *count* persist beyond conflicts. Additionally, upon invalidation, transactions send their (1) identities so order-capture can track the dependencies (Section 3.3) and (2) timestamps for cycle detection (Section 3.4). If a cycle occurs, at least one of the conflicting transactions aborts. The other case, where a transaction accesses a block that has been written by another transaction is similar. The accessor sets the block's *C* bit, *count* to 1, and the L1 *R* or *W* bit. Observe that the *count* is the number of accessors that have evicted or invalidated the block; accesses to L1-resident blocks are denoted by the L1 *R* and *W* bits. We emphasize that to support acyclic dependencies, the conflict-state applies to *all* blocks, delinquent or not. Thus, Figure 3 in Section 2.2 shows that all conflicting transactional accesses set the *C* bit (step 11) and all transactional accesses set the L1 *R* and *W* bits (step 14). The *R*, *W*, and *C* bits and *count* are the L1 transactional state in Figure 2.

Because coherence involves only L1s with resident blocks, transactions will not be notified of accesses to evicted blocks. Accordingly, WnGTM pushes the conflict-state to all memory hierarchy levels, like TokenTM. Upon eviction, to ensure future accessors detect conflicts, WnGTM sets the *C* bit in the L2 if the block's *C* or *W* bit is set and adds the evicted *R* or *W* bit to *count*. The L2 transactional state (two state bits and *count*) is stored with the directory (Figure 2).

Once the conflict-state has been set at L1 or L2, any other transaction's access to the block will see the state, detect a conflict, and trigger order-capture and timestamp cycle detection. At aborts or commits (which, due to the conflicts, are slow commits), the software handler clears the *R* and *W* bits for L1-resident blocks, decrements *count* for non-L1-resident blocks, and, if *count* reaches zero, clears the *C* bit to indicate that the block is conflict-free.

3.3 Order-capture: Ordering dependencies in WnGTM

As explained in Section 2.2.4, going past conflicts requires dependent transactions to commit and abort in the data dependence order

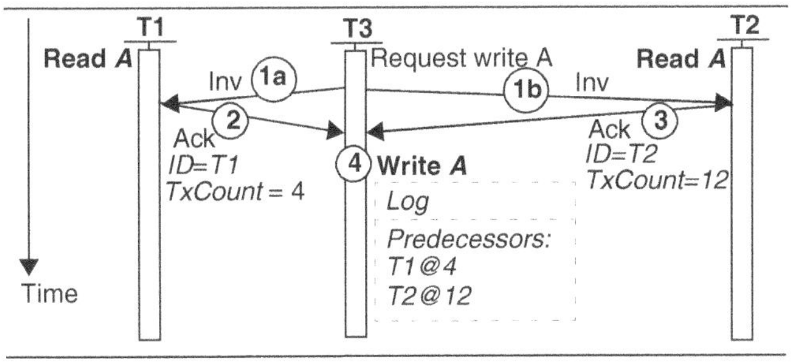

Figure 8. Order-capture

for correct serializability. That is, a transaction may commit only after all its predecessors have committed and must abort if a predecessor aborts (cascaded abort) but must do so only after all the transaction's successors have aborted. Ordering with WnGTM's timestamps would serialize all transactions, not just dependent ones, strictly based on numeric values. To limit serialization, we propose *order-capture* which scalably and explicitly tracks data dependencies so that commits and aborts wait only for predecessors and successors, respectively.

To track dependencies, conflict block accessors (i.e., *C* bit is set) log the predecessor transactions' identities (thread identifier and per-thread dynamic transaction count mentioned in Section 2.1 and shown in Figure 2); the accessing transaction is the successor because other transactions' accesses occurred earlier. Because predecessors may not be notified upon conflicts (e.g., the block is not in the L1), only the successor logs. In the simple, common case of conflicts on L1-resident blocks, hardware provides the predecessors' identities (piggybacked on coherence messages). In Figure 8, transaction *T3*'s write to block *A* conflicts with prior reads by *T1* and *T2*, so *T3* sends invalidations to *T1* and *T2* (steps 1a and 1b). *T1* and *T2* then piggyback their identities on their invalidation acknowledgements to *T3* (steps 2 and 3) which then logs *T1's* and *T2*'s identities (step 4), as also shown in Figure 3, step 11. In the uncommon, more-difficult case of conflicts via evicted blocks, where the predecessors are unknown, the conflicting access raises an exception (Figure 3, step 10). The exception handler performs an all-log walk to determine the predecessors' identities, which are logged upon the original access's retrial (Figure 3, step 11). In contrast to this distributed, scalable, method for identifying predecessors, DATM globally broadcasts conflicts so that all transactions can record the dependence ordering.

Rarely, a race may arise during an all-log walk: A new predecessor thread may join after the all-log walk has checked the thread's log but before the original conflicting access is complete, causing the all-log walk to miss the new predecessor. Consequently, the conflicting access and all-log walk must occur atomically. To this end, we employ a new per-block transactional (not coherence) state, *log-walk state*, to force concurrent block accessors to wait during a previous access's all-log walk. The log-walk state, which consists of a single *LW* bit, is set in the log-walking thread's L1 (Figure 9, step 1) and, like the conflict-state, is piggybacked on coherence to ensure that other concurrent accesses see the state. Accesses encountering the log-walk state except and wait on the state in their exception handlers. Upon completing the all-log walk (Figure 9, step 2), the access retries and clears the *LW* bit in hardware (Figure 9, step 3), thereby releasing the waiting accesses. Because all other concurrent accesses wait, only the original (log-walking) access's retry is guaranteed to clear the *LW* bit from all copies (located by the directory); the state clearing does not introduce races.

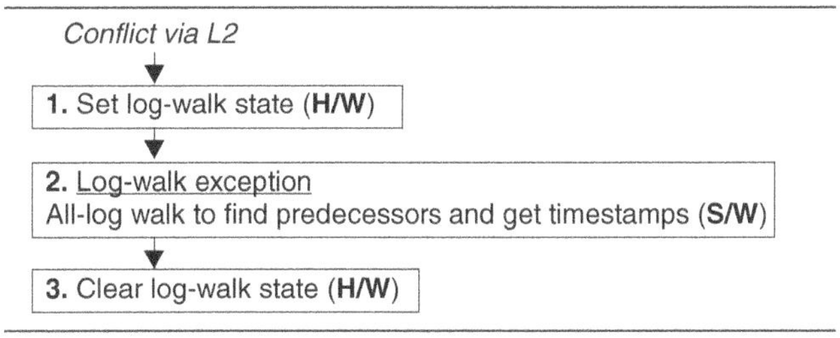

Figure 9. Log-walk

A transaction that has proceeded past a conflict slow-commits in software via an exception (like TokenTM), during which the transaction uses its log to wait for its predecessors to commit. Conflict-free transactions do not wait at commit. Analogously, an aborting transaction waits in its abort handler for all its successors to abort. However, because transactions only log predecessors, successors are not known. Consequently, aborting transactions trigger all-log walks to check all transactions' predecessor lists and abort those transactions for which the aborting transaction is a predecessor.

3.4 Timestamps: Detecting cycles in WnGTM

Both waiting and proceeding past conflicts induce inter-transaction dependencies so WnGTM requires cycle detection to ensure serializability. To this end, we employ timestamps, as mentioned previously in Section 2.1 and Section 2.2. Prior schemes detect cycles using static timestamps which are assigned at transaction start [23]. Such static timestamps cause false cycles among independent transactions due to coincidental numerical ordering among the timestamps. To minimize false cycles, WnGTM adopts Timetraveler's post-dated timestamps [30] which are adjusted dynamically to allow transactions' timestamps to slide flexibly and independently with respect to each other. As any conflict (delinquent or not) may close a cycle and as conflicts occur fairly frequently, we use hardware to generate timestamps and detect cycles in the simple, common case of conflicts on L1-resident blocks. We resort to software to detect cycles in the rare and more difficult case of L1-evicted block conflicts. Also, as CIST waiting already occurs in software, we detect waiting cycles in software. Crucially, cycle detection is independent of the WnG policy, ensuring that mispredictions cannot corrupt the timestamps.

Post-dating creates a timestamp window between a smaller *current* timestamp (*CTS*) and a larger *post-dated* timestamp (*PTS*). The timestamps are stored in hardware registers, as shown in Figure 2. To capture a dependence, a successor and predecessor transaction adjust their windows to make the successor's *CTS* strictly greater than the predecessor's *PTS*. To preserve existing dependencies, a *PTS* may only decrease and a *CTS* may only increase. This invariant guarantees that a successor's *CTS* is always strictly more than a predecessor's *PTS* even if the timestamps are adjusted dynamically and independently; a violation of this guarantee indicates a cycle. Because the strictly-more-than relationship is transitive, post-dating detects cycles through an arbitrary number of transactions.

We illustrate post-dating in Figure 10. To maximize window flexibility, transactions *T1*, *T2*, and *T3* begin with their *CTS* and *PTS* set to *NULL* (indicating no timestamp has been set) and upon conflicts, select the largest possible windows. Upon a conflict, if the successor's *CTS* is *NULL*, as shown for conflict #1 between *T1's Wr A* and *T2's Rd A*, the predecessor (*T1*) sets its *PTS* to its CTS + *post-dating offset* (e.g., 100); the successor (*T2*) sets its *CTS* to the predecessor's (*T1*'s) *PTS*+1. Conflict #2 between *T2* and *T3*

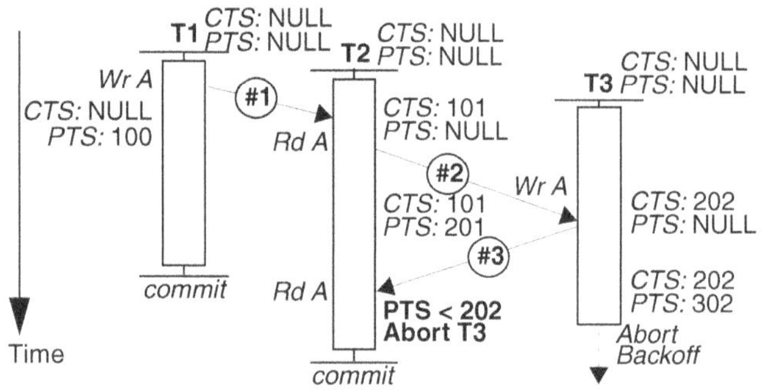

Figure 10. Timestamps

also falls in this case. If either the predecessor's or successor's *CTS* or *PTS* are set, any overlap in the CTS-to-PTS windows are removed by splitting the overlap, as done in [30]. If a conflict causes a transaction's *CTS* to exceed its *PTS*, a cycle is declared and the younger transaction (with a larger *PTS*) aborts, like [9]. Thus, in Figure 10, upon conflict #3, *T2*'s *CTS-PTS* window is 101-201 and *T3*'s window is 202-NULL. Because *T2* cannot increase its *CTS* above *T3*'s *PTS* (which cannot be set below 202), a cycle is declared.

Transactions exchange timestamps by piggybacking on coherence in the simple, common case of L1-resident block conflicts (Figure 3, step 11). For the more-difficult case of L1-evicted block conflicts, we exploit order-capture's software all-log walks for identifying predecessors (Section 3.3) to exchange timestamps in software (Figure 3, step 10). In contrast to this software approach, Timetraveler places a single coarse-grain timestamp at each L2 bank to reduce space overhead. Using such coarse-grain timestamps for WnGTM would cause many false cycles.

Additionally, CIST waiting, as mentioned in Section 2.2, may cause cycles if transactions encounter CISTs in different orders (e.g., transaction *T1* waits behind *T2* at CIST *A*, *T2* waits behind *T1* at CIST *B*). Cycles can be avoided if transactions wait in a single, global order (e.g., timestamp order). However, transactions that wait for CISTs while executing another CIST (as done for read-only CISTs in Section 2.2.5) may do so in different orders. To reduce the number of waiting cycles and to detect waiting cycles, respectively, transactions wait in timestamp order and update their timestamps to reflect the dependence between the waiting transaction (successor) and the predecessor executing the CIST. Because CIST waiting occurs *before* a delinquent block is accessed and our hardware can update the timestamps only upon an access, we leverage the CIST-Enter exception (Section 2.2.1) to update the timestamps in software (Figure 4, steps 2, 3). Further, though waiting transactions do not make transactional accesses, the transactions' timestamps may change due to conflicts with transactions that are not waiting. However, such changes can cause new waiting cycles only when another transaction enqueues or dequeues, at which point the CISTqueue can be re-ordered if necessary and any cycles can be detected. Thus, our timestamps seamlessly detect both waiting and data dependence cycles, and are updated in hardware in the simple case and in software in the more-difficult case. In contrast, DATM detects cycles using snooping and global broadcast which degrade scalability.

Finally, to keep the timestamps small and flexible, they are reset at commit and abort. Such resetting repeals a transaction's seniority which may lead to repeated aborts and starvation. We did not observe starvation, likely because WnG reduces instances of repeated aborts. Still, if starvation occurs, a transaction may avoid further aborts by setting its *PTS* low for the next retrial.

3.5 Hardware complexity and other overhead

Although serializing in-flight, dependent transactions is invariably involved, we carefully divide the labor between hardware and software such that hardware handles only simple cases in the policy and mechanisms, such as updating the CPT and detecting conflicts via L1-resident blocks. Software performs the more difficult tasks such as serializing CISTs and handling conflicts via L1-evicted blocks (where coherence cannot be leveraged). Most importantly, WnGTM does not change coherence.

WnGTM's hardware, shown in Figure 2, consists of a per-core 32-entry CPT, two 2-byte timestamp registers, and one 4-byte dynamic transaction count register. The CPT holds less than 500 bytes (4 bytes each for address, *CISTend,* and *CISTbegin*; 2-byte *TxID*; and two 2-bit counters per entry). Further, WnGTM adds nothing to TokenTM's modest 3% transactional state space overhead (TokenTM's state subsumes WnGTM's state). The CPT is looked up on every access and its power overhead is comparable to that of a small TLB (e.g., 3-13% of core power [29]) whereas WnGTM avoids many aborts, eliminating 48% of all dynamic instructions and their power (accounting for WnGTM's exception instructions). Furthermore, complex CPT operations (e.g., identifying overlapping CISTs) are pushed to software. Finally, TokenTM incurs a modest 2-3% coherence-traffic overhead for piggybacking (1) transactional state on data blocks and (2) thread ids and age-priority timestamps [9] upon L1-resident conflicts. WnGTM adds another 3-4% due to gossip, order-capture, and post-dated timestamps.

We push the more difficult actions to software. For our policy, software exceptions (Section 2.2) handle CIST serialization including identifying overlapping CISTs, waiting at CISTs, and releasing waiting transactions at CIST exit. Because most transactions have only one CIST (possibly an overlapping set), each incurs the performance overhead of only two exceptions. On the mechanism side, WnGTM resorts to software all-log walks for identifying predecessors upon L1-evicted block conflicts. Each STAMP benchmark incurs fewer than 10 all-log walks, except *labyrinth* which has long, contentious transactions and incurs all-log walks in 70% of its transactions. Our full-system simulations include WnGTM's exception overhead in the execution time. However, as we show in Section 6.1, WnGTM's fewer cyclic aborts more than compensates for this performance overhead.

3.6 WnGTM-wait: A simpler variant of WnGTM

The WnG policy allows a successor transaction to proceed concurrently with a predecessor transaction once the predecessor exits the CIST. While it increases concurrency, WnG necessitates the complexity of tracking the predecessor-successor data dependence via order-capture and of enforcing the dependence order to ensure serializability via all-log walks and the log-walk state. To avoid some of this complexity, we consider a variant policy, called *WnG-wait*, where the successor simply waits until the predecessor commits or aborts. That is, CISTs are still serialized but the serialization is elongated until the transaction end instead of the CISTend. In this variant, because the successor waits at the CIST entry *before* accessing a delinquent block, there is no predecessor-successor data dependence and the associated complexity of order-capture and the log-walk state. However, WnGTM-wait still has to detect (1) CISTs via CIST prediction, (2) conflicts via the conflict state, and (3) waiting cycles via timestamps, like WnGTM. We note that WnG-wait is different from always-wait because WnG-wait avoids most CIST-induced aborts by waiting at the CIST entry *before* accessing the delinquent block whereas always-wait waits upon a conflict usually *after* multiple accesses to the delinquent block making cyclic waiting, and hence aborts, inevitable. Finally, WnGTM-wait's lower complexity than WnGTM comes at the cost of (1) slower CIST learning due to the extra waiting and (2) lower predecessor-successor concurrency. We evaluate WnGTM-wait's complexity-performance trade-off in our results.

4. Related Work

WnG's CIST prediction is inspired by memory dependence prediction [24]. WnG generalizes the centralized scheme for sequential programs in [24] to a distributed scheme for parallel, TM programs. Current HTMs (as discussed in Section 1) force conflicting transactions to wait for the others to commit or abort (*always-wait*), abort the transactions (*always-abort*), or allow the transactions to proceed, forcing commits and aborts in the conflict-induced dependence order (*always-go*).

LogTM [23], LogTM-SE [33], and UFO [4] use always-wait with logical timestamps to detect deadlocks and trigger aborts. Bobba et al. in [9] reduce (cyclic) waiting in always-wait by prioritizing older transactions over younger ones. The always-wait HTMs wait in hardware via nacks, requiring changes to coherence. While these HTMs do not pre-empt waiting threads, Blake et al. [5] propose a variant of always-wait which serializes *entire* repeatedly-conflicting transactions by swapping-out some of the conflicting threads until the remaining thread commits and swapping-in other threads. However, the other threads also run into conflicts which causes excessive serialization of entire transactions.

Many HTMs [3,6,8,11,19,25,28] use always-abort. UTM [3], PTM [11], and TokenTM [8] use age priority to abort younger transactions upon conflicts. Other TMs use the amount of work done, instead of age, to prioritize conflicting transactions (e.g., [6,19,25]). TokenTM employs always-abort to avoid coherence changes. OneTM [6] and MetaTM [19] can be configured to use always-wait or always-abort. SigTM [22] employs always-abort but switches to always-wait if a transaction aborts repeatedly.

As discussed before, DATM uses always-go to increase concurrency and uses coherence changes and broadcasts for dependence tracking and cycle detection. Recently, RETCON [7] uses always-go but employs slice re-execution to repair incorrect memory state instead of imposing dependence order on commits and aborts. Because such repair is hard in the general case, RETCON is limited to simple cases, such as counter increments. RETCON shows performance improvements only for the STAMP benchmarks re-configured to include simple counters (e.g., hash table occupancy counters) and no improvements with the normal configuration. Lazy conflict resolution (e.g., TCC [17]), a special case of always-go, postpones conflict detection until commit and then attempts to serialize conflicting transactions. While TCC avoids some acyclic aborts, it incurs late, cyclic aborts. Further, lazy conflict resolution requires lazy version management and therefore, hardware write buffers (eager versioning is not possible). These buffers incur complexity and performance degradation when transactions exceed the buffers' finite size. Finally, to correctly detect conflicts at commit and atomically update the memory system with committed write values, transactions' commits are serialized.

In summary, always-wait waits upon conflicts until transactions end — well past the CISTs — incurring long delays, whereas WnG serializes only the CISTs. While always-abort incurs frequent aborts and always-go inevitably incurs late aborts due to cyclic dependencies, WnG avoids many aborts by serializing the CISTs. Unlike RETCON, WnG can handle CISTs comprising arbitrary computation.

Finally, while WnG prediction specifically targets cyclic conflicts, there has been some work on general prediction of conflicts. Blake et al. [5], mentioned above, learn repeated conflicts to avoid scheduling conflicting transactions in parallel. Waliullah et al. [31] learn repeated conflicts and take checkpoints during transactions when a potentially conflicting block is accessed. On aborts, the transaction uses the checkpoints to reduce the extent of rollback. While this scheme reduces lost work upon an abort, WnG avoids aborts, thereby reducing not only lost work but also roll-back, backoff, and waiting.

Table 1. Hardware parameters

Cores	16, in-order issue
Private L1	32K, 4-way, 64 byte blocks, 1-cycle latency
Shared L2	8M, 8-way, 64 byte blocks, 34-cycle latency
Memory	8 GB, 448-cycle latency
Coherence	Directory MESI with full bit-vector sharer list
TokenTM	State bits per block (5 in L1 and 2 in L2) + 14-bit thread id/count per L1 & L2 block
Wait-n-GoTM	*C, LW* bits per L1 & L2 block (+ TokenTM's 14-bit id/count), 32-entry CPT, *instability-threshold = 1.6 (Section 2.2.5)*

5. Methodology

We implement WnGTM by extending TokenTM in the Wisconsin GEMS HTM simulator [21] which uses Simics [20] for full-system simulations. We simulate a SPARC-based multicore running Solaris 10. Table 1 summarizes the simulated system's parameters. Using GEMS's user-level exception handlers, we simulate *CIST-Enter* and *CIST-Exit* exceptions and order-capture's all-log walks, as well as TokenTM's slow commits and aborts.

We evaluate WnGTM using STAMP [10], as shown in Table 2. We select small or medium input datasets based on simulation feasibility. The table also shows the fraction of TokenTM's execution time spent in transactions (*%tx time*), the transaction length described quantitatively as the number of instructions per transaction (*#instrs/tx*) and qualitatively (*tx length*), the amount of contention expressed quantitatively as the number of aborts per commit in TokenTM (*#aborts/commit*) and qualitatively (*contention*), and the base-case performance shown as 16-core TokenTM's speedups over sequential runs (*TokenTM vs. Single*). *Labyrinth*'s speedup does not scale beyond 8 cores without early-release [10]. The data mostly match those in [10] and show that STAMP covers a wide spectrum of transactional behavior. To account for statistical variations, we use enough randomly-perturbed runs to achieve 95% confidence [2].

6. Experimental Results

We first compare the conflict resolution policies, always-abort, always-wait, and always-go, against the WnG policy. To explain the performance differences we provide an execution time breakdown. Next, we show CIST and delinquent block statistics. We then isolate the performance impact of our various optimizations for WnG. Finally, we show sensitivity to the CPT size.

6.1 Performance

To compare the conflict resolution policies, we run WnGTM, TokenTM (always-abort), LogTM-SE (always-wait), and DATM (always-go). While these HTMs' policies differ, their hardware mechanisms also differ significantly (e.g., LogTM-SE and DATM require coherence changes and LogTM-SE's Bloom filter incurs false positives, whereas TokenTM and WnGTM incur exception overhead to avoid coherence changes but do not have Bloom filter

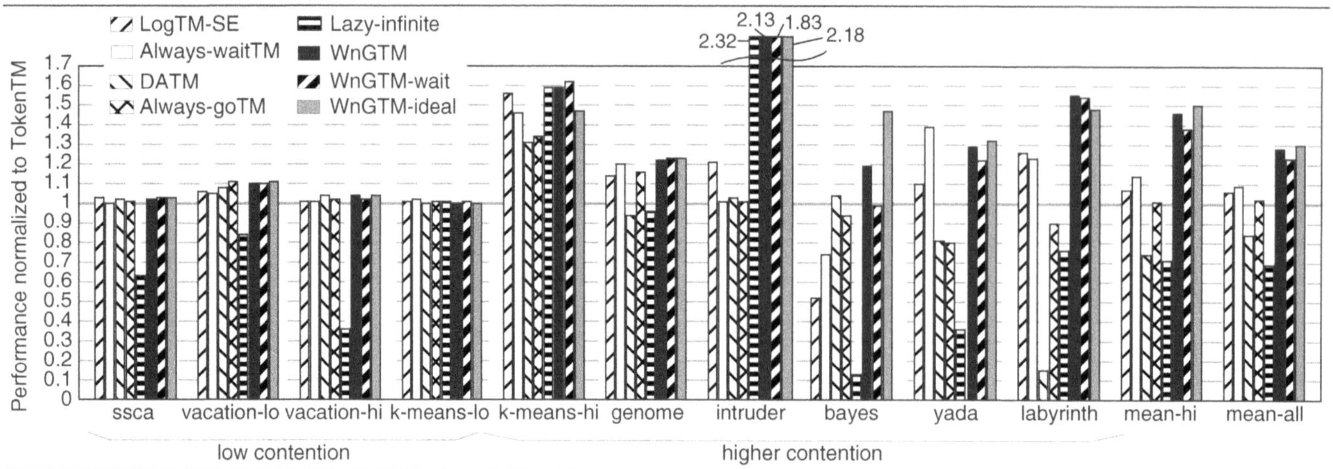

Figure 11. Performance

drawbacks). To isolate the policies' impact, we show always-wait (*Always-waitTM*) and always-go (*Always-goTM*) implemented using WnGTM's hardware mechanisms. The always-abort variant is identical to TokenTM. We also compare to a TCC-like, idealized lazy scheme which uses lazy conflict detection and lazy versioning with an infinite write buffer, called *lazy-infinite*. Further, we include *WnGTM-wait*, a simpler variant of WnGTM that avoids data dependencies among in-flight transactions (Section 3.6). Additionally, we show an idealized WnGTM, called *WnGTM-ideal*, which waits in hardware via coherence nacks to avoid CIST exception overheads and uses perfect dependence information without log-walk overhead and timestamp-induced false cycles. Finally, we compare to always-wait with thread pre-emption [5], shown separately later due to methodology differences. We implemented each of these schemes (except lazy-infinite and LogTM-SE which are part of the GEMS simulator) and ensured that our results are in line with published results.

For a fair comparison, we use good configurations for each HTM, as discussed in Section 4: age-based priority for TokenTM; 2K-entry Bloom filters and age-based priority for LogTM-SE; perfect broadcasts, perfect cycle detection, and perfect aborts for DATM; and 2K-entry Bloom filters and infinite write buffers for lazy-infinite. For WnGTM, we use (1) CIST-Enter and CIST-Exit exceptions for waiting, (2) order-capture to identify dependencies (including all-log walks upon L1-evicted block conflicts), and (3) post-dated timestamps with the potential for false cycles.

Figure 11 shows the speedups over TokenTM (Y axis) for LogTM-SE, Always-waitTM, DATM, Always-goTM, lazy-infinite, WnGTM, WnGTM-wait, and WnGTM-ideal (X axis). The X axis groups the low- and higher-contention benchmarks (the medium- and high-contention benchmarks in Table 2, column 5), and shows the averages for the higher-contention benchmarks and for all benchmarks, denoted as *mean-hi* and *mean-all*, respectively. Table 3 gives the number of aborts per commit.

Figure 11 shows that most conflict resolution policies perform similarly for the low-contention benchmarks but differ significantly for the higher-contention benchmarks. LogTM-SE incurs generally fewer aborts than TokenTM (Table 3, columns 1, 2) but on average, performs similarly due to significant waiting. By avoiding Bloom filters' false conflicts and static timestamps' false cycles, Always-waitTM aborts less often than LogTM-SE in *intruder* and *bayes* (Table 3, columns 2, 3). While Always-

Table 2. Benchmarks

Benchmark (input)	1 %tx time	2 #instrs / tx	3 tx length	4 #aborts / commit	5 conten-tion	6 TokenTM vs. Single
ssca2 (m)	8	22	short	~0	low	6.2
vacation-lo (m)	95	2015	med	~0	low	13.3
vacation-hi (m)	96	2730	med	~0	low	13.9
k-means-lo (m)	5	155	short	0.1	low	7.3
k-means-hi (m)	44	155	short	0.5	med	7.6
genome (m)	44	1237	med	0.4	med	3.5
intruder (m)	95	212	short	3.2	high	1.7
bayes (s)	94	41978	long	4.0	high	2.7
yada (s)	98	6263	long	1.7	high	3.7
labyrinth (s)	99	249450	long	10.4	high	0.6

Table 3. Aborts per commit

Benchmark	1 TokenTM	2 LogTM-SE	3 Always-waitTM	4 DATM	5 Always-goTM	6 Lazy-infinite	7 WnGTM	8 WnGTM-wait	9 WnGTM-ideal
ssca2	~0	~0	~0	~0	~0	~0	~0	~0	~0
vacation-lo	~0	~0	~0	~0	0	2.5	0	0	0
vacation-hi	~0	~0	~0	~0	~0	2.6	~0	~0	~0
k-means-lo	0.1	~0	~0	0.1	~0	0.1	~0	~0	~0
k-means-hi	0.5	0.1	0.2	0.4	0.4	0.3	0.1	~0	0.1
genome	0.4	0.2	~0	0.2	0.1	0.2	~0	~0	~0
intruder	3.2	3.7	3.0	1.4	1.5	0.6	0.5	0.6	0.4
bayes	4.0	3.9	2.9	2.1	2.1	3.0	1.2	0.7	1.2
yada	1.7	0.7	0.6	1.1	1.1	1.1	0.4	0.3	0.5
labyrinth	10.4	8.8	8.7	22.4	8.9	8.0	2.1	1.5	2.2

waitTM's fewer aborts in *bayes* translate to better performance, Always-waitTM's exception overhead for waiting negates the abort advantage in *intruder* (LogTM-SE waits via coherence nacks). As expected, the always-go HTMs (DATM, Always-goTM, and lazy-infinite) incur fewer aborts than TokenTM (Table 3, columns 1, 4, 5, 6) by allowing acyclic dependencies but incur numerous CIST-induced late aborts. *Labyrinth* performs much worse with DATM due to especially late aborts. Lazy-infinite performs worse than TokenTM in some cases (e.g., *vacation-hi* and *yada*) and better in others (e.g., *k-means-hi* and *intruder*). Recall that lazy-infinite uses an infinitely-large write buffer and therefore does not incur any eviction-related overheads such as exceptions and log walks while the other schemes include these overheads. Therefore, lazy-infinite performance is an upper bound and should be not be used to compare directly against the other schemes. *Vacation*'s higher abort rate stems from its moderate number of acyclic conflicts. Lazy-infinite's serialized commits extend the time that a transaction is active in *vacation*, increasing the likelihood of acyclic conflicts and aborts. Lazy-infinite's late, cyclic aborts significantly hurt *bayes* and *yada*. In contrast, WnGTM avoids acyclic aborts and many cyclic aborts in TokenTM to achieve better performance (Table 3, columns 1, 7). WnGTM-wait's extra waiting (Section 3.6) reduces aborts over WnGTM in all the higher-contention benchmarks except *intruder* where WnGTM-wait's slower learning results in more aborts (Table 3, columns 7, 8).

On average, the always-wait HTMs, LogTM-SE and Always-waitTM, perform better than TokenTM with Always-waitTM achieving 14% and 9% improvements for the higher-contention benchmarks and all the benchmarks, respectively (*mean-hi* and *mean-all* in Figure 11). Among the always-go HTMs, Always-goTM performs similar to, whereas DATM and lazy-infinite perform worse than, TokenTM. WnGTM achieves significant improvements of 46% (*mean-hi*) and 28% (*mean-all*) over TokenTM, respectively. WnGTM's high speedup for *intruder* comes from incurring far fewer aborts than TokenTM (Table 3, columns 1, 7). WnGTM lags behind only Always-waitTM for *yada* — due to *yada*'s unstable delinquent block set — and lazy-infinite for *intruder* — because WnGTM incurs some abort overhead whereas lazy-infinite's aborts are overhead-free; however, the lag is under 9% in both cases. By serializing the CISTs, WnGTM drastically reduces the abort rate (Table 3, column 7) and performs significantly better than the previous policies, including Always-waitTM which is the best previous policy. Thus, WnGTM achieves its goal of increasing concurrency while avoiding many cyclic aborts. By trading-off concurrency for complexity, WnGTM-wait performs worse than WnGTM, with significant degradation in *intruder, bayes,* and *yada*. Thus, WnGTM-wait sacrifices some performance to eliminate some complexity. Nevertheless, WnGTM-wait performs 39% better than TokenTM for the higher-contention benchmarks, illustrating the importance of avoiding cyclic aborts via CIST-prediction. WnGTM-wait is a viable option for designers who wish to reap the benefits of CIST prediction while avoiding the complexity of order-capture and the log-walk state. WnGTM-ideal is only 2% better than WnGTM and has a similar abort rate (Table 3, columns 7, 9), indicating that the performance overhead from CIST exceptions, all-log walks, and timestamp-induced false cycles is small. In two cases, *k-means-hi* and *labyrinth*, WnGTM-ideal performs slightly worse than WnGTM. In *k-means-hi*, WnGTM's exception overhead spaces conflicting transactions apart in time, so that the transactions are more likely to reach commit in their dependence order and thereby avoid waiting at commit. This spacing is absent in WnGTM-ideal causing extra waiting. In *labyrinth*, WnGTM-ideal's infinite CPT

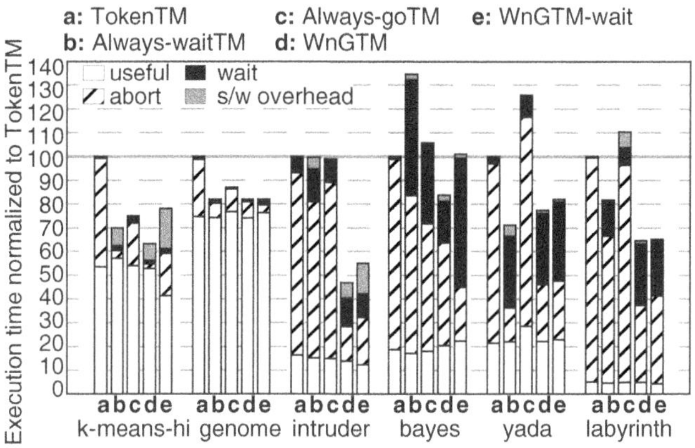

Figure 12. Execution time breakdown

serializes an excessive number of CISTs, increasing waiting. Both programs' waiting is due to program dependencies which cannot be removed in WnGTM-ideal.

While WnGTM avoids acyclic aborts and many cyclic aborts, Table 3 (column 7) shows that WnGTM still experiences some aborts in the higher contention benchmarks. In *intruder*, these aborts stem primarily from delinquent read-only blocks transitioning to read-write and from learning-related aborts. Learning-related aborts include aborts before all conflicting transactions have learned a block to be delinquent and aborts from accessing a delinquent block beyond its current CISTend (Section 2.1). *Bayes*' aborts are also primarily learning-related. *Yada*'s unstable delinquent block set leads to many cyclic aborts through non-delinquent blocks. *Yada* additionally incurs aborts due to learning and to rushing, where a transaction that is a predecessor to another transaction for one CIST reaches a later CIST after its successor has entered that later CIST. Finally, *labyrinth* incurs learning-related and rushing-induced aborts.

To explain WnGTM's performance, Figure 12 shows an execution time breakdown for TokenTM (representing always-abort), Always-waitTM, Always-goTM, WnGTM, and WnGTM-wait, normalized to TokenTM. We break total time into useful (includes non-transactional work), abort (includes lost transactional work, futile waiting, roll back of log, and back-off), wait (includes fruitful waiting and waiting to commit or abort), and software overhead (CIST exceptions, slow commits, and log walks). We show only the higher-contention benchmarks where conflict resolution matters. From Figure 12, we see that TokenTM (always-abort) loses a significant fraction of time to aborts, mostly due to back-off. Although Always-waitTM and Always-goTM abort less than TokenTM (Table 3, columns 1, 3, and 5), the policies lose a significant amount of time to late, cyclic aborts, which lead to futile waiting (Always-waitTM) and lost work (Always-goTM). WnGTM loses a smaller amount of time to aborts compared to TokenTM, Always-waitTM, and Always-goTM, which correlates with WnGTM's fewer aborts (Table 3, columns 1, 3, 5, and 7). Still, WnGTM loses a moderate amount of time to aborts, for the reasons stated above. Further, WnGTM waits mostly less than Always-waitTM because WnGTM waits only for conflicting delinquent-block accesses and only until the CISTend, whereas Always-waitTM waits for all conflicting accesses and until the transaction end. Moreover, Figure 12 confirms our previous claim that WnGTM's software overhead, including CIST exceptions, is small. WnGTM-wait incurs more aborts than WnGTM due to slower learning (Table 3, columns 7, 8) and hence loses more time to aborts in *intruder*. In *bayes* and *yada*, WnGTM-wait's waiting

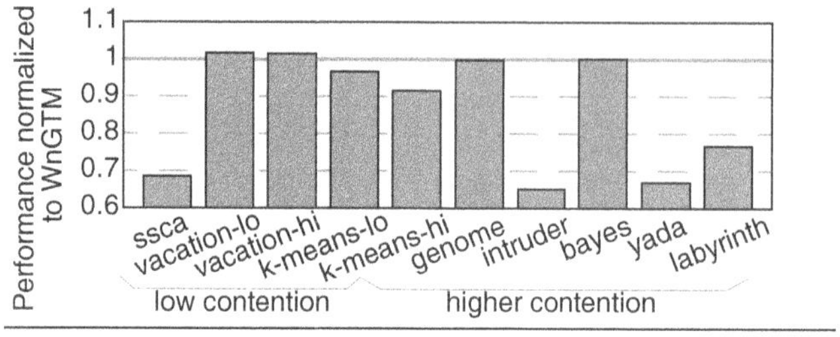

Figure 13. WnGTM versus wait-pre-empt

until the transaction end instead of the CISTend results in longer waiting.

Finally, we compare WnGTM to always-wait with thread preemption, called *wait-pre-empt*, which learns repeated conflicts in software to pro-actively serialize entire transactions at their start [5]. Wait-pre-empt switches out long transactions or stalls short transactions that are predicted to conflict. Because changing the thread scheduler's preemption policy is involved, we simulate the effect in hardware: an 8-core wait-pre-empt running 16 threads executes on 16 cores and stalls/unstalls cores so that exactly 8 cores are unstalled at a time. While normal thread switching incurs software and cold-cache overhead, our thread switching is zero-cost, favoring wait-pre-empt. Figure 13 shows wait-pre-empts' performance normalized to WnGTM's for 8 cores. Because the switched-in threads also run into conflicts, causing excessive serialization of entire transactions, wait-pre-empt performs worse than or at par with WnGTM for all the benchmarks. Though *ssca2* has few conflicts, it has many transactions and the per-transaction overhead of checking the prediction in software worsens performance.

6.2 CIST statistics

Table 4 describes CISTs using the number of all and read-only delinquent blocks per benchmark (*#delinquent blks* and *#rd-only delinq blks*), the fraction of dynamic transactions that contain CISTs (*%tx with CISTs*), read-only CISTs (*%tx with rd-only CISTs*), and overlapping CISTs (*%tx with overlap CISTs*), the average number of all and overlapping CISTs per transaction containing CISTs (*#CISTs/tx* and *#overlap CISTs/tx*), the average number of CISTs per set of overlapping CISTs (*#CISTs/overlap set*), and the average predicted and real CIST lengths in number of instructions (*predicted/real CIST length*). We omit *ssca2*, *vacation-lo*, and *vacation-hi* as they do not have delinquent blocks.

Most higher-contention benchmarks have only a few delinquent blocks (Table 4, column 1), a small subset of which are read-only (column 2). Nevertheless, a substantial fraction of the transactions contain CISTs (column 3), correlating with the high number of aborts (Table 3) and highlighting the need to serialize CISTs. *Genome* is the only exception where many aborts are due to non-delinquent blocks. *Intruder* and *labyrinth* have considerable fractions of transactions containing read-only CISTs (Table 4, column 4), making the read-only optimization (Section 2.2.5) important for these benchmarks. Over a third of *intruder*'s and *labyrinth*'s transactions contain overlapping CISTs (Table 4, column 5) so handling overlapping CISTs helps these benchmarks to some extent.

Although many transactions contain CISTs, individual transactions contain fewer than two CISTs (Table 4, column 6), except for *labyrinth* whose long transactions contain many (mostly overlapping) CISTs (Table 4, columns 7, 8). Because transactions have few CISTs, the likelihood of multiple CISTs forming cyclic dependencies is small. Predicted and real CIST lengths (Table 4, column 9) are similar, indicating the CISTend prediction is accurate. *Intruder* and *labyrinth* are exceptions and the difference is almost fully due to read-only CISTs (not shown). Finally, because the CISTs are much shorter than the transactions (Table 2, column 2 vs. Table 4, column 9), WnG exploits concurrency outside CISTs, unlike always-wait. At the same time, transactions and CISTs comprise many instructions, making special-case optimizations like RETCON unlikely to be effective broadly. Though we show only the average CIST lengths and the individual CIST lengths vary, the above two points hold for individual CISTs as well.

Table 4. CIST statistics

	1	2	3	4	5	6	7	8	9
Benchmark	**#delinquent blks**	**#rd-only delinq blks**	**%tx with CISTs**	**%tx with rd-only CISTs**	**%tx with overlap CISTs**	**#CISTs/tx**	**#overlap CISTs/tx**	**#CISTs/overlap set**	**predicted / real CIST length**
k-m-lo	10	0	25	0	0	1	0	-	2/1.2
k-m-hi	16	0	27	0	0	1	0	-	6/5
genome	11	1	1	~0	0	1	~0	-	153/92
intruder	240	22	77	60	35	1.5	0.5	2	43/12
bayes	23	8	64	3	6	1.2	0.1	2.3	3.5K/2.9K
yada	85	4	34	~0	2	1	~0	2.3	382 /157
labyrinth	41	40	84	32	41	11	0.5	20	11.4K/ 2.2K

6.3 Impact of optimizations

In Figure 14 we isolate the impact of our optimizations for handling overlapping CISTs (Section 2.2.2), handling read-only CISTs (Section 2.2.5), gossiping CIST information (Section 2.1), and handling unstable delinquent-block sets (Section 2.2.5). The Y axis shows WnGTM's performance as we add each of these optimizations, beginning with WnGTM without optimizations (*none*) and ending with the complete WnGTM (*unstable delinquent set*). Performance is normalized to that of the complete WnGTM. The X axis shows the benchmarks (only higher-contention).

Each optimization impacts a few benchmarks. While both *intruder* and *labyrinth* have many overlapping CISTs (Table 4, column 5), *labyrinth* responds well to our overlap optimization whereas *intruder* does not because it has only two CISTs per overlapping set (Table 4, column 8). *Intruder* and *labyrinth* have many read-only CISTs (Table 4, column 4), and gain with the read-only optimization. Gossip accelerates CIST learning, aiding both *k-means-hi* and *labyrinth*. Finally, *yada*—and, to a lesser extent,

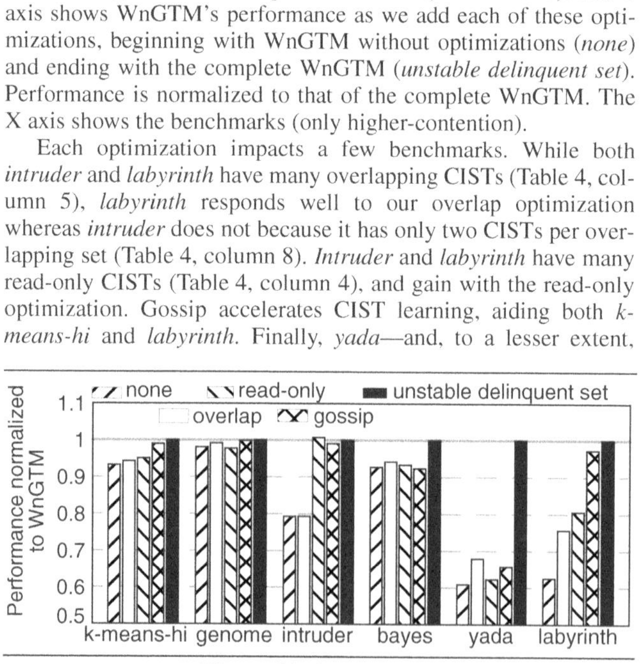

Figure 14. Optimizations

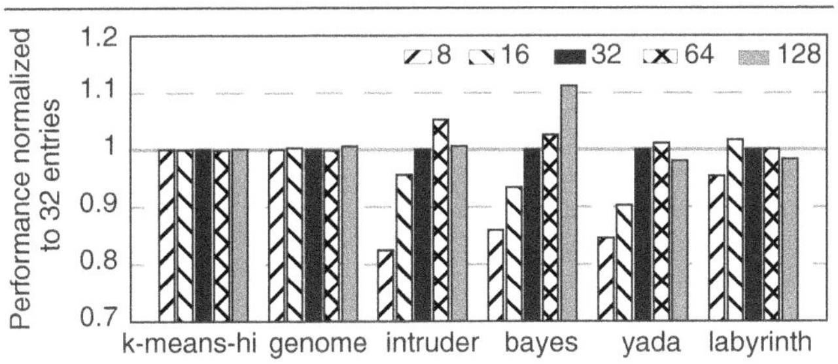

Figure 15. CPT size sensitivity

bayes—have unstable delinquent-block sets and improve with the corresponding optimization.

6.4 Sensitivity to CPT

Figure 15 shows WnGTM's sensitivity to the CPT size for the higher-contention benchmarks. The Y axis shows WnGTM's performance with the CPT size varying as 8, 16, 32, 64, and 128 entries, normalized to that of WnGTM with a 32-entry CPT (default). WnGTM's performance improves with larger CPTs for *intruder*, *bayes*, and *yada* which have many delinquent blocks (Table 4, column 1). *Labyrinth* also has many delinquent blocks, but accesses only a few at a time, so does not benefit from larger CPTs. Overall, even 16 entries would work reasonably well, and little benefit is seen beyond 32 entries.

7. Conclusion

Conflict resolution policies significantly impact TM performance. While previous policies, always-abort, always-wait, and always-go have their advantages, they degrade performance in the presence of contention by limiting concurrency (always-abort, always-wait) or by incurring late aborts (always-go). Further, none of the policies avoid aborts due to cyclic dependencies. We stipulated that conflict resolution policies should increase concurrency while avoiding cyclic aborts. To that end, we proposed Wait-n-GoTM (WnGTM) based on the key observation that most cyclic dependencies (and hence aborts) are caused by threads interleaving accesses to a few heavily-read-write-shared *delinquent* data cache blocks. We referred to the section of code containing all accesses to a particular delinquent block as a *cycle inducer section* (*CIST*). The Wait-n-Go (WnG) policy employs a CIST predictor in hardware to predict when transactions need to be serialized (i.e., upon entering a CIST) and for how long to avoid many cyclic aborts (i.e., until exiting a CIST). To implement WnG, we proposed WnGTM which adds three mechanisms to previous HTMs: (1) a new transactional state, *conflict-state*, to allow multiple readers and writers; (2) *order-capture*, to scalably identify data dependencies among transactions; and (3) an adaptation of a hardware timestamp scheme to detect cycles. To keep the complexity manageable, WnGTM handles in hardware only the simple cases in both the policy and mechanisms (e.g., updating the predictor and handling L1-resident blocks) and pushes the more-difficult cases to software (e.g., serializing CISTs and handling L1-evicted blocks).

Using 16-core simulations of STAMP, we showed that WnGTM achieves, on average, 46% and 28% speedups over always-abort (TokenTM) for the higher-contention benchmarks and all the benchmarks, respectively, with low-contention benchmarks remaining unchanged. In comparison, always-go (DATM) and always-wait (LogTM-SE), perform worse than and 6% better than TokenTM, respectively.

To combat the programmability issues with locks, HTM support has begun to appear in commercial products and many STMs are being developed. Because WnG is applicable to HTMs and STMs, WnG is likely to be important for improving TM performance and performance robustness.

Acknowledgements

We thank the anonymous reviewers and our shepherd, Adam Welc, for their valuable comments. Gwendolyn Voskuilen was supported by an NSF Graduate Fellowship.

Appendix

The code in Figure 16 shows a CIST in *intruder* from STAMP [10]. The CIST occurs in transaction #2 and the block pointed to by `queuePtr` is delinquent. For brevity, we show only the lines of code (with line numbers) pertaining to the CIST.

```
[1]    BEGIN_TRANSACTION(2)
[2]      TMdecoder_process(decoderPtr,...);
[3]    END_TRANSACTION(2)

[1]    TMdecoder_process(decoderPtr,...) {
           :
         // check for errors and allocate memory
           :
[153]    decodedQueuePtr = decoderPtr->decodedQueuePtr;
           :
         // CIST BEGIN
[154]    TMqueue_push(decodedQueuePtr,...);
         // CIST END
           :
[159]    return;
[160] }

[1]    TMqueue_push(queuePtr,...) {
[2]      pop = queuePtr->pop;
[3]      push = queuePtr->push;
[4]      capacity = queuePtr->capacity;
           :
[11]     if (newPush == pop) { // resize if needed
             :
           // malloc newElements array
             :
[19]       elements = queuePtr->elements;
             :
           // populate newElements array
             :
[36]       queuePtr->elements = newElements;
[37]       queuePtr->pop = newCapacity - 1;
[38]       queuePtr->capacity = newCapacity;
             :
[42]     } // end if resize
[43]     elements = queuePtr->elements;
           :
[46]     queuePtr->push = newPush;
           :
[48]     return;
[49]   }
```

Figure 16. Real CIST in *intruder*

References

[1] A.-R. Adl-Tabatabai, B. T. Lewis, V. Menon, B. R. Murphy, B. Saha, and T. Shpeisman. Compiler and runtime support for efficient software transactional memory. In *Proceedings of the 2006 ACM SIGPLAN Conference on Programming Language Design and Implementation*, pages 26–37. 2006.

[2] A. R. Alameldeen and D. A. Wood. Variability in architectural

simulations of multi-threaded workloads. In *Proceedings of the 9th International Symposium on High-Performance Computer Architecture*, page 7. 2003.

[3] C. S. Ananian, K. Asanovic, B. C. Kuszmaul, C. E. Leiserson, and S. Lie. Unbounded transactional memory. In *Proceedings of the 11th International Symposium on High-Performance Computer Architecture*, pages 316–327. 2005.

[4] L. Baugh, N. Neelakantam, and C. Zilles. Using hardware memory protection to build a high-performance, strongly-atomic hybrid transactional memory. In *Proceedings of the 35th Annual International Symposium on Computer Architecture*, pages 115–126, 2008.

[5] G. Blake, R. G. Dreslinski, and T. Mudge. Proactive transaction scheduling for contention management. In *Proceedings of the 42nd Annual IEEE/ACM International Symposium on Microarchitecture*, pages 156–167,2009.

[6] C. Blundell, J. Devietti, E. C. Lewis, and M. M. K. Martin. Making the fast case common and the uncommon case simple in unbounded transactional memory. In *Proceedings of the 34th Annual International Symposium on Computer Architecture*, pages 24–34, 2007.

[7] C. Blundell, A. Raghavan, and M. M. Martin. RETCON: transactional repair without replay. In *Proceedings of the 37th Annual International Symposium on Computer Architecture*, pages 258–269, 2010.

[8] J. Bobba, N. Goyal, M. D. Hill, M. M. Swift, and D. A. Wood. TokenTM: Efficient execution of large transactions with hardware transactional memory. In *Proceedings of the 35th Annual International Symposium on Computer Architecture*, pages 127–138, 2008.

[9] J. Bobba, K. E. Moore, H. Volos, L. Yen, M. D. Hill, M. M. Swift, and D. A. Wood. Performance pathologies in hardware transactional memory. In *Proceedings of the 34th Annual International Symposium on Computer Architecture*, pages 81–91. 2007.

[10] C. Cao Minh, J. Chung, C. Kozyrakis, and K. Olukotun. STAMP: Stanford transactional applications for multi-processing. In *Proceedings of the IEEE International Symposium on Workload Characterization*, 2008.

[11] W. Chuang, S. Narayanasamy, G. Venkatesh, J. Sampson, M. Van Biesbrouck, G. Pokam, B. Calder, and O. Colavin. Unbounded page-based transactional memory. In *Proceedings of the 12th International Conference on Architectural Support for Programming Languages and Operating Systems*, pages 347–358, 2006.

[12] J. Chung, L. Yen, S. Diestelhorst, M. Pohlack, M. Hohmuth, D. Christie, and D. Grossman. ASF: AMD64 extension for lock-free data structures and transactional memory. In *Proceedings of the 43rd Annual IEEE/ACM International Symposium on Microarchitecture*, pages 39–50, 2010.

[13] C. Click. Azul's experiences with hardware transactional memory. In *Transactional Memory Workshop*, 2009.

[14] Intel Corporation. Intel architecture instruction set extensions programming reference, 319433-012a edition. 2012.

[15] P. Damron, A. Fedorova, Y. Lev, V. Luchangco, M. Moir, and D. Nussbaum. Hybrid transactional memory. In *Proceedings of the 12th International Conference on Architectural Support for Programming Languages and Operating Systems*, pages 336–346, 2006.

[16] D. Dice, Y. Lev, M. Moir, and D. Nussbaum. Early experience with a commercial hardware transactional memory implementation. In *Proceedings of the 14th International Conference on Architectural Support for Programming Languages and Operating Systems*, pages 157–168, 2009.

[17] L. Hammond, V. Wong, M. Chen, B. D. Carlstrom, J. D. Davis, B. Hertzberg, M. K. Prabhu, H. Wijaya, C. Kozyrakis, and K. Olukotun. Transactional memory coherence and consistency. In *Proceedings of the 31st Annual International Symposium on Computer Architecture*, pages 102-113, 2004.

[18] M. Herlihy and J. E. B. Moss. Transactional memory: Architectural support for lock-free data structures. In *Proceedings of the 20th Annual International Symposium on Computer Architecture*, pages 289–300. 1993.

[19] O. S. Hofmann, C. J. Rossbach, and E. Witchel. Maximum benefit from a minimal HTM. In *Proceedings of the 14th International Conference on Architectural Support for Programming Languages and Operating Systems*, pages 145–156. 2009.

[20] P. S. Magnusson, M. Christensson, J. Eskilson, D. Forsgren, G. Hallberg, J. Hogberg, F. Larsson, A. Moestedt, and B. Werner. Simics: A full system simulation platform. *IEEE Computer*, 35(2):50–58, Feb. 2002.

[21] M. M. K. Martin, D. J. Sorin, B. M. Beckmann, M. R. Marty, M. Xu, A. R. Alameldeen, K. E. Moore, M. D. Hill, and D. A. Wood. Multifacet's general execution-driven multiprocessor simulator (GEMS) toolset. *SIGARCH Computer Architecture News*, 33(4):92–99, 2005.

[22] C. C. Minh, M. Trautmann, J. Chung, A. McDonald, N. Bronson, J. Casper, C. Kozyrakis, and K. Olukotun. An effective hybrid transactional memory system with strong isolation guarantees. In *Proceedings of the 34th Annual International Symposium on Computer Architecture*, pages 69–80, 2007.

[23] K. E. Moore, J. Bobba, M. J. Moravan, M. D. Hill, and D. A. Wood. LogTM: Log-based transactional memory. In *Proceedings of the 12th International Symposium on High-Performance Computer Architecture*, pages 254–265. 2006.

[24] A. Moshovos, S. E. Breach, T. N. Vijaykumar, and G. S. Sohi. Dynamic speculation and synchronization of data dependences. In *Proceedings of the 24th Annual International Symposium on Computer Architecture*, pages 181–193, 1997.

[25] R. Rajwar, M. Herlihy, and K. Lai. Virtualizing transactional memory. In *Proceedings of the 32nd Annual International Symposium on Computer Architecture*, pages 494–505, 2005.

[26] H. E. Ramadan, C. J. Rossbach, and E. Witchel. Dependence-aware transactional memory for increased concurrency. In *Proceedings of the 41st Annual IEEE/ACM International Symposium on Microarchitecture*, pages 246–257, 2008.

[27] N. Shavit and D. Touitou. Software transactional memory. In *Proceedings of the 14th ACM Symposium on Principles of Distributed Computing*, pages 204–213. 1995.

[28] A. Shriraman, S. Dwarkadas, and M. L. Scott. Flexible decoupled transactional memory support. In *Proceedings of the 35th International Symposium on Computer Architecture*, pages 139–150. 2008.

[29] A. Sodani. Race to exascale: Opportunities and challenges. In *Keynote at the Annual IEEE/ACM 44th Annual International Symposium on Microarchitecture*, 2011.

[30] G. Voskuilen, F. Ahmad, and T. N. Vijaykumar. Timetraveler: exploiting acyclic races for optimizing memory race recording. In *Proceedings of the 37th Annual International Symposium on Computer Architecture*, pages 198–209, 2010.

[31] M. Waliullah and P. Stenstrom. Intermediate checkpointing with conflicting access prediction in transactional memory systems. In *Proceedings of the 2008 IEEE International Symposium on Parallel and Distributed Processing*, pages 1 –11, 2008.

[32] A. Wang, M. Gaudet, P. Wu, J. N. Amaral, M. Ohmacht, C. Barton, R. Silvera, and M. Michael. Evaluation of Blue Gene/Q hardware support for transactional memories. In *Proceedings of the 21st International Conference on Parallel Architectures and Compilation Techniques*, pages 127–136, 2012.

[33] L. Yen, J. Bobba, M. M. Marty, K. E. Moore, H. Volos, M. D. Hill, M. M. Swift, and D. A. Wood. LogTM-SE: Decoupling hardware transactional memory from caches. In *Proceedings of the 13th International Symposium on High-Performance Computer Architecture*, pages 261–272. 2007.

Volition: Scalable and Precise Sequential Consistency Violation Detection

Xuehai Qian, Josep Torrellas
University of Illinois, USA
{xqian2, torrella}@illinois.edu
http://iacoma.cs.uiuc.edu

Benjamin Sahelices
Universidad de Valladolid, Spain
benja@infor.uva.es

Depei Qian
Beihang University, China
depeiq@buaa.edu.cn

Abstract

Sequential Consistency (SC) is the most intuitive memory model, and SC Violations (SCVs) produce unintuitive, typically incorrect executions. Most prior SCV detection schemes have used data races as proxies for SCVs, which is highly imprecise. Other schemes that have targeted data-race cycles are either too conservative or are designed only for two-processor cycles and snoopy-based systems.

This paper presents *Volition*, the first hardware scheme that detects SCVs in a relaxed-consistency machine precisely, in a scalable manner, and for an arbitrary number of processors in the cycle. Volition leverages cache coherence protocol transactions to dynamically detect cycles in memory-access orders across threads. When a cycle is about to occur, an exception is triggered. Volition can be used in both directory- and snoopy-based coherence protocols. Our simulations of Volition in a 64-processor multicore with directory-based coherence running SPLASH-2 and Parsec programs shows that Volition induces negligible traffic and execution overhead. In addition, it can detect SCVs with several processors. Volition is suitable for on-the-fly use.

Categories and Subject Descriptors C.1.2 [*Processor Architectures*]: Multiple Data Stream Architectures (Multiprocessors) - Parallel Processors

Keywords Memory Consistency, Sequential Consistency, Parallel Programming, Shared-Memory Multiprocessors

1. Introduction

When programmers write and debug applications with shared-memory threads, they intuitively assume the Sequential Consistency (SC) model. SC requires that the memory operations of a program appear to execute in some global sequence, as if the threads where multiplexed on a uniprocessor [17]. In practice, however, processors and memory systems overlap, pipeline, and reorder the memory accesses of threads. As a result, the execution of a parallel program can violate SC.

As an example, consider Figure 1(a). Processor P_0 initializes variable *p* and then sets flag *OK*; later, P_1 tests *OK* and, if it is set, uses *p*. While the interleaving in Figure 1(a) produces the expected results, the interleaving in Figure 1(b) does not. Here, while the two writes in A0 and A1 are retired in order, they complete out of order: the first one after B0 and B1, and the second one before B0 and B1. In this interleaving, P_1 ends up using an unitialized *p*. This order is an SC Violation (SCV).

While this example is trivial, SCVs often appear under subtle thread interleavings and timing conditions, even in popular codes. For example, Muzahid et al. [24] discovered SCVs in the Pthread and Crypt libraries of glibc. SCVs are often found in double-checked locking constructs [27], some synchronization libraries, and code for lock-free data structures. In Section 2, we show a typical example of SCV.

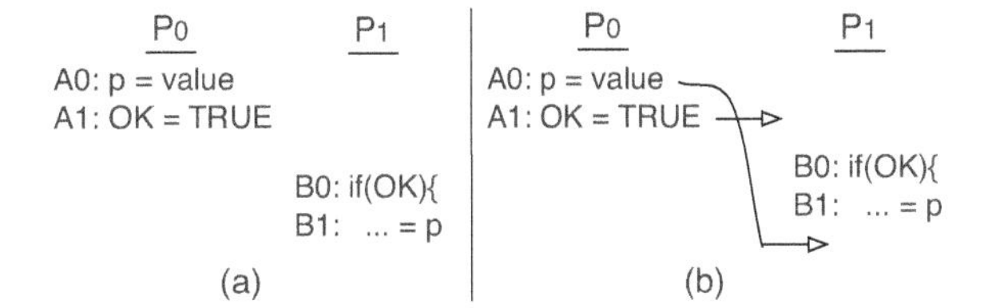

Figure 1. Example of an SC violation.

From the hardware perspective, an SCV occurs only when multiple conditions are met. First, there needs to be two or more data races — e.g., the races on variables *p* and *OK* in Figure 1. Second, these races must overlap in time. Finally, the order of the references in these races has to form a cycle at runtime [28].

Specifically, for two threads, an SCV requires a pattern like that in Figure 2(a) where, if we follow program order, the two threads reference the same two variables in opposite orders, and each variable is written at least once. Moreover, the references in these two racing pairs have to form a cycle as shown in Figure 2(b) — where we have arbitrarily picked reads and writes. Specifically, A1 must occur before B0, and B1 must occur before A0. This what happens in Figure 1(b), where *y* is *OK* and *x* is *p*.

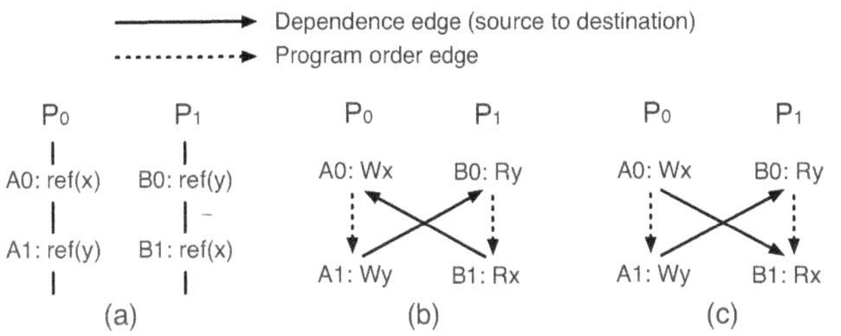

Figure 2. SC violation pattern.

However, if the timing at runtime is such that at least one of the two dependence arrows occurs in the opposite direction, there is no SCV. For example, Figure 2(c) shows the case when A1 executes before B0, but A0 executes before B1. Since there is no cycle, SC is not violated. This case corresponds to the timing in Figure 1(a).

It is important to detect SCVs because, in virtually all cases, SCVs are programming mistakes — as shown in Figure 1(b), they are the result of memory-access orders that contradict a programmer's intuition. In addition, given their subtlety, they can potentially cause great harm to the program without being obvious to the programmer. Finally, the programmer cannot reproduce them using a single-stepping debugger, and has to largely rely on mental analyses of interleavings to uncover them.

Most prior work has attempted to find SCVs by focusing on detecting data races (e.g., [3, 8, 14, 15, 21, 22, 31]). However, using data races as proxies for SCVs is very imprecise. As discussed

ASPLOS'13, March 16–20, 2013, Houston, Texas, USA.

above, the specific race pattern and interleaving required for an SCV is not necessarily common. In large codes, race-detection tools typically flag a very large number of data races, often causing the programmer to spend time examining races that are much less likely to cause code malfunctioning than SCVs [12, 25].

A second reason for not using data races as proxies is that we may want to uncover SCVs in codes that have intentional data races — perhaps in lock-free data structures. We may want to debug such codes for SCVs, while being less concerned about non-SC-violating races. Here, a race-detection tool would not be a good instrument to use. If we want to detect SCVs, we need to precisely zero-in on the data races and interleavings that cause them.

Given the importance of these bugs and the difficulty in isolating them, there have been two recent proposals for hardware-supported detection of data-race cycles [20, 24]. The first one, by Lin et al. [20], focuses on detecting overlapping data races, even if they involve disjoint sets of processors. Hence, the approach is fairly conservative, resulting in false positives. However, false positives are not a problem because the goal of that approach is to avoid SCVs (by flushing the processor pipeline) rather than to detect them and report them to the programmer.

The second appoach, by Muzahid et al. [24] detects cycles that cause SCVs, precisely. However, it is only designed to work for two-processor cycles and relies on a broadcast-based cache coherence protocol in the machine. We compare our work to these two approaches in Section 8.

In this paper, we advance the state of the art by proposing the first hardware scheme that detects SCVs in a relaxed-consistency machine precisely, in a *scalable* manner, and for an *arbitrary* number of processors in the cycle. We call our scheme *Volition*. Volition leverages cache coherence protocol transactions to dynamically detect cycles in memory-access orders across threads. When a cycle is about to occur, an exception is triggered, providing information to debug the SCV. Volition can be used in both directory- and snoopy-based coherence protocols; it does not rely on any property of snoopy protocols such as the broadcast ability.

The current Volition design does not consider speculative loads from mispredicted branch paths. In addition, it is unconcerned with SCVs due to compiler transformations; it only reports SCVs due to hardware-initiated access reordering. Within these constraints, and with large-enough hardware structures, Volition suffers neither false positives nor false negatives for a given execution.

In our experiments, we simulate Volition in a 64-core multicore with a directory-based protocol under either the Release Consistency (RC) or the Total Store Order (TSO) model. Our results running SPLASH-2 and Parsec applications show that Volition induces negligible network traffic and execution time overhead. Moreover, by removing fences from several concurrent programs, we show that Volition can detect SCVs with several processors. Overall, Volition's preciseness, scalability and low overhead make it suitable for on-the-fly use in a variety of environments.

This paper is organized as follows: Section 2 gives a background; Section 3 shows the basic Volition mechanisms; Section 4 extends Volition to work with multiple-word cache lines; Sections 5 and 6 discuss implementation and other issues; Section 7 evaluates Volition; and Section 8 discusses related work.

2. Background

An SCV occurs when the memory accesses of a program have executed in an order that does not conform to any SC interleaving. It is virtually always a programming mistake, since it involves an unintuitive interleaving. Given its subtlety, an SCV can potentially cause great damage to the program and not be obvious to the programmer. Finally, an SCV cannot be reproduced using a single-stepping debugger, and has to be identified with mental analyses of possible interleavings.

Shasha and Snir [28] showed what causes an SCV: overlapping data races where the dependences end up ordered in a cycle. Recall that a data race occurs when two threads access the same memory location without an intervening synchronization and at least one is writing. Figure 2 showed the required program pattern and order of dependences at runtime for two threads. We arbitrarily assigned reads and writes to the references.

An SCV is avoided by placing one fence instruction between the two references that participate in the cycle in each thread. For example, in Figure 2, we need a fence between A0 and A1, and another between B0 and B1. The algorithm that finds where to put the fences is called the Delay Set [28].

SCVs are very subtle. A major source of SCVs is the commonly-used Double-Checked Locking (DCL) [27]. This is a programming technique to reduce the overhead of acquiring a lock by first testing the locking criterion without actually acquiring the lock. Only if the test indicates that locking is required does the actual locking logic proceed. Figure 3(a) shows a DCL example. The code checks variable x in access B0 and, if it is not null, it reads its field $x \rightarrow m$ in B1. If, instead, x is null, we grab a lock, check again and, if x is null, allocate a new object and assign it to x in A1. As part of the constructor, in A0, the field of the object is initialized.

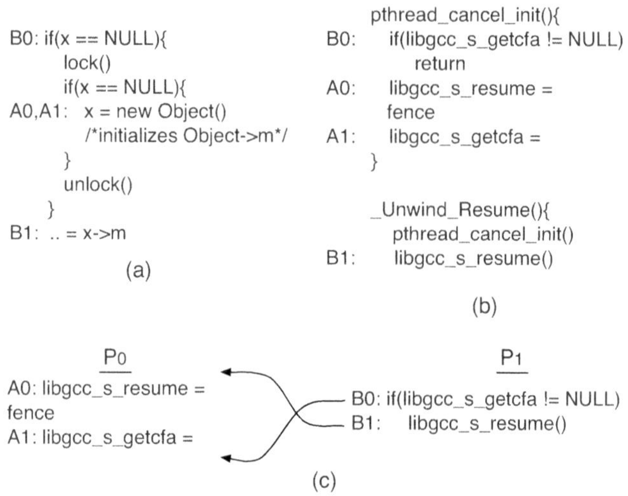

Figure 3. SCV uncovered by Muzahid et al. [24] in the Pthread library.

The DCL code has a structure like in Figure 1(a), with equivalent A0, A1, B0, and B1 references. In Figure 3(a), A0 sets the field *Object→m*, and then A1 assigns *Object* to x. Unfortunately, the updates of the accesses A0 and A1 can get reordered. This causes the same problem as in Figure 1(b). According to our discussion, to guarantee SC execution, the software needs to place a fence between A0 and A1, and another between B0 and B1. Unfortunately, because the code is typically complicated, such fences end up occasionally missing.

As an example, Muzahid et al. [24] found one of such fences missing in the Pthread and Crypt libraries of glibc. The Pthread code is shown in Figure 3(b). It shows two subroutines that construct a DCL pattern. We mark the references A0, A1, B0, and B1. We see that the code has a fence between A0 and A1, but not between B0 and B1. Since the second fence is missing, an erroneous reorder with an SCV can happen. This is shown in Figure 3(c), where we picked the four relevant references. The SCV occurs when the condition in B0 is predicted true by the branch predictor (although it is currently false) and B1 is executed before A0.

After A0 and A1 execute, the B0 branch resolves, confirming that B1 is in the correct path. However, B1 used the old value and the code crashes. To fix this, we put a fence between B0 and B1.

Given the importance of SCVs, there has been significant work in this area. Most prior work has attempted to find SCVs by detecting data races, which is very imprecise. There are several software-based approaches, but they typically have high overhead. Finally, there are two recent hardware-supported schemes to detect data-race cycles [20, 24]. However, they are either too conservative or are designed only for two-processor cycles and snoopy-based systems. We discuss the work in Section 8.

3. Volition: Scalable and Precise SCV Detection

In this section, we present the basic design of Volition. For now, we assume a cache line size equal to the granularity of processor accesses — e.g., one word. In Section 4, we extend the design to support multi-word cache lines.

3.1 Design Goals and Basic Assumptions

We are interested in an always-on hardware monitoring scheme usable for production runs. The scheme should detect all the SCVs that occur in the current dynamic execution, rather than attempting to find all the potential SCVs in the code. As a result, for a given binary, the scheme may detect different SCVs in different runs on the same machine and on different machines. Based on this usage model, an ideal SCV detection scheme has four traits.

1. Precise. The scheme should report SCVs, not conservative estimates of SCVs such as data races. Moreover, it should have no false positives or false negatives for a particular run.

2. Scalable. The scheme should not rely on any specific property of snoopy coherence protocols, which have limited scalability. It should be applicable to both snoopy- and directory-based protocols. In addition, the size of the hardware structures should increase only slowly with the processor count.

3. Low overhead. The scheme should have low overhead in terms of execution time and network bandwidth consumption.

4. Decoupled from the coherence protocol. Since the coherence protocol is difficult to design and verify, the SCV detection scheme should be decoupled from it.

In our design, we assume a multicore with directory-based coherence (although our scheme can also work with a snoopy-based protocol) and a relaxed memory consistency model, such as RC or TSO. We assume an MSI coherence protocol, which has a clean state (S, the line is coherent with memory and can be in multiple caches) and a dirty state (D, the line is not coherent and can be in only one cache). Each core is an out-of-order superscalar. For stores, the value is only written to the cache after retirement. Retired stores are held in the store buffer while they are being globally performed. They enter the store buffer in program order but may update the cache out-of-order. Reads can get their value before retiring. When an SCV is detected, an exception is raised.

The compiler can itself induce SCVs with certain optimizations [30]. However, Volition is a pure hardware scheme and, as a result, is not able to detect those. Hence, in this paper, we assume that the compiler does not perform SCV-inducing transformations, and we are only concerned with hardware-induced reorderings that cause SCVs. We leave the problem of preventing SCVs cooperatively by the compiler and hardware as future work.

3.2 Basic Insight to Identify an SCV

Volition detects an SCV by continuously trying to identify the pattern of Figure 2(b) across two or more processors. Such a pattern involves an interaction between processors on different memory addresses. In general, it is challenging to identify such a pattern, since the information is distributed. However, the insight of Volition is to start by first detecting a special access pattern that is a necessary condition for an SCV to subsequently occur. Such a pattern is called *Suspicious Pattern (SP)*. It can be detected locally within a processor and inexpensively. When a processor detects an SP, it piggybacks a small amount of local state information with the response coherence message. If a true SCV eventually occurs, the processors involved in the cycle will detect it. Before describing our solution, we define some terms.

Completion of a memory operation. A load completes when it gets its value from the memory system and no store from any processor can alter it; a store completes when its value updates the memory system and no load from any processor can return the value before the store. In relaxed memory consistency, memory operations from a thread can complete out of order.

Active access. A memory access *A* is *Active* when either itself or an older local access (according to program order) have not completed, *or* they are the destination of a data dependence from a remote access that is still active. For example, in Figure 4(a), B1 is active while B1 is not completed, or B0 is not completed, or (following the A1→B0 dependence) A1 is active.

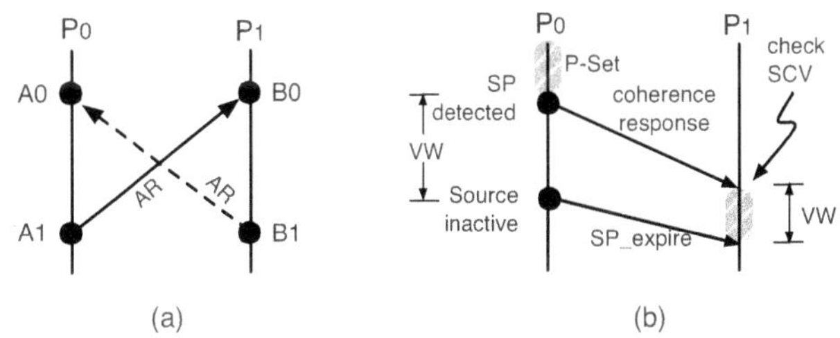

Figure 4. Basic ideas in Volition.

Pending set (*P-Set*). The *P-Set* of an access is the set of older local accesses that are still active.

Active Data Race (AR). An AR is a data race where the source access is active. We refer to the source and destination processors of an AR as AR_s and AR_d, respectively.

Suspicious Pattern (SP). A processor detects an SP when the processor is the source of an AR. The processor identifies the SP locally, when it responds to a coherence event (i.e., it provides and/or invalidates a cache line). If the local access involved in the transaction is active, then an SP is identified. For example, in Figure 4(a), assume that A1 is completed and A0 is not. Hence, A1 is active. When the dependence A1→B0 occurs, it is an AR and, therefore, P_0 detects an SP. As a result, in the response coherence message, AR_s piggy-backs some information that AR_d will need to detect an SCV, if it ever occurs. When A1 ceases to be active, then the SP is considered *expired*. At that point AR_s informs AR_d.

SCV pattern. An SCV occurs when multiple ARs form a cycle across two or more processors. Figure 4(a) shows a two-AR cycle.

Vulnerability Window (VW). Given an AR, the VW is the global physical time period during which an SCV is possible. In the AR_s processor, the VW is from the time when it identifies the SP until when the source access of the AR becomes inactive. In AR_d, the VW is from the time when it is notified about the SP (by AR_s) to when it receives the SP expiration notification by AR_s.

Volition works as follows. When an AR occurs, AR_s includes in its coherence response to AR_d some information about the *P-Set* of the AR's source access. Then, AR_d checks its local state against the information received, to flag if this AR closes a cycle. When the SP induced by this AR expires, AR_s notifies AR_d via a small *SP_expire* message so that AR_d no longer tries to check for a cycle. Figure 4(b) shows a timeline of the VWs and *SP_expire* message.

3.3 Volition Hardware Structures

To support the algorithm described, we need structures to (i) represent the local execution state, and to (ii) detect and record ARs.

3.3.1 Representing the Local Execution State

In Volition, each processor assigns a monotonically increasing *Sequence Number (SN)* to every memory access as it is issued. The SN reflects the order of local accesses in program order. If the access produces a network transaction, its SN is piggy-backed in the request message. With the proper way to handle the occasional wrap-around of SN (Section 5), the SN does not need to be very long.

The main hardware structure in Volition is the per-processor *Active Table (ACT)*. The ACT is in the core, and maintains state for all of the local accesses that are currently active. An ACT entry is allocated for each access in program order as it is issued. When an access ceases to be active and is the oldest access in the ACT, it is deallocated. At any time, the ACT may contain some entries that are completed and some that are not.

The goal of the ACT is to help record ARs. As shown in Figure 5(a), the ACT entry for an access contains its SN, the address of the location it loads or stores (*Addr*), a bit to specify whether the access is completed (*C*) and a writeback bit (*wb*). The functionality of *wb* is described later. The granularity of *Addr* (byte, half-word, word, etc.) depends on the granularity of the access. In our evaluation, we will assume word granularity only.

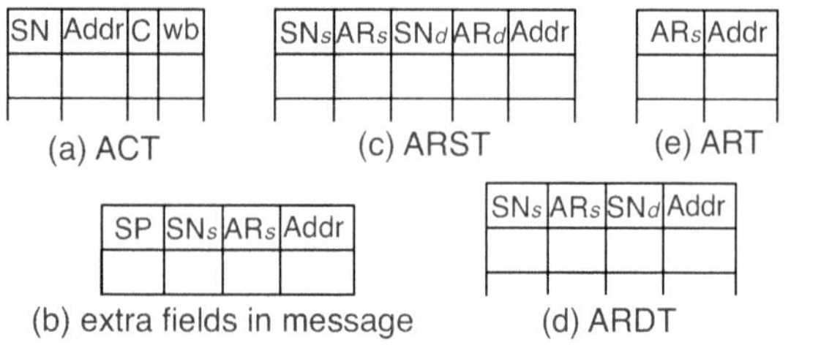

Figure 5. Hardware structures in Volition.

3.3.2 Detecting and Recording ARs

A processor detects an AR as follows. When it receives a request from the network, it checks the ACT for a race. We will later see how to avoid most of the unnecessary checks. The ACT is scanned from younger to older access, trying to find the first completed local access to the address of the request. If such an entry *E* is found, we have detected an AR. The *P-Set* is the set of accesses in the ACT that precede *E*. However, the *P-Set* is effectively encoded with the SN of *E*, which we represent as SN_s.

If an AR is found, the Volition hardware performs two actions. First, it appends the information in Figure 5(b) to the response coherence message. Such information is a bit (SP) to indicate that this is an SP, the SN of the source of the AR (SN_s), the processor ID (AR_s), and the memory address of the dependence (*Addr*).

In addition, Volition records the AR information in a local table called the *AR Source Table (ARST)*. As shown in Figure 5(c), an ARST entry contains: the AR source's SN (SN_s) and processor ID (AR_s), the AR destination's SN (SN_d) and processor ID (AR_d), and the memory address (*Addr*). AR_s obtained the values of SN_d and AR_d from the incoming message. We will explain later why we need to store AR_s: in a cycle with more than two processors, AR_s may not be the ID of the local processor.

When the destination processor of the dependence receives a coherence response with SP=1, Volition records the AR information in a local table called the *AR Destination Table (ARDT)*. As shown in Figure 5(d), an ARDT entry contains: the AR source's SN (SN_s) and processor ID (AR_s), the AR destination's SN (SN_d) and the memory address (*Addr*). We do not need to store the processor ID of the AR destination because it is the local processor.

3.3.3 Ensuring Correct Monitoring for ARs

For Volition to work correctly, a processor *P* with an ACT entry for address *Addr* has to be able to see subsequent coherence transactions to *Addr* that can cause ARs. Unfortunately, this is not guaranteed without additional support. Specifically, consider a line in state Dirty (D) in *P*'s cache that is written back to the shared cache — either (i) because it is evicted from *P*'s cache or (ii) because another processor reads it. In the first case, *P* will not be sharer in the directory anymore and, therefore, will be unable to see future reads or writes to the line; in the second case, *P* will still be a sharer in the directory, but will be unable to see future reads.

To solve this problem, when *P* writes back a D line for which it has ACT entries, Volition allocates an entry in the directory's *AR Table (ART)*. As shown in Figure 5(e), the entry contains the processor ID (AR_s) and the line address (*Addr*). In addition, *P* sets the *wb* bit in its youngest ACT entry for *Addr*.

From then on, when reads to the *Addr* by other processors reach the directory, the directory will read the ART entry and inform *P*. *P* will check its ACT and possibly send a message like the one in Figure 5(b) to the reader, informing it of an AR. Similarly, when the first write to *Addr* by another processor reaches the directory, the directory will read the ART entry and add *P* to the list of sharers that need to be notified. The ART entry will then be removed. The sharers (including *P*) may send messages like the one in Figure 5(b) to the writer if they find ARs.

When the entry in *P*'s ACT that had the *wb* bit set becomes inactive, *P* sends an *SP_expire* message to the processors it has informed of ARs, and to the directory. The latter deallocates the ART entry if it still exists.

Note that if *P* evicts a clean shared (S) line from its cache, it requires no action. The reason is that the directory is not updated, and still records *P* as a sharer.

3.3.4 Table Operations

Table 1 shows how the tables described are used. Specifically, for each of the ACT, ARST, ARDT, and ART, the table shows: (i) the condition for inserting an entry, (ii) the actions when an entry is inserted, (iii) the condition for deleting an entry, and (iv) the actions when an entry is deleted.

In the ACT, an entry is inserted when a memory instruction is issued. An entry is removed only when it satisfies the following three conditions: it is at the head of the ACT, its access is completed, and its access is not the destination of any AR. The latter means that its SN is not the SN_d of any local ARDT entry.

When an entry is deleted from the ACT, three actions need to be taken (Table 1). First, if the entry's *wb* field is set, it means that the corresponding line in L1 had been written back and, therefore, an *SP_expire* message is now to be sent to the ART to deallocate the entry. Second, the ARST is checked for entries that need to be removed; these are the entries representing ARs whose source is the removed ACT entry. Their AR_s and SN_s are equal to the local processor ID and to the SN of the removed ACT entry, respectively. Finally, Volition tries to delete the new entry at the head of the ACT, repeating the process above.

In the ARST, an entry is inserted when a new AR is detected whose source is a local access. In addition, when we discuss cycles with more than two processors (Section 3.5), we will see that we also allocate an ARST entry when an AR is *propagated* from another processor to the local one. In either case, when an ARST entry is allocated, Volition sends a message with SP=1 (format in Figure 5(b)) with information on the new AR to the AR_d processor.

Action/Condition	Active Table (ACT)	AR Source Table (ARST)	AR Destination Table (ARDT)	AR Table (ART) in dir.
Insert Condition	Memory instruction is issued (in program order)	(i) When an AR is detected locally or (ii) When a predecessor AR is propagated (cycles with >2 cores)	When a message with SP=1 is received	When a dirty cache line is written back from a cache whose processor has the line's address in its ACT
Actions on Insert		Send information on the (local or propagated) AR to the AR_d in a message with SP=1		
Delete Condition	When an entry with SN satisfies these three conditions: (i) Head of ACT (ii) Completed (C=1) (iii) SN is not the SN_d of any ARDT entry	(i) When an AR source is deleted from the ACT or (ii) When an *SP_expire* is received from a predecessor AR (cycles with >2 cores)	When an *SP_expire* is received for an AR	When directory receives: (i) either an *SP_expire* for the entry (ii) or a write request for the line in the entry
Actions on Delete	(i) If *wb*=1, then send *SP_expire* to the ART (ii) Check if any ARST entries need to be deleted (iii) Check if the ACT next top entry also needs to be deleted	Send an *SP_expire* for the (local or propagated) AR to the AR_d	Check if an ACT entry can be deleted	

Table 1. Table operations in Volition.

An ARST entry representing an AR is deleted in two cases. One is when the source reference of the AR has been removed from the ACT, as discussed above. The other is when, in environments with cycles with more than two processors (Section 3.5), an *SP_expire* message for the AR is propagated from another processor to the local one. Finally, when an entry is deleted from the ARST, an *SP_expire* message for the AR is sent to the AR_d processor.

In the ARDT, an entry is inserted when the processor receives a message with SP=1 from the source of the AR. An entry is deleted when an *SP_expire* message for the AR is received. Finally, when an ARDT entry is deleted, Volition checks if the entry at the head of the ACT can now be removed; this will be possible if the reference at the ACT head is the destination of the removed AR and of no other existing AR.

We insert an entry in the ART in the directory module when a dirty cache line is written back from a cache whose processor has the line's address in its ACT. Moreover, an entry is deleted from the ART when the directory receives (i) either an *SP_expire* message for the entry (ii) or a write request for the line in the entry.

Figure 6 repeats the information in the table for the ACT, ARST, and ARDT in the form of a state diagram. We use the diagram to describe the examples below.

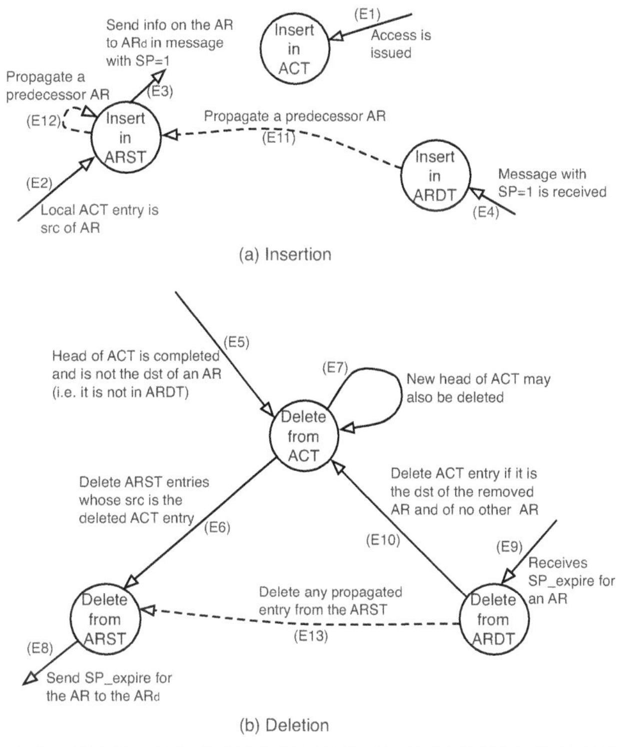

Figure 6. State diagrams for insertion and deletion of table entries. The transitions with dashed lines will be discussed later.

3.3.5 Examples

To better understand the operations, we consider several example access streams in Figure 7. In the streams, *w* and *r* are writes and reads, and arrows are data races. Moreover, white, gray, and black circles indicate incompleted accesses, completed but active accesses, and inactive accesses, respectively.

In Figure 7(a), assume that P_1 issues r1. This causes the insertion of an entry in P_1's ACT (edge (E1) in Figure 6(a)). Since r1 reads the value produced by w1 in P_0, and w1 is active because w0 is incompleted, P_0 detects an AR. Hence, P_0 inserts an entry in its ARST ((E2) in Figure 6(a)) and responds to P_1 with a message with SP=1 ((E3) in Figure 6(a)). When P_1 receives the message with SP=1, it inserts an entry in its own ARDT ((E4) in Figure 6(a)).

Later, as shown in Figure 7(b), assume that w0 in P_0 has completed and been deleted from P_0's ACT. At this point, w1 is completed and at the head of P_0's ACT. Since w1 is not the destination of any AR (it has no associated entry in P_0's ARDT), it is deleted from P_0's ACT (edge (E5) in Figure 6(b)). Such removal causes the deletion of any entry in P_0's ARST whose source is the deleted ACT entry ((E6) in Figure 6(b)). Hence, in our example, we delete the ARST entry corresponding to the AR that goes from w1 to r1. After removing the ARST entry, P_0 sends an *SP_expire* message to P_1 ((E8) in Figure 6(b)). At the same time, P_0 also tries to remove its next entry in the ACT, which is w2 ((E7) in Figure 6(b)). When P_1 receives the *SP_expire*, it deletes the entry for this AR in its ARDT ((E9) in Figure 6(b)). Immediately after this, P_1 has to check its ACT — to see if the deletion of the ARDT entry makes the entry at the head of its ACT eligible for deletion ((E10) in Figure 6(b)). In the example, P_1 can remove r1's entry in the ACT.

Figure 7(c) augments 7(b) with another processor (P_2) that also had an AR whose destination is r1 in P_1. In this case, after the deletion of P_1's ARDT entry for the w1→r1 AR, P_1 cannot yet

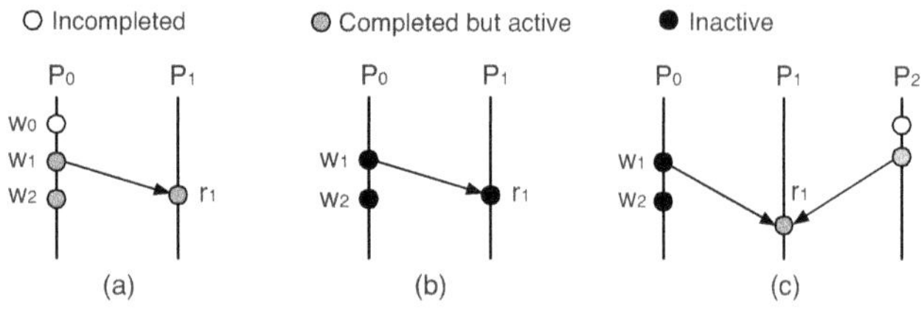

Figure 7. Examples of access streams.

remove r1's entry from the ACT. It can only be deleted when both races have ceased to be active.

3.4 Detecting SCVs between Two Processors

An SCV between two processors occurs when there are two ARs in the opposite directions forming a cycle as in Figure 8. The cycle requires that, in each of the processors, the source access of the outgoing AR is equal to or younger than the destination access of the incoming AR. Hence, the condition for an SCV is determined in a processor *locally* by comparing the local ARST and ARDT. Specifically, we are looking for an entry *arst* in ARST and an entry *ardt* in ARDT that satisfy all of the following four conditions:

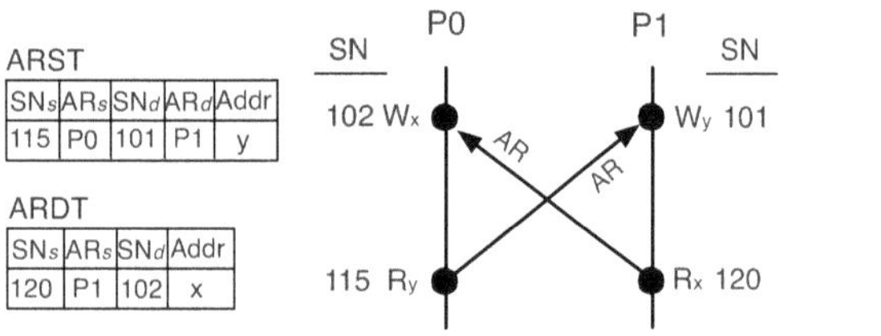

Figure 8. Detecting an SCV between two processors.

• The source processor in *arst* is the local processor. This is always the case based on our discussion so far. However, it may not be the case in cycles with more than two processors (Section 3.5).

$arst[AR_s]$=Local_PID

• The destination processor in *arst* is the same as the source processor in *ardt*.

$arst[AR_d]=ardt[AR_s]$

• The SN of the source access in *arst* is equal to or larger than the SN of the destination access in *ardt*.

$arst[SN_s]\geq ardt[SN_d]$

• The SN of the source access in *ardt* is equal to or larger than the SN of the destination access in *arst*.

$ardt[SN_s]\geq arst[SN_d]$

Figure 8 shows the entries in P_0's ARST and ARDT for the example shown. We see that the entries satisfy the four conditions listed above. Specifically, from top to bottom, the conditions find: P_0, P_1, $115\geq 102$, and $120\geq 101$. For simplicity, Figure 8 does not show P_1's ARST and ARDT. Using such tables, the conditions are also show to be satisfied in P_1.

In each processor, the condition for SCV is locally checked every time that a new entry is added to its ARST or to its ARDT. Specifically, when a new entry is added to the ARST, it is checked against those currently in the ARDT, and vice-versa.

With this approach, when an SCV occurs, both processors detect it. Like in Vulcan [24], the timing of the detection depends on the relative timing of the ARs. If the two writes in Figure 8 complete at approximately the same time, both processors detect the SCV when their write transaction receives the response and causes the allocation of an ARDT entry. However, if one write (say *Wy* in Figure 8) is already completed by the time its processor receives the invalidation from the other write (at the point of *Rx* in the figure), then this processor (P_1) detects the SCV as receives the invalidation. The other processor (P_0) detects the SCV as it gets the invalidation acknowledgement.

In either case, when each processor detects the SCV, it raises an exception. As in Vulcan [24], the exception may not provide the exact architectural state at the point of the SCV-causing accesses. Specifically, the information that is available to the debugger in the interrupted processor at the destination of an AR is the address being accessed, the instruction's PC and the ID of the other processor. If the destination reference of the AR is a read, the exception gets the precise processor state. If it is write, it is not generally possible to get the precise state at the reference because the write is in the store buffer and later operations may have already retired and completed. The information available to the debugger in the interrupted processor at the source of the AR is the address accessed, the ID of the requesting processor, and if we augment the ACT with PCs, the instruction's PC. The exception in the source processor is not precise because newer instructions may have finished.

Execution can potentially continue after reporting the SCV in the exception handlers. It requires that Volition explicitly remove one the ARs participating in the cycle, by sending an *SP_expire* for the AR to the AR's destination processor. Otherwise, the four accesses involved in the SCV would remain active and no entry would ever be removed from the tables.

3.5 Detecting SCVs Among Any Number of Processors

In this section, we discuss the mechanism to detect SCVs involving an arbitrary number of processors. We start with some examples, describe the concept of AR propagation, and then define the conditions for an SCV.

3.5.1 Motivating Examples

Figure 9(a) shows an SCV involving three processors. The cycle is composed of active races AR0, AR1, and AR2. Although Volition can find the three ARs, our previous conditions for SCV cannot find the SCV.

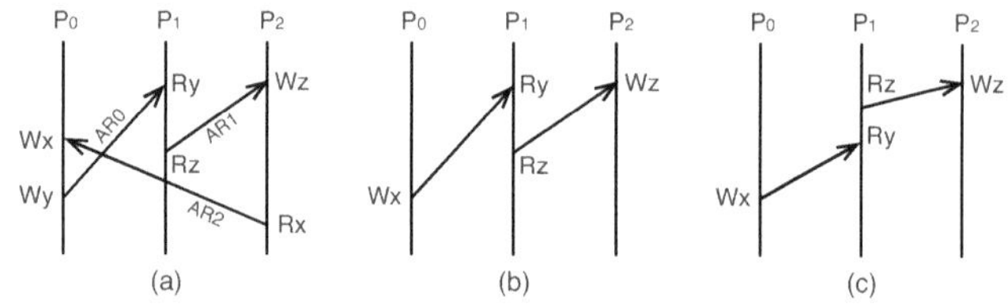

Figure 9. Finding SCVs across more than two processors.

To be able to detect the SCV, we use the insight that two ARs transitively imply another AR that combines them. For example, in Figure 9(a), ARs Wy→Ry and Rz→Wz transitively imply Wy→Wz. If P_0 and P_2 have such information, they can easily detect the SCV.

As we attempt to transitively combine ARs, we need consider the order of the local accesses of the ARs. Specifically, in a processor, the destination of one AR *has to precede* the source of the other AR. This is seen in Figure 9(b) for P_1. If the opposite is the case, as in P_1 in Figure 9(c), the two ARs cannot be combined.

3.5.2 Propagation of Active Races

To understand how Volition transitively combines two ARs, Figure 10(a) shows two ARs with the SNs of their accesses. We name these ARs from the point of view of the processor that sees them both, namely P_j: the *Predecessor* AR (AR_{pred}) is the one whose destination is in P_j, and the *Successor* AR (AR_{succ}) is the one whose source is in P_j. Such terminology does not imply the relative time of when the ARs were identified. The goal of Volition is to generate AR_{trans}, the AR in dashes in Figure 10(b), which connects the source of the predecessor AR (SN_i) to the destination of the successor AR (SN_k).

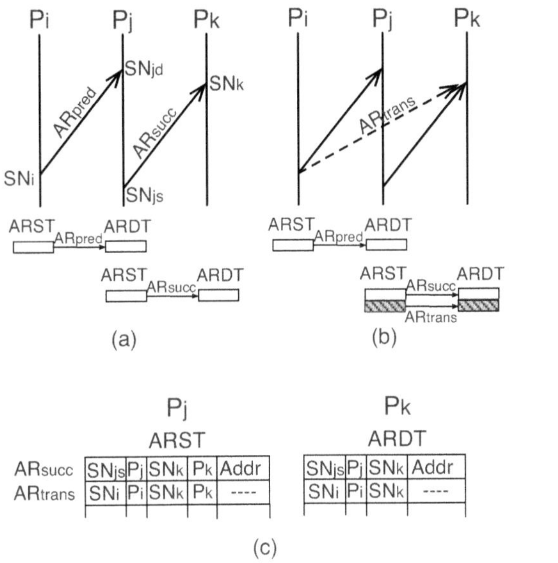

Figure 10. Propagating active races.

Figure 10(a) also shows that AR_{pred} has an entry in P_i's ARST and one in P_j's ARDT. Similarly, AR_{succ} has one in P_j's ARST and one in P_k's ARDT. Figure 10(b) shows how Volition will represent the new AR_{trans}: with a new entry in P_j's ARST and one in P_k's ARDT. They are shown as shaded. The new entries will combine information of P_i and P_k, and contain no information on P_j, even though one of the entries is in P_j.

Specifically, the new entries for AR_{trans} are shown in Figure 10(c), together with those existing for AR_{succ} for comparison. Consider the ARST for AR_{trans}. It contains source information from AR_{pred} (SN_i and P_i) and destination information for AR_{succ} (SN_k and P_k); the address field is unused. Similarly, the ARDT for AR_{trans} contains source information from AR_{pred} (SN_i and P_i) and destination information for AR_{succ} (SN_k). P_k will be unable to distinguish transitive ARs from direct ones; P_j will distinguish transitive ARs because the source information is from another processor. It appears as if Volition had "propagated" the information from P_i to P_j. Hence, we refer to the operation of transitively combining two ARs as AR *Propagation*.

3.5.3 Table Operations

To propagate ARs, the state diagrams of Figure 6 are augmented with the three transitions with dashed lines. Consider insertion first. Assume that, in Figure 10(a), P_j has already recorded AR_{pred} and now it detects AR_{succ}. After inserting the usual ARST entry, P_j observes that P_j is the destination of an AR that can be transitively combined. Hence, it creates a new entry in its ARST and sends a second message with SP=1 to the destination of AR_{succ}. This message contains the information in Figure 10(c): SN_i, P_i, and SN_k). This operation is shown in edge (E12) in Figure 6(a).

Consider, instead, that in Figure 10(a), P_j has already recorded AR_{succ} and now it detects AR_{pred}. After inserting the usual ARDT entry, P_j observes that P_j is also the source of an AR that can be transitively combined. Therefore, it performs the same operations as described above. This operation is shown in edge (E11) in Figure 6(a).

Finally, consider removal. Among AR_{pred} and AR_{succ}, the one that must become inactive first is AR_{pred}. Hence, P_i sends an *SP_expire* message to P_j. After P_j deletes its ARDT entry corresponding to (P_i, SN_i), it now has to check for an entry in its ARST with the same source (P_i, SN_i). If it finds one, it is a propagated AR. Therefore, it deletes it and sends an *SP_expire* message for it to its destination, which is P_k. This operation is shown in edge (E13) in Figure 6(b). On reception of the *SP_expire*, P_k removes its entry from ARDT.

3.5.4 SCV Condition

With the AR propagation operations, the SCV is detected when one of the created transistive ARs ends up having the same processor as source and destination. This event occurs when Volition creates a new ARDT entry in a processor, such that the AR source is also the current processor and the AR source SN is larger than the AR destination SN. Specifically, the new ARDT entry *ardt* is such that:

• The source processor in *ardt* is the local processor. Recall that there is no destination processor in *ardt* because it is always the local one.

$$ardt[AR_s]\text{=Local\_PID}$$

• The SN of the source access in *ardt* is equal to or larger than the SN of the destination access in *ardt*.

$$ardt[SN_s] \geq ardt[SN_d]$$

Figure 11 shows an example with three processors. Charts (a)-(f) show snapshots of the transitive ARs as they are generated; Chart (g) shows a timeline of events. Consider Chart (a), which corresponds to time t_0. At this time, AR (1) and AR (2) have been used to generate transitive AR (i). The timeline in Chart (g) shows that, at time t_0, processor P_1 took predecessor AR (1) and successor AR (2) and generated AR (i), creating an ARST entry in P_1 and an ARDT entry in P_2.

Chart (b) shows that, at time t_1, AR (3) is detected. There are now enough ARs to creat a cycle. It will be uncovered by creating transitive ARs.

Specifically, Chart (c) corresponds to time t_2 in P_0, when P_0 generates AR (ii). The timeline in Chart (g) shows that, at time t_2, processor P_0 took AR (3) and AR (1) and generated AR (ii), creating an ARST entry in P_0 and an ARDT entry in P_1. Chart (d) is also at the same logical time t_2 in P_2, when P_2 generates AR (iv) and AR (v). As shown in Chart (g), at time t_2, processor P_2 took AR (2) and AR (3) and generated AR (iv), augmenting the ARST in P_2 and the ARDT in P_0. P_2 also took AR (i) and AR (3) and generated AR (v), recording it in the ARST in P_2 and the ARDT in P_0. This ARDT entry causes the detection of the SCV in P_0.

Potentially while this is taking place, Chart (e) shows time t_3 in P_1, where AR (iii) is created. Specifically, as shown in Chart (g), at time t_3, P_1 takes AR (ii) and AR (2) and generates AR (iii), recording it in the ARST in P_1 and the ARDT in P_2. This ARDT entry causes the detection of the SCV in P_2. Moreover, Chart (f) shows time t_4 in P_0, where (vi) is created. Specifically, as shown in Chart (g), at time t_4, processor P_0 takes AR (iv) and AR (1) and generates AR (vi), recording it in the ARST in P_0 and the ARDT in P_1. This ARDT entry causes the detection of the SCV in P_1.

When a processor detects the condition for the SCV, we envision Volition to trigger an exception. The processor then obtains the SN_s and SN_d from the offending ARDT entry. These are the local SNs of the two local accesses involved in the SCV. The processor can then read its ACT and obtain the addresses for these two accesses. Moreover, if the ACT is augmented with the program counters (PC) of the instructions, then it can also obtain the local PCs of the accesses.

From the example, we see that all of the processors involved in the cycle eventually detect the SCV. However, the actual timing and order is not deterministic. Hence, we can think of different usage modes for Volition. In one mode, as soon as the first processor detects the SCV, the processor dumps the addresses and PCs of

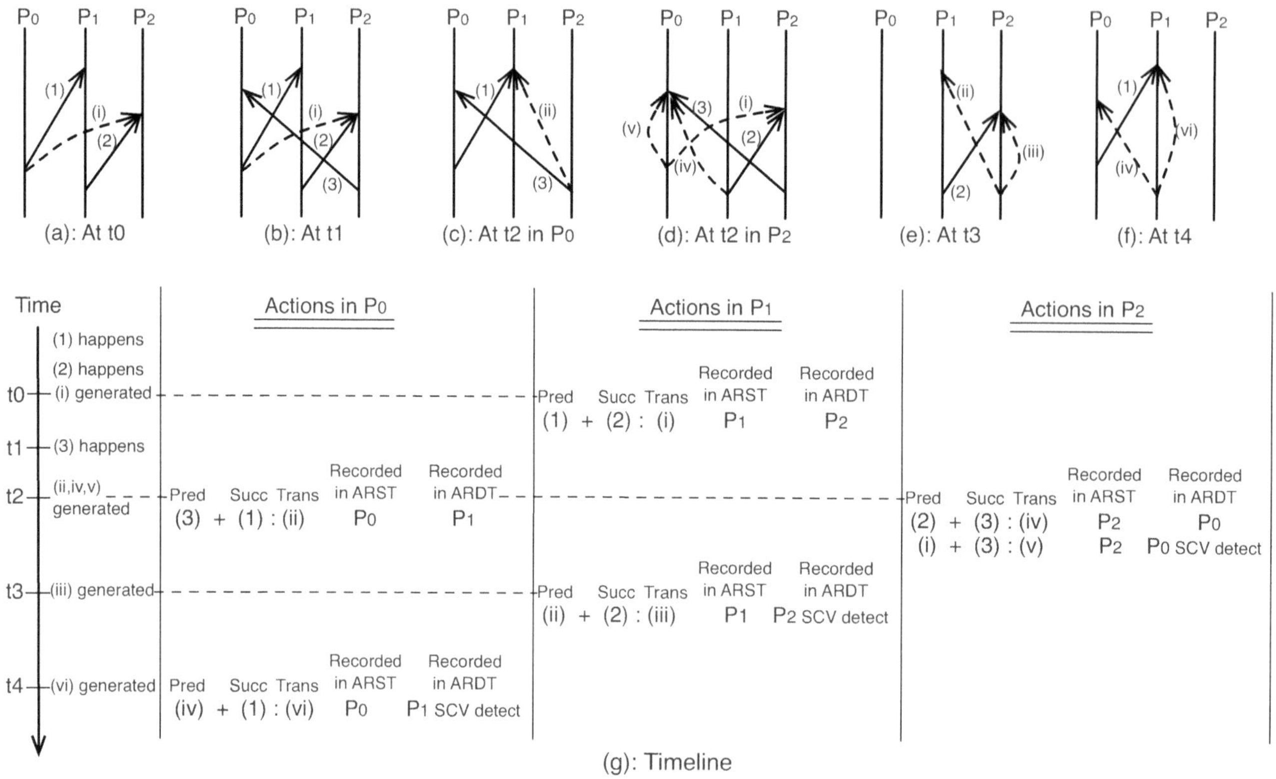

Figure 11. Detecting an SCV with three processors.

the local accesses, and then stops all other processors. In a second mode, we let each processor involved in the SCV find the SCV, dump the information, and continue. With this approach, we will get a better picture of the SCV, but the Volition tables of the processors involved in the SCV will eventually fill up and the processors will stop. Finally, in a third mode, as soon as the first processor detects the SCV, it reports it in a log file and sends an *SP_expire* for one of the ARs participating in the SCV. This will break the cycle and allow the processors to continue execution. This mode is attractive when the program runs in a non-interactive mode. The log can later be examined. However, it is not guaranteed that all the processors in the SCV will suffer an exception.

The approach described is applicable irrespectively of the number of processors participating in the SCV. In particular, it works in cycles with only two ARs, where one AR is arbitrarily chosen as predecessor and one successor. Hence, this approach supersedes the one in Section 3.4, which was presented to ease the explanation.

4. Supporting Multi-Word Cache Lines

4.1 The Problem

With single-word cache lines, every inter-processor dependence (not affected by cache displacements) induces a coherence transaction — which Volition uses for AR recording. In multi-word cache lines, the fact that all of the words in a line have to have the same state, may cause a simple design to miss some ARs (false negatives) or to falsely report some ARs (false positives). For example, in Figure 12, where *a* and *b* are in the same line, there is only one coherence action, at Wa. The Rb access is silently satisfied from the local cache. However, in reality, there are two races in the example. The opposite case, where there are no races but the protocol induces transactions, can occur due to false sharing. Hence, we must extend the Volition scheme of Section 3. In the rest of the discussion, we assume that, although the coherence protocol is line-based, coherence transactions include the address of the word accessed within the line.

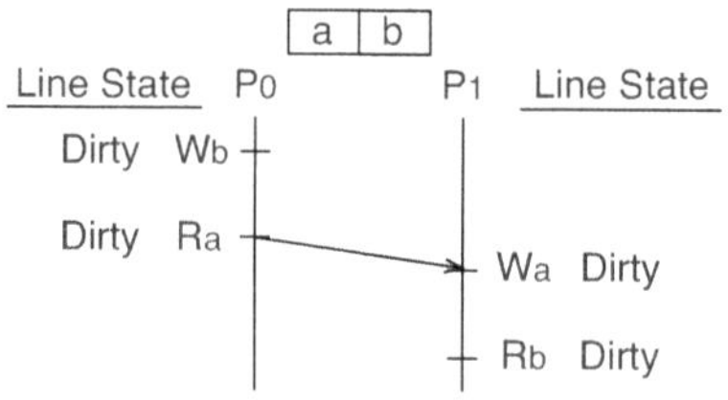

Figure 12. Missing an AR with multi-word cache lines.

4.2 Approach: Metadata Transactions

To solve this problem, we use the general approach proposed in Vulcan [24]. It involves augmenting a cache line with some information on recent accesses performed by processors to each of the words in the line. Such information should be enough to tell a processor that is referencing the line whether or not it needs to check for ARs in other processors. If it needs to, but the protocol will not generate a coherence transaction, Volition triggers a *Metadata Transaction*. Such transaction checks and updates the Volition metadata in other processors, possibly recording ARs. However, it involves no data transfer or cache coherence transition. Hence, the cache coherence protocol is unmodified.

In Volition, the information that needs to be associated with a line in a cache is the set of accesses from any processor to any of the words in the line that are currently active — i.e., that are in the Active Table (ACT) of any processor. With this information, when a processor accesses a line, it can check, for the relevant word, whether any AR can be created. In particular, we need the following information for each word:

• The most recent active write (if any).
• The set of active reads (if any) that follow the most recent active write (if there is one) or that currently exist (if there is no active write).

This information is needed when a processor issues a read or a write to the word, to indentify a potential AR. Note that all of the accesses before the most recent active write are irrelevant because they cannot source any future race.

Consequently, our basic design augments some of the cache lines with the information shown in Figure 13, which we call *Summary of Active Information* (SAI). For each word in the line, it contains: (i) the ID of the processor that has issued the most recent active write (if any), and (ii) the IDs of the processors that have issued the active reads (if any) that follow the most recent active write (if there is one) or that just currently exist (if there is no active write). Note that there is room for only a few readers. Hence, like in limited directory schemes [2], we keep space for only very few readers; if more are needed, we set a Broadcast bit. Since most of the words in a line are likely to need little or no information, the SAI should be encoded to use little space. The SAI has to travel with the line in the cache hierarchy and must be kept up to date.

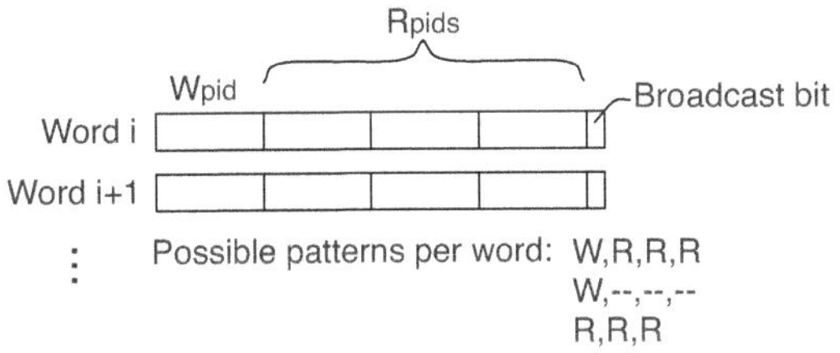

Figure 13. Structure of an SAI associated with a cache line.

When a processor accesses a line in its cache that has an SAI, Volition checks the SAI for the word accessed. If it finds that there are active accesses to this word in other processors that can create an AR with the current access, it needs to communicate with such processors. The communication automatically happens if the current access causes a coherence transaction with such processors; it simply requires including the updated SAI. Otherwise, Volition explicitly triggers a metadata transaction with the updated SAI directed to the processors that can potentially generate ARs. The arrival of the coherence or metadata transaction at these processors triggers Volition operations there.

4.3 Basic Operation

To describe the operation of Volition, we initially assume that all the cached lines have SAI entries, and that there are no cache line evictions. These assumptions will be removed later.

With these assumptions, the main challenge of the design is how to keep a line's SAI information correct. A SAI is associated with a copy of the line, and when such a copy is accessed, its SAI is updated with appropriate read or write information. If the multiprocessor cache hierarchy contained at most a single copy of a line, then keeping the SAI up to date would be easy. In reality, however, in the MSI protocol that we use in this paper (Section 3.1), a line repeatedly moves between a situation where there is a single (D or S) copy of the line in the system, and one where the caches have multiple S copies of the line that are identical.

Figure 14 shows the transition diagram for the system-wide state of a cache line in our protocol. When there is a single D or S copy of the line (leftmost circle in Figure 14), there also a single copy of the SAI. Such line may be accessed by the local processor or may receive an external write, in which case it moves to another cache, followed by its up-to-date SAI.

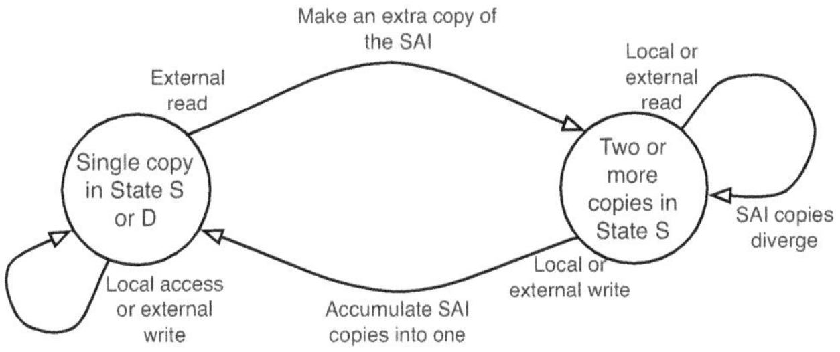

Figure 14. Transition diagram for the system-wide state of a cache line.

When an external read occurs, an extra copy of both the line and its SAI is made (rightmost circle in Figure 14). At this point, these two (or more) processors may repeatedly read words in the line. As they do so, each updates its local SAI copy, which starts to diverge from the other SAI copies. However, their divergence only consists of reader IDs, and can only induce RAW metadata transactions with the single recent-most writer of the word.

When one processor (among the sharers or otherwise) writes any of the words of the line, the state transitions back to the leftmost circle in Figure 14. As invalidation coherence messages are sent to all the sharers (which potentially record ARs), the current SAI copies are all returned to the writer. The writer accumulates the information from all of the SAI copies, and now keeps the single SAI entry for the line. The SAI information for the particular word written is reset to have a single writer ID, namely the writer processor, and no reader IDs.

We now consider several issues, namely which cache lines have SAI entries, how is the information removed from SAI entries as accesses become inactive, and the interaction with line eviction from caches.

4.4 Allocation of SAI Entries

SAI entries are only needed for lines that are being *actively* shared between processors. If a line is accessed by a single processor, it does not need an SAI. Even for a shared line, as accesses to it become inactive, Volition progressively removes information from its SAI; when the SAI contains no information, the SAI can be deallocated. Overall, at any given time, only very few lines in a multiprocessor cache hierarchy have SAI entries.

Specifically, as a processor misses on a line, if there are no sharers or the sharers do not have an SAI, then the line is read into the local cache without an SAI. Note that we also require that there is no information in the directory from a past eviction, as we will see in Section 4.6. If, instead, an SAI needs to be allocated, it is allocated in a small table in the cache controller called the Summary Active Table (SAT) (Figure 15).

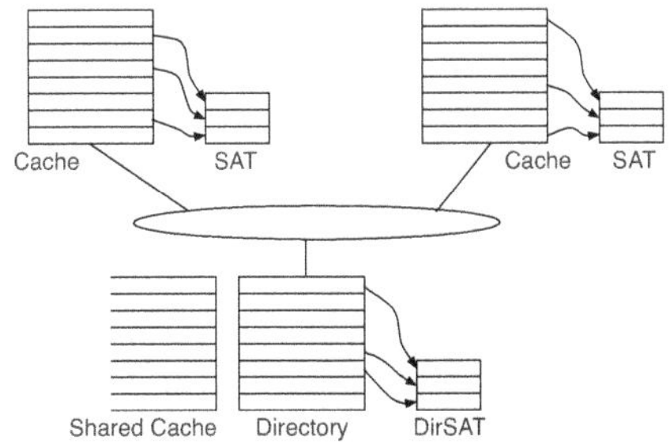

Figure 15. Storing SAI information in the system.

As a processor accesses the line, Volition attempts to update the line's SAI. However, it only does it if it finds one. As local accesses to the line become inactive, Volition attempts to remove information from the line's SAI, if it exists. Section 4.5 discusses this operation in detail. As soon as the line's SAI becomes empty, it is deallocated from the SAT.

Finally, there are situations when a processor with a line without a SAI needs to build a SAI for it. This occurs when the processor has active accesses to the line in its ACT, and either it receives a coherence transaction for the line, or its cache wants to evict the line. In these cases, Volition allocates the SAI, updates it with information on the current local active accesses, and includes it with the coherence response or with the evicted line.

4.5 Removal of Information as Accesses Become Inactive

As an active access (by a processor *P*) to a line becomes inactive, *P*'s information should be removed from the line's SAI entries. This is because we do not want to keep querying *P* for ARs anymore in any future access by other processors.

To see how information is removed from an SAI entry, consider four possible cases. The first, trivial case is when the line is in *P*'s cache but has no SAI; in this case, no action is taken. The second case is when the line state tells us that the line is present only in *P*'s cache; in this case, Volition simply removes *P*'s ID from the SAI's write or the read area (for a write or read, respectively).

A third case occurs when the line is present in *P*'s cache and potentially in other caches as well. If *P*'s access is a read, its information is simply removed from the local SAI. It may be that other copies of the line also have the read's information, which now becomes redundant. A subsequent write will trigger an unnecessary metadata transaction to *P*'s cache. However, to miminize overall traffic, Volition takes no further action now.

However, if the now-inactive access by *P* is a write, both the local and all of the remote SAIs are updated. Volition removes the write PID from all of the SAIs to prevent future reads by other processors from initiating unnecessary metadata transactions to *P*'s cache. Hence, after Volition removes *P*'s ID from the local SAI, it initiates a metadata transaction to the directory, which is forwarded to all of the sharers of the line. All the SAI versions are updated.

Finally, the fourth case is when the line is not present in *P*'s cache — because it has been invalidated or it has been evicted. In this case, for both reads and writes, Volition initiates a metadata transaction to the directory, which is forwarded to all of the sharers of the line and removes *P*'s ID from all SAIs. This is done to avoid future unnecessary metadata transactions.

4.6 Cache Eviction of Lines with SAI Entries

When a line with SAI information is evicted from a cache, its SAI needs to be saved. The reason is that the SAI may contain unique information: the complete SAI information if this was the only cached copy of the line in the system, or unique reader PIDs otherwise. Hence, Volition stores the evicted SAI in a table in the directory controller called Directory SAT (DirSAT) (Figure 15). The DirSAT subsumes the ART structure in Section 3.3.3, which worked for single-word lines only.

Subsequent metadata transactions, as they reach the directory on their way to check for ARs in the relevant processors, they must read the dirSAT. If they find an SAI entry for the line accessed, they read its information (combining it with the information in the transaction's own SAI). Similarly, messages from processors that indicate that a certain access has become inactive, as they reach the directory, they remove the relevant bits from the SAI entry in the DirSAT.

Multiple evictions of a line's SAI from multiple caches simply accumulate their state in a single DirSAT entry. Moreover, when a line (with SAI) that is dirty in a processor is read by a second one, as the line and SAI are provided to the reader, the DirSAT also collects a copy of the SAI. The reason is that future read misses on the line will read directly from memory (since the line is not D in any cache), and they also need to obtain a copy of the SAI.

Eventually, as bits for inactive accesses are removed form an SAI entry in the DirSAT, the entry may lose all of its information and be deallocated. In addition, an SAI entry in the DirSAT is also deallocated on any write to the line. Specifically, as a write coherence transaction invalidates all copies of the line in the system and collects (and accumulates) all the SAIs for the line, it also collects and removes the SAI entry in the dirSAT.

Overall, we see that Volition manages multi-word cache lines without modifying the cache coherence protocol.

5. Implementation Issues

5.1 Wrap-Around of SNs

The wrap-around of SNs could confuse SCV detection because a number that is supposed to be comparable to another is now much smaller. While this problem occurs infrequently with our 4-Byte SN, we still need to handle it. Specifically, we use the most significant bit of the 4-Byte SN as a detector of wrap-around. When the Volition logic compares two SNs and finds that the most-significant bit of one has changed, it knows that it is a larger number that has wrapped. The range of SNs is large enough that a processor is very highly unlikely to wrap around a second time before all the other processors have wrapped around once. If this event appears to be possible, as the SN reaches a certain watermark, all processors are interrupted and the starting point of SNs is reset.

5.2 Reducing the Cost of ACT Scan

To avoid searching a processor's ACT for every incoming coherence message, we follow Vulcan's design [24] and use a counting Bloom filter (CBF) [4] to represent the current set of addresses in the ACT. If the incoming address does not hit in the CBF, we know the address is not in the ACT. We need to use a CBF because addresses need to be removed from the filter when they are deallocated from the ACT.

5.3 Region Expiration to Reduce Bandwidth

As discussed in Section 3.3, Volition causes a processor to send an *SP_expire* message when a local AR expires. While ARs are not generally very common, we can optimize this operation and save some network bandwidth when there are many clustered ARs. Specifically, rather than sending a message to the destination processor (AR_d) with the AR's SN_s immediately when the AR expires, Volition can wait for a small time. At regular intervals, when a few ARs have expired, it can multicast the *SP_expire* message with the maximum of the expired ARs' SN_s to all of the AR_ds. If ARs cluster in time, and there are only very few different AR_ds, we can save bandwidth. In practice, for our applications, we do not find this optimization beneficial.

6. Discussion

The current Volition design largely attains the design goals of Section 3.1. First, Volition detects SCVs involving an arbitrary number of processors, in a precise manner, and with no false positives or false negatives. Of course, the hardware design has to be adapted to support the finest granularity of program accesses (e.g., bytes). The current design has assumed word-level accesses.

One limitation of the current design is that it does not consider speculative loads from mispredicted branch paths. To be able to support them, we need to extend Volition, possibly delaying the recording of an AR until the source load becomes non-speculative, and discarding an AR whose destination load is proven to be in the wrong path. We consider this extension to be our future work.

Note also that Volition is not concerned with the impact of compiler optimizations on SCVs. It simply takes the executable that the compiler provides to the hardware and reports SCVs due to hardware-initiated reference reordering. Similarly, since Volition is a dynamic scheme, it only provides information for the actual performed runs.

A second goal attained is to have a scalable design. Volition works with a scalable directory-based cache-coherence protocol. In addition, the size of its hardware structures increases only moderately with the processor count, and Volition does not need all-to-all structures.

A third goal is to have low overhead. As we show in Section 7.4, Volition incurs little execution time and bandwidth overhead.

The final goal is to be decoupled from the coherence protocol. The Volition hardware is substantial and often fairly involved. However, all of the additional messages used to manage the metadata for SCV detection are largely decoupled from the existing cache coherence protocol. Hence, the coherence protocol should not have to be revalidated.

7. Evaluation

7.1 Evaluation Setup

We focus the evaluation on three aspects, namely, (1) the ability of Volition to detect SCVs, (2) the characteristics of SCVs, and (3) the overhead and scalability of Volition.

We implement Volition in the SESC [26] cycle-level architectural simulator. We model a multicore with 64 cores and an MSI directory-based cache coherence protocol. The hardware uses either the Release Consistency (RC) or the Total-Store-Order (TSO) memory consistency model. We use different store buffer sizes to see their impact on access reordering. For comparison, we also implement the Conflict Ordering scheme of Lin et al. [20]. We name it *CO*. Such scheme, as we describe in Section 8, enforces SC. When a potential SCV is about to occur, CO avoids it by squashing and replaying certain instructions. The configuration of the simulated machine is shown in Table 3.

Architecture	Multicore chip with 64 cores
Core width; ROB size	4-issue; 128 entries
Consistency	RC or TSO
Store buffer	32 entries
Private L1 cache	32KB WB, 4-way, 2-cycle round trip
Shared L2 cache	1MB module/proc. Module: WB, 8-way
Latency to L2	Local module: 11-cycle round trip
Cache line size	32 bytes
Cache coherence	Directory-based MSI protocol
Network	2-D mesh with 7-cycle hop latency
Main memory	200-cycle round trip
Volition parameters	SN size: 4 bytes; ACT size: 256 entries per-node ARST, ARDT: 40 entries each; per-node SAT: 100 entries

Table 3. Architecture parameters.

We run the applications shown in Table 4. They include several small codes with concurrent algorithms, a kernel with a double-checked lock (DCL), and SPLASH-2 and Parsec applications. The codes with concurrent algorithms were mostly obtained from [1], which in turn comes from CheckFence [5]. They are small C-code programs where threads share data structures without synchronization, and rely on explicit fences to maintain correct access ordering. Many of these programs insert and remove elements from a linked list. In addition, we added two well-known algorithms for mutual exclusion, namely Dekker (which only runs with two threads) and Peterson.

We use the codes with the concurrent algorithms and DCL to check the ability of Volition to detect SCVs. Specifically, we explicitly remove all of their fences and run each code 100 times. We count the total number of SCVs detected. Note that many of the executions are now incorrect, but they help us understand Volition's effectiveness. Finally, we use the SPLASH-2 and Parsec codes to evaluate the overheads and scalability of Volition.

Set	Application	Description
Conc. Algo.	Aharr	Variant of Harris
	Dekker	Algorithm for 2 proc. mutual exclusion
	Harris	Non-blocking set
	Lazylist	List-based concurrent set
	Moirbt	Non-blocking sync. primitives
	Moircas	Non-blocking sync. primitives
	Ms2	Two-lock queue
	Msn	Non-blocking queue
	Mst	Non-blocking queue
	Peterson	Algorithm for N proc. mutual exclusion
	Snark	Non-blocking double-ended queue
Bug	DCL	Double-checked lock without fence
Full Apps	SPLASH-2	12 programs
	Parsec	4 programs

Table 4. Applications executed.

7.2 Ability to Detect SCVs

To assess Volition's ability to detect SCVs, we take each of the small codes stripped of fences and run them 100 times. We use the simulator to count the number of SCVs observed with Volition — even if the SCVs repeat across runs. When a processor dectects an SCV, it sends an *SP_expire* to remove one of the ARs and ensure that the program continues execution. We model either RC or TSO.

Table 2 shows, for each consistency model, the number of SCVs detected with full Volition support (*# of SCVs*). It also shows the SCVs detected when Volition does not keep per-word access information (*# of Line-SCVs*). This environment is missing the SAT support from Section 4 that records which words of the line have been accessed by the processor. In this case, there are no metadata transactions — only the transactions generated by the coherence protocol occur. Hence, Volition misses SCVs. Finally, the table shows the number of active races detected (*# of ARs*). Intuitively, these are the races between largely concurrent accesses. They roughly capture the types of races recorded by DRFx [22] and Conflict Exceptions [21].

Looking at the RC columns, we see that Volition detects many SCVs in these codes. If metadata transactions are disabled (*Line-SCVs*), about half of the SCVs are missed. Hence, we need full Volition support. We also see that the number of ARs is very high — on average, over two orders of magnitude higher than the number of SCVs. This shows that ARs are not good proxies for SCVs.

The number of SCVs detected changes with the memory model. Typically, the more relaxed RC model causes more SCVs and Line-SCVs than the TSO model. However, in some applications, the opposite is the case.

Finally, the table shows the number of replays required to enforce SC in CO from Lin et al. [20], running on RC. We can see that the number of replays is lower than the number of ARs. However, it is, on average, one order of magnitude higher than the number of SCVs in Volition. Therefore, we conclude that, while CO is more precise than just reporting active races, it is much less precise than Volition in its detection of SCVs.

7.3 Characteristics of SCVs

In this section, we characterize the SCVs observed. Figure 17 takes the SCVs reported for each code and memory model in Table 2 and classifies them based on the number of processors participating in

Appl.	# of Runs	RC			TSO			CO
		# SCVs	# Line-SCVs	# ARs	# SCVs	# Line-SCVs	# ARs	# Replays
Aharr	100	166	20	4097	29	29	7035	2443
DCL	100	122	48	8529	61	55	9570	3984
Dekker	100	316	140	2653	675	235	7758	763
Harris	100	123	56	11752	43	39	9023	4061
Lazylist	100	49	26	11688	85	76	11535	2402
Moirbt	100	127	37	9408	92	61	12618	2824
Moircas	100	90	41	9522	14	14	12467	2969
Ms2	100	98	93	26252	256	176	26563	5891
Msn	100	355	251	15277	393	204	22717	1689
Mst	100	2288	1048	110293	875	618	181644	8589
Peterson	100	31	23	2028	40	24	2860	615
Snark	100	174	103	213082	276	60	196909	16432
Average	100	328	157	35381	236	132	41724	4388

Table 2. Volition's ability to detect SCVs.

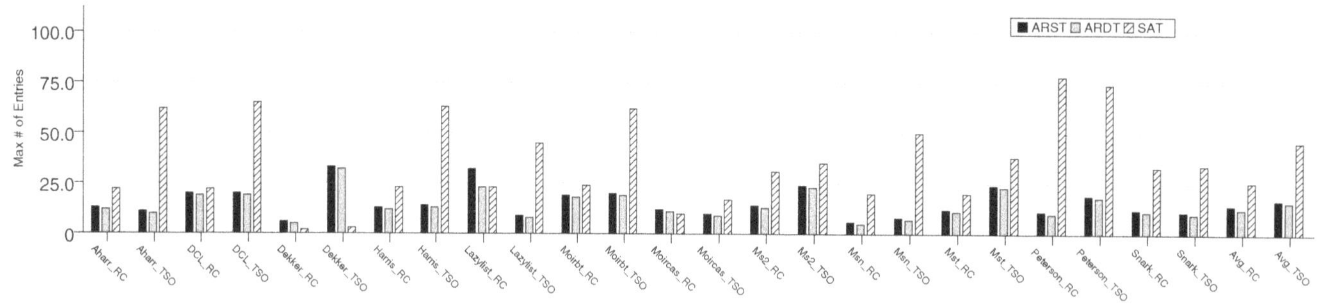

Figure 16. Table size requirements.

the SCV cycle. Specifically, we have cycles with 2 processors, 3 processors, and 4 or more processors. For each code, the number of SCVs is normalized to the number under RC.

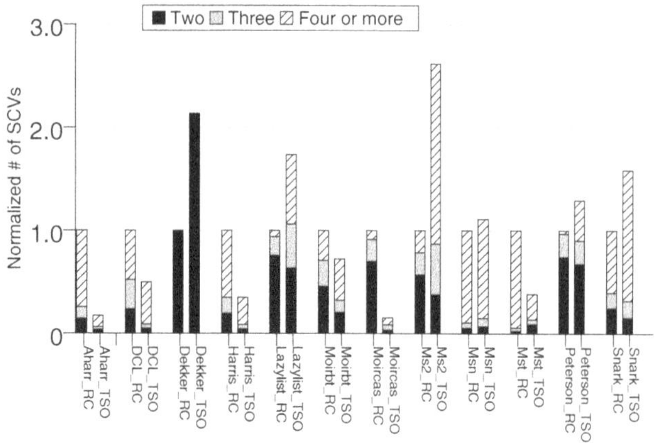

Figure 17. Number of processors involved in an SCV.

The figure shows that, in these sharing-intensive, fence-free codes, cycles appear with a variety of processor counts. While two-processor SCVs dominate in some applications (e.g., Moircas for RC), four-and-more processor SCVs are dominant in others (e.g., Msn). Hence, Volition's ability to detect cycles with an arbitrary number of processors is useful for the bug conditions represented by these fence-free codes. Note that Dekker can only have 2-processor cycles.

Figure 16 shows the use of the Volition hardware tables. Specifically, it shows, for each program and memory model, the maximum number of entries in use in each of the per-node ARST, ARDT, and SAT. We can see that these sizes are modest. In most cases, the maximum number of entries used in the ARST and ARDT is less than 25. For the SAT, it is less than 75. Therefore, our proposed sizes of 40 entries for the ARST and ARDT, and 100 entries for the SAT (Table 3) are more than enough.

Figure 18 shows the sensitivity of the number of SCVs to the size of the store buffer. For each program under RC, the figure shows the number of SCVs with store buffers of 4, 8, 16, and 32 entries. The latter is the default size. For each program, the bars are normalized to the number of SCVs for 4-entry buffers and are broken down into the number of processors per cycle.

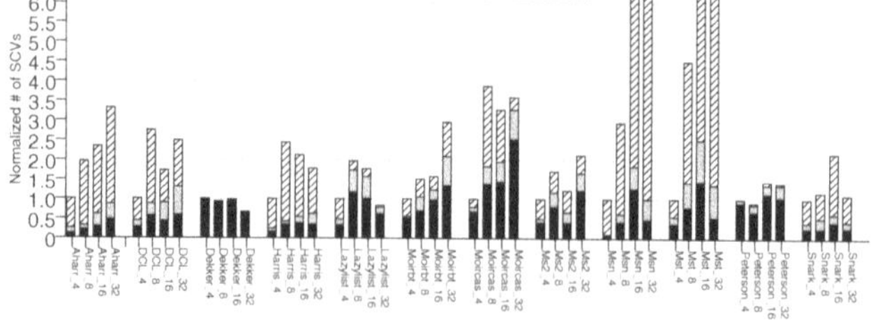

Figure 18. Sensitivity to the size of the store buffer.

Intuitively, larger store buffers should induce more SCVs because they allow more store reordering. While this is the general trend, there are several programs where smaller buffers induce more SCVs. The reason is that smaller buffers also affect the timing of execution significantly, by introducing more access stalls due to full buffers.

7.4 Overheads of Volition

We consider two overheads of Volition, namely the increase in network traffic and the increase in program execution time. Figure 19 shows the total number of bytes transferred in the network of the machine for different programs and memory consistency models. The figure also includes bars for the average of the SPLASH-2 applications and the average of the Parsec codes. We break down the bytes transferred into those from memory access requests (*MemAcc*), data transferred in a read (*Read*) or write (*Write*), coherence activity in invalidations, acknowledgements, or forwarding to the owner cache (*Coh*), and additional traffic due to Volition (*Overhead*). The latter includes messages such as *SP_expire*, AR propagation in cycles with more than two processors, or SAI information transfer. The sum of the first four categories is normalized to 100. From the figure, we see that, even with 64 processors, the additional traffic induced by Volition (*Overhead*) is largely negligible. For fewer processor counts, it is even smaller.

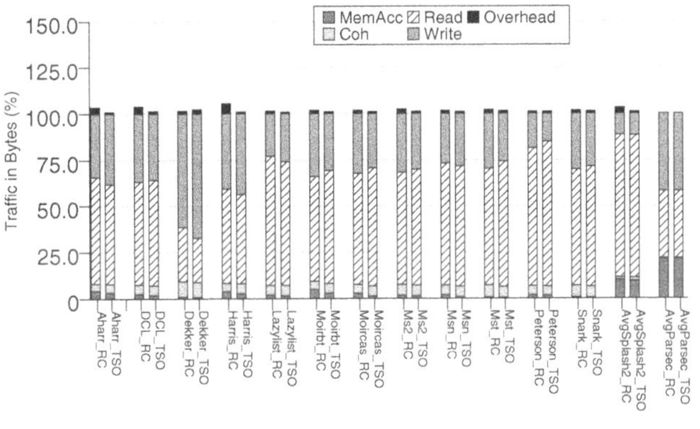

Figure 19. Network traffic overhead of Volition.

Finally, we consider the execution time overhead of Volition in Figure 20. The figure shows the execution time of the different applications under the RC memory model on a multiprocessor without Volition (Baseline) and on one with Volition. We show bars for all the small programs, their average, the average of SPLASH-2, and the average of Parsec. For each application, the bars are normalized to the Baseline.

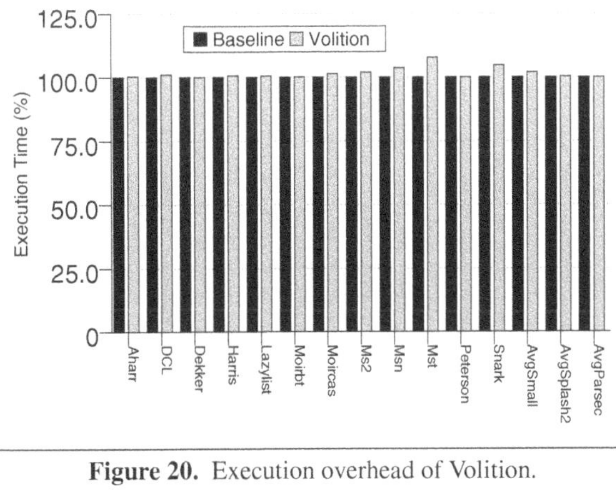

Figure 20. Execution overhead of Volition.

The main source of execution overhead in Volition is the stall due to a full ACT. We use a 256-entry ACT, and we can see that, for most applications, the execution time overhead of Volition for 64 processors is negligible. Some of the applications with visible overhead are those with many SCVs which, according to Table 2 include Mst and Msn. Still, for the large applications (SPLASH-2 and Parsec), there is no visible overhead. For the small applications, the average overhead is only about 2%.

Overall, based on the results of the traffic and execution time overheads, we conclude that Volition has low overhead and good scalability.

8. Related Work

We discuss related work in architecture, compilation, testing, and hardware verification. In architecture, the most related work is Vulcan by Muzahid *et al.* [24] and Conflict Ordering (CO) by Lin *et al.* [20]. Both works are based on identifying SCVs in hardware using Shasha and Snir [28] delay sets.

Vulcan [24] is the most similar work to Volition. It is a hardware scheme to detect SCVs at runtime, in programs running on a relaxed-consistency machine. It also leverages the cache coherence transactions to detect dependence cycles between processors and, from there, SCVs. It also supports multiple-word cache lines. While it has similar metadata structures as Volition, it works differently. It relies on a snoopy-based coherence protocol. Moreover, the design presented only operates with 2-processor SCVs. With Volition, we have taken a different approach, focusing on scalability and on handling SCV cycles with an arbitrary number of processors. The resulting Volition design is scalable, as it works with a scalable directory-based cache-coherence protocol and its hardware does not need all-to-all structures. In addition, it works seamlessly for any number of processors in the SCV cycle.

CO [20] is a technique that detects upcoming SCVs and enforces SC in a relaxed-consistency machine. As a potential SCV is about to occur, CO avoids it by squashing and replaying certain instructions. Although it is an SC enforcement scheme, it can be used as an SCV detection scheme if it reports the SCV when the replay is needed to retain SC semantics. However, CO has substantial false positives, which are fine in an SC enforcement approach but not in an SCV detection scenario. To see why, consider Figure 21. Initially, there is a race between P_0 and P_1 on variable x. When CO sees this, it gets from the directory the set of pending writes. In this example, it gets the writes to variables y and z. If P_1 then tries to access y or z, CO conservatively assumes an SCV is about to occur, and causes a replay. Clearly, these dependences do not cause a cycle; we need a new dependence between P_1 and P_0 for a cycle.

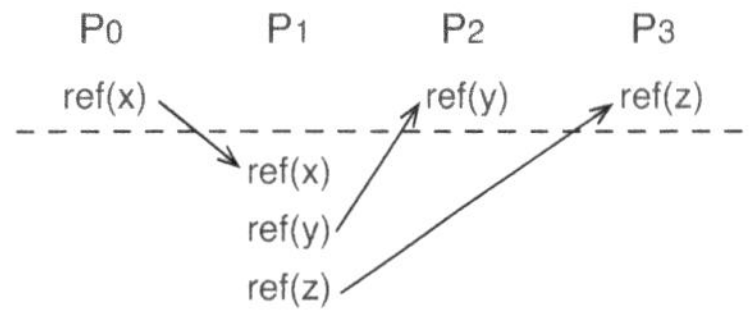

Figure 21. Operation of CO.

CO also requires the serialization of some of the accesses from the same processor to operate correctly. Finally, it is unclear how CO works for a distributed directory design: since a processor gets the pending sets asynchronously from the directory modules, the information seen by different processors can easily become inconsistent.

Other work has focused on identifying data races as proxies for SCVs. However, data races and SCVs are very different, and programs have more data races than SCVs. Specifically, one line of work detects incoming coherence messages on data that has local outstanding loads or stores. This work includes that of Gharachorloo and Gibbons [14] and many aggressive speculative designs (e.g., [3, 8, 15, 31]). Another line of work detects a conflict between two concurrent synchronization-free regions. This includes DRFx [22] and Conflict Exceptions [21]. In general, all of these works look for a data race with two accesses that occur within a short time — but still, only a single race. Overall, while focusing on these races may be a good way to discard many irrelevant ones, it is still a very different problem than focusing on uncovering SCVs.

There are compiler techniques to identify race pairs that could cause SCVs, typically using the Delay Set algorithm, and then insert fences to prevent cycles (e.g., [13, 16, 18, 29]). They are conservative because they only use static information, and typically cause large slowdowns. Lin *et al.* [19] can hide some of the resulting fence delay with architectural support. Duan *et al.* [11] use a race detector to construct a graph of races dynamically. Then, off-line, they traverse the graph to find potential SCVs. Our work differs in that: (1) it is an on-the-fly scheme, while Duan's SCV detection is off-line; (2) it needs no software support; and (3) it has no false positives, while Duan's scheme may point to SCVs that never occur.

The software testing community has proposed static and off-line techniques to check for SCVs (e.g., [5–7]). While promising, these techniques are not designed for on-the-fly SCV detection in large codes with negligible overhead. The hardware verification community has designed techniques to verify if a memory system hardware is correctly implemented (e.g., [9, 10, 23]). While related, these works have a different goal: we focus on debugging software as it runs on a relaxed-consistent machine; they focus on verifying that the hardware correctly implements a memory model.

9. Conclusions

This paper proposed Volition, the first hardware scheme that detects SCVs in a relaxed-consistency machine precisely, in a scalable manner, and for an arbitrary number of processors in the cycle. Volition uses cache coherence protocol transactions to detect cycles in memory-access orders across threads. When a cycle is about to occur, an exception is triggered. For the conditions considered in this paper, Volition suffers neither false positives nor false negatives. We simulated Volition on a 64-processor multicore with directory-based coherence and 32-byte cache lines, running some small codes and SPLASH-2 and Parsec applications. Our results showed that Volition induces negligible network traffic and execution time overhead and is scalable. In addition, it detects SCV cycles with several processors. Volition is suitable for on-the-fly use.

Acknowledgements

This work was supported in part by NSF grants CCF-1012759 and CNS-1116237; Intel under the Illinois-Intel Parallelism Center (I2PC); Spanish Gov. & European ERDF under grants TIN2010-21291-C02-01 and Consolider CSD2007-00050; and NSF China grants 61073011 and 61133004.

References

[1] CheckFence at SourceForge. `http://sourceforge.net/projects/checkfence/`.

[2] A. Agarwal, R. Simoni, J. Hennessy, and M. Horowitz. An Evaluation of Directory Schemes for Cache Coherence. In *International Symposium on Computer Architecture*, May 1988.

[3] C. Blundell, M. M. Martin, and T. F. Wenisch. InvisiFence: Performance-Transparent Memory Ordering in Conventional Multiprocessors. In *Int. Symp. on Computer Architecture*, 2009.

[4] F. Bonomi et al. An Improved Construction for Counting Bloom Filters. In *Ann. Euro. Symp. on Algo.*, Sep 2006.

[5] S. Burckhardt, R. Alur, and M. M. K. Martin. CheckFence: Checking Consistency of Concurrent Data Types on Relaxed Memory Models. In *Programming Language Design and Implementation*, Jun 2007.

[6] S. Burckhardt and M. Musuvathi. Effective Program Verification for Relaxed Memory Models. In *Computer Aided Verification*, Jul 2008.

[7] J. Burnim, K. Sen, and C. Stergiou. Sound and Complete Monitoring of Sequential Consistency for Relaxed Memory Models. In *Tools and Algo. for the Const. and Ana. of Sys.*, July 2011.

[8] L. Ceze, J. M. Tuck, P. Montesinos, and J. Torrellas. BulkSC: Bulk Enforcement of Sequential Consistency. In *International Symposium on Computer Architecture*, June 2007.

[9] Y. Chen, L. Yi, W. Hu, T. Chen, H. Shen, P. Wang, and H. Pan. Fast Complete Memory Consistency Verification. In *International Symposium on High Performance Computer Architecture*, Feb 2009.

[10] A. Deorio, I. Wagner, and V. Bertacco. DACOTA: Post-silicon Validation of the Memory Subsystem in Multi-core Designs. In *International Symposium on High Performance Computer Architecture*, Feb 2009.

[11] Y. Duan, X. Feng, L. Wang, C. Zhang, and P.-C. Yew. Detecting and Eliminating Potential Violations of Sequential Consistency for Concurrent C/C++ Programs. In *Code Gen. and Opt.*, Mar 2009.

[12] J. Erickson, M. Musuvathi, S. Burckhardt, and K. Olynyk. Effective Data-race Detection for the Kernel. In *Operating System Design and Implementation*, Feb 2010.

[13] X. Fang, J. Lee, and S. P. Midkiff. Automatic Fence Insertion for Shared Memory Multiprocessing. In *International Conference on SuperComputing*, Jun 2003.

[14] K. Gharachorloo and P. B. Gibbons. Detecting Violations of Sequential Consistency. In *Symp. on Par. Alg. and Arch.*, Jul 1991.

[15] C. Gniady, B. Falsafi, and T. N. Vijaykumar. Is SC + ILP = RC? In *International Symposium on Computer Architecture*, May 1999.

[16] A. Krishnamurthy and K. Yelick. Analyses and Optimizations for Shared Address Space Programs. *Jour. Paral. Dist. Comp.*, Nov 1996.

[17] L. Lamport. How to Make a Multiprocessor Computer that Correctly Executes Multiprocess Programs. *IEEE Tran. on Comp.*, July 1979.

[18] J. Lee and D. A. Padua. Hiding Relaxed Memory Consistency with a Compiler. *IEEE Trans. Comput.*, Aug 2001.

[19] C. Lin, V. Nagarajan, and R. Gupta. Efficient Sequential Consistency using Conditional Fences. In *Parallel Architecture and Compilation Techniques*, Sep 2010.

[20] C. Lin, V. Nagarajan, R. Gupta, and B. Rajaram. Efficient Sequential Consistency via Conflict Ordering. In *Architectural Support for Programming Languages and Operating Systems*, Mar 2012.

[21] B. Lucia, L. Ceze, K. Strauss, S. Qadeer, and H.-J. Boehm. Conflict Exceptions: Simplifying Concurrent Language Semantics with Precise Hardware Exceptions for Data-races. In *International Symposium on Computer Architecture*, Jun 2010.

[22] D. Marino, A. Singh, T. Millstein, M. Musuvathi, and S. Narayanasamy. DRFx: A Simple and Efficient Memory Model for Concurrent Programming Languages. In *Programming Language Design and Implementation*, June 2010.

[23] A. Meixner and D. J. Sorin. Dynamic Verification of Sequential Consistency. In *Int. Symp. on Comp. Arch.*, Jun 2005.

[24] A. Muzahid, S. Qi, and J. Torrellas. Vulcan: Hardware Support for Detecting Sequential Consistency Violations Dynamically. In *International Symposium on Microarchitecture*, December 2012.

[25] S. Narayanasamy, Z. Wang, J. Tigani, A. Edwards, and B. Calder. Automatically Classifying Benign and Harmful Data Races using Replay Analysis. In *Prog. Lang. Des. and Impl.*, Jun 2007.

[26] J. Renau, B. Fraguela, J. Tuck, W. Liu, M. Prvulovic, L. Ceze, S. Sarangi, P. Sack, K. Strauss, and P. Montesinos. SESC Simulator, January 2005. http://sesc.sourceforge.net.

[27] D. C. Schmidt and T. Harrison. Double-Checked Locking: An Optimization Pattern for Efficiently Initializing and Accessing Thread-safe Objects. In *Patt. Lang. of Prog. Des. Conf.*, 1996.

[28] D. Shasha and M. Snir. Efficient and Correct Execution of Parallel Programs that Share Memory. *ACM Transactions on Programming Languages and Systems*, 10(2):282–312, April 1988.

[29] Z. Sura, X. Fang, C.-L. Wong, S. P. Midkiff, J. Lee, and D. Padua. Compiler Techniques for High Performance Sequentially Consistent Java programs. In *Prin. and Pract. of Para. Prog.*, Jun 2005.

[30] J. Ševčík. Safe Optimisations for Shared-memory Concurrent Programs. In *Prog. Lang. Des. and Impl.*, Jun 2011.

[31] T. F. Wenisch, A. Ailamaki, B. Falsafi, and A. Moshovos. Mechanisms for Store-wait-free Multiprocessors. In *International Symposium on Computer Architecture*, June 2007.

Hardware Support for Fine-Grained Event-Driven Computation in Anton 2

J. P. Grossman,[1,†] Jeffrey S. Kuskin,[1] Joseph A. Bank,[1] Michael Theobald,[1]
Ron O. Dror,[1] Douglas J. Ierardi,[1] Richard H. Larson,[1] U. Ben Schafer,[1]
Brian Towles,[1] Cliff Young,[1] David E. Shaw[1,2,†]

[1] D. E. Shaw Research, New York, NY 10036, USA.
[2] Center for Computational Biology and Bioinformatics, Columbia University, New York, NY 10032, USA.
[†] Correspondence: JP.Grossman@DEShawResearch.com and David.Shaw@DEShawResearch.com

Abstract

Exploiting parallelism to accelerate a computation typically involves dividing it into many small tasks that can be assigned to different processing elements. An efficient execution schedule for these tasks can be difficult or impossible to determine in advance, however, if there is uncertainty as to when each task's input data will be available. Ideally, each task would run in direct response to the arrival of its input data, thus allowing the computation to proceed in a fine-grained event-driven manner. Realizing this ideal is difficult in practice, and typically requires sacrificing flexibility for performance.

In Anton 2, a massively parallel special-purpose supercomputer for molecular dynamics simulations, we addressed this challenge by including a hardware block, called the dispatch unit, that provides flexible and efficient support for fine-grained event-driven computation. Its novel features include a many-to-many mapping from input data to a set of synchronization counters, and the ability to prioritize tasks based on their type. To solve the additional problem of using a fixed set of synchronization counters to track input data for a potentially large number of tasks, we created a software library that allows programmers to treat Anton 2 as an idealized machine with infinitely many synchronization counters. The dispatch unit, together with this library, made it possible to simplify our molecular dynamics software by expressing it as a collection of independent tasks, and the resulting fine-grained execution schedule improved overall performance by up to 16% relative to a coarse-grained schedule for precisely the same computation.

Categories and Subject Descriptors C.1.3 **[Processor Architectures]**: Other Architectural Styles—*data-flow architectures*; C.1.4 **[Processor Architectures]**: Parallel Architectures; C.3 **[Special-Purpose and Application-Based Systems]**; D.1.3 **[Programming Techniques]**: Concurrent Programming—*parallel programming*

General Terms Performance, Design

Keywords Event-driven, task scheduling, parallel, dispatch unit, Anton 2

1. Introduction

Many scientific computations naturally decompose into small tasks that can be assigned to different processors when the application is parallelized. Examples of such tasks include modifying individual positions and velocities within a particle simulation, or updating the local state variables of a Navier-Stokes fluid dynamics model. When the number of tasks per processor is large and the data is readily available, the tasks can be efficiently executed in a series of tight loops, each of which evaluates a single type of task for many different data inputs. The overhead of invoking these loops is small compared to the total compute time. When there are few tasks per processor, however, or when the tasks must wait for the arrival of data from other processors, the overheads of communication latency and synchronization can become a significant portion of the overall computation time, and it is much more challenging to keep the processors busy with useful work.

The problem of scheduling tasks to minimize these overheads can be divided into three parts: determining *when* a task is ready to run, deciding *where* a task should be executed, and choosing an *order* for the tasks that are ready. Previous work on task scheduling has primarily concentrated on software and hardware mechanisms for dynamically assigning tasks to cores within a chip multiprocessor (e.g., [7,12,14,17,19,24,27]). In a massively parallel machine with highly non-uniform memory access, however, tasks must be co-located with their data in order to maximize performance. As such, there is less flexibility in assigning tasks to cores, so the focus of task scheduling shifts to detecting and prioritizing tasks that are ready to run. Our work addresses these challenges.

Much of the difficulty arises from the often-unpredictable order in which data arrives at a processor. If an oracle were to provide this order in advance, then an optimal schedule for the tasks could be pre-determined. This would allow a processor to efficiently detect the next input datum (for example by polling a single memory location) and immediately begin the appropriate computation when it arrives. In reality, processors must be able to handle an unknown arrival order and dynamically schedule tasks accordingly. Coarse-grained scheduling—waiting for and processing large chunks of data at once—is the simplest approach, but reduces the overlap of communication with computation because it requires waiting for an entire data chunk to arrive before processing any of it.

In theory, we can improve processor utilization by allowing each task to run as soon as its input data is available, that is, by formulating the computation in a fine-grained event-driven manner. This is reminiscent of dataflow computing [4] and is similar to data-driven multithreading [28], but with scheduling performed

```
wait for data for task A
for i = 0 ... a.size() - 1
    a[i].eval()
wait for data for task B
for i = 0 ... b.size() - 1
    b[i].eval()
```

(a)

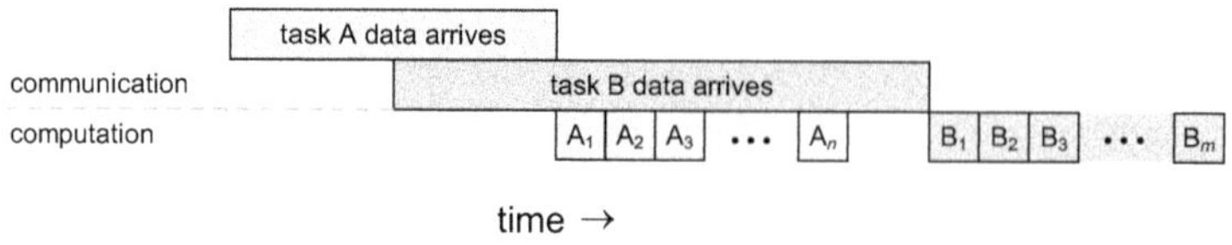

(b)

Figure 1. (a) Procedural implementation of an application with two types of computational tasks. (b) Execution schedule arising from this implementation.

```
void handleA (A *a)
    a->eval();

void handleB (B *b)
    b->eval();
```

(a)

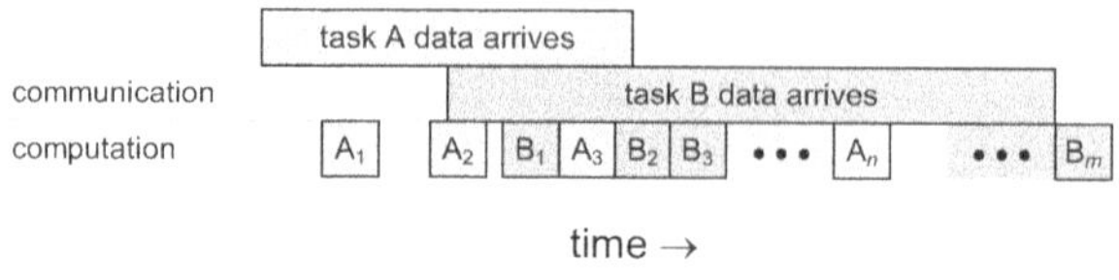

(b)

Figure 2. (a) Event-driven implementation of an application with two types of computational tasks. (b) Possible execution schedule arising from this implementation.

at the task level rather than at the instruction or basic-block levels. This form of task scheduling is challenging in practice because it can be expensive to check for the presence of multiple smaller chunks of data and choose an execution order for the tasks whose data has arrived. Some amount of flexibility must generally be sacrificed in order to arrive at a practical implementation; message-driven architectures, for example, impose a one-to-one mapping from messages to tasks and schedule tasks in strict first-in-first-out order (e.g., [11,16,21]).

We faced these considerations in designing the hardware and software for Anton 2, a massively parallel special-purpose supercomputer for molecular dynamics simulations. Like its predecessor (referred to here as Anton 1) [26], Anton 2 maps part of the computation to hardwired pipelines and performs the remainder on programmable cores. This remaining computation has several characteristics that make it difficult to schedule: each core handles a small, heterogeneous set of fine-grained (tens to hundreds of instructions) tasks, the cores receive input data for these tasks via Anton 2's communication network, the arrival order of this data is unpredictable, and some of the input data is consumed by multiple tasks. Anton 1, which dramatically accelerated molecular dynamics relative to the previous state of the art, employed a batch processing model, using coarse-grained hardware synchronization counters to detect the arrival of input data for the next group of tasks. One of the ways in which Anton 2 seeks to further improve performance is by reformulating molecular dynamics as a fine-grained event-driven computation, resulting in a more aggressive task execution schedule.

To this end, we introduced the *dispatch unit*—a hardware block with support for flexible dependency tracking and task dispatching. The dispatch unit differs from previous hardware accelerators for task scheduling by offering an arbitrary many-to-many mapping from incoming data to a set of hardware synchronization counters, providing the ability to categorize tasks by type and query for a subset of these types, and supporting flexible prioritization of different task types. The dispatch unit's support for fine-grained event-driven computation arises from the ability to use a separate synchronization counter to track the arrival of input data for each task, but the fixed number of hardware counters raises the issue of how to support applications with arbitrarily many tasks. We address this problem with a software library that hides hardware resource limitations, allowing programmers to treat Anton 2 as an idealized machine containing infinitely many synchronization counters.

The dispatch unit, together with this software library, makes fine-grained event-driven computation practical from both an architectural and a software standpoint. It allowed us to achieve an improved task execution schedule for our molecular dynamics application, increasing overall performance by up to 16% relative to a coarse-grained schedule for the same computation. Equally important, the dispatch unit and associated library made it possible to simplify our application software by expressing it as a collection of independent tasks, with most of the task sequencing logic moved into the hardware.

2. Event-Driven Programming Model

Consider a parallel application with two different types of computational tasks—call them A and B—each of whose input data arrives over some communication network. A conventional batch-mode procedural implementation of the application waits for all task A data to arrive, evaluates all instances of task A, then repeats this process for task B. Pseudocode for this implementation, along with the resulting execution schedule, is shown in Figure 1.

While straightforward, this implementation makes suboptimal use of the processor, which sits idle waiting for all the task A data to arrive, and then again waiting for all the task B data to arrive. We can achieve better processor utilization by adopting an event-driven programming model in which each individual task runs in response to the arrival of its input data.[1] An event-driven implementation consists of a collection of event handlers, as shown in Figure 2 alongside a hypothetical execution schedule. Because individual tasks are allowed to execute as soon as their data arrives, this implementation achieves better overlap of communication with computation, resulting in improved processor utilization and faster overall execution.

When multiple events are waiting to be handled, some scheme is required to determine the order in which the handlers run. The simplest approach is to handle the events in the order that they occur, for example, by keeping track of events within a first-in, first-out queue. This may not be optimal, however. In the previous

[1] Here we use the term "event" to refer to the arrival of a task's input data; events are handled by executing the appropriate task.

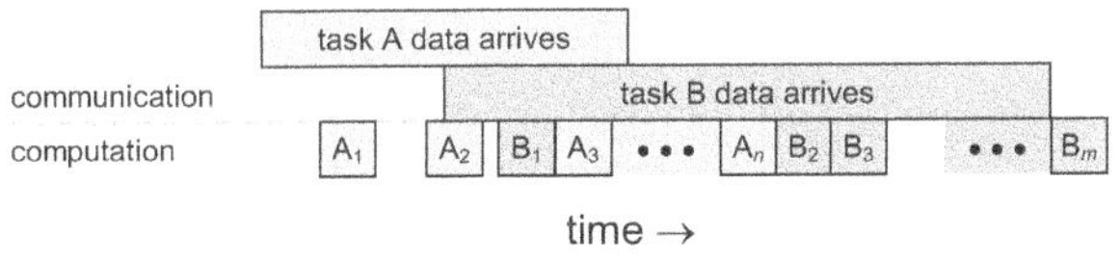

Figure 3. Modified execution schedule with task A statically prioritized over task B.

example, suppose that task A is in the critical path of the overall computation, whereas task B is not. In this case, performance can be improved by statically prioritizing task A over task B. Figure 3 shows how the execution schedule in Figure 2b changes with this prioritization. While the processor utilization stays the same, the last instance of task A finishes sooner, shortening the critical path.

3. Support for Event-Driven Programming in Anton 2

The previous section leaves some important questions unanswered. How are events detected? How are events mapped to their handlers? How are the event handlers scheduled? Anton 2 has been designed so that each of these activities can be performed within the dispatch unit. A full description of the Anton 2 architecture will be presented elsewhere; here we focus on the aspects related to event-driven computation.

Anton 2 comprises a set of identical application-specific integrated circuits (ASICs), which are directly connected to form a three-dimensional torus. The ASIC is a tiled architecture with two types of computational tiles connected by an on-chip mesh network: High Throughput Interaction Subsystem (HTIS) tiles, which contain special-purpose datapaths for computing particle interactions, and Flexible Subsystem (flex) tiles, which each contain several programmable cores called *Geometry Cores* (GCs), 256 KB of local SRAM, a network interface, and a dispatch unit (Figure 4). The fundamental unit of data in Anton 2 for all communication and memory accesses is a 128-bit quad word, which we will refer to as a *quad* for brevity.

Any flex tile can read or write the SRAM within any other flex tile. There is no memory hierarchy associated with this SRAM; in particular all addresses are physical and uncached, so Anton 2 is effectively a distributed, shared physical address machine. Anton 2 supports *counted remote writes* [10], which are remote writes of quads directly into another flex tile's SRAM that cause a synchronization counter to be incremented upon receipt. Counted remote writes form the basis of event detection: after a counted remote write is processed by SRAM, the address is forwarded to

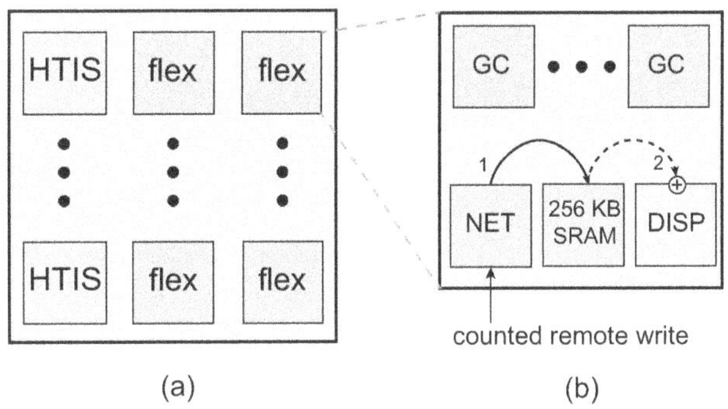

Figure 4. (a) The Anton 2 ASIC contains two types of computational tiles. (b) A flex tile comprises several GCs, local SRAM, a network interface, and a dispatch unit. Counted remote writes are first handled within SRAM (1), then forwarded to the dispatch unit to increment a synchronization counter (2).

the dispatch unit so that it can be mapped to a synchronization counter (Figure 4b). The synchronization counter is incremented; an event occurs when a counter reaches its threshold, indicating that all data required for a task has arrived.

Each counter has a programmer-specified event type that can be used to dynamically select and prioritize events. When a GC queries the dispatch unit for work (this is referred to as a *dispatch operation*), it specifies the set of types that it is willing to accept in up to four priority levels. The dispatch unit selects a synchronization counter of an appropriate type that has reached its threshold (if one exists) and returns to the GC some programmer-specified data associated with the counter. This data is used to describe the event and includes a function pointer to the event handler, which is then invoked by the GC. The intended programming model is for each GC to run an event handling loop, alternately issuing a dispatch operation to fetch the next event and then handling the event (Figure 5). All of the GCs within a flex tile query the same dispatch unit for work, providing dynamic load-balancing across the flex tile.

To summarize, in Anton 2 events are detected using hardware synchronization counters, events are mapped to their handlers via function pointers associated with these counters, and event handers are scheduled by prioritizing event types within dispatch operations. Events must also be assigned to synchronization counters; the dispatch unit is primarily designed to support this assignment for applications in which the set of events is known in advance (so that counters can be initialized before the application

```
void event_loop ()
{
    while (1)
    {
        data = dispatch();
        (*data.handler)(data);
    }
}
```

(a)

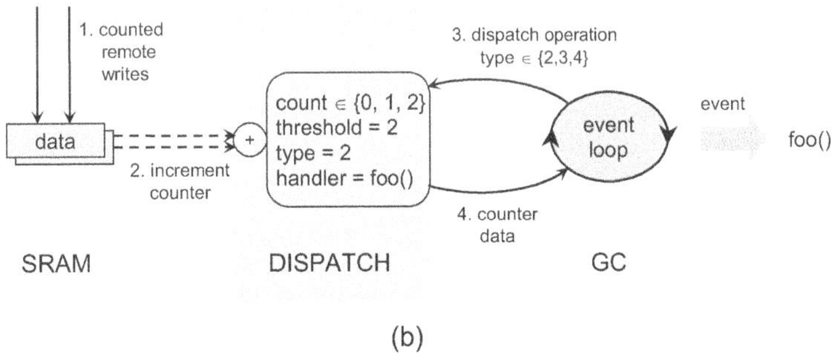

Figure 5. (a) Simplified version of the event loop that runs on each GC. (b) Sequence of events leading to the execution of an event handler: (1) input data is received via counted remote writes; (2) a counter starts at zero and is incremented by one with each counted remote write until it reaches its threshold; (3) a GC's event loop issues a dispatch operation specifying a set of types that includes the counter's type; (4) The dispatch unit responds with the counter's data, which includes a pointer to the handler; (5) The GC invokes the handler.

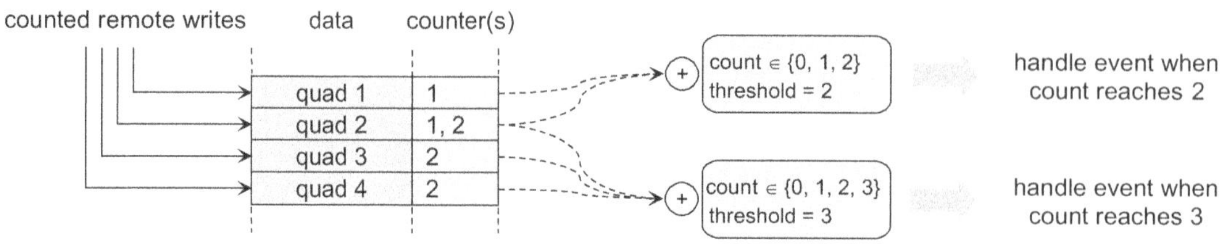

Figure 6. SRAM quads can be mapped to either individual counters or lists of counters.

runs) and repeats many times over the course of a computation (in particular, counters are automatically reset to zero upon reaching their threshold in preparation for the next occurrence of the same event). Dynamic events can be supported by introducing a level of indirection, for example by embedding a pointer within the counted write data to a secondary function that is called by the initial event handler. When necessary, it is also possible modify the counters and their SRAM associations at run time.

4. Dispatch Unit Implementation

The previous section outlined the general operation of the dispatch unit; here we provide some additional details related to its implementation within Anton 2.

4.1 Counters and counter lists

A dispatch unit contains 128 hardware synchronization counters, each of which has a 32-bit count, a 32-bit threshold, a 5-bit type, and a quad of programmer-specified counter data that forms the result of a dispatch operation. A key feature of the dispatch unit is its ability to arbitrarily map the SRAM quad addresses of counted remote writes to synchronization counters. This reduces the amount of global information that must be shared and communicated between tiles, since the sender of a counted remote write only needs to know the destination address and does not need to specify a counter ID.

It is possible for multiple tasks to depend on the same input data, in which case it becomes desirable to increment multiple counters in response to a single counted remote write. The dispatch unit provides efficient support for this operation via 128 counter lists. Each counter list specifies an arbitrary subset of the 128 counters; an SRAM quad can be mapped to either a single counter or a counter list (Figure 6). The mapping uses eight bits per SRAM quad—one bit to select a counter versus a counter list, and seven bits to specify one of the 128 counters or counter lists—representing a ~6% overhead for the flex tile SRAM.

4.2 Dispatch operations

When a counter reaches its threshold it is marked as "active" and becomes a candidate for selection when a dispatch operation is processed. A GC issues a dispatch operation by atomically exchanging a quad with a special memory address, so in particular no hardware support for dispatch operations is required within the GCs beyond the ability to perform 128-bit atomic exchanges with memory. The request quad sent from the GC to the dispatch unit specifies the event types that the GC can accept in up to four priority levels.

If a dispatch operation succeeds (i.e., at least one active counter's type matches the request), then the dispatch unit selects one of the highest-priority matching counters and returns that counter's data quad to the GC. If a dispatch operation fails, then it stalls until a matching counter becomes active, at which point the operation completes successfully. This blocking behavior obviates the need to run a polling loop on the GCs, and can cut the expected latency between counter activation and event handling roughly in half relative to a standard polling loop. Figure 7 illustrates the sequence of events involved in a blocking dispatch operation.

4.3 Error detection

There are a number of ways in which software errors and race conditions can lead to incorrect operation in the form of counters that become active prematurely or never at all. The dispatch unit contains three hardware error detectors designed to catch the majority of these errors, which would otherwise be extremely difficult to diagnose.

1. ***Counter overflow.*** This error is generated when a counter is incremented past its threshold, which can be caused by a misconfigured threshold, or an errant counted remote write (one that should have been omitted or that was directed to the wrong SRAM address).
2. ***Phase mismatch.*** Every counted remote write includes a software-generated single-bit *phase* that is generally expected to alternate in value between consecutive activations of a single counter. For example, a counter with threshold five expects five phase 0 counted remote writes, after which it becomes active and is reset to zero in preparation for five phase 1 counted remote writes. A *phase mismatch* error is generated when a counted remote write is received with the wrong phase, indicating a software race condition.

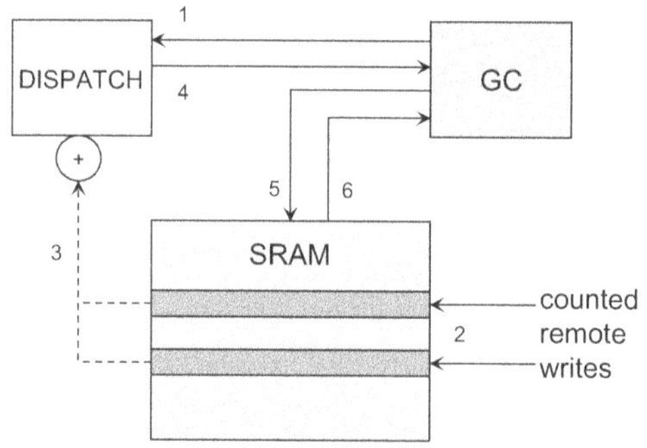

Figure 7. Typical blocking dispatch operation. (1) A GC issues a dispatch operation to the dispatch unit; no active counter is available so the operation stalls. (2) Counted remote writes are received from the network containing the data required for a task. (3) The SRAM addresses are forwarded to the dispatch unit. The task's counter is incremented, causing it to reach its threshold and become activated. (4) The dispatch unit returns the counter's data quad to the GC. (5,6) The GC reads the data from SRAM when it handles the event.

3. ***Repeated activation.*** An active counter must be processed by a dispatch operation before it can become active again, since the dispatch unit does not maintain a queue of pending events, but simply keeps track of which counters are active. If an active counter reaches its threshold again before being dispatched then a *repeated activation* error is generated, indicating a software race condition.

5. Software Support

The raw dispatch hardware presents a difficult resource allocation problem: software must manage cases where there are more tasks than counters, the counters must be partitioned among the various task types, and only 128 counter lists are available when in principle each of the 16,384 SRAM quads could be associated with a different set of counters. To ease the burden on the programmer, we implemented a higher-level software library that abstracts away the finite hardware resources, allowing arbitrarily many events and counter-SRAM associations to be defined when the application is initialized. In addition, we reduced the run-time overhead of event handler dispatching by prefetching data from SRAM and employing a form of tail recursion.

5.1 Prefetching task data

The counter data quad returned from a dispatch operation is passed to the event handler in order to describe the corresponding task. In particular, if the task requires some SRAM data (which is generally the case), then the quad must include a pointer to this data. A simple convention for event handlers would be to accept a single argument (the counter data quad), and begin by reading the required data from SRAM (Figure 8). The drawback to this approach is that SRAM reads are expensive, requiring over 20 cycles to complete, so most event handlers will immediately stall for a significant amount of time.

To reduce this overhead, we adopt the (slightly more complicated) convention of always prefetching the first data quad from SRAM *before* the event handler is called, and passing this "prefetch" quad as a second argument using a register calling convention (Figure 9). This allows some of the latency of the SRAM read to be hidden behind the latency of invoking the event handler (which is at least seven cycles). In some cases the prefetch quad is the only SRAM data that is required; in other cases additional quads must be read, but the latency of these reads can often be hidden behind computation involving the prefetch quad.

```
void some_handler (quad counter_data)
{
    task_data = sram_read(counter_data.task_data);
    process the task data
}
```

Figure 8. An event handler could take a single argument (the counter data quad) and begin by reading data from SRAM.

```
void some_handler (quad counter_data, quad prefetch_data)
{
    possibly read additional quads from SRAM
    process the prefetch quad
}
```

Figure 9. Our software convention for event handlers prefetches the first SRAM data quad so that the SRAM read latency can be partially hidden.

```
void event_loop ()
{
    while (1)
    {
        quad counter_data = dispatch();
        quad prefetch_data = sram_read(counter_data.task_data);
        (*counter_data.handler)(counter_data, prefetch_data);
    }
}
```

Figure 10. An event loop repeatedly fetches the next event and invokes the event handler.

5.2 Tail recursion for event handlers

Conceptually, the software runs an event loop that invokes the event handlers, as shown in Figure 10. In order to reduce the overhead between handlers, we introduced a compiler transformation that modifies the end of a handler to jump directly to the next handler. This is essentially tail recursion for event handlers, and it eliminates the overhead of returning to an event loop.

To enable this transformation, the programmer marks the handler with a special attribute and places a dispatch operation at the end of the handler. The compiler then inserts code after this dispatch operation to clean up the stack (as if it were about to return from the handler), load the prefetch quad from SRAM, and jump to the next handler, using registers to pass the counter data quad and the prefetch quad as arguments. In addition to obviating the need for an explicit event loop, placing the next dispatch operation directly in the handler gives the compiler the opportunity to schedule it earlier so that some of the dispatch latency can be hidden. In our molecular dynamics software, we observed that the compiler was able to schedule the dispatch operation 20 cycles before the end of some handlers, reducing the time between back-to-back event handlers from 46 cycles to as little as 26 cycles.

5.3 Allocating and initializing counters

The software library virtualizes the counter hardware, presenting the programmer with a seemingly unlimited number of counters and counter lists. The application software can allocate a separate virtual counter for each discrete task. A virtual counter is initialized with a software task type and the counter data quad, which contains a function pointer to the event handler, an SRAM pointer to the task data (of which the first quad is prefetched), and 64 bits of arbitrary user data (Figure 11).

The software task type is assigned by the programmer and is used by the library to categorize tasks. It is more general than the 5-bit hardware event type associated with each physical counter. Software task types are mapped to hardware event types (as specified by the programmer), but this mapping can be many-to-one, so there is no limit on the number of software task types. Our molecular dynamics software, for example, uses over 70 distinct software task types. Different hardware event types are only required for tasks that are prioritized differently within dispatch operations.

A counter can be associated with any data quad in SRAM by specifying the quad's address as well as the total expected remote write count from that quad (Anton 2 supports accumulation into

127 … 64	64 … 32	32 … 0
user data	task data	handler

Figure 11. Structure of the counter data quad that forms the result of a dispatch operation. The first 32-bit word is a function pointer to the event handler. The next 32-bit word is a pointer to the task data in SRAM. The remaining 64 bits can contain arbitrary event-specific information.

```
// initialization time
void initialize_adder (sram_ptr pa, sram_ptr pb, sram_ptr psum)
{
    cntr = cntr_new(ADDER_EVENT, adder_handler, pa /*task data*/, make_user_data(pb,psum) /*user data*/);
    cntr->attach_to_sram(pa, 1 /*expected count*/);
    cntr->attach_to_sram(pb, 1 /*expected count*/);
}

// run time
void adder_handler (quad counter_data, quad prefetch_data /*=a*/)
{
    quad b = sram_read(counter_data.user_data[0]);
    quad sum = prefetch_data + b;
    sram_write(counter_data.user_data[1], sum);
}
```

Figure 12. Simple counter example for a two-input adder. The counter is incremented by one with the arrival of each input data quad, so its threshold is two. In the run-time handler the first input is prefetched; the pointers to the second input and the sum are stored in the user data portion of the counter data quad.

SRAM quads, so multiple counted writes may be directed to a single quad in order to add their values, resulting in multiple counter increments). The counter's threshold is the sum of these expected counts. Figure 12 shows a very simple example for a task that adds two quads. The counter data is initialized with three SRAM pointers: two for the source operands, and one for the sum.

5.4 Mapping virtual counters to physical counters

Once the virtual counters have been allocated, they must be assigned to physical counters. A virtual counter's flex tile is implicitly specified by the counter's task data pointer and SRAM associations (which must all resolve to the same flex tile). When at most 128 virtual counters are assigned to a flex tile, they can each be mapped to a separate physical counter. When a flex tile has more than 128 virtual counters, however, its physical counters must somehow be shared amongst them.

In some cases it is possible to time-multiplex a physical counter between multiple virtual counters, for which the software library does provide some support, but doing so safely requires very specific knowledge of the application's dataflow, as well as appropriately timed dynamic modifications to the counter state. More typically, time multiplexing is not an option because it is difficult or impossible to place restrictions on when a given task's input data will arrive. Instead, we allow a group of tasks of the same type to use a single physical counter, coarsening the event granularity: an event occurs when the input data for all tasks in the group has arrived.

Tasks can be grouped in this manner by assigning their virtual counters to the same physical counter. Their thresholds are added together, and the data for the individual tasks is stored in a linked list (Figure 13). The handler is responsible for iterating over the linked list to execute each of the tasks.

While it is possible to perform this counter assignment manually, doing so is tedious and forms a difficult optimization problem. The library automates the process using *counter pools*, which are collections of tasks that all have the same type. The programmer can explicitly create a counter pool of a given type and add arbitrarily many tasks to this pool. The library decides how many physical counters to allot for each counter pool (assigning more physical counters to pools with more tasks), then within each counter pool partitions the tasks among the physical counters.

Some care must be taken to avoid introducing deadlock. In particular, if two tasks are assigned to the same physical counter but one of them has an input dependency on the other, then the counter will never reach its threshold. The library prevents such deadlocks by imposing the restriction that any two tasks of the same type must be *independent*, that is, none of a task's input data can be generated by another task of the same type. The programmer is responsible for ensuring that this is the case, so that it is safe to assign multiple tasks from a counter pool to a single physical counter.

5.5 Counter lists

The programmer can arbitrarily associate virtual counters with SRAM quads without having to explicitly create or manage counter lists. Once the virtual counters have been mapped to physical counters, the library automatically creates a counter list for any SRAM quad associated with two or more physical counters. The number of such implicitly generated counter lists may exceed the hardware limit of 128, however, in which case the library auto-

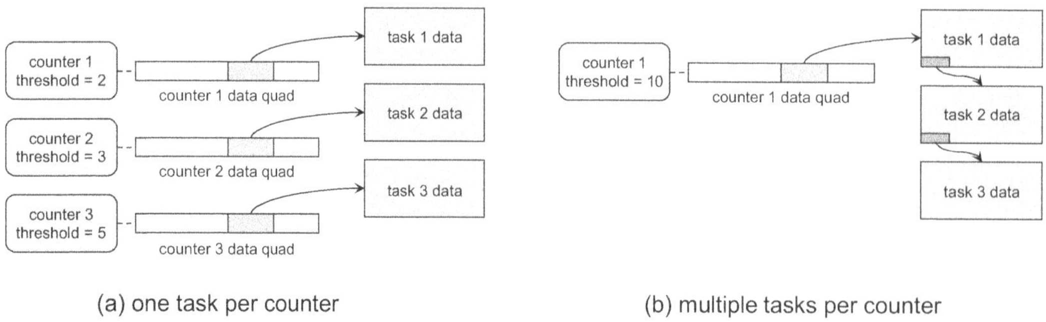

Figure 13. When multiple tasks are assigned to the same physical counter (b), the thresholds are added and the data for the tasks is stored as a linked list in SRAM.

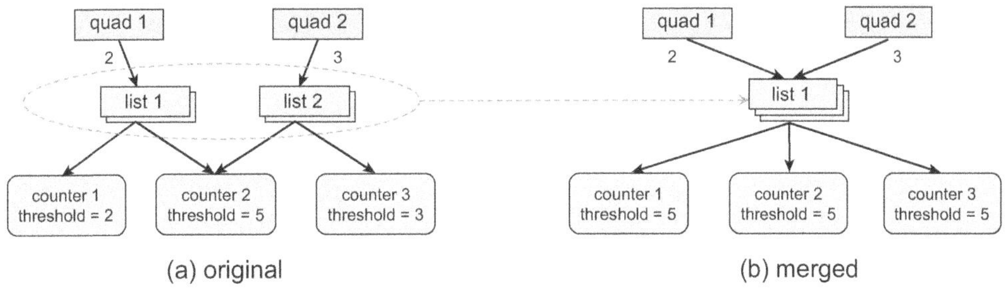

Figure 14. Counter lists are merged by replacing two lists with their union. (a) The programmer specifies that counters 1 and 2 will receive two increments from quad 1, while counters 2 and 3 will receive three increments from quad 2, which implicitly defines two counter lists. (b) If the two lists are merged, then all three counters will receive two increments from quad 1 and three increments from quad 2.

matically merges certain groups of counter lists so that a smaller number of "union lists" are required (Figure 14).

This operation preserves all original dependencies: a counter associated with an SRAM quad still depends on that quad for activation. It also introduces false dependencies that were not originally specified by the programmer. For example, the merged list in Figure 14b causes counter 1 to depend on quad 2 and counter 3 to depend on quad 1. The counter thresholds are automatically adjusted to account for the false dependencies, but there is another complication: false dependencies can lead to deadlock. In the same example, if the event triggered by counter 1 is responsible for sending data to quad 2, then merging the lists creates a circular dependency and none of the counters will ever reach their thresholds. To avoid this situation, the library only merges lists whose tasks are of the same type, again leveraging the restriction that any two tasks of the same type must be independent. In the extreme case, a single list is used for all counters of a given task type, so that none of the counters will be activated until the data for all the tasks of that type has arrived.

The algorithm for merging counters lists on a given flex tile begins by counting, for each event type t, the number N_t of distinct lists of type-t counters. The 128 physical counter lists are then partitioned among the types such that the number L_t of physical lists allotted for type t is proportional to N_t. The task of merging lists for type t until only L_t remains can be formulated as the following covering problem: given N_t lists and an integer $L_t < N_t$, find L_t "covering lists" such that each of the original lists is contained in one of the covering lists. We then merge each group of lists contained within a common covering list.

The goal is to find covering lists that approximate the original lists as closely as possible. To define this metric more precisely, observe that whenever a list is contained in a covering list with more counters, the "extra" counters in the covering list lead to false dependencies as described above. The covering lists are generated using a greedy heuristic that attempts to minimize the total number of false dependencies. For example, two possible 2-coverings of the lists {[0,1], [0,2], [3,4]} are {[0,1], [0,2,3,4]} and {[0,1,2], [3,4]}; of these, the latter is preferred as the covering lists contain fewer extra entries.

6. Event-Driven Implementation of Molecular Dynamics

A molecular dynamics (MD) simulation models the motions of individual atoms as a chemical system (e.g., a protein surrounded by water) evolves. The simulation steps through time, alternating between a force calculation phase that determines the force acting on each simulated atom, and an integration phase that advances the positions and velocities of the atoms according to the classical laws of motion. Each iteration through these phases is referred to as a *time step*. On Anton 2, the chemical system to be simulated is spatially divided into a regular grid of boxes, with each box assigned to one ASIC.

There are several reasons that MD is well-suited to an event-driven implementation in general, and the Anton 2 dispatch unit in particular:

- An MD computation naturally consists of a large number of fine-grained tasks, which are known in advance and repeated in each time step, and can therefore be statically mapped to counters within the dispatch unit.
- When a simulation runs on a large parallel machine, there may only be zero or one instances of a given task type executed on a given core, so a batch processing model (executing many tasks of the same type in a tight loop) is ineffective.
- Statically scheduling these tasks when MD is parallelized is challenging, because the order in which input data arrives is unpredictable.
- Prioritization is important when the tasks are dynamically scheduled because some affect the critical path more than others.

Figure 15 shows the dataflow of an MD simulation. The force calculation phase consumes atom positions and produces forces; the integration phase consumes forces and produces updated atom positions and velocities. The force calculation phase has three major components: various specific interactions that are computed by hardware within the HTIS tiles; bond terms, which involve small groups of atoms connected by one or more covalent bonds; and a three-dimensional fast Fourier transform (FFT), which forms part of an algorithm to efficiently compute long-range interactions. The bond terms, FFT, and position/velocity updates are computed within the flex tiles and are implemented in an event-driven manner, as described in the following sections.

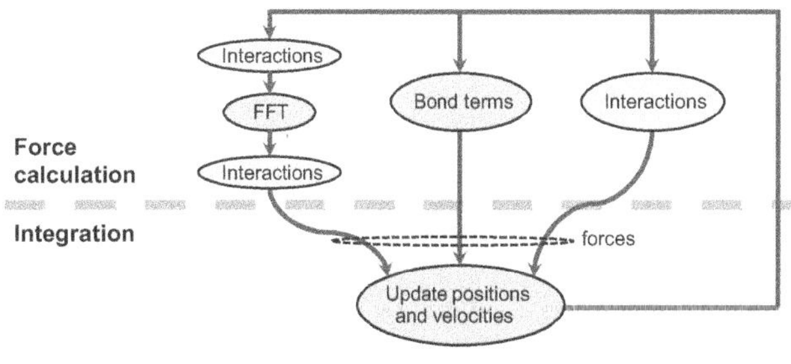

Figure 15. Dataflow of a molecular dynamics simulation.

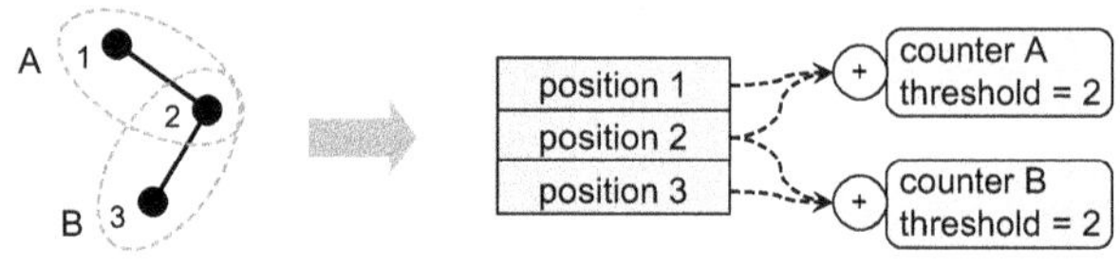

Figure 16. Two bond terms (A, B) involving three atoms (1, 2, 3) are assigned to a flex tile. Three SRAM quads are allocated to receive the atom positions; the two bond term counters are incremented as the positions arrive. Atom 2 participates in both bond terms, so a counter list is used to increment both counters when its position arrives.

6.1 Bond terms

The set of bond terms does not change during the course of a simulation: on each time step, positions for the same groups of atoms must be brought together to compute forces. On Anton 2, this is accomplished by statically mapping the computation for each bond term to a task on a fixed flex tile. Each atom has an associated list of flex tiles to which its position must be sent using counted remote writes; the dispatch units track the arrival of these positions to determine when each bond term can be evaluated. An atom can participate in multiple bond terms mapped to the same tile, so counter lists are used to update the appropriate set of counters as each atom position is received (Figure 16). Bond term tasks are created within a pool; the software library automatically partitions them among the available physical counters.

6.2 Three-dimensional FFT

The FFT comprises six "rounds" of computation. Rounds 1–3 perform one-dimensional FFTs in each dimension, round 3 also performs a Fourier-space computation with the transformed data, then rounds 4–6 perform one-dimensional inverse FFTs. There is a communication phase between pairs of consecutive rounds, in which the output from the previous round is scattered over Anton 2's communication network to the appropriate flex tiles for the next round. The FFT is mapped to exactly six counters per flex tile (one for each round); each round is triggered by the arrival of its input data (Figure 17).

The FFT tends to affect the critical path more than bond terms because additional HTIS work is required to convert the output of the FFT into forces, as shown in Figure 15. We therefore statically prioritize FFT events above bond events within dispatch operations. This allows the GCs to work on bond terms during the communication phases of the FFT, then resume FFT work once all data has arrived for the next round. Without hardware support for this type of fine-grained prioritized event interleaving, the easiest way to give the FFT absolute priority over bond terms would be to wait for all rounds to complete before starting the bond computations. This would place the bond terms on the critical path following the FFT, degrading performance.

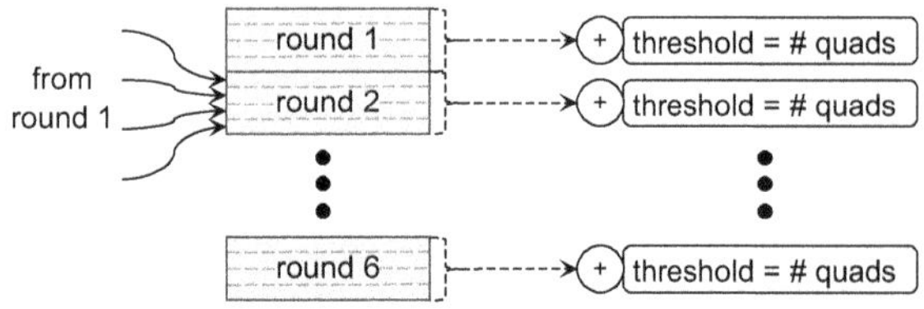

Figure 17. Six arrays of SRAM quads are allocated to receive the input data for the six FFT rounds. A single counter is used for each round, whose threshold is the number of quads in the corresponding array.

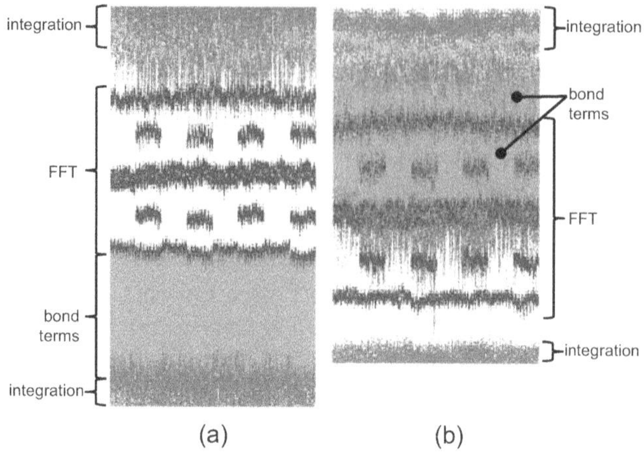

Figure 18. GC activity during force calculation. The communication phase between rounds 3 and 4 of the FFT is very short, causing these rounds to appear merged in the activity plots. (a) Bond events are delayed until the FFT has completed. (b) Prioritized event types are used to handle bond events in the background during the FFT.

Figure 18 shows GC activity for a single force calculation phase across all flex tiles that participate in the FFT. In Figure 18a, FFT events are given absolute priority over bond events by delaying the bond work until the FFT has completed. In Figure 18b, the bond event handlers are dynamically interleaved with the FFT event handlers using prioritized event types. Even though this interleaving causes the FFT to finish slightly later, the overall force calculation is accelerated as the majority of the bond work is removed from the critical path.

6.3 Integration

During the integration phase, small groups of 1–4 atoms (referred to as *constraint groups*) have their velocities and positions updated according to Newton's laws of motion and certain rigid-body constraints. Each constraint group is mapped to a task within a counter pool, and depends on the accumulation (in SRAM) of forces for all atoms within the group. When a constraint group counter is associated with a force quad in SRAM, the total expected count for that quad is greater than 1, because the total force for an atom is the sum of multiple partial forces from bond terms and HTIS tiles (Figure 19). Each partial force arrives as a separate counted remote accumulation with the same destination address. Constraint groups are disjoint, so no counter lists are required.

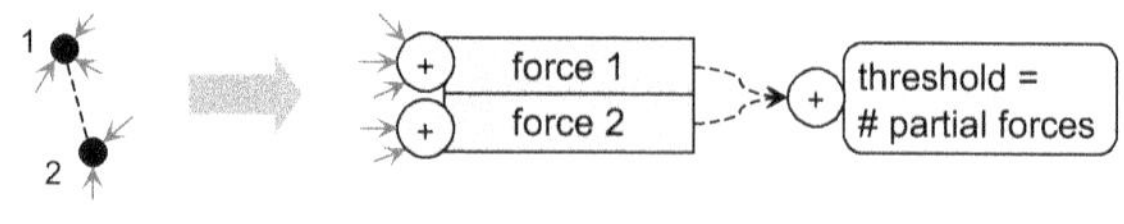

Figure 19. Two SRAM quads are allocated to accumulate the partial forces (small arrows) for a constraint group with two atoms (1, 2). The constraint group's counter is incremented as each partial force is accumulated, and its threshold is the total number of partial forces for both atoms.

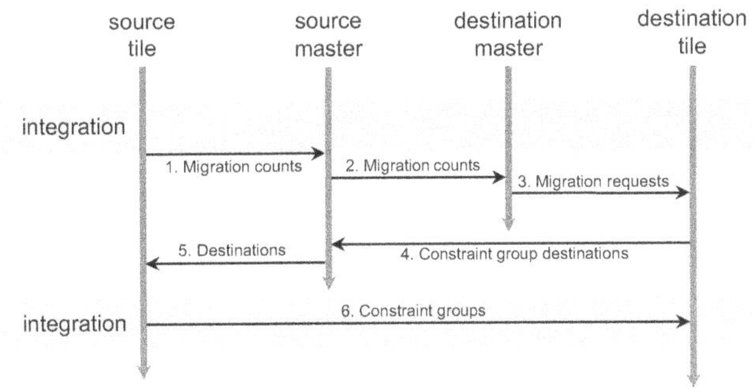

Figure 20. Constraint groups are migrated from a source tile on one ASIC to a destination tile on another ASIC using a six-stage algorithm involving migration "masters," which coordinate all migrations into and out of an ASIC.

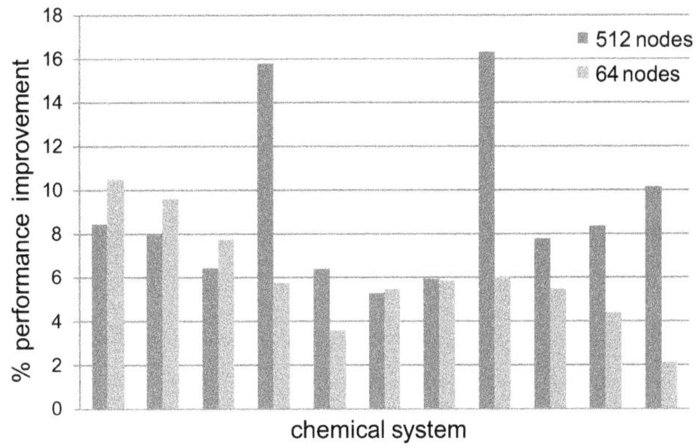

Figure 21. Percentage performance improvement relative to a coarse-grained task execution schedule.

6.4 Migration

Because the simulation is spatially subdivided among the ASICs, as the system evolves and atoms move through space it becomes necessary to periodically migrate constraint groups from one ASIC to another. We implement migration using a six-stage algorithm, shown in Figure 20. The first three stages propagate migration requests from source tiles to destination tiles via "master" tiles, which coordinate all migrations into and out of an ASIC. The destination tiles allocate SRAM storage and return destination addresses to the source tiles in stages four and five. Finally, the constraint groups are sent to these destination addresses in stage six. Each stage in the migration algorithm uses a distinct counter.

Migration is pipelined across two integration phases: the decision to migrate a constraint group is made during the first phase, but the actual migration does not occur until the second. This allows the majority of the migration communication and synchronization to be overlapped with force computation, removing it from the critical path. Migration events are given lower priority than the bond and FFT events so that they can be handled in the background. No software is required to schedule or sequence the stages; each event is simply handled once its data has arrived and there are no pending bond or FFT events. Without the dispatch unit, it would be necessary to explicitly schedule the migration stages in software, and it would be difficult to overlap the migration work with force computation.

7. Performance Evaluation

For our performance experiments, we used 11 sample chemical systems with varying characteristics: some are proteins surrounded by water while others are proteins embedded in membranes; the relative amount of bond and FFT work differs from system to system; and the overall sizes range from 23,558 atoms to 147,683 atoms (this represents a typical range for long-timescale molecular dynamics simulations; Anton 2 will also support much larger simulations). We measured the average number of cycles required to complete a single time step (one force phase and one integration phase) for each system on simulated 512-node and 64-node Anton 2 machines (these are two of the physical configurations that will be supported).

The performance advantages of the dispatch unit stem from its ability to dynamically generate an efficient execution schedule for a heterogeneous set of fine-grained tasks. To quantify this effect, we ran our molecular dynamics software using two different execution schedules: the more aggressive schedule enabled by the dispatch unit, and a coarse-grained schedule that fixes the order of task types within a time step, and executes all tasks of a given type as a single batch (by waiting for all of their input data to arrive before execution begins). This schedule is suitable for machines that provide a limited number of synchronization counters but no other hardware support for task scheduling.

Figure 21 shows the result of this comparison. The performance improvement afforded by the dispatch unit generally ranges from 2% to 10%, but is larger (~16%) on a 512-node machine for two systems in which bond terms constitute a higher fraction of the overall work. For these two systems, the primary advantage of the dispatch unit is the ability to dynamically interleave bond terms with FFT computation. On a 64-node machine this effect is much less pronounced because the bond terms represent a larger fraction of the total computation time (the FFT computation is communication-limited and takes about the same amount of time on 64- and 512-node machines), so there is less advantage to interleaving them with the FFT.

One of the important design parameters of the dispatch unit is the number of physical counters. A certain minimum number of counters is required to support the set of distinct task types within an application (which, for our molecular dynamics software, is around 48). Beyond this minimum number we generally expect performance to improve with additional counters, since this permits finer-grained task scheduling.

In Figure 22 we vary the number of counters per dispatch unit from 48 to 128, showing the performance improvement relative to 48 counters. Most of the performance gains occur in the first half of this range (48–88 counters); using more than 88 counters confers little additional performance advantage. This indicates that 128 counters are more than sufficient for our target application. More generally, it demonstrates that using only a limited number of counters, we can achieve the performance of a hypothetical machine with enough resources to assign each task to a distinct counter. Note that on a 512-node machine the smaller systems do not benefit at all from additional counters since few GCs have more than one task of any given type. For these systems, the primary benefit of the dispatch unit is the ability to dynamically schedule tasks of different types based on priority and the availability of input data.

One specific performance advantage of the dispatch unit's fine-grained scheduling is its support for efficiently processing background tasks using prioritized event types. The various migration events are given a lower priority, for example, and will be handled only when no higher-priority events are ready. Migration

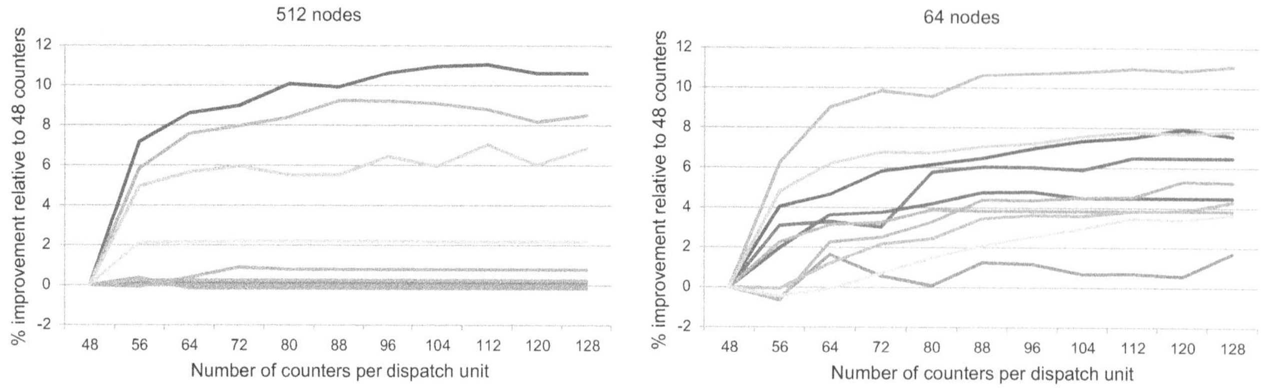

Figure 22. Percentage performance improvement relative to a dispatch unit with only 48 counters.

uses a complex multi-stage algorithm with many different events, so one might expect it to have a significant performance impact. In Figure 23, however, we see that the maximum performance overhead (measured by running a small number of time steps both with and without migration) is just over 4%, and is less than 1.4% on average. By contrast, the migration overhead in Anton 1—which does not have a dispatch unit and thus needs to explicitly schedule all migration activities in software—is typically closer to 10%.

8. Related work

At the extreme end of fine-grained event-driven computation are static and dynamic dataflow machines [4], in which every single instruction is triggered by the arrival of its operands. Scheduling every instruction independently incurs significant overhead [22], so hybrid architectures have been described in which small groups of instructions are executed together, combining the dynamic parallelism of a dataflow architecture with the efficiency of sequential execution [3,13,23,28]. These architectures are geared towards chip multiprocessors and leverage basic-block-level dependencies that can be discovered by the compiler; they are less suitable for large parallel machines with explicit messages used to initiate user-defined task.

Early work on hardware and software mechanisms for creating tasks in response to messages within a parallel machine, often referred to as *active messages*, dates back to the nineties [11,16,21]. These message-driven architectures assume a one-to-one mapping from messages to tasks and always schedule tasks in the order that the corresponding messages were received. By contrast, the dispatch unit supports many-to-many mappings from messages to tasks as well as dynamic prioritization of tasks, both of which are important for our event-driven implementation of molecular dynamics.

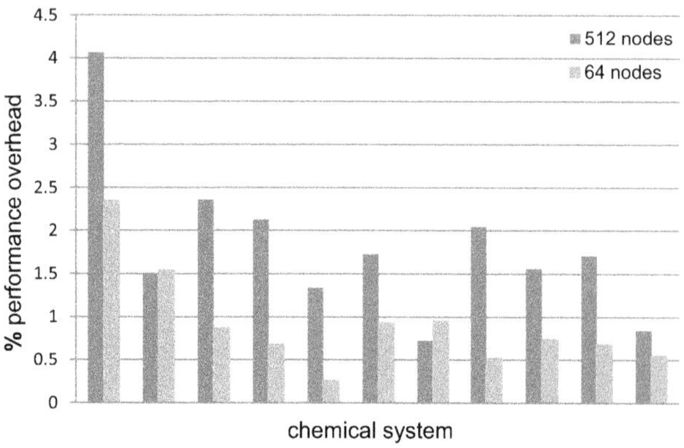

Figure 23. Percentage performance overhead of migration.

More recent work on task creation has focused on scheduling tasks among the cores of a chip multiprocessor using variations of *work stealing* [2,6,7,9,14,15,17]. This approach assigns a local task queue to each processor, but improves load-balancing of irregular algorithms by allowing processors to "steal work" from other queues once they complete their local tasks. Performing work stealing entirely in software is inefficient for fine-grained tasks because the overhead of task migration becomes comparable to the run time of each task, so several hardware mechanisms have been proposed to reduce this overhead [1,19,24,27]. The dispatch unit does not provide hardware support for task migration (which is undesirable in Anton 2 since each task's data resides in SRAM on a specific flex tile), but it does provide some dynamic load balancing by virtue of being shared among the GCs within a flex tile.

Software is typically responsible for determining when a task can be executed, although hardware mechanisms have also been proposed that perform this function by tracking inter-task dependencies [1,12,27]. While this approach is effective for tasks that communicate via shared memory in a cache-coherent single-chip multiprocessor, Anton 2 must directly track data dependencies across the nodes of a parallel machine, since most tasks receive their input data via counted remote writes.

The dispatch unit provides flexible support for tracking counted remote writes by allowing one or more hardware counters to be associated with every quad of SRAM. Word-level synchronization mechanisms have appeared previously in various architectures; examples include I-structures in the Tagged Token Dataflow Machine [5], presence tags in the J-Machine [21], message queue control words in the Cray T3E [25], and register-mapped hardware receive queues in the Tile Processor [29]. Using a separate set of counters introduces a level of indirection that supports more powerful synchronization primitives. Hamlyn, Anton 1 and Blue Gene/P each allow incoming packets to be mapped to receiver synchronization counters [8,18,20]. In these architectures, however, the receiver can only poll individual synchronization counters rather than poll for any event within a set of types, so they are less suitable for fine-grained event-driven computation.

9. Conclusion

Event-driven computation is a powerful paradigm, but is difficult to realize efficiently due to the overheads of synchronization, scheduling, and task creation. Hardware support can reduce these overheads, but carries the additional challenge of mapping arbitrarily many tasks to a finite set of synchronization counters. The dispatch unit represents a practical event-driven architecture that improves both the performance and the programmability of Anton 2. Performance is improved by executing tasks as soon as their input data is available and scheduling non-critical-path tasks in the background with a lower priority. Programmability is enhanced by allowing applications to be formulated as a set of independent tasks, largely eliminating the need to perform task scheduling and prioritization in software, and enabling the use of algorithms with many fine-grained tasks and/or communication rounds (such as constraint group migration).

Our software library simplifies the development of event-driven applications and addresses the problem of supporting a potentially large number of tasks with a small set of synchronization counters. By virtualizing the counters, providing a counter pool mechanism and automatically generating counter lists, the library presents an abstraction with unbounded resources and insulates the programmer from low-level details of counter and counter list allocation. The programmer simply creates a virtual counter for each task, initialized with the appropriate SRAM associations.

Although the overheads of synchronization and task creation are much smaller in Anton 2 than in commodity processors, there is still room for improvement. More than 40 machine cycles are required to start a new task in the worst case. With typical task durations measured in hundreds of cycles, this overhead represents a significant fraction of the overall compute time. It may be possible to reduce this overhead by replacing the dispatch operation with a mechanism that pushes tasks directly to the GCs. We chose not to pursue this design in Anton 2 because of the additional complications that it introduces, such as deciding which GC should receive a task and what to do when a GC cannot process a task it receives.

The motivation for the dispatch unit was specifically to accelerate molecular dynamics simulations, but the design consists of general primitives for event-driven computation. Other applications with similar characteristics—namely those that comprise a large, static set of fine-grained tasks whose input data is received in an unpredictable order from other processors—may be able to benefit from similar hardware mechanisms.

Acknowledgments

We thank the anonymous reviewers for their helpful suggestions and Mollie Kirk for editorial assistance.

References

[1] Ghiath Al-Kadi and Andrei Sergeevich Terechko, "A hardware task scheduler for embedded video processing," *4th International Conference on High Performance Embedded Architectures and Compilers* (HiPEAC '09), Paphos, Cyprus, January 25–28, 2009, pp. 140–152.

[2] Nimar S. Arora, Robert D. Blumofe and C. Greg Plaxton, "Thread scheduling for multiprogrammed multiprocessors," *10th Annual ACM Symposium on Parallel Algorithms and Architectures* (SPAA '98), Puerto Vallarta, Mexico, June 28–July 2, 1998, pp. 119–129.

[3] Joseph M. Arul and Krishna M. Kavi, "Scalability of scheduled dataflow architecture (SDF) with register contexts," *5th International Conference on Algorithms and Architectures for Parallel Processing* (ICA3PP 2002), Beijing, China, October 23–25, 2002, pp. 214–221.

[4] Arvind and David E. Culler, "Dataflow architectures," *Annual Review of Computer Science*, Volume 1, June, 1986, pp. 225–253.

[5] Arvind and Rishiyur S. Nikhil, "Executing a program on the MIT tagged-token dataflow architecture," *IEEE Transactions on Computers*, Volume 39, Issue 3, March, 1990, pp. 300–318.

[6] Robert D. Blumofe, Christopher F. Joerg, Bradley C. Kuszmaul, Charles E. Leiserson, Keith H. Randall and Yuli Zhou, "Cilk: an efficient multithreaded runtime system," *Journal of Parallel and Distributed Computing*, Volume 37, Issue 1, August, 1996, pp. 55–69.

[7] Robert D. Blumofe and Charles E. Leiserson, "Scheduling multithreaded computations by work stealing," *Journal of the ACM*, Volume 46, Number 5, September, 1999, pp. 720-748.

[8] Greg Buzzard, David Jacobson, Milon Mackay, Scott Marovich and John Wilkes, "An implementation of the Hamlyn sender-managed interface architecture," *2nd USENIX Symposium on Operating System Design and Implementation* (OSDI '96), Seattle, WA, October 28–31, 1996, pp. 245–259.

[9] David Chase and Yossi Lev, "Dynamic circular work-stealing deque," *17th Annual ACM Symposium on Parallelism in Algorithms and Architectures* (SPAA 2005), Las Vegas, NV, July 18–20, 2005, pp. 21–28.

[10] Ron O. Dror, J.P. Grossman, Kenneth M. Mackenzie, Brian Towles, Edmond Chow, John K. Salmon, Cliff Young, Joseph A. Bank, Brannon Batson, Martin M. Deneroff, Jeffrey S. Kuskin, Richard H. Larson, Mark A. Moraes and David E. Shaw, "Exploiting 162-nanosecond end-to-end communication latency on Anton," *International Conference on High Performance Computing, Networking, Storage and Analysis* (SC10), New Orleans, LA, November 15–18, 2010.

[11] Thorsten von Eicken, David E. Culler, Seth Copen Goldstein and Klaus Erik Schauser, "Active messages: a mechanism for integrated communication and computation," *19th International Symposium on Computer Architecture* (ISCA 1992), Gold Coast, Australia, May 19–21, 1992, pp. 430–440.

[12] Yoav Etsion, Felipe Cabarcas, Alejandro Rico, Alex Ramirez, Rosa M. Badia, Eduard Ayguade, Jesus Labarta and Mateo Valero, "Task superscalar: an out-of-order task pipeline," *43rd Annual IEEE/ACM International Symposium on Microarchitecture* (MICRO '43), Atlanta, Georgia, December 4–8, 2010, pp. 89–100.

[13] Mark Gebhart, Bertrand A. Maher, Katherine E. Coons, Jeff Diamond, Paul Gratz, Mario Marino, Nitya Ranganathan, Behnam Robatimili, Aaron Smith, James Burrill, Stephen W. Keckler, Doug Berger and Kathryn S. McKinley, "An evaluation of the TRIPS computer system," *14th International Conference on Architectural Support for Programming Languages and Operating Systems* (ASPLOS 2009), Washington, D.C., March 7–11, 2009, pp. 1–12.

[14] Danny Hendler and Nir Shavit, "Non-blocking steal-half work queues," *21st Annual ACM Symposium on Principles of Distributed Computing* (PODC 2002), Monterey, CA, July 21–24, 2002, pp. 280–289.

[15] Ralf Hoffmann, Matthias Korch and Thomas Rauber, "Performance evaluation of task pools based on hardware synchronization," *ACM/IEEE Conference on High Performance Networking and Computing* (SC04), Pittsburgh, PA, November 6–12, 2004.

[16] Laxmikant V. Kale and Sanjeev Krishnan, "CHARM++: a portable concurrent object oriented system based on C++," *8th Annual Conference on Object-Oriented Programming Systems, Languages, and Applications* (OOPSLA 1993), Washington, D.C., September 26–October 1, 1993, pp. 91–108.

[17] Matthias Korch and Thomas Rauber, "A comparison of task pools for dynamic load balancing of irregular algorithms," *Journal of Concurrency and Computation: Practice & Experience*, Volume 16, Issue 1, December, 2003, pp. 1–47.

[18] Sameer Kumar, Gabor Dozsa, Gheorghe Almasi, Dong Chen, Mark E. Giampapa, Philip Heidelberger, Michael Blocksome, Ahmad Fa-

raj, Jeff Parker, Joseph Ratterman, Brian Smith and Charles Archer, "The deep computing messaging framework: Generalized scalable message passing on the Blue Gene/P supercomputer," *22nd International Conference on Supercomputing* (ICS '08), Island of Kos, Greece, June 7–12, 2008, pp. 94–103.

[19] Sanjeev Kumar, Christopher J. Hughes and Anthony Nguyen, "Carbon: architectural support for fine-grained parallelism on chip multiprocessors," *34th International Symposium on Computer Architecture* (ISCA 2007), San Diego, CA, June 9–13, 2007, pp. 162–173.

[20] Jeffrey S. Kuskin, Cliff Young, J.P. Grossman, Brannon Batson, Martin M. Deneroff, Ron O. Dror and David E. Shaw, "Incorporating flexibility in Anton, a specialized machine for molecular dynamics simulation," *14th International Symposium on High Performance Computer Architecture* (HPCA-14), Salt Lake City, UT, February 16–20, 2008, pp. 343–354.

[21] Michael D. Noakes, Deborah A. Wallach and William J. Dally, "The J-Machine multicomputer: an architectural evaluation," *20th International Symposium on Computer Architecture* (ISCA 1993), San Diego, CA, May 16–19, 1993, pp. 224–235.

[22] Gregory M. Papadopoulos and Kenneth R. Traub, "Multithreading: a revisionist view of dataflow architectures," *18th Annual International Symposium on Computer Architecture* (ISCA 1991), Toronto, Canada, May 27–30, 1991, pp. 342–251.

[23] Shuichi Sakai, Yoshinori Yamaguchi, Kei Hiraki, Yuetsu Kodama and Toshitsugu Yuba, "An architecture of a dataflow single chip processor," *16th Annual International Symposium on Computer Architecture* (ISCA 1989), Jerusalem, Israel, June, 1989, pp. 46–53.

[24] Daniel Sanchez, Richard M. Yoo and Christos Kozyrakis, "Flexible architectural support for fine-grain scheduling," *15th International Conference on Architectural Support for Programming Languages and Operating Systems* (ASPLOS 2010), Pittsburgh, PA, March 13–17, 2010, pp. 311–322.

[25] Steven L. Scott, "Synchronization and communication in the T3E multiprocessor," *7th International Conference on Architectural Support for Programming Languages and Operating Systems* (ASPLOS 1996), Cambridge, MA, October 1–5, 1996, pp. 26–36.

[26] David E. Shaw, Martin M. Deneroff, Ron O. Dror, Jeffrey S. Kuskin, Richard H. Larson, John K. Salmon, Cliff Young, Brannon Batson, Kevin J. Bowers, Jack C. Chao, Michael P. Eastwood, Joseph Gagliardo, J.P. Grossman, C. Richard Ho, Douglas J. Ierardi, István Kolossváry, John L. Klepeis, Timothy Layman, Christine McLeavey, Mark A. Moraes, Rolf Mueller, Edward C. Priest, Yibing Shan, Jochen Spengler, Michael Theobald, Brian Towles and Stanley C. Wang, "Anton, a special-purpose machine for molecular dynamics simulation," *34th Annual International Symposium on Computer Architecture* (ISCA 2007), San Diego, CA, June 9–13, 2007, pp. 1–12.

[27] Magnus Själander, Andrei Terechko and Marc Duranton, "A look-ahead task management unit for embedded multi-core architectures," *11th Euromicro Conference on Digital System Design Architectures, Methods and Tools* (DSD 2008), Parma, Italy, September 3–5, 2008, pp. 149–157.

[28] Kyriakos Stavrou, Costas Kyriacou, Paraskevas Evripidou and Pedro Trancoso, "Chip multiprocessor based on data-driven multithreading model," *International Journal of High Performance Systems Architectures*, Volume 1, Number 1, 2007, pp. 24–43.

[29] David Wentzlaff, Patrick Griffin, Henry Hoffmann, Liewei Bao, Bruce Edwards, Carl Ramey, Matthew Mattina, Chyi-Chang Miao, John F. Brown III and Anant Agarwal, "On-chip interconnection architecture of the Tile Processor," *IEEE Micro*, Volume 27, Issue 5, September, 2007, pp. 15–31.

Author Index